MITCHELL BEAZLEY

THE **WINE ATLAS** OF

ITALY

AND TRAVELLER'S GUIDE

TO THE VINEYARDS

by

BURTON ANDERSON

MITCHELL BEAZLEY

THE WINE ATLAS OF
ITALY
AND TRAVELLER'S GUIDE
TO THE VINEYARDS

— by —

BURTON ANDERSON

The Wine Atlas of Italy
Edited and designed by Mitchell Beazley
part of Reed Consumer Books Limited
Michelin House, 81 Fulham Road,
London SW3 6RB
and Auckland, Melbourne, Singapore
and Toronto

A CIP catalogue record for this book is
available from the British Library.

The author and publishers will be grateful for
any information which will assist them in
keeping future editions up to date. Although all
reasonable care has been taken in the
preparation of this book neither the publishers
nor the author can accept any liability for any
consequences arising from the use thereof or
from the information contained herein.

Editor Alison Melvin
Art Editor Gaye Allen
Map Editors Paul Drayson, Zoë Goodwin
Index Marie Lorimer
Production Ted Timberlake
Managing Editor Chris Foulkes
Senior Art Editor Tim Foster

Photographs Alan Williams
Illustrations Madeleine David

ISBN 0 85533 793 1

Typeset in Century Old Style by
Servis Filmsetting Ltd, Manchester, England.
Reproduction by Mandarin Offset, Hong Kong.
Printed in China

Contents

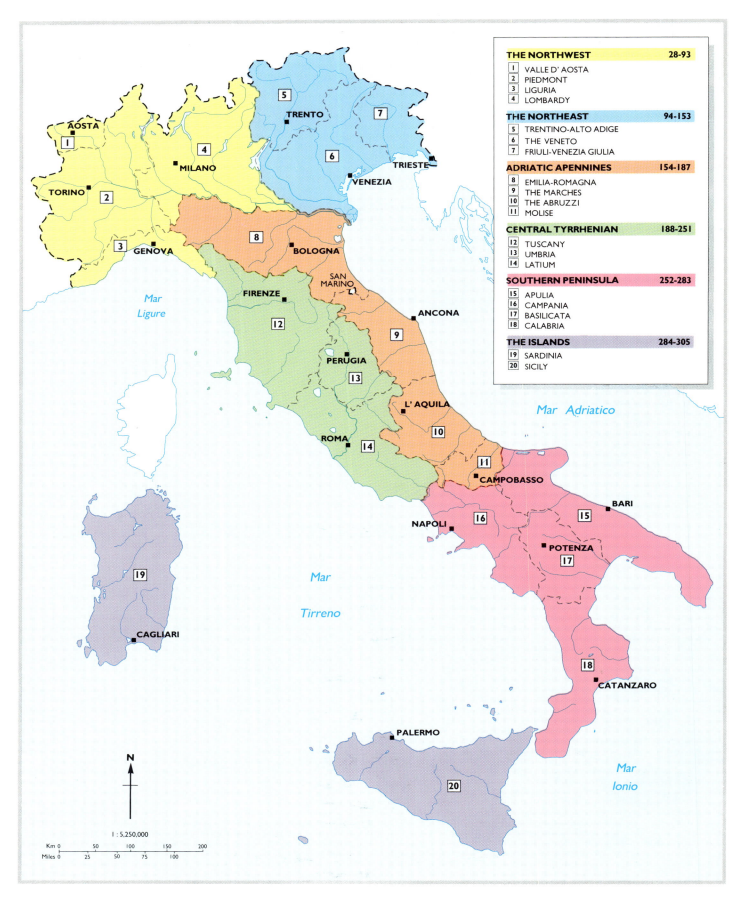

THE NORTHWEST   **28-93**
1	VALLE D' AOSTA
2	PIEDMONT
3	LIGURIA
4	LOMBARDY

THE NORTHEAST   **94-153**
5	TRENTINO-ALTO ADIGE
6	THE VENETO
7	FRIULI-VENEZIA GIULIA

ADRIATIC APENNINES   **154-187**
8	EMILIA-ROMAGNA
9	THE MARCHES
10	THE ABRUZZI
11	MOLISE

CENTRAL TYRRHENIAN   **188-251**
12	TUSCANY
13	UMBRIA
14	LATIUM

SOUTHERN PENINSULA   **252-283**
15	APULIA
16	CAMPANIA
17	BASILICATA
18	CALABRIA

THE ISLANDS   **284-305**
| 19 | SARDINIA |
| 20 | SICILY |

AOSTA

TRENTO

MILANO

TORINO

GENOVA

BOLOGNA

VENEZIA

TRIESTE

Mar Ligure

SAN MARINO

FIRENZE

ANCONA

PERUGIA

Mar Adriatico

L' AQUILA

ROMA

CAMPOBASSO

BARI

NAPOLI

POTENZA

Mar Tirreno

CATANZARO

CAGLIARI

PALERMO

Mar Ionio

N

1 : 5,250,000

| Km 0 | 50 | 100 | 150 | 200 |
| Miles 0 | 25 | 50 | 75 | 100 |

Introduction

The aim of this book, ambitious as it may sound, is to put Italian wines on the map. Not all Italian wines, but those whose individual virtues or collective stature have earned them a place in the sun. Singling out the worthy from the rest is no routine matter in a country that makes more wine than any other but has never managed to count let alone categorize all the types. The need to concentrate information into a reasonably comprehensive text on a subject of such scope and diversity made it clear from the start that *The Wine Atlas of Italy* would be different from the earlier volumes on Germany and France in the series. My critical perspective brings a measure of subjectivity to a book that more than an atlas and traveller's guide is designed to serve as a basic reference to the current state of Italian wine. Mapping the nation's vineyards presented a challenge that, however determined the effort, could only be met to a degree. For beyond the limits of time, space, and finances, the results relied on data that in places had to be extracted from sketchy or contradictory accounts. But even if the picture isn't always complete, this Atlas with its original series of maps, words, and photographs sheds new light on the contours of an ancient but by no means antiquated land of wine.

Over a period of 4,000 years Italians have woven together a nationwide tapestry of *Vitis vinifera* unequalled for colour and texture. Vineyards have been planted in most places where function permits and in many where practicability was not a prime consideration: across the foothills of the Alps, down along the Apennines to the toe of the boot-shaped peninsula, and out on the islands of Sicily and Sardinia. Vines suit the nature of a country whose cultivable land between the limits of mountain and sea supplies the basics of what has come to be known as the Mediterranean diet. But wine goes beyond material sustenance to nourish the spirit of a people whose highest form of culture might be described as the art of living. Italy today moves at a modern pace, but within the context of a history that rather than a tired record of the past remains an active element of life. Every corner of the country has its own variations of old and new lending a special flavour to each of its cities, its hill towns and seaports, its art and music, its cooking and its wines.

Travellers in Italy often take to the local wines as nonchalantly as their hosts do, drinking freely without paying much attention. The names, so melodically easy to listen to on the spot, can be maddeningly hard to recall back home. Apart from such popular types as Chianti, Soave, and Frascati, Italy's fine wines have rarely made as much impact abroad as they might. The average consumer may complain that they are too many and too varied. Experts on other nations' wines often find Italy's difficult to follow, probably because they lack the basic references of vineyards charted with due devotion to detail. Or so it seemed to me as a map-minded foreigner when I began searching out the wines of Italy in the early 1960s, and so it seemed when I began work on this book.

In the old days people often got around by following what road signs there were and asking directions along the way. The formal wine tour hadn't been conceived, nor has it been developed much today. But the lack of meaningful maps to Italy's wine zones puzzled me from the start. There were exceptions. The late Renato Ratti mapped the vineyards of Barolo and Barbaresco, and devised a chart dividing Italy into wine sectors similar to those followed in this Atlas. But most wine maps available, the sketchy regional outlines and posters with cartoon figures cavorting along the Italian boot, were all too much in keeping with the image being projected abroad. Serious wine drinkers found it hard to take Italy seriously.

We who criticized knew where to lay the blame. Producers themselves had been guilty first of lapses in vineyards and cellars, second of failing to convince even their compatriots let alone foreigners that they followed their laws, and third of neglecting to let the world know that, despite everything, they possessed a wealth of good wines waiting to be discovered. After saturating international markets with cheap wines in gimmicky bottles, they wondered why the dignified reds, the nobles, were so slow to acquire status. They reminded us that the ancient Greeks called the country Oenotria, the land of wine, while striving to grasp the concepts of marketing, the art of PR, that in a utopian tomorrow were to make their wines as prestigious and profitable as those of their long envied neighbours the French. It seems strange that a country noted since antiquity for its aptitude to vines is still struggling to convince the world of the worthiness of its wines.

But responsibility doesn't lie within the industry alone. Missing along with the maps is a popular literature of wine in Italy, where periodicals and books circulate mainly within the establishment. There is no lack of scholarly texts, but they are rarely read beyond research centres and technical high schools (a university degree in oenology is a recent innovation). Some old publications seemed more to the point. A manual entitled *Vade-Mecum del Commerciante di Uve e di Vini in Italia*, published in 1903, was a compendium of each province's wines and vines, vinification methods, producers, distillers, even barrel makers. It proved to be more useful in my research than did most books in print today. There is no reliably up-to-date publication on the wines of *denominazione di origine controllata* (DOC), so details in this Atlas have been drawn from various sources. Cited in the Bibliography are a few well researched books and useful guides to producers, but they are exceptions.

At the international level the literature is scarcer still. Only a handful of publications, including a couple of my own, have covered Italian wine in much depth in recent years. Curiously, none of the world's recognized experts on wine has confronted Italy in a profound way since Cyril Ray with his pioneering work in the 1960s. I've often wondered why it took so long for writers from afar to arrive with their notebooks and spit buckets to analyse the nuances of Barolo or Brunello on the spot. Or why importers took so long to find their way past Italy's wine factories and start knocking at estate doors. More than complacency, I suspect, it was fear of the unknown. Even today many people who write about wines or sell them abroad have only vague ideas about where Italy's come from.

Perhaps learning about wine in the country led me to approach the subject in a different way. For to me no wine, however satisfying to drink, could be complete without a curriculum vitae: who made it, when, how, and, the fundamental question, where? In Italy, where every hillside has its own look and feel, the lay of the land, the texture of the soil, and the variables of climate are the keys to a wine's personality. For with few exceptions fine wines tell more about the vineyards they were born in than the cellars where they were raised. This Atlas might be considered a substitute for visiting the vineyards, but it should prove even more useful as a working manual for those who arrive. As a travel guide it offers tips on how to get around the wine zones. As a reference work it provides clues to why the wines of each place are the way they are. If read carefully, it may raise more questions than it answers – part of the learning process in a field where deep knowledge is scarce. But even if visiting might involve more time and trouble than in other countries, Italy's vineyards are worth getting to know.

The text follows a geographical order often used before – moving from northwest to northeast, then southeast down the peninsula to conclude

7

on the islands. The country is divided into six sectors, though that does not mean that the regions included in each are closely linked to one another. Italy is delightfully heterogeneous. However you divide it – 20 regions, 94 provinces, 8,090 communes – the units contrast. This variety accounts for local colour and mass confusion. How many wines are there in Italy? How many grape varieties? Figures have been given, but nobody knows. What is certain, though, is that there are far fewer varieties and far fewer types of wine than there were before.

Yet too much wine is made today in a country that on the one hand boasts of its prodigiousness and on the other frets over surpluses. The wines that really matter – and rate most attention in this book – are at the tip of an iceberg in a sea of anonymity. Those that have earned official status are at the peak of a pyramid of a classification system that Italy has been building slowly and improbably from the top down. Yet my emphasis in every region is on the wines that come from identifiable places, mainly from the 232 zones that have qualified as DOC or the highest "guaranteed" category of DOCG. Basic details of each are given, along with a description that may be a phrase or an essay, depending on the weight they carry. Also reviewed are many unclassified *vini da tavola*, which in some cases outclass the delimited wines in prestige and value. Hundreds of producers are listed with a wine or wines, sometimes with notes about vineyards and techniques, along with comments about what sets them apart.

But why this emphasis on the DOC/DOCG wines that account for only 10-12 percent of the total? The laws have been so downgraded in Italy that some foreign experts have been led to believe that the country's best wines are not delimited. And, indeed, a growing number of fine bottles, including some that might qualify as DOC or DOCG, are issued with individual names and higher prices. In some regions, notably Tuscany,

these upmarket "table wines" lead the wave of the future. They are often products of advanced technology or creative flair, but what they represent above all else is the winemaker's sacred freedom of expression.

Some such renegades have earned special status while reinforcing the view that any wine's ultimate guarantee is its producer's integrity. But consumers abroad can hardly be expected to keep track of labels that might carry names of vineyards, poems, musical instruments, flowers, birds, ancestors, or loved ones. Such enterprise may express an honest sense of independence, but what began about 15 years ago as a refreshing trend has taken on the air of a mass ego trip. Winemakers who believe that their every whim will be greeted as a masterpiece and command a commensurate price are either arrogant or shortsighted. This avalanche of fanciful nomenclature threatens not only to bury DOC but to smother the hard-earned credibility of fine Italian wines in general.

The laws clearly need revision, but DOC, despite its battered image, has given a home and a definition to a majority of Italy's fine wines. For even if it represents only a tenth of the quota, that's still more than 7 million hectolitres a year, more wine than most countries produce in total. Once the surplus is trimmed away – the masses destined for blending or distillation – it turns out that, absurd as it seems, less than half of all Italian wine is designed to be consumed in its original state anyway. By now the recognized zones of origin cover nearly all the prime vineyard areas of the country and most quality wines, whether classified or not, are made within them. In other words, DOC, for all its flaws, really does indicate where the good wines originate.

The prime example can be seen in the chain of DOC zones that extends, with never any more than a river valley as a break, from the outskirts of Turin in Piedmont to just short of the heel of the boot in Apulia's Salento (*see* the DOC map on page 23). Along this stretch that never deviates far from the Apennines the climate ranges from cool and damp to torridly dry; terrains vary radically in form and content; some 200 different vines are grown under nearly every method known to viticulture. Yet there is something, however abstract, that links the vineyards along the way. It might be the world's most extensive classified wine territory.

Italy's wine industry seems to be moving ahead with more momentum than any other nation's – or, at least, it is shifting gears at a faster rate. Keeping track of activities at the tip of the iceberg has been a full-time job. The scenes recorded are based on findings from yet another tour of the vineyards, though references often date to earlier moments of an odyssey that has covered nearly 30 years. Valuable sources of information are mentioned in the text or acknowledgments, but most of the research and all of the conclusions it led to are my own. Over time I've learned that things in Italy are not always what they seem to be on first glance, or even on second or third, so data has been carefully checked but not flatly guaranteed. Opinions, especially when they range beyond conventional views about Italian wine, have been expressed after due contemplation. Criticism is meant to be constructive, though the text is not supposed to read like a travelogue or a dithyramb on the wonders of Oenotria.

Wines are evaluated throughout. But this is not a collection of tasting notes or ratings of wines, producers, or vineyards with numbers or stars. Vintages are often mentioned but not charted in a book intended to be referred to over time. Wines evolve, sometimes rapidly, according to how they are stored, shipped, and served. Tasting notes provide useful insights into a wine at a moment in its life. But perhaps too much attention is paid to temporary ratings these days and not enough to the enduring factors that determine a wine's value over time: terrain and climate, vine varieties, vineyard maintenance, and the techniques of vinification and ageing.

This Atlas emphasizes the enduring factors by focusing on Italy's main wine zones and, where warranted, mapping the vineyards in detail. But I have not presumed to classify such a complex and diverse array. For in only a few places where vines grow in Italy can continuing evidence of special worth be attached to zones, communes, hillsides or single plots. Veteran growers often know where the best wine of their village comes (or came) from, though some vineyards have been neglected or abandoned. The great deterrent to quality over the last hundred years or more has been the emphasis on productivity. Since only a small minority of Italy's estimated 1,200,000 growers make commercial wine directly, the majority in many regions has aimed for the greatest quantity attainable (or the highest sugar/alcohol level) in supplying grapes to wine houses or cooperatives. There were always exceptions, but only over the last 20 years or so have many producers insisted on growing their own grapes or controlling cultivation and on making estate or single vineyard wines.

Producers throughout Italy now cite vineyard names on labels. The practice often respects the superiority of terrains and indicates devotion to detail. But in some cases it is pure opportunism, for there is no way yet of officially confirming that a name applies to a genuine *cru* rather than the figment of an active imagination. Tempting as it might be to rank vineyards, the realities work against such endeavours. For one thing the emphasis on premium quality is so recent in so many parts of the country that it isn't always clear whether a wine's superiority is due more to a vine's affinity to a terrain or to a winemaker's mastery of techniques. Still, with each good vintage the endowments of certain vineyards become more evident, particularly in places such as Piedmont where traditional vines prevail.

Complicating the issue in many regions is the rise of varieties not native to Italy: Chardonnay, the Pinots, and Sauvignon Blanc for white wines; the Cabernets, Merlot, and Pinot Noir for reds. Although Italians can pick from a vast array of admirable native vines, they often have

reason to prefer the foreigners. They know that the French vines due to careful clonal selection are often more reliable than multi-faceted Italian natives that have rarely been treated like nobles. Also their universally recognized names and flavours in theory mean greater market potential.

Despite the fact that all the prominent foreign vines have been grown in Italy for well over a century, the upsurge in varietal wines from them is often criticized abroad. Optimists have been predicting that in the not too distant future Italy's unique, even exotic wines will gain in stature while the imitation Claret, Burgundy, and Fumé Blanc made on six continents will suffer from over-exposure. But market performances seem to back the pessimists' view of a world of ever more standardized tastes. It remains to be seen whether wine drinkers beyond clubs and cliques will ever heed the wisdom of George Saintsbury in *Notes on a Cellar Book* and learn "the appreciation of difference without insisting on superiority".

Italy has slowly impressed on the world that it can make outstanding wines from both native and foreign varieties, but it has failed to convince doubters that it exercises rigid control over them. The DOC/DOCG system, with its multitude of appellations, needs to become more broadly based to identify fine wines now made outside the norms. It also needs to become more flexible to allow for the creativity, the sacred freedom of expression that has engendered some of the nation's most artistic wines. One way to bring prominent outsiders into the system would be to create niches for them within the base of regional appellations. In other words, to recognize each of Italy's 20 regions as a primary DOC zone whose name would be required on all wines that meet basic requirements of origin and exceed a set quality standard.

Consumers abroad could more easily deal with the names of 20 regions than with the nuances of the current 232 appellations that range in scope from a territory nearly as extensive as Bordeaux (Chianti) down to zones that cover part of a commune (Torgiano, for example). It's worth noting that Italy's regions of prime importance – Piedmont, Tuscany, the Veneto, Friuli-Venezia Giulia and Trentino-Alto Adige – are as few as France's and with the right promotion could become similarly recognizable.

A regional DOC system is one possible solution; there may well be others. But it's essential that the world's largest wine industry comes to grips with a meaningful production code and that this time it be designed with foreign consumers in mind. Italian disregard for DOC has done incalculable damage to the image of the country's wines abroad. This flaw needs to be corrected before it becomes fatal. For more than ever before the success of Italian wine depends on its performance abroad, where credible competition mounts steadily.

Patterns of Italian viticulture have been revitalized over the last 20 years or so to show new patterns of form and colour, though overall the work lacks harmony and the finishing touches that could lend it splendour. The time has come for the artists and patrons of Italy's renaissance in wine to envision a grand design. For it would be a shame to see such a rich and varied tapestry, woven and spliced together over 4,000 years, once again start coming apart at the seams.

History and Legend

Italians were not the first of the world's peoples to make wine, but through 40 centuries or perhaps more of practice they have shown the most natural aptitude for the craft. Some wild strains of *Vitis vinifera* originated in Italy, as noted in vine fossils dating to the early days of man. Peoples up and down the peninsula grew grapes and no doubt made wine before the dawn of history; among them were the Raeti and Salassi in the northwest, the Veneti in the northeast, the Piceni and Praetutti along the central Adriatic, and the Oscan and Samnite tribes that dominated the south. Phoenicians, who arrived in Apulia around 2000 BC, found an active if rudimentary wine industry there. The Liguri, who learned from the Greeks, carried viticulture across the Apennines to Piedmont and north to Valtellina in the Alps, and also west as far as France's Rhône valley.

The early peoples, as they were conquered by Greeks and Romans and assimilated into their societies, contributed more to Italian civilization than is generally acknowledged. Their names often remained attached to places and it is said that their physical features and even traces of their languages and cultures can be detected in local populations. The vines they grew were at best vaguely noted, and, as now, the wines they made must have varied radically from place to place. Yet many of the early vines that went on to prominence in Italy seem to have been brought from elsewhere across the Mediterranean.

As the Greeks settled in the southern peninsula and Sicily they introduced varieties that are still grown today: Muscat or Moscato, Malvasia, those species known as Greco or Grecanico, and the noblest of southern vines Aglianico. Herodotus and other historians came to refer to Magna Graecia as Oenotria. The name may first have referred to the Oenotri tribe of Apulia or, as some say, to the stakes used to train vines close to the ground, a system they found in use all over the southern peninsula. But, even if the original Oenotria was the south, all of Italy eventually came to be known as the land of wine.

As the Greeks imposed their standards on the south, Etruscans, who also seem to have arrived from the east, advanced their methods in the heart of the peninsula. Italy's most ambitious early vintners built a wine trade from their Tyrrhenian ports that reached at least as far as ancient Gaul. Curiously, even today the basic concepts of vine training in the country are sometimes referred to as *greco* (for the short pruning that originally took the form of a bush) and *etrusco* (for the high pergolas or arbours that evolved from the age-old habit of draping vines over trees).

Opportunistic Romans learned from both systems and moved beyond. They developed new types of viticulture, including cane pruning of vines trained along wooden rods and poles in much the same way as they are fixed to wires in the vertical systems prevalent in Italy today. They devised oenological methods so ingenious that some feats weren't matched again until the seventeenth or eighteenth centuries when Europeans began to look beyond the mysteries of God and nature to view wine as a science. Roman texts on the subject were both poetic (from the pens of Virgil, Horace, and Ovid) and profound (from the erudite tomes of Pliny the Elder, Cato, Varro, and Columella). Yet, as Hugh Johnson points out in *The Story of Wine*, their writing was "teasingly rich in detail, always ambiguous in conclusion".

At first the Romans favoured hot climes for vineyards, such as the coast south towards Naples, where the vaunted Falernian and Caecuban originated. But later they looked beyond their home territories to assess the qualities of wine from the vineyards that became history's first *grands crus*. These ranged beyond Falernum and Caecubum to include Mamertinum in Sicily, Praetutium on the Adriatic coast, Lunense on the Ligurian coast, and Rhaeticum in the central Alps. The ruins of Pompeii and Herculaneum are showcases of the Roman mastery of wine. Although they used resin, honey, spices, herbs, and sea water to flavour and stablize wines for ageing, they also made naturally dry or lightly sweet types that might have appealed to modern palates. They even knew how to keep wines bubbly by immersing amphorae sealed with corks into cold well water to arrest fermentation.

The cult of Bacchus spread through the Roman empire with the growing commerce in wine. The Romans planted vines in France, Spain, North Africa, and even as far north as Germany and England as they developed a thriving trade in wine between the colonies. Most was shipped in amphorae, but from people in northern Italy they also learned the use of wooden barrels for transporting and, as a consequence, ageing wine. Like modern producers, they occasionally overdid things. When a surplus developed in the first century AD, the Emperor Domitian ordered the widespread uprooting of vines – an ominous precedent to current official policy. But no other people in history have done so much as the Romans to advance the culture of wine.

That great heritage was practically forgotten as the empire declined and fell. Though winemaking survived during the Dark Ages in Apulia and scattered parts of the south, in much of Italy viticulture was kept alive at monastic orders and wine was used mainly for religious or medicinal purposes. Not until the late Middle Ages did wine re-emerge as daily sustenance, or, for those who could afford the best, the most civilized of drinks. The few reliable accounts that have been passed down through the ages indicate that at least some wines that met the then almost universal requirement of sweet were fine indeed. But the fact that Italy wasn't a unified country from the end of the Roman empire to the Risorgimento meant that nothing like a national history of wine, or other matters, was kept. Events which occurred in the regions and provinces – the city republics, papal states, kingdoms, principalities, duchies, and family-run fiefs – were recorded or interpreted in often contradictory ways. A scholarly exception was Petrus de Crescentiis, known as Pier de' Crescenzi in Italian, whose research into vines and wines in the fourteenth century matched the early Romans for thoroughness.

Even during the Renaissance, when wine was a familiar subject of paintings and poems, it was rarely treated in a learned way in writing. Leading chroniclers of Italian wines in the sixteenth and seventeenth centuries were Sante Lancerio, official bottler for Pope Paul III, and the physicians Andrea Bacci and Francesco Redi. But their assessments were mainly eulogies, often in verse. Still, there is little question that winemaking standards had improved to meet growing demand for quality from well-to-do Italians and even from northern Europeans.

Today the literature of Italian wine often dwells on the past, on the legend of Oenotria, the Roman feats, and the odes of Renaissance poets. Yet the history of what might be described as wine in a modern context began only in the last century in those few parts of Italy where valid traditions developed. Perhaps the first signs of its emergence were in the Grand Duchy of Tuscany in the eighteenth century under the enlightened leadership of the House of Lorraine. Principal wine zones, including Chianti, were defined and protected and the Georgofili academy set standards of viniculture that were, in theory at least, as advanced as any of Europe. But overall in a land ruled by foreigners and tyrants, ravaged by wars, and depressed by poverty, meditated patterns of winemaking had little chance to develop. Already the French, though they lacked the natural advantages of Oenotria, had confirmed their supremacy with wine.

Above: detail from a Roman floor mosaic depicting the head of Autumn in the Cirencester Museum, Gloucestershire, England.

The Frenchman André Jullien in a catalogue of wines published in 1816 wrote of Italy: "One could believe that this country produces the best wines of Europe; but while the people of less favoured lands are busy choosing the best vines to suit their intemperate seasons, the Italians accustomed to seeing the vine grow almost spontaneously, and everywhere give ripe fruit, never even try to maximize their advantages." He noted that "bad quality comes not only from neglect in cultivation, but even more from sheer bad winemaking." A century and a half later the American professors M.A. Amerine and V.D. Singleton practically echoed Jullien's conclusions when they wrote that "...the wines of Italy are made from small vineyard holdings in mountainous areas in promiscuous culture, and the many untrained winemakers use rather primitive techniques. The wines do not enjoy sufficient distribution among critical consumers either inside or outside Italy to force an improvement in quality."

Yet between 1816 and 1966 when the new DOC laws gave impetus to what is sometimes called the modern renaissance of wine, Italy's vineyards and cellars were swept by change. Dry red wines for ageing had emerged in the middle of the nineteenth century as Italians learned French techniques brought to Barolo by Louis Oudart and adjusted to Chianti by Bettino Ricasoli. A sparkling wine industry grew around Asti when Carlo Gancia introduced methods from Champagne. Earlier the Englishman John Woodhouse had devised the formula for Sicily's Marsala whose popularity came to rival port and sherry in Victorian England.

After decades of struggle, the Risorgimento culminated in a unified Italy that seemed to herald a new era for its wines. Producers in Tuscany, Piedmont, the Veneto, and other key regions honed styles with an eye to international tastes as markets expanded in Italy and abroad for wines in bottles or flasks. By the late nineteenth century wine once again had become a subject of scholarly research in literature that was sometimes more precise than it is today.

But just as Italian wines began to reach new levels of prestige, oidium and phylloxera swept Europe's vineyards and dealt the new concepts of quality crippling blows. The scourges from America deprived the nation of uncountable local vines whose ultimate worth will never be known since winemaking up to then rarely realized top results. Foreign varieties, primarily French, largely replaced native vines in parts of the country. Many worthy traditional vines were salvaged, but the emphasis turned to productive varieties of indifferent quality to meet growing demands in Europe for blending wines. New vineyards were developed to supply them, especially in the south.

In this century most of Italy's vineyards have been converted from mixed cropping to monoculture, a process that reached peaks in the 1960s and 1970s and provided a working base for the modern wine industry. But through it all growers in most regions have continued to choose varieties and clones that helped them raise yields, reasoning correctly that quantity is – or, at least, was – more profitable than quality. In most regions, grapes were sold by weight for wines priced according to alcoholic strength. Large-scale cellars were built by private interests and, increasingly, by growers grouped in cooperatives equipped mainly to process inexpensive wines for indiscriminate drinkers.

In the decades following World War II, Italy overtook France to become the world's largest wine producer. During this time the nation also became the leading purveyor of what is sometimes referred to as plonk. This bargain *vino* was often sold in bottles of outlandish forms and sizes, generating profits for shippers while projecting a farcical image of Italian wine that still haunts the industry.

The average Italian consumer was accustomed to spending about the same for his daily wine as his daily bread, though if he had access to a decent *vino da contadino* – whose virtues depended on the luck of the latest vintage, the farmer's integrity, and the time of year – he might have drunk better than average anyway. Over time rustic country wines have largely given way to homogeneous beverages of collective cellars. But the lack of demand for quality deprived aspiring premium wine producers of a home base from which to build prestigious markets abroad. Some exceptionally good wines were made nonetheless by estate owners and vintners who until quite recently in Italy seemed almost a heroic breed apart.

Over the last quarter century the advent of DOC and a renewed sense of value among wine drinkers willing to pay the price of a fine bottle have inspired estate owners, merchants, and even some cooperatives to aim higher. Dramatic improvements have been accomplished by a generation of winemakers who have studied techniques elsewhere in Europe and abroad and translated them into distinctively Italian styles. Some new wave wines from international varieties have been highly acclaimed. But what should prove to be more important in the long run are the wines from worthy native vines that have been steadily upgraded in class.

It is now said that Italian wine has never been better, which if true, as it no doubt is, might shed new light on the past. To hear some tell it there is hardly a wine in the country that isn't the result of a long and sacred tradition. But in looking back over 40 centuries or more to the legends that arose at the moments when things went right, it might be wise to reflect on the events that recurred in the eras when things went wrong. Recent progress has brought new respect for the potential of a land of wine whose vineyards on the one hand have been avidly exploited and on the other scarcely tapped.

Climate and Geography

A relief map of Italy illustrates why uniformity is not a national trait, for the physical features of this long, narrow Mediterranean land vary as frequently as do its vines and wines. The fundamental infrastructure of the Alps and Apennines has been transfigured by landslides, glaciers, winds, and flowing water, as well as the earthquakes and volcanos that still provide dramatic effects. Terrains vary in angle, colour, texture, and components of soils whose origins range through the geological epochs. Yet amidst the often chaotic morphology of the peninsula and islands the weather shifts in patterns that are more or less predictable.

The Alps form a wall that fends off cold currents from the north and the Apennines serve as a weather barrier from Piedmont to Sicily with only a brief break at the Straits of Messina. The mountains influence the intensity of sunshine, heat, and precipitation in vineyards within their ranges. The Mediterranean is the other main determinant of weather, though there's a substantial difference in whether the nearest sea is the upper Adriatic or the lower Tyrrhenian. Rivers, lakes, plains, and forests govern local microclimates. Yet between the 47th parallel that crosses the Alps and the 35th parallel that passes beneath Sicily's island of Lampedusa, conditions range between subarctic and subtropical. That's because in a country that is 39.7 percent mountains and 38.7 percent hills altitude often has more to do with climate than latitude.

Nature's variables give grape growers and winemakers a wealth of options that some have learned to play with enviable dexterity. Yet it has often been said that the very ease of viticulture explains why Italian wine has so rarely achieved potential greatness. That theory, however, only holds true in places, for most of Italy's vineyards are on slopes, some so precariously situated that their maintenance is little short of heroic.

When the Greeks dubbed southern Italy Oenotria they were admiring the way vines thrived along the Ionian and Adriatic coasts, where ample sunshine and generous soils assured full ripening of grapes for strong, sweet wines. The early Romans, too, preferred hot climes for their Falernian and Caecuban, but eventually they ventured north across the Apennines to the lower slopes of the Alps where Liguri, Etruscans, and other peoples had planted vines on cooler slopes. That such climates enhanced aromas and flavours in wine did not escape the Romans' notice, but it wasn't until much later that growers in Italy began to appreciate how much vines can benefit from a struggle with the elements.

That concept has gained credence lately as more winemakers advance the cause of premium quality. Today, of course, with sweet and strong flavours less in fashion, cooler climates are generally considered superior for wines that meet modern notions of taste. So even if vines have spread across plains, a vast majority of Italy's fine wines come from hills. In general vineyards in high places throughout the country are cooler, damper and more subject to the threats of frost, hail, and incomplete ripening than in the plains. But the advantages outweigh the risks. Vines on well exposed slopes absorb the sun's rays directly and benefit from air currents and natural drainage that prevent mildew and rot. Vineyards in the hills feel the change of seasons, as well as day-night temperature fluctuations, factors that heighten aromas and flavours.

Most of Italy's prime vineyard hill zones lie within climatic bands considered ideal for vines, where annual mean temperatures are between 12-16°C, rainfall (or snow) is sufficient in winter and early spring, and summers are warm to hot with sunshine continuing into mid-autumn. But microclimates vary radically from place to place and the weather can change capriciously from one year to the next. So there is no truth to the once accepted notion that every vintage in Italy is the same.

As a rule, grapes for white wines mature earlier than those for red, so a cooler climate slows ripening and helps maintain primary aromas, acidity, and fresh fruit flavours. Two key white wine regions are Friuli-Venezia Giulia and Trentino-Alto Adige along the Alps to the northeast, where annual mean temperatures on hillsides range as low as 10°C, close to the lower limits that wine grapes can tolerate. Both native and foreign varieties do well there, though slopes as far south as Sicily have similarly favourable conditions, if rarely as deftly exploited. Italy's noblest red varieties also do well in temperate conditions. Yet the best vintages in such prime hilly areas as Piedmont's Langhe, Tuscany's Chianti, and Campania's Avellino are in hot, dry seasons when grapes ripen fully and wines develop the essential power for ageing.

But even in the best of hill zones class depends on factors that have not always been well understood or appreciated because the emphasis on top quality is so recent. Dedicated growers are learning the importance of selecting the right varieties and clones of vines grafted on to the proper rootstock for balanced yields. Many have modified traditional methods of vine training as well as pruning and thinning to further reduce production. Some are experimenting with greater plant density, increased from the usual 2,000-3,000 vines per hectare to as much as 7,000-10,000, as in Burgundy, or sometimes even more. But since each variety has its own prerequisites and since experiments are often recent, definitive results remain to be seen. Had growers in the past concentrated on such matters in more systematic ways, Italian wine might have

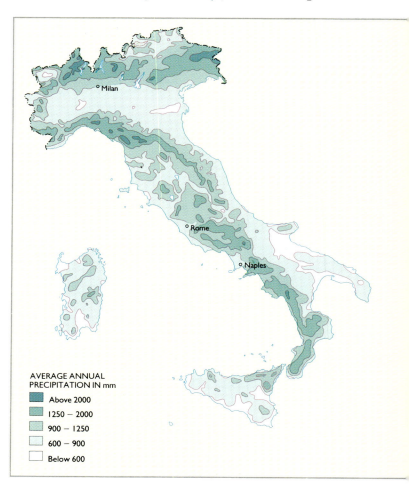

AVERAGE ANNUAL
PRECIPITATION IN mm

- Above 2000
- 1250 – 2000
- 900 – 1250
- 600 – 900
- Below 600

moved ahead of the field long ago.

But even today the markets for quality wine in Italy are much more restricted than for bulk. The most productive regions – Apulia and Sicily in the south, the Veneto and Emilia-Romagna in the north – have ample plains or easily rolling contours where vines thrive in hot, often irrigated conditions. In some places yields can reach as high as 300-400 quintals of grapes per hectare, or about four times the normal rate for quality wines from most species of vines. Much production from the plains is for blending into ordinary table wines or, in recent times, for distillation. But each of these regions also makes wines of distinctive personality on low-lying, hot terrains. Examples are the rich Marsala of Sicily's western coast, the delicate rosés of Apulia's Salento peninsula, the vivacious Lambrusco of Emilia's plains, and the soft, fruity Merlot of the Veneto's coastal flats of Piave and Lison-Pramaggiore.

Climate is the arbiter of quality, but the character of the finest of wines derives from the soil. In most zones vines have been selected by man or through mutation to suit the nature of the terrain, or of a precise *terroir*, as the French put it. But just why certain varieties thrive in certain conditions isn't always known. As a rule, fertile land does not favour class because vines tend to overproduce. The relatively poor soils found in so many hilly zones, but also on plains, are usually better. At least as important as the chemical makeup of the topsoil are the physical aspects of the subsoil, which should be well drained so that roots are forced to burrow deep for moisture. This favours slow ripening that results in firmer, better balanced fruit and richer aromas and flavours.

Some vines adapt remarkably well to different soils and climates. Versatility and steady productivity have made Trebbiano Toscano and Barbera among the most popular Italian varieties. But others, such as Piedmont's Nebbiolo and Trentino's Teroldego are extremely sensitive to environment. Nebbiolo reaches heights in the marly calcareous clays of the Langhe hills, though there are marked differences in the styles of wine from the two sides of the Barolo zone and between most of Barolo and Barbaresco. Nebbiolo also makes fine wines in glacial moraine of northern Piedmont around Gattinara and in siliceous clays on terraces of Lombardy's Valtellina, but personalities are different. The mysterious Teroldego seems to do well only in the gravelly Rotaliano plain along the Adige river north of Trento. When planted on hillsides it never performs as well. Sangiovese's various subvarieties have been widely diffused, but its noblest levels have been attained in parts of Chianti, Montalcino, and Montepulciano in Tuscany where special clones and diverse soil and climatic conditions account for distinct differences in the wines.

Some leading foreign varieties are enviably adaptable. For instance, Cabernets and Merlot dominate along the upper Adriatic in gravelly coastal plains (as in Bordeaux), but when moved to the hills of Friuli, the Veneto, Tuscany, and some other regions they often show the same basic character traits but more refined style. Chardonnay, like white Pinot, has by now been planted in all regions, and in most its vines do well, though best results seem to be in calcareous soils on cool hillsides of the north and centre.

Observations about how vines respond to different climates and terrains appear under each region's wine zones and elsewhere. But conclusions about why a variety might thrive in one vineyard and wither in a plot just down the slope are largely avoided. For even the French, or the Piedmontese, who have had more experience than others in such matters, like to describe the nature of each *terroir* in terms of its own peculiar magic.

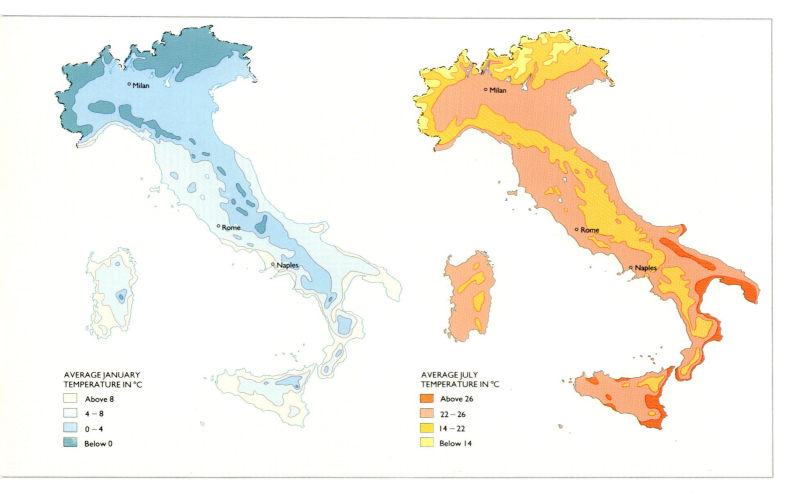

AVERAGE JANUARY
TEMPERATURE IN °C

- Above 8
- 4 – 8
- 0 – 4
- Below 0

AVERAGE JULY
TEMPERATURE IN °C

- Above 26
- 22 – 26
- 14 – 22
- Below 14

Vineyards and Grape Varieties

Italy ranks third among nations in area under vine (after Spain and the Soviet Union), but it surpasses all others in number of grape varieties and volume of wine. Yet statistics about viticulture have been largely guesswork up to now, for only in 1990 after decades of sweeping change did the government schedule a long-awaited census of vineyards. Estimates are that 1 million hectares of vines are divided between 1,200,000 growers, for an average of 0.83 hectare per property (much less than the 4.4 hectare average of France). In many regions this fragmentation has prevented effective formation of wine estates.

Modern Italy's vineyards are more uniform than ever, though on the hillsides where they prevail they never look monotonous. A majority has been converted from mixed cropping (*promiscuo*) to monoculture (*specializzato*). As late as 1975 about half the vineyards were mixed, but *promiscuo*, which still adds colour to the hill country scenery, is estimated at less than a quarter and fading. The change has made viticulture more scientific, putting new emphasis on clonal selections, cross breeding, plant density, use of fertilizers and sprays, and determination of the rootstocks onto which nearly all vines have been grafted since phylloxera. This research has brought a net improvement in quality in places, but perhaps its main contribution so far has been to greater productivity.

Over the last 30 years, vineyards in the plains have increased from about 20 to 40 percent of Italy's total. Overall yields have risen by about a third as growers have continued to favour prolific varieties. The average of just over 70 hectolitres of wine per hectare is the highest among major vineyard nations, though France is a close second. Yields vary sharply from one region to the next, however. It is no coincidence that those most noted for premium wines – Tuscany, Piedmont, and Friuli-Venezia Giulia – have yields as low as the prime vineyard areas of France.

Italian vine training methods represent a medley of types. Their bases have been traced to Etruscans, who trained vines up and over trees, and Greeks, who kept them close to the ground. The Romans drew upon both concepts and came up with systems that foretold many of the variations in use today. Each region's systems are discussed in the Atlas, but to provide an idea of what to expect, the following are the three basic categories of vine training used in Italy today.

1. Head-trained vines are known as *alberello* in Italy because they resemble a low "bush" due to short spur pruning. The Greek system has variations in which a mature vine may be free standing or supported by stakes. *Alberello* long prevailed in southern Italy in dry, hot places where moderate yields built strength in grapes for sweet or blending wines, but it is fading there, as well as in the northwest.

2. High horizontal canopy systems and tilted pergolas evolved from the Etruscan *alberate*, the tree training still seen along the length of the Apennines. In the north, the *pergola trentina* with a single, tilted pole arm dominates on slopes of the Adige valley, though south of Verona across the Po valley double pergolas typical of Lambrusco prevail. Variations are seen in the wood-beamed arbours of Valle d'Aosta and Carema and in strikingly similar structures of the Amalfi coast south of Naples. Vineyards on the irrigated plains of the south and islands are now often planted in *tendone*, a high trellis formed by crossed wires. Though shading slows ripening and lowers alcohol for better balance in table wines, growers often exploit *tendone* for high yields in both wine and table grapes. Experts sometimes blame the lingering Etruscan influence for excessive yields that inhibit potential quality.

3. Cordon or vertical training is generally known as *cordone* or *spalliera*, though specific names are used for the different ways of attaching vines to wires strung along rows of posts. Variations on Guyot, which keeps the fruiting canes low and foliage high, are used most often on Piedmont's slopes, as well as in much of central Italy and other zones where quality is the goal. Alternatives include the double arched *cappuccina* of Friuli and *doppio capovolto* of Tuscany and Umbria, the higher Sylvoz, and the Casarsa devised for mechanical harvesting.

Italy still grows an uncountable range of grape varieties, despite drastic reductions since oidium and phylloxera struck in the last century. Among well over a thousand vines recorded, nearly 400 are either recommended or approved in the various regions. These include a virtually complete array of western European vines. Not included are many local vines that have proved to be eccentric or unproductive and seem headed for extinction, though experiments with some could lead to revivals.

The following listing of vines in regular use refers to most varieties (or distinct subvarieties or clones) in the region where they are regarded as being native or are more prominent than elsewhere and where they are described. Varieties or families of vines that have come to be associated with more than one region are discussed below. These include such groups as Malvasia and Moscato, which have the most variations in types, and the Trebbiano and Sangiovese families, which are Italy's most diffused. Also described are principal foreign varieties, such as Chardonnay, currently the most popular, and Merlot, Cabernet, and the Pinots which have been prominent in Italy for well over a century. In each region there are also references to vines officially recommended or authorized, including some scarcely in use. There are also references to remaining curiosities among the thousands of vines recorded over the ages. The descriptions are observations culled from various sources and updated – an attempt to relate vines in actual use with their wines and, where discernible, their places of origins and families.

Abbuoto. Latium.

Aglianico. This gift of the Greeks (the name is a corruption of Hellenico or Ellenico from *Vitis hellenica*) may have been planted as early as the seventh century BC, apparently first in Basilicata and then in Campania. What may have been used by the Romans in Falernian is still considered southern Italy's noblest vine. Key zones are Basilicata's Vulture and Campania's Taurasi, but it shows promise elsewhere in the Mezzogiorno.

Albana. Emilia-Romagna.

Albarola. Liguria.

Aleatico. The origins of this ever rarer vine are uncertain. It may have come from Greece, as a dark mutation of Muscat, or it may be a native of Tuscany, where it makes sweet red wines mainly on Elba. DOC under Aleatico di Gradoli (Latium) and Aleatico di Puglia (Apulia).

Alicante. Synonym in Calabria, Tuscany, and elsewhere for Granacha or Grenache (*see*). The French Alicante Bouschet, a cross of Grenache and Petit Bouschet, is used sparingly in Italy.

Ancellotta. Emilia-Romagna.

Ansonica. Sicily's Inzolia is also called Ansonica or Anzonica there and along the Tuscan coast and islands where it is used in white table wines.

Arneis. Piedmont.

Asprinio or **Asprino**. Campania.

Barbarossa. Diverse vines in Liguria and Emilia-Romagna (*see*).

Barbera. This native of Piedmont (*see*) is Italy's second most diffused red wine variety after Sangiovese and one of few native vines prominent abroad (notably California). Noted for steady productivity and adaptability to different conditions, it makes varietal wines in Piedmont,

Lombardy, and Emilia, but in other regions is used mainly for blending. There is also a Barbera Sarda in Sardinia and a white Barbera Bianca.

Bellone. Latium.

Berzemino or **Barzemino**. Synonyms for Marzemino (*see* Trentino-Alto Adige) used mainly in northern Italy.

Biancame or **Bianchello** or **Passerina**. An ancient vine, probably an offshoot of Trebbiano, grown along the Adriatic between Romagna and Abruzzi and in Umbria. In the Marches it makes the sprightly Bianchello del Metauro DOC. Known as Passerina in the Marches and Abruzzi.

Bianchello. Marches. *See* Biancame.

Bianchetta Genovese. Liguria.

Bianco d'Alessano. Apulia.

Biancolella. Campania.

Blanc de Morgex or **Blanc de Valdigne**. Valle d'Aosta.

Bombino Bianco. Apulia. *See* also Pagadebit (Emilia-Romagna), Campolese (Abruzzi).

Bombino Nero. Apulia.

Bonarda. A native of Piedmont (*see* Bonarda Piemontese and Novarese), its name is often used for Croatina in Lombardy and Emilia.

Bosco. Liguria.

Bovale Grande, Bovale Sardo. Sardinia.

Brachetto. Piedmont.

Brunello di Montalcino. Clone of Sangiovese (*see* Tuscany).

Buzzetto. *See* Lumassina in Liguria.

Cabernet/Cabernet Franc/Cabernet Sauvignon. Vines in the Cabernet-Merlot family were known to the ancient Romans as Biturica after a tribe in France's Gironde. It isn't clear whether they remained in Italy afterwards, but what was known in eighteenth-century Tuscany as *uva francesca* was probably a Cabernet. In the nineteenth century, vines were planted in much of Italy, though after phylloxera they remained mainly in the northeast where the productive Cabernet Franc was favoured. Today Cabernet Sauvignon is often preferred in the northeast and other regions for distinctive varietal wines and used in Bordeaux blends with Merlot and Malbec, as well as with native varieties, notably Sangiovese in Tuscany.

Cagnina. Name used for a varietal wine in Emilia-Romagna (*see*) from Friuli's Terrano or Refosco del Carso vine.

Calabrese or **Nero d'Avola**. Sicily.

Campolese. Abruzzi.

Canaiolo Bianco. Tuscany; also Umbria as Drupeggio.

Canaiolo Nero. Native of Tuscany (*see*) for use in Chianti, it is often grown elsewhere in central Italy.

Cannonau. Sardinia.

Carignano. Sardinia.

Carricante. Sicily.

Catarratto Bianco. Sicily.

Cesanese di Affile, Cesanese Comune. Latium.

Chardonnay. The native of Burgundy was noted in Italy early in the century, though the first vines may have been brought from Champagne for use in sparkling wines. But growers, mainly in the northeast and Lombardy considered it another Pinot, calling it *giallo* (yellow) to distinguish it from the Pinot Bianco with which it often shared vineyards. Only in 1978 was the variety recognized and only in the 1980s was it qualified as DOC under various appellations. It has rapidly become the nation's most fashionable white wine variety and, according to soundings, is the second most diffused after Trebbiano Toscano. It is still used often in sparkling wines based on Champagne clones or medium to light bodied still wines. But some growers have selected Burgundy clones for fuller, richer Chardonnay that takes well to oak ageing.

Chiavennasca. Name for Nebbiolo in Lombardy's Valtellina.

Ciliegiolo. Native of Tuscany (*see*) often grown elsewhere.

Cinsaut. *See* Ottavianello (Apulia).

Clairette. White variety of southeastern France is used occasionally in blends in Sardinia, Tuscany, and Adriatic regions.

Cococciola. Abruzzi.

Coda di Volpe. Campania. An apparently unrelated vine of the name is planted in Emilia's Colli Piacentini.

Colorino. Tuscany.

Cornallin. Valle d'Aosta.

Cortese. Native of Piedmont (*see*) is also prominent in white wines in Lombardy.

Corvina Veronese. Veneto.

Croatina. An ancient vine of uncertain origin is the popular source of soft red wines on its own or in blends with Barbera in Lombardy's Oltrepò Pavese and Emilia's Colli Piacentini, where it is called Bonarda. It is also grown in Piedmont's Novara-Vercelli hills, where it is often blended with Nebbiolo and true Bonarda.

Damaschino. Sicily.

Dolcetto. Piedmont; *see* also Ormeasco in Liguria.

Drupeggio. Name for Canaiolo Bianco in Orvieto (Umbria).

Durella. Veneto.

Erbaluce. Piedmont.

Falanghina. Campania.

Favorita. Piedmont.

Fiano or **Fiano di Avellino**. Campania.

Forastera. Campania.

Fortana or **Fruttana** or **Uva d'Oro**. Emilia-Romagna.

Franconia or **Blaufränkisch** or **Limberger**. Friuli-Venezia Giulia.

Frappato di Vittoria. Sicily.

Freisa. Piedmont.

Fumin. Valle d'Aosta.

Gaglioppo. Calabria.

Gamay. The Beaujolais vine is grown here and there (Valle d'Aosta, Veneto, Friuli, Tuscany, Umbria) though it rarely performs more than satisfactorily and never makes wines comparable to the original.

Garganega. Italy's second most diffused native white variety after Trebbiano Toscano is best known as the source of Soave (*see* Veneto).

Gewürztraminer or **Traminer Aromatico**. Though linked to Tramin, a village in Alto Adige, it assumed nobility in Alsace, where the prefix *gewürz* (spicy) assumes full meaning. In Italy its honey-pink grapes yield less than the dark-skinned Traminer, though Gewürztraminer can be convincing in the South Tyrol. Elsewhere, as Traminer Aromatico, it makes more delicately scented whites. (*See* also Traminer.)

Girò. Sardinia.

Goldmuskateller/Moscato Giallo. Trentino-Alto Adige.

Granacha or **Grenache**. The vines widely planted in Spain and France are known in Italy as Cannonau (Sardinia), Granaccia (Liguria), Guarnaccia (Campania), as well as Alicante.

Grauvernatsch/Schiava Grigia. Trentino-Alto Adige.

Grecanico or **Grecanico Dorato**. Sicily.

Grechetto. Umbria; also prominent in Tuscany and Latium.

Greco. Ancient Greek vines, possibly in the Aminea family, were diffused in Italy with names such as Greco, Grecanico, Grechetto. Though often white, there are also dark varieties, but they aren't necessarily all related. They may be linked to the Falanghina of Falernum and to vines that evolved into the Trebbiano family, Verdicchio, and others. There is also evidence that vines of the name were introduced by Venetians to northeastern Italy and by the ancient Liguri in Piedmont and the northwest.

Greco Bianco. Calabria.

Greco di Tufo. Campania.

Greco Nero. Dark variety grown in Calabria and Sardinia.

Grignolino. Piedmont.

From left to right. Among the many vine training systems used in Italy, these are some of the most noted: the low head-trained alberello; *the* pergola trentina *of the Adige valley; the vertical systems known as* cordone *or* spalliera *or* Guyot *which now prevail in many regions; and the high trellis* tendone *which is common on hot plains.*

Grillo. Sicily.

Groppello. Lombardy.

Grossvernatsch/Schiava Grossa. Trentino-Alto Adige.

Impigno. Apulia.

Incrocio Bruni 54. Marches.

Incrocio Manzoni 6.0.13. This cross of Riesling Renano x Pinot Bianco is perhaps the most prominent of many developed in Italy, especially in the northeast at Conegliano Veneto and San Michele all'Adige. Incrocio Manzoni 2.15 is Prosecco x Cabernet Sauvignon.

Incrocio Terzi N.1. Lombardy.

Inzolia or **Insolia**. Sicily; *see* also Ansonica.

Lacrima (di Morro d'Alba). Marches.

Lacrima Nera. *See* Gaglioppo (Calabria).

Lagrein. Trentino-Alto Adige.

Lambrusco. From the Apennine species *Vitis vinifera silvestris*, most Lambrusco is planted in Emilia-Romagna and Lombardy, though subvarieties are found as far afield as Trentino, Apulia, and Sicily.

Lambrusco a Foglia Frastagliata. Trentino-Alto Adige.

Lambrusco di Sorbara, also **Lambrusco Grasparossa, Maestri, Marani, Montericco, Salamino**. Emilia-Romagna.

Lambrusco Viadanese. Lombardy; also Emilia-Romagna.

Lumassina. Liguria.

Maceratino. Marches.

Magliocco Canino. Calabria.

Malbec. The Bordeaux variety is planted mainly in the eastern Veneto and Friuli, where it is also called Malbech or Malbeck, for use in blends with Cabernet and Merlot, and occasionally in varietal wines. It is also planted elsewhere, as far south as Apulia.

Malvasia. The family of vines that may have originated in Asia Minor took the name of the Greek city of Monemvasia to become Malvasia in Italian, Malvoisie in French, Malvasier in German, and Malmsey in English. Apparently related to the Moscato/Muscat, they were noted by the Romans in the category of sweet grapes known as Apianae. Among many varieties called Malvasia in Italy grapes range in colour from pale green to nearly black. Their wines vary from crisp, dry, and pale white to golden, pink, or dark red and sweet. The wines tend to be stronger in the south and lighter in the north and centre, but rules don't always hold.

Malvasia Bianca di Candia. This white variety is prominent in Latium, where it is also known as Malvasia Rossa, but is planted in many regions. A distinct strain known as Malvasia di Candia *aromatica*.

Malvasia del Chianti or **Malvasia Toscana**. Tuscany.

Malvasia di Casorzo. Piedmont.

Malvasia di Lipari. Sicily.

Malvasia di Schierano. Piedmont.

Malvasia Istriana. Friuli-Venezia Giulia.

Malvasia Nera. The name is often applied to dark skinned Malvasia of various types, including Alto Adige's Roter Malvasier.

Malvasia Nera di Brindisi/Lecce. Apulia.

Malvasia Rossa/Roter Malvasier. Trentino-Alto Adige.

Malvasia Sarda or **di Sardegna**. Sardinia.

Malvoisie de Nus. Valle d'Aosta; *see* also Pinot Grigio.

Mammolo. Once popular variety is now found mainly in Tuscany (*see*).

Mantonico or **Montonico Bianco**. Calabria.

Mantonico or **Montonico Nero**. *See* Gaglioppo in Calabria.

Marzemino. Once widely planted in the north, production is now centred in Trentino.

Mayolet. Valle d'Aosta.

Merlot. The Bordeaux native ranks third among red varieties planted in Italy after Sangiovese and Barbera, a tribute to steady productivity noted in Italy since the mid-nineteenth century. It thrives on plains of the Veneto's Piave and Lison-Pramaggiore and Friuli's Grave for light, fruity wines, though when yields are restrained, particularly in hill vineyards, it can rival Cabernet Sauvignon in class and add elegance to blends. As popularity declines in the north, it has gained stature in central Italy as a varietal or in blends with Cabernets and Sangiovese.

Molinara. Veneto.

Monica. Sardinia.

Montepulciano or **Montepulciano d'Abruzzo**. Though widely planted in central and southern Italy, this red is mainly associated with the Abruzzi (*see*).

Montù or **Montuni**. Emilia-Romagna.

Moscadello or **Moscadelletto di Montalcino**. Tuscany.

Moscatello or **Moscatellone**. Large berried Moscato grapes are known by this synonym for Muscatel in various parts of Italy.

Moscato. Muscat vines are ubiquitous in Italy in different forms, colours, and styles, though what tends to unite them is a grapey, slightly musky aroma. Of antique origin, probably in Asia Minor, they were brought to Italy by Phoenicians and Greeks and mutated into distinct varieties or clones, usually white but also dark. The Romans put them with Malvasia in the Apianae vine family noted for sweet wines, though there are some dry types of Moscato. The basic types are the large-berried Alexandria variety (also known as Zibibbo), which are normally table grapes but when dried make rich, sweet golden to amber wines, sometimes fortified, and the small-berried Moscato Bianco that can make lighter whites and pale golden wines, often sparkling. But there are numerous other variations that carry the name.

Moscato Bianco. This seems to apply to several types, but the most prominent by far is that of the Asti area where it is also known as Moscato di Canelli (*see* Piedmont).

Moscato di Chambave or **Muscat de Chambave**. Valle d'Aosta.

Moscato di Scanzo or **Merera**. Lombardy.

Moscato di Terracina. Latium.

Moscato di Trani or **Moscato Reale**. Apulia.

Moscato Giallo/Goldmuskateller. Trentino-Alto Adige.

Moscato Nero. Dark-skinned Moscato of various types are used for sweet red wines or as table grapes.

Moscato Rosa/Rosenmuskateller. Trentino-Alto Adige.

Mostosa. White variety used in blends along the Adriatic and in Latium.

Müller Thurgau. The cross of Riesling x Sylvaner that dominates German vineyards has caught on in northern Italy in wines that are often more gracefully refreshing than their counterparts from points north. Vines excel in high points of Trentino-Alto Adige, but Friuli and other regions also make notable wines of the name.

Nasco. Sardinia.

Nebbiolo. Piedmont's noble variety is also known by the synonyms Pugnet, Picutener (or Picotendro), Spanna, and (in Lombardy's Valtellina) Chiavennasca.

Negrara or **Negrara Trentina**. Veneto.

Negroamaro or **Negro Amaro**. Apulia.

Nerello Cappuccio, Nerello Mascalese. Sicily.

Neretta or **Neretto**. Piedmont.

Nero Buono di Cori. Latium.

Nero d'Avola or **Calabrese**. Sicily.

Neyret. Valle d'Aosta.

Nieddera. *See* Bovale Grande in Sardinia.

Nocera. Calabria, Sicily.

Nosiola. Trentino-Alto Adige.

Nuragus. Sardinia.

Olivella or **Olivella Nera**. Synonym for Sciascinoso (*see*).

Ormeasco. Type of Dolcetto (*see* Liguria).

Ortrugo. Emilia-Romagna.

Ottavianello. Apulia.

Pagadebit or **Pagadebito**. Emilia-Romagna.

Pampanuto. Apulia.

Passerina or **Passarina**. Synonym for Biancame (*see* Marches).

Pecorello. Calabria.

Pecorino. Marches.

Pelaverga. Piedmont.

Perricone or **Pignatello**. Sicily.

Petit Rouge. Valle d'Aosta.

Petite Arvine. Valle d'Aosta.

Picolit. Friuli-Venezia Giulia.

Picutener or **Picotendro**. Nebbiolo cultivar used in Valle d'Aosta and Piedmont's Carema.

Piedirosso or **Per'e Palummo**. Campania.

Pigato. Liguria.

Pignoletto. Emilia-Romagna.

Pignola Valtellinese. Lombardy.

Pignolo. Friuli-Venezia Giulia.

Pinot. The three pillars of the family – Noir, Blanc, and Gris – were brought from Burgundy and Champagne over the last two centuries to enhance Italian viticulture. Besides the basic Nero, Bianco, and Grigio and their German synonyms in Alto Adige, the family takes in the Meunier subvariety and Pinot Auxerrois.

Pinot Bianco or **Pinot Blanc**. This white mutation of Pinot Noir has been planted in Italy since the early nineteenth century. It has often been blended and confused with Chardonnay in still and sparkling wines, mainly in the northeast, reaching peaks in Friuli and Trentino-Alto Adige. Yet even if experts often consider its wines finer, Pinot Bianco can't match Pinot Grigio's popular appeal. Synonyms include Borgogna Bianco and Weissburgunder in Alto Adige.

Pinot Grigio or **Pinot Gris**. Wines from this bluish grey-skinned mutation of Pinot Noir have probably reached world peaks of popularity from Italy, where it is widely planted in the Tre Venezie, Lombardy, and increasingly elsewhere. It is used mainly for a white varietal wine but also for blends, particularly of *spumante*. Known as Ruländer in Alto Adige. A clone is called Malvoisie de Nus in Valle d'Aosta.

Pinot Meunier or **Meunier**. If rarely accredited, this Champagne vine grows alongside related Pinots and Chardonnay in northern Italy, lending fruit and acidity to sparkling wines.

Pinot Nero or **Pinot Noir**. It isn't certain when Pinot Noir arrived in Italy, though it might have been long before it was prominently recorded in the nineteenth century. Some say it is the same as a vine known in Lombardy as Pignuolo, noting similarities in its clusters' resemblance to pine cones and its opulent red wines that were praised as early as 1304. But in modern times Pinot Nero has succeeded mainly as a base for sparkling wines from clones selected in Champagne. Though some good red wines have been made in the Venezie and Lombardy, few resembled good Burgundy until recently after some growers selected clones there.

Pollera Nera. Liguria.

Prié Blanc, Prié Rouge. Valle d'Aosta.

Primitivo or **Primativo**. Apulia.

Procanico. Clone of Trebbiano found in Umbria and maritime Tuscany. Though used interchangeably with and even called Trebbiano Toscano, growers in Orvieto consider it superior.

Prosecco. Veneto.

Prugnolo Gentile. Clone of Sangiovese (*see* Tuscany).

Raboso. Veneto.

Rebo. Cross of Marzemino x Merlot used mainly in Trentino.

Refosco. Friuli-Venezia Giulia; *see* also Cagnina in Emilia-Romagna.

Rheinriesling. *See* Riesling Renano.

Ribolla Gialla, Ribolla Nera. Friuli-Venezia Guilia.

Riesling Italico. The origins of this vine, which is not related to the "true" Riesling of the Rhine, are uncertain, though, despite the name, Italy seems unlikely. It is widely planted in central Europe, especially Austria where it is known as Welschriesling, as in Alto Adige. High yields make it useful in northern Italy in light, finely scented whites.

Riesling Renano. The White (or Rhine or Johannisberg) Riesling native to the Rhine has been planted in northeastern Italy for decades, though it has never become really popular anywhere. It makes notably perfumed, dry whites in Alto Adige, where it is called Rheinriesling, as well as in Friuli, though they never match the full-blown style of Rieslings of Germany and Alsace.

Rondinella. Veneto.

Rosenmuskateller/Moscato Rosa. Trentino-Alto Adige.

Rossese. Liguria.

Rossignola. Veneto.

Rossola Nera or **Rossara**. Lombardy.

Roter Malvasier/Malvasia Rossa. Trentino-Alto Adige.

Roussanne. The Rhône valley variety is used occasionally in whites in

Tuscany and Liguria.

Ruchè or **Rouchet** or **Roche**. Piedmont.

Ruländer. *See* Pinot Grigio.

Sagrantino. Umbria.

Sangiovese or **Sangioveto**. The Sangiovese family takes in several clones and many subvarieties planted through central and southern regions and parts of the north to rival Trebbiano Toscano as Italy's most diffused vines. Presumably a *Vitis vinifera silvestris* native to Tuscany, it may have been grown by Etruscans, though it was first noted in the sixteenth century as Sangiogheto. It was usually called San Gioveto (Saint Jove) or Sangioveto in Tuscany and Romagna (which also claims its origin) until the nineteenth century. The name Sangiovese is now applied to various vines differentiated by grape size. The medium-large to large Sangiovese or Sangioveto *grosso* types include Brunello di Montalcino, Montepulciano's Prugnolo, and one sort of Sangiovese di Romagna, though different clones of each produce distinct wines. Sangiovese *piccolo* is typified by the small-berried Sangioveto of Chianti, though there are variations. Despite class of certain clones, Sangiovese shows nobility mainly in central Tuscany, though Romagna's finest is distinctive. Elsewhere it serves mainly as a workaday variety, though it rarely succeeds outside Italy. *See also* Brunello di Montalcino, Prugnolo Gentile, Sangioveto (Tuscany), and Sangiovese di Romagna.

Sauvignon. The name of this classical white variety of the Gironde and Loire is usually given without a modifier in Italy, even though Sauvignon Blanc (as opposed to Vert and others) is the type generally planted. Up till now its best wines have come from Friuli and Alto Adige but it can excel in Tuscany, Piedmont, Umbria, and other regions as well. Sauvignon has clear personality, but since top producers are experimenting styles vary somewhat between the flinty *fumé* of the Loire and the cool crispness of dry white Bordeaux. Blends with Sémillon and use of oak barrels are adding dimensions to a variety that can rival Chardonnay in some places and in more than a few surpass it. Known as Spergola in Emilia.

Schiava/Vernatsch. The dominant variety of Trentino-Alto Adige (*see*) is also found in Lombardy and the Veneto, usually in blends.

  Schiava Gentile/Kleinvernatsch or **Mittervernatsch**, also **Schiava Grossa/Grossvernatsch, Schiava Grigia/Grauvernatsch**, and **Tschaggele**. Trentino-Alto Adige.

Schioppettino or **Ribolla Nera**. Friuli-Venezia Giulia.

Sciascinoso. Dark variety, also known as Olivella or Olivella Nera, used in Campania's Vesuvio *rosso* and for blending in Latium.

Semidano. Sardinia.

Sémillon. Though rare in Italy, the Bordeaux variety is used in blends to round out Sauvignon and alone in sweet and dry wines.

Serprina. Synonym for Prosecco (Veneto).

Somarello. Apulia.

Spanna. Synonym for Nebbiolo in northern Piedmont.

Spergola. Name used for Sauvignon Blanc in Emilia.

Susumaniello. Apulia.

Sylvaner Verde/Grüner Silvaner. Trentino-Alto Adige.

Syrah. The variety associated with the Rhône but probably of Middle Eastern origin (its alternate name is Shiraz) is grown sparingly in Italy, though signs are that it could do as well as some other French nobles.

Tazzelenghe or **Tacelenghe**. Friuli-Venezia Giulia.

Teroldego. Trentino-Alto Adige.

Terrano. *See* Refosco in Friuli-Venezia Giulia.

Tocai Friulano. Friuli-Venezia Giulia.

Tocai Italico. Though considered a table grape variety related to Tocai Friulano, it is used in wines in the Venezie, notably the Veneto.

Tocai Rosso. Veneto.

Torbato. Sardinia.

Traminer. The South Tyrolean village of Tramin inspired the name, though the vine may have come from Greece and brought north by the Romans. The name Traminer alone refers to a productive vine whose red berries make white wines that are less esteemed than Gewürztraminer.

Traminer Aromatico. *See* Gewürztraminer.

Trebbiano. Vines called Trebbiano, though not all strictly related, occupy about 100,000 hectares in Italy, considerably more than Sangiovese. Pliny the Elder cited a *Vinum trebulanum* from a place called Trebulanis in Campania. Origins could be Greek, since some vines called Greco seem to be related, or Etruscan, since that people made wine in Campania before the Greeks arrived. It could have originated at an Etruscan place called Trebbiano in the Luni hills at the border of Liguria and Tuscany or the Trebbia valley of Emilia-Romagna. But apparently various lines developed independently. Most Trebbiano makes light, zesty whites whose neutrality is useful in blends. Rarely do they show much character. Ancient strains must have been different, since Pier de' Crescenzi in the fourteenth century described Trebbiano as "a noble wine that keeps well". Vines of the name and numerous synonyms are planted through Italy and abroad, notably in France, where they are called Ugni Blanc in the Midi, St-Emilion in Cognac. The Trebbiano family probably makes more wine worldwide than any other, as Jancis Robinson wrote in *Vines, Grapes and Wines*. Not because it occupies most space (Granacha-Grenache is more heavily planted, mainly in Spain and France) but because its yields are so prolific. In Italy, Trebbiano Toscano is most diffused, followed by Trebbiano Romagnolo, Trebbiano Giallo, and Trebbiano di Lugana or Soave. In addition to subvarieties cited below, *see* Biancame/Bianchello, Lumassina (Liguria), Greco, Procanico.

Trebbiano d'Abruzzo. Abruzzi.

Trebbiano di Lugana. Lombardy, the same as Trebbiano di Soave or Veronese in the Veneto.

Trebbiano Giallo. Latium.

Trebbiano Modenese. Emilia-Romagna.

Trebbiano Romagnolo or **di Romagna**. Emilia-Romagna.

Trebbiano Spoletino/di Spoleto or **Trebbiano Verde**. Umbria.

Trebbiano Toscano. Tuscany.

Tschaggele. *See* Vernatsch/Schiava in Alto Adige.

Ughetta. Lombardy; *see* Vespolina in Piedmont.

Uva di Troia. Apulia.

Uva d'Oro. *See* Fortana in Emilia-Romagna.

Uva Rara. Synonym for Bonarda Novarese in Lombardy.

Veltliner. Trentino-Alto Adige; also Abruzzi.

Verdea. Emilia-Romagna; also Lombardy.

Verdeca. Apulia.

Verdello. The name of apparently unrelated vines in Sicily and Umbria.

Verdicchio. Marches.

Verdiso. Veneto.

Verduzzo Friulano. Friuli-Venezia Giulia.

Verduzzo Trevigiano. Veneto.

Vermentino. Possibly in the Malvasia family, it may have originated in Madeira, reaching Italy via the Spanish mainland and Corsica. It makes distinctive whites in Liguria and Sardinia (though some say clones are different) and is used increasingly along the Tuscan coast. Possibly related to Piedmont's Favorita (*see*). There is also a Vermentino Nero.

Vernaccia di Oristano. Sardinia.

Vernaccia di San Gimignano. Tuscany.

Vernaccia di Serrapetrona or **Vernaccia Nera**. Marches.

Vernatsch/Schiava. Trentino-Alto Adige.

Vespaiola. Veneto.

Vespolina. Piedmont; *see* also Ughetta in Lombardy.

Vien de Nus. Valle d'Aosta.

Weissburgunder. *See* Pinot Bianco.

Welschriesling. *See* Riesling Italico.

Zibibbo. Sicily.

Zinfandel. *See* Primitivo in Apulia.

How to Use this Atlas

As a basic reference to the wines of Italy, this Atlas provides a new fund of knowledge in words, maps, and pictures that can be studied or consulted at home. It is also designed to be used as a travel guide with entirely new maps of the wine zones that suggest scenic routes through the vineyards. Though not as convenient to carry around as a pocket guide, it takes a much more thorough look at the infinite particulars that make Italian wines unique. It focuses in depth on the vineyards, describing the lay of the land and the climate and soil, while providing insights into each zone's winemaking practices and to which producers use them most effectively. For the traveller it also suggests restaurants, hotels, and places of interest to visit along the way.

The book is designed to appeal to both the student of wine and the casual drinker. The text may be read following a north to south geographical sequence through Italy's 20 regions, which have been grouped into six general wine sectors (see the map on page 6). Or it may be referred to intermittently to find out more about a certain region or vineyard area or to get an idea of what to expect from the bottle to be opened at dinner. The Atlas can also be used as a buyer's manual, but only in a general way, since its lasting value as a reference does not permit it to be an up to the minute guide to vintages and prices.

Each region is introduced by an overview of wines and production trends, with notes on the landscapes, history, customs, and foods that give it a special flavour. Then comes information on the vineyards and grape varieties and a survey of the geographical conditions of wine zones shown on the accompanying regional map. The wines of each area within the region are discussed following a geographical order, though when there are many DOC zones to cover, as in Piedmont and Tuscany, paths may cross frequently. The descriptions, which include both praise and critical appraisals, mix fact and opinion in a fashion designed to enlighten without being pedantic. Details of each of the many types of wine produced in the 232 classified zones of Italy are also given. The fine points behind DOC and DOCG convey the technical side of winemaking, but even casual readers might be curious to know how grape varieties and such factors as yields, alcohol strength, acidity, and ageing determine a wine's type and style.

Italy consists of a long, mountainous peninsula extending from the Alps into the Mediterranean, whose many islands within the national boundaries include Sicily and Sardinia, the largest in the sea. The nation is made up of 20 regions subdivided into 94 provinces, each of which produces wine. Since each may also have its own wines and winemaking traditions, it is not easy to generalize about the wines of a single region let alone those of any larger unit. So the division of Italy into six wine sectors in this book is more a matter of editorial convenience than an attempt to show viticultural cohesion within the blocks. Yet, even if the exceptions outweigh the rules, extraregional patterns of winemaking can be detected here and there.

Vineyards are planted throughout Italy, though their distribution varies markedly from region to region. Apulia has 133,000 hectares under vine and produces an average of nearly 12 million hectolitres of wine a year, whereas Valle d'Aosta has 900 hectares of vineyards and makes about 40,000 hectolitres annually. But since the focus is on quality, the emphasis in every region is on zones and producers noted for premium wines, whether classified or not. That is why Piedmont, Tuscany, Friuli-Venezia Giulia, and Trentino-Alto Adige are paid more attention than some regions that produce considerably more wine. In each region, recommended producers of each important area or individual DOC zone are differentiated by estates, merchants, or cooperatives, each listed with a location. An entry might consist of a mere mention or a brief description of the vineyards, wines, and performances by winemakers who merit special attention.

The maps

The maps vary widely in scope and detail, depending on the complexity of the wine zones in each region or area. The four levels of maps used in the Atlas are as follows:

National maps. The Introduction (pages 1-27) has maps showing the six geographical sectors, the nationwide distribution of DOC zones, average temperatures and rainfall, and major routes.

Sectional maps. These correspond to the six sectors of Italy followed in geographical order in the Atlas. These maps show the broad geography of the sector, with roads, railways, and physical features. They also show regional boundaries thus acting as a key to the regional maps.

Regional maps. Each of the 20 regions has a general map with two inset maps. One shows the region within an outline of Italy and the second the different wine areas within it, which are colour coded to correspond with the geographical wine zones in the text. For example, in Emilia-Romagna there are four such wine zones: Emilia's plains, Emilia's hills, Romagna's plains, and Romagna's hills, each with its own colour.

The regional map shows all DOC/DOCG areas and these are marked by coloured boundaries. Where DOCs overlap, the individual boundaries are outlined in distinct colours and these are also used to underline the DOC/DOCG names. Where possible the names are indicated on the map, but if space doesn't permit, the wine area is given a number in a box and the name is indicated by the side (underlined in the distinct colour). When numbers are used, they are colour coded to correspond with the relevant area on the inset map. This is to help locate DOCs on the map and to relate them to the wine zones discussed in the text.

Some DOC/DOCG appellations consist of a large area with several subzones within it. The borders of subzones are indicated by a dotted line, but where no subzone is indicated then this is used to refer to a proposed DOC. This means a DOC zone has been determined but not officially approved at the time of going to press.

Detailed maps. Italy's most important DOC zones are shown in varying degrees of detail, giving the locations of recommended producers and noted vineyard areas or in some cases individual vineyards (eg Barolo, Barbaresco). To check the precise location of an individual DOC area, you can refer back to the regional map which locates all DOC wine zones within the region's boundaries. Where possible the names of producers, vineyards, and recognized *vini da tavola* are given on detailed maps. But, if space doesn't permit, they are numbered on the map and listed in a north to south order. The suggested wine routes shown on maps lead through vineyard areas of special interest.

As a key to reading the regional and detailed maps, names of physical or geographical points (eg towns, mountains, rivers) are in black type and wine data (eg producers, noted vineyards, recognized *vini da tavola*) are in red. In addition, different type styles are used to distinguish between wine producers and noted vineyard areas on the detailed maps.

All the boundaries for DOC/DOCG areas have been compiled from the most authoritative and up-to-date information available. Each map (except for those in the introductory pages) is enclosed by a lettered and numbered grid. Important points on the maps (towns, producers, DOC/DOCGs) have a grid reference so they can be easily located. These grid references are listed in the index and gazetteer.

Laws and Labels

Italy has been making wine laws since Roman times, but they have not always been conscientiously heeded. Through much of this century norms were ignored as Italian wines of questionable pedigree reached the world's markets. Responsible producers had strived for decades to protect their wines' authenticity, but not until 1963 when the *denominazione di origine controllata* laws were pushed through the Italian Parliament did things begin to improve. Modelled after the French *appellation contrôlée* that had taken effect in the 1930s, DOC brought a new sense of purpose to a wayward industry and has been the key to the improved status of Italian wine.

But the system has been under seige almost from the start. The laws were composed before modern concepts of winemaking prevailed in Italy, so the traditions they respect are too often backward and the mentality behind production too often favours quantity over quality, or popularity over excellence. There are now 232 DOC or DOCG (the "G" for guaranteed) zones. Yet they represent a mere 10-12 percent of Italy's total – a far lower proportion than in other European countries under the category of VQPRD (for quality wine produced in determined regions).

DOC performances in Italy are uneven. For instance, Trentino-Alto Adige classifies about 55 percent of its production, while Campania designates 0.5 percent of its total as DOC. Nearly everyone agrees that the laws need changing. Some say they're too restrictive, preventing progress from within, others that they're too loose in controlling quality, which in some zones is as variable as price. Another complaint is that there are too many small DOCs. The lack of broad-based identities has prevented such prestigious regions as Tuscany, Piedmont, or Friuli from making the sort of impact abroad that led to the early success of Bordeaux, Burgundy, or Alsace. But, whatever the reasons, Italy has failed to create a comprehensible and credible system of controls. For what is often neglected in the domestic quarrels over DOC is that its real purpose is to guide consumers worldwide towards wines they can identify and trust.

The Italian government, under pressure from internal interest groups and its EEC partners, has vowed to reform the DOC laws as part of a national program to bring other categories of wine into line with European standards. The mandate is to raise DOC/DOCG production to 20 percent, while building up the new group of *vini tipici* to account for another 40 percent of the total. Unclassified table wines, or *vini da tavola*, make up the theoretical remaining 40 percent. But roughly a fifth of Italian wine is distilled into industrial alcohol under EEC programs. Also production of blending wines and concentrated musts remains active in a country that does not permit the use of sugar to raise alcohol levels. So only a part of the wine that represents the lower end of the scale actually ends up on Italian tables. Among that which does is table wine with a geographical indication, a loose category that takes in an array of ordinary types along with some of the gems of Italian viticulture.

Production of all wine, whether DOC or not, is governed by national, regional, and provincial authorities in compliance with EEC policies. Any wine exported, whatever its category, must be certified by chemical analysis and, if bottled, its label must meet the standards of the importing nation. The legal steps involved from planting vines (only those approved by the province) to making wine and selling it have become increasingly burdensome to producers – in part because of stricter law enforcement after the methanol scandal of 1986. The approach of the single European market in 1992 has further confused matters as new EEC regulations come into effect. By 1990, in the midst of a rapidly changing scene, the following categories have been created,

moving up the ladder from unclassified table wine to DOCG.

Vini da tavola

This applies to table wines of any provenance. If bottled, labels may not cite grape variety, vintage, or geographical names. Much wine sold for blending is included, as is most of that distilled into industrial alcohol. In general, a wine labelled simply *vino da tavola* with no other reference is not to be trusted, though there are some exceptions.

Vini da tavola con indicazione geografica

The category differentiates wines made in designated areas from generic *vini da tavola*. The territories may cover a region, province, commune, or even part of a commune, or an area such as a range of hills or a river valley. Labels, which may state the vintage, give the place name with colour or grape variety and type (*frizzante, amabile, novello* etc.). Most *vini da tavola* (abbreviated as vdt) cited in the Atlas have a geographical indication. Authenticity and typology are not controlled, but the category takes in many of the new-style single vineyard wines of Tuscany and other regions that are backed by their producers' reputations – in a sense the highest recommendation possible. Many wines in this category are destined to become *vini tipici*.

Vini tipici

The Italian equivalent to the French *vin de pays* and German *Landweine* was initiated in 1989 after years of delay. The category of *vini tipici* will be created by identifying some of the geographical table wines described above with a distinct typology – not as being typical in the sense of run of the mill. Norms, to be determined individually (no wines had qualified at the time of writing), will be less specific and demanding than for DOC. Like *vins de pays*, they might qualify under the European category of VDQS (for *vini di qualità superiore*). However, some critics fear that *vini tipici* could become a catch all for hundreds of diverse wines, rather than representing whole regions or provinces like their French and German counterparts. An extended new list of wine names might further confuse consumers already daunted by the numbers of DOC.

Denominazione di origine controllata (DOC)

The essential classification, in effect since 1966, applies to wines from prescribed grape varieties grown in approved vineyards within clearly defined geographical zones that may vary in scope from an entire region or province to the confines of a commune or a place within it. By early 1990 there were 232 DOC zones (including the six DOCGs), though the numbers depend on how they are calculated, since, for example, Valle d'Aosta, though it has 18 wines in its regional appellation, has been counted as one, as has Chianti, which has seven subdistricts. More than 850 types of wine are covered by the various appellations, though, again, the figures depend on how they are counted, or on how nuances are interpreted. Some zones are divided between Classico (a historical area) and the rest or into subzones determined along other lines. Details of each DOC are worked out by growers and producers who may form a voluntary consortium. The candidacy, if approved by the local Chamber of Commerce (which eventually supervises control) and regional officials is presented to the national DOC committee appointed by the Ministry of Agriculture. If approved, the production code is confirmed by presidential decree and published as an addition to the original DOC law.

Some DOC zones produce only one wine, but others have multiple types that may be defined by colour or grape variety or by such descriptive terms as *spumante* (sparkling), *frizzante* (fizzy), *liquoroso* (fortified or naturally strong), or *passito* (from semidried grapes), among many alternatives. Rules for each type prescribe which grape or grapes are used and in what percentages, while setting maximum permitted yields in both grapes and wine. (The limits, however, may be exceeded by as much as 20 percent in what are referred to as "exceptional years"). In some cases the method of vinification is specified as is length of ageing, sometimes in wood, for wines that qualify as *vecchio* or *riserva* after a set period of months or years. The term *superiore* usually indicates a wine that meets standards of higher alcohol or longer ageing than normal.

Each type of wine must meet standards of appearance, colour, odour, and flavour as controlled by tasting commissions, which became obligatory in 1990. They must also pass chemical analysis for minimum levels of alcohol by volume, total acidity, and net dry extract. Some wines have minimum or maximum limits on residual sugars for degrees of sweetness, moving up the scale from the semisweet *abboccato* to *amabile*, to *dolce*, the most frequently used terms among many. These often rather rigid rules favour quality but don't assure it. Many recent changes in individual codes seem aimed more at raising yields or adding new types of wine than at making significant improvements in class.

Despite the profusion of DOCs, those that really count are not so many. Two-thirds of all classified wine comes from 20 zones. At the other end of the scale, some 50 zones report production of less than a third of vineyard potential. Not only are many DOCs obscure or neglected, a few are practically non-existent. Sicily's Moscato di Siracusa is one of several zones that for years has recorded no production. Though it might make sense to abolish the underachievers, no DOC has yet been rescinded.

Denominazione di origine controllata e garantita (DOCG)

By early 1990 six wines of "particular esteem" had been promoted to this top level of DOC, which through rigid controls theoretically guarantees authenticity. They are Barolo and Barbaresco in Piedmont, Brunello di Montalcino, Vino Nobile di Montepulciano, and Chianti in Tuscany, and Albana di Romagna. Several others were approaching recognition, among them Tuscany's Carmignano, Umbria's Orvieto and Torgiano Rosso Riserva, Piedmont's Gattinara and Latium's Frascati. Though DOCG has been perceived as an honour, many producers of Chianti, Vino Nobile, and Albana have been subject to the disgrace of having their wines rejected by tasting commissions which award the coloured strips that go over the capsule or cork. So even if heavily criticized, particularly after the arrival of Albana, DOCG has served the purpose of eliminating inferior wines and thereby raising general quality standards.

Special categories

Certain wines qualify to be labelled with special terms defining their typology under either national or EEC rules.

Vini novelli. Any wine labelled as *novello* (the equivalent of the French *nouveau*) whether DOC, *vino tipico*, or vdt of geographical indication, cannot be sold before November 6 of the year of harvest but must be bottled by December 31. At least 30 percent of the wine must be vinified by carbonic maceration, have a minimum alcohol grade of 11 and contain no more than 10 grams per litre residual sugar.

Vini spumanti. Sparkling wine that meets basic standards of alcohol content and pressure is entitled to be labelled simply *vino spumante*. Higher standards, including six months minimum ageing for tank method and nine months for bottle fermented wines, are set for *vino spumante di qualità* and *DOC spumante*, which qualifies for the initials VSQPRD. In these categories degrees of sweetness are defined from the driest to the sweetest depending on residual sugars, as extra brut, brut, extra dry, *secco* or *asciutto*, *abboccato*, and *dolce*.

Vini frizzanti. Lightly bubbly wines are usually labelled as *frizzante*,

meaning that they meet certain standards which the Italians have been campaigning to have recognized through the EEC.

Labelling of all wines, DOC and otherwise, is restricted to pertinent data in which the wording and in some cases even the size of the type is controlled. Required on all labels are the wine name and category (DOC, *vino da tavola di Toscana*, *vino spumante di qualità*, etc.); the producer or bottler's name and commune of bottling; quantity of wine contained (a standard 750 ml bottle must carry the letter **e**); and the alcohol grade by volume. Labels may also carry a vintage date (obligatory for most DOCG and many DOC wines, but not permitted on ordinary vdt), plus a trademark, coat of arms, and consortium seal. DOC and DOCG wines sometimes give the number of bottles produced. Other information may be given on the back labels or attached cards or scrolls, but this should be verifiable and cannot include such terms as *riserva*, *speciale*, *superiore*, etc., unless the wine qualifies for them under DOC or DOCG.

Wine exported outside the EEC must state "Product of Italy" on the bottle and, if destined for the United States, the type (red table wine, etc.) and the official INE red export seal, as well as that country's unique warnings about health.

Abbreviations

Abbreviations for terms frequently used in the text include the following:

DOC/DOCG	Denominazione di origine controllata, and garantita, the essential classifications of wine of controlled, and guaranteed, authenticity.
Vdt	Vino da tavola, table wine, usually with a geographical reference.
CS	Cantina Sociale, or cooperative cellar, also abbreviated in Alto Adige as K for Kellereigenossenschaft in German.
Alc	Alcohol by volume (ie Alc 12) as minimum grade permitted for DOC wines.
Res sugar	Residual sugar in sweet wines under DOC, expressed either in percentage of volume (res sugar 4%) or in grams per litre (res sugar 40 gr/l).
Acd	Acidity, expressed in total or fixed acids by units per hundred (ie Acd 0.5) as minimum for DOC wines.
Ag	Ageing required (ie Ag 3 yrs) for DOC wines.
Yld	Yield, expressed as the maximum permitted per hectare both in volume of wine in hectolitres and weight of grapes in quintals (100 kilograms) under DOC. For example, Yld 70/100 means that 70 hectolitres of wine could come from a maximum of 100 quintals of grapes, the equivalent of 9,333 standard bottles or 777 cases. Permitted yields run as high as 140/200 and as low as 28/40.

Measures

The metric system is used in the text. To aid readers who are still more familiar with traditional systems in the UK and US, here are some basic metric measures (with abbreviations) and their equivalents.

Length:	
Kilometre (km)	0.621 mile (1 mile = 1.609 km)
Metre (m)	3.281 feet or 39.37 inches
Centimetre (cm)	(1/100 of a metre)
Millimetre (mm)	(1/1000 of a metre)
Area:	
Square kilometre	0.386 square mile
Hectare (ha)	(10,000 square metres) 2.471 acres
Weight:	
Metric Ton	(1,000 kilograms) 1.016 UK long tons or 1.102 US short tons
Quintal	(100 kilograms) 220.46 pounds
Kilogram (kg)	(1,000 grams) 2.2046 pounds
Gram (g)	0.03527 ounces (1 ounce = 28.349 grams)
Liquid Capacity:	
Hectolitre (hl)	(100 litres)
Litre (l)	1.76 UK pints or 1.057 US quarts (1 imperial gallon = 4.546 litres, 1 US gallon = 3.785 litres)
Centilitre (cl)	(1/100 of a litre) 0.338 fluid ounces
Millilitre (ml)	(1/1,000 of a litre) 0.0338 fluid ounces

The Contemporary Scene

Over the last 25 years Italy's vineyards and cellars have undergone the most radical transformation ever recorded by a single nation's wine industry. Steady progress has been made with new style premium wines, both red and white, as well as with light and bubbly types for popular consumption. But, perhaps more important in the long run is the improved class and style of traditional wines. Still, Italy has only begun to realize its potential for quality. For the fact that the country makes so much wine in such variety from so many different growers and producers has in some ways hindered planning and progress.

Italy surpassed France as the world's largest producer in the 1960s and maintains the position, though surpluses make leadership a dubious distinction. The country ranks third in vineyard area after Spain and the Soviet Union, but, as in France, wine production has been increased by raising vine yields. In the late 1960s and 1970s, the EEC financed vast plantings of vines, especially in southern Italy where income was needed. But declining wine consumption led to surpluses that have been soaked up through distillation. Today farmers are paid premiums to uproot vines on fertile, flat land that had always been better suited to other crops anyway. The folly of European wine policy has gone full circle.

The fortunes of Italian wine on world markets have followed mercurial patterns. Production rose steadily in the 1970s as exports spiralled and analysts predicted growing consumption worldwide. From an average of 70 million hectolitres in the late 1960s, output reached a peak of 86.5 million hectolitres in 1980. Exports rose from about 2 million hectolitres in 1965 to a high of 19.4 million hectolitres in 1982. Some two-thirds of the wine shipped abroad was in bulk for blending, mainly to France and Germany.

By the mid-1980s supply had far exceeded demand in Italy, as wine consumption declined from 110 litres per capita annually in 1966-70 to 90 litres in 1976-80 to what is now calculated at less than 70 litres. Meanwhile, markets have failed to grow as expected in Europe and North America. To make matters worse for the Italians, competition has increased, as wines from the Americas, Australia and New Zealand, and Eastern Europe claim space on the world's shelves. In most years Italy has exported more wine than France, but earnings have been less than half the price per litre of the French. The methanol scandal of 1986 caused exports to drop back to levels of the mid-1970s. But in the late 1980s they rose again, both in quantity and value. Meanwhile, the 1988 and 1989 harvests have averaged just over 60 million hectolitres, a decline that has eased the pinch as Italy and the EEC work on programs to stabilize production.

Distillation in the 1980s has claimed as much as a quarter of total output – a far greater share than in France and other countries. In some years Italy has distilled more than twice as much wine as it classified as DOC/DOCG. Since only 10-12 percent of production is classified, most wine in Italy is sold in the anonymous category of *vino da tavola*. But much of the wine isn't consumed directly. Besides distillation, many cellars, especially in Apulia and Sicily, specialize in blending wines for export. Another active market is in concentrated musts to raise alcohol levels in Italy, where the use of sugar isn't permitted as it is in most other EEC countries. Many producers in northern and central Italy consider sugar a more refined solution than musts which can alter a wine's character. Yet those who use sugar face the prospect of jail for a practice that is routine in the making of fine French and German wines. This is just one of the discrepancies of EEC policy that needs to be clarified.

Italy's mandate is to raise DOC/DOCG to 20 percent of total output, while building the new category of *vini tipici* (similar to France's *vin de pays*) to account for another 40 percent, though many observers doubted that these quotas could be met. The quality oriented segment of the Italian wine industry has been hindered by a fragmented production base on the one hand and uncertain consumer trends on the other. The country has an estimated 1,200,000 registered vineyards covering about 1 million hectares (an average of 0.83 hectares compared with 4.4 hectares in France). Some 340,000 cellars produce wine, of which about 50,000 bottle and sell it. Cooperatives make about two thirds of Italy's wine, though a good share of production is sold to private firms for bottling under their labels.

Statistics on wine production in Italy are only indicative, however, since many small producers don't file reports as required and direct sales to consumers go unrecorded. Only about 11,000 estates or growers are estimated to bottle and sell their own wine, or about 15 percent of the total. More than 700,000 growers work less than half a hectare of vines, so many are at best amateur winemakers with little knowledge or interest in quality. A majority of consumers seem equally indiscriminate. Surveys indicate that fewer than 15 percent of Italians regularly buy wine in bottles with corks and that many believe they are better assured of authenticity from demijohns than from labelled bottles. This lack of trust has hindered development of quality wine in many parts of Italy, where producers are unable to build the essential base of a strong local market.

Among Italian wines that have built a reputation, the most respected abroad are noble reds, exemplified by Barolo, Barbaresco, Brunello and reserve Chianti. But markets for aged red wines have been confined to connoisseurs, as production has shifted towards brighter, better balanced, more immediate reds and, even more noticeably, towards fresher, fruitier, more fragrant whites. The home market's craving for the light, crisp and bubbly has misled foreigners who seek more pronounced character in whites than they had been getting from Soave, Frascati, Verdicchio or Orvieto. But models of depth and personality have come forth recently to dispel the myth that Italy can't produce world class dry white wines.

Two fast-growing fields in Italy are dry sparkling wines and *vini novelli* (usually red, as in Beaujolais Nouveau). Most sparkling wine is made in the north, in the Tre Venezie, Lombardy and Piedmont, which also specialize in the bottle-fermented *metodo classico* types. The main centres of *vini novelli* are Tuscany and the Tre Venezie. Emilia-Romagna is a major producer of lightly bubbly wines, both red Lambrusco and whites, though by now *frizzante* and *vivace* are popular everywhere.

Italy's vast heritage of vines connotes both benefits and burdens. It permits the country to produce a greater range of distinctive wines than any other. The curious could spend a lifetime exploring the nation's vineyards and still not experience everything. But to the casual consumer the scope is staggering. Economic problems have slowed the pace, forcing winemakers to invest more prudently and respond more decisively to world markets. But the crisis hasn't dulled the vaunted Italian sense of individuality or spirit of adventure. The choices between native or foreign vines and traditional or avant-garde methods give winemakers in Italy more options than the others. Their challenge is to convey the assets of this infinite variety to a world of increasingly standardized tastes.

DOC areas
International boundary
Regional boundary
Regional capital

AOSTA

TRENTO

MILANO

TRIESTE

TORINO

VENEZIA

GENOVA

BOLOGNA

SAN MARINO

FIRENZE

Mar Ligure

ANCONA

Mar Adriatico

PERUGIA

Elba

L'AQUILA

ROMA

CAMPOBASSO

Sardegna

BARI

NAPOLI

Ischia

POTENZA

Capri

Mar Tirreno

CAGLIARI

CATANZARO

Isole Eolie o Lipari

PALERMO

Sicilia

Mar Ionio

N

1 : 5,250,000

Km 0   50   100   150   200
Miles 0   25   50   75   100

Pantelleria

Regional Wine Production

The Northwest

VALLE D'AOSTA

Number of DOCs: **1**
Total vineyard area: **926 ha**
DOC vineyard area: **73 ha**
Annual wine production: **39,500 hl**
Total DOC annual wine production: **2,500 hl**
Individual DOC annual wine production: Valle d'Aosta 2,500*.
*Based on early vintages for the regional DOC that incorporated the earlier Donnaz and Enfer d'Arvier.

PIEDMONT

Number of DOC/DOCGs: **37**
Total vineyard area: **70,460 ha**
DOC/DOCG vineyard area: **34,930 ha**
Annual wine production: **4,060,000 hl**
Total DOC/DOCG annual wine production: **1,050,000 hl**
Individual DOC/DOCG annual wine production: Barbaresco (DOCG) 20,000, Barbera d'Alba 40,000, Barbera d'Asti 120,000, Barbera del Monferrato 82,000, Barolo (DOCG) 45,000, Boca 300, Brachetto d'Acqui 1,700, Bramaterra 900, Caluso/Erbaluce and Passito 4,000, Carema 800, Colli Tortonesi 13,000, Cortese dell'Alto Monferrato 9,000, Dolcetto d'Acqui 8,000, Dolcetto d'Alba 48,000, Dolcetto d'Asti 6,000, Dolcetto delle Langhe Monregalesi 200, Dolcetto di Diano d'Alba 6,000, Dolcetto di Dogliani 12,000, Dolcetto di Ovada 17,000, Fara 900, Freisa d'Asti 5,000, Freisa di Chieri 500, Gabiano 200, Gattinara 4,000, Gavi 40,000, Ghemme 1,500, Grignolino d'Asti 14,000, Grignolino del Monferrato Casalese 9,000, Lessona 300, Malvasia di Casorzo d'Asti 1,300, Malvasia di Castelnuovo Don Bosco 1,600, Moscato d'Asti/Asti Spumante 520,000, Nebbiolo d'Alba 12,000, Roero/Arneis di Roero 5,000*, Rubino di Cantavenna 400, Ruchè di Castagnole Monferrato –, Sizzano 400.
*Roero production does not include the recently approved Arneis.

LIGURIA

Number of DOCs: **4**
Total vineyard area: **6,305 ha**
DOC vineyard area: **288 ha**
Annual wine production: **330,000 hl**
Total DOC annual wine production: **7,000 hl**
Individual DOC annual wine production: Cinqueterre 4,500, Colli di Luni –, Riviera Ligure di Ponente –, Rossese di Dolceacqua 2,500.

LOMBARDY

Number of DOCs: **13**
Total vineyard area: **30,392 ha**
DOC vineyard area: **12,888 ha**
Annual wine production: **2,070,000 hl**
Total DOC annual wine production: **388,000 hl**
Individual DOC annual wine production: Botticino 1,000, Capriano del Colle 1,000, Cellatica 1,500, Colli Morenici Mantovani del Garda 3,500, Franciacorta 34,000, Lambrusco Mantovano –, Lugana 19,000*, Oltrepò Pavese 260,000, Riviera del Garda Bresciano 15,000, San Colombano al Lambro 1,500, Tocai di San Martino della Battaglia 4,000*, Valcalepio 2,500, Valtellina 45,000.
*Excludes wine produced in the Veneto's province of Verona.

The Northeast

TRENTINO-ALTO ADIGE

Number of DOCs: **12**
Total vineyard area: **13,850 ha**
DOC vineyard area: **10,590 ha**
Annual wine production: **1,350,000 hl**

Total DOC annual wine production: **735,000 hl**
Individual DOC annual wine production: Alto Adige/Südtiroler 160,000, Caldaro/Kalterersee 215,000, Casteller 65,000, Colli di Bolzano/Bozner Leiten 3,000, Meranese di Collina/Meraner Hügel 11,000, Santa Maddalena/St. Magdalener 30,000, Sorni 2,000, Teroldego Rotaliano 22,000, Terlano/Terlaner 11,000, Trentino 115,000, Valdadige/Etschtaler 92,000*, Valle Isarco/Eisacktaler 9,000.
*Excludes production of Valdadige from the Veneto's province of Verona.

THE VENETO

Number of DOCs: **13**
Total vineyard area: **90,680 ha**
DOC vineyard area: **33,800 ha**
Annual wine production: **9,000,000 hl**
Total DOC annual wine production: **1,700,000 hl**
Individual DOC annual wine production: Bardolino 210,000, Bianco di Custoza 65,000, Breganze 25,000, Colli Berici 47,000, Colli Euganei 32,000, Gambellara 55,000, Lessini Durello –, Lison-Pramaggiore 55,000*, Lugana 6,000**, Montello e Colli Asolani 8,000, Piave 135,000, Prosecco di Conegliano-Valdobbiadene 140,000, Soave 500,000, Tocai di San Martino della Battaglia 100**, Valdadige 52,000**, Valpolicella (Recioto della Valpolicella/Amarone) 370,000.
*Excludes Lison-Pramaggiore DOC produced in Friuli-Venezia Giulia.
**Lugana and Tocai di San Martino della Battaglia are centred in Lombardy; Valdadige in Trentino-Alto Adige. Figures are for production in Verona province only.

FRIULI-VENEZIA GIULIA

Number of DOCs: **7**
Total vineyard area: **21,026 ha**
DOC vineyard area: **11,800 ha**
Annual wine production: **1,120,000 hl**
Total DOC annual wine production: **433,000 hl**
Individual DOC annual wine production: Aquileia 25,000, Carso 700, Colli Orientali del Friuli 70,000, Collio 80,000, Grave del Friuli 190,000, Isonzo 54,000, Latisana 9,000, Lison-Pramaggiore 4,300*.
*For the part of the Lison-Pramaggiore zone, centred in the Veneto, that extends into Friuli.

Adriatic Apennines

EMILIA-ROMAGNA

Number of DOC/DOCGs: **15**
Total vineyard area: **76,250 ha**
DOC/DOCG vineyard area: **26,070 ha**
Annual wine production: **8,635,000 hl**
Total DOC/DOCG annual wine production: **711,000 hl**
Individual DOC/DOCG annual wine production: Albana di Romagna (DOCG) 35,000, Bianco di Scandiano 8,000, Bosco Eliceo –, Cagnina di Romagna –, Colli Bolognesi 13,000, Colli di Parma 7,000, Colli Piacentini 95,000, Lambrusco di Sorbara 90,000, Lambrusco Grasparossa di Castelvetro 45,000, Lambrusco Reggiano 195,000, Lambrusco Salamino di Santa Croce 65,000, Montuni del Reno –, Pagadebit di Romagna –, Sangiovese di Romagna 98,000, Trebbiano di Romagna 60,000.

THE MARCHES

Number of DOCs: **10**
Total vineyard area: **31,230 ha**
DOC vineyard area: **9,742 ha**
Annual wine production: **2,386,000 hl**
Total DOC annual wine production: **292,000 hl**
Individual DOC annual wine production: Bianchello del Metauro 18,000, Bianco dei Colli Maceratesi 4,000, Falerio dei Colli Ascolani 10,000, Lacrima di Morro d'Alba 500, Rosso Cònero 21,000, Rosso Piceno 46,000, Sangiovese dei Colli Pesaresi 16,000, Verdicchio dei Castelli di Jesi 160,000, Verdicchio di Matelica 15,000, Vernaccia di Serrapetrona 1,500.

THE ABRUZZI

Number of DOCs: **2**
Total vineyard area: **30,200 ha**
DOC vineyard area: **8,358 ha**
Annual wine production: **4,000,000 hl**
Total DOC annual wine production: **280,000 hl**
Individual DOC annual wine production: Montepulciano d'Abruzzo 196,000, Trebbiano d'Abruzzo 84,000.

MOLISE

Number of DOCs: **2**
Total vineyard area: **9,355 ha**
DOC vineyard area: **106 ha**
Annual wine production: **531,000 hl**
Total DOC annual wine production: **2,830 hl**
Individual DOC annual wine production: Biferno 2,830, Pentro di Isernia 0.

Central Tyrrhenian

TUSCANY

Number of DOC/DOCGs: **23**
Total vineyard area: **86,787 ha**
DOC/DOCG vineyard area: **29,022 ha**
Annual wine production: **3,895,000 hl**
Total DOC/DOCG annual wine production: **1,200,000 hl**
Individual DOC/DOCG annual wine production: Bianco della Valdinievole 2,000, Bianco dell'Empolese –, Bianco di Pitigliano 30,000, Bianco Pisano di San Torpè 15,000, Bianco Vergine Valdichiana 33,000, Bolgheri 2,500, Brunello di Montalcino (DOCG) 25,000, Candia dei Colli Apuani 500, Carmignano 4,000, Chianti (DOCG) 950,000* (Classico 275,000; Colli Aretini 25,000; Colli Fiorentini 35,000; Colli Senesi 145,000; Colline Pisane 6,000; Montalbano 20,000; Rufina 19,000), Colli di Luni –**, Colline Lucchesi 7,400, Elba 6,000, Montecarlo 9,500, Montescudaio 8,000, Morellino di Scansano 17,000, Moscadello di Montalcino 100, Parrina 3,000, Pomino 4,000, Rosso di Montalcino 13,000, Rosso di Montepulciano –, Val d'Arbia 7,000, Vernaccia di San Gimignano 39,000, Vino Nobile di Montepulciano (DOCG) 24,000.
*Chianti DOCG is the total of the seven zones plus 425,000 hl without a zone name.
**The Colli di Luni zone is centred in Liguria.

UMBRIA

Number of DOCs: **7**
Total vineyard area: **22,220 ha**
DOC vineyard area: **5,335 ha**
Annual wine production: **1,115,000 hl**
Total DOC annual wine production: **164,000 hl**
Individual DOC annual wine production: Colli Altotiberini 6,000, Colli del Trasimeno 20,000, Colli Martani –, Colli Perugini 8,000, Montefalco 5,000, Orvieto 110,000*, Torgiano 15,000.
*Excludes Orvieto DOC made in Latium.

LATIUM

Number of DOCs: **16**
Total vineyard area: **65,625 ha**
DOC vineyard area: **16,550 ha**
Annual wine production: **5,380,000 hl**
Total DOC annual wine production: **532,000 hl**
Individual DOC annual wine production: Aleatico di Gradoli 500, Aprilia 30,000, Bianco Capena 5,000, Cerveteri 25,000, Cesanese del Piglio 5,000, Cesanese di Affile 0, Cesanese di Olevano Romano 2,000, Colli Albani 95,000, Colli Lanuvini 15,000, Cori 2,500, Est! Est!! Est!!! di Montefiascone 22,000, Frascati 195,000, Marino 80,000, Montecompatri-Colonna 4,500, Orvieto 20,000, Velletri 30,000, Zagarolo 500.

Southern Peninsula

APULIA

Number of DOCs: **24**
Total vineyard area: **133,000 ha**
DOC vineyard area: **16,630 ha**
Annual wine production: **11,900,000 hl**
Total DOC annual wine production: **185,000 hl**
Individual DOC annual wine production: Aleatico di Puglia 150, Alezio 1,400, Brindisi 2,000, Cacc'e Mmitte di Lucera 3,500, Castel del Monte 40,000, Copertino 5,000, Gioia del Colle –, Gravina 2,000, Leverano 3,500, Lizzano –, Locorotondo 35,000, Martina Franca 12,000, Matino 1,500, Moscato di Trani 250, Nardò 1,500, Orta Nova 150, Ostuni 3,000, Primitivo di Manduria 1,500, Rosso Barletta 1,500, Rosso Canosa 2,000, Rosso di Cerignola 500, Salice Salentino 10,000, San Severo 55,000, Squinzano 4,000.

CAMPANIA

Number of DOCs: **10**
Total vineyard area: **46,843 ha**
DOC vineyard area: **1,117 ha**
Annual wine production: **2,594,000 hl**
Total DOC annual wine production: **14,500 hl**
Individual DOC annual wine production: Aglianico del Taburno –, Capri 300, Cilento –, Falerno del Massico –, Fiano di Avellino 600, Greco di Tufo 4,500, Ischia 800, Solopaca 3,500, Taurasi 1,300, Vesuvio 3,500.

BASILICATA

Number of DOCs: **1**
Total vineyard area: **16,300 ha**
DOC vineyard area: **1,436 ha**
Annual wine production: **452,000 hl**
Total DOC annual wine production: **7,400 hl**
Individual DOC annual wine production: Aglianico del Vulture 7,400.

CALABRIA

Number of DOCs: **8**
Total vineyard area: **31,600 ha**
DOC vineyard area: **3,227 ha**
Annual wine production: **1,146,000 hl**
Total DOC annual wine production: **39,000 hl**
Individual DOC annual wine production: Cirò 29,500, Donnici 100, Greco di Bianco 100, Lamezia 1,700, Melissa 1,400, Pollino 2,000, Sant'Anna di Isola Capo Rizzuto 200, Savuto 4,000.

The Islands

SARDINIA

Number of DOCs: **18**
Total vineyard area: **65,899 ha**
DOC vineyard area: **8,674 ha**
Annual wine production: **2,185,000 hl**
Total DOC annual wine production: **104,000 hl**
Individual DOC annual wine production: Arborea –, Campidano di Terralba 1,000, Cannonau di Sardegna 10,000, Carignano del Sulcis 5,000, Girò di Cagliari 200, Malvasia di Bosa 300, Malvasia di Cagliari 500, Mandrolisai 800, Monica di Cagliari 200, Monica di Sardegna 25,000, Moscato di Cagliari 1,000, Moscato di Sardegna 300, Moscato di Sorso-Sennori 100, Nasco di Cagliari 600, Nuragus di Cagliari 35,000, Vermentino di Gallura 15,000, Vermentino di Sardegna –, Vernaccia di Oristano 9,000.

SICILY

Number of DOCs: **9**
Total vineyard area: **164,500 ha**
DOC vineyard area: **19,543 ha**
Annual wine production: **11,140,000 hl**
Total DOC annual wine production: **257,000 hl**
Individual DOC annual wine production: Alcamo 24,000, Cerasuolo di Vittoria 1,500, Etna 8,000, Faro 50, Malvasia delle Lipari 250, Marsala 220,000, Moscato di Noto 50, Moscato di Pantelleria 3,500, Moscato di Siracusa 0.

(Production figures have not been recorded for some recently approved DOCs.)

Travel Information

Italy's eternal knack for attracting visitors, friend and foe alike, is all the more remarkable when you consider that the country was not, until quite recently, all that easy to reach. Foreigners since the ancient Greeks and before have found the country irresistible, worth the challenge of crossing mountains or seas to get to. Today, of course, getting there is easy. Even the most remote corner of Italy, from the snow covered Alps to the sunny Mediterranean isles, can be reached in hours by land, sea, or air.

Tourism, as the nation's leading industry, focuses on Rome, Florence, and Venice, as well as on the amplitude of seaside settings and the multitude of mountain resorts. Italian food, whether it adheres strictly to the Mediterranean diet or not, is also a major attraction. But perhaps because Italians seem to take both wine and tourism so casually in their stride, they have rarely exploited the obvious affinity the two have for each other. In the past, travellers knew that they could count on a glass or carafe of local wine anywhere in Italy. When combined with a tasty pasta and a charming setting, almost any *vino* seemed palatable. Vinous spontaneity was one of the joys of wandering through the countryside.

But things are no longer so quaint. As visitors are noting, perhaps with mixed feelings, the approach to wine has become more businesslike than it once was in Italy. The rise of smartly bottled wines has reminded managers of restaurants, hotels, and bars not only of their pride in the national beverage but also of the profits that can be made from selling it. Until not long ago it was rare indeed to find a host who offered more than a perfunctory choice between *bianco* or *rosso*, with maybe a nod towards the dozen or so popular brands in bottle gathering dust on a shelf – as a sop to anyone so uppity to refuse his own. But today in places where people who care about wine gather, most waiters, who may also be trained sommeliers, can offer well chosen bottles from their own regions and beyond.

Still, Italians haven't begun to match the coordinated style of wine tourism encountered in France or Germany and raised to enterprising heights by Californians. But the fact that Italy's wine regions aren't always formally organized for touring is no reason to avoid a visit. A good way to start might be to join one of the tours of Italian wine regions sponsored by clubs or travel agencies in other countries. Some even offer biking or hiking trips through the vineyards, and there are no more stimulating ways to get the feel of the wine country. But the experienced traveller with atlas and road maps in hand may well prefer a car as the quickest and most convenient way to get around. Language may seem a problem, but when wine enthusiasts get together that barrier has a way of breaking down. Many winemakers in Italy are pleased to greet visitors and provide tastings and tours either spontaneously or on short notice. Often a phone call from a nearby hotel or restaurant is enough to arrange a visit.

Restaurants and hotels

The restaurants and hotels cited in the Atlas represent a casual choice. Those mentioned are located either in or near wine zones. The listings are by no means complete nor are they intended to replace or upstage existing guides. Restaurants are recommended for quality of food and availability of good wines, as recognized either through direct experience or else by a consensus of published comments about them. Choices were also made with an eye to how well the menu and wine list represent the region. The author does not pretend to have eaten in all restaurants or to have inspected the kitchens, surroundings, and facilities of every establishment.

It is always wise to phone or write in advance to reserve rooms or tables, particularly at weekends or during the height of the tourist season. As for prices, many restaurants and hotels in Italy today are more expensive than they deserve to be by both national and international standards. So don't expect to eat, drink, or sleep like a prince without paying a princely sum. But don't forget that in much of Italy even the common man is accustomed to eating and drinking well at affordable prices. An invitingly simple *trattoria* or *osteria* is often a better bet than a trendy *ristorante*.

Wine shops/Enoteche

Public displays of wine or noted retail wine shops, often known as *enoteche*, are recommended in most regions, though some are much better equipped than others. Each of Piedmont's major wine zones has a special *enoteca*, usually with a restaurant. A well-supplied *enoteca* is often the best place to browse when learning about an area's wines. It can also double as a research centre when wines are available by the glass.

Suggested wine routes

A number of suggested wine routes are noted on the maps in the Atlas, though not all of the itineraries are marked with road signs. As might be expected, Piedmont has the most thorough network of wine routes. The original wine route was Lombardy's Oltrepò Pavese, though the most travelled is probably the Weinstrasse that runs through some of Alto Adige's most scenic vineyards. Also noteworthy are the Chiantigiana route through Chianti Classico south of Florence, the Strada del Vino through the Prosecco zone north of Venice, and the road that winds through the hills of Collio in Friuli-Venezia Giulia. But nearly any route through Italy's vineyards, whether marked or not, will be scenic.

Wine activities

Italians sponsor so many wine activities – tastings, fairs, seminars, local festivals, and international conventions – that it is impossible to keep track of them all. But the one not-to-be-missed gathering of the national wine establishment is Vinitaly, the event held each April in Verona. Nearly all wines of importance have a fraternal order or society of admirers to exalt them, though most activities are by invitation only. Harvest festivals are held in September or October in many Italian wine towns. Space doesn't permit for all such events to be mentioned, but since they are mainly local celebrations, coming upon them by chance only adds to the fun.

	Autostrada
	Main road
	Main railway
	Principal ferry service
⊕	Principal airports
	International boundary
	Regional boundary
■	Regional capital
•	Provincial capital

Aosta

Bolzano

Sondrio
Trento
Belluno
Udine
Varese
Como
Bergamo
Pordenone
Gorizia
Novara
Brescia
Treviso
Vicenza
Trieste
Vercelli
Milano
Verona
Padova
Venezia
Torino
Pavia
Cremona
Rovigo
Asti
Piacenza
Mantova
Alessandria
Ferrara
Cuneo
Parma
Modena
Reggio
nell' Emilia
Bologna
Genova
Ravenna
Savona
Forlì
La Spezia
Massa
Pistoia
Pesaro
Imperia
Lucca
Pisa
Firenze
SAN
MARINO
Ancona
Livorno
Arezzo
Macerata
Piombino
Siena
Perugia
Grosseto
Ascoli Piceno
Elba
Viterbo
Terni
Teramo
Pescara
Rieti
Chieti
L'Aquila
Civitavecchia
ROMA
Frosinone
Isernia
Campobasso
Foggia
Latina
Bari
Caserta
Benevento
Napoli
Avellino
Matera
Potenza
Brindisi
Ischia
Salerno
Capri
Taranto
Lecco

_Mar
Ligure_

_Mar
Adriatico_

_Mar
Tirreno_

Porto
Torres
Olbia
Sassari

Sardegna

Nuoro

Oristano

Cagliari

Cosenza

Catanzaro

_Isole Eolie
o Lipari_

Milazzo
Reggio di
Calabria

_Mar
Ionio_

Trapani
Palermo
Messina

Marzara del
Vallo
Sicilia
Catania
Enna
Caltanissetta
Agrigento
Siracusa
Ragusa

Pantelleria

N

1 : 5,250,000

Km 0   50   100   150   200
Miles 0   25   50   75   100

27

Above: manicured vineyards cover the slopes of Barbaresco in the Langhe hills of southern Piedmont.

The Northwest

The Alps of northwestern Italy form a wall along the border of Switzerland and France that links with the Apennines above the Ligurian Sea in a great arc over the upper basin of the Po. Within the elongated semicircle lies a vast stretch of the Pianura Padana, whose fertile fields support a major share of the nation's agriculture and whose ample water powers the industry centred around Turin and Milan. Vines, which were once festooned onto trees across the plains as they had been since Etruscan times, are now mainly confined to rolling hills within the enclosure or along the often steep valleys of rivers flowing down from the Apennines and the Alps.

The ancient Liguri, who were divided into tribes scattered along the Mediterranean from the Apuan Alps of Tuscany to Marseilles in southern France, also controlled much of the territory north of the Apennines in what are now Piedmont, Lombardy, and Emilia. They might have grown the wild vines of the Apennines that became known as Lambrusco, though their greatest contributions to viticulture came after they learned about winemaking from the Greeks around 600 BC. The Liguri are credited with planting vines using a Greek type of low training along the northern flank of the Apennines. They might have even established the terraced vineyards of the alpine Valtellina before they, like the Etruscans, relinquished their lands to the Celts of Cisalpine Gaul.

Some of Italy's most renowned wine zones lie in the northwest, in Piedmont's Langhe, Monferrato, and Novara-Vercelli hills, and in Lombardy's Oltrepò Pavese, Valtellina, and Franciacorta. The four regions vary to extremes in size and nature, as well as in their peoples' historical attitudes towards vines and wines, yet each, for reasons of its own, seems to have taken an increasingly elitist view of viniculture.

None of the four is a big producer, not even Piedmont, the largest region of mainland Italy. Yet even if it ranks only sixth among the twenty in volume, Turin's region is a giant in stature. Piedmontese have an abiding faith in native vines that finds its highest expression in Barolo and Barbaresco from Nebbiolo grown in the Langhe hills to the south around Alba. Neighbouring Asti has attached its name to the most popular of sweet *spumanti* from Moscato. Dolcetto is a growing favourite among red wines and Gavi from the Cortese grape continues to rise among whites, but the Barbera that dominates in the vast Monferrato hills and elsewhere in the northwest remains the choice of growers for steady productivity. Nebbiolo wines from the Novara-Vercelli hills were once more prized than Alba's, but Gattinara and company have faded in both quantity and prestige.

Lombardy, which is nearly as large as Piedmont and even more industrialized and populous, has steadily reduced vineyards to rank only twelfth among the regions in production. Its choice slopes include some of the most dramatically positioned in the Valtellina, the alpine stronghold of Nebbiolo. But the cosmopolitan Milanese, like other Lombardians, pay little heed to traditional wines or native vines. The region has become a major producer of sparkling wine by the *champenoise* method from Pinot and Chardonnay grown mainly in Franciacorta to the east and in the Oltrepò Pavese to the southwest adjacent to Piedmont. The latter zone, Lombardy's most productive, is also a major source of red wine from Barbera and Bonarda.

The mountain walls of Valle d'Aosta and Liguria have been carved since Roman times or before into terraces that represent some of the most challenging conditions for vines anywhere. Apart from the lack of space, hardship has reduced winemaking in both places to token levels. Liguria

ranks nineteenth among the regions in production and Valle d'Aosta is a distant last in every category except fortitude. For there are few places in Italy or anywhere else where viticulture could be so aptly described as heroic. Although Valle d'Aosta was long a part of Piedmont under the Savoy regime, growers there work mainly with their own vines. Names echo the French dialect spoken in Italy's smallest region: Petit Rouge and Blanc de Morgex, the latter from Europe's highest vineyards near the foot of Mont Blanc. In Genoa's region, remaining *vignaioli* of Cinque-terre's seaside terraces still make some white wine to satisfy tourists in the eastern riviera. But Liguria's strongpoints are the soft red Rossese di Dolceacqua and the distinctive white Vermentino and Pigato from the western riviera.

The weather in the four regions can be as variable as the landscape. Piedmont and Lombardy stretch over mountains and plains, so local climates range from temperate and breezy in the hills to hot and foggy in the lowlands. In winter snow often falls in the hills and normally blankets the mountains. The Alps present the most trying conditions, in the Valtellina where vines are planted on terraces facing south along the Adda river, and in Valle d'Aosta, where they are confined to the narrow gap cut by the Dora Baltea river from Mont Blanc to Piedmont. Coastal Liguria alone has a truly Mediterranean climate for vines to thrive with enviable regularity, but since the Apennines drop directly into the sea at most points, the challenge has always been to find, or create, a place flat enough to plant them.

▪ Wines from vines grown in such diverse conditions vary widely in type, quality, and price. Yet natural elements are not always as important to a wine's success as economic factors. Land values have risen steadily to become too precious for vineyards in many places – in the fertile Po flatlands, for example, or around the expanding cities. Since hill vineyards are for the most part tiny and often hard to work, growing grapes can only be rewarding if wine prices reflect the effort involved. As a rule consumers in this most prosperous part of the country are drinking less but demanding higher quality. Throughout the northwest wine has become less a staple than a luxury.

The result has been new emphasis on quality in vineyards and cellars. Striking examples of change are Franciacorta and Gavi. Twenty years ago those zones were neglected sources of wine but today they rank with the most sophisticated DOCs of Italy. Their producers have proved that even in places with little previously noted aptitude, investments in equipment and knowhow can lead to achievements. But it may be even more reassuring to note the progress in places where the the aptitude has never been doubted. The best example is in the Langhe hills of Piedmont where after an era of transition and doubt Barolo and Barbaresco have reaffirmed their stature not only as the noblest of Italy's red wines but as the most honourably made.

Above: the terraces of Cinqueterre in southeastern Liguria. The dramatic man-made landscape has inspired writers from Petrarch to Lord Byron, but today vineyards are in decline in a zone whose white wine is sold mainly to tourists.

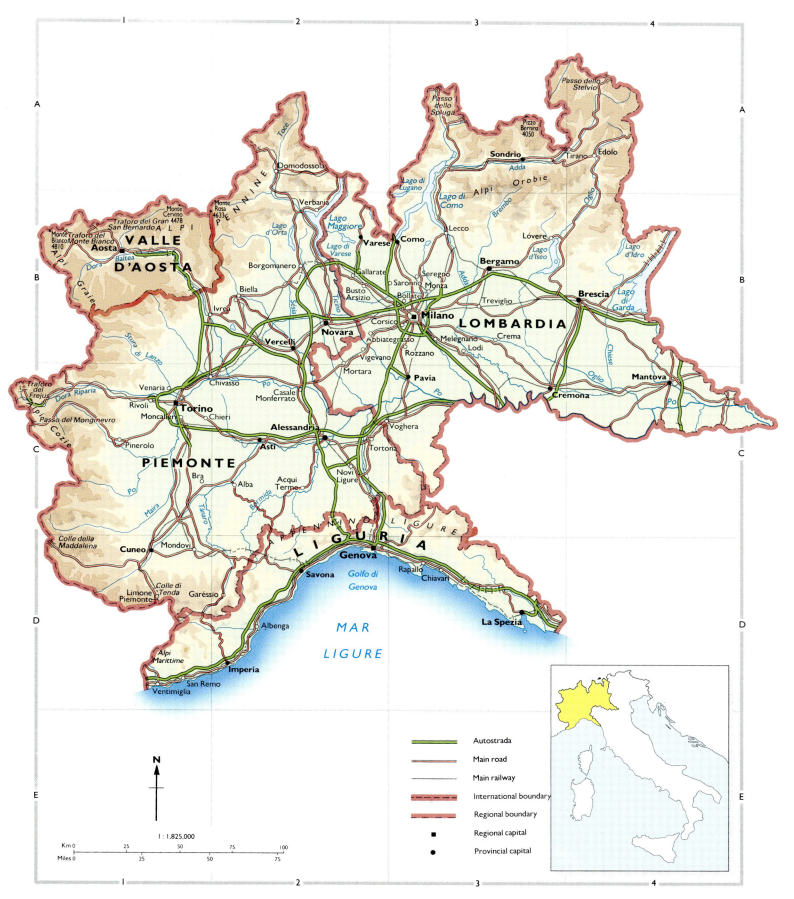

Passo dello Stelvio
Passo dello Spluga
Pizzo Bernina 4050
Sondrio
Tirano
Edolo
Adda
Alpi
Orobie
Oglio
Domodossola
Toce
Lago di Lugano
Lago di Como
Lecco
Lóvere
Lago d'Idro
Verbania
Brembo
Lago d'Orta
Lago Maggiore
Lago di Varese
Varese
Como
Bergamo
Lago d'Iseo
Oglio
Monte Cervino 4478
Traforo del Gran San Bernardo
Monte Rosa 4633
VALLE
Borgomanero
Gallarate
Busto Arsizio
Saronno
Monza
Seregno
Treviglio
Brescia
Lago di Garda
Monte Bianco 4810
Traforo del Monte Bianco
Aosta
D'AOSTA
Biella
Bollate
Milano
LOMBARDIA
Dora Baltea
Ivrea
Sesia
Ticino
Corsico
Crema
Graie
Novara
Abbiategrasso
Melegnano
Lodi
Stura di Lanzo
Vercelli
Vigevano
Rozzano
Chiese
Oglio
Mantova
Venaria
Chivasso
Po
Mortara
Pavia
Cremona
Po
Traforo del Frejus
Dora Riparia
Rivoli
Casale Monferrato
Po
Torino
Moncalieri
Chieri
Alpi Cozie
Passo del Monginevro
Pinerolo
Alessandria
Voghera
Tortona
Asti
PIEMONTE
Bra
Alba
Acqui Terme
Novi Ligure
Po
Bórmida
Maira
Tanaro
APPENNINO LIGURE
Colle della Maddalena
Cuneo
Mondovi
LIGURIA
Genova
Rapallo
Chiavari
Savona
Golfo di Genova
La Spezia
Limone Piemonte
Colle di Tenda
Garéssio
Albenga
MAR
Alpi Marittime
LIGURE
Imperia
San Remo
Ventimiglia

N

Km 0   25   50   75   100
Miles 0   25   50   75

1 : 1,825,000

━━━	Autostrada
━━━	Main road
───	Main railway
━━━	International boundary
━━━	Regional boundary
■	Regional capital
●	Provincial capital

Valle d'Aosta

Capital: Aosta.
Province: Aosta (AO).
Area: 3,262 square kilometres (twentieth).
Population: 113,000 (twentieth).

The Alps with their pinnacles along the borders of France and Switzerland give Italy's smallest region its measure of magnitude. But the mountains so dominate Valle d'Aosta – or Vallée d'Aoste in the provincial French – that human habitation is confined to a few available spaces. Most are found along the valley of the Dora Baltea river, which flows down from its sources in Mont Blanc's glaciers through the city of Aosta and on to Piedmont to join the Po. Nearly all vineyards are planted on slopes and terraces along its 90-kilometre path across the region, but all the wine made from them – about 40,000 hectolitres a year – wouldn't fill the tanks of some large cellars of Asti. The 18 wines covered by the region's comprehensive DOC account for less than 3,000 hectolitres between them, a volume surpassed by some single wineries that in other places might be considered "boutiques". Yet Valle d'Aosta's *vignerons* protect their heritage of vines with gallant perseverance.

To back them the government of this autonomous, bilingual region willingly channels funds into viticultural research and development. Cooperative cellars have been outfitted with the ultimate in equipment, but even producers who go their own ways are encouraged to excel. Most wines come from a dozen vines that are either indigenous or so well acclimatized that they have assumed local names and traits, though even Nebbiolo or Dolcetto from Piedmont or Pinot Noir or Gamay from France show unique features here. Some wines are still quaintly individual, but others have style that could give them wide appeal if they were made in quantity. As it is, supplies don't begin to meet the demands of the local population, let alone the tourists who frequent some of Europe's most popular alpine resorts.

The terraced vineyards of Valle d'Aosta are as treasured a part of the scenery as are the castles that guard the valley's historic access routes or the forests of beech, spruce, and fir that reach to the timberline of the Matterhorn, Monte Rosa, and Gran Paradiso. Along the steep river banks rocks have been piled to form dry walls upon which carved stone columns support wood beams for pergolas that testify to an age-old devotion to viticulture rarely equalled for ardour or for visual effects.

Vines may have been grown here by the Salassi, a prehistoric people who controlled the approaches to the two St. Bernard passes. They were conquered by the Romans, whose colony of Augusta Praetoria became known as Aosta. A winemaking tradition begun in the early Christian era was maintained at monasteries during the dominions of Goths, Franks, Longobards, and the Dukes of Burgundy. The clergy continued to guide winemaking when the region came under the rule of the Savoy in the ninth century and long after as the family ascended to Italy's throne and made Aosta a province of Piedmont. In 1947 Valle d'Aosta became one of five "autonomous" regions with special privileges due to the prominent ethnic group that speaks a Savoyard version of French.

The valley's priests have remained active in wine. The late Abbé Alexandre Bougeat led the drive to revive Blanc de Morgex a couple of decades ago when Europe's highest vineyards were threatened with abandonment. Production of the rare Malvoisie de Nus was for years the handiwork of Don Augusto Pramotton. The Institut Agricole Régional has become the leading influence on modern winemakers under the enlightened guidance of Canon Joseph Vaudan. As a result more young Aostans have made wine a career. Their presence in the vineyards, even if part time, means that clergymen should never again have to fight alone to safeguard the region's heritage of vines and wines.

Valle d'Aosta's Vineyards

A century ago Valle d'Aosta had 3,000 hectares of vineyards but today just over 900 hectares are registered. Curiously, though, current wine production is slightly greater than before phylloxera. This is not because modern grape yields are high (on the contrary the average rate is among northern Italy's lowest), but because in those places where monoculture is possible it has largely replaced the mixed cropping of old. Vineyards are owned by more than 4,000 *vignerons*, most of whom work them part time, since the size of an average plot is the smallest of any region. Training systems have also evolved. The high pergolas used in the past are kept functioning for aesthetic reasons, but new planting is usually in the low pergolas, typical of Morgex, or vertical systems, such as Guyot. Here and there the low head or spur training typical of France is seen.

Even if Valle d'Aosta has much fewer vineyards than other regions, nowhere else are so many varieties grown in such a compact space. The official registry of 22 doesn't list some old vines cultivated by a few growers, nor does it include recent imports that haven't been approved – such as Cabernet Sauvignon, Sauvignon Blanc, and Riesling. Successful outside varieties include Gamay, Pinot Noir, Pinot Gris, Müller Thurgau, and recently Chardonnay. But most vines are native. Some minor varieties are Prié Blanc, Prié Rouge, and the grey-skinned Cornallin and Mayolet, besides the more prominent following varieties.

Blanc de Morgex. The variety, also known as Blanc de Valdigne or de La Salle, is considered indigenous to the upper Aosta valley, though some link it to a vine of the Swiss Valais. It can be grown without rootstock since phylloxera never reached the Morgex area where it has been planted as high as 1,400 metres.

Fumin. A dark variety sometimes used in blends can make an interesting red on its own.

Malvoisie de Nus. This localized clone of Pinot Gris makes rare sweet wines at Nus, where it is known as Malvoisie, though it is not a Malvasia.

Moscato di Chambave/Muscat de Chambave. This clone of white Muscat grown at Chambave makes both sweet and dry whites of character, though Moscato Bianco is also permitted under DOC.

Neyret. Native vine used in blends of Donnaz and Arnad-Montjovet.

Petit Rouge. The worthiest of native dark varieties makes wine of distinctive character in Torrette, Enfer d'Arvier, and Chambave. It may be related to the nearly extinct Rouge de Valais of Switzerland.

Petite Arvine. The variety, apparently the Swiss Arvine, makes a singular pear-scented white called Vin du Conseil.

Picutener/Picotendro. Cultivar of Nebbiolo grown mainly in the southeast for use at Donnaz and Arnad-Montjovet.

Vien de Nus. A native of Nus is used in that town's DOC red and in blends of several others.

Other varieties

For red (or rosé): Dolcetto, Freisa, Gamay, Merlot, Nebbiolo, Pinot Nero, Prié Rouge, Syrah.

For white: Chardonnay, Cornallin, Mayolet, Moscato Bianco, Müller Thurgau, Pinot Bianco, Pinot Grigio, Prié Blanc.

Valle d'Aosta's Wine Zones

Valle d'Aosta is so engulfed in the Alps that the only easy access to the outside world is along the Dora Baltea river into Piedmont. Otherwise there are high mountain passes – the Great St. Bernard into Switzerland and the Little St. Bernard into France – and the long tunnel under Europe's highest peak, the 4,810-metre Mont Blanc. Its glaciers are the source of the Dora Baltea river which crosses the region through a long, narrow valley that supports most of the population and all of their limited sources of wine. Yet despite the scarcity of arable land, some of the steep and often terraced slopes have exceptional conditions for vines in prevalently sandy soils on a glacial base or, lower down, in alluvial sandy clays and gravel.

Winters are cold with ample snowfall in the mountains, but at some points along the valley summer days can be extremely hot and nights relatively cool. Precipitation in the central valley around Aosta is among the lowest in central Europe (500-600 millimetres annually). This apparent anomaly is due to the enclosed position and the effect of the so-called *föhn*, hot Mediterranean currents that lose their moisture before they reach the valley. To the north lie the highest Alps in Mont Blanc, Cervino (the Matterhorn), and Monte Rosa. To the south rises the mass of Gran Paradiso. The Dora Baltea's tributaries form lateral valleys which lead to alpine resorts too high for vines.

The upper valley or Valdigne

The upper valley of the Dora Baltea river between Mont Blanc and the gorge at Runaz has vineyards around Morgex and La Salle which are reputedly the highest of Europe (between 900 and 1,300 metres) where the vines of Blanc de Valdigne trained onto low pergolas make delicately perfumed whites with light, zesty flavours.

The central valley

The unusually dry, hot summer climate of Aosta's central valley between Avise and Saint-Vincent favours reds of some body and finesse from Petit Rouge (Enfer d'Arvier, Torrette, Chambave Rouge), as well as the vaunted sweet wines from Malvoisie de Nus and Muscat de Chambave, though conditions in vineyards at 500-700 metres are well suited to Pinot Noir, Müller Thurgau, Gamay, and other varieties.

The lower valley

The broader valley between Saint-Vincent and Piedmont is noted above all for Nebbiolo in vineyards at 300-400 metres for lean but sometimes attractive red Donnaz and Arnad-Montjovet.

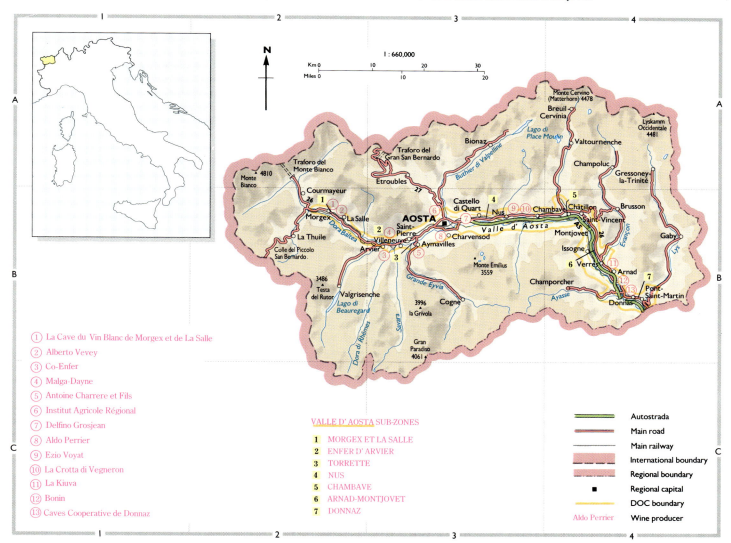

1 La Cave du Vin Blanc de Morgex et de La Salle
2 Alberto Vevey
3 Co-Enfer
4 Malga-Dayne
5 Antoine Charrere et Fils
6 Institut Agricole Régional
7 Delfino Grosjean
8 Aldo Perrier
9 Ezio Voyat
10 La Crotta di Vegneron
11 La Kiuva
12 Bonin
13 Caves Cooperative de Donnaz

VALLE D'AOSTA SUB-ZONES

1 MORGEX ET LA SALLE
2 ENFER D' ARVIER
3 TORRETTE
4 NUS
5 CHAMBAVE
6 ARNAD-MONTJOVET
7 DONNAZ

Autostrada
Main road
Main railway
International boundary
Regional boundary
Regional capital
DOC boundary
Aldo Perrier   Wine producer

Wines of Valle d'Aosta

Aosta's elite wines have a built-in market among citizens and tourists, though visitors often find the unique vine varieties and French names confusing. But at least here, under the nation's first comprehensive regional program, most wines could carry a mark of authenticity as Valle d'Aosta or Vallée d'Aoste DOC. The system potentially covers all wines made from approved grape varieties, while identifying historical types and their vineyard areas. Up till now, winemakers here have seemed content if their bottles reached a few noted restaurants and *enoteche* in northern Italy. But this is merely for prestige, since no qualified producer has problems selling at home. The new DOC seems to offer the possibility of building markets if producers comply in numbers to give the name Valle d'Aosta wider impact. That remains to be seen. In a nation of variegated and often undisciplined wine production, this DOC might become a model of organization for other regions to follow. But it seems more likely to stand as an isolated monument to the advantages of being small.

Valle d'Aosta/Vallée d'Aoste (1986)

(Incorporating the DOCs of Donnaz, 1971, and Enfer d'Arvier, 1972, into a regional appellation that covers 18 categories and seven subzones.)

The regional DOC opened a new era for Aosta's wines, though their modern styles are only gradually becoming evident as producers improve techniques. In theory, practically all of the region's dry wines could be covered under the basic Bianco/Blanc, Rosso/Rouge, and Rosato/Rosé categories, which can be made from any of the 22 approved grape varieties grown throughout the zone. This universal status also applies to the three main imported varieties: Müller Thurgau, Gamay, and Pinot Nero/Pinot Noir, the latter as either red or white and sparkling. Crisp, delicately aromatic Müller Thurgau shows promise here.

Gamay only vaguely resembles Beaujolais, though the hearty Aostan style has found admirers. Pinot Noir as a red shows class from the Institut Agricole Régional and Grosjean, though the wines should not be compared with those of Burgundy.

The crux of the DOC code is the identification of traditional wines and their subzones in the region's three main vineyard areas: the upper, central, and lower valleys. The upper valley, or Valdigne, is the home of Blanc de Morgex et de La Salle, whose name does not have an Italian equivalent, reasonably enough, since this part of the region is French speaking. The fame of this coveted white is due to the height and setting of its vineyards in full view of Mont Blanc, whose mass blocks cold northern currents and influences what at times seems to be an almost Mediterranean microclimate. But frosts are a recurring threat at altitudes over 1,000 m. The wine's pristine fragility can be exquisite when tasted at Morgex or La Salle, or even at nearby Courmayeur, though when sipped in less lofty places this white could be mistaken for a Trebbiano.

The central valley extends from Avise east to Châtillon and takes in four subzones with a mix of dry red wines and rare sweet whites. West of Aosta is the village of Arvier, where steep slopes enclosed by rock walls become so hot that the area's wine is called Enfer (inferno). The microclimate accounted for heavy, thick, rather bitter wines from past vintages, though new techniques may give Enfer some of the finesse of neighbouring Torrette, whose subzone extends east of Aosta as far as Quart. Both wines derive from the admirable Petit Rouge blended with others. Torrette from classical vineyards around Saint-Pierre, Villeneuve, Sarre, and Aymaville tends to be lighter in colour, body, and flavour, though from some producers it develops remarkably deep bouquet with age. East of Aosta lies the village of Nus, known for a rustic red based on the local Vien de Nus and a lightly sweet white which may be Italy's most unusual interpretation of Pinot Grigio, though it is better known as Malvoisie. The preferred version comes from semidried grapes known as *passito* in Italian or *flétri* in French, though the golden wine made for years by the village priests is exceedingly rare. Gradually, though, the cooperative La

Crotta di Vegneron seems to be bringing it back. The nearby village of Chambave has an admirable red based on Petit Rouge and two versions of Moscato, one almost dry of a pale gold colour and the other rather sweet of golden to amber hues. La Crotta di Vegneron also makes them well. Ezio Voyat, the acknowledged master of Chambave, now issues his wines with special names as vdt.

The lower valley between Saint-Vincent and the border of Piedmont is broader and flatter than the others with vineyards in sandy clay soils that favour Nebbiolo in a local clone known as Picutener or Picotendro. The prime wine is Donnaz or Donnas, made in limited quantities from around the town of that name. It tends to be austere when young, mellowing after four or five years of ageing. It is often likened to its Piedmontese neighbour Carema, though it rarely compares in class. The adjacent subzone of Arnad-Montjovet has a Nebbiolo-based red similar to Donnaz in its superior version, though the wine is rarely seen beyond the environs.

Zone: The entire viticultural area of Aosta province in 38 communes along the Dora Baltea valley between Morgex and the border of Piedmont. Vineyards along the river's right bank may range up to 800 m high, along the left bank up to 850 m between Nus and the Piedmontese border, up to 1,000 m between Avise and Quart, and up to 1,300 m at Morgex and La Salle. The seven subzones of Morgex e La Salle, Enfer d'Arvier, Torrette, Nus, Chambave, Arnad-Montjovet, and Donnaz are described below.

Bianco/Blanc Dry white, sometimes vivace. Grapes: approved white varieties. Yld 84/120, Alc 9, Acd 0.5, Ag 6 mths.

Rosso/Rouge Dry red. Grapes: approved red varieties. Yld 84/120, Alc 9.5, Acd 0.5, Ag 6 mths.

Rosato/Rosé Dry rosé. Grapes: as rosso. Yld 84/120, Alc 9.5, Acd 0.5, Ag 6 mths.

Gamay Dry red. Grapes: Gamay; other reds up to 10%. Yld 84/120, Alc 11, Acd 0.5, Ag 6 mths.

Müller Thurgau Dry white. Grapes: Müller Thurgau; other whites up to 10%. Yld 77/110, Alc 10, Acd 0.4, Ag 3 mths.

Pinot Nero (Bianco)/Pinot Noir (Blanc) Dry white. Grapes: Pinot Nero; other reds up to 10%. Yld 59.5/85, Alc 11.5, Acd 0.5, Ag 3 mths.

Pinot Nero (Rosso)/Pinot Noir (Rouge) Dry red. Grapes: Pinot Nero; other reds up to 10%. Yld 59.5/85, Alc 11.5, Acd 0.45, Ag 6 mths.

Left: La Salle in the upper Aosta valley is one of two villages of the Blanc de Morgex et de La Salle appellation. A cooperative cellar has been built in the zone to encourage growers to continue making wine in one of Europe's few phylloxera free vineyard areas.

Morgex et La Salle subzone

Slopes up to 1,300 m in the communes of Morgex and La Salle in the Valdigne, the upper Dora Baltea valley between Mont Blanc and the gorge of Pierre Taillée.

Blanc de Morgex et de La Salle Dry white, often lightly frizzante. Grape: Blanc de Morgex. Yld 63/90, Alc 9, Acd 0.55, Ag 3 mths.

Enfer d'Arvier subzone

Slopes in the commune of Arvier on the right bank of the Dora Baltea river and the localities of Monbet and Bouse on the left bank.

Enfer d'Arvier Dry red. Grapes: Petit Rouge; Dolcetto/Gamay/Neyret/Pinot Nero/Vien de Nus up to 15%. Yld 49/70, Alc 11.5, Acd 0.5, Ag 6 mths.

Torrette subzone

Slopes up to 1,000 m along the left bank of the Dora Baltea river and up to 800 m along the right bank in the communes of Quart, Saint-Christophe, Aosta, Sarre, Saint-Pierre, Charvensod, Gressan, Jovençan, Aymavilles, Villeneuve, and Introd.

Torrette Dry red, either youthful or aged as superiore or supérieur. Grapes: Petit Rouge; Dolcetto/Gamay/Fumin/Neyret/Pinot Nero/Vien de Nus up to 30%. Yld 70/100, Alc 11; superiore 12, Acd 0.45; superiore 0.5, Ag 6 mths; superiore 8 mths in wood.

Nus subzone

Slopes up to 850 m along the left bank of the Dora Baltea river in the communes of Nus, Verrayes, Quart, Saint-Christophe, and Aosta.

Nus Pinot Grigio or **Malvoisie/Pinot Gris** Dry, golden white. Grape: Malvoisie de Nus (Nus Pinot Grigio). Yld 56/80, Alc 12, Acd 0.45, Ag 3 mths.

Nus Pinot Grigio passito or **Malvoisie flétri/Pinot Gris flétri** Lightly sweet wine, copper to amber. Grape: Malvoisie de Nus semidried. Yld 28/80, Alc 16.5 (res sugar 2%), Acd 0.5, Ag 2 yrs.

Nus Rosso/Rouge Dry red. Grapes: Vien de Nus at least 50%, Petit Rouge/Pinot Nero at least 40%. Yld 56/80, Alc 11, Acd 0.55, Ag 6 mths.

Chambave subzone

Slopes up to 750 m on the left bank of the Dora Baltea river and up to 700 m on the right in the communes of Chambave, Saint-Vincent, Pontey, Châtillon, Saint-Denis, Verrayes, and Monjovet.

Chambave Moscato/Muscat Delicately dry, aromatic white. Grape: Moscato di Chambave. Yld 75/100, Alc 11, Acd 0.5, Ag 3 mths.

Chambave Moscato passito/Muscat flétri Sweet wine, golden to amber. Grape: Moscato di Chambave semidried. Yld 35/100, Alc 16.5 (res sugar 3.5%), Acd 0.7, Ag 2 yrs in barrels.

Chambave Rosso/Rouge Dry red. Grapes: Petit Rouge at least 60%, Dolcetto/Gamay/Pinot Nero at least 25%.

Arnad-Montjovet subzone

Slopes up to 700 m in Aosta's lower valley in

Left: vineyards at Chambave are noted for a dry Rouge and two types of Moscato, or Muscat, one sweet and the other nearly dry.

Right: Ezio Voyat in his cellars at Chambave where he produces the classical wines of the town but sells them under individual names. The Passito Le Muraglie from semidried Moscato grapes can be outstanding.

the communes of Arnad, Montjovet, Verrès, Issogne, Challand-Saint-Victor, Hône, and Champdepraz.

Arnad-Montjovet Dry red, either youthful or aged as superiore or supérieur. Grapes: Nebbiolo; Dolcetto/Freisa/Neyret/Pinot Nero/ Vien de Nus up to 30%. Yld 56/80, Alc 11; superiore 12, Acd 0.6; superiore 0.55, Ag 8 mths; superiore 2 yrs.

Donnaz subzone
Slopes up to 700 m on the left bank of the Dora Baltea river in the communes of Donnas, Perloz, Pont-Saint-Martin, and Bard and on the right bank on the rise known as Grand Vert.

Donnaz or **Donnas** Dry red. Grapes: Nebbiolo; Freisa/Neyret/Vien de Nus up to 15%. Yld 49/70, Alc 11.5, Acd 0.55, Ag 2 yrs.

Other wines of note
Most wines of Aosta are still unclassified, though gradually more are coming under DOC. Ezio Voyat sells the classics of Chambave under individual names. The Institut Agricole Régional has recently made promising Chardonnay and Syrah to add to its impressive array of DOC and vdt. A few other vdt of note are mentioned with their producers.

ESTATES/GROWERS

Bonin, Arnad (AO). Arnad-Montjovet and Müller Thurgau DOC.
Antoine Charrère et Fils, Aymavilles (AO). Constantin Charrère makes the long respected red La Sabla vdt based on Petit Rouge and the light red Premetta from the rare vine of that name.
Delfino Grosjean, Quart (AO). Good Torrette and Pinot Noir in *barrique*, along with the unusual vdt Blanc d'Ollignan.
Malga-Daynè, Villeneuve (AO). Marisa Daynè makes promising Torrette and Müller Thurgau from her few vines.
Aldo Perrier, Charvensod (AO). Gamay and other DOC.
Alberto Vevey, Morgex (AO). From various plots above Morgex and La Salle, the late Alberto Vevey's sons make the most admired of the zone's renowned Blanc.
Ezio Voyat, Chambave (AO). Voyat and family make the classic wines of Chambave but sell them with special names: La Gazzella (dry Moscato), Passito Le Muraglie (Moscato passito), and Rosso Le Muraglie (red). The *passito* can be outstanding.

WINE HOUSES

Institut Agricole Régional, Aosta. The school directed for years by Joseph Vaudan leads the region's revival in viticulture while producing admirable wines under oenologist Grato Praz. Vineyards of the Prieuré de Montfleury at Cossan make impressive Pinot Noir and other DOCs, as well as the sprightly Blanc de Cossan, from dark Grenache, and the rich, perfumed Vin du Conseil. That wine, from Petite Arvine, a variety of uncertain origin, is aged in wood to become Aosta's most consistently impressive dry white.

COOPERATIVES

La Kiuva, Arnad (AO). Arnad-Montjovet DOC.
Co-Enfer Arvier, Arvier (AO). Enfer d'Arvier DOC.
La Crotta di Vegneron, Chambave (AO). The cellars directed by Yves Burgay have emerged with an impressive range of DOC from Chambave and Nus and promise of more and better things to come.
Caves Cooperative Donnaz, Donnas (AO). Donnaz and other DOC from growers with 10 ha.
La Cave du Vin Blanc de Morgex et de La Salle, Morgex (AO). The name announces the speciality from growers with 15 ha of vines. Recent improvements in quality should be heightened as the elaborate new cellars financed by the region come into operation.

Travel Information

RESTAURANTS/HOTELS

Cavallo Bianco, 11100 Aosta. Tel (0165)362214. Brothers Paolo and Franco Vai have made this antique post house in the heart of Aosta into a showcase of creative cooking with an inspired selection of wines.
Maison de Filippo, 11013 Entreves de Courmayeur (AO). Tel (0165)89968. The Garin family provides bountiful Aostan food and its own red Torrette in this warmly rustic, if rather touristy, mountain retreat.
Dora, 11026 Pont-Saint-Martin (AO). Tel (0125)82035. An inviting small town inn with good cooking and wines.
Casale, 11020 Saint-Christophe (AO). Tel (0165)541203. Fulvio and Ugo Casale and family offer gracious hospitality and fine regional cooking in this comfortable small hotel near Aosta.

WINE SHOPS/ENOTECHE

La Cave Valdotaine at Aosta and Enoteca La Crotta at Courmayeur have studied choices of wines from the Valle d'Aosta and other regions.

PLACES OF INTEREST

Visiting Valle d'Aosta's vineyards is mainly a matter of following the Dora Baltea river from one end of the valley to the other and stopping wherever strikes your fancy. The vineyards are more accessible from the old road (marked as Route des Vins) than the *autostrada*, which runs from Aosta into Piedmont. Aosta has remnants of its Roman past, though the most imposing reminders of the valley's history are the castles and fortresses at Montjovet, Issogne, Saint-Pierre, Aymaville, and Fénis, among other strategic points. A popular valley resort is Saint-Vincent, with restful parks and a casino near the vineyards of Chambave. Courmayeur is noted for ski runs on the south face of Mont Blanc. Nearby are Europe's highest vineyards at Morgex and La Salle. The lateral valleys also lead to winter resorts, including the fashionable Breuil-Cervinia beneath the Matterhorn. They also lead to remote villages where people speak the curious patois of Savoyard French and country inns serve mountain food of thick soups, smoked and air dried meats and sausages, and the local *fonduta* or fondue based on fontina cheese. Meals may end with a gesture of friendship, the passing of the *grolla*, a hand-carved, covered wooden bowl with spouts from which diners sip coffee "corrected" with grappa.

Piedmont (Piemonte)

Capital: Torino (Turin).
Provinces: Alessandria (AL), Asti (AT), Cuneo (CN), Novara (NO), Torino (TO), Vercelli (VC).
Area: 25,399 square kilometres (second).
Population: 4,395,000 (fifth).

Much of Piedmont, as the name suggests, lies either in the mountains or at their feet, an impression heightened on clear days when the vast arc of the snow-covered Alps and Apennines looms from every vantage point. Turin on the Po commands the region's commerce and industry now as it did for centuries under the Savoy, who joined Piedmont's great statesman Camillo Benso di Cavour in the drive for unity that made them kings of Italy and him its first prime minister. Reminders of the Savoy splendour can be seen in the city's palaces, churches, and museums, and in the cafés where the Torinesi sip their habitual vermouths. But as home to Fiat, Europe's largest car manufacturer, modern Turin has the air of an overextended metropolis that has little time for the past.

Piedmont's proud customs are best preserved in country villages where people still speak Savoyard dialects and where the chill of autumn brings fog with the scents of wood smoke and fermenting wine. That's when white truffles arrive to be shaved over pasta and emit the most beguiling of the earth's odours to mingle with the heady bouquets of Barolo and Barbaresco. Those red wines, like truffles, come from near Alba, from Nebbiolo vines planted in tidy rows on the steep south-facing slopes and rounded crests of the Langhe hills. No other wines of Italy carry themselves with such aplomb, yet Alba's reds are sometimes portrayed as old world aristocrats threatened by the revolutionary zeal that has swept the industry. Cabernet and Chardonnay have arrived on hillsides where Nebbiolo had ritually pre-empted the choicest vineyards, the *sorì*, from Dolcetto and Barbera. The return of foreign varieties to Piedmont has hastened the trend towards new-style table wines, especially white, which are welcomed by producers in need of alternatives. But perhaps the most useful purpose served by the novelties has been to reinforce Piedmontese faith in native vines and a heritage of wine that no other Italians can rival for strength or solidarity.

Piedmont's reaffirmation of leadership with red wines is a tribute to the energy and ideas of a new generation of winemakers who didn't need to abandon their fathers' ways to prove that they could do things better. Barolo and Barbaresco, both distinguished as DOCG, have reached historical heights in the 1980s, due in part to a series of outstanding vintages but maybe even more to the application of techniques that have practically ended the long-standing dispute between the old school of winemaking and the new. Traditional Nebbiolo wines survive, but the concepts behind them have been revised even by those who might deny it. Dolcetto has also improved markedly. Even the omnipresent Barbera has taken on style that had been long hidden behind rustic vigour. Gattinara, Carema, Ghemme, and the other Nebbiolo-based reds of northern Piedmont had been losing ground for years, but lately they have shown at least modest signs of a comeback.

Erudite interest in Alba and Nebbiolo tends to obscure the fact that most of the region's red wines are made from other varieties in the provinces of Asti and Alessandria to the east. Yet, even if 75 percent of Piedmont's total production is red, a majority of the DOC is white. Production of Asti Spumante under the broad appellation of Moscato d'Asti has increased to 520,000 hectolitres a year to rank as the nation's second DOC in volume after Chianti and the world's second sparkling wine after Champagne. Most Asti is made on a large scale by wineries centred in the town of Canelli that export a majority of production. Italians often prefer the gentler, more fragrant Moscato d'Asti made on a small scale, usually by estates. As Italy's major *spumante* producer, Piedmont also makes dry types often based on Pinot and Chardonnay from Lombardy and Trentino-Alto Adige. Some *spumante* houses also make vermouth, for which the Turin houses of Martini & Rossi and Cinzano are world leaders. The rapid rise of Gavi, from Alessandria province, has brought Piedmont new distinction in the unfamiliar field of dry white wine. Arneis from Alba's Roero hills is following a similar course to success.

But Piedmontese still habitually drink red wines through meals. That may explain why they devised so many different types, ranging from soft Dolcetto to austere Barolo, from hearty Barbera to svelt Grignolino to mellow Ruchè, from fizzy dry Freisa to sweet and bubbly Brachetto and Malvasia. Nebbiolo represents a small minority of the region's production. Barbera, which covers nearly half of the vineyards, is the source of most everyday wines, but it also accounts for more than 250,000 hectolitres a year of DOC, much of it under the Asti and Monferrato appellations. Dolcetto in its seven DOCs also surpasses the volume of all Nebbiolo wines combined. Outsiders sometimes find Piedmont's other red wines strange, yet Freisa and Grignolino, which had faded in popularity, seem to be coming back. Even the sweet red Brachetto and Malvasia, which had always been drunk close to home, have found a few followers elsewhere.

The Monferrato and Langhe hills are among the most intensively cultivated vineyard areas of northern Italy, yet overall Piedmont is a moderate wine producer. It ranks sixth among the regions both in vineyard area and volume of wine produced, but third after the Veneto and Tuscany in output of classified wine, which represents about a quarter of its total. Piedmont has more DOC or DOCG zones than any other region – 37 geographical areas with 42 distinct types of wine – though each of the three Venezie has more types covered by the multi-faceted appellations.

What numbers could never describe is wine's role in Piedmontese culture, the sense of history that has not only preserved the native vines but elevated them to new heights. Nowhere is this faith more eloquently expressed than in the Langhe hills and the wines of Nebbiolo. A century ago Gattinara often overshadowed Alba's reds, but today the supremacy of Barolo and Barbaresco in Piedmont is beyond dispute. Their producers feel the competition from Tuscany, from Brunello di Montalcino, the best of Chianti Classico, and the so-called Super Tuscan table wines from Cabernet and Sangiovese. But for collective class the Nebbiolo wines of the Langhe are unrivalled in Italy. Technology has improved them, but their basic strength is tradition, the Piemontese respect for the vine in its time-honoured habitat that is rarely witnessed outside the most privileged vineyard areas of France.

Piedmont's links to France are legendary. Barolo's history as a dry wine began in the mid-nineteenth century when the French oenologist Louis Oudart applied techniques of vinification and barrel ageing to the Nebbiolo previously used for sweet wines. Asti Spumante emerged after 1870 when Carlo Gancia introduced bottle fermentation methods from Champagne. Long before that vines were grown by the Taurini, a Celtic

37

Above: vineyards in the Langhe hills with the Alps in the background.

people who left their name to Turin, and the Liguri, who learned winemaking from the Greeks. The Romans planted vines at Gattinara and noted other wines, but none of Piedmont ranked among their favourites. References to Nebbiolo, Moscato, Dolcetto, and other vines date to the Middle Ages, when the usual succession of bards, minstrels, and papal aides-de-camp passed through and praised the local nectars. But Piedmont didn't achieve real distinction with wine until the nineteenth century when French methods became the rule and the Savoy and other landowners had time to turn their attention to vineyards and cellars. It was then that Barolo became "king of wine and wine of kings".

But in recent times Barolo and Barbaresco have tended to divide the experts between those who found their power and complexity unrivalled and those who found their tannic toughness and unfamiliar flavours hard to swallow. A new school emerged in the 1970s, led by Renato Ratti and sustained by, among others, the Ceretto brothers, whose big but balanced wines were palatable at an early age. Conservatives protested, but the enlightened among them made those few concessions to modernity that further enhanced their styles.

French *barriques* soon arrived at Alba and at nearby Asti where Giacomo Bologna discovered their unexpected virtues in Barbera. But their leading advocate has been Angelo Gaja of Barbaresco, whose genius and drive have made him a messianic figure in the Langhe. He introduced Chardonnay and Cabernet there amidst protests and proved their worth amidst praise and imitation. But Gaja's faith in Nebbiolo never wavered as he pushed his single-vineyard Barbaresco towards the pinnacles of price and prestige while acquiring an estate in Barolo to further his ambitions. His feats have drawn notice in the international

press and helped focus attention on the dramatic improvements in Alba's classic wines realized by progressives and traditionalists alike. Today more than ever Barolo and Barbaresco seem to rate a place among the world's great wines, but as always they stand with their own kind of majesty a few steps apart from the crowd.

Piedmont's Vineyards

The modern quality of Piedmont's wines owes much to old concepts of viticulture, a stubborn preference for native varieties, and a healthy conviction that vineyards belong on hills and not plains. The DOC codes reflect the habit of sensibly restrained yields, which on average are among the lowest of Italy. But the will to preserve a heritage also partly explains why Piedmont's vineyards have decreased by nearly a third in 20 years. An hereditary system that fragments land ownership has reduced most vineyards to less than a hectare on often steep slopes, so few growers can make a living on grapes from one plot alone. Yet they became attached to their parcels of land, referring to them proudly as *sorì* or *sörì* (for sunny), *bricco* or *bric* (for hillcrest), and other dialect terms.

Many different vine training systems have been used in Piedmont over the centuries, varying according to conditions and variety. The early Liguri introduced Greek-style low training to southern areas, but eventually Etruscan festoons over trees found their way here. Still, as the author Pier de' Crescenzi recorded, a Greek method of twisting the vines to halt growth and allow grapes to overripen was used around Asti in the fourteenth century. Short training was also used in northern Piedmont for Nebbiolo, whose synonym there of Spanna apparently referred to vines being trained a hand's span from the ground. Another system that developed around Gattinara was the inverse pyramid known as *quadretti maggiorini*, though by now vertical systems with training on wires prevail. In the Langhe and Monferrato hills the prevalent system is a high arched Guyot that lets grape bunches hang close to the ground. The most colourful exception to modern training methods is Carema's high pergolas supported by round stone columns.

Barbera was prevalent a century ago, as now, though Nebbiolo, Dolcetto, Moscato, Freisa, Bonarda, Grignolino, and Erbaluce were also well noted. Cortese and Arneis, which have gained space lately, were little noticed then. Some Piedmontese seem scandalized by the arrival of foreign vines, yet Cabernet, the Pinots, and other French varieties were widely planted in the mid-nineteenth century. At that time Marchese Leopoldo Incisa della Rocchetta catalogued 374 varieties grown in the Asti area alone, including virtually all important French vines, though he said he had omitted many minor types. Curiously, though, after phylloxera the foreign vines never recovered, or not until recently when Chardonnay has gained ground. Phylloxera struck a crippling blow to such locally appreciated vines as Doux d'Henry, Avanà, Durasa, Averengo, Timorasso, Lambrusca di Alessandria, Plassa, and Carica l'Asino which are still grown but scarcely noticed. The following varieties are prevalently Piedmontese.

Arneis. Reference to this vine native to Alba's Roero date to the fifteenth century as Renesium and later as Ornesio. It was used mainly for sweet wines or for blending with Nebbiolo until its recent revival in a dry white that has attracted enough attention to encourage heavy planting.

Barbera. Several versions exist about the origins of the vine native to Monferrato and planted in nearly half of Piedmont's vineyards, usually for use alone in red wines ranging from robust and aged to light and youthful. One dates to seventh century Longobards, but the first confirmed citation was in 1799. It was known elsewhere as *Vitis vinifera Montisferratensis*. Adaptability and steady productivity have made Barbera a favourite throughout Italy, though away from the northwest it is more often used in blends than varietal wines. There is also a Barbera Bianca.

Bonarda or **Bonarda Piemontese**. True Bonarda, once widely planted, is used mainly in DOC blends with Nebbiolo in the north (where clones are called Novarese and di Gattinara) or on its own in table wines. Confusingly, the Croatina of Lombardy's Oltrepò Pavese and Emilia's Colli Piacentini is often called Bonarda.

Brachetto. Apparently a native of Bellet near Nice in Provence, where it is known as Braquet, Brachetto is planted in the Acqui area where it is coming back as a source of sweet, bubbly red wines.

Cortese. Noted as Curteisa in 1798, this native of Alto Monferrato thrives at Gavi as the source of Piedmont's most prized dry white. It is also grown in the Colli Tortonesi, Lombardy's Oltrepò Pavese, and Verona where it is called Bianca Fernanda.

Dolcetto. The name refers to the sweet grapes of this early ripening variety whose wines were often *amabile* in the past but today are invariably dry and increasingly appreciated. References to origins were noted as early as the sixteenth century and possibly even the fourteenth in Alba's Langhe, though the vine known as "Dosset" was confirmed in the eighteenth century by Conte Nuvolone. Dolcetto has various clones, but local variations in style may be due to soil and climate since, like Nebbiolo, the vine is sensitive to environment. It is known as Ormeasco in Liguria.

Erbaluce. This source of the dry white and golden *passito* wines of Caluso may be of Greek origin. The name refers to the ripe grapes' roseate coppery colour. It has faded recently, due to irregular yields.

Favorita. The vine found mainly in Alba's Roero may be related to Liguria's Vermentino. It makes light, fragile white wines.

Freisa. A prolific variety widely planted in the past, when it was also known as Fresa or Fresia, it supposedly dates to the eighteenth century when *piccola* and *grossa* clones were noted. After fading from vogue, it is enjoying a comeback in usually bubbly wines both dry and sweet that are DOC in Asti and Torino's Chieri and vdt in the Langhe.

Grignolino. A native of Monferrato has been reduced to secondary status, a victim of shy yields. It makes pale, delicate wines oddly out of step among Piedmont's bold reds, but they are so distinctive that growers are determined to maintain it. Origins are obscure, though evidence of a vine known as Barbesino for light red or *chiaretto* was noted in the thirteenth century. The name seems to refer to *grignare* (smile or laugh in dialect).

Malvasia di Schierano/Malvasia di Casorzo. Vigorous dark Malvasia associated with Schierano and Casorzo in Asti's Basso Monferrato are used in sweet reds under Casorzo d'Asti and Castelnuovo Don Bosco DOCs.

Moscato Bianco or **Moscato di Canelli**. Noted in the Asti area in the sixteenth century, or possibly much earlier, this white Moscato came to be associated with Canelli, centre of the *spumante* industry. It is planted mainly in the steep Langhe hills of Asti and Cuneo and the Alto Monferrato around Acqui and Strevi. It was well noted a century ago as the base for aromatic *spumante* and also rich *passito* wines, which have started to come back. It was also an ideal base for vermouth, though now it is considered too expensive.

Nebbiolo. Italy's noblest red wine variety has been grown in Piedmont since at least the thirteenth century when a document at Rivoli mentioned a vine called "Nibiol". But other reference have placed its origins in the Novara hills and there are suggestions that it was already known in Roman times. The name refers to *nebbia*, after the fogs that are normal during its late October harvest. Extremely late ripening and sensitive to environment, it thrives only in certain places, most notably around Alba in Barolo and Barbaresco and the Roero hills, but also in the north between Carema and Gattinara and in Lombardy's Valtellina. Attempts to plant it elsewhere, from Tuscany to Oregon to Australia, have been mostly disappointing. Research on the Alba subvarieties called Lampia, Michet, Rosé, and Bolla have led to the supposition that rather than distinct clones it develops mutations determined by habitat. In northern Piedmont cultivars are known as Picutener or Picotendro (for tender stems), Pugnet (for fist-like bunches), and Spanna. In Valtellina it is called Chiavennasca.

Neretta or **Neretto**. Dark varieties known as Neretta Cuneense, Neretto di Bairo, or simply Neretto, or in Valle d'Aosta Neyret seem to have a common background, though they now play minor roles in wines.

Pelaverga. An ancient vine of Saluzzo, on Cuneo's plain, it is found in the Barolo zone around Verduno where it makes pale ruby wines of sharp flavour.

Ruchè. Origins are uncertain, though the vine is considered a native of Asti's Castagnole Monferrato, where it makes unique red wines also known as Rochè or Rouchet. Cultivation had declined due to sparse yields, but a recent DOC has made Ruchè one of Piedmont's most sought after reds.

Vespolina. The variety, apparently native to the Novara-Vercelli hills, is sometimes used in blends with Nebbiolo DOC reds there. It is also used in Lombardy's Oltrepò Pavese, where it is known as Ughetta.

Other varieties

Other varieties recommended or approved in the region include:

For red (or rosé): Aleatico, Ancellotta, Avanà, Averengo, Cabernet Franc, Cabernet Sauvignon, Croatina, Durasa, Lambrusca di Alessandria, Mèrlot, Moscato Nero, Pinot Nero, Sangiovese, Uva Rara.

For white: Barbera Bianca, Chardonnay, Müller Thurgau, Pinot Bianco, Pinot Grigio, Riesling Italico, Riesling Renano, Sauvignon, Sylvaner Verde, Timorasso, Traminer Aromatico.

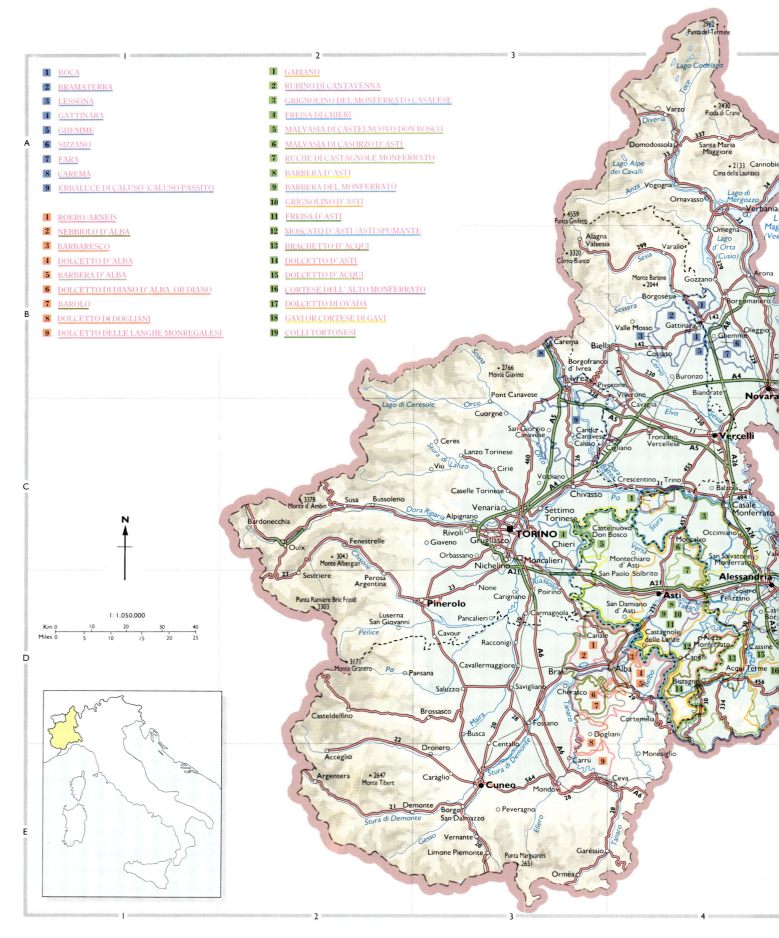

1 BOCA
2 BRAMATERRA
3 LESSONA
4 GATTINARA
5 GHEMME
6 SIZZANO
7 FARA
8 CAREMA
9 ERBALUCE DI CALUSO /CALUSO PASSITO

1 ROERO /ARNEIS
2 NEBBIOLO D' ALBA
3 BARBARESCO
4 DOLCETTO D' ALBA
5 BARBERA D' ALBA
6 DOLCETTO DI DIANO D' ALBA OR DIANO
7 BAROLO
8 DOLCETTO DI DOGLIANI
9 DOLCETTO DELLE LANGHE MONREGALESI

1 GABIANO
2 RUBINO DI CANTAVENNA
3 GRIGNOLINO DEL MONFERRATO CASALESE
4 FREISA DI CHIERI
5 MALVASIA DI CASTELNUOVO DON BOSCO
6 MALVASIA DI CASORZO D' ASTI
7 RUCHE DI CASTAGNOLE MONFERRATO
8 BARBERA D' ASTI
9 BARBERA DEL MONFERRATO
10 GRIGNOLINO D' ASTI
11 FREISA D' ASTI
12 MOSCATO D' ASTI /ASTI SPUMANTE
13 BRACHETTO D' ACQUI
14 DOLCETTO D' ASTI
15 DOLCETTO D' ACQUI
16 CORTESE DELL' ALTO MONFERRATO
17 DOLCETTO DI OVADA
18 GAVI OR CORTESE DI GAVI
19 COLLI TORTONESI

N

1 : 1,050,000

Km 0   10   20   30   40
Miles 0   5   10   15   20   25

Piedmont's Wine Zones

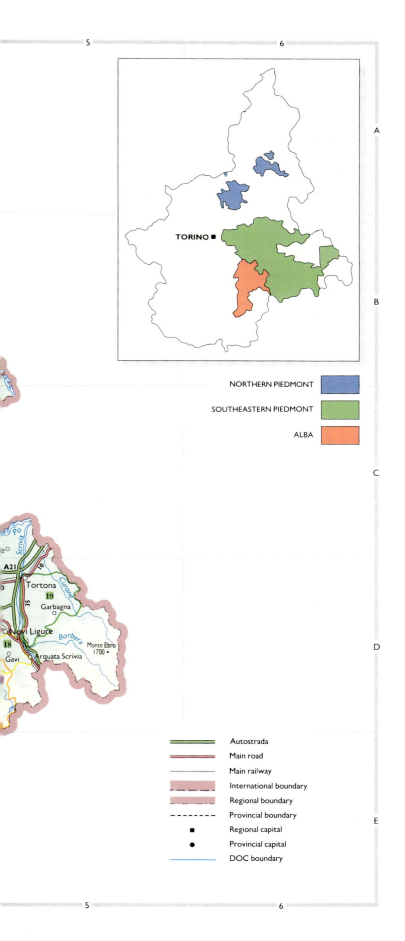

NORTHERN PIEDMONT

SOUTHEASTERN PIEDMONT

ALBA

Autostrada
Main road
Main railway
International boundary
Regional boundary
Provincial boundary
Regional capital
Provincial capital
DOC boundary

Piedmont is the largest region of the Italian mainland, but since 43 percent of its area is mountains and 27 percent plains there is no surplus of space for growers who insist on positioning vineyards on just the right angles of the hills. The walls of the Alps, which form the borders with Switzerland, Valle d'Aosta, and France to the north and west, were sheered by glaciers in a way that left few of those finely sculpted slopes that vines desire. But part of the Apennines, which link with the Maritime Alps to the south, have been eroded by streams into suitably sloping hills along a sort of promontory that juts northwards to the banks of the Po as it curves past Turin and flows eastwards into Lombardy. There the ranges known as Monferrato to the north and east and Langhe to the southwest produce 90 percent of the region's wine under conditions that vary from almost easy to arduous. What is described as a continental climate is in theory cold and damp in winter, when growers want snow, and warm or hot in summer, when they need sunshine, but the weather is whimsical even in autumn when grapes are supposed to ripen slowly in the protective mists. In the past vines were more prominent in the alpine foothills than they are today, as well as in the Po flatlands south of Turin around Saluzzo. But as vineyards diminished, production became concentrated in the Monferrato hills around Asti and Alessandria and the Langhe around Alba and Canelli. Terrains in both ranges are prevalently calcareous, but their elements, like their microclimates, vary in subtle ways. Barbera thrives nearly everywhere, but others – Dolcetto, Grignolino, Moscato, and the temperamental Nebbiolo – have to choose their sites to prosper.

Piedmont's wine zones are clearly divided into two major areas: the alpine foothills to the north and the Monferrato and Langhe hills to the south between the Po and the Apennines. But since the southern hills are so vast and varied they have been further divided into southeastern Piedmont, which covers the provinces of Asti and Alessandria, and Alba which covers the Roero hills and most of the Langhe in Cuneo province.

Northern Piedmont takes in the alpine foothills and glacial basins north of the Po in two sectors: Carema and Canavese along the Dora Baltea river to the west in Torino province and the hills of Vercelli and Novara provinces to the east between Biella and Lake Maggiore, where Nebbiolo-based wines are made in seven DOC zones.

Southeastern Piedmont covers the Monferrato range, extending over much of Asti and Alessandria provinces and into Turin's hills. The Tanaro river divides the range into Basso Monferrato to the north and Alto Monferrato to the southeast. The area, which also includes Asti's share of the Langhe hills, has 19 of the region's 37 DOCs covering a majority of the classified wines in a series of overlapping and interlocking zones. The Moscato d'Asti-Asti Spumante zone, though centred in Asti province, also takes in a share of Alba's Langhe hills. Also included are the Colli Tortonesi, at the border of Lombardy, and the Freisa di Chieri zone of Turin's hills.

Alba is most noted as the centre of Nebbiolo production from a territory divided into two distinct vineyard areas: the Roero hills, which link with the Monferrato range northwest of the Tanaro, and the Langhe hills that extend into the Apennines to the south. Apart from Barolo and Barbaresco, DOCs there also cover Barbera, Dolcetto, and Nebbiolo.

Carema and Canavese

Carema's Nebbiolo vines are planted mainly on terraces where stone columns support cross beams known as *topie*. The crystalline glacial terrain in vineyards between 350-450 metres high renders notably refined and durable wines. The Caluso zone is in the hills of the Canavese glacial basin enclosing the Dora Baltea river between Ivrea and the Po in sandy clays on a gravel base conducive to delicate dry white from Erbaluce and a rich Caluso Passito.

The Vercelli and Novara hills

The northern outpost of Nebbiolo (or Spanna) covers seven DOC zones in the alpine foothills and high plains on either side of the Sesia river north of Vercelli and Novara. The climate is tempered by the play of currents between the Po flatlands and the Alps above lakes Maggiore and Orta. The soils, largely glacial moraine, vary in contents of minerals that can be decisive factors in the quality of wines. West of the Sesia are the Vercelli hills with Lessona, Bramaterra, and Gattinara, whose vineyards are the focal point of production. To the east are the Novara hills with Boca, Ghemme, Sizzano, and Fara, wines that are often lightened by blends with Vespolina and Bonarda, though some Ghemme can rival Gattinara.

Monferrato Casalese

Alessandria's share of Basso Monferrato consists of hills south of the Po in the area of Casale. Sandy calcareous clays are especially noted for fragrant Grignolino, though Barbera in both the Monferrato and Asti appellations also thrives in those soils in both light wines and types suitable for ageing.

Colli Tortonesi

The hills adjacent to Lombardy's Oltrepò Pavese produce mainly Cortese and Barbera which can be light and tasty but rarely distinguished.

Gavi and Ovada

The adjacent DOC zones of Gavi and Ovada lie in the easternmost Monferrato hills where the climate is tempered by breezes crossing the Ligurian Apennines from the Mediterranean. Cortese thrives in Gavi's hills in calcareous clays mixed with tufaceous and siliceous rock and where hot, dry summers are favourable to Piedmont's favourite dry white. Dolcetto is a tradition at Ovada where the arid climate and poor tufaceous soils inhibit yields in wines noted for strength and longevity.

Acqui and Alto Monferrato

Acqui Terme is at the heart of Alto Monferrato, the Apennine foothills of Alessandria province drained by the Bormida river. Barbera is the prime variety there as elsewhere, but vineyards in calcareous soils of the relatively cool hills traditionally supplied Dolcetto, Brachetto for a sweet red, and Moscato of rich texture and restrained aromas, notable around Strevi in *passito* wines.

Asti and Turin's hills

Each of Asti's vines has preferred areas delineated by DOC zones. Barbera is universal, but its prime area for robust wines is south of the Tanaro in hills extending down across the Belbo valley. Basso Monferrato to the north has calcareous terrains where clay is often lightened by sands favourable to Grignolino, dark Malvasia, and the Freisa which also does well at Chieri in Turin's hills. The rare red Ruchè is noted at Castagnole Monferrato. Dolcetto in Asti's Langhe hills rarely matches wines from Alba. Moscato grapes for Asti Spumante are grown in Alto Monferrato as far east as the Bormida valley in Alessandria province, but most vineyards lie around Canelli in the Langhe and to the west towards Alba. The eastern Langhe are high and steep with cool conditions that account for full aromas in Moscato. The southern Monferrato hills are somewhat lower and more gradually sloped with a slightly warmer climate that accounts for richer Moscato wines.

Above: vineyards in the Barolo zone, where Nebbiolo is usually planted on south-facing slopes, or sorì, *and other vines take less privileged positions.*

Alba's Roero

The hills north of the Tanaro have fairly sandy calcareous soils that render Nebbiolo of a lighter, fruitier style than in the Langhe. Wines may be either Nebbiolo d'Alba or the separate DOC of Roero. Conditions are also favourable for Arneis, a rising white variety. Barbera is also prominent around Govone and the commune of Alba.

Alba's Langhe hills

The Langhe hills take in the Barolo zone southwest of Alba and Barbaresco to the east, though the range extends beyond Barolo to cover the Dolcetto zone of Dogliani and Langhe Monregalesi and further east on slopes considered ideal for the gentle Moscato d'Asti. Soils are prevalently marly calcareous clays, though even slight variations in components as well as in microclimates on the steep hillsides can account for telling differences in the wines. These natural phenomena supposedly explain why Barolo from different sides of the zone varies in structure and character, and also why Barolo overall is slightly more robust than Barbaresco. But rules don't always hold. Barbera can do well in the Langhe when planted in favourable positions. The favoured variety for everyday wines is Dolcetto, which thrives in higher, cooler places than Nebbiolo, though its character also varies from place to place. Some Freisa and Grignolino planted here make distinctive table wines.

NORTHERN PIEDMONT

Only a tenth of Piedmont's wine comes from north of the Po, yet the lower flank of the Alps between the Dora Baltea and Sesia river valleys is Nebbiolo's second home after the Langhe and Roero hills of Alba. Northern Nebbiolo differs markedly from Barolo and Barbaresco, in part because the alpine foothills have particular climatic conditions. But perhaps the greatest difference is in soils: the acidic glacial terrains that give Nebbiolo a stamp so distinct from wines of the alkaline calcareous clays and marls of the Langhe. In the north, the Nebbiolo cultivars called Picutener, Pugnet, and Spanna are often blended with other varieties that further alter the wines' personalities. Yet at times in the past the wines of Carema, Ghemme, Lessona, and especially Gattinara were considered rivals to Barolo in quality, longevity, and status. No longer. Production has so declined that many winemakers are involved in an uphill battle to rebuild their wines' prestige. But there are encouraging signs issuing from Gattinara and, on a limited scale, from other places. Northern Piedmont's wine zones are generally divided into two sectors. Towards the west along the Dora Baltea valley in Torino province are Carema and the hilly glacial basin called Canavese, home of the white Erbaluce di Caluso and Caluso Passito. Towards the east in the alpine foothills on either side of the Sesia river in the provinces of Vercelli and Novara are the seven zones that make most of the northern Nebbiolo.

Wines of Carema and Canavese

The prosperous little city of Ivrea lies between Carema to the north and Caluso to the south, towns whose wines were better known in the past than they are today. Carema's terraces on the steep lower face of the Alps provide an annual endurance test for Nebbiolo that can result in wines that are durable and refined, if rare. Caluso lies in the Canavese basin whose northeastern edge is La Serra d'Ivrea, the largest glacial bank in Europe. Vineyards amidst Canavese's gentle hills grow Erbaluce for both a crisp dry white and a lusciously sweet Caluso Passito. Historical citations for both wines date back to the Middle Ages, though vineyards were probably planted in Roman times. But recently viticulture has faded as vineyard owners have taken jobs connected with Ivrea's industries and find little time to devote to vines or wines. Were it not for Luigi Ferrando and a few other producers determined to build on what remains of their heritage, the wines of Carema and Caluso would be even more obscure than they already are.

Carema (1967)

A wine made in minute quantities and rarely sold outside the environs is sometimes lauded as one of Piedmont's grandest reds. But critics who have seen Carema's 40 ha of vineyards divided into about 100 plots might be excused for treating it more kindly than other northern Nebbiolos. On the steep slopes above the town, rocks were piled to form terraces and to reflect the sun's rays onto the vines during the day and hold the heat into the night. Heavy round columns of cut stone or mortar support cross beams known as *topie*, trellises onto which vines are tied down firmly to keep them from being broken by the winds that whip through the Dora Baltea valley with a fury. The microclimate in vineyards ranging from 350 m to nearly double that height is relatively cool and dry in summer, but weather is inconsistent, meaning that fine vintages are rare. Still, the Nebbiolo known here as Picutener does excellently in places, even if in the best of years yields are sparse. Grapes are often harvested from ladders and baskets relayed down the slopes by hand. In the past, it took days to fill a vat with grapes, meaning that the earlier batches were already fermenting when the last arrived. The result was a rudimentary form of carbonic maceration that was said to give the wine an attractive youthful quality. Today, however, it must be aged four years before being sold as Carema, which means that much of the town's wines from Nebbiolo, as well as Dolcetto and Neretto, are consumed earlier.

Most Carema comes from the cooperative Produttori Nebbiolo di Carema and Luigi Ferrando, both of whom rely on oenologist Gaspare Buscemi to direct harvesting and vinification. When the season permits full ripening, wines are more refined and better balanced than before; otherwise high acidity is a problem. Carema tends to be lighter and leaner than other Nebbiolos, though from fine vintages such as 1985, 1982, 1979, and 1978 it shows the same elaborate shadings of bouquet with graceful nuances of flavour. Ageing brings out its best, yet even such special bottlings as Ferrando's black label and the Produttori's Carema Carema cost little more than half that of a fine Barolo or Barbaresco. Hardship has made viticulture a part-time occupation for growers, but some seemed determined to stick it out in the hopes that the wine of this alpine enclave will some day receive not only written compliments but the prices such sacrifices deserve.

Zone: The commune of Carema in Torino province where most vineyards are on terraced hillsides facing southwest above the Dora Baltea river valley adjacent to Valle d'Aosta. Dry red. Grape: Nebbiolo (Picutener/ Pugnet/Spanna). Yld 56/80, Alc 12, Acd 0.55-0.8, Ag 4 yrs (2 in oak or chestnut barrels no larger than 40 hl).

Erbaluce di Caluso or Caluso (1967)

The Erbaluce grape can make attractive dry whites and *spumante*, though Caluso and the hills of Canavese have been noted since the Middle Ages for sweet golden wines. But today neither the dry Erbaluce di Caluso or luscious Caluso Passito has anything more than token markets. Much of Canavese's dry whites are sold in inexpensive bottles or bulk by producers who blame Erbaluce's sharp acidity for its lack of wide appeal. But that theory has been discredited by Francesco Orsolani, who excels with dry versions in both still and *champenoise* of real finesse. Colombaio di Candia also makes good dry Erbaluce. Luigi Ferrando leads the mild revival of sweet wines with unclassified versions that show new possibilities for Erbaluce. He has also guided Vittorio Boratto to heights with Caluso Passito of rich golden amber colour, velvety texture, and flavours reminiscent of toasted hazelnuts. Though exceedingly rare, Boratto's is deservedly ranked among Italy's best sweet wines. The *liquoroso* is capable of long ageing, but little is available. Some of the rest of what is sold as "Passito" in the area tastes more like Sicilian Moscato.

Zone: The Canavese glacial basin drained by the Dora Baltea river in hills extending from north of Ivrea to southeast of the town of Caluso and taking in 32 communes in Torino province and three in Vercelli. Most vineyards are around Lake Candia to the south and Lake Viverone to the east along the glacial bank of La Serra.

Erbaluce di Caluso Dry white. Grape: Erbaluce. Yld 84/120, Alc 11, Acd 0.7.

Caluso Spumante Sparkling dry white. Grape: Erbaluce. Yld 84/120, Alc 11.5, Acd 0.65.

Caluso Passito Golden to amber dessert wine. Grapes: Erbaluce; Bonarda up to 5%. Yld 42/120 (from semidried or passito grapes), Alc 13.5, Acd 0.65, Ag 5 yrs (a blend of different vintages is permitted).

Caluso Passito liquoroso Golden to amber fortified sweet wine. Grapes: as passito. Yld 42/120 (from semidried or passito grapes), Alc 17.5, Acd 0.6, Ag 5 yrs (a blend of different vintages is permitted).

Other wines of note

Red vdt from Nebbiolo and Barbera may carry the name Canavese. The towns of Roppolo and Viverone also make respectable red vdt.

ESTATES/GROWERS

Renato Bianco, Caluso (TO). Respected Erbaluce and Passito Macellio.

Vittorio Boratto, Piverone (TO). Veteran oenologist Boratto as a hobby makes the one remaining Caluso Passito worthy of fame, but he only does so in certain vintages from grapes selected in a 0.3-ha plot. Sometimes they are infected by botrytis cinerea that adds intriguing dimensions. His few hundred expensive bottles go to choice restaurants and *enoteche*.

Colombaio di Candia, Candia Canavese (TO). Good dry Erbaluce Vigneto Colombaio and a late harvest *riserva* in *barrique*.

Orsolani, San Giorgio Canavese (TO). Francesco Orsolani makes fine dry Erbaluce La Rustia, whose name means "roasted" in reference to selected ripest grapes. His Caluso Spumante *champenoise* indicates that Erbaluce has unexpected potential in the sparkling field.

WINE HOUSES/MERCHANTS

Luigi Ferrando, Ivrea (TO). Ferrando makes exemplary Carema and avant-garde wines from Erbaluce. His 3 ha at Carema are in four plots – Laure, Silanc, Siei, Piolei – used for a special black label bottling and a youthful red vdt from Nebbiolo and Neretto called Tupiun. In the Caluso zone he has 3 ha at Piverone for the unclassified sweet wines of Vigneto Cariola and the late harvested, *barrique*-aged Solativa. He sells these rarities and other wines at his *enoteca* in Ivrea.

COOPERATIVES

Produttori Nebbiolo di Carema, Carema (TO). Luciano Clerin presides over this admirable winery whose 45 members supply grapes for about two-thirds of DOC, including the choice Carema Carema.

CS di Piverone, Piverone (TO). Erbaluce di Caluso DOC Bianco della Serra.

Wines of the Vercelli and Novara hills

Gattinara is the focal point of the seven small but historically significant wine zones grouped in the last waves of alpine foothills on either side of the Sesia river in the provinces of Vercelli and Novara. To the west towards Biella are the Colli Vercellesi with Lessona, Bramaterra, and Gattinara. Along the river's eastern bank are the Colli Novaresi with Boca, Ghemme, Sizzano, and Fara. The hills and high plains of glacial moraine have an unusual climate in which the heat and damp of the Po flatlands (often flooded for rice fields) are alleviated by air currents from the Alps and the lakes of Maggiore and Orta to the north. The Romans planted vineyards there, though it was probably not until the late Middle Ages that Nebbiolo or Spanna began to play a role in wines. By the mid-nineteenth century Gattinara was often rated above Barolo as a dry red. A survey of Italian wines entitled *Carta Vinicola d'Italia* published in 1887 noted that Ghemme, Lessona, and Gattinara could outlast Barolo and that after five to ten years of age they were used in Lombardy as tonics for convalescents. Longevity has been attributed in part to Nebbiolo's naturally high acidity from glacial soils whose elements vary from one point to another. Gattinara and Lessona made from practically pure Nebbiolo were noted in the past as being more generous, austere, and perfumed than wines from the other side of the Sesia valley, where grapes from the more productive Vespaiola and Bonarda were often blended in, then as now, to soften and lighten flavours.

The northern Nebbiolos are at their best from hot, dry years – such as 1988, 1985, 1982, 1978, 1974, and 1970 – when fruit and extract subdue acidity. Well-aged wines here may be distinguished from Barolo or Barbaresco by a hint more of violets and tar on the nose and broader, softer textures with a somewhat bitter sensation at the finish. The class of wines of the Vercelli-Novara hills depends not only on the ratio of Nebbiolo in the blend but also on the exposure, altitude, and soil mix of vineyards. Gattinara has what are considered the area's best natural conditions, though growers rarely exploit them to the full. Vineyards in the Vercelli-Novara hills have declined through much of the century due to vine maladies and migration of farmers to the cities. Still, Gattinara remained widely admired in Italy until a couple decades ago, when too much wine of the name became available at suspiciously low prices. Even as new vineyards were planted in response to DOC, the once active market in nearby Milan began to fail, hailing a general decline. Some cellars in the area bottled vdt Spanna that tasted more like Aglianico or other southern wines than Nebbiolo. Although a few such wines were unexpectedly refined, their low prices undermined markets for Gattinara and other DOCs. These days the Gattinara legend seems to be more plausible abroad since exports surpass domestic sales. Recently, though, producers seem to have pointed Gattinara towards a slight revival that could carry over to other wines. But since the seven DOCs of the Vercelli-Novara hills account for about 8,000 hectolitres a year, or little more than a million bottles between them, their stories often have more to do with past glories than with the isolated individual achievements of the present.

Lessona (1976)

Lessona was known for wines in abundance as early as the 14th century, and later for a Nebbiolo that was often compared with Gattinara. But today the Sella family, which has had an estate there since the 17th century, seems to be alone in making an austerely aristocratic wine.

Zone: The commune of Lessona in Vercelli province on hillsides with soils and exposure deemed suitable for vines. Dry red. Grapes: Nebbiolo (Spanna); Bonarda/Vespolina up to 25%. Yld 56/80, Alc 12, Acd 0.55, Ag 2 yrs (1 in wood).

Bramaterra (1979)

The Sella family produces what is generally considered to be a simpler wine than Lessona or the adjacent Gattinara, but from normal vintages their Bramaterra, which includes some Croatina, is often more attractively drinkable than either. Luigi Perazzi regularly matches their feats.

Zone: Hills in seven communes of Vercelli province, though the few vineyards are mainly around Roasio and Villa di Bosco on wooded slopes at a place called Bramaterra. Dry red. Grapes: Nebbiolo (Spanna) 50-70%, Croatina 20-30%. Bonarda/Vespolina up to 20%. Yld 49/70, Alc 12, Acd 0.5, Ag 2 yrs (18 mths in wood); riserva 3 yrs (2 in wood).

Gattinara (1967)

History relates that the Romans planted the town's first vineyards and that Cardinal Mercurino Arborio, the native son who became chancellor of Charles V, served the wines at Europe's royal courts. Yet Gattinara came to be distinguished not by myths but by the fact that almost to the present day experts considered it to be one of Piedmont's and Italy's great red wines. It was known as the most robust and long lived of the northern Nebbiolos, and also the most luxurious. From all accounts, its fame was merited. Part of the blame for its decline has been attributed to unscrupulous bottlers who blended wine from other places and sold it as "Gattinara". But even much genuine Gattinara of recent times has failed to live up to the name. It isn't clear whether the fault lies more with vineyard practices or cellar techniques.

Whatever the reasons, honest producers seem tired of offering excuses for a failing image. Most admit that wines could be improved, though they don't always agree about how. Nebbiolo may be used alone in the wine, but some who make the ten percent correction to tone down Spanna's high acidity would prefer Vespolina to the permitted Bonarda. Many feel that the four years of required ageing are too much for a modern wine. Where they do seem to agree is that a change is needed to restore Gattinara's reputation. That probably explains why they requested DOCG. Critics may argue that Gattinara does not warrant promotion on the strength of its performance as a DOC. But recent interpretations of the law indicate that the "guarantee" rather than a mark of achievement is a mandate to improve. In Chianti and Albana di Romagna, DOCG has raised standards by eliminating unworthy wines. So if producers of Gattinara are willing to commit their current half million bottles a year to a survival test perhaps they deserve credit. Their numbers have declined during the crisis, so remaining producers represent a workable group, some of whom have already raised standards. Le Colline seems to have excelled most often over the last decade with Monsecco. Travaglini and the house of Nervi also perform admirably, but the most dynamic winemaker is Rosanna Antoniolo with markedly improved single vineyard wines.

Gattinara has the advantage of an easily controllable vineyard zone, since there are only about 90 ha registered on slopes facing south on what is virtually a single hill northwest of the town. Veteran growers know the best plots amidst the crests and hollows and call each by a name in the peculiar local dialect, though they have also been translated into Italian. A few vineyards are worth citing since they are sources of recognized Gattinara. Antoniolo has vines at Osso San Grato, San Francesco, and Castelle (where a roofless tower that was once part of a castle stands as a symbol of Gattinara). Nervi makes the vaunted *crus* of Molsino and Valferana, an area where Le Colline also has vines for Monsecco. It remains to be seen whether other vineyards on the hill will return to the prominence they enjoyed in Gattinara's more active and illustrious past.

Zone: South-facing slopes in the commune of Gattinara in Vercelli province. Dry red. Grapes: Nebbiolo (Spanna); Bonarda di Gattinara up to 10%. Yld 63/90, Alc 12, Acd 0.55-0.85, Ag 4 yrs (2 in wood).

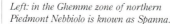

Left: in the Ghemme zone of northern Piedmont Nebbiolo is known as Spanna.

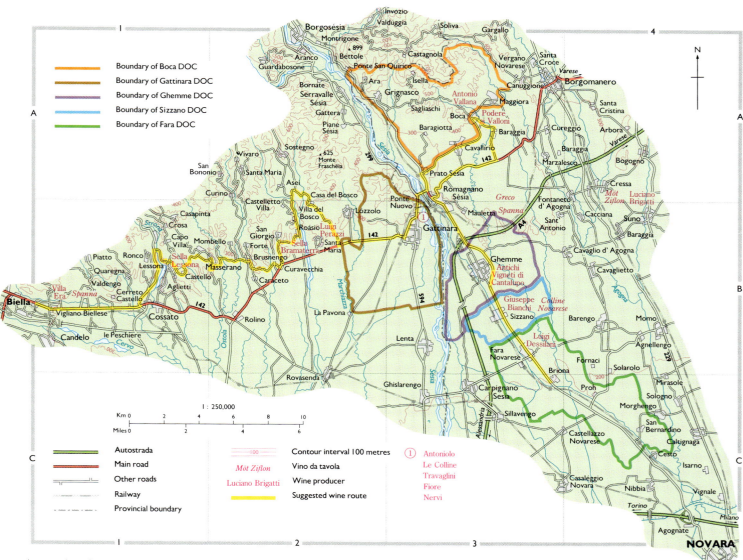

Boundary of Boca DOC
Boundary of Gattinara DOC
Boundary of Ghemme DOC
Boundary of Sizzano DOC
Boundary of Fara DOC

1 : 250,000

Km 0   2   4   6   8   10
Miles 0   2   4   6

Autostrada
Main road
Other roads
Railway
Provincial boundary

Contour interval 100 metres
Möt Ziflon Vino da tavola
Luciano Brigatti Wine producer
Suggested wine route

① *Antoniolo*
Le Colline
Travaglini
Fiore
Nervi

Boca (1969)

The towns of Boca and Maggiora in the wooded hills between the Sesia valley and Lago d'Orta had been known for wines since Roman times, but today this DOC represents a rarity that is rarely seen in commerce.

Zone: Slopes no higher than 500 m facing south in the commune of Boca and parts of Maggiora, Cavallirio, Prato Sesia, and Grignasco in Novara province. Dry red. Grapes: Nebbiolo (Spanna) 45-70%, Vespolina 20-40%; Bonarda Novarese (Uva Rara) up to 20%. Yld 63/90, Alc 12, Acd 0.6, Ag 3 yrs (2 in wood).

Ghemme (1969)

The commune directly across the river from Gattinara made wines that were often likened to its neighbour's in the past, though so little Ghemme is produced now that it is hard to compare. Still, the Arlunno brothers of Antichi Vigneti di Cantalupo make a Ghemme Collis Breclemae that ranks with the finest of Nebbiolos and Le Colline produces a Ghemme that from some vintages matches its Gattinara.

Zone: Slopes facing south in the commune of Ghemme and the part of Romagnano Sesia known as Mauletta in Novara province. Dry red. Grapes: Nebbiolo (Spanna) 65-85%, Vespolina 10-30%; Bonarda Novarese (Uva Rara) up to 15%. Yld 70/100, Alc 12, Acd 0.6, Ag 4 yrs (3 in wood).

Sizzano (1969)

Moving south along the Sesia the ratio of Spanna to other varieties lessens and wines become lighter and more youthfully appealing, as in the Sizzano and Ghemme of Giuseppe Bianchi.

Zone: The commune of Sizzano in Novara province on slopes facing south in suitable soils. Dry red. Grapes: Nebbiolo (Spanna) 40-60%, Vespolina 15-40%; Bonarda Novarese (Uva Rara) up to 25%. Yld 70/100, Alc 12, Acd 0.55, Ag 3 yrs (2 in wood).

Fara (1976)

This is often the lightest of Vercelli-Novara wines, though Dessilani's Caramino sometimes shows the class and staying power of a fine Gattinara. The CS di Fara Novarese is also reliable.

Zone: The communes of Fara and Briona in Novara province on gentle slopes facing south. Dry red. Grapes: Nebbiolo (Spanna) 30-50%, Vespolina 10-30%; Bonarda Novarese (Uva Rara) up to 40%. Yld 77/110, Alc 12, Acd 0.55, Ag 3 yrs (2 in wood).

Other wines of note

Spanna lost much of its mysterious allure when the house of Antonio Vallana stopped using vineyard and estate names for table wines, though some bottles of Campi Raudii and Traversagna from the 1960s are still extraordinarily drinkable, if hard to find. The most admired authentic Spanna today comes from Villa Era. Another unclassified wine of special interest is Luciano Brigatti's Möt Ziflon from Nebbiolo with Bonarda and Vespolina, though many estates and all of the merchants hereabouts make vdt in addition to DOC. Colline Novaresi is a recognized vdt for red, white, and rosé, as are the town names of Barengo, Briona, Maggiora, Romagnano Sesia, and Suno in Novara province.

ESTATES/GROWERS

Antichi Vigneti di Cantalupo, Ghemme (NO). Alberto and Maurizio Arlunno uphold the good name of Ghemme with Collis Breclemae and Colli Carellae meticulously selected from 20 ha of vines, along with the vdt red Agamium, from the Roman name for Ghemme.

Antoniolo, Gattinara (VC). Rosanna Antoniolo is a driving force behind the recovery in Gattinara with her remarkably improved single vineyard bottlings of Osso San Grato, San Francesco, and Castelle from 12 ha.

Giuseppe Bianchi, Sizzano (NO). Sizzano and Ghemme DOC.

Luciano Brigatti, Suno (NO). Lone producer of the vdt Möt Ziflon, from Nebbiolo with Bonarda and Vespolina, Brigatti also makes Bonarda from 5 ha of vines.

Le Colline, Gattinara (VC). Bruno Cervi runs the estate made famous by the Ravizza family, with the Monsecco that has been the most acclaimed Gattinara of recent times. Le Colline's

45

18 ha of vineyards include estates at Ghemme for that DOC and at Treiso (Cascina Bordino) for Barbaresco and Moscato d'Asti.

Luigi Perazzi, Roasio (VC). Fine Bramaterra and the vdt red La Sassaia.

Podere ai Valloni, Boca (NO).

Sella, Lessona (VC). Fabrizio Sella and family have 11 ha on the San Sebastiano allo Zoppo estate for Lessona and the vdt red Piccone, and 9 ha on the wooded estate at Roasio for Bramaterra and the vdt Orbello. The Sella production is among the most admired of northern Piedmont's wines.

Travaglini, Gattinara (VC). From 17 ha, Giancarlo Travaglini produces admired Gattinara.

Villa Era, Vigliano Biellese (VC). Roberto Rivetti makes vdt Spanna di Vigliano that often surpasses the class of northern Nebbiolo DOCs.

WINE HOUSES/MERCHANTS

Guido Barra, Gattinara (VC). Gattinara.

Luigi Dessilani, Fara Novarese (NO). The winery run by Enzio Lucca makes

Gattinara, Ghemme, and a bit of the fine Fara DOC called Caramino – always of excellent value.

Umberto Fiore, Gattinara (VC). Dependable producer-bottler of Gattinara and other wines of Piedmont.

Luigi & Italo Nervi, Gattinara (VC). The respected house is run by Giorgio Aliata, who selects from 21 ha for Gattinara, including single vineyard bottlings of Molsino (5 ha) and Valferana (6 ha).

Antonio Vallana, Maggiora (NO). The house long noted for Spanna with exotic labels and amazing life spans has evolved into a reliable low-profile producer of Boca and other wines.

COOPERATIVES

CS di Fara Novarese, Fara Novarese (NO). Reliable producer of Fara DOC and vdt.

CS di Gattinara, Gattinara (VC). Cellars make nearly a third of Gattinara.

CS di Ghemme e Sizzano, Sizzano (NO). Ghemme and Sizzano DOCs.

SOUTHEASTERN PIEDMONT

The provinces of Asti and Alessandria together produce about two thirds of the region's wine from vineyards mainly in the Monferrato hills that range between the Apennines and the Po over most of southeastern Piedmont. The 19 DOC zones covered here include all of those two provinces plus Freisa di Chieri, which lies in an extension of Monferrato in Torino province. The zones vary radically in scope. Barbera del Monferrato covers most of Alessandria and Asti provinces and Barbera d'Asti is only slightly more restricted in area. Moscato d'Asti (Asti Spumante) extends across parts of both and into Cuneo province. At the other end of the scale is Gabiano, which covers parts of two communes. The zones overlap and intermingle in patterns that correspond to geographical or historical criteria, or at least to some noteworthy local custom. But on the map they can give the impression of an impenetrable maze. Any logic behind them reveals itself as they are explored.

The range is divided by the Tanaro river into Alto Monferrato towards the Apennines and Basso Monferrato towards the Po. Terrains are mostly calcareous, though mixtures of sand and clay vary as decisively as do microclimates from one valley to the next. Nearly all vines are native and each has its favoured areas, even Barbera, which grows everywhere but expresses itself in different ways. Its often rustic wines had always met the everyday needs of Piedmontese until changing tastes forced it to become more contemporary. Today most Barbera, whether medium bodied or well structured for ageing, can qualify as a normal red wine by universal standards. So can Dolcetto, which does well at points in both provinces, notably at Ovada in Alessandria. But Monferrato's other reds – Freisa, Grignolino, Brachetto, Malvasia, and Ruchè – are so eccentric or rare that they could only reach limited audiences. Curiously, the little Nebbiolo planted in Monferrato has never thrived as it does in Alba's hills.

Producers, who still have to struggle to sell their red wines, have no such problem with whites, since Asti Spumante has international status and Gavi and other whites from Cortese are popular in Italy. Much Moscato for *spumante* is grown in Alto Monferrato, but the most prized grapes come from around Canelli in high parts of the Langhe hills in the provinces of Asti and Cuneo. Gavi comes from Cortese grown in a remote southern part of Alessandria province near the border of Liguria. Across the Scrivia valley from Gavi are the Colli Tortonesi, a range connected with Lombardy's Oltrepò Pavese.

Southeastern Piedmont is among the most intensely cultivated vineyard areas of northern Italy, but the territory is so vast and wine zones so varied that they are a challenge to approach. The following sequence goes by province, taking first Alessandria and the zones that lie entirely in its territory or where producers make a greater share of a DOC wine, and then moving on to Asti and Chieri. In Alessandria, estates and wine houses are listed by general areas, but in Asti, where producers often make several different DOCs, there is a single listing.

Wines of Monferrato Casalese

Alessandria's share of Basso Monferrato extends along the Po between the town of Casale Monferrato and the border of Asti province through often steep hills noted historically for Barbera and, above all, Grignolino. Since both wines have lost some of their former popularity, viticulture has suffered here, though a dozen or so producers who have persisted with quality seem to be weathering the crisis. The special appellations of Gabiano and Rubino di Cantavenna, created to satisfy local interests, remain obscure.

Barbera del Monferrato (1970)

Piedmont's most extensive DOC offers growers through most of Monferrato the closest thing to a universal appellation for Barbera, though about two-thirds of production is in Alessandria province. In the past Barbera del Monferrato was often rustically sharp or sluggish and insipid. But producers are making wines that are increasingly well balanced and easy to drink, whether robust and aged or light and lively, as favoured by trends. *Superiore* from certain winemakers can stand with Piedmont's finest. The code also permits a lightly sweet type.

Zone: Nearly the entire Monferrato overlapping all other DOC zones in Asti province and all but Gabiano, Rubino di Cantavenna, Gavi, and Colli Tortonesi in Alessandria province. The zone also includes low hills along the Po around Valenza northeast of Alessandria. Dry red, also abboccato and frizzante. Grapes: Barbera 85-90%, Freisa/Grignolino/Dolcetto 10-15%. Yld 70/100, Alc 12; superiore 12.5, Acd 0.6, Ag superiore 2 yrs.

Grignolino del Monferrato Casalese (1974)

Among Piedmont's diverse red wines Grignolino may be the hardest to define, since it isn't so much a red as a rust-coloured *chiaretto* of gentle fragrance. Yet the wine, despite its delicate appearance, is rich in tannins that can clamp a pretty tight grip on the tongue. Admirers of that peculiar sensation like to compare nuances in wines from the villages of what is considered the classical area of the Basso Monferrato straddling the provinces of Asti (discussed under Grignolino d'Asti) and Alessandria in the Monferrato Casalese zone. Noted vineyards in what are generally light, sandy soils lie at Olivola, Terruggia, Treville, and especially Vignale Monferrato, where the Gaudio family and Nuova Cappelletta are admired growers. The regional *enoteca* there permits extensive research into this uncommon wine.

Zone: Hills of Monferrato Casalese in 34 communes of Alessandria province. Dry, pale red. Grapes: Grignolino; Freisa up to 10%. Yld 45/75, Alc 11, Acd 0.55.

Rubino di Cantavenna (1970)

A Barbera-based red created in recent times by a small cooperative is made in minuscule quantities and rarely seen outside the area.

Zone: Hills along the south bank of the Po in the communes of Cantavenna, Gabiano, Moncestino, Camino, and Villamiroglio in Alessandria province. Dry red. Grapes: Barbera 75-90%, Grignolino/Freisa up to 25%. Yld 70/100, Alc 11.5, Acd 0.6, Ag 1 yr.

Gabiano (1983)

The Castello di Gabiano's red wines from Barbera were noted in past decades for power and depth with exceptional ageing potential, but production seems to have faded since DOC was created for the town of Gabiano.

Zone: Hills along the south bank of the Po in the communes of Gabiano and Moncestino in Alessandria province. Dry red. Grapes: Barbera 90-95%, Grignolino/Freisa 5-10%. Yld 56/80, Alc 12; riserva 12.5, Acd 0.5, Ag riserva 2 yrs.

Other wines of note

Colle Manora's Sauvignon is a rare example of a foreign variety succeeding in an area that uses mainly traditional varieties for both DOC and vdt.

ESTATES/GROWERS

Giulio Accornero & Figli, Terruggia (AL). Barbera, Grignolino, Freisa, and Malvasia di Casorzo d'Asti.

Augustus, Alfiano Natta (AL). Barbera and Grignolino.

Cascina Alberta, Vignale Monferrato (AL). Barbera and Grignolino.

Castello di Gabiano, Gabiano (AL). The long noted estate of the Marchesi Cattaneo Adorno family makes the ever rarer Gabiano DOC.

Castello di Salabue, Ponzano Monferrato (AL). From 16 ha, Carlo Cassinis makes admired Barbera, Grignolino and vdt Rubello di Salabue.

Colle Manora, Quargnento (AL). Barbera d'Asti and admirable Sauvignon Mimosa and Cabernet.

Il Mongetto, Vignale Monferrato (AL). Barbera and Grignolino.

La Tenaglia, Serralunga di Crea (AL). From 12 ha, Delfina Quattrocolo makes good Barbera and Grignolino.

Ermenegildo Leporati, Casale Monferrato (AL). The estate, which specializes in Grignolino and Barbera has made wine since the 13th century.

Nuova Cappelletta, Vignale Monferrato (AL). From 36 ha, the noted

Grignolino La Collina and Barbera La Guerra and Montalbava.

Poderi Bricco Mondalino, Vignale Monferrato (AL). From 7 ha, Amilcare Gaudio and son Mauro produce the outstanding Grignolino Il Mondalino and Barbera d'Asti Il Bergantino.

WINE HOUSES/MERCHANTS

Livio Pavese, Treville Monferrato (AL). Admired producer of Grignolino,

Brachetto d'Acqui, and other wines of Monferrato, including a fine Barbera del Monferrato Podere Sant'Antonio and Barbera d'Asti.

COOPERATIVES

CS di Rubino, Cantavenna di Gabiano (AL). Small production of the rare Rubino di Cantavenna.
CS di Vignale, Vignale Monferrato (AL). Grignolino and Barbera.

Wines of Tortona's hills

The town of Tortona lies on the Scrivia river in the easternmost part of Piedmont on the edge of the range of Apennine foothills that link up with the Oltrepò Pavese. The Colli Tortonesi wines come from Barbera and Cortese grown in an area that seems more Lombardian than Piedmontese.

Colli Tortonesi (1973)
Production had been dominated by fizzy white Cortese for a while, but the traditional Barbera, both still and bubbly, remains the base. Some wines can compare with those from Monferrato or Oltrepò Pavese.

Zone: The lower Apennine foothills southeast of Tortona between the Scrivia river and the border of Lombardy in 30 communes of Alessandria province.
Barbera Dry red, often vivace. Grapes: Barbera; Freisa/Bonarda/Dolcetto up to 15%. Yld 63/90, Alc 12; superiore 12.5, Acd 0.6, Ag superiore 2 yrs (1 in oak or chestnut barrels).
Cortese Dry white, often vivace, also spumante. Grape: Cortese. Yld 70/100, Alc 10.5; spumante 11.5, Acd 0.55.

ESTATES/GROWERS

Fratelli Massa, Monleale (AL). Colli Tortonesi DOC.

WINE HOUSES

Cantine Volpi, Tortona (AL). Specialists in Colli Tortonesi bubbly wines, along with DOCs of Monferrato.

Wines of Gavi and Ovada

The neighbouring wine towns of Gavi and Ovada lie in the easternmost reaches of the Monferrato hills at the foot of the Ligurian Apennines. Names of towns often take the suffix Ligure in an area that was historically linked to Genoa and still feels the Mediterranean influence in customs, speech, and climate. Despite the similar geographical features of the adjacent DOC zones, Gavi and Ovada specialize in different types of wine. Ovada has long been noted for Dolcetto, which develops unique character there, but Gavi only recently made its mark with Cortese in what has rapidly become Piedmont's favourite dry white.

Gavi or Cortese di Gavi (1974)
The rapid rise of Gavi as the paragon of modern Italian white wine has brought Piedmont distinction in a field where it never before stood out. Viticulture had been noted in Gavi since 972 on hillsides of beige coloured calcareous clays where the climate is tempered by breezes crossing the Apennines from the Mediterranean. But until the recent boom, Cortese was grown there mainly for use in base wines for Asti's *spumante* industry. There was little evidence of serious winemaking in the zone until the 1950s, when Vittorio Soldati at the La Scolca estate launched the Gavi dei Gavi that became Italy's most vaunted – and expensive – dry white of the 1960s and 1970s. That inspired investments by others in a zone that has become a model of the sort of enterprise that typifies other businesses in the industrial triangle but is rarely seen in wine. Production has nearly tripled in the 15 years that Gavi has been fashionable, but the 30 or so estates that make the wine back their often high prices with what is virtually a warranty of good workmanship. Several houses from other parts of Piedmont issue Gavi of respectable standards, though not all brands from what are estimated to be more than 200 bottlers are reliable.

The virtues of what might be considered a typical Gavi are cleanly refined scent and acutely dry flavour with pronounced acidity countered by a vague sensation of fruit. In short, an exemplary fish wine distinguished from most of the rest of the field by slicker style. Success in Italy stimulated exports, led by the American-owned Villa Banfi with Principessa Gavia from its own vineyards. Other estates have developed limited foreign markets and

Below: Parodi Ligure in the Gavi DOC zone of southeastern Piedmont.

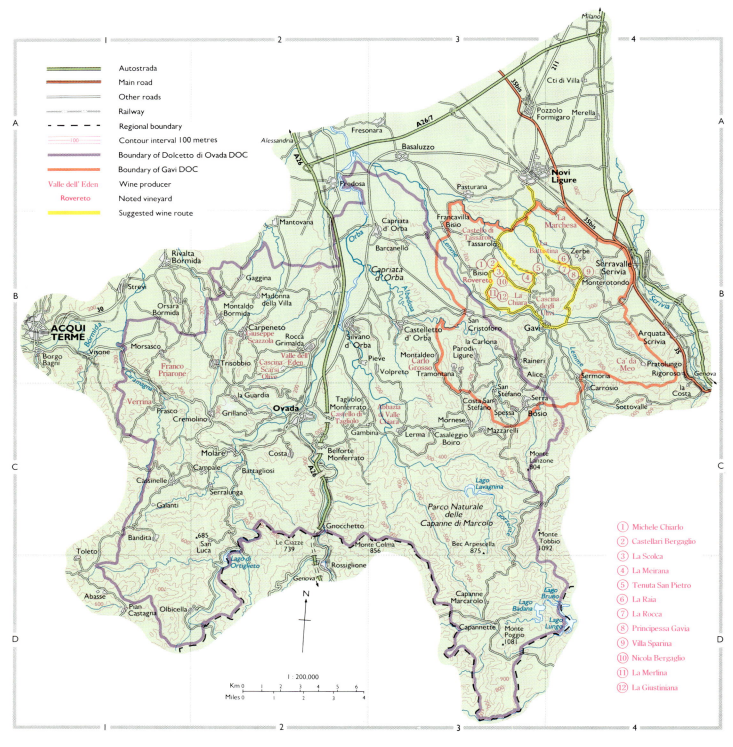

Legend:

- Autostrada
- Main road
- Other roads
- Railway
- Regional boundary
- Contour interval 100 metres
- Boundary of Dolcetto di Ovada DOC
- Boundary of Gavi DOC

Valle dell' Eden Wine producer

Rovereto Noted vineyard

Suggested wine route

1 Michele Chiarlo
2 Castellari Bergaglio
3 La Scolca
4 La Meirana
5 Tenuta San Pietro
6 La Raia
7 La Rocca
8 Principessa Gavia
9 Villa Sparina
10 Nicola Bergaglio
11 La Merlina
12 La Giustiniana

1 : 200,000

Km 0   1   2   3   4   5   6
Miles 0   1   2   3   4

many producers or bottlers of other Piedmontese wines include a Gavi in their export lines. Yet foreign experts, perhaps more than Italian, have raised doubts about Gavi's attributes after searching in vain for those aromas, textures, and flavours that usually distinguish costly white wines. Several producers, perhaps in response to what they interpret as international tastes, age Gavi in *barriques*. Yet, even if wine from Cortese is unusually rich in tannins for a white, the oak as so far

applied seems if anything to mask the already meagre measure of fruit.

Some of La Scolca's past vintages were memorable perhaps because wines seemed more like white Burgundy in style than they do today. Castello di Tassarolo's Vigneto Alborina shows tone in what seems the least typical among current examples of Gavi. Cortese's customary role in sparkling wines was somewhat neglected during the rise of the still version, but more producers have been making *spumante*,

following La Scolca's lead with its Pados *champenoise*. That estate retains its cachet, though it no longer towers over the competition as it did when its black label bottling was called "Gavi dei Gavi" – a connotation of superiority no longer permitted. Now it is "Gavi di Gavi" like other wines from the commune. La Scolca is in the Rovereto area where the most noted vineyards are located, though wines from plots along the slopes north of the town as far as Monterotondo and Tassarolo can

equal them. Still, it is often said that terrains are less of a quality factor than oenological techniques in the production of modern white wines. And, indeed, Gavi's continuing triumphs would seem to owe more to well-financed winemaking and marketing skills than to the innate class of Cortese.

Zone: Hills west of the Scrivia river extending from Novi Ligure into the Apennines to the border of Liguria in 11 communes in Alessandria province. Though most vineyards are located near the town of

Gavi on slopes between 200-450 m and in the hills towards Tassarolo, Serravalle Scrivia, and Pratolungo. Dry white, also spumante. Grape: Cortese. Yld 70/100, Alc 10.5, Acd 0.5.

Dolcetto di Ovada (1972)

Dolcetto is so well established on the slopes along the upper Orba valley that its grapes used to be known throughout the province as Uva di Ovada. Wines from there are often considered the closest rivals to fine Dolcettos of Alba and Dogliani in class, though typology is different. Dolcetto di Ovada is noted for sturdy structure combined with unusually high levels of alcohol, acidity, and tannins that permit it to age for a few years as its grapey scent and fleshy fruit flavours become composed enough to be described as graceful. This character may be due in part to the different clones of Dolcetto planted there. But the key points seem to be that Ovada, which feels constant winds from Liguria, has a drier climate than Alba and that soils are considerably less productive. Noted vineyards lie around the hill towns of Rocca Grimalda, Carpeneto, Montaldo, Morsasco, Prasco, and Cremolino west of the Orba, and Tagliolo and Lerma to the east. A leading exponent of the aged style is Giuseppe Ratto with wines from the Cascina Scarsi Olivi at Rocca Grimalda. But the death of his neighbour Giuseppe Poggio has meant that the most prized wine of the zone, Bricco Trionzo, is no longer produced. Most producers sell their wines young, when they may show precocious charm, though even the modern style of Dolcetto di Ovada can age with a dignity that sets it apart from the rest.

Zone: Often steep hills in the southeastern part of Alto Monferrato extending along both sides of the Orba valley from the border of Liguria north past Ovada to Capriata d'Orba and including 22 communes in Alessandria province. Dry red. Grape: Dolcetto. Yld 56/80, Alc 11.5; superiore 12.5, Acd 0.5, Ag superiore 1 yr.

ESTATES/GROWERS

Abbazia di Valle Chiara, Lerma (AL). Actress Ornella Muti owns the 14th-century abbey where a promising Dolcetto di Ovada is being made.
Nicola Bergaglio, Rovereto di Gavi (AL). Respected Gavi includes the single vineyard La Minaia.
Ca' da Meo, Pratolungo di Gavi (AL). Maurizio Vilona makes good Gavi and a vdt Dolcetto Bricco della Croce.
Cascina degli Ulivi, Gavi (AL). Stefano Bellotti makes improving Gavi.
Cascina Scarsi Olivi, Rocca Grimalda (AL). Giuseppe Ratto, a confirmed nonconformist, believes that Dolcetto di Ovada needs years to reach prime; his Gli Scarsi and Le Olive from 5 ha back his stand.

Castellari Bergaglio, Rovereto di Gavi (AL). From 7 ha of her Belvedere estate, Wanda Castellari Bergaglio has choice vineyards for Gavi.
Castello di Tagliolo, Tagliolo Monferrato (AL). Oberto Pinelli Gentile makes respected Dolcetto di Ovada, Barbera, and Cortese.
Castello di Tassarolo, Tassarolo (AL). The Marchesi Spinola and winemaker Giancarlo Scaglione produce fine Gavi with more style than Cortese usually shows in Vigneto Alborina.
Carlo Grosso & Figli, Montaldeo (AL). Dolcetto di Ovada.
La Battistina, Novi Ligure (AL). From 22 ha, Giuseppe Terragno makes respected Gavi, including the barrel-aged Bricco Battistina.
La Bollina, Serravalle Scrivia (AL). The estate with 60 ha of vines is owned by Guido Berlucchi of Franciacorta in Lombardy, which sells a Gavi under the estate name and uses Cortese in its *champenoise cuvées*.
La Chiara, Vallegge di Gavi (AL). Respected Gavi from Ferdinando and Roberto Bergaglio.
La Guardia, Morsasco (AL). The Priarone family makes fine Dolcetto di Ovada Bricco Riccardo and Bricco Lencino from 30 ha of vines.
La Giustiniana, Rovereto di Gavi (AL). From 30 ha around the former Benedictine monastery come the single vineyard Gavi di Lugarara, Montessora, and Centurionetta (from the oldest vines), along with a *champenoise*.
La Marchesa, Novi Ligure (AL). Besides a bit of Gavi under the label, the estate's 36 ha supply several bottlers with good quality Gavi.
La Meirana, Gavi (AL). Gian Piero Broglia strives for excellence from 30 ha where he makes La Meirana, Vigna Fasciola, and the gold label Gavi di Gavi from selected grapes.
La Merlina, Rovereto di Gavi (AL). Fausto Gemme makes admired Gavi from 10 ha of choice vineyards.
La Raja, Novi Ligure (AL). Gavi DOC.
La Rocca, Monterotondo di Gavi (AL). From 10 ha, the Coppo brothers make a good Gavi.
La Scolca, Rovereto di Gavi (AL). The estate where Vittorio Soldati launched Gavi in the 1950s is run by his son Giorgio Soldati, who draws from some 20 ha of vines on the property and another 30 under contract for the black label Gavi di Gavi as well as a fine Pados *champenoise*.
Santa Seraffa, Colombare di Gavi (AL). Promising Gavi di Gavi from Filippo Rusca.
Principessa Gavia, Monterotondo di Gavi (AL). Villa Banfi has vineyards and cellars here for a widely respected Gavi.
Giuseppe Scazzola, Carpeneto (AL). Dolcetto di Ovada.
Tenuta San Pietro, Gavi (AL). Maria Rosa Gazzaniga makes admired Gavi

from 15 ha of vineyards at San Pietro.
Valle dell'Eden, Rocca Grimalda (AL). Dolcetto di Ovada.
Verrina, Prasco (AL). Dolcetto di Ovada.
Villa Sparina, Monterotondo di Gavi (AL). Gavi di Gavi La Villa and a good Villa Sparina Brut *champenoise*.

WINE HOUSES/MERCHANTS

Michele Chiarlo, Calamandrana (AT). Chiarlo has cellars at Rovereto for Gavi

from vineyards in key zones, including the barrel-aged Fior di Rovere.

COOPERATIVES

Cantina Produttori del Gavi, Gavi (AL). Major supplier of Gavi to bottlers and shippers.
Tre Castelli, Montaldo Bormida (AL). Good Dolcetto di Ovada among a range of DOC and vdt.

Wines of Acqui and Alto Monferrato

Alto Monferrato refers to the area south of the Tanaro, though the name is more specifically applied to the higher part of the range in the Apennine foothills of Alessandria province. Barbera is the prime variety there as elsewhere, but vineyards in the hills along the Bormida valley traditionally supplied the wine centres of Acqui Terme and Strevi with Moscato and Brachetto, as well as Dolcetto.

Cortese dell'Alto Monferrato (1979)

As a somewhat lighter and less expensive alternative to Gavi this Cortese has gained ground. Trends favour bubbly versions over still.

Zone: Hills through much of Alto Monferrato extending from the edge of the Gavi zone west across the Orba and Bormida valleys as far as Canelli in numerous communes of Alessandria and Asti provinces. Dry white, also frizzante or spumante. Grapes: Cortese; other whites up to 15%. Yld 70/100, Alc 10, Acd 0.6.

Brachetto d'Acqui (1969)

The old Piedmontese custom of bubbly sweet red wines is epitomized in Brachetto, which is returning to favour after its vines (related to the Braquet of Provence) had practically disappeared. A century ago Brachetto was more prized than Moscato in the Alto Monferrato in wines made in quantities adequate for export. But its vines weren't as productive as Barbera and as dry white sparkling wines came into fashion Brachetto went out. A few growers around Strevi stuck with it, providing the base for a revival that began in the 1970s. Early versions were rustic, but Brachetto has taken on style from Marenco and Ivaldi whose wines have a Muscat-like aroma enhanced by what are often described as scents of violets and roses. Brachetto's cause has been taken up by Villa Banfi at its Strevi cellars with a sparkling wine that enjoys some fashion around Italy. Though nearly always *frizzante* or *spumante*, it can also become a luscious light ruby *passito*, as made by Forteto della Luja at Loazzolo, and even a dry vdt of singular class in Scarpa's Brachetto di Moirano. Both are cited with Asti's producers on page 54.

Zone: Hills around Acqui Terme, Strevi, and six other communes of the Bormida valley in Alessandria province, extending west to the Belbo valley through 18

communes in Asti province. Sweet red usually frizzante or spumante. Grapes: Brachetto; Aleatico/Moscato Nero up to 10%. Yld 56/80, Alc 11.5 (res sugar 5.5%), Acd 0.5.

Dolcetto d'Acqui (1972)

Dolcetto from the hills along the Bormida often show the opulent fruity qualities typical of wines from around Alba. But some have a sturdiness reminiscent of Dolcetto from the adjacent Ovada zone. Villa Banfi's Argusto, smoothed by some barrel ageing, is an example of the latter type.

Zone: Hills of Alto Monferrato extending along the Bormida valley from the border of Liguria north past Acqui to Sezzadio and including 23 communes in Alessandria province. Dry red. Grape: Dolcetto. Yld 56/80, Alc 11.5; superiore 12.5, Acd 0.5, Ag superiore 1 yr.

Other wines of note

Non-DOC Moscato of Strevi is distinctive enough to be considered apart from Moscato d'Asti, both in the bubbly version and the *passito* of Ivaldi.

ESTATES/GROWERS

Ca' del Mauri, Acqui Terme (AL). Dolcetto d'Acqui.
Il Cascinone, Moirano d'Acqui (AL). Respected producer of Acqui and Asti DOCs from 50 ha.
Domenico Ivaldi, Strevi (AL). Giovanni Ivaldi fashions fine Brachetto d'Acqui, Moscato di Strevi, and the praised Moscato *passito* Casarito.
La Baccalera, Acqui Terme (AL). Dolcetto d'Acqui.
Villa Banfi, Strevi (AL). The American firm's Piedmontese base produces Asti Spumante, Brachetto d'Acqui, and the barrel-aged Dolcetto d'Acqui Argusto, along with the *champenoise* Banfi Brut and *charmat* Brut Pinot. The 55 ha include vineyards at Gavi for Principessa Gavia.

WINE HOUSES/MERCHANTS

Ca' Bianca, Alice Bel Colle (AL). Good range of Asti wines and Brachetto d'Acqui, mainly from 20 ha of company vines.

Marenco, Strevi (AL). Fine Brachetto d'Acqui Pineto, Dolcetto d'Acqui Marchesa, Moscato d'Asti Scrapona.

COOPERATIVES

Viticoltori dell'Acquese, Acqui

Terme (AL). Dolcetto d'Acqui, Barbera, and Grignolino.

Vecchia CS di Alice Bel Colle, Alice Bel Colle (AL). Paolo Ricagno directs the cellars with a wide and reliable range of Asti, Monferrato, and Acqui DOCs.

CS di Cassine, Cassine (AL). Acqui and Monferrato DOCs.

CS di Ricaldone, Ricaldone (AL). Range of Acqui, Asti, and Monferrato DOCs.

Top: in Piedmont and much of northern Italy boiled corn meal is known as polenta.
Bottom: vineyards at Rocchetta Palafea in the southern part of Asti province.

Wines of Asti and Turin's hills

Asti may signify *spumante* to the rest of the world, but the red wines that also carry its name are a more integral part of the provincial culture. Barbera, Grignolino, and Freisa are not Piedmont's most honoured wines, but they, too, have their histories, their myths, and their partisans who would rather drink them than Barolo or Barbaresco. Red wine varieties dominate, yet Asti's wine industry built fame and fortune on the white Moscato planted in little more than ten percent of Monferrato's vineyards. *Spumante* production is concentrated around Canelli and Nizza Monferrato along the Belbo valley to the south. Moscato grapes are grown in the Alto Monferrato as far east as the Bormida valley in Alessandria province, but the most noted vineyards lie around Canelli in the Langhe hills, which extend into the Alba area where much of the fine Moscato d'Alba is made on estates. Most Asti Spumante is produced on an industrial scale by houses that also make dry sparkling wines, often based on Pinots from Lombardy and Chardonnay from Trentino-Alto Adige. Canelli is also a centre of vermouth production, part of an industry founded in Turin where Piedmont's largest houses – Martini & Rossi and Cinzano – are based.

Many estates of Asti's Monferrato make red wines from Barbera and other varieties. Cooperatives and *negociants* also work well. Each of Asti's reds has preferred vineyard areas that are often clearly delineated. The best Grignolino and Freisa come from north of the Tanaro in the Basso Monferrato that extends into the hills of Torino province where Freisa di Chieri is made. Two other peculiar varieties of Basso Monferrato are the dark Malvasia for sweet, bubbly wines around Casorzo and Castelnuovo Don Bosco, and Ruchè, which makes a dry red at Castagnole Monferrato. Limited amounts of Dolcetto d'Asti come from the province's share of the Langhe hills. Barbera is ubiquitous, but its classical area for wines of the size and structure for ageing is south of the Tanaro in hills extending through the Belbo valley.

Available terrains for Moscato have nearly reached their limits, so new planting in the province is largely in Chardonnay for both sparkling and still wines. But growers who haven't forgotten Monferrato's heritage of red wine have been stimulated to renew vineyards of Barbera and other varieties and improve winemaking techniques. Newly inspired reds being produced by estates and small merchant houses have reminded Asti's wine industry that *spumante* need not be its only source of profits.

Barbera d'Asti (1970)

It once seemed that Barbera's versatility, its adaptability to almost any environment, would be its downfall. Growers took advantage, planting it in their poorest plots and stretching yields. Their rustic wines were sometimes robust, sometimes spare, sometimes sinewy, usually tart (due to naturally high acidity), and as often as not bubbly. There was also a trend to make white wine from it. Even dignified Barbera, which ranked as the outstanding value among Piedmont's reds, was a challenge to sell. Customers were often confused and disappointed. Ironically, the methanol scandal of 1986, which involved bottles labelled "Barbera", prompted changes that seem to have pointed the wine back towards respectability. An ambitious campaign by producers' consortiums of Asti, Alessandria, and Alba promotes "La rosa dei Barbera" – not for rosé, as the name suggests, but for youthful red wines, often *vivace*. Most are made by cooperatives and large houses which, unlike in the old days, reward growers for quality grapes. Temperature controlled processing helps maintain fruitiness and fragrance in wines that now undergo malolactic fermentation early to lower acidity and make them softer and rounder. There is also *novello*, which has its fans, though wines with the substance to last a year or two longer, even if bubbly, show a

mellow harmony in scents and flavours that have been winning over even former enemies of Barbera.

Some producers had been making Barbera d'Asti of depth and character for years. Among others, Scarpa's single vineyard bottlings often have had the class and durability to rival all but the finest Barolo and Barbaresco from top vintages. But Barbera's quality potential was rarely noted by opinion leaders until Giacomo Bologna released the *barrique*-aged Bricco dell'Uccellone in the early 1980s. The wine, edified by French oak (like Gaja's influential Barbera d'Alba Vignarey) was a revelation, as were the deluxe prices Bologna got for bottles of a vdt that, like his more recent Bricco della Bigotta, is labelled as Barbera di Rocchetta Tanaro. Other producers have stayed with DOC in Barbera d'Asti of style, such as Trinchero's Vigna del Noce, Carnevale's Il Crottino, Chiarlo's Valle del Sole, Coppo's Camp du Rouss, and Rabezzana's Il Bricco. More wines are emerging from the area historically noted for Barbera in hills south of the Tanaro down across the Belbo valley past Nizza Monferrato to Castel Boglione towards the east and Costigliole d'Asti towards the west. Noted wine towns include Rocca d'Arazzo, Rocchetta Tanaro, Belveglio, Mombercelli, Vinchio, Incisa Scapaccino, Castelnuovo Calcea, Moasca, Agliano, Mombercelli,

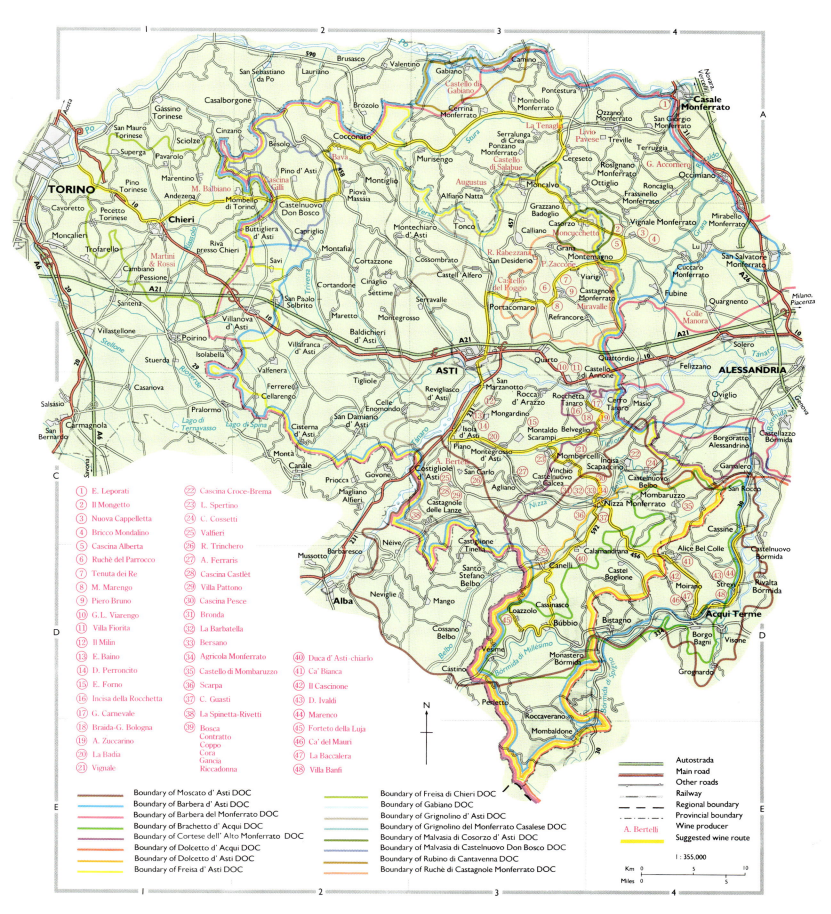

① E. Leporati
② Il Mongetto
③ Nuova Cappelletta
④ Bricco Mondalino
⑤ Cascina Alberta
⑥ Ruchè del Parrocco
⑦ Tenuta dei Re
⑧ M. Marengo
⑨ Piero Bruno
⑩ G.L. Viarengo
⑪ Villa Fiorita
⑫ Il Milin
⑬ E. Baino
⑭ D. Perroncito
⑮ E. Forno
⑯ Incisa della Rocchetta
⑰ G. Carnevale
⑱ Braida-G. Bologna
⑲ A. Zuccarino
⑳ La Badia
㉑ Vignale

㉒ Cascina Croce-Brema
㉓ L. Spertino
㉔ C. Cossetti
㉕ Valfieri
㉖ R. Trinchero
㉗ A. Ferraris
㉘ Cascina Castlèt
㉙ Villa Pattono
㉚ Cascina Pesce
㉛ Bronda
㉜ La Barbatella
㉝ Bersano
㉞ Agricola Monferrato
㉟ Castello di Mombaruzzo
㊱ Scarpa
㊲ C. Guasti
㊳ La Spinetta-Rivetti
㊴ Bosca
  Contratto
  Coppo
  Cora
  Gancia
  Riccadonna

㊵ Duca d'Asti-chiarlo
㊶ Ca' Bianca
㊷ Il Cascinone
㊸ D. Ivaldi
㊹ Marenco
㊺ Forteto della Luja
㊻ Ca' del Mauri
㊼ La Baccalera
㊽ Villa Banfi

Boundary of Moscato d' Asti DOC
Boundary of Barbera d' Asti DOC
Boundary of Barbera del Monferrato DOC
Boundary of Brachetto d' Acqui DOC
Boundary of Cortese dell' Alto Monferrato DOC
Boundary of Dolcetto d' Acqui DOC
Boundary of Dolcetto d' Asti DOC
Boundary of Freisa d' Asti DOC

Boundary of Freisa di Chieri DOC
Boundary of Gabiano DOC
Boundary of Grignolino d' Asti DOC
Boundary of Grignolino del Monferrato Casalese DOC
Boundary of Malvasia di Cosorzo d' Asti DOC
Boundary of Malvasia di Castelnuovo Don Bosco DOC
Boundary of Rubino di Cantavenna DOC
Boundary of Ruchè di Castagnole Monferrato DOC

Autostrada
Main road
Other roads
Railway
Regional boundary
Provincial boundary
A. Bertelli   Wine producer
        Suggested wine route

1 : 355,000

Km 0 10
Miles 0 5

51

Vigliano, Montegrosso, and Mongardino. Growers there and in other parts of the zone have found that by lowering yields and selecting grapes from good plots they can make wine of character with or without *barriques* and ask a respectable price for it.

Zone: Hills throughout Asti province, as well as Monferrato Casalese and part of Alto Monferrato in Alessandria province. Dry red, also vivace, rarely amabile. Grape: Barbera. Yld 63/90, Alc 12; superiore 12.5, Acd 0.6, Ag superiore 1 yr in oak or chestnut barrels.

Freisa d'Asti (1972)

Wines from Freisa, being uncompromisingly unique, seem to arouse strong feelings either for or against. King Victor Emmanuel wouldn't dine without Freisa on the table. But an 18th century Piedmontese poet denounced the wine's "damaging effects" and tried in vain to have the variety legally banned. Freisa's apparent duplicity might be due to the fact that vines are so sensitive to conditions that they can produce different types of grapes in various parts of the same vineyard. Wines may be dry or sweet or still or sparkling with colour and flavours often associated with raspberries, though some tasters also detect a dash of salt on the tongue in the dry version. Though once widely planted in Piedmont, Freisa had been fading for decades as its *amabile* wines went out of fashion. But lately the dry, *frizzante* type has come into favour so Freisa's star seems to be once again on the rise in Asti province and even in Alba's hills where it is vdt.

Zone: Hills throughout Asti province in calcareous or sandy clay soils, excluding the communes of Cellarengo d'Asti and Villanova d'Asti. Garnet to cherry-hued red, dry or amabile, often frizzante, also spumante. Grape: Freisa. Yld 56/80, Alc 11; superiore 11.5, Acd 0.65, Ag superiore 1 yr.

Freisa di Chieri (1974)

The Colli Torinesi just east of Turin have been noted for Freisa for centuries, though today so little is made that there seems to be just one producer of note in Balbiano.

Zone: The Colli Torinesi around Chieri and 11 other communes in Torino province. Garnet to cherry-hued red, dry or amabile, often frizzante, also spumante. Grape: Freisa. Yld 56/80, Alc 11 (amabile res sugar 4%); superiore 11.5, Acd 0.5, Ag superiore 1 yr.

Grignolino d'Asti (1973)

Grignolino does well in several places in the province, but it attains a spring-like fragrance and a delicate balance of flavour that can be almost elegant in the hills northeast of Asti. Noted vineyards are at Casorzo, Castagnole Monferrato, Calliano, Grazzano Badoglio, and Moncalvo, though the

choicest plots are reputed to be those of Migliandolo, a village in the commune of Portacomaro, where several small estates make wine of notable class. The fact that Zonin of the Veneto has invested heavily in the vast vineyards of Castello del Poggio whose speciality is Grignolino is perhaps the surest indication that the wine has potential not only to survive but to prosper.

Zone: Hills north and south of Asti in 35 communes in the centre of the province, though vines thrive in prevalently sandy, calcareous soils north of the Tanaro in the Basso Monferrato. Dry, pale red. Grapes: Grignolino; Freisa up to 10%. Yld 52/80, Alc 11, Acd 0.5.

Malvasia di Casorzo d'Asti (1968)

Italy's mosaic of Malvasias includes this pale cherry hued, softly sweet bubbly wine served mainly in the area as a pleasant alternative to Asti Spumante.

Zone: Hills of calcareous clay northeast of Asti in the communes of Casorzo d'Asti and Grazzano Badoglio in its province and Altavilla Monferrato, Olivola, Ottiglio, and Vignale Monferrato in Alessandria province. Sweet, aromatic red or rosé, usually frizzante or spumante. Grape: Malvasia Nera di Casorzo; Barbera/Freisa/Grignolino up to 10%. Yld 77/110, Alc 10.5 (res sugar min 3.5%); spumante 11, Acd 0.5-0.8.

Malvasia di Castelnuovo Don Bosco (1974)

Don Giovanni Bosco, the 19th-century priest who founded the Salesian order to aid orphans, is known as a saint at his home town of Castelnuovo. They say that he encouraged his parishioners to make wine and instructed them in techniques of viticulture and oenology. The gem of local wines, then as now, was dark Malvasia. It reached heights from vineyards on a hill called Schierano, which also gave its name to the local clone of Malvasia. Today Bava makes enough of this blushing pink bubbly wine to have found some followers in other parts of Italy. But most is drunk on the spot by pilgrims who come to pay homage to Don Bosco.

Zone: In Basso Monferrato northwest of Asti around Castelnuovo Don Bosco and five other communes in its province along the border of Torino province. Sweet, aromatic red or rosé, usually frizzante or spumante. Grape: Malvasia di Schierano; Freisa up to 15%. Yld 77/110, Alc 10.5 (res sugar min 4.2%); spumante 11, Acd 0.5.

Right: the hill town of Calamandrana overlooks the Belbo valley at the heart of the Moscato d'Asti zone.

Vermouth is a Piedmontese speciality, which by law must contain at least 70 percent wine in intricate and often secret blends with herbs, spices, and other flavourings, along with sweetening components and grape spirits to bring alcohol to 16 degrees. The industry started in Turin in the 18th century when the firm of Carpano began selling vermouth, whose name came from the German Wermut, for wormwood or Artemisia absinthium, a major ingredient of the early blends. Other firms based in Turin followed, notably Martini & Rossi and Cinzano, which are the largest and best known brands today. The industry also grew in Asti province, particularly around Canelli, which was the centre of spumante production from Moscato grapes. The firms of Cora and Gancia were early leaders there. Traditionally, Moscato was the base wine in blends, but today white wines from other regions, notably Sicily, are more often used. Among various types on the market today, flavours can range from practically dry to quite sweet, though always with a sense of bitter. The dry types are usually white, and the sweeter versions red or amber, though each house has its own styles and trademarks for what is one of Piedmont's most successful wine-based products.

Ruchè di Castagnole Monferrato (1987)

Families at Castagnole made Grignolino and Barbera for everyday use but kept Ruchè for special occasions because it often had a hint of aromatic sweetness and with age took on traits that reminded some of old Nebbiolo and others of Marsala. Mario Pesce of Scarpa began bottling a dry red table wine called Rouchet in the 1970s. Some vintages aged well, others didn't, but Rouchet drew attention to the variety and stimulated growers to cultivate what was known locally as Ruchè and make wine from it. Retired village priest Don Giacomo Cauda, a *vignaiolo* himself, has led the revival that resulted in DOC and a growing fashion for bottles that sometimes carry the price of rarity. The rules don't require ageing, but most producers let Ruchè season in casks for a while, even if it has attractively full aroma and flavour when bottled young. With age its basic ruby-violet colour takes on hints of orange as the bouquet, which reminds some of violets and roses, evolves with the flavours in unpredictable ways. The ageing question isn't settled, but Ruchè at whatever stage of development can

offer wine drinkers in quest of them new sensations.

Zone: Hills northeast of Asti in the communes of Castagnole Monferrato, Grana, Montemagno, Portacomaro, Refrancore, Scurzolengo, and Viarigi in Basso Monferrato. Dry red. Grapes: Ruchè; Barbera/Brachetto up to 10%. Yld 63/90, Alc 12, Acd 0.5.

Dolcetto d'Asti (1974)

Dolcetto is second to Barbera in popularity among Asti's vines. Yet, even if conditions seem right in the eastern Langhe, where most is planted, Dolcetto d'Asti rarely equals the best of Alba for full, ripe fruit qualities.

Zone: Hills of the Langa Astigiana and part of Alto Monferrato in 23 communes in Asti province. Dry red. Grape: Dolcetto. Yld 56/80, Alc 11.5; superiore 12.5, Acd 0.5, Ag superiore 1 yr.

Moscato d'Asti/Asti Spumante (1967)

Moscato was noted in Piedmont as early as 1203, but its rich aromatic wines became prominent only in the 17th century after Giovan Battista Croce, jeweller to the Dukes of Savoy, refined the difficult techniques of viticulture and vinification. White Moscato thrived in the steep, cool Langhe hills on either side of the Belbo valley around Canelli, which gave its name to the vine. It was there in about 1870 that Carlo Gancia introduced the Champagne method and became the father of Asti Spumante. An industry grew around sparkling Asti, whose production took various twists and turns over the decades as winemakers experimented with techniques more

practical than bottle fermentation for wines that needed to retain residual sugars. The challenge was to block the alcoholic fermentation while keeping the fine balance between sweet, fragrant, and sparkling. Even early tank methods were difficult, since they involved repeated fining of the wine through cloth sack filters to remove active yeasts before bottling. Some producers maintained high standards, but many bottlers didn't, and in the competition for national and international markets that developed after World War II the quality of what was sold as "Asti Spumante" was often as low as the price.

The combination of DOC and self-imposed discipline by mainly large producers have brought about the steady gains that have elevated Asti from its role as "the poor man's Champagne" to the staus of a dignified sparkling wine whose refined aromas and suavely sweet flavours are inimitable. Yet the wine still may not be as esteemed as it deserves to be. Over the last decade DOC production has increased from an average of 350,000 to 520,000 hl a year to surpass Soave as Italy's most voluminous classified wine after Chianti. Asti outsells Champagne in Britain and the USA, where wine drinkers have a noted weakness for the sweet and bubbly. Another attraction is price, which after sharp rises has been contained over the last few years. This is partly because producers and growers agreed to cost controls for Moscato grapes, which had been Italy's most expensive from past vintages. Asti is less successful on the home

market, where dry sparkling wines have gained. Italian cognoscenti often prefer the softer, fruitier, more subtly effervescent Moscato to fully sparkling Asti. Although they are covered by the same DOC, there are differences between the two.

Both types have been improved by methods that rely on regulating temperatures in stainless steel tanks. Grapes are usually picked earlier than before to maintain higher acidity and they are processed quickly to avoid oxidation – key factors in maintaining vital aromas. The normal process for Asti involves soft crushing of grapes and settling of the juice which is centrifuged and filtered. The purified musts are pumped into storage tanks and chilled to near freezing temperatures so that they can't ferment. This enables producers to make batches of wine to meet demands, which are heaviest for the year-end holidays. Unlike methods for Champagne and most other sparkling wines that involve an induced secondary fermentation of the blended cuvées, Asti Spumante is made in a single phase that takes about six weeks between fermentation and bottling. The musts are inoculated with selected yeasts and fermented in large sealed tanks in which natural carbon dioxide is retained during the process. The fermentation is stopped by rapid chilling when the wine reaches the desired ratio of alcohol (7-9 degrees) to residual sugar (3-5 percent), though sweetness depends on each house's style. After filtering and bottling with the wired down cork like Champagne, Asti is usually shipped immediately to

its destination by producers who strive to deliver the freshest wine possible. Carbon dioxide is a natural preservative, but problems can arise if the wine is stocked in warehouses or left on shelves. Since Asti is rarely vintage dated, customers have no way of knowing its age. That is why it is often safest to choose a well known brand with active international distribution – such as Gancia, Contratto, Fontanafredda, Martini & Rossi, Cinzano, or Riccadonna. But careful chemical and taste examinations by the consortium control the quality of wines leaving the cellars of all producers.

Moscato d'Asti is made mainly by small wineries from select batches of grapes. But since it is fragile and much in demand it is consumed largely in Italy. Most producers follow steps similar to those for spumante, except that some do only a light filtering of the juice to retain more fruit in aromas and flavours. By now most have the tanks that allow them to keep musts in cold reserve so that they can do two or three bottlings a year. Another difference is that the fermentation is usually stopped when alcohol reaches 5 or 6 degrees and the carbon dioxide pressure is still low – in the range between frizzante and crémant. Moscato d'Asti is usually bottled with an ordinary cork and with the vintage stated on the label and sold immediately to enoteche and restaurateurs who make a point of serving it at its freshest. It is so in demand that producers follow the trend to bottle the new wine for Christmas, but this means that fermentations are rushed. The wine is best when allowed to ferment slowly and express its full aromas at their prime in the spring. Despite fragility, Moscato d'Asti has managed to create an elite market abroad.

Fine Moscato is made at several places in the zone, but the most prized of recent times comes from the Langhe west of Santo Stefano Belbo around the towns of Castiglione Tinella, Camo, Mango, Valdivilla, Moncucco, and Neviglie in Cuneo province and Castiglione Lanze and Coazzolo in Asti. Leading producers in that part of the zone include Rivetti, Dogliotti, Saracco, Bera, Traversa, Gatti, Carbonere, and I Vignaioli di Santo Stefano, all of which work on a small scale. Moscato d'Asti's success has prompted some large wineries to get into the act, even if a few have wisely resisted the temptation, fearing that their presence could spoil the wine's elite image.

The Moscato d'Asti-Asti Spumante DOC zone ranges from the Langhe to the Alto Monferrato through vineyard areas where wines had been noted historically for somewhat different traits. Four subzones are often delineated. The first, already mentioned, lies west of Santo Stefano Belbo mainly in Cuneo province where vineyards on cool slopes as high as 550 m at Mango are generally planted on steep, south-facing *sorì*. Almost half of DOC production is from Cuneo province. The second subzone is in the Canelli area in Asti's Langhe north and south of the Belbo, where most grapes for *spumante* come from slopes between 200-350 m, though higher points in the area, such as Calosso and Loazzolo, are known for fine, well-scented Moscato. The third subzone lies across the Belbo in Alto Monferrato. The relatively low hills around Calamandrana, Castel Boglione, Castel Rocchero, and Monteruzzo in Asti province and Alice Bel Colle and Ricaldone in Alessandria are known for rich, smooth Moscato. The area west of the Bormida in Alessandria province between Acqui Terme and Cassine is the warmest subzone. Vineyards on slopes of 150-200 m around Strevi produce rich Moscato of fine aroma that often seems better suited to *passito* than *spumante*.

Strevi was known in the past for Moscato that some producers feel still deserves a local appellation, as might wines from other towns or areas with their own traditions. At Loazzolo, for instance, producers have requested a DOC for a Moscato *passito* based on customs that predated production of sparkling wine in these hills. This tendency to return to the past seems to offer new promise to winemakers who are realizing that there can be more to Moscato's future than Asti Spumante.

Zone: Often steep hills of the Langhe and Alto Monferrato covering 29 communes in Asti province, nine in Alessandria (west of the Bormida river), and 15 in Cuneo, where it overlaps the Barbaresco zone east of Alba and includes a section of Barolo at Serralunga and of Roero around Santa Vittoria d'Alba.

Moscato d'Asti Sweet, aromatic white, usually frizzante. Grape: Moscato Bianco. Yld 82.5/110, Alc 10.5 (res sugar min 3.5%), Acd 0.5.

Asti Spumante or **Asti** or **Moscato d'Asti Spumante** Semisweet to sweet sparkling white. Grape: Moscato Bianco. Yld 82.5/110, Alc 12 (res sugar 2.5-5%), Acd 0.5.

Other wines of note

Asti province produces quantities of unclassified wine, much of it sold locally for everyday consumption. Large producers mainly in Monferrato have developed light, popular wines based on red varieties: the fizzy white Verbesco and the soft and sometimes bubbly red Arengo. Canelli is a major centre of sparkling wine production by both tank and bottle fermentation, but since grapes often come from other

Right: the ancient craft of barrel making is still active around Asti.

regions, no local appellations are anticipated. Some dry *spumanti* are mentioned with their producers, as are numerous vdt from Barbera, Chardonnay, and other varieties or blends.

ESTATES/GROWERS

(Moscato d'Asti producers in Cuneo province are listed under Alba.)

Agricola Monferrato, Nizza Monferrato (AT). Notable Barbera d'Asti.

Emilio Baino, Mongardino (AT). Good Barbera d'Asti.

Balbiano, Andezeno (TO). Producer of the rare Freisa di Chieri and Malvasia di Castelnuovo Don Bosco.

A. Bertelli, San Carlo di Costigliole d'Asti (AT). From their Giarone vineyards, Aldo and Alberto Bertelli produce fine Barbera d'Asti and convincing barrel-fermented Chardonnay, along with a Traminer called Plissé.

Alfiero Boffa, San Marzano Oliveto (AT). Fine Barbera d'Asti Vigna Ronco.

Bronda, Nizza Monferrato (AT). Barbera d'Asti.

Piero Bruno, Castagnole Monferrato (AT). Good Ruchè Bricco delle Donne.

Cascina Castlét, Costigliole d'Asti (AT). From 4 ha of vines, Maria Borio makes Barbera d'Asti Vigna Malabaila and two noted vdt from Barbera: Policalpo and Passum.

Cascina Gilli, Castelnuovo Don Bosco (AT). Freisa d'Asti Vigna del Forno.

Cascina La Barbatella, Nizza Monferrato (AT). Angelo Sonvico makes a promising Barbera vdt in *barrique* called Vigna dell'Angelo and Grignolino.

Cascina La Spinetta-Rivetti, Castagnole Lanze (AT). The Rivetti family makes the most praised of modern Moscato d'Asti from Bricco Quaglia, as well as good Barbera d'Asti Ca' di Pian.

Cascina Pesce, Nizza Monferrato (AT). Mario Pesce of Scarpa brings his usual flair to a full range of Asti and Acqui wines from 15 ha.

Castello del Poggio, Portacomaro (AT). Zonin of the Veneto makes DOC Grignolino, Barbera, Moscato d'Asti, and other wines from 90 ha of vines on this former Bersano estate.

Castello di Mombaruzzo, Mombaruzzo (AT). Asti DOCs and Cortese dell'Alto Monferrato.

Achille Ferraris, Agliano (AT). First-rate Barbera d'Asti Vigneto Nobbio.

Enzo Forno, Montaldo Scarampi (AT). Good Barbera and Grignolino d'Asti.

Forteto della Luja, Loazzolo (AT). Noted oenologist Giancarlo Scaglione, encouraged by Giacomo Bologna, blends tradition with innovation in making one of Italy's most acclaimed sweet wines at his small farm in hills south of Canelli. In vineyards nearly 500 m high with a plant density of 10,000 per ha, Moscato grapes are left to dry on the vine and develop botrytis cinerea before being crushed in a hand operated press. The wine is fermented for about 18 months in small barrels and racked frequently before being filtered through cloth to stop the fermentation with about 13 percent of alcohol and 4 percent residual sugar. The wine blends the luxury of pourriture noble with Moscato's exquisite flavours and textures – results that inspired other growers to follow and request a special DOC for Loazzolo.

They are Giuseppe Galliano with Borgo Maragliano, Armando Satragno with Borgo Sambui, and Giuseppe Laiolo with Bricchi Mej.

Incisa della Rocchetta, Rocchetta Tanaro (AT). Maria Incisa della Rocchetta (whose brother Mario originated Sassicaia in Tuscany), makes Barbera and Grignolino at the family estate in Piedmont.

Il Milin, San Marzanotto d'Asti (AT). Fratelli Rovero make Barbera Giustin and Grignolino Casa Lina, along with the *barrique*-aged Barbera vdt Rouvé from 11 ha on this estate.

La Badia, Montegrosso d'Asti (AT). Luigi Pia makes good Barbera.

Massimo Marengo, Castagnole Monferrato (AT). Noted Ruchè.

Miravalle, Refrancore (AT). Ruchè.

Moncucchetto, Casorzo d'Asti. Pietro and Carlo Biletta make fine Barbera d'Asti, Freisa, Grignolino, and Ruchè from 14 ha at Cascina Moncucchetto.

Domenico Perroncito, Mongardino (AT). Good Barbera d'Asti.

Renato Rabezzana, San Desiderio d'Asti. The owner of an *enoteca* in Turin has an estate for Grignolino and the fine Barbera d'Asti Il Bricco.

Fratelli Renosio, Montaldo Scarampi (AT). Good Barbera d'Asti Vigna Castellazzo.

Ruchè del Parrocco, Castagnole Monferrato (AT). Don Giacomo Cauda makes noted Ruchè, Barbera, Grignolino.

Luigi Spertino, Mombercelli (AT). Fine Barbera and an interesting late harvested Grignolino called Vendemmiatardiva.

Tenuta dei Re, Castagnole Monferrato (AT). Grignolino d'Asti.

Renato Trinchero, Agliano (AT). Fine Barbera d'Asti Vigna del Noce.

Above: the ingenious Giacomo Bologna in his cellars at Rocchetta Tanaro, where he created Bricco dell'Uccellone, a Barbera aged in small oak barrels.

Fratelli Vignale, Belveglio (AT). Good Barbera and Grignolino d'Asti.

Villa Fiorita, Castello d'Annone (AT). Fine Grignolino and Barbera d'Asti.

Villa Pattono, Costigliole d'Asti (AT). Renato Ratti's sons Giovanni and Piero with Massimo Martinelli make the persuasive vdt Villa Pattono from Barbera, Freisa, and Uvalino in *barriques*.

Piero Zaccone, Grana Monferrato (AT). Good Barbera d'Asti.

Agostino Zuccarino, Rocchetta Tanaro (AT). Good Barbera d'Asti.

WINE HOUSES/MERCHANTS

Antica Casa Vinicola Scarpa, Nizza Monferrato (AT). Mario Pesce has made Scarpa a model of reliable class with wines from southern Piedmont, including its own Poderi Bricchi di Castelrocchero and Moirano, source of unique dry vdt Brachetto and Freisa. Asti DOCs and vineyards include Barbera (Banin dell'Annunziata, Bogliona, Possabreno), Grignolino (San Defendente), and the Ruchè known as Rouchet (Bricco Rosa, Varolino). From Alba come Barolo (Le Coste di Monforte, Tettimorra), Barbaresco (Barberis, Tettineive), and Nebbiolo d'Alba (Moirane).

Antiche Cantine Brema, Incisa Scapaccino (AT). Reliable range of Asti wines, led by Barbera, including single vineyard bottlings in part from the Brema family's Cascina Croce.

Bava, Cocconato d'Asti (AT). The Bava family makes a full range of Asti wines of sound quality enhanced by the "Quintetto" labels showing musical instruments, as well as a popular Malvasia di Castelnuovo Don Bosco. Among other wines produced is a Barolo from their own vineyards.

Bersano, Nizza Monferrato (AT). The Bersano family developed the Antico Podere Conti della Cremosina with a spirit that made them leaders in Asti, as recorded in the museum compiled by Arturo Bersano that honours local winemaking traditions. After a period of uncertainty under Seagram's control, Bersano seems to be recovering under Italian ownership with improving wines from Asti and Alba, plus Gavi from leased vineyards of the Marchese di Raggio.

Bosca, Canelli (AT). The Bosca group recently sold its firm of Canei, for popular wines, to the French Pernod Ricard. Among other projects, Bosca, long a producer of vermouth and *spumanti* (also under the Tosti label), is developing nearly 150 ha of vineyards for quality wines.

Braida-Giacomo Bologna, Rocchetta Tanaro (AT). Giacomo Bologna, more than an accomplished *negoçiant*, is a creative force in Piedmontese wine, a man of uncommon foresight, wit, and drive, blessed with the charisma to put his ideas across. His Bricco dell'Uccellone and Bricco della Bigotta from vineyards above Rocchetta Tanaro gave Barbera and its producers new standards and inspiration. The house wines, made with the aid of oenologist Giancarlo Scaglione, include exemplary Barbera La Monella, Grignolino, and Moscato d'Asti.

Giorgio Carnevale, Cerro Tanaro (AT). Giorgio and Alessandro Carnevale produce a range of Asti wines of unerring class, led by the fine Barbera Il Crottino.

Cinzano, Torino. The firm founded in 1757 is a major producer of vermouth and Asti at its main cellars at Santa Vittoria d'Alba, along with the respected *champenoise* Cinzano Brut and Marone Cinzano Pas Dosé and other *spumanti* such as Pinot Chardonnay and Principe di Piemonte Riserva. It also owns Col d'Orcia in Montalcino for Brunello and Rosso and with the Illva group of Saronno controls the largest producer of Marsala in Savi Florio. The company has numerous subsidiaries abroad.

Cocchi, Asti. Rare Asti *spumante* *champenoise* and Barolo Chinato.

Giuseppe Contratto, Canelli (AT). The family house founded in 1867 was noted for bottle-fermented Asti, though Alberto Contratto has enhanced its reputation with *champenoise* (including Brut Riserva, Bacco d'Oro, Imperial Riserva Sabauda, Reserve for England, and Riserva Novecento) and choice DOCs of Asti and Alba. The firm also has estates for Barolo (Cascina Secolo) and Barbaresco (Cascina Alberta).

Coppo, Canelli (AT). Brothers Piero, Gianni, Paolo, and Roberto Coppo have brought new lustre to their established *spumante* house with wines from the estate of La Galleria near Asti (Grignolino Il Rotondino, the *barrique*-aged Barbera d'Asti Camp du Rouss, and the Chardonnay-based Monteriolo), Gavi from La Rocca, and the *champenoise* Brut Riserva Coppo.

Cora, Canelli (AT). The ancient vermouth house also makes *spumanti*.

Clemente Cossetti & Figli, Castelnuovo Belbo (AT). Barbera Cascina Salomone and other Asti DOCs, in part from 12 ha of vineyards.

Michele Chiarlo-Cantine Duca d'Asti, Calamandrana (AT). Chiarlo and oenologist Roberto Bezzato in cellars at Calamandrana, Gavi, and Barolo have developed an array of invariably well made DOC wines from Monferrato and Alba, along with *spumanti* and vdt. Prestige bottlings include Barbera d'Asti Valle del Sole, Gavi Fior di Rovere, Grignolino San Lorenzo, Moscato d'Asti Rocca delle Uccellette, Barolo Vigna Rionda di Serralunga, Rocche di Castiglione and Cannubi, Barbaresco Rabajà, and the vdt Barilot from Nebbiolo and Barbera.

Fratelli Gancia, Canelli (AT). The house founded in 1850 by Carlo Gancia remains a leader with *spumanti* and vermouth while expanding interests under director Vittorio Vallarino Gancia into cellars and estates in Piedmont and Apulia. Production of about 20 million bottles annually based at the Santo Stefano Belbo cellars includes Asti as well as the popular Pinot di Pinot and the more recent Gancia dei Gancia and Castello Gancia dry sparkling wines. Investments in the Torrebianco estate and Rivera (*see* under Apulia) have been complemented by an interest in Cantine Sebaste and bottling of other Piedmontese wines under the Mirafiore brand and Barolo Chinato under Castello di Canelli. Gancia also distributes Castello Vicchiomaggio Chianti and Castello di Tassarolo Gavi.

Gilardino, Canelli (AT). Carlo Micca Bocchino, noted distiller, also makes commendable wines from Asti and Alba.

Clemente Guasti & Figli, Nizza Monferrato (AT). Asti DOCs in part from own vineyards.

Martini & Rossi, Torino. Founded in 1863 in Turin, Martini & Rossi Ivlas is the Italian base of an international conglomerate known as the General Beverage Corporation that leads the world in production of vermouth in its main plant at Pessione and branches in major European countries, North and South America, Japan, and Australia. The company, headed by the Rossi di Montelera family descendants of Luigi Rossi, one of the founders, also leads in production of Asti Spumante with about 17 million bottles annually from its cellars at Santo Stefano Belbo, along with sparkling Riesling Oltrepò Pavese from Lombardy and the *champenoise* Riserva Montelera Brut. The company's wine museum at Pessione contains a fascinating collection of relics from the Piedmontese tradition as well as Greek and Roman.

Riccadona, Canelli (AT). The firm headed by Ottavio Riccadonna is a major producer of vermouth, Asti Spumante, and dry sparkling wines, including the popular President Reserve and the *champenoise* Conte Balduino Extra Brut and Riserva Privata Angelo Riccadonna. The company also has controlling interest of Valfieri (*see* under Alba) and a share of Bersano.

Scrimaglio, Nizza Monferrato (AT). Reliable producer with a notable Barbera Croutin.

Terre da Vino, Moriondo (TO). Expanding *negoçiant* operation with DOCs selected from various zones of Piedmont.

G.L. Viarengo, Castello di Annone (AT). Barbera and Grignolino d'Asti.

COOPERATIVES

Antiche Terre dei Galleani, Agliano (AT). Small cellars specialize in Barbera.

Antica Contea di Castelvero, Castel Boglione (AT). From growers with 650 ha, a sound range of Asti wines led by Barbera Collina Croja.

CS di Castelnuovo Calcea, Castelnuovo Calcea (AT). Specialists in Barbera.

I Vignöt, Costigliole d'Asti (AT). Good Barbera and Grignolino d'Asti.

CS di Mombercelli, Mombercelli (AT). Barbera and Grignolino d'Asti.

CS Sette Colli, Moncalvo (AT). Asti DOCs.

CS di Nizza Monferrato, Nizza Monferrato (AT). Good Barbera d'Asti and Acqui DOCs.

CS di Rocchetta Tanaro, Rocchetta Tanaro (AT).

CS di Vinchio e Vaglio Serra, Vinchio d'Asti (AT). Oenologist Giuliano Noë makes exemplary Asti and Monferrato DOCs of good value.

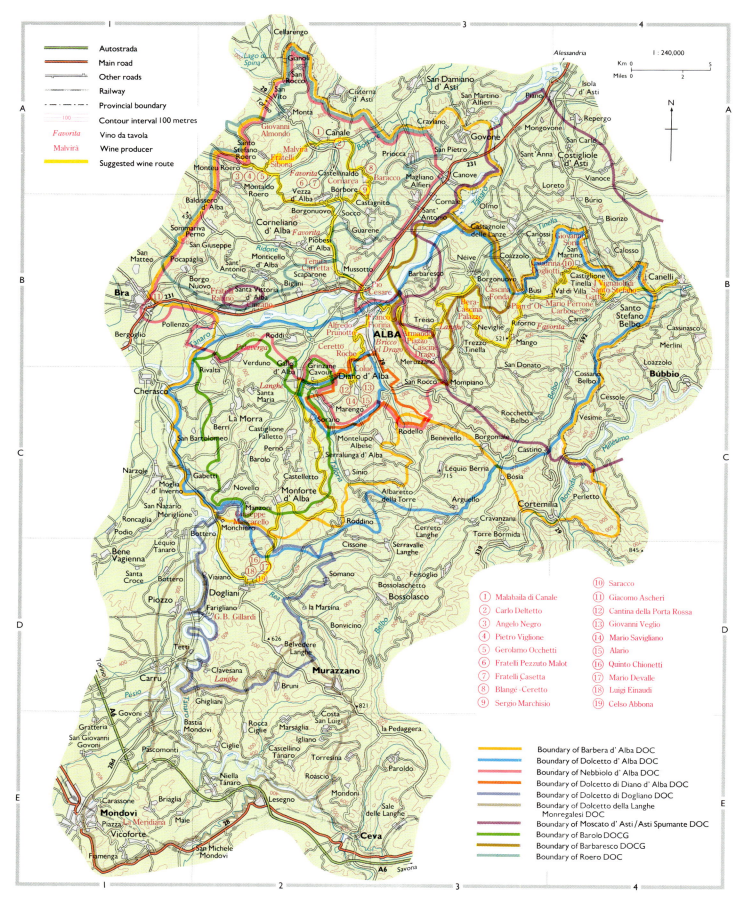

Legend

- Autostrada
- Main road
- Other roads
- Railway
- Provincial boundary
- *100* Contour interval 100 metres
- *Favorita* Vino da tavola
- *Malvirà* Wine producer
- Suggested wine route

1:240,000

① Malabaila di Canale
② Carlo Deltetto
③ Angelo Negro
④ Pietro Viglione
⑤ Gerolamo Occhetti
⑥ Fratelli Pezzuto Malot
⑦ Fratelli Casetta
⑧ Blangé-Ceretto
⑨ Sergio Marchisio
⑩ Saracco
⑪ Giacomo Ascheri
⑫ Cantina della Porta Rossa
⑬ Giovanni Veglio
⑭ Mario Savigliano
⑮ Alario
⑯ Quinto Chionetti
⑰ Mario Devalle
⑱ Luigi Einaudi
⑲ Celso Abbona

- Boundary of Barbera d' Alba DOC
- Boundary of Dolcetto d' Alba DOC
- Boundary of Nebbiolo d' Alba DOC
- Boundary of Dolcetto di Diano d' Alba DOC
- Boundary of Dolcetto di Dogliani DOC
- Boundary of Dolcetto della Langhe Monregalesi DOC
- Boundary of Moscato d' Asti / Asti Spumante DOC
- Boundary of Barolo DOCG
- Boundary of Barbaresco DOCG
- Boundary of Roero DOC

ALBA

By political standards Alba, a town of 30,000 inhabitants on the Tanaro river, isn't important enough to rate a province of its own, so it serves as overseer of the eastern part of "la pruvincia granda" of Cuneo, Italy's largest such territory. But by epicurean standards Alba has earned sovereignty as Piedmont's capital of red wine and the world's capital of white truffles. Vines and truffles have found an exceptional environment in Albese, Alba's dominion which extends through most of the two ranges of hills known as the Langa or Langhe to the south and east of the Tanaro and Roero or Roeri to the north and west. Alba, whose location in the valley gave it relatively easy access to Asti and Turin, emerged as a wine centre in the late nineteenth century as farmers who had acquired vineyards through land reform sold grapes to merchants in the town. In those days growers rarely made wine to sell, since their plots were small and they lacked the equipment and experience for vinifying and ageing. So vintners in the hill towns and the few estates that made their own wine gravitated towards the markets of Alba.

The town's reputation grew as Barolo and Barbaresco rose to become Italy's most prestigious red wines. They went on to achieve DOCG, yet these classics of Italian wine often seem less compatible with local tastes than the Dolcetto, Barbera, and other reds from Nebbiolo grouped under Alba's seven DOCs. Foreign palates, too, often find the heavy tannins and chewy textures of the traditional Nebbiolo wines hard to deal with. An easier approach to the variety is through the lighter Nebbiolo d'Alba or the DOC red of Roero. New winemaking techniques have helped give Barolo and Barbaresco mellower flavours and more immediate appeal than before, but even around Alba they aren't considered wines for everyday. Barbera clearly is, however, though some growers who have planted vines in favoured sites and restricted yields from them have made wines of real interest in the DOC zone that extends over the Roero and much of the Langhe. Dolcetto with its rich yet softly bittersweet flavours is the favourite in the Langhe, where it thrives in high vineyards of the Barolo and Barbaresco zones (as Dolcetto d'Alba), as well as at Dogliani and Diano d'Alba and on the distant rises of the Langhe Monregalesi. Although they don't rate DOC, Freisa and the rare Grignolino of Albese sometimes show more than the classified wines of Asti.

Alba's vineyards are fairly evenly distributed between Nebbiolo, Barbera, and Dolcetto, though production from the first two varieties seems to have levelled off while Dolcetto's popularity is increasing. Yet the prevalent variety for DOC wines is Moscato d'Asti, mainly from vineyards in the Langhe between the Barbaresco zone and Santo Stefano Belbo. Alba had never been noted for dry whites, but the revival of Arneis in Roero and the emergence of persuasive vdt Chardonnay, Sauvignon, and Pinot have raised doubts about the adage that Albese is by nature red wine country.

Other attitudes are also changing in what is still often regarded as Italy's most conservative wine area even if leading producers have set new standards that have little to do with the complacent patterns of the past. Alba's wine industry was long commanded by merchants and *negoçiants* whose control of grape and wine prices made it hard for small estates or independent growers to create markets. Most wines, including Barolo and Barbaresco from different vineyards, were blended and bottled with a brand and the general denomination on the label. Some houses in the Alba area, as well as in Asti province, built reputations for reliability or even excellence. But some bottlers and shippers located on the fringes of the zone or in other areas sold cheap wines that aroused suspicions about origins, even after DOC was introduced in the late-1960s. Some were merely continuing an old practice of blending in strong southern wines to enrich locally produced Nebbiolo or other varieties from inadequate vineyards or poor years. But the presence of those questionable bottles on the market did nothing for the status of Alba's wines.

In a move to uphold individual integrity, several producers who had regularly made wines from certain vineyards began identifying them on labels – a normal practice in Burgundy and other parts of France. Some even used the term "cru" until European authorities reminded them that that was reserved for the French. But the concept, encouraged by Renato Ratti when he was director of the Barolo and Barbaresco producers' consortium and promoted by the wine writer Luigi Veronelli, gained momentum. At first it was used mainly for Barolo and Barbaresco by small-scale vineyard owners and *negoçiants*, but it has come to apply to a majority of Alba's premium wines bottled by estates and merchants alike. The practice, which so far relies on each producer's sense of honour, has no doubt been abused by some who know that there is still no way of verifying that grapes come from a particular *bricco* or *sorì*. Nor has the idea been accepted by producers who insist that blending of grapes from different places results in wines of better balance and complexity.

But single vineyard bottlings, more than a trend, are a confirmed reality. In putting new emphasis on special plots they have significantly increased both land values and wine prices. The movement seems to have heightened the competitive spirit in an area where company rivalries, family feuds, and personal conflicts were already common-place when winemaking was a tranquil occupation. It has helped to break down the

patriarchal structure of Alba's wine trade as production has become decentralized. Many merchants have acquired vineyards or estates and growers have equipped cellars to make wines under their own names and labels. An important result of the revolution is that it has encouraged young people, often graduates of Alba's prestigious school of oenology, to establish their own careers in wine rather than work for a company. Not long ago vineyards in the area were readily available at relatively low cost, even in Barolo and Barbaresco, but lately there has been a rush for choice land among winemakers increasingly convinced that the only way to assure quality is to grow their own grapes.

Below: a truffle hunter and his dog.

Wines of Roero

Nebbiolo in the Roero or Roeri hills is different from the rest: lighter in colour and body, fruitier and livelier. The typology is attributed to the sandy siliceous clay soils on slopes, often cleaved by fissures and ravines, that more resemble those of the adjoining Monferrato hills of Asti than the Langhe. Roero's vineyards, rarely higher than 300 to 350 metres, are slightly warmer than Barolo's heights, so grapes ripen earlier for wines that don't need long cask ageing to become buoyantly drinkable. Nebbiolo d'Alba made mainly from vineyards in Roero had a style that found admirers beyond Piedmont. But the appellation, shared with wines from the fringes of the Barolo and Barbaresco zones across the river, seemed to suggest second class status to the bigger Nebbiolo wines. So producers in the hills requested and were granted a DOC of their own called simply Roero. Meanwhile, the Arneis that had been grown there for softening Nebbiolo suddenly came into its own as a varietal white whose unexpected success prompted a recent addition to the DOC. But the increasing popularity of Roero's simplistic Favorita perhaps more than anything else indicates Alba's serious shortage of native white varieties.

Nebbiolo d'Alba (1970)

The appellation applies to Nebbiolo grown on both sides of the Tanaro river, excluding the Barolo and Barbaresco zones, but production has always been centred in Roero and the commune of Alba. When dry (there are also sweet and bubbly versions) and aged for a spell in casks, Nebbiolo d'Alba can show the variety's innate nobility with enviably drinkable style. Leading examples are Bruno Giacosa's Valmaggiore, Prunotto's Occhetti, Ratti's Ochetti, Scarpa's Moirane, Gaja's Vignaveja, and Ceretto's Lantasco. Producers north of the Tanaro tend to distinguish between Nebbiolo d'Alba as a wine for moderate ageing and Roero for a more youthful style.

Zone: Hills in 25 communes of Cuneo province, extending northwest of the Tanaro in an area that overlies the entire Roero zone and south of the river in the communes of Alba, Montelupo Albese, Sinio, Roddino, and

Monchiero and parts of Verduno, Roddi, Grinzane Cavour, Diano d'Alba, Monforte d'Alba, and Novello that aren't included in Barolo. Dry red, sometimes sweet and spumante. Grape: Nebbiolo. Yld 63/90, Alc 12, Acd 0.5, Ag secco 1 yr.

Roero/Arneis di Roero (1985, Arneis 1989)

The name Roero alone on a label denotes the red from Nebbiolo whose production has risen steadily to approach a million bottles a year. But before Roero could establish its own clear identity it had already been upstaged by Arneis. That vine was noted in the hills as early as the 15th century as Renesium, but not long ago it had practically disappeared. Its grapes were good to eat and its wines were useful for blending down Nebbiolo to make it lighter and softer in its youth. But Arneis, whose name means "rascal" in dialect because of its unpredictable behaviour, was so lightly regarded that it was planted amidst Nebbiolo because it ripened first and its sweet grapes drew bees away from the more prized dark bunches. Some growers made simple dry whites from it before the 1970s when Vietti and Bruno Giacosa did limited bottlings that drew attention.

The arrival of the Ceretto brothers in Roero, first in collaboration with Cornarea and then with their own estate of Blangé, increased the momentum that has also led to planting of Arneis across the river in the Langhe. But Roero's terrains seem better suited to this dry white of scant scent but lively fruit flavours which in well made versions last long enough to mingle with the almondy aftertaste. Blangé wins the prize for stylish packaging but Giacosa's Arneis, if sometimes described locally as atypical, has drawn the highest praise from foreign experts. The American critic Robert Parker once wrote in *The Wine Advocate* that "Arneis seems to be Italy's most distinctive indigenous white wine grape." Even some of its producers seem to doubt that potential, but it's comforting to note that Chardonnay isn't the only rising star among Alba's whites.

Zone: The Roero or Roeri hills extending north from the stretch of the Tanaro river between Alba and Bra through 19 communes in Cuneo province, including Canale, Monteu Roero, Santo Stefano Roero, and Vezza d'Alba where production is most intense.

Roero Dry red. Grapes: Nebbiolo, Arneis 2-5%; other varieties up to 3%. Yld 56/80, Alc 11.5; superiore 12, Acd 0.5, Ag 8 mths.
Roero Arneis or **Arneis di Roero** Dry white, also spumante. Grape: Arneis. Yld 70/100, Alc 10.5; superiore 11.5, Acd 0.5, Ag superiore 1 yr.

Other wines of note

Many producers of Roero also make Barbera d'Alba, whose zone overlies the hills. Moscati d'Asti DOC can be produced in the commune of Santa Vittoria d'Alba, where Cinzano has its main cellars. Roero DOC does not include the traditional sweet Arneis from *passito* grapes, though several producers make it as unclassified wine. The Favorita grown in Roero may be related to Liguria's Vermentino, but its white wines seem to lack distinguishing character. It is a recognized vdt from the communes of Corneliano, Piobesi, and Vezza. Montà also has a recognized vdt for its red, white, and rosé.

ESTATES/GROWERS

Giovanni Almondo, Montà (CN). Roero and Arneis.
Blangé-Ceretto, Castellinaldo (CN). The exhilarating flavours of Arneis

from 4 ha of vineyards on the Blangé estate and 10 ha on a second property, shows Marcello Ceretto's style with white wine.
Cornarea, Canale (CN). From 18.5 ha of vines Francesca Rapetti makes respected Roero and Arneis, including a *passito* called Tarasco.
Malabaila di Canale, Canale (CN). From 8 ha, respected Arneis Pradvaj, Roero Bric Volta, and Nebbiolo d'Alba Bric Merli.
Malvirà, Canale (CN). Roberto and Massimo Damonte make good single vineyard Arneis, Roero, Favorita, and a promising vdt San Guglielmo from Barbera with Nebbiolo and Bonarda in *barrique*.
Angelo Negro & Figli, Monteu Roero (CN). Roero and Arneis.
Gerolamo Occhetti, Monteu Roero (CN). Fine soft, fruity Roero.
Fratelli Pezzuto Malot, Vezza d'Alba (CN). Arneis and Roero.
Fratelli Rabino, Sant Vittoria d'Alba (CN). Fine Nebbiolo d'Alba, along with Roero, Arneis, and other Alba wines at reasonable prices.
Fratelli Sibona, Santo Stefano Roero (CN). Roero and Arneis.
Tenuta Carretta, Piobesi (CN). From properties on both sides of the Tanaro, good Roero, Arneis, Nebbiolo d'Alba, and vdt Brachetto as well as Barolo from Cannubi.
Pietro Viglione & Figlio, Monteu Roero, (CN). Roero and Arneis in a dry version called Bricula and a sweet type called Rivat Dus.

WINE HOUSES/MERCHANTS

Baracco, Castellinaldo (CN). Reliable Alba reds, including the Nebbiolo Baracco di Baracho.
Fratelli Casetta, Vezza d'Alba (CN). Among a range of Alba wines, Arneis and Roero Vigna Pioiero.
Carlo Deltetto, Canale (CN). Along with good Roero and dry Arneis comes the enticingly sweet version of Arneis called Bric Tupin.
Sergio Marchisio, Castellinaldo (CN). Roero and Arneis.
(Other producers of Arneis are listed under the Langhe.)

COOPERATIVES

Produttori Montaldesi Associati, Montaldo Roero (CN). Roero and Arneis.

Wines of the Langhe

The Maritime Alps meld with the Apennines along the border of Liguria, forming the watershed from where the Tanaro, Belbo, and Bormida rivers flow north into Piedmont through the hills known as the Langhe. There, in vineyards planted since the Middle Ages, Nebbiolo has asserted supremacy over other vines. But, having a primadonna's temperament, it needed the proper stages to perform, and with time it found them on *sorì* of calcareous marl around Alba where the wines came to be called after the villages of Barolo and Barbaresco. The climate in the lower Langhe is moderated by currents from the Tanaro valley that provide ventilation in summer and bring mists in autumn that allow Nebbiolo grapes to ripen slowly and develop the extract and intensity of fruit to balance the ample acids and tannins in the wines.

In the early days winemaking in the Langhe was largely the concern of patrician landowners, whose domains surrounded villages marked by towering castles or churches of architectural designs that expressed a remarkable diversity of tastes. Even today each town along the dome-like crests and sculpted promontories of the range has its own peculiar mix of medieval and modern and its own personality that carries over into the wines it produces. The silhouettes of these motley citadels stand out against the Langhe's steep slopes which, being free of surface rocks, permit planting of vines in rows of regimental order. This uniformity belies the fact that vineyards are fragmented into often minuscule plots whose owners sometimes seem to have memorized property lines rather than mark them. Here function generates its own kind of splendour that stands out on those autumn mornings when the hills tinted with the auburn of turning vine leaves loom like islands in a sea of fog. For visual effects the Langhe may not equal the sheer drama of the heights of Etna or the upper Adige valley nor can it match the Renaissance glamour of Chianti or Orvieto. But no other landscape of Italy so conveys how deeply vines and wines are rooted in a people's culture.

In an era when alternative varieties triumph elsewhere in wines uninhibited by DOC,

Above: vineyards in Barolo where subtle variations in components of the calcareous clay soils account for marked differences in wines from either side of the zone.

Above: the village of Castiglione Falletto has an 11th-century castle and some prime vineyards for Barolo in Monprivato, Villero, and Rocche di Castiglione.

winemakers of the Langhe maintain an abiding faith in Nebbiolo and the ultimate worth of Barolo and Barbaresco as DOCG. Some look for inspiration to Burgundy, a region often compared with their own. And, indeed, the *vignaioli* of the Langhe often show traits in common with the *vignerons* of the Côte d'Or: in the deep attachment to parcels of land, the proud, even stubborn sense of tradition, the keen competitive spirit, and that gleam in the eye that tells you that theirs is the nonpareil of wines. Yet none of this seems to affect their outward simplicity of manner.

The Langhe's ancient wines, if usually sweet, seem to have been more individualistic than the modern. Not until the nineteenth century did any emerge with more than a local appellation. Barolo gained prominence in the 1840s after Victurine Colbert, the French-born wife of the Marchese Falletti, scion of the town, hired compatriot Louis Oudart as winemaker. His conversion of previously sweet Nebbiolo into a dry wine aged in barrels was such a revelation that Piedmont's Prime Minister Cavour hired him to do the same at his castle at nearby Grinzane. Members of the Savoy family created their own royal estates as vineyards for Barolo spread through other villages in the hills southwest of Alba. Nebbiolo's class was also well known at Barbaresco, a village to the northeast, but the wine of the name didn't emerge until the 1890s when Domizio Cavazza, founder of Alba's wine school, organized a cooperative of growers from the area.

But Nebbiolo didn't thrive everywhere. Even in Barolo and Barbaresco it reacted sensitively to diverse conditions. Subvarieties were singled out as Michet, Lampia, and Rosé, as now specified in production codes, but studies suggest that Nebbiolo is subject to local mutations that determine the sizes and shapes of clusters and grapes and that these differences are not necessarily clonal. Even in the best of sites it yields less than other local varieties, which is why its value to growers depends on how well wine markets are moving. Where conditions aren't right, they often plant Dolcetto, which ripens early and does well on higher, cooler plots, or else Barbera, which prefers a *sorì*

but being accommodating by nature will produce ripe fruit even on a north-facing slope.

Dolcetto in the Langhe becomes the most stylish of Piedmont's everyday wines, but typology varies from place to place. In the Alba DOC zone that spans Barolo and Barbaresco its wines' vibrantly fruity qualities draw all too frequent comparisons to Beaujolais with which it really has little in common. In the Dogliani zone, Dolcetto's firmer structure requires time to show style. At Diano d'Alba, Dolcetto is distinguished as the first DOC with all vineyards recognized by name. Barbera, too, when it isn't relegated to its usual minor role, can shine in the Langhe, both in single vineyard DOC and *barrique*-aged vdt. The other major variety is Moscato, planted mainly in the steep hills between Alba and Santo Stefano Belbo. Its production is described under Moscato d'Asti (*see* page 53), though producers of Albese are listed with those of the Langhe.

Barolo and Barbaresco tower over the other wines in prestige, but if anything this aura of nobility has inhibited popular appeal. Some Italian experts who routinely rank them at the top of the national hierarchy only rarely drink them. And some foreign critics who seem to feel obliged to call them great might confess in private to not really understanding them.

Their true admirers – if divided first between devotees of Barolo or Barbaresco and then between advocates of traditional or contemporary styles – don't seem to mind that they're considered wines for experienced palates. The fact that neither resembles Bordeaux or Burgundy or Brunello di Montalcino only weighs in their favour. They are probably too widely known to qualify as cult wines, but acquiring a taste for their rich, warm, intriguing but uncompromising characters is better considered a privilege than an obligation.

If Barolo has the bigger reputation, Barbaresco is often considered the more agreeable of the two. But many producers of the Langhe would rather do away with the stereotypes and have their wines judged on actual merits. The combination of scientific winemaking and a series of fine vintages has improved quality dramatically while making both wines more approachable. But, in Italy at least, Barolo and Barbaresco are looked upon as being stuffy, an image that dates to the era when other wines were evolving and they seemed to be standing still.

The vinification methods that prevailed for decades in the area involved fermentation in contact with the skins of very ripe grapes for up to two months in wooden vats to extract tannins and build substance. The wines were then placed in large oak or chestnut casks to undergo malolactic fermentation gradually and age for years to lose their initial toughness. From fine vintages some Barolo and Barbaresco reserves achieved monumental stature with uniquely elaborate bouquets and austerely complex flavours. But they didn't always age as well as their producers pretended they did and if the workmanship wasn't right – and too often it wasn't – they oxidized, developing peculiar odours and flavours with which even veteran imbibers couldn't always contend.

A run of mediocre vintages in the 1970s kept skilled traditionalists from reaching top form and blocked emerging progressives from showing new styles. Markets were further confused by the presence of bottlers' innocuous blends on store shelves and by the sale of thick, heavy wines from *cantine* in the zones – all carrying the noble names. Many Italians decided that Barolo and Barbaresco weren't right for their modern palates and turned to other sources for lighter, easier reds. By the late 1970s, sales, which had never been rapid, slowed to crisis levels. The wines retained some loyalist followings in Italy and abroad, but their only real gains for years were in the German and Swiss markets. German-speaking wine drinkers, in becoming the leading customers for Barolo and Barbaresco, have given them a decisive lift towards new heights of quality and prestige.

Behind the scenes the Langhe's wine industry has changed more profoundly and rapidly than is generally perceived. Most wineries large and small are now directed by oenologists who strive to bring out the best of the temperamental Nebbiolo whatever the challenge. Grapes are often picked earlier when their components are in better balance. Fermentations – both alcoholic and malolactic – are now usually conducted under controlled temperature, which might be the most significant improvement to date. Even traditionalists consider stainless steel fermenting vats essential and most have shortened contact with the skins to less than a month, important factors in the more accessible styles of wines that manage to maintain size and structure while showing better harmony of bouquet and flavour.

Progressives limit skin contact to as little as ten days, on the theory that that is long enough to extract the so-called soft tannins and leave behind the hard tannins that account for sharp, gritty flavours. The other point of contention is wood ageing, which some producers of reserve wines extend for years in large oak casks but progressives often hold to the minimum two years for Barolo and one for Barbaresco. More and more producers round out their wines in *barriques* – a practice studiously avoided by the old school. Wines made in the new way tend to be a shade lighter and softer than the old with fresher scents and more vital fruit flavours that can make them drinkable after just a year or two in bottle. Yet producers insist that they will outlast the old because they have better balance. The Langhe's most visible producers, Gaja and Ceretto, have developed personalized techniques for Barbaresco and Barolo that have proved to be on target for international tastes. Gaja's methods, which rely on *barriques*, have made a resounding impact on other winemakers of the Langhe, the young in particular, who are eagerly honing styles of their own.

Still, even if critics like to point to models of the old school and the new, the wines aren't always as discernible as their advocates suggest. For after the essential differentiations are made between vintages and vineyards, what sets the Langhe's wines most emphatically apart from one another is not the philosophy behind them but the talent. Basic methods can only be advanced to a point after which skilled craftsmanship, or, in some cases, artistic touches, play a determining role. The quality of grapes from low yielding vines is fundamental, though it is often said here that top winemakers are distinguished by good performances in off years. Recently they have had little chance to prove it, though, since the Langhe has enjoyed a series of outstanding harvests in the 1980s. After 1982 was greeted with superlatives, 1985 was hailed as the vintage of the century. Small but mostly favourable crops in 1986 and 1987 were followed by such extraordinary harvests in 1988 and 1989 caused some producers to wonder if they hadn't spoken too soon of the '85.

Emerging vintages of Barolo and Barbaresco have generated enough international attention to have reawakened interest among Italians who had been ignoring the wines for years. But what some producers hail as the dawn of a golden age for the wines of the Langhe is not without doubts. Growers, who acknowledge that the unusually long recent periods of heat and drought aided the great vintages, worry about the long-term effects of stress on the vines. Several winters passed with little snow, which normally falls heavily in the hills and in melting seeps moisture deep into the soil to sustain vines over the summer.

Nor are markets steady. Grape prices rose through the decade, a factor reflected in the wines. But most remain within reasonable limits for fine wines that are still not

Above: Marcello (left) and Bruno Ceretto, are leading innovators with Alba's wines.

international favourites. Collectors seem willing to pay for individual achievements, as they have for Barbaresco from Gaja and Barolo from Ceretto that have reached price levels close to those of the elite châteaux of France. Some other producers have tried to follow, but most resist the temptation, perhaps realizing that the DOCG of Barolo and Barbaresco does not carry anywhere near the weight of the classified growths of Bordeaux and Burgundy.

Alba's winemakers, with their links to France, know how important *crus* can be in building an image, as illustrated by the single vineyard wines they have been issuing for years. Many producers, but not all, support the drive to systematically identify the vineyards of Barolo and Barbaresco. Solid bases exist for such recognition, not only in current records but in annals dating back over a century. In 1879, Lorenzo Fantini, assessor of agriculture and an estate owner in Barolo, compiled a remarkable ledger listing each vineyard of the Barolo and Barbaresco zones with, where merited, the notation "posizione scelta" or "buona", or, rarely, "sceltissime". Many of his evaluations still hold, even if some names have changed or vanished and new vineyards have been created. Renato Ratti personally mapped both zone's major vineyards and in Barolo singled out those of "first category" and "historical vocation" before he died in 1988. Other writers have listed more vineyards and even presumed to rank them.

National and regional officials discourage such initiatives, perhaps fearing controversies. But in 1986 the commune of Diano d'Alba recognized 77 vineyards, or *sorì*, for its Dolcetto DOC. That move was backed by the provincial agriculture board and the consortium of Alba wine producers, who use it as a model in miniature for more ambitious projects in Barolo and Barbaresco. The aim is to individuate vineyards of proven worth for authorized use on labels, but not to classify them. For even if Barolo and Barbaresco are in many ways the most qualified of Italy's wine zones, the criteria for rating their vineyards are still inadequate.

But that does not deny that the basic worth of vineyards in each zone is generally known. The legends of Cannubi in the commune of Barolo, Bussia in Monforte d'Alba, Rocche in Castiglione Falletto, and Rabajà and Asili in Barbaresco aren't just folklore. Some *negoçiants* who buy grapes in those places can recite the performance records of each plot year to year. Yet if any ten were asked to rank Barolo's vineyards in order they would come up with ten different classifications. Ratings by writers might be even more unpredictable. It comes down to a matter of taste, of individual preference, pride, and prejudice. French classifications were based mainly on the market value over time of wines from certain vineyards or estates. But in Barolo and Barbaresco single vineyard bottlings are too recent to follow that guideline.

Nor does the historical status of a vineyard guarantee that it will produce the best of modern wines. In the past a *sorì* was often designated in winter as the place on a hillside where the snow melted first, meaning that ample sunshine would assure early and complete ripening of grapes. That was a clear advantage when wine prices were based on alcoholic strength and Barolo and Barbaresco were often judged more on power than finesse. A sun-drenched plot in a hot year renders grapes with plenty of sugar, tannins, and extract but wines can lack fruit and aroma. Lately some producers have preferred Nebbiolo from cooler positions where the slower ripening heightens primary aromas in more balanced, elegant wines. Even if certain vineyards have been noted for over a century, others have only recently acquired the name of a *sorì*, *bricco*, or just plain *vigneto* with no known historical value. These wines haven't been in evidence long enough to conclude whether their class owes more to the terrain or the winemaker. But anyone tempted to classify their vineyards might do well to remember that up to now some of the grandest *crus* of Barolo and Barbaresco have been of a human nature.

Barolo (DOCG 1980, DOC 1966)

Barolo, cast in its role of king, has had to maintain regal bearing through an era when wine was supposedly becoming democratic. Other wine drinkers used to be reminded rather loftily that Barolo's noble austerity was an acquired taste to be revered in the company of roast game, braised beef, or aged cheese. A wine for the cold months, they were assured, when a fire in the hearth could warm it gradually to the temperature of the room, if not the soup. The rituals meant something when Piedmont's dining rooms weren't centrally heated and when its cellars emitted odours of faded vintages and damp earth. But most Italians stopped buying the line – and the wine – some time ago. Or, at most, they kept a few bottles around for those special occasions that never seemed to occur. Rather than a king, the wine was often treated like a sacred monster.

Barolo could never be a commoner, but its producers might feel more comfortable if they could forget about the *noblesse oblige*. Some try, and their winemaking styles have evolved past the point where they need to feel apologetic for having substituted grandfathers' blackened chestnut casks with French *barriques*. But perhaps too great an issue has been made over differences in cellar methods in a zone where even the most advanced technicians trace their wines' typology to the nature of terrains.

The Barolo zone extends over a large area of often sharply inclined hills southwest of Alba. Most vineyards are oriented towards the south on slopes either along the central valley that includes the town of Barolo or the eastern valley overlooked by Serralunga. Since Nebbiolo is planted mainly in favoured sites, its registered vineyards cover only 1,179 ha split into 1,163 different plots. (The Barbera and Dolcetto d'Alba zones overlie Barolo, so there are also extensive vineyards for those varieties, along with Moscato d'Asti at Serralunga and Freisa and Chardonnay for table wines.) The fragmentation partly explains the variations in style of Barolo among a production that fluctuates between four and seven million bottles a year.

Young wines often show intense ruby or even blackberry colour, though Barolo's essential shading after a few years of age is medium garnet with a warm brick red rim. The wine often used to be tough and astringent until tannins relented, but now it can be round and harmonious with a bracingly firm edge and it can conjure up sensations to the nose and palate rarely equalled by other wines. Often detected are violets, wild berries, tar, tobacco, vanilla, chocolate, mint, licorice, and all manner of spices. Truffles were

Above: a newly planted vineyard beneath the chapel of Santo Stefano at Perno in the Barolo zone.

customarily part of the array, though some modernists omit them since *funghi* don't fit the clean-cut image they've been striving to give the wine. Yet, whatever the nuances, winemakers and experts alike often narrow down Barolo to two basic types that originate in the divergent soils on either side of the zone.

To the east around Monforte, Serralunga, and Castiglione Falletto they insist that theirs is the real Barolo (the heroic type), but to the west around La Morra they argue that the historically true Barolo (the graceful type) comes from their side of the soil barrier. Partisans dispute the differences, though producers in the town of Barolo, where it all began, sometimes rise above the battle by claiming to excel with both types of wine. Together those five communes make an overwhelming share of Barolo, which is one reason why their producers tend to agree that Nebbiolo from the other six communes doesn't deserve the name. Barring exceptions, they have a point, but some of the area's best Dolcetto comes from the fringes of the Barolo zone.

Geologists, who confirm that the soil barrier exists, trace the dividing line through the central valley along the stream known as Rio Bussia south of the town of Barolo and Rio Talloria dell'Annunziata to the north. West of the line on the steep slopes of the amphitheatre of hills between Barolo and La Morra the soil is called tortonian. To the east on the rises of

Monforte and Castiglione Falletto and across the valley at Serralunga it is called helvetian. Both are calcareous marls of marine origin, but tortonian, which has a bluish tint, is rich in magnesium and manganese, while helvetian, of a chalky beige colour, contains more iron. There is more to it than that, but basically vineyards in tortonian soils make more fragrant, elegant, and early maturing Barolo than do helvetian soils, which are noted for stronger wines with more colour, body, and ageing potential.

The different types were less noticeable in the days when most Barolo was made by merchant houses that blended wines from the areas, as some still do. But the emphasis on single vineyard wines has called attention to typology in relation to precise places of origin, or *crus*. Barolo's vineyards are concentrated in the five communes on sites along the two main valleys. Terrains vary considerably in altitude (from about 250-450 m) as well as incline in a zone of unpredictable climate where even subtle variations in position and exposure to sun and winds can cause sharp differences in the wines. In a normal decade growers expect to have two or three top vintages, three to five good to satisfactory, and the rest mediocre to disastrous due to cold, damp, and hail. The key to success is a dry, warm September that allows the extremely late ripening Nebbiolo to develop for the late October harvest. But, at least until recently, success depended on

vineyards' exposure to the sun. Growers differentiate between the basic *sorì*, which faces due south, and those that face the morning sun to the east (*sorì del mattino*) or the evening sun to the west (*sorì della sera*).

Such subtleties make Barolo's vineyards fascinating to contemplate but nearly impossible to explain. The map indicates historical vineyard areas, including those with distinct individual plots, as well as some sites which have gained prominence recently or are emerging. Since some vineyards are divided among growers into small parcels, their owners couldn't be indicated on the map. Estates or cellars located in the zone are shown, though some merchant houses noted for Barolo – such as Prunotto, Bruno Giacosa, Pio Cesare, Scarpa, Michele Chiarlo – are in other places. Recommended producers of Barolo are listed, mainly under the Langhe, along with notable single vineyard wines. The following survey of the major communes calls attention to highlights of current production.

La Morra. The large commune possesses the most vineyards of the zone – located mainly in the *conca*, the slopes that curve beneath the heights of La Morra towards Barolo – and it accounts for about a third of total production. Good Barolo here is among the most perfumed and graceful of Nebbiolo wines, reaching peaks from the Brunate, Cerequio, and Rocche di La Morra vineyards that Renato Ratti ranked as *prima categoria*. Also well regarded are Monfalletto, La Serra (above Brunate), and Rocchette (adjoining Rocche). Many small wineries are located in the commune, where Ratti, Cordero di Montezemolo's Monfalletto, Elvio Cogno's Marcarini, and Fratelli Oddero have been leaders for years. Roberto Voerzio and Elio Altare are bright young winemakers. Vinicola Piemontese, Accomasso, Gianni Voerzio, and Rocche Costamagna have solid reputations. Also in the commune is Batasiolo, a resurgent house with choice vineyards in the zone.

Barolo. The town where Barolo originated in the cellars of the Marchesi Falletti is noted for wines that share characteristics of both soil zones and when blended combine elegance with power. The latter traits are well expressed in one of the zone's most vaunted vineyards, Cannubi, which is adjacent to the town and further subdivided into Boschis, Muscatel, Boschetti, and Valletta. The Zonchetta, Sarmassa (or Sarmazza), and Costa di Rose vineyards are also well rated, as are the parts of Brunate and Cerequio that Barolo shares with La Morra. The commune, which produces about 12 percent of the DOCG total, is the home of the historical Marchesi di Barolo firm and numerous medium or small wineries. Long admired among them are Bartolo Mascarello, Barale, and the two Rinaldi families. Emerging winemakers of special note are Luciano Sandrone, Vajra, Cantina Sebaste, and Scarzello.

Castiglione Falletto. The small commune makes less than ten percent of Barolo, whose wines are noted for rich bouquet and velvety texture in a range from medium bodied to powerful. Prime vineyards are Monprivato, Villero (source of Monfalletto's Enrico VI), and Rocche di Castiglione, at whose crest Ceretto created Bricco Rocche. The estate's single vineyard Bricco Rocche, noted for modern styling, has been the highest priced Barolo of recent years. The small house of Vietti is noted for outstanding traditional Barolo from Rocche and other vineyards. Other noteworthy producers are Paolo Scavino, Azelia, Brovia, and Cavallotto.

Monforte d'Alba. The commune, with a number of newly prominent estates, is a rising force in Barolo. Wines of potent structure and uncommon depth of flavour are constantly improving in class. Monforte makes about a sixth of Barolo's production from vineyards in the highly regarded Bussia area, as well as the re-emerging Santo Stefano di Perno, Castelletto, Ginestra, and Mosconi. Also notable are the Arnulfo, Dardi, Le Coste, Manzoni, and Fontanin areas. In the 1970s the only well known producers were Giacomo Conterno, with the massive Monfortino, and Aldo

Conterno, who has confirmed his leadership with Barolo from Bricco Bussia. Valentino Migliorino has reconstructed Rocche dei Manzoni into a major Barolo estate with stylish wines from vineyards at key points in the commune. Clerico stands out among recently established producers. Grasso, Parusso, and Conterno-Fantino are rapidly on the rise.

Serralunga d'Alba. Fontanafredda has established international fame from its vast former royal estate in a commune whose vineyards had long been favoured by *negoçiants* as the source of powerful, long-lived Barolo, often used for blending. But the recent arrival of Angelo Gaja with purchase of the Marenca-Rivette property has drawn new attention to Serralunga's extended bank of southwest facing slopes that some say could become Barolo's Côte-de-Nuits. The commune, which produces about a sixth of the DOCG wine, has vineyards of historical importance in Lazzarito, Gabutti, Parafada, Baudana, Ceretta (Prapò), Vigna Rionda, and the Fontanafredda complex of sites. Also noted are Giovanni Conterno's Cascina Francia, Gigi Rosso's Cascina Arione, Pio Cesare's Ornato, and Batasiolo's Boscareto and Briccolina. Eredi Virginio Ferrero is a respected small estate, Cappellano a re-emerging vintner.

Much of the territory to the north and west of the Barolo zone is not well suited to Nebbiolo. Few vineyards are noted in the communes of Verduno, Roddi, Cherasco, Grinzane Cavour, Diano d'Alba, and Novello, though the latter two are known for Dolcetto.

Zone: The Langhe hills southwest of Alba in 11 communes of Cuneo province, though most respected vineyards are situated on often steep slopes oriented towards the south around the towns of Barolo, Castiglione Falletto, Serralunga d'Alba, Monforte d'Alba, and La Morra. Barolo from the communes of Diano d'Alba, Grinzane Cavour, Roddi, Cherasco, Novello, and Verduno rarely equals wine from the others. Dry red. Grape: Nebbiolo. Yld 56/80, Alc 13, Acd 0.55-0.8, Ag 3 yrs (2 in wood); rìserva 5 yrs.

Barolo Chinato is permitted under DOCG as a bitter *digestivo* made by steeping china (quinine, the bark of the cinchona tree) in the wine.

PRODUCERS IN THE VILLAGE OF BAROLO

Barale	Giorgio Scarzello
Bartolo Mascarello	Giuseppe Rinaldi
Brezza	Luciano Sandrone
Cantina Sebaste	Marchesi di Barolo
Enrico Pira	Serio & Battista Borgogno
Francesco Rinaldi	G. D. Vajra
Giacomo Borgogno	

PRODUCERS IN THE VILLAGE OF LA MORRA

Accomasso	Luigi Viberti
Aurelio Settimo	Marcarini
Batasiolo	Molino
Corino	Monfalletto
Elio Altare	Renato Ratti
Fratelli Ferrero	Roberto Voerzio
Fratelli Oberto	Rocche Costamagna
Fratelli Oddero	Silvio Grasso
Gianfranco Bovio	Vinicola Piemontese
Gianni Voerzio	

1 Castello di Verduno
2 G. B. Burlotto
3 Bel Colle
4 Terre del Barolo
5 Gigi Rosso
6 Giuseppe Cappellano
7 Azelia
8 Brovia
9 Paolo Scavino
10 Cavallotto
11 Eredi Virginia Ferrero
12 Vietti
13 Bricco Rocche-Ceretto
14 Parusso
15 Aldo Conterno
16 Gaja
17 Giuseppe Massolino
18 Josetta Safirio
19 Elio Grasso
20 Conterno-Fantino
21 Renzo Seghesio
22 Rocche dei Manzoni
23 Giacomo Conterno
24 Pira
25 Clerico

26 (Rocche Marcenasco)
  (Vigna Francesco)
  (Vigna Riccardo)
27 (Vigneto Arborina)
28 (Bianca)
  (Gallaretto)
  (Gattinera)
  (La Rosa)
  (San Pietro)
29 (Bricco Boschis)
30 (Bric del Fiasc)
31 (Momprivato)
32 (Briacca)
  (Rocche dei Brovia)
33 (Vigna Cicala)
  (Vigna Colonello)
34 (Coste di Rose)
35 (Bricotto Bussia)
  (Vigna Mesdi)
  (Vigna Romirasco)
36 (Collina Rionda)
  (Sori Vigna Riunda)
37 (Madonna Assunta di Castelletto)
38 (Casa Matè)
  (Ciabot Mentin Ginestra)
  (Sori Ginestra)
  (Vigna del Gris)
39 (Vigna d' la Roul)

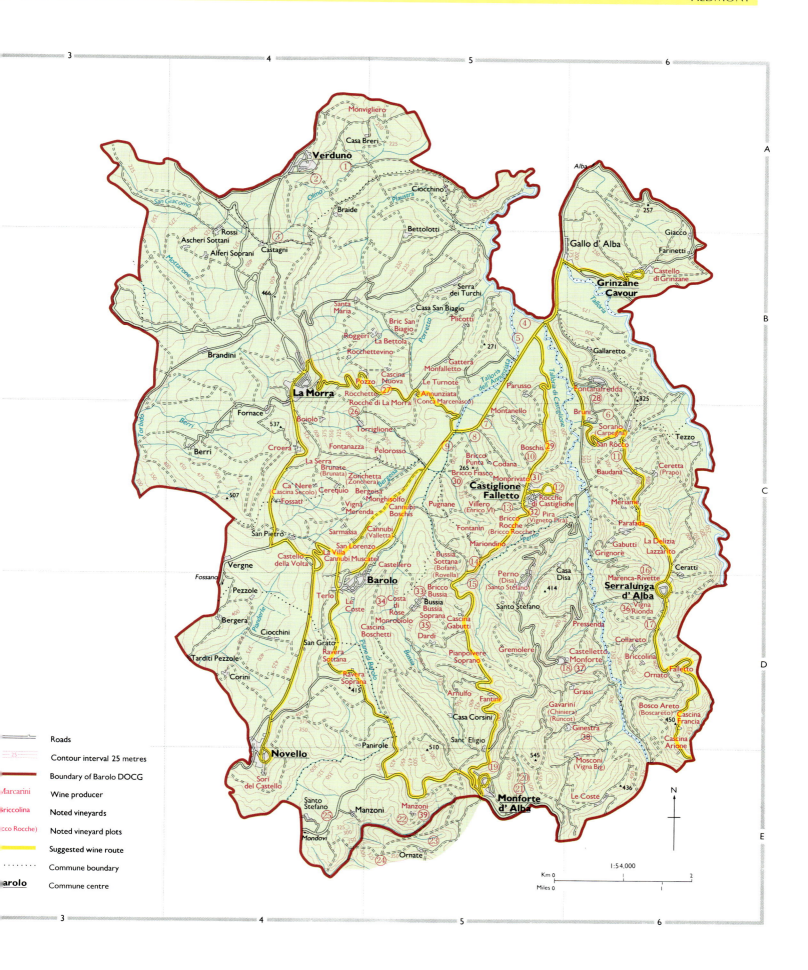

Roads

Contour interval 25 metres

Boundary of Barolo DOCG

Marcarini   Wine producer

Briccolina   Noted vineyards

(Bricco Rocche)   Noted vineyard plots

Suggested wine route

Commune boundary

Barolo   Commune centre

Km 0   1:54,000   2

Miles 0   1

N

Barbaresco (DOCG 1980, DOC 1966)

At times Barbaresco seems to have overcome its status as Barolo's perennial junior partner. Writers and connoisseurs in Italy not only praise it but drink it more than occasionally. They seem to agree with foreign experts who find Barbaresco easier on the palate than Barolo and more consistent in type and quality. It has even been called Italy's finest classified wine. Leading producers – Bruno Giacosa, Marchesi di Gresy, Ceretto, Castello di Neive, and the cooperative Produttori del Barbaresco – have built sterling reputations. But it took Angelo Gaja with his *sorì* bottlings to send prices and prestige soaring.

The name Gaja came to be better known than the appellation in the international wine circles which he frequents with such charismatic energy. But deep down he always knew that Barbaresco as a wine didn't command the authority of Barolo and that its name didn't ring with the same resound. His family had stopped making Barolo long ago for the creditable reason that it didn't have vines in the zone. But in 1988 Gaja bought the run down Marenca-Rivette estate at Serralunga d'Alba and resumed production of Barolo. The move was greeted elsewhere as a boon to Barolo's fortunes, though some of Gaja's neighbours feared that it might tend to move their wine back into the shadows. But Barbaresco so far seems to be holding its own against Barolo in price and prestige.

Production varies from year to year, but Barbaresco's average of about 2.5 million bottles is less than half of Barolo's. The zone, which reaches almost to Alba in the west and fronts directly on the Tanaro, has 490 ha of Nebbiolo in 482 registered vineyards, though the presence of Dolcetto, Barbera, and Moscato, as well as Chardonnay, Sauvignon, and Cabernet gives growers a well-rounded variety. The slopes around the village of Barbaresco with its landmark tower are among the most intensely cultivated of the Langhe. Major vineyards are at somewhat lower levels (200-350 m) than Barolo's, on hills with steep slopes and gently rounded crests. The proximity of the Tanaro valley makes the climate slightly warmer and drier than in Barolo, so grapes ripen sooner and often with more regularity. In this environment Nebbiolo renders wines of slightly less strength and structure than the robust type of Barolo and with less of those threatening tannins that mean,

Right: slopes in the commune of Barbaresco are among the most densely planted of the Langhe, though vineyards are divided into often minuscule plots.

in theory, that it needs less wood ageing to reach its prime. The differences are often attributed to soils, which are basically the same calcareous marls as in Barolo, though micro-elements vary in ways that have still not been well explained.

But light isn't the word for Barbaresco. At its best it combines the power and depth of Nebbiolo with uncommon grace, but differences between it and Barolo are not as dramatic as they may seem. Barolo from around La Morra can be gentler than Barbaresco from around Neive; even producers who make both can't always tell them apart. Some who excel with both, such as Bruno Giacosa, Marcello Ceretto, and Prunotto's Beppe Colla, lean towards Barolo as the greater wine of the two, while admitting that it is more of a challenge to produce, partly because it takes longer, and in Italy at least it is often harder to sell than Barbaresco.

Winemakers of Barbaresco, perhaps more than in Barolo, often rely on sophisticated cellar techniques to shape the final results. Gaja's single vineyard wines, sculpted in *barriques*, are considered masterpieces of modern winemaking. Marchesi di Gresy is also a widely admired stylist.

But some critics regard their wines as being too worldly to stand alongside Barbaresco of the grand tradition. Bruno Giacosa is the master of that species with Barbaresco whose Barolo-like structure has earned him the description of "barolista" and accolades as one of Italy's, and the world's, great winemakers. The debate continues, but in the meantime many qualified producers in the zone seem content to remain in the middle with Barbaresco

of sound quality and sensible price. Leading values over the years have been the single vineyard reserves of Produttori del Barbaresco.

As in Barolo, the map of Barbaresco indicates historical vineyard areas, including those with distinct individual plots, as well as sites which have recently gained prominence or are emerging. Since some vineyards are divided among growers into small parcels, their owners couldn't be indicated on the map. Estates or cellars located in the zone are shown, though some houses noted for Barbaresco – such as Prunotto, Vietti, Ratti, Fontanafredda, Pio Cesare, Scarpa, Michele Chiarlo – are in other places. Most recommended producers of Barbaresco are listed under the Langhe, along with single vineyard wines. The following survey of the three main communes calls attention to highlights of recent production.

Barbaresco. The quiet village where Domizio Cavazza made the first wine called Barbaresco in the 1890s remains the focal point of the zone with nearly half the vineyards including the most prestigious sites. The key area is just south of the village on undulating slopes where noted vineyards are practically linked in two series: first Secondine, San Lorenzo, Ghiga, and Paglieri, then Pora, Asili, Rabajà, and Martinenga. To the east are Ovello, Montefico, and Montestefano. Another key grouping south towards Alba takes in Roccalini, Como, Rio Sordo, Roncaglia, and Roncaglietta with Costa Russi and Sorì Tildin. The three largest wineries – Gaja, Produttori del Barbaresco, and Marchesi di Gresy, which claims all of Martinenga – are widely respected. Among numerous

small wineries of note are Luigi Bianco, Cortese, De Forville, La Spinona, Moccagatta, Bruno Rocca, Roagna's I Paglieri, and Ceretto's Bricco Asili.

Treiso. The village that used to be part of Barbaresco is now a commune with some of the zone's highest vineyards, which are as well known for Dolcetto as Nebbiolo. Prime sites lie along the road between Treiso and Barbaresco in places known as Giacosa, Casotto, Marcarini, and (the most esteemed) Pajorè. Also notable are the vineyards of Ausario, Bernardotti, Rizzi, Valeriano, Contratto's Cascina Alberta, Le Colline's Bordino, and Marchesi di Gresy's Monte Aribaldo (for Dolcetto). Noted producers in the commune include Pelissero, Eredi Lodali, Meinardi, Nada, Rizzi, Vezza, and the cooperative I Vignaioli Elvio Pertinace.

Neive. Though the commune wasn't part of the Barbaresco zone at first, it was already noted in the mid-19th century for Nebbiolo wines made by the Frenchman Oudart at Castello di Neive, which has re-emerged as a top estate. Highly regarded historical vineyard areas are Albesani-Santo Stefano, Gallina, Chirrà, and Cottà, though other sites of note include Basarin, Messoirano, Masseria, Tetti, Gaia, Marcorino, Serraboella (with Sorì Paitin), and Bricco di Neive. Among local winemakers Bruno Giacosa is a towering figure. Other noted houses include Fratelli Giacosa, Cantina del Glicine, and Accademia Torregiorgi. Growers who make Barbaresco of outstanding character are Fratelli Cigliuti, Pasquero-Elia, Gastaldi, Punset, and Busso.

The zone also extends into a small section of the commune of Alba, where a couple vineyards are noted, but no

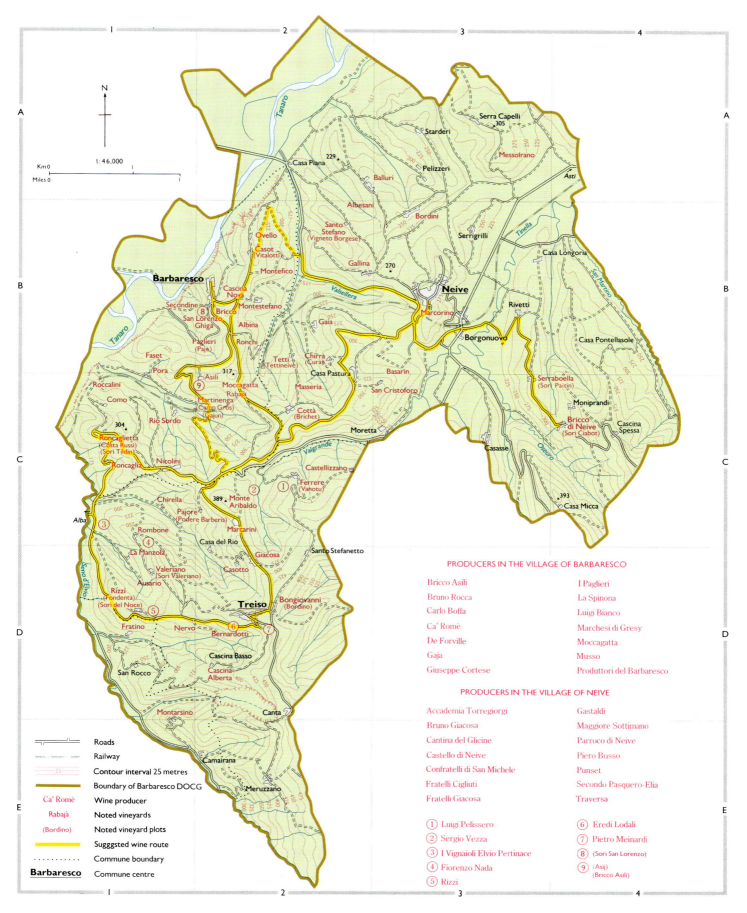

N

Km 0
Miles 0

1:46,000

PRODUCERS IN THE VILLAGE OF BARBARESCO

Bricco Asili	I Paglieri
Bruno Rocca	La Spinona
Carlo Boffa	Luigi Bianco
Ca' Romè	Marchesi di Gresy
De Forville	Moccagatta
Gaja	Musso
Giuseppe Cortese	Produttori del Barbaresco

PRODUCERS IN THE VILLAGE OF NEIVE

Accademia Torregiorgi	Gastaldi
Bruno Giacosa	Maggiore Sottimano
Cantina del Glicine	Parroco di Neive
Castello di Neive	Piero Busso
Confratelli di San Michele	Punset
Fratelli Cigliuti	Secondo Pasquero-Elia
Fratelli Giacosa	Traversa

① Luigi Pelissero   ⑥ Eredi Lodali
② Sergio Vezza   ⑦ Pietro Meinardi
③ I Vignaioli Elvio Pertinace   ⑧ (Sori San Lorenzo)
④ Fiorenzo Nada   ⑨ (Asij)
⑤ Rizzi   (Bricco Asili)

Legend:
- Roads
- Railway
- Contour interval 25 metres
- Boundary of Barbaresco DOCG
- *Ca' Romè*   Wine producer
- *Rabajà*   Noted vineyards
- *(Bordino)*   Noted vineyard plots
- Sugggsted wine route
- Commune boundary
- **Barbaresco**   Commune centre

65

outstanding producers of Barbaresco are located there.

Zone: The communes of Barbaresco, Treiso, and Neive in the Langhe hills east of Alba and including the village of San Rocco Senodelvio in its commune in Cuneo province. Dry red. Grape: Nebbiolo. Yld 56/80, Alc 12.5, Acd 0.5, Ag 2 yrs (1 in wood); riserva 3 yrs.

Barbera d'Alba (1970)
Renewed interest in this long downtrodden variety has yielded wines of such unexpected class that Barbera d'Alba for the first time in memory seems almost on the verge of becoming chic. When treated with respect on the Langhe's slopes it can perform at least as well as in its native Monferrato around Asti. A number of growers had made good Barbera around Alba for years, but they often ended up sharing it with friends. Even some respected estates and merchants that made fine Barbera d'Alba at reasonable prices rarely managed to convince devotees of Nebbiolo and Dolcetto. In the late 1970s, Angelo Gaja tried ageing his Barbera Vignarey in *barriques* and found that it came out rounder and more interestingly complex than in standard casks. Though he didn't push it, Vignarey drew new admiration to Barbera and sparked a trend towards carefully styled wines from it that has taken hold in Alba and Asti. Some winemakers use *barriques*, others prefer casks. Some label their wines Barbera d'Alba, others prefer vdt. Increasingly popular are blends of Barbera with Nebbiolo. The net effect is that Barbera is coming back in rich, smooth, durable wines that at their finest concede little to a top Barolo. Examples of fine Barbera d'Alba DOC include Aldo Conterno's Conca Tre Pile, Prunotto's Pian Romualdo, Vietti's Bussia, and Bruno Giacosa's Altavilla.

Zone: Most of Alba's vineyard area in 54 communes of Cuneo province, extending over the entire Roero area north of the Tanaro and much of the Langhe, excluding the sector south from Dogliani. Dry red. Grape: Barbera. Yld 70/100, Alc 12; superiore 12.5, Acd 0.6, Ag superiore 1 yr in oak or chestnut casks.

Dolcetto d'Alba (1974)
Among the Langhe's uncompromisingly distinctive red wines, the taste for Dolcetto may be the easiest to acquire. Its popularity seems due to the youthfully grapey, mouth-filling qualities it offers in contrast with the rather severe aspects of aged wines from Nebbiolo and Barbera. Not everyone likes it, but some admirers consider Dolcetto the paragon of everyday wines and an ideal foil to the pungent flavours of regional cooking. When young, as Dolcetto d'Alba is preferred, it has a deep mulberry colour

and a hint of newly fermenting grapes on the nose with rich but mellow fruit flavours of almost chocolate-like sweetness offset by a mouth tingling bitter undertone. Dolcetto thrives in high, cool vineyards of the Langhe where grapes ripen early but in unpredictable ways. Improvements in the difficult techniques of vinifying grapes with ample tannins but low acidity have resulted in smooth, balanced wines that are by far the most popular among Piedmont's seven Dolcetto DOCs. Though devotees know that the wine defies comparison, it is often likened to Beaujolais. Some winemakers, who seem to have taken such jests seriously, have made Dolcetto to drink soon after the harvest, proving that it doesn't work as *nouveau*. Many producers of Barolo and Barbaresco make fine Dolcetto; a number of single vineyards bottlings are mentioned under their names.

Zone: The northern sector of the Langhe hills in 35 communes of Cuneo province, including the Barolo and Barbaresco zones and the commune of Alba, but excluding the other Dolcetto DOC zones of Diano d'Alba, Dogliani, and Langhe Monregalesi. Dry red. Grape: Dolcetto. Yld 63/90, Alc 11.5; superiore 12.5, Acd 0.5, Ag superiore 1 yr.

Dolcetto di Diano d'Alba or Diano (1974)
The hilltop town of Diano is surrounded by sloping vineyards for a Dolcetto that stands apart from others of Alba not so much in character as in rank. For in a sense the commune's 77 *sorì* are the first *crus* not only of Alba but of Italy. The status was conferred through a communal effort to determine which lands were suitable for vines and to officially designate each vineyard of proven worth by name. They are not classified in order and probably will not

be, but any vineyard named on a label of Diano (the preferred appellation) is an authentic *cru*. Diano's system serves as a model for producers in other zones. The town, which overlooks Alba from the south, is noted for some of the area's finest Dolcetto, as proved by wines from Colué, Porta Rossa, Fontanafredda, Gigi Rosso, Savigliano, Casavecchia, and Veglio.

Zone: Slopes in the commune of Diano d'Alba in Cuneo province. Dry red. Grape: Dolcetto. Yld 56/80, Alc 12; superiore 12.5, Acd 0.5, Ag superiore 1 yr.

Dolcetto di Dogliani (1974)
Dogliani, self proclaimed birthplace and capital of Dolcetto (both honours disputed), has had to undergo a revival to restore its good name as a wine town. Documents indicate that Dolcetto was planted around Dogliani on slopes facing west along the Tanaro valley in the 16th century. But a legend has it that in 1303 the Marchese di Clavesana issued an edict from his castle in the zone ordering that only Dolcetto be planted in his vast territories with the warning that violators would be beheaded. Early in this century Dogliani developed a reputation for Dolcetto after Luigi Einaudi, who later became president of Italy, founded a winery there. But over time other elements of the local industry developed a market for cheap and questionable wines. A few producers, including Einaudi's estate, continued to make respectable Dolcetto from the zone. But Dogliani's wines didn't draw much praise until the early 1980s when young Andrea Chionetti made single vineyard Dolcetto that some critics judged to be the finest of the name. Before his untimely death, Chionetti inspired other winemakers, including his father Quinto, to realize Dogliani's long

Above: Castellinaldo is noted for a light style of Nebbiolo called Roero.

neglected potential for Dolcetto that with time develops fragrance rarely sensed in more forward wines from around Alba. Besides Chionetti and Einaudi, other producers who succeed admirably are Gillardi and Pira.

Zone: Slopes of the Langhe extending from the edge of the Barolo zone south along the eastern bank of the Tanaro river as far as Cigliè and including ten communes of Cuneo province, though production is centred in Dogliani, Clavesana and Farigliano. Dry red. Grape: Dolcetto. Yld 56/80, Alc 11.5; superiore 12.5, Acd 0.5, Ag superiore 1 yr.

Dolcetto delle Langhe Monregalesi (1974)
The steep hills of the southern Langhe on either side of the Tanaro near Mondovì were once noted for Dolcetto, but only 17 ha are planted for a wine that, where available, is noted for its fragrant, fruity qualities.

Zone: Slopes of the upper Langhe in 11 communes of Cuneo province, extending along the eastern edge of the Dogliani zone from Murazzano to Castellino and along the western side of the Tanaro as far south as Mondovì and Vicoforte, where most of the slight production is centred. Dry red. Grape: Dolcetto. Yld 49/70, Alc 11; superiore 12, Acd 0.55, Ag superiore 1 yr.

Other wines of note
Classified wines are so dominant in the Langhe, where DOCG or DOC represent nearly two-thirds of production, that there is little space for up market table wines of the sort that have made an impact elsewhere. But there are trends. Gaja started one with oak-aged Chardonnay, though his achievements with Cabernet Sauvignon and

Sauvignon Blanc haven't been widely imitated. Valentino Migliorini created the Nebbiolo-Barbera blend of Bricco Manzoni which has inspired others. Aside from Moscato d'Asti, some good dry *spumanti* are made in the area, though base wines often come from elsewhere. The name Langhe may be applied to 22 different varieties ranging from native Freisa and Grignolino to some increasingly familiar French varieties. An approved vdt is Bricco del Drago for a special red from near Alba. Pelaverga is a pale ruby wine of spicy scent and bracing flavour from an ancient variety grown mainly around Verduno. Several producers make the prized bitter Barolo Chinato.

ESTATES/GROWERS

Celso Abbona, Dogliani (CN). Dolcetto di Dogliani.

Accomasso, La Morra (CN). Lorenzo Accomasso makes exemplary Barolo from vines at Rocchette.

Alario, Diano d'Alba (CN). Emerging small estate with good Diano.

Elio Altare, La Morra (CN). One of Alba's most inspired winemakers has 5 ha of vines on his Cascina Nuova estate near L'Annunziata for highly praised Barolo Vigneto Arborina, Dolcetto La Pria, and two fine *barrique*-aged vdt: Vigna Larigi from Barbera and Vigna Arborina from Nebbiolo.

Azelia, Castiglione Falletto (CN). From 10 ha of vines, Lorenzo and Alfonso Scavino make Barolo Bricco Fiasco and Bricco Punta, plus Dolcetto.

Fratelli Barale, Barolo (CN). Sergio and Carlo Barale make good traditional Barolo Castellero, Barbaresco Rabajà, and Dolcetto Coste di Rose from 19 ha.

Bera-Cascina Palazzo, Neviglie (CN). The Bera brothers, Valter and Attilio, produce some of the finest Moscato and Asti Spumante, along with Barbera and Dolcetto d'Alba from 17 ha.

Luigi Bianco & Figlio, Barbaresco (CN). Good Barbaresco Faset, Rabajà, and Ronchi, along with Dolcetto and Barbera.

Carlo Boffa & Figli, Barbaresco (CN). Sound Barbaresco Casot and Vitalotti, along with Dolcetto.

Pietro Boschis, Dogliani (CN). Dolcetto di Dogliani.

Gianfranco Bovio, La Morra (CN). The owner of the noted Belvedere restaurant makes fine Barolo Gattera and Dolcetto Dabbene and Firagnetti from his estate near L'Annunziata.

Brezza, Barolo (CN). The Brezza family restaurant is supplied with Barolo from its own vineyards of Bricco Sarmassa, Cannubi, and Castellero, along with good Barbera, Dolcetto, and vdt Nebbiolo.

Bricco Asili, Barbaresco (CN). Ceretto has 1.2 ha of vines and a small cellar on this choice site for Barbaresco Bricco

Asili, Faset (from a 1-ha site), and Asij, from a leased vineyard.

Bricco Rocche, Castiglione Falletto (CN). Ceretto built hilltop cellars to make artistically styled Barolo from the 1-ha plot of Bricco Rocche, as well as from 5 ha of Brunate at La Morra and 3 ha of Prapò at Serralunga. The limited bottling of Bricco Rocche has been the highest priced Barolo from recent top vintages.

Fratelli Brovia, Castiglione Falletto (CN). The Brovia family makes reds of noted weight in Barolo Rocche dei Brovia, Dolcetto Solatio dei Brovia and Ciabot del Re, and Barbera Sorì del Drago.

Piero Busso, Neive (CN). Emerging grower with distinctive Barbaresco from Vigna Borgese in Neive's Albesani area.

Carbonere, Santo Stefano Belbo (CN). Amerio Agostino's Bricco Carbonere is a revelation among recent releases of Moscato d'Asti.

Cascina Fonda-Barbero, Mango (CN). Massimo Barbero makes good Moscato d'Asti.

Cascina Pian d'Or-Barbero, Mango (CN). Walter Barbero makes fine Moscato d'Asti.

Cascine Drago, San Rocco Seno d'Elvio (CN). Luciano De Giacomi, Gran Maestro of the Ordine del Tartufo e dei Vini d'Alba, makes good Dolcetto, along with Barbera, Freisa, and Nebbiolo, though his speciality is the long-lived Bricco del Drago, a vdt from Dolcetto with Nebbiolo.

Castello di Neive, Neive (CN). In the castle where the Frenchman Oudart made prize-winning wines in the 1860s, Italo and Giulio Stupino select from 25 ha for highly admired bottlings of Barbaresco Santo Stefano, Messoirano, and Gallina; Dolcetto Basarin, Messoirano, and Bric Valtorta; Barbera Messoirano and Santo Stefano; Moscato d'Asti Marcorino; along with vdt Arneis and Rocca del Mattarello, a pure Barbera aged in *barrique*.

Castello di Verduno, Verduno (CN). The former estate of King Carlo Alberto is owned by the Burlotto sisters, who make Barolo and Pelaverga.

Caudrina Dogliotti, Castiglione Tinella (CN). Redento and Romano Dogliotti make widely respected Moscato La Galeisa, along with Dolcetto d'Alba and Freisa from 14 ha.

Fratelli Cavallotto, Castiglione Falletto (CN). Olivio and Gildo Cavallotto make noted Barolo from 15 ha of their Bricco Boschis estate, along with Barbera and Dolcetto.

Quinto Chionetti & Figlio, Dogliani (CN). Chionetti continues to make Dolcetto di Dogliani that ranks with the most admired wines of the Langhe, despite the loss of his son, Andrea, who created the single vineyard Briccolero, San Luigi, and Le Coste.

Fratelli Cigliuti, Neive (CN). Renato Cigliuti and family make Barbaresco of Barolo-like proportions, along with rich Barbera and Dolcetto from 3 ha of meticulously tended vineyards at Serraboella.

Clerico, Monforte d'Alba (CN). Domenico Clerico is a rising star in the Langhe with first-rate Barolo Ciabot Mentin Ginestra and Bricotto Bussia, as well as Barbera, Dolcetto, Freisa, and the vdt Arte of Nebbiolo in *barrique*.

Colué, Diano d'Alba (CN). Massimo Oddero is noted as a pioneer in single vineyard bottlings of Diano with his Dolcetto Vigna Tampa. He also makes Barolo Cannubi and Barbaresco Sorì Valeriano.

Aldo Conterno, Monforte d'Alba (CN). One of the Langhe's most admired winemakers has high vineyards at Bricco Bussia for Barolo from Vigna Cicala and Vigna Colonello, combined in top years as Gran Bussia. Barolo plantings reached 11 ha with the adjacent Vigna Romirasco. Also from Nebbiolo comes the fine *barrique*-aged vdt Favot. Conterno makes superb DOC Barbera Conca Tre Pile and Dolcetto Bussia Soprana. Langhe vdt Freisa and Grignolino will soon be joined by Arneis and Chardonnay.

Giacomo Conterno, Monforte d'Alba (CN). Giovanni Conterno, Aldo's brother, has kept the family winery a bastion of tradition, noted for the mighty Barolo Monfortino (which despite the allusion to Monforte seems to come from 13 ha of vines at Cascina Francia in Serralunga). Conterno also makes solid Barbera and Dolcetto.

Conterno-Fantino, Monforte d'Alba (CN). The Conterno and Fantino families have 14 ha at Ginestra and Bricco Bastia for Barolo Sorì Ginestra and Vigna del Gris, along with Dolcetto, the Nebbiolo vdt Ginestrino, and a Nebbiolo-Barbera *barrique* wine called Monprà.

Corino, La Morra (CN). Renato Corino is emerging with fine Dolcetto.

Giuseppe Cortese, Barbaresco (CN). Good Barbaresco Rabajà and Dolcetto.

Mario Cozzo, Dogliani (CN). Dolcetto di Dogliani from Cascina Lasagna.

De Forville, Barbaresco (CN). Paolo and Walter De Forville make respected Barbaresco, Dolcetto, and Chardonnay in part from their own 10 ha.

Mario Devalle, Dogliani (CN). Dolcetto di Dogliani Bric sur Pian.

Luigi Einaudi, Dogliani (CN). The firm founded by Einaudi, who became the first president of the Italian Republic, has 24 ha of vines divided between the estate at Dogliani, where a sturdy Dolcetto is made, and the Terlo plot at Barolo for an exceptionally durable Barolo.

Eredi Virginia Ferrero, Serralunga d'Alba (CN). Barolo of unusual depth and staying power from vineyards at San Rocco.

Fratelli Ferrero, La Morra (CN). Promising Barolo and Dolcetto.

Gaja, Barbaresco (CN). Angelo Gaja has transformed the family cellars founded in 1859 into Piedmont's most dynamic estate winery. Though noted above all for Barbaresco Sorì Tildin, Sorì San Lorenzo, and Costa Russi, Gaja and oenologist Guido Rivella also use creative styling with *barriques* for Cabernet and Chardonnay and have begun making Barolo on the Marenca-Rivette estate at Serralunga. That purchase in 1988 brought total vineyards in the Alba area to 85 ha. Of those 29 are for Barbaresco, including 8.8 ha of Cascina San Lorenzo (where the 3.9-ha Sorì San Lorenzo is located) and 13.3 ha of Cascina Roncagliette (3.4 ha at Sorì Tildin and 4.4 ha at Costa Russi). Cellars are being built and 10 ha of vineyards replanted with other varieties at the Barolo estate, which will be given a new name before wines are released. Gaja, whose average production of about 300,000 bottles a year comes exclusively from family vineyards, also makes the stylish Alba wines of Nebbiolo Vignaveja, Dolcetto

Above: Angelo Gaja, the most dynamic and discussed of Piedmont's producers, is the leading influence on recent winemaking styles in the Alba area.

Vignabajla, and Barbera Vignarey. The elite vdt are Darmagi (a Cabernet Sauvignon from the Bricco plot at Barbaresco), Chardonnay Gaia & Rey and Rossj-Bass from Treiso, and Sauvignon Blanc Alteni di Brassica from Treiso. Though all are high priced, Gaja's policy is to keep single vineyard Barbaresco (and eventually Barolo) at the top of his list. He also produces a *novello*, called Vinòt, from Nebbiolo. His firm called Gaja Distribuzione imports and distributes prestigious wines from France and California as well as glassware and other wine accessories.

Gastaldi, Neive (CN). Bernardino Gastaldi makes promising Barbaresco and outstanding Dolcetto d'Alba Moriolo from vines at Rodello.

Gatti, Santo Stefano Belbo (CN). Piero Gatti makes fine Moscato d'Asti from his Moncucco vineyards.

Gillardi, Farigliano (CN). Giovanni Battista Gillardi, oenologist at Ceretto, makes a fine Dolcetto di Dogliani.

Elio Grasso, Monforte d'Alba (CN). Steadily improved techniques have enhanced Grasso's single-vineyard Barolo Rüncot, Chiniera, and Case Matè from the Gavarini, Ginestra, and Grassi areas, which are also sources of first-rate Dolcetto, Barbera, and Nebbiolo.

Silvio Grasso, La Morra (CN). Improving Barolo and Dolcetto from vineyards at L'Annunziata.

I Paglieri, Barbaresco (CN). Alfredo Roagna was an early exponent of a lighter, more refined style of Barbaresco from vines at Pajè and Asili, which combine in the singular Crichet Pajè. Opera Prima is a pure Nebbiolo vdt blended from different vintages and aged in *barriques*. The Dolcetto is also admirable.

La Meridiana, Vicoforte (CN). From 4 ha, Vittorio Tesio provides a rare taste of Dolcetto delle Langhe Monregalesi.

La Spinona, Barbaresco (CN). Pietro Berutti has 20 ha of vines for sound Barbaresco (from Faset, Albina, and Ghiga), Dolcetto, Barbera, and vdt.

Marcarini-Cogno, La Morra (CN). A pioneer of contemporary style in Barolo, Elvio Cogno makes wines of voluptuous Burgundy-like style from 9 ha of Brunate and La Serra, vineyards owned by Anna Marcarini. He also makes first-rate Dolcetto from Fontanazza, Nassone, and the pre-phylloxera vines of Boschi di Berri.

Bartolo Mascarello, Barolo (CN). The best evidence that the old school of winemaking lives on in the Langhe is Bartolo Mascarello, whose cramped cellars in the heart of Barolo contain no concession to modernity: no stainless steel tanks, no *barriques*, no telephone. Yet the wines that emerge from his wizened casks show a polish that has won praise from writers who sometimes idolize this philosophical *vignaiolo*. He

has vines at Cannubi and other preferred plots, but Mascarello labels his wines simply Barolo, Dolcetto d'Alba, and Nebbiolo delle Langhe.

Giuseppe Massolino-Vigna Rionda, Serralunga d'Alba (CN). The 10 ha of the vaunted Rionda site are used for a hefty Barolo called Sörì Vigna Riunda, as well as Barbera and Dolcetto.

Pietro Meinardi, Treiso (CN). Good Dolcetto and Barbaresco.

Moccagatta, Barbaresco (CN). Franco and Sergio Minuto make improving Barbaresco, along with Chardonnay and Barbera in *barriques*.

Molino, La Morra (CN). Mauro Molino makes fine Barolo Vigna Conca and Dolcetto from L'Annunziata.

Monfalletto-Cordero di Montezemolo, La Morra (CN). Giovanni and Enrico Cordero are building on the proud tradition begun by their father Paolo with Barolo and Dolcetto from 16 ha at Monfalletto (near L'Annunziata) and 2.2 ha at Villero in Castiglione Falletto, source of the admirable Barolo Enrico VI.

Musso, Barbaresco (CN). Walter Musso makes Barbaresco from the Pora and Rio Sordo plots, also good Dolcetto.

Fiorenzo Nada, Treiso (CN). Good Barbaresco and Dolcetto.

Fratelli Oberto, La Morra (CN). Andrea Oberto makes a good Dolcetto and a promising Barolo from Rocche vineyards at L'Annunziata.

Fratelli Oddero, La Morra (CN). The established family winery has 23 ha of choice vineyards in the Alba area from which grapes had been blended for Barolo and Barbaresco. Recently Luigi Oddero and daughter Cristina have begun selecting for single vineyard bottlings that promise greater things.

Parroco di Neive, Neive (CN). Don Giuseppe Cogno and brother Achille, winemaker, had once made Neive's church cellars into an inspiration for Barbaresco producers, though recent vintages have been less inspiring.

Armando Parusso, Monforte d'Alba (CN). Young Marco Parusso has revived the winery with Barolo from Bussia and Mariondino in Castiglione Falletto, along with Barbera Pagliana and Dolcetto Mariondino.

Secondo Pasquero-Elia, Neive (CN). From 6 ha between Serraboella and Bricco di Neive, the Pasquero family makes persuasive Barbaresco from Sörì Paitin, along with Barbera and Dolcetto, and from Vigna Elisa Moscato d'Asti and Chardonnay.

Luigi Pelissero, Treiso (CN). Good Barbaresco Vanotu from vineyards in the Ferrere area, along with Dolcetto and Barbera.

Mario Perrone, Santo Stefano Belbo (CN). Moscato d'Asti Ca' del Re and Cascina Galletto.

Pianpolvere Soprano, Monforte d'Alba (CN). Riccardo Fenocchio makes

impressive Barolo, Barbera, Dolcetto, and Grignolino at this estate.

Armando Piazzo, San Rocco Seno d'Elvio (CN). Piazzo, a renowned figure known as Mugiòt, makes a range of Alba wines from some 50 ha of vineyards in various zones.

Pira, Monforte d'Alba (CN). Emerging producer of Dolcetto both of Alba and Dogliani from Bricco dei Botti.

Enrico Pira, Barolo (CN). The small estate, where the Pira brothers crushed grapes with their feet and said so on the labels, made acclaimed Barolo in the 1960s and 1970s. It is now owned by the Boschis family, who are trying to rebuild the reputation.

Punset, Neive (CN). Marina and Renzo Marcarino make notably improved Barbaresco, Dolcetto, and Barbera.

Francesco Rinaldi & Figli, Barolo (CN). Luciano Rinaldi continues a tradition with Barolo from Cannubi and Brunate that gains finesse only with time, along with Dolcetto Roussot.

Giuseppe Rinaldi, Barolo (CN). Traditional Barolo from Le Coste and Brunata (part of Brunate), as well as Dolcetto. The Rinaldi family still ages some Barolo in large bottles – one secret of their longevity.

Rizzi, Treiso (CN). Ernesto Dellapiana makes Barbaresco Fondenta and Sörì del Noce and Alba DOCs from 25 ha in the Cascina Rizzi area.

Bruno Rocca-Cascina Rabajà, Barbaresco (CN). Rocca makes good Barbaresco, Dolcetto, and vdt Nebbiolo from the original Cascina Rabajà, for which the vineyard area is named.

Rocche Costamagna, La Morra (CN). Claudia Ferreresi Locatelli revived the winery with 4 ha of vines at Rocche di La Morra for Barolo Vigna Francesco and Vigna Riccardo. Also Dolcetto, Barbera, and vdt Nebbiolo.

Rocche dei Manzoni, Monforte d'Alba (CN). Valentino Migliorini is Barolo's leading innovator, but as an outsider (from Emilia) his wines are less praised locally than elsewhere. Various vineyards cover 46 ha, much for opulent Barolo made only in top years (Vigna d'la Roul at Manzoni, Vigna Big at Mosconi, Vigna Mesdì at Bussia Soprana) and the replanted historic sites of Santo Stefano at Perno and Madonna Assunta at Castelletto. Migliorini and oenologist Sergio Galetti brought *barriques* to the zone for Bricco Manzoni, the imitated Nebbiolo-Barbera blend, and later for Barolo, as well as Chardonnay and Pinot Nero. The latter varieties are also used in a *champenoise* Valentino Brut Riserva Elena.

Josetta Safirio, Monforte d'Alba (CN). Fine Barolo from a plot at Castelletto.

Luciano Sandrone, Barolo (CN). Long experience at another winery has helped Sandrone and his brother Luca to turn Barolo from 1.2 ha at Cannubi Boschis into one of the most praised of

the zone. Dolcetto is also admirable. A Barbera is in the works.

Saracco, Castiglione Tinella (CN). Giovanni Saracco and sons Paolo and Roberto make both a refined new-style light Moscato and an old-style rich version from very ripe grapes. Connoisseurs often lean to the latter.

Mario Savigliano, Diano d'Alba (CN). Small production of good Diano Dolcetto Sörì del Sot.

Giorgio Scarzello & Figli, Barolo (CN). Giorgio and Gemma Scarzello have notably improved Barolo from Vigna Merenda. Also good Dolcetto.

Paolo Scavino, Castiglione Falletto (CN). Enrico Scavino makes fine Barolo Cannubi and Bric dël Fiasc, along with Dolcetto and Barbera.

Aurelio Settimo, La Morra (CN). Barolo from vines at Rocche and Rocchette at L'Annunziata.

Giovanni Soria, Castiglione Tinella (CN). Good Moscato d'Asti.

Tenute Cisa Asinari dei Marchesi di Gresy, Barbaresco (CN). Alberto di Gresy, amiable scion of a noble family, has vineyards at two major estates in Barbaresco: Monte Aribaldo at Treiso, source of notable Dolcetto and barrel-aged Chardonnay, and La Martinenga, source of some of the most elegant of all Nebbiolo wines. Gresy and winemaker Piero Ballario produce Barbaresco La Martinenga from most vintages, selecting in best years from the two best plots for Gajun, which is partly aged in *barriques*, and Camp Gros. From the family estate at Cassine in Asti province Marchesi di Gresy makes Moscato d'Asti La Serra.

Traversa, Neive (CN). Giuseppe and Flavio Traversa make good Moscato d'Asti and Barbaresco Sörì Ciabot.

G.D. Vajra, Barolo (CN). Aldo Vajra has built his reputation with Barolo from the Fossati area and what he calls Bricco delle Viole, along with fine Barbera and Dolcetto.

Giovanni Veglio & Figlio, Diano d'Alba (CN). Fine Diano Dolcetto Sörì Ubart and Puncia d'l Bric.

Sergio Vezza & Figlio, Treiso (CN). Respectable Barbaresco.

Luigi Viberti, La Morra (CN). Fine Barbera and Dolcetto from Santa Maria.

Gianni Voerzio, La Morra (CN). The family winery is noted for fresh, young Dolcetto, Freisa, Barbera, and Arneis, though from top years Barolo from La Serra is also noteworthy.

Roberto Voerzio, La Morra (CN). One of Alba's bright young winemakers has new cellars in which to hone style on the always persuasive Barolo La Serra, and emerging *crus* from Brunate and Cerequio. He draws from 8 ha of vines, partly his own, for a range of impeccably made wines: Dolcetto Priavino and San Francesco Croera, the promising Nebbiolo-Barbera vdt Vigna Serra, Freisa Boiolo-Pozzo, and Arneis.

WINE HOUSES/MERCHANTS

Accademia Torregiorgi, Neive (CN). Mario Giorgi selects in top years for Barbaresco Messoirano, Barolo Carpegna, Barbera, and Dolcetto.

Giacomo Ascheri, Bra (CN). Reliable Alba and Roero wines.

Batasiolo, La Morra (CN). The former Kiola and Fratelli Dogliani has begun anew with winemaker Marco Monchiero developing potential from 120 ha of vines on seven estates in Barolo known as "I Beni di Batasiolo". They include Boscareto and Briccolina at Serralunga, Bofani at Bussia Sottana in Monforte, and Cerequio at La Morra. Vineyards at Serralunga also produce Moscato for Asti. Other specialities are Dolcetto Bricco di Vergne and Chardonnay Morino from La Morra.

Bel Colle, Verduno (CN). Specialist in Pelaverga, along with good Dolcetto and a vdt Nebbiolo called Monvijé.

Giacomo Borgogno & Figli, Barolo (CN). The house, once a pillar of Barolo, is owned by the Boschis family, whose 20 ha of vines include choice plots in Cannubi.

Serio & Battista Borgogno, Barolo (CN). This long-noted Barolo house with vines in Cannubi has faded recently.

G.B. Burlotto, Verduno (CN). Historical house is noted for Barolo from Monvigliero and Cannubi.

Ca' Romé, Barbaresco (CN). Romano Marengo makes classic wines only in top years, exemplified by the limited bottling of Barbaresco Maria di Brun.

Calissano, Alba (CN). The cellars, as an adjunct of Gruppo Italiano Vini, bottle Alba wines and others.

Cantina del Glicine, Neive (CN). Adriana Marzi and Roberto Bruno achieve consistent class with Barbaresco Marcorino and Curà from their own vines and selections.

Cantina della Porta Rossa, Diano d'Alba (CN). Among a selection of Alba and other Piedmontese wines, the Dolcetto crus of Diano stand out. Barolo from La Delizia at Serralunga and Barbaresco Faset are also good.

Cantina Sebaste, Barolo (CN). Mauro Sebaste, backed by Gancia, has built this house into a leader with Barolo from his own vines at Bussia Soprana, along with fine Dolcetto and vdt Freisa, Arneis, and Bricco Viole, from Barbera and Nebbiolo aged in barriques. The Sylla Sebaste label is used.

Giuseppe Cappellano, Serralunga d'Alba (CN). The house that made the first Barolo Chinato is run by Teobaldo and Roberto Cappellano, who are striving to bring new style and prestige to Barolo and other select wines.

Ceretto, Alba (CN). Bruno Ceretto is the strategist behind the purchase of properties that have converted a patriarchal merchant house into a specialist in single vineyard wines.

Brother Marcello is the chief winemaker whose innovative touches have earned worldwide prestige for Bricco Rocche in Barolo, Bricco Asili and Faset in Barbaresco, and Blangé in Roero. Besides the estate wines, Ceretto also makes Barolo Zonchera (from Zonchetta), Barbaresco Asij, Nebbiolo d'Alba Lantasco, and Dolcetto d'Alba Rossana from leased vines under their control. They direct the Moscato d'Asti group known as I Vignaioli di Santo Stefano. Ceretto has leased the splendid La Bernardina estate just outside Alba where it has headquarters and is planting new varieties, including Chardonnay, Cabernet, Merlot, and Riesling.

Pio Cesare, Alba (CN). The house founded by Pio Cesare in 1881 is run by Pio Boffa, whose revisions include purchase of vineyards and the addition of new style wines to the traditional line. The house Barolo, Barbaresco, Nebbiolo, Barbera, and Dolcetto are still blended from different vineyards in line with the policy to avoid crus. The firm owns the 8.5-ha Ornato plot in Barolo at Serralunga and the 8-ha Cascina Bricco in Barbaresco at Treiso (source of barrel-fermented Chardonnay Piodilei). Winemaker Paolo Fenocchio also makes a youthful Nebbiolo called Il Nebbio, along with other Piedmontese wines.

Eredi Lodali, Treiso (CN). Rita Lodali makes good Barbaresco and Dolcetto.

Fontanafredda, Serralunga d'Alba (CN). The striped cellars of Tenimenti di Barolo e Fontanafredda are the landmark of this house founded in 1878 by Conte Emanuele Guerrieri, son of King Victor Emmanuel II and Contessa Rosa di Mirafiori e Fontanafredda, known as La Bela Rosin. The complex, owned by the Monte dei Paschi di Siena bank, includes 70 ha of vines for Alba DOC, vdt, and spumanti, though Fontanafredda produces and bottles other wines as well. Since the 1982 vintage, Barolo has been issued from eight vineyards. Adjacent to the cellars are Vigna Bianca, Gallaretto, Gattinera, La Rosa, and San Pietro. Vigna La Delizia and Lazzarito (the biggest and most durable wine) are near the village of Serralunga. Vigna La Villa is in the Cannubi area. Winemaker Livio Testa has brought Barbaresco, Diano Vigna La Lepre, Barbera, Nebbiolo, and vdt Pinot to admirable levels, along with Asti and the refined champenoise Contessa Rosa Brut and Rosé and Gattinera Brut.

Franco Fiorina, Alba (CN). The firm owned by Elsa Franco and Giuseppe Fontana is a reliable source of Alba wines. The steady hand of oenologist Armando Cordero is evident in the long-lived Barolo and Barbaresco, as well as Nebbiolo, Dolcetto, and Barbera.

Bruno Giacosa, Neive (CN). Giacosa has built his reputation for the

Above: Bruno Giacosa uses stainless steel tanks to enhance his wines' style.

enlightened traditional style shown in Barolo and Barbaresco of power, depth, and finesse. He selects grapes from top vineyards in Barbaresco (from Santo Stefano, Gallina, and Rio Sordo) and Barolo (from Bussia, Villero, Rocche di Castiglione Falletto, and Collina Rionda in Serralunga). Other Alba wines also stand out – Nebbiolo from Valmaggiore, Dolcetto from Basarin, Barbera from Altavilla, Arneis from Roero – as do Grignolino and Freisa. He also makes one of Italy's finest champenoise in Bruno Giacosa Extra Brut of Pinot Nero and Chardonnay from Oltrepò Pavese.

Fratelli Giacosa, Neive (CN). Valerio and Renzo Giacosa have steadily improved quality with Barbaresco Vigneto Roncaglie and Roccalini, Barolo Vigneto Pira (from Castiglione Falletto), good Dolcetto, and a fine vdt Barbera in barrique called Maria Gioana.

Marchesi di Barolo, Barolo (CN). The winery, in whose cellars the original Barolo was supposedly made under the Marchesi Falletti, is living up to its name again after a lapse. Emphasis on quality is evident in six single-vineyard Barolo – Cannubi, Cannubi Muscatel, Sarmassa, Coste di Rose, Valletta, and Brunate – from 35 ha. There is also a good Dolcetto (Madonna di Como), along with an assortment of DOC and vdt. The winery is among the few with a stock of old vintages available, some dating to when the cellars belonged to a society known as Opera Pia.

Giuseppe Mascarello & Figlio, Monchiero (CN). Mauro Mascarello is a master of traditional style Barolo, the most esteemed of which comes from his plot of Monprivato in Castiglione Falletto. He also buys grapes at Villero, from Bussia and Dardi in Monforte, and from La Francia. He makes Barbaresco (Bernadotti and Marcarini), Barbera (Fasana and Ginestra), and Dolcetto (Gagliassi) of notable class.

Alfredo Prunotto, Alba (CN). Giuseppe Colla, one of the wisest selectors of Alba's crus, continues as winemaker at this prestigious house in which controlling interest has been acquired by the Antinori-Whitbread

firm of A&W Investments. Colla respects tradition with style in single vineyard Barolo (Bussia, Cannubi), Barbaresco (Montestefano, Rabajà), Barbera d'Alba (Pian Romualdo), Dolcetto d'Alba (Mosesco), and Nebbiolo d'Alba (Occhetti).

Renato Ratti-Antiche Cantine dell'Abbazia dell'Annunziata, La Morra (CN). Renato Ratti's genius went beyond the operation of this small but renowned house, where sons Piero and Giovanni have joined his nephew Massimo Martinelli in making wines with habitual flair. His belief that Alba's wines could maintain character and suit modern palates is exemplified in Barolo from vineyards around the desanctified Benedictine abbey next to the cellars: at Marcenasco, Rocche-Marcenasco, and Conca-Marcenasco. Deft selections include Barbaresco and reds that use the label themes of 19th-century Piedmontese soldiers, for Barbera Altavilla, Dolcetto Campetto Colombé, and Nebbiolo Ochetti di Monteu. The family also owns the Villa Pattono at Costigliole d'Asti. The museum he assembled in the abbey testifies to Ratti's passion for the Langhe and its wines.

Roche, Alba (CN). The cellars on an estate with 22 ha of vines is being developed by Raffaele Ferrero, whose Dolcetto Vigna a Mano, Barbera Crotin, and Nebbiolo Mesdì show promise.

Gigi Rosso, Castiglione Falletto (CN). Luigi Rosso, who has headed the Alba wine consortium has 32 ha for the noted Barolo Cascina Arione from Serralunga and Diano Moncolombetto.

Renzo Seghesio, Monforte d'Alba (CN). Barolo and Dolcetto.

Maggiore Sottimano, Neive (CN). Barbaresco Brichet and Dolcetto Cottà.

Valfieri, Alba (CN). The company headed by Rosangela Riccadonna has cellars at Costigliole d'Asti for Alba and Asti DOCs as well as at Cortina all'Adige for Alto Adige DOCs.

Vietti, Castiglione Falletto (CN). Alfredo Currado, daughter Elisabetta, and son-in-law Mario Cordero combine talents in wines highly praised in Italy and perhaps even more abroad for power and elegance. Vineyard selections vary according to vintage, but notable have been Barolo (Rocche di Castiglione, Villero, Bussia, and Briacca), Barbaresco (Masseria), Dolcetto (Bussia, Castelletto, Disa, and Pugnane), Barbera (Bussia and Pian Romualdo), and Nebbiolo (San Michele). They also make good Freisa and a vdt red Fioretto from Barbera and Nebbiolo with Neyrano. Vietti was a pioneer of modern Arneis.

Vinicola Piemontese, La Morra (CN). Marco Ferrero selects from 10 ha of vines of the former Tenuta Cerequio for highly regarded Barolo, along with Barbaresco and Dolcetto.

COOPERATIVES

Produttori del Barbaresco, Barbaresco (CN). Italy's most admired cooperative was founded in 1958 on the base of the original town cellars started in 1894 by Domizio Cavazza, the father of Barbaresco. Celestino Vacca directs the group of 65 growers that offers outstanding quality at reasonable price in wines selected from an honour roll of the town's vineyards: Asili, Montefico, Montestefano, Rio Sordo, Ovello, Rabajà, Moccagatta, and Pora. Another half million bottles a year is taken up by a Nebbiolo vdt of the Langhe.
Terre del Barolo, Castiglione Falletto (CN). Growers with 800 ha in Barolo and environs are leading suppliers to bottlers, but they also make good Dolcetto, Barbera, Nebbiolo, and Barolo, including a single vineyard bottling from the Castello di Grinzane plot.
Cantina del Dolcetto di Dogliani, Dogliani (CN). Good values in Dolcetto.
Confratelli di San Michele, Neive (CN). Barbaresco, Dolcetto, and Barbera.
I Vignaioli di Santo Stefano, Santo Stefano Belbo (CN). Growers with 25 ha of vines make good Moscato and Asti.
I Vignaioli Elvio Pertinace, Treiso (CN). Mario Barbero leads growers whose Barbaresco includes Treiso's *crus* – Casotto, Castellizzano, Marcarini, and Nervo – at reasonable prices.

Travel Information

RESTAURANTS/HOTELS

Da Cesare, 12050 Albaretto della Torre (CN). Tel (0173)520141. Cesare Giaccone's mercurial temperament provides the high and low points of the Langhe's cuisine.
Gener Neuv, 14100 Asti. Tel (0141)57270. Piero and Giuseppina Fassi serve Asti's food and wines in a warmly rustic setting.
Da Guido, 14055 Costigliole d'Asti. Tel (0141)966012. Guido and Lidia Alciati and sons have elevated Piedmontese cooking and wines to their ultimate levels in a basement setting of restrained elegance.
Il Cascinalenuovo, 14057 Isola d'Asti. Tel (0141)958166. The Ferretto family deftly combines tradition and innovation in cooking with impeccably chosen wines in this hotel restaurant.
Belvedere, 12064 La Morra (CN). Tel (0173)50190. Gianfranco Bovio has the knack for feeding hundreds of guests well on traditional Langhe fare. Try his own Dolcetto and Barolo.
Giardino da Felicin, 12065 Monforte d'Alba (CN). Tel (0173)78225. The classical setting for food and wines of Barolo, as knowingly interpreted by Giorgio and Rosina Rocca and son Nino. Rooms with views.
La Contea, 12057 Neive (CN). Tel (0173)67126. The gregarious warmth of old Piedmont is summed up in this hostelry where Tonino Verro chooses the Barbaresco and truffles to go with wife Claudia's artistic cooking.
Locanda San Martino, 15060 Pasturana (AL). Tel (0143)58444. Michele Bergaglio does delicious interpretations of Gavi's cooking.
Al Sorriso, 28018 Soriso (NO). Tel (0322)983228. Country elegance in food, wine, and setting in the smiling hills between Gattinara and Lago d'Orta.
Falstaff, 12060 Verduno (CN). Tel (0172)459244. Franco Giolitto cooks with youthful inspiration in this quiet corner of the Barolo zone.
La Pergola, 12040 Vezza d'Alba (CN). Tel (0173)65178. Maria Occhetti's cooking and Piermario Bergadano's wines provide fine dining in Roero.

WINE SHOPS/ENOTECHE

The region sponsors eight *enoteche* with permanent displays. In the Alba area they are located in the castle of Grinzane Cavour (for surrounding zones), in the castle of Barolo (for Barolo), in Barbaresco's old church of San Donato (for Barbaresco), and in the castle of Mango (for Moscato d'Asti). The castle at Costigliole d'Asti has a range of Asti's wines. The Palazzo Calleri at Vignale Monferrato has wines of Monferrato Casalese. The Palazzo Robellini at Acqui Terme displays wines from the Acqui area and Asti. The castle at Roppolo emphasizes wines of Torino, Vercelli, and Novara provinces. Restaurants at Grinzane Cavour, Costigliole, Vignale Monferrato, and Roppolo are all recommended. Also many communes sponsor a shop – often known as Bottega del Vino – with the local wines.

Piedmont has many fine privately owned wine shops with selections that range beyond regional specialities to the classics of other parts of Italy and France. A few of note are La Mia Crota at Biella, Ferrando at Ivrea, and Vivian at Novara. Near the Swiss border are the Enoteca Bava and Conca d'Oro at Cannobio. Good *enoteche* in Turin are Borio and Il Vinaio, which provides a rare collection of old vintages of Barolo and Barbaresco, as well as Brunello and Bordeaux.

PLACES OF INTEREST

Piedmont's numerous treasures of art and history are centred in Turin with its memories of the Savoy dynasty. Its alpine resorts, notably Sestriere, are renowned and the scenery around the lakes of Maggiore and Orta is hard to beat. But where Piedmont stands out from the rest of Italy is in its organization of wine tourism, which here can be a serious endeavour and not just the lark that it is almost everywhere else. The first destination is Alba with Barolo and Barbaresco, but some less glorified wines also come from lovely places. The suggested routes marked on maps provide itineraries, but nearly all the winding roads of the Langhe and Monferrato hills are suited to wandering through vineyards, woods, and high pastures with panoramas from the Apennines to the Alps.

Alba: Barolo and Barbaresco. The Langhe are attractive any time of year, but they are irresistible in autumn when the harvest is underway and truffles are in season. The white tartufi d'Alba are considered the most exquisite of the breed. Alba holds its annual truffle fair in October, but the *trifolai*, who scratch them from the earth after they've been sniffed out by hounds, known that they really reach their prime in mid-November after the frosts set in. That's also the time when the vines turn red and yellow and the fogs creep up the valleys creating dramatic views from such high spots as La Morra in Barolo and Treiso in Barbaresco. Both zones have well-marked wine routes running through them, leading to prominent estates and cellars. Not to be missed in Barolo are the Ratti wine museum at L'Annunziata below La Morra, the Castle at Barolo, and the Castle of Grinzane, where Cavour kept a vineyard and where the Cavalieri del Tartufo e dei Vini d'Alba, the most prominent of Piedmont's wine-related fraternal orders, meet. The road from Alba to Neive crosses the Barbaresco zone through a panoply of sloping vineyards. Both zones have fine restaurants and quiet hotels, though when truffles are in season there are never enough rooms to host the crowds that arrive from across the Alps. So it's best to book well in advance. Routes through the Roero, Diano, and Dogliani zones are scenic, though the high vineyards of Moscato between Neive and Canelli are Alba's most picturesque.

Canelli, Monferrato, and Turin's hills. Asti isn't really a wine town, but Canelli to the south is the capital of *spumante*, so the slopes along the Belbo are covered with Moscato vines. Roads through the hills between the Belbo and Tanaro rivers cross the classic vineyards of Barbera d'Asti. The Bersano museum at Nizza Monferrato displays the traditional tools of the local winemaking craft. North of the Tanaro is the Basso Monferrato where Grignolino is planted on sweeping slopes between Portacomaro and the Monferrato Casalese hills south of the Po. The other popular variety is Freisa, planted mainly to the west on hills extending into the Turin area at Chieri. At nearby Pessione are the main cellars of Martini & Rossi, worth a visit by admirers of vermouth. But the main attraction is the wine museum with an outstanding collection of artefacts ranging from the great Piedmontese tradition to the Romans, Etruscans, and Greeks.

Gavi, Ovada, and Acqui. The hills of southeastern Piedmont along the Bormida, Orba, and Scrivia rivers on the edge of the Apennines are known as Alto Monferrato. Vineyards there are noted on the one hand for sweet Moscato and Brachetto, which thrive around Acqui Terme and Strevi, and on the other for dry Dolcetto and Cortese, which reach peaks at Ovada and Gavi. Towns in the Gavi zone have a look and feel of Liguria about them that dates to when they were part of Genoa's domain. And, indeed, among Piedmont's vast array of wines, zesty white Gavi seems the most Mediterranean in nature.

The north: Carema to Gattinara. Carema's vineyards on terraces with pergolas supported by stone columns are as dramatically poised as any of adjacent Valle d'Aosta. Just to the south in the Canavese glacial basin below Ivrea are the vineyards of Erbaluce for the dry and sweet whites of Caluso. From there the drive through Biella east to the Sesia valley passes vineyards of the northern Nebbiolo and the wine towns of Lessona, Ghemme, and Gattinara. Perhaps the best place to enjoy the wines is in restaurants with views over the nearby lakes of Maggiore and Orta.

Liguria

Capital: Genova (Genoa).
Provinces: Genova (GE), Imperia (IM), La Spezia (SP), Savona (SV).
Area: 5,416 square kilometres (eighteenth).
Population: 1,770,000 (eleventh).

Above: Riomaggiore, one of the five villages of Cinqueterre on the Ligurian Sea.

Genova la Superba, northern Italy's busiest port, is the axis of a slender strip of a region that clings to the walls of the Maritime Alps and Apennines as they arch over the Ligurian Sea between Provence and Tuscany. The Italian Riviera, called Ponente west of Genoa and Levante to the east, is a marvel of contrasts between mountain and sea and a major source of tourist income. But the sheer harshness of its slopes has always posed a challenge to viticulture. Were it not for the legends that surround its vineyards, Liguria's wines would be lost in the national deluge. The terraces carved out of the cliffs of Cinqueterre, for example, tell more about wine's historical value in Liguria than statistics ever could.

The region makes less than half of one percent of the nation's wine and classifies just over two percent of its own total. Until lately the only DOC zones were Cinqueterre and Dolceacqua, though the promotion of Riviera Ligure di Ponente and Colli di Luni will raise the quota. Ligurians also consume less wine than their neighbours in the north, slightly less than the estimated annual national rate of 65 litres per capita. What the figures reveal, though, is not an aversion to wine but a natural sense of restraint, of healthy moderation. For over the centuries those Ligurians who did not keep a vineyard themselves certainly had a relative or friend whose toil as a *vignaiolo* made them treasure their limited allotments.

Early Greek traders might have introduced vines and the techniques of working them to the Liguri, whose various tribes inhabited the territory. The Liguri later planted vineyards across the Apennines in Piedmont, Lombardy, and Emilia, and even in the Alps at Valtellina. The Etruscans kept vineyards in the Luni hills along the Magra valley, and possibly even near the sea at what became Cinqueterre. In those sites of eastern Liguria the Romans made Lunense and Corneliae, the latter in reference to the wine from the village of Corniglia, one of the "five lands".

But if the wines of the Riviera di Levante won most early praise, those of the Riviera di Ponente have prevailed in later days as Genoa became a major sea power whose loyalties were often linked to France. The Rossese of Dolceacqua, a favourite of Napoleon, is still the most prized red, though the Ponente version of Dolcetto known as Ormeasco can be equally tasty. Liguria lost its former lands to the north where Gavi has become the leading white of Piedmont. But many experts are convinced that the Ponente's Pigato makes wines of more class and character than Gavi, even if Ligurians often prefer the Vermentino grown along both rivieras. The dry white of Cinqueterre has faded from favour, but the sweet version Sciacchetrà has built hopes for a small revival.

Ligurians were more deeply involved with wine in the past than they are today. Migration to Genoa, Savona, La Spezia, and other cities reduced the rural population, which often finds it more profitable to grow flowers or vegetables in green houses than tend vines. Reminders of the fading cult of home winemaking can be spotted on the outskirts of Genoa, where solitary vines grow on patches of earth not yet conceded to concrete and steel. More moving still is the sight of those precipitous terraces of Cinqueterre overgrown with brush and scrub where vines have been abandoned. But perhaps the neglect of this unique heritage was to be expected in a region where wine has become such an incidental that the authorities have no maps of their latest DOC zones.

Wine's loss of ground as both business and leisure has taken with it many old-time examples of local colour and taste. Yet some 85 types of wine are still made in Liguria from about 100 grape varieties, many either indigenous or thoroughly localized. Some view this miscellany as a triumph of individuality, others as an obstacle to a regional identity with wine. But Liguria, due to the physical distance from one end to the other, has always had a split personality. The rivalry between Ponente and Levante is felt keenly in the wines. Grape varieties differ, as do practices of winemaking. To the west most wines are pure varietals as in Piedmont; to the east they are more often blends as in Tuscany.

Until quite recently the Apennines shielded Liguria from its neighbours, leaving towns and villages dependent on produce from the surrounding hills and the sea. But laboriously tunnelled *autostrade* have improved access, increasing the market for wines from other parts of Italy and France. Ligurian wine drinkers have gained something from their new eclecticism: an awareness of quality judged by international standards rather than parochial tastes. Some producers have realized that given the limited grape yields from their difficult terrains, they must make wines of superior class to make an impact beyond local markets. The temperate, breezy Mediterranean hill climate favours their quest. But growers, many of whom work small plots part time, have been reluctant to update their methods and, just as important, the mentality that could lead their wines towards greater recognition.

Liguria's Vineyards

In a region where most wine is still made at artisan or family levels, growers have developed an amazing range of individual styles in working their vineyards. Their loyalty to local vines and time tested methods of training them makes their wines as distinctive in personality as they are variable in quality and style. Vineyards are similarly diversified. Custom favoured pergolas to the east in Cinqueterre, and *alberello*, low head or spur training, to the west where the French influence is felt. But many growers find it easier to maintain vertical, wire-trained systems, such as Guyot or their own interpretations thereof.

Among an estimated 85 identifiable grape varieties grown in the region, only a half dozen are at all prominent. The most diffused is Dolcetto, better known as Ormeasco on the Riviera di Ponente where it prevails, followed at a distance by Rossese and Sangiovese among red wine varieties. The common Albarola, prevalent on the Riviera di Levante, leads white wine varieties, though the admirable Vermentino

has gained on both sides of Genoa. Cinqueterre's Bosco and Trebbiano Toscano occupy more space than Pigato, though the latter seems to be gaining as the source of the Ponente's most dignified whites. Several vines that once enjoyed some prominence have practically disappeared, among them Barbarossa, Rollo, and Greco (which may have arrived from Greece via Calabria). Scattered interest has been shown in Cabernet and Merlot, as well as Chardonnay and Sauvignon, but overall foreign varieties seem to have made less progress here than in any other region of Italy. The following varieties are proudly local.

Albarola. This characterless component of the Cinqueterre blend and anonymous table wines is also called Erbarola.

Bianchetta Genovese. Once prominent white variety in the Coronata and Val Polcevera areas near Genoa, it is fading along with the vineyards there.

Bosco. Brought from Genoa to Cinqueterre in the last century, the prolific variety has become the mainstay there. If it has personality traits they are hard to define.

Granaccia. Ligurian version of Granacha or Grenache or Cannonau used for a light red at Quiliano near Savona.

Lumassina. The vine, perhaps a Trebbiano, grows around Savona for use in zesty white wines, notably at Quiliano where it is called Buzzetto.

Ormeasco. A Dolcetto clone that apparently came from the Piedmontese town of Ormea in the Apennines across the border from where the wine called Ormeasco is now made in a subzone of the Riviera di Ponente DOC. There is some evidence that Dolcetto was planted in both Piedmont and Liguria as early as the fourteenth century.

Pigato. The vine possibly of Greek origin has grown since at least the seventeenth century in Liguria, mainly around Albenga, where it excels in whites of body and tone. The name comes from the dialect term *pigau* in reference to its blotchy skins.

Pollera Nera. Ancient variety of the Riviera di Levante, where it figures in Colli di Luni Rosso. It is also planted across the border in Tuscany.

Rossese. Origins of this prized but unprolific vine are uncertain, though some say it came from France. Noted in Liguria in the sixteenth century, it is now planted mainly in the extreme west around Dolceacqua where it makes medium-bodied, fruity reds. Another clone known as Savonese or di Campochiesa makes lighter reds around Albenga.

Vermentino. The vine which apparently arrived in the fourteenth century from Spain via Corsica has developed local traits to admire in varietal whites in the Riviera di Ponente and Colli di Luni DOCs, as well as in Cinqueterre.

Other varieties

Other varieties recommended or authorized in Liguria include:

For red (or rosé): Alicante, Barbera, Cabernet Franc, Canaiolo, Ciliegiolo, Dolcetto, Merlot, Sangiovese.

For white: Albana, Greco, Malvasia Bianca Lunga (or del Chianti), Moscato Bianco, Trebbiano Toscano

Liguria's Wine Zones

Its privileged position along the southern flank of the Maritime Alps and Apennines permits Liguria alone among northern regions to bask in Mediterranean warmth. But any advantages for agriculture in the mild climate are offset by the ruggedness of the terrain. Farming surpassed subsistence levels in Liguria because slopes were terraced and valleys banked until man's handiwork became the hallmark of the landscape. But lately vineyards and olive groves have lost ground to brush and scrub. In places along the 343 kilometres of coast, mountains rise directly from the sea. In others rockfalls and alluvial deposits of gravel and sand have formed beaches and level stretches suitable for planting crops or building. Streams coursing south from the mountain watershed cut gorges and valleys whose banks are sometimes gradual enough for unterraced vineyards. But the only sizeable spreads of vines are along the Arroscia valley to the west and around the Magra valley to the southeast. The northern side of the mountain chain is the source of such rivers as the Tanaro, Bormida, and Scrivia flowing into Piedmont and the Trebbia into Emilia-Romagna, but few vines grow in their cool valleys.

Breezes waft the coast, where summers are usually sunny and dry and winters pleasantly mild. But microclimates vary to extremes in the cooler, damper interior, where clashing air currents can cause violent winds and sudden changes of weather. Still, throughout Liguria the main deterrent to a good vintage is drought.

The western riviera

Most of the Riviera di Ponente is new DOC territory, but the proven zone is Dolceacqua in the extreme west where Rossese grows on the warm lower slopes of the Nervia and Crosia valleys. The reddish calcareous clays there, as along much of the coast, are also well suited to white varieties, notably for rich Pigato from around Imperia and Albenga and fine Vermentino from Finale and other points. The upper Arroscia valley is noted for red Ormeasco, a Dolcetto that shows singular personality on those cool slopes.

The eastern riviera

Vines are planted along much of the Riviera di Levante, though the noted zones lie to the southeast near La Spezia. Cinqueterre's once vaunted whites come from sandy calcareous soils on terraces that benefit from a gentle maritime climate. The lower Magra and Vara valleys have calcareous clay soils in the region's most productive vineyard area, the home of Colli di Luni, a new DOC for promising whites based on Vermentino and a red based on Sangiovese.

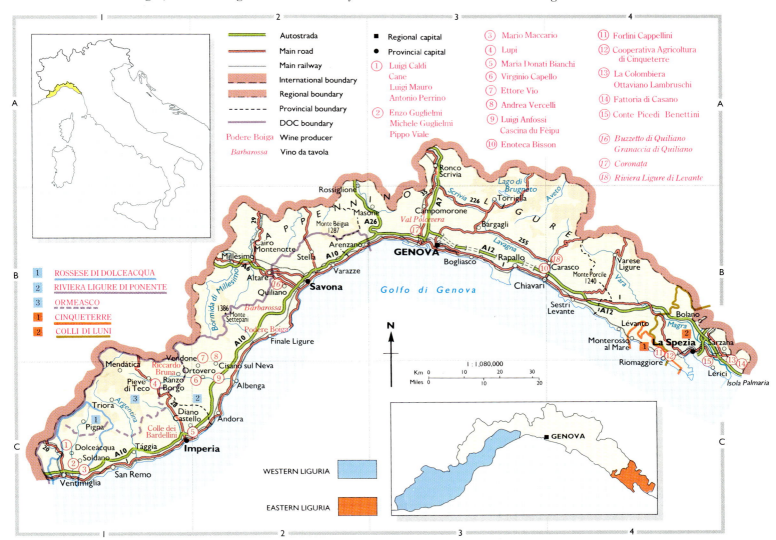

Wines of the western riviera

The Riviera di Ponente's sundry vines over time found havens of their own on rugged rises along the coast and up through the valleys of the Apennines and Maritime Alps. The challenge of working hillsides so intricately variable in form and weather accounts for the diversity, the individual specialization that has made the wines of western Liguria modest in volume but bold by nature. Some admirable wines have come and gone – the legendary Moscatello of Taggia, for instance, and the pale red Barbarossa of Pietra Ligure. Many others have faded. Today, the varieties regarded as important have been reduced to four: the red Rossese and Ormeasco and the white Pigato and Vermentino. Rossese di Dolceacqua has long stood as Liguria's premier red. But the other varieties only came under DOC in 1988 in Riviera Ligure di Ponente, which also attempted to define their historical vineyard areas. Pigato can be one of Italy's most distinctive native whites, though some experts rate the popular Vermentino just as highly. Ormeasco, a Ligurian Dolcetto, can sometimes match the class of its counterparts from Piedmont and almost invariably outlast them. A few estates of the western riviera were already noted for traditional wines; a few others have emerged with convincing modern styles. But if these slight stirrings of activity could be described as a revival, it is being led by the house of Lupi, whose selections of Ormeasco, Pigato, Vermentino, and Dolceacqua set Liguria's standards. Despite some replanting of white varieties, vineyards in the area continue to diminish, a trend that, if not reversed, seems destined to make the precious wines of the western riviera ever more confined to their sanctuaries.

Rossese di Dolceacqua or Dolceacqua (1972)

Although grown along the riviera as early as the 16th century, Rossese came into its own after a visit by Napoleon I in 1805 to the Doria family's castle in Dolceacqua. Finding exquisite what was probably then a sweet wine, he reportedly told his hosts "from now on I authorize you to call it by my name". Few producers ever did. Maybe they, too, had heard that the Emperor's palate was no match for his ego. Still, Rossese became the leading red of the riviera, the wine gourmets seek out when menus switch from fish to the upland specialities of game birds or rabbit stewed with olives.

Rossese from Dolceacqua is considered the finest: fuller and softer with more depth of flavour and bouquet and richer ruby colour than wines from points east. Some producers strive for a supple Beaujolais style in wines to drink in a year or two. Others use wood ageing to build complexity in the *superiore*, whose flavours can become warm and velvety with a few years in bottle. Rossese's modern heights were reached by the late Emilio Croesi, though wines from Vigneto Curli at Perinaldo have not been the same since his passing. Nor have many other recent examples been impressive in a zone where vineyards are declining and soils in many places seem better suited to white wines than red. Much Rossese is thin, pale, and tends to oxidize. But several producers make attractive wines of good body, colour, and balance. Noted vineyards at Dolceacqua include Arcagna (where Cane has vines), Morghe, and Pozzuolo. The Crosia valley has choice plots at Soldano (Enzo Guglielmi and Viale) and San Biagio della Cima (Maccario). Lupi is always reliable with selections of small batches from vineyards in several parts of the zone.

Zone: Often steep slopes adjacent to the French border, extending from near the coast at Ventimiglia and Bordighera into the Ligurian Alps in 13 communes of Imperia province, though vineyards which cannot be higher than 600 m are mainly in the lower Nervia and Crosia valleys around Dolceacqua, Apricale, Perinaldo, and Soldano. The Riviera Ligure di Ponente zone overlaps Dolceacqua, where growers have the option of declaring Rossese for either DOC. Dry red. Grapes: Rossese; other reds up to 5%. Yld 63/90, Alc 12; superiore 13, Acd 0.45, Ag superiore 1 yr.

Riviera Ligure di Ponente (1988)

Most of western Liguria is covered by this zone, whose stunning green hillsides produce some fine Pigato and Vermentino and a lightweight Rossese, each of which may cite one of three subdenominations on its labels. Ormeasco, a singular type of Dolcetto, is made in a subzone that includes traditional vineyards in the Arroscio valley and the town of Pornassio, where it reaches peaks of finesse and durability from Lupi. Ormeasco also makes a coral-hued rosé known as Sciac-trà, for "schiacciare e trarre" in reference to crushing the grapes and drawing the juice off the skins.

The subdenominations apply to vineyard areas of historical note for certain wines, but use of the names for Pigato, Rossese, and Vermentino is optional under the confusing DOC code. The key to recognition is the varietal wine name, obligatory on labels after the appellation Riviera Ligure di Ponente.

Below: the town of Dolceacqua is the production centre of Rossese, Liguria's best known red wine.

Albenga or **Albenganese**. Refers to the coastal hills around Albenga and Andora noted above all for Pigato. There it becomes rich and velvety with a sunny yellow colour, a hint of wild fennel in its ample aroma, and refined fruitiness on the palate. Cascina du Fèipu and Anfossi are leaders in the Albenga area, which is also known for a Rossese from a distinct clone in wines that often seem closer to rosé than red.
Finale or **Finalese**. Refers to Finale Ligure and the coastal areas around Pietra Ligure and Noli noted for Vermentino that combines fragrant delicacy with firmness in body and flavour. Boiga makes an example of the style, though good Vermentino is also made at other points along the coast.
Riviera dei Fiori. Takes in the entire "Coast of Flowers" from Imperia to the French border and also, for convenience, all other parts of Imperia province, including Ormeasco. The Imperia-Diano hills are noted for fine Vermentino, exemplified by Colle dei Bardellini. Notable Pigato is made by Riccardo Bruna.

Zone: A vast tract of western Liguria extending from the edge of the commune of Genova to the French frontier and ranging through often rugged terrain of the Ligurian Alps and Apennines across the upper Arroscio valley to the border of Piedmont. The territory, which comprises 67 communes in Imperia province, 46 in Savona, and 2 in Genova, includes a subzone for the wine of Ormeasco in the upper valleys of the Arroscio, Impero, Carpasina, Argentina, and Nervia streams in 21 communes of Imperia province. There are also three areas in which Pigato, Rossese, and Vermentino are entitled to a subdenomination: Albenga or Albenganese from Albenga and 19 other communes in Savona province; Finale or Finalese from Finale Ligure and 15 other communes in Savona province; Riviera dei Fiori from all communes in Imperia province, including those of Ormeasco. The Riviera

Ligure di Ponente zone also overlaps Dolceacqua, where growers have the option of declaring Rossese for either DOC.
Ormeasco Dry red. Grapes: Ormeasco (Dolcetto); other reds up to 5%. Yld 63/90, Alc 11; superiore 12.5, Acd 0.5, Ag superiore 1 yr.
Ormeasco Sciac-trà Dry rosé. Grapes: as Ormeasco. Yld 63/90, Alc 11, Acd 0.5.
Pigato Dry white. Grapes: Pigato; other whites up to 5%. Yld 77/110, Alc 11, Acd 0.5.
Rossese Dry red. Grapes: Rossese; other reds up to 5%. Yld 63/90, Alc 11, Acd 0.5.
Vermentino Dry white. Grapes: Vermentino; other whites up to 5%. Yld 77/110, Alc 11, Acd 0.5.

Other wines of note

Most wines made along the coast are unlabelled and sold locally, though there are never enough to satisfy demands during the tourist season. The majority is white and light, epitomized by the often fizzy Lumassina that may seem to have the same effect as lemonade, though gastronomes choose it as the ideal match for pasta with pesto. Lumassina is known as Buzzetto at the town of Quiliano near Savona, where the red Granaccia is also issued in bottles from several growers who use a standard label. Genoa, at the axis of the two rivieras, has its own wines in the white Coronata and red and white Val Polcevera, though bottles are hard to find. But most wines are presented as *bianco*, *rosso*, or *rosato*, guaranteed to be local, or course, in a happy go lucky sort of way.

ESTATES/GROWERS

Luigi Anfossi, Bastia d'Albenga (SV). Notable Pigato and bright Rossese.
Maria Donati Bianchi, Diano Castello (IM). Vermentino.
Riccardo Bruna, Ranzo Borgo (IM). Tiny production of some of the finest Pigato.

Luigi Caldi, Dolceacqua (IM). Good Rossese.
Cane, Dolceacqua (IM). Giobatta Cane has a tiny production of highly regarded Rossese from the Vigneti d'Arcagna area.
Virginio Capello, Ortovero (SV). Good Pigato.
Cascina du Fèipu, Bastia d'Albenga (SV). From 2.3 ha of densely planted head-trained vines at Massaretti, Pippo and Bice Parodi have created a legend with their Pigato di Albenga, a white of uncommon stature, along with a bit of flowery fresh Rossese.
Colle dei Bardellini, Sant'Agata di Imperia. From less than 6 ha of terraces on this model estate overlooking Imperia, fine Vermentino, including the *riserva* U Munte, along with tasty Rossese.
Enzo Guglielmi, Soldano (IM). From 2 ha in the Zona Pini, Guglielmi makes Rossese di Dolceacqua that ranks consistently near the top.
Michele Guglielmi, Soldano (IM). Sound Dolceacqua from a tiny plot.
Mario Maccario, San Biagio della Cima (IM). Outstanding potential for Dolceacqua still to be realized in the wine.

Left: the village of Apricale in the Rossese di Dolceacqua zone lies along the Nervia valley at the foot of the Maritime Alps.

Luigi Mauro, Dolceacqua (IM). Grower emerging with Dolceacqua.
Antonio Perrino, Dolceacqua (IM). Good Dolceacqua.
Podere Boiga, Finale Ligure (SV). Domenico Boiga makes good DOC Vermentino, along with an enticing vdt Lumassina.
Andrea Vercelli, Cisano sul Neve (SV). Good Vermentino from Tenuta La Conca at Cenesi.
Pippo Viale, Soldano (IM). Consistently good Dolceacqua.
Ettore Vio, Vendone (SV). Improving Pigato.

WINE HOUSES/MERCHANTS

Cantine Calleri, Albenga (SV). Riviera di Ponente DOC.
Lupi, Pieve di Teco (IM). In running their *enoteca* at Imperia, brothers Tommaso and Angelo Lupi noticed that good local grapes were too often being turned into defective wines, so in 1977 they built cellars and became producers themselves. They selected small batches of grapes from choice vineyards around the Riviera di Ponente and with oenologist Donato Lanati have steadily progressed to become the region's leading wine house. Their long-lived Ormeasco di Pornassio is exemplary, as are Pigato Le Petraie, Vermentino Le Serre, Rossese di Dolceacqua, and the vdt red Le Braje (Ormeasco in *barrique*). The vdt white Vignamare is a deft blend of Pigato and Vermentino.

Below: Pippo and Bice Parodi produce a noted Pigato di Albenga at their Cascina du Fèipu.

Wines of the eastern riviera

Wine had such a glorious past along the Riviera di Levante that winemakers might be excused for lapses in the present. But developments in the new DOC zone of Colli di Luni indicate that eastern Liguria's wines might yet hold some hope for the future. Etruscans may have planted the first vines in the hills along the Gulf of La Spezia and the Magra valley where the Romans founded the town of Luni. But the wine that always dominated the scene was Cinqueterre, from the "five lands", the five fishing villages nestled into inlets along the coast above La Spezia. Roman slaves might have hewn the first terraces out of the rock walls there and transported the soil by hand. That labour continued at painstaking intervals until the eighteenth century when growers apparently decided that it was enough just to maintain vines there. The man-made landscape inspired writers from Petrarch to Lord Byron, and the wines, which were usually sweet and amber, were admired in France and even North America.

Early visitors arrived by foot or, more conveniently, by boat, since there were no tunnelled railways or winding roads as there are now. They must have been spellbound by the sight of terraces scaling the cliffs from a stone's throw above the sea to heights where even gulls decline to soar. If they came during the harvest, they could have watched pickers relaying baskets of grapes down the slopes to fishermen in waiting boats. And they might have savoured the wine known as Vernaccia. That name, from the village of Vernazza, is no longer used, though unrelated vines called Vernaccia make wines in Tuscany, the Marches, and Sardinia. Those wines of Cinqueterre's golden days might not have been so different from today's sweet Sciacchetrà. But there is little of that to taste. Even the dry wine that dominates production has relinquished its primary position among the region's whites. The legend, too, has lost its lustre as *vignaioli* find fewer incentives for continuing their historic endeavours and the terraces of Cinqueterre become overgrown with brush. Yet, despite the saddening trend, some growers remain attached to their *pàstini*, the precipitous parcels of land where they prune and hoe and pick and maybe dare to hope that some day a miracle will revive one of the most enchanting places where vines have ever grown.

Cinqueterre (1973)

The vanishing vineyards may be a sad inevitability, but the decline of Cinqueterre's wines to secondary status seems an inexcusable shame. Most of the blame falls on the backward or makeshift winemaking practised in many small cellars in the zone. The 140 ha of vineyards registered for DOC render enough for about half a million bottles of the dry white and perhaps 6,000 of the sweet Sciacchetrà. Among an estimated 400 producers, some do well enough to have a steady clientele, but others are notoriously lax in their methods, knowing that tourists will buy wine called Cinqueterre whether bottled or not. Another problem is that grapes in the DOC blend seem to have been chosen for productivity rather than proven class. The primary Bosco and optional Albarola make dry wines of little colour and faint, almost neutral odour and flavour. Since both oxidize easily, most dry Cinqueterre is light and fragile to be drunk in a year or so before it begins to turn to amber. The other optional variety, Vermentino, makes wines of fine texture and aroma and livelier fruit flavours when yields are restrained, so producers who seek character tend to use it at the maximum 40 percent – or sometimes more.

Still as production declines, more producers in Cinqueterre do seem to be seeking character. Forlini Cappellini's fragrant dry white has drawn praise from experts. Among those who sell wines mainly locally the names of Silvano Cozzani, Vittorio Arpe, Benito

Fossani, and Rollandi are often singled out. But the leader in the uphill drive to preserve a heritage is Nello Capris of the Cooperativa Agricola di Cinqueterre. His quiet quest of integrity attracts little notice beyond the zone, but examples of good dry whites that carry vineyard names have influenced other producers. Even more persuasive is the cellar's Sciacchetrà. That name refers to an antique system of crushing the semidried grapes and drawing the juice off the skins after 24 hours. Then the wine was regularly racked from barrel to barrel and bottled with the March moon before the fermentation was complete to retain sugars. The old methods are still used, but more modern techniques seem to enhance this wine whose rich tawny colour shows enticing orange highlights and whose aromas and flavours vary as subtly as do degrees of sweetness. This unexpected luxury explains the growing conviction that if Cinqueterre is to regain some of its former prestige it will do so with Sciacchetrà.

Zone: Steep, terraced hillsides along the Ligurian Sea west of La Spezia and including part of its commune and three others in its province: Monterosso, Riomaggiore, Vernazza, Corniglia, and Manarola are the "five lands". Dry white. Grapes: Bosco at least 60%; Albarola/Vermentino up to 40%. Yld 63/90, Alc 11, Acd 0.5.

Sciacchetrà Amber wine, amabile or dolce naturale, also liquoroso. Grapes: as Cinqueterre but passito. Yld 31.5/90, Alc 17 (res sugar 3.5%; dolce naturale min 4%); liquoroso 16, Acd 0.6, Ag 1 yr.

Colli di Luni (1989)

The elevation to DOC reconfirmed a way with wine that had been known along the Magra valley and the Gulf of La Spezia since the Romans settled in Luni. But Liguria's most productive vineyard area had been overshadowed in later eras by Cinqueterre. Even before DOC, estates had been making good red wines from blends based mainly on Sangiovese and whites from Vermentino that outshone most Cinqueterre and could rival the best of the Riviera di Ponente. Since leading winemakers have invested in equipment and knowhow and seem determined to improve, the zone could acquire some renown. But at the moment most good wines are consumed in a resort area popular with the Milanese.

Zone: Hills on both sides of the Magra river extending from La Spezia north to Calice al Cornoviglio, south along the Gulf to Bocca di Magra and east into Tuscany, comprising 15 communes in La Spezia province and Aulla, Fosdinovo, and Podenzana in Massa e Carrara province.

Rosso Dry red, also riserva. Grapes:

Sangiovese 60-70%, Canaiolo/Pollera Nera/Ciliegiolo Nero at least 15%; other reds up to 25% except Cabernet up to 10%. Yld 70/100, Alc 11.5; riserva 12.5, Acd 0.5, Ag riserva 2 yrs.

Bianco Dry white. Grapes: Vermentino at least 35%, Trebbiano Toscano 25-40%; other whites up to 30%. Yld 70/100, Alc 11.5, Acd 0.5.

Vermentino Dry white. Grapes: Vermentino; other whites up to 10%. Yld 70/100, Alc 11, Acd 0.5.

Other wines of note

More than two-thirds of Liguria's wine is made east of Genoa, mainly in La Spezia province, but only a fraction comes under its two DOCs. A bid to use Riviera Ligure di Levante for vdt was blocked when producers on the other side protested that the name would be confused with their DOC. So until another solution is found, the many wines of eastern Liguria remain localized. Nearly every town along the coast has something to offer, not only from familiar local varieties but also Barbera, Cabernet, Merlot, Malvasia,

Travel Information

Above: Manarola in Cinqueterre was once accessible mainly by sea.

RESTAURANTS/HOTELS

Palma, 17021 Alassio (SV). Tel (0182)40314. Silvio and Fiorita Viglietti bring unusual refinement to Liguria's food and wines.

Paracucchi-Locanda Dell'Angelo, 19031 Ameglia (SP). Tel (0187) 64391. Itinerant chef Angelo Paracucchi commutes between Liguria and his **Carpaccio** restaurant in Paris, but home is this comfortably modern inn dedicated to the fine art of Italian cooking. Also 37 rooms.

Gino, 18030 Camporosso Mare (IM). Tel (0184)291493. Classical Ligurian food and wines on a relaxing terrace.

Nannina, 18100 Porto Maurizio-Imperia. Tel (0183)20208. Owner Mimmo Canna's wife Lucette lends a French hand to Ligurian dishes in this cordial restaurant at Imperia's port.

Ca' Peo, 16040 Leivi (GE). Tel (0185)319090. Franco and Melly Solari have created a rustic paradise on the heights of Leivi with personalized touches in Ligurian country cooking and a most astute choice of wines for the restaurant and *enoteca*. Five roomy apartments have views.

Splendido, 16034 Portofino (GE). Tel (0185)269551. A hotel that lives up to its name: luxurious, expensive, unforgettable. The restaurant and wine list equal the surroundings.

Taverna del Corsaro, 19025 Portovenere (SP). Tel (0187)900622. Pasquale and Angela Maietta cook seafood as masterfully as son Angelo chooses wines from Cinqueterre, Colli di Luni, and farther afield for the restaurant and *enoteca* by the sea.

Balzi Rossi, 18039 Ponte San Ludovico (IM). Tel (0184)38132. Whether you consider it the first chance to eat fine Ligurian food on leaving France or the last on leaving Italy, this luxurious border post is worth the stop.

WINE SHOPS/ENOTECHE

Liguria has several fine wine shops, some specializing in the region's bottles with selections from other parts of Italy and France. In Genoa, the leaders are the Enoteca Bar Sola (which also provides local dishes) and Mantelli. The Enoteca Lupi at Imperia offers the best of the Riviera di Ponente. The Enoteca Internazionale at Monterosso offers a range of Cinqueterre and more, as does the Enoteca Baroni at Lerici.

PLACES OF INTEREST

Genoa with its old port, narrow walkways, and memories of favourite son Christopher Columbus, has treasures of art and architecture, but Liguria's main attraction is its sweeping vistas of mountain and sea. The coast is marked by promontories and inlets that alternate as settings for ports and resort towns adorned by gardens surrounded by palms, umbrella pines, and cypresses. Rapallo and Santa Margherita are the always chic settings of the Levante. The flower of the Ponente is San Remo, where the beaches are rocky but the casinos and nightclubs lively.

The interior hills along the Alps and Apennines have their own charms, not the least of which are the absence of summer crowds and tourist prices. There olive groves and terraced vineyards mix with the ilex, broom and heather to frame the pastel towns in perennial shades of green. Liguria is famous for its restaurants, a few of which are mentioned. The cooking based on pasta, vegetables, herbs, nuts, cheese, olive oil, and fresh seafood may be the most glorious expression of the Mediterranean diet. Few tourists travel to Liguria just for the wines, unless they come to Genoa in March for the Bibe fair, which displays bottles from other regions and abroad. But whatever the reason for a visit to Liguria, the wine zones are worth seeing.

Riviera di Ponente and Dolceacqua. Liguria has no specified wine roads, but the coastal route from Finale past Albenga to Imperia passes many vineyards for Pigato and Vermentino. A drive from Imperia or Albenga up the Arroscia valley to Pieve di Teco and Pornassio reaches the high vineyards of Ormeasco. Dolceacqua, with its medieval castle and graceful arched bridge, provides a quiet contrast to the fast pace of the riviera. A drive from Bordighera or Ventimiglia up through the hills along the Nervia valley and lunch at a country *trattoria* provide a taste of rural Liguria.

Cinqueterre. The seaside villages with their incomparable vineyards can be reached by local trains leaving regularly from La Spezia (with stops at Riomaggiore, Manarola, Corniglia, Vernazza, and Monterosso) or to some degree by car (from La Spezia to Riomaggiore and Manarolo or from the Genoa-Livorno *autostrada* exit of Deiva Marina to Monterosso). But the best way to see the real Cinqueterre is to hike along the footpaths that link the villages.

---

and more. Vdt made in the Colli di Luni, under the names Ameglia, Arcola, Bolano, Camporegio, Linero, Poggialino, and Sarticola, may qualify as DOC, as might the fine red Terrizzo. Other notable wines along the Riviera are the Vermentino di Verici from near Chiavari

ESTATES/GROWERS

Nanni Barbero, Fravizzola-Fosdinovo (MS). From vineyards in Tuscany but within the Colli di Luni DOC zone, Barbero makes big, old-style Vermentino and Rosso del Fornello.

Conte Picedi Benettini, Baccano di Arcola (SP). Good Colli di Luni Vermentino del Chioso.

Fattoria Casano, Ortonovo (SP). Colli di Luni Vermentino.

Forlini Cappellini, Manarola (SP). From 5,100 vines the Forlini Cappellini family makes a full-bodied, fragrant Cinqueterre that stands out.

La Colombiera, Castelnuovo Magra (SP). Young Francesco Ferro leads the revival in Colli di Luni with a fine Vermentino and the vdt white Albachiara and red Terizzo, from Sangiovese and Cabernet.

Ottaviano Lambruschi, Castelnuovo Magra (SP). Good Colli di Luni Vermentino.

WINE HOUSES/MERCHANTS

Enoteca Bisson, Chiavari (GE). Pier Luigi Lugano and wife Wally make fine Vermentino di Verici.

COOPERATIVES

Cooperativa Agricola di Cinqueterre, Riomaggiore (SP). Oenologist Nello Capris directs growers in making dry white Cinqueterre of consistent quality, including the single vineyard Costa da' Posa, Costa de Campu, and Costa di Sèra, though perhaps the best of the range is the refined Sciacchetrà.

Lombardy (Lombardia)

Capital: Milano (Milan).
Provinces: Bergamo (BG), Brescia (BS), Como (CO), Cremona (CR), Mantova (MN), Milano (MI), Pavia (PV), Sondrio (SO), Varese (VA).
Area: 23,856 square kilometres (fourth).
Population: 8,882,000 (first).

Lombardians may be moderate wine producers compared to other Italians, but as consumers they are second to none. Milan, or Milano, capital of industry and finance, is also the nation's most active wine market, the pacesetter in matters of food and drink. This influence has contributed to Lombardy becoming the leader in production of sparkling wine by the *champenoise* method, of which Franciacorta and the Oltrepò Pavese are the main centres. But otherwise the Milanese show a worldly nonchalance about wines from the home region, often turning to Piedmont, Tuscany, or Bordeaux for reds, Friuli, Trentino-Alto Adige, or Burgundy for whites, and Champagne for sparkling wines for special occasions.

In Italy's most populous and industrialized region the chancy craft of winemaking is not one of the more gainful pursuits. But the relative dearth of vineyards is also a question of geography. The ample plains of the Po are better suited to field crops and livestock than modern viticulture. Mountains claim a large share of space, as do the lakes of Maggiore, Lugano, Como, and Garda, where tourism has left little room for vineyards. Still, between the cool heights of the Alps and Apennines and the hot valley floor, Lombardy does have hillsides where vines excel. There are three major areas of wine production. In the southwest lies the Oltrepò Pavese, one of northern Italy's most luxuriant vineyard zones and Lombardy's most productive. But as a perennial supplier of everyday wines to Milan and other cities, its status is not nearly as high as it might be, despite the improved quality of its reds and whites, as well as classical *spumante*. In the north is the alpine Valtellina, which rivals Barolo as the largest source of red wines from Nebbiolo, exemplified by the *superiore* types of Valgella, Sassella, Inferno, and Grumello. But since the Swiss own a fair share of the terraced vineyards and import much of the wine, bottles are easier to find in Zurich than Milan. In the east are the provinces of Brescia, with seven of the region's thirteen DOC zones, flanked by Bergamo (with Valcalepio) and Mantova (with Colli Morenici Mantovani del Garda and Lambrusco Mantovano). Just west of Brescia is Franciacorta, which has emerged as Italy's most prestigious producer of *champenoise*. To the east along the shores of Lake Garda are the Lugana and Riviera del Garda Bresciano zones. Quality standards seem as high on Lombardy's side of the lake as they do on the Veneto's, but as a wine centre Brescia continues to be overshadowed by Verona.

Lombardy's first wines may have been made at Garda by lake dwellers who were known to have grown *vinifera* vines. They might have set the precedent for the wine the Romans knew as Rhaetic, though the Valtellina in the Rhaetian Alps also stakes claims to its origins. The name seems to have applied to various wines made where the ancient Raeti people dwelled in the alpine arc from Como to Verona. Other early vintners were Ligurians, who might have built the Valtellina's first terraces, and Etruscans, who grew vines over trees along the Po.

Milan, at the upper end of the plains, became a commercial centre under the Romans, who opened trade routes along rivers and lakes and over alpine passes into Switzerland and France. After serving as capital of the Western Empire, Milan fell to Barbarian invaders, among whom the Longobards or Lombards left the region with a name and a basis for cohesion under the Lombard League. Milan re-emerged as northern Italy's main city under the Visconti and Sforza families between the

fourteenth and sixteenth centuries. Then came foreign domination, including a period as capital of the Kingdom of Italy under Napoleon, before the battles for independence from Austria culminated in Lombardy's emergence in a unified Italy.

Historical chroniclers had nice things to say about wines of the Valtellina, Garda, Pavia, Bergamo, Mantua, Como, and even Milan. But with time Lombardy's viticulture became geared more towards quantity than quality. The Po valley flourished with vines until oidium and phylloxera influenced the switch to more reliable crops. Many hill vineyards have also been abandoned, in the Brianza north of Milan, and around Lake Como, where good everyday wines were once made.

But as production dimininishes some wines of Lombardy have taken a turn for the better. The brightest examples have come from the *champenoise* of Franciacorta, where Guido Berlucchi proved the potential for growth and Ca' del Bosco and Bellavista, among the elite estates, showed that Italy really can offer valid alternatives to Champagne. They and others followed with equally noble reds for ageing and whites of a certain stature – as often as not from French varieties. But wines from native vines also have won favour – the white Lugana, for instance, and even some of the Oltrepò Pavese's red variations on Barbera and Croatina. Yet, despite improvements, many winemakers of Lombardy may have to aim still higher if they expect to reach the upper echelon of the home market and capture the nation's most demanding clientele.

Lombardy's Vineyards

Viticulture has changed radically over the last century in a region where rational use of available space has reduced the historical abundance of the Po valley and brought new standards to the hills. In the mid-nineteenth century, the Oltrepò Pavese grew some 260 varieties, though there as elsewhere phylloxera spelled the doom of many. Ensuing selections favoured such prolific varieties as Barbera, Croatina, and Riesling Italico. Around Brescia and Bergamo the once popular Marzemino (called Berzemino or Barzemino) and Schiava have diminished. Nebbiolo reigned in the Valtellina and Lambrusco along the Po.

Lombardians followed early trends towards vines of French origin with Cabernet Franc, Merlot, and the Pinots, more recently with Cabernet Sauvignon and Chardonnay. The region has steadily increased Pinot Nero for sparkling wines, notably in Oltrepò Pavese which seems to have Italy's heaviest plantings. (There is even a theory that Burgundy's Pinot Noir derived from the Pignuolo of Lombardy, though that would be hard to verify since that vine identified in the fourteenth century is no longer found.) Chardonnay has gained for both sparkling and still wines, checking the earlier popularity of Pinot Bianco and Grigio.

But some traditions remain. The Valtellina is still a stronghold of Nebbiolo on high terraces where vines are trained in a low arched cordon to benefit from the soil's heat. The antique varieties known as Brugnola or Prugnola, Pignola Valtellinese, and Rossola Nera also remain in limited use there. The flatlands of Mantova province still have Lambrusco, but as in adjacent Emilia the high arbour Raggi or Bellussi has largely replaced *alberate*, the training of vines onto stunted elms or other trees used since Etruscan times. Around Brescia and Lake Garda

Above: the village of Poggiridenti in northern Lombardy's Valtellina.

vines were customarily trained onto pergolas like those of the Adige valley, but most recent plantings are in low vertical systems in increased density, notably at Franciacorta. The Oltrepò Pavese, like Piedmont, uses mainly variations on Guyot in its often steep hills. Lombardy's catalogue has been reduced to a few true native vines, though plenty of local synonyms have been created for varieties from elsewhere.

Bonarda. Name for Croatina in Oltrepò Pavese and San Colombano al Lambro, where it is confused with the true Bonarda of Piedmont.

Chiavennasca. Name used for Nebbiolo in Valtellina.

Groppello. Worthy variety today mostly confined to the Valtènesi in the Riviera del Garda zone, where it is used in the blends of DOC red and *chiaretto* or alone in table wines. Subvarieties include Groppello di Mocasina, di Santo Stefano, and Gentile, as well as Groppellone.

Incrocio Terzi N.1. Cross of Barbera and Cabernet Franc used in reds of Brescia and Bergamo provinces.

Lambrusco Viadanese. This Lambrusco subvariety refers to the town of Viadana in Lombardy. It is also prominent in Emilia.

Moscato di Scanzo or **Merera**. This dark variety apparently in the Muscat family is grown near Bergamo for a rare dessert wine.

Rossola Nera. A worthy native of Valtellina is now used sparingly. The vine, also called Rossara, is apparently the original Roter Veltliner, which makes white wines in the Alto Adige's Isarco valley.

Trebbiano di Lugana. Though considered part of the Trebbiano family, the species seems to have evolved into something special at Lugana, south of Lake Garda, where it makes a white of notable personality. It is known as Trebbiano di Soave or Veronese around Verona and Trebbiano Nostrano around Mantua. It may be related to the Verdicchio of the Marches.

Ughetta. Name used in Oltrepò Pavese for Piedmont's Vespolina.

Uva Rara. Oltrepò Pavese synonym for Piedmont's Bonarda Novarese.

Other varieties

Other varieties recommended or approved in the region include:

For red (or rosé): Ancellotta, Barbera, Bonarda Piemontese, Cabernet Franc, Cabernet Sauvignon, Corvina Veronese, Dolcetto, Fortana, Franconia, Freisa, Lambrusco di Sorbara, Lambrusco Grasparossa, Lambrusco Marani, Lambrusco Maestri, Lambrusco Salamino, Marzemino, Merlot, Molinara, Montepulciano, Nebbiolo, Negrara Trentina, Pignola Valtellinese, Pinot Nero, Rondinella, Sangiovese, Schiava Gentile, Schiava Grigia, Schiava Grossa, Schiava Lombarda, Vespolina.

For white: Chardonnay, Cortese, Garganega, Incrocio Manzoni 6.0.13, Invernega, Malvasia Bianca di Candia, Malvasia Istriana, Moscato Bianco, Müller Thurgau, Pinot Bianco, Pinot Grigio, Prosecco, Riesling Italico, Riesling Renano, Sauvignon, Tocai Fruilano, Trebbiano Giallo, Trebbiano Romagnolo, Trebbiano Toscano, Verdea.

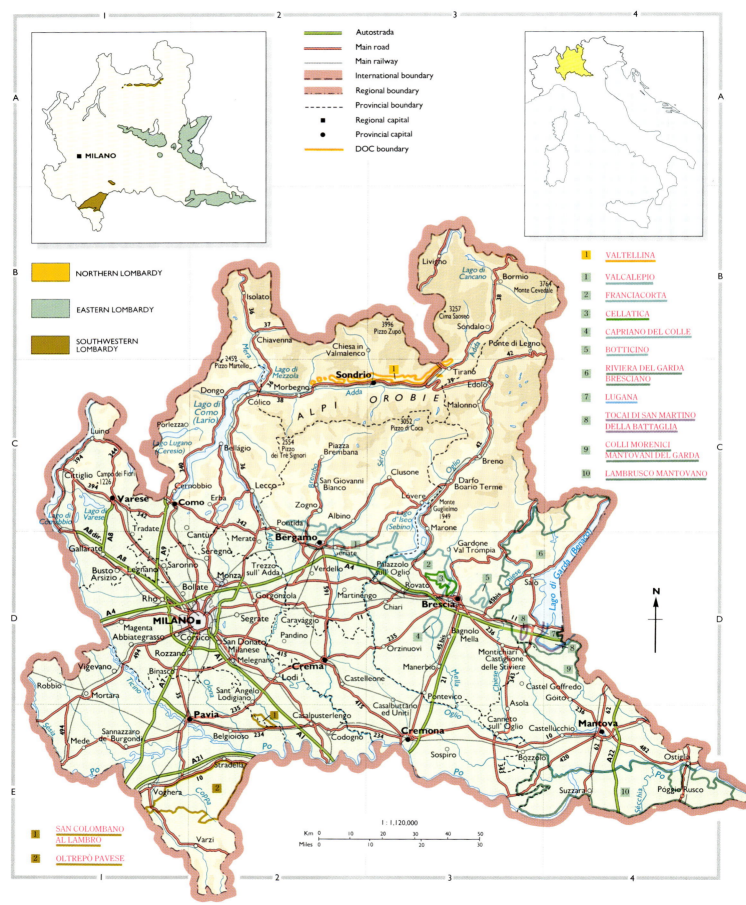

Autostrada
Main road
Main railway
International boundary
Regional boundary
Provincial boundary
Regional capital
Provincial capital
DOC boundary

NORTHERN LOMBARDY
EASTERN LOMBARDY
SOUTHWESTERN LOMBARDY

1 VALTELLINA

1 VALCALEPIO
2 FRANCIACORTA
3 CELLATICA
4 CAPRIANO DEL COLLE
5 BOTTICINO
6 RIVIERA DEL GARDA BRESCIANO
7 LUGANA
8 TOCAI DI SAN MARTINO DELLA BATTAGLIA
9 COLLI MORENICI MANTOVANI DEL GARDA
10 LAMBRUSCO MANTOVANO

1 SAN COLOMBANO AL LAMBRO
2 OLTREPÒ PAVESE

1 : 1,120,000

Km 0   10   20   30   40   50
Miles 0   10   20   30

Lombardy's Wine Zones

The essence of Lombardy's thriving industry and agriculture is water from the Alps, the Lepontine and Retiche (or Rhaetian) ranges along the Swiss border and the Orobie range between the Valtellina and Bergamo and Brescia. The scenic benefits are the lakes that give the region a major base of tourism. The large lakes have rivers flowing from them: Maggiore the Ticino, Como the Adda, Iseo the Oglio, and Garda the Mincio. These and other tributaries of the Po supply power for factories and irrigation for farms in the fertile lower plains. But the damp has its drawbacks; the Padana is one of Europe's foggiest places in the cold months. The region has a neat balance between mountains and plains, but the hills that cover only an eighth of the surface offer the best conditions for vineyards. The main stretch of hills follows the southern flank of the Alps east-west from Garda past Iseo and Como to Maggiore. The lakes have a favourable influence on microclimates, though only the lower glacial basins of Garda and Iseo have important vineyards. An exceptional alpine wine zone is the Valtellina to the north along the upper Adda valley near Sondrio. Lombardy has a short stretch of Apennines in the extreme southwest in Pavia province, but a majority of its wine, both DOC and otherwise, comes from the Oltrepò Pavese.

Oltrepò Pavese and San Colombano

The Oltrepò Pavese hills that rise abruptly south of the Po towards the Apennines have a relatively mild climate, characterized by a hot, dry spell in late summer and autumn that favours full ripening in a range of red and white varieties. The soils, variations on clay with calcareous or chalky formations, vary as widely as microclimates in these pretty hills whose quality potential has never been fully exploited. Much of the dominant Barbera and Croatina for reds come from the northeast around Stradella, Broni, and Rovescala. Higher vineyards along the upper Versa valley and Rocca de' Giorgi are key sources of Pinot Nero for sparkling wines, as well as Moscato. The chalky soil around Montalto Pavese and Oliva Gessi favours fragrant whites, mainly from Riesling Italico, though red varieties do well on lower slopes towards Casteggio. Gentle slopes rising from the hot Po valley around San Colombano have calcareous clay soils suited to a hearty red from Croatina and Barbera, though white varieties can also do well.

Valtellina

The upper Adda valley is walled between the Retiche and Orobie Alps in a long enclosure with a unique habitat for Italy's northernmost wines from Nebbiolo. The Valtellina DOC zone stretches above Sondrio across terraces exposed to the south on pebbly soils of siliceous clays. Day-night temperature fluctuations can be sharp in summer, notably at heights of up to 800 metres. But air currents from Lake Como have a moderating effect that most years allows for slow, even ripening in durable reds that need age to round out and develop bouquet. Hail, heavy rains, and landslides have ruined some recent harvests, though the usual threat to a good vintage is a cool alpine summer.

Bergamo's Valcalepio

The province's lone DOC takes its name from the valley where the Oglio river flows out of Lake Iseo and applies it to most of Bergamo's vineyards. A red from Merlot and Cabernet does well in light calcareous clays of the original Valcalepio zone, as do Pinot Bianco and vdt Chardonnay. Elsewhere wines are ordinary.

Brescia's hills and Franciacorta

Most vineyards around Brescia are in the Franciacorta DOC zone in the glacial moraine of the lower Iseo basin where breezes crossing the lake from the Aprica range of the Alps create a special climate for *spumante* and still wines, red and white. Some of Italy's finest *champenoise* comes from the west around Corte Franca and the slopes of Monte di Erbusco, where vdt reds from Cabernet, Merlot, and Pinot Nero and whites from Chardonnay also show uncommon class. The often steep, rocky hills adjacent to Brescia have the DOC zones of Cellatica to the west and Botticino to the east, both long noted for light reds. The Capriano del Colle zone on a hill south of the city makes simple reds and whites.

Lake Garda's riviera

Most of the western and southern shores of Lake Garda are in Brescia province in the vast Riviera del Garda zone which overlaps Lugana and Tocai di San Martino della Battaglia to the south. Vineyards for the Riviera's hearty *rosso* and zesty *chiaretto* are centred in the Valtènesi to the southwest where steep slopes seem equally suited to still unclassified whites. The Lugana and San Martino zones cover plains and low hills of the Garda basin. The heavy terrain of calcareous clays on a bed of glacial moraine is evidently better suited to Trebbiano for the admired white Lugana than to the obscure Tocai of San Martino.

Mantova's hills and plains

The Colli Morenici Mantovani are an extension of Garda's glacial terrain through broadly rolling hills west of the Mincio river where light, tasty reds, whites, and rosés are made. Lambrusco Mantovano comes from two sectors of the flatlands north and south of the Po, where wines can compare with their Emilian neighbours.

Below: backpack baskets known as portini *are used by grape pickers on the steep slopes of the Valtellina.*

Wines of southwestern Lombardy

The plains washed by the Po and Ticino end abruptly some 50 kilometres south of Milan in the Apennine foothills of the Oltrepò Pavese, whose name refers to the location across the Po from Pavia. This southwestern corner of Lombardy, wedged between Emilia and Piedmont, was once part of the latter region and is still sometimes called Antico Piemonte. But Lombardians have good reason to feel possessive about the Oltrepò, whose lovely hills, topped by villages and castles built by the Sforza, Visconti, and Malaspina families, support the region's most prodigious stand of vines. The Milanese still get much of their daily wine from here, yet it might be that proximity to the big city has done the Oltrepò Pavese's reputation more harm than good. For along with the robust reds and lightly scented whites and *spumante* that qualify for DOC comes a steady flow of ordinary wine bought up by outsiders in what accounts for the bulk of commerce. There is also an active market for grapes and musts from the area that grows more Pinot Nero for sparkling wines than any other. But outside producers, based mainly in Piedmont, rarely acknowledge the source on labels. San Colombano al Lambro, which dominates one of the rare rises in Milan's foggy hinterland, boasts a hard-won DOC – a credit to its few resourceful producers.

Oltrepò Pavese (1970)

The zone produces about 1.2 million hl of wine a year, more than half of Lombardy's total, classifying some 260,000 hl as DOC, about two-thirds of the region's quota. Yet, despite the enormous potential of these sweeping hillsides that are comparable to privileged parts of Piedmont, the wines of the Oltrepò Pavese have a lacklustre image. Some criticize the prominence of "utilitarian" grape varieties in the principal wines: Barbera, Croatina (for Bonarda), Riesling Italico, and Moscato. Even the Pinot Nero prominent here (along with some Pinot Grigio and Bianco) was chosen mainly for use in *spumante* rather than in still wines. Others blame the continuing custom of supplying regional markets with inexpensive everyday wine, more often red than white. Even restaurateurs who insist on DOC wines in bottles shop for bargains in the Oltrepò.

Much production is centred in cooperatives, which offer premium wines among their variable selections. Most of the zone's approximately 9,000 vineyard owners are part-time grape. growers rather than winemakers, understandable since plots average less than 1.5 ha each. Yet a number of estates have emerged with wines that have enhanced their own status and, perhaps indirectly, that of the Oltrepò. Giorgio Odero pioneered the estate concept with the Frecciarossa wines that had an international following as early as the 1930s. The wines of Angelo Ballabio at Casteggio were once admired by Italian experts, in particular the Clastidium Gran Riserva, a white from Pinot Nero and Grigio that reached peaks after years in barrel and bottle. Estates that have made their marks over the years are Monsupello, Montelio, Mairano, and Luigi Valenti. Lately others have won praise – Tenuta Mazzolino, Doria, Tronconero, Cella di Montalto, Pietro Vercesi, and the tiny La Muiraghina, among them.

The best-selling DOC is Barbera, which when made with skill can be among the finest of that varietal anywhere. The softer Bonarda, often *frizzante*, has its own sort of appeal. Pinot Nero in red wine was rarely impressive until Tenuta Mazzolino came up with its vdt called Noir from clones selected in Burgundy. But overall the most distinctive red of the Oltrepò is the traditional *rosso*. When the blend is right, the sinewy strength of Barbera is enveloped by the mellow fruit of Croatina, while Uva Rara and Ughetta lend useful complexity to the whole. Some wines show pleasing tone in their first year, though from top

Below: the Oltrepò Pavese in the southeast is Lombardy's most productive wine zone.

vintages the *riserva*, after ageing in wood, can gain finesse for a decade or so. Examples of the aged version are unfortunately hard to find.

Two variations on *rosso* known as Buttafuoco and Sangue di Giuda come from a restricted area within the zone. These colourfully named wines – the first from the dialect *buta'me'lfogh* ("sparks like fire") and the other translated as "Judas's blood" – have largely local appeal. They are often *frizzante*, like Barbarcarlo, which was removed from the DOC rolls when its original producer, Lino Maga, won a ruling recognizing it as a proprietary wine.

White wine varieties have gained ground lately, especially Chardonnay which is often used with Pinot Nero in *spumante*. Rieslings are widely planted, though the Renano is often outclassed by the dominant Italico, whose subtle scents and flavour can be exquisite. Pinot Grigio occasionally matches its counterparts from the Venezie, though vdt Müller Thurgau and Chardonnay are often more impressive. Home

production of *champenoise* sparkling wines has increased, following the lead of the cooperative at Santa Maria della Versa with its widely hailed La Versa Brut. But lately bottlings from Fontanachiara and Anteo, among a growing number of local producers, have rivalled or surpassed it. Tank method *spumanti* from Pinots and Chardonnay as well as Riesling can be convincing, though markets in Lombardy, as elsewhere, are becoming saturated with inexpensive bubbly wines.

Soil conditions vary markedly in a large zone where altitude and exposure are important quality factors. The classical area for Oltrepò Rosso is on lower slopes of calcareous clay between Stradella, Broni, and Canneto Pavese, in the restricted areas for Buttafuoco and Sangue di Giuda. Barbera does well in several places, though some of the best Croatina (Bonarda) comes from the east around Rovescala and San Damiano. The upper reaches towards the south around Santa Maria della Versa and Rocca de' Giorgi are noted for Pinot

Nero and Moscato. The hills between Casteggio and Montalto Pavese are noted for several types of wine, though the lower slopes seem better suited to reds, while Riesling Italico and other whites thrive in chalky terrain within the triangle formed by Oliva Gessi, Montalto, and Calvignano. But it can be a mistake to generalize too much about aptitudes in the scenic hills coursed by what was Italy's first designated wine route. Good wines can emit from nearly any place where growers show dedication – even from the western reaches where a hint of sulphur in aromas apparently derives from the soil around the spas there.

Reformists in the Oltrepò look forward to the day when Chardonnay, Sauvignon Blanc, Cabernet Sauvignon, and Pinot Noir clones from Burgundy come into their own in still wines matured in *barriques*. But most producers continue to work with traditional varieties, while cautiously experimenting with alternatives that have aroused some optimism for the future. The active consortium has

achieved recognition for the trademark Classese (from Classico and Pavese) for sparkling *champenoise* under the DOC. But, despite their promotional efforts, the name Oltrepò Pavese doesn't carry the weight that a potential giant of Italian wine could wield.

Zone: The Apennine foothills south across the Po from Pavia and taking in 42 communes in its province in a large, triangular territory between the borders of Piedmont and Emilia-Romagna. The wines of Buttafuoco and Sangue di Giuda come from a subzone covering the communes of Broni, Stradella, Canneto Pavese, Montescano, Castana, Cigognola, and Pietra de' Giorgi to the northeast. Other wines may come from throughout the zone.

Rosso Dry red, sometimes vivace, also riserva. Grapes: Barbera up to 65%, Uva Rara/Ughetta (Vespolina) up to 45%, Croatina at least 25%. Yld 71.5/110, Alc 11.5; riserva 12, Acd 0.5, Ag riserva 2 yrs.

Rosato Dry rosé, sometimes vivace. Grapes: as rosso. Yld 71.5/110, Alc 10.5, Acd 0.5.

Buttafuoco Dry red, usually frizzante. Grapes: Barbera up to 65%, Uva Rara/Pinot Nero/Ughetta (Vespolina) up to 45%, Croatina at

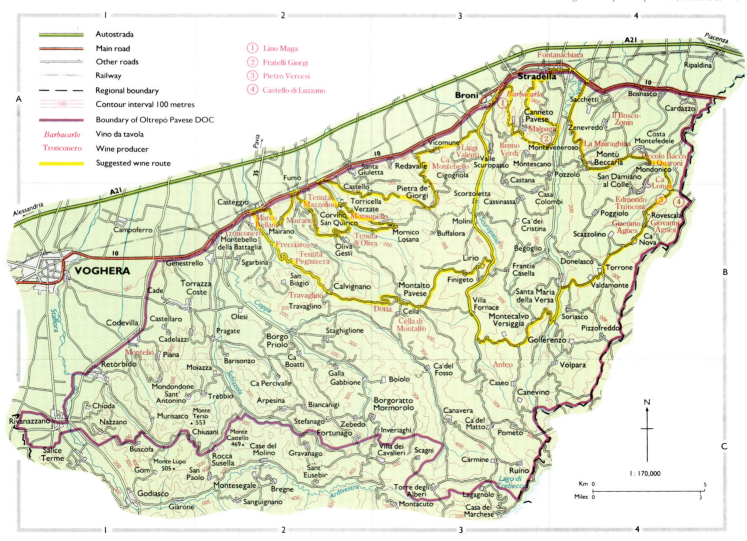

least 25%. Yld 68/105, Alc 12, Acd 0.5.

Sangue di Giuda Dry red, usually frizzante, also abboccato, amabile, or dolce. Grapes: as Buttafuoco. Yld 68/105, Alc 12 (res sugar abboccato or amabile min 18 gr/l; dolce min 50 gr/l), Acd 0.5, Ag 6 mths.

Barbera Dry red, also frizzante. Grapes: Barbera; other reds up to 15%. Yld 84/120, Alc 11.5, Acd 0.5.

Bonarda Dry red, often frizzante, also abboccato, amabile, or dolce. Grapes: Bonarda (Croatina); other reds up to 15%. Yld 68/105, Alc 11 (res sugar abboccato or amabile min 18 gr/l; dolce min 50 gr/l), Acd 0.5.

Cortese Dry white, also frizzante, spumante. Grapes: Cortese; other whites up to 15%. Yld 71.5/110, Alc 10.5 (spumante res sugar max 20 gr/l), Acd 0.6.

Moscato White either abboccato, amabile, or dolce, also spumante. Grapes: Moscato Bianco; Malvasia di Candia up to 15%. Yld 77/110, Alc 10 of which min 5.5 fermented (res sugar abboccato or amabile min 18 gr/l; dolce min 50 gr/l); spumante 10 of which min 6 fermented (res sugar min 50 gr/l), Acd 0.6.

Moscato liquoroso Golden to amber fortified wine, lightly sweet as secco or "dry", and sweet as dolce naturale. Grapes: as Moscato. Yld 77/110, Alc secco or dry 18-22 (res sugar max 40 gr/l); dolce naturale 17.5-22 (res sugar min 50 gr/l), Acd 0.45.

Pinot Grigio Dry white, also frizzante. Grapes: Pinot Grigio; Pinot Nero/Pinot Bianco/Riesling Italico/Riesling Renano up to 15%. Yld 65/100, Alc 10.5, Acd 0.5.

Pinot Nero Dry red, also rosé or white which can be frizzante. Grapes: Pinot Nero; other reds up to 15%. Yld rosso or rosato 65/100; bianco 60/100, Alc 10.5 (rosato and bianco res sugar max 10 gr/l), Acd 0.6.

Pinot Nero spumante Dry sparkling rosé or white. Grapes: Pinot Nero; Pinot Grigio/Pinot Bianco/Riesling Italico/Riesling Renano up to 15%. Yld rosato 65/100; bianco 60/100, Alc 11.5 (res sugar max 15 gr/l), Acd 0.6.

Riesling Italico Dry white, also frizzante or spumante. Grapes: Riesling Italico; Riesling Renano up to 15%. Yld 71.5/110, Alc 10.5 (spumante res sugar max 25 gr/l), Acd 0.6.

Riesling Renano Dry white, also frizzante or spumante. Grapes: Riesling Renano; Riesling Italico up to 15%. Yld 58.5/90, Alc 11 (spumante res sugar max 25 gr/l), Acd 0.6.

Other wines of note

Many good wines of the Oltrepò, both still and sparkling, remain unclassified, sometimes because they don't qualify under the regulations, sometimes because their producers prefer individual identities. Lino Maga's Barbacarlo is the most conspicuous exception to DOC among the several cited with their producers.

San Colombano al Lambro or San Colombano (1984)

The only classified wine of Milan's province is a rustic red reminiscent of the Oltrepò's but somewhat softer and fuller in colour, perhaps from a larger dose of Croatina (Bonarda) and the greater heat generated by the plains surrounding the 144-m height of Colle di San Colombano. Though recommended young and cool, some bottles can age and hold their flavour, which is noted for a lightly bitter finish. Producers are due credit for having kept alive a long winemaking tradition around San Colombano and for striving to build on it.

Zone: The gentle rises of the Colle di San Colombano 35 km southeast of Milano and including parts of the communes of San Colombano al Lambro, Graffignana, and Sant'Angelo Lodigiano in its province and Miradolo Terme and Inverno e Monteleone in Pavia. Dry red. Grapes: Croatina 30-45%, Barbera 25-40%, Uva Rara 5-15%; other reds up to 15%. Yld 77/110, Alc 11, Acd 0.5.

Other wines of note

Growers at San Colombano work with varieties that go beyond the DOC, including the traditional white Verdea and Chardonnay. Some examples are mentioned below.

ESTATES/GROWERS

(Those cited without comment are recommended for wines under Oltrepò Pavese DOC.)

Giacomo Agnes, Rovescala (PV). Oltrepò Rosso and the vdt Gaggiarone from Bonarda and Barbera.

Giovanni Agnes-Poggiopelato, Rovescala (PV).

Anteo, Rocca de' Giorgi (PV). The estate managed by Trento Cribellati has the base to become a leader in sparkling wine of the Oltrepò. From 33 ha in Pinot Nero and Chardonnay, consultant Beppe Bassi makes *champenoise* Anteo Brut Rocca de' Giorgi and Nature, as well as good *charmat*.

Marco Bellani, Casteggio (PV).

Ca' Longa, San Damiano al Colle (PV).

Ca' Montebello, Cigognola (PV). Good range of Oltrepò DOC.

Castello di Luzzano, Rovescala (PV). Sisters Giovannella and Maria Giulia Fugazza have 60 ha in the Oltrepò, where they specialize in red wines of notable class. They also produce Colli Piacentini wines in Emilia.

Cella di Montalto, Montalto Pavese (PV). From 25 ha, the Canegallo family concentrates on fine Riesling Italico while providing an inviting setting for *agriturismo* in the former Benedictine monastery.

Doria, Montalto Pavese (PV). Brothers Adriano and Bruno Doria with Beppe Bassi are building the 20 ha Cascina Vermietta into an exemplary estate with an impressive Pinot Nero (from Burgundy clones) matured in *barriques*, notable DOC red Roncorosso and Bonarda, good Riesling, and a refined *charmat* Querciolo.

Fontanachiara, Stradella (PV). From 20 ha near Stradella and 10 ha at Bosnasco mainly in Pinot Nero and Chardonnay Marco Maggi and consultant Beppe Bassi fashion some of the zone's finest *champenoise* in Fontanachiara Brut and Riserva, the latter from base wines partly aged in wood.

Frecciarossa, Casteggio (PV). The dignified "Red arrow" estate belonging to the Odero family had been a leader for decades, though its Oltrepò DOCs from 15 ha of vines no longer stand alone.

Fratelli Giorgi, Canneto Pavese (PV).

La Muiraghina, Montù Beccaria (PV). Anna Gregorutti moved from Friuli's Collio to the Oltrepò where she has turned wines from her tiny estate into some of the zone's most noticed bottlings, all vdt of Montù Beccaria, in uncommonly scented Malvasia and Riesling, hearty Barbera, and Il Felicino, a red from local varieties, one type of which is aged in *barriques*.

Lino Maga, Broni (PV). The estate that originated the wine called Barbacarlo (from uncle Carlo in dialect) won back exclusive rights to the name after owner Lino Maga contested its inclusion in Oltrepò Pavese DOC. That publicized case won the wine from Croatina with Uva Rara, Ughetta, and Barbera a following willing to pay a lofty price for what is reputedly the most durable of local *vivace* reds. Maga also makes Oltrepò Rosso DOC.

Mairano, Casteggio (PV). Fernando Bussolera makes a good range of Oltrepò DOC from 25 ha of vines. The wines, sold under the trademark Le Fracce, are led by Cirgà Rosso.

Malpaga, Canneto Pavese (PV).

Monsupello, Torricella Verzate (PV). From 12 ha, Carlo Boatti makes a classic Oltrepò Rosso, the fine Classese Monsupello Brut, and the delightfully fizzy Pinot Nero called I Germogli.

Montelio, Codevilla (PV). Owner Anna Maria Mazza and winemaker Mario Maffi make good traditional style Oltrepò wines and Müller Thurgau from 28 ha of vines.

Stefano Panigada, San Colombano al Lambro (MI). Hearty San Colombano DOC along with light red, white, and rosé vdt called Banino.

Piccolo Bacco dei Quaroni, Montù Beccaria (PV). Long noted specialists in Oltrepò reds.

Pietrasanta, San Colombano al Lambro (MI). Besides a tasty San Colombano DOC, Carlo Pietrasanta makes an ambitious range of vdt including red, white, and pink wines della Costa and even a *champenoise*.

Riccardi, San Colombano al Lambro (MI). Enrico Riccardi makes San Colombano DOC and a respectable white vdt Verdea della Tonsa.

San Zeno *See* Tenuta Il Bosco.

Tenuta di Oliva, Oliva Gessi (PV). The estate has 29 ha of vines in chalky soil that lends finesse to some of the zone's finest Riesling.

Tenuta Il Bosco, Zenevredo (PV). Zonin of the Veneto produces Oltrepò DOC and various sparkling wines from 110 ha at this estate and San Zeno at Stradella.

Tenuta Mazzolino, Corvino San Quirico (PV). Roberto Piaggi and consultant Giancarlo Scaglione produce a fine range of Oltrepò DOCs including the Pinot Guarnazzola and the red Terrazze di Mazzolino, and the outstanding vdt called Noir, from Pinot Nero deftly matured in *barriques*.

Tenuta Pegazzera, Casteggio (PV).

Travaglino, Calvignano (PV).

Tronconero, Casteggio (PV). Good Oltrepò DOC led by a sumptuous Bonarda, along with fine Chardonnay vdt.

Edmondo Tronconi, Rovescala (PV).

Luigi Valenti, Cigognola (PV). Specialist in always enjoyable Buttafuoco and Sangue di Giuda under the name Monterucco.

Pietro Vercesi, Rovescala (PV). Fine Bonarda and *rosso*.

Bruno Verdi, Canneto Pavese (PV).

WINE HOUSES/MERCHANTS

Angelo Ballabio, Casteggio (PV). The house, long famous for its extraordinary Clastidium Gran Riserva and other wines, seems a shadow of its former self.

(Many Piedmontese houses buy grapes or base wines for spumante in the zone. Fontanafredda, Gancia, and Martini & Rossi are among the few which cite Oltrepò Pavese DOC on labels of certain wines.)

COOPERATIVES

CS di Casteggio, Casteggio (PV). **CS di Santa Maria della Versa**, Santa Maria della Versa (PV). The large and diversified cellars presided over by Antonio Duca Denari draw from growers with some 2,000 ha to produce more than 70,000 hl of wine a year, including Oltrepò DOC in part under the Donelasco label. The most noted product is Gran Spumante La Versa Brut, an early example of locally made *champenoise*.

CS Torrevilla, Torrazza Coste (PV). Sound DOC wines, *spumante*, and vdt from the communes of Codevilla and Torrazza.

Wines of northern Lombardy

North of Milan plains give way to rolling hills of the Brianza towards Como and the Varesotto towards Varese, areas where any rural charms have narrowly escaped being overrun by the sprawl of the Lombardian megalopolis. Tourism and residential development have checked the growth of industry around the lakes of Como and Varese and along the shores of Maggiore and Lugano which Italy shares with Switzerland. But few vines remain on hillsides that were once known for light local wines: around Angera on Lake Maggiore, Bellagio at the fork of Lake Como, and Montevecchia in Brianza, whose vineyards are still sometimes noted as the closest to Milan. The Alps dominate the landscape above the lakes to the north and east of Como, where high valleys are better suited to making cheeses than wines. The one place where vineyards thrive in the north is on steep slopes along the Adda river near Sondrio in the Valtellina. Were it not for the perseverance of growers in that awe inspiring wine zone, viticulture in northern Lombardy would for all practical purposes be dead.

The story of Valtellina's emergence as the only major producer of Nebbiolo wines outside Piedmont seems a fascinating one, though some of the background details aren't clear. The valley's first vines may have been planted by the ancient Liguri, who had experience building terraces back home, or even by Etruscans. It seems likely that native varieties – including the still active Rossola, Pignola, and Brugnola – preceded Nebbiolo's arrival, which some accounts put in the late Middle Ages and others during Napoleon's conquest in the late eighteenth century. Whatever the case, it came to be called Chiavennasca and developed some local traits. The name seems to refer to the nearby town of Chiavenna, but insiders say that it comes from the dialect term *ciù vinasca*, or "most vinous" because of its grapes' suitability for wine. Among the peoples who possessed the Valtellina, the Swiss have kept a standing claim. Not only do they own a good share of the vineyards but they consume much of the wine, which can be brought across the border duty free. That is why the Valtellina is sometimes alluded to as a binational wine zone.

Valtellina/Valtellina Superiore (1968)

The Valtellina is hard to reach from any direction, though the road that follows the Adda river eastwards from where it enters Lake Como is the most frequented by skiers and moutaineers. Just after Morbegno the road crosses the river to the north bank as the view opens onto a panorama of steeply sloping vineyards against a backdrop of the perenially white-capped Pizzo Bernina at 4,050 m in the Retiche or Rhaetian Alps. The mountains serve as a protective barrier against cold northern currents, trapping heat in the narrow valley walled to the south by the Orobie Alps and to the west by the Adamello, enabling vines planted mainly on terraces facing south to grow at heights up to 800 m. Some slopes are so steep that grapes are relayed down in backpack baskets called *portini* or buckets attached to cabled rigs. Lately, tiny monorail trains have been used to speed the grapes to the wineries. For passersby the sight of vines clinging to the mountain walls continues past Sondrio as far as Tirano, where the road climbs towards the Stelvio pass and Switzerland. Some compare the scenery to Trentino, Alto Adige, or Valle d'Aosta, others to the Swiss Valais, but the Valtellina and its wines show the sort of individuality that could only have developed over the ages in an isolated alpine place.

Only red wines based on Nebbiolo qualify for DOC, though the zone's two-level appellation applies to various types. Normal Valtellina, which may include a good share of other varieties, is a sturdy wine in the everyday category best to drink within two or three years. A robust alternative is Sforzato, or Sfursat in dialect, in reference to the drying of grapes to concentrate sugar and extract. Sfursat at its best is a rich, mellow wine reminiscent of the Amarone of Valpolicella in the Veneto.

Valtellina Superiore applies to about a third of the total production of wines made almost exclusively from Nebbiolo and aged in wood for at least a year, usually longer. Most *superiore* carries the name of one of four subdistricts: Grumello (after a medieval castle); Inferno (from a rocky area known as the valley's hottest); Sassella (after the chapel of Sassella); or Valgella (the zone's longest expanse of vineyards). Differences can be noted among the wines, of which Sassella is most often considered the finest, though when well made from good vintages each can be distinguished. Most vineyards are planted in pebbly, siliceous clay soils, which in some cases have been carried up from the valley floor to fill in the grades of terraces or spaces between boulders. Landslides are a frequent problem, as in 1987 when torrential rains washed away sections of vineyards and flooded the valley. The hardship and expense of tending vineyards by hand are key factors in declining production, which among DOC wines has gone from an annual average of about 60,000 hl a decade ago to about 45,000 hl today. Studies are underway into ways to make viticulture more scientific and efficient without destroying the unique appearance of hillsides carved by man over thousands of years. Leading the research is the Fondazione Fojanini under Alberto Baiocchi.

The Valtellina's production is centred in wine houses, which often have vineyards of their own augmented by grapes from growers. The best known is Nino Negri, a winery run until the late 1970s by the founder's son Carlo, known as "sciur Carlúcio", a legendary figure whose Castel Chiuro and Fracia labels built the Valtellina name in Italy. But as production has declined so has the prestige of a zone whose wines are for the most part exported to Switzerland, as well as Austria, Germany, and Great Britain. Several wineries are based in Switzerland and much wine is consumed in the neighbouring canton of Grigioni (Grisons or Graubünden) where tourists

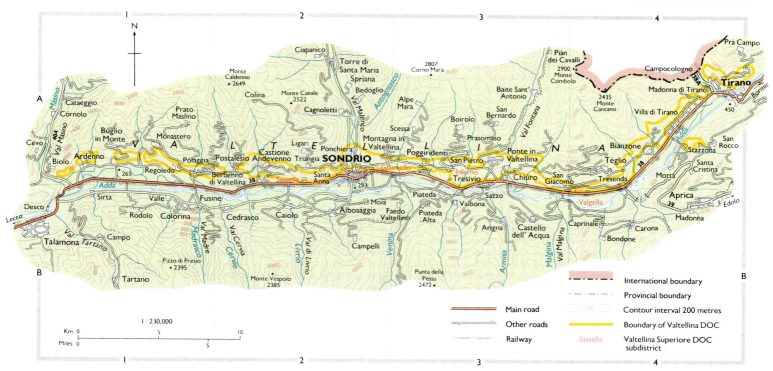

▬▬▬ Main road	▬·▬·▬ International boundary
▬▬ Other roads	········ Provincial boundary
········ Railway	▬ Contour interval 200 metres
	▬▬▬ Boundary of Valtellina DOC
Sassella	Valtellina Superiore DOC subdistrict

1 : 230,000

consider it local. The Valtellina wines are rarely prized in Italy even if the best can show enviable style: from Negri, Enologica Valtellinese, and Fondazione Fojanini's La Castellina, for example. Only recently have growers come forward with estate wines of their own. Among names to look for in the zone are Leusciatti for Sassella and Marsetti for Grumello, though bottles are limited.

The Valtellina wines differ from Barolo or Barbaresco in their leaner structures, paler garnet-orange colours, and more austere constitutions, attributed to the mountain atmosphere. But hints of anaemia can be deceptive, for some *superiore* has the stamina to outlast its Piedmontese cousins. With age flavours soften and expand and bouquets become richer with scents of what are often described as alpine flowers and herbs. Still, though the Valtellina wines are sometimes suggested as the best introduction to the Nebbiolo family, they are too variable to recommend universally. Some are awkwardly taut and tannic even when aged; others seem thin and wither rapidly after excessive time in cask. Backward methods are one cause of defects, though expedient winemaking is another, particularly when grapes come from lower slopes where yields can be surprisingly high. But indications are that the nucleus of producers are determined to further improve quality and restore prestige to a wine zone that, if for no other reason than its growers' sheer tenacity, deserves to be better appreciated both at home and abroad.

Zone: Slopes up to 800 m high where most vineyards are planted on terraces facing south along the Adda river in a 45-km stretch between Ardenno and Tirano and including Sondrio and parts of 12 other communes in its province. Valtellina Superiore comes from subzones along the north bank of the Adda within which wines of four distinct areas may carry the names: Sassella (between Castione Andevenno and Sondrio); Grumello (between Sondrio and Montagna); Inferno (between Poggiridenti and Tresivio); Valgella (between Chiuro and Teglio).

Valtellina Dry red. Grapes: Chiavennasca (Nebbiolo) 70%; Pinot Nero/Merlot/Pignola Valtellinese/Rossola/Brugnola up to 30%. Yld 84/120, Alc 11, Acd 0.5-0.75, Ag 1 yr.

Sforzato or **Sfursat** Strong, dry red. Grapes: as Valtellina but passito. Yld 84/120, Alc 14.5, Acd 0.5-0.75, Ag 1 yr.

Valtellina Superiore Dry red, also riserva. Grapes: Chiavennasca (Nebbiolo); other reds up to 5%. Yld 70/100, Alc 12, Acd 0.5-0.7, Ag 2 yrs (1 in wood); riserva 4 yrs.

Other wines of note

Among the many unclassified wines of the Valtellina are whites from Nebbiolo and reds from some of the antique varieties alone. Experiments are also underway with Pinot Nero and Merlot, as well as foreign white varieties that could thrive in the alpine environment.

ESTATES/GROWERS

Sandro Fay, San Giacomo di Teglio (SO). Good Valgella Ca' Moréi.
Fondazione Fojanini, Sondrio. The foundation dedicated to research and development in aid of growers in the Valtellina is run by Alberto Baiocchi, who from 8 ha makes a fine Sassella sold as La Castellina.

WINE HOUSES/MERCHANTS

Franco Balgera, Sondrio. Emerging with good Valtellina Superiore.
Fratelli Bettini, San Giacomo di Teglio (SO).
Enologica Valtellinese, Sondrio. Respected Valtellina Superiore under the Tre Leghe label, as well as the reserves Antica Rhaetia and Paradiso, the vdt white from Nebbiolo called Roccascissa, and the rare red Rossola.
Nino Negri, Chiuro (SO). The zone's largest cellars now belong to the Gruppo Italiano Vini, which also owns the Arturo Pelizzatti house used for commercial standard wines. Careful selection from 42 ha of vines and advanced technology under Casimiro Maule have kept the name Negri in the forefront with the *riserve* issued as "Le Botti d'Oro". The firm no longer uses the Castel Chiuro and Fracia labels.
Nera, Chiuro (SO). Giampiero Silvestrini makes Valgella, Sassella, and the *riserva* Signorie, along with a Sfursat from grapes dried on the vine.
Fratelli Polatti, Sondrio. Champions of tradition in Valtellina Superiore.
Rainoldi, Chiuro (SO). Valtellina Superiore, mainly for export.
Tona, Villa di Tirano (SO).
Fratelli Triacca, Madonna di Tirano (SO). The winery run by Domenico and Gino Triacca has invested heavily in vineyards and equipment for notably improved Valtellina wines that sell mainly in Switzerland.
(The houses of Pola and Plozza make wine bottled and sold in Switzerland.)

COOPERATIVES

Cantina Cooperativa Villa Bianzone, Villa di Tirano (SO). Valtellina DOCs.

Left: the Valtellina DOC zone. Top: pickers use hand scales to weigh baskets of grapes. Most of the zone's wine is made by merchant houses which sell a major share of production in nearby Switzerland.

Wines of Bergamo

Above: vineyards in the lower part of the valley whose special climate provides a unique habitat for Italy's northernmost Nebbiolo vines.

Bergamo's heritage of wine, noted in documents from the twelfth century, had slumped almost as sadly as in the neighbouring provinces of Milano and Como. But in recent times growers in the hills that run from northwest of the city to the edge of Lake Iseo have staged a revival of sorts by substituting the once prominent traditional varieties of Groppello and Marzemino with fashionable French vines. The resulting wines have never quite restored the old glory, but they have given Bergamo a DOC. Meanwhile, the singular red Moscato di Scanzo from around Scanzorosciate in the Serio valley east of Bergamo refuses to disappear, though it seems too esoteric to rate official recognition.

Valcalepio (1976)

The name comes from the valley formed by the Oglio river flowing from Lake Iseo where the Conti Calepio had their domain. Wines from the area adjacent to Franciacorta have long been considered Bergamo's finest, but DOC extended Valcalepio northwest to take in most of the province's remaining vineyards. The blend of Merlot and Cabernet Sauvignon works well at Tenuta Castello and La Cornasella in the original Valcalepio, though elsewhere wines sometimes show the grassy, bitter traits typical of Bordeaux varieties in northern Italy. The white from Pinot Bianco and Grigio is rarely more than just refreshing.

Zone: Alpine foothills and adjacent slopes extending from the Valcalepio (where the Oglio river flows out of Lake Iseo past Sarnico, Castelli Calepio, and Grumello del Monte) northwest across the Serio and Brembo valleys as far as Almenno and taking in part of Bergamo and 46 other communes in its province.

Bianco Dry white. Grapes: Pinot Bianco 55-75%, Pinot Grigio 25-45%. Yld 58.5/90, Alc 11.5, Acd 0.45.

Rosso Dry red. Grapes: Merlot 55-75%, Cabernet Sauvignon 25-45%. Yld 65/100, Alc 12, Acd 0.5, Ag 2 yrs.

Other wines of note

Moscato di Scanzo, though made in minute quantities, is admired beyond Bergamo for its inimitable character. It has a warm mahogany colour and aromas that bring to mind spices, exotic fruits, and burnished wood. Its restrained sweetness and smooth texture can't hide the rusticity that seems to be part of its appeal. Recommended producers are Celinate Ronchello at Celinate di Scanzo and Il Cipresso at Scanzorosciate. Good sparkling wines are also made in the Valcalepio.

ESTATES/GROWERS

La Cornasella, Grumello del Monte (BG). Alessandro Geroli makes good Valcalepio and fine Moscato di Scanzo on his small property.

Le Corne, Grumello del Monte (BG). Valcalepio DOC, along with vdt Chardonnay and *champenoise* Cuvée Perletti Brut.

Tenuta Castello, Grumello del Monte (BG). Carlo Zadra makes what are often considered the best wines of Valcalepio under the Colle del Calvario label, along with an impressive wood-aged Chardonnay called Aurito.

WINE HOUSES/MERCHANTS

Perlage, Grumello del Monte (BG). Zadra of Tenuta Castello makes three types of classical *spumante* of Chardonnay, Pinot Nero, and Pinot Bianco from Trentino-Alto Adige. Carlozadra Brut and Nondosato are dry and drier; the more recent Carlozadra Tradizione is a velvety soft *demisec* made by traditional Champagne methods.

Wines of Brescia

Brescia, an industrious city at the foot of the Alps, has always been better known for its precision firearms than wines, even if it had an active trade in economical bottlings from its side of Lake Garda as well as Verona's. Its own wines were mainly reds or rosés from combinations of the local Groppello or the long present Marzemino or Schiava with Nebbiolo or Barbera or Cabernet Franc or Merlot or even Sangiovese. Those curious blends, if tasty, were not of a calibre to give Brescia the reputation with wines that it had with rifles and revolvers. Then came the *champenoise* of Franciacorta and Brescia entered Italy's premium wine field with what might be described as a bang. A zone that two decades ago was an obscure source of country reds now makes a major share of Italy's Champagne method wines, including some of its most prestigious. The enterprise shown by Franciacorta's producers might serve as a model for others to follow in a province with seven of Lombardy's thirteen DOC zones scattered through the Garda and Iseo glacial basins. But so far only a few winemakers of Lugana, a persuasive white from Garda's southern shores, have shown any similar initiative. The only other established white is Tocai di San Martino della Battaglia from a zone that practically coincides with Lugana but whose wine doesn't rival it. Garda's steep western litoral is Lombardy's largest DOC zone, though most red and *chiaretto* of Riviera del Garda Bresciana come from a small area where vineyards are in decline. Capriano del Colle, on the last hill south of Brescia toward the Po, makes simple red and white rarely seen elsewhere. Even Brescia's time-honoured local reds of Botticino and Cellatica have had to fight for survival against the city's expansion.

Franciacorta (1967)

The area south of Lake Iseo may have been called Franciacorta from the Latin Francae Curtes, the tax exempt status of convents and monasteries, though there are other versions of how it got its name. Gentle hills there have been noted since ancient times for a blissful climate and a certain propensity for wine. But the miracle of Franciacorta, as it is sometimes called, is a modern event that occurred in two phases. The first was the invention of a *champenoise* in a zone where it didn't previously exist by a young oenologist named Franco Ziliani, who later built the house of Guido Berlucchi into Italy's largest producer. That feat inspired the second part of the phenomenon, the transformation of the once bucolic villas and farms of Franciacorta into the châteaux of a miniature Champagne. The DOC also applies to an often impressive still white and a blended red that can be pleasant, but its acknowledged forte is *champenoise* which here, unlike in any other major zone of Italy or France, is made primarily by estates.

Guido Berlucchi was still an estate in the mid-1950s when Franco Ziliani convinced the owner that the Pinot in his vineyards might make bottle-fermented sparkling wine to rival Champagne. Though early experiments left doubts, when the first 3,000 bottles were released in 1960, Ziliani already had the firm's future mapped out. His learn-by-doing strategy had taken him to Epernay where he was inspired by Moët & Chandon's formula for success of large volume, consistent quality, and competitive prices. By 1975, Cuvée Imperiale Berlucchi had become Italy's best-selling *champenoise* and Ziliani realized that local vineyards couldn't supply all his needs. So he turned to

sources in Trentino-Alto Adige, Oltrepò Pavese, and Gavi in Piedmont for his cuvées, thereby reducing the share from Franciacorta to about a quarter of the total and losing the right to DOC. In 1990, the house of Berlucchi has projected sales of 5 million bottles of *champenoise*, or roughly a third of the nation's production.

Franciacorta's other wineries account for a mere 1.3 to 1.5 million bottles of *spumante* between them, but the zone's soaring prestige has been acquired largely by estates. The first to emerge prominently was Ca' del Bosco, where Maurizio Zanella began as a teenager to make and market wines that became national standards. After creating Italy's most praised and expensive *champenoise* with French cellarmaster André Dubois, Zanella followed with some of the finest non-DOC still wines from Cabernet and Merlot, Pinot Nero, and Chardonnay. Comparable creations have built the names of the nearby estates of Bellavista and Cavalleri. Among Franciacorta's 70 wineries that bottle, including 33 that produce *spumante*, at least a dozen make wines that are highly regarded and, more important, continue to improve. But since so much activity is recent, Franciacorta's full potential remains to be seen.

The lower Iseo basin consists of glacial moraine in gentle hills where breezes wafting down the lake from the Aprica range of the Alps create a mild climate held in check by the mass of Monte Orfano to the south. Most estates are in the western part of the zone in two adjacent areas. The rises of Monte di Erbusco have what are considered the most privileged conditions around the villages of Erbusco, Adro, and Capriolo. There *champenoise* is noted for fragrance and finesse and still

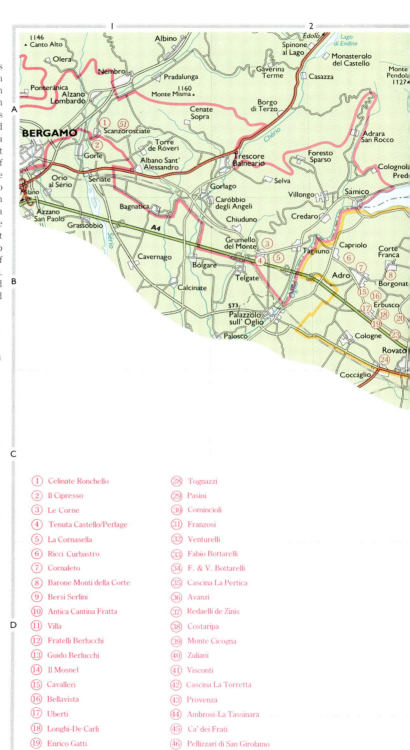

1. Celinate Ronchello
2. Il Cipresso
3. Le Corne
4. Tenuta Castello/Perlage
5. La Cornasella
6. Ricci Curbastro
7. Cornaleto
8. Barone Monti della Corte
9. Bersi Serlini
10. Antica Cantina Fratta
11. Villa
12. Fratelli Berlucchi
13. Guido Berlucchi
14. Il Mosnel
15. Cavalleri
16. Bellavista
17. Uberti
18. Longhi-De Carli
19. Enrico Gatti
20. Ca' del Bosco
21. Monte Rossa
22. Catturich-Ducco
23. Principe Banfi
24. Montorfano
25. Bolzoni Mestriner
26. Pasolini
27. Bonetti
28. Tognazzi
29. Pasini
30. Comincioli
31. Franzosi
32. Venturelli
33. Fabio Bottarelli
34. F. & V. Bottarelli
35. Cascina La Pertica
36. Avanzi
37. Redaelli de Zinis
38. Costaripa
39. Monte Cicogna
40. Zuliani
41. Visconti
42. Cascina La Torretta
43. Provenza
44. Ambrosi-La Tassinara
45. Ca' dei Frati
46. Pellizzari di San Girolamo
47. Hirundo
48. Zenegaglia
49. Fattoria Colombara
50. Gianni Boselli
51. *Moscato di Scanzo*
52. *Groppello*
53. *Alto Mincio*

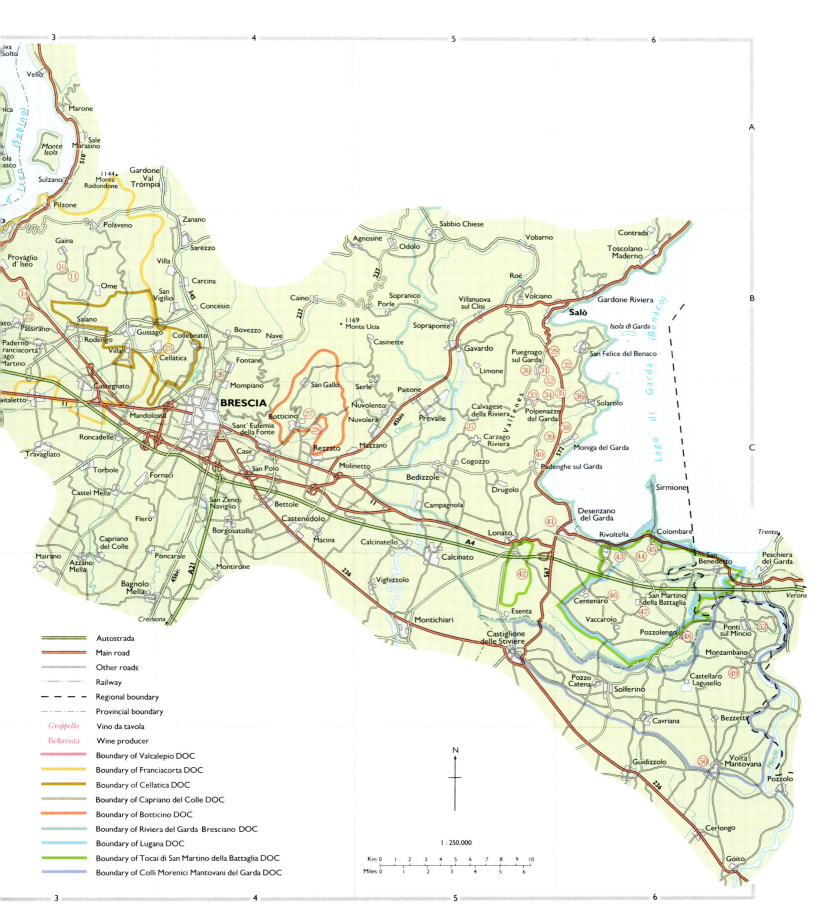

Legend:
- Autostrada
- Main road
- Other roads
- Railway
- Regional boundary
- Provincial boundary
- *Groppello* — Vino da tavola
- *Bellavista* — Wine producer
- Boundary of Valcalepio DOC
- Boundary of Franciacorta DOC
- Boundary of Cellatica DOC
- Boundary of Capriano del Colle DOC
- Boundary of Botticino DOC
- Boundary of Riviera del Garda Bresciano DOC
- Boundary of Lugana DOC
- Boundary of Tocai di San Martino della Battaglia DOC
- Boundary of Colli Morenici Mantovani del Garda DOC

N

1 : 250,000

Km 0 1 2 3 4 5 6 7 8 9 10
Miles 0 1 2 3 4 5 6

wines, both red and white, show marked character. Estates there include Ca' del Bosco, Bellavista, Cavalleri, Uberti, Enrico Gatti, Cornaleto, and Ricci Curbastro. The Corte Franca area makes nicely balanced *champenoise* in the relatively fertile rolling terrain between the lake and Passirano. Estates there include Monte Rossa, Bersi Serlini, Fratelli Berlucchi, Il Mosnel, and vineyards of Guido Berlucchi. Monte Orfano's calcareous slopes are noted for Pinots of good aroma and acidity, though no major estates are located there. The eastern part of the zone, with its epicentre at Monticelli, has few noted vineyards, though the Villa estate makes respected *spumante*.

It might be that Franciacorta doesn't have Italy's best natural conditions for Pinots and Chardonnay, as Franco Ziliani has observed in creating his *cuvées*. Yet no other zone equals the general class of its *champenoise*, which has been steadily enhanced by vineyard improvements and cellar techniques that are clearly in the vanguard. Several producers now age part of their base wines in barrel, which helps fill out body and texture and lower acidity that had been annoyingly excessive in early examples of Italian *champenoise*. But apart from *spumante*, Franciacorta's best still wines from noble varieties are rarely matched in other zones of Italy.

Credit goes to producers who have invested, often heavily, in estates where experts control the complete cycle from planting vineyards to selling wine. Since they had no strong traditions to contend with, some pursue their goals with a lack of inhibition and a competitive business sense that seem more Californian than European. And, indeed, a few wineries of Franciacorta would look right at home in the Napa Valley. But the villas surviving from the days when Brescia's nobility summered in the hills give this ultramodern wine zone touches of old world splendour. In two decades registered vineyards have increased tenfold while DOC production has reached 35,000 hl, of which white (including *spumante*) now accounts for two thirds. The red continues to decline. Franciacorta Bianco, which was called Pinot until the alternative Chardonnay was introduced, shows tone that from top winemakers can approach elegance. The *rosso* relies on a bizarre blend based on Cabernet Franc. Though often rustic, some producers use deft oak ageing for wines of some complexity and style.

Right: vineyards in the Franciacorta zone where enterprising producers now make a major share of Italy's sparkling wine by the Champagne method.

Zone: Rolling hills of the so-called Iseo morainic amphitheatre between Lake Iseo, Monte Orfano, and Brescia, which is one of the 22 communes of its province in the zone, though noted vineyards lie mainly to the west around Corte Franca, Erbusco, Adro, Capriolo, and Passirano.

Bianco Dry white. Grapes: Pinot Bianco/ Chardonnay. Yld 85/125, Alc 11, Acd 0.55.
Spumante Sparkling white. Grapes: Pinot Bianco/Chardonnay; Pinot Grigio/Pinot Nero up to 15%. Yld 85/125, Alc 11.5 (res sugar max 20 gr/l), Acd 0.6.
Rosato spumante Sparkling rosé. Grapes: Pinot Bianco/Chardonnay, Pinot Nero obligatory up to 15%; Pinot Grigio up to 15%. Yld 85/125, Alc 11.5 (res sugar max 20 gr/l), Acd 0.6.
Rosso Dry red. Grapes: Cabernet Franc 40-50%, Barbera 20-30%, Nebbiolo 15-25%, Merlot 10-15%; other reds up to 15%. Yld 87.5/125, Alc 11, Acd 0.5-0.7, Ag 8 mths.

Cellatica (1968)

The tasty light red of Cellatica, which has been a favourite around Brescia since at least the 16th century, in times past drew comparisons with Claret, but not today. Its lively fruit and lightly bitter finish make it best within a couple years of the harvest.

Zone: Hills adjacent to Brescia on the northeast, extending through the communes of Cellatica, Collebeato, Gussago, and Rodengo-Saiano and overlapping part of the Franciacorta zone. Dry red. Grapes: Schiava Gentile 35-45%, Barbera 25-30%, Marzemino 20-30%, Incrocio Terzi N. 1 10-15%. Yld 84/ 120, Alc 11.5, Acd 0.55-0.75, Ag 11 mths.

Botticino (1968)

Brescia's other local red seems a bit more robust and durable than Cellatica, due perhaps to the slightly warmer climate of the Valverde, though it would take a sharp palate to tell the difference. Recommended producers are Miro Bonetti and Benedetto Tognazzi.

Zone: Slopes of the Valverde just east of Brescia and taking in part of its commune as well as Botticino and Rezzato. Dry red. Grapes: Barbera 30-40%, Schiava Gentile 20-30%, Marzemino 15-25%, Sangiovese 10-20%. Yld 84/120, Alc 12, Acd 0.5-0.7, Ag 11 mths.

Capriano del Colle (1980)

The name when used alone applies to a vivacious red based on Sangiovese and Marzemino, though the little known zone also has a tartly dry white Trebbiano. Both are consumed for the most part locally. A recommended producer is Botti Cantine.

Zone: Low slopes of Monte Netto southwest of Brescia around the communes of Capriano del Colle and Poncarale on the edge of the Padana plain. Dry red. Grapes: Sangiovese 40-50%, Marzemino 35-45%, Barbera 3-10%; Merlot/ Incrocio Terzi N.1 up to 15%. Yld 87.5/125, Alc 11, Acd 0.5.
Trebbiano Dry white. Grapes: Trebbiano di Lugana (or Soave)/Trebbiano Toscano. Yld 85/125, Alc 11, Acd 0.55.

Riviera del Garda Bresciano or Garda Bresciano (1967)

Lombardy's largest DOC zone covers most of the western flank of Lake Garda, including the riviera between Salò and Limone where the road had to be tunnelled through cliffs along the lake. But the few vines that grew on that dramatic stretch of shoreline have nearly all disappeared. Meanwhile, to the southwest in the Valtènesi, which was always the preferred wine area, production of the DOC *rosso* and *chiaretto* has dropped sharply as vineyards that once covered 800 ha are down to 150 ha. *Chiaretto*, cherry pink and buoyantly refreshing, has an enthusiastic summer following along the lake, but it rarely sells away from it. The *rosso* can be good, though the basic Groppello, which can make an impressive vdt on its own, is often lost among the other varieties in the bizarre DOC blend. Some experts maintain that the Valtènesi is Garda's best vineyard area, superior to Bardolino Classico, because its steep slopes of glacial moraine in which large, rounded boulders emerge from the soil are generally better exposed to the sun and the effects of breezes off the lake. But some suggest that this nature is better suited to white wine than red or *chiaretto*. To that end a request has been made to add a white DOC based on Riesling (Renano and/or Italico), though there are doubts that those varieties are as well suited to the ambience as are the proven local Trebbiano di Lugana or the Chardonnay and Sauvignon that have shown promise in vdt. The bid would

also change *chiaretto* to *rosato* and add a *spumante* version, while providing for a red *novello* – no doubt inspired by the success of those types at Bardolino.

Zone: Often steep hills along the western and southern shores of Lake Garda in 30 communes of Brescia province, though most production is in the Valtènesi to the southwest around Moniga, Manerba, Puegnago, Polpenazze, San Felice, Soiano, and Padenghe in vineyards no higher than 350 m. The southern part of the zone overlaps Lugana and San Martino della Battaglia.

Rosso Dry red. Grapes: Groppello 30-60%, Sangiovese 10-25%, Barbera 10-20%, Marzemino 5-30%; Nebbiolo, Schiava, Cabernet Franc, Trebbiano or others up to 10%. Yld 85/125, Alc 11; superiore 12, Acd 0.5, Ag superiore 1 yr.

Chiaretto Dry light red to pink. Grapes: As rosso. Yld 85/125, Alc 11.5, Acd 0.55.

Lugana (1967)

The rise of Lugana as one of Lombardy's few white wines that count defies doctrine since it comes from a species of Trebbiano and much of its vineyards are on flat, rather heavy soil. Its success has been attributed to the fact that it is white and comes from the well-frequented Garda resort of Sirmione, but the real point in its favour is its graceful personality that appeals both to novices and to people who take wine seriously. Steady growth in vineyards attests to faith in the future by growers, including owners of large estates where investments have been notable. Trebbiano di Lugana is so different from other vines of the family that some admirers would prefer to have it called simply Lugana in the way that its apparent relative Verdicchio has been distinguished in the Marches. It seems to have evolved to fit the conditions of the Garda basin in a zone that stretches from the lakeside plain into low hills to the south in soils of calcareous clay on a bed of glacial moraine. The lake has a moderating effect on ripening in a variety that reaches maturity unusually late. When grapes are picked young, wines have the acidity suited to the sparkling wines, usually by tank method, that are increasingly popular here. But Lugana is best as a still white of good body and texture that gains poise after a year or two in bottle when most Trebbiano would have faded. Two consistently fine producers are the estate of Ca' dei Frati and the house of Visconti, though a majority of wineries have made the investments that assure wines of reliable quality. The Lugana judged best of the year in a rigorous tasting is given the award known as Gran Priorato.

Zone: The glacial basin at the south of Lake Garda, extending from the peninsula of Sirmione and the plains in the part of its commune known as Lugana into rolling hills in the communes of Desenzano, Lonato, and Pozzolengo in Brescia province and Peschiera del Garda in Verona. The zone coincides with Tocai di San Martino della Battaglia and part of Riviera del Garda. Dry white, also spumante. Grapes: Trebbiano di Lugana (Veronese); other non-aromatic whites up to 10%. Yld 87.5/125, Alc 11.5; spumante 12, Acd 0.5; spumante 0.6.

Tocai di San Martino della Battaglia (1970)

Friuli's Tocai transplanted to Garda's southern shores is rarely distinguished, though it makes a pleasant enough little wine of sunny yellow colour and a zesty suggestion of citrus and almonds that goes down well in summer. Producers in the zone that was named after the site of a Piedmontese victory over Austria in 1859 have requested to have the DOC name shortened to simply San Martino della Battaglia and add a sweet *liquoroso*.

Zone: The glacial basin at the south of Lake Garda centred in the village of San Martino della Battaglia in the commune of Desenzano in an area almost identical to that of Lugana, except that it also includes an isolated sector just south of Lonato. It also coincides with the southern part of Riviera del Garda Bresciano. Dry white. Grape: Tocai Friulano. Yld 81/125, Alc 12, Acd 0.5.

Other wines of note

The decline of Brescia's traditional reds partly explains why producers have been creating new styles with Cabernet Sauvignon and Pinot Nero – notably at Franciacorta which has proved that it can make world class wines in categories other than sparkling. The Pinots and Chardonnay are used increasingly for whites in several areas. Prominent DOCs, including Pasolini's Ronco di Mompiano, are listed with their producers.

ESTATES/GROWERS

Ambrosi-La Tassinara, Rivoltella del Garda (BS). Good Lugana, including a *champenoise*.

Barone Monti della Corte, Cortefranca (BS). Franciacorta Brut.

Bellavista, Erbusco (BS). Owner Vittorio Moretti and winemaker Mattia Vezzola have built this estate into Franciacorta's nearest rival to Ca' del Bosco with sparkling and still wines of enviable style. Five types of *champenoise* dominate production from nearly 50 ha. Only Chardonnay is used in Cuvée Bellavista and Gran Cuvée Crémant Millesimato, which some consider the cream of its category. Chardonnay is combined with Pinot Nero in Gran Cuvée Brut Millesimato, Gran Cuvée Pas Operé Millesimato, and Gran Cuvée Rosé Millesimato. Still wines designed to be elegantly drinkable have further enhanced Bellavista's reputation in Solesine from Cabernet Sauvignon and Merlot, Casotte from Pinot Nero, and the oak-aged Chardonnay Uccellanda. The estate, which awards annual prizes for published works on Franciacorta, also makes good DOC *rosso* and *bianco*.

Fratelli Berlucchi, Borgonato di Cortefranca (BS). An early leader with Franciacorta's still wines and *champenoise* from 32 ha of vines.

Bersi Serlini, Timoline di Cortefranca (BS). Sound Franciacorta Brut.

Fabio Bottarelli & Figlio, Polpenazze (BS). Riviera del Garda DOC.

Franco & Valerio Bottarelli, Picedo di Polpenazze (BS). Riviera del Garda DOC.

Ca' dei Frati, Sirmione (BS). From 10 ha in the heart of Lugana, Pietro Dal Cero and family make what is regularly regarded as one of the best wines of the name, along with good Riviera del Garda DOC.

Ca' del Bosco, Erbusco (BS). The Zanella family's wooded property has been converted into one of Italy's most elaborate estates with 60 ha of vines and extraordinary underground cellars, including a cathedral-like dome built in stone like the adjoining arched caves where *champenoise* ages in ideal conditions. Maurizio Zanella began with former cellarmaster André Dubois to make what became Italy's most admired range of sparkling wines in Brut, Crémant, the exquisite Dosage Zero, and the opulent Brut Millesimato, whose base wine comes from grapes crushed in a hand-operated wooden basket press. The basic Franciacorta Rosso and especially the Bianco have improved markedly, but most acclaim has been won by vdt from French varieties that can match the elite of Bordeaux and Burgundy in style and price. First was the Maurizio Zanella signature wine from Cabernet Sauvignon and Merlot, then barrel-fermented Chardonnay, then Pinèro, a Pinot Noir from Burgundy clones. Zanella honed his style with Californian Brian Larky for a time, but winemaking feats are decidedly his own.

Cascina La Pertica, Picedo di Polpenazze (BS). Ruggero Brunori is starting to realize ambitions in Riviera del Garda DOC and vdt under the Il Colombaio and Le Sincette labels, as well as in the convincing barrel-aged Chardonnay Le Zalte Bianco.

Cascina La Torretta-Spia d'Italia, Lonato (BS). Reliable Tocai di San Martino and Riviera del Garda, along with vdt Chardonnay Carato Bianco.

Catturich-Ducco, Camignone (BS). Franciacorta DOC.

Cavalleri, Erbusco (BS). Giovanni Cavalleri commands an increasingly admired family enterprise in Franciacorta with 16 ha of vines for first-rate *champenoise* Brut, Pas Dosé, and Rosé, with a high point in the Millesimato from Chardonnay with Pinot Nero. Equally impressive is the array of French-style bottlings: Tajardino (Cabernet-Merlot) and barrel-fermented Chardonnay Seradina. The Franciacorta Rosso and Bianco, including the Chardonnay-Pinot blend called Rampaneto, are good value.

Comincioli, Puegnago (BS). Unsung producer of some of the most consistently impressive Riviera del Garda DOC.

Cornaleto, Adro (BS). From 18 ha of vines, Luigi Lancini makes a fine Franciacorta Rosso, along with admired *champenoise*.

Costaripa, Moniga del Garda (BS). From 4 ha, Bruno Vezzola and sons

Above: a section of the elaborate cellars at Ca' del Bosco in Franciacorta where Maurizio Zanella uses oak barrels for ageing some of Italy's most admired still wines as well as bases for highly acclaimed champenoise.

Imer and Mattia make Riviera del Garda DOC, led by a fresh and fragrant Chiaretto di Moniga, along with a red vdt Groppello.

Bruno Franzosi, Puegnago (BS). Riviera del Garda DOC.

Enrico Gatti, Erbusco (BS). Young Lorenzo Gatti and Enzo Bazzarini are emerging with impressive Franciacorta DOC.

Il Mosnel, Camignone di Passirano (BS). Emanuela Barboglio Barzanò and family make respected Franciacorta DOC from 27 ha of vines.

Longhi-De Carli, Erbusco (BS). Franciacorta DOC.

Monte Cicogna, Moniga del Garda (BS). Good Riviera del Garda DOC from 18 ha of vines.

Monte Rossa, Bornato (BS). Paola Rovetta and son Emanuele Rabotti make fine Franciacorta *champenoise* from 16 ha of vines, including Brut, Non Dosato, Rosé, and Extra Brut dei Rossa Millesimato.

Pasini Produttori, Raffa di Puegnago (BS). Diego Pasini makes Riviera del Garda DOC, along with the red vdt Groppello and the impressive San Gioan from Groppello and Marzemino.

M. Pasolini, Brescia. Mario Pasolini's Ronco di Mompiano vdt from Marzemino and Merlot is a legend around Brescia with a label to match.

Pellizzari di San Girolamo, Desenzano (BS). Reliable Lugana, Tocai di San Martino, and Riviera del Garda DOC.

Principe Banfi, Villa di Erbusco (BS). Franciacorta *champenoise* from the estate called Podere Pio IX Principe Banfi.

Provenza, Rivoltella del Garda (BS). Dependable Lugana from vineyards of Cascina Maiolo.

Ragnoli, Colombaro (BS). Long admired producer of Franciacorta Rosso.

Redaelli de Zinis, Calvagese Riviera (BS). Riviera del Garda DOC and vdt Groppello di Mocasina.

Ricci Curbastro, Capriolo (BS). Small production of respected Franciacorta Rosso, Bianco, and *champenoise*.

Uberti, Erbusco (BS). From 11 ha, the Uberti brothers make Franciacorta DOC, including the *champenoise* Francesco 1° Brut and Pas Dosé, along with the vdt called Rosso dei Frati Priori from Cabernet Sauvignon.

Villa, Monticelli Brusati (BS). From 15 ha of vines, Alessandro Bianchi makes Franciacorta DOC, including *champenoise* brut, rosé, and pas dosé.

Italo Zuliani, Padenghe (BS). Riviera del Garda DOC.

WINE HOUSES/MERCHANTS

Antica Cantina Fratta, Monticelli Brusati (BS). Guido Berlucchi and Franco Ziliani use this lovely villa with

Above: the gate of a villa in the Franciacorta zone where ultramodern winemaking is practised amidst touches of old world splendour.

ageing cellars in Franciacorta for 200,000 bottles a year of their alternate brand of *champenoise*.

Avanzi, Manerba (BS). Riviera del Garda DOC.

Barbi, Roncadelle (BS). Marina and Claudio Barbi, owners of Decugnano de Barbi in Orvieto, also make Cellatica at the family wine house here.

Guido Berlucchi, Borgonato di Cortefranca (BS). The house founded by Guido Berlucchi has been built by the dynamic Franco Ziliani into Italy's largest producer of *champenoise*. The firm has 70 ha of vines in Franciacorta but *cuvées* for production of some 5 million bottles a year include Pinot Nero from the Oltrepò Pavese, Chardonnay from Trentino and Alto Adige, and Cortese from the company's La Bollina estate in Piedmont's Gavi. The best-selling Cuvée Imperiale Berlucchi Brut heads a line that includes Brut millesimato, Grand Cremant, Pas Dosé, and Max Rosé. There is also a still Bianco Imperiale from Chardonnay with the Pinots at 400,000 bottles a year. The firm also owns the Antica Cantina Fratta cellars.

Folonari, Persico Dosimo (CR). From a base in Brescia the Folonari family winery grew into a giant with some 350,000 hl a year of DOC (mainly Veronese) and vdt. Now part of Gruppo Italiano Vini, its main cellars are located near Cremona.

Hirundo, San Martino della Battaglia (BS). Lugana DOC.

Montorfano, Coccaglio (BS). Domenico De Filippo makes good Franciacorta *champenoise* Brut Nature from purchased grapes.

Premiovini, Brescia. The firm in the Folonari family selects and bottles wines from various parts of Italy under

different brand names: San Grato for Brescia, Pègaso for Verona, Plauto for Romagna, Contessa Matilde for Lambrusco, Nozzole for Chianti Classico, Torre Sveva for Castel del Monte and Aglianico del Vulture, Anforio for Alba and Asti Spumante, and Della Staffa for Alto Adige. Quality is always reliable and sometimes excellent.

Vigneti Venturelli, Raffa di Puegnago (BS). Riviera del Garda and Lugana DOC, in part from own vineyards.

Villa Mazzucchelli, Ciliverghe (BS).

Piero Giacomini makes admired *champenoise* Brut, Pas Dosé, and Riviera del Conte.

Visconti, Desenzano (BS). The winemaking skills of Franco Visconti and oenologist Gianfranco Tonon are consistently evident in Lugana, from the basic Collo Lungo to Lugana di Lugana and, ultimately, to the single vineyard Sant'Onorata. The house also makes good *spumante* and Riviera del Garda DOC.

Zenegaglia, Pozzolengo (BS). Reliable Lugana.

Wines of Mantova

The Romans spoke of Rhaetic from the Morenici hills in the Garda basin, but ancient Mantua earned its title of "la gloriosa" from endeavours other than wine. Still, between the hills and the flatlands along the Po, Mantova province manages to make nearly as much wine as Brescia. Most of the limited production of DOC and large quantities of table wines are drunk locally.

Colli Morenici Mantovani del Garda (1976)

Vineyards are a minor part of the crop mix on the sweeping hillsides of this peaceful farm country, where the influence of Verona is evident in the usually simple but often tasty red, white, and rosé.

Zone: Rolling hills at the south of Garda's glacial basin in Mantova province, extending from the Mincio valley in the communes of Ponti sul Mincio, Monzambano, and Volta Mantovano, west through Cavriana and Solferino to Castiglione delle Stiviere.

Bianco Dry white. Grapes: Trebbiano Giallo/Trebbiano Toscano 20-50%, Garganega 20-40%, Trebbiano Nostrano/Pinot Bianco 10-35%; Riesling Italico/Malvasia di Candia up to 15%. Yld 65/100, Alc 11, Acd 0.6.

Rosso or **Rubino** Dry red. Grapes: Rondinella 20-50%, Merlot 20-40%, Rossanella (Molinara) 20-30%; Negrara/Sangiovese up to 15%. Yld 65/100, Alc 11, Acd 0.5.

Rosato or **Chiaretto** Dry rosé. Grapes: as rosso. Yld 65/100, Alc 11; Chiaretto 11.5, Acd 0.5.

Lambrusco Mantovano (1987)

The province's newer DOC acknowledges the long tradition of Lambrusco in Mantova's stretch of the Po valley adjacent to the more noted areas of Modena and Reggio in Emilia. The Lambrusco subvariety of Viadanese comes from the town of Viadana, source of a robust version of the wine, though the sandy flatlands to the east are noted for lighter, zestier wines. Both can compare with their Emilian counterparts.

Zone: The Padana flatlands in two sectors at the southern part of Mantova province: the Viadanese to the west between the Po and Oglio rivers around Viadana, Sabbioneta, and four other communes; the Oltre Po Mantovano to the east between Suzzara and Sermide and in 13 other communes between the Po and the border

of Emilia-Romagna. Dry red, frizzante, also amabile. Grapes: Lambrusco Viadanese and other subvarieties; Ancellotta/Fortana (Uva d'Oro) up to 15%. Yld 97.5/150, Alc 10.5, Acd 0.65.

ESTATES/GROWERS

Gianni Boselli, Volta Mantovana (MN). Colli Morenici DOC

Fattoria Colombara, Monzambano (MN). Colli Morenici DOC, along with vdt Chardonnay, Cabernet, and Merlot.

COOPERATIVES

CS Colli Morenici Alto Mantovano, Ponti sul Mincio (MN). Sound wines of the Colli Morenici and vdt Alto Mincio.

CS di Quistello, Quistello (MN). Lambrusco Mantovano to rival the best of Modena and Reggio.

Travel Information

RESTAURANTS/HOTELS

Dal Pescatore, 46013 Canneto sull'Oglio (MN). Tel (0376)70304. The Santini family has carried the cooking of the Po valley to the ultimate but always with respect for its origins and always with wine to match.

Miramonti l'Altro, 25062 Concesio (BS). Tel (030)2751063. Mauro Piscini directs this comfortable restaurant with refined food and wines that range beyond the specialiies of nearby Brescia.

Al Bersagliere, 46044 Goito (MN). Tel (0376)60007. The Ferrari family continues to perfect this temple of Lombardian gastronomy and Italian wines beside the Mincio.

Sassella, 23033 Grosio (SO). Tel (0342)845140. Tempting choices of Valtellina dishes and wines in a tastefully appointed villa with rooms.

Le Maschere, 25049 Iseo (BS). Tel (030)9821542. Vittorio Fusari and associates created this fine restaurant as an alternative to the simpler pleasures of their nearby **Il Volto**, Tel (030)981462. The wine lists have the best of Franciacorta and other places.

Vecchia Lugana, 25010 Lugana di Sirmione (BS). Tel (030)919012.

Pierantonio Ambrosi and family set Garda's culinary standards at this lakeside restaurant and the even more romantic **Villa Fiordaliso** (with rooms) up the shore at Gardone Riviera, Tel (0365)20158.

Albergo del Sole, 20076 Maleo (MI). Tel (0377)58142. In this small town inn (with rooms) Franco and Silvana Colombani have brought new definitions of taste and integrity to the concept of regional cooking and wines.

Al Pino da Mario, 27040 Montescano (PV). Tel (0385)60479. A pleasant place in the Oltrepò Pavese with inspired cooking and good local wines.

Cerere, 23026 Ponte in Valtellina (SO). Tel (0342)482294. The singular specialities of the Valtellina are served with the best of local wines.

L'Ambasciata, 46026 Quistello (MN). Tel (0376)618255. The Tamani family interprets the traditional cooking of the Bassa Mantovana in ways that can match the good local Lambrusco or the best of Italian wines.

WINE SHOPS/ENOTECHE

Milan may be some distance from noted sources of wine, but its cellars are well stocked with bottles from Lombardy and beyond. Choice wine lists in Milan and other cities are to be found in restaurants, though there are too many good ones to mention (the previous references are to a few in or near wine zones). Shops with outstanding selections include Solci, Cotti, Ronchi, Vino-Vino, and N'Ombra de Vin in Milan, and nearby Meregalli at Monza and Enoteca 77 at Meda. Elsewhere in the region are Al Portico at Ponte San Pietro (Bergamo), Malinverno at Isola Dovarese (Cremona), Rocco Lettieri at Cantù (Como), and Regno di Bacco and Zocchi at Ponte Tresa (Varese).

PLACES OF INTEREST

Each of Lombardy's major wine zones has a look and feel of its own, an atmosphere that photographs can only hint at. And, except for the Valtellina, they are all easy to reach by car from Milan or other cities.

Oltrepò Pavese. Drivers heading south from Milan might begin a tour at the monumental Certosa di Pavia, where the adjacent Enoteca Lombarda displays a cross section of the region's wines with emphasis on the Oltrepò Pavese. The zone, also accessible from the Torino-Piacenza *autostrada* (exit at Stradella or Casteggio), was the first of Italy to chart wine routes through its scenic hills.

Valtellina. The terraced vineyards along the Adda with the Alps in the background are worth the drive up past Lake Como or across the high passes from Switzerland to see. Even though the remote valley has been increasingly frequented by tourists in recent years, its old alpine customs and unique local delicacies can still be savoured. Among several ski resorts in the area, Bormio is the most famous.

Franciacorta. The rolling countryside south of Lake Iseo has a genteel air about it that seems to find its way into the renowned sparkling wines. Most estates of Franciacorta are too small to accept visitors without appointments, but the largest producer, Guido Berlucchi, provides tours and tastings. The zone is crossed by the Milano-Verona *autostrada* (exit at Palazzolo or Rovato).

Riviera del Garda and Lugana. Wine is just one of the attractions that make Garda the most touristy of the Italian lakes. It may be worth braving the summer crowds to sip Lugana on the Sirmione peninsula or *chiaretto* at Gardone Riviera, but a tour along the quiet back roads that lead to their vineyards should increase the pleasure.

Below: San Pietro in the Valtellina with the Alps in the background.

Above: the South Tryolean town of Tramin, or Termeno, in the Adige valley gave its name to the Gewürztraminer vine.

The Northeast

The three regions of the northeast are known collectively as the Venezie or Tre Venezie due to ancient links with the Republic of Venice. Vineyards were planted there by Etruscans before the Romans knew the Rhaetic grown along the Adige valley or the wines of the Colli Euganei or the Pulcinum of Carso. Venice's influence was stronger on the flourishing plains and hills that cross its primary domain of the Veneto and the Adriatic basin of Friuli-Venezia Giulia than in the alpine provinces of Trentino and Alto Adige (formerly the Austrian South Tyrol). Teutonic and Slavic minorities remain in places, as do ancient ethnic groups who speak Friulano and Ladin, adding colour and contrasts to local ways of life.

This cultural intermingling contributed to a collection of vines that may be unequalled in numbers anywhere. The diverse nature of the vineyards that climb from the hot plains along the Po to cool terraces in the Dolomites is another factor behind the variety. Many native vines remain, augmented by some rare species from neighbouring lands. But the base for what has come to be considered a common heritage of wine in the Venezie is that dozen or so varieties planted not only here but through much of the world. Some are so well established that growers call them "Merlott", "Pinott", "Cabernett", maybe not knowing, or not caring, that elsewhere they're considered French.

But folklore means less and less in the sector of Italy that first turned wine into a profitable modern business. Each region – or, more precisely, each province – takes its own approach to wine, but between them the Venezie set the nation's pace. They produce about 15 percent of Italian wine, but account for more than 35 percent of the DOC. The Veneto leads all regions in production of classified wine, largely on the strength of Verona's Soave, Valpolicella, and Bardolino. Space is more limited in Trentino-Alto Adige and Friuli-Venezia Giulia, but those regions rank first and second in the proportion of DOC wines produced. The northeast also leads in exports of premium wine, thanks to traditional trade links with German-speaking countries and to effective marketing by the Veneto's wineries in Britain and the United States.

The three regions produce an indisputable majority of Italy's fine white wines, epitomized by the stylish estate bottlings of Friuli from both native varieties, such as Tocai and Ribolla, and the international elite.

95

Cool conditions along the southern flank of the Alps heighten aroma in whites, notably from Alto Adige, and lend finesse to sparkling wines from Pinots and Chardonnay, a speciality of Trentino. Soave is still Italy's best known dry white abroad, though Pinot Grigio and Chardonnay from the Venezie are more in demand at home. Bubbly Prosecco, a favourite in Venice, is also gaining rapidly beyond the Veneto.

Still, though it might not seem that way, the three regions make more red wine than white. Valpolicella and Bardolino, from blends of native grapes, are rivalled in volume by Merlot and Cabernet from the eastern Veneto and Friuli. Schiava (or Vernatsch) prevails in Trentino-Alto Adige in the pale reds of Kalterersee (Caldaro) and St. Magdalener (Santa Maddalena). Trends favour the light and fruity in *vini novelli* and spritzy reds, as well as rosé and *chiaretto*. But all regions also make reds of durable class from native vines: Alto Adige's Lagrein, Trentino's Teroldego, Friuli's Refosco and Schioppettino, and Verona's Amarone, whose mellowed corpulence contrasts with the youthful vigour of its kindred Valpolicella. Despite wide diffusion in the Venezie, the Bordeaux varieties rarely make wines that might be considered "world class". Whether they consist of Cabernet or Merlot alone or in blends, they are often criticized for grassy, bitter flavours that have been attributed to the nature of their terrains but might as well be due to big yields. In the past

vine nurseries based mainly in Friuli-Venezia Giulia often propagated locally selected Cabernet Franc and Merlot to meet demands for productivity, though a recent emphasis on French clones, Cabernet Sauvignon in particular, has led to notable improvements from certain producers in all three regions.

White wine varieties are gaining ground steadily throughout the Venezie. The trend picked up momentum with Pinot Grigio, whose fortunes may owe less to breed than to a name that conveys the notion that a Pinot can be uniquely Italian. Then came Chardonnay, a pleasant surprise to growers who had it in their vineyards but thought it was just another Pinot. Much Chardonnay, like so many of the Venezie's whites, has a fresh, easy manner that may explain both why it pleases Italians and why doubts have been raised about its authenticity abroad. Few of the bargain-priced early versions resembled the amply structured, oaked wines from France or California. Recently, though, some producers have approached international levels for Chardonnay in both quality and price by using clones from Burgundy and maturing the wines in barrels of French oak.

Yet wood is no prerequisite for most of the Venezie's fine whites. Friuli's wines have won growing praise abroad for a purity of line and harmony of components that takes more talent to create than a mouthful of liquid oak. Growers there showed that white wines crafted artistically from select batches of grapes or individual vineyards command a deservedly high price since yields in Friuli's hills are among the lowest in Italy. By contrast, growers in the Veneto and Trentino-Alto Adige, despite sterling records with DOC, average about 100 hectolitres of wine

Above: a vineyard in Trentino illustrates the pergola trentina *used for centuries along the Adige valley.*

per hectare. That rate is surpassed only in the Abruzzi and Emilia-Romagna, but nowhere else, not even in bulk wine strongholds of the south. The Veneto might explain that two-thirds of its vineyards are on plains, where it is hard to practice restraint. But in Trentino-Alto Adige, whose cramped hillsides should be reserved only for privileged vines, excess may be the main reason why the region isn't making its potential share of Europe's finest wines.

Gradually, though, more producers in the corner of the country with the most modern and efficient wine industry are becoming convinced that selection and care on a limited scale pays off in quality and prestige. So even in the regions with the best records for achievement, there is plenty of room for improvement.

Trentino-Alto Adige

Capital: Trento.
Provinces: Bolzano/Bozen (BZ), Trento (TN).
Area: 13,620 square kilometres (eleventh).
Population: 880,000 (sixteenth).

The Adige, Italy's second longest river, rises in an alpine lake and flows for a third of its 410-kilometre course to the Adriatic through the South Tyrol, where it is known in German as the Etsch. South of Bozen (or Bolzano), it follows a valley between the Rhaetian Alps and the Dolomites down the Südtiroler Unterland into the province of Trento, past apple orchards and terraces of trellised wine gardens kept with a tidiness that everywhere in this Arcadian ambience seems more Teutonic than Latin. Yet the provincial boundary that crosses the river between Salurn (or Salorno) in what most Italians call Alto Adige and Roverè della Luna in Trentino divides two alpine enclaves that no hyphen could ever unite.

The South Tyrol, ceded to Italy by Austria after World War I, is the province of Bolzano, whose autonomy makes it officially bilingual and gives citizens certain privileges. But its German-speaking majority represents a discordant minority within the region which encompasses the autonomous province of Trento. This union is also awkward to the people of Trentino, whose perennial buffering between two contrasting cultures has left them with a somewhat ambivalent sense of identity. South Tyroleans have not adjusted well to being Italian, even if most speak the language and shun the independence drive by fanatics whose terrorist acts are the events that draw the most attention from the outside world to this otherwise peaceful place. Though few German-speaking citizens hold any hope of returning to Austria, many cling proudly to old country ways.

The South Tyrol is the oldest wine zone of German-speaking Europe. There the Romans supposedly discovered the use of wooden barrels for ageing and transporting wine, including Rhaetic. They also found vines trained onto wood frames (rather than trees), forerunners of the *pergola trentina* still used from the South Tyrol to Verona. Trentino traces its viticulture to the Etruscans, as symbolized by the *situla*, a wine vase found in the Cembra valley that was used for homages to the gods in the sixth or seventh century BC. The area's wines were lauded during the sixteenth-century Council of Trent, a highlight in a long and fruitful heritage.

Today, even if growers go their own ways, Trentino and Alto Adige do have common bonds, such as a full range of native and foreign vines and enviable efficiency in making and selling wines from them. On paper, at least, the region has the nation's top standards. About 55 percent of wine is DOC and more than a third is exported outside Italy. The wine schools at San Michele all'Adige and Laimburg are among the most active and admired. Yet, whatever the records, it might be argued that both provinces are chronic underachievers with wine, for steady good quality isn't enough from terraces hewn from rock and bedecked with pergolas that represent some of the wine world's most elaborate and costly engineering feats. These alpine slopes boast conditions for refined reds and, even more clearly, for graceful whites that could rank with Europe's elite.

Both Trentino and Alto Adige are known elsewhere in Italy, and increasingly abroad, for Pinot Grigio and Chardonnay whose popularity shows no sign of ebbing. Yet, despite demand for those and other whites, the emphasis remains on reds, for which the region serves as central Europe's bargain basement. In Austria, Switzerland, and Germany, the Südtirol signifies fleeting reds in big bottles with metal caps. Trentino bolsters the flow north, much of it in tankers. So in valleys so cramped for space that there should be no alternative to the quest of excellence, the leading vines are Vernatsch in the South Tyrol and a native strain of Lambrusco in Trentino. Vernatsch, or Schiava, can make delectable reds, best expressed in what are known in German as Kalterersee and St. Magdalener. Trentino's Marzemino is also nicely quaffable, though the native Teroldego, like the South Tyrol's Lagrein, shows more authority. At best, both are more distinctive than the Cabernet, Merlot, and Pinot Nero that are only rarely outstanding here. But domination by red varieties contradicts the growing conviction that Trentino-Alto Adige ought to be white wine country.

A reluctance to strive for the optimum may reflect producers' doubts that customers used to bargains would pay the price of excellence. Wine houses have trouble acquiring top quality grapes, since growers hesitate to reduce yields below the often excessive permitted DOC levels, even when favourable prices are offered. Farmers often find it easier and more profitable to grow apples, of which the region is a prime producer. Many growers have joined forces in Italy's most efficient collective wineries, which in the province of Trento account for three-quarters of production and in Bolzano nearly two-thirds. In Trentino most of the marketing is coordinated by Càvit, whose selections set the standards for the province's producers. In Alto Adige the consortium of cooperatives chooses wines to be labelled with vineyard or estate names. Both provinces maintain dignified standards that reflect a broad base of technical proficiency. But rare indeed are examples of the stellar quality that should be achieved here regularly.

Chardonnay was the region's dominant white variety even before the name became popular over the last decade. But since much is grown in valley vineyards exploited for big yields, and since clones were originally chosen for sparkling wines, it often tends to be tastily anonymous. Lately, though, several producers in both provinces have indicated that a Burgundy style – with or without wood – is within reach. Some of Italy's better Pinot Grigio comes from here, though the light and bright type seems more saleable than the traditional ripe and fruity. Pinot Bianco can show more class, particularly in well aged bottles from those few producers who have kept the faith in longevity. This unexpected ageing capacity also characterizes Italy's most sumptuous aromatic wines from the heights of the South Tyrol and Trentino's Cembra area: Gewürztraminer, Riesling, Sylvaner, and Müller Thurgau, which is sometimes most impressive of all.

Yet arguably the finest whites to date have been *champenoise*, as pioneered by Giulio Ferrari of Trento early in the century and today made expertly in both provinces. Here the basic Chardonnay comes into its own in convincing Blanc de Blancs, though some winemakers prefer the structure and complexity built by adding Pinot Nero, Bianco, and Meunier. A revelation is Trentino's Vino Santo from Nosiola grown in the Valle dei Laghi, a rarity that ranks as one of Italy's most opulent dessert wines.

The still whites of Trentino-Alto Adige continue to trail those of Friuli in price and prestige. Despite the desire to move up market, many producers still rely on earnings from bottles of a litre or more. Some of the

Top: the Santa Maddalena or St. Magdalener classical zone is on steep hillsides above Bolzano. The heights above the city can be reached by a cable car that provides views over the vineyards to the Dolomites.
Bottom: the abbey of Novacella or Neustift near Bressanone has cellars for the white wines of the Isarco or Eisack valley, whose high vineyards are among the most northerly of Italy.

most inspired wines in both provinces emanate from merchant houses, which even when large can be admirably selective. But the habit of trying to suit everyone's taste – one South Tyrolean house lists 34 types of wine – means that oenologists' attention spans are stretched to the limits. Here, too, it is stylish to identify properties on labels, often with a reference to "maso" in Trentino or the suffix "hof" in the South Tyrol. Yet neither Trentino nor Alto Adige has developed a nucleus of estates that could give wine real status. Few large properties exist in the South Tyrol, where less than five percent of wine is bottled by growers. Since land is formidably expensive and prosperous small farmers refuse to sell anyway, producers who have tried to build estates have found it practically impossible to put together a coherent spread of vines. In Trentino, only six percent of production is estate bottled, though the field does include a number of respected names among winemakers who just lately have shown more enterprise than their cautious and insular neighbours to the north.

Trentino-Alto Adige's Vineyards

The *pergola trentina* has typified viticulture in Trentino and the South Tyrol for centuries. Though expensive to build and maintain, the wooden pole arms, which are usually single on steep slopes and double on flatter terrain, permit lavish growth in the dominant Vernatsch and Lambrusco. The arbours form tunnels through which wafts the *ora*, the daily breeze

Below: grape pickers in vineyards near Trento.

from Lake Garda, drying grapes and foliage and preventing rot even in irrigated vineyards. White varieties seem to benefit from the leaf shading that slows ripening. Disadvantages of the pergola, apart from cost, are that it promotes excess if growth isn't controlled and that the shading can hinder ripening in some red varieties, perhaps accounting for the grassy, bitter flavours often noted in Cabernet and Merlot. But, even if some growers have switched to standard vertical systems of vine training, the pergola prevails with its canopies of green decorating hillsides from Merano to Verona.

Both provinces have healthy mixes of international varieties to complement native vines, which here, as elsewhere, have been steadily reduced. Of the 56 vines noted in the region a century ago, about 20 remain, but the only prominent natives are the South Tyrol's Vernatsch, Traminer, and Lagrein, and Trentino's Teroldego, Marzemino, and Nosiola. Vernatsch in its various clones covers two-thirds of the South Tyrol's vineyards. In Trentino, where it is known as Schiava, it figures in minor DOCs and vdt reds and rosés, though the even commoner Lambrusco a Foglia Frastagliata outweighs it. Cabernet, Merlot, and Pinot Nero, grown here since the mid-nineteenth century, seem to be losing ground in both provinces, though Cabernet Sauvignon has begun to replace the long prevalent Cabernet Franc.

The rise in white varieties is led by Chardonnay, dominant in Trentino and gaining in the South Tyrol, where vines were normally mixed with Pinot Bianco and Grigio. The Chardonnay for use in sparkling wines was selected primarily in Champagne; the Burgundy clones for richer still wines seem to have arrived only recently. Traminer, which may have originated at the Tyrolean village of Tramin, is much more diffused in the region than Gewürztraminer or Traminer Aromatico, though the two are often blended. Other Germanic varieties of Riesling Renano, Sylvaner Verde, Müller Thurgau, and Veltliner thrive in the South Tyrol's high vineyards, where they generally perform better than anywhere else in Italy. Though Sauvignon Blanc excels in places, it is still surprisingly rare.

The Agricultural Institute at San Michele all'Adige, a national leader in vine research, has been studying methods of mountain viticulture using compact, efficient machines to reduce the manual labour that has forced growers to abandon high vineyards, despite their superior quality potential. Among vines developed at the school is Rebo, a cross between Marzemino and Merlot. Oddities in Alto Adige include Weisserterlaner, which was the base of Terlan whites until Pinot Bianco and Chardonnay took over, and Blauer Portugieser, the Austrian vine used in Vinschgau or Val Venosta for vdt reds. Kerner, the German cross by pollination of Riesling and Vernatsch (or Trollinger) is sometimes used in white vdt and blends. The rare Rotberger, a cross of the same vines, has dark grapes used for light reds or rosés. The following varieties are associated primarily with Trentino or Alto Adige:

Lagrein. The vine was cited in the seventeenth century by Benedictines at the monastery of Muri on the edge of Bolzano at Gries, where it still reaches peaks, though the name suggests origins in Trentino's Lagarina valley. Prized in the South Tyrol in dark, robust Dunkel and fragrant Kretzer (one of Italy's best rosés), it also does well in Trentino's Rotaliano plain.

Lambrusco a Foglia Frastagliata. This "slashed leaf" Lambrusco seems to be a native of Trentino and unrelated to Emilian varieties of the name. As the province's most heavily planted red variety, it figures in blends of Casteller and Valdadige Rosso, as well as table wines.

Marzemino. Probably of Austrian origin, the vine, also known as Berzemino among many synonyms, has been widely planted in northern Italy since the sixteenth century. Today it is most at home in Trentino's Vallagarina, where it makes reds of rustic tang, usually drunk young. Elsewhere in the Tre Venezie, Lombardy, and Emilia-Romagna it is used mainly for blending.

Above: vineyards near the lake of Caldaro are noted for their picturesque settings and their light red wine known in German as Kalterersee.

Moscato Giallo or **Goldmuskateller**. This yellow or golden Muscat, though one of a vast family, is grown almost exclusively in the region for a bit of aromatic sweet golden wine and very little dry white.

Moscato Rosa or **Rosenmuskateller**. This rare dark Muscat, which apparently came from Yugoslavia's Dalmatia, makes exquisitely fragrant pink dessert wines that are DOC in Alto Adige, where it reaches peaks, and Trentino. It is occasionally found in Friuli.

Nosiola. The apparently indigenous Nosiola Trentina or Spinarola is the source of Vino Santo and distinctive dry whites in Trentino, where it is found almost exclusively.

Roter Malvasier. The fading source of a DOC red in Alto Adige may be related to dark Malvasia of Apulia or other places, though origins are uncertain.

Sylvaner Verde or **Grüner Silvaner**. The vine, once widely planted in German-speaking countries, in Italy is found mainly in the South Tyrol's Isarco valley, where it makes steely dry whites, sometimes of real character.

Teroldego. Origins are uncertain, though the name might derive from Tiroler Gold or the German word "Teer" (meaning tar because of its characteristic flavour), or from an apparently unrelated vine of Verona known as Terodola. What is certain is that Teroldego, which was cited in 1480 and mentioned in literature at the sixteenth-century Council of Trent, makes noble red wines only in Trentino's Rotaliano plain.

Veltliner. The early ripening Roter (red) Veltliner, used sparingly for fleeting whites in the Isarco valley, is not to be confused with Austria's Grüner Veltliner, which is rarely seen in Italy. It probably originated in Lombardy's Valtellina where it is called Rossola Nera.

Vernatsch or **Schiava**. Origins may be Slavic, but Vernatsch's home is the South Tyrol as the base for St. Magdalener, Kalterersee, Meraner Hugel, Bozner Leiten, Alto Adige Vernatsch/Schiava, as well as vdt. It is also essential in Trentino Schiava, Casteller, and Valdadige Rosso. The most popular subvariety is Grossvernatsch (Schiava Grossa) due to steady high yields. The greyish-hued Grauvernatsch (Schiava Grigia) makes finer wines but yields less and is prone to maladies. The small-berried Kleinvernatsch and Mittervernatsch (both Schiava Gentile in Italian) ripen early and yield little but their wines are noted for bouquet. The clone called Tschaggele, which produces small bunches of large berries, makes good wines but ripening is irregular. Schiava is also planted in northern Lombardy and around Verona. In Germany's Württemberg, Grossvernatsch is called Trollinger, from Tirolinger, in reference to the Tyrol.

Other varieties

Other varieties recommended or approved in Trentino-Alto Adige include:

For red (or rosé): Cabernet Franc, Cabernet Sauvignon, Merlot, Negrara Trentina, Pavana, Pinot Nero, Portoghese/Blauer Portugieser, Rebo.

For white: Bianchetta Trevigiana, Chardonnay, Incrocio Manzoni 6.0.13, Kerner, Müller Thurgau, Pinot Bianco, Riesling Italico, Riesling Renano, Sauvignon, Trebbiano Toscano.

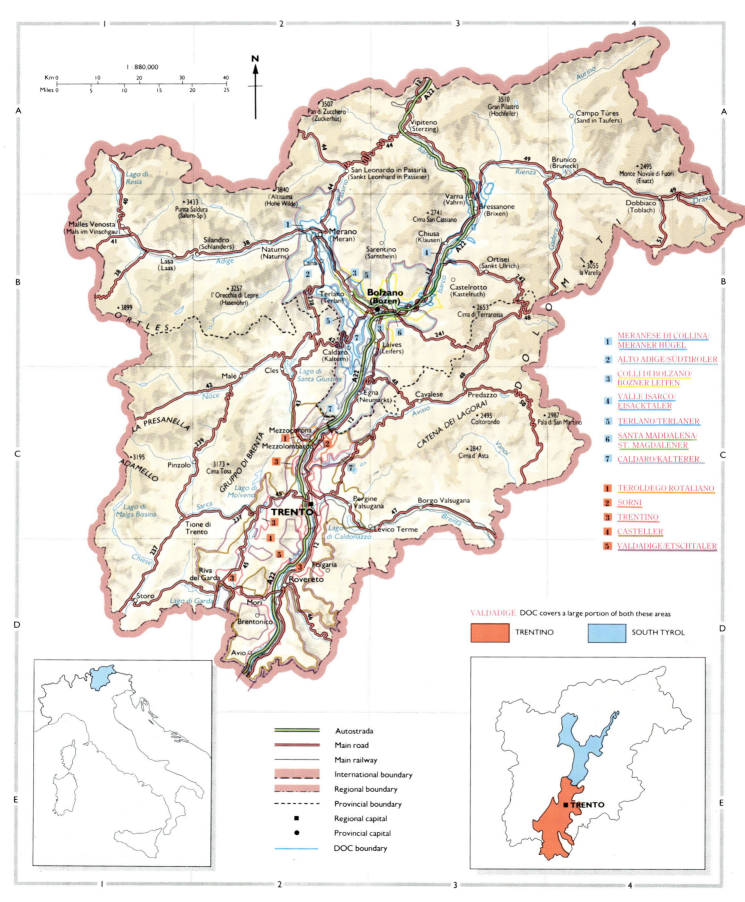

Km 0   10   20   30   40
1 : 880,000
Miles 0   5   10   15   20   25

N

▲3507
Pan di Zucchero
(Zuckerhút)

▲3510
Gran Pilastro
(Hochfeiler)

Campo Túres
(Sand in Taufers)

Vipiteno
(Sterzing)

49

Brunico
(Bruneck)

▲2495
Monte Novale di Fuori
(Eisatz)

San Leonardo in Passiria
(Sankt Leonhard in Passeier)

Varna
(Vahrn)

Rienza

49

Dobbiaco
(Toblach)

Drava

▲3840
l'Altissima
(Hohe Wilde)

Bressanone
(Brixen)

▲3433
Punta Saldura
(Salurn-Sp.)

Merano
(Meran)

▲2741
Cima San Cassiano

Chiusa
(Klausen)

Malles Venosta
(Mals im Vinschgau)

Silandro
(Schlanders)

Naturno
(Naturns)

Sarentino
(Sarnthein)

Ortisei
(Sankt Ulrich)

Lasa
(Laas)

Adige

Lana

Terlano
(Terlan)

Castelrotto
(Kastelruth)

▲3257
l'Orecchia di Lepre
(Hasenöhrl)

Bolzano
(Bozen)

▲2653
Cima di Terrarossa

▲3899

ORTLES

Caldaro
(Kaltern)

Laives
(Leifers)

Cles

Lago di
Santa Giustina

Male

Egna
(Neumarkt)

Cavalese

Predazzo

Noce

▲2495
Coltorondo

▲2987
Pala di San Martino

LA PRESANELLA

Mezzocorona

Avisio

CATENA DEI LAGORAI

Mezzolombardo

Pinzolo

Cima Tosa
▲3173

GRUPPO DI BRENTA

▲2847
Cima d'Asta

Vanoi

ADAMELLO

▲3195

Lago di
Molveno

Sarca

Pergine
Valsugana

Borgo Valsugana

Lago di
Malga Bissina

TRENTO

Brenta

Tione di
Trento

Levico Terme

Lago di
Caldonazzo

Chiese

Folgaria

Riva
del Garda

Rovereto

Storo

Mori

Lago di Garda

Brentonico

Avio

DOC areas

VALDADIGE DOC covers a large portion of both these areas

■ TRENTINO   ■ SOUTH TYROL

Legend

━━━ Autostrada
━━━ Main road
──── Main railway
▬▬▬ International boundary
▬▬▬ Regional boundary
---- Provincial boundary
■ Regional capital
● Provincial capital
━━━ DOC boundary

TRENTO

Trentino-Alto Adige's Wine Zones

Italy's northernmost region is enveloped by the Alps, whose slopes were sculpted mainly by glaciers and mountain streams until man built the terraces that testify to his fortitude. Agriculture here is an age-old challenge, since only about five percent of land lies below 500 metres and only 15 percent of the rocky surface is cultivable. Most vineyards lie along the few flat shoulders of the Adige and Sarca rivers or on arboured terraces that reach vertiginous heights in the Isarco and Cembra valleys. Terrains are based on dolomite and limestone in glacial or alluvial deposits of gravel, sand, or clay. Though not fertile, they are usually light and well drained, so almost ideal for vines. The splendid green colours of these valleys in summer is due to ample rainfall or irrigation from alpine springs. Weather varies from sub-arctic at the heights of the Ortles and Dolomites to practically Mediterranean at the northern tip of Lake Garda. The alpine cold, usually with plenty of snow in winter, can bring damaging spring frosts. Summers, normally warm and sunny, can be torrid on the valley floors. Temperature fluctuations, also from day to night, heighten flavour and aroma in wines. All but remote areas benefit from the drying and cooling effects of the *ora*, the breeze that wafts from Garda up the valleys as far as Merano and Bressanone.

Alto Adige/South Tyrol

Nearly all vineyards are along the Adige and Isarco valleys on south-facing slopes or terraces. Yet confinement does not limit options at altitudes ranging from 250 metres at Bolzano to 1,000 metres above Bressanone and at Fennberg, creating dramatically diverse conditions in the five main DOC zones.

The Isarco/Eisack valley

Italy's most northerly DOC zone, Valle Isarco/Eisacktaler, also has some of the highest vineyards in gravelly soil between Bolzano and Vahrn, north of Bressanone. Cool, often damp conditions favour white varieties, notably Sylvaner, though Müller Thurgau also thrives. Pergolas are lower here, to take advantage of ground heat, though vertical training in some vineyards allows grapes to ripen in direct sunlight.

Merano/Meran

Hills above the city are noted mainly for Vernatsch under the DOC Meraner Hügel, though cool conditions on slopes above the Adige also favour white varieties and Pinot Nero. To the west is the Vinschgau or Venosta valley, which makes a bit of rare red and white vdt.

Terlano and the Bolzano basin

The whites of Terlano/Terlan, including fine Sauvignon and Pinot Bianco, come from gentle slopes along the Adige northeast of Bolzano, though the zone extends south past the lake of Caldaro/Kaltern. The Bolzano basin, at the confluence of the Adige, Isarco, and Talvera rivers, is often the hottest point in the province. The city is noted primarily for the red St. Magdalener, whose classical area is on steep slopes just to the north. A simpler Vernatsch wine is Colli di Bolzano/Bozner Leiten. Vaunted Lagrein comes from sandy flats at Gries on the edge of town. Towards Terlano lies Siebeneich, source of sometimes outstanding Merlot.

Überetsch and Caldaro/Kaltern

Überetsch, the rolling high plain across the Adige from Bolzano, makes a giant share of the province's wine from densely planted vineyards around Appiano/Eppan, Caldaro/Kaltern, and Cornaiano/Girlan. Vernatsch prevails in Kalterersee from the classical area around the lake, but vineyards are also a key source of Alto Adige/Südtiroler DOC wines often processed in large wineries. Though overall quality is admirable, the habit of big yields here has inhibited production of what might be some of northern Italy's finest whites and reds.

The Südtiroler Unterland

Below Caldaro the Adige valley widens into the Südtiroler Unterland, with noted wine towns and vineyard sites along the steep edges and even in the plains. Tramin is known for Gewürztraminer that was named for the town and thrives at Söll on slopes above it. Also on the western side is Cortaccia/Kurtatsch, whose steep terraces climb to Fennberg at 1,000 metres where Müller Thurgau excels. The villages of Magrè/Margreid and Cortina/Kurtinig are on gravelly plains that render Pinots and Chardonnay for sparkling wines, as well as good Cabernet. Across the river above Egna/Neumarkt lie the villages of Montan, Pinzon, and Mazzon, all noted for Pinot Nero and Gewürztraminer, though other white varieties also thrive. Growers of Salorno/Salurn specialize in the Pinots and Chardonnay, which excel from high vineyards around the village of Buchholz.

Trentino

The province's vineyards, mainly along the Adige and Sarca valleys, are on average somewhat lower and warmer than Alto Adige's, and slightly more productive, due to the prevalence of Lambrusco, though growers have been raising standards with nobler varieties.

Campo Rotaliano

The broad plain where the Noce river meets the Adige is known for Teroldego, which is unsurpassed from the sandy lime soils on a gravel base around Mezzolombardo and Mezzocorona. Lagrein and white varieties also do well. Just above the plain around Roverè della Luna, vineyards are noted for Chardonnay and Pinot used in sparkling wines.

Sorni and the Cembra valley

The hills east of the Adige between San Michele and Lavis in the Sorni DOC zone have a mixture of soils and microclimates favourable to a range of red and white varieties. High points around Faedo make notable Müller Thurgau, Nosiola, and Chardonnay. The spectacular terraces of the Cembra valley between Giovo and Faver were carved out of masses of purple-hued porphyritic rock on which Schiava prevails, though Pinots, Chardonnay, and Müller Thurgau give results of a higher order.

Vallagarina and Isera

Vallagarina between Trento and the Veneto is the province's largest vineyard area with diverse natural conditions to account for the mix of vines. Marzemino thrives in the dark basalt soils of Isera, across the Adige from Rovereto. Chardonnay and the Pinots are planted nearly everywhere from the sandy banks of the Adige to terraces ascending the rocky mountain walls. Cabernet and Merlot do well in places, though Lambrusco and Schiava claim more of the valuable space.

The Valle dei Laghi

The influence of Lake Garda makes the valley of the Sarca and the lakes of Cavedine, Toblino, and Santa Massenza mild enough for lemons and olives as well as most of the province's vines. Many varieties do well in the calcareous terrain where vineyards are wafted not only by the daily *ora* but also the nightly *pelér*. The speciality is Vino Santo from Nosiola, whose long drying process is favoured by the cool, dry microclimate in the northern sector around Calavino, Santa Massenza, and Lasino.

Wines of the South Tyrol

The sense of order that has made the South Tyrol Italy's most proficient source of classified wine is the positive side of a heritage that in other ways holds the industry back. A majority of the province's impeccable vineyards furnish German-speaking neighbours with inexpensive reds, even if wine drinkers elsewhere would be willing to pay more for perfumed whites. The stubborn preference for Vernatsch over nobler vines is just one of the ambiguities that make this gorgeous alpine province hard for outsiders – including other Italians – to understand. Even foreigners who can point to it on a map may take a while to grasp that Alto Adige, the South Tyrol or Südtirol, and the province of Bolzano or Bozen are one and the same. Labels are equally confusing, since they may be in either of two languages or both, with appellations given as DOC, VQPRD, or QbA (for Qualitätswein bestimmter Anbaugebiete, the only zone outside West Germany that may use the term). The province is often likened to Alsace, due to their similarities in wines, language, and political histories. But there is nothing else quite like the South Tyrol, splendidly isolated within its mountain walls, as if defying the rest of the world to come and find it.

That challenge is worth the trip, for there are few other places where young wines flow so freely or where vineyards boast backdrops as majestic as the Dolomites. A hefty share of wine is drunk by tourists who cross the Brenner or Reschen passes to bask in the southern alpine sun and propose toasts of "Prosit!" in the warm, wood-panelled Weinstüben. Italy's most travelled wine road must be the Südtiroler Weinstrasse that winds through dense vineyards in the Überetsch, the rolling hills across the Adige from Bolzano, and the Unterland, the mountainsides and plains along both sides of the river from Tramin south to Trentino. But even visitors who understand the Austrian dialect may be baffled by the multitude of varieties or the intermingling appellations that cover them and return to the old reliable Vernatsch reds of Kalterersee and St. Magdalener. Few wines are so enchanting when drunk amidst their vineyards on arbours around the jewel-like lake of Caldaro (or Kaltern) and on steep terraces around the church of St. Magdalena above Bolzano. Other reds pack more wallop, notably Cabernet, Merlot, and Bolzano's other favourite Lagrein. Sometimes even Pinot Nero can be impressive.

But, as growers admit (if reluctantly), the wave of the future favours whites. Yet those blossomy examples that in the 1970s began to draw interest from the previously ignored Italian market have rarely reached the pinnacles expected. The unshakeable habit of big yields and the expedient of robot-like technology combine in wines that are

Below: the vineyards of Alto Adige produce the nation's highest percentage of DOC in wines whose names are given in both Italian and German.

always acceptable but rarely extraordinary. Opportunistic blending in supposedly pure varietals (chiefly "Pinot Grigio") has further compromised character. Natural conditions here seem unsurpassed for some white varieties, but selection of clones and vineyard sites often have been haphazard. So evidence of superiority is the exception rather than the rule: in wines from the brilliant but erratic Giorgio Grai; from the shrewd but cautious Herbert Tiefenbrunner; from Paolo Foradori at Hofstätter; Werner Walch at Wilhelm Walch; Dieter Rudolph at Castel Schwanburg; Franz Stocker at the cooperative of Terlan. Finally, though, Alois Lageder, young namesake of an old family winery, seems to be giving the South Tyrol the leadership it lacked. His prestige wines, all DOC, are Chardonnay and Cabernet Sauvignon Löwengang, Sauvignon Lehenhof, Pinot Grigio Benefizium Porer, and Pinot Bianco Haberlehof. They not only name the estates or *crus*, they back them with the kind of class that ranks them with the nation's elite. Lageder might be a star of Italian wine if he lived closer to the mainstream. But, since he has few vineyards of his own, he relies on purchased grapes. This means that he, like the few other imaginative and inspired producers here, has to pursue his aims with uncommon patience.

Alto Adige has the nation's best record with DOC, which accounts for about two-thirds of volume, though it could be more since nearly all of the province's vineyards are registered. The bulk is Kalterersee, a wine rarely seen under its Italian name of Caldaro. The basic appellation is Alto Adige or Südtiroler with 19 types of wine from a zone that covers most of the vineyard area except Isarco/Eisacktaler. Varieties are duplicated in zones it overlaps: in Terlano/Terlan, which is noted for whites; in the Vernatsch wines of Kalterersee, St. Magdalener, Bozner Leiten, and Meraner Hügel; as well as the extra-regional category of Valdadige/Etschtaler (*see* Trentino). Most growers stick to their specialities, but wine houses and cooperatives – many of which also make both up-market and ordinary table wines – have more options than they can comfortably deal with. The frenzy of harvesting and vinifying so many different varieties separately means that in some wineries quality varies sharply from year to year. In the following DOCs, Italian names and terms are given first in keeping with the national code, though labels are still primarily in German.

Alto Adige/Südtiroler (1975)

This wide-ranging zone provides many of the South Tyrol's fine whites, as well as the only classified reds from Lagrein, Cabernet, Merlot, Pinot Nero, Malvasier, and Moscato Rosa. Most vineyards lie south of Bolzano, in the Überetsch, the Caldaro/Kaltern area, and the Südtiroler Unterland, though the zone also reaches northeast from the Bolzano basin along the Adige past Merano. Most terraces are devoted to Vernatsch, particularly around Caldaro, Bolzano, and Merano. Though quantities are limited, Italy's finest Gewürztraminer, Riesling Renano, and Goldmuskateller originate

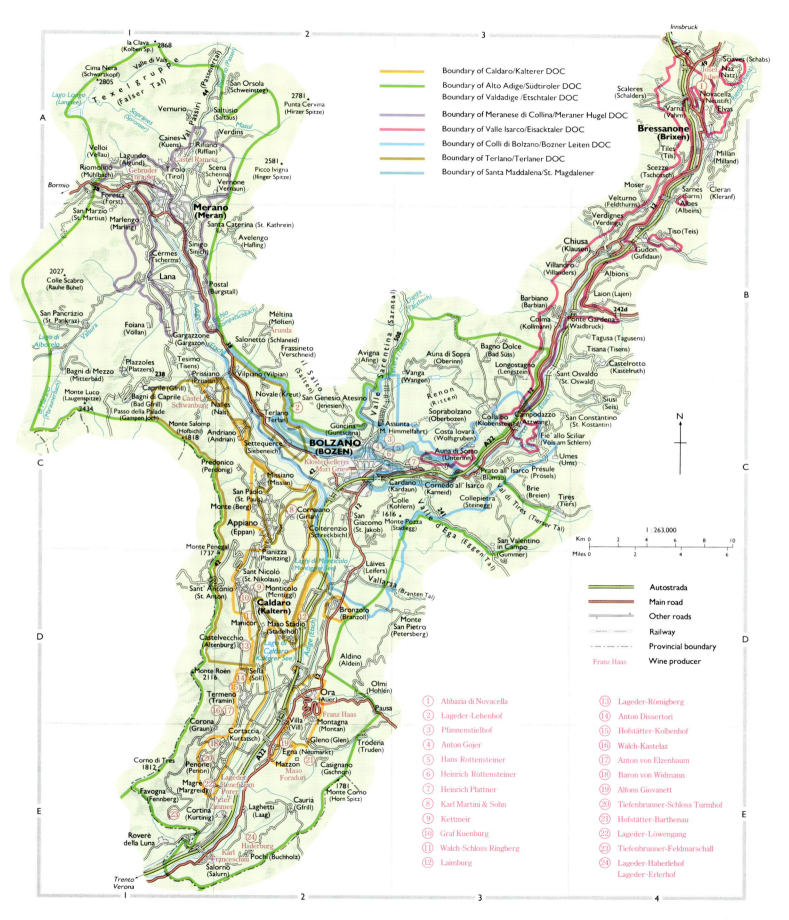

Boundary of Caldaro/Kalterer DOC

Boundary of Alto Adige/Südtiroler DOC
Boundary of Valdadige /Etschtaler DOC

Boundary of Meranese di Collina/Meraner Hügel DOC

Boundary of Valle Isarco/Eisacktaler DOC

Boundary of Colli di Bolzano/Bozner Leiten DOC

Boundary of Terlano/Terlaner DOC

Boundary of Santa Maddalena/St. Magdalener

1 : 263,000

Km 0   2   4   6   8   10
Miles 0   2   4   6

Autostrada

Main road

Other roads

Railway

Provincial boundary

Franz Haas   Wine producer

① Abbazia di Novacella
② Lageder-Lehenhof
③ Pfannenstielhof
④ Anton Gojer
⑤ Hans Rottensteiner
⑥ Heinrich Rottensteiner
⑦ Heinrich Plattner
⑧ Karl Martini & Sohn
⑨ Kettmeir
⑩ Graf Kuenburg
⑪ Walch-Schloss Ringberg
⑫ Laimburg

⑬ Lageder-Römigberg
⑭ Anton Dissertori
⑮ Hofstätter-Kolbenhof
⑯ Walch-Kastelaz
⑰ Anton von Elzenbaum
⑱ Baron von Widmann
⑲ Alfons Giovanett
⑳ Tiefenbrunner-Schloss Turmhof
㉑ Hofstätter-Barthenau
㉒ Lageder-Löwengang
㉓ Tiefenbrunner-Feldmarschall
㉔ Lageder-Haberlehof
    Lageder-Erlerhof

here, along with first-rate Müller Thurgau. Their delicate, flowery aromas and refined flavours give them unexpected affinity with food. But their special character seems to limit their appeal, since other Italians often find them too aromatic and wine drinkers elsewhere resist them because they rarely show the full-blown qualities of their counterparts from Alsace. Pinot Bianco, better known as Weissburgunder, may be the most consistently good white of the province, though its firmness often needs time to show the style that Giorgio Grai expounds. The more immediate and voluptuous Pinot Grigio/Ruländer remains in vogue, thanks to the aggressive marketing of Santa Margherita. Chardonnay, when not made to be anonymous, combines subtle varietal traits with enviable drinkability, notably in Tiefenbrunner's Turmhof. But so far the most convincing barrel-aged versions of Chardonnay are Lageder's Löwengang and Portico dei Leoni.

Among dark varieties, Lagrein from Bolzano's vineyards at Gries stands out. The Dunkel is a muscular red of pronounced character and the Kretzer is a gracious rosé, but neither type has caught on elsewhere. Cabernet here had long been noted for bitter, grassy flavours that some described as *goût de terroir*, others attributed to incomplete ripening under the arbours, and still others blamed on the dominance of the Franc subvariety. Yet some fine Cabernet had been made over the years, by Giorgio Grai and, in a potent style, by Castel Schwanburg. Lately, more Cabernet Sauvignon has been planted, not only along the gravelly banks of the Adige but up on the hills, and a few producers – notably Lageder with Löwengang – have achieved a more refined, international style. Merlot, as elsewhere, is too often pushed for high yields, yet certain vintages from Siebeneich (near Terlano) have shown undeniable class. Pinot Nero or Blauburgunder is appreciated locally, though only rarely does it resemble good Burgundy, most often in Hofstätter's Villa Barthenau from vineyards at the village of Mazzon. The red that has drawn most praise is Moscato Rosa or Rosenmuskateller, whose ruby rose colour, flowery aroma, and exquisitely fruity sweetness are exemplified by Kuenburg's Schloss Sallegg.

Zone: Slopes and stony plains through much of the viticultural area in 33 communes of Bolzano province. The territory overlaps all other DOC zones except Valle Isarco/Eisacktaler. Vineyards may not be higher than 700 m for red varieties or 900 m for white. Lagrein from the commune of Bolzano may be called Gries (the classical area) or Grieser Lagrein. Pinot Nero/

Blauburgunder from the village of Mazzon may use that name or Mazzoner.
The 19 types include 17 varietals of at least 95%, possibly complemented by other DOC grapes of the same colour. Schiava/ Vernatsch may consist of any or all subvarieties at 85% and other DOC red grapes up to 15%.
Cabernet (Cabernet Sauvignon/Cabernet Franc) Dry red. Yld 77/110, Alc 11.5, Acd 0.45, Ag riserva 2 yrs.
Chardonnay Dry white. Yld 91/130, Alc 11, Acd 0.5.
Lagrein Rosato/Lagrein Kretzer Dry rosé. Yld 98/140, Alc 11.5, Acd 0.45.
Lagrein Scuro/Lagrein Dunkel Dry red. Yld 98/140, Alc 11.5, Acd 0.45, Ag riserva 1 yr.
Malvasia/Malvasier Dry red. Yld 77/110, Alc 11.5, Acd 0.45.
Merlot Dry red. Yld 91/130, Alc 11, Acd 0.45, Ag riserva 1 yr.
Moscato Giallo/Goldenmuskateller or **Goldmuskateller** Sweet white. Yld 56/80, Alc 11, Acd 0.5.
Moscato Rosa/Rosenmuskateller Sweet rosé. Yld 39/60, Alc 12.5, Acd 0.55.
Müller Thurgau or **Riesling Sylvaner** Dry white. Yld 91/130, Alc 11, Acd 0.45.
Pinot Bianco/Weissburgunder Dry white, also spumante/Sekt. Yld 91/130, Alc 11, Acd 0.5.
Pinot Grigio/Ruländer Dry white, also spumante/Sekt. Yld 91/130, Alc 11.5, Acd 0.45.
Pinot Nero/Blauburgunder Dry red, also white or rosé as spumante/Sekt. Yld 84/120, Alc 11.5, Acd 0.45, Ag riserva (rosso only) 1 yr.
Riesling Italico/Welschriesling Dry white. Yld 91/130, Alc 11, Acd 0.5.
Riesling Renano/Rheinriesling Dry white. Yld 84/120, Alc 11, Acd 0.5.
Sauvignon Dry white. Yld 84/120, Alc 11.5, Acd 0.5.
Schiava/Vernatsch Dry red. Yld 98/140, Alc 10.5, Acd 0.4.
Spumante Sparkling white. Grapes: Pinot Bianco/Chardonnay 70%, Pinot Nero/Pinot Grigio up to 30%. Yld 91/130, Alc 11, Acd 0.45.
Sylvaner Dry white. Yld 91/130, Alc 11, Acd 0.5.
Traminer Aromatico/Gewürztraminer Dry white. Yld 84/120, Alc 11.5, Acd 0.45.

Valle Isarco/Eisacktaler (1974)

No wines speak more eloquently of the Alps than the whites of Isarco. Sylvaner, the dominant grape variety, with some ageing can rival the German Franken wines at heights in which Müller Thurgau also shows its best. Pinot Grigio and Gewürztraminer can show uncommon finesse. The bit of Veltliner, unique in Italy, is delicate and sprightly. Each shows its own style, yet they share a purity of line in rarefied aromas and brisk flavours unattainable in lower vineyards. This class, though by no means an annual feat, represents a triumph over natural hardships that few growers anywhere else would be

willing to put up with. The abbey of Novacella/Neustift is the symbolic winery in the classical zone above Bressanone, where the tiny Pacherhof excels with Müller Thurgau. Lower in the valley, the cooperative at Chiusa/ Klausen is noted for Müller Thurgau and Sylvaner.

Zone: Slopes as high as 800 m along both sides of the Isarco/Eisack river, extending from the edge of Bolzano northeast through 11 communes as far as Varna/Vahrn and Naz-Sciaves/Natz-Schab. Wines may carry the name Bressanone/Brixen (also Brixner) if they come from that commune or neighbouring Varna/Vahrn.
The five types are all pure varietals.
Müller Thurgau Dry white. Yld 91/130, Alc 10.5, Acd 0.5.
Pinot Grigio/Ruländer Dry white. Yld 70/100, Alc 11, Acd 0.5.
Sylvaner Dry white. Yld 91/130, Alc 10.5, Acd 0.5.
Traminer Aromatico/Gewürztraminer Dry white. Yld 70/100, Alc 11, Acd 0.5.
Veltliner Dry white. Yld 84/120, Alc 10.5, Acd 0.5.

Meranese di Collina/Meraner Hugel or Meranese/Meraner (1971)

Merano's long-standing tipple seems a bit more plump and perfumed than other Vernatsch reds. Perhaps that's because much of it comes from vineyards high on the "Hügel" (hill) around the castle from which the counts of Tyrol ruled in the Middle Ages when the territory was united. This accounts for the reference to wines from vineyards in the former county of Tirol as Burggräfler – "Burg" refers to the castle, "Grafen" to the counts – or Burgravio in Italian.

Zone: Slopes between 300-650 m exposed to the south and southwest around Merano and extending on either side of the Adige valley south to Lana and Gargazzone/ Gargazon through 13 communes in Bolzano province. Wines from vineyards in the former county of Tirol/Tirolo are entitled to the designation Burggräffler or Burgravio. Dry red. Grapes: Schiava (Grossa/Media/Piccola/ Gentile/Grigia/Tschaggele). Yld 87.5/125, Alc 10.5, Acd 0.4.

Terlano/Terlaner (1975)

Terlan has long been synonymous with white wine, primarily the Weissburgunder that used to represent the blend of Pinot Bianco and Chardonnay before those varieties were given separate status – though they still often grow together in the vineyards. An earlier speciality was Weisserterlaner, from a vine prone to maladies that has practically disappeared, to the regret of those old enough to remember its tasty wines. But the most promising variety of the zone, if grown in still limited quantities, is Sauvignon Blanc. The cooperative at Terlan succeeds admirably with that

and other varieties, as does Castel or Schloss Schwanburg at Nalles. Though Lageder's single-vineyard Terlaner Sauvignon Lehenhof, from high vineyards at Montigl, seems ever more clearly in a class by itself.

Zone: Slopes on both sides of the Adige river northwest of Bolzano in the communes of Terlano/Terlan, Nalles/Nals, and Andriano/ Andrian (the historical zone). The territory extends east to Meltina/Mölten and San Genésio/Jenesien and south to Appiano/ Eppan and Caldaro/Kaltern. Wines from Terlano may be called Classico or Klassischer, a privilege reserved for certain types from Nalles and Andriano.
The eight types include seven varietals of at least 90%, possibly complemented by other DOC grapes of the same colour, and the blend known as Terlano or Terlaner, which may also be spumante.
Chardonnay Dry white. Yld 91/130, Alc 11, Acd 0.5.
Müller Thurgau Dry white. Yld 91/130, Alc 11, Acd 0.45.
Pinot Bianco/Weissburgunder Dry white. Yld 91/130, Alc 11, Acd 0.5.
Riesling Italico/Welschriesling Dry white. Yld 91/130, Alc 10.5, Acd 0.5.
Riesling Renano/Rheinriesling Dry white. Yld 91/130, Alc 11.5, Acd 0.45.
Sauvignon Dry white. Yld 91/130, Alc 12, Acd 0.5.
Sylvaner Dry white. Yld 91/130, Alc 11.5, Acd 0.5.
Terlano/Terlaner Dry white, also spumante. Grapes: Pinot Bianco 50%, Riesling Italico/ Riesling Renano/Sauvignon/Sylvaner/Müller Thurgau up to 50%, other whites up to 5%. Yld 91/130, Alc 11.5, Acd 0.45.

Colli di Bolzano/Bozner Leiten (1975)

Bolzano's hillsides ("Leiten") supply the city with its spritzig red tavern wine. Though described as the poor man's St. Magdalener, whose zone it entirely surrounds, Bozner Leiten can upstage its famous neighbour as a thirst quencher.

Zone: Hills in seven communes in the Bolzano basin, on the east side of the Adige between Laives/Leifers and Terlano/ Terlan, and extending from the city south of the Isarco past Cornedo/Karneid to Fiè allo Sciliar/Vols am Schlern and north to San Genésio/Jenesien and Renon/ Ritten. Dry red. Grapes: Schiava; Lagrein/ Pinot Nero up to 10%. Yld 91/130, Alc 11, Acd 0.4.

Santa Maddalena/St. Magdalener (1971)

The queen of Vernatsch – there could hardly be a king of a group of vines whose Italian name means "slave girl" – has long reigned over the South Tyrol's reds. Though dainty like the others, St. Magdalener is fuller in colour and body, with more fruit in the flavour and less of that tell-tale almondy aftertaste. The finest – no grower seems

Above: the fortified rotunda of the chapel of St. Michael is part of the abbey of Novacella, whose vineyards climb the slopes.

more inspired than Heinrich Rottensteiner – comes from the so-called Klassisches Ursprungsgebiet, the classic vineyards whose terraced hillsides form an amphitheatre above Bolzano with the Rosengarten peaks of the Dolomites glowing from pink to purple in the background. Producers gained protection from imitators in 1931, a decade before the Fascist regime proclaimed Santa Maddalena one of Italy's three outstanding red wines. But even the Swiss, who buy most of it and rate it "Extra Class", might question that status today.

Zone: Slopes climbing from the edge of Bolzano into parts of the communes of Renon/Ritten, San Genésio/Jenesien, and Terlano/Terlan, though only wines from the historical vineyards east of the Talvera/Talfer river in the localities of St. Magdalena, St. Justina, St. Peter, Leitach, and Kosten all in Bolzano's commune may be called Classico or Klassischer. Dry red. Grapes: Schiava (Grossa/Media/Grigia/Tschaggele); Lagrein/Pinot Nero up to 10%. Yld 87.5/125, Alc 11.5, Acd 0.4.

Caldaro/Kalterer or **Lago di Caldaro/Kalterersee (1970)**

The most popular member of the Vernatsch clan and the region's most voluminous DOC, this perky pale red to garnet pink beverage is known to most admirers as Kalterersee. Its home base is the lake that glistens amidst terraces of vines – a mecca for wine lovers and windsurfers – though its vineyards range much farther afield. Kalterersee may well be dismissed by a Feinschmecker (a German-speaking gourmet), but when young and fresh it's as quaffable as a red wine can be, with an undeniable affinity for local dishes, such as sausages and sauerkraut, the dumplings called "Knödel", and the smoked bacon known as "Speck". At best it can match St. Magdalener in style. The Classico/Klassischer area has been stretched too far to mean much and *superiore* merely indicates that the wine has the basic level of alcohol. *Auslese* or *scelto*, which suggests special selection, really means only that the wine is pure Vernatsch and a half degree stronger than normal.

Zone: Slopes around the lake of Caldaro/Kalterersee in the Überetsch and part of the Unterland in the nine communes of Bolzano province where wines may be called Classico or Klassischer. The territory also extends north as far as Nalles and south into Trentino to the Rotaliano plain and the Cembra valley in eight communes in Trento province. Dry red. Grapes: Schiava Grossa/Schiava Gentile/Schiava Grigia; Pinot Grigio/Lagrein up to 15%. Scelto or Auslese must be pure Schiava. Yld 98/140, Alc 10.5 (scelto or Auslese 11), Acd 0.4.

Other wines of note

Despite its record with DOC, a fair share of South Tyrolean wine manages to remain unclassified. One example is Feldmarschall, the Müller Thurgau from Tiefenbrunner, whose vineyards are too high to be approved. A number of up-market bottlings, mainly reds, are vdt because they consist of blends. Some are cited under producers. Others, mainly from Vernatsch, come in outsized bottles for everyday drinking. An example is the vdt known as Tiroler Leiten, popular in Switzerland. The only vineyard area outside DOC is Vinschgau or Val Venosta, along the upper Adige, where local reds from Portugieser and whites can be tasty.

ESTATES/GROWERS

(Those estates listed without comment are recommended for at least one type of Alto Adige DOC.)

Baron Georg von Widmann, Cortaccia/Kurtatsch (BZ). Andreas von Widmann makes good Cabernet and Lagrein from various family plots in choice sites.

Anton Dissertori-Plattenhof, Termeno/Tramin (BZ). Noted Gewürztraminer from vineyards at Söll.

Karl Franceschini, Salorno/Salurn (BZ).

Anton Gojer-Glögglhof, Bolzano. Good St. Magdalener from the heart of the zone, as well as *barrique*-aged Lagrein Dunkel.

Haderburg, Salorno/Salurn (BZ). The Ochsenreiter family makes respected Haderburg Brut and Nature *champenoise* from their own vineyards at Buchholz, where they have also begun work on promising still wines.

Josef Huber-Pacherhof, Bressanone/Brixen (BZ). Excellent Müller Thurgau from vineyards high above Novacella/Neustift.

Graf Eberhard Kuenburg-Schloss Sallegg, Caldaro/Kaltern (BZ). Kuenburg selects from several plots for a range of wines vinified in the cellars of the splendid castle. The speciality is a late harvest Rosenmuskateller, which when right is the most exquisite of its name. Kalterersee from the Bischofsleiten and Lotterbrunnen vineyards is also fine.

Maso Foradori, Mazzon (BZ). Foradori of Mezzolombardo in Trentino makes a fine Gewürztraminer from vineyards here.

Pfannenstielhof, Bolzano. Eduard Pfeifer makes good St. Magdalener.

Heinrich Plattner, Bolzano. St. Magdalener from Waldgrieshof vineyards at St. Justina.

Heinrich Rottensteiner, Bolzano. A grower of uncommon dedication and integrity makes St. Magdalener as it was meant to be from classical vineyards at Obermoserhof.

Gebrüder Torggler, Merano (BZ). Meraner Hügel from Haisreiner vineyards.

WINE HOUSES/MERCHANTS

Abbazia di Novacella/Stiftskellerei Neustift, Varna/Vahrn (BZ). The abbey, a landmark in the scenic Isarco valley, bottles classical Müller Thurgau and Sylvaner entitled to the designation Brixner.

Arunda/Vivaldi, Meltina/Mölten (BZ). Josef Reiterer makes exemplary *champenoise* Brut and Extra Brut under the Vivaldi label at his home in an alpine village in what may be the highest cellars anywhere at 1,150 m.

Josef Brigl, Cornaiano/Girlan (BZ).

Castel/Schloss Rametz, Merano (BZ). The imposing castle was long noted as a quality leader in the region. Today the firm makes a range of modern DOCs and *champenoise* Castel Monreale and Schloss Königsberg Brut.

Castel/Schloss Schwanburg, Nalles/Nals (BZ). At his lovely old family castle Dieter Rudolph produces admired Terlano and Alto Adige DOCs, as well as the *barrique*-aged vdt Castel Schwanburg from Cabernet and Merlot. Most grapes come from 27.5 ha of vines on slopes below the landmark castle, though some are bought in.

Alfons Giovanett-Castelfeder, Egna/Neumarkt (BZ). A solid producer of Alto Adige DOCs is most noted for Gewürztraminer.

Giorgio Grai, Bolzano. Italy's paladin of the palate now bottles wines with his own signature rather than under the Bellendorf, Herrnhofer, and Kehlburg labels of the past. He tutors selections of the Tyrol's classics to exhibit more flavour and aroma than the norm and, above all, to improve with time. Pinot Bianco and Cabernet have often stood out, though Grai never makes a dull wine. But since he has more pressing things to do than distribute them, the only sure place to taste the wines are at his Edy Bar on Bolzano's Walther Platz. Grai is constantly on the move due to commitments with Gancia and the many cellars he advises, if often more in spirit than letter – owners, however, never hesitate to drop his name.

Franz Haas, Montagna/Montan (BZ). Emerging producer with good wines, led by a Pinot Nero, partly from his own Ordenthal vineyards.

Hirschprunn, Magrè/Margreid (BZ).

J. Hofstätter, Termeno/Tramin (BZ). Paolo Foradori runs this admired old family winery in the heart of Tramin, with 35 ha of vines in choice plots supplemented by grapes purchased from another 160 ha. Hofstätter is noted for Gewürztraminer from Kolbenhof above Tramin and Barthenau at Mazzon. Pinot Nero from Barthenau has often ranked with Italy's best. Kolbenhofer is a fine Vernatsch, De Vite a charming white from Kerner.

Kettmeir, Caldaro/Kaltern (BZ). The noted family house is still run by Franco Kettmeir, who sold controlling interest to Santa Margherita. A full range of regional wines is sold under the Kettmeir label, along with *spumante*.

Klosterkellerei Muri Gries, Bolzano. The cellars of the Benedictine monastery at Gries on the edge of Bolzano are noted for Lagrein, which invariably ranks with the finest, along with Alto Adige and Terlano DOCs.

Alois Lageder, Bolzano. The large family winery was founded in 1855 by the great-grandfather and namesake of

Above far left: Alois Lageder has built his long established family wine house in Bolzano into the province's leader with a series of single vineyard bottlings that carry his signature as well as the name Löwengang from the cellars at Magrè. Above: Giorgio Grai, one of Italy's most renowned oenologists, in his Edy Bar on Bolzano's Walther Platz where he serves a range of his own wines.

the current owner, who has made it the modern leader in the South Tyrol. Alois Lageder, sister Wendel, and brother-in-law and winemaker Luis von Dellemann select from 20 ha of their own, around Magrè/Margreid and Caldaro, and from growers with about 400 ha. Wines, nearly all DOC, are vinified and barrel-aged at the Löwengang cellars in Magrè and bottled at headquarters in Bolzano. The two prestige lines are Löwengang – for *barrique*-aged Chardonnay from Buchholz and Magrè, and Cabernet Sauvignon from Magrè and Caldaro – and the Alois Lageder single-vineyard wines: Terlaner Sauvignon Lehenhof (at Montigl), Pinot Bianco Haberlehof (at Buchholz), Pinot Grigio Benefizium Porer (at Magrè), and Chardonnay Erlerhof (at Buchholz). Other single vineyard bottlings are Kalterersee Auslese Römigberg, St. Magdalener Oberingramhof, Lagrein Dunkel Lindenburg, and Terlaner Tannhammerhof. *See also* Portico dei Leoni.

Laimburg, Ora/Auer (BZ). The agricultural school puts out good wines under the Laimburg label from 31 ha of vines.

Anton Lindner, San Michele-Appiano/St. Michael-Eppan (BZ).

H. Lun, Bolzano. Full range of wines, some under the name Sandbichler.

Karl Martini & Sohn, Cornaiano/Girlan (BZ). Among a range of DOCs, good Kalterersee from the Felton and Justina vineyards.

Josef Niedermayr, Cornaiano/Girlan (BZ).

Portico dei Leoni, Magré/Magreid (BZ). Alois Lageder and Luis von Dellemann are joined by Maurizio Castelli, a winemaker in Tuscany, in this *negoçiant-éléveur* type operation, which makes a fine barrel-fermented Chardonnay.

Praeclarus, San Paolo-Appiano/St. Pauls-Eppan (BZ). Johann Ebner makes noted *champenoise* Praeclarus Brut and Extra Brut at his Kledona cellars.

Hans Rottensteiner, Bolzano. Good St. Magdalener from Premstallerhof among a sound range of DOCs, in part from 16 ha of his own vines.

J. Tiefenbrunner-Schloss Turmhof, Cortaccia/Kurtatsch (BZ). Herbert Tiefenbrunner and son Kristof draw from their own vineyards near the family's castle at Entiklar for a share of some of the South Tyrol's most widely praised wines. Much Pinot Grigio, Chardonnay, and Pinot Bianco are shipped to Britain and the USA, though visitors to the *Stübe* and gardens of Schloss Turmhof often prefer the aromatic whites and fruity reds with plates of sausage or *Speck* (smoked bacon). The whites are noted for heightened aromas in Gewürztraminer, Riesling, Sylvaner, the bone-dry vdt Goldmuskateller, and, above all, the Müller Thurgau vdt Feldmarschall from the region's highest vineyard: 1,000 m at Fennberg. Chardonnay is selected for a barrel-aged type and the rich but un-oaked Turmhof. Among reds are a range of soft Vernatsch types, good Lagrein and Cabernet, and Kristof's unique Linticlarus, which combines the latter two with Pinot Nero.

Vinicola Santa Margherita, Caldaro/Kaltern (BZ). The Veneto firm has created a new winery beside Kettmeir as a base for Alto Adige DOCs, particularly Pinot Grigio, of which it is by far the largest bottler, as well as Chardonnay and the vdt Luna dei Feldi from Chardonnay, Müller Thurgau, and Traminer grown at Roverè della Luna in Trentino.

Anton von Elzenbaum, Termeno/Tramin (BZ). Noted Gewürztraminer and other wines, partly from own 15 ha.

Karl Vonklausner, Bressanone/Brixen (BZ). Good Valle Isarco whites.

Wilhelm Walch, Termeno/Tramin (BZ). Werner Walch makes a full range of increasingly admired DOCs, partly from 20 ha of his own for the estate-bottled Kastelaz and Schloss Ringberg.

Reinhold Waldthaler, Ora/Auer (BZ). Specialist in Lagrein.

Peter Zemmer, Cortina/Kurtinig (BZ). Helmuth Zemmer makes a good range of DOCs.

COOPERATIVES

(K stands for Kellereigenossenchaft, German for cooperative.)

CS Andriano/K Andrian, Andriano/Andrian (BZ).

CS San Michele/K St. Michael, Appiano/Eppan (BZ). Hans Terzer directs the cellars with a good range of Alto Adige DOCs, Kalterersee, vdt, and *spumante*, some sold under the Castel San Valentino/St. Valentin label.

CS San Paolo/K St. Pauls, Appiano/Eppan (BZ).

CS/K Gries, Bolzano.

CS Santa Maddalena/K St. Magdalener, Bolzano.

CS/K Baron Josef Di Pauli, Caldaro/Kaltern(BZ).

CS Caldaro/K Kaltern, Caldaro/Kaltern (BZ).

Prima & Nuova Cantina/Erste & Neue KG, Caldaro/Kaltern (BZ).

CS Valle d'Isarco/K Eisacktaler, Chiusa/Klausen (BZ). Noted specialists in Müller Thurgau and Sylvaner.

CS Colterenzio/K Schreckbichl, Cornaiano/Girlan (BZ). Luis Raifer leads this go-ahead group of 360 growers with 450 ha in the Überetsch and prime points elsewhere for a range of Alto Adige, Terlano, St. Magdalena, and Kalterersee DOCs, including single vineyard bottlings. Trade names are Greifenstein, Praedium, and Cornell. The latter, from the Cornellhof vineyards at Siebeneich, is used for selected wines aged in *barriques*. Cornelius is a vdt from Merlot and Cabernet.

CS Cornaiano/K Girlan, Cornaiano/Girlan (BZ). Steady quality from growers with 235 ha in the Überetsch is due to veteran winemaker Hartmuth Spitaler, whose speciality is Kalterersee but whose selections under the Optimum label include good Riesling, Gewürztraminer, and Pinot Nero.

CS Magrè-Niclara/K Margreid-Entiklar, Magrè/Margreid (BZ).

CS Nalles/K Nals, Nalles/Nals (BZ). Terlano DOCs.

CS Terlano/K Terlan, Terlano/Terlan (BZ). Franz Stocker is a legendary *Kellermeister*, known for the solid quality of Alto Adige and Terlano DOCs, notably Sauvignon, though growers with 155 ha also supply prized base wines for *spumante*. The collection of well-preserved bottles includes a remarkable 1947 Müller Thurgau.

CS Termeno/K Tramin, Termeno/Tramin (BZ).

(Cooperative wines are sold by the Consorzio Viticoltori Alto Adige or Verband der Kellereigenossenschaften Südtirols, with an admirable selection of estate and single-vineyard bottlings at reasonable prices.)

Wines of Trentino

A quiet revolution is taking place in the vineyards and cellars of Trentino after years in which the wine industry seemed to coast along as its former vanguard standards became routine. An exception has been *champenoise*, where Ferrari's feats drew followers and enhanced the image of Trentino. But, before the recent stirrings of revival, inspired winemaking in these splendid valleys was all too rare. Over the last couple of decades, many growers opted for the security (and anonymity) of cooperatives, knowing that they could push up quantities and still get a decent price for grapes. Wine technicians became adept at skimming off the cream of the crop, as both private and collective cellars met demands for the new-style whites – mainly Pinot Grigio and Chardonnay – to offset the slow decline in sales of bulk reds from Lambrusco and Schiava. Tasty red Teroldego, Cabernet, Merlot, and Marzemino complemented the light and fruity whites. The DOC record, if not up to Alto Adige's, stood out from the rest of the country's. Markets moved because prices were right, so perhaps complacency was excusable. But, apart from the sparkling, few Trentino wines won raves from the experts.

The revival is slowly but surely raising Trentino's status. Each vintage confirms that a more worldly concept of premium quality is taking hold, not only among estates and merchants, but even amidst the sometimes massive workings of cooperatives. Càvit, which groups most cellars, supplies international markets with a cross section of white, red, and *spumante*. Lately, some individual cellars have set out to build their own names. One is LaVis, whose select Ritratti wines may be Trentino's most important recent innovation.

The enterprise shown by the Lunelli brothers in building the name Ferrari has spread to other wine houses. The *champenoise* field has been strengthened by a growing number of producers, inspired by the Ferrari prototypes or their own preferences in Champagne. Some have succeeded on a small scale: Equipe Trentina, Le Brul, Abate Nero, and Giuseppe Spagnolli among them. To promote their interests producers have formed the consortium of Spumante Trento Classico. A new sense of style is coming across in still wines, too, from such small merchant houses as Bolognani, Battistotti, Pisoni, and Sebastiani, and larger houses such as Gaierhof and I Vini del Concilio.

Yet, even if wine estates now represent a fraction of production, they seem to hold the key to Trentino's fortunes. Not long ago, as the ranks of grower-bottlers dwindled, some prominent family properties seemed in decline. But, while making the difficult adjustment to modern concepts of winemaking and marketing, Guerrieri Gonzaga's San Leonardo, Bossi Fedrigotti's Foianeghe, Baroni a Prato, and Barone De Cles seem to have recovered some of their former prestige. Other established family estates – Conti Martini, De Tarczal, Foradori, among them – made a smoother transition.

In the meantime a new generation of *vignaioli* has emerged with attitudes enviably free of burdensome legacies. The early pacesetters, Pojer & Sandri, showed that certain whites of Trentino could match Friuli's elite in style and price. Other growers followed, adding such names as Zeni, Simoncelli, Calovi, Fanti, Maso Cantanghel, and Poli to smart wine lists. The studied techniques at Longariva, Madonna della Vittoria, and Vallarom promise to add new lustre to the rolls of estates. The Istituto Agrario Provinciale at San Michele all'Adige qualifies in a sense as an estate, but it might be better described as the reference point for Trentino's wine. A decade ago, the school's bottlings ranked with the best of the province, but then quality inexplicably slipped. With the 1988 vintage they returned to form, setting the standard for the region's winemakers (many of them graduates) to follow.

The basic DOC is Trentino, whose territory overlaps the restricted zones of Teroldego Rotaliano and Sorni, as well as the extended Casteller zone. Trento also supplies the bulk of the interregional category of Valdadige.

Trentino (1971)

Trentino is a blanket DOC that covers the whole province and nearly all the varietals, red and white, along with some classified *spumante* and a bit of extraordinary Vino Santo. Vineyards are concentrated in four main areas between which distinctions can be drawn. The first lies to the north around Roverè della Luna and the Campo Rotaliano, where Teroldego merits a special appellation and red and pink Lagrein also do nicely. This exceptional plain along the Adige is a prime source of Chardonnay and Pinots for sparkling wines, though still whites from Zeni, Conti Martini, Gaierhof, and Foradori also show finesse.

The second area lies east of the Adige on rises above San Michele and Lavis coinciding with the DOC zone of Sorni and stretching back through the high terraces of the Cembra valley. A full range of varieties thrives on the lower slopes in vineyards that supply the Istituto Agrario, LaVis, Maso Poli, Fanti, and Bolognani. Notable Nosiola, Pinot Bianco and Grigio, and Chardonnay originate there, along with flavourful Cabernet and pleasant Pinot Nero. The heights at Faedo, Giovo, Cembra, Faver, and Segonzano were traditionally dominated by Schiava for Caldaro and other simple reds, but

Müller Thurgau, Chardonnay, and Pinot Nero have proved to be more inspiring to growers such as Pojer & Sandri, Remo Calovi, and Baroni a Prato.

The third and largest vineyard area of Trentino is the Vallagarina, the vast gorge stretching from just south of Trento along the Adige into the Veneto. Variations in soils and temperatures between the river banks and the mountainsides permit a wide range of vines. The sentimental favourite is Marzemino, sung of in Mozart's *Don Giovanni*. Its plump, grapey-almondy flavours and youthful fragrance are best expressed in the volcanic soil of Isera, west of the Adige, and around Mori, Nomi, Nogaredo, and Marano. Producers in the area include De Tarczal, Enrico Spagnolli, Letrari, Bossi Fedrigotti, Battistotti, and CS di Isera. Marzemino also does well farther up the valley at Aldeno and across the river around Calliano, Volano, and Rovereto. Producers have formed a special consortium to promote Marzemino from the historical vineyards. Vallagarina is also a major source of Chardonnay and the Pinots for sparkling and still wines, as well as Nosiola, Cabernet, and Merlot. Simoncelli excels with all. Other growers of note in the Rovereto area are Giuseppe Spagnolli, Longariva, and Raffaelli. Down the valley around Ala and Avio are La Cadalora, San Leonardo, and Vallarom.

The Valle dei Laghi, which opens north of Lake Garda along the Sarca river and around the lakes of Cavedine, Toblino, and Santa Massenza, has the same viticultural versatility as the Adige valley and a similar range of wines. But as the warmest and best ventilated area, its special microclimate is uniquely suited to the rich Vino Santo. To make it, ripe Nosiola grapes are left on cane trays (*solèri*) or, if rarely, nets (*arèle*) in airy lofts to dry for five or six months, the *infavatura* process that induces an internal "noble rot" known as *muffa larvata*. The thick musts were usually left in small oak barrels for two or three years to undergo a slow and intermittent fermentation and ageing process that results in a copper-amber wine of lingering, velvety sweetness. Yet perhaps the finest current Vino Santo, from Giovanni Poli, is made in stainless steel tanks by a method that seems to retain more vital flavours and aromas. A half dozen producers form still another consortium within the Trentino zone; between them they account for much of the roughly 30,000 litres a year, most sold in half bottles. Though painstaking and expensive to make (the finished wine is equal to about a sixth of the original weight of the grapes), growing acclaim for this luscious "holy wine" seems to promise increasing

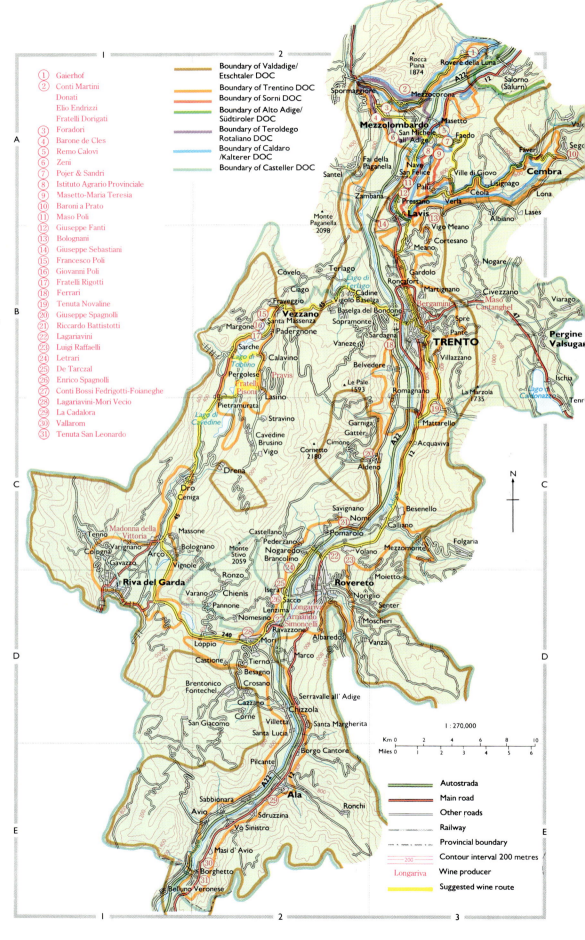

1   Gaierhof
2   Conti Martini
    Donati
    Elio Endrizzi
    Fratelli Dorigati
3   Foradori
4   Barone de Cles
5   Remo Calovi
6   Zeni
7   Pojer & Sandri
8   Istituto Agrario Provinciale
9   Masetto-Maria Teresia
10 Baroni a Prato
11 Maso Poli
12 Giuseppe Fanti
13 Bolognani
14 Giuseppe Sebastiani
15 Francesco Poli
16 Giovanni Poli
17 Fratelli Rigotti
18 Ferrari
19 Tenuta Novaline
20 Giuseppe Spagnolli
21 Riccardo Battistotti
22 Lagariavini
23 Luigi Raffaelli
24 Letrari
25 De Tarczal
26 Enrico Spagnolli
27 Conti Bossi Fedrigotti-Foianeghe
28 Lagariavini-Mori Vecio
29 La Cadalora
30 Vallarom
31 Tenuta San Leonardo

Boundary of Valdadige/Etschtaler DOC
Boundary of Trentino DOC
Boundary of Sorni DOC
Boundary of Alto Adige/Südtiroler DOC
Boundary of Teroldego Rotaliano DOC
Boundary of Caldaro/Kalterer DOC
Boundary of Casteller DOC

1 : 270,000

Km 0   2   4   6   8   10
Miles 0   1   2   3   4   5   6

Autostrada
Main road
Other roads
Railway
Provincial boundary
Contour interval 200 metres
Longariva   Wine producer
Suggested wine route

production. The best Nosiola Spinarola grapes for Vino Santo come from hillsides to the north around Calavino, Toblino, and Santa Massenza, where Giovanni Poli has vineyards. Other producers of note are Francesco Poli at Santa Massenza, Pisoni at Pergolese Sarche, Rigotti at Padergnone, and the Toblino cooperative. Pravis makes a fine, dry Nosiola at Lasino. The promising new Madonna della Vittoria estate near Arco produces a range of Trentino wines.

Zone: Slopes and plains along the Adige, Avisio (Cembra), and Sarca valleys, and around the lakes of Caldonazzo and Levico, covering practically the entire viticultural area of Trento province in 47 communes. Marzemino is restricted to 13 communes in the Vallagarina along the Adige between Aldeno and the Veneto. Wines from the Isera area may use the name on labels. Vino Santo is restricted to 11 communes in the Valle dei Laghi between Vezzano and Lake Garda.

The 20 types include 17 pure varietals, plus Bianco, Rosso, and Vino Santo.

Bianco Dry white. Grapes: Chardonnay 50-85%, Pinot Bianco 15-50%. Yld 105/150, Alc 11, Acd 0.45.

Cabernet (Cabernet Sauvignon/Cabernet Franc) Dry red. Yld 91/130, Alc 11; riserva 11.5, Acd 0.45, Ag riserva 2 yrs.

Cabernet Franc Dry red. Yld 91/130, Alc 11; riserva 11.5, Acd 0.45, Ag riserva 2 yrs.

Cabernet Sauvignon Dry red. Yld 91/130, Alc 11; riserva 11.5, Acd 0.45, Ag riserva 2 yrs.

Chardonnay Dry white, also spumante. Yld 105/150, Alc 11, Acd 0.5.

Lagrein Dry red or Dunkel, also rosé or Kretzer. Yld 98/140, Alc 11; riserva 11.5, Acd 0.45, Ag riserva (red only) 2 yrs.

Marzemino Dry red. Yld 91/130, Alc 11; riserva 11.5, Acd 0.45, Ag riserva 2 yrs.

Merlot Dry red. Yld 105/150, Alc 11; riserva 11.5, Acd 0.45, Ag riserva 2 yrs.

Moscato Giallo Sweet white, also liquoroso. Yld 84/120, Alc 11.5; liquoroso 14, Acd 0.5.

Moscato Rosa Sweet rosé, also liquoroso. Yld 70/100, Alc 12.5; liquoroso 14, Acd 0.5.

Müller Thurgau Dry white. Yld 98/140, Alc 11, Acd 0.45.

Nosiola Dry white. Yld 98/140, Alc 10.5, Acd 0.45.

Pinot Bianco Dry white, also spumante. Yld 105/150, Alc 11, Acd 0.5.

Pinot Grigio Dry white, also spumante. Yld 98/140, Alc 11, Acd 0.45.

Pinot Nero Dry red, also rosé or white as spumante. Yld 84/120, Alc 11.5; riserva 12, Acd 0.45, Ag riserva (red only) 2 yrs.

Riesling Italico Dry white. Yld 105/150, Alc 10.5, Acd 0.5.

Riesling Renano Dry white. Yld 98/140, Alc 11, Acd 0.5.

Rosso Dry red. Grapes: Cabernet 50-85%, Merlot 15-50%. Yld 98/140, Alc 11.5, Acd 0.5.

Traminer Aromatico Dry white. Yld 98/140, Alc 11.5, Acd 0.5.

Vino Santo Sweet white. Grape: Nosiola semidried or passito. Yld 42/140, Alc 16 (res sugar max 6%), Acd 0.6, Ag 3 yrs.

Teroldego Rotaliano (1971)

Teroldego thrives only on the gravel-based soils of the Campo Rotaliano, where double canopied pergolas mesh in a field of green framed by the Alps in what has been described as "the loveliest wine garden of Europe". Elsewhere, Trentino's prince of wines becomes a pauper. Permitted yields were recently raised to excessive levels, apparently to back the tendency to make Teroldego light and youthful, a style Zeni exemplifies with a supple, fruity red from the Pini plot. It also makes a tasty rosé. But what insiders know as the true Teroldego is a dark ruby red of aristocratic bearing with the structure and substance to become fascinating with age. Though grown in vineyards of uniform appearance through the plain, Teroldego shows distinguished traits from certain plots, chiefly to the west around Mezzolombardo where they feel the cooling effects of the massive Paganella. The Cantina Cooperativa Rotaliana takes the prize for consistency in Teroldego, rivalled by Conti Martini. Past peaks were reached by Barone de Cles with Maso Scari. But over the last couple of decades the noblest versions have come from Foradori, whose Vigneto Morei would seem to rank first among Teroldego's *crus*.

Zone: The Campo Rotaliano, the broad plain at the confluence of the Adige and Noce rivers in the communes of Mezzolombardo, Mezzocorona, and San Michele all'Adige's frazione of Grumo. Dry red. Grape: Teroldego. Yld 119/170, Alc 11.5; superiore 12, Acd 0.45, Ag superiore 2 yrs.

Rosato or **Kretzer** Dry rosé. Grape: Teroldego. Yld 119/170, Alc 11.5, Acd 0.45.

Sorni (1979)

The light, fragrant wines are appreciated locally for their enticingly fresh and fruity qualities when young. Maso Poli sets the standard, though the LaVis cooperative is also steadily reliable. The term *scelto* (selected) for the red indicates slightly higher alcohol.

Zone: Slopes northeast of the point where the Avisio river meets the Adige in the communes of Giovo, San Michele all'Adige, and Lavis, of which the village of Sorni is a frazione.

Bianco Dry white. Grapes: Nosiola: Müller Thurgau/Sylvaner Verde/Pinot Bianco up to 30%. Yld 98/140, Alc 10, Acd 0.5.

Rosso Dry red. Grapes: Schiava (Gentile/Grigia/Grossa) at least 70%, Teroldego 20-30%; Lagrein up to 10%. Yld 98/140, Alc 10.5 (scelto 11), Acd 0.45.

Casteller (1974)

This all-purpose rosy red, originally named after a village near Trento, is now made through much of the province, though it is rarely seen outside. Like the Vernatsch wines of the South Tyrol it can be enviably quaffable.

Zone: Slopes no higher than 600 m and gravelly plains along the Adige river from the border of the Veneto north to Lavis (just above Trento) and covering 27 communes in the province. Dry light red, also amabile. Grapes: Schiava Grossa/Schiava Gentile at least 30%, Lambrusco a Foglia Frastagliata up to 60%; Merlot/Lagrein/Teroldego up to 20%. Yld 112/160, Alc 10.5; superiore 11.5, Acd 0.45.

Valdadige/Etschtaler (1975)

The category is the lowest rung on the ladder of the Adige valley's DOCs,

Above: a cellarman at Ferrari in Trento performs the rémuage *used for sparkling wines from Chardonnay and Pinot grapes. Ferrari and other leading producers belong to a consortium that sells wines as Spumante Trento Classico.*

though it does provide wine drinkers in Italy and points north with sanctified bargains. Much Pinot Grigio flows through here, sometimes tasty, sometimes unidentifiable. The other wines rarely have points to distinguish them, but some producers are raising standards. The province of Trento dominates production, followed by Verona. Growers around Bolzano scarcely bother.

Zone: Slopes and plains along the Adige from Merano in the South Tyrol south through Trentino to Sant'Ambrogio di Valpolicella in the Veneto, covering 38 communes in Trento province, 33 in Bolzano, and four in Verona.

Bianco Dry white, also amabile. Grapes: Pinot Bianco/Pinot Grigio/Riesling Italico/Müller Thurgau/Chardonnay at least 20%; Bianchetta Trevigiana/Trebbiano Toscano/Nosiola/Vernaccia up to 80%. Yld 98/140, Alc 10.5, Acd 0.5.

Rosso Dry red, also amabile. Grapes: Lambrusco a Foglia Frastagliata at least 30%; Schiava (various subvarieties) at least 20%; Merlot/Pinot Nero/Lagrein/Teroldego/Negrara up to 70%. Yld 98/140, Alc 11, Acd 0.45.

Rosato Dry rosé, also amabile. Grapes: As rosso. Yld 98/140, Alc 10.5, Acd 0.45.

Pinot Grigio Dry white, also amabile. Grapes: Pinot Grigio; other non-aromatic whites up to 15%. Yld 98/140, Alc 10.5, Acd 0.5.

Schiava Dry red. Grapes: Schiava (Grossa/Gentile/Grigia); other reds up to 15%. Yld 98/140, Alc 10.5, Acd 0.45.

Above: a castle in Trentino's Valle dei Laghi, where vineyards around lakes and along the Sarca river valley are most noted for Nosiola grapes used for the area's rare Vino Santo.

Other wines of note

The DOCs may seem to cover everything, but well over half of Trentino's wine is unclassified, including some of the finest. Most of the often sterling sparkling wines could qualify as Trentino Spumante DOC, but few do. However, the Spumante Trento Classico group of 15 houses imposes its own rigorous standards. Several admirable producers do not belong. The many red vdt made using variations on Cabernet and Merlot would now qualify under Trentino Rosso DOC, but so far few producers have complied. Wines in both categories are cited in producer entries. Some respected growers, Pojer & Sandri among them, prefer to leave wines unclassified. A few others make special wines outside the norms.

Growers in the lower Vallagarina are attempting to build a market for light vdt from the predominant Lambrusco. A century ago vineyards covered nearly all of Trentino's valleys, but today the Valsugana and the lofty Val di Non and Val di Sole are among marginal areas that produce wines mainly for local consumption.

ESTATES/GROWERS

(Those listed without comment are recommended for Trentino DOC.)

Barone de Cles, Mezzolombardo (TN). From 25 ha in the Rotaliano plain, Michele and Leonardo de Cles make long noted Teroldego from Maso Ischia and Maso Scari, along with other Trentino DOCs

Baroni a Prato, Segonzano (TN). From 5 ha of the noble estate high in the Cembra valley, Chardonnay, Pinot Nero, and Cabernet.

Bergamini, Cognola di Trento (TN).

Remo Calovi, Faedo (TN). Good Chardonnay and sometimes excellent Müller Thurgau from the tiny Palai dei Siori plot.

Conti Martini, Mezzocorona (TN). The old family estate directed by Lucia Cristina Martini makes fine Teroldego and Lagrein, along with good whites, including a perfumed, dry Moscato Bianco.

De Tarczal, Marano d'Isera (TN). From 16 ha, Ruggero and Gèza Dell'Adami de Tarczal make an admirable range of Trentino DOCs, exemplified by Marzemino d'Isera, plus the vdt Cabernet-Merlot blend of Pragiara.

Donati, Mezzocorona (TN). Sound Teroldego and Trentino DOCs.

Elio Endrizzi, Mezzocorona(TN). Often good Teroldego.

Giuseppe Fanti, Pressano di Lavis (TN). Good Chardonnay, though Fanti's name is linked to fine dry Nosiola.

Foradori, Mezzolombardo (TN). From 12 ha in the Campo Rotaliano, Gabriella Foradori and daughter Elisabetta select from low yielding vines for their exemplary Teroldego Vigneto Morei, while making good Trentino DOCs and a fine Alto Adige Gewürztraminer from their Maso Foradori at Mazzon. Granato is a novel vdt based on Teroldego.

Istituto Agrario Provinciale, San Michele all'Adige (TN). The agricultural school resumed as Trentino's model with whites from 1988 that showed winemaking professor Salvatore Maule's touch. The 40 ha include special plots: Rauti for Pinot Grigio and Riesling Renano, San Donà for Chardonnay (including a barrel-fermented version), Giaroni for Pinot Bianco, Fontane Alte for Sauvignon Blanc, Pozza for Castel San Michele in both white (from Incrocio Manzoni 6.0.13) and red (from Cabernet-Merlot).

La Cadalora, Ala (TN). From 4 ha, Marzemino, Pinots, and Chardonnay.

Letrari, Nogaredo (TN). From 9 ha, Leonello Letrari makes notable Marzemino and the Cabernet-Merlot vdt Maso Lodron.

Longariva, Rovereto (TN). Marco Manica's estate at Borgo Sacco makes admired DOCs from 11 ha of the Graminè, Perer and Alle Pergole plots, plus a Cabernet-Merlot vdt called Tre Cesure and a rich, coppery Ruländer.

Madonna della Vittoria, Arco (TN). Iginio Mandelli's new textbook estate has considerable promise to live up to with a range of Trentino DOCs.

Masetto, San Michele all'Adige (TN). Trento Classico Maria Teresia Brut

Maso Cantanghel, Civezzano (TN). Piero Zabini working with Salvatore Maule fashions fine barrel-fermented Chardonnay Vigna Piccola and Pinot Nero from 2 ha.

Maso Poli, San Michele all'Adige (TN). Luigi Togn selects from 10 ha on this ancient estate for good Sorni Bianco, palatable Pinot Nero, and other DOCs.

Fratelli Pisoni, Pergolese Sarche (TN). The house Vino Santo stands out among the range that includes Pisoni Brut Trento Classico.

Pojer & Sandri, Faedo (TN). Trentino's pioneers of premium small estate wines, the perenially youthful Mario Pojer and Fiorentino Sandri continue to seek the ultimate from 12 ha at the 750-m heights of the Molini estate. The wines, entirely vdt, take in renowned Müller Thurgau from the Palai plot, Nosiola, Chardonnay (including a special bottling called Fayè), Pinot Nero, and *champenoise*. Vin dei Molini is a taut rosé from Rotberger, a cross of Schiava and Riesling.

Francesco Poli, Santa Massenza (TN). Vino Santo.

Giovanni Poli, Santa Massenza (TN). The speciality, Vino Santo, is luscious and elegant, a model of the genre, though aged only in stainless steel tanks.

Pravis, Lasino (TN). Valle dei Laghi vdt include a good, dry Nosiola Le Frate.

Luigi Raffaelli, Volano (TN). Good range of Trentino DOCs, plus the vdt Salengo from Cabernet-Merlot.

Fratelli Rigotti, Padergnone (TN). Notable Vino Santo.

Armando Simoncelli, Navicello di Rovereto (TN). A leading grower makes fine Marzemino among the DOCs, along with Simoncelli Brut Trento Classico, and one of Trentino's better Cabernet-Merlot blends in Navesel.

Giuseppe Spagnolli, Aldeno (TN). Spagnolli and son Francesco, professor at San Michele, blend Chardonnay with plenty of Pinot Nero in the outstanding *champenoise* Spagnolli Brut.

Tenuta Novaline, Mattarello (TN). Trentino DOCs and Novaline Brut.

Tenuta San Leonardo, Avio (TN). The Marchesi Guerrieri Gonzaga estate at Borghetto was once Trentino's leader with hearty Cabernet, but pronounced varietal traits seemed to jar modern palates. After experiments with 15 ha of vines, Carlo Gonzaga has used *barriques* to bring new finesse to Cabernet Sauvignon and the Cabernet-Merlot blend of Campi Sarni.

Vallarom, Avio (TN). The family estate of viticulturist Attilio Scienza, director of San Michele, has drawn praise for Marzemino, Pinot Nero, Merlot, and Cabernet Sauvignon, though a late harvest Chardonnay is the most admired wine. Scienza also grows traditional Trentino vines without grafting onto American rootstock.

Roberto Zeni, Grumo di San Michele (TN). From 4 ha on the edge of the Rotaliano plain, Roberto and Andrea Zeni make widely admired single-

Right: Mario Pojer (on the right) and Fiorentino Sandri are leading producers of premium small estate wines in Trentino from high vineyards at Faedo. They are shown in the distillery where they make grappa from the pomace of wine grapes.

vineyard bottlings: Pinot Bianco Sortì and Seipergole, Müller Thurgau La Croce, Chardonnay Zaraosti, a youthful Teroldego Pini, and the sweet Moscato Rosa from a plot called Rosa.

WINE HOUSES/MERCHANTS

Abate Nero, Gardolo (TN). Abate Nero Brut is first-rate *champenoise*.

Riccardo Battistotti, Nomi (TN). Range of DOCs includes fine Marzemino.

Bolognani, Lavis (TN). Nilo Bolognani has rapidly emerged as a quality leader in Trentino with fine white Nosiola, Müller Thurgau, and Chardonnay.

Cassina, Trento.

Cesarini Sforza Spumanti, Trento. Specialist in Trento Classico.

Conti Bossi Fedrigotti-Foianeghe, Rovereto (TN). The Bossi Fedrigotti family continues an ancient tradition with a range of Trentino DOCs and vdt from 40 ha in the Isera valley. Best

known are the Foianeghe vdt *rosso* from Merlot and Cabernet, and *bianco* from Chardonnay and Traminer.

Fratelli Dorigati, Mezzocorona (TN). Franco and Carlo Dorigati make good Teroldego, Trentino DOCs, and the interesting red vdt Rebo and Grener (from Teroldego with Cabernet), in part from 5 ha of their own vines in the Campo Rotaliano. *See* also Metius.

Fratelli Endrizzi, San Michele all'Adige (TN). Trentino DOCs and Teroldego.

Équipe Trentina Spumante, Mezzolombardo (TN). The long-admired Équipe 5 Brut and Riserva are pillars of Trento Classico.

Ferrari, Trento. The firm, founded in 1902 by Giulio Ferrari, still leads the *champenoise* field under the Lunelli brothers – Franco, Gino, and Mauro. From 20 ha of their own *masi* around Trento – Pianizza, Montalto, ai Palazzi, and Villa Margon – and a network of faithful growers, they make about

75,000 cases a year, mainly Brut, along with the acclaimed Brut de Brut (pure Chardonnay), Extra Brut (pas dosé), Brut Rosé, and the outstanding Giulio Ferrari Riserva del Fondatore. The cellars are at Ravina, though headquarters are now in the handsomely restored Villa Gentilotti-Ferrari in Trento.

Gaierhof, Roverè della Luna (TN). Luigi Togn and oenologist Enrico Paternoster make a vast and varied array of DOC and vdt of consistent quality and reasonable price. Togn, a leader in Trentino's wine circles, also owns Maso Poli and the house of Lechthaler, which bottles Torre di Luna Pinot Grigio and Merlot.

Girelli, Trento. Vast range of Trentino DOC, vdt, and *spumanti*.

Lagariavini-I Vini del Concilio, Volano (TN). An array of imaginatively labelled DOCs is complemented by Mori Vecio, a Cabernet-Merlot from vineyards at Mori, Grand Bleu Pinot *frizzante*, and Concilio Brut Trento Classico.

Le Brul, Mezzocorona (TN). Salvatore Maule, Trentino's leading consultant in the field, has his own elite production of Gran Le Brul *champenoise*.

Malpaga, Faedo (TN).

Metius, Mezzocorona (TN). Enrico Paternoster and the Dorigati brothers make a *champenoise* called Methius of extraordinary finesse from Pinot Nero and Chardonnay.

Fratelli Pedrotti, Trento. Established house makes a range of DOCs, the red vdt Morlacco, and Trento Classico Pedrotti Brut.

San Rocco, Trento. Creator of the fine Novecento Brut *champenoise*.

Giuseppe Sebastiani, Lavis (TN). Solid range of DOCs.

Enrico Spagnolli, Isera (TN). Reliable range of Trentino DOC wines include fine Marzemino and Müller Thurgau.

COOPERATIVES

La Vinicola Sociale, Aldeno (TN). Range of Trentino DOCs, San Zeno vdt from Merlot with Cabernet, and Degli Aldii Brut Trento Classico.

CS Isera, Isera (TN). Specialists in Marzemino.

CS Lavis-Sorni-Salorno, Lavis (TN). A group of 770 growers on prime slopes east of the Adige between Lavis and Salorno have made LaVis an increasingly admired cooperative trademark. Progetto Qualità is an ambitious program to guide growers in planting suitable varieties and clones and limiting yields. The Ritratti line of Trentino Chardonnay, Cabernet Sauvignon, and Pinot Nero is selected by winemaker Fausto Peratoner and sold with labels depicting classical art. Also produced are Sorni, Caldaro, and

Casteller DOCs, and the *champenoise* Arcade.

Cantina Produttori Mezzocorona, Mezzocorona (TN). Trentino DOCs, Teroldego, and Caldaro.

Cantine MezzaCorona, Mezzocorona (TN). Trentino DOCs and Teroldego, as well as Rotari Brut Trentino Classico.

Cantina Cooperativa Rotaliana, Mezzolombardo (TN). The cellars make Teroldego of consistent class, along with Lagrein and Trentino DOCs.

Cantina di Toblino, Sarche (TN). Range of Trentino DOCs includes fine Vino Santo.

Càvit, Trento. Càvit (for Cantina Viticoltori) groups 15 cooperatives in marketing a major share of Trentino's

select wine under the direction of Giacinto Giacomini. A complete range of always reliable and often exemplary DOCs is supplemented by the Cabernet-Merlot vdt Quattro Vicariati and a line of sparkling wines topped by the Trentino Classico Graal Ducale (Chardonnay-Pinot Nero) and Firmato (pure Chardonnay). In collaboration with the Istituto Agrario Provinciale, the group is developing a series of estate wines under the program "Progetto il Maso".

Above: the Mareccio or Maretsch castle at Bolzano houses an enoteca *with the South Tyrol's wines.*

114

Travel Information

RESTAURANTS/HOTELS

Alto Adige/South Tyrol

Elefante, 39042 Bressanone/Brixen (BZ). Tel (0472)32750. The inviting 16th-century inn with gardens is noted for its elephant platter, which anyone who has finished it will never forget. Restful rooms.

Villa Mozart, 39012 Merano (BZ). Tel (0473)30630. Andreas Hellrigl's luxury *pensione* provides creative Tyrolean cooking in a refined Austrian-style setting, though the owner is often away at the **Palio** in New York, where he is the chef known as Andrea di Merano.

Pichler, 39037 Rio di Pusteria/Mühlbach (BZ). Tel (0472)49458. Local gastronomes rate this small restaurant near Bressanone one of the South Tyrol's best.

Trentino

Maso Cantanghel, 38045 Civezzano (TN). Tel (0461)858714. Piero and Lucia Zabini have shaped this cosy retreat ten minutes from Trento into the consummate alpine trattoria. The inspired wine list is headed by their own fine Chardonnay and Pinot Nero.

Al Borgo, 38068 Rovereto (TN). Tel (0464)436300. Rinaldo Dalsasso's artistic cooking gets good reviews from well beyond Rovereto. The wine list matches the high standards.

Da Silvio, 38010 San Michele all'Adige (TN). Tel (0461)650324. The Manna family has made this roadside chalet into an inviting modern restaurant with appetizing food at sensible prices and a studied choice of wines.

Chiesa, Via San Marco 64, 38100 Trento. Tel (0461)985577. Sergio Chiesa provides options between old and new. Good wine list.

WINE SHOPS/ENOTECHE

The South Tyrol's wines are displayed at the regional *enoteca* in the Castel Mareccio, which also has a restaurant at Via Claudia de' Medici 12 in Bolzano. Two attractive shops with wine bars are the Vinoteque Alois Lageder at Viale Druso 235 in Bolzano and the Enoteca Johnson & Dipoli at Egna/Neumarkt. At Trento, the Enoteca Lunelli at Largo Carducci 12 has the owner's Ferrari *spumanti* and a good choice of other Trentino wines.

PLACES OF INTEREST

As the gateway to Italy for the German-speaking world, Trentino-Alto Adige has become a haven of tourism. The prime attraction is the Dolomites in two massive blocks on either side of the Adige. The main group lies to the east between Bolzano and Cortina d'Ampezzo, with the chimney peaks of the Catinaccio or Rosengarten, Sella, and Marmolada, and the splendid Gardena valley, where some natives speak the antique Ladin. To the west is the Brenta massif, whose axis is Madonna di Campiglio, amidst lakes, ski slopes, and hiking trails.

But there are more than alpine sports to enjoy in this multi-faceted region. The South Tyrol is a major centre of wine tourism. Some visitors begin by hiking up from the centre of Bolzano to the terraces of St. Magdalener or taking the cable car from Merano up to the Tirol castle, where wines may be called Burgräffler. But the focal point for wine buffs is the lake of Kaltern/Caldaro amidst the boundless vineyards of the Überetsch and Unterland. There the busy wine road runs through villages with Gothic spires and German names that end with "auf der Weinstrasse".

Staid Trento, with its memories of the Council of Trent, is the hub of a network of valleys whose crumbling hilltop fortresses and majestic castles attest to an eventful past. Trentino's chief wine areas are the Vallagarina around Rovereto and the Campo Rotaliano, adjacent to San Michele with its noted wine school. The Cembra valley's precipitous terraces provide dramatic scenery. Equally picturesque is the drive through the Valle dei Laghi from Lake Garda along the Sarca river to the symbolic castle on an island in the lake of Toblino.

Both provinces hold wine fairs that practically coincide in late April/early May: the Bozner Weinkost, which has been held since 1896 in the centre of Bolzano, and the Mostra dei Vini Trentini in Trento. Both provide extensive tastings of recent vintages. Though the events are aimed chiefly at the wine trade, the public can also take part for a nominal fee.

Below: fruit vendors in a market at Bolzano sell their produce in two languages. The South Tyrol is a major producer of apples and other fruit, which thrive in the alpine climate just as grapes do.

Veneto

Capital: Venezia (Venice).
Provinces: Belluno (BL), Padova (PD), Rovigo (RO), Treviso (TV),
Venezia (VE), Verona (VR), Vicenza (VI).
Area: 18,364 square kilometres (eighth).
Population: 4,371,000 (seventh).

Maritime Venice is the hub of a bountiful land of vines. The plains that stretch from the Adriatic shores of the Venetian mainland through the fertile farmland north of the Po provide even more space for vineyards than do the hills that flank the alpine wall from Lake Garda to Vittorio Veneto. Still, the region's winemakers have often managed to combine quantity with quality over the last couple of decades as they transformed the antiquated craft of winemaking into a modern business. The Veneto ranks third after Apulia and Sicily in volume of wine, but has no rivals in DOC output with 1.7 million hectolitres a year – more than a fifth of the nation's total. Two-thirds of this comes from Verona, where

Above: vineyards of Prosecco at Col San Martino near Valdobbiadene north of Venice.

the classical trio of Soave, Valpolicella, and Bardolino has been joined by Bianco di Custoza. The province alone makes nearly as much classified wine as does the entire region of Tuscany and considerably more than Piedmont.

Verona had been known as a privileged place for wine since Etruscan times. The Romans were fond of the Rhaetic of the Adige valley, a wine that is sometimes said to have been the forerunner of the grandiose Reciotos. Vines around Verona are still usually trained onto pergolas and grapes for the sweet Recioto and its richly dry counterpart Amarone are still dried on racks in airy lofts as they have been for centuries. Winemaking in the region can be traced back to around 1000 BC, when the Veneti settled there, though evidence of grape pressings around Lake Garda and the Berici and Euganei hills to the southeast suggests an even earlier beginning. Vines prospered under the Venetian Republic, known as la Serenissima, whose civilized style of life lingers in the region's small cities and the villas and gardens of the countryside.

The Veneto's prodigiousness with wine seems to have developed in recent times as viticulture expanded from the hills to the plains and yields were gradually raised to the highest levels of northern Italy. Growers around Verona followed the trend by extending their wine zones beyond the historical limits, but unlike so many others of the Veneto, they remained loyal to native vines and traditional blends. Verona's wines reached peaks of popularity in the 1970s. Their special appeal to foreigners may have been as much due to drinkable styles and affordable prices as to lyrical names and romantic places of origin in the surrounding hills. Smooth and easy Soave, linked to the house of Bolla, surpassed even Chianti to become the best-selling DOC wine in America, while hearty Valpolicella held sway among Italian reds in Britain. Many producers of Bardolino's breezy red and pink *chiaretto* also make the white of Custoza from adjacent vineyards. Verona built an industry around these wines while developing a marketing strategy that made them fixtures in Italian restaurants around the world.

Producers elsewhere in the Veneto followed the lead. Santa Margherita launched the Pinot Grigio that became synonymous with its name, while Zonin, Europe's largest private winery, added estates in prime regions of Italy and even in the United States to its family empire. Enterprising producers of Conegliano and Valdobbiadene have made Prosecco into one of Italy's most requested bubbly wines. Yet, despite the increase in foreign white varieties and the continuing dominance of Merlot and Cabernet, few other producers east of Verona have made much impact with their wines outside the region. A conspicuous exception is Maculan of Breganze, who produces outstanding Cabernet and dry whites, along with some of Italy's most prized dessert wines.

On the map the region's wine zones appear to be split into two major groupings east and west of the Brenta river that flows down from the Alps past Bassano del Grappa and Padova. The eastern Veneto covers four zones between the Brenta and the western edge of Friuli-Venezia Giulia. But to the west, even though the DOC zones are practically linked from Padova to Lake Garda, distinctions can be drawn between the wines of Verona and those of Vicenza and Padova in what is often referred to as the central Veneto. The division is primarily geographical, since climate and soil around Verona differ from those of the central zones of Breganze, Gambellara, Colli Berici, and Colli Euganei. But the split may also be considered philosophical, since Verona's wines derive almost entirely from native vines while foreign varieties prevail from the central hills eastwards.

Italy's heaviest concentration of Merlot is in the eastern Veneto's Adriatic plains in the DOC zones of Piave and Lison-Pramaggiore, the latter extending into Friuli. Most Merlot there, like the popular Cabernet, is for everyday drinking. The Prosecco of Treviso's hills is the prime attraction among white varieties, followed by Tocai and the rapidly emerging Chardonnay. Guidance from the respected vine research centre at Conegliano Veneto has raised standards in an area where industrial-scale wineries and cooperatives account for a major share of production. But, for reasons hard to explain, the eastern Veneto seems to lack the sort of inspired winemaking on a small scale that makes neighbouring Friuli so admired. Still, some historical estates have maintained their dignity, among them Loredan Gasparini of Venegazzù and Castello di Roncade, both of which built status a couple of decades ago with reds from Bordeaux blends.

Verona's wine industry seems if anything to have lost ground lately. This might be because it grew so rapidly on the strength of moderately priced exports in the 1970s that it failed to keep up with the domestic market's move up-market in the 1980s. Producers there, apparently lulled by the success of Soave, responded late to the competition from varietal whites of Friuli and Trentino-Alto Adige. The traditional red wines seemed out of step with Italian tastes. Valpolicella was neither light enough to be trendy nor luxurious enough to rival the new-style reds from Tuscany and Piedmont. Amarone faced a different sort of dilemma. Though it comes from the same grapes as Valpolicella, concentrated by drying, Amarone is almost too much of a luxury for palates not attuned to its port-like opulence. Among Verona's red wines, only Bardolino seemed to be gaining after producers devised Italy's first classified *novello* and introduced sparkling *chiaretto*. Demand for white wines has kept some wineries active, especially those which make Soave and Bianco di Custoza sparkling to keep up with current tastes. But the wines of Verona seem to be in the midst of an identity crisis as more than a few houses struggle to make a profit.

Trends seem to favour small, serious producers who make wines from special vineyards. In Soave, Pieropan and Anselmi have defied what had become a virtual cartel of large producers to create a newly elite concept of the wine. In Valpolicella, the family wineries of Allegrini, Quintarelli, Speri, Tedeschi, Tommasi, Tramanal, and Le Ragose have gained stature. The tendency there has been to scale down Amarone to more drinkable dimensions while giving Valpolicella more weight and better balance. Winemakers often use the pomace of Amarone to referment Valpolicella in a process known as *ripasso* that gives the wine greater structure and character.

Masi, the house that revived *ripasso* in the 1970s with Campo Fiorin, set Verona's standards in the 1980s with Amarone and Recioto, partly from its own vineyards, as well as from the estate of Serègo Alighieri. Bolla has successfully offset the slump in Verona by diversifying into new style wines from other places. Lately, the established family houses of Bertani and Guerrieri-Rizzardi seem to be reasserting leadership. Their efforts to realize the ultimate from choice vineyards in the classical zones could be the key to revival of Verona's wines in the 1990s, and an example for other industrious Veneto winemakers to follow.

The Veneto's Vineyards

Standards for Italian viticulture may be set at Conegliano, but growers do not always follow the scholarly leads. The Veneto's vines cover an enormous range, from antique natives to voguish imports, from the most pedestrian national types to exotic local varieties and even *non-vinifera* species from America. It may seem odd that a wine region as industrial-minded as the Veneto would maintain more than 80 authorized types of vines grown on 116,000 properties whose vineyards average less than a hectare each. But both the number of vineyards and the space devoted to vines have been sharply reduced as monoculture replaced mixed cropping and standard varieties, often of foreign origin, have taken the place of traditional vines.

Native vines prevail in places, most notably in the Verona area where Corvina and Rondinella hold sway in Valpolicella and Bardolino, and where Garganega has gained ground in Soave and neighbouring zones. Planting of Prosecco has increased steadily in Treviso's hills to meet demand for its bubbly whites. Other white varieties such as Tocai, Verduzzo, and Durella seem to be holding their own, though the dark Raboso, once prominent in the eastern Veneto, has been far outdistanced by Merlot, the region's most heavily planted variety, as well as by Cabernet.

But Merlot and Cabernet are not considered foreign in much of the Veneto, where they have been grown for so long that their wines have acquired local traits. Still, their continuing prominence, coupled with the rapid rise of Chardonnay, the Pinots, and Sauvignon, have hastened many local varieties into obscurity. The Venetian strain of Marzemino, once prevalent in the central hills, is now found occasionally around Conegliano. Other old favourites – such as Bianchetta Trevigiana, Pavana, Pinella, Turca, and Trevisana Nera – remain on the official lists though they are rarely more than curiosities. Fading with them are the North American vines called Clinton and Uva Fragola, which were brought in because of their immunity to phylloxera and remained popular long after. But they have been banned for not being *Vitis vinifera*. Meanwhile, crosses of different varieties developed at Conegliano have gained favour with growers.

Vine training systems cover a full range. Around Verona, the traditional double-canopied *pergola veronese* is used in low hills and plains, though the single-armed pergola and vertical systems are more common in the hills to the east. In the flatlands of the eastern Veneto and along the Po and Adige, growers favour the Raggi or Belussi pergola that prevails in Emilia-Romagna. The trellised *tendone* is also used in the plains.

The following varieties are associated primarily with the Veneto.

Corvina Veronese. Verona's most admired red wine variety is not only the key component of Bardolino and Valpolicella, but is sometimes used almost exclusively in Recioto and Amarone, since the drying process seems to bring out its best. Selections are being made from more than 200 clones of Corvina, which is also known as Corvinone and Cruina.

Durella. Once prominent in the west-central Veneto, where its sharp acidity and taut fruit flavours made it a favourite in blends. Today it is the base of the white DOC Lessini Durello, most noted as *spumante*.

Garganega. When treated with respect in hill vineyards, the vine gives Soave noted personality. Its steady productivity is appreciated in light whites through the Veneto in Gambellara, Bianco di Custoza, Colli Berici, Colli Euganei, in eastern Lombardy, and occasionally elsewhere.

Incrocio Manzoni 2.15. A cross of Prosecco and Cabernet Sauvignon developed by Giovanni Manzoni at Conegliano, its productive nature seems best suited for light reds.

Incrocio Manzoni 6.0.13. Professor Manzoni's most noted cross, Riesling Renano x Pinot Bianco, has gained favour in the Venezie, and occasionally elsewhere, in refined whites.

Molinara. A minor component in the Bardolino and Valpolicella blends, it is noted for light, fruity qualities. Synonyms are Rossara, Rossanella.

Negrara. This once prominent family of vines is fading, though Negrara Trentina may still figure in blends of Valpolicella and Bardolino.

Prosecco. The Prosecco Bianco (or Tondo or Balbi) of Treviso's hills apparently originated at the village of Prosecco in Friuli's Carso, where the ancient Romans praised a wine from it called Pulcinum. Today it is prized for softly bubbly whites in the eastern Veneto but is seldom found in Friuli, where it is also called Glera. Another theory is that it originated in the Colli Euganei, where it is known as Serprina.

Raboso. Of the two distinct varieties, Raboso del Piave is preferred in the dark, sharply flavoured red of the eastern Veneto's plains, though the more productive Raboso Veronese is often preferred for blending. The Piave type is also known as Friularo.

Rondinella. The prolific second variety (after Corvina) of Bardolino and Valpolicella, it adds colour, body, and acidity to the blend.

Rossignola. A native of Valpolicella, its lively acidity was appreciated in youthful Verona reds, though its use is now optional.

Tocai Rosso. Though origins are uncertain, this dark Tocai has nothing to do with white varieties of the name, though some experts cite similarities to Sardinia's Cannonau and a possible link to the Granacha or Grenache family. It makes lively light reds in the Colli Berici.

Trebbiano di Soave. The same as Lombardy's Trebbiano di Lugana, around Verona it is nearly always blended with Garganega in DOC

Soave, Bianco di Custoza, and table wines. Also known as Trebbiano Veronese.

Verdiso. Though once prominent in Treviso's hills, it is used sparingly for sharp, skittish bubbly whites or, more often, in blends with Prosecco.

Verduzzo Trevigiano. Though not related to Verduzzo Friulano, and probably not native to Treviso as the name suggests, it makes light, dry whites in the Piave area.

Vespaiola. The vine, also called Bresparolo and Vesparola, is used for a dry white under Breganze DOC, though it gives more luxurious results in unclassified sweet wines known as Torcolato and Acininobili.

Other varieties

Other varieties recommended or authorized in the Veneto include:

For red (or rosé): Ancellotta, Barbera, Cabernet Franc, Cabernet Sauvignon, Ciliegiolo, Croatina, Fertilia, Freisa, Groppello Gentile,

Italica, Lagrein, Lambrusco a Foglia Frastigliata, Lambrusco di Sorbara, Malbec, Marzemino, Merlot, Nigra, Pavana, Pinot Nero, Prodest, Refosco dal Peduncolo Rosso, Schiava Gentile, Schiava Grigia, Schiava Grossa, Teroldego, Trevisana Nera, Turca, Wildbacher.
For white: Bianchetta Trevigiana, Chardonnay, Cortese, Flavis, Incrocio Bianco Fedit 51 C.S.G., Malvasia Bianca di Candia, Malvasia del Chianti, Malvasia Istriana, Moscato Bianco, Moscato Giallo, Müller Thurgau, Nosiola, Pinella, Pinot Bianco, Pinot Grigio, Riesling Italico, Riesling Renano, Sauvignon, Sémillon, Sylvaner Verde, Tocai Friulano, Traminer Aromatico, Trebbiano Giallo, Trebbiano Romganolo, Trebbiano Toscano, Veltliner, Verduzzo Friulano.

Above: the Valpolicella Classico zone where vineyards on the hillsides overlooking Verona produce Corvina and other varieties for the popular red wine of the name as well as Recioto and Amarone from semidried grapes.

The Veneto's Wine Zones

The Veneto is clearly divided between mountain and plain. The Alps which cover a third of the region to the north along the borders with Trentino-Alto Adige, Austria, and Friuli-Venezia Giulia, give way rather abruptly to the broad flatlands formed by the Po, Adige, Astico, Brenta, Piave, and Livenza rivers along their courses to the Adriatic. Venice is the axis of the Pianura Veneta, whose fertile soils and warm climate make it the most bountiful source of wine in northern Italy. The Adriatic serves as a moderating influence on the coastal plains, though the interior can be hot in summer, even suffering from occasional drought. Most of the Veneto's fine wines come from the alpine foothills and high plains between Lake Garda and Conegliano (north of Venice) and the Berici and Euganei ranges rising from the plains near Vicenza and Padova. The alpine barrier traps heat in the Adriatic basin and induces rainfall in the hills. Excessive damp and hail can create problems in some vintages. Yet, despite nature's occasional deterrents, the Veneto normally manages to produce ample quantities of both premium and ordinary wines.

Verona's Lake Garda: Bardolino and Custoza

Bardolino and Bianco di Custoza occupy the rolling hills in the eastern part of the Garda glacial basin. The area has an unusually mild climate for northern Italy, thanks to the lake's direct influence and protection from northern air currents provided by the mass of Monte Baldo to the north. Bardolino, in both red and *chiaretto*, comes from a blend of Veronese grape varieties based on Corvina, Rondinella, and Molinara, similar to that of Valpolicella. Yet Bardolino's red is lighter as a rule. This characteristic is said to derive from the sandy, gravelly soils in the classical zone to the north, though where clay is prominent wines tend to have more body and colour. Bianco di Custoza comes from a blend of Trebbiano, Garganega, and Tocai grown in rolling morainic hills. Its southern sector along the Mincio valley feels the summer heat from the Padana, but cooler air from Garda helps give the wines vitality.

Verona's Lessini hills: Valpolicella, Soave, and Durello

Monte Lessini, the volcanic massif that dominates Verona, has been moulded by glaciers and sliced by streams towards the south into valleys whose often steep slopes support the province's major vineyards of Valpolicella and Soave. Valpolicella covers much of the lower slopes, though its Classico area is limited to the southwestern corner where breezes from Lake Garda have a temperate effect on the terraced hillsides. There red wines based on Corvina and Rondinella are noted for a youthful heartiness, though their *passito* versions – the sweet Recioto and dry Amarone – can show uncommon power if dry, cold weather allows the grapes to concentrate through autumn and winter. Valleys to the east have similar mixtures of tufaceous and calcareous soils, but apart from some wines of the Valpantena, Valpolicella from the eastern valleys rarely equal those of Classico. Differences in Soave can be even more pronounced, since Classico covers the hills and most other vines stretch across plains to the southwest towards the Adige. Soave Classico's noted vineyards lie along a crest between the communes of Soave and Monteforte d'Alpone. Sites there are generally exposed to the south, benefiting from mountain currents and sharp day-night temperature fluctuations that account for the heightened aromas and flavours in well-made wines based on Garganega and Trebbiano. The new Lessini DOC zone covers the eastern slopes of the range in a large territory extending from the edge of Soave and Valpolicella into Vicenza province. Reddish calcareous soils in choice vineyards there are said to account for a steely quality in white Durello. The marked acidity in wines from Durella grapes is also due to cool temperatures in the high vineyards.

The central hills: Vicenza and Padova

Vicenza province has three distinct wine areas. Breganze lies on high plains formed by the Agno, Astico, and Brenta rivers and the foothills of the Asiago plateau, whose protection from the north accounts for the mild climate. Vineyards in glacial moraine along the Astico and volcanic soil in the hills make reds of stature from Cabernet and whites of tone from Tocai, the Pinots, and Vespaiolo. Gambellara lies to the extreme southeast of the Lessini range adjacent to Soave, but subtle variations in terrains and microclimates in the low hills account for notable differences in the white wines, which also include Recioto and Vino Santo. South of Vicenza are the Colli Berici, hills formed by volcanic eruptions like the nearby Colli Euganei southwest of Padova. Both ranges have relatively fertile volcanic soils with calcareous deposits. Cabernet, Merlot, and whites from Garganega, Tocai and other varieties show balance from high vineyards in the Colli Euganei and from slopes around San Germano and Villaga in the Colli Berici, though wines from the plains in both zones are rarely noteworthy.

Treviso's hills

Two distinct ranges north and south of the Piave river are noted for wine. The hills between Valdobbiadene and Conegliano have a gentle climate protected by the alpine wall to the north, though soil variations account for somewhat different styles in the prevalent Prosecco. Wines from pebbly calcareous terrain on the warmer Conegliano side to the east tend to be softer and fruitier than those from the higher slopes to the west around Valdobbiadene, where the most refined wines come from calcareous sandy clays on steep slopes at a place called Cartizze. The Montello e Colli Asolani rises to the south are slightly warmer and damper due to the prevalence of woods around Asolo that create a microclimate noted as much for mushrooms as wine. Prosecco prevails in this DOC zone, too, though Merlot and Cabernet can attain stature in the iron rich clays slopes of Montello.

The Venetian plains: Piave and Lison-Pramaggiore

The alluvial plains formed by the Piave, Livenza, and Tagliamento have a warm maritime climate favourable to red wines that can show marked personality, as well as to light, often spritzy whites. Piave is Italy's major source of Merlot, which thrives in mixed soils of sand and clay on a gravel base to the north and in finer loam towards the Adriatic. Cabernet, Raboso, Verduzzo, and Chardonnay are also prominent. Lison-Pramaggiore, which stretches north into Friuli between the Livenza and Tagliamento, has well-drained calcareous clay soils rich in minerals that seem to lend a touch of distinction to the prevalent Cabernet, Merlot, and Tocai.

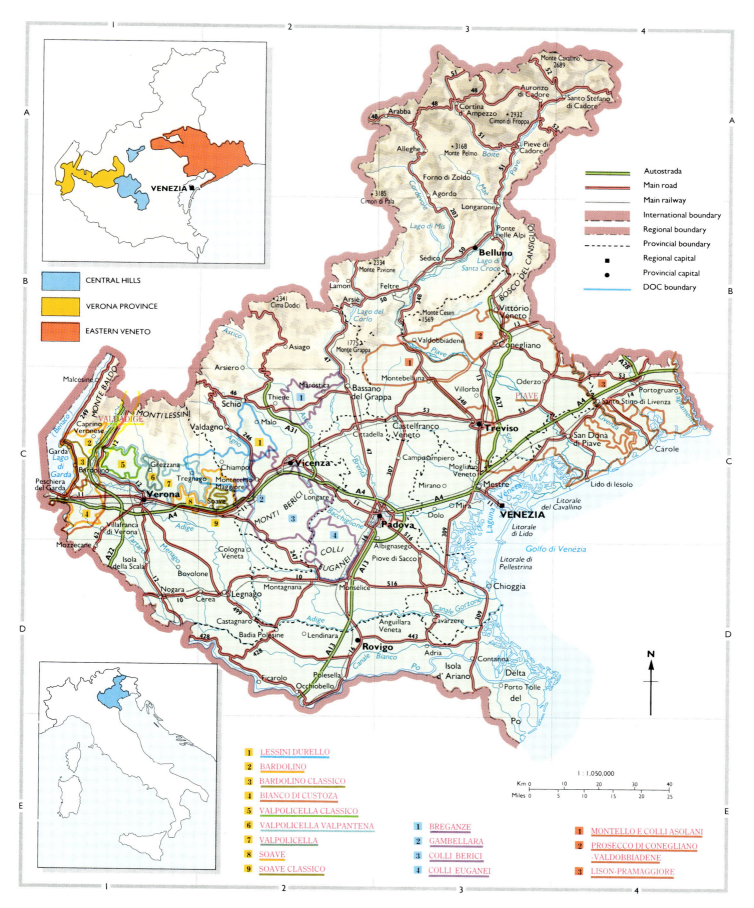

CENTRAL HILLS

VERONA PROVINCE

EASTERN VENETO

VENEZIA

Autostrada
Main road
Main railway
International boundary
Regional boundary
Provincial boundary
■ Regional capital
● Provincial capital
DOC boundary

1 LESSINI DURELLO

2 BARDOLINO

3 BARDOLINO CLASSICO

4 BIANCO DI CUSTOZA

5 VALPOLICELLA CLASSICO

6 VALPOLICELLA VALPANTENA

7 VALPOLICELLA

8 SOAVE

9 SOAVE CLASSICO

1 BREGANZE

2 GAMBELLARA

3 COLLI BERICI

4 COLLI EUGANEI

1 MONTELLO E COLLI ASOLANI

2 PROSECCO DI CONEGLIANO
-VALDOBBIADENE

3 LISON-PRAMAGGIORE

1 : 1,050,000
Km 0   10   20   30   40
Miles 0   5   10   15   20   25

N

Wines of Verona

Verona is Italy's most active wine centre, its leading source of DOC, and the host each April to Vinitaly, the quintessential trade fair. Vineyards practically surround the walled city on the Adige whose wines come from places as attractive as their names along the shores of Lake Garda and the lower slopes of the Monti Lessini. Soave is the easiest to reach, since the hillside town with its sprawling castle is adjacent to the Milan-Venice *autostrada*. Bardolino, a Lake Garda resort, is the centre of a gently hilly wine zone joined to the south by Bianco di Custoza. Also parts of the Lugana and Tocai di San Martino della Battaglia DOC zones extend into the province from Lombardy, giving the area's producers even more options. Valpolicella's steep terraces afford marvellous views over Verona from the north – for those who manage to find their way through the city's industrial suburbs to reach them. For there, as elsewhere, tourists who come to sip the wines amidst the vineyards are given little guidance about how to find them and few signs of welcome when they do arrive. It sometimes seems that the city of Romeo and Juliet has forgotten about its wines' romantic heritage.

The fading of local colour is just one symptom of the change that has swept the wine industry here. Verona, situated between the Alps and the Padana plains, enjoys a special climate, influenced by the reflection of sunlight and cooling air currents from Lake Garda that supposedly account for the wines' perennial fragrance and verve. The hills abound in those privileged sites known as *capitelli*, but the Veronese, in their rush to meet market demands, have too often ignored the proverb that good wine is made in the vineyard. To keep their wines competitive during the boom of the 1970s and after, the large houses and cooperatives that prevail here held grape prices down. So growers, who were rarely rewarded for quality, were forced to raise quantities. As a consequence, many choice hill vineyards were abandoned while vines chosen for productivity spread across the plains. Improved oenology raised the quality level for a time, but critics often complain that the wines of Verona, so long noted for their uniquely native personalities, have become increasingly standardized.

As exports of DOC wines declined in the 1980s, many large houses turned to popular types to take up the slack – mainly Pinot Grigio and Chardonnay from neighbouring regions, as well as *frizzanti* and *spumanti*. Some have managed to move up market with new styles of Soave, Valpolicella, and Amarone, as well as table wines. But since many producers here have become more adept at selling wine than making it, that strategy hasn't always worked. For the fact is that there aren't enough of those esteemed old *capitelli* in active production to meet the demands of increasingly sophisticated consumers. Only a few wineries have managed to notably improve class and build prestige – almost invariably those which possess or have direct access to good vineyards.

Their quest has been aided by experiments on native varieties being carried out at the State Agricultural Institute at San Floriano in Valpolicella. While leading research into clonal selections and improved vineyard methods, the school is training a new generation of winemakers in the techniques of viticulture and oenology that augurs well for the future.

Apart from scattered plantings of Chardonnay and Cabernet, leading growers have concentrated on improving native vines and making wines that express the old-time character but in more contemporary styles. That aim is not easy to achieve, but the wines of a number of estates in Valpolicella and Soave have been winning critical acclaim. Their success has inspired a flush of new "crus" from wineries large and small. But some of those vineyards are imaginary, carrying names that might have struck their bottlers' fancies as they perused the map. This opportunism aroused the indignation of honest growers, who as a group have begun to demand verification of vineyard and estate bottlings. Their movement may be without precedent in Italy. If it succeeds, it could help to restore some dignity and pride to a wine community that, after years of neglecting its intrinsic advantages, seems somewhat short of both.

Below: vineyards in the Bardolino Classico zone near Lake Garda, whose special microclimate is said to contribute to a spicy quality in the light reds and bright pink chiaretto. The wines carry the name of the lakeside town of Bardolino.

Bardolino (1968)

Classical Bardolino, whether of a tenuous ruby-garnet colour or boldly pink *chiaretto*, had enticing fragrance and a subtle dose of cherry-like fruit offset by a slightly bitter finish. At its sprightly best in either version it was praised as *salato* (literally "salty", or, more to the point, "spicy") which to admirers around Lake Garda meant that they couldn't get enough of it. Originally, Bardolino came from the hilly environs of the lakeside town and the neighbouring villages that now comprise Classico. There wines from vineyards in glacial gravel and sand showed youthful redolence and verve, though where clay prevails they tended to be more robust and durable. The grape composition is nearly identical to Valpolicella, yet Bardolino, if by nature lighter, is not necessarily a lesser red. The rosé – which, according to local expert Zeffiro Bocci, was traditionally known as Chiaretto del Garda – was admired both as a refreshing summer wine and the ideal match for Garda's sumptuous lake trout. Gradually, though, Bardolino's vineyards spread southwards through the rolling countryside now shared with the DOC of Bianco di Custoza and away from the valuable land near the lake. Growth did little for quality. A decade ago, Bardolino's fortunes were in decline, as styles fluctuated between the old and the new. But in the mid-1980s producers, led by Lamberti, found a formula for success in Italy's first officially sanctioned *novello*. That imitation of Beaujolais Nouveau has been so successful that grape prices in Bardolino, for the first time in memory, surpassed those of Valpolicella. Sparkling *chiaretto* has also been in vogue. Those who fondly recall the old Bardolino can rest assured that a few estates, notably the perennial leader Guerrieri-Rizzardi, still make wines of classical dimensions with breed never found amidst the commercial novelties. Some producers even consider Bardolino Classico Superiore from top vintages a wine to lay away for a few years to develop the same sort of mellow warmth sensed in certain aged Valpolicella. But such bottles aren't for modern markets, so their main admirers are the winemakers themselves.

Zone: Hills and rolling plains between the southeastern shore of Lake Garda and the Adige river, extending from Torre del Benaco south past Peschiera del Garda to Valeggio sul Mincio and Sommacampagna and comprising 16 communes in Verona province. The lakeside town of Bardolino is the heart of the Classico zone, which also encompasses the neighbouring villages of Affi, Cavaion Veronese, Costermano, Garda, and Lazise.

Dry red, sometimes frizzante. Grapes:

Above: the popular Garda resort town of Bardolino holds an annual festival to celebrate the grape harvest and the promise of vini novelli, wines that are issued in November like Beaujolais Nouveau.

Corvina Veronese 35-65%, Rondinella 10-40%, Molinara 10-20%; Negrara up to 10%, Rossignola/Barbera/Sangiovese/Garganega up to 15%. Yld 91/130, Alc 10.5; superiore 11.5, Acd 0.5, Ag superiore 1 yr.

Chiaretto Dry rosé, also spumante. Grapes: as rosso. Yld 91/130, Alc 10.5; spumante 11.5, Acd 0.5; spumante 0.6.

Novello Youthful dry red that must be bottled before the end of the year of harvest. Grapes: as rosso. Yld 91/130, Alc 10.5, Acd 0.55.

Bianco di Custoza (1971)

The wine once considered a white version of Bardolino or a cheaper alternative to Soave has surpassed original expectations. Though it hasn't matched the peaks of Soave Classico, the current standard of Bianco di Custoza seems a shade higher than that of its famous neighbour. The reason might be that the vanguard of estate owners has invested not only in vineyards and cellars but also in the knowhow that can make the difference between an ordinary white wine and an interesting one. Bianco di Custoza, despite its mix of not particularly illustrious varieties grown in softly rolling hills of Garda's glacial basin, is at its best a wine of some style and individuality. Estate bottlings of note come from Arvedi d'Emilei, Cavalchina, Fraterna Portalupi, Gorgo, and Le Vigne di San Pietro.

Zone: Low hills and rolling plains between the Adige river and Lazise on the southeastern shore of Lake Garda, extending south between the Mincio river and Villafranca through seven communes in Verona province. The name comes from the village of Custoza, a battle site in Italy's war for independence. Much of the area coincides with the southern part of Bardolino. Dry white, also spumante. Grapes: Trebbiano Toscano 35-45%, Garganega 20-40%, Tocai Friulano 5-30%, Cortese/Riesling Italico/Malvasia Toscana 20-30%. Yld 97.5/150, Alc 11, Acd 0.45.

Valpolicella/Recioto della Valpolicella/Amarone (1968)

The wines closest to Verona's heart come from steeply terraced hillsides overlooking the city in an area known historically as Valpolicella. The name originally applied to the southwestern corner of the Monti Lessini in the valleys formed by the Fumane, Marano, Negrar, and Novare streams. Breezes from Lake Garda and the plains along the Adige flowed into the valleys creating microclimates favourable not only to ripening of grapes for young red wines but to their drying in autumn and winter for the sweet Recioto and richly dry Amarone. When the DOC was conceived, Valpolicella was extended eastwards across the Valpantena and other valleys where producers were in the habit of using the name. Natural conditions along those gorges are similar, yet with few exceptions the best wines of all types originate in what came to be known as Valpolicella Classico.

Valpolicella has long rivalled Chianti in popularity abroad, notably in Britain, where it is often served as the house wine in Italian restaurants. A warm, hearty, cheerful red, it is appreciated for its lack of pretention and affordable price. The blend – in which the weight of Corvina and Rondinella are balanced by the lighter, spicier Molinara and sometimes the traditional Negrara and Rossignola – is best suited to wines of refreshing grapey flavour that rarely benefit from more than a year or two of ageing.

Recently, leading producers have made more robust and durable versions of the wine by refermenting the basic Valpolicella with the pomace of Amarone, which relies most of all on the admirable Corvina. Nino Franceschetti, who updated *ripasso* from a rustic practice of the past, described it as the marriage of a king and a commoner. Yet the Campo Fiorin, which he created at Masi, set a noble precedent in adding a welcome dimension to the red wines of Verona. Confusingly, though, some such wines are labelled as Valpolicella Superiore, while others become special table wines. *Ripasso* deserves a special category within the DOC to distinguish its plush, poised wines from the youthful Valpolicella and even from the slightly aged *superiore*, which isn't necessarily the same thing.

Equally deserving of differentiation – from the rest of Valpolicella and from one another – are Recioto and Amarone, even though they come from the same vines in the same zone. Both wines are categorized as Recioto della Valpolicella, though the dry version is usually called just Amarone. It has been said that the name Recioto comes from Retico (the Roman Rhaetic), but it

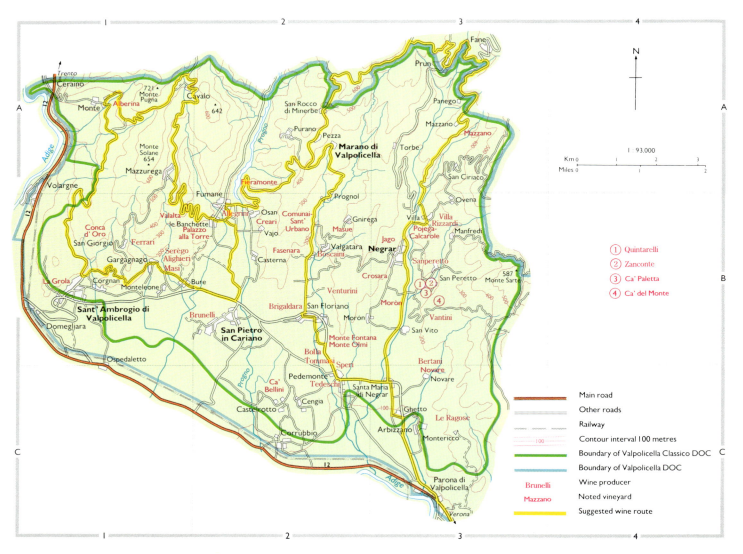

Quintarelli
Zanconte
Ca' Paletta
Ca' del Monte

Main road
Other roads
Railway
Contour interval 100 metres
Boundary of Valpolicella Classico DOC
Boundary of Valpolicella DOC
Brunelli Wine producer
Mazzano Noted vineyard
Suggested wine route

probably derives from *recie* (dialect for the "ears" of the bunches with the ripest, sweetest grapes).

Today grapes for Recioto usually come from vineyards facing southwest, where they develop more sugar, while those for Amarone are selected in eastern-oriented plots where slower ripening results in better balance of components. Both wines are painstaking to make, since a good vintage is the result not only of high quality grapes but of a prolonged streak of luck in drying them on racks in airy lofts. The success of this *appassimento* depends on dry, cool weather from the harvest until January, when Amarone grapes are pressed, and a couple months longer for Recioto. In the past, when the sweet type prevailed, the shrivelled grapes usually developed botrytis cinerea that gave Recioto the nuances of flavour still desired by some. But leading producers of Amarone try to avoid this noble rot, since it can lessen acidity and colour and cause premature ageing.

Amarone was supposedly created by error when the fermentation of a Recioto didn't stop as expected and the wine came out dry with that bitter undertone, the *amaro* that is one element of its complex flavour and the reason for its name. The finest Amarone deserves most of the superlatives applied to great red wines for ageing, yet the sheer grandeur that places it somewhere between, say, Barolo and port, leave people wondering when and with what to drink it. Should it be served on special occasions with the prescribed game dishes and strong cheeses, or should it be sipped after dinner by the fireside? Some Amarone producers are trying to reduce its strength to the same level as other dry red wines without losing the extraordinary range of flavours that set it apart. Sweet Recioto is even more like port. Though a fortified type is permitted, the best is naturally rich and velvety. There is also a sparkling version appreciated around Verona.

Some producers predict a comeback

for both types of wine, though they now have to work hard to sell the total of about 1.5 million bottles a year. Whatever the future holds in store, they deserve the separate recognition as Recioto della Valpolicella and Amarone della Valpolicella which has long been sought by the producers consortium.

Valpolicella's array of diverse types is as confusing as the attitudes that lie behind their production. The rivalry between the estates and what are often called commercial interests goes beyond a mere division between the small and the large, however. Some large houses, notably Bertani and Bolla, have made some of the best Valpolicella and Amarone from certified vineyards over the years, while some small producers have performed less than gallantly.

The *cru* controversy may begin to sort out differences, since growers who vinify their own grapes have more at stake in Valpolicella than do merchant houses that merely bottle the wines. Some estates are clearly on the move. Giuseppe Quintarelli, the champion of

artisans, makes wines that often outweigh the rest while ranging beyond them in rustic complexity, but more producers seem to be following the contemporary lines set by Masi and reinforced by Tedeschi, Speri, Tommasi, Vantini, and Ferrari. Among a dozen or so admirable estates in Valpolicella, Allegrini seems to be setting the current pace, by acquiring more choice vineyards and honing techniques to give newly artistic definitions to the wines.

The renewed emphasis on vineyards has raised the controversial question about whether names refer to real plots or to places where vines have been abandoned or indeed never grew. Rumours about pretenders may be better left to producers in the zone to verify. But inquiries among experienced growers have arrived at an informal consensus about which vineyard areas of Valpolicella are superior, either in results or potential, and might be considered the nucleus for official recognition in the future. To the west in the commune of Sant'Ambrogio lie the Alberina area near Monte, the largely abandoned Conca d'Oro at San Giorgio, and the newly thriving La Grola, an uncontested top growth. In the next valley over in the commune of Fumane are Valalta, Palazzo della Torre, Fieramonte, and the nearly adjacent Creari and Comunai-Sant'Urbano. In the valley below Marano, adjacent to Valgatara, is Fasenara. On the lower slopes in the commune of San Pietro in Cariano are Ca' Bellini at Castelrotto and, above Pedemonte, Monte Fontana and Monte Olmi. The Negrar valley to the east boasts several of Classico's most esteemed vineyards. Just northwest of Negrar are Masue and Jago (Alto and Basso), and to the south Crosara and Moròn. Along the eastern flank of the Negrar valley, from north to south, are Mazzano, Pojega (or Poiega) and Calcarole, Ca' Paletta and Ca' del Monte, Tramanal, and Novare. High above Arbizzano are the restored terraces of Le Ragose and Le Sassine, which, like other of Valpolicella's nearly forgotten *capitelli*, are slowly re-establishing their own rank.

Zone: The often steep inclines along the lower valleys of the Monti Lessini above Verona, extending from the banks of the Adige and the area known historically as Valpolicella east across the Pantena, Squaranto, and Ilasi valleys to Montecchia di Crosara in the Alpone valley north of Soave. Of the 19 communes in Verona province included in the zone, Classico takes in Fumane, Marano, Negrar, San Pietro in Cariano, and Sant'Ambrogio. Valpantena

(between Verona and Grezzana) may also be cited on labels. Dry red, usually youthful, sometimes aged as superiore or ripasso. Grapes: Corvina Veronese 40-70%, Rondinella 20-40%, Molinara 5-25%; Negrara Trentina/Rossignola/Barbera/Sangiovese up to 15%. Yld 84/120, Alc 11; superiore 12, Acd 0.5, Ag superiore 1 yr.

Recioto della Valpolicella Sweet red, sometimes spumante or liquoroso. Grapes: as Valpolicella but semidried or passito. Yld 48/120, Alc 14 (res sugar 2%); liquoroso 16, Acd 0.55.

Recioto della Valpolicella Amarone or **Amarone** Dry red, sometimes with a sweet vein. Grapes: as Valpolicella but semidried or passito. Yld 48/120, Alc 14 (res sugar max 0.4%), Acd 0.55.

Valpolicella-Valpantena May be used by all types grown in the Pantena valley.

Left: grapes of both Valpolicella and Soave are partly dried for use in the strong sweet wines known as Recioto. The process depends on having dry, cold weather during the four to six months after the harvest when they are left to shrivel on racks in well ventilated rooms. Dampness can cause rot and spoil wines whose quality depends to a great extent on luck.

Below: the town of Fumane lies along one of five valleys in the area that was historically called Valpolicella and which today is recognized as Classico in the extensive DOC zone. Vineyards on the steep and often terraced hillsides are noted as the sources of the finest wines of the name, both as Classico Superiore and as the rich, dry Amarone.

Soave (1968)

Soave is easily accessible from the Milan-Venice *autostrada*, which while crossing flat fields of vines east of Verona provides inviting vistas of the hillside town. The landmark is a medieval castle, whose crenellated ramparts join the town's walls and reach into the first hill vineyards. A symbolic greeting on the approach from the motorway is provided by a modern plant with a large sign that reads "Soave Bolla". The name Soave seems to have come from the Swabians who settled there in the Middle Ages. It also happens to mean suave in Italian, a term often used to describe the wine and explain its wide appeal. The Englishman Charles G. Bode captured the essence of Soave in 1956 when he wrote, "It tastes as a very clear, sunny sky might taste if one could drink it!" His book, *Wines of Italy*, preceded the technological transformation that enabled enormous growth in exports during the 1970s. That boom also encouraged the spread of vines from the hills of Soave Classico southwest across the plains towards the Adige, during which the basic Garganega and Trebbiano di Soave were supplemented by the more productive Trebbiano Toscano. Soave, in a sense, ushered Italian white wine into the modern era, setting the precedent for the national stereotype of light, fresh, fruity, consistent, and affordable. Bolla built such a widespread reputation that many foreigners seemed to think Soave was a company trademark. But over time the bottlers and shippers who added to Soave's flow abroad have also contributed to a decline in popularity. Reasonable price and a steady increase in sparkling versions have kept Soave's markets alive. But, at least until recently, tasters in Italy tended to routinely dimiss Soave as too bland, too standardized, too commercialized to be taken seriously. Some foreign experts, who decided years ago that Italy wasn't capable of making whites of heightened personality, may have been lulled into thinking that Soave was the best the country could do. But any who have bothered to taste the current range would be aware that some Soave Classico rates an honourable position among the nation's new hierarchy of white wines.

Soave Classico's superiority is clear cut, since it covers most of the hill vineyards in a zone where nearly three quarters of the grapes come from the plains. Differences in soils and microclimates are telling, but equally important is the work of several vineyard owners who have found more satisfying ways to make a living than growing grapes for mass production. Leonildo Pieropan bottled the first single-vineyard Soave Classico, Vigneto Calvarino, in 1971, followed by Vigneto La Rocca in 1978. He also made Soave's first modern Recioto, Le Colombare, from grapes selected and dried on racks to be pressed into an elegantly restrained sweet wine. Roberto Anselmi advanced the *cru* concept with Capitel Foscarino, while devising Capitel Croce and sweet Recioto dei Capitelli whose acclaimed styles derive in part from *barriques*. Anselmi has planted choice plots with traditional clones of low yielding Garganega in heavy density (10,000-13,000 vines per ha) because he believes that the drive to realize the ultimate in Soave depends more on ideal vineyard conditions than on dazzling cellar feats. He has decided that Garganega, complemented by the worthy local Trebbiano, should remain the base, despite the temptations of Chardonnay and other varieties. Pieropan quietly pioneered the drive for greater quality and integrity in Soave to which Anselmi, with his infectious exuberance, drew nationwide attention. They alone among producers opposed a recent bid to raise permitted grape yields for Soave, a change rejected by the national DOC committee by a single vote. This earned the enmity of fellow growers who seem reluctant to admit that Anselmi and Pieropan have done more to build a newly respectable image of Soave than all the others combined.

But they are not the only respected producers of Soave Classico. Bertani and Guerreri-Rizzardi have vineyards there for wines of unerring dignity. Bolla's noted standards for Soave Classico are surpassed by its special

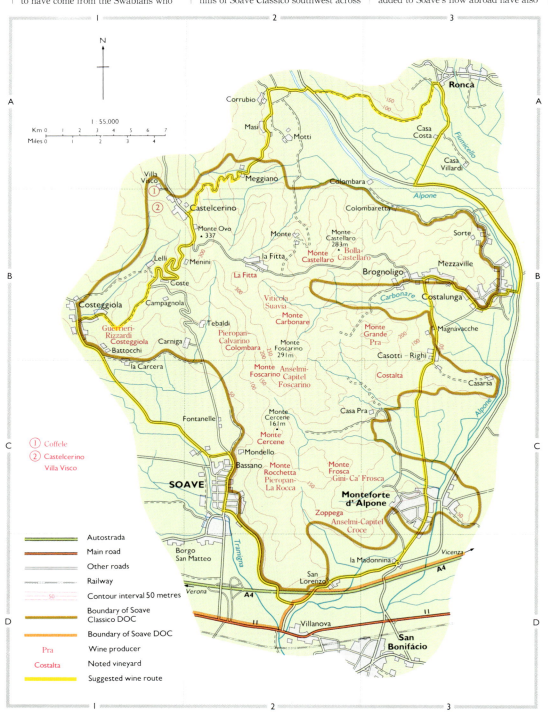

Map legend

- ① Coffele
- ② Castelcerino
  Villa Visco

- Autostrada
- Main road
- Other roads
- Railway
- Contour interval 50 metres
- Boundary of Soave Classico DOC
- Boundary of Soave DOC
- Pra — Wine producer
- Costalta — Noted vineyard
- Suggested wine route

Above: the town of Soave east of Verona with its castle on the hillside where the Classico zone begins, though vineyards are also planted on the plains.

wine from Castellaro, though limited quantities prevent it from making the impact it deserves. The largest producer, the Cantina Sociale, has access to some of the best vineyards, from which selections are made for special bottlings. Several growers – Viticola Suavia, Graziano Pra, and Gini – make well-rated single vineyard wines. Others supply producers elsewhere with respectable Soave Classico, even if the *crus* named on labels don't always correspond with the facts. Here, as in Valpolicella Classico, moves are afoot to certify single vineyard wines as the first step towards meaningful recognition.

All of Soave's vineyards whose worth has been verified over time are situated in the Classico area along the often steep rises near the crests that form the divide between the communes of Soave and Monteforte d'Alpone. Vines are usually exposed to the south or southwest at altitudes between 100-350 m. Soils vary from calcareous clays to tufaceous formations, with often heavy glacial deposits of rounded stones useful for building dry walls around vineyards. Experienced growers have distinguished 13 areas that could be rated as superior, beginning with

Monte Foscarino, whose central position makes it the zone's point of reference. South of it lie Monte Cercene, Monte Frosca, Zoppega, and Monte Rocchetta, adjacent to Soave's castle. To the east lie Monte Grande and Costalta, and to the west Colombara and the village of Costeggiola. To the north are Monte Carbonare, Monte Castellaro, and the slopes adjacent to the villages of La Fitta and Castelcerino.

Still it would be incorrect to state that all good Soave Classico comes from those vineyards alone, since grapes are often mixed in wines of respectable quality. But most Soave still deserves its reputation as standardized and commercial, an image that has not been enhanced by the recent increase of dry *spumante* made by tank methods or the sweet Recioto, which is clearly not suited to bubbles.

Zone: Often steep hills east of Verona above the towns of Soave and Monteforte d'Alpone, where wines from vineyards between the Tramigia and Alpone valleys may be called Classico. Also included are eight other communes in Verona province, mainly on plains north of the Adige where vineyards flank the Verona-Venice autostrada. Dry white, also spumante. Grapes: Garganega; Trebbiano di Soave/

Trebbiano Toscano up to 30%. Yld 98/140, Alc 10.5; superiore 11.5, Acd 0.5, Ag superiore 8 mths.

Recioto di Soave Sweet white, also spumante and liquoroso. Grapes: as Soave but semidried or passito. Yld 56/140, Alc 14 (res sugar 2.5%), liquoroso 16, Acd 0.55.

Lessini Durello (1987)

Soave's new DOC neighbour to the north in the Lessini hills is based on a vine long respected in the area as a source of *spumante*, though wines from the zone, which extends into Vicenza province, are scarcely known. The grape name is feminine, the wine masculine, but both Durella and Durello connote hardness, probably in reference to a steely edge that gave the rustic whites of the Lessini hills a refreshing tang. Its sturdy texture and sharp acidity are what makes Durella ideal in blends of *spumante*, a style of Durello which seems most likely to succeed as a DOC.

Zone: The southeastern slopes of the Monti Lessini extending from the edge of the Soave and Gambellara zones north nearly to Schio and including 21 communes in Vicenza province and seven in Verona. Dry white, also spumante. Grapes: Durella; Garganega/Trebbiano di Soave/Chardonnay/Pinot Nero up to 15%. Yld 112/160, Alc 10; superiore and spumante 11, Acd 0.7; spumante 0.8.

Other wines of note

Wines of the other DOC zones that extend into Verona province are discussed elsewhere: Lugana and Tocai di San Martino della Battaglia in Lombardy and Valdadige in Trentino-Alto Adige. Verona abounds in unclassified wines. Some of the most worthy, such as *ripasso* reds of Valpolicella and other special wines from native varieties, along with promising Cabernets and Chardonnays, are listed with their producers. In Valpolicella, unclassified sweet whites from Allegrini, Masi, Quintarelli, and Tedeschi can rival fine Recioto di Soave. There has also been steady growth in sometimes respectable *spumanti* and *frizzanti*. The most publicized of the Veneto's popular wines are called Turà, light, fizzy white and rosé made by the Gruppo Italiano Vini under various labels.

ESTATES/GROWERS

Allegrini, Fumane (VR). The estate founded by the late Giovanni Allegrini is run by children Walter, Marilisa, and Franco, whose cellars at Corte Giara produce increasingly admired wines from about 50 ha of choice plots in Valpolicella Classico. Single-vineyard wines are Valpolicella La Grola and Palazzo alla Torre (a *ripasso*), and Amarone Fieramonte. Gardane is a Recioto, Fiorgardane a sweet white *passito*. La Poja is a promising pure Corvina vdt from La Grola. Pelara is a red vdt from a pre-phylloxera vine.

Anselmi, Monteforte d'Alpone (VR). Roberto Anselmi has proved Soave's unexpected class and versatility, drawing upon his own 25 ha of vines at Monte Foscarino, Monte Cercene, and Zoppega as well as from growers with 30 ha under his control. Soave Capitel Foscarino and barrel-fermented Capitel Croce from Zoppega express new styles, though his regular Soave Classico is exemplary. Recioto dei Capitelli, seasoned in *barriques*, is one of Italy's most admired dessert wines. He makes a soft, refined Cabernet Sauvignon vdt called Realda and buys grapes in Valpolicella for Amarone.

Arvedi d'Emilei, Cavalcaselle (VR). Pietro Arvedi and family make good Bianco di Custoza and Bardolino from 30 ha around their ancient estate.

Brigaldara, San Floriano (VR). Noted for Valpolicella and Amarone.

Giuseppe Brunelli, San Pietro in Cariano (VR). Valpolicella and vdt.

Ca' del Monte, Negrar (VR). Luigi Zanconte makes good Valpolicella and Amarone.

Cavalchina, Sommacampagna (VR). Good Bianco di Custoza and Bardolino.

Coffele, Soave (VR). Giuseppe Coffele's Villa Visco at Castelcerino has some of Soave's best vineyards, but potential is not fully expressed.

Colle dei Cipressi, Calmasino di Bardolino (VR). Bardolino from 26 ha.

Ferrari, Gargagnago (VR). Aleardo Ferrari makes good Valpolicella and often excellent Recioto and Amarone.

Fongaro, Roncà (VR). Good Lessini Durello from the Motto Piane estate.

Fratelli Fraccaroli, San Benedetto di Lugana (VR). Good Lugana.

Fraterna Portalupi, Custoza (VR). Distinctive Bianco di Custoza and Bardolino.

Umberto Giarola, Palazzolo (VR). Bardolino and Bianco di Custoza.

Gini, Monteforte d'Alpone (VR). Producer of single vineyard Soave Classico Ca' Frosca from Monte Frosca and a Recioto called Col Foscarin.

Girasole, Lazise (VR). Good Bardolino and Valpolicella.

Gorgo, Custoza (VR). Roberto Bricolo makes good Bianco di Custoza and Bardolino from 30 ha.

Guerrieri-Rizzardi, Bardolino (VR). From their lakeside villa, Cristina Guerrieri-Rizzardi and family coordinate production of some of Verona's most gracious wines from 150 ha in Bardolino, Valpolicella, and Soave, each vinified in separate cellars. Single-vineyard bottlings are Bardolino (Tacchetto), Soave (Costeggiola), and Valpolicella (Villa Rizzardi Poiega), as

well as the vdt red Castello Guerrieri (from mainly forgotten local varieties), the white Bianco San Pietro (Chardonnay, Sémillon, Garganega, Tocai), and the medium dry Moscato called Dògoli.

Il Maso, Negrar di Valpolicella (VR). Zonin's estate for Valpolicella Classico and Amarone.

Le Fraghe, Affi (VR). Bardolino from 20 ha.

Le Ragose, Arbizzano di Negrar (VR). Maria Marta and Arnaldo Galli make widely admired Valpolicella Classico, Amarone, and sparkling Recioto from 12 ha of high, carefully terraced vineyards, along with the vdt Le Ragose Bianco and the reds Le Piane and Le Sassine.

Le Tende, Lazise (VR). Bardolino and Bianco di Custoza.

Le Vigne di San Pietro, Sommacampagna (VR). Young Carlo Nerozzi makes fine Bardolino and Bianco di Custoza (also *champenoise*), though his pride is a Cabernet Sauvignon vdt called Refolà from 5 ha.

Marcato, Roncà (VR). Good Soave from vineyards at Barche, along with impressive Lessini Durello, both still and *champenoise*.

Antonio Menegotti, Villafranca (VR). Bianco di Custoza and Bardolino.

Montecorno, Sona (VR). Good Bardolino and Bianco di Custoza from 23 ha.

Pieropan, Soave (VR). Leonildo Pieropan distinguished his Soave from the masses with the first single-vineyard wine in Vigneto Calvarino and the first modern Recioto in Le Colombare, both from 8 ha at Colombara. The Vigneto La Rocca, from 3 ha at Rocchetta, is often rated as his top Soave. Other family plots and grapes from trusted growers in the hills are sources of good regular Soave Classico and Riesling Italico vdt. The wines often show more colour, structure, and flavour than others, partly because they come from low yielding vines, but also because Pieropan and his wife Teresita use a minimum of filtering and other interventions in pursuing their ideals of what Soave ought to be.

Fratelli Poggi, Affi (VR). Good Bardolino from 40 ha.

Graziano Pra, Monteforte d'Alpone (VR). Emerging grower in Soave Classico with fine single-vineyard Monte Grande.

Quintarelli, Cerè di Negrar (VR). Gentle Giuseppe Quintarelli is a folk hero in Valpolicella due to quaint methods that include long fermentation of wines in old casks with little racking and no filtration. His Valpolicella (a *ripasso*), Recioto, and Amarone from Monte Ca' Paletta are praised, or sometimes criticized, for being so individualistic that variations can be noted from one bottle to the next – possibly because each is filled from a hand-operated tube. But when all goes right, Quintarelli's wines are unmatched for richness, complexity, and price – not only the reds, but Amabile di Cerè, a golden *passito* made from Garganega and other grapes selected one by one. He has been criticized locally for using Cabernet Franc in Valpolicella blends and for a vdt called Alzero. But Quintarelli explains rather cryptically that that's his only concession to international taste.

Sanperetto, Negrar (VR). From 7 ha of choice vineyards, Roberto Mazzi makes Valpolicella Poiega, Recioto Le Calcarole, and Amarone Punta di Villa.

Serègo Alighieri, Gargagnago (VR). From 30 ha around a villa that has been a Valpolicella landmark for centuries, Pieralvise Serègo Alighieri, a descendant of Dante Alighieri, grows grapes for wines made by Masi. Some of the finesse of Serègo Alighieri Valpolicella, Amarone Vaio Armoron, and Recioto Casal dei Ronchi comes from ageing in cherry wood casks.

Fratelli Speri, Pedemonte (VR). Carlo Speri has some 40 ha of vines in choice parts of the zone for Valpolicella Classico and Amarone from the Comunai-Sant'Urbano and Monte Fontana vineyards.

Fratelli Tedeschi, Pedemonte (VR). Renzo Tedeschi draws from family vines and growers to make some of Verona's best wines at sensible prices: Valpolicella Capitel delle Lucchine and Capitel dei Nicalò, Soave Monte Tenda, and the vdt Capitel San Rocco Bianco and Rosso delle Lucchine, as well as the luscious white Vin de la Fabriseria. Top of the line are the select blend of Amarone della Fabriseria, Amarone Capitel Monte Olmi, and Recioto Capitel Monte Fontana.

Tommasi, Pedemonte (VR). From 35 ha of vines, Dario Tommasi specializes in Valpolicella, Recioto, and an Amarone which can rival the finest, along with Soave, Bardolino, and Bianco di Custoza. He also owns the Villa Girardi label.

Left: Giuseppe Quintarelli during the harvest at his estate at Cerè di Negrar in Valpolicella Classico. His wines, regular Valpolicella and Recioto and Amarone, are noted for their remarkable individuality due to his personalized cellar techniques.

Tramanal, Arbizzano di Negrar (VR). Domenico Vantini, a physician, has turned his tiny estate into one of the most admired of Valpolicella, noted for Amarone whose *goût de terroir* suggests marasca cherries and eucalyptus.

Massimo Venturini, San Floriano (VR). Valpolicella and Amarone in part from vineyards at Masue.

Viticola Suavia, Soave (VR). From 10 ha, Giovanni Tessari makes an admired single-vineyard Soave Monte Carbonare.

WINE HOUSES/MERCHANTS

Bertani, Verona. The house, founded by Cavaliere G.B. Bertani in 1857, remains a pillar of Veronese wine under Gaetano and Giovanni Bertani. Their reputation is based on unerring Secco-Bertani Valpolicella-Valpantena, fine Soave Le Lave, and, in particular, on outstanding Amarone from vintages dating back decades. They might have followed the trend and made the Amarone a *cru*, since its base is family vineyards at Novare, among the best sites of Valpolicella. But because it may also be blended, the Bertani showed customary integrity in keeping its traditional house label. The Verona DOCs vinified at the original cellars at Grezzana di Valpantena, as well as in Valpolicella and at Monteforte d'Alpone in Soave, are models of reliability. They are complemented by a vdt red *ripasso* called Catullo and a promising Chardonnay in *barrique*.

Bolla, Verona. The name is still synonymous with Soave in much of the world, though the family firm founded in 1883 has diversified under Giuseppe Bolla and nephew Pierluigi Bolla to become a growing national force in the wine trade with more than 2.5 million cases sold a year. Two cellars process Soave, including the fine Castellaro and Vigneti di Frosca, and a third at Pedemonte is used for the respected Valpolicella Classico Jago and Amarone Cantina del Nonno, among other wines. Grapes come largely from a "club" of more than 400 growers who receive benefits from the Fondazione Sergio Bolla, aimed at improving local viticulture. Valdo, a fully owned subsidiary, makes sparkling wines at Valdobbiadene. Bolla's alternative wines are headed by the *barrique*-aged Creso red from Cabernet Sauvignon and Corvina and white based on Chardonnay. The firm also makes Valdadige DOC Retico and selects Gavi from Piedmont and Trebbiano d'Aprilia from Latium, among other wines shipped mainly to the USA, where it has its own importing company.

Paolo Boscaini & Figli, Valgatara (VR). The large family winery is run by Dario Boscaini, who also directs Verona's respected Agricultural Institute. The range of Verona DOCs includes Bardolino Le Canne; Soave Monteleone; Valpolicella, Recioto, and Amarone Marano; Recioto Ca' Nicolis; Amarone Ca' de Loi. The firm also makes Alto Adige Chardonnay and Pinot Grigio.

Fratelli Farina, Pedemonte (VR). Good Valpolicella and Amarone.

Lamberti, Lazise (VR). This large producer of Verona DOCs is part of the Gruppo Italiano Vini. Special bottlings include Bardolino Le Primule, Valpolicella Le Primule, and Soave I Ciliegi, in part from company vines. A pioneer of Bardolino *novello*, Lamberti also makes Lugana and Riviera del Garda DOC and the vdt Turà.

Masi, Gargagnago (VR). Sandro Boscaini heads the winery that has been in the family for generations and set Verona's pace throughout the 1980s. In 1989, the noted oenologist Lanfranco Paronetto replaced winemaker Nino Franceschetti. The latter had revived *ripasso* in Campo Fiorin and styled special Amarone (Mazzano, Campolongo di Torbe), Recioto (Mezzanella), and the sweet white Campociesa. Masi has 40 ha of vines in Valpolicella, and leased land at Pertica di Costermano for Bardolino La Vegrona and Monteforte d'Alpone for Soave Col Baraca. The line includes ordinary and light DOCs and the stylish vdt white Masianco (Garganega-Sauvignon). Masi also makes the wines of Serègo Alighieri. The Masi International Award is given for achievements in wine.

Giacomo Montresor, Verona. Large bottler of Verona DOC and vdt.

Fratelli Pasqua, Verona. The established family house has introduced "new generation" wines, in part from 85 ha, including bottlings labelled Soave Costalunga, Amarone Vigneti Casterna, and Cabernet vdt Morago.

Santa Sofia, Pedemonte (VR). The once legendary estate has become a trademark for Verona DOCs, including a Valpolicella called Montegradella.

Santi, Illasi (VR). A.G. Santi, now an adjunct of Gruppo Italiano Vini, bottles a range of Verona wines, including Valpolicella Castello d'Illasi, Bardolino Ca' Bordenis, Soave Monteforte, Botte Regina Amarone, Carlo Santi Brut *champenoise*, and Turà.

Sartori, Negrar (VR). Large and reliable bottler of Verona wines.

Scamperle, Fumane di Valpolicella (VR). Large bottler of Verona wines.

Fratelli Zeni, Bardolino (VR). Bardolino, Valpolicella, and Amarone, partly from own vineyards.

Zenato, San Benedetto di Lugana (VR). Verona DOC wines and Lugana, in part from 16 ha of vines.

COOPERATIVES

CS Valpolicella, Negrar (VR). Despite access to some of Valpolicella's best vineyards, quality is rarely noteworthy.

CS di Soave, Soave (VR). Verona's largest cellars draws from 630 growers with 2,500 ha of vines to make 300,000 hl of wine annually, led by Soave sold both under its own labels and, more frequently, others. Selected bottlings of Soave Costalta, Monte Foscarino, and Castelcerino are reliable. It also makes other Verona DOC, vdt, and *spumanti*.

Left: vineyards around the villa of Serègo Alighieri at Gargagnago in Valpolicella Classico, where descendants of Dante Alighieri have grown grapes for centuries. Pieralvise Serègo Alighieri has recently planted more vines for wines made by Masi.

Wines of the central hills: Vicenza and Padova

Verona's success with native blends has had little influence on winemaking in the neighbouring provinces of Vicenza and Padova, where foreign vines and varietal wines are prominent. Only Soave's Garganega, which may have been shared from the start with growers in adjacent Gambellara, has made much impact in the Veneto's central hills. Verona and Vicenza also share the white Durello from the Lessini hills that straddle the provinces. The Berici and Euganei ranges that loom over the Venetian plain trace their viticultural background to the Bronze Age, but little from that heritage seems to have been retained. Vicenza has some local vines of special interest in the Vespaiola of Breganze and the red Tocai of the Colli Berici, though the once prominent Raboso and Marzemino are rarely seen today. Growers in Padova's Colli Euganei have clung to the Serprina which they insist is the real Prosecco, while meeting local demands for sweet wines with the Veneto's only classified Moscato. But otherwise trends favour international varieties: the long familiar Merlot and Cabernets, as well as Pinots, Sauvignon, and the still unclassified Chardonnay. Few producers in the Veneto – or anywhere else in Italy – work as convincingly with the elite varieties as Maculan, who in doing so has enhanced the name of Breganze. Elsewhere, scattered results have been encouraging, especially in the Colli Euganei, though the central Veneto has all too few of those go-ahead estates that build prestige. Much production is centred in cooperatives, including what may be Europe's largest such cellars at Lonigo in the Colli Berici, though few have made an impact in the quality field. Vicenza also has Italy's largest privately owned wine house in Zonin of Gambellara, which has proved that class can be achieved on a large scale.

Breganze (1969)

Breganze's wines emerged from obscurity over the last decade, thanks more than anything else to the energetic genius of Fausto Maculan, a name increasingly respected in Italy and abroad. Other producers have improved their own standards with the traditional white Vespaiolo (from Vespaiola), and what is considered a local clone of Tocai, as well as Pinot Bianco and the red DOCs. But, if anything, Maculan seems to have widened the gap with the competition, not only with the DOCs, including the single vineyard Cabernets of Fratta and Palazzoto, but with some outstanding vdt and dessert wines. He has overcome doubts in showing that the terrains and microclimates in vineyards at the foot of the Asiago plateau offer advantages to winemakers inspired to follow his lead.

Zone: Low hills and gravelly plains at the foot of the Asiago plateau, extending south along the Astico valley to Montecchio Precalcino and east past the towns of Breganze and Maróstica to the banks of the Brenta opposite Bassano del Grappa, taking in 13 communes in Vicenza province. Besides Bianco and Rosso there are five pure varietals; Cabernet may consist of Cabernet Franc or Cabernet Sauvignon or both.

Bianco Dry white. Grapes: Tocai; Pinot Bianco/Pinot Grigio/Riesling Italico/Sauvignon/Vespaiola up to 15%. Yld 91/140, Alc 11, Acd 0.55.

Rosso Dry red. Grapes: Merlot; Marzemino/Groppello Gentile/Cabernet Sauvignon/Cabernet Franc/Pinot Nero/Freisa up to 15%. Yld 91/140, Alc 11, Acd 0.6.

Cabernet Dry red. Yld 84.5/130, Alc 11.5; superiore 12, Acd 0.6.

Pinot Bianco Dry white. Yld 84.5/130, Alc 11.5; superiore 12, Acd 0.55.

Pinot Grigio Dry white. Yld 84.5/130, Alc 10.5; superiore 12, Acd 0.55.

Pinot Nero Dry red. Yld 84.5/130, Alc 11.5; superiore 12, Acd 0.55.

Vespaiolo Dry white. Grape: Vespaiola. Yld 84.5/130, Alc 11.5; superiore 12, Acd 0.55.

Gambellara (1970)

The wines of Gambellara, though often considered substitutes for Soave, deserve separate status. For despite the similarities in grape varieties, wines from the adjacent zones have distinct personalities that experienced tasters supposedly never mistake. It might be that there has rarely been enough Gambellara available outside the zone to provide for comparisons. Gradually, though, production of bottled Gambellara is increasing, gaining some long lost ground on Soave. The leading producer, Zonin, makes both an estate-bottled dry Il Giangio and a Recioto *spumante*, whose crisp, *demi-sec* style, though hardly traditional, has been winning followers. Gambellara also has one of the few examples of Vin Santo outside central Italy. The rich, raisiny dessert wine has been traditional here since the 17th century, though today it is only made in token amounts.

Zone: Rolling hills of the lower Lessini range and plains southwest of Vicenza in the communes of Gambellara, Montebello Vicentino, Montorso Vicentino, and Zermeghedo. Dry white. Grapes: Garganega; Trebbiano di Soave/Trebbiano Toscano up to 20%. Yld 98/140, Alc 10.5; superiore 11.5, Acd 0.5.

Recioto di Gambellara Sweet white, also spumante. Grapes: as the dry white but semidried or passito. Yld 56/140, Alc 12, Acd 0.5.

Vin Santo di Gambellara Golden to amber dessert wine. Grapes: as the dry white but semidried or passito. Yld 56/140, Alc 14, Acd 0.5, Ag 2 yrs.

Colli Berici (1973)

It might be that the people of Vicenza have tried to keep the Berici hills a secret for fear that tourism would spoil their charms. That certainly seems to be the case with the wines, which are not often seen outside the environs of the city of Palladio. A couple of estates had provided exceptions: Conti da Schio at Costozza, long noted for Cabernet, and Alfredo Lazzarini's Villa dal Ferro, widely acclaimed for Merlot and Pinot Nero. But local taste has been focused on Garganega and Tocai Rosso, which is DOC only in this zone. Garganega (or Garganego) can bear a family resemblance to Soave, but Tocai Rosso, whose colour of ripe raspberries carries over to its vivacious aroma and flavour, is *sui generis*. Visitors may be amused by the lack of presumption in so many of the wines, but some might wonder why these pretty hills aren't used for greater things. The Cabernet of Costozza now seems to be just one of the crowd and even Villa dal Ferro's reds no longer stand out from the nationwide competition. Though some estates have started to move – Ca' Bruzzo, among others – nearly total domination of production by the giant complex called Cantine dei Colli Berici has resulted in a mass of wine of ordinary standards.

Zone: Slopes and broad valleys extending from the edge of Vicenza to the south around the rises of the Monti Berici between Longare and Lonigo and west of the city around Montecchio Maggiore, Sovizzo, and Monteviale, taking in 28 communes in the province.

Cabernet Dry red. Grapes: Cabernet Sauvignon/Cabernet Franc. Yld 78/120, Alc 11; riserva 12.5, Acd 0.45, Ag riserva 3 yrs.

Garganega or **Garganego** Dry white. Grapes: Garganega; Trebbiano di Soave up to 10%. Yld 98/140, Alc 10.5, Acd 0.55.

Merlot Dry red. Grape: Merlot. Yld 91/130, Alc 11, Acd 0.55.

Pinot Bianco Dry white. Grapes: Pinot Bianco; Pinot Grigio up to 15%. Yld 78/120, Alc 11, Acd 0.5.

Sauvignon Dry white. Grapes: Sauvignon; Garganega up to 10%. Yld 78/120, Alc 11, Acd 0.5.

Tocai Bianco Dry white. Grapes: Tocai Bianco; Garganega up to 10%. Yld 84/120, Alc 11, Acd 0.55.

Tocai Rosso Dry red. Grapes: Tocai Rosso; Garganega up to 15%. Yld 78/120, Alc 11, Acd 0.5.

Colli Euganei (1969)

The domed rises of the Colli Euganei, which tower so majestically over Padova's flatlands, have been noted since ancient times for an enchanted quality that poets also noted in its wines. Some found a hint of fire in them that supposedly derived from the volcanic soil of the hills, where conditions are clearly superior to the plains. Among endorsements through the ages, perhaps the most lasting came from the 14th-century poet Petrarch, who late in his life settled in the hills to grow vines.

In recent times wines have tended towards the soft and bubbly in styles aimed largely at local tastes (which can be taken to include Venetian). The most popular types, the Bianco, Rosso, and the sweet Moscato, are often sparkling. Even the usually dry Cabernet, Merlot, Pinot Bianco, and Tocai may hint at *abboccato*. The Bianco combines the traditional varieties of Serprina (Prosecco) and Pinella with Garganega and international varieties. The *rosso* is basically a Bordeaux blend with the unusual complements of Barbera and Raboso. Quality seems to be improving in the Colli Berici at a faster rate than in other zones of the central Veneto, thanks in part to efforts by a strong producer consortium. Some estates in the hills – such as Villa Sceriman, La Montanella, and Cecilia Baone – seem to be aiming part of their production at more sophisticated audiences.

Zone: Slopes of the Euganean range, whose focal point is the 603-m Monte Venda southwest of Padova, though vineyards in 17 communes in the province also extend into the Venetian plain.

Besides the white and red wines, there are five varietals, which may be supplemented by grapes of the same colour.

Bianco Dry white, also amabile, spumante. Grapes: Garganega 30-50%, Serprina (Prosecco) 10-30%, Tocai Friulano/Sauvignon 20-40%; Pinella/Pinot Bianco/Riesling Italico/Chardonnay up to 20%. Yld 84/120, Alc 10.5; superiore 12; spumante amabile 11 and secco 12, Acd 0.5.

Rosso Dry red, also amabile, spumante. Grapes: Merlot 60-80%, Cabernet Sauvignon/Cabernet Franc/Barbera/Raboso Veronese 20-40%. Yld 98/140, Alc 11; superiore and spumante 12, Acd 0.55.

Cabernet Dry red. Grapes: Cabernet Franc/Cabernet Sauvignon at least 90%. Yld 84/120, Alc 11.5; superiore 12.5, Acd 0.55, Ag superiore 1 yr.

Merlot Dry red. Grape: Merlot at least 90%. Yld 98/140, Alc 11; superiore 12, Acd 0.55, Ag superiore 1 yr.

Moscato Sweet white, also spumante. Grape: Moscato Bianco at least 95%. Yld 78/120, Alc 10.5, Acd 0.55.

Pinot Bianco Dry white, also abboccato. Grape: Pinot Bianco at least 90%. Yld 84/120, Alc 11; superiore 12, Acd 0.5.

Tocai Italico Dry white, also abboccato. Grape: Tocai Italico at least 90%. Yld 84/120, Alc 11; superiore 12, Acd 0.5.

Other wines of note

The central Veneto has a wealth of unclassified wines, ranging from the bulk type, which are often *frizzante*, to fine *spumanti*, variations on the Bordeaux varieties, Chardonnay, and the outstanding sweet wines of Maculan. The Colli Euganei specialize in the bubbly sweet Moscato Fior d'Arancio. Rovigo province in the plains along the Po produces no DOC and only a bit of vdt for local consumption.

ESTATES/GROWERS

Ca' Bruzzo, San Germano dei Berici (VI). From 17 ha, Aldo Bruzzo and American wife Sarah Wallace make persuasive Tocai Rosso among a solid range of Colli Berici DOC, complemented by vdt Chardonnay and the surprising light pink "California Blush".

Castello di Belvedere, Villaga (VI). Colli Berici DOC.

Cecilia di Baone, Terralba di Baone (PD). Emerging estate with a well publicized array of Colli Euganei DOCs, Don Noè Spumante Brut, and Moscato Fior d'Arancio.

Conti A. & G. da Schio, Costozza di Longare (VI). From 17 ha on their historical estate in the Colli Berici, Alvise and Giulio da Schio make Costozza Cabernet Franc, which is no longer as admired as it once was, along with Pinot Bianco and vdt.

Il Giangio, Gambellara (VI). Zonin estate for Gambellara DOC.

La Montanella, Monselice (PD). From 13 ha, good Colli Euganei DOC and Moscato Fior d'Arancio.

Maculan, Breganze (VI). Fausto Maculan and sister Franca make some of the Veneto's most inspired wines from 30 ha of family vines and grapes supplied by growers. The most impressive Breganze DOC is the Cabernet from the 1-ha Fratta vineyard where old vines evenly divided between Cabernet Sauvignon and Franc make a soaringly rich wine of grand style, though it can be nearly matched by the pure Cabernet Sauvignon Palazzotto. Other DOCs are Bianco (Breganze di Breganze), Rosso (Brentino), Pinot Bianco, and dry Vespaiolo. Vdt, led by the newly released Ferrata Chardonnay and Cabernet Sauvignon, include the white Prato di Canzio (Tocai-Pinot Bianco) and an exquisite Pinot Noir rosé Costa d'Olio. There is also a *charmat* Accademia Brut. But Maculan's top achievements to date have been with unclassified sweet wines from semidried Vespaiola grapes: Torcolato, a type of *recioto* aged in *barriques*, and the even more sumptuous Acininobili, from grapes selected for botrytis cinerea – different from great Sauternes but no less delicious for it. Dindarello is

Above: Vespaiola grapes are draped from the ceiling of a drying room at the Maculan winery in Breganze. They are used for the renowned sweet wines of Torcolato and Acininobili, from grapes selected after they develop botrytis cinerea, or noble rot.

a bracingly sweet white from Moscato Fior d'Arancio.

Alessandro Piovene, Villaga (VI). Colli Berici DOC and vdt Bianco Toara from Garganega.

Villa dal Ferro, San Germano dei Berici (VI). Alfredo Lazzarini brought a new concept of class to the Colli Berici in the 1970s with wines that often rank with Italy's best of breed from 12 ha around his ancient villa. All varietals carry vineyard names: Bianco del Rocolo (Pinot Bianco), Busa Calcara (Riesling Renano), Campo del Lago (Merlot), Costiera Granda (Tocai), Le Rive Rosse (Cabernet), Rosso del Rocolo (Pinot Nero). Though formerly unclassified, all are now covered by DOC.

Villa Magna, Sandrigo (VI). Breganze DOC from 45 ha.

Villa Sceriman, Vó Euganeo (PD). The Soranzo family has made this estate with 25 ha a widely respected leader in Colli Euganei with fine DOCs and *spumanti* from Moscato Rosa, Moscato Fior d'Arancio, Marzemino, and Prosecco.

WINE HOUSES/MERCHANTS

Zonin, Gambellara (VI). The Zonin family, established at Gambellara since 1821, expanded first through mass production and then through estate development to become the largest privately owned wine complex in Italy. The Zonin brothers – Gianni (president), Giuseppe (general manager), and Gaetano (sales manager) – direct production of 3.2 million cases of wine a year, of which about a third is exported. A quarter of production comes from ten independently operated estates with 730 ha of vines in northern regions and Tuscany. (Zonin also owns Barboursville Vineyards, which in the 1970s became the first commercial winery in Virginia, USA.) The main cellars at Gambellara produce a range of DOCs and vdt varietals, and *spumanti*, including the *champenoise* Riserva Domenico Zonin. Domenico Valentini heads a staff of 16 oenologists who make the wine at the estates: Il Giangio in Gambellara, Il Maso in Valpolicella, Ca' Bolani and Ca' Vescovo in Friuli's Aquileia, Castello del Poggio in Piedmont's Asti province, Il Bosco and San Zeno in Lombardy's Oltrepò Pavese, Castello d'Albola in Tuscany's Chianti Classico, and Abbazia Monte Oliveto and Il Palagio in Tuscany's San Gimignano.

COOPERATIVES

Bartolomeo da Breganze, Breganze (VI). From growers with 1,200 ha Breganze DOC and vdt.

CS di Gambellara, Gambellara (VI). Large production of Gambellara and Colli Berici DOC and vdt.

Cantina dei Colli Berici, Lonigo and Barbarano (VI). The unification in 1989 of the Colli Berici's two cooperatives created what is proclaimed as Europe's largest wine production unit with about 750,000 hl annually from about 4,000 ha of vines. But the fraction that qualifies as Colli Berici DOC had little to distinguish it among the masses of vdt and *spumanti*.

CS Cooperativa dei Colli Euganei, Vò Euganeo (PD). Large production includes reliable Colli Euganei DOC, vdt, and *spumanti*.

Wines of the eastern Veneto: Venice and Treviso

The eastern Veneto, from the Brenta river to the border of Friuli, is Venice's domain. It covers the provinces of Venezia, which is nearly all flat; Belluno, which is mostly mountainous; and Treviso, which has ample hills and dales. Venice's formal wine lists are drawn from wide-ranging sources to satisfy eclectic clienteles, but when Venetians themselves sip the pick-me-ups known as *ombrette*, they usually ask for something local. It's true that the canal city doesn't look like a wine town, but its hinterland – the plains that stretch along the coast towards Friuli and the hills that roll towards the Alps above Treviso – proliferates in vines for wines that Venetians like to call their own. The favourite *ombretta* is Prosecco, a casually dry to subtly sweet white, usually bubbly, from the hills of Conegliano and Valdobbiadene and the nearby rises of Montello and Colli Asolani. Most Venetian red wines, and a growing share of whites, come from flatlands of the sort that Italians usually reserve for corn. Merlot prevails in the Piave and Lison-Pramaggiore zones, followed at a distance by Cabernet. The best reds there show reasonable class and durability, yet, if appreciated locally, they are rarely praised outside the Veneto orientale. Cabernet and Merlot have been criticized for flavours and scents tending towards the vegetal, but even wines that don't show such traits rarely match the best of breed from the Médoc, California, or Tuscany. Bordeaux type blending of Cabernet and Merlot with minor varieties isn't as common here as it might be, since the most refined reds over time – Venegazzù della Casa and Castello di Roncade Villa Giustinian – have been blends. Recently, Chardonnay, the Pinots, and Sauvignon have gained space on the plains alongside the veteran Tocai and Verduzzo, but even if their names are international, their spritzy styles are unmistakably Venetian.

Prosecco di Conegliano-Valdobbiadene (1971)

Gentle Prosecco so suits the joyous nature of the hills of Conegliano and Valdobbiadene that it would seem to have flowed there forever. The Colli Trevigiani had been known for wines since the early days of the Venetian Republic and the vine had been praised by the ancient Romans as the source of Pulcinum in nearby Friuli. But Prosecco was still a secondary variety here late in the last century after the Counts Balbi Valier rescued it from phylloxera. Success finally came when the wine acquired bubbles. The father of modern Prosecco was Antonio Carpenè, who introduced the Champagne method to Conegliano and founded Carpenè Malvolti, the house that carried the wine's fame to Venice and beyond. Carpenè also inspired the viticultural centre and wine school that have made Conegliano a reference point for Italian wine. The industry that grew up around Prosecco developed methods of bottle and tank fermentation more economical than *champenoise*, which is now used here mainly for wines from Chardonnay and Pinot. Prosecco's basic style has gradually shifted from a softly sweet *frizzante* of sunny golden hue to a practically dry, clear, full-fledged *spumante*. The wine retains a natural softness against a light almondy background that may not appeal to admirers of Champagne, but its distinct personality and attractive price have won devotees well beyond the Veneto. Production in the Conegliano-Valdobbiadene zone has reached 140,000 hl a year, making Prosecco second to Asti Spumante among Italian sparkling wines. Growing popularity in

Italy has left little available for export.

Labels may carry the names of both towns, but they seldom do since Prosecco's domain is divided by the Soligo stream into two areas whose wines are the subject of local pride and joy. Slopes to the east open towards the warm plains, supposedly accounting for a soft, almost creamy fruitiness in wines that take the name of Conegliano. Towards the west, though microclimates vary on the often sharp inclines, Prosecco assumes the delicate, dry, crisp qualities associated with Valdobbiadene. Partisans argue about which is best – while some neutral observers insist that there isn't much difference – but few dispute that Cartizze is indeed *superiore*. That is, superior when it really comes from the 108 ha of steep banks within the triangle defined by the villages of San Pietro di Barbozza, Santo Stefano, and Saccol on the edge of Valdobbiadene, and when growers carefully limit yields. Those privileged vineyards might be considered a rare officially recognized *cru*, though demand is so great that Cartizze – or what is passed off as such – far exceeds the annual limits of just over a million bottles.

In the past, Prosecco made by bottle fermentation methods was usually *frizzante* and *amabile*, though the intensity of bubbles and sweetness varied from year to year. Now that tank fermentation is the rule, often in the so-called "charmat lungo" that leaves the wine in long contact with the lees, Prosecco is most often *spumante* and either *brut* or just hinting at sweet. *Amabile* and *dolce* are permitted but rarely seen. Some producers, responding to local sentiments, lean

towards the old style, exemplified by Primo Franco's Rustico. The insistence on bubbles means that only a little of the still, dry Prosecco is made, though it can be one of northern Italy's more persuasive native white wines. The Colli Trevigiani are among Italy's best organized zones for wine tourism, with a well-marked Strada del Vino Prosecco that leads to wine bars and shops along the way and a wealth of festivals and promotional activities, such as the annual Mostra Nazionale dello Spumante at Valdobbiadene.

Zone: Hills northwest of Treviso extending from Valdobbiadene east to Conegliano and Vittorio Veneto between the Alps and the Piave in 15 communes in the province. Prosecco may take both names or Conegliano or Valdobbiadene alone. Wine from specified vineyards at San Pietro di Barbozza in the commune of Valdobbiadene

may be called Superiore di Cartizze or Cartizze. Dry white, also amabile or dolce, usually frizzante or spumante. Grapes: Prosecco; Verdiso/ Pinot Bianco/Pinot Grigio/ Chardonnay up to 15% or Verdiso alone up to 10%. Yld 84/120, Alc 10.5; spumante 11 (dolce res sugar max 6%), Acd 0.5.

Superiore di Cartizze or **Cartizze** All types from the delimited area have the same norms as Prosecco, except that alcohol is 11 for still wine and frizzante and 11.5 for spumante.

Montello e Colli Asolani (1977)

Well-to-do Venetians kept villas in these hills, not only to escape the stifling summers by the lagoon but also to provide them with fresh produce and wine. The prettiest sites were on the wooded slopes around Asolo and Maser. But vines seem to do even better on the gentle inclines of Il Montello,

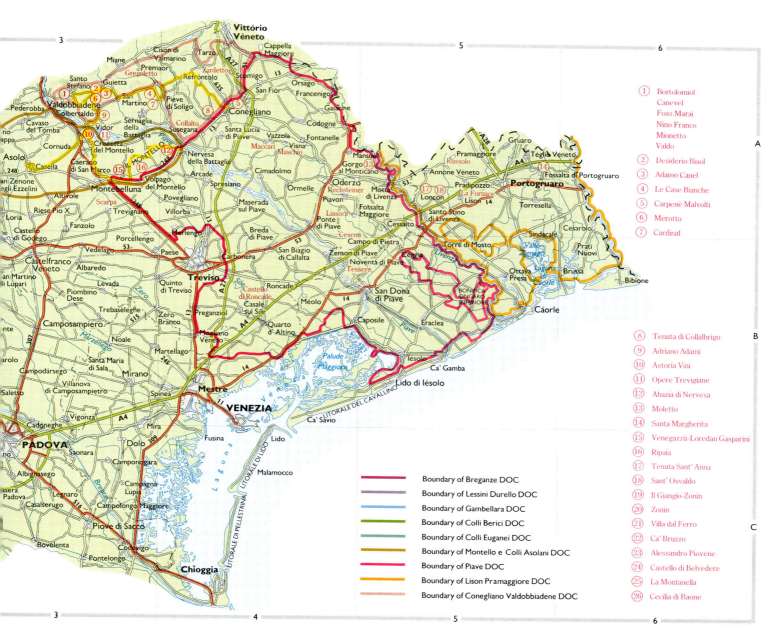

where the Loredan Gasparini family built the villa at Venegazzù that remains the most renowned of the area's wine estates. Newcomers worth watching are Abazia di Nervesa and Fernando Berta. But overall the appellation hasn't lived up to its promise.

Zone: Slopes of two ranges flanking Montebelluna between the Piave river and the plains, Il Montello (above Volpago, Giavera, and Nervesa della Battaglia) and Colli Asolani (between Cornuda and Monte Grappa with the axis in Asolo), taking in 17 communes in Treviso province.

Cabernet Dry red. Grapes: Cabernet Franc/Cabernet Sauvignon; Malbec up to 15%. Yld 70/100, Alc 11.5; superiore 12, Acd 0.5, Ag superiore 2 yrs (1 in wood).

Merlot Dry red. Grapes: Merlot; Cabernet Franc/Cabernet Sauvignon/Malbec up to 15%. Yld 84/120, Alc 11; superiore 11.5, Acd 0.5, Ag superiore 2 yrs (1 in wood).

Prosecco Dry white, usually frizzante or spumante. Grapes: Prosecco; Pinot Bianco/Pinot Grigio/Riesling Italico/Verduzzo Trevigiano/Bianchetta Trevigiana up to 15%. Yld 84/120, Alc 10.5; spumante 11, Acd 0.5.

Piave (1971)

The broad banks of the Piave river are Italy's main font of Merlot, as well as fluent sources of Cabernet. The Bordeaux varieties, familiar for more than a century around Oderzo, Motta di Livenza, Roncade, Monastier, and Ponte di Piave, make wines of marked personality. But the area's most distinctive red is often the native Raboso. Deep violet to bright garnet, warm and earthy, it can become almost smooth when time tames its tannic sharpness. Among whites, the prevalent Verduzzo and Tocai have snappy acidity to offset their youthful fruitiness. Piave's French connection was strengthened by the addition to the DOC list of the three Pinots, whose wines tend to show more fragrance and freshness from the gravelly terrains to the north than from the sandy clays towards the Adriatic. The research centre at Conegliano has helped raise standards here, yet nothing in the current array of red wines seems to show the depth and complexity of certain old vintages of Castello di Roncade Villa Giustinian, a blended vdt. On these prolific plains it seems to be more profitable to cater to popular tastes than to strive for splendid individuality.

Zone: Plains of the Piave basin reaching from the banks of the Adriatic north past Conegliano between the Livenza river and Treviso, including 50 communes in its province and 12 in Venezia.

The eight types are varietals of at least 95%.

Cabernet (Cabernet Franc/Cabernet Sauvignon) Dry red. Yld 77/110, Alc 11.5; riserva 12.5, Acd 0.5, Ag riserva 3 yrs.

Merlot Dry red. Yld 91/130, Alc 11; vecchio 12.5, Acd 0.48, Ag vecchio 3 yrs.

Pinot Bianco Dry white. Yld 84/120, Alc 11, Acd 0.5.

Pinot Grigio Dry white. Yld 77/110, Alc 11.5, Acd 0.48.

Pinot Nero Dry red, also amabile. Yld 84/120, Alc 11.5; riserva 12.5, Acd 0.48, Ag riserva 2 yrs.

Raboso (Raboso del Piave/Raboso Veronese) Dry red. Yld 91/140, Alc 11.5, Acd 0.65, Ag 3 yrs.

Tocai Italico Dry white. Yld 77/110, Alc 11, Acd 0.5.

Verduzzo (Verduzzo Trevigiano/Verduzzo Friulano) Dry white. Yld 84/120, Alc 11, Acd 0.5.

Lison-Pramaggiore (1986)

(Incorporating Tocai di Lison and Pramaggiore Cabernet and Merlot DOCs, 1971, while adding new types.)

Lison and Pramaggiore might have remained obscure farm towns on the Venetian plains had it not been for the enterprise shown by local wine producers. Pramaggiore had been linked to Cabernet and Merlot, which were tasty and conveniently priced, but what put the town on the map was the hosting of an annual wine fair at which medals were awarded freely to bottles from all over Italy. Lison's Tocai rarely matched the tone of Friuli's finest, yet it managed to become a classic nonetheless. In 1986, the coinciding zones were joined in a tandem DOC, with a string of trendy varietals added to the original three. Perhaps to be sure they didn't miss any markets, all 12 types were given the option of being bubbly – even the three Cabernets. Yet, to give them their due, Lison-Pramaggiore often ranks a cut above other wines of the plains. The reds (now including Refosco) often seem richer and more durable and the whites (Tocai and the newer Chardonnay, Pinots, and Sauvignon) sleeker than the competition. This quality is partly due to the well-drained calcareous clay soils that support vast tracts of vineyards between the Tagliamento and Livenza streams. But the key may be the skilled winemaking practised hereabouts, evident on a large scale at Santa Margherita and in a more artisan way at Russolo. A point not to be ignored these days is that wines here are usually good value. They are available at the Enoteca Regionale Vini Veneti at Pramaggiore – the latest in a series of local initiatives.

Zone: Plains in the easternmost Veneto between the Tagliamento and Livenza rivers, extending from the Adriatic litoral north into Friuli-Venezia Giulia, and including 11 communes in Venezia province, two in Treviso, and five in Pordenone. Lison and Pramaggiore are small wine centres near the town of Portogruaro. Tocai di Lison Classico is from the traditional zone.

The 12 types are varietals of 90%, possibly complemented by other grapes of the same colour, except for Tocai di Lison Classico, which must be pure Tocai. All types, white and red, may also be spumante.

Cabernet (Cabernet Franc/Cabernet Sauvignon) Dry red. Yld 84/120, Alc 11; riserva 11.5, Acd 0.5, Ag riserva 3 yrs.

Cabernet Franc Dry red. Yld 84/120, Alc 11; riserva 11.5, Acd 0.5, Ag riserva 3 yrs.

Cabernet Sauvignon Dry red. Yld 84/120, Alc 11; riserva 11.5, Acd 0.5, Ag riserva 3 yrs.

Chardonnay Dry white. Yld 91/130, Alc 11, Acd 0.5.

Merlot Dry red. Yld 91/130, Alc 11; riserva 11.5, Acd 0.45, Ag riserva 2 yrs.

Pinot Bianco Dry white. Yld 84/120, Alc 11, Acd 0.5.

Pinot Grigio Dry white. Yld 70/100, Alc 11, Acd 0.5.

Refosco (Refosco dal Peduncolo Rosso) Dry red. Yld 84/120, Alc 11, Acd 0.5.

Riesling Italico Dry white. Yld 84/120, Alc 11, Acd 0.5.

Sauvignon Dry white. Yld 84/120, Alc 11, Acd 0.5.

Tocai Italico Dry white. Yld 84/120, Alc 11; Tocai di Lison Classico 11.5, Acd 0.5.

Verduzzo Dry white. Yld 91/130, Alc 11, Acd 0.5.

Other wines of note

The eastern Veneto specializes in bubbly wines that range beyond Prosecco to take in *champenoise* from Pinots and Chardonnay, as well as an array of *frizzante* and *vivace* bottlings from virtually all varieties. Everyday wines represent good value, whether bottled and shipped or sold locally in large containers. The once prominent Marzemino has faded, but growers at Refrontolo near Conegliano have requested a DOC as a first step towards reviving it. Among curiosities are spritzy white Verdiso, semisweet Buschino, as well as the dry red Wildbacher. Malbec or Malbech, which plays minor roles in Bordeaux, approaches star status here; Santa Margherita's outclasses most DOC varietal Cabernets and Merlots. Some other individual vdt are cited with producers. The province of Belluno has no DOC, though vineyards in the Cadore area along the Piave and beneath the Dolomites towards Cortina d'Ampezzo make some Prosecco, Merlot, and other vdt from vines that include Pavana, Nera, and Turca.

ESTATES/GROWERS

Abazia di Nervesa, Nervesa della Battaglia (TV). Promising Cabernet and Merlot and good Prosecco from an estate being revived in Montello e Colli Asolani DOC.

Castello di Roncade, Roncade (TV). From 30 ha, Vincenzo Ciani Bassetti is reviving a long-noted family tradition with Villa Giustinian Riserva, from a classical Bordeaux blend, along with Piave DOC and *spumante*.

Collalto, Susegana (TV). A large and varied production with good Piave Cabernet.

Fattoria di Ogliano, Ogliano (TV). Gianni Spinazzè goes his own way in Conegliano's hills with vdt red Capo del Monte and white Campitello.

La Fornace, Lison (VE). Lison-Pramaggiore DOC.

Le Case Bianche, Pieve di Soligo (TV). From 45 ha, Alvise Orlandi makes Prosecco di Conegliano Brusolè among sparkling wines and interesting vdt Wildbacher and Camoi (Cabernet Sauvignon-Wildbacher). He also sells estate wines under the Orlandi label.

Liasora, Ponte di Piave (TV). From 40 ha, Piave DOC and the curious semisweet white Buschino, from an indigenous vine of the name.

Moletto, Motta di Livenza (TV). Piave DOC.

Rechsteiner, Piavon di Oderzo (TV). From 45 ha, the estate of the Baroni Stepski-Doliwa makes some of the best Piave DOC and Chardonnay vdt.

Ripaia, Selva di Montello (TV). Fernando Berta's vdt Roveto comes from Cabernet Franc.

Above: the ombra *or* ombretta *is the tiny glass of white wine sipped by Venetians as an aperitif or at intervals during the day. The name refers to the shade of St. Mark's bell tower in whose shadow were the bars that started the pleasant custom.*

Scarpa, Trevignano (TV). Tobia and Afra Scarpa make Corbulino Bianco (Pinot Bianco-Chardonnay) and Rosso (a Bordeaux blend with Pinot Nero) bearing the stamp of friend Giorgio Grai.

Tenuta di Collalbrigo, Conegliano (TV). Alberto Cosulich uses the Museo del Vino label for still Prosecco and vdt Rosso di Collalbrigo (Cabernet-Merlot).

Tessere, Noventa di Piave (VE). Piave DOC.

Venegazzù-Conte Loredan Gasparini, Venegazzù di Volpago (TV). From 60 ha on Il Montello at the former estate of the Loredan Gasparini family, which gave Venice two doges, come some of the Veneto's most renowned wines. The classical Venegazzù della Casa, from a Bordeaux blend, may carry a white label or the more prestigious black "Etichetta Nera" for the reserve from vines 40-45 years old. Also notable from this estate owned by Giancarlo Palla are Cabernet, Pinot Bianco, Pinot Grigio, and a good *champenoise* Loredan Gasparini Brut.

WINE HOUSES/MERCHANTS

Adriano Adami, Colbertaldo di Vidor (TV). Respected specialist in Prosecco di Valdobbiadene (Vigneto Giardino) and Superiore di Cartizze.

Astoria Vini, Crocetta del Montello (TV). Prosecco, Cartizze, and the *champenoise* Astoria Brut.

Desiderio Bisol & Figli, Santo Stefano di Valdobbiadene (TV). The house is widely known for fine Prosecco FOL, Cartizze, and *champenoise* Bisol Brut Riserva.

Bortolomiol, Valdobbiadene (TV). Prosecco and Cartizze.

Adamo Canel & Figli, Col San Martino (TV). Good Prosecco and Cartizze, partly from own vines.

Canevel, Valdobbiadene (TV). Reliable Prosecco and Cartizze.

Cantina Sant'Osvaldo, Loncon di Annone Veneto (VE). Lison-Pramaggiore and other wines.

Cantine Torresella *See* Santa Margherita.

Cardinal, Pieve di Soligo (TV). Winemaker Gianni Bignucolo puts personalized style into Prosecco and Cartizze DOC, sparkling Pinot Bianco, and the emblematic bright pink Cardinal Brut from Lagrein.

Carpenè Malvolti, Conegliano (TV). Founded in 1868 by Antonio Carpenè, the firm still run by the family remains a symbolic leader of Prosecco di Conegliano. Production of some 300,000 cases at two cellars includes the respected Carpenè Malvolti Brut *champenoise*.

Enoteca Prof. Cescon, Campo di Pietra (TV). Ivan Cescon's studied techniques seem best expressed in a durable Piave Raboso.

Foss Marai, Valdobbiadene (TV). Prosecco and Cartizze.

Nino Franco, Valdobbiadene (TV). Winemaker Primo Franco gets attractive style into his Cartizze and Prosecco, both bubbly and still, while amusing admirers of traditionally rustic Prosecco with Rustico.

Gregoletto, Premaor di Miane (TV). Good Prosecco di Conegliano.

Maccari, Visnà (TV). Piave DOC.

Maschio, Visnà (TV). Large production of vdt and sparkling wines includes Prosecco DOC and the *champenoise* Maschio dei Cavalieri.

Merotto, Col San Martino (TV). Admirable Prosecco and Cartizze, along with Merotto Brut *champenoise*.

Mionetto, Valdobbiadene (TV). Prosecco and Cartizze.

Opere Trevigiane, Crocetta del Montello (TV). Opere is a fine *spumante classico* from this expanding firm owned by the Moretti family, which also makes Prosecco DOC and other wines under the trademark La Gioiosa.

Russolo, Pramaggiore (VE). Iginio Russolo's creativity shines in the vdt Borgo di Peuma (Cabernet-Merlot-Refosco) and Casali Bearzi (Raboso-Malbec), in addition to good DOC primarily of Lison-Pramaggiore.

Santa Margherita, Fossalta di Portogruaro (VE). The fortunes of this house founded by the Marzotto family began with the 1960 launching of Pinot Grigio, with which its name became synonymous, followed by equally popular Chardonnay. The firm run by Arrigo Marcer also owns Cantine Torresella, which makes a complete range of wines from the eastern Veneto and the Venezie. Santa Margherita also has a controlling interest in Kettmeir in Alto Adige, for a combined production of about 700,000 cases a year of a wide range of wines from the Venezie. Both DOC and vdt made under chief winemaker Giorgio Mascarin are noted for sound quality and remarkable consistency.

Tenuta Sant'Anna, Loncon di Annone Veneto (VE). Lison-Pramaggiore and Grave del Friuli DOC and sparkling wines in part from company vines.

Valdo, Valdobbiadene (TV). The cellars owned by Fratelli Bolla of Verona make Prosecco, Cartizze, and other sparkling wines.

Zardetto, Scomigo di Conegliano (TV). Pino Zardetto, leading exponent of *charmat lungo*, proves his theory with fine Prosecco di Conegliano and Cartizze (including a semisweet "Dry"), and Zardetto Brut (from Pinot).

COOPERATIVES

CS Montelliana e del Colli Asolani, Caonada di Montebelluna (TV). Reliable range of local DOC and vdt.

CS di Ponte a Piave (TV), Ponte a Piave (TV). Piave DOC.

CS di Valdobbiadene, San Giovanni di Bigolino (TV). Good value in Prosecco and Cartizze.

Left: this distillery in the eastern Veneto is equipped to make grappa on a rather large scale, though much of the crafting of this uniquely Italian eau-de-vie is done by artisans. Grappa differs from brandy in that it derives from the liquidy grape pomace removed during fermentation and not from finished wine – and in that sense it bears a resemblance to French marc. But grappa, which had long been associated with cheap bottles sold by the distillers across the alpine arc of the country, has recently become prized by connoisseurs, and not only in Italy. Its admirers favour those from noble grape varieties grown at noted estates or vineyards and distilled in small batches using the traditional copper alembics or pot stills. When skillfully made, the individual grappas can be as distinctively scented as wines. The preference has been for clear, unaged grappa over slightly coloured wood-aged types. The most prestigious producer of any size in Italy is Nonino of Friuli, whose range of varietals includes a rare Picolit. But by now distillers of note are to be found not only in such old strongholds as the Venezie and Piedmont but also in Tuscany and points south. Prices, which sometimes exceed those for famous aged brandies and liqueurs, may seem exorbitant. But price doesn't seem to matter to those admirers who covet cru grappa as avidly as others collect old Cognacs and Armagnacs.

Travel Information

RESTAURANTS/HOTELS

Villa Michelangelo, 36057 Arcugnano (VI). Tel (0444)550300. Lovely villa with comfortable rooms and a good restaurant in the peaceful Colli Berici.

La Montanella, 35032 Arquà Petrarca (PD). Tel (0429)718200. Tasty country food and wines with enchanting views over the Colli Euganei.

Villa Cipriani, 31011 Asolo (TV). Tel (0423)55444. Venetian grace in a Renaissance villa in a charming hill town. Deluxe food, wine, and prices.

Aurora, 37011 Bardolino (VE). Tel (045)7210038. Lake fish and local wines with views over Garda.

Da Lino, 31053 Pieve di Soligo (TV). Tel (0438)82150. Lino Toffolin adds personal touches to Treviso's vaunted cuisine, wining and dining large groups well and at reasonabe prices. Comfortable rooms.

Dalla Rosa Alda, 37010 San Giorgio Valpolicella (VR). Tel (045)7701018. This gathering spot for Valpolicella's winemakers offers well-prepared Veronese country food and classic wines.

Alfredo-Relais El Toulà, Via Collalto 26, 31100 Treviso. Tel (0422)540275. The original El Toulà and in theory still the best of the series of rustically chic restaurants created by Alfredo Beltrame.

Ca' Masieri, 36070 Trissino (VI). Tel (0445)962100. Delightful country inn where Angelo Vassena and Gianni Zarantonello serve the creations of chef Gianfranco Minuz and choice wines of Vicenza and Verona. Restful rooms.

Antica Locanda Mincio, 37067 Borghetto di Valeggio sul Mincio (VR). Tel (045)7950059. Romantic spot for lunch under a pergola beside the rushing Mincio river. Good Bianco di Custoza and other local wines.

Il Desco, Via Dietro San Sebastiano 7, 37121 Verona. Tel (045)595358. Verona's top ranking restaurant matches the inspired cooking of Elio Rizzo with Natale Spinelli's choices of wine in an artistically original setting.

WINE SHOPS/ENOTECHE

The Enoteca Regionale Veneto at Pramaggiore displays a large selection of bottles and provides other activities promoting the region's wine and food. Recommended among the many private *enoteche* around the region are Angelo Rasi at Padova, La Caneva at Jesolo, Istituto Enologico Italiano at Verona, and Al Volto at Venice.

PLACES OF INTEREST

Venice draws the crowds to Italy's most visited region, though the Veneto has more to offer than the exotic pleasures of the canal city. Its outlying towns possess some of northern Italy's most treasured works of art and architecture and provide relaxing settings to enjoy them in. The countryside varies to physical extremes, though everywhere, high and low, are those villas designed by Palladio and other masters that are the hallmark of Venetian rural civilization. Overlooking the lush flatlands of the Adriatic basin are the wooded hills of Treviso, Padova, and Vicenza, and beyond them the Alps with Cortina d'Ampezzo and other winter resorts within view of the Dolomites. Vineyards are planted widely through northern Italy's most productive wine region, though the following have the most to offer.

Verona. The city becomes Italy's wine capital each April when the colossal Vinitaly fair is held and bottles from around the country and the world are available for tasting. Verona province leads all others in premium production, but visitors who come to taste Soave, Valpolicella, and Bardolino where they are made may have to improvise with map in hand since wine tourism here has not been developed. Still the scenery in the classical sectors of all three zones is worth witnessing.

Colli Berici and Colli Euganei. Visitors to Vicenza and Padova may find excursions through the nearby hills stimulating, as much for the scenery as the wines. Vicenza's Colli Berici have striking villas set amidst wooded slopes. Padova's Colli Euganei are noted for thermal springs, castles and monasteries, and the medieval town of Arquà Petrarca, where Petrarch spent his later years.

Treviso's hills. The Conegliano-Valdobbiadene zone is well organized for wine tourism, with clearly marked routes through the vineyards and indications of shops and taverns where Prosecco and other wines of the area can be sampled. A tour of these pretty hills could be extended to take in the Montello and Colli Asolani zone, south of the Piave, where the main attraction is Palladio's Villa Barbaro at Maser.

Left: despite its location on the lagoon, Venice is the axis of a bountiful land of vines that grow on the plains and hillsides of its hinterland.

Friuli-Venezia Giulia

Capital: Trieste.
Provinces: Gorizia (GO), Pordenone (PN), Trieste (TS), Udine (UD).
Area: 7,847 square kilometres (seventeenth).
Population: 1,220,000 (fifteenth).

Friuli-Venezia Giulia stepped to the front when the new technology came along and showed a doubting world that Italy can make white wine of eminence after all. But if Friuli has become the sanctuary of *vino bianco*, the credit goes as much to human resourcefulness as to the auspicious nature of its gentle hills along the border of Yugoslavia. For the southern flank of the Alps has more than a few such havens for vines across the top of Italy, but nowhere else have winemakers shown the foresight, versatility, and grit of Friulians in coaxing the optimum from them.

What Italians esteem as the Friuli style emerged in Collio Goriziano in the early 1970s with the handcrafted wines of Mario Schiopetto. Their varietal traits might now seem rather linear, but their fresh fragrance, crisp fruit, suave textures, and vital personalities were revelationary. Larger wineries, such as those of brothers Marco and Livio Felluga and Vittorio Puiatti's EnoJulia (now EnoFriulia), propagated the style through Italy and, here and there, abroad. Pinot Grigio popularized the mode, but Chardonnay, Sauvignon, Pinot Bianco, and the sentimental favourites Tocai Friulano and Ribolla Gialla can show more character. Dessert wines – the legendary if overrated Picolit and rejuvenated Verduzzo – and the growing ranks of *spumanti* also show a Friulian touch. Even some red wines, which were habitually soft and fruity, are taking on the weight and complexity that should appeal to more sophisticated audiences.

The ferment prompted small-scale winemakers in Collio to sharpen skills. Growers called Gradnik, Jermann, Gravner, Princic – names that echo the Slavic and Austrian presence in this meridional corner of Central Europe – joined Collio's galaxy of stars whose supplies never equal demands. The working base rapidly widened from Collio to adjacent and equally privileged Colli Orientali del Friuli. Nor are nature's gifts confined to the hills. The emergence of Isonzo, on the plain adjoining Collio, has helped make Friuli's eastern front into one of the nation's major wine areas. Some producers of Grave del Friuli, Aquileia, and Latisana in the broad Adriatic basin have further enhanced the region's image.

The Friuli style, if evolving, remains distinct. Most exponents still consider their whites too graceful to benefit from the softening effects of malolactic fermentation or even from wood, and instead seek what they define as a natural expression of the grapes. The fine-tuned balance is hard to achieve, because it depends on fruit at the perfect point of ripeness vinified by a creative tactician able to pay minute attention to detail. When it works – and when the vintage is right – few white wines anywhere are as exquisite as those of Friuli. When it doesn't, wines can seem light and anonymous to palates attuned to bolder tastes.

Since Friuli's finest bottles are expensive by Italian standards, this delicacy has cost them points abroad, especially with raters who consider oak an essential component of a world class white wine. Some producers, led by Walter Filiputti, who has revitalized several estates in Colli Orientali and Collio, use *barriques* to give new dimensions to whites as well as reds from Cabernet, Merlot, and native vines. Impressive examples include table wines that blend varieties in imaginative ways. Yet this quest for more depth and nuance holds little danger of spilling over into excess, or resulting in the oaky and overbearing varietal wines that Californians are still trying to forget. No such blockbusters for Friulians, who insist that their wines be thoroughly drinkable and at their best with food.

Friuli-Venezia Giulia, one of five "autonomous" regions, represents a recent political union. Both Friuli and Giulia refer to Julius Caesar, whose armies conquered the territory after a long struggle and made the military outpost of Aquileia the second city of the empire. Friuli (from the Latin Forum Julii, now Cividale) comprises the large provinces of Udine and Pordenone between the Adriatic and Austria. It was historically populated by the ethnically distinct Friulani people, whose language is related to Ladin and Romansch. Venezia Giulia, the former Byzantine territory that became the coastal sector of the Venetian Empire, now covers the small provinces of Gorizia and Trieste to the southeast. Its population includes a prominent Slovenian minority.

Ethnic contrasts are a way of life in a region whose relatively easy access by land and sea subjected it to conquests since tribes of ancient Veneti and Celts settled there in the sixth and fifth centuries BC. After the Romans, Byzantines and various barbarians, the dominant influence became Venetian. But before becoming part of a unified Italy in 1866, the region was part of the Austro-Hungarian Empire that made Trieste its gateway to the Mediterranean. World War II left the fate of Trieste hanging in the balance until 1954, when it was returned to Italy. But the Italian-speaking Istrian peninsula had already been ceded to Yugoslavia, along with much of the province of Gorizia and some of Collio's best vineyards.

Wines of Friuli enjoyed moments of glory in the past – when Pliny the Elder praised Pulcinum, the apparent predecessor of Prosecco, and the courts of eighteenth-century Europe savoured Picolit, then exported by a certain Fabio Asquini at the rate of 100,000 small bottles a year. But for most producers who have achieved it, success is a modern phenomenon. A few watched their grandfathers replant vineyards after the devastation of World War I, and many helped their fathers peddle flasks and demijohns to local *osterie*. Now some can marvel over how their bottles generate the peninsula's tidiest profits. For it was Friulians who introduced the concept that good young white wine could, indeed should, be expensive.

Other Italians emulate the style, if rarely with equal success. Yet even in Friuli only an enlightened minority regularly excels. Here, too, producers tend to make too many types of wine to devote full attention to each. The mania in Italy for drinking whites within months of the harvest means that wines are often bottled and sold before they are ready and drunk up before they reach their primes. Since prices remain high even in off years, and since unworthy producers profit from the lofty image, Friuli's wines often meet resistance, and even resentment, from consumers and restaurateurs. Yet the stocks from elite producers of Collio and Colli Orientali are often sold out before being bottled. When accused of pushing up prices, they argue that quick returns enable them to reinvest in better equipment and, more essential, to give greater care to vineyards, in choosing the right clones, limiting yields, and picking selectively – the fine points that make the difference between adequate and excellent wines.

But not everyone prospers. Most Friulian wine originates in the broad

Adriatic plain between the Veneto and the eastern hills. More red than white is made there, much of it for everyday. Still, even in the flatlands, Friulians have an enviable reputation for seriousness. Grave del Friuli accounts for nearly half of the region's DOC wine, much of it Merlot, though there, too, white varieties are gaining rapidly. Wines of the coastal zones of Aquileia and Latisana also show merit in both reds and whites that can occasionally rival those of the hills.

A share of credit for Friuli's emphasis on quality goes to the direction provided by the regional centre for the development of viticulture and oenology based in Udine, where it maintains a "Casa del Vino" with educational and promotional facilities. The centre, headed by Piero Pittaro, who is also a winemaker and president of the Italian association of oenologists, is one of the most active and influential regional forces in wine. Nearly 40 percent of Friuli's production is DOC, a rate surpassed only by Trentino-Alto Adige. Yields are among Italy's lowest – 53 hectolitres per hectare overall, less than 40 hectolitres per hectare in the seven DOC zones. These rates, which are much lower than those of Trentino-Alto Adige and the Veneto, reflect the care given to vineyards by producers who for the most part work with grapes from their own estates. These factors also explain why Friuli-Venezia Giulia has managed to project an image of class that its neighbours rarely achieve.

The region is the nation's leader in viticultural research and diffusion. More than half of the vines planted in Italy originate in Friuli, mainly at the Vivai Cooperativi di Rauscedo, the world's largest nursery, which prepares about 20 million rooted cuttings a year. Nurseries have often been blamed for propagating the varieties that increased production throughout Italy at the expense of class. But recently Rauscedo and others have followed more rigid standards in providing growers with varieties and clones of certified origins selected from vineyards in Italy, France, and Germany.

Friuli-Venezia Giulia's Vineyards

The Veneti, among other early peoples, grew vines here long before the Romans knew Pulcinum, which seems to have been the progenitor of the Prosecco now so popular in the Veneto. The Romans also enjoyed a red wine that may have been Refosco. In the Middle Ages, Benedictine monks recorded varieties that have survived, including Ribolla, Pignolo, Malvasia Istriana, and Verduzzo. The rare red Schioppettino and Tazzelenghe are also considered native. But the origins of the beloved Tocai Friulano, with its intriguing Hungarian connection, have never been adequately explained. Nor is it clear from whence came the fabled Picolit.

The region's aptitude for viticulture was confirmed in the sixteenth century when the governor of Venice banned the removal of vines, citing wine production as "the principal strength and sustenance of the magnificent city of Udine and of the whole land of Friuli". Vines are still worked with uncommon care, perhaps because most wine is made directly by growers. Only about a quarter of the vineyards are on hillsides, which are often terraced and yield less than those on the plains. Growers in Collio and Colli Orientali have tended to increase plant density above the average 3,200 per hectare, while reducing yields – telling factors in favour of quality. Friuli's main systems of vine training is the *cappuccina*, an arched double cordon used chiefly in the hills. A system used increasingly in Italy for mechanical harvesting was developed at Casarsa, in the plains, and carries the name of that town.

It might seem odd that foreign varieties prevail in a region with a rich history of vines considered more or less indigenous. But then, in Friuli, as in the rest of the Venezie, Merlot, Cabernet, and Pinot have been in the vintner's vocabulary since the last century. Before phylloxera the region recorded 217 native vines and 139 imported. Today there are only a dozen natives in regular use and about double that number of imports.

At the turn of the century, red varieties dominated, but today space is evenly divided with white. Merlot still covers about a third of the region's vineyards, though it has lost ground lately, as have Cabernet Franc (to which Cabernet Sauvignon is increasingly preferred), and Refosco. White varieties, which now account for nearly two-thirds of DOC wine, are sharply on the rise. Tocai covers a fifth of the vineyards, but it has lost space to Chardonnay, Pinots, and Sauvignon. The native varieties of Ribolla Gialla, Schioppettino, and Pignolo are coming back. There is even some interest in Prosecco, known as Glera in Collio. The following varieties are associated primarily with Friuli-Venezia Giulia.

Franconia. The Blaufränkisch or Limberger probably native to Croatia is common in Austria and Yugoslavia, but in Italy as Franconia it is found mainly in Friuli, where it makes a bright red with raspberry like flavour.

Malvasia Istriana. Part of the widespread Mediterranean family, the clone grown in Istria and Friuli since the Middle Ages can make fine dry whites with only a hint of that typical Malvasia almond and apricot flavour.

Picolit. Almost certainly Friulian, possibly dating to Roman times, it was once grown through the hills as the source of the region's most vaunted dessert wine. Glory was greater in the past than today, though scarce yields due to floral abortion are offset by hefty prices for wines. The name probably refers to its small (*piccoli*) grapes or bunches.

Pignolo. Cited in the eighteenth century for its excellent red wines, it was nearing extinction until growers in the Colli Orientali began reviving it. This Pignolo, which makes fruity, fragrant wines, is not related to vines of the name (also Pignol, Pignola, Pignolone) grown mainly in Lombardy.

Refosco. Vines in the family probably made wines in Carso and Istria in Roman times. As a source of tastily durable reds, Refosco has been popular for centuries. Of the subvarieties, Refosco dal Peduncolo Rosso (referring to its red stalks) is considered worthier than Refosco Nostrano or Terrano. In Romagna, where Refosco may have been planted by Byzantines, it is known as Cagnina. In France's Savoie it is Mondeuse Noire. Refosco is also planted in North and South America.

Ribolla Gialla. After decades of decline, the variety is making a strong comeback in Collio and Colli Orientali in medium-bodied whites of sunny yellow colour and citrus-like acidity, growing softer and richer with age. Though considered native, since it was cited in the thirteenth century, it is also found in Yugoslavia as Rebula and in Greece as Robola. Ribolla Verde is rare. Ribolla Nera is better known as Schioppettino.

Schioppettino. The ancient Ribolla Nera is called Schioppettino in the Colli Orientali, where it is coming back after a serious decline. The name means gunshot, in reference to the way the still fermenting young wine seemed to burst forth on the palate. New-style red wines can become smooth, even elegant with age.

Tazzelenghe or **Tacelenghe.** Another curiosity, this variety makes red wine of such sharp acidity that it is said to cut the tongue, hence the name. A few producers in the Colli Orientali have admirably tamed it.

Terrano. The Carso version of Refosco Nostrano, known locally as Terran.

Tocai Friulano. An enigma whose vines and name may (or may not) have come from Hungary, Tocai is no mystery to Friulians, who have made it their preferred white. Friuli's Tocai (the name means "here" in Slavic) is definitely not related to vines that make Tokay d'Alsace (Pinot Gris) or Tokaji in Hungary (mainly Furmint). Yet it is speculated that Furmint, which is also grown in Piedmont and France's Midi, was brought to Hungary from Friuli by the Formentini family. Tocai Friulano is at its best in Collio and Colli Orientali, in fresh, crisp whites of marked personality, though it is also prominent in the Veneto (which also uses the related Tocai Italico and the rare and unrelated Tocai Rosso) and Lombardy. It is found as far south as Latium.

Verduzzo Friulano. This ancient vine has two distinct clones, the

verde (green) used for dry, lemony wines in the plains, and the *giallo* (yellow) or Verduzzo di Ramandolo, used for golden dessert wines in the Colli Orientali. The Veneto's Verduzzo Trevigiano is apparently not related.

Other varieties

Other varieties recommended or authorized in Friuli-Venezia Giulia include:

For red (or rosé): Ancellotta, Cabernet Franc, Cabernet Sauvignon, Gamay, Lambrusco Maestri, Malbec, Marzemino, Merlot, Moscato Rosa, Piccola Nera, Pinot Nero, Raboso Piave, Raboso Veronese.

For white: Chardonnay, Garganega, Malvasia Lunga del Chianti, Moscato Giallo, Müller Thurgau, Pinot Bianco, Pinot Grigio, Prosecco, Riesling Italico, Riesling Renano, Sauvignon, Sémillon, Sylvaner Verde, Traminer Aromatico.

Above: vineyards at Rosazzo in the Colli Orientali del Friuli zone lie within view of the Alps, which generate currents that combine with those from the nearby Adriatic Sea to create what is sometimes described as an air conditioned climate. The hills, like neighbouring Collio Goriziano, are known primarily for white wines, though reds can also be notable.

1:690,000

Km 0 ... 10 ... 20 ... 30
Miles 0 ... 10 ... 20

1 COLLI ORIENTALI DEL FRIULI
2 COLLIO
CARSO SUB-ZONE
3 TERRANO DEL CARSO

① San Cipriano
② Vigneti Le Monde
③ Isola Augusta
④ Sergio Pevere
⑤ Ca' Bolani
⑥ Obiz
⑦ Ca' Vescovo

ADRIATIC BASIN

EASTERN FRONT

Autostrada
Main road
Main railway
International boundary
Regional boundary
Provincial boundary
Regional capital
Provincial capital
DOC boundary
Plozner   Wine producer

Friuli-Venezia Giulia's Wine Zones

Friuli-Venezia Giulia is neatly divided across the middle. The mountains to the north (the Carnic and Julian Alps, which cover 43 percent of the land) open like an amphitheatre onto the Adriatic basin (the Pianura Veneta which covers 38 percent). In between are slopes at 100-500 metres, the elite zones of Collio and Colli Orientali, as well as the Carso plateau along the Yugoslavian frontier. The upper plains, coursed by the Tagliamento and Isonzo rivers, take in the vast Grave del Friuli zone and the best of Isonzo. The lower plains along the Adriatic include most of Aquileia and Latisana, plus the bit of Lison-Pramaggiore that extends into Friuli from the Veneto. The play of currents between the Alps and the Adriatic creates a mild, sometimes damp, climate, breezy enough to be referred to by growers in the hills as "air conditioned". Yet microclimates vary markedly, depending on altitude, exposure to sun and air currents. The Carnic Alps have Italy's heaviest rainfall, contributing to the regional average of 1,600 millimetres, well above the national median of 960 millimetres. Summers can be fairly hot and dry in the coastal plains, though prolonged drought is uncommon. Winters in the wine zones are not usually severe, except when the *bora* winds blast past Trieste from the Balkans and the *tramontana* sweeps down from the Alps, which are capped by snow for about six months each year. Snow falls occasionally in the hills, less frequently in the plains. Spring frosts are rarely late enough to cause problems to growers.

Colli Orientali del Friuli

Vineyards are often terraced in these soft hills where flysch – layers of crumbly marl and sandstone – prevails, though in the valleys clay is often mixed with sand and gravel. Microclimates vary notably between the southerly hills around Corno di Rosazzo and Buttrio, which feel the Adriatic influence, and the cooler, damper alpine foothills to the north above Cividale and Nimis. The southern sector has the greatest concentration of vineyards in a zone that produces about twice as much white wine as red. Dry whites – Tocai, Ribolla, the Pinots, Chardonnay, and Sauvignon – do well in most places in conditions that favour notable aromas in wines that gain stature with some ageing. The renowned area for sweet Picolit is Rocca Bernarda and the hills of Bosco Romagno and Prepotto in the southern part of the zone, but some of the finest wines of the past came from Savorgnano del Torre to the northwest. Today little Picolit of real interest is made anywhere. The classic Verduzzo comes from Ramandolo in the extreme north. Colli Orientali's reds often show greater weight and colour than in adjacent Collio, notably in combinations of Cabernet and Merlot from the southern hills, though Schioppettino from Prepotto and a few other places is even more distinctive.

Collio Goriziano

The hills are similar to Colli Orientali in form and soil content, though the zone is more compact and its better vineyards are almost entirely in the marl and sandstone around the town of Cormons, known as flysch di Cormons. The crumbly, well-drained terrain contains a mix of minerals favourable to perfumed, harmonious whites of unusual finesse, as well as agreeably soft, scented reds. The climate is fairly uniform, though the southerly rises at about 100 metres between Gorizia, Farra d'Isonzo, and Cormons are warmer and drier than the heights along the Yugoslavian border, reaching 276 metres at San Floriano. White wines account for a vast majority of production, led in quantity by Tocai but strongly supported by Pinot Bianco and Grigio and increasingly by Chardonnay and Sauvignon. The red Cabernet Franc and Merlot are usually mellow and fruity, though some wines improve with age.

Isonzo

The terrain varies sharply between the gravelly and calcareous high plains coinciding with southernmost Collio and easternmost Grave del Friuli and the alluvial deposits of the Isonzo river basin near Monfalcone. The mild maritime climate is slightly cooler with more rain in the north. Both red and white wines from the upper reaches can show remarkable fragrance and, in general, more personality than other wines from the plains. The range of grape varieties is similar to Collio's in wines that can sometimes rival those of the hills in class.

Carso

The plateau consists largely of chalk-white limestone, mixed with sandy marl in the south around Trieste. The porous terrain, drained by underground streams which have formed networks of caves and potholes, is a geological formation referred to in Italy as *carsico*. The climate varies from mild on the cliffs along the Gulf of Trieste to often harsh and windy along the Yugoslavian border with heights of 200-500 metres in the restricted Terrano del Carso area. The weather can change abruptly. The wines, the reds from Terrano or Refosco and the white from Malvasia, are reputed to have medicinal properties due to the soil's mineral contents.

Grave del Friuli

Vineyards in this vast zone lie almost entirely on the high plain, though the glacial-alluvial terrain varies from prevalently gravel along the Tagliamento river and east towards Udine to sandy loam in much of the western sector around Pordenone. The eastern part, which reaches into the alpine foothills, is also cooler and damper than the maritime climate to the west. The large production is dominated by reds of medium-light to medium-heavy structure, though whites are on the increase. Quality ranges from common to very good, with superior wines often coming from the broad river bed of the Tagliamento, in particular from the *magredi*, the heavy, low-yielding soils on the beds of gravel that give the zone its name.

Aquileia

Glacial and alluvial terrains vary from gravelly clay in the north to sandy loam in the south around the town of Aquileia, though better wines often come from calcareous soils. The mild maritime climate is slightly cooler in the north. Red and white wines tend to be enviably drinkable, fruity and well-scented.

Latisana

Soils consist mainly of sandy loam, sometimes mixed with gravel, partly on reclaimed land jutting out into the Adriatic. The maritime climate and rather fertile terrain seem to favour light and easy Merlot, Cabernet, and Refosco over whites.

Wines of the eastern front: Collio and Colli Orientali

The hills extending from Gorizia along the border of Yugoslavia northwest to Tarcento are at centre stage of Friuli's theatre of wine. Collio Goriziano steals the show, denying an equal share of the spotlight even to its twin Colli Orientali del Friuli. The lead role is not a legacy but an honour won by a new generation of winemakers who, if still a bit star struck by success, have little doubt about their domain's primacy for whites. Still, the notion that Colli Orientali is in some way second class is unfounded. Collio got its DOC first, makes more of the glamorous whites than its neighbour, and has attracted more attention – not to mention profits – in selling them. But its main advantage may be that the short version of its name is so easy to remember. Gradually, though, producers of Colli Orientali are building an image that seems potentially even more dignified. They are already acknowledged by the experts to be able to match their neighbours with most dry white wines, but they also make Friuli's finest Picolit and Verduzzo, and have shown clear supremacy with reds for ageing. The names of both zones have risen steadily in prestige as winemakers, who usually have the advantage of growing their own grapes, compete among themselves with apparently little concern about potential rivals from elsewhere in Italy.

Though split by provincial boundaries with Collio Goriziano towards Gorizia and Colli Orientali del Friuli towards Udine, the zones share a common terrain with its own peculiar form and content. Geologists trace the morphology to the Eocene period, but any visitor can sense the special nature of these rises, in the ochre-amber hues of the pebbly soil supporting vines that scale the slopes towards *cucuzzoli*, the gentle, tree-clumped crests. Superior vineyards grow in flysch, a Germanic term for the strata of

marl and sandstone rich in calcium from fossils deposited before the land rose from the sea. Geologists further distinguish the rather loose flysch di Cormons from the more compact flysch di Stregna, both named after towns in these hills. Farmers make it simpler, describing the crumbly earth as *ponca*. Though blessedly easy to work, the soil tends to slip away with winter rains, so terraces have been built, creating a neatly cultivated appearance but adding to maintenance costs. The terraces, usually oriented towards the south, are known in Friulian as *ronchi* (singular *ronco* or in dialect *ronc*) terms that lend a favourable connotation to vineyards or estates.

The climate, tempered by the exchange of breezes between the Julian Alps and the northern Adriatic, varies intricately as it shifts over and around the slopes. The eclectic range of vines gives growers a wealth of options, which some have learned to play with enviable dexterity. Yet, the stress involved in following many wines through each vintage has influenced some producers to reduce and concentrate on the best. The local preference for whites over reds once followed the fortunes of golden Tocai, Friuli's favourite tipple, or *tajut*. But lately it reflects demand for modern Chardonnay, Pinot Grigio and Bianco, Sauvignon, and Ribolla Gialla. In Collio, white varieties occupy nearly five times as much land as reds. In Colli Orientali, where evidence mounts that red wines could challenge white supremacy, the ratio is not quite two to one. Despite the success of varietals in two of Italy's most privileged DOC zones, some of the most admired wines are unclassified blends. Jermann's Vintage Tunina was the prototype for the up-market *vini da tavola* that sometimes outclass single varietals and nearly always cost more.

Below: vineyards of Collio Goriziano, or simply Collio, are often planted on terraces known as ronchi, *which have a favourable connotation when connected with the name of a vineyard or estate.*

Collio Goriziano or Collio (1968)

It seems hard to imagine that two decades ago most growers of Collio supplied grapes to industrial cellars or sold homemade wine in demijohns. For a growing number of the prosperous little estates that grace these terraced slopes would figure in any *Who's Who* of Italian wine. This is the home of Tocai Friulano, which still commands a patriarchal share of the vineyards. But many outsiders learned the name Collio through Pinot Grigio when it gained international attention as a crisp, pale white a decade or so ago. Its success surprised Friulians, who rank Pinot Grigio as one of their lesser varieties, perhaps remembering the copper-tinged *ramato* before its broad flavours went out of vogue. Mario Schiopetto, who in his quiet way first made Collio chic, has always shown more style with Pinot Bianco, giving it velvety opulence rarely achieved elsewhere.

The younger generation seems to favour Chardonnay, though it isn't DOC yet, even if Vittorio Puiatti recalls bottling a wine of the name in 1972. Yet some unclassified Chardonnay shows world class – for example, from Josko Gravner, who relies on late picking, small barrels, and uncommon devotion to reach similar heights with Sauvignon Blanc. Though not yet as trendy as Chardonnay, some observers consider Sauvignon better suited to these rises, where some versions show the full-blown varietal character of Sancerre, others the subtlety of white Graves. Although red wines are a sideline for many producers, Merlot is rarely as plush and quaffable as from Marco Felluga's Russiz Superiore.

The focus on international varieties has distracted attention from the natives, yet Tocai can still arouse more than local sentiment. When closely cropped and vinified with respect, its wines can be as racy as their rivals with foreign names. Admirers are not just old timers. Young Nicola Manferrari of Borgo del Tiglio has mastered Tocai's secrets with Ronco della Chiesa, distinguished by what tasters note as pear, licorice, herbs, and citrus. But by now it seems safe to assume that nearly any respectable variety would thrive in Collio, even if much of the best land of the range lies in Yugoslavia. A few growers manage to bring grapes across the border, but most wines of what is known in Slovenian as Brda are so shabbily made that they're hardly fit to sell in jugs.

Still, the Italian share of Collio could be put to better use. The current line-up of varieties includes some eccentric choices. For instance, why Cabernet Franc to the exclusion of Cabernet Sauvignon? Why Riesling Italico and not the true Riesling of the Rhine? Why common Traminer instead of the worthier Gewürztraminer? Where are those worthy natives Ribolla Gialla, Verduzzo, Picolit, Refosco, Schioppettino, and Pignolo? Why are there no categories to allow prestigious blends to qualify, instead of parading as *vini da tavola*? It seems a shame that Collio which has lent such lustre to DOC has excluded so many fine wines, more often by necessity than choice.

Current ratings of Collio wines probably give more credit to winemaking skill than to the proven worth of individual terrains or estates. Public identification of *crus* has been so recent that time is needed to determine their real value on the market. More will be known over the next decade or two as new investments in vineyards of notable size come to fruition and established plots are put to better use through denser planting and lower yields. Still, without presuming to rank them, it is worth pointing out specific areas, estates, and vineyards that have shown a predilection for quality.

Collio divides into two tiers north and south of an imaginary line between the crests of Monte Quarin (above Cormons) and Monte Calvario (above Gorizia). Slopes to the south vary somewhat in terrain where flysch di Cormons mixes with irregular deposits of marl, sand, and quartz. But climate is fairly uniform in vineyards between 50-120 m high. Adriatic air favours early budding and ripening for whites of rich flavour and texture and reds of ample body and colour. The greatest concentration of estates is on the southern slopes of Colle della Croce, between Cormons and Capriva,

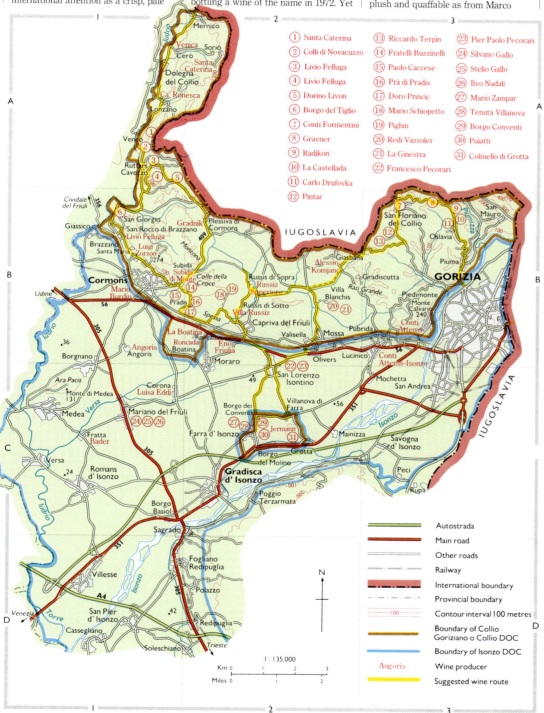

1 Santa Caterina
2 Colli di Novacuzzo
3 Livio Felluga
4 Livio Felluga
5 Dorino Livon
6 Borgo del Tiglio
7 Conti Formentini
8 Gravner
9 Radikon
10 La Castellada
11 Carlo Drufovka
12 Pintar
13 Riccardo Terpin
14 Fratelli Buzzinelli
15 Paolo Caccese
16 Prà di Pradis
17 Doro Princic
18 Mario Schiopetto
19 Pighin
20 Redi Vazzoler
21 La Ginestra
22 Francesco Pecorari
23 Pier Paolo Pecorari
24 Silvano Gallo
25 Stelio Gallo
26 Ilvo Nadali
27 Mario Zampar
28 Tenuta Villanova
29 Borgo Conventi
30 Puiatti
31 Colmello di Grotta

1:135.000

Km 0   1   2   3
Miles 0   1   2

Legend:
- Autostrada
- Main road
- Other roads
- Railway
- International boundary
- Provincial boundary
- 100 Contour interval 100 metres
- Boundary of Collio Goriziano o Collio DOC
- Boundary of Isonzo DOC
- *Angoris* Wine producer
- Suggested wine route

extending from Pradis (Princic, Caccese, Prà di Pradis) east past Spessa (Castello di Spessa, Schiopetto, Pighin) to Russis di Sopra (Russiz Superiore) and Russis di Sotto (Villa Russiz). To the south, the isolated rise of Monte Fortin has vineyards of undeniable class (Jermann, Borgo Conventi, Tenuta Villanova). Other points of note are at Blanchis above Mossa (Vazzoler and La Ginestra); Lucinico at the foot of Monte Calvario (Attems); and in the vicinity of Cormons.

The northern tier has two main sectors, one to the east on the heights above Gorizia and the other to the west between Cormons and Mernicco adjacent to Colli Orientali. Flysch with calcareous deposits is fairly uniform in vineyards. Generally higher altitudes and the influence of mountain currents, particularly to the east, make these slopes somewhat damper and cooler, so grapes tend to ripen later, heightening primary aromas in whites. The eastern rises between 100-275 m high have points of note around Oslavia (Gravner, La Castellada, Radikon) and between

San Floriano and Gradiscuta (Formentini, Komjanc, Pintar). To the west, at heights between 100-200 m along the Judrio valley, points of interest are above Brazzano (Borgo del Tiglio), at Plessiva (Gradnik), Ruttars and Vencó (Livio Felluga, Livon, Santa Caterina), and Dolegnano (Ca' Ronesca, Venica).

Zone: Hills along the southern edge of the Collio (Brda) range against the border of Yugoslavia between the Isonzo and Judrio rivers in the province of Gorizia. The main sector extends from the commune of Oslavia west through San Floriano del Collio, Gorizia, Mossa, San Lorenzo Isontino, Capriva del Friuli, and Cormons, curving north to Dolegna del Collio. An isolated sector covers the rise of Monte Fortin at Farra d'Isonzo, eight km southwest of Gorizia.

Among the 11 types, all are pure varietals, except Collio Bianco.

Cabernet Franc Dry red. Yld 77/110, Alc 12, Acd 0.5-0.75.

Collio Bianco Dry white. Grapes: Ribolla Gialla 45-55%, Malvasia Istriana 20-30%, Tocai 15-25%. Yld 77/110, Alc 11, Acd 0.5-0.75.

Above: the Collio DOC zone occupies the southern sector of a range that is centred in Yugoslavia where it is known as Brda and where some of the best vineyard sites are located.

Malvasia Dry white. Yld 77/110, Alc 11.5, Acd 0.45-0.75.

Merlot Dry red. Yld 77/110, Alc 12, Acd 0.5-0.7.

Pinot Bianco Dry white. Yld 77/110, Alc 12.5, Acd 0.45-0.7.

Pinot Grigio Dry white. Yld 77/110, Alc 12, Acd 0.5-0.75.

Pinot Nero Dry red. Yld 77/110, Alc 12.5, Acd 0.45-0.65.

Riesling Italico Dry white. Yld 77/110, Alc 12, Acd 0.5-0.75.

Sauvignon Dry white. Yld 77/110, Alc 12.5, Acd 0.5-0.75.

Tocai Friulano Dry white. Yld 77/110, Alc 12, Acd 0.4-0.65.

Traminer Dry white. Yld 71.5/110, Alc 12, Acd 0.5-0.7.

Other wines of note

Collio has a number of notable blends and outstanding unclassified varietals, but most producers maintain a nucleus of DOC wines. The leading exception is

Jermann, who followed up on his revelationary Vintage Tunina by making all his wines vdt, including approved varietals. Most other top producers have a vdt or two as listed below. Sparkling wines have emerged with some prominence, most based on Chardonnay and Pinots, though other varieties, such as Ribolla, may also be used. Two of special note are the *champenoise* Puiatti Extra Brut and the *charmat* Livio Felluga Brut. Collio's most original wine is Vino della Pace made by the cooperative at Cormons from more than 400 varieties from around the world planted in a single vineyard. Adorned by labels designed each year by three famous artists, it is sent to heads of state as a gesture of peace and goodwill.

ESTATES/GROWERS

Borgo Conventi, Farra d'Isonzo (GO). From 12 ha, Gianni Vescovo has built a reputation for good Sauvignon and barrel-aged Braida Nuova Rosso vdt. He also issues a commercial line of Isonzo DOC and vdt under his name.

Borgo del Tiglio, Brazzano di Cormons (GO). From 3 ha, Nicola Manferrari makes outstanding Tocai from the Ronco della Chiesa plot, fine Malvasia and a good vdt Rosso della Centa from Merlot and Cabernet.

Mario Burdin, Cormons (GO). Sound Collio and Isonzo DOC.

Fratelli Buzzinelli, Cormons (GO). Collio DOC and Müller Thurgau vdt.

Ca' Ronesca, Dolegna del Collio (GO). Sergio Comunello has vineyards in both Collio and Colli Orientali from which winemaker Fabio Coser makes persuasive whites, exemplified by the Sauvignon di Ipplis. Also impressive is the red vdt Sariz, based on Merlot.

Paolo Caccese, Pradis di Cormons (GO). From 3 ha, Collio whites and reds.

Castello di Spessa, Spessa di Capriva (GO). Re-emerging estate with potential.

Colli di Novacuzzo, Vencó (GO).

Conti Attems, Lucinico (GO). From 30 ha around Piedimonte del Calvario, Douglas Attems, longtime head of the Collio producers' consortium, collaborates with Collavini in making good Collio and Isonzo DOC, the latter labelled with the name Podgora.

Conti Formentini, San Floriano del Collio (GO). The estate was founded in 1520 by the Formentini family, which supposedly introduced to Hungary the vine that became known as Furmint – the base of Tokaji. From more than 100 ha, Michele Formentini makes Collio DOC and *spumante*. The estate also has a restaurant, hotel, wine museum, and 9-hole golf course.

Carlo Drufovka, Oslavia (GO).

Livio Felluga, Brazzano di Cormons (GO). From 15 ha in Collio (Ruttars and Vencó) and 89 ha in Colli Orientali (Rosazzo and Oleis), Livio Felluga and sons Maurizio and Andrea at their Brazzano cellars make wines whose full style has won international acclaim. DOCs include fine Tocai, the single vineyard Sauvignon di Rolat from Collio, and a rare Pinot Grigio *ramato* from the Colli Orientali. Most esteemed is the white vdt Terre Alte (Tocai, Pinot Bianco, Sauvignon from a plot at Rosazzo). Livio Felluga Brut is an unusually refined tank method sparkler.

Gradnik, Plessiva di Cormons (GO). The late Gradimir Gradnik built a name for quality in wines from 9 ha, a tradition carried on with flair by daughter Wanda. Beyond fine Collio DOCs, she makes a Picolit.

Gravner, Oslavia (GO). From 11 ha of manicured vines, including plots straddling Yugoslavia, Josko Gravner makes oustanding Collio DOCs, along with the vdt red Rujno of Cabernet and Merlot and the curious white vdt Vinograd Breg, from Glera (a local name for Prosecco), Ribolla, Malvasia, and Pagadebit. Most of his wines are aged in wood, including Chardonnay and Sauvignon with the strength of character and personalized style to rank with Italy's finest. But his favourite is Ribolla Gialla, which he treats not as a lightweight but as a structured white for ageing.

Jermann, Villanova di Farra (GO). Silvio Jermann, who works 23 ha on Monte Fortin, is the soft-spoken heretic of Collio. As a youth in the mid-1970s he invented Vintage Tunina, from late-picked Sauvignon and Chardonnay with Ribolla, Malvasia, and Picolit, now grown in a 3-ha plot. It influenced the fashion of some fine blended whites among other producers, but rarely equal to the prototype. His vineyards face north, east, and west, but not south like most others, meaning that grapes ripen later. He has renounced DOC for varietals that rank with the best of Collio. Other innovations are Engelwhite (pure Pinot Nero), Vinnae (Ribolla with Riesling and Malvasia), and the sweet pink Vigna Bellina from Moscato Rosa. His long aversion to barrel-aged whites ended with a blend of '86 and '87 Chardonnay called "Where the Dreams have no end", which even some English-speaking admirers found hard to interpret.

Il Carpino, San Floriano del Collio (GO).

Alessio Komjanc, San Floriano del Collio (GO).

La Boatina, Cormons (GO).

La Castellada, Oslavia (GO). Giorgio and Nicolò Bensa have made this one of Collio's most promising small estates.

La Ginestra, Mossa (GO).

Dorino Livon *See* Colli Orientali.

Francesco Pecorari, San Lorenzo Isontino (GO). From vineyards divided between Collio and Isonzo, Pecorari does well with both.

Pighin, Capriva del Friuli (GO). Livio and Fernando Pighin have 27 ha of vines at Capriva where they make their well known Collio DOCs and a vdt white Soreli from Tocai, Pinot Bianco, and Sauvignon. They have another estate for Grave del Friuli wines.

Pintar, San Floriano del Collio (GO).

Prà di Pradis, Pradis di Cormons (GO). An emerging estate to watch.

Doro Princic, Pradis di Cormons (GO). Sandro Princic, who has long made notable Tocai and Pinot Bianco DOC on the family farm, combines them with Ribolla in a fine vdt called Vedute di Pradis.

Radikon, Oslavia (GO). Collio DOCs and a vdt called Slatnik from Chardonnay, Tocai, and Sauvignon.

Roncada, Cormons (GO). From 17 ha, Silvia and Lina Mattioni make Collio DOC and a rare Franconia vdt red.

Above: Josko Gravner has the latest in winemaking equipment at his small cellars near Oslavia in Collio, but he insists that the quality of wines that have won increasing critical acclaim is due primarily to devotion to vineyards that straddle the border of Yugoslavia.
Right: producers in the Collio zone, as elsewhere in Friuli, often make several types of wine, white and red from native and foreign vines.

Russiz Superiore, Capriva (GO). The enterprising Marco Felluga and son Roberto have created some of Collio's most stylish wines from 60 ha of terraced vines on this model estate at Russis di Sopra. The classical whites and easy reds from Merlot, Cabernet Franc, and Pinot Nero show unerring class. Two white vdt have drawn acclaim, the dry Roncuz from Pinot Bianco, Tocai, Sauvignon, and Riesling Italico, and a lightly sweet, oak-kissed Verduzzo.

Santa Caterina, Scriò di Dolegna (GO). From 50 ha at Scriò and Vencó, Gianfranco Fantinel makes impressive Collio DOC and vdt Franconia, Picolit, Ribolla Gialla, and Schioppettino.

Mario Schiopetto, Spessa di Capriva (GO). A living legend in Collio for his pioneering with white wines, the philosophical Schiopetto continues to strive for greater finesse and purity in wines from 16 ha leased from the Archbishopric of Gorizia. His passion for viticulture and almost stoical patience in the cellar enable him in good vintages to excel with up to a dozen wines. Among DOCs, Pinot Bianco and Tocai seem to stand out more often than the others. The array of vdt includes fine Ribolla and Riesling Renano, the singular Blanc des Rosis (Tocai, Pinot Bianco, Ribolla), and Rivarossa (Cabernet Sauvignon, Merlot, Pinot Nero).

Subida di Monte, Cormons (GO). Sound DOCs from 7 ha.

Tenuto Villanova, Farra d'Isonzo (GO). From 80 ha, the ancient estate makes DOCs of Isonzo and Collio, the

Top: Mario Schiopetto, a pioneer of the Friuli style with white wines that set standards for others to follow, continues to strive for perfection on his Collio estate.

latter under the Montecucco label.

Riccardo Terpin, San Floriano del Collio (GO).

Redi Vazzoler, Mossa (GO). From 15 ha at Blanchis, Redento Vazzoler makes notably improved Collio DOCs under Walter Filiputti's guidance. He also produces a fine vdt white called Ghiaie Bianche from Tocai, Pinot Bianco, and Müller Thurgau sold by Cinzano-Col d'Orcia of Montalcino in Tuscany.

Venica, Dolegna del Collio (GO). An admirable range of Collio wines is led by Sauvignon. All are served in the Venica family's trattoria at Cerò.

Villa Russiz, Capriva (GO). The Istituto A. Cerutti is an orphanage partly supported by proceeds from good Collio wines made by director Edino Menotti from 30 ha around the historical estate.

Luigi Zorzon, Brazzano di Cormons (GO).

WINE HOUSES/MERCHANTS

Fabio Berin, Mossa (GO).
Collavini *See* Colli Orientali.
Comini, Cormons (GO). Collio, Colli Orientali, and Aquileia DOC.
EnoFriulia, Capriva del Friuli (GO). Vittorio Puiatti was a pioneer of the Friuli style at EnoJulia, founded in 1967. Now as EnoFriulia, the firm makes a range of wines, usually vdt, from Friuli's hills and other choice parts of the Tre Venezie – always of good quality and reasonable price. *See* Puiatti.

Marco Felluga, Gradisca d'Isonzo (GO). The impressive line of Collio DOCs sold under the Marco Felluga label comes from grapes bought under long-term contracts from growers with 150 ha of vines. A new white vdt is called Marco Felluga.

Puiatti, Farra d'Isonzo (GO). Vittorio Puiatti, one of Italy's most astute winemakers, turned the family estate into an elite wine house, where he and son Giovanni select grapes for Collio DOC and vdt of notable style. They use Chardonnay, Pinot Bianco, and Pinot Nero in the white vdt Nuvizial and Puiatti Bianco (which combines different vintages) as well as the fine *champenoise* Puiatti Extra Brut.

Giovanni Scolaris, San Lorenzo Isontino (GO).
Valle *See* Colli Orientali.
Vinicola Udinese *See* Colli Orientali.

COOPERATIVES

Cantina Produttori Vini del Collio e dell'Isonzo, Cormons (GO). From growers in Collio and Isonzo, large production of DOC, *spumanti*, and vdt. The cooperative also makes Aquileia DOC from the agricultural school of Villa Chiozza. Cellarmaster Luigi Soini created the unique Vino della Pace.

Brda Cooperativa Viticoltori, San Floriano del Collio (GO).

Bottom: the gradual slopes around Capriva del Friuli in the southern tier of Collio has vineyards noted for whites of rich flavour and texture and reds of ample body and colour.

Colli Orientali del Friuli (1970)

Winemakers here take offence at the suggestion that Colli Orientali is an annex of Collio. The zone is more spread out and, therefore, less uniform, true enough, but most Colli Orientali *crus* are in the southern hills, which have nearly identical conditions to adjacent Collio. Impartial observers generally concede that the several whites the two have in common – Tocai, the Pinots, Sauvignon – are of comparable class, but for the competitive growers of Colli Orientali that isn't enough. They may first point out that they have more types of red – including the indigenous Schioppettino and the regional stalwart Refosco – and that their Merlot and Cabernet (both types) have more power and durability. As for whites, Colli Orientali has classified the prized, if overpriced, Picolit, as well as the native Ribolla Gialla, plus Chardonnay and Riesling Renano, and it boasts the ultimate Verduzzo in Ramandolo Classico. So it might be conceded that only an inopportune twist of fate (a provincial boundary) placed these worthy oriental hills on what the misinformed perceive to be an inferior position.

The estates of Colli Orientali seem to be flourishing nonetheless. But even if their top whites may be priced with the cream of Collio, the collective image isn't the same. Leadership is lacking, especially since the shake-up in 1989 at Abbazia di Rosazzo, the antique abbey that Walter Filiputti had built into the go-ahead estate. Filiputti is an influential figure in these hills, not only as an author and journalist but as a winemaker and manager. He was deprived of his post not only at Abbazia di Rosazzo, but also at the boutique wineries of Ronco del Gnemiz and Vigne dal Leon. Italian acclaim for the wines of those estates had begun to echo abroad, none with such resound as Ronco delle Acacie, the abbey's singular barrel-aged white. Filiputti, like his neighbours, had succeeded admirably

1 Coos
2 Giovanni Dri
3 Rieppi
4 Giuseppe Toti
5 Ca' Ronesca-Ipplis
6 Vigne dal Leon
7 I Moros
8 Rocca Bernarda
9 I Poderi-Angoris
10 Torre Rosazza
11 Specogna
12 Ronco Noax-Marin
13 Buiatti
14 Valle
15 Marina Danieli
16 D' Attimis Maniago
17 Bandut-Colutta
18 Fornaci di Manzano
19 Ronchi di Manzano
20 Ronco del Gnemiz
21 Dorino Livon
22 Abbazia di Rosazzo
23 Livio Felluga
24 La Viarte
25 Nascig
26 Valentino Butussi
27 Gigante
28 Collavini

Main road
Other roads
Railway
International boundary
Provincial boundary
Contour interval 100 metres
Boundary of Colli Orientali del Friuli DOC
Bosco Romagno   Wine producer
Ramandolo   Noted vineyards
Suggested wine route

with the international elite. But what he worked hardest at was reviving the natives – Ribolla Gialla, Verduzzo, Picolit, Schioppettino, Tazzelenghe, Pignolo – vines that give Colli Orientali a unique stamp in the world of wine. Filiputti's latest mandate is to make a leader of the Torre Rosazza estate, which seems to have the vineyards and finances to succeed.

Colli Orientali's versatility is also partly due to the climate, which ranges from the mild Adriatic influence along the southern flank to cooler and damper in the alpine foothills to the north. For example, Manzano has an annual average of 1,436 mm of rain and Ramandolo, 25 km to the north, records about 2,000 mm. Even if vineyards are concentrated in the south on terraced *ronchi* with flysch similar to adjacent Collio, telling differences exist in the wines.

The best vineyards of Colli Orientali's southern flank cover three distinct groups of hills. One lies to the west above Manzano and Buttrio, where conditions favour balance and finesse in both whites and reds. Producers there include Dorigo, Valle, Marina Danieli, Fornaci di Manzano, Ronchi di Manzano, Buiatti, and D'Attimis Maniago. The central rise between San Giovanni al Natisone and Ipplis around the crest of Monte Santa Caterina takes in the renowned vineyards of Rosazzo, Rocca Bernarda, and Ipplis. Though historically noted for Picolit, Friuli's biggest Merlot also originates in the environs, along with fine dry whites. Prominent there are Abbazia di Rosazzo, Torre Rosazza, Vigne dal Leon, Ronco del Gnemiz, Specogna, Livio Felluga's Oleis and Rosazzo properties, Ca' Ronesca's Ipplis vineyards, Rocca Bernarda, Marin's Ronco Noax, I Moros, and the Angoris I Poderi plots. The eastern rise is larger, extending from Corno di Rosazzo north through the vineyard areas of Gramogliano and Novacuzzo (noted for full-bodied reds and whites), Bosco Romagno (noted for Picolit), Prepotto and Albana (which specialize in Schioppettino). Growers of note are Nascig, Gigante, Butussi, and Lui at Gramogliano; La Viarte at Novacuzzo; Arzenton and Bosco Romagno at Bosco Romagno; Rubini and Rodaro at Spessa; Colli Sant'Anna at Sant'Anna; and Riepi and Toti at Albana. From that village north, prime vineyards are scattered – at Cialla (Ronchi di Cialla), Fornalis (Marin's Ronco Fornaz), and above Cividale at Togliano where Volpe Pasini makes outstanding wines. The only real concentration of vineyards in the north is at Ramandolo, a village that gives its name to the sweet wine from Verduzzo Giallo. The DOC was modified to give growers there the exclusive right to call their wine

Ramandolo Classico, but, confusingly, producers throughout Colli Orientali still have the right to call their sweet or *amabile* Verduzzo simply Ramandolo. Vineyards at Savorgnano del Torre were noted for Picolit in the past, though little is made there today.

Zone: Low hills in an elongated tract that curls around the plain of Udine from Buttrio and Manzano east to the Judrio river, north to Cividale, and northwest along the foothills of the Julian Alps to Tarcento, taking in 14 communes in Udine province. The majority of vineyards lie in the southern area adjacent to Collio. The subdistrict of Ramandolo Classico is confined to parts of the communes of Nimis and Tarcento in the extreme north.

The 20 types include 17 varietals of at least 90%, possibly complemented by other DOC grapes of the same colour. Ramandolo must be 90% Verduzzo Friulano. Rosato 90% Merlot.

Cabernet (Cabernet Franc/Cabernet Sauvignon) Dry red. Yld 77/110, Alc 11, Acd 0.5, Ag riserva 2 yrs.

Cabernet Franc Dry red. Yld 77/110, Alc 11, Acd 0.5, Ag riserva 2 yrs.

Cabernet Sauvignon Dry red. Yld 77/110, Alc 11, Acd 0.5. Ag riserva 2 yrs.

Chardonnay Dry white. Yld 77/110, Alc 11, Acd 0.5.

Malvasia Istriana Dry white. Yld 77/110, Alc 11, Acd 0.6.

Merlot Dry red. Yld 77/110, Alc 11, Acd 0.5. Ag riserva 2 yrs.

Picolit Dessert white, amabile or dolce. Yld 28/40, Alc 15, Acd 0.5, Ag riserva 2 yrs.

Pinot Bianco Dry white. Yld 77/110, Alc 11.5, Acd 0.5.

Pinot Grigio Dry white. Yld 77/110, Alc 11.5, Acd 0.5.

Pinot Nero Dry red. Yld 77/110, Alc 11, Acd 0.5, Ag riserva 2 yrs.

Ramandolo/Ramandolo Classico Dessert white, amabile or dolce. Yld 56/80, Alc 14, Acd 0.5.

Refosco dal Peduncolo Rosso Dry red. Yld 77/110, Alc 11, Acd 0.5.

Ribolla Gialla Dry white. Yld 77/110, Alc 11, Acd 0.5.

Riesling Renano Dry white. Yld 77/110, Alc 11, Acd 0.5.

Rosato Dry rosé. Yld 77/110, Alc 11, Acd 0.5.

Sauvignon Dry white. Yld 77/110, Alc 11.5, Acd 0.5.

Schioppettino Dry red. Yld 77/110, Alc 11, Acd 0.5.

Tocai Friulano Dry white. Yld 77/110, Alc 11, Acd 0.45.

Traminer Aromatico Dry white. Yld 71.5/110, Alc 11, Acd 0.5.

Verduzzo Friulano Dry white, also amabile or dolce. Yld 77/110, Alc 11.5, Acd 0.5.

Other wines of note

The gradual comeback of the natives Pignolo and Tazzelenghe, like the outsider Franconia, has added a touch of old spice to the recipes for modern vdt. Livio Felluga's Terre Alte and Abbazia di Rosazzo's Ronco delle

Acacie are widely admired, though by now most producers have their own creations, some of which are cited below. Also notable are sparkling wines, where Collavini stands out in a growing field that consists of the usual standard Pinots and Chardonnay but also includes some novelties.

ESTATES/GROWERS

Abbazia di Rosazzo, Manzano (UD). From 12 ha around the 11th-century abbey come noted DOCs plus the unique vdt whites Ronco delle Acacie (Tocai, Pinot Grigio, Ribolla), Ronco di Corte (Sauvignon, Pinot Bianco), red Ronco dei Roseti (Franconia, Tazzelenghe, Refosco, Cabernet, Merlot), and a bit of Pignolo. After Walter Filiputti's departure in 1989, Silvano Formigli and Franco Bernabei, both noted for work in Tuscany, became manager and winemaker.

Mario Arzenton, Cividale (UD). Good DOCs from 11 ha at Bosco Romagno.

Bandut, Manzano (UD). Wines are issued under the Colutta label.

Bosco Romagno, Spessa di Cividale (UD).

Livio & Claudio Buiatti, Buttrio (UD).

Valentino Butussi, Corno di Rosazzo (UD).

Colli Sant'Anna, Spessa di Cividale (UD).

G.B. Comelli, Torlano (UD). Noted for Ramandolo Classico.

Fratelli Coos, Ramandolo (UD). Noted for Ramandolo Classico.

Marina Danieli, Buttrio (UD). Re-emerging estate around the sumptuous Villa Florio Maseri where Marina Danieli, tutored by Giorgio Grai, makes Colli Orientali and Grave DOC of distinct style, along with vdt red Faralta (Cabernet-Tazzelenghe), Müller Thurgau, and bubbly Brut Mus.

Gianfranco D'Attimis Maniago, Buttrio (UD). The Tenuta Sottomonte has produced respected wine for centuries.

Below: vineyards on the lower slopes of Colli Orientali del Friuli near Manzano are in the warmest, driest part of a zone that extends north into the foothills of the Alps.

Girolamo Dorigo, Vicinale di Buttrio (UD). Girolamo Dorigo has invested heavily in 18 ha of vines and cellars designed to carry him to the top in Friuli. Quality is good and improving, but names are confusing. Montsclapade applies to a vdt red (Cabernet, Merlot, Malbec), a *champenoise*, and several Colli Orientali DOC. Ronc di Juri applies to a vdt white (Ribolla, Tocai, Sauvignon, Chardonnay), several DOC, and vdt Pignolo and Tazzelenghe.

Giovanni Dri, Ramandolo (UD). From 6 ha, Dri makes the most admired Ramandolo Classico, along with a bit of Picolit and Refosco, and the vdt Roncat Bianco from Verduzzo and Picolit.

Livio Felluga *See* Collio.

Fornaci di Manzano, Manzano (UD).

Arturo & Adriano Gigante, Corno di Rosazzo (UD).

I Moros, Rocca Bernarda (UD).

I Poderi *See* Angoris under Isonzo.

La Viarte, Novacuzzo (UD). Giuseppe Ceschin makes an admirable range of DOC at this estate, whose Sauvignon can rank with the finest.

Le Due Terre, Prepotto (UD). Emerging with wines of power and finesse.

Dorino Livon, Dolegnano (UD). From choice vineyards in Colli Orientali (Masarotte and Cumini), Collio (Ruttars, Cavezzo, and Trussio), and Grave (Medeuzza), Livon has 3 cellars for wines of remarkable quality and reasonable price, including DOC and *spumante*.

Giovanni Marin, Fornalis di Cividale (UD). From 20 ha at Ronco Fornaz and Ronco Noax, Giovanni Marin makes fine DOC and vdt under the vineyard names.

Nascig, Corno di Rosazzo (UD). Angelo and Giuseppe Nascig make admirable DOC and vdt Franconia from Prà di Corte and Vigna del Broili at Gramogliano.

Lina & Paolo Petrucco, Buttrio (UD). Emerging estate.

Rieppi, Albana di Prepotto (UD). Specialist in Schioppettino.

Rocca Bernarda, Rocca Bernarda (UD). The estate, famous for Picolit when it belonged to the Perusini family, is now run by the Knights of Malta.

Paolo Rodaro, Spessa di Cividale (UD).

Ronchi di Cialla, Cialla di Prepotto (UD). The estate of Paolo and Dina Rapuzzi has drawn praise for Verduzzo and Schioppettino from 8 ha.

Ronchi di Manzano, Manzano (UD).

Ronco del Gnemiz, San Giovanni al Natisone (UD). From 6 ha, owner Enzo Palazzolo makes good DOCs, plus vdt Müller Thurgau, fine barrel-fermented Chardonnay, and Ronco del Gnemiz from Cabernet Sauvignon and Franc.

Rubini, Spessa di Cividale (UD). The long-established estate run by Leone Rubini has 40 ha of vines on properties at Spessa and Borgo Centa near Prepotto. The two lines of wines, mainly DOC, represent some of the best quality for price in Friuli's hills.

Specogna, Rocca Bernarda (UD). Picolit stands out from the DOC assortment.

Torre Rosazza, Poggiobello di Manzano (UD). The historical Poggiobello estate with 84 ha of prime vineyards is being developed by the Generali insurance group with Walter Filiputti in charge of wine. Early issues of DOC were promising, as was the vdt Ronco della Torre from Cabernet and Merlot. Novelties in *barriques* are the white Ronco delle Magnolie (Pinot Bianco and Chardonnay) and L'Altromerlot, a pure varietal.

Giuseppe Toti, Albana di Prepotto (UD). Schioppettino and Franconia.

Valle, Buttrio (UD). Luigi Valle makes a bit of everything Colli Orientali and Collio have to offer, including DOC and vdt mainly from 65 ha of his own vines. He has a normal, reasonably priced range, and the select Araldica, which includes the vdt Araldo Rosso from Cabernet, Merlot, and Refosco.

Vigne dal Leon, Rocca Bernarda (UD). From 6 ha, Tullio Zamò makes admired white DOCs, plus vdt of Schioppettino, Tacelenghe, and Rosso di Vigne dal Leon from Merlot and Cabernet. The Tullio Zamò signature wine is a fine oak-matured Pinot Bianco.

Volpe Pasini, Togliano di Torreano (UD). The Volpe Pasini family makes some of Colli Orientali's finest wines from 30 ha surrounding the estate that was once the summer residence of the patriarchs of Aquileia. The name Zuc di Volpe is used for select DOCs, of which Tocai and Pinot Bianco often stand out. Fine vdt are white Le Roverelle (Tocai, Sauvignon, Pinot Bianco, Verduzzo) and red Le Marne (Cabernet with Refosco and Pinot Nero).

WINE HOUSES/MERCHANTS

Collavini, Corno di Rosazzo (UD). Artistic *negoçiant* Manlio Collavini and sons make always reliable DOC from Colli Orientali, Collio, and Grave, along with vdt Conte di Cuccanea, a barrel-aged white from Chardonnay, Ribolla, and Pinot Bianco. Three sparkling wines stand out: the *charmat lungo* Ribolla Gialla and Il Grigio (based on Pinot and Chardonnay) and the *champenoise* Applause Nature (from Chardonnay and Pinot Nero). Collavini recently took over production and commerce of the Conte Attems Collio estate.

Vinicola Udinese, Udine. Sound selections of Colli Orientali, Grave, Collio, and Carso DOC, plus vdt and *spumante*.

Wines of the eastern front: Isonzo and Carso

Along Friuli's eastern front between Gorizia and Trieste lie two more DOC zones that slightly overlap but are profoundly different from one another. First comes Isonzo, which follows the river from Gorizia almost to its mouth at the Gulf of Trieste. Though vineyards lie mainly on level land, parts of Isonzo have features that distinguish its wines from others of the plains. Its fragrant reds and whites sometimes outclass even those of adjacent Collio. Carso is something else again. The chalky plateau extending from the banks of the Isonzo down past Trieste holds vineyards of an ancient strain of Refosco known as Terrano, source of what might rank as Friuli's most peculiar wine.

Isonzo or **Isonzo del Friuli (1975)**
Isonzo owes its rising status to growers who refuse to believe that lowlands are innately inferior to highlands. The zone had been known for some of Friuli's most seductive Merlot and Cabernet. But the whites, led by gregarious Tocai, just didn't have the natural poise of their Collio cousins. Or so it seemed until the Chardonnay and Sauvignon of Stelio Gallo began to sway expert opinions. Even now, as other growers rise to the challenge, observers often credit their success to hard work in overcoming the natural handicaps of the plains. But another explanation might be that parts of Isonzo enjoy privileged conditions that growers bent on volume had previously neglected. The northern sector – above where the Isonzo intercepts its Judrio and Torre tributaries – lies adjacent to Collio's southern tier and enjoys a kindred climate. The terrain is decidedly diverse, however, nearly deprived of flysch or rich organic matter. Yet the best land is arable and well-drained on a gravel base and the calcareous topsoil contains some iron, which gives the earth a reddish hue and supposedly

Above: vines in the Carso DOC zone near Trieste.

lends a touch of vigour to the wines.

The recent extension of the DOC to include 20 types left producers with more options than they could sensibly deal with. Here, as in the hills, future success may depend on how wisely they narrow the field in a zone where French varieties seem to outperform natives. Some of Isonzo's best Merlot and Cabernet have regularly come from the northwest corner below Cormons and Capriva and around Monte di Medea. Whites, exemplified by Sauvignon, Chardonnay, and the Pinots, seem best suited to gravelly soils found along the Isonzo's northern flank. Estates of note are at Lucinico (Attems), San Lorenzo Isontino (Francesco and Pier Paolo Pecorari), on the lower slopes of Monte Fortin (Colmello di Grotta, Tenuta Villanova, Zampar), and especially around Mariano del Friuli (Stelio and Silvano Gallo). Vineyards are dense as far south as Sagrado and Villesse, where wines tend to be light but attractive. Wines of the sandy river basin west of Monfalcone have little to

recommend them beyond fleeting drinkability. The strip that overlaps Carso to the east takes in Redipuglia and Cave di Selz, where calcareous soils lend themselves to fresh, easy whites and soft, well-scented reds.

Zone: The Isonzo river basin between the Adriatic litoral and Gorizia covering 20 communes in its province. The northern plains are interrupted by Monte Fortin and Monte di Medea. The alluvial flatlands to the south give way to the edge of the Carso plateau towards the east.

The 20 types include 17 pure varietals, plus Bianco, Rosso, and Pinot Spumante.

Bianco Dry white, also amabile, frizzante. Grapes: Tocai Friulano 40-50%, Malvasia Istriana/Pinot Bianco 25-30%, Chardonnay 25-30%. Yld 91/130, Alc 10.5, Acd 0.45.

Cabernet (Cabernet Franc/Cabernet Sauvignon) Dry red. Yld 84/120, Alc 11, Acd 0.5.

Cabernet Franc Dry red. Yld 84/120, Alc 11, Acd 0.5.

Cabernet Sauvignon Dry red. Yld 84/120, Alc 11, Acd 0.5.

Chardonnay Dry white. Yld 84/120, Alc 11, Acd 0.45.

Franconia Dry red. Yld 84/120, Alc 11, Acd 0.5.

Malvasia Istriana Dry white. Yld 91/130, Alc

10.5, Acd 0.45.

Merlot Dry red. Yld 91/130, Alc 10.5, Acd 0.5.

Pinot Bianco Dry white. Yld 84/120, Alc 11, Acd 0.45.

Pinot Grigio Dry white. Yld 84/120, Alc 11, Acd 0.45.

Pinot Nero Dry red. Yld 84/120, Alc 11, Acd 0.5.

Pinot Spumante Sparkling white, dry or amabile. Grapes: Pinot Bianco, Pinot Nero/Chardonnay up to 15%. Yld 84/120, Alc 11, Acd 0.5.

Refosco dal Peduncolo Rosso Dry red. Yld 84/120, Alc 11, Acd 0.5.

Riesling Italico Dry white. Yld 84/120, Alc 11, Acd 0.45.

Riesling Renano Dry white. Yld 84/120, Alc 11, Acd 0.45.

Rosso Dry red, also amabile, frizzante. Grapes: Merlot 60-70%, Cabernet Franc/Cabernet Sauvignon 20-30%, Refosco dal Peduncolo Rosso/Pinot Nero up to 20%. Yld 91/130, Alc 11, Acd 0.5.

Sauvignon Dry white. Yld 84/120, Alc 11, Acd 0.45.

Tocai Friulano Dry white. Yld 91/130, Alc 10.5, Acd 0.45.

Traminer Aromatico Dry white. Yld 84/120, Alc 11, Acd 0.45.

Verduzzo Friulano Dry white. Yld 91/130, Alc 10.5, Acd 0.45.

Other wines of note

The expanded DOC would seem to cover everything, though some producers have sold their up-market Chardonnays as vdt up till now.

ESTATES/GROWERS

Angoris, Cormons (GO). The vast Tenuta Angoris run by Luciano Locatelli has 120 ha of vines for Isonzo DOC, vdt, and *spumante*, including plots at Rocca Bernarda for its "I Poderi" line of Colli Orientali DOC.

Bader, Romans d'Isonzo (GO).

Colmello di Grotta, Farra d'Isonzo (GO). New estate with 7 ha for Isonzo DOC.

Conti Attems *See* Collio.

Luisa Eddi, Corona di Mariano (GO). Tasty Cabernet and Merlot from 12 ha.

Silvano Gallo, Mariano del Friuli (GO). From 5 ha, fine Isonzo reds and whites of good value.

Stelio Gallo, Mariano del Friuli (GO). Stelio Gallo's son Gianfranco, who, like Mario Schiopetto and Josko Gravner of Collio, knows that fine white wines are made in the vineyard, has turned 5 ha of flat land into a model of what can be achieved in Isonzo. His densely planted vines (up to 7,000 per ha), yield much less than permitted limits in whites whose virtues are rarely exceeded in the hills. The Isonzo DOCs and vdt Chardonnay are exemplary, though the outstanding wine in recent years has often been the Sauvignon from the Pière plot. The American giant Gallo contested use of the family name on labels of the few cases sold in the USA, so the trademark Masut is used there.

Ilvo Nadali, Mariano del Friuli (GO).
Francesco Pecorari *See* Collio.
Pier Paolo Pecorari, San Lorenzo Isontino (GO). From 6 ha adjacent to Collio, Pecorari makes some of Isonzo's most impressive DOCs and a good vdt Chardonnay.
Sant'Elena, Gradisca d'Isonzo (GO).
Tenuta Villanova *See* Collio.
Mario Zampar, Farra d'Isonzo (GO).

WINE HOUSES/MERCHANTS

Gianni Vescovo, Farra d'Isonzo (GO). The owner of Borgo Conventi in Collio sells Isonzo DOC and vdt under his own name, partly from his own vines.

COOPERATIVES

Cantina Produttori Vini del Collio e dell'Isonzo *See* Collio.

Carso (1986)

This most exotic of the region's DOCs consists of two tart, sturdy, ruby violet wines from the native Terrano, or Terran (a strain of Refosco), and a zesty Malvasia that takes on a harmonious suggestion of honey and almonds here. The higher part of the plateau, strewn by limestone boulders and drained by tunnels cut by subterranean streams, is often cool and windy, and vineyards, some of the best of which lie in Yugoslavia, yield sparsely. Maritime conditions along the Isonzo river and the Gulf of Trieste favour usually modest reds, though Malvasia also thrives in places. Terrano was the usual

accompaniment to *gulasch* and *schnitzel* when Trieste was the Mediterranean port of Austria and Hungary. But its piercing acidity, though appreciated locally, can sting uninitiated palates. Still, the wines, which used to be prescribed to treat anaemia because of their wealth of minerals, are capable of more than blood building. The classic of this earthy breed is Terrano del Carso, whose vines share brush and scrubland around solemn Slavic villages along the border. It takes on scents of wild flowers and currants and, though taut on the tongue, is a lively foil for the hearty local cuisine. Edy Kante is Carso's leader with DOC and other whites.

Zone: The western edge of the Carso plateau by the border of Yugoslavia, extending from the Isonzo river below Gorizia (where it slightly overlaps Isonzo), southeast past Monfalcone and along the Gulf of Trieste south of the city to the edge of the Istrian peninsula, covering six communes in Gorizia province and six in Trieste. The Terrano subzone covers parts of the communes of Aurisina, Monrupino, Sgonico, and Trieste.

Carso Dry red. Grapes: Terrano (Refosco Nostrano) 70%; other reds up to 30%. Yld 70/100, Alc 10.5, Acd 0.6.

Terrano del Carso Dry red. Grapes: Terrano (Refosco Nostrano) 85%; Piccola Nera/Pinot Nero up to 15%. Yld 70/100, Alc 10, Acd 0.7.

Malvasia del Carso Dry white. Grapes: Malvasia Istriana 85%; other whites up to 15%. Yld 70/100, Alc 10.5, Acd 0.55.

ESTATES/GROWERS

Teodora Gabrovec Incante, Prepotto di Duino (TS).
Edy Kante, San Pelagio (TS). Promising Carso DOC along with fine vdt Sauvignon and the curious white Vitovska, from an indigenous variety.
Daniele Lupinz, Prepotto di Duino (TS).
Giusto Vodopivec, Coludrofa di Sgonico (TS).

Wines of the Adriatic basin

The Pianura Friulana, the plain stretching from the Veneto across the Tagliamento river east to the Isonzo, produces most of the region's wine. Flat vineyards there may look regimented, but the diverse geological formations of the terrains explains why wines are by no means monotonous. The upper plains towards the Alps are cooler, damper, and contain more glacial or alluvial rock and gravel than the sandy stretches towards the Adriatic in the Aquileia and Latisana zones. But favourable conditions do not always translate into superior wines. Red varieties prevail, but their once clear domination has been trimmed to a vanishing edge, as trendy whites take over stretches of land that had been strongholds of Merlot. Vineyards here tend to be larger, more prolific, and easier to work than the *ronchi* of the eastern hills. Production is often centred in cooperatives and industrial-scale wineries. But more than a few estates have distinguished their wines from the masses. (The Lison-Pramaggiore DOC zone which extends into Pordenone province is discussed in the Veneto.)

Grave del Friuli (1970)

Grave del Friuli is a wellspring of affordable wine. The zone, by far Friuli's largest, produces about two-thirds of the region's total and more than half of the DOC, some of which can contend in class, if rarely in price, with the gems of the eastern hills. Merlot still makes up nearly half of the total, followed among the reds by Cabernets. When treated with respect, the Bordeaux varieties can show more than ordinary class, as can the native Refosco. Tocai's prime position among whites is being eroded by Pinot Grigio, Sauvignon, and, of course, Chardonnay, which here became DOC for the first time in Italy. Even Riesling Renano and Traminer Aromatico do well in cool spots on the upper plains. Pinot Nero, seldom gambled with in reds, has found a welcome place in the growing array of sparkling wines, usually made by tank methods.

Grave, like the Graves of Bordeaux, is noted for its gravelly terrain. Here it is mainly glacial moraine washed down from the Alps and accumulated along the paths of the Tagliamento, Livenza, Meduna, Torre, Judrio, and Natisone rivers. The zone sprawls across the plains and into the alpine foothills, but the slopes are rarely hospitable to vineyards. Vines flourish in fields of loam to the southwest, but wines there are often common. The prized terrains of Grave are its poorest, *the magredi*, where gravel is topped by a meagre layer of dusky topsoil that peals and cracks like old paint when it dries. Though shunned as too frugal for other crops, the *magredi* account for the top growths of the upper plains. Most lie close to the broad river bed of the Tagliamento within the triangle defined by the towns of Spilimbergo, Bertiolo, and Casarsa. Along the west bank in the province of Pordenone, *magredi* of note are found around San Martino, San Giorgio della Richinvelda, Tauriano, Barbeano, and Rauscedo. Along the east bank in the province of Udine they are concentrated around Codroipo, Bertiolo, and Rivolto. Whites can be remarkably fresh and fruity there,

sometimes with virtues that would draw praise in Collio. La Delizia is the delightful name of the otherwise undramatic flats around Casarsa, where the cooperative makes large measures of convincing Merlot.

West of the Tagliamento, where sandy clay prevails, the climate is warmer and drier due to the proximity of the Adriatic Sea. Wines there rarely show the style of the best *magredi*. But there are exceptional spots, such as the gravelly stretches near to where the Meduna river flows into the Livenza around the villages of Ghirano and Villanova.

Zone: A vast territory, bisected by the Tagliamento river, which covers much of Friuli's upper plains and parts of the alpine foothills in 58 communes in Udine province and 36 in Pordenone.

The 15 types include 14 varietals and Rosato. Varietals may include 15% of other DOC grapes of the same colour. Reds may also include Refosco Nostrano. Wines with at least 1% more alcohol than the minimum may be labelled superiore.

Cabernet (Cabernet Franc/Cabernet Sauvignon) Dry red. Yld 84/120, Alc 11, Acd 0.5.

Cabernet Franc Dry red. Yld 84/120, Alc 11, Acd 0.5.

Cabernet Sauvignon Dry red. Yld 84/120, Alc 11, Acd 0.5.

Chardonnay Dry white. Yld 91/130, Alc 10.5, Acd 0.5.

Merlot Dry red. Yld 91/130, Alc 11, Acd 0.5.

Pinot Bianco Dry white. Yld 84/120, Alc 11, Acd 0.5.

Pinot Grigio Dry white. Yld 91/130, Alc 11, Acd 0.5.

Pinot Nero Dry red. Yld 84/120, Alc 11, Acd 0.5.

Refosco dal Peduncolo Rosso Dry red. Yld 91/130, Alc 11, Acd 0.5.

Riesling Renano Dry white. Yld 84/120, Alc 11, Acd 0.5.

Rosato Dry rosé. Grapes: Merlot 70-80%, Cabernet Franc/Cabernet Sauvignon/Refosco dal Peduncolo Rosso/Pinot Nero 20-30%. Yld 84/120, Alc 11, Acd 0.5.

Sauvignon Dry white. Yld 84/120, Alc 11, Acd 0.45.

Tocai Friulano Dry white. Yld 91/130, Alc 11, Acd 0.5.

Traminer Aromatico Dry white. Yld 84/120, Alc 11, Acd 0.5.

Verduzzo Friulano Dry white, also amabile, dolce, frizzante. Yld 91/130, Alc 11, Acd 0.5.

Other wines of note

A few unclassified wines that stand out amidst quantities of everyday vdt and *spumanti* are mentioned along with their producers. The vdt Truola and Fondreta of San Cipriano are unique.

Aquileia or Aquileia del Friuli (1975)

Aquileia, named after the Roman city on whose site now stands a modest country town, consists of broad plains that look better suited to field crops than vines. But, here and there, like rectangular oases of green in the amber fields of grain, are vineyards whose wines can rise to the occasion. Noted plots lie between Aquileia and the Venice-Trieste *autostrada* in an extensive stretch of sand and clay mixed with pebbly limestone, soil more generous than its jaundiced colour might indicate. Most sites of proven value – Ca' Bolani, Ca' Vescovo, Borgo Gortani – lie close to Cervignano. But even reclaimed land near the lagoon can render wines of unexpectedly bright aroma. The part of the zone that overlaps Grave on cooler plains to the north promises more than it delivers. The wines of Aquileia rank between lightweight and middleweight in size, though a few are contenders in their class. Merlot is the people's choice in pleasant wines by no means lacking punch, though Cabernet and Refosco can surpass them in weight and durability. Here, uniquely, Tocai does not dominate whites. It has been upstaged by Pinot Bianco, though Pinot Grigio, Chardonnay, and Sauvignon are also coming up.

Zone: Plains extending from the Grado lagoon north through Aquileia, Cervignano del Friuli, Palmanova, and 14 other communes in Udine province.
Of the 14 types 13 are varietals that may include 10% of other DOC grapes of the same colour.
Cabernet (Cabernet Franc/Cabernet Sauvignon) Dry red. Yld 84/120, Alc 11, Acd 0.5.
Cabernet Franc Dry red. Yld 84/120, Alc 11, Acd 0.5.
Cabernet Sauvignon Dry red. Yld 84/120, Alc 11, Acd 0.5.
Chardonnay Dry white, also spumante brut. Yld 84/120, Alc 11; spumante 12, Acd 0.5.
Merlot Dry red. Yld 91/130, Alc 10.5, Acd 0.5.
Pinot Bianco Dry white. Yld 84/120, Alc 11, Acd 0.5.
Pinot Grigio Dry white. Yld 91/130, Alc 10.5, Acd 0.5.
Refosco dal Peduncolo Rosso Dry red. Yld 91/130, Alc 10.5, Acd 0.5.
Riesling Renano Dry white.Yld 91/130, Alc 10.5, Acd 0.5.

Rosato Dry rosé. Grapes: Merlot 70-80%, Cabernet Franc/Cabernet Sauvignon/Refosco Nostrano/Refosco dal Peduncolo Rosso 20-30%. Yld 91/130, Alc 10.5, Acd 0.5.
Sauvignon Dry white. Yld 84/120, Alc 11, Acd 0.45.
Tocai Friulano Dry white. Yld 91/130, Alc 10.5, Acd 0.45.
Traminer Aromatico Dry white. Yld 70/100, Alc 11, Acd 0.45.
Verduzzo Friulano Dry white. Yld 84/120, Alc 11, Acd 0.5.

Other wines of note

Chardonnay and Pinot make *spumanti* that do not always qualify as DOC.

Latisana or Latisana del Friuli (1975)

Vines prosper in maritime conditions where some varieties could no doubt double permitted yields in the sandy clay. Some growers hold back and meet the challenge of DOC with the modest grace and good humour that make their wines attractive. Whites are grown in gravelly soils rich in calcium and magnesium along the Tagliamento river from Varmo south past Latisana to Pertegada. Reds, which seem to weather the summer with more aplomb than the whites, thrive in the clay around Palazzolo della Stella, Muzzana, and Teòr. The favoured Merlot can be fleshy, Cabernet and Refosco firmer, though they are all best in their youth. Reliable Tocai makes a pleasant summer sipper, as do the breezy Pinots, though Verduzzo here is rarely more than a vinous alternative to lemonade.

Zone: Plains extending from the reclaimed marshland along the Adriatic litoral at Lignano north along the Tagliamento river past Latisana to Gradiscutta and east across the Stella river to the Cormors canal, taking in 12 communes in Udine province.
The 13 types include 12 varietals and Rosato.
The varietals may include 15% of other varieties of the same colour.
Cabernet (Cabernet Franc/Cabernet Sauvignon) Dry red. Yld 84/120, Alc 11, Acd 0.5.
Cabernet Franc Dry red. Yld 84/120, Alc 11, Acd 0.5.
Cabernet Sauvignon Dry red. Yld 84/120, Alc 11, Acd 0.5.
Chardonnay Dry white. Yld 84/120, Alc 11, Acd 0.5.
Merlot Dry red. Yld 91/130, Alc 10.5, Acd 0.5.
Pinot Bianco Dry white. Yld 91/130, Alc 11, Acd 0.45.
Pinot Grigio Dry white. Yld 84/120, Alc 10.5, Acd 0.5.
Refosco dal Peduncolo Rosso Dry red. Yld 91/130, Alc 10.5, Acd 0.5.

Rosato Dry rosé. Grapes: Merlot 70-80%, Cabernet Franc/Cabernet Sauvignon/Refosco Nostrano/Refosco dal Peduncolo Rosso 20-30%. Yld 91/130, Alc 10.5, Acd 0.5.
Sauvignon Dry white. Yld 84/120, Alc 11, Acd 0.45.
Tocai Friulano Dry white. Yld 91/130, Alc 10.5, Acd O.45.
Traminer Aromatico Dry white. Yld 84/120, Alc 11, Acd 0.45.
Verduzzo Friulano Dry white. Yld 91/130, Alc 10.5, Acd 0.45.

Other wines of note

Many producers make *spumanti* and vdt as plain and prolific as their vineyards.

ESTATES/GROWERS

Borgo Magredo, Tauriano (PN). From about 100 ha in classical *magredi*, the Generali insurance group, with Walter Filiputti, is developing a new line of Grave DOC.
Ca' Bolani, Cervignano del Friuli (UD). Zonin of the Veneto owns this vast estate, which once belonged to the Conti Bolani, along with the nearby Ca' Vescovo. Together they have 180 ha of vines, mainly for Aquileia DOC which is widely noted for style. Ca' Bolani makes a Müller Thurgau vdt, Chardonnay *frizzante*, Pinot Brut, and the *champenoise* Conte Bolani Brut Riserva.
Ca' Vescovo *See* Ca' Bolani.
Cantoni, Tricesimo (UD). Grave DOC.
Marina Danieli *See* Colli Orientali.
Duchi Badoglio Rota, Codroipo (UD). Francesco Badoglio, grandson of Marshal Pietro Badoglio, who led Italy in the post-Mussolini period, makes sound DOC and *spumante* from 110 ha.
Durandi, San Giorgio della Richinvelda (PN). Grave DOC.
Giacomelli, Pradamano (UD). Grave DOC.
Isola Augusta, Palazzolo della Stella (UD). From 40 ha the Bassani family makes sound Latisana reds and Tocai, plus *spumante*.
Obiz, Cervignano del Friuli (UD). From 20 ha, Aquileia DOC and Obiz Brut *spumante*.
Sergio Pevere, Palazzolo della Stella (UD). Latisana DOC.
Pighin, Risano (UD). From 170 ha, sound Grave DOC and the vdt red Baredo (Cabernet, Merlot, Refosco) to complement the Pighin Collio estate production.
Plozner, Barbeano (PN). The Grave estate is better known abroad than in Italy as a pioneer producer of Chardonnay, now DOC, and good Cabernet and Pinot Grigio.
Valderie, Teòr (UD). Latisana DOC.
Vigneti Le Monde, Fagnigola (PN). The Pistoni family makes good Cabernet Sauvignon among Grave DOCs.

Vigneti Pittaro, Rivolto di Codroipo (UD). Piero Pittaro, president of the Associazione Enotecnici Italiani and the regional development board, has 52 ha for Grave DOC, *champenoise*, the singular vdt Agresto (red based on Cabernets with local varieties), and Apicio (sweet white based on Chardonnay).

Aldo Zaglia, Latisana (UD). Latisana DOC.

WINE HOUSES/MERCHANTS

Antonutti, Colloredo di Prato (UD). Grave and Collio DOC and vdt.

Cantine Bidoli, San Daniele del Friuli (UD). Grave DOC.

Fantinel, Pradamano (UD). Grave DOC, vdt, and *spumante*, in part from 50 ha of company vines. The firm also owns the respected Santa Caterina estate in Collio.

Mangilli, Flumignano di Talmassons (UD). Grave, Collio, and Colli Orientali DOC.

Pradio, Bicinicco (UD). Grave DOC.

San Cipriano, Sacile (PN). The Lot family makes Grave DOC along with a bit of the white Truola and red Fondreta named for vines grown only around Sacile and the ancient Castella del Livenza.

Villa Frattina, Ghirano (PN). Grave DOC.

(Other producers of Grave DOC include Collavini, Valle, and Vinicola Udinese in Udine province and Russolo, Santa Margherita, and Tenuta Sant'Anna in the Veneto.)

COOPERATIVES

Viticoltori Friulani-La Delizia, Casarsa della Delizia (PN). Noè Bertolin directs annual production of 120,000 hl from growers with 1,500 ha for Grave as well as Aquileia DOC, vdt, and *spumanti* of good quality and price. Among wines labelled La Delizia, the Merlot often stands out.

CS Cooperativa del Friuli Orientali, Cervignano del Friuli (UD). The cellars account for a major share of Aquileia's output, along with vdt and *spumanti*.

CS di Codroipo, Codroipo (UD). Grave DOC.

Travel Information

RESTAURANTS/HOTELS

Zorutti, Borgo Ponte 9, 33043 Cividale del Friuli (UD). Tel (0432)731100. A classic Friulian restaurant for grilled meats and dishes based on mushrooms.

Al Cacciatore della Subida, 34071 Subida di Cormons (GO). Tel (0481)60531. A converted hunting lodge with fine country cooking and Collio wines. Also quiet rooms.

Felcaro, 34071 Cormons (GO). Tel (0481)60214. Refined Friulian dishes served in a former Hapsburg villa with gardens and pleasant rooms.

Al Giardinetto, 34071 Cormons (GO). Tel (0481)60257. The Zoppolatti family has made this inviting trattoria a favourite with Collio's winemakers.

Da Toni, 33030 Gradiscutta di Varmo (UD). Tel (0432)778003. Elegant country cooking with good house wines and the best of the rest of Friuli.

Bidin, 33054 Lignano Sabbiadoro (UD). Tel (0431)71988. Fresh fish from the Grado lagoon, expertly prepared, with a good choice of wines.

Carso da Bozo, 34016 Monrupino (TS). Tel (040)227113. In the heart of Carso, good Slovenian-Italian cooking with local and regional wines.

Trattoria Blanch, 34070 Mossa (GO). Tel (0481)80020. Good local dishes and Collio wines in a pleasant wooded setting.

Del Doge, 33033 Passariano del Codroipo (UD). Tel (0432)906591. The setting in the Villa Manin, lavish country residence of Venetian doges, upstages the otherwise fine cooking and wines.

Antica Trattoria Boschetti, 33019 Tricesimo (UD). Tel (0432)851230. An antique post house elegantly restored by Giorgio Trentin is the critics' choice as Friuli's finest restaurant. Superb wine list. Comfortable rooms.

WINE SHOPS/ENOTECHE

The Enoteca La Serenissima at Gradisca d'Isonzo provided Italy's first public display of regional wines. The carefully chosen array is available for tasting by the glass. At Udine, the recently opened Casa del Vino has become the regional headquarters of wine activities with an enoteca and library at Via Vittorio Veneto 65.

Private wines shops of note include the Enoteca Volpe Pasini at Via Rialto 12 in Udine and the Enoteca Bere Bene at Viale Ippodromo 2/3b in Trieste.

PLACES OF INTEREST

Visitors in search of wine will no doubt head straight for the hills of Collio and Colli Orientali, which, like all the region's DOC zones, have wine routes running through them. Cormons, the hub of the hill zones, is a quiet wine town with good *trattorie* and country inns in the neighbourhood. Nearby are Udine with its Venetian Renaissance-style Piazza della Liberta, Cividale del Friuli with its Byzantine Romanesque temple called the Tempietto, and what remains Italian of Gorizia. Other wine zones have more dramatic attractions. Carso has the exotic old port of Trieste. Grave del Friuli has the hill town of San Daniele with sweeping views and a *prosciutto* sometimes held more delectable than Parma's. Aquileia has the remnants of the once great Roman city and the shallow Grado lagoon with its islets where makeshift eateries serve *boreto alla gradese* (a fish chowder) and seafood fresh from the grill. Latisana has one of the Adriatic's most popular beach resorts in Lignano Sabbiadoro. But perhaps the most inviting regional feature is life in the country towns.

Friulians are solid folk known for their happy capacity to stash away wine and *grappa* with or without meals. The *tajut* is the little glass of Tocai, sipped in the *osterie*, those taverns which, beyond the dispensing of wine, spirits, coffee, and gossip, still serve as the centres of village life. Cheering the ambience of many an inn is the open fireplace (the *fogolar*) whose circular chimney is draped with a dainty curtain, a friendly spot to warm one's hands in the winter while watching the host work the grill. Most *trattorie* serve essential country fare, but when the accents of neighbouring lands are added, with the likes of gulasch, dumplings, paprika, and strudel, the local cuisine becomes almost cosmopolitan.

Right: street market in Udine.

153

Above: Loreto Aprutino in the Abruzzi, whose peaceful hills have vineyards noted for Montepulciano and Trebbiano.

Adriatic Apennines

It might seem far-fetched to suggest that four regions strung out over more than half the length of the peninsula could constitute a wine alliance. What does Emilia's Piacenza, which peers across the Po towards Lombardy, have to do with Molise's Campobasso, which shares weather patterns with Apulia? Parochial identities, like customs and patterns of speech, change at each region's border and often at points between. Yet, despite the apparent dissimilarities, the four do have geographical bonds.

They lie along the Apennines, whose Adriatic flank is drained by a series of relatively short, straight rivers in an almost symmetrical ribbed formation that contrasts with the haphazard contours on the Tyrrhenian side. Calcareous clay prevails through the span of foothills, though other key components vary from place to place. Still, nearly every slope is favourable to vines, as evidenced by the chain of DOC zones that extends from Emilia's Colli Piacentini to Molise's Biferno with never more than a river valley to break the link.

The Apennines act as a buffer that holds the weather under the Adriatic influence, meaning that rainfall and temperatures do not vary as much as expected in the drop from the forty-fifth to the forty-second parallel. Altitude, exposure to sun and wind, and soil components are quality factors that go beyond variables in grape varieties and training methods. Higher vineyards are cooler and damper, yet even in such mountain retreats as the Marches' Matelica and the Abruzzi's province of L'Aquila conditions are rarely inhospitable. Adriatic winters can be harsh when winds from the Balkans blast across the sea and accumulate moisture that turns to snow, but summers are often benign. If drought is not prolonged, yields can be notoriously high, reaching Italy's maximum levels in the southeastern Abruzzi and Emilia-Romagna's plains.

Cooperatives make a major share of the four regions' wine, notably in Emilia-Romagna where they account for 70 percent, reaching giant proportions in Emilia's Riunite and Romagna's Corovin. Gruppo Coltiva, a national association of cooperatives, has annexed the privately owned cellars of Gruppo Italiano Vini to become one of the world's largest wine aggregates. Still, more and more growers in these Apennine foothills aim for premium quality with both native and foreign varieties. Though standards have improved, sometimes remarkably, few winemakers have

Above: vineyards are an essential part of the traditional crop mix on small farms of the Abruzzi, such as this one near Bisenti in the northern province of Teramo.

yet achieved the potential offered by the favourable natural factors.

But allusions to unity among these four regions could be stretched too far. The only vines they share to any significant degree are Sangiovese, Trebbiano, and Malvasia – names that reverberate through the centre and south. But distribution is uneven. Sangiovese, which thrives in Romagna and parts of the Marches, is ignored in Emilia and gets short shrift in the Abruzzi, where it is outclassed by the native Montepulciano. Malvasia has star status in Emilia, but acts as a back-up elsewhere. Trebbiano is never more than Trebbiano whatever the modifier, except in the Abruzzi where one producer has turned it in to something special.

When Renato Ratti drew his original *Carta Enografica d'Italia*, he put the Marches, Abruzzi, and Molise (with Apulia) under "Vini Adriatici" and secluded Emilia-Romagna under "Vini Centrali". He knew that Emilia and Romagna are as awkward to relate to other places as they are to one another. The region, which ranks fourth in volume in Italy, makes 60 percent of the wine along the Adriatic Apennine corridor, but growers in the two sectors go their own ways. Emilia is in Italy's northern sphere, which gravitates towards Milan, so its viticulture has points in common with Lombardy's Oltrepò Pavese. But a couple of oddities set it apart: a vine called Lambrusco that grows mainly on the plains, and a penchant

for bubbles in wines of all colours. Independent-minded Romagnans are not merely joking when they refer to "Pianeta Romagna". Their planet has its own species of Sangiovese and Trebbiano, but the leading light is supposedly Albana, despite shadows cast upon it by its dubious choice as Italy's first DOCG white wine.

The Marches, the Abruzzi, and Molise are technically part of central Italy, though in the past they managed well enough as separate entities. In the Marches, Verdicchio has re-emerged as one of Italy's most promising white wines from a native variety, but its class remains almost as secret as that of the underrated Rosso Cònero. The Abruzzi's choice of vines is basic: Montepulciano for sometimes laudable red and rosé and Trebbiano in rarely inspired whites. Like Molise, which was long annexed to it, the Abruzzi leans towards the south in attitudes to wine.

The briefest link in the Adriatic Apennine vineyard chain is the republic of San Marino *see* page 170.

Autostrada
Main road
Main railway
International boundary
Regional boundary
■ Regional capital
● Provincial capital

Emilia-Romagna

Capital: Bologna.
Provinces: Bologna (BO), Ferrara (FE), Forlì (FO), Modena (MO), Parma (PR), Piacenza (PC), Ravenna (RA), Reggio Emilia (RE).
Area: 22,124 square kilometres (sixth).
Population: 3,940,000 (eighth).

Emilia and Romagna have enough in common to be united by a hyphen, but their peoples insist on diversity. If you polled the citizens of Bologna, the capital which lies between the two, most would call themselves Emilians, a few Romagnans, but no one would consider himself both. Even the wines are divisive. Emilia, west of Bologna to Piacenza, is known as the Red Belt because of its politics, but it might also be called the Bubble Belt since Lambrusco and nearly everything else bottled there is effervescent. Romagna, east of Bologna to the Adriatic, is the Republic of Sangiovese to red wine drinkers, though white wine has stolen the show with Albana's improbable rise to DOCG.

Outsiders may consider them all strange, but Emilians and Romagnans cherish their wines and make no excuses to anybody. It isn't known exactly when they set off on their disparate paths, but the Liguri (early inhabitants of the woodlands between the Po and the Apennines) were known to have made wine in the west and the Umbri probably did so in the east. The Etruscans tamed the wild vines that culminated in Lambrusco, leaving a legacy that persists in the arbours and pergolas that proliferate in what are now the open spaces of the Padana.

The Romans gave names to both sectors: Romagna because of their long dominion and Emilia after their road from Rimini to Piacenza. As a perennial trade route, the Emilian Way gave the region a lifeline when it was split into far more political factions than today. Emilia prospered during the Renaissance under family dynasties. Romagna, after Ravenna's decline as capital of Byzantium, splintered into tiny states that battled for centuries against Tuscans, Venetians, and armies of the Pope. Among Romagnans, perhaps more than Emilians, this spirit lingers on.

Cooperative domination has not compromised either area's sense of identity with its wines. If regional DOCs ever come into being, each deserves separate recognition. Romagna for the most part already has it with the wines that carry its name: Albana, Sangiovese, Trebbiano, and the recent Cagnina and Pagadebit. Their five overlapping zones are oriented towards the hills, placing them a cut above Bosco Eliceo, whose seaside site seems better suited to strawberries or resort development than vines. The hill wines are tutored by the Ente Tutela Vini Romagnoli, whose political influence was shown by the elevation of Albana di Romagna. This event, which made Emilia-Romagna the third region with a DOCG after Piedmont and Tuscany, raised eyebrows in the still deprived Venezie and protests in the press. But Albana backers view the guarantee as a foundation on which to build a new image of Romagna as a producer of serious wines.

Emilian wine drinkers pay little heed to colour or place of origin, since nearly everything called *vino* is fizzy. Lambrusco dominates the DOCs from four zones on the plains, though wines from the Apennine foothills often have more to distinguish them. Today many hill wines are dry, or almost, where in the past they were most often *amabile*. But still wines of any sort are unusual.

Emilians adore Lambrusco because it is fun and easy to drink, and also because it contains elements reputed to aid digestion and inhibit cholesterol – useful in a place with a diet based on pasta, prosciutto, salami, sausages, butter, cream, and cheese. Even though most of the Lambrusco drunk here is dry, the sweet variety was not invented solely for export to the United States, as is sometimes said. Both styles had been made since the thirteenth century and whether it was sweet, dry or vinegary often depended on its phase of development. But it is true that Lambrusco amabile, with only a gentle twist or two of tradition, was revived in response to American tastes. In the early 1980s, three out of every ten bottles of wine imported into the United States originated in Emilia, much of it from the cooperative cellars of Riunite. But by the decade's end Lambrusco and its bubbly cohorts had lost ground to coolers and wine-based fruit beverages.

Emilia-Romagna deserves praise for reducing its vineyards in recent years but much production is still centred on the plains. Most vineyards there, apart from Lambrusco, furnish the industry with concentrated musts, grape juice, and base wines for blending, vermouth, and brandy. But only the hills, if not always discernible through the haze from the valley floor, provide a vision of hope to winemakers who have begun to realize that they too can aspire to international class.

Emilia-Romagna's Vineyards

The distinct heritages of Emilia and Romagna are reflected in their vines. Traces of the Greek-Ligurian influence are evident in western Emilia and remnants of ancient Rome abound everywhere, especially in Romagna. The Etruscans' love of abundance shines through in vine training methods used through the lowlands – even if these vary in different areas. Emilians shifted from *alberate* (tree training) to the equally lofty Raggi or Bellussi, the double-armed pergola of Lambrusco. The latter is now being replaced by the less costly Geneva Double Curtain, with a single pole arm in the shape of a "T". Romagnans devised their *pergoletta* with a cross-like pole arm. All systems favour big yields; the region's average of 113 hectolitres per hectare is second only to the Abruzzi. Still, vineyards have increased in the hills, where vertical systems are mainly variations on Guyot or cordon.

Among red varieties, Lambrusco prevails in Emilia, Sangiovese in Romagna, though like Barbera and Croatina (Bonarda) they are losing ground to white. Trebbiano Romagnolo, backed by the even more prolific Trebbiano Toscano, dominates whites, though Malvasia di Candia stands unchallenged in Emilia's hills. There has been a trend back to Sauvignon, the Pinots, and Riesling (mainly Italico), as well as Cabernet, all of which have been planted here since the last century, or in some cases earlier. But the rising star is Chardonnay. Few regions have rehabilitated so many aged local varieties. Romagna's Pagadebit, Cagnina, Canina, Malise, Barbarossa, and Albana Nera are examples. Marsanne has been grown for ages in the Colli Piacentini, where it is still called Champagne, as were its bubbly wines until rules forbade it. But such varieties as Alionza, Aleatico di Bertinoro, Biancale di Rimini, Fogarina, Occhio di Gatto, Negretto, and Rossola are no longer approved. The following varieties are associated primarily with Emilia-Romagna.
Albana. The origins of Romagna's premier white variety are uncertain, though it might have been brought by the Romans from Latium's Alban hills. Among more than 20 clones, Gianfranco Bolognesi, an authority on Romagna's wines, cites the preferred Gentile, along with della Bagarona, della Compadrona, della Gaiana, and della Serra. Experts are studying new cultivars since the vine, which develops enormous bunches of light

Above: a vineyard at Marzeno near Faenza in Romagna, whose hills are renowned for red wines from Sangiovese and whites from Albana.

golden grapes, is prone to maladies. Despite new status as Albana di Romagna DOCG, its wines, if sometimes distinctive in sweet versions, rarely show much class when dry. There is also a rare Albana Nera.

Ancellotta. This dark variety of Emilia adds colour to Lambrusco.

Barbarossa. Isolated at Bertinoro, where it makes a convincing red wine. The name "red beard" refers to its bunches and to the Holy Roman Emperor Frederick I. Not related to the fading Barbarossa of Liguria.

Bonarda. Name for Croatina used in Colli Piacentini and Colli di Parma.

Cagnina. Elevated to DOC as Cagnina di Romagna, the vine, possibly brought by Byzantines, is the same as Friuli's Terrano or Refosco. Often confused with the unrelated Canina (or Canena) Nera.

Fortana or **Fruttana** or **Uva d'Oro**. In Emilia Fortana or Fruttana is said to be a native of Piacenza or Parma, while in Romagna, where it is often known as Uva d'Oro, it is said to come from Burgundy's Côte d'Or. Its rustically sharp red wines include Bosco Eliceo DOC Fortana.

Lambrusco. The name derives from the Latin *labrusca* or *lambrusca*, a species of *Vitis vinifera silvestris*, wild vines of the Apennines recorded by the Romans and probably first grown by Etruscans or Liguri. The Lambrusco family has several subvarieties, usually but not always used for bubbly wines. Most respected are: **Sorbara** (from the village near Modena); **Grasparossa** (named for its red stalks, from Castelvetro south of Modena); **Salamino** (for its salami-shaped bunches, from the village of Santa Croce near Carpi). **Maestri**, **Marani**, and **Montericco** are noted for abundance. **Viadanese** is Lombardian. **Lambrusco a Foglia Frastagliata** grows mainly in Trentino. The term *Vitis labrusca*, used for North American vines, comes from the same Latin base as Lambrusco but they are not related.

Malvasia di Candia aromatica. Of Greek origin, this variety makes whites of distinct aroma in the hills of Piacenza and Parma. The ordinary Malvasia di Candia, linked to Latium, is less prized here.

Montuni or **Montù**. Indigenous vine used between Bologna and Modena for white Montuni del Reno. Known in Romagna as Bianchino.

Ortrugo. Respectable variety of Colli Piacentini, where it makes a bubbly dry varietal white wine. The name is dialect for *altra uva* (other grape), because it is normally blended with Malvasia.

Pagadebit or **Pagadebito**. Revived in Romagna in a new white DOC, this is the same as Apulia's Bombino Bianco. The name refers to consistent yields that enable farmers to "pay debts" when other crops fail. Vines are found along the Adriatic under various names.

Pignoletto. White variety of Colli Bolognesi, which may be indigenous or, according to some, may have originated in the Rhine as a relative of Riesling, to which its light, fizzy wines bear a faint resemblance.

Sangiovese di Romagna. "Sanzves" is so adored by Romagnans that they dispute the vine's reputed Tuscan origins, contending that it came from Monte Giove at Sant'Arcangelo di Romagna. The two prominent Romagnan clones (one large berried, one small) are distinct from the native Tuscan varieties of Chianti, Montalcino, and Montepulciano, so the two strains seem to have developed independently. Old-style Sangiovese was fairly rough-and-tumble, but some recent examples have shown unquestionable breed perhaps due to wider use of Tuscan clones.

Spergola. Name traditionally used in Emilia for Sauvignon Blanc.

Trebbiano Modenese. Used around Modena in wine and also as a base for *aceto balsamico* in place of the once prominent Trebbiano di Spagna.

Trebbiano Romagnolo. Though lineage has been traced to antiquity, Romagna's Trebbiano is a distinct but little distinguished member of the family. Its big yields have made it second to the Toscano clone in nationwide popularity. Besides its role in Trebbiano di Romagna DOC and in blends, it makes respected bases for brandy and vermouth.

Verdea. White variety of Colli Piacentini, apparently related to Romagna's Paradisa and Tuscany's Colombana.

Other varieties

Other varieties recommended or approved in Emilia-Romagna include: For red (or rosé): Canina Nera, Ciliegiolo, Dolcetto, Marzemino, Montepulciano, Pinot Nero, Raboso Veronese, Sgavetta, Tosca. For white: Bervedino, Biancame, Moscato Bianco, Mostosa, Müller Thurgau, Pinot Bianco, Pinot Grigio, Ribolla Gialla, Tocai Friulano, Trebbiano Toscano.

Emilia-Romagna's Wine Zones

The Po, which forms much of the northern border with Lombardy and the Veneto, is Emilia-Romagna's jugular vein. From the Val Padana it is easy to forget that the region has the longest stretch of Apennines (290 kilometres forming borders with Liguria and Tuscany) or that more than half of it is over 100 metres high (culminating in the 2,165-metre Monte Cimone). Yet two-thirds of vineyards are in the lowlands, foggy and cold in winter and stifling in summer, when in places the only available shade is beneath corridors of Lambrusco. The cooler hills have clear-cut quality potential in places, though production is less consistent.

Emilia's plains

The Val Padana between Piacenza and Bologna may look monotonous on the surface but the soil varies enough to distinguish top growths from also-rans. Most Lambrusco vineyards lie in the clay soil around Modena and Reggio on beds of alluvial sand and gravel. The zones of Sorbara, Salamino di Santa Croce and much of Reggiano lie to the north towards the Po. Sorbara is the classic source of deep ruby to bright pink wines noted for freshness and finesse. The Grasparossa di Castelvetro and Reggiano zones extend south into low hills of sandy, calcareous terrain where Lambrusco often has more colour, aroma, and structure.

Emilia's hills

The hills of Piacenza, Parma, Reggio, and Bologna have a fairly uniform climate, with cold winters and hot summers, yet slight variations in the sandy clay terrain account for differences in wines. Each Colli Piacentini valley has its specialities. The calcareous soils of the Val Tidone around Ziano abound in Barbera and Bonarda for Gutturnio. The Val Trebbia grows white Malvasia and Ortrugo on the left bank's gravelly slopes from Rivergaro to Bobbio, notably at Travo. In the Val d'Arda, the same vines make fragrant Monterosso and other whites in lean, low acid soils of Castell'Arquato, Bacedasco, and Vigoleno. In the Colli di Parma, Sala Baganza's sandy slopes are noted for aromatic Malvasia. South of Reggio, Sauvignon shows atypical softness in Bianco di Scandiano. Wines from Colli Bolognesi's often sheer slopes range from zesty whites to elegant reds from choice plots rich in marl.

Romagna's plains

The hot, alluvial Po delta is a prolific source of dull if useful wines for blends or distillates. Most of Trebbiano di Romagna DOC lies in flats southwest of Ravenna, where wines can be lively if grapes are picked early. Bosco Eliceo is noted for a pungent red.

Romagna's hills

Growers have only begun to explore the potential of these slopes that abound in agreeable vineyard sites. The best wines come from slopes 10-25 kilometres from the sea, where temperature fluctuations heighten aromas. Variables in the basic marly or sandy clay delineate the best areas. The finest Albana comes from vineyards along the so-called *spungone romagnolo* – a calcareous vein rich in marine fossils and organic residue in low hills from Bertinoro west to Imola. Sangiovese's *superiore* area covers all but the lower and upper reaches of the zone, but its vigorous and best wine comes from hills drained by the Ronco, Rabbi, and Montone streams, the so-called Rocche above Forlì, Faenza, and Cesena as far west as the Rubicone. Wines from east of the Rubicone and west of the Montone are generally lighter but can show finesse.

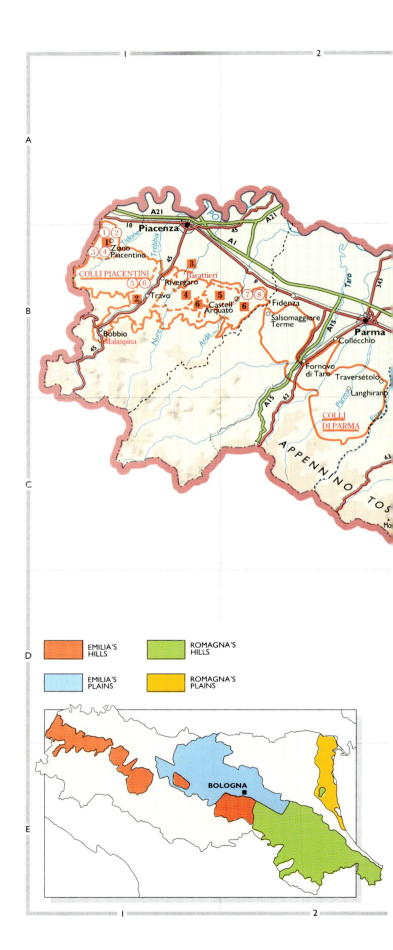

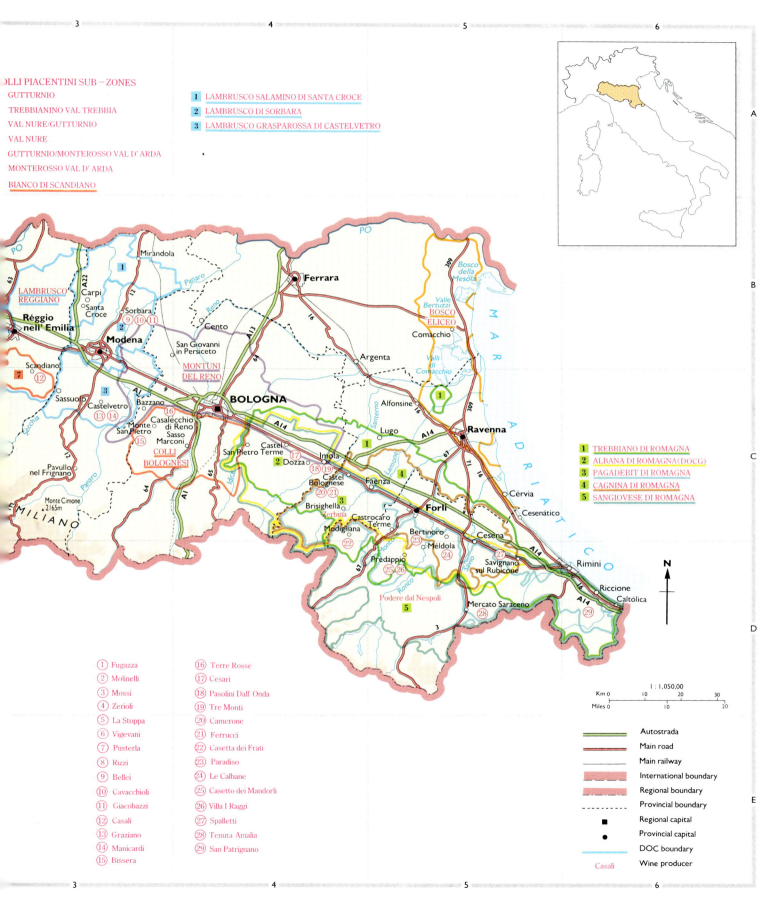

COLLI PIACENTINI SUB – ZONES

GUTTURNIO

TREBBIANINO VAL TREBBIA

VAL NURE/GUTTURNIO

VAL NURE

GUTTURNIO/MONTEROSSO VAL D' ARDA

MONTEROSSO VAL D' ARDA

BIANCO DI SCANDIANO

1 LAMBRUSCO SALAMINO DI SANTA CROCE

2 LAMBRUSCO DI SORBARA

3 LAMBRUSCO GRASPAROSSA DI CASTELVETRO

1 TREBBIANO DI ROMAGNA

2 ALBANA DI ROMAGNA (DOCG)

3 PAGADEBIT DI ROMAGNA

4 CAGNINA DI ROMAGNA

5 SANGIOVESE DI ROMAGNA

LAMBRUSCO REGGIANO

BOSCO ELICEO

MONTUNI DEL RENO

COLLI BOLOGNESI

① Fugazza
② Molinelli
③ Mossi
④ Zerioli
⑤ La Stoppa
⑥ Vigevani
⑦ Pusterla
⑧ Rizzi
⑨ Bellei
⑩ Cavacchioli
⑪ Giacobazzi
⑫ Casali
⑬ Graziano
⑭ Manicardi
⑮ Bissera

⑯ Terre Rosse
⑰ Cesari
⑱ Pasolini Dall' Onda
⑲ Tre Monti
⑳ Camerone
㉑ Ferrucci
㉒ Casetta dei Frati
㉓ Paradiso
㉔ Le Calbane
㉕ Casetto dei Mandorli
㉖ Villa I Raggi
㉗ Spalletti
㉘ Tenuta Amalia
㉙ San Patrignano

1 : 1,050,00

Km 0   10   20   30
Miles 0   10   20

———— Autostrada
———— Main road
———— Main railway
▨▨▨ International boundary
▨▨▨ Regional boundary
- - - - Provincial boundary
■ Regional capital
● Provincial capital
———— DOC boundary
Casali Wine producer

Wines of Emilia's plains

Lambrusco reigns over the Emilian plains from its capital of Modena, a prosperous town within whose province lie three DOC zones: Sorbara, Grasparossa di Castelvetro, and Salamino di Santa Croce. But Reggio Emilia, with its DOC Lambrusco Reggiano, not only dominates production and exports but rivals Modena's crown of quality. Yet in the end, every local gastronome has his own source of *Lambròsc*, and it is not likely to have come off a production line. Still traditional bottle fermentation has been largely replaced by tank methods that leave the wines stable but too often lacking personality. The downturn in exports of Lambrusco and other bubbly wines has affected the fortunes of such giant producers as Cantine Riunite and Giacobazzi, while persuading farmers to replace vines with more lucrative crops. But an upturn in sales to Germany, Britain, and to some extent in Italy has prevented what might have been a catastrophic decline.

Lambrusco di Sorbara (1970)
The classic Lambrusco was noted in the past for its ruby to purple colour and its depth of aroma and flavour, though styles seem to be evolving to suit current tastes. Traditionalists stick to the standard type, but the leading progressives, Francesco Bellei and Cavacchioli (with Vigna del Cristo), make blushing pink, fruity wines of unabashed freshness. The *amabile* is largely produced for export.

Zone: Plains in ten communes just north of Modena centred around the village of Sorbara. Bubbly red or rosé, dry or amabile. Grapes: Lambrusco di Sorbara 60%, Lambrusco Salamino 40%. Yld 98/140, Alc 11, Acd 0.7.

Lambrusco Salamino di Santa Croce (1970)
Though usually ruby to purple, the trend is for lighter, fresher wine tending towards pink. The best Lambrusco here is hard to distinguish from wines of the adjacent Sorbara zone.

Zone: Plains north of Modena extending to the border with Lombardy taking in 11 communes in the province, though the name comes from the village of Santa Croce near Carpi. Bubbly red, dry or amabile. Grapes: Lambrusco Salamino; other Lambrusco subvarieties or Uva d'Oro up to 10%. Yld 105/150, Alc 11, Acd 0.7.

Lambrusco Grasparossa di Castelvetro (1970)
Though volume is the smallest of the four DOCs, bottles from producers who work on a small scale here appeal to those who like to think of Lambrusco as a genuine red wine with deep colour, robust body, and full aroma, and not just a fizzy beverage. This explains why the wines of Graziano, Manicardi, and Villa Barbieri are almost invariably sold out.

Zone: Plains between Modena and the Apennine foothills taking in the communes of Castelvetro, Castelfranco Emilia, Maranello, Sassuolo, Spilamberto, Vignola, and eight others in the province. Bubbly red, dry or amabile. Grapes: Lambrusco Grasparossa; other Lambrusco subvarieties or Uva d'Oro up to 15%. Yld 98/140, Alc 10.5, Acd 0.6

Lambrusco Reggiano (1971)
The most heavily produced Lambrusco can vary radically in type. Much wine from the plains is on the pink side with an *amabile* produced for export, but from higher vineyards around Scandiano, Quattro Castella, and Sant'Ilario d'Enza, it can be full and round with class to match the more vaunted *crus* of Modena. Leading small producers are Venturini Baldini and Moro. Riunite dominates the quantity field.

Zone: Plains and low hills of 20 communes in Reggio Emilia province. Bubbly red or rosé, dry or amabile. Grapes: Lambrusco Marani/Lambrusco Salamino/Lambrusco Montericco/Lambrusco Maestri; Ancellotta up to 20%. Yld 97.5/150, Alc 10.5, Acd 0.7.

Montuni del Reno (1988)
Usually spritzy little white wine of local appeal, whether dry or semisweet.

Zone: Vast tract of plains drained by the Reno river and its tributaries in Bologna province and five communes in Modena. Dry or amabile white, also frizzante. Grapes: Montuni; other non-aromatic whites up to 15%. Yld 126/180, Alc 10.5, Acd 0.65.

Below: high-trained Lambrusco vines in late autumn after the harvest at San Prospero near Modena in Emilia's plains.

Other wines of note

Besides the flow of non-DOC *amabile* from commercial cellars, there is also Lambrusco from Parma and Bologna provinces though rarely of note. The cutting edge flavours of Parma's dark, bubbly Fortana take getting used to. Some producers make sparkling white Lambrusco of unexpected class as *champenoise*. Among the area's invariably fizzy whites come Alionza from the grape of the same name and variations on Malvasia, Sauvignon, Chardonnay, and other varieties that usually do better in the hills.

ESTATES/GROWERS

Francesco Bellei, Bomporto (MO). Giuseppe Bellei makes highly regarded Lambrusco di Sorbara DOC and Pinot-Chardonnay *champenoise* from 15 ha.
Vittorio Graziano, Castelvetro (MO). Graziano's Lambrusco Grasparossa DOC and vdt Bianco di Castelvetro from 3 ha have a cult following.
Enzo Manicardi, Castelvetro (MO). Justly acclaimed small producer of Lambrusco Grasparossa DOC.
Moro, Sant'Ilario d'Enza (RE). Rinaldo Rinaldini makes fine Lambrusco Reggiano DOC and the admired Picòl Ross.
Venturini & Baldini, Roncolo di Quattro Castella (RE). Fine, full-bodied Lambrusco Reggiano and Cuvée di Pinot *champenoise* from 35 ha of vines.
Villa Barbieri, Savignano sul Panaro (MO). Casimiro Barbieri makes recherché Lambrusco Grasparossa di Castelvetro DOC from Magazzeno plot.

WINE HOUSES/MERCHANTS

Cavacchioli, San Prospero (MO). Large and admired producer of various Lambrusco DOCs, including the Vigna del Cristo of Sorbara, as well as Lambrusco Bianco *champenoise*.
Chiarli 1860, Modena. The original Lambrusco house with classic bottlings of the DOCs, in part from own 70 ha.
Colombini, Castelvetro (MO). Medium-large house respected for Lambrusco.
Gruppo Coltiva-Gruppo Italiano Vini, Modena. The Gruppo Coltiva consortium of cooperative wineries acquired Gruppo Italiano Vini in 1986 to become one of the world's largest wine conglomerates. Coltiva members produce more than 7 million hl annually, or about 10% of Italy's wine, from a network of 107 cellars with about 45,000 growers. Of the 3 million hl of bottled wine, there are 150 different types, including 50 DOCs representing most Italian regions. Gruppo Italiano Vini (the former Winefood) represents more than 20 private firms, including the well-known trademarks Folonari, Fontana Candida, Bigi, Melini, Conti Serristori, Lamberti,

Negri, and Santi.
Contessa Matilde, Modena. Established Lambrusco house now part of the Premiovini group.
Fini, Modena. Lambrusco DOC and other wines are selected for the family restaurant in Modena and to complement a range of fine food.
Giacobazzi, Nonantola (MO). Giant producer and bottler of Lambrusco DOC and other wines, mainly light and fizzy. Once second to Riunite in exports to the USA, but today diversifying in other markets.
Oreste Lini & Figli, Correggio (RE). Lambrusco DOC and other bubbly wines, including the rapturous pink Labrusca.

COOPERATIVES

CS di Castelfranco Emilia, Castelfranco Emilia (MO). Lambrusco DOC and fizzy white Alionza.
CIV-Consorzio Interprovinciale Vini, Modena. Immense quantities of wine from the region are bottled at this centre, which selects Lambrusco, as well as other DOC and vdt wines.

Gruppo Coltiva *See* Wine Houses.
Riunite, Reggio Emilia. Cantine Riunite, the cooperative operation which accounts for about half the Italian wine sold in the United States, led the boom in sweet Lambrusco and other bubbly wines that reached a peak of more than 11 million cases exported in 1981. But recent sales have reflected the slump of Italian wine in the USA. Lambrusco accounted for less than one fifth of Riunite's exports in the late 1980s, as wine-based fruit beverages competed with wine coolers to take up some of the slack felt by its highly publicized wines. Under President Walter Sacchetti, who has worked with America's largest importer Villa Banfi since the late 1960s, Riunite sustained losses by building new markets in Europe, yet overall production had slipped from 1,226,000 hl in 1984/85 to around 1 million hl recently. In addition to Lambrusco Reggiano (mainly sweet), Lambrusco di Sorbara (dry), and Bianco di Scandiano DOC, Riunite makes white and rosé vdt and *spumante*.
CS di Sorbara, Sorbara (MO). Lambrusco di Sorbara DOC.

Left: Emilia's most cherished product of the grape is vinegar, even if true aceto balsamico *might better qualify as a condiment, or even a liqueur or tonic, as it is still sometimes served. The oldest – 50, 100, 150 years or more – would rank among the most expensive comestibles, rivalling ancient wines and spirits in value. But they are rarely sold. The term* balsamico *came to refer to its balmy wood odours in the mid-18th century when the Este family ruled Modena and Reggio. Today, the* acetaia, *the drafty loft with its tiny barrels and crocks, is the pride of hundreds of households here. More than just a traditional craft, to some* aceto balsamico *is an art, a passion, a way of life. Recently, Aceto Balsamico Tradizionale of Modena and Reggio Emilia became Italy's first vinegar DOC under a code requiring that it be made not from wine but from cooked grape musts following intricate methods that permit no additives and involve at least 12 years of ageing in wooden barrels. The result is a dense, dark amber to ebony liquid whose essence of resin strikes an exotic sweet-sour note. DOC distinguishes the traditional or natural product from imitations made by blending wine vinegar with caramelized sugar, herbs, and other flavourings. Devotion to the most extraordinary of vinegars culminates in the Palio held each year in June in the town of Spilamberto. Certified master tasters work their way through more than 700 entries to find the winner which is announced on the feast day of San Giovanni.*

Wines of Emilia's hills

The Apennine foothills south of Piacenza, Parma, Reggio, Modena, and Bologna are known for a genial air that lends succulence to the prosciutto and salami seasoned there. The gentle slopes and terraced hillocks seem equally hospitable to vines, yet most wines, though esteemed locally, are too happy go lucky for today's serious wine drinkers. The surprise isn't that they fizzle, but that even red "table wines" here can be sweet. Apart from fragrant Malvasia and bracing Barbera, the pillars of the hills, the likes of Sauvignon, Merlot, Pinot Grigio, and Pinot Nero may also be *frizzante*. In the Colli Piacentini, for example, a dry wine is usually known as *amaro* (bitter) and a still wine as *morto* (dead). Despite this frivolity, supply can't keep up with demand. Colli Bolognesi and Colli Piacentini were among the few zones of Italy granted an EEC dispensation to plant new vines. A few radical producers, exemplified by the Vallania family of the Colli Bolognesi, have broken the mould to make dry, still wines of undeniable stature. But that doesn't mean that lovers of the eccentric can't still enjoy a glass of foaming Cabernet Sauvignon or sweet Chardonnay here.

Colli Piacentini (1984)

(Incorporating the earlier DOCs of Gutturnio dei Colli Piacentini, 1967, Monterosso Val d'Arda, 1974, and Trebbianino Val Trebbia, 1975, with the newly approved Val Nure and seven varietals.)

Piacenza stands above the crowd in Emilia since its vineyards lie only in hills and its enduring ways began when it was part of Antico Piemonte, which also took in the adjacent and similar Oltrepò Pavese of Lombardy. Its history dates back to the Liguri, whose winemaking was influenced by the Greeks, though it was the Romans who left behind a silver pitcher known as a *gutturnium*, from which came the name of the premier red Gutturnio. A blend of Barbera and Bonarda, Gutturnio used to be sweet and bubbly, though now it is often still and dry. As varietals, Barbera is always dry and Bonarda is invariably medium dry. Yet the astonishing popularity of the Colli Piacentini has been built not on red wines but on lively whites from the aromatic Malvasia di Candia and Ortrugo. Trebbianino Val Trebbia and Monterosso Val d'Arda are the established names, but Malvasia alone, whether DOC or not, is the people's choice. Here most wines, whether white

or red, are *vivace* (lively) and *morbido* (softly sweet). But what outsiders regard as weird tastes may be due to quirks of nature. A mysterious factor related to soil and yeasts prevents many wines from fermenting completely, so residual sugar and bubbles are normal. Go-ahead estates – La Stoppa, Vigevani, Fugazza – make dry, still wines of class, but their example isn't widely followed. The appeal of soft, lively wines is growing and even if they rarely go beyond Bologna or Milan, they invariably sell out before the next harvest. So any change to more universal styles would have more to do with prestige than economic necessity.

Zone: Slopes in the Apennine valleys formed by the Tidone, Trebbia, Nure, and Arda rivers flowing towards the Po in Piacenza province. There are four subzones: Gutturnio (in three sectors and nine communes in the Tidone, Nure, Chero, and Arda valleys); Monterosso Val d'Arda (in six communes, including Castell'Arquato, in the Arda valley); Trebbianino Val Trebbia (in the communes of Bobbio, Coli, Travo, Rivergaro, and Gazzola along the Trebbia); Val Nure (in the communes of San Giorgio Piacentino, Vigolzone, and Ponte dell'Olio in the Nure valley).

Gutturnio Dry or amabile red, also frizzante. Grapes: Barbera 55-70% and Bonarda (Croatina). Yld 78/120, Alc 12, Acd 0.55.

Monterosso Val d'Arda Dry or amabile white, also frizzante and spumante. Grapes: Malvasia di Candia aromatica 30-50%, Trebbiano Romagnolo/Ortrugo 20-35%, Moscato Bianco 10-30%; Bervedino/Sauvignon up to 20%. Yld 63/90, Alc 11, Acd 0.55.

Trebbianino Val Trebbia Dry or amabile white, also frizzante and spumante. Grapes: Ortrugo 35-50%, Malvasia di Candia aromatica/Moscato Bianco 10-30%, Trebbiano Romagnolo/Sauvignon 15-30%; other whites up to 15%. Yld 63/90, Alc 11, Acd 0.5; spumante 0.55.

Val Nure Dry or amabile white, also frizzante and spumante. Grapes: Malvasia di Candia aromatica 30-50%, Ortrugo 20-35%, Trebbiano Romagnolo 20-35%; other whites up to 15%. Yld 70/100, Alc 11, Acd 0.55.

Barbera Dry red, also frizzante. Grapes: Barbera; other reds up to 15%. Yld 85/130, Alc 11.5, Acd 0.6.

Bonarda Dry, amabile or dolce red, also frizzante. Grapes: Bonarda; other reds up to 15%. Yld 85/130, Alc 11, Acd 0.55.

Malvasia Dry, amabile or dolce white, also frizzante and spumante. Grapes: Malvasia; other whites up to 15%. Yld 84/120, Alc 10.5, Acd 0.55.

Ortrugo Dry white, also frizzante and spumante. Grapes: Ortrugo; other whites up to 15%. Yld 77/110, Alc 10.5, Acd 0.55.

Pinot Grigio Dry white, also frizzante and spumante. Grapes: Pinot Grigio; other whites up to 15%. Yld 63/90, Alc 11, Acd 0.55.

Pinot Nero Dry red, also frizzante and spumante (either white or rosé). Grapes: Pinot Nero; other reds up to 15%. Yld 63/90, Alc 11, Acd 0.55.

Sauvignon Dry white, also frizzante. Grapes: Sauvignon; other whites up to 15%. Yld 70/100, Alc 11, Acd 0.55.

Colli di Parma (1983)

The notion that Parma's exquisite prosciutto goes best with effervescent white wine originated in these gentle hills. Though the ham is understandably more renowned than

the wine, local Malvasia can rival the best of the Colli Piacentini for its finesse. Here, too, demand outstrips supply. The *rosso*, which bears a family resemblance to Gutturnio, also has its fans, though the Sauvignon is too scarce to reach more than a few of the many fine restaurants in the province.

Zone: Apennine foothills drained by the Stirone, Taro, Baganza, Parma, and Enza rivers crossing Parma province through 14 communes, including Salsomaggiore Terme, Medesano, Collecchio, Sala Baganza, Felino, Langhirano, and Traversetolo.

Rosso Dry red, also frizzante. Grapes: Barbera 60-75%, Bonarda (or Croatina) 25-40%; other dark varieties up to 15%. Yld 70/100, Alc 11, Acd 0.65.

Malvasia Dry white, also amabile and spumante. Grapes: Malvasia di Candia aromatica; Moscato Bianco up to 15%. Yld 71.5/110, Alc 10.5, Acd 0.6.

Sauvignon Dry white, also frizzante. Grape: Sauvignon. Yld 49/75, Alc 11.5, Acd 0.6.

Bianco di Sandiano (1977)

Sauvignon, planted here for so long that it goes under the nickname of Spergola, makes a simple bubbly wine that seems to have more allure in the sweet versions than the dry. Much of the moderate output is exported.

Zone: Low hills and plains at the southern edge of the Po valley around Scandiano south of Reggio and taking in five other communes in its province.

Frizzante Bubbly white, secco, and dolce or amabile. Grapes: Sauvignon (Spergola); Malvasia di Candia or Trebbiano Romagnolo up to 15%. Yld 84.5/130, Alc 10.5 (amabile min 5.5% alcohol with the rest in res sugar), Acd 0.65.

Spumante Sparkling white, secco or brut, and semisecco. Grapes: As frizzante. Yld 84.5/130, Alc 11, Acd 0.65.

Colli Bolognesi-Monte San Pietro/Castelli Medioevali (1975)

A decade or so ago the wines of the Colli Bolognesi were hard to sell, even in Bologna. Since most were bubbly

with a hint of sweetness, they were regarded as impish hill versions of Lambrusco. Gradually, though, discerning Bolognesi realized that these often oblique rises can produce dry, still wines of real stature. Credit goes to the late Enrico Vallania, whose wines from the Terre Rosse estate conquered both local and national markets. The Colli Bolognesi varietals take in the indigenous Pignoletto, which makes a white vaguely reminiscent of a light Rhine wine, even when it fizzes. The similar Riesling Italico is the most popular variety, assuming poise in Terre Rosse's late harvest version called Elisabetta Vallania. Sauvignon, Pinot Bianco, and Pinot Grigio can also produce stylish wines. Hearty Barbera dominates red wines, though Terre Rosse's Cabernet Sauvignon reigns supreme in these hills.

Zone: The Apennine foothills adjacent to Bologna, extending east-west from the Zena river to the Panaro and south on either side of the Reno valley to Marzabotto, taking in 13 communes in Bologna province and Savignano sul Panaro in Modena. Colli Bolognesi may be referred to as Monte San Pietro, the hill town that is the historic centre of the zone, or Castelli Medioevali, the state road running from Casalecchio di Reno through Bazzano.

Barbera Dry red, also riserva. Grapes: Barbera; Sangiovese up to 15%. Yld 84/120, Alc 11.5; riserva 12.5, Acd 0.5, Ag riserva 3 yrs (1 in wood).

Bianco Dry white, also amabile. Grapes: Albana 60-80%, Trebbiano Romagnolo at least 20%; other whites up to 20%. Yld 91/130, Alc 11 (amabile res sugar 4-20 gr/l), Acd 0.5.

Cabernet Sauvignon Dry red, also riserva. Grapes: Cabernet Sauvignon; Merlot up to 15%. Yld 70/100, Alc 12; riserva 12.5, Acd 0.45, Ag riserva 3 yrs (1 in wood).

Merlot Dry to medium dry red. Grapes: Merlot; other dark varieties up to 15%. Yld 84/120, Alc 11.5 (res sugar max 5 gr/l), Acd 0.5.

Pignoletto Dry white, also amabile and frizzante. Grapes: Pignoletto; other whites up to 15%. Yld 84/120, Alc 11 (amabile res sugar 4-20 gr/l), Acd 0.5.

Pinot Bianco Dry to medium dry white. Grapes: Pinot Bianco; Trebbiano Romagnolo up to 15%. Yld 77/110, Alc 12 (res sugar max 5 gr/l), Acd 0.45.

Riesling Italico Dry to medium dry white. Grapes: Riesling Italico; Riesling Renano/Trebbiano Romagnolo up to 15%. Yld 84/120, Alc 12 (res sugar max 5 gr/l), Acd 0.45.

Sauvignon Dry to medium dry white. Grapes: Sauvignon; Trebbiano Romagnolo up to 15%. Yld 84/120, Alc 12 (res sugar max 5 gr/l), Acd 0.5.

Other wines of note

Besides DOC versions, *spumanti* and *frizzanti* wines are made through the hills from nearly every available grape variety and by every method of achieving bubbles. Leading estates in Colli Piacentini (La Stoppa and Vigevani) and Colli Bolognesi (Terre Rosse) make vdt of note. There are also many curiosities, including sweet wines such as Vin Santo di Vigoleno, made from Coda di Volpe and Santa Maria varieties in the Colli Piacentini.

ESTATES/GROWERS

Al Pazz, Monteveglio (BO). Colli Bolognesi DOC.
Conte Otto Barattieri, Vigolzone (PC). From 40 ha of vines, good Colli Piacentini DOC and vdt.
Calzetti, San Vitale Baganza (PR). Colli di Parma Malvasia and Sauvignon.
Cantine Romagnoli, Villò di Vigolzone (PC). From more than 90 ha of vines a complete range of Colli Piacentini DOC, plus vdt and *spumanti*.
Casali, Pratissolo di Scandiano (RE). Bianco di Scandiano and Lambrusco DOC plus vdt.
Fugazza, Ziano Piacentino (PC). Giovanna and Maria Giulia Fugazza make Gutturnio from vineyards in Colli Piacentini. *See* also Castello di Luzzano in Oltrepò Pavese, Lombardy.

La Stoppa, Ancarano di Rivargaro (PC). A leader in Colli Piacentini owned by Raffaele Pantaleoni. From 24 ha comes a bit of DOC, but more impressive vdt red La Stoppa and the *champenoise* Pantaleoni Brut.
La Tosa, Vigolzone (PC). Stefano Pizzamiglio makes good Colli Piacentini wines at this emerging estate.
Alberto Lusignani, Vigoleno di Vernasca (PC). Colli Piacentini DOCs, Chardonnay and a rare Vin Santo di Vigoleno.
Malaspina, Bobbio (PC). Colli Piacentini wines and Cabernet from 23 ha.
Giancarlo Molinelli, Ziano Piacentino (PC). Range of Colli Piacentini wines, *spumanti* and even a sweet Picolit.
Mossi, Ziano Piacentino (PC). Luigi Mossi makes fine Malvasia in an array of Colli Piacentini DOC, vdt and sparkling wines.
Pusterla, Vigolo Marchese (PC). Traditional style in Gutturnio and Monterosso under Colli Piacentini DOC.
Fratelli Rizzi, Castell'Arquato (PC). Good Monterosso Val d'Arda.
Tenuta Bissera, Monte San Pietro (BO). Bruno Negroni makes good Colli Bolognesi DOC and *spumanti*.
Terre Rosse, Zola Predosa (BO). Enrico Vallania introduced premium dry, still wines in Bologna's hills in the 1960s and 1970s, planting 19 ha in reddish calcareous clay known as *terra rossa*. His Cabernet Sauvignon was a perennial winner, though it never went into wood. His Chardonnay, Pinot Bianco and Grigio, and Sauvignon easily rivalled their counterparts from the Venezie. His widow Adriana, son Giovanni, and daughter Elisabetta have come up with creations of their own. Cuvée Enrico Vallania is a Cabernet selected in special years, like the late harvest Riesling Italico called Elisabetta Vallania. Chardonnay, which is not permitted in the hills, is called Giovanni Vallania and a sweet Malvasia is known as Adriana Vallania.

Vigevani/Tenuta Castello di Ancarano, Ancarano di Rivergaro (PC). The Colli Piacentini estate owned by the Vigevani family is supervised by the Viticultural Department of Piacenza's Università del Sacro Cuore under Professor Mario Fregoni. He leads experiments in 25 ha of vines in five plots, which include standard DOC varieties as well as Chardonnay and Müller Thurgau. Cabernet Sauvignon and Franc, Malbec, and Merlot are blended in both still and *frizzante* reds. Cellars are equipped for such vanguard techniques as cellular fermentation of whole grapes exposed to radical heat changes (a form of carbonic maceration) and use of aerated chambers for rapid drying of grapes for *passito* wines, including Cabernet. Commercial bottlings include Vigevani Brut by *charmat lungo* from Pinot Nero and Chardonnay and a youthful Cabernet called Annibale.
Vigneto Bagazzana, Zola Predosa (BO). Carlo Gaggioli makes good Colli Bolognesi DOC from 7 ha.
Zerioli, Ziano Piacentino (PC). From 56 ha, Arrigo Zerioli and family carry on a century-old tradition with a complete range of Colli Piacentini DOCs, vdt, and the *champenoise* Zerioli Brut.

COOPERATIVES

Cantina Cooperativa Colli di Scandiano, Scandiano (RE). Bianco di Scandiano DOC.

From left to right: Italy's most famous cheese is Parmigiano Reggiano, or Parmesan, used everywhere for grating over pasta but at home often eaten in bite-sized chunks with Lambrusco and other wines. Made in a delimited zone between Parma, Reggio, Modena, Bologna, and Mantova in Lombardy, its production methods and two years of required ageing are as strictly controlled as those of DOC wines.

Wines of Romagna's plains

Most growers in the flats of Ravenna and Ferrara are content to grow grapes for blending wines or brandy. Still, the reclaimed marshland around the Comacchio lagoon was once a thick wood (*bosco*) where a red wine from Fortana vines grown on the fringes enjoyed some renown. The woods and the wine have largely disappeared, but the legend was persuasive enough to qualify Bosco Eliceo as one of the humblest of recent DOCs. Much Trebbiano di Romagna DOC grows in the plains, too, but since the zone extends into the Apennines, it is discussed under Romagna's hills.

Bosco Eliceo or **Bosco (1989)**
This grapey red from Fortana (or Uva d'Oro) develops a rustically tannic bite that has made it the customary match with plump eels from the Comacchio lagoon. Merlot seems out of place in this curious seaside zone, though Sauvignon might prove to be more stimulating than the Bianco.

Zone: Dunes and reclaimed marshland of the Adriatic litoral between the Po and Ravenna, though production is centred in the Bosco della Mésola and the Bertuzzi and Comacchio lagoons in six communes in Ferrara province and two in Ravenna.

Bianco Dry white, also frizzante or vivace, abboccato or amabile. Grapes: Trebbiano Romagnolo; Sauvignon/Malvasia di Candia up to 30%. Yld 105/150, Alc 10.5, Acd 0.6.
Fortana Dry red, also frizzante or vivace, abboccato or amabile. Grapes: Fortana; other dark varieties up to 15%. Yld 105/150, Alc 10.5, Acd 0.6.
Merlot Dry red, also vivace. Grapes: Merlot; other dark varieties up to 15%. Yld 105/150, Alc 10.5, Acd 0.5.
Sauvignon Dry white, also frizzante or vivace, abboccato or amabile. Grapes: Sauvignon; other whites up to 15%. Yld 105/150, Alc 11, Acd 0.6.

Wines of Romagna's hills

Romagnans are spirited people with a partiality for their native produce. The traditional hill wines – vigorous Sangiovese and languid Albana – were usually pleasant to drink on the spot, even if few tasters beyond Bologna or Rimini found cause to rave about them. Lately, though, wines from some producers have moved up-market due to their improved methods and new respect for higher vineyards, where lower yields result in greater size, fragrance, and grace. Though Sangiovese usually seemed to offer more than Albana, the Ente Tutela Vini Romagnoli rallied behind the white in an uphill battle for DOCG. The amusement that greeted Albana's candidacy years ago turned to shock in 1987 when it actually made it. Suddenly a wine that non-partisans considered pleasant at best had become, on paper at least, Italy's premier white. Credit for this unlikely success was due primarily to persistence on the part of the consortium, whose symbol is the Passatore, a bearded nineteenth-century brigand in cocked hat, noted for his rakish defiance of authority. Critics, who suspected political motives behind the choice, charged that it discredited the DOC/DOCG system. But Romagnans, who could be accused of nothing more than excessive zeal, view Albana's elevation as a vital step towards building prestige – and sales – for all their wines, including Sangiovese and Trebbiano and the recent DOCs of Cagnina and Pagadebit di Romagna. Their goals are far from realized, but few consortiums can equal their ambition. The Ente Tutela Vini Romagnoli have been striving for years to make Romagna a centre for wine tourism with a number of marked routes through the DOC vineyards and *enoteche* that double as taverns for sampling wines (*see* Travel Information on page 170). The exclusive Club Viticoltori di Romagna grants a neck label for member estates' wines.

Albana di Romagna (DOCG 1987)
(The earlier DOC, 1967, now applies to spumante only.)
Despite Albana's new status, legends suggest that its distant past may have been more splendid than its recent. One tale has it that Albana prompted Galla Placidia, daughter of a 5th-century Roman Emperor, to exclaim that she would like to "berti in oro!" (drink you in gold) – the enchanted version of how the wine town of Bertinoro got its name. Reliable accounts of Albana date to the late Middle Ages, when Pier de' Crescenzi described it as "very potent and of noble flavour, well suited to ageing and middlingly subtle". Bertinoro remains Albana's garden, though there are other privileged pockets in the hills between Imola and Cesena. Until recently, almost every *contadino* crafted a little Aibàna, usually a touch sweet with a hint of *pétillance* to give it a lift on a summer afternoon. But modern methods have changed all that. DOCG has put Albana on the spot, challenging producers not only to show what is so special about it but what its true character is. So far, few have responded, maybe because they have too many options open to them. Dry versions rarely measure up. At best they have a pleasant peachy scent with soft fruit on the palate that fades to a vague sensation of toasted almonds; at worst they are flat with an overbearing odour of marzipan. The wine is especially prone to oxidation, though cold processing reduces the risk. Albana grapes, which ripen late in heavy golden bunches, have been described as "sugar machines", generating ample sucrose no matter what the yields. The permitted 91 hl/ha may seem excessive, but too much pruning and thinning inhibits normal vegetation. Though Albana Gentile was known as the best cultivar, experts have singled out the clinical L19 as the promising clone. The key to quality is the siting of vines. High vineyards, where yields are moderate and grapes ripen slowly, favour balanced expression of primary aromas. Overall, sweetness seems to best suit Albana's delicate nature. De Crescenzi's "middlingly subtle" description is apt for today's slightly sweet versions, which are perhaps most successful when still or *frizzante* rather than fully sparkling. But the revelation is Fattoria Zerbina's velvety *passita* from vineyards at Marzeno Faenza, where autumn mists induce botrytis cinerea. Though the wine called Scaccomatto defies the tradition because it is fermented and aged on the lees in small barrels and is redolent of noble rot, this is one Albana guaranteed as worthy of drinking in gold.

Zone: Hills extending from the Via Emilia into the low Apennines between Ozzano dell'Emilia on the outskirts of Bologna southeast to Savignano sul Rubicone, west of Rimini, and taking in 21 other communes in Bologna, Ravenna, and Forlì provinces. Bertinoro and hills above Forlì are noted for Albana amabile, while the secco has been poular to the west as far as Dozza. Grape: Albana.
Secco Dry white, also spumante*. Yld 91/140, Alc 11.5, Acd 0.5.
Amabile Slightly sweet white, also spumante*. Yld 91/140, Alc 12 (res sugar 12-45 gr/l), Acd 0.5.
Dolce Sweet white. Yld 91/140, Alc 12 (res sugar 45-80 gr/l), Acd 0.5.
Passita Semisweet to sweet, golden to amber. Yld 70/140, Alc 15.5 (res sugar min 15 gr/l), Acd 0.45, Ag 6 mths.
* Spumante secco and amabile may be classified as DOC but not DOCG.

Sangiovese di Romagna (1967)
Romagna's dauntless red covers the divisions from light heavyweight down, though even welterweights can pack a tannic punch. In the past, the local favourite succeeded more on vigour than style, but lately some bottlings have indicated that Tuscany has no monopoly of graceful Sangiovese. *Superiore* is too extensive to mean much, for within its confines lie five distinct areas in hills adjacent to Cesena, Faenza, Forlì, Imola, and Rimini. Each has its so-called *rocche*,

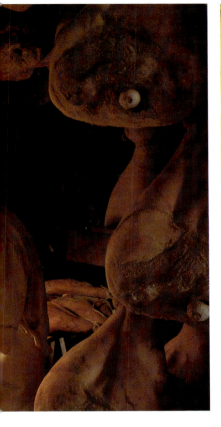

Left: the hills above Parma have a mild climate ideal for the production of the air-cured ham or prosciutto di Parma made following methods that require at least a year of ageing in well-ventilated rooms. Emilians often eat the succulent pink ham, sliced paper thin, with melon or figs as an antipasto accompanied by the soft, lightly bubbly Malvasia of the Colli di Parma.

towns known for their wines. The Rocche Forlivesi – Bertinoro, Predappio, Civitella, Meldola, and Castrocaro – stand out for "Sanzves" of deep ruby colour, power and endurance, led by Fattoria Paradiso's Vigna delle Lepri. The Rocche Faentini – Castelbolognese, Faenza, Brisighella, and Modigliana – can be nearly as big and equally stylish, as evidenced by the wines of Fattoria Zerbina and Ferrucci. The Rocche Cesenati – Savignano and Mercato Saraceno – make wines of balanced refinement, epitomized by Spalletti's Rocca di Ribano. Though Imola and Rimini are noted for lighter, easier wines, the exceptions can be interesting. Romagna's wine roads lead to four types of Sangiovese – *allegro*, *gentile*, *forte*, and *nobile* (see page 170).

Zone: Hills extending from the outskirts of Bologna southeast almost to the Adriatic border with the Marches, covering 42 communes in Bologna, Ravenna, and Forlì provinces. Superiore applies to wines of at least 12% alcohol from an area covering much of the DOC zone, excluding the plains north of the Via Emilia and the upper reaches of the Apennines. Dry red, also superiore and riserva. Grape: Sangiovese. Yld 71.5/110, Alc 11.5; superiore 12, Acd 0.5, Ag 6 mths; riserva 2 yrs.

Trebbiano di Romagna (1973)

With Albana struggling to move up market, Trebbiano is more than ever Romagna's everyday white. Its breezy

Above: the main piazza in Bologna, the capital city of Emilia-Romagna.

style goes down well in fish restaurants along the Adriatic, where the sparkling version also has fans. The few wines from the hills carry hints of flowers and fruit beyond the acidic nip. The best that can be said for most Trebbiano from the flatlands (the majority of production) is that it is clean tasting and unobtrusive.

Zone: A vast tract extending from the low Apennines into the Po flatlands north of Lugo in an area flanking the Via Emilia from the outskirts of Bologna southeast almost to the Adriatic border with the Marches, covering 54 communes in Bologna, Forlì, and Ravenna provinces, including the isolated Isola di Savarna in the commune of Ravenna. Dry white, also dry, semisweet, or sweet spumante. Grape: Trebbiano Romagnolo. Yld 84/140, Alc 11.5, Acd 0.5.

Cagnina di Romagna (1989)

The revival of this softly sweet violet to purple wine is due to a sprightly freshness and a mouth-cleansing tannic-acid bite that come across best within months of the harvest when most is sold. Though Cagnina is the same as Friuli's Terrano clone of Refosco, it develops a warmer, fleshier style in Romagna, where it is considered the ideal match for roasted chestnuts.

Zone: Hills and plains on either side of the Via Emilia between Castel Bolognese and the Rubicone river, covering 16 communes in Forlì province and five in Ravenna. Slightly sweet to sweet red. Grapes: Cagnina (Terrano/Refosco); other varieties up to 15%. Yld 84.5/130, Alc 11 (res sugar min 40 gr/l), Acd 0.5.

Pagadebit di Romagna (1989)

When dry, this gentle white can show as much class as Albana, with more fruit to offset the almondy background. The *amabile* is delicate enough to drink as an aperitif. Pagadebit's traditional home, Bertinoro, rates as a special subdenomination.

Zone: Low hills south of the Via Emilia from Imola southeast to Cattolica on the border with the Marches, covering 24 communes in Forlì province and five in Ravenna. Wine of at least 11.5% alcohol produced in the commune may cite Bertinoro on the label. Grapes: Pagadebit (Bombino Bianco); other whites up to 15%. **Secco** Dry white, also frizzante. Yld 98/140, Alc 10.5; Bertinoro 11.5, Acd 0.45; Bertinoro 0.5.

Amabile Slightly sweet white, also frizzante. Yld 98/140, Alc 11; Bertinoro 11.5 (res sugar both max 40 gr/l), Acd 0.45; Bertinoro 0.5.

Other wines of note

Every estate makes one or two special vdts, often inspired and invariably original. Prime examples are Fattoria Paradiso's unique Barbarossa, Fattoria Zerbina's Marzeno di Marzeno and Vicchio, Ferrucci's Domus Caia, Cesari's Liano and Malise, Le Calbane's Calbanesco, Podere dal Nespoli's Borgo dei Guidi, and Casetta dei Frati's Rosso della Trafila. Romagna has become a major source of *novelli*, some of which are even good. There are far too many ordinary vdt and *frizzanti* to document, but as new wines emerge, visitors to the area may come across some as yet undisclosed treasures.

ESTATES/GROWERS

Camerone, Castelbolognese (RA). From 18 ha at Biancanigo, Giuseppe Marabini makes a good range of Romagna DOCs and *spumante*.

Casetta dei Frati, Modigliana (FO). Good Sangiovese and the unique Rosso della Trafila from an unknown variety found in 10 ha of vines.

Casetto dei Mandorli, Predappio Alta (FO). Good range of Romagna DOCs, including Sangiovese and Cagnina.

Castelluccio, Modigliana (FO). Despite doubts about the estate's future, Gianmatteo Baldi has been making some of Romagna's finest wines in the single vineyard red vdt Ronco Casone, Ronco dei Ciliegi, and Ronco delle Ginestre (all from the Tuscan clones of Sangiovese) and the Sauvignon Blanc Ronco del Re.

Cesari, Castel San Pietro Terme (BO). Umberto Cesari draws from 60 ha of vines on his Parolino and La Macolina properties as well as buying in grapes for his admirable Romagna DOCs, vdt, and *spumanti*. He recently issued a signature range for Albana Colle del Re and the vdt red Liano (from Sangiovese and Cabernet) and white Malise, which blends that rare variety with

Chardonnay, Pignoletto, and Trebbiano.

Colombina, Bertinoro (FO). Romagna DOCs.

Fratelli Conti, Faenza (RA). Romagna DOCs and *spumanti*.

Fattoria Paradiso, Bertinoro (FO). Mario and Rina Pezzi have been the spiritual leaders of Romagna's gradual revival with exemplary DOC and vdt, mostly from single plots among 18 ha of vines. Their Sangiovese Superiore Vigna delle Lepri and Albana, both dry and *amabile*, are long-standing models. Barbarossa, isolated in the vineyards years ago, makes a robust red vdt. Mario Pezzi is also credited with rediscovering Pagadebit and bringing the long-neglected Cagnina back to respectability (and DOC).

Fattoria Zerbina, Marzeno Faenza (RA). Vincenzo Geminiani and daughter Cristina, guided by oenologist Vittorio Fiore, are creating wines from varieties both traditional and new that seem destined to reshape quality concepts in Romagna. Their Albana passita '87 has dimensions that exceed anything to

Above: Brisighella with its medieval castle lies along a valley with a microclimate conducive to vines.

date from that dubious DOCG. Called Scaccomatto (Checkmate), it was issued in late 1989 along with Marzeno di Marzeno '87, from Sangiovese with a little Cabernet, which should become a pacesetter among vdt reds. From 33 ha, the estate makes good Albana dolce, Trebbiano, and Sangiovese Superiore (including the occasional riserva Pietramora), as well as a promising white vdt called Vicchio, from Chardonnay with Trebbiano.

Stefano Ferrucci, Castelbolognese (RA). From 12 ha of vines around Domus Caia, the restored Roman way station now the focus of the estate, Ferrucci crafts wines of style and originality. Besides fine DOC Sangiovese and a promising Albana passita, he uses semidried Sangiovese grapes for the Amarone-like Domus Caia and has devised a white from the nearly extinct Bianchino and a red

novello from the rare Albana Nera.
Guarini Matteucci, Forlì. Full range of Romagna DOC, vdt, and *spumante*.
Le Calbane, Meldola (FO). Cesare Raggi makes good Sangiovese Superiore, but his pride is a vdt, the dark, warm, austere Calbanesco, from a mystery variety discovered in the vineyards of his small estate.
Roberta Nanni, Rimini (FO). Romagna DOCs.
Nicolucci, Predappio (FO). Sangiovese di Predappio vdt.
Pasolini Dall'Onda, Imola (BO). Sound Romagna DOCs from 30 ha at Montericco source of a fine semisweet Albana vdt Villa Montericco.
Picchi, San Colombano di Meldola (FO). Romagna DOCs.
Podere dal Nespoli, Civitella di Romagna (FO). Fine Sangiovese Superiore and Trebbiano from Vigna del Prugneto, along with the red vdt Borgo dei Guidi from Sangiovese, Cabernet Sauvignon, and Raboso.
San Patrignano, Ospedaletto di Coriano (FO). Young people at a drug rehabilitation centre make good Sangiovese Superiore and Trebbiano, as well as vdt and *spumanti* from 45 ha.
Spalletti-Tenuta di Savignano, Savignano sul Rubicone (FO). The Colonna Spalletti family is a perennial top producer of Sangiovese Superiore from 36 ha of vines, including the prized Rocca di Ribano and the red vdt Villa Rasponi.
Tenuta Amalia, Villa Verrucchio (FO). Good Sangiovese Superiore and vdt from 60 ha.

Tenuta del Monsignore, San Giovanni in Marignano (FO). Romagna DOCs and vdt from 25 ha.
Tre Monti, Imola (BO). The Tarsallo label is used for good Albana, including an *amabile* called Vitalba, a Sangiovese-Cabernet vdt called Boldo, and Tarsallo Brut from Chardonnay and Albana grown on 20 ha.
Treré, Faenza (RA). Romagna DOCs and vdt from 23 ha.
Villa I Raggi, Predappio Alta (FO). Sangiovese Superiore.

WINE HOUSES/MERCHANTS

Carla Foschi, Cesena (FO). Fine Sangiovese Superiore.
Samorì, Bertinoro (FO). Promising new house with Romagna DOCs selected from vineyards around Bertinoro.
Luciano Tamburini, Santarcangelo di Romagna (FO). Romagna DOCs.

COOPERATIVES

Corovin, Forlì. Romagna's consortium of cooperatives has enormous reserves of DOC, vdt, and sparkling wines available from cellars supplied by 35,000 growers.
CS di Forlì, Forlì. Noteworthy Sangiovese Superiore DOC.
Cantina Produttori Predappio, Predappio (FO). Sangiovese Superiore.
CS Ronco, Ronco (FO). Large production of Romagna DOCs, including single vineyard bottlings and vdt.

Travel Information

RESTAURANTS/HOTELS

Gigiolè, 48013 Brisighella (RA). Tel (0546)81209. Tarcisio Raccagni's talents have made this a noted inn in the town of Brisighella, where its worth spending the night to also sample the food and wine at brother Nerio's **La Grotta** Tel (0546)81829 the next day.
La Frasca, 47011 Castrocaro Terme (FO). Tel (0543)767471. Gianfranco Bolognesi, the leading authority on Romagna's wines, chooses just as deftly from elsewhere in Italy and France to complement wife Bruna's inspired variations on Romagnan cooking.
Picci, 42025 Cavriago (RE). Tel (0522)57201. Raffaele Piccirilli's touches with mushrooms, *aceto balsamico*, and wines makes for splendid variations on Reggio's cooking.
Villa Maria Luigia-di Ceci, 43044 Collecchio (PR) Tel (0521)805489. Local specialities of Parma, including prosciutto and wines from adjacent slopes, served in a villa with gardens.
San Domenico, 40026 Imola (BO). Tel (0542)29000. Gian Luigi Morini and chef Valentino Marcattilii have created one of Italy's most admired restaurants and wine cellars with a branch in New York.
Ristorante della Piazza, 29029 Rivergaro (PC) Tel (0523)958155. Home

cooking from Giuseppina, whose pasta is delectable, and Germano, who knows about Colli Piacentini wines.
Osteria di Rubbiara, 41015 Rubbiara (MO). Tel (059)549019. Italo Pedroni and family make superb pasta and *aceto balsamico*, highlights of this inn in Lambrusco country.
Locanda della Colonna, 40020 Tossignano (BO). Tel (0542)91006. Interesting combinations of old and new dishes with a first-rate wine list.

PLACES OF INTEREST

The Via Emilia runs close to most of the region's DOC zones, though less congested routes provide better views of the vineyards. Lambrusco grows almost entirely in the plains, in arboured stretches that resemble orchards with roads marked through the Sorbara, Castelvetro, and Santa Croce zones. The prettiest vineyards are in the hills, which, when approached from the plains, provide relief from a summer heat wave or a winter fog.
Emilia's hills. Roads follow rivers into the Apennine foothills, some of which rise abruptly from the valley floors into knolls topped by castles among stands of pines and cypresses or hamlets clinging precariously to clifftops. In the

Below: a vineyard on the slopes of Romagna's Apennine foothills with the town of Brisighella in the background.

Colli Piacentini, the Val Tidone contains some of Italy's most intensively cultivated vineyards; the Arda and Trebbia valleys are picturesque. Local wines can be tried at the *enoteca* in the handsome medieval town of Castell'Arquato. Parma is noted for opera (Verdi and Toscanini came from there), as well as patrician villas and its prosciutto, salami, and Parmesan cheese. Villages in the hills south of Reggio, Modena, and Bologna provide a tranquil contrast to the bustle of the valley towns.

Romagna's hills. The Romagnans' exuberance for wine, food, and music makes them the most convivial of hosts. The Ente Tutela Vini Romagnoli has created a system of wine roads and *enoteche* unmatched anywhere outside of Piedmont. The marked routes follow themes: Albana Amabile (around Bertinoro and Forlì); Albana Secca (between Forlì and Dozza); Sangiovese Allegro (between Faenza and Dozza); Sangiovese Forte (through hills above Forlì); Sangiovese Nobile (from Forlimpopoli to Savignano sul Rubicone); Sangiovese Gentile (from Sant'Arcangelo past San Marino to Cattolica). Emilia-Romagna's largest public display of wine is the Enoteca Regionale in the castle at Dozza. There are also a number of Romagnan taverns (Ca' in dialect) that serve wine and sometimes food. In the hills are Ca' de Be' at Bertinoro and Ca' de Sanzves at Predappio Alta. There are also Ca' de Passador at Cesenatico, Ca' de Ven at Ravenna, and Chesa de Ven at Rimini.

Wines of San Marino

San Marino's wines were once almost as joked about as the postage stamps that keep "the world's oldest republic" thriving. But that was before growers in this nation whose 60 square kilometres are mainly perpendicular decided to move up market. The majority belong to the Consorzio Vini Tipici di San Marino, in whose modern cellars consulting oenologist Vittorio Fiore directs production of much of the republic's nearly 20,000 hectolitres of wine a year from about 225 hectares of vines. The Consorzio alone may issue *vini a identificazione di origine* of San Marino with the varietal names of Sangiovese, Biancale, and Moscato, after a government appointed tasting commission has approved the wines. Sangiovese is the stalwart in three versions, comprising an ordinary red, as well as *superiore* and *rosato*. The local Biancale di Rimini is a superior type of Trebbiano. But emphasis is increasingly on sweet bubbly Moscato, experiments are under way with ouside varieties such as the Pinots and Chardonnay. Over the last decade, quality has risen to compare with adjacent DOCs in Romagna and the Marches, though Fiore says the republic's conditions are generally superior to its neighbours. San Marino's wines in bottles (which have largely replaced the traditional demijohns) seem to enjoy greater success. Wine has become San Marino's major export, reaching other European nations and even Japan. But most of the wine produced travels no farther than the Adriatic resorts visible from the jagged heights of Monte Titano.

Marches (Marche)

Capital: Ancona.
Provinces: Ancona (AN), Ascoli Piceno (AP), Macerata (MC), Pesaro e Urbino (PS).
Area: 9,694 square kilometres (fifteenth).
Population: 1,426,000 (thirteenth).

Gentle seems an adjective designed for the Marches, in the way it defines the landscape, the climate, the rhythm of life. The wines show composure as well, though the notion that the popular Verdicchio is docile has been questioned by the emergence of a hidden personality that might better be defined as genteel. Rosso Cònero also seems to be undergoing metamorphosis, though on such a limited scale that it is hardly ever publicized as the region's – and one of Italy's – best reds.

Even everyday wines here show class beyond their implausibly low prices. It is probably no coincidence that the Marchigiani drink more wine per capita and live longer than other Italians, though there may be other factors behind their healthy glow. The weather is agreeable in these quiet hills. Even when it rains or snows, breezes from the Adriatic or Apennines offset the dampness. The diet, balanced between produce from land and sea, is prepared with the deftest of Mediterranean touches. Still, even if the pace of life is relaxed, old-timers may remind you that it's those regular doses of *vino* that work wonders for body and soul.

It is not known when the inhabitants of the Marches first made wine, though fossils of *Vitis vinifera* dating to the Iron Age have been found around Ascoli Piceno. Etruscan-style agriculture thrived here before the Roman conquest of the third century BC. Previously the Senone Gauls occupied the territory north of the Esino (now the river of Verdicchio) and the Piceni dominated the south. The Romans, who admired the wines of Picenum, especially the Praetutian made in the southern Marches and northern Abruzzi, marvelled over the productivity of the chalky clay soil. The Greeks, impressed by the natural harbour, founded what is now the capital of Ancona. They shipped wines in clay amphorae, whose shape, many centuries later, inspired the bottle that made Verdicchio famous.

A Verdicchio legend was built around Alaric, king of the Visigoths, who in the fourth century AD encouraged his troops with the wine as they crossed the Apennines to sack Rome. More credible accounts trace Verdicchio's origins to the fourteenth century, after the feudal domains known as *marche* had been unified under the Holy Roman Empire.

Verdicchio attracted attention over the centuries, including praise as the nonpareil of fish wines. But it didn't make an international impact until the 1950s when Fazi-Battaglia, still the market leader, devised the green amphora bottle with the scroll (*cartoglio*) curled around its neck. That ingenious container soon became a fixture in Italian restaurants around the world, where candles flickered over chequered table cloths and fishnets dangled from the ceilings. Imitations flourished. Even if the wines weren't always memorable, the bottles were hard to forget.

But by the late 1970s serious wine drinkers shunned the amphora as pointedly as the Chianti flask. Sales began to slip. Producers, faced with surpluses from vineyards planted when the export boom began, realized that things had to change. The leading producers, to their credit, rather than relying on sales campaigns, set about improving quality in the long term. Some have succeeded beyond expectations, raising suspicions that central Italy has a noble native vine for white wine after all. Today, all the large wineries and some of the small ones make a special version of Verdicchio sold in standard bottles. Quality has risen so steadily that even the wine still sold in amphorae seems a cut above the general level. Verdicchio has another advantage over its competitors: it excels as a base for sparkling wines by both bottle and tank fermented methods.

Verdicchio's turnaround has revitalized a wine industry that was faltering in the early 1980s. Yet, even if the region's white wines are gaining, or holding their own, red wines are in decline. Sangiovese, whose dominance is best expressed in Rosso Piceno, rarely shows style in the Marches, perhaps because the cultivars aren't the best. Montepulciano, base of the sometimes superb Rosso Cònero, is less productive than Sangiovese and seems destined to become even more elite.

Aggressive marketing might do wonders for the Marches' wines, but the hard sell doesn't seem to be in their producers' nature. Maybe that's just as well. The amiable people of the Marches need to keep most of those good wines themselves to drink to their enduring good health.

The Marches' Vineyards

Verdicchio, though it seems to dominate, covers less than ten percent of the region's vineyards, surpassed by the red Sangiovese and Montepulciano, and the white Trebbiano Toscano. But in the central hills between Jesi and Matelica, Verdicchio is clearly gaining, with increasing attention being paid to clones and rootstocks.

Growing emphasis on white wine goes beyond Verdicchio and the relentless Trebbiano to Biancame and Malvasia. Regional authorities are also encouraging plantings of Pinot Bianco and Grigio and the still not approved Chardonnay and Sauvignon. But the red varieties of Sangiovese and the less productive Montepulciano are falling from favour. Not only has the market for DOC reds declined, but the use of these varieties for blending in Tuscany and northern regions has fallen off.

Training is almost entirely vertical, mostly in the *doppio capovolto* or double arch system that gives Verdicchio space to flourish. Though Castelli di Jesi's permitted yields of 105 hectolitres per hectare have been criticized as excessive, experts agree that a threshold below 85-90 hectolitres per hectare is impractical, since short pruning may force excessive foliage and encourage what is known as berry expulsion. Not long ago, vines trained onto trees or scatterered among other crops were a familiar sight, but picturesque "coltura promiscua" has all but disappeared in the conversion to monoculture. Only in southern areas adjacent to the Abruzzi is *tendone* or canopy used – mainly for Trebbiano. The following varieties are associated primarily with the Marches.

Bianchello. Local name for Biancame in Bianchello del Metauro DOC.
Incrocio Bruni 54. Cross between Verdicchio and Sauvignon that rarely shows the best of either, so it is used sparingly.
Lacrima (di Morro). Some say this dark variety is an Aleatico, though origins are uncertain. It has been planted since the eighteenth century in the Marches, where it makes the fragile Lacrima di Morro d'Alba DOC. Also known as Galloppo or Gallioppa.
Maceratino. Declining variety, possibly in the Greco family or a clone of Verdicchio, used in the blend of Bianco dei Colli Maceratesi DOC.
Passerina. Synonym for Biancame in the Marches, Romagna, and Latium. It may figure in Falerio dei Colli Ascolani and Rosso Piceno DOC.
Pecorino. Fading variety whose high acidity and smooth fruitiness once made tasty whites, though now it plays a minor role in Falerio dei Colli Ascolani DOC. Also found in Abruzzi (as Pecorino Bianco to distinguish it from the dark Pecorino), as well as Umbria and Latium.

Verdicchio. A varied species whose dozen or so cultivars seem to have derived from the antique Greco-Trebbiano family. Today most Verdicchio Bianco and related clones are planted in the Marches, mainly in the Castelli di Jesi and Matelica zones, where it reaches heights unequalled elsewhere. Though subject to maladies, its grapes are in demand so it is favoured by growers. Clonal studies have led to selections which seem certain to further improve quality. Verdicchio seems to be related to the Trebbiano of Lugana (Lombardy) and Soave (Veneto). It is sometimes confused with the unrelated Verdeca, Verdone, Verdello, and Verduzzo, whose names also refer to their greenish skins.

Vernaccia di Serrapetrona or **Vernaccia Nera**. Once prominent as a source of red sparkling wines in the hills of Macerata province, it survives as a curiosity around Serrapetrona, where it has a DOC.

Other varieties

Among outsiders are the predictable Barbera and Merlot, but curiously there is no provision yet for Cabernet Sauvignon, Chardonnay, or Sauvignon Blanc, which are catching on here as in neighbouring regions. Other varieties recommended or approved in the Marches include:

For red (or rosé): Aleatico, Alicante, Cabernet Franc, Canaiolo Nero, Carignano, Ciliegiolo, Gaglioppo, Maiolica, Pinot Nero.

For white: Albana, Bombino Bianco, Grechetto, Malvasia Bianca di Candia, Malvasia Toscana or Chianti, Montonico or Mantonico Bianco, Mostosa, Pinot Bianco, Pinot Grigio, Riesling Italico, Tocai Friulano, Vermentino.

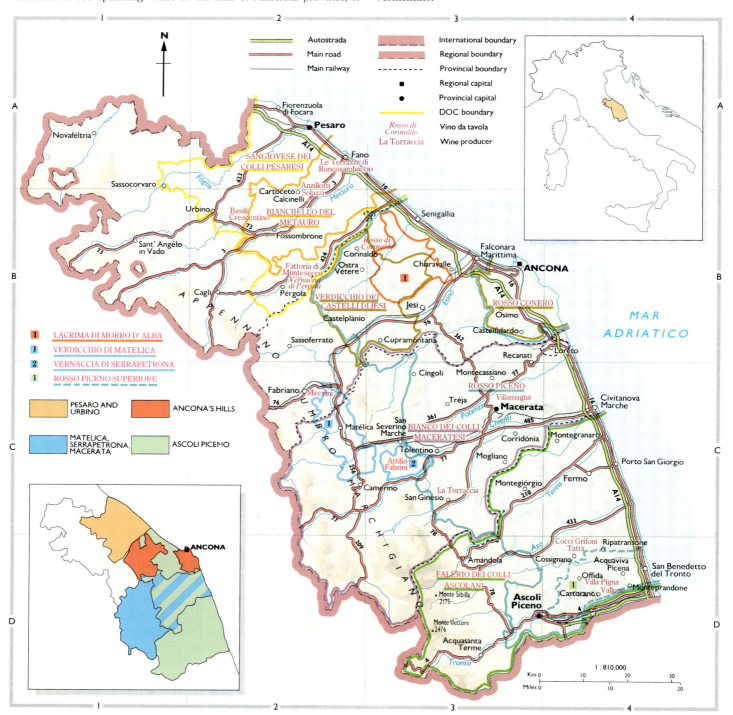

The Marches' Wine Zones

The map of the Marches suggests symmetry even though a third of the surface is hilly and the rest mountainous. Between the wall of the Umbro Marchigiano Apennines to the west and the dunes along the Adriatic lies a strip of hills about 30 kilometres wide on average that support most of the vineyards. Though the higher slopes can be precipitous, there is a soft harmony to these hills drained by a dozen rivers at such regular intervals that their short courses to the sea give the cartographic impression of stripes on a waving banner. Two key wine zones lie slightly apart from this strip: Verdicchio di Matelica, which basks within a pocket of the Apennines, and Rosso Cònero, whose massif forms what the Greeks noted as an elbow at Ancona, the only relief along the 173 kilometres of otherwise straight, flat coast. Marly or sandy clay dominates in these rises, which are well suited to viticulture, though variations in rock, fossil, and mineral content, as well as exposure, account for differences in quality. The climate is enviably reliable, though high slopes, often covered by snow in winter, can be cool and damp. In the summer, the sunny, mild Adriatic-Apennine ambience can be shattered by violent storms, hail, or withered by a long drought.

Pesaro e Urbino

Sangiovese dei Colli Pesaresi DOC covers the province's hills, though noted vineyards lie on coastal rises below the border with Romagna near Fiorenzuola di Focara, Pesaro, and Fano, and along the Foglia and Metauro valleys. Warm, dry conditions in the sandy clay soil suit hearty Sangiovese, though wines from the cooler hills around Urbino and the Montefeltro range tend to be lighter and sharper. Bianchello del Metauro extends through the river valley on sunny slopes of clay mixed with sand and gravel, where Biancame grapes render light, fresh whites.

Ancona's hills

The extensive Verdicchio dei Castelli di Jesi zone reaches to within ten kilometres of the Adriatic at Morro d'Alba, whose arid slopes also produce the curious red Lacrima. But the classic vineyards for Verdicchio lie west of Jesi 20-30 kilometres from the sea in two groups of hills 200-500 metres high on either side of the Esino river. Calcareous clay prevails, though the presence of sand, fossils, and minerals can be decisive quality factors. Equally important are exposure, which in higher places is generally towards the south to assure full ripening, and moisture retention of the soil in an area subject to drought. The proximity of the Apennines increases chances of hail, which affects certain places more than others. Some growers have vines in different areas to reduce the risk of losing an entire crop. The Rosso Cònero DOC zone covers most of the 572-metre massif and adjacent hills, though vines are planted on slopes protected from Adriatic winds. The chalky clay soil is rich in lime, so Montepulciano does well nearly everywhere in sunny, dry microclimates. But since much of the area is a suburb of Ancona, vineyards are scattered through what farmland remains.

Matelica, Serrapetrona, and Macerata

The Matelica zone covers a broad valley between two ridges of the Apennines in what was once a closed saltwater sea. Hence the sandy clay is rich in mineral salts, as well as active limestone, iron, and magnesium. The best vineyards lie east of the Esino on gradual slopes at 300-450 metres. Despite the altitude, summers can be hot, though air currents channelled up from the high Potenza and Chienti valleys to the south

Above: lavender growing on the slopes of the Cònero massif near Ancona in the Rosso Cònero DOC zone.

prevent problems with mountain moisture. Average rainfall in this zone, which lies 50-60 kilometres from the Adriatic, is 1,250-1,500 millimetres, slightly more than Castelli di Jesi, whose nearest point is less than 20 kilometres to the northeast. Matelica's conditions favour Verdicchio of ample strength and acidity with accented fruit and aroma. Serrapetrona lies southeast of Matelica along the Chienti in hills that were once renowned for wine. But little of the dark Vernaccia remains. Macerata's hills are planted in Sangiovese, which may be used for Rosso Piceno, and in Trebbiano and Maceratino for the simple Bianco dei Colli Maceratesi and other whites. Verdicchio does well in the sandy clay soil, but wines of special class are rare.

Ascoli Piceno

The hills between the Adriatic and the Sibillini range of the Apennines (with the Marches' highest peak, Monte Vettore, at 2,476 metres) have a majesty about them. The author Giovanni Poli described them as affable, with "vineyards that ascend in parade formation". They are also fertile, rendering more than half of the region's wine, sometimes from canopied vines, though vertical systems prevail. Rosso Piceno Superiore is from a restricted area between Ascoli and the sea. Falerio dei Colli Ascolani covers a wider area. But the sandy clay slopes, which are normally baked dry in summer, are no longer noted for much class from Sangiovese and Trebbiano, which overwhelm the worthier Montepulciano and Pecorino.

Wines of the north: Pesaro e Urbino province

The hills between the port of Pesaro and the art centre of Urbino have an agrestic appeal that contrasts with the resort atmosphere along the coast. The wines, which resemble the reds and whites of adjacent Romagna, if anything seem more rustic, particularly Sangiovese dei Colli Pesaresi. Bianchello del Metauro nonetheless has found itself in growing demand as a fish wine in restaurants along the coast. In terms of creativity, some unconventional *vino da tavola* made around Pergola especially from the Fattoria di Montesecco offer more than the DOCs.

Sangiovese dei Colli Pesaresi (1972)

An unsung cousin of Sangiovese di Romagna, at best it reveals a mellow core to its grapey heartiness, but it can be lean and raspy. The *consorzio* label carries a portrait of Pesaro's favourite son, the opera composer and bon vivant Gioacchino Rossini.

Zone: Hills between the Adriatic and the Montefeltro range of the Apennines covering much of Pesaro e Urbino province, though noted vineyards are in hills along the Adriatic or in the Foglia and Metauro valleys. Dry red. Grapes: Sangiovese; Ciliegiolo/ Montepulciano up to 15%. Yld 77/110, Alc 11.5, Acd 0.5.

Bianchello del Metauro (1969)

This white is unabashedly popular, maybe because its lemony zest appeals to summer tourists. But it need not always be taken lightly. Some producers – Anzillotti Solazzi and Giovanetti, for example – give it an understated sort of style. It is increasingly sold further afield, even overseas, where it seems to be accepted as a sprightly alternative to Verdicchio.

Zone: Low hills along the Metauro river in 18 communes in Pesaro e Urbino province. The better vineyards face the river from the north. Dry white. Grapes: Biancame (called Bianchello); Malvasia Toscana up to 5%. Yld 98/140, Alc 11.5, Acd 0.55-0.8.

Other wines of note

The remote vineyards of Pergola might have gone unheeded were it not for the bravura of Massimo Schiavi, whose offbeat wines from the Fattoria di Montesecco have attracted attention nationally. Nearby are the Fattoria Ligi-Montevecchio and the Fattoria Sant'Onofrio, which produce good examples of the once renowned red Vernaccia di Pergola.

ESTATES/GROWERS

Anzillotti Solazzi, Fano (PS). Noted Bianchello del Metauro DOC from vineyards at Calcinelli.
Basili Crescentino, Canavaccio di Urbino (PS). Bianchello and Sangiovese DOC.
Ciardiello & Evalli, Gradara (PS). Sangiovese dei Colli Pesaresi DOC.
Fattoria di Montesecco, Montesecco di Pergola (PS). Massimo Schiavi uses ingeniously natural methods to make three inimitable white wines, all vdt: the dry Tristo di Montesecco, the aromatic Jubilè, and the luscious Gallia Togata, which might be described as an agrestic Sauternes.
Fattoria Ligi-Montevecchio, Pergola (PS). Vernaccia di Pergola vdt.
Fattoria Mancini, Pesaro. Sangiovese dei Colli Pesaresi DOC.
Fattoria Sant'Onofrio, Pergola (PS). Vernaccia di Pergola vdt.
Le Terrazze di Roncosambaccio-Giovanetti, Fano (PS). Tasty Bianchello and Sangiovese DOC.

COOPERATIVES

CS dei Colli Pesaresi, Colbordo (PS). Sangiovese dei Colli Pesaresi DOC.
Cooperativa Vitivinicola Colli Metaurensi (COVIM), Montemaggiore al Metauro (PS). Bianchello and Sangiovese DOC.

Below: Rosso Cònero from Montepulciano vines has won increasing praise from critics, though production has decreased because vineyards such as this one on the outskirts of Ancona are on valuable land for building.

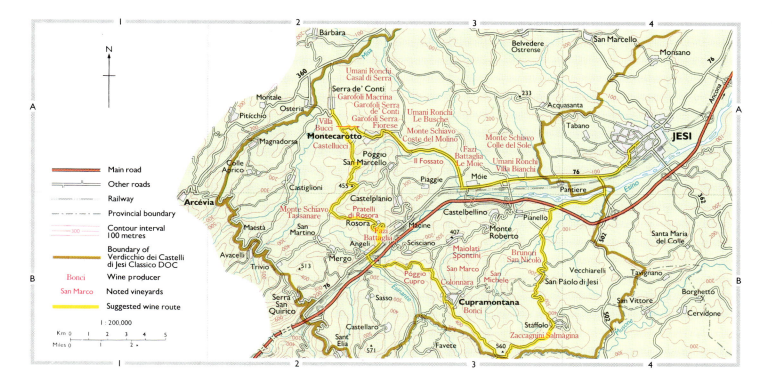

Wines of Ancona's hills: Castelli di Jesi and Monte Cònero

Ancona's status as a wine town has risen rapidly with the revival of Verdicchio dei Castelli di Jesi and the emergence of Rosso Cònero from obscurity. Though neither wine ranks among Italy's elite yet, each in its own way can aspire to a high position. The zones are divided with Monte Cònero on the coast next to Ancona and Jesi 30 kilometres to the west along the Esino river but in several cases they share producers who lead the quest for quality. Part of the Verdicchio di Matelica zone is in the province of Ancona, but the centre is in Macerata. The Rosso Piceno zone rambles across the province, though little wine of note is made as growers have concentrated on raising yields. Curiosity seekers may perhaps be amused by the exotic Lacrima di Morro d'Alba DOC.

Verdicchio dei Castelli di Jesi (1968)

Verdicchio's fate has followed that of Fazi-Battaglia through the boom and slump and now the revival that seems destined to last, since other houses are equally committed to attaining new heights of prestige. Even the wine in amphora, whose nostalgia value persists, has improved markedly over a decade. The first step was cool fermentation, which brought out more fragrance and fruit. But diligent producers have gone further by reducing yields, picking grapes at balanced primes, crushing immediately, leaving Malvasia and Trebbiano out of the blend, and vinifying at temperatures neither so warm as to kill primary aromas nor so cool as to stunt character development. Some practise late harvesting or cold maceration with the skins to build structure and nuance. There has even been some barrel fermenting and ageing *sur lie*, as with Muscadet, a wine with which

Verdicchio, due to its affinity with fish, is too often compared.

Several of the larger houses have introduced Verdicchio from single vineyards or special *cuvées*, invariably sold in standard bottles of varying type. Among them are Fazi-Battaglia's Le Moie, Garofoli's Macrina and Serra del Conte, Umani Ronchi's Casal di Serra and Villa Bianchi, Monte Schiavo's Coste del Molino and Il Pallio di San Floriano. Small producers have also made an impact, first Brunori with the *cru* San Nicolò, then Fratelli Bucci with the widely acclaimed Villa Bucci, and recently Fratelli Zaccagnini with Salmàgina.

These wines seem to be improving with each good vintage. Though strikingly individual, they share an unmistakable varietal character. Yet this emerging personality is not easy to pinpoint, since Verdicchio can range from light and crisp with faint greenish-yellow tones to full and richly textured with a golden hue. Alcohol may be held

to 11%, but the fruit-acid balance seems better at 12-12.5%, and can sometimes climb another degree without destroying freshness. To the nose Verdicchio may recall ripe apples or peaches, quince, kiwi, or even orange marmalade, but the aromas defy clichés since they don't strike you like those of a Riesling or Sauvignon but hang back like those of a Chardonnay or Pinot Bianco. This characteristic has been referred to as *aroma di bocca*, because it is best expressed on the palate. However defined, it also comes across winningly in sparkling versions, whether tank fermented or the result of the *méthode champenoise*, which was first employed by Garofoli. Here bubbles are true to tradition and not just a whim, since Verdicchio was nearly always *frizzante* in the past. At Cupramontana, where the cult of bubbles thrives, they claim to have produced bottle-fermented sparkling wine before it was made in Champagne.

Some tasters are impressed by Verdicchio aged in wood. First there was Villa Bucci, lightly seasoned in casks of Yugoslavian oak, more recently Garofoli's Serra Fiorese, aged in French *barriques*, and Umani Ronchi's Le Busche, fermented and aged on the lees in small barrels. But it's too early to say whether wood will acquire a key role here. Already Verdicchio has gained more than occasional recognition as one of Italy's most promising – or at least most surprising – white wines from a native variety.

But perhaps the most encouraging point about Verdicchio is that producers seem to agree that even better things lie ahead.

Zone: Hills lying mainly west of Jesi as far as the Apennine foothills, extending through 23 communes in Ancona province. The Classico zone covers all but the area above the Miso and Triponzio rivers, though the best vineyards lie at 200-500 m in hills on either side of the Esino river between Serra de' Conti and Staffolo. Dry white, also spumante. Grapes: Verdicchio; Malvasia Toscana/Trebbiano Toscano up to 15%. Yld 105/150, Alc 11.5, Acd 0.5-0.7.

Lacrima di Morro d'Alba (1985)

Although rescued from collapse by DOC, this purple-crimson wine with its slightly foxy berry-like odour and ripe plum flavour seems destined to remain a local peculiarity. Since it fades quickly, oenologists are studying its prospects as a *novello*.

Zone: Hills in the communes of Morro d'Alba, Belvedere Ostrense, Monte San Vito, Ostra, San Marcello, and Senigallia in Ancona province. Dry red, sometimes semisweet or bubbly. Grapes: Lacrima; Montepulciano/Verdicchio up to 15%. Yld 98/140, Alc 11, Acd 0.5.

Rosso Cònero (1967)

Montepulciano's supremacy over Sangiovese along the Adriatic comes to the fore in this red. As Ancona's perennial tipple, Rosso Cònero was known for vigour with a deep ruby colour and full, round flavour laced by tannins that allowed it to keep for years. Among the remaining producers, Mario Marchetti remains the doyen of tradition, insisting that Sangiovese has no place in the blend – a view now generally accepted by serious winemakers. Recently, wines from the massif have shown more splendour in bouquet and flavour than anyone had reason to expect. Garofoli's Piancarda set the early standard for a smattering of single vineyard bottlings. Rosso Cònero's reputation was given a surprise boost by the coup scored by Umani Ronchi's Cùmaro at London's International Wine Challenge of 1988. Among 2,480 entries in what was billed as the world's largest comparative tasting, Cùmaro '85 emerged as one of three wines (and the only red) to win trophies – special recognition above the medal categories. The result may have amazed the British, but the current class of Rosso Cònero indicates that Cùmaro's triumph was no fluke. Fine estate bottlings from Alessandro Moroder and Le Terrazze point to a bright future for growers tenacious enough to hang on to their precious plots and keep the faith in Montepulciano.

Zone: The Cònero massif and adjacent slopes in the communes of Ancona, Camerano, Offagna, Sirolo, Numana, Osimo, and Castelfidardo in Ancona province. Dry red, also superiore. Grapes: Montepulciano; Sangiovese up to 15%. Yld 98/140, Alc 11.5; superiore 12.5, Acd 0.6-0.8, Ag superiore 2 yrs.

Other wines of note

Though Verdicchio dei Castelli di Jesi and Rosso Cònero dominate, a few table wines deserve special notice. Montepulciano also makes fine rosé, as proved by Garofoli's prize-winning Kòmaros and the champenoise called Donna Giulia from Le Terrazze. Among innovations with new-style reds, Villa Bucci's Tenuta di Pongelli from Sangiovese, Montepulciano, and Cabernet may set a precedent. Merlot shows class from some vintages in the Cantina Sociale Val di Nevola's Rosso di Corinaldo. Most wineries meet the regional demand for everyday wines, often of commendable quality, in large economy bottles.

ESTATES/GROWERS

Fratelli Bonci, Cupramontana (AN). Verdicchio Classico, also *spumante*.
Fratelli Bucci, Ostra Vetere (AN). Ampelio Bucci, with help from Giorgio Grai, makes widely esteemed Verdicchio Classico, the best of which carries the Villa Bucci label. The 12 ha of vines are also the source of the unique red Tenuta di Pongelli vdt.
Castellucci, Montecarotto (AN). Verdicchio Classico.
Le Terrazze, Numana (AN). Paolo Terni makes good Rosso Cònero and the perfumed Donna Giulia, the Marches' answer to pink Champagne.
Marchetti, Ancona. Mario Marchetti makes respected traditional Rosso Cònero from 6 ha on the outskirts of Ancona near a place called Pinocchio, though son Maurizio is more progressive with Villa Bonomi Rosso Cònero, *spumante*, and vdt.
Moroder, Montacuto (AN). Alessandro Moroder produces increasingly stylish Rosso Cònero from a small estate on the edge of Ancona.
Fratelli Zaccagnini, Staffolo (AN). Verdicchio Classico, including the single vineyard Salmàgina, from 15 ha of vines.

WINE HOUSES/MERCHANTS

Bianchi See Umani Ronchi.
Brunori, Jesi (AN). Giorgio Brunori, assisted by father Mario, makes prized Verdicchio at the cellars recently moved from behind the family wine shop at Jesi to San Paolo di Jesi, adjacent to their 3.5 ha of vines. Plots include the 1.2-ha San Nicolò, an early Verdicchio *cru* for about 12,000 bottles a year. Four growers supply grapes to bring output of ordinary Verdicchio Classico to 50,000 bottles.
Fazi-Battaglia "Titulus", Castelplanio Stazione (AN). Founded in 1949, the firm introduced the amphora in the 1950s and has been the market leader ever since. Complete revision of the cellars has aided steady improvement in quality, a key factor in Verdicchio's resurgent status. The company owns cellars and vineyard holdings of about 250 ha, mainly in Verdicchio Classico. Additional grapes are purchased to bring Verdicchio production to more than 3,500,000 bottles, of which roughly 40% are exported. The top of the range Le Moie, the most renowned single vineyard bottling of Verdicchio, is selected from a 36-ha plot at Moie. The firm also produces Rosso Cònero and Rosso Piceno DOC and vdt.
Gioacchino Garofoli, Castelfidardo (AN). The family firm is a quality leader with Rosso Cònero from its own vineyards and Verdicchio mainly acquired under contract with growers and processed at cellars at Serra de' Conti. Winemaker Carlo Garofoli excels with the single vineyard Verdicchio Macrina and oak-aged Serra Fiorese, as well as sparkling versions by both tank and bottle fermented methods, of which Garofoli Brut Riserva is the model. The 21-ha Piancarda plot produces Rosso Cònero, including the cask-aged Piancarda, though the barrique-aged Grosso Agontano and the youthful Guasco are also admirable. Montepulciano is used for a good rosé vdt called Kòmaros.
Mecvini, Fabriano (AN). Enzo Mecella produces wines from various parts of the region, including DOC Verdicchio from Matelica and Jesi, Rosso Cònero, and a wood-aged Verdicchio known as Antico di Casa Fosca.
Serenelli, Ancona. Alberto Serenelli makes typical Rosso Cònero, plus a special selection known as Varano aged in small oak barrels.
Umani Ronchi, Osimo Scalo (AN). Founded by Gino Umani Ronchi, the winery makes fine Verdicchio and Rosso Cònero under brothers Massimo and Stefano Bernetti, whose separate family firm owns 80 ha in Castelli di Jesi and 20 ha on Cònero. Verdicchio from 10 ha at Casal di Serra stands out, though Villa Bianchi from 15 ha at Moie, and even the amphora wines are exemplary. The barrel-fermented Le Busche is promising. Verdicchio is vinified at Castelbellino, Rosso Cònero at the main winery at Osimo. The firm has three admirable versions of Rosso Cònero: Casal di Serra; San Lorenzo from a 6-ha plot, and the revelation called Cùmaro (the Greek name for Cònero) from a 3-ha plot. The firm also bottles Bianchello del Metauro and Montepulciano d'Abruzzo DOC. Wines are exported under the trade name Bianchi.

COOPERATIVES

Vinimar, Camerano (AN). The trademark used by the Associazione delle Cantine Cooperative delle Marche on wines, often of good value, from cooperative cellars throughout the region.
CS Val di Nevola, Corinaldo (AN). Verdicchio Classico and Rosso Piceno DOC and vdt, including Rosso di Corinaldo.

① Umani Ronchi San Lorenzo
② Umani Ronchi Cùmaro

Map legend:
- Autostrada
- Main road
- Other roads
- Railway
- Provincial boundary
- Contour interval 100 metres
- Boundary of Rosso Conero DOC
- Marchetti Wine producer
- Suggested wine route

1:240,000

Colonnara, Cupramontana (AN). From nearly 300 ha of vineyards around Cupramontana, winemaker Carlo Pigini Campanari makes good *champenoise* and *charmat*, as well as a still Verdicchio Classico DOC called Cuprese.

Monte Schiavo, Moie di Maiolati Spontini (AN). This uncommon cooperative, backed by the farm machinery manufacturing firm of Pieralisi, functions as ably as top private wineries with which it competes in quality. From 35 growers with 145 ha come Verdicchio Classico and *spumante*, as well as a Rosso Cònero. The amphora Verdicchio is enhanced by special bottlings: the 30-ha Colle del Sole, 18-ha Coste del Molino, Il Pallio di San Floriano (from late harvested grapes in the 23-ha Il Fossato plot), and the tank fermented Vigna Tassanare *spumante* (from the 30-ha Tassanare plot.

Cantina Cooperativa tra Produttori del Verdicchio, Montecarotto (AN). Sound Verdicchio Classico includes the Moncaro label.

Wines of Matelica, Serrapetrona, and Macerata

The province of Macerata climbs from a narrow strip of coast to a large chunk of Apennines, on whose foothills, almost concealed from the prying eyes of wine buffs, lie the vineyards of the scarce Verdicchio di Matelica and the almost obsolete Vernaccia di Serrapetrona. Macerata's short wine list takes in the unheralded Bianco dei Colli Maceratesi and a share of Rosso Piceno, including a couple of its better examples. But only a few producers in the province have established a name for themselves outside the district.

Verdicchio di Matelica (1967)

This second Verdicchio zone is smaller and more isolated than Castelli di Jesi and produces only a fraction as much wine. But Matelica's token supplies are coveted. Verdicchio from the two zones bears a family resemblance, though the Matelica version seems to wield more weight. That's probably why admirers who remember the past insist that the real Verdicchio – with depth of flavour and staying power from high acidity – came from Matelica. Their views are hard to verify as there has been so little of it in recent years. Fratelli Bisci's wondrous '82 might have settled the issue, if later vintages had kept up the pace. La Monacesca leads the race in Matelica with Verdicchio of consistent quality, though Cavalieri di Benedetti is also progressing rapidly. If these three neighbours manage to hit their stride together, they could move ahead of their competitors from Jesi.

Zone: The high Apennine valley between Fabriano and Camerino and including six other communes in Macerata and Ancona provinces, with top vineyards near the towns of Matelica and Cerreto d'Esi on slopes facing southwest along the Esino river. Dry white, also spumante. Grapes: Verdicchio; Malvasia Toscana/Trebbiano Toscano up to 15%. Yld 91/130, Alc 12, Acd 0.5-0.7.

Vernaccia di Serrapetrona (1971)

Bubbly red from dark Vernaccia was once prominent in the western Marches, but today is rare outside the environs of Serrapetrona, where it has been made since the 15th century. Traditionally sweet, which still seems the most successful style, it may also be dry. But in either case, it has a fairly deep purple crimson colour and a balmy aroma with a bitter edge to its otherwise broad, soft flavour. Attilio Fabrini uses *méthode champenoise* for both types to achieve the most impressive results in a limited and otherwise rustic production.

Zone: Hills around Serrapetrona and parts of the communes of Belforte del Chienti and San Severino Marche in Macerata province. Sparkling dry red, also amabile or dolce. Grapes: Vernaccia di Serrapetrona; Sangiovese/Montepulciano/Ciliegiolo up to 15%. Yld 70/120, Alc 11.5 (amabile or dolce res sugar min 16 gr/l), Acd 0.55.

Bianco dei Colli Maceratesi (1975)

Light and elusive, this white can be refreshing in its infancy.

Zone: Hills not exceeding 450 m above sea level throughout Macerata province and in the commune of Loreto in Ancona. Dry white. Grapes: Trebbiano Toscano at 50-70% with Maceratino; Malvasia Toscana/Verdicchio up to 15%. Yld 98/140, Alc 11, Acd 0.55.

Other wines of note

Attilio Fabrini's Verdicchio Pian delle Mura, both still and sparkling, and Villamagna's Verdicchio di Montanello and Monsanulus stand out from an otherwise uninspiring array of table wines.

ESTATES/GROWERS

Fratelli Bisci, Cerreto d'Esi (AN). Occasionally astonishing Verdicchio proves that the Bisci brothers might have the base on which to build a legend from their vineyards amidst Matelica's high meadows.

Attilio Fabrini, Serrapetrona (MC).

Fabrini draws deftly upon methods old and new in crafting his prized Vernaccia di Serrapetrona. From the 14-ha Pian delle Mura plot near San Severino, he also grows Verdicchio for a worthy *champenoise* and a still vdt, along with a little Bianco dei Colli Maceratesi DOC.

Fattoria dei Cavalieri di Benedetti, Matelica (MC). Improving producer of Verdicchio di Matelica from 18 ha, including the single vineyard Podere Fornacione.

Fattoria La Monacesca, Matelica (MC). Young Aldo Cifola has installed a high-tech cellar on the family estate as part of his ambition to raise his Verdicchio di Matelica to unprecedented levels. Plans call for gradual revision of 18 ha of vineyards through experiments with clones and plant density. Though vinified at Matelica, the wine is bottled at Civitanova Marche.

La Torraccia, Passo Sant'Angelo (MC). Piero Costantini, who runs an *enoteca* in Rome and makes the fine Villa Simone Frascati, also manages to produce a good Rosso Piceno at his estate in the Marches.

San Biagio della LI.RA., Matelica (MC). Verdicchio di Matelica.

Villamagna, Montanello di Macerata. From 15 ha of vines on the ancient estate at the edge of Macerata, Valeria Compagnucci Compagnoni produces perhaps the finest Rosso Piceno, even if its location prevents it from being labelled *superiore*. Her Bianco dei Colli Maceratesi DOC, however, is clearly outclassed by Verdicchio di Montanello and Monsanulus vdt.

COOPERATIVES

CS di Matelica e di Cerreto d'Esi, Matelica (MC). Verdicchio di Matelica.
Produttori Vitivinicoli di Matelica, Matelica (MC). Verdicchio di Matelica.

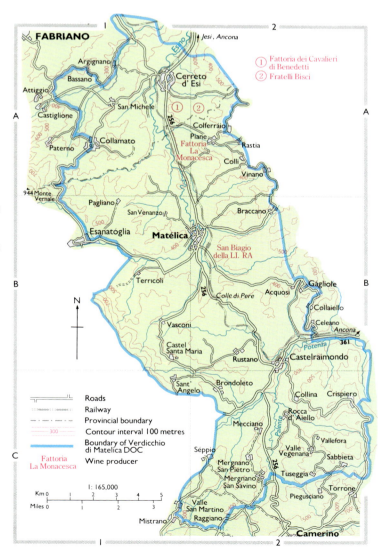

177

Above: the limited quantities of Verdicchio from high vineyards near Matelica can rival the class of the more popular wines from the Castelli di Jesi zone.

Wines of Ascoli Piceno

The stark but stately hills in the province of Ascoli Piceno produce more than half of the Marches' wine, but little of it deserves adulation. The Rosso Piceno DOC zone, which sprawls northwards through much of the region, is *superiore* only in a restricted area east of Ascoli. The white Falerio dei Colli Ascolani makes no claims to superiority.

Rosso Piceno (1968)

The region's largest DOC zone with the wine ranking second to Verdicchio dei Castelli di Jesi in production, though one needs to search for worthy bottles. Sangiovese dominates the blend, but when Rosso Piceno shows class it is usually due to a telling dose of Montepulciano. Sadly, though, that variety is fading in a territory where productivity has proved to be more profitable than prestige. Still Villa Pigna, Cocci Grifoni, and Tattà make *superiore* of good quality for price, though over the last decade the best wine of the name has come from Villamagna, which is nowhere near the alleged promised land.

Zone: Hills between the Adriatic and the Apennines extending from the border with the Abruzzi north past Senigallia in Ascoli Piceno, Macerata, and Ancona provinces,

excluding the DOC zones of Rosso Cònero and Lacrima di Morro d'Alba. Superiore applies to 13 communes in the hills north of the Tronto river between Ascoli and the coast. Dry red, also superiore. Grapes: Sangiovese at least 60%, Montepulciano up to 40%; Passerina/Trebbiano up to 15%. Yld 84/140, Alc 11.5; superiore 12, Acd 0.55-0.8, Ag superiore 1 yr.

Falerio dei Colli Ascolani (1975)

This white might have shown distinction if it had been based on Pecorino, which was once prized locally, and not the all-too-convenient Trebbiano Toscano. Still, it can sometimes be a respectable if skittish fish wine.

Zone: Hills throughout Ascoli Piceno province. Dry white. Grapes: Trebbiano Toscano up to 80%, Passerina/Verdicchio/ Pecorino/Pinot Bianco up to 25%/Malvasia

Toscana up to 7%. Yld 84/140, Alc 11.5, Acd 0.5.

Other wines of note

Villa Pigna's Vellutato, a pure Montepulciano vdt, often outshines its Rosso Piceno DOC. That estate has increased its production of sparkling wines, as have other producers, to meet the growing demand from local restaurants.

ESTATES/GROWERS

Cocci Grifoni, San Savino di Ripatransone (AP). Guido Cocci Grifoni has progressed steadily with Rosso Piceno Superiore and Falerio from 25 ha of vines on the family's handsome estate.

Tattà, Porto San Giorgio (AP). Good Rosso Piceno and Montepulciano vdt from vineyards at Cossignano and Ripatransone.

Vallone, Monsampolo del Tronto (AP). Rosso Piceno Superiore and Falerio.

Villa Pigna, Offida (AP). The

charismatic Costantino Rozzi and brother Elio own this vast 250-ha estate, producing good Rosso Piceno Superiore, the even better Vellutato vdt from Montepulciano, Falerio, and *champenoise* and tank-fermented *spumanti*. Rozzi, industrialist and president of Ascoli's perennial Cinderella soccer club, considers Villa Pigna more a hobby than a business, though winemaker Pasquilino Gabriele takes his work seriously. Costantino Il Grande, as he is known around Ascoli, gives away much of the wine to friends, celebrities, journalists, politicians. "It's my calling card", he says. "Did you know that the President of Italy serves Villa Pigna wines at lunch?"

COOPERATIVES

Consorzio Agrario Provinciale, Ascoli Piceno. Rosso Piceno Superiore and Falerio sold under the trademark Picenum.

Travel Information

RESTAURANTS/HOTELS

Symposium, 61030 Cartoceto (PS). Tel (0721)898320. Lucio Pompili offers innovative cooking and fine wines in an old farmhouse.

Da Ilario, 60015 Falconara Marittima (AN). Tel (071)9160005. Creative dishes and regional wines selected by Ilario Berardi.

Villa Amalia, 60015 Falconara Marittima (AN). Tel (071)912045. Lamberto Ridolfi carefullly selects wines from the Marches and elsewhere to go with Adriatic seafood in both traditional and innovative styles prepared by his wife and his mother Amalia.

Osteria dell'Arancio, 63013 Grottammare (AP). Tel (0735)631059. Light meals or snacks are served with a range of fine wines.

Ristorante Floriani, 62100 Montanello di Macerata. Tel (0733)429267. Tasty country cooking with the wines of adjacent Villamagna.

Emilia, 60020 Portonovo (AN). Tel (071)801145. Fine fish and Verdicchio in an inviting hillside hotel with pool, tennis courts, and good views.

Fortino Napoleonico, 60020 Portonovo (AN). Tel (071)801124. A pentagonal fortress has become a seaside hotel with a fine restaurant managed by Gualberto Compagnucci, recent Italian champion sommelier.

Riccardone's, 60019 Senigallia (AN). Tel (071)64762. Riccardo Gigli matches seafood and other delicacies with the region's top wines.

WINE SHOPS/ENOTECHE

Enoteca Internazionale Bugari, Lungalbula Montello 18, San Benedetto del Tronto (AP). The scholarly Teodoro Bugari combines the best of the Marches and the Abruzzi with an array from elsewhere in a wine library equipped for serious browsing.

Enoteca dei Vini Marchigiani, sponsored by the region, in the historical centre of Jesi.

PLACES OF INTEREST

The Marches' main attraction is its sandy beaches, which though not as commercialized as those around Rimini can be congested all the same. But just across the dunes lie hills with villages linked by winding roads through pastures, woods, and vineyards, providing relief from the crowds. Wine tourism hasn't been developed here yet, but samples are readily available at cellars, shops, or roadside inns. Along the way, each town will have a monument, a relic, or a work of art worth discovering.

Castelli di Jesi. Two wine routes cover the hills of Verdicchio's classic zone, as suggested by Ivano Carotti and Mario Livieri in their guide to the "castles" (or towns) of Jesi. One climbs the rises on the right or south bank of the Esino through San Paolo di Jesi, Staffolo, Cupramontana, Maiolati Spontini, and Castelbellino. The other stays on the left bank with a circuit from Moie up through Montecarotto and Serra de' Conti before returning to the valley at Castelplanio and Serra San Quirico, then climbing again to Arcevia. From there they suggest a visit to the Grotte di Frasassi, one of Italy's most spectacular caverns. Not far away is the other Verdicchio DOC zone of Matelica, nestled picturesquely in the mountains.

Monte Cònero. The vineyards of Rosso Cònero are just part of the attraction of the massif. Also worth visiting are Portonovo with its harbour at the foot of the cliffs and the Badia di San Pietro with views along the Adriatic from Ancona to Loreto and out across the hills to the Apennines.

Urbino. Of all the region's hill towns this is the most artistic. The displays at the Palazzo Ducale and the National Gallery include works by native sons Raffaello Sanzio and Donato Bramante. Nearby is Acqualagna, the busiest autumn white truffle market outside of Alba in Piedmont.

Abruzzi (Abruzzo)

Capital: L'Aquila.
Provinces: L'Aquila (AQ), Chieti (CH), Pescara (PE), Teramo (TE).
Area: 10,749 square kilometres (fourteenth).
Population: 1,250,000 (fourteenth).

Above: the Abruzzi's hills have some of the most prolific vineyards of the peninsula.

The Abruzzi's highlands are not easy to get around in, which may explain why its inhabitants were known as stubborn hill people or gritty mountain folk (here you were one or the other) until the advent of the car and the mass media made them over. They are descended from a miscellany of tribes whose Italianized names still apply in places: Aequi, Marsi, Paeligni, Vestini, Marrucini, and Sabines. The Praetuttii, the Piceni peoples who inhabited the coastal hills, seem to have been the source of the term Aprutium, from which came Abruzzi (Abruzzo in Italian). The wine known as Praetutian was regarded by the Romans as a sort of *grand cru*.

Though hard to unite, the Abruzzesi usually defied later arrivals who attempted to rule them – be they Greeks, Romans, Swabians, Aragonese, or Bourbons. Still, long Spanish dominion imposed from the south registered its effects. In speech, manners, and diet, the Abruzzesi seem closer to their neighbours in the Mezzogiorno than to those across the mountains to the north and west. Viticulture here has much in common with that of Apulia, which lies just across Molise's easy contours. In other words, the growing of grapes in abundance as just another fruit crop still offers more attractive prospects than does the making of premium wine. The shame of it is that the Abruzzi's sunny hills could make outstanding wines, not only from the native Montepulciano but from many other noble vines.

Few winemakers have even tried to produce serious wines; fewer still have succeeded. Though a dozen or so cellars have earned a measure of respect, only one producer has consistently made superior wines that stand the test of time. Edoardo Valentini's Montepulciano may have an occasional rival from a top vintage, but his golden Trebbiano is so patently in a class by itself that it is surrounded by the wildest sort of gossip, not only among rivals but even among admirers. Valentini laughs off rumours as befits a man known as the "Lord of the Vines".

Since farmers here were traditionally grape growers rather than winemakers, most have found it convenient to join cooperatives. These account for about two thirds of the Abruzzi's wine, yet only two such cellars – Cantina Tollo and Casal Thaulero – have made a mark in the quality field. The Abruzzi's average yields are Italy's highest – 133 hectolitres per hectare – though much of the surplus originates south of Chieti, which ranks in the nation's top five provinces in volume of wine.

Growers take advantage of irrigation on those sunny slopes to force production well beyond the limits of quality. Examples of abundance are glaring. In fewer vineyards registered for wine grapes than the Marches, the Abruzzi on average makes two-thirds again more wine. With less than half the vineyards of Tuscany or Piedmont, it often surpasses both

Above: amidst barren landscape near Atri are vineyards for Montepulciano.

in annual output. But behind the excess lies a curious fact: table grapes are permitted here in wines to drink (and not just for distillation).

Although classified wine represents a fraction of the total, there are points to admire in what was Italy's first regional DOC system. The names of the two varietal wines are easy to remember. And if one concedes that Trebbiano d'Abruzzo is rarely memorable and that the pink Cerasuolo is unfortunately scarce, that leaves red Montepulciano almost alone to admire. Some producers would like to have the regional appellation divided into zones to distinguish those of proven worth. Their goal is admirable, even if so far what could be one of Italy's most prominent red wines of class is too often compromised by high yields or inadequate winemaking. Luckily, Montepulciano tends to be pleasant by nature, because for the time being the Abruzzi has little else to offer.

The Abruzzi's Vineyards

Grape growing has long been profitable in the Abruzzi's coastal hills, thanks to prolific vineyards which are now most often expanded in the high canopy *tendone* but before phylloxera were kept mainly low and dense in *alberello*. The admirable native Montepulciano is still by far the leading variety, not only for DOC red and Cerasuolo but also for blending

into northern wines. Trebbiano Toscano has gained favour as a source of Trebbiano d'Abruzzo DOC and in light table wines. The next most planted variety is Sangiovese, which is usually blended with Montepulciano since it rarely performs well on its own.

The province of Chieti achieves some of Italy's most exorbitant yields, not only from Montepulciano and Trebbiano, but also from the table varieties of Regina and Regina dei Vigneti, which are authorized here for wine. Canopies now prevail, except in the high interior and hills to the north where cooler conditions have made vertical training systems with lower yields – and, in theory, superior quality – a must. The traditional *testucchio* (training onto stunted trees) is now only rarely seen in the hills. In the past, numerous local vines were popular, notably the white Campolese and Cococciola, though the few remaining natives now play a minor role in the region's oenology. Montonico (or Mantonico) is believed to have originated in the province of Teramo, though vines of the name are now more often found in Calabria. The white Pecorino of the Marches is called Pecorino Bianco here to distinguish it from the dark variety also called Pecorino. Two centuries ago, various types of Moscato were prominent in sweet wines, but today none is approved in the region. Authorities have made much of experiments with Cabernet and Merlot for reds, Chardonnay, Sauvignon, Pinot Bianco and Grigio, and Riesling for whites, but, despite promise, noteworthy wines have yet to be made from them. The following varieties are associated primarily with the Abruzzi.

Campolese. *See* Trebbiano d'Abruzzo.

Cococciola. Once respected variety plays an auxiliary role in Trebbiano d'Abruzzo.

Montepulciano or **Montepulciano d'Abruzzo**. The name links it confusingly to the Tuscan town that is home to Vino Nobile. But the theory that it was a Sangiovese brought from Tuscany and transmuted over time has been proved false by biochemical analysis, lending weight to the argument that Montepulciano originated in the Abruzzi and was named by Tuscan wool traders. Its red wines are admired for full, mellow qualities due to low acidity, though some are tannic and capable of long ageing. It also makes the cherry pink Cerasuolo. The vine, prominent in the Marches, Molise, Apulia, and Latium, is also gaining favour in the south. Montepulciano ranks seventh among vines planted in Italy with 36,500 hectares (about half in the Abruzzi) and fifth among red varieties after Sangiovese, Barbera, Merlot, and Negroamaro.

Passerina or **Passarina**. The local name for Biancame, this once important blending variety is optional in Trebbiano d'Abruzzo.

Trebbiano d'Abruzzo. Some people say this phantom vine is the same as what was known in the past as Campolese, but that would link it to Apulia's Bombino Bianco, which seems unlikely. Edoardo Valentini, who makes the only distinguished wine of the name, says it was traditionally grown in family vineyards at Loreto Aprutino, where local conditions account for its unique character. Since he guards his vines jealously, ampelographers have not been able to trace its origins. Nor is it certain that the true Trebbiano d'Abruzzo (whatever it might be) is even a Trebbiano.

Other varieties

Abruzzi's official list of vines is fairly extensive, but rarely do outsiders play a prominent role in a wine. Varieties recommended or approved in the Abruzzi include:

For red (or rosé): Barbera, Ciliegiolo, Dolcetto, Maiolica, Malbec (or Malbeck), Merlot, Pinot Nero.

For white: Bombino Bianco, Malvasia del Chianti, Montonico (or Mantonico) Bianco, Mostosa, Pecorino Bianco, Pinot Bianco, Pinot Grigio, Riesling Italico, Riesling Renano, Sylvaner Verde, Tocai Friulano, Traminer Aromatico, Veltliner, Verdicchio Bianco.

The Abruzzi's Wine Zones

The Abruzzi is dominated by the Apennines, which reach their highest peaks in the 2,914-metre Corno Grande in the Gran Sasso d'Italia group and the 2,795-metre Monte Amaro in the Maiella range. The entire region qualifies as an upland of 65 percent mountains and 35 percent hills. Even its few flat stretches – the Tirino valley between Sulmona and Ofena and, most extensively, the Piana di Fucino – are comfortably above sea level. The region is physically walled off by the Abruzzesi Apennines from Latium and Umbria to the west and divided by the Tronto river and its gaping valley from the Marches to the north. Conditions vary from cool and damp in the lofty interior, which feels the Mediterranean influences from both sides, to steadily warmer and drier towards the 129 kilometres of Adriatic coast. Some vines grow in high places, where warm, sunny days and cool nights can heighten wines' aromas. But most vineyards are planted in tapered hills of calcareous clay along the Adriatic, which provides ventilation even during the usual summer drought. Since the emphasis is on quantity, vineyards are concentrated in the gentle coastal hills of Chieti province to the southeast, where irrigated canopies proliferate in the heat.

Teramo province

The northern province boasts favourable conditions for Montepulciano with soils of siliceous clay, rich in lime and iron. Wines from the hills between the Tronto and Vibrata valleys around Torano Nuovo, Controguerra, Ancarano, Colonella, Corropoli, and Nereto are usually bigger than the rest in colour, body, alcohol, and tannins, though they can be slow to mature. The hills between Teramo and Roseto degli Abruzzi around Notaresco and Morro d'Oro produce slightly lighter Montepulciano. Growers concerned about quality often prefer vertical training to the canopied *tendone*, which prevails along the coast. Good white wines were reputedly made here in the past, though today's Trebbiano gives little evidence of potential.

Pescara province

The slopes around Città Sant'Angelo and the higher hills at Penne have been praised for their wines, though the best results are regularly achieved at Loreto Aprutino by Valentini. His triumphs with Trebbiano and Montepulciano may be due as much to a personal style of

winemaking as to advantages of the moderately cool hill climate and calcareous clay soil. To the south, slopes of sandy clay and gravel along the Pescara river valley at Scafa, Torre de' Passeri, Tocco da Casauria, and Bolognano also show aptitude for fine Montepulciano.

Chieti province

Vast stretches of canopied vines in the often loose, pebbly clay soil of the coastal hills behind Ortona between Tollo and Lanciano are among Italy's most productive. But few producers make agreeable wines from Montepulciano and Trebbiano. Wines from the Agro di Vasto between the Sangro and Trigno rivers may have commercial value but rarely show interesting flavour in a hot, dry area that seems best suited to table grapes.

L'Aquila province

Viticulture in the Apennines is a fading craft, even if the southern slopes of the Morrone range in the Peligna valley and the stony terraces around Navelli and Ofena have long been famous for fresh, perfumed Cerasuolo. Remaining vines, whether head trained, vertical, or trellised are kept low to soak up heat from the gravelly, calcareous and dolomitic soils, though sheltered spots at Ofena can get so hot that it is known as the *forno* (oven) of the Abruzzi. The rarefied conditions of the high Fucino plain, the Marsica plateau, and the Aterno river valley favour interesting wines, but methods are often rustic.

Wines of the Abruzzi

Montepulciano d'Abruzzo (1968)

Producers who get things right can make rather majestic Montepulciano, sometimes suited to long ageing. At best it has a deep ruby colour with a robust structure and ample tannins softened by a supple roundness rare in central Italian reds. The scarce Cerasuolo can be one of Italy's more convincing rosés, and perhaps the only wine that can stand up to the Abruzzi's piquant cuisine, with dishes such as *maccheroni* laced with hot peppers or vegetable soup simmered with vinegar and onions.

Zone: Slopes in all four provinces of the Abruzzi, though vineyards may not be higher than 500 m above sea level, except for those facing directly south, which may be up to 600 m. Though most Montepulciano comes from Chieti, the finest red versions originate in Teramo and Pescara provinces, and the limited quantities of good Cerasuolo come from high valleys around L'Aquila. Dry red, also vecchio. Grapes: Montepulciano; Sangiovese up to 15%. Yld 98/140, Alc 12; vecchio 13.5, Acd 0.5-0.75, Ag 4 mths; vecchio 2 yrs.

Cerasuolo Dry rosé. Grapes: As rosso. Yld 98/140, Alc 12, Acd 0.5-0.75.

Trebbiano d'Abruzzo (1972)

Most examples of this DOC fall into the stereotype of Trebbiano as a lacklustre white to drink young and cold with seafood. Then there's that wine from Valentini which seems to have everything a Trebbiano isn't supposed to have: colour, body, complex aromas, depth and length of flavours, and an uncanny capacity to age. For lack of anything to compare it with hereabouts, it is often likened to white Burgundy which it resembles more in class than personality.

Zone: Slopes in all four provinces, though vineyards may range higher than those of Montepulciano d'Abruzzo, even if qualitative differences from one place to another are less discernible. Dry white. Grapes: Trebbiano d'Abruzzo and/or Trebbiano Toscano; Malvasia Toscana/Cococciola/Passerina (Biancame) up to 15%. Yld 122/175, Alc 11.5, Acd 0.5.

Other wines of note

The predominance of Montepulciano and variations on Trebbiano have left little room for novelties in the Abruzzi, even if every cellar of any size or ambition makes table wines and something bubbly for local consumption. The most important are listed with producers. The tradition of sweet wines from Moscato has practically expired, as has the once thriving *vin cotto* (cooked wine) made by boiling down musts and fermenting them with freshly pressed grapes to achieve a syrupy liquid of burnished amber colour and caramel-like flavour. Though *vin cotto* has been banned from sale, it is still occasionally savoured in homes as a *digestivo*.

Left: Emidio Pepe ages Montepulciano and Trebbiano entirely in bottles rather than casks at the cellars of his estate at Torano Nuovo.

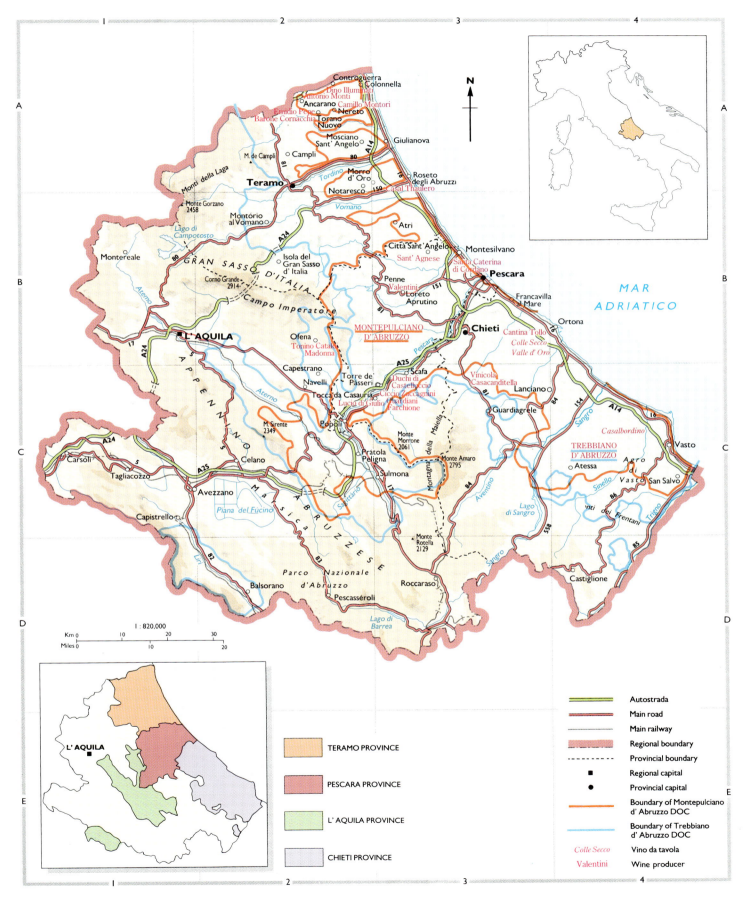

Controguerra
Colonnella
Dino Illuminati
Antonio Monti
Ancarano   Camillo Montori
Emidio Pepe   Nereto
Barone Cornacchia   Torano
Nuovo
Mosciano
Sant' Angelo
Giulianova
M. de Campli   Campli
80
A14
Morro
d'Oro
Roseto
degli Abruzzi
Tordino
Teramo
150
Casal Thaulero
Notaresco
16
Monte Gorzano
2458
Montório
al Vomano
Vomano
Monti della Laga
81
A24
Atri
Lago di
Campotosto
Isola del
Gran Sasso
d' Italia
Citta Sant' Angelo
Montesilvano
80
GRAN SASSO D'ITALIA
Sant' Agnese
Santa Caterina
di Cordiano
Montereale
Corno Grande
2914
Campo Imperatore
Penne
Valentini
Pescara
151
MAR
ADRIATICO
Aterno
Loreto
Aprutino
Francavilla
al Mare
L'AQUILA
Ofena
Tonino Cataldi
Madonna
MONTEPULCIANO
D'ABRUZZO
81
Chieti
Ortona
17
A24
Capestrano
Navelli
Torre de' Passeri
Pescara
Cantina Tollo
Colle Secco
Valle d' Oro
Aterno
Tocca da Casauria
A25
Scafa
Duchi di
Castelluccio
Ciccio Zaccagnini
Lucio di Giulio   Guardiani
Farchione
Vínicola
Casacanditella
Lanciano
84
154
A14
APPENNINO
M. Sirente
2349
Popoli
Monte
Morrone
2061
Guardiagrele
16
Casalbordino
Carsoli
A24
5
Celano
A25
Pratola
Peligna
Montagna della Maiella
Monte Amaro
2795
TREBBIANO
D'ABRUZZO
Vasto
Atessa   Agro
di
Vasto
San Salvo
Tagliacozzo
MARSICA
Avezzano
Sulmona
Aventino
84
Sangro
Sinello
Monti dei Frentani
Trigno
Piana del Fúcino
Sagittario
17
Lago
di Sangro
86
Capistrello
Liri
82
ABRUZZESE
83
Monte Rotella
2129
558
Sangro
85
Castiglione
Balsorano
Parco   Nazionale
d'Abruzzo
Roccaraso
Pescassèroli
Lago di
Barrea

1 : 820,000

Km 0   10   20   30
Miles 0   10   20

N

	TERAMO PROVINCE
	PESCARA PROVINCE
	L' AQUILA PROVINCE
	CHIETI PROVINCE

L'AQUILA

	Autostrada
	Main road
	Main railway
	Regional boundary
	Provincial boundary
■	Regional capital
●	Provincial capital
	Boundary of Montepulciano d' Abruzzo DOC
	Boundary of Trebbiano d' Abruzzo DOC
Colle Secco	Vino da tavola
Valentini	Wine producer

ESTATES/GROWERS

Barone Cornacchia, Torano Nuovo (TE). Traditional DOCs from 30 ha.
Tonino Cataldi Madonna, Ofena (AQ). Tiny production of Montepulciano DOC includes a fine Cerasuolo.
Lucio Di Giulio, Tocco di Casauria (PE). Montepulciano DOC Cantalupo.
Duchi di Castelluccio, Scafa (PE). Montepulciano and Trebbiano DOC.
Guardiani Farchione, Tocco di Casauria (PE). Montepulciano DOC.
Dino Illuminati, Contraguerra (TE). From 60 ha of the Fattoria Nicò comes a complete range of DOC, along with vdt white Ciafré and red Nicò, fizzy Nicolino, and the *champenoise* Diamante d'Abruzzo.
Antonio Monti, Contraguerra (TE). Good Montepulciano DOC.
Camillo Montori, Contraguerra (TE). From 30 ha of vines an admirable range topped by the Poderi di Fonte Cupra Montepulciano DOC.
Emidio Pepe, Torano Nuovo (TE). Sometimes monumental Montepulciano DOC and uncommon Trebbiano made by Pepe's singular methods. This involves crushing grapes by foot and ageing wines entirely in bottle.
Sant'Agnese, Città Sant'Angelo (PE). Montepulciano DOC and vdt.
Santa Caterina di Cordano, Montesilvano Colle (PE). Montepulciano.
Valentini, Loreto Aprutino (PE). From about 60 ha of vines in places called Castelluccio, Camposacro, and Colle Cavaliere, Edoardo Valentini makes sumptuous aged Montepulciano, hearty Cerasuolo, and perhaps the only Trebbiano ever described as great. His wines' unbending individuality begins in the vineyards, where he devised his own style of *tendone*, after trying various methods. Valentini lives with his vines and wines in a relationship so intimate that he sometimes seems reluctant to part with bottles. The average of 10,000 Montepulciano, 25,000 Trebbiano, and 5,000 Cerasuolo is roughly 5% of potential (most grapes are sold). In 1989, he still offered '77 and '79 Montepulciano and had switched from '84 to '85 Trebbiano. He records every nuance of his eccentric operation in hand-written ledgers piled in the studio of his family *palazzo*, whose otherwise stately hallways and staircases are lined with stacks of bottles from vintages waiting to be ready. In the cellars underneath he hones wines through processes that he vows are based as much on ancient Roman knowhow as on anything he has learned from modern texts.
Ciccio Zaccagnani, Bolognano (PE). A small but increasingly admired estate run by Marcello Zaccagnini, whose Castello di Salle has emerged in the front ranks of the Abruzzi's Montepulciano. He also makes a rare Nebbiolo vdt known as Capsico.

WINE HOUSES/MERCHANTS

Vinicola Casacanditella, Casacanditella (CH). Giuseppe Di Camillo strives for modern styles in Montepulciano DOC Rosso and Rosa della Quercia, as well as vdt known as Angelo Bianco and Rosso.

COOPERATIVES

Casal Thaulero, Roseto degli Abruzzi (TE). Winemaker Giulio Silvestri achieves sound quality in Montepulciano DOC, including the special bottlings of Orsetto Oro. Abbazia di Propezzano vdt is a pure Montepulciano aged in small barrels.
Cantina Tollo, Tollo (CH). Constant progress under oenologist Umberto Svizzeri has made this large cooperative a model of reliability with highly drinkable Montepulciano (Rocca Ventosa stands out) and Trebbiano DOCs, plus a range of decent vdt under the Valle d'Oro and Colle Secco labels.

Travel Information

RESTAURANTS

Venturini, 66100 Chieti. Tel (0871)65863. Deft use of vegetables in imaginative Abruzzesi dishes. Good wine list.
Beccaceci, 64022 Giulianova Lido (TE). Tel (085)8003550. Temple of seafood in a popular Adriatic resort.
Tre Marie, Via Tre Marie 3, 67100 L'Aquila. Tel (0862)20191. The capital's monument to the Abruzzo's food and wines.
La Bilancia, 65014 Loreto Aprutino (PE). Tel (085)8289321. Hearty pasta and grilled meats in a rustic setting.
Il Corsaro, 66054 Porto di Vasto (CH). Tel (0873)50113. Claudio and Michela Crisci serve quintessential seafood and choice white wines in a clandestinely romantic seaside setting.

WINE SHOPS/ENOTECHE

Enoteca Templi Romani, Via Priscilla 13, 66100 Chieti. Adriano Scioli and Roberta Giannini select wines from the Abruzzi and elsewhere with uncompromising rigidity.

PLACES OF INTEREST

The Abruzzi has treasures of art and architecture scattered through its hill towns and mountain villages, monasteries, abbeys, and country churches. The mountains are the prime tourist attraction: skiing or hiking on the Gran Sasso or Maiella massifs, which are more or less accessible from the lofty scenic capital of L'Aquila. Spotting Italy's few remaining wolves and bears in the Abruzzi National Park may inspire some, but searching out the few remaining mountain wines could be even more of a challenge. Look for bracingly rustic Cerasuolo around the villages of Navelli and Ofena. Adriatic resorts – some with sandy beaches, some set on rocky promontories or cliffs – can be relaxing, if you avoid the August crush.

Far left: Montepulciano d'Abruzzo grapes. Left: Edoardo Valentini is known as the Abruzzi's "Lord of the Vines".

Molise

Capital: Campobasso.
Provinces: Campobasso (CB), Isernia (IS).
Area: 4,438 square kilometres (nineteenth).
Population: 334,000 (nineteenth).

Molise, which until 1963 was an appendix of the Abruzzi, is still regarded as an afterthought. The region has been so habitually neglected, that even the origins of its name are uncertain – though one version is that it came from a prominent early medieval family. Evidence exists that people have inhabited these hills for 700,000 years. The Samnites, whose Oscan language was spoken through much of the southern peninsula before the Romans finally conquered them, originated around Isernia in what are known as the Sannio hills.

References to the wines of Sannio date back to Pliny the Elder, but little of note seems to have come out of Molise's vineyards since. Through the ages the hill people kept their rustic wines to themselves. The advent of DOCs Biferno and Pentro added official status in the 1980s, a step up from the almost total obscurity of a decade earlier. But considering the favourable conditions for vines on the sunny hillsides between the Apennines and the Adriatic, ample room remains for improvement.

A single estate, Masseria Di Majo Norante, has given Molise a dot on modern Italy's wine map. Its national (and to some extent international) status might seem an anomaly, since the vineyards are located south of Termoli in hot, fertile plains previously considered unsuitable for viticulture. But admirable cellar techniques have overcome the odds to produce wines that are rarely matched for class in more prodigious neighbouring regions. Few other growers seem to have a clear idea of what premium production involves. So wines that aren't consumed locally are often destined for the blending vats of Abruzzi or Apulia.

Molise's DOC zones reflect a provincial division – Biferno in Campobasso and Pentro in Isernia. Biferno is the river that flows northeastwards through Campobasso province. The name Pentro derives from the Pentri, a Samnite tribe that dominated Isernia's hills.

Molise's Vineyards

As a slowly crumbling bastion of family hill farming, Molise has some rustic vines of its own, though their names are no longer recorded in official annals. Vineyards are so fragmented – more than 90 percent cover less than half a hectare and only two estates are reported to have more than 20 – that it's difficult to say what grows where and in what quantities. Montepulciano is, however, known to hold a commanding lead among red wine varieties over Sangiovese, Barbera, Bombino Rosso, and Aglianico. Trebbiano Toscano dominates whites, followed by Bombino Bianco, Malvasia Bianca, and the officially ignored Falanghina.

Most vineyards are now planted in *tendone*, which prevails in new plantings along the coast, where viticulture has expanded, as well as in the hills, where trellises have largely replaced traditional *alberello*.

Other varieties recommended or approved in Molise include:
For red (or rosé): Bovale Grande, Cabernet Franc, Cabernet Sauvignon, Ciliegiolo, Pinot Nero.
For white: Incrocio Manzoni 6.0.13, Garganega, Malvasia del Chianti, Moscato Bianco, Pinot Bianco, Pinot Grigio, Riesling Italico, Riesling Renano, Sauvignon, Sylvaner Verde, Traminer Aromatico, Veltliner.

Molise's Wine Zones

Much of Molise's interior is the rugged and stark Sannio range of the Apennines, which forms a watershed between the Adriatic and the Tyrrhenian. The Apennines reach a height of 2,000 metres in the Matese range on the western border with Latium in the province of Isernia, where the climate is relatively cool and damp, but the high plain towards Venafro opens into Campania's Volturno valley, which feels the warming Tyrrhenian influence. To the northeast, the Trigno, Biferno, and Fortore rivers have tapered the Frentani and Daunia hills into gentle slopes enjoying a mild climate in the province of Campobasso. The short stretch of coastal plain near Termoli adjoins Apulia's Capitanata, which can be witheringly hot and dry in summer. Although more than half of the region is mountainous, the hills boast auspicious but largely neglected vineyard sites. Most recent plantings have been in fertile coastal flats.

Isernia province

Modern viticulture has yet to develop in the province of Isernia with its unknown Pentro DOC. Clay and schist contain calcareous deposits in the Sannio hills, though the valleys along the upper Sangro, Trigno, and Verrino streams to the north and the plains formed by the Volturno and

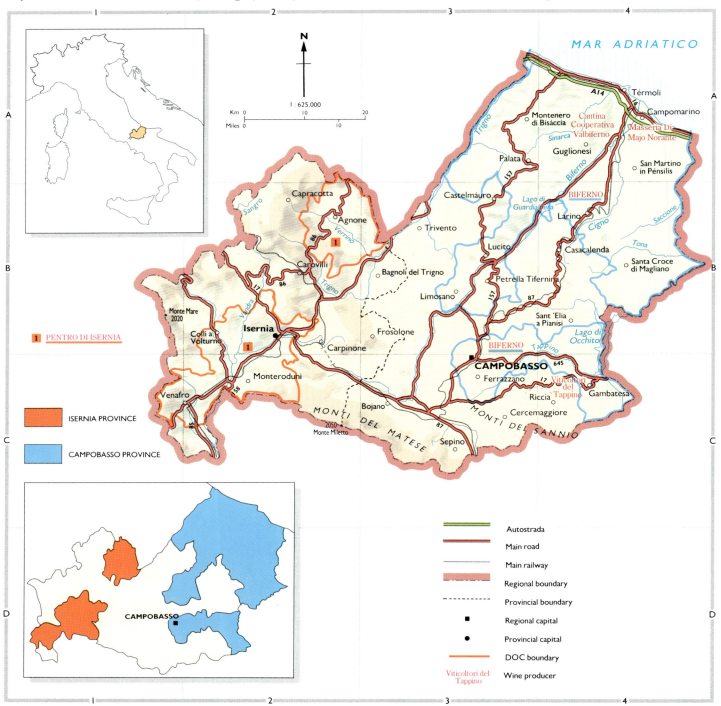

1 PENTRO DI ISERNIA

ISERNIA PROVINCE

CAMPOBASSO PROVINCE

────	Autostrada
────	Main road
────	Main railway
────	Regional boundary
- - - -	Provincial boundary
■	Regional capital
●	Provincial capital
────	DOC boundary
Viticoltori del Tappino	Wine producer

its tributaries to the south have deposits of alluvial sand and gravel. Summers are mild and dry, but winters can be bitterly cold.

Campobasso province

The lower hills of Campobasso province are fairly uniform in shape and terrain – mixtures of clay, sand, and calcareous rock – well suited to premium wine. But despite the advent of Biferno DOC, quality has yet to emerge on a notable scale. The climate is mild in the interior, becoming hot and dry near the coast. Reservoirs on the Biferno and Fortore rivers provide irrigation for trellised vines in the sandy clay of the alluvial plains. Most impressive results so far have come from red Montepulciano, though white varieties could no doubt thrive in the hills.

Travel Information

RESTAURANTS/HOTELS

Squalo Blù, 86039 Termoli (CB). Tel (0875)83203. One of the best seafood restaurants along the Adriatic coast and improving, thanks to the genial cooking of Bobo and Rita Vincenzi and smart choice of wines by Mario D'Aurizio.

PLACES OF INTEREST

Molise might be considered a haven for escapists. Even the sandy Adriatic beaches are rarely crowded. The hills and mountains are blessedly free of tourist traffic all year round. Remnants of Samnite and Roman civilizations can be witnessed at Sepino, Venafro, Larino, and Pietrabbondante.

Above: harvest on the leading Di Majo Norante estate at Campomarino.

Wines of Molise

Biferno (1983)

The stil limited output indicates good potential in the hills, though so far the only wines of note come from the seaside plains at Campomarino, where Di Majo Norante's Rosso is outstanding. The rosé might prove to be refreshing but there is little hope for anything out of the ordinary from the white.

Zone: In 42 communes in Campobasso province coursed by the Biferno river in four separate areas of hills no higher than 500 m for red and rosé, and 600 m for white.

Bianco Dry white. Grapes: Trebbiano Toscano 65-70%, Bombino Bianco 25-30%, Malvasia Toscana 5-10%. Yld 78/120, Alc 10.5, Acd 0.6.

Rosso Dry red, also riserva. Grapes: Montepulciano 60-70%, Trebbiano Toscano 15-20%, Aglianico 15-20%; other varieties up to 5%. Yld 84/120, Alc 11.5; riserva 13, Acd 0.5, Ag riserva 3 yrs.

Rosato Dry rosé. Grapes: As rosso. Yld 60/120, Alc 11.5, Acd 0.6.

Pentro di Isernia or Pentro (1984)

So far no producers have classified their wines as Pentro DOC, so any evidence of modern quality is a well-kept local secret.

Zone: Hills of two separate areas, one in the high Verrino valley to the north, the other in the upper Volturno valley to the southwest in 16 communes in Isernia province.

Bianco Dry white. Grapes: Trebbiano Toscano 60-70%, Bombino Bianco 30-40%; other varieties up to 10%. Yld 71/110, Alc 10.5, Acd 0.6.

Rosso Dry red. Grapes: Montepulciano 45-55%, Sangiovese 45-55%; other varieties up to 10%. Yld 77/110, Alcl 11, Acd 0.5.

Rosato Dry rosé. Grapes: As rosso. Yld 55/110, Alc 11, Acd 0.6.

Other wines of note

The region's most promising wines seem destined to remain outside DOC: Di Majo Norante's Montepulciano del Molise, Ramitello Bianco from Falanghina, and an experimental red from Aglianico. The Vernaccia di San Gimignano grape has proved to be clearly superior to Trebbiano in Vernaccia di Serra Meccaglia. Most other unclassified wines, including the occasional bubbly and sweet examples, are for local consumption.

ESTATES/GROWERS

Masseria Di Majo Norante-Ramitello, Campomarino (CB). This vast property owned by Luigi Di Majo and managed by son Alessio contains the only established private winery in Molise. Selections from 50 ha of irrigated vines result in 200,000 bottles a year of wine whose unexpected style bears the stamp of consultant Giorgio Grai. The estate range is split between the Molì brand for Biferno DOC Bianco and Rosso and the Ramitello brand with the prestigious Montepulciano del Molise riserva vdt. Ramitello Rosso is a Biferno DOC, whose full, supple qualities derive from Montepulciano. Ramitello Bianco vdt comes from Falanghina, one of the south's few dry whites of real character. Due out is a red from Aglianico, which showed intense aroma and flavour from early vintages.

COOPERATIVES

VI.TA.-Viticoltori del Tappino, Gambatesa (CB). Ambitious group produces Biferno DOC with the Serra Meccaglia and Rocca del Falco brands, as well as Vernaccia di Serra Meccaglia white and other vdt and *spumante*.
Cantina Cooperativa Valbiferno, Guglionesi (CB). Biferno DOC and vdt.

Above: the medieval town of Pitigliano in Tuscany's Grosseto province is known for its white wine.

Central Tyrrhenian

The Apennines arch gracefully away from the Tyrrhenian over Tuscany, Umbria, and Latium, making space for an aggregate of hills whose lack of uniformity only begins to explain their splendour. The Etruscans, the early vintners, made the most of the rocky rises, but the Romans knew better, shunning them in favour of warmer plains. Only later was it realized that the hills between Rome and Florence are as well endowed for fine wines as any of the peninsula. But vines need to be treated with dedication and restraint, sacrifices that few growers were willing to make. That probably explains why Italy's heartland, its perennial wellspring of the arts, politics, and religion, has not always lived up to expectations with wine.

Even today amidst the chorus of oaths to quality, performances in the Central Tyrrhenian regions are glaringly uneven. Sometimes it seems as if Tuscans alone are convinced that excellence pays. They have surged to the forefront of Italian oenology by shedding the burden of tradition and first imitating, then inventing modern styles of wine. Their personalized table wines have drawn attention to a region whose premium production comes largely from estates. But novelty isn't all, for the key to success has been the improved class of the venerable reds: Chianti, Brunello di Montalcino, Vino Nobile, and Carmignano. The revival even owes something to group spirit, a trait that had never been considered Tuscan.

Scattered achievements elsewhere are for the most part individual. Latium's wines, mainly white along the lines of Frascati, retain a bland image that seems all too easy to explain. The region, whose production is centred in cooperatives, has only three-quarters as much vineyard space as Tuscany, yet makes 40 percent more wine, the most of central Italy. Even Umbrians, who on a smaller scale could match Tuscan prowess, have been rather lax, though Orvieto has regained some of its old status. Production figures illustrate the differences. Tuscany classifies more than a third of its wine as DOC, Umbria less than a sixth, and Latium less than a tenth.

But, then, each region has habitually gone its own way. Latium has been eternally dominated by Rome, the ancient and modern capital of Italy and Catholicism. Tuscany, from the Florence of the Medici, engendered the Renaissance that enlightened the western world. Umbria, the "green heart of Italy", is the home of Francis of Assisi, the nation's

patron saint. Yet, despite the apparent spiritual ties, the three regions probably had more in common in Roman or even Etruscan times than they do today.

The core of Etruscan territory was between the Arno and Tiber rivers and the sea, from where they moved north across the Apennines and south to rival the Greek colonists in Campania. The Romans, who subdued and absorbed them, honoured them in names. Tuscany came from Tuscia, Latin for Etruria. Tyrrhenian signifies the Etruscan sea. They also left their mark in a type of viticulture that favoured abundance. Much of the picturesque back country is still adorned by vines draped over stunted willows and poplars surrounding planted fields. Big yields are impractical on steep and stony slopes, which in the interior – much of Umbria and Tuscany's central hills – can also be cool and damp. Still, where abundance was possible, mainly in the fertile and rather flat country south of Rome, it had long been envied.

Other Etruscan legacies, though accounts don't all agree, seem to be Trebbiano and Sangiovese, vines whose vigour has helped them conquer the peninsula. Trebbiano, whatever its merits doesn't aim at the heights. The various Malvasias regularly planted alongside it can show character, both in dry wines and Vin Santo. Umbria's Grechetto shows distinctive style. But safer bets for white wines are Chardonnay, Sauvignon, and Pinots, which are gaining ground everywhere.

Sangiovese, on the other hand, is often described as noble, at least in its clones of Brunello, Sangioveto, and Prugnolo Gentile, all natives of Tuscany. Elsewhere – with exceptions in Umbria and Romagna – Sangiovese tends to be a workaday variety, useful mainly for blending.

Above: the Tuscan countryside has a look of self-sufficiency about it on farms that still supply most of their owner's needs, from livestock, fruit, and vegetables to olive oil and wine.

Umbria's Sagrantino and Latium's Cesanese can outclass it on their home grounds. Montepulciano d'Abruzzo is also widely planted, though it rarely performs as well on the Tyrrhenian side of the Apennines as it does on the Adriatic. The problem is that conditions can vary so radically on these irregular rises that what thrives in one vineyard may wither in a plot just over the hill.

The often fickle showings of native red varieties have hastened the rise of Cabernet Sauvignon and, more recently, Merlot. Cabernet has done well in all three regions in wines of depth and balance with little of the grassy, bitter traits that mar it in much of northern Italy. The vine has adjusted so well to parts of Tuscany that, ironic as it seems, growers may be closer to realizing its upper limits than they are with Sangiovese. Winemaking has improved overall in a way that has left little to chance in the cellars, though room remains for more artistry. But the real deterrent to class in the Central Tyrrhenian regions has been a casual approach to viticulture. The challenge facing growers who don't opt for the easy route with Cabernet and Chardonnay, is to select native vines that harmonize with the habitat. For in the hills of the heartland the most one could ask of a wine is that it equal its surroundings.

APPENNINO

Pontremoli

Massa

Pietrasanta

Montecatini Terme

Pistoia

Viareggio

Lucca

Prato

Campi Bisenzio

Sesto Fiorentino

San Giuliano Terme

Pisa

Empoli

Scandicci

Firenze

Cascina

Pontedera

Arno

Livorno

Poggibonsi

Montevarchi

Sansepolcro

Arezzo

Città di Castello

Rosignano Marittimo

TOSCANA

Cécina

Colline Metallifere

Siena

Cortona

Tevere

Chiascio

San Vincenzo

Perugia

Assisi

Lago Trasimeno

Foligno

UMBRIA

Nera

Chiana

Todi

Spoleto

Grosseto

Fiora

Orvieto

Tevere

Golfo di Follónica

Isola d' Elba

Bruna

Ombrone

Albegna

Lago di Bolsena

Terni

Velino

Archipelago Toscano

Isola Pianosa

Montefiascone

Rieti

Lago del Salto

Maremma

Viterbo

Monti Sabini

Isola di Montecristo

Isola del Giglio

Marta

Lago di Vico

Turano

Isola di Giannutri

Lago di Bracciano

Civitavecchia

Monterotondo

ROMA

Tivoli

Aniene

MAR

TIRRENO

LAZIO

Marino

Albano Laziale

Velletri

Sora

Pomézia

Cisterna di Latina

Monti Lepini

Aprília

Frosinone

Anzio

Latina

Cassino

Liri

Fórmia

Lago di Sabaudia

Terracina

Gaeta

Golfo di Gaeta

Legend:
- Autostrada
- Main road
- Main railway
- Regional boundary
- ■ Regional capital
- ● Provincial capital

N

1 : 1,675,000

Km 0   25   50   75

Miles 0   25   50

Tuscany (Toscana)

Capital: Firenze (Florence).
Provinces: Arezzo (AR), Firenze (FI), Grosseto (GR), Livorno (LI), Lucca (LU), Massa Carrara (MS), Pisa (PI), Pistoia (PT), Siena (SI).
Area: 22,992 square kilometres (fifth).
Population: 3,577,000 (ninth).

Above: the landscape south of Siena has vast sweeps of vineyards enclosed by hills.

After eras of complacently turning out Chianti, Tuscany has become Italy's most dynamic innovator in wine. The focus of change is in the hills of Florence and Siena, in vineyards interspersed with olive groves and woods around castles and villas where man and nature harmonize in the archetypal Italian landscape. The renaissance, as it is often described, began as Tuscans realized that their patriarchal wine industry was impossibly out of date, though much of the money and drive behind it have come from outside. Estates large and small have changed hands as oenologists trained in Piedmont or the Venezie, or even France or California, meet a new demand for artistic styling in wines, whether they be originals or regenerated classics.

Change has come at the expense of a once proud heritage built around Chianti, whose straw flask made the world aware that Italy, too, in its peculiar way was a wine country. The *fiasco* like the folklore has faded. Chianti remains the nucleus of Tuscan viniculture, still the most voluminous of Italy's classified wines. But attention has shifted to the rise of Brunello di Montalcino, to the resurrection of Vino Nobile di Montepulciano, to the rejuvenation of whites such as Vernaccia di San Gimignano, perhaps most of all to the surge of those arrogantly independent table wines sometimes known as "Super Tuscans".

Members of a wine establishment who grew up praising Sangiovese and Trebbiano and the blessings of ancient casks now compare notes on Cabernet and Chardonnay and degrees of "toast" of the French *barriques* that mount steadily in their cellars. But the revolution has also caused soul searching among Tuscans, who can justly state that at times in history their oenology was second to none. The role of prominent families in wine attests to an epic past. Ricasoli traces its tradition to 1141, Frescobaldi to 1300. Antinori has 600 years behind its reputation as Italy's most admired modern wine house.

The Etruscans built a flourishing wine trade here which the Romans, who preferred heavier stuff from the south, let slide before generations of invaders obliterated the cult of Bacchus. Monks reawakened viticulture in the wooded hills, as wine became a part of everyday life in the medieval towns and burgeoning cities of Florence, Siena, Pisa, Lucca, and Arezzo. The spread of the Renaissance from Florence through Europe radiated Tuscan wines. Exports of "Florence Red" and Vermiglio were complemented by sweet whites, including the prized Vin Santo. Francesco Redi's dithyrambic ode *Bacchus in Tuscany* (1685) flattered them all with enduring endorsements, though rarely so effusive as fellow poet Fulvio Testi's tribute to the "Etruscan Chianti" that "kisses you and bites you and makes you shed sweet tears".

In 1716, the Grand Duchy of Tuscany decreed what may have been Europe's first official wine zones in Carmignano, Chianti, Pomino, and Val d'Arno di Sopra. The Georgofili Academy and the scholar Giovan Cosimo Villifranchi advanced methods of viticulture, fermentation, and ageing to levels unsurpassed anywhere. But in the nineteenth century, despite Bettino Ricasoli's new designs for Chianti and Ferruccio Biondi Santi's creation of Brunello di Montalcino, the French took a lead in prestige that they never relinquished. Instead of blossoming into Italy's Bordeaux, as admirers aspired, Chianti, corrupted by popular appeal, became the worldwide symbol of *vino* in all its rambunctious excess.

Demand prompted growers to increase white varieties in the blend with Sangiovese, while bottlers stretched volume with wine from other places. A decade ago, after an era of expansion, Chianti lapsed into a crisis as supply exceeded demand. Remedial measures, marked by the advent of DOCG, cut volume and redirected the best of Chianti back towards respectability. But recovery is far from complete. It may be argued that vineyards should never have spread beyond the original Chianti in the Classico zone near Siena. The change of habitat altered character almost as much as did opportunistic blending by bottlers. But questions of origin are by now academic. Chianti is officially sanctioned in seven zones that span Tuscany's interior, taking in Carmignano, Pomino, Rufina, San Gimignano, Montepulciano, and Montalcino, where the historical value of other wines has been reasserted.

In an era of of sometimes frantic diversification, few producers rely on Chianti alone. Large wineries promote popular items: white Galestro, ruby-hued *novello*, refrigerator red Sarmento. But assembly line wines have limits in a region whose modest yields on rugged contours rank it only eighth in quantity. Many fine wines are made by estates with stately villas fashioned from abbeys, fortresses, or farmhouses.

The emphasis on quality shines through the statistics. Tuscany ranks second to the Veneto in volume of classified wines and boasts three of the nation's six DOCGs in Chianti, Brunello, and Vino Nobile. Carmignano and Pomino have re-emerged as elite DOCs, while more zones have been sanctioned beyond the prime central hills to cover the region's coastal flank from the northwest around Massa-Carrara and Lucca down past Pisa and Livorno to the island of Elba and Grosseto's Maremma.

Brunello, backed by legends of longevity and high prices, has risen to challenge Barolo as the king of Italian reds. Vino Nobile, which the poet Redi proclaimed king of all wines, has begun to live up to its name again after decades of degeneracy. But, despite heavy stakes in their futures, markets for these regal reds have proved painstaking to build. Italians, who seem non-plussed by DOCG, have little time for monarchs, so producers have turned abroad. But foreigners, if impressed by improved quality, seem perplexed by rising prices and a lack of clear guidelines to style and type. Since many estates and vineyards in Tuscany's official zones are new or radically revised, their real values are still unknown.

Cult wines, meanwhile, triumph. Sassicaia, a pure Cabernet with no official status, may have done more to convince the world that Italy can make noble red wines than have the majestic Brunellos and Barolos that foreign palates sometimes struggle to understand. Sassicaia's success inspired Antinori's Sangiovese-Cabernet blend of Tignanello, which launched a new style of red wine. They in turn led to Cabernet-Sangiovese blends and the ever more stylish pure Sangiovese or Sangioveto, as well as Merlot, Pinot Noir, and whites from Chardonnay, Sauvignon, Vernaccia, and even Trebbiano – all, of course, in *barriques*.

Many estates, even tiny ones, have hired one of the new itinerant winemakers to create a *vino da tavola* from a special vineyard or select batches of grapes. They give it a catchy name, adorn it with the ultimate in heavy bottles, designer labels, and wooden crates, and price it at the top of the list, well above DOCG Chianti. A few superb wines have emerged along with a number of promising bottles, but all that stands out about some impromptu "grands crus" are their costumes and their cost. Still, fashion-minded Italians can't seem to get enough of them. It seems doubtful that these virtuosos can dazzle the crowds forever.

Above: vineyards are still noted mainly for red wines from native Sangiovese.

Even advocates of change seem hesitant to move too far towards new horizons, realizing that eventually the renegades will have to be brought into line with official appellations. In seeking them, it might be well to remember that the first purpose of the renaissance is the restoration of Chianti, the one name in Tuscan wine that everybody knows.

Tuscany's Vineyards

Despite nearly complete revision of vineyards over the last 25 years, much of rural Tuscany still looks invitingly antiquated. That may be because the practice of allotting about a tenth of estate land to vines has often been continued, meaning that olives and other crops keep their share. Since traditional *fattorie* tend to be big, Tuscan growers have the most vineyard space per unit (1.15 hectares compared with the national average of 0.83). That figure is diminished by stubborn *vignaioli* who still believe that small is beautiful and, sometimes, that the best grapes come from vines trained up trees in the manner of their Etruscan ancestors.

Only recently, as earlier vineyard errors became evident, has much attention been paid to varieties or clones. The predominant Sangiovese is often described as noble, even if some branches of this widespread and often nondescript family are rather ill bred. But serious attempts at selection are underway as extensive replanting begins in elite zones. Chianti's Sangioveto is in vogue, as are Montalcino's Brunello and Montepulciano's Prugnolo. But other native reds have faded, mainly Canaiolo Nero, Sangiovese's habitual partner in Chianti, along with Colorino and Ciliegiolo. Meanwhile, Cabernet Sauvignon, which shows undeniable class in many places, continues its rise, followed by Merlot. Among whites, the irrepressible Trebbiano Toscano thrives as a source of light wines in the Galestro mould, defying the trend to exclude it and the worthier Malvasia del Chianti from red wine blends. Vernaccia has been revived in San Gimignano, though Chardonnay and the equally promising Sauvignon Blanc are widely preferred for premium whites. The Pinots, Rieslings, and Traminer are used mainly for blending.

Through its history Tuscany has maintained an amazing assortment of both native vines and varieties imported long ago. Grand Duke Cosimo III de' Medici, a passionate wine man, was credited with importing 150 varieties of the 211 listed in Tuscany in the mid-eighteenth century. Among them was Cabernet, which was known in Carmignano as *uva francesca*. Research at San Felice in Chianti turned up about 250 minor varieties that farmers refer to jokingly as *i viziati* (like undisciplined children). Many are oddities with comical names, but a few show enough to warrant planting as possible sources of unique wines in the future.

Vine training in Tuscany is almost entirely vertical, using mainly Guyot or cordon in the arched *capovolto* or low, single-cane systems typical of Chianti. Some new planting is in Casarsa, notably at Villa Banfi in Montalcino where it was intended for mechanical harvesting. But that has proved to be impractical since two or three pickings are required to catch grapes at peaks of ripeness. Etruscan-style vine rows are still seen here and there. In maritime areas until not long ago vines were often trained low onto cane poles set tepee style, a system still seen on Elba. Average vine density in most of Tuscany is 2,000-3,000 per hectare, though some estates are experimenting with 4,000-8,000 or more. Most native varieties, red and white, mature late, so harvesting may last from late September to late October in parts of Chianti, until mid-October in Montalcino and Montepulciano, and to the end of September along the

Above: the rural way of life continues in the Tuscan hill towns.

coast. The following varieties are associated primarily with Tuscany.

Brunello di Montalcino. This Sangioveto or Sangiovese *grosso*, whose name refers to the dark or dusky brown colour of ripe grapes, was noted around 1840 at Montalcino, where it was isolated and used alone for red wine by Ferruccio Biondi Santi. Over time various "Brunello" vines have emerged. Recently, four clones were selected in Biondi Santi's vineyards and one, known by its initials as BBS11, is being propagated. This Brunello has medium-small, tightly packed clusters of medium-large grapes whose thick skins give the wine ample body, tannins, polyphenols, and colouring. The late-ripening vine is vigorous and resistant to disease, so close cropping and thinning are practised by top growers.

Canaiolo Bianco. Once popular white Canaiolo is rarely seen today, except in Umbria's Orvieto, where it is known as Drupeggio.

Canaiolo Nero. Known as Canaiuolo or Canajolo in the eighteenth century when it was more important in Chianti than Sangioveto. But since it is neither so productive or assertive, it became a blender used widely in central Italy. Though fading, it may be revived yet for *vini novelli* to which its natural softness seems better suited than Sangiovese.

Ciliegiolo. Once popular variety whose name refers to its cherry coloured skins is used sparingly in central Italy and the south.

Colorino. Dark, thick-skinned grapes were dried for use in the *governo* in Chianti, to which it gave colour and body without dominating, but this admirable, low yielding blending variety is nearly obsolete.

Malvasia del Chianti. Generous white Malvasia has been long noted in sweet wines and Vin Santo and as a softener for Chianti, though when treated with respect it can make dry wine of character. It ranks among the most diffused whites with more than 12,000 hectares planted, mainly in central and southern Italy. Also known as Malvasia Toscana.

Mammolo. Vines of the name, which refers to the aroma of violets (*mammole*), have been noted in Tuscany since the seventeenth century. Today they play a small role in Vino Nobile and sometimes still in Chianti. Also known as Mammolo Nero and Mammolone di Lucca.

Moscadello. Ancient strain of Moscato long noted as source of sweet Moscadello or Moscadelleto of Montalcino, where little remains since the recent DOC ignored it in favour of the Piedmontese Moscato Bianco.

Prugnolo Gentile. This Sangiovese was noted at Montepulciano in the

Below: sunset in the hills of Siena province with Monte Amiata in the distance.

early eighteenth century as the source of red wine which came to be called Vino Nobile. Though full, tannic wines often show traits distinctive from other Sangiovese, it isn't certain whether it is *grosso* (as generally believed) or *piccolo*. Studies may soon decide the issue. The Montepulciano d'Abruzzo vine has been mistaken for a Prugnolo, but this is due to confusion in the names, since there is no connection. Synonyms include Prugnolo Rosso, Pignolo, Tignolo, and Uva Canina.

Sangioveto. The name Sangioveto or San Gioveto preceded Sangiovese for vines evidently native to Tuscany, both the *piccolo* or *forte* and the *grosso* or *dolce* – though reference to the size of grapes or bunches is not consistent. Indiscriminate use of the names, coupled with heavy planting of Sangiovese di Romagna and other subvarieties, has led to confusion. Producers in Chianti Classico (some of whom have formed a Club del Sangioveto) favour selection and use of the *piccolo* type, whose best clones have thick skins which give wines colour and substance. The more prevalent *grosso* takes in Brunello.

Trebbiano Toscano. This clone, known for reliability and high yields, has swept from Tuscany through Italy. Wines on their own tend to be thin and neutral, but blend conveniently with aromatic varieties. Some Trebbiano (Tribbiano, etc.) was noted for wines of good colour, body, and aroma, often softly sweet, as in the prized whites of the Val d'Arno di Sopra in the early eighteenth century. Since phylloxera, the emphasis has been on productivity, for which this seems to be world champion.

Vernaccia di San Gimignano. Recorded at San Gimignano since the thirteenth century, this Vernaccia's origins are uncertain, possibly Greek but not related to other vines of the name in Sardinia, the Marches, or Liguria. Wines were noted more for ageing capacity in the past than today. Modern whites can have good body and tone, but they rarely show clear varietal traits in aroma or flavour. Capable of ample yields, Vernaccia has also been planted in central Italy and the south.

Other varieties

Tuscany's once vast inventory of vines has been rapidly reduced, though the region maintains more minor varieties than most. Two that were once prominent, the dark Marzemino and the white San Colombano (which was noted for Vin Santo) are no longer on the official lists. Other varieties recommended or approved in Tuscany's nine provinces include:

For red (or rosé): Aleatico, Alicante, Alicante Bouschet, Ancellotta, Barbera, Barsaglina, Bonamico, Bracciola Nera, Cabernet Franc, Cabernet Sauvignon, Caloria, Canina Nera, Colombana Nera, Foglia Tonda, Gamay, Groppello di Santo Stefano, Groppello Gentile, Malvasia Nera di Brindisi, Malvasia Nera di Lecce, Mazzese, Montepulciano, Pinot Nero, Pollera Nera, Schiava Gentile, Syrah, Teroldego, Vermentino Nero.

For white: Albana, Albarola, Ansonica, Biancone di Portoferraio, Clairette, Chardonnay, Durella, Grechetto, Greco, Livornese Bianca, Malvasia Bianca di Candia, Moscato Bianco, Müller Thurgau, Pinot Bianco, Pinot Grigio, Riesling Italico, Riesling Renano, Roussanne, Sémillon, Sylvaner Verde, Traminer Aromatico, Verdea, Verdello, Verdicchio Bianco, Vermentino or Vermentino Bianco.

Below: the town of San Gimignano is noted for its medieval towers and its white wine.

Legend

- Autostrada
- Main road
- Main railway
- Regional boundary
- Provincial boundary
- Regional capital ■
- Provincial capital ●
- DOC boundary
- *Val di Cornia* Vino da tavola
- Sorbaiano Wine producer

Km 0 10 20 30
Miles 0 10 20
1 : 1,100,000

① Fattoria di Fubbiano
② La Badiola
③ Tenuta di Maria Teresa
④ Carmignani G. 'Fuso'
   Cerruglio
   Fattoria del Buonamico
   Fattoria Maionchi
   Fattoria Michi
   Franceschini
   Vigna del Greppo
⑤ Il Colle

⑥ Chigi Saracini
⑦ Sestano
⑧ Sassicaia-Tenuta San Guido
⑨ Ornellaia
⑩ Antinori-Belvedere
⑪ Grattamacco
⑫ Avignonesi-La Selva
⑬ Mario Baldetti
⑭ *Alta Valle della Greve*
⑮ *Colline fra Siena e Firenze*

1 BIANCO DELLA VALDINIEVOLE
2 BIANCO DELL' EMPOLESE
3 CARMIGNANO
4 POMINO
5 VERNACCIA DI SAN GIMIGNANO
6 BIANCO VERGINE VALDICHIANA
7 BRUNELLO DI MONTALCINO
   ROSSO DI MONTALCINO
   MOSCADELLO DI MONTALCINO
8 VINO NOBILE DI MONTEPULCIANO
   ROSSO DI MONTEPULCIANO

1 CANDIA DEI COLLI APUANI
2 COLLINE LUCCHESI
3 MONTECARLO
4 BIANCO PISANO DI SAN TORPE
5 MONTESCUDAIO
6 BOLGHERI
7 MORELLINO DI SCANSANO
8 BIANCO DI PITIGLIANO
9 PARRINA

Isola d' Elba
ELBA
Aleatico di Portoferraio

CENTRAL HILLS COASTAL FLANK

Tuscany's Wine Zones

Tuscany sprawls between mountain and sea over hills as variable in form as in flora. Yet, despite incongruities, the ensemble shows extraordinary harmony. The Tosco-Emiliano stretch of the Apennines, with points over 2,000 metres, arches over the top from Liguria to the Marches. The so-called counter Apennine rises, which peak in the 1,738-metre Monte Amiata, range from the Monti del Chianti south along the borders with Umbria and Latium to the Argentario promontory. The hills trap heat and damp in the basins of the Chiana, Ombrone, and Arno valleys (Florence can be torrid in summer). But two-thirds of the region's surface lies between 100-500 metres on slopes wafted by currents even during the usual summer drought. Italy's vintage hill country encircles Florence and Siena, where vines and olives are essentials of the habitual crop mix. But even if vineyards blanket parts of Chianti Classico, Montalcino, and Montepulciano, woods are usually more prominent on Tuscan slopes. Nor do vines proliferate along the Tyrrhenian flank, the 578 kilometres of coast (including Elba and the other six islands of the Tuscan archipelago). Parts of the central hills, which are generally cooler than the coast, have exemplary conditions for vines, whether traditional or recently introduced. Points along the coast have realized unexpected potential. But some areas have practically no vines of note. Apart from the mountains and the bit of low plains, these include the rocky Colline Metallifere, much of the Maremma's arid brushland, and the clay moors of the *crete* southeast of Siena. Nearly everywhere viticulture seems to have become more elitist, as growers face up to the fact that on these historic hillsides only quality pays.

The text follows a basic division in Tuscany's wine zones between the central hills and the coastal flank. The central hills take in the Chianti zones of Classico, Colli Fiorentini, Rufina, Montalbano, Colli Aretini, and Colli Senesi. Within the vast territory lie the zones of Valdinievole mainly in Pistoia province; Carmignano, Pomino, and Bianco Empolese in Firenze province; Montalcino, Montepulciano, San Gimignano, and Val d'Arbia in Siena province; and Valdichiana mainly in Arezzo province. The coastal flank covers zones in the five provinces along the Ligurian and Tyrrhenian seas. To the northwest in Massa province is Colli Apuani and in Lucca the Colline Lucchesi and Montecarlo. Pisa has Chianti Colline Pisane, San Torpè, and Montescudaio. Livorno includes Bolgheri and the island of Elba. Grosseto has the Scansano, Parrina, and Pitigliano zones. The regional map shows Chianti Classico, though the other six Chianti subzones are indicated as a unit due to limited space.

Florence's hills: Montalbano-Carmignano, Rufina-Pomino

Conditions vary radically, though slopes opening onto the broad valleys of the lower Arno and its tributaries the Elsa and Pesa are more exposed to the maritime influence than are the often steep, wooded hills east of Florence along the upper Arno and Sieve. Wines from sandy clay soils of the western arm of Colli Fiorentini and Montalbano tend to be light, but there are exceptions. Chianti from calcareous terrain at Barberino and Tavarnelle, as well as at Impruneta, just outside Florence, can show stature as *riserva*. Carmignano, on the cooler eastern flank of Montalbano, is renowned for reds of poise and durability. Due east of Florence, against the Apennine wall of the Mugello, lie the sandy calcareous slopes of Colli Fiorentini and Rufina, where Chianti reaches heights of size and

longevity rivalled only in privileged parts of Classico. Pomino, a lofty niche within Rufina, makes reds and whites of uncommon finesse. Further up the Arno, where it slices between the Pratomagno and Monti del Chianti after crossing the gaping Valdarno Superiore, wines from the heavier clay soils tend to be leaner and harsher. The Valdinievole zone in the province of Pistoia ranges from the fertile Arno floor well into the Apennine foothills, but the *bianco* from all levels is simplistic.

Chianti Classico

Wines, like microclimates and terrains, vary markedly from one place to another on often steep slopes between 250-550 metres. The biggest, longest-lived wines generally come from the southern area, the original Chianti around Castellina, Gaiole, and Radda. Soils there are mainly stony calcareous, though the lower fringes around Siena were once under a lake where sand and clay are mixed with mineral-rich residue, rendering wines of uncommon stature. The northern and eastern sectors in Firenze province tend to be cooler and damper and soils are more varied between lime, sand and clay, various schists, flysch, and the desirable flaky marl known as *galestro*. Though the Greve valley and nearby hills were generally noted for fruity flask wines, refined *riserve* can also be produced, notably around the village of Panzano. Weather can vary violently in these hills, where the prime threat to crops is hail. Besides the traditional Chianti varieties, conditions have proved to be first rate for Cabernet, Chardonnay, Sauvignon, and even Pinot Noir.

Colli Senesi and Val d'Arbia

Chianti Colli Senesi ranges over much of Siena province, through various soils and microclimates (*see* also San Gimignano, Montalcino, and Montepulciano zones below). Overall, the better Chianti comes from calcareous or sandy tufaceous terrains, where clay is not heavy (as it is in the *crete* hills southeast of Siena, excluded from the zone). Most light whites of the Val d'Arbia come from the southern part of Chianti Classico

Right: vineyards in Montalcino are renowned for their long-lived red Brunello.

Above: rows of vines and olives are still sometimes interspersed on estates that produce extra virgin olive oil as well as wine.

in warm, dry conditions better suited to reds, though the zone extends into the *crete* and west of Siena to the rocky rises of Montagnola, where little wine is made.

San Gimignano

The well exposed hills of the commune consist largely of light, almost chalky beige to grey soils where calcareous clays and tufa prevail, or else of yellow terrain where sand dominates. Studies have located superior sites around the town in the highest part of the zone, though notable Vernaccia also comes from warmer slopes towards the Elsa valley where marine deposits make a difference. Chardonnay is promising, but the town's age old reputation for white wine may be upstaged by improving Chianti, and, recently, by first-rate pure Sangiovese and Cabernet.

Montalcino

The extensive commune is an upland of broad slopes encircled by the Orcia and Ombrone valleys, which merge at the southwest corner of the zone, some 40 kilometres from the sea. The temperate hill climate feels the Tyrrhenian influence in hot, dry summers, while the nearby mass of Monte Amiata protects vineyards from hail and violent storms in what is considered an exceptional ambience for vines. Several vineyard areas stand out. The cooler upper reaches (400-550 metres) around the fortress town are most noted for Brunello of great longevity. Soils are largely *galestro* in the noted vineyards of Il Greppo, Barbi, and Colle al Matrichese, as well as in the lower Montosoli and Canalicchio, where wines tend to be even more robust. Much new planting has been in the hotter southwest corner of the commune around Sant'Angelo in Colle, Pian delle Mura, Argiano, and Camigliano. Sandy clay soils there are often mixed with limestone and *galestro*, favouring strong, well

structured Brunello. In the old days, wines of different places were often blended, but today most estate bottlings reflect individuality. Among many varieties planted in the commune, Brunello still stands out.

Montepulciano

The commune straddles the southern Chiana valley, whose broad basin opening east towards Umbria's Lake Trasimeno and protected by mountains on the west is warm but well ventilated – a habitat long noted for vines. Most vineyards for Vino Nobile are planted on gradual, open slopes rising from about 250 metres on the valley's edge to about 600 metres around the town of Montepulciano. The terrain, chiefly sandy clays, is rich in marine deposits in such prized areas as Argiano, Cervognano, Gracciano, and Caggiole, where wines show strength and structure. Higher vineyards at Pietrose produce wines of rich bouquet. Vineyards across the valley at Valiano make Vino Nobile of notable balance and finesse.

Colli Aretini and Valdichiana

Chianti Colli Aretini and Bianco Vergine Valdichiana occupy broad valleys which are hot in summer and cold in winter and often fairly damp. The rolling hills along the Arno and the Chiana canal have mainly sandy clay soils with marine sediment and alluvial deposits washed down from the hills. Both were noted in the past for delicate whites from Trebbiano and Malvasia, but today only Bianco Vergine typifies the tradition. Sangiovese for Chianti sometimes fails to ripen fully in the Colli Aretini on the cool slopes of the Pratomagno and eastern side of the Chianti range.

The northwest: the Apuan hills and Lucca

The Apuan Alps confine the hot maritime climate to the coast, where some soft white Vermentino for Candia dei Colli Apuani and Tuscany's share of Liguria's Colli di Luni grows in mineral-rich sandy clays amidst the marble quarries around Massa and Carrara. Currents from the hot Arno valley waft Lucca, giving the Colline Lucchesi a gentle climate where sandy soils produce light, scented *rosso* and *bianco*. Montecarlo is lower and warmer with vineyards on sandy calcareous slopes generally exposed south, so ripening is steady for sound whites and sometimes refined reds.

Maritime hills: Colline Pisane, Bolgheri, and Elba

Pisa's hills, around Casciana Terme, are the warmest of Chianti's seven zones, so wines from the sandy clay soil tend to be lighter than the rest. The overlapping Bianco Pisano di San Torpè comes mainly from alluvial land along the Arno where a hot climate renders light, fleeting white. Montescudaio's temperate hills consist of sandy clays rich in minerals, favouring fragrant, medium-bodied reds and whites. Bolgheri produces the finest wines of the coast in Sassicaia, Ornellaia, and Grattamacco. Soils there are largely stony, medium-textured calcareous clays, rich in lime and marine fossils, favouring reds of uncommon size and finesse, particularly from Cabernet. Vintages are unusually even in the warm maritime climate, though the position of Elba influences winds in a way that can cause damaging droughts. Elba's iron-rich soils and island climate result in reds and whites of marked strength of character, notably the sweet Aleatico.

Grosseto's Maremma

In the Maremma south of Grosseto, the prevalently calcareous terrain of Parrina and Morellino di Scansano gives way to volcanic soils in the Bianco di Pitigliano zone, just north of the crater lake of Bolsena. Parrina is hot and dry, accounting for a sturdy character in the wines. The cooler climate in the higher interior around Scansano and Pitigliano seems to give bouquet and complexity to reds and heighten the scent of whites.

THE CENTRAL HILLS

Chianti, the eternal pillar of Tuscan wine, wobbles under the weight of invention. But at least some winemakers seem determined to keep it standing. Beyond the historical value of the name is the magical physiognomy of the place, those hills around Florence and Siena that still look like backdrops for Renaissance paintings. The name Chianti, which may have come from an Etruscan family, first applied to the area around Radda, Gaiole, and Castellina in the southern part of what is now the Classico zone. Feudal lords who formed the thirteenth-century Chianti League no doubt had vineyards there, but the first known reference to a wine of the name came in 1404 when Francesco Datini, the merchant of Prato, bought a white at Vignamaggio to the north of the historical area. As Chianti's popularity spread earlier in this century, vineyards extended north past Greve and San Casciano, which are now in the Classico zone, to burgeon through the hills of Florence east to Arezzo, south well past Siena, and west almost to the Tyrrhenian coast near Pisa. In the process, Chianti's identity as a place was corrupted by the use of its name for a type of wine, exclusively red, produced in a vast territory comprising seven subzones and fringes.

But Chianti as a wine doesn't stand alone in Tuscany's central hills. Its domain overlies or adjoins other DOC or DOCG zones where growers may also declare vineyards for other wines. These include Carmignano, Pomino, Vernaccia di San Gimignano, Val d'Arbia, Montepulciano, Montalcino, and Bianco Vergine Valdichiana, all of which have provisions for various types which may range beyond the basic dry to include *spumante* and Vin Santo. The many classified wines of the central hills will be discussed in geographical order, descending from the provinces of Florence and Pistoia down through Chianti Classico to the provinces of Siena and Arezzo. Most producers also make table wines, some of which carry a collective name such as Galestro or Sarmento or Predicato, but many of which refer to vineyards or places, though their names could just as well be fantasy. These individualistic vdt will be cited with the producer entries.

The multitude of options has diverted the focus from Chianti, a wine as elusive today as it has been through most of its chequered career. Producers still haven't decided whether Chianti should be as dignified as aged Pauillac or as blithe spirited as young Beaujolais, so customers often have to take their pick from a medley of types in between. It derives from a composite dominated more than ever by Sangiovese or Sangioveto, along with dark Canaiolo, and the controversial and increasingly ignored white varieties of Malvasia and Trebbiano. The ancient practice of using white grapes in red wine was confirmed by Barone Bettino Ricasoli when he arrived at the long-respected formula for Chianti at his Castello di Brolio in the mid-nineteenth century. The Iron Baron noted that Malvasia toned down the vigour of Sangioveto for wines to drink young. Other growers took the cue to use the more productive Trebbiano to stretch Chianti of all types. Another curious Tuscan custom was *governo*, which consisted of adding dried grapes (or their rich musts) to the newly fermented wine to induce a secondary fermentation. Most producers used *governo all'uso toscano* to make young Chianti sweeter and rounder with a prickle, though some used it to reinforce wines for ageing. Practices which made sense once upon a time may seem eccentric today, yet white varieties are still required in the blends and *governo* has enjoyed a mild comeback. Some oenologists insist that it makes wines richer and sturdier though doubts remain about ageing capacities.

It's a wonder that Chianti and company are as good as they often are, considering the errors and oversights that typified the conversion of vineyards in the 1960s and 1970s. A decline in Chianti's popularity paralleled the phasing out of the flask, which in 1970 held more than three-quarters of the wine sold and today carries less than a tenth. The crisis peaked a decade or so ago as critics noted that much of what was supposed to have been newly dignified Chianti in Bordeaux bottles lacked substance and stature — partly due to the coming to fruition of hastily planted vineyards. Improvement since is a credit to better winemaking and in part to Chianti's elevation to DOCG in 1984. Volume was sharply reduced by banning unsuitable vineyards, lowering yields (and percentages of white grapes in the blends), and commissioning tasters to reject atypical and substandard wines. Some producers also took it as a cue to include Cabernet in the blend to build colour and body, though others have hesitated, realizing that even a small portion can pervade bouquet and flavour and alter authentic typology. Just recently there seems to be a reawakening of native pride with a trend towards making *riserva* from practically pure Sangiovese.

The main benefactors of DOCG have been growers of Chianti Classico, whose preferred status is a historical privilege. Prices for their grapes and wines have risen far more than have the others. Most Chianti Classico producers and bottlers belong to the consortium known as Gallo Nero after its black rooster emblem. Many in other zones belong to the confederation called Putto after its symbolic cherub. But membership is optional. The large houses of Antinori, Ricasoli, and Ruffino belong to neither. Producers of Chianti Classico, whose estate wines tend increasingly towards the full-bodied types best expressed in *riserva*, are seeking a separate DOCG as a definitive break from the pack. For most of the rest of Chianti the *guarantee* hasn't improved things much at all.

The Putto consortium has been encouraging youthful styles in members' wines, including adaptations of *governo*, perhaps recalling those cheerier days when Chianti came in flasks.

Below left: a farmhouse in the hills near Pienza in the Chianti Colli Senesi zone. Below right: the black rooster, or gallo nero, *is the symbol of the Chianti Classico consortium.*

Chianti (DOCG 1984, DOC 1967)

Chianti is a single appellation with multiple ramifications. Approved wine from one of the seven subzones may specify Classico, Colli Aretini, Colli Fiorentini, Colli Senesi, Colline Pisane, Montalbano, or Rufina. Or, if it originates in those zones or anywhere else within the broader DOCG area, it may be labelled simply Chianti. Generic Chianti must meet regulations given below for percentages of grapes, yield, alcohol, and ageing. In the subzones some rules are more restrictive. Producers of Classico and Rufina normally meet the requirements and cite the geographical name, but since this is not obligatory, many in other subzones don't bother. Each of the seven subzones is discussed in geographical order with its regulations.

Zone: Slopes up to 550 m (in exceptional cases up to 650 m) in five provinces and 103 communes (19 in Arezzo, 34 in Firenze, 16 in Pisa, 8 in Pistoia, 26 in Siena). Dry red. Grapes: Sangiovese 75-90%, Canaiolo Nero 5-10%, Trebbiano Toscano/Malvasia del Chianti 5-10%. Yld 70/100, Alc 11.5; riserva 12.5, Acd 0.5, Ag 6 mths; riserva 3 yrs. Wines made using "governo all'uso del Chianti" must refer to the fact on labels and be sold within a year of the harvest.

Vin Santo

Tuscany's most cherished nectar of the grape is Vin Santo, the golden or amber "holy wine" made with pride at nearly every farm, not so often to sell as to sip on special occasions. Though some insist that real Tuscan Vin Santo is dry, or nearly so, sweet versions were no doubt more suitable for use in the Mass when served to young and old alike. But since styles are steadfastly individual and arrived at as often by chance as design, dry or sweet or shadings in between are acceptable. The elaborate process begins when bunches of grapes (usually white Malvasia, Trebbiano, or Grechetto, though other varieties, including red, can be used), are selected for drying on racks or by hanging from rafters. This *appassimento*, during which mouldy grapes should be discarded but are not always, concentrates sugar and extract. Some time after Christmas, grapes are crushed and the juice is placed in small chestnut or oak barrels called *caratelli* usually with a bit of *madre* (thick residue from a previous batch) to feed it yeasts and guide it through the long fermentation. This takes place in *vinsantai*, airy lofts that feel the heat of summer and cold of winter – essential to the ageing that can go on for 2-6 years. Traditionally, *caratelli* were

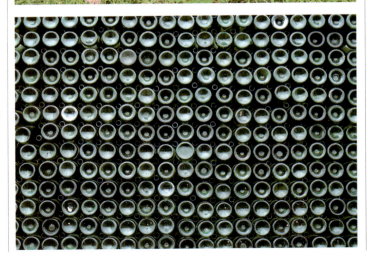

Centre right: the town of Sorano in southern Tuscany is in the Bianco di Pitigliano wine zone.

sealed with cement to be broken only when the wine was ready (or had turned to vinegar). But some oenologists prefer to control the process by having access to the barrels. Whisky or brandy butts or even new *barriques* may also be used.

When all goes well, Vin Santo can be a sumptuous aperitif or dessert wine, habitually served with almond biscuits called *cantucci*, which are dipped into it. Avignonesi's extraordinarily concentrated Occhio del Pernice leads the field, though other small producers make exquisite versions. Brolio, Frescobaldi, and Antinori make it admirably on a fairly large scale. But imitations – usually based on Sicilian Moscato – abound. Homemade Vin Santo can range from surprisingly refined to disgustingly coarse. Since Vin Santo is already DOC in seven zones – Carmignano, Pomino, Montescudaio, San Torpè, Valdinievole, Val d'Arbia, and Empolese – approval under the impending Colli dell'Etruria Centrale would make it the closest thing to a regional classification. Still, though it seems to be gaining again after a period of decline, production of the real article is too painstaking and expensive to reach significant commercial levels.

Other wines of note

Colli dell'Etruria Centrale is designed to give producers of DOCG Chianti the options of light, fresh, dry wines and Vin Santo under DOC. Four types have been approved in a territory that overlaps much of Chianti in the provinces of Arezzo, Firenze, Pistoia, and Siena. These are:

Rosso Dry red. Grapes: Sangiovese at least 75%; Canaiolo/other reds up to 25%, Cabernet/Merlot up to 10%. Yld 84/120, Alc 10.5-11.5, Acd 0.5.

Rosato Dry rosé. Grapes: As rosso. Yld 78/120, Alc 10.5, Acd 0.5.

Bianco Dry white. Grapes: Trebbiano Toscano/Malvasia del Chianti/Vernaccia di San Gimignano at least 50%, Pinot Bianco and Grigio/Chardonnay/Sauvignon 10-50%. Yld 78/120, Alc 9.5, Acd 0.55.

Vin Santo Golden to amber dessert wine, secco or amabile. Grapes: As bianco but passito. Yld 42/120, Alc 16, Acd secco 0.4; amabile 0.45.

Production of a share of Tuscany's commercial type vdt has been supervised by the Ente Tutela Vini dei Colli della Toscana Centrale, a consortium of large houses and cooperatives, as well as a number of estates. The wines, made following regulations similar to DOC, must be approved by tasting commissions before being sold under the names. They include the simple Rosso and Bianco dei Colli della Toscana Centrale, as well as Galestro and Sarmento, all of which might qualify under the DOC Colli dell'Etruria Centrale. Galestro, a white of no more than 10.5 alcohol, must be processed at cool temperatures. Though based on Trebbiano, it may include up to 40% of other varieties such as Chardonnay, the Pinots, Sauvignon, and Riesling, which heighten aroma and flavour. Sarmento, its red equivalent based on Sangiovese and Canaiolo, is designed to be served cool. The more prestigious category of Predicato would not qualify under the new DOC. Ambrogio Folonari of Ruffino led formation of the group in an attempt to bring the most definable of the new-style wines into line for official recognition. But despite admirable examples from Ruffino, Frescobaldi, and San Felice, among others, participation had been less than hoped. Though some Predicato (for merit) wines sold well, consumers seem confused by the names of archaic significance applied to four categories.

Predicato del Muschio for white from Chardonnay or Pinot Bianco with up to 20% Riesling, Müller Thurgau, or Pinot Grigio.

Predicato del Selvante for white from Sauvignon Blanc with the same complementary varieties as Muschio.

Predicato di Biturica for red from Cabernet with up to 30% Sangiovese and 10% other red grapes.

Predicato di Cardisco for red from Sangiovese with up to 10% other red grapes.

Tuscany, which leads in production of *vini novelli*, was the first region to regulate vinification and sales under an association that included five of the nation's ten largest producers: Antinori, Villa Banfi, Frescobaldi, Ruffino, and Castello d'Albola.

(Recommended producers of generic Chianti and various vdt are cited throughout.)

Wines of Florence's hills

Florence, founded by the Romans on a plain along the Arno, built its reputation as a wine town in the hills that practically surround it. When the Grand Duchy singled out four elite wine zones in 1716, three were in the domain of Florence: Carmignano, Pomino, and Val d'Arno di Sopra. The fourth, Chianti, was still confined to the area close to Siena; only later did it expand into the colossus that reaches right up to Florence's walls. In recent times, Florence has been overshadowed as a wine centre by Siena, with DOCG Brunello, Vino Nobile, and a major share of Chianti Classico in its province. But Florentines, never bowing to their archrivals, have rallied to restore the old lustre to Carmignano and Pomino, while elevating some Rufina and Colli Fiorentini to the front ranks of Chianti. The treasured sweet white of the upper Arno valley has vanished, alas, but most of its former territory is now the Valdarno Superiore in the province of Florence's other old nemesis Arezzo. The Montalbano range, home of Carmignano and the Chianti that carries its name, extends into Pistoia province around Montecatini where the inconsequential Bianco della Valdinievole is made.

Chianti Colli Fiorentini

In the days when wine came in unlabelled flasks and the majority of Florence's inhabitants were real Florentines, most of what was called Chianti there came from the city's enchanted hills. The numerous noble families and bourgeoisie maintained *fattorie* to supply them not only with wine but olive oil and fresh produce. Each Florentine *trattoria* had its special "Chianti", guaranteed (verbally, not with a government seal) to be *genuino*, and that was what you drank with your *bistecca* and beans. The changes in Florentine life style, like the crisis that persists for Chianti that isn't Classico, have changed all that. These days producers need to be not only shrewd but diligent to make money from wine in Florence's hills. But the revolution, which drained the local *fattorie* of the old colour, has improved the wines overall. The best of Colli Fiorentini – now in bottles, of course – is among Chianti's leading values.

Zone: Hills fanning out from Florence to cover 14 other communes in its province, ranging northeast above Fiesole and southeast on both sides of the Arno to Figline and Pian di Scò, then following a strip south of the city along the northern part of Chianti Classico, west as far as Montelupo and south between the Pesa and Elsa valleys as far as Barberino. Slopes of the western arm are relatively open and tend to be warmer and drier than the often steep, wooded hills above the upper Arno valley. Dry red. Grapes: Sangiovese 75-90%, Canaiolo Nero 5-10%, Trebbiano Toscano/Malvasia del Chianti 5-10%, other reds up to 10%. Yld 56/80, Alc 11.5; riserva 12.5, Acd 0.5-0.75, Ag 8 mths; riserva 3 yrs.

Other wines of note

Most estates produce vdt whites on the order of Galestro, along with some rosé and *spumante*. Fattoria Montellori, Il Corno, and Carla Guarnieri are among those showing style with special table wines.

Right: terraced hillsides with vines and olives in the Carmignano and Chianti Montalbano zone west of Florence.

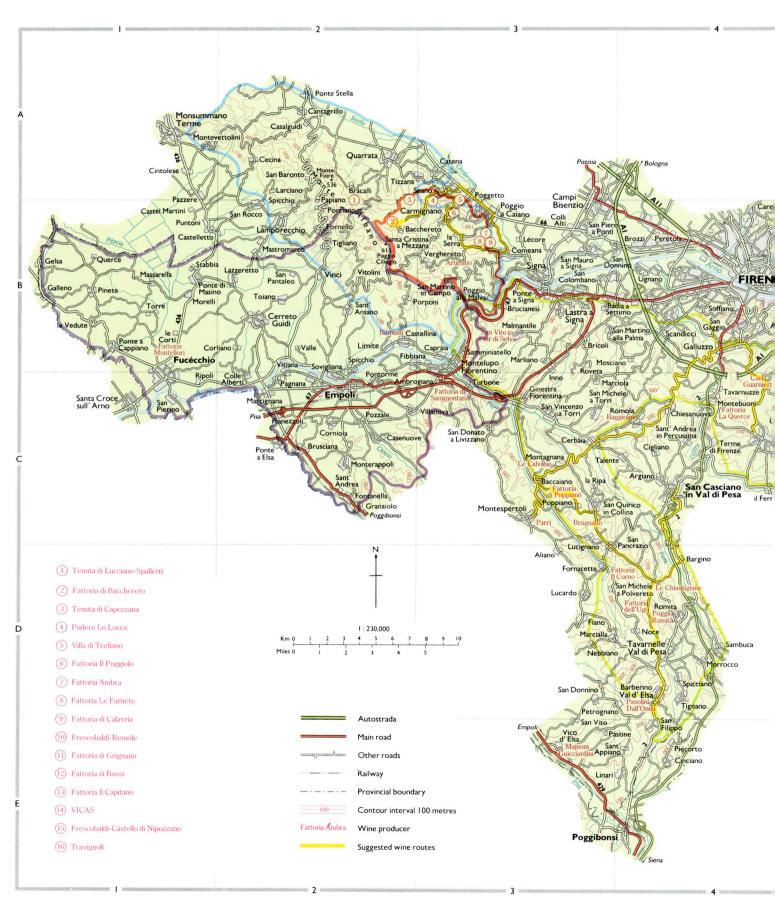

① Tenuta di Lucciano-Spalletti

② Fattoria di Bacchereto

③ Tenuta di Capezzana

④ Podere Lo Locco

⑤ Villa di Trefiano

⑥ Fattoria Il Poggiolo

⑦ Fattoria Ambra

⑧ Fattoria Le Farnete

⑨ Fattoria di Calavria

⑩ Frescobaldi-Remole

⑪ Fattoria di Grignano

⑫ Fattoria di Bossi

⑬ Fattoria Il Capitano

⑭ VICAS

⑮ Frescobaldi-Castello di Nipozzano

⑯ Travignoli

▬▬▬	Autostrada
▬▬▬	Main road
▬▬▬	Other roads
┄┄┄	Railway
▬·▬·▬	Provincial boundary
―600―	Contour interval 100 metres
Fattoria Ambra	Wine producer
▬▬▬	Suggested wine routes

1 : 230,000

Km 0 1 2 3 4 5 6 7 8 9 10
Miles 0   1   2   3   4   5

N

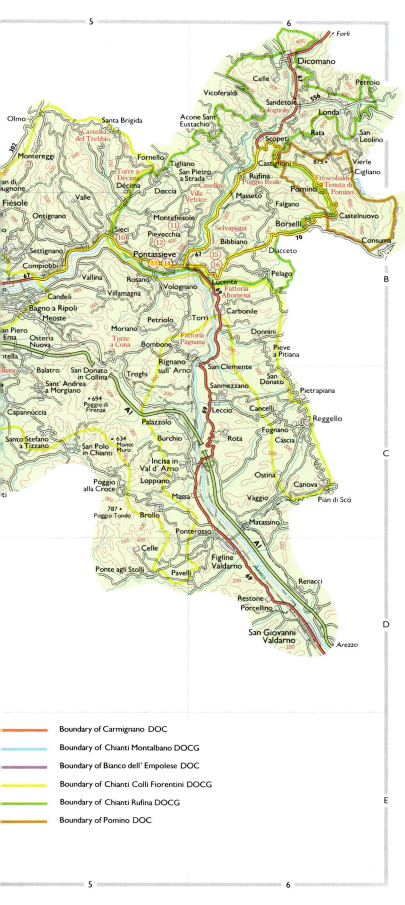

Boundary of Carmignano DOC

Boundary of Chianti Montalbano DOCG

Boundary of Bianco dell' Empolese DOC

Boundary of Chianti Colli Fiorentini DOCG

Boundary of Chianti Rufina DOCG

Boundary of Pomino DOC

Chianti Montalbano

Chianti varies in nature between the sun-drenched western flank of the Montalbano range and the higher, more wooded eastern edge. From the west around Vinci wines were noted in the past for extraordinary size and strength, but producers now usually aim at soft, fruity Chianti to drink fairly young. Carmignano's excellence is expressed in a separate category, but even if Chianti is second choice there, it can be charming.

Zone: Slopes of Montalbano, an appendix of the Apennines extending southeast towards the Arno, in the communes of Carmignano, Capraia e Limite, and Vinci in Firenze province, and Larciano, Monsummano Terme, Serravalle Pistoiese, and Pistoia in the latter province. Dry red. Grapes: Sangiovese 75-90%, Canaiolo Nero 5-10%, Trebbiano Toscano/Malvasia del Chianti 5-10%, other reds up to 10%. Yld 70/100, Alc 11.5; riserva 12.5, Acd 0.5-0.75, Ag 6 mths; riserva 3 yrs.

Carmignano (1975, Rosato and Vin Santo 1983)

Carmignano was known for wine centuries before the Grand Duke's decree of 1716. In the 14th century, Francesco Datini, the merchant of Prato, and companion Ser Lapo Mazzei preferred "sparkling Carmignano", among the most admired and costliest reds of Florence. Especially prized over the centuries was the wine of Capezzana, one of several Medici villas in this balcony of hills overlooking Florence from the west. But, like the others, Carmignano was eventually overwhelmed by Chianti and only recently, under the leadership of Capezzana's Ugo Contini Bonacossi, has its good name been restored. What set Carmignano apart early from other Tuscan reds from Sangiovese was the inclusion of Cabernet, evidently planted here in the 18th century as *uva francesca*. The name Carmignano alone on a label refers to the red, which has been joined under DOC by rosé and Vin Santo. When young, the red resembles supple Chianti, but with age from top vintages it acquires shadings of finesse reminiscent of old Pauillacs. Carmignano has been called Italy's most reliable DOC, since only wine approved by experts at an annual public judging can carry the name. Maximum production of the red (rarely reached) is half a million bottles from 11 estates. Carmignano Rosato may also be called Vin Ruspo, which implies rustic or improvised, in reference to the peasant trick during the harvest of spilling a little juice from dark grapes into demijohns to ferment into a lively pink wine at home. Some of Tuscany's best classified Vin Santo comes from Capezzana, Bacchereto, and Il Poggiolo. Producers may also use grapes for the red to make a lighter wine called Barco Reale to be sold earlier at a lower cost. Since they are seeking what would be a well-deserved DOCG for Carmignano, Barco Reale could become an alternative DOC.

Zone: Slopes on the eastern flank of Montalbano within limits of the domain of the Medici Barco Reale (originally surrounded by a 32-mile wall) in the commune of Carmignano and part of Poggio a Caiano in Firenze province. Dry red. Grapes: Sangiovese 45-65%, Canaiolo Nero 10-20%, Cabernet Franc/Cabernet Sauvignon 6-10%, Trebbiano Toscano/Canaiolo Bianco/Malvasia del Chianti 10-20%, other varieties up to 5%. Yld 56/80, Alc 12.5, Acd 0.5, Ag 20 mths; riserva 3 yrs (2 in oak or chestnut casks). **Rosato** Dry rosé. Grapes: As rosso. Yld 77/110, Alc 11.5, Acd 0.50. **Vin Santo** Golden to amber dessert wine, secco, semisecco, or dolce. Grapes: Trebbiano Toscano 65-75%, Canaiolo Bianco/Malvasia del Chianti 15-35%, other whites up to 10% (semidried before vinification). Yld 38.5/110, Alc 17 (res sugar secco 3%; semisecco 4%; dolce 5%), Acd 0.6, Ag 3 yrs in wood (caratelli no larger than 2 hl) in vin santo lofts.

Bianco dell'Empolese (1989)

Another unknown white from Trebbiano Toscano joins the rolls, this one from the hills around Empoli. The production code also allows for Vin Santo.

Zone: Slopes on both sides of the lower Arno in the communes of Empoli, Cerreto Guidi, Fucecchio, Vinci, Capraia e Limite, and Montelupo Fiorentina in Firenze province. Dry white. Grapes: Trebbiano Toscano at least 80%; other whites up to 20%, Malvasia del Chianti up to 8%. Yld 84/120, Alc 10.5. Acd 0.55. **Vin Santo** Golden to amber dessert wine, dry or amabile. Grapes: As bianco but passito. Yld 42/110, Alc 17, Acd 0.55, Ag 3 yrs in caratelli.

Bianco della Valdinievole (1976)

The lack of success of the dry white and Vin Santo from the Montecatini area indicates that those who come to take the waters can afford more distinguished wines.

Zone: Hills between the Nievole and Pescia rivers opening into the Arno valley west of Montalbano around Montecatini Terme and including eight other communes in Pistoia province. Dry white. Grapes: Trebbiano Toscano at least 70%, Malvasia del Chianti/Canaiolo Bianco/Vermentino up to 25%, other whites up to 5%. Yld 75/130, Alc 11, Acd 0.48. **Vin Santo della Valdinievole** Amber dessert wine, secco, semisecco, or dolce. Grapes: As bianco but semidried. Yld 45/130, Alc 17 (res sugar secco 3%; semisecco 4%; dolce 5%), Acd 0.48, Ag 3 yrs in caratelli.

Other wines of note

Most producers of Chianti Montalbano and Carmignano also make vdt, none so prominently as Tenuta di Capezzana (*see* page 205). Carmignano's light red Barco Reale is a candidate for DOC.

Chianti Rufina

Long before it became Chianti, Rufina's red wine was noted as having greater strength, extract, and structure – and a better disposition for travel – than most other Tuscan wines. This superiority can be explained by premium conditions on the sandy calcareous lower slopes of the Apennines in an enclosure that gets hot in the daytime and cool at night. The habit of blending southern wines and concentrates into their so-called Chianti nearly ruined the reputation, but lately growers have recalled the advantages of making authentic estate wines and Rufina has regained stature as what is undoubtedly one of Tuscany's most privileged vineyard areas. The smallest of the seven Chianti zones ranks as next in the class after Classico, as other producers follow the historical lead provided by Frescobaldi at Castello di Nipozzano. It was there and at the nearby Tenuta di Pomino in the 1840s that the scholarly Marchese Vittorio degli Albizi planted Cabernets and Pinots to complement local varieties, while following new ideas of viticulture. His wines not only travelled but won prizes abroad. The Frescobaldi, who acquired the properties through marriage, have continued the tradition with some of the most admired Chianti, including the *riserva* Montesodi from a small plot at Nipozzano. Other estates, most notably Francesco Giuntini's Selvapiana and the now sadly defunct Poggio Reale of Spalletti, have proved that Rufina's class is not an isolated phenomenon but a factor that could make this enclave even more elite. Producers ought to be having second thoughts about calling their wine Chianti, when it could stand, proudly backed by past performances, as Rufina alone.

Zone: The valley of the Sieve as it courses south along the Mugello past Dicomano to meet the Arno at Pontassieve. Rufina is the centre of this enclave whose slopes reach towards the Apennines around Londa and Pelago in Firenze province. Dry red. Grapes: Sangiovese 75-90%, Canaiolo Nero 5-10%, Trebbiano Toscano/Malvasia del Chianti 5-10%, reds up to 10%. Yld 56/80, Alc 11.5; riserva 12.5, Acd 0.5-0.75, Ag 8 mths; riserva 3 yrs.

Right: vineyards in the Chianti Rufina zone in the Apennine foothills east of Florence.

Pomino (1983)

The recent resurrection of this parcel of history is a credit to the Frescobaldi, whose Tenuta di Pomino monopolizes production of some of Tuscany's most drinkable modern wines from perhaps its highest vineyards. The Ducal decree of 1716 defined Pomino as an area east of the Sieve taking in much of the modern Chianti Rufina, but the new DOC is restricted to the village of Pomino where land belongs mainly to Frescobaldi. Attempts by other growers to widen the zone to its historical size have failed. The 1716 decree, like the poetry that eulogized Pomino earlier, certified the excellence of wines from the *galestro* soils without specifying grape varieties. Vittorio degli Albizi's intuition about French vines has been deftly exploited by the Frescobaldi. They let Pinot and Chardonnay command in the *bianco*, including Pomino Il Benefizio, which seems to have been Tuscany's first barrel-fermented modern white. They fill out the Sangiovese-based *rosso* with Cabernet, Merlot, and Pinot Nero. The same varieties are used in the two types of Vin Santo, including the rare red, whose style doesn't seem to have suffered at all from this twist of tradition.

Zone: Slopes up to 700 m facing southwest beneath the Consuma pass of the Apennines around the village of Pomino in the commune of Rufina in Firenze province.
Bianco Dry white. Grapes: Pinot Bianco/ Chardonnay 60-80%, Trebbiano Toscano up to 30%, other whites up to 15%. Yld 73.5/ 105, Alc 11, Acd 0.55.
Rosso Dry red. Grapes: Sangiovese 60-75%, Canaiolo Nero/Cabernet Sauvignon/ Cabernet Franc 15-25%, Merlot 10-20%, other reds up to 15%. Yld 73.5/105, Alc 12; riserva 12.5, Acd 0.55, Ag 1 yr; riserva 3 yrs (18 mths in oak or chestnut barrels).
Vin Santo bianco Golden to amber dessert wine, secco, semisecco, or dolce. Grapes: As bianco but semidried. Yld 31.5/105, Alc 15.5, Acd 0.55, Ag 3 yrs in *caratelli*.
Vin Santo rosso Garnet red dessert wine, secco, semisecco, or dolce. Grapes: As rosso but semidried. Yld 31.5/105, Alc 15.5, Acd 0.55, Ag 3 yrs in *caratelli*.

Other wines of note

Frescobaldi has kept its wines where possible within the classified ranks, though from such a diversified range several inevitably remain outside. Most other producers make the usual variations on vdt and Vin Santo. The vdt della Val di Sieve (*indicazione geografica*) applies to *bianco*, *rosato*, and *rosso*.

ESTATES/GROWERS

Chianti Colli Fiorentini

(Estates cited without comment are recommended for Chianti.)

Baggiolino, La Romola (FI). Ellen Fantoni Sellon makes good Chianti and the vdt Poggio Brandi from 15 ha.
Brugnano, San Casciano Val di Pesa (FI). Good Chianti from the estate of Conte Lodovico Guicciardini.
Castello del Trebbio, Santa Brigida (FI). The legendary castle of the Pazzi family continues to make Chianti and other wines from 100 ha.
Castello di Poppiano, Montespertoli (FI). Ferdinando Guicciardini makes good Chianti at this historical estate.
Castelvecchio, San Casciano Val di Pesa (FI).
Fattoria Altomena, Pelago (FI).
Fattoria dell'Ugo, Tavarnelle Val di

Pesa (FI). From 38 ha, Franco Amici Grossi produces admirable young Chianti.

Fattoria di Petriolo, Rignano sull'Arno (FI).

Fattoria di Sammontana, Montelupo Fiorentino (FI). From 30 ha at Sammontana, long noted for its wines, Andrea and Michele Dzieduszycki produce popular Chianti.

Fattoria Il Corno, San Casciano Val di Pesa (FI). From 60 ha surrounding their imposing villa, Antonio and Maria Teresa Frova make good Chianti and vdt, including the pure Sangiovese in *barriques* called Fossespina.

Fattoria La Chiusura, Montelupo Fiorentino (FI).

Fattoria La Querce, Impruneta (FI). From 7.6 ha, always good and occasionally outstanding Chianti.

Fattoria La Tancia, Tavarnelle Val di Pesa (FI).

Fattoria Lucignano, San Casciano Val di Pesa (FI).

Fattoria Montellori, Fucecchio (FI). From 50 ha at Cerreto Guidi, Giuseppe Nieri and son Alessandro vie over traditional versus modern styles.

Besides a good Chianti, there are promising *barrique*-aged Castelrapiti Rosso (Cabernet-Sangiovese) and Bianco (Chardonnay), and a *champenoise* Montellori Brut.

Fattoria Pagnana, Rignano sull'Arno (FI).

Carla Guarnieri, Pozzolatico (FI). From 12 ha of the Antiche Terre de' Ricci estate, Chianti and a vdt Sangiovese called Terricci of style.

I Mori, Ginestra Fiorentina (FI).

Le Calvane, Montagnana Val di Pesa (FI). From 14 ha, good Chianti Il Quercione and white vdt Sorbino.

Lilliano, Antella (FI). Historical estate with 21 ha makes often good Chianti.

Majnoni Guicciardini, Vico d'Elsa (FI). From 21 ha Chianti and vdt.

Parri, Montespertoli (FI). Luigi Parri makes good Chianti from the estates of Ribaldaccio, Il Monte, and Corfecciano Urbana.

Pasolini Dall'Onda-Enoagricola, Barberino Val d'Elsa (FI). From 60 ha, the Pasolini family makes Chianti, including a notable *riserva*, Montòli, and vdt.

Poggio Romita, Tavarnelle Val di Pesa (FI). Angiolo Sestini makes fine Chianti.

San Jacopo, Reggello (FI).

San Vito in Fior di Selva, Montelupo Fiorentino (FI). From 22 ha, Laura and Roberto Drighi make tasty Chianti and vdt whites.

Sant'Isidoro, Impruneta (FI).

Tenuta di Calzaiolo, San Casciano Val di Pesa (FI). From 14 ha, Chianti Colli Fiorentini and vdt.

Torre a Cona, San Donato in Collina (FI). Improving Chianti from 11 ha beneath the extraordinary villa owned by the Rossi di Montelera family of Martini & Rossi.

Torre a Decima, Molino del Piano (FI). From 150 ha, sometimes outstanding Chianti and vdt.

Montalbano and Carmignano
(Estates cited without comment are recommended for Carmignano.)

Artimino, Carmignano (FI). The Medici Villa Ferdinanda with its 100 chimneys is the administrative headquarters of this renowned estate, which has 75 ha of vines for Carmignano and Chianti, along with vdt.

Bibbiani, Capraia e Limite (FI). Good Chianti Montalbano from a villa with magnificent gardens and a history dating to 8th-century Longobards.

Fattoria Ambra, Carmignano (FI). From 6 ha, the Rigoli family makes good Carmignano.

Fattoria di Bacchereto, Carmignano (FI). From vines around a former Medici hunting lodge, the Bencini Tesi family

Above: Florence's traditional wine bars are called vinerie, *holes in the wall where Chianti is served by the glass over marble counters. Among the most noted are the* vinerie *in Piazza dell'Olio, Via dei Cimatori, Via dei Neri, and under the arch of San Pierino.*

makes Carmignano, including Le Vigne di Santuaria riserva, and Chianti Montalbano, served with home cooking at the Cantina di Toia, an inn on the property.

Fattoria di Calavria, Carmignano (FI).

Fattoria Il Poggiolo, Carmignano (FI). From 32 ha, Giovanni Cianchi Baldazzi makes fine Carmignano, Vin Ruspo, and Vin Santo.

Fattoria Le Farnete, Carmignano (FI).

Podere Lo Locco, Seano di Carmignano (FI). The Pratesi family makes token quantities of good Carmignano.

Tenuta di Capezzana, Seano di Carmignano (FI). Ugo Contini Bonacossi and family produce the classics of Carmignano from 106 ha on hillsides around their Medici villa. Cellars hold reserve reds and Vin Santo dating back over half a century, but the family, which makes Carmignano at two estates – Villa di Capezzana and Villa

di Trefiano – is equally noted for innovation. Contini Bonacossi, who founded the nationwide group of estates called VIDE, has been called the "King of Carmignano" for his enlightened leadership. He created the rosé Vin Ruspo and red Barco Reale, names shared with other producers, while introducing outside varieties. Ghiaie della Furba (the name refers to its vineyard's gravel along the Furba stream) combines Cabernet and Merlot in a red sometimes compared to a Graves. Chardonnay is used for both a still white varietal and in the blend of the *champenoise* Villa di Capezzana Brut.

Tenuta di Lucciano-Spalletti, Quarrata (PT). From 45 ha, Chianti Montalbano and vdt.

Villa di Trefiano *See* Tenuta di Capezzana.

Chianti Rufina and Pomino

(Estates cited without comment are recommended for Chianti Rufina.)

Casellino, Rufina (FI).
Castello di Nipozzano, Montesodi, Remole, Tenuta di Pomino *See* Marchesi de' Frescobaldi under Wine Houses.
Colognole, Rufina (FI). The Marchesa Spalletti, formerly of Poggio Reale, makes good Chianti Rufina at this old family estate.
Fattoria di Bossi-Marchese Gondi, Pontassieve (FI). From 16.5 ha, the Marchesi Gondi make good Chianti Rufina, Vin Santo, and vdt.
Fattoria di Grignano, Pontassieve (FI). Part of the once immense estate of the Marchesi Gondi has 40 ha for Chianti Rufina.
Fattoria di Vagliano, Rufina (FI).
Fattoria Il Capitano, Pontassieve (FI).
Le Coste, Rufina (FI). From 10 ha, Antonio Grati makes Chianti Rufina.
Selvapiana, Rufina (FI). Steady

evolution in style by owner Francesco Giuntini and winemaker Franco Bernabei has put this Rufina estate in the front ranks of all Chianti, both in class and value. Giuntini holds yields to meager levels in his quest for quality from 27 ha. The new style is expressed in the *riserva* Bucerchiale, though vintages dating back decades show a persuasive traditional stamp. Vdt include good *rosato* and Borro Lastricato, a white from Pinot Bianco and Grigio, as well as a fine Vin Santo.
Tenuta di Poggio, Rufina (FI). From 25 ha, Vittorio Spolveri makes good Chianti Rufina.
Travignoli, Pelago (FI). Giampiero and Giovanni Busi make good Chianti Rufina.
Villa Vetrice, Rufina (FI). From 100 ha of the Galiga and Vetrice estate, Grato and Umberto Grati make fine Chianti Rufina and Vin Santo under the Villa Vetrice label.

Right: vineyards surround the villa of the Selvapiana estate where a noted Chianti Rufina is made to be sold along with olive oil and other produce at a roadside shop (below). Above: the doorway of the Medici villa at the Tenuta di Capezzana.

WINE HOUSES/MERCHANTS

Chianti Rufina and Pomino

Marchesi de' Frescobaldi, Firenze. The illustrious Florentine family, in the wine business since 1300, has estates in Rufina and Pomino among eight properties with more than 500 ha of vines that provide nearly all of its diverse array of wines. Brothers Vittorio, Ferdinando, and Leonardo Frescobaldi divide duties in a firm steadily regaining prestige under winemaker Luciano Boarino after the slump that set back so many Chianti houses. The prime property is Castello di Nipozzano, whose 125 ha make Chianti Rufina riserva, including the praised single vineyard Montesodi. The 75-ha Tenuta di Pomino, revitalized by

Pomino DOC, produces a fine red and two white versions, including Il Benefizio. Remole produces a lighter Chianti Rufina from 55 ha at Pontassieve adjacent to the plant where all wines, including regular Chianti, are bottled. The Frescobaldi are also leaders in the table wine field with Predicato di Biturica Mormoreto and Predicato del Selvante Vergena, as well as Galestro, Sarmento and the popular *novello* Nuovo Fiore. The fine *champenoise* Frescobaldi Brut is processed in Trentino-Alto Adige from Pinot and Chardonnay grown there. The firm also owns the Castelgiocondo estate at Montalcino.
I. L. Ruffino *See* Chianti Classico. This large house has its headquarters at Pontassieve.

Spalletti, Rufina (FI). The historic house, until recently controlled by Cinzano, has been forced to close. The Spalletti family also lost the splendid villa of Poggio Reale, which gave its name to the long admired Chianti Rufina riserva. The villa's wine museum has been maintained.

COOPERATIVES

VICAS, Pontassieve (FI). From grapes conferred by 190 growers in the Sieve and Arno valleys, director Carlo Casadei began by making vdt white and rosé to complement Chianti. But since 1986 the winery has made impressive Rufina sold under the Montulico label, drawing mainly from such noted estates as Parga, Doccia,

Valiano, Monte, and Terra Rossa.
Le Chiantigiane, Tavarnelle Val di Pesa (FI). Group of 10 cooperatives with combined production of about 135,000 hl, bottling Chianti, including a bit of Chianti Classico, other DOCs and vdt, including Galestro.
Cantine Leonardo, Vinci (FI). From growers with about 500 ha, Chianti and vdt, including Galestro, under the Leonardo trademark.

Right: a street market in the centre of Florence.

Wines of Chianti Classico

The long-contested middle ground between Florence and Siena is the realm of Chianti Classico and, to judge from its appearance, the enchanted ground of Italian wine. Yet, though castles and manors match the most elaborate notions of *châteaux*, life in Chiantishire (as it was dubbed by resident English) has a rustic air about it that seems enviably relaxed. Less than a tenth of the 70,000 hectares is under vine. And even where viticulture might be called intense, there are none of those hillsides carpeted in a single hue of green as in Piedmont or Burgundy. Chianti's vast tracts of woods and rocky brushland can be crossed without spotting a vine. But the casual appearance can be deceptive, for some of those cellars noted only yesterday as antiquated now seethe with inventive oenology.

Not so long ago the possessors of those storybook estates cursed the fates of Chianti, as the wine lost its identity, its pride, and its markets. As the crisis deepened, properties were sold, and producers looked desperately for ways to survive in the wine business. Some found an answer in up-market table wines. The prototype was Antinori's Tignanello, the Sangiovese-Cabernet blend named after a plot on the Santa Cristina estate in Chianti Classico. That brainchild of Piero Antinori and oenologist Giacomo Tachis was actually not so novel, since blending of *bordelaise* varieties with Sangiovese was practised in Tuscany at the turn of the century. But Tignanello, more than any other wine, escorted in the new style in Italian reds aged in small, usually French, oak barrels. It also led to the frequent if controversial inclusion of Cabernet in Chianti itself. Antinori followed with Solaia, where Cabernet Sauvignon dominated Sangiovese, a formula that also reaches heights in Castello dei Rampolla's Sammarco.

More than a few producers in Chianti have been won over by the wonders of Cabernet. But others felt that exploiting the French variety's universal attributes might be less rewarding in the long run than exploring the still unattained upper limits of Sangioveto. Growers willing to reduce yields and select from their best plots have rediscovered the native's noble tendencies. The revival dates to 1977, when Sergio Manetti of Monte Vertine devised Le Pergole Torte, the first pure Sangioveto in *barrique*. Others followed, none more dynamically than the estates where Maurizio Castelli, Vittorio Fiore, and Franco Bernabei took charge and built their reputations as the region's star winemakers. Soon other oenologists and producers established their own marks by raising Sangiovese/Sangioveto to new levels, not least of all in more stylish versions of Chianti.

Chianti Classico recovered quickly from the crisis. Since DOCG took effect in 1984, prices for grapes and wine have risen so sharply that merchant houses are reluctant to deal with them. Antinori, for example, stopped using its well known Santa Cristina label for Chianti Classico, preferring wider ranging and more reasonable sources for a vdt. But some estates have stuck gallantly with Chianti. Castello di Ama set an admirable example by putting its best Sangioveto into Chianti riserva from single vineyards, whose prestige and prices rival those of special vdt, and whose class surpasses most of them. Producers now find themselves in the enviable position of having to choose between DOCG and the renegades whose ranks have been swelled by Merlot, Pinot Noir, Chardonnay, Sauvignon Blanc, and more. So with Chianti Classico on the rise again and no end in sight to the vogue for Super Tuscans, the squires of Chiantishire seem to be enjoying the best of both worlds.

Chianti Classico

Classico ranks a cut above the rest of Chianti, thanks not only to history but to closer organization and generally better quality. The bid for a separate DOCG can be justified not as a gesture of superiority but as a chance to prove the substance behind the status. The problem is that Chianti Classico is not a single wine but a multitude. In theory, DOCG might define and evaluate the nature of wines from different places. But, much as such guidelines are needed, the law is not designed to differentiate the typology or relative value of wines from different communes, hillsides, estates, or vineyards. As the DOC fathers remind advocates of classification, Italy is not France, Tuscany is not Bordeaux, and Chianti Classico is not the Haut-Médoc. Yet, beyond the fleeting indications offered by comparative tastings and

summary ratings, there are ways of distinguishing one Chianti from another.

First come history and geography. The real Chianti was and in a sense still is the area covered by the communes of Radda, Gaiole, and Castellina in the province of Siena. Within this domain of the ancient Chianti League, Barone Bettino Ricasoli determined the enduring formula for blending the wine at Brolio, one of many castles or hamlets historically noted for vineyards. Chianti "Storico" or "Geografico" has soils prevalently in the lime-rich *alberese* and flaky *galestro* prized by growers. Its slopes open towards the vast Siena basin, once covered by a lake, where the warm, dry Tyrrhenian influence favours full, even ripening. This environment accounts for a major share of the biggest and longest-lived reserves. The annexation

of Castelnuovo Berardenga to the south added resources of Chianti Classico with equally desirable traits. Stratiform sands and marine deposits are said to account for the heightened bouquets of Chianti from around San Gusmé to the east and Vagliagli to the west. Nor could classical status be denied to the southern part of the commune of Greve in the province of Florence, since it was there at Vignamaggio that the first wine called Chianti, a white, was sold and at nearby Lamole that Sangioveto *piccolo* may have originated. Estates at Greve's neighbouring village of Panzano make some of the most complex and refined reserve Chianti, due to a moderate climate and favourable soil on slopes facing southwest above the Pesa stream.

Purists contested the extension of Classico to the northern arc of the zone. This takes in the area above Greve from Dudda and San Polo in the Monti del Chianti west past Strada and Mercatale to San Casciano, Tavarnelle, and Barberino, all in the province of Florence. That broad sector, somewhat closed in by hills rising between the Pesa, Greve, Ema, and Arno valleys, tends to be cooler and damper than the Storico area and has long been noted for wines of a different stamp. At the turn of the century, wines from the historical Chianti area were distinguished from the "more coloured and rustic" reds of the Val di Greve. But conditions vary markedly from one place to another in the broadened Chianti Classico zone, whose irregular contours contain soils with a myriad of macro- and micro-elements. Their effect on quality is not always understood, but the northern reaches also have areas where vines prosper.

Nature's variables are rarely as capricious as the human factor in Chianti. It has been said that wines were more individualistic in the old days than now, though the distinctions probably reflected defects as often as virtues. The overworked term tradition was too often synonymous with backwards or slipshod winemaking. The rules of the old oenology weren't necessarily bad, but their interpretation was often ruinous: overheated fermentations with uncontrolled yeasts and bacteria, long ageing in old and unhygienic casks. The charge that the new oenology has standardized Chianti is nonsense. Besides greater convenience, science has expanded horizons, giving producers with imagination and artistic sense (and few qualms about bending outmoded rules) more options than ever before.

The most glaring errors have occurred in Chianti's vineyards. Through the chaotic planting of recent

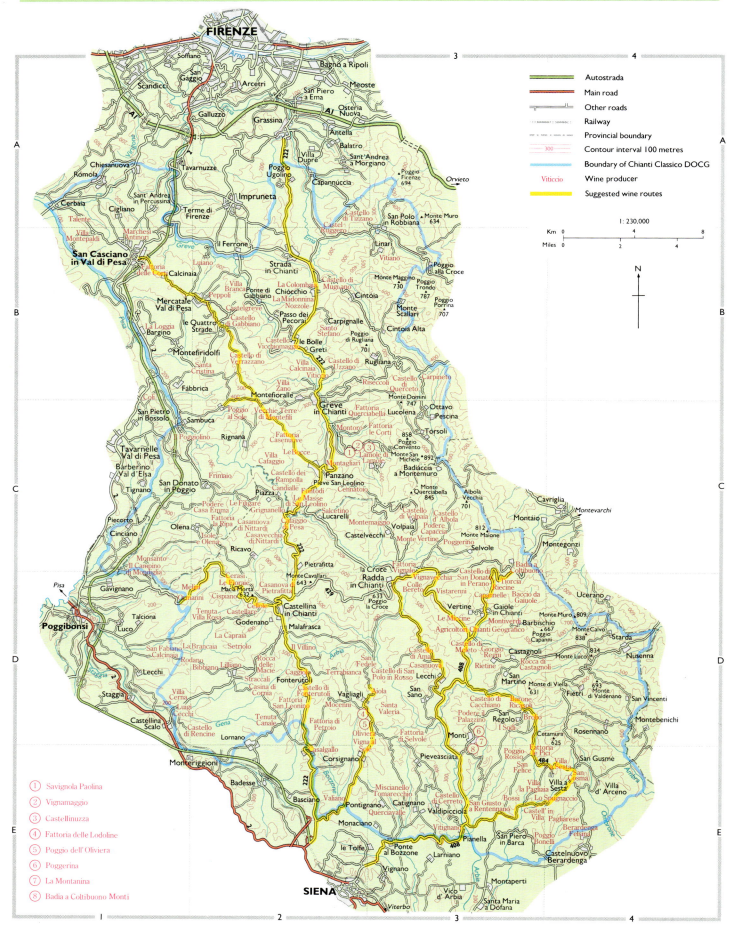

FIRENZE

Soffiano
San Gaggio
Scandicci
Arcetri
Meoste
Bagno a Ripoli
San Piero a Ema
Osteria Nuova
A1
Gallúzzo
Grassina
Antella
Balatro
Sant'Andrea a Morgiano
Villa Dupré
Capannúccia
Poggio Firenze 694
Orvieto
Chiesanuova
Rómola
Tavarnuzze
Poggio Ugolino
Castello di Tizzano
San Polo in Robbiana
Monte Muro 634
Cerbáia
Sant'Andrea in Percussina
Terme di Firenze
Impruneta
Castel Ruggero
Linari
Talente
Cigliano
il Ferrone
Strada in Chianti
Vitiano
Poggio alla Croce
Villa Montepaldi
Marchesi Antinori
San Casciano in Val di Pesa
Calcinaia
Luiano
Villa Branca
La Colombáia
Castello di Mugnano
Monte Maggio 730
Poggio Trondo
Poggio Porrina 787
Fattoria delle Corti
Peppoli
Ponte di Gabbiano
Chiócchio
La Madonnina Nozzole
Cintoia
Mercatale Val di Pesa
Castelgreve
Passo dei Pecorai
Santo Stefano
Carpignalle
Monte Scallari
Cintoia Alta
le Quattro Strade
Castello di Gabbiano
le Bolle
Greti
Poggio di Rugliana
Montefiridolfi
Castello di Vicchiomaggio
Monte 701
La Loggia Bargino
Castello di Verrazzano
Villa Calcinaia
Viticcio
Castello di Uzzano
Rugliana
Santa Cristina
Villa Zano
Fábbrica
Montefioralle
Castello di Riseccoli
Castello di Querceto
Carpineto di Querceto
Poggio al Sole
Vecchie Terre di Montefili
Greve in Chianti
Montoro
Fattoria Querciabella
Monte Domini 747
Ottavo
San Pietro in Bossolo
Poggiolino
Rignana
Fattoria le Corti
Lucolena
Pescina
Torsoli
Sambuca
Fattoria Casenuove
858 Poggio Convento
Tavarnelle Val di Pesa
Villa Cafaggio
le Bocce
Montagliari
Lamole di Lamole
Monte San Michele 892
Badiáccia a Montemuro
Barberino Val d'Elsa
Castello dei Rampolla
Panzano
Pieve San Leolino
Cennatoio
Candialle
Fontodi
Monte Querciabella 845
San Donato in Poggio
Tignano
Piazza
Le Filigare
Grignanello
le Masse di San Leolino
Lucarelli
Montemaggio
Albola Vecchia 701
Cavríglia
Podere Casa Emma
Salcetino
Volpaia
Montevarchi
Piecorto
Fattoria la Ripa
Casanuova di Nittardi
Cafaggio Pesa
Podere Capaccia
Castello d'Albola
Montaio
Olena
Casavecchia di Nittardi
Monte Vertine
Poggerino
Isole e Olena
Ricavo
Monte Maione 812
Montegonzi
Cinciano
Pietrafitta
la Croce
Monte Vertine
Selvole
Monsanto Il Campino di Mondiglia
Cerasi
Monte Cavallari 643
Fattoria Vignale
Badia a Coltibuono
Pisa
Gavignano
Le Fioraie
Macia Morta
Casanova di Pietrafitta
Radda in Chianti
Vignavecchia
Castello di San Donato in Perano
Nusenna
Melini
Cispiano
633 Poggio la Croce
Colle Bereto
Vistarenni
San Donato in Perano
Riecine
Baccio da Gaiuole
Ucerano
Tenuta Villa Rosa
Castellare
Cellole
Castellina in Chianti
459
Capannelle
Monte Muro 809
Poggibonsi
Godenano
Malafrasca
Le Miccine
Vertine
Gaiole in Chianti
Barbischio
Luco
La Capraia
Setriolo
Il Villino
Agricoltori Chianti Geografico
Montiverdi
Poggio Capanni 667
Monte Calvo 838
Starda
San Fabiano Calcinaia
La Brancaia
Rodano
Lilliano
Rocca delle Mácie
Caggiole
Terrabianca
Castello di Meleto
Castello di Giorgio Regni
Castagnoli
Monte Luco 834
Nusenna
Lecchi
Staggia
Bibbiano
Straccali
Casina di Corsia
Fonterutoli
Castello di San Polo in Rosso
Castello di Fonterutoli
Lecchi
Rietine
Rocca di Castagnoli
Villa Cerna
Luigi Cecchi
Fattoria San Leonino
Vagliagli
Aiola
San Sano
San Martino
Monte di Viella 631
Monte di Valdenano 693
San Vincenti
Castellina Scalo
Castello di Rencine
Tenuta Canale
Mocenni
Santa Valeria
Castello di Cacchiano
Barone Ricásoli
Fietri
Montebenichi
Lornano
Fattoria di Petroio
Fattoria di Selvole
Monti
Podere il Palazzino
San Régolo
Brolio
Rosennano
Cetamura 625
Olíviera Vigna al Pino
Pieveasciata
Poggio Rosso
San Felice
Villa la Pagliáia
484 Villa Sesta
San Gusme
Monteriggioni
Casalgallo
Corsignano
Villa a Sesta
San Cosma
Badesse
Miscianello Tomarecchio
Castello di Cerreto
San Giusto a Rentennano
Bossi
Lo Spugnáccio
Villa d'Arceno
Basciano
Valiano
Catignano
Querciavalle
Valdipicciola
Vitignano
"Castell'in Villa"
Berardenga Felsina
Pagliarese
Pontignano
San Piero in Barca
Poggio Bonelli
Monaciano
Ponte al Bozzone
Pianella
Castelnuovo Berardenga
le Tolfe
408
Larniano
Vignano
Montaperti
SIENA
Viterbo
Vico d'Arbia
Santa Maria a Dófana

Legend

Autostrada
Main road
Other roads
Railway
Provincial boundary
300 Contour interval 100 metres
Boundary of Chianti Classico DOCG
Viticcio Wine producer
Suggested wine routes

1: 230,000

Km 0 4 8
Miles 0 2 4

N

times some estates have retained the Sangioveto native to Chianti, others have planted Sangiovese *grosso*, particularly Brunello. Yet it is estimated that the dominant subvariety in Chianti today is Sangiovese di Romagna, which rarely performs as well as in the warmer climes back home. But since nearly two-thirds of Chianti Classico's vineyards are due to be replanted over the next decade, growers have a chance to start anew and, it might be hoped, to get it right this time around. Still, despite all, steady improvements have come about through closer cropping and selective harvesting. The growing number of fine estate wines demonstrates notable progress. But Chianti Classico at its finest will be the privilege of future generations to enjoy.

Through the coming era, though, wines seem sure to be subjected to ever greater scrutiny as consumers insist on guidelines. Producers might help by mentioning communes on labels of all estate-bottled Chianti Classico. But this would provide only a hint, since communal confines were often drawn along political rather than geographical lines and wines made within each can vary to extremes. A more meaningful breakdown would be by estates, as in the Haut Médoc, where relative values have been assigned to *crus*. But Chianti Classico with all its revisions and novelties isn't ready for that. Until it is, admirers will be left to rely on their own palates or on the experts' ratings and tasting notes.

Zone: A tract of hills extending from just south of Florence to just north of Siena between the Monti del Chianti to the east and the Pesa and Elsa valleys to the west, taking in all or part of nine communes: Greve, San Casciano, Tavarnelle, and Barberino in Firenze province; Radda, Gaiole, Castellina, Castelnuovo Berardenga, and Poggibonsi in Siena. Dry red. Grapes: Sangiovese 75-90%, Canaiolo Nero 5-10%, Trebbiano Toscano/Malvasia del Chianti 2-5%, other reds up to 10%. Yld 52.5/75, Alc 12, riserva 12.5, Acd 0.5, Ag 8 mths; riserva 3 yrs.

Other wines of note

The Val d'Arbia DOC zone covers the southern flank of Chianti Classico and ranges through Siena's hills, where it is described. Some producers of Bianco and Vin Santo Val d'Arbia will be noted in the following list, which also cites numerous vdt with more emphasis on the fine than the common.

ESTATES/GROWERS

(Estates cited without comment are recommended for Chianti Classico.)

Aiola, Vagliagli (SI). Senator Giovanni Malagodi owns this estate with 26 ha producing Chianti, Bianco Val d'Arbia, and a Sangiovese vdt Logaiolo.
Baccio da Gaiuole, Gaiole (SI).
Badia a Coltibuono, Gaiole (SI). The estate of Piero Stucchi-Prinetti and family comprises the 11th-century abbey and cellars at Coltibuono, where some of Chianti's earliest wine was made, and 60 ha of vines among Chianti's oldest at Monti, 15 km away. Manager Roberto Stucchi-Prinetti, a graduate of the University of California Davis, and consultant Maurizio Castelli make Chianti riserva whose uncommon ageing capacity may be surpassed by the virile vdt Sangioveto. Also fine Vin Santo. Coltibuono Bianco, Rosato, and Rosso usually include purchased wines. A trattoria on the estates serves typical dishes with wines.
Badia a Passignano *See* Marchesi L. & P. Antinori under Wine Houses.
Berardenga-Fattoria di Felsina, Castelnuovo Berardenga (SI). Manager Giuseppe Mazzocolin and winemaker Franco Bernabei have earned this estate the accolade of the Margaux of Chianti. From 50 ha come opulent Chianti, exemplified by the *riserva* Vigneto Rancia, and the Sangiovese vdt Fontalloro, which gains stature from Bernabei's form of *governo*. Also in the front rank of its category is the barrel-fermented Chardonnay I Sistri.
Bibbiano, Castellina (SI).
Bossi, Castelnuovo Berardenga (SI).
Brolio or **Castello di Brolio**, Gaiole (SI). At the castle Chianti was regenerated by Barone Bettino Ricasoli and some of the noblest wines of former times were produced. The Iron Baron's namesake, Bettino Ricasoli, still owns the castle and vineyards, whose 250 ha include some of Chianti's choicest plots. He is a shareholder and president of the corporation that owns the Brolio and Barone Ricasoli trademarks.
Cafaggio di Pesa, Castellina (SI).
Caggiolo, Castellina (SI). Overworked brothers Ezio and Pietro Rivella manage to make sometimes superb Chianti here as a sideline.

Below: the ancient abbey of Badia a Coltibuono is a landmark of Chianti Classico and headquarters of one of its leading estates.

Above: Alceo Di Napoli at his desk in the Castello dei Rampolla, an estate known for Chianti as well as the Cabernet-Sangiovese blend of Sammarco.

Left: a roadside chapel near Badia a Passignano in Chianti Classico.

Right: the hamlet of Volpaia where the estate of Castello di Volpaia has vineyards that are among the highest in the Chianti Classico area.

Candialle, Panzano (SI). From 3 ha, Swiss owner Gerd von Bentheim makes fine Chianti.

Capannelle, Gaiole (SI). Raffaele Rossetti has just over 2 ha of vines for recherché vdt Capannelle Rosso, Bianco, and Chardonnay. Gold and silver labels raise the values of often genteel but overpriced wines.

Casalgallo, Quercegrossa (SI).

Casanova di Pietrafitta, Castellina (SI).

Casanuova, Lecchi (SI).

Casanuova di Nittardi, Castellina (SI).

Casavecchia di Nittardi, Castellina (SI). Noted Chianti from just over 2 ha on a farm that once belonged to the family of Michelangelo Buonarotti.

Casina di Cornia, Castellina (SI). From 5 ha, Antoine Luginbuhl and Duccio Fontani makes wholesome Chianti.

Castellare (di Castellina), Castellina (SI). Publisher Paolo Panerai and wife Fioretta have brought lustre to this estate with strikingly labelled wines made by Maurizio Castelli. From 20 ha come fine Chianti and the highly regarded vdt I Sodi di San Niccolò, from Sangioveto with Malvasia Nera. Vin Santo is notable, as are promising new vdt Chardonnay Canonico and

Sauvignon Blanc Spartito. Governo di Castellare is a snappy young red.

Castellinuzza, Lamole-Greve (FI).

Castell'in Villa, Castelnuovo Berardenga (SI). From 54 ha of choice vines, Greek-born Princess Coralia Pignatelli della Leonessa makes excellent Chianti even in off years, along with Bianco Val d'Arbia, Vin Santo, and the impressive Sangiovese vdt Balsastrada.

Castello d'Albola or **Pian d'Albola**, Radda in Chianti (SI). From 52 ha around the 10th-century castle owned by Zonin of the Veneto come Chianti, Bianco Val d'Arbia, and the *novello* Sant'Ilario.

Castello dei Rampolla, Panzano (FI). From 36 ha at 350-400 m around the princely castle at Santa Lucia in Faulle, Alceo Di Napoli and family select for always good Chianti, though their pride is the Cabernet-Sangiovese blend Sammarco, sometimes cited as a rival to Sassicaia or Mouton Rothschild.

Castello di Ama, Lecchi (SI). The estate directed by Silvano Formigli has assumed a lead role in Classico by putting prime emphasis on Chianti while also creating vdt of unsurpassed class. From 85 ha around the hamlet of Ama, long noted for its wines, oenologist Marco Pallanti selects for the

excellent single vineyard Chianti riserve of Bellavista, La Casuccia, and San Lorenzo. Vdt use the appellation Colline di Ama in fine Sauvignon, Pinot Grigio, and Chardonnay. Benefitting from occasional tips from Mouton-Rothschild's Léon Patrick, Pallanti has made impressive Merlot Vigna l'Apparita and Tuscany's best Pinot Noir to date in Vigna Il Chiuso, though the young winemaker promises still better things.

Castello di Cacchiano, Gaiole (SI). The castle near Brolio, in the Ricasoli-Firidolfi family since 1150, has 30 ha of vines where Elisabetta Ricasoli Balbi Valier and Giovanni Ricasoli make persuasive Chianti (the second label is Castello di Montegrossi) and a fine red vdt Vigneto Selice.

Castello di Cerreto, Pianella (SI). Fashion designer Emilio Pucci owns this estate whose extraordinary potential is largely neglected.

Castello di Fonterutoli, Castellino (SI). Lapo Mazzei, long president of the Gallo Nero consortium, heads this eminent estate in the family since 1435. From 34 ha, sons Filippo and Francesco and oenologist Franco Bernabei have recently brought the wines to unprecedented levels with fine Chianti, exemplified by the *riserva* Ser Lapo

from the Siepi vineyard, and the vdt Concerto, one of Tuscany's best Cabernet-Sangiovese blends.

Castello di Gabbiano, Mercatale Val di Pesa (FI). Winemaker Franco Bernabei has realized good Chianti, lately upstaged by two vdt – the pure Sangiovese Ania and R & R, which blends Sangiovese with Cabernet and Merlot. Also impressive is the Chardonnay Ariella.

Castello di Meleto, Gaiole (SI). The towered castle with 190 ha of choice vineyards could be one of Chianti's top estates, but potential has been squandered by the Viticola Toscana/Le Storiche Cantine group, which also controls Castello di Monterinaldi/La Pesanella, and Castello di San Donato in Perano, none of whose wines are recommended.

Castello di Monterinaldi See Castello di Meleto.

Above: The charismatic Piero Antinori has made the ancient Florentine house of Marchesi L. & P. Antinori a leader in Italian wine with a worldwide reputation for combining tradition with innovation. The family has estates in Tuscany and Orvieto in Umbria for production of both regions' classics and such influential table wines as Tignanello, Solaia, and Cervaro della Sala.

Castello di Mugnana, Greve (FI).
Castello di Querceto, Greve (FI). From 45 ha around this Longobard castle near the Sugame pass, Alessandro François makes refined Chianti and vdt Sangiovese La Corte, white Le Giuncaie, and Vin Santo.
Castello di Rencine, Castellina (SI).
Castello di San Donato in Perano *See* Castello di Meleto.
Castello di San Polo in Rosso, Gaiole (SI). From 22 ha, Cesare and Katrin Canessa and oenologist Maurizio Castelli make fine Chianti and the prized pure Sangioveto vdt Cetinaia, as well as Bianco and Rosato d'Erta.
Castello di Tizzano, San Polo (FI).
Castello di Uzzano, Greve (FI). From 47 ha at this historical estate, Briano Castelbarco Albani Masetti and Marion de Jacobert have updated the style of Chianti, but more impressive is a red vdt Vigna Niccolò da Uzzano.

Castello di Verrazzano, Greve (FI). From 42 ha around the manor where the explorer Giovanni da Verrazzano was born, the Cappellini family makes Chianti and a red vdt Sassello.
Castello di Volpaia, Radda in Chianti (SI). Carlo and Giovannella Stianti Mascheroni have converted cellars and vineyards at the medieval hamlet of Volpaia into one of Chianti's most unique and talked about estates. From 37 ha of some of the zone's highest vines at 430-600 m, Maurizio Castelli makes wines noted for scented refinement. Besides Chianti, there are the admired red vdt Coltassala (from Sangioveto and Mammolo) and Balifico (from the same grapes with Cabernet). The oak-aged Sauvignon-Sémillon Torniello is a revelation. Also Bianco Val d'Arbia and good Vin Santo.
Castello Vicchiomaggio, Greve (FI). From 22 ha around the towering castle,

English owner John Matta and Vittorio Fiore make noted Chianti, including the *riserve* Prima Vigna and Vigna Petri, along with vdt Ripa delle More (Sangiovese with Cabernet) and Ripa delle Mimose (Chardonnay).
Castel Ruggero, Antella (FI).
Cellole *See* San Fabiano Calcinaia.
Cennatoio, Panzano (FI). From 8.3 ha, Leandro Alessi and winemaker Alfonso Garberoglio produce notable Chianti. They also buy Chianti and bottle it under the Luca della Robbia label.
Cerasi-Fattoria Concadoro, Castellina (SI).
Cispiano, Castellina (SI).
Colle Bereto, Radda (SI). From 6 ha, Chianti and a Sangiovese-Cabernet vdt called Il Tòcco.
Fattoria Casenuove, Panzano (FI). From 24 ha Pietro Pandolfini makes well known Chianti.
Fattoria delle Corti, San Casciano

Val di Pesa (FI). Modest Chianti from more than 50 ha at the historical Principe Corsini estate.
Fattoria delle Lodoline, Vagliagli (SI).
Fattoria di Petroio, Quercegrossa (SI). From 15 ha, Pamela and Gian Luigi Lenzi make notably improved Chianti.
Fattoria di Selvole, Vagliagli (SI).
Fattoria La Ripa, San Donato in Poggio (FI).
Fattoria Le Corti, Greve (FI). From 7 ha, modest Chianti and a promising red vdt Masso Tondo.
Fattoria Le Pici, San Gusmé (SI). From 9 ha, Gunnar Lüneburg makes fine Chianti.
Fattoria Querciabella, Greve (FI). Chianti and good red vdt Camartina.
Fattoria San Leonino, Castellina (SI). Lionello Marchesi acquired this property with 50 ha of vines and good potential, to become the first owner of estates in Chianti Classico, Montalcino (Val di Suga), and Montepulciano (Trerose).
Fattoria Vignale, Radda (SI). From 18 ha, fine Chianti from the estate owned by Roberto Bracali that also houses a comfortable hotel (Relais Fattoria Vignale) and a centre for historical studies of the zone. An expensive restaurant serves Vignale wines.

Fontodi, Panzano (FI). The estate run by Marco and Giovanni Manetti and oenologist Franco Bernabei excels with Chianti riserva Vigna del Sorbo and makes admired vdt from 33 ha. These include what may be the most acclaimed pure Sangioveto to date in Flaccianello della Pieve, named after the nearby chapel of San Leolino, as well as unique barrel-aged whites Meriggio, from Traminer, Pinot Bianco, and Sauvignon, and Solstizio, an opulent late harvest version.

Frimaio, San Donato in Poggio (FI).

Grignanello, Castellina (SI).

Il **Campino di Mondiglia**, Barberino Val d'Elsa (FI).

Il **Poggiolino**, Sambuca Val di Pesa (FI). From 6 ha, Carlo and Maria Grazia Pacini make improving Chianti and a good Sangiovese vdt Roncaia.

Il **Villino**, Castellina (SI).

I Sodi, Gaiole (SI).

Isole e Olena, Barberino Val d'Elsa (FI). Passionate Piedmontese manager Paolo De Marchi makes fine Chianti from his 36 ha, along with the admired pure Sangiovese vdt Cepparello, and excellent Vin Santo. He uses the Collezione De Marchi label for a good Chardonnay and a recently conceived Cabernet Sauvignon. He may have been the first in Chianti to plant Syrah, for which the first vintage was 1989.

La Brancaia, Castellina (SI). From 5 ha, Bruno and Brigitte Widmer make fine Chianti.

La Capraia, Castellina (SI). Owner Calogero Calì is reviving this estate for Chianti and other wines vinified at Rocca di Castagnole.

La Colombaia, **La Madonnina**, Chiocchio (FI). The Triacca brothers and Oliviero Masini, who call their association Notorius, make good

Chianti at these estates with 80 ha between them.

La Loggia, Montefiridolfi (FI). From 12 ha, Giulio Baruffaldi makes Chianti called Terra dei Cavalieri, noteworthy for its horse inspired labels, along with vdt and *spumante*.

La Montanina, Monti (SI).

Lamole di Lamole, Greve (FI). The Antiche Fattorie Fiorentine group of the Toscano family makes sometimes convincing Chianti, including the *riserva* Campolungo, and Vin Santo from 22 ha of the Pile e Lamole estate once as renowned for its wines as was neighbouring Vignamaggio. They also bottle Classico from the Salcetino estate at Lucarelli and regular Chianti called Marsilio Ficino from the Il Poggio estate at Gaville.

Le Bocce, Panzano in Chianti (FI). Good Chianti from 16 ha.

Le Filigare, San Donato in Poggio (FI). From 7 ha, winemaker Gabriella Tani makes good Chianti and a stylish red vdt called Podere Le Rocce.

Le Fioraie, Castellina (SI).

Le Masse, Panzano-Greve (FI). From 3 ha, Scotsman Norman Bain makes a highly praised Chianti with help from Franco Bernabei.

Le Miccine, Gaiole (SI).

Lilliano, Castellina (SI). This venerable estate of the Berlingieri and Ruspoli families could be one of Chianti's true *châteaux*, but wines from nearly 50 ha don't quite measure up.

Lo Spugnaccio, Castelnuovo Berardenga (SI).

Luiano, Mercatale Val di Pesa (FI).

Miscianello Tomarecchio, Vagliagli (SI). From 7 ha, good Chianti and Bianco Val d'Arbia.

Mocenni, Vagliagli (SI). From 18 ha, good Chianti and Bianco Val d'Arbia.

Monsanto, Barberino Val d'Elsa (FI). From 45 ha, Milanese Fabrizio Bianchi makes distinguished Chianti, including the *riserva* Il Poggio from a 5-ha plot, a wine that has often stood above the crowd, and the long-lasting Sangioveto Grosso from the Vigneti di Scanni.

Monsanto's special vdt reds are the Sangiovese-Cabernet Tinscvil, and the pure Cabernet Nemo. The estate also makes good Vin Santo.

Montagliari, Panzano (FI). From 40 ha, Giovanni Cappelli makes a nice Chianti, a middling red vdt Brunesco di San Lorenzo, and often excellent Vin Santo that carries his name. He also runs So.Co.Vi.Ch., which bottles Chianti La Quercia. A trattoria on the property serves local specialities.

Monte Vertine, Radda (SI). Iconoclast Sergio Manetti, with veteran consultant Giulio Gambelli, made Tuscany's first pure Sangioveto in *barriques* in 1977: Le Pergole Torte from 1977, followed by Il Sodaccio, which contains some Canaiolo. From 8 ha or so of slowly expanding vineyards he makes only vdt, since he dropped use of the term Chianti Classico in favour of Monte Vertine alone. Like the others, Vin Santo is first rate. At last report, Manetti was abandoning *barriques* (too popular) for larger barrels and had planted the nearly extinct Colorino trained onto dried chestnut trees – just like old times.

Montemaggio, Radda (SI). Publisher Giampaolo Bonechi has 13 ha of high vineyards where oenologist Vittorio Fiore makes Chianti labelled Montemaggio and, from purchases, Castello di Radda.

Montiverdi, Gaiole (SI).

Montoro, Greve (FI).

Nozzole, Greve (SI). The estate owned by the Folonari family has 75 ha for Chianti, including Podere della Forra, distributed by Premiovini.

Oliviera, Vagliagli (SI). Mario Bandini makes good Chianti from 3 ha.

Ormanni, Poggibonsi (SI).

Pagliarese, Castelnuovo Berardenga (SI). From 25 ha, the Sanguineti family and consultant Vittorio Fiore make noted Chianti, Bianco Val d'Arbia, Vin Santo, and the red vdt Camerlengo.

Peppoli, Mercatale Val di Pesa (FI). Antinori uses the 60 ha of the former Villa Terciona for a Chianti that carries the tradition of Sangiovese and Canaiolo seasoned in large casks to peaks of harmony and drinkability.

Podere Capaccia, Radda (SI). From 3 ha, good Chianti and Sangioveto vdt Querciagrande, which shows winemaker Vittorio Fiore's touch.

Podere Casa Emma, Barberino Val d'Elsa (FI). Good Chianti from 11 ha.

Podere Il Palazzino, Monti (SI). From 6 ha, Alessandro and Andrea Sderci make fine Chianti and the deservedly acclaimed pure Sangioveto vdt Grosso Senese, plus Vin Santo.

Poggerina, Monti (SI). Good Chianti made by Francesco Giorgi at the smallest registered vineyard (0.1375 ha) in the Gallo Nero consortium.

Poggerino, Radda (SI).

Poggio al Sole, Sambuca Val di Pesa (FI). From 7 ha, Aldo Torrini and oenologist Gabriella Tani make noted Chianti, Vin Santo, and the white vdt from Gewürztraminer called Vino della Signora.

Poggio Bonelli, Castelnuovo Berardenga (SI).

Poggio dell'Oliviera, Vagliagli (SI). Brunaldo Bandini makes good Chianti from 2.2 ha.

Poggio Rosso, Castelnuovo Berardenga (SI). On a *podere* belonging to San Felice, Enzo Morganti selects Sangioveto for an excellent Chianti riserva.

Querciavalle, Vagliagli (SI). From 10 ha, the Losi brothers make fine Chianti and Bianco Val d'Arbia.

Giorgio Regni-Fattoria Valtellina, Gaiole (SI). From 2.2 ha, Giorgio and Giuseppina Regni make good Chianti and vdt red Convivio.

Riecine, Gaiole (SI). Englishman John Dunkley and Italian wife Palmina bought this *podere* in 1971 and turned its 2.2 ha of high vineyards into one of Chianti's most respected *crus*. Consultant Carlo Ferrini helps make exemplary Classico and pure Sangioveto vdt La Gioia di Riecine, along with a bit of Bianco.

Rietine, Gaiole (SI).

Riseccoli, Greve (FI).

Rocca delle Macie, Castellina (SI). The corporation headed by film producer Italo Zingarelli bases operations on 220 ha of vines in Chianti, but production ranges farther afield. Top of the line is Chianti Fizzano riserva and the red vdt Ser Gioveto. Orvieto Classico comes from Podere di Caiano. Vdt includes Galestro and the light red Rubizzo and Decembrino.

Rocca di Castagnoli, Castagnoli (SI). Owner Calogero Calì and manager Walter Filiputti (of Fruli) make fine Chianti from nearly 150 ha of vines here and at La Capraia. Production, which includes Val d'Arbia and Chardonnay, will soon be enhanced by pure Sangiovese and Cabernet vdt.

Rodano, Castellina (SI). From 18 ha, Vittorio Pozzesi makes fine Chianti.

Salcetino See Lamole di Lamole.

San Cosma, San Gusmè (SI). Bent Myhre makes good Chianti from 6 ha.

San Fabiano Calcinaia, Poggibonsi (SI). Winemaker Giuseppe Bassi fashions increasingly fine Chianti from two estates: 20 ha for San Fabiano Calcinaia and 15 ha for Cellole near Castellina. Promising vdt are called Cerviolo, the red from Cabernet and the white from Chardonnay with Sauvignon.

San Fedele, Radda (SI).

San Felice, Castelnuovo Berardenga (SI). The estate owned by the Agrel corporation occupies an ancient hamlet with 190 ha of vines where experiments in native clones have been carried out. Some of the zone's finest reds are styled by young oenologist Leonardo Bellaccini: Chianti and *riserva* Il Grigio, the pure Sangioveto Vigorello, and Predicato di Biturica. Whites include Bianco Val d'Arbia and Vin Santo, plus a vdt Chardonnay. San Felice under director Enzo Morganti also sells the fine Chianti Poggio Rosso riserva and the markedly improved Chianti of Villa La Pagliaia. The firm uses the Pagni label for a commercial Chianti.

San Giusto a Rentennano, Monti (SI). From 24 ha around a former Cistercian monastery, Francesco Martini di Cigala and family make notable Chianti and some 8,000 bottles of Percarlo, the most virile pure Sangioveto, selected from two distinct plots and aged in *barrique*. Vin Santo is among the authentic best.

Santa Cristina, Montefiridolfi (FI). The Antinori estate whose name, long used for Chianti Classico, is now applied to a red vdt. The original Tignanello and Solaia plots are amongst more than 100 ha of vineyards (*see* Marchesi L. & P. Antinori).

Santa Valeria, Vagliagli (SI). From 6 ha in a privileged spot, fashion designer Alberto Procovio and adviser Carlo Ferrini make fine Chianti.

Santo Stefano, Greve (FI).

Savignola Paolina, Vagliagli (SI). The death of venerable *vignaiola* Paolina Fabbri left the future of this tiny estate in doubt.

Setriolo, Castellina (SI). Desmond and Antoinette Crawford make good Chianti from 2 ha.

Talente, San Casciano Val di Pesa (FI). Good Chianti from 3 ha.

Tenuta Canale, Castellina (SI). From 7 ha, Andrea Aiello makes Chianti Tenuta Canale and bottles more under the Aiello label.

Tenuta Villa Rosa, Castellina (SI). From 37 ha, the Lucherini family makes sometimes good Chianti.

Terrabianca, Vagliagli (SI). From 15 ha, Swiss owner Roberto Guldener and Vittorio Fiore make Chianti Scassino and Vigna della Croce, vdt Campaccio (Cabernet-Sangiovese) and Piano della Cappella (Chardonnay).

Tiorcia, Gaiole (SI). Angelo Acconcia makes a bit of *simpatico* Chianti.

Valiano, Vagliagli (SI). Decent Chianti from 56 ha.

Vecchie Terre di Montefili, Greve (FI). Roccaldo Acuti and winemaker Vittorio Fiore have developed one of the most admired small estates with 11 ha for fine Chianti, the acclaimed red vdt Bruno di Rocca, and the novel white vdt Vigna Regis, from Chardonnay with Sauvignon Blanc and Traminer.

Vigna al Sole, Vagliagli (SI). From 3 ha, Ademo Bandini makes good Chianti.

Vignamaggio, Greve (FI). New owner Gianni Nunziante is renewing cellars and 32 ha of vines and with winemaker Franco Bernabei is heading the historical estate (where Mona Lisa was

Above: a farmhouse near Castellina.

born) back to the front ranks of Chianti. A pure Sangiovese vdt Gherardino is promising.

Vignavecchia, Radda (SI). From 24 ha, the Beccari family makes Chianti and vdt red Canvalle.

Villa Antinori. Brand name of Marchesi L. & P. Antinori whose image is based on an estate near Florence that no longer belongs to the family.

Villa a Sesta, San Gusmè (SI). The estate around a lovely hamlet recently changed ownership. Good potential for Chianti.

Villa Branca, Mercatale Val di Pesa (FI). Modest Chianti Santa Lucia from 60 ha at the estate of the Branca family that originated Fernet Branca.

Villa Cafaggio, Panzano (FI). From some 30 ha, Stefano Farkas makes noted Chianti and the respected red vdt Solatio Basilica and San Martino.

Villa Calcinaia, Greve (FI). The estate in the Capponi family since 1523 makes modest Chianti and vdt from 40 ha.

Villa Cerna, Castellina (SI). Luigi Cecchi and family use this ancient residence with 80 ha of vines for their top Chianti riserva and the vdt Spargolo, a Predicato di Cardisco.

Villa Montepaldi, San Casciano Val di Pesa (FI). The former Medici villa makes middling Chianti from 33 ha.

Villa Zano, Greve (FI). The Ruffino-Folonari estate with 76 ha is the prime source of Chianti Aziano and Riserva Ducale.

Vistarenni, Gaiole (SI). The estate with 40 ha of vines surrounding the splendid villa is owned by the Tognana family. Director Elisabetta Tognana and Friulian oenologist Gaspare Buscemi make respected Chianti and Bianco and Vin Santo Val d'Arbia, along with the vdt red Codirosso.

Vitiano, San Polo in Chianti (FI).

Viticcio, Greve (FI). From 15 ha, Chianti and pure Sangioveto vdt Prunaio.

Vitignano, Pianella (SI). The estate with 19 ha of vines for Chianti has notable potential, largely undeveloped.

WINE HOUSES/MERCHANTS

Barone Ricasoli-Brolio, Gaiole in Chianti (SI). The Ricasoli family has made wine since 1141 at Castello di Brolio, which might qualify as the world's oldest winery. Fame came after Barone Bettino Ricasoli devised the formula in the mid-1800s that made Brolio Chianti's leader for more than a century. After a lapse due to an ill-starred affiliation with Seagram's, new mangement under Englishman Roger Lambert has led to marked improvement in the firm's wines under chief oenologist Luigi Casagrande. The fine Chianti Classico labelled Brolio and other wines come from the estate, whose vineyards include a plot called Torricella for the cask-aged white that ranks with the best of Malvasia. Besides Chianti, there is fine Vin Santo and the vdt Brolio Bianco and Rosato. The Barone Ricasoli label applies to a young Chianti called San Ripolo and other wines from Brolio vineyards or elsewhere. Recent additions include white vdt Nebbiano from Sauvignon Blanc and Riesling Italico and rosé Tramonto. The range also includes Orvieto, Vernaccia di San Gimignano, and Barone Ricasoli Brut, a *champenoise* from Oltrepò Pavese.

Carpineto, Dudda (FI). Giovanni Carlo Sacchet is a reliable purveyor of Chianti, Orvieto, and other wines.

Luigi Cecchi & Figli, Castellina Scalo (SI). The firm owned and run by Luigi Cecchi and sons Cesare and Andrea processes some 50,000 hl a year, including Chianti, Brunello, Vino Nobile, Vernaccia, Orvieto, along with Galestro, Sarmento, and other vdt.

Coli, Tavarnelle Val di Pesa (FI). Chianti Classico under the Coli and Della Badessa labels.

Conti Serristori, Sant'Andrea in Percussina (FI). The firm, owned by Gruppo Italiano Vini and directed by Nunzio Capurso, has headquarters at the ancient estates of the Conti Serristori with the Albergaccio where the Florentine statesman Niccolò Machiavelli lived in exile. His name figures in the Machiavelli riserva from the 22 ha Vigna di Fontalle and the red vdt Ser Niccolò. The range also includes Vernaccia di San Gimignano.

Fossi, Compiobbi (FI). Andrea and Gianfranco Fossi make 300-500 hl of Chianti Classico, including some of the most admired *riserve*.

Marchesi L. & P. Antinori, Firenze. The family firm, which celebrated its 600th anniversary in 1985, has become Italy's most admired wine house under the enlightened leadership of Piero Antinori. His father Niccolò built a foundation with Chianti and Orvieto of unerring reliability. But what carried Antinori to the top were the inventive and widely imitated vdt of Tignanello and Solaia, following the successful marketing of Sassicaia in the early 1970s. Recent lustre has been added by the white vdt of Cervaro and Borro from Castello della Sala at Orvieto in Umbria. Headquarters are the Renaissance Palazzo Antinori in the centre of Florence, but chief winemaker Giacomo Tachis bases operations at the San Casciano cellars in Chianti Classico. The Santa Cristina estate (where Tignanello and Solaia originated) now lends its name to a vdt, though the trademark Villa Antinori with its Riserva del Marchese and the newly developed Peppoli have kept Antinori in the forefront of Chianti Classico. Leased vineyards and cellars of the magnificent Badia a Passignano near Sambuca Val di Pesa have further increased the scale. Another property at Bolgheri provides a DOC rosé. The respected Villa Antinori Bianco, Galestro "Capsula Viola", Sarmento, and Italy's most popular *novello* San Giocondo round out the sound range of

Below: the Ricasoli family's Castello di Brolio is a monument of Chianti.

vdt. Antinori Brut Nature, and the prestigious brown label *riserva*, come from Chardonnay and Pinot from Trentino-Alto Adige.

Melini, Poggibonsi (SI). The house owned by the Gruppo Italiano Vini and directed by Nunzio Capurso has 126 ha of vines as a base for Chianti Classico that carry the proprietary names of La Selvanella and Terrarossa, as well as the vdt red Coltri and Chardonnay Granaio. The range includes Vino Nobile, Vernaccia, and vdt.

I. L. Ruffino, Pontassieve (FI). The firm, founded by Ilario and Leopoldo Ruffino, has belonged to the Folonari family of Brescia since 1913. It is among the largest producer-bottlers of Chianti Classico (including the venerable Riserva Ducale Oro and Aziano) as well as Chianti (including the *governo* type Torgaio di San Salvatore). But a recent surge in prestige has come from other wines, including Predicato del Muschio Vigneto La Pietra and Biturica Vigneto Il Borgo, both sold under the Cabreo brand, as well as an impressive Pinot Nero known as Nero del Tondo. Ruffino has four properties in Chianti Classico, as well as the family owned Nozzole estate. Ambrogio Folonari, the force behind Predicato, supervises winemaking, which extends through Galestro, Sarmento, and the popular Rosatello, to the vdt Libaio (Chardonnay with Sauvignon) from San Gimignano. The firm also makes Brunello Il Greppone Mazzi and bottles Orvieto Classico.

Straccali, Castellina (SI).

Vinattieri, Gaiole (SI). The *négociant-éleveur* operation of Maurizio Castelli and Roberto Stucchi-Prinetti specializes in vdt Vinattieri Rosso (Sangioveto-Brunello) and Rosso II (with Cabernet), as well as the Chardonnay based Vinattieri Bianco from Alto Adige.

COOPERATIVES

Agricoltori Chianti Geografico, Gaiole (SI). Admirable group of growers with 300 ha producing about 20,000 hl of Chianti Classico, from which winemaker Vittorio Fiore selects for bottlings of Contessa di Radda and the *riserva* Tenuta Montegiachi. Other wines include Vernaccia di San Gimignano and Bianco Val d'Arbia DOC and vdt Galestro and Sarmento.

Castelgreve/Castelli del Grevepesa, Mercatale Val di Pesa (SI). From growers with 650 ha, some 30,000 hl of Chianti Classico are made annually, some bottled and sold under the Catelgreve label, others in select batches as Lamole, Monte Firidolfi, Panzano, Sant'Angelo Vico L'Abate, and Selezione Vigna Elisa. The red vdt Coltifredi is a Predicato di Cardisco.

Above: ancient Siena is sometimes known as Italy's wine capital.

Wines of Siena's hills

Siena reigns demurely as Italy's capital of wine. Not even Piedmont's Alba, where Barolo and Barbaresco hold forth, can quite match the honours bestowed upon the wines of Siena's historic domain. Chianti originated in its province, as did Brunello di Montalcino, Vino Nobile di Montepulciano, and Vernaccia di San Gimignano. Its status has been reinforced by the recent DOC reds of Montepulciano and Montalcino (which also boasts the revived Moscadello), and the white of the Val d'Arbia. Some of Italy's most lauded table wines have been created in the surrounding hills, whose potential for greatness has rarely been tested beyond the habitual variations on Sangiovese. Among other points in its favour, the city lies near the centre of the peninsula with a fluent tourist trade. Yet, as visitors may observe, apart from a dutiful display of bottles at the Enoteca Italiana in the basement of the Medici Fortress, Siena hardly seems to be a wine town at all. The Sienese don't seem to get as excited about their bottled treasures as they do about their marvels of art or that most bizarre of horse races the Palio, which is run twice each summer in the ancient Piazza del Campo.

Chianti Colli Senesi

The Colli Senesi could make Chianti to compare with the biggest and best, but the proof is hard to find. In Montalcino, Montepulciano, and San Gimignano, producers' top efforts almost invariably go into the prime wines that carry the town names, leaving Chianti as an afterthought. Still, among the seven Chianti zones, Colli Senesi is second to Classico in volume. In the few places in these hills where it doesn't get short shrift, Chianti does rather well, even inspiring some producers to mention Colli Senesi on the label.

Zone: The most extensive Chianti district is split into three sectors that cover hills in 23 communes in Siena province. One reaches from San Gimignano southeast past

Poggibonsi and Siena along the southern flank of Chianti Classico to Castelnuovo Berardenga. The second stretches from Murlo south of Siena down to cover Montalcino. The third reaches from Sinalunga southeast along the Valdichiana past Montepulciano and Chianciano Terme to Chiusi. Dry red. Grapes: Sangiovese 75-90%, Canaiolo Nero 5-10%, Trebbiano Toscano/Malvasia del Chianti 5-10%, other reds up to 10%. Yld 70/100, Alc 11.5; riserva 12.5, Acd 0.5-0.75, Ag 6 mths; riserva 3 yrs.

Val d'Arbia (1986)

The Arbia's moment of notoriety came in 1260 when the armies of Siena and Florence battled at Monte Aperti and, as Dante Alighieri noted, its waters ran

red with blood. Today this otherwise unassuming stream, whose bed is normally dry in summer, lends its name to a DOC that for the most part provides producers of southern Chianti Classico with official status for a white of slick simplicity along with a bit of Vin Santo. The zone covers two other diverse sectors – the barren clay moors known as the *crete* southeast of Siena and the wooded hills west of the city around Sovicille and Monteriggioni – though production is limited there. Producers are cited under Chianti Classico and Colli Senesi.

Zone: A broad basin of slopes drained by the Arbia and other tributaries of the Ombrone river around Siena, extending from the Chianti Classico communes of Radda, Gaiole, Castellina, and Castelnuovo Berardenga, south through Asciano, Monteroni d'Arbia, Murlo, and Buonconvento and reaching through hills west of Siena to Monteriggioni and Sovicille. **Bianco** Dry white. Grapes: Trebbiano Toscano 75-85%, Malvasia del Chianti 15-25%, other whites (except Moscato Bianco) up to 15%. Yld 84.5/130, Alc 11, Acd 0.55. **Vin Santo** Amber dessert wine, secco, semisecco, or dolce. Grapes: As bianco but semidried. Yld 45.5/130, Alc 17, (res sugar secco 3%; semisecco 4%; dolce 5%), Acd 0.55, Ag 3 yrs in *caratelli*.

Other wines of note

Among unclassified wines of Siena's hills, those of La Suvera, which lies outside the DOC zone at Pievescola, are most unusual.

ESTATES/GROWERS

(Listed below are those producers whose prime emphasis is on Chianti or vdt. Producers of Montalcino, Montepulciano, San Gimignano, and Chianti Classico are listed separately.)

Amorosa, Sinalunga (SI). From vineyards around the medieval hamlet that houses his restaurant/hotel, Carlo Citterio makes full-bodied Chianti, a potent Sangioveto vdt called Borgo Amorosa as well as light Amorosa Bianco.

Castello di Monteriggioni, Monteriggioni (SI). From 41 ha, Chianti Colli Senesi and Classico.

Castelpugna, Valdipugna, Siena. From 11 ha on the edge of the town of Siena, Conti Fumi Cambi Gado make admirable Chianti.

Chigi Saracini, Castelnuovo Berardenga (SI). From 40 ha on the estate owned by the Chigiana Musical Academy of Siena, good Chianti and Bianco Val d'Arbia.

Fattoria Montemorli, Poggibonsi (SI). From 16.5 ha, Sergio Conforti makes respected Chianti.

Fattoria Roscarter, Colle Val d'Elsa (SI). From 55 ha, Chianti Rosso di Casavecchia.

Ficomontanino, Chiusi (SI). From 3.5 ha, oenologist Gabriella Tani makes fine Chianti Colli Senesi.

Il Poggiolo, Monteriggioni (SI). From 19 ha, Federico and Francesco Bonfio make refined Chianti, including special bottlings of Le Portine and Villa Poggiolo.

La Muraglia, Monteriggioni (SI). Chianti.

La Suvera, Pievescola (SI). From 9 ha of *terra rossa* on the property of Marchesi Ricci Paracciani Bergamini, winemaker Vittorio Fiore fashions the Chianti-like vdt Rango Rosso and Rango Bianco, a remarkably durable white from Trebbiano and Malvasia, along with the sparkling Cuvée Italienne Brut.

Sestano, Castelnuovo Berardenga (SI). From 23 ha around this handsome estate, Chianti Terra della Ragnaia.

Tenuta Trecciano, Sovicille (SI). From 15 ha, Pietro Rivella makes good Chianti and vdt.

Left and below: many of Siena's steep and narrow streets lead to the Piazza del Campo, where the bell tower of the town hall affords views over the city and surrounding countryside. Twice each summer a horserace known as the Palio is run around the piazza, whose sloping contours in the form of a seashell make it difficult for horses to manoeuvre and jockeys, who ride bareback, to stay mounted. The fierce competition between the city's contrade, *each of which sponsors a horse and rider, builds this sporting event into a festival in medieval dress that has no equal for colour, passion, and drama.*

Wines of San Gimignano

Vernaccia di San Gimignano (1966)

If this stands out among Tuscany's DOC whites, it's not just because Vernaccia ranks a cut above other local varieties but because the town it comes from towers over the rest. Otherwise, the image of Vernaccia di San Gimignano might not be so lofty. Rapid growth in production since it was tapped as Italy's first DOC in 1966 (from about 700 hl to 40,000 hl annually) has been backed by gradual improvements in the cellars. Yet, while a few producers strive for real class, the general trend is to expand vineyards and raise yields to capitalize on a marketable name. Much of the wine is sold to tourists who flock to the town with its medieval skyscrapers. Vernaccia has been grown at San Gimignano since at least 1286, when its wines were recorded as commanding higher prices than Greco and others. Michelangelo Buonarotti the Younger wrote in 1643 that Vernaccia "kisses, licks, bites, slaps, and stings". Yet after centuries of epithets, the current jumble of styles suggests that it still isn't clear what Vernaccia's personality is or how it is best expressed. Experts allow that the vine outclasses Trebbiano, but that hardly makes it noble. Much needed clonal selection is lacking, but there is no shortage of rumours among growers about competitors who build quantities with Trebbiano or compromise typicality with Chardonnay. Studies indicate that the best terrains lie in the immediate vicinity of the town and at Pietrafitta, the venerable estate whose Vernaccia riserva took on traits reminiscent of Vin Santo. But in San Gimignano winemaking skills seem to have become more important than vineyard locations. The most acclaimed (and most expensive) Vernaccia, Teruzzi & Puthod's Terra di Tufo, which gains complexity in French barrels, comes from outside the privileged area, as does the impressive wood-aged *riserva* of the ancient Cusona estate of Roberto Guicciardini and Girolamo Strozzi. Most producers aim for harmonious modern styles, which Riccardo Falchini achieved first, and which Montenidoli, Pietraserena, and Le Colonne express admirably. *Spumante* is increasingly popular, though results, usually by tank method, are rarely inspiring. Vernaccia is often upstaged by fine non-DOC wines emerging in the area. A split in the consortium has meant that many producers are going their own ways but that hasn't prevented them from requesting DOCG. Much Vernaccia sold in Italy and abroad under various labels comes from the large cooperative. It is

not clear what effect the development of estates by large houses such as Zonin of the Veneto and Cecchi (*see* Chianti Classico) might have on national and international markets. But as long as the tourists keep coming, most producers of Vernaccia will probably be content with local sales.

Zone: Hills no higher than 500 m in the commune of San Gimignano. Dry white. Grape: Vernaccia di San Gimignano. Yld 77/110, Alc 11, Acd 0.5, Ag riserva 1 yr.

Spumante Sparkling dry white. Grapes: Vernaccia di San Gimignano, Chardonnay/Pinot Bianco/Pinot Nero up to 15%. Yld 77/110, Alc 11.5, Acd 0.65.

Other wines of note

Many Vernaccia producers make Chianti, sometimes called Colli Senesi and sometimes of class. Among the emerging vdt, those made by Riccardo Falchini, Fattoria di Cusona, Teruzzi & Puthod, and Montenidoli are most noteworthy.

ESTATES/GROWERS

(All estates are in the commune of San Gimignano.)

Abbazia Monte Oliveto. Zonin has been developing this and Fattoria Il Palagio for Vernaccia sold under the former label, as well as for Chianti and the *novello* Sant'Ilario.

Castello di Montauto. This estate with 30 ha of vines has been acquired by Luigi Cecchi as a base for an increasingly active market in Vernaccia.

Castelvecchio di Libaio. Ruffino grows Chardonnay and Sauvignon Blanc here for its popular vdt Libaio.

Riccardo Falchini-Il Casale. From a base of admired Vernaccia and Chianti, Falchini has expanded cellars and vineyards to 32 ha to make vdt, as well as the *champenoise* Falchini Brut (from Vernaccia, Pinots, and Chardonnay), and fine Vin Santo. The red Paretato from Sangiovese with Cabernet is surpassed by Predicato del Muschio (oak-aged Chardonnay) and an outstanding pure Cabernet Sauvignon called Campora. Vigna a Solatio is the

second label for Vernaccia.

Fattoria di Cusona. The estate, which dates to the 10th century, was known for Vernaccia as early as the 15th, when it was owned by the Bardi before passing to another prominent family, the Guicciardini. Today it is owned by Roberto Guicciardini and Girolamo Strozzi. Prodded by winemaker Vittorio Fiore, Strozzi, who manages the operation, is revitalizing 70 ha of vines and the ancient cellars for improving Vernaccia (the youthful San Biagio and smooth, barrel-aged *riserva*), Chianti, Vin Santo, *spumante*, and an impressive pure Sangiovese vdt called Sòdole.

Fattoria di Pancole. Vernaccia and Chianti from 17 ha.

Fattoria Il Paradiso. From 13 ha, Graziella and Vasco Cetti make Vernaccia, Chianti, and pure Sangiovese vdt Paterno II.

Giulio Frigeni. From 14 ha, Vernaccia and Chianti.

Le Colonne. From 3.5 ha, Sergio Picciolini and oenologist Vittorio Fiore make a promising barrel-fermented Vernaccia riserva.

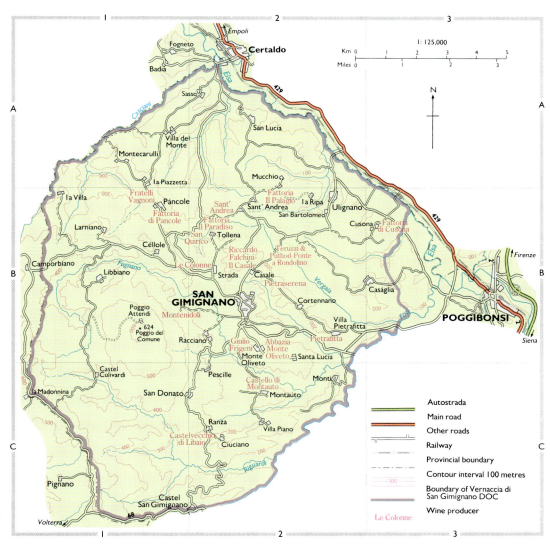

Left: San Gimignano stands out among Tuscan hill towns because of its skyline. Today only 14 towers remain of the 72 that were built when prominent families competed to construct the tallest.

Montenidoli. From 6 ha, the indefatigable Elisabetta Fagiuoli makes a Vernaccia of real finesse, good Chianti Colli Senesi called Sono Montenidoli, the vdt white Vinbrusco, and *rosato*.

Pietrafitta. From 40 ha on the estate long noted for wines of the traditional stamp, oenologist Sergio Conforti is aiming for better balance and freshness in Vernaccia and Chianti.

Pietraserena. From 16.5 ha, good Vernaccia led by the outstanding Vigna del Sole.

San Quirico. From 33 ha at Pancole, Andrea Vecchioni makes sometimes impressive Vernaccia.

Sant'Andrea. Vernaccia and Chianti.

Teruzzi & Puthod. Milanese Enrico Teruzzi and wife Carmen Puthod brought high-tech winemaking to San Gimignano, followed by the even more revolutionary concept of creative marketing. From 34 ha at Ponte a Rondolino and La Ripa, and 3.5 ha leased, Teruzzi fashions Vernaccia, one of which carries the name Carmen and the other Terra di Tufo. The latter, whose appeal comes from a kiss of oak and a label the size of a postage stamp, is the most expensive and most sought after Vernaccia. The vdt include the red Terra Peperino (from Sangiovese, Montepulciano, and Colorino), a Galestro "for the rich", and the *champenoise* Sarpinello. Perhaps uniquely in Italy, all wines are presold before the harvest.

Fratelli Vagnoni. From 15 ha at Pancole, Vernaccia and Chianti Colli Senesi.

WINE HOUSES/MERCHANTS

(Vernaccia must be vinified in the commune, though houses outside the zone bottle the wine under their labels. These include Luigi Cecchi, Barone Ricasoli, Melini, Conti Serristori, and the cooperative Agricoltori del Chianti Geografico.)

COOPERATIVES

Società Cooperativa Cantina di San Gimignano, San Gimignano (SI). Major supplier of Vernaccia to bottlers.

Bottom left: the town of San Gimignano is known for its white Vernaccia, which comes from vineyards such as this one on the estate of Abbazia Monte Oliveto.

Wines of Montalcino

Tuscany's premier wine town has a defiant air about it, an aloofness born of distance and distrust that has kept it splendidly isolated from the mainstream. It first gained prominence as a fortress, due to its position astride a crest with vistas over the lonely sweeps of the Orcia and Ombrone valleys and the Via Cassia running north from Rome past Monte Amiata towards Siena. Behind its walls the last refugees of the Sienese Republic held out against the Florentines and Spaniards until a treaty brought the town into the Tuscany of the Medici. Then attention was turned to wines, which were once described as black, vermillion, and purple, though most plaudits went to the gold, or to what the poet Francesco Redi described as that "gracious, so divine Moscadelletto". The Brunello clone of Sangiovese *grosso* was noted here in 1842, decades before Ferruccio Biondi Santi made a wine of the name. Fame was slow in coming, for it was not until the 1960s, when word spread about the extraordinary Biondi Santi vintages of 1888 and 1891, that Brunello drew much acclaim. Then came the revolution, as other growers took up the cause and outside investors created estates. Vast tracts of new vineyards have altered the landscape, most dramatically in the southwestern corner of the commune where the American-owned Villa Banfi moved hills to establish a winery that resembles a swatch of California stretched across a tapestry of bucolic stone hamlets, castles, and farms. In two decades, Montalcino's vineyards have multiplied. Yet, by defying the uncontrolled growth that could have diluted the wine and upset the market, producers have cautiously expanded sales of Brunello, gradually building stature while largely upholding prices. They have usefully diversified into Rosso di Montalcino, a younger alternative to Brunello from the same vines, while creating a series of up-market table wines. Even Moscadelletto, which had practically disappeared, has made a mild comeback as Moscadello di Montalcino DOC. The extensive commune has shown exceptional aptitude for wine on slopes where vineyards still claim less space than pastures, grain fields, and woods of ilex, the evergreen holm oak which figures in its name (from the Latin *Mons Ilcinus*) and decorates its coat of arms. Vine varieties now take in the world's elite, though none of them, not even Cabernet Sauvignon, has yet rivalled Brunello's supremacy here. Wine, perhaps more than anything else, has broken down Montalcino's barriers, bringing a once dwindling populace new pride and prosperity while extending to the growing numbers of outsiders who come in quest of Brunello a welcome, not always lavish but sincere.

Brunello di Montalcino (DOCG 1980, DOC 1966)

The wine projects an image of majesty and mystery that heightens its allure to some but to others makes it seem untouchable. This aura was cultivated by the Biondi Santi family, who long claimed Brunello di Montalcino as a birthright. Ferruccio Biondi Santi isolated the Brunello clone of Sangioveto *grosso* in his vineyards at Il Greppo and in 1888 and 1891 made wines that are still admired today. The foundation was created by his maternal grandfather Clemente Santi who in 1865 won a prize for a "Vino rosso scelto (brunello)". Ferruccio's son Tancredi built the Brunello legend in Italy earlier in this century, not by pushing but by patiently letting experts taste the old vintages. Yet wide renown came only in the last generation, as Tancredi's son Franco quietly raised the price until the wine world had to take notice. His Brunello was greeted with wonder, praised for power and durability, criticized for cost, but rarely condemned, since tasters who failed to grasp its grandeur were reminded that the *riserve* required a quarter of a century to show their stuff. Other estates had begun bottling Brunello in the 1950s and 1960s. The alternatives offered by Giovanni Colombini at Barbi, Emilio Costanti at Colle al Matrichese, and Tenuta Il Poggione sometimes surpassed the original. But as recently as the mid-

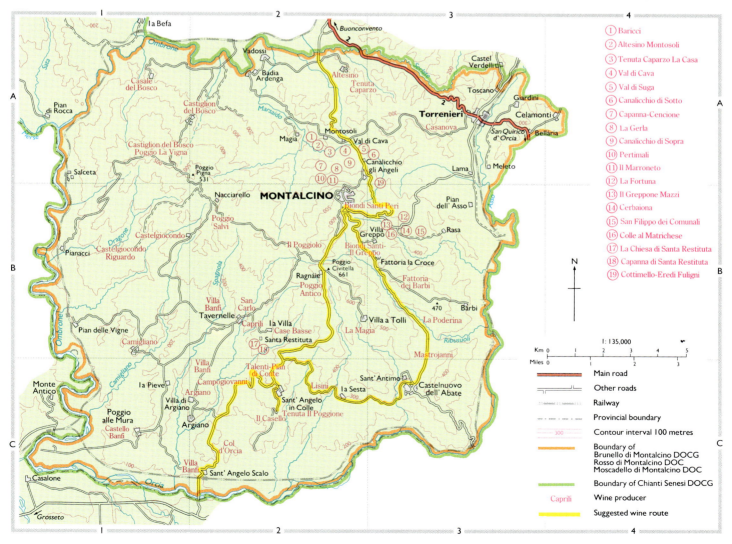

1. Baricci
2. Altesino Montosoli
3. Tenuta Caparzo La Casa
4. Val di Cava
5. Val di Suga
6. Canalicchio di Sotto
7. Capanna-Cencione
8. La Gerla
9. Canalicchio di Sopra
10. Pertimali
11. Il Marroneto
12. La Fortuna
13. Il Greppone Mazzi
14. Cerbaiona
15. San Filippo dei Comunali
16. Colle al Matrichese
17. La Chiesa di Santa Restituta
18. Capanna di Santa Restituta
19. Cottimello-Eredi Fuligni

1: 135,000

| Km 0 | | 1 | 2 | 3 | 4 | 5 |
| Miles 0 | 1 | | 2 | | 3 | |

Main road
Other roads
Railway
Provincial boundary
Contour interval 100 metres
Boundary of
Brunello di Montalcino DOCG
Rosso di Montalcino DOC
Moscadello di Montalcino DOC
Boundary of Chianti Senesi DOCG
Caprili Wine producer
Suggested wine route

1970s, the token amounts of Brunello sold outside Tuscany were more often than not from Biondi Santi.

Yet vineyard and estate development was already underway. Plantings of Brunello increased from less than 80 ha in 1968 to nearly 1,000 ha in 1988, as production rose from 2,000 hl to nearly 40,000 hl (though not all is bottled and sold as DOCG). The new competition increasingly gives Biondi Santi and the old guard a run for the money. Consumers may complain about prices, but Montalcino is a rare place where growers can afford (or can't afford not) to make the sacrifices in vineyards and cellars that lead to class. Along with the influx of outside capital at such vast estates as Villa Banfi, Col d'Orcia, and Castelgiocondo, there has been a proliferation of small wineries owned and run by farmers or by local business people or, increasingly, by refugees from the city who prefer the country air. Despite confusion created by the rush of new labels, Brunello seems to be winning over experts, including some who had expressed earlier doubts. First Il Poggione, then Villa Banfi, and lately others have expanded markets for fine Brunello of tolerable price. The emerging estates of Lisini, Altesino, Tenuta Caparzo, Talenti-Pian di Conte, Baricci, Caprili, and Mastrojanni have won high praise, though none so extravagant as the tiny Case Basse, whose Brunello often gets top marks

Above: the town of Montalcino, a medieval stronghold, today ranks as Tuscany's premier wine town. Left: the Poggio alle Mura castle became Castello Banfi after its purchase by the American-owned Villa Banfi.

from raters. Yet, despite rapid progress, Brunello is not destined to become a widely accessible commodity. The market for big, long-lived red wines has proved to have strict limits. Sales seem to be levelling off at around 1.5 million bottles a year, little more than half the quota of Barbaresco and a quarter of Barolo, Piedmont's veterans in the field. Meanwhile, though, Rosso di Montalcino, the lower-priced alternative, has surpassed Brunello in volume, giving producers welcome early returns on their often sizeable investments.

Brunello stands out from other Sangiovese-based Tuscan reds, perhaps most of all because it is a thoroughbred, while Chianti and Vino Nobile, officially at least, are composites. Montalcino, being closer to the sea, is generally warmer and drier than Montepulciano, Chianti Classico, or Rufina, so ripening is earlier and vintages more consistent. Brunello usually has greater body, structure, and colour than the others, and it has a reputation for lasting longer, though few estates have proved it. Admirers of Chianti and Vino Nobile may contend that their *riserve* have greater complexity and finesse, and that their wines are better value. Oenologists have criticized the obligatory cask ageing for Brunello of 3.5 years, compared with two years in wood for Vino Nobile and none for Chianti. They say that this too often causes the wine to fade prematurely, to dry out, particularly from middling vintages. Villa Banfi's Ezio Rivella, a man with no time for dust-covered myths, was one of the first to speak out against lengthy wood ageing, though now even Biondi Santi would reduce the required time. But traditionalists, who seem to feel nostalgia for those wizened veterans of antique casks, resist change.

The commune of Montalcino is extensive enough to offer diverse conditions in its hills, yet uniform enough to give wines from the various clones called Brunello a distinctive stamp. The territory, whose outline resembles a square formed by the Ombrone, Orcia, and Asso rivers, has four major slopes that rise like the sides of a pyramid to the crest of the 667-m Poggio Civitella. The zone lies just across the Maremma hills from the Tyrrhenian, whose breezes temper the dry heat of summer. The mass of nearby Monte Amiata protects the slopes from hail and violent storms. Since so many vineyards are new, *crus* will be revealed only gradually. Still, if classification is unthinkable for the present, certain areas, estates, and plots have shown superior aptitude.

First, of course, is Biondi-Santi's Il Greppo, just southeast of the town, where vines at 400-500 m are among the zone's highest. Costanti and Barbi are neighbours on this sometimes steep terrain, which consists largely of *galestro*. Cool conditions favour slow ripening in Brunello noted for austere structure that requires long ageing to develop rich bouquet. Two increasingly noted vineyard areas, Montosoli and Canalicchio, lie to the north and east of the town on much lower slopes where wines develop full, ripe qualities. Most new planting has been in the southwestern corner around Sant'Angelo in Colle, Argiano, Pian della Mura, and Camigliano. The large properties of Villa Banfi, Il Poggione, Castelgiocondo, and Col d'Orcia are located there, as are several small but respected estates, including Case Basse amidst a grouping around the church of Santa Restituta. The soils, prevalently clay and sand mixed with limestone, often contain maritime deposits, though *galestro* prevails at higher points. Elsewhere, though clay is often heavy, particularly to the north, deposits of marl and sandy limestone have created favourable conditions in isolated places such as Castelnuovo

dell'Abate, Altesino, and Castiglione del Bosco.

Brunello di Montalcino, backed by a couple dozen estates whose wines show inherent class, increasingly asserts its supremacy among Tuscany's classified wines. Yet growth has been so rapid and change so radical that the wine should be considered not so much for what it has been but for what it seems destined to be. Its prices range higher than those of even the most sought after Super Tuscans and, since it has a proven past and fits a well-defined category, its future would seem to be more secure. To that end, one might ask who will make a Brunello this year that will be good to drink in 2090? As a tip to anyone who thinks he might be around to collect the bet, the smart money is on Biondi Santi.

Zone: Slopes in the extensive commune of Montalcino in Siena province. Dry red. Grape: Brunello di Montalcino. Yld 56/80 (52/80 after ageing), Alc 12.5, Acd 0.55, Ag 4 yrs (3.5 in oak or chestnut casks); riserva 5 yrs.

Top: Brunello vines on the Poggio Antico estate. Bottom: the Villa Banfi cellars are a model of advanced technology.

Rosso di Montalcino (DOC 1984)

As Italy's first alternative appellation to DOCG, this gives growers the option of using grapes from the same vineyards for either Brunello or this younger DOC. So in good years they may select superior grapes for wine to be aged as Brunello, while declaring the rest as Rosso di Montalcino. From mediocre harvests they can produce Rosso alone. Since it can be sold after a year and at lower price, it gives producers a quicker turnover of capital and consumers a chance to taste the basic goodness of the Brunello grape without spending a fortune. Indeed, some Rosso di Montalcino is more enjoyable to drink. The prototype came from Il Poggione, a red whose unharnessed vigour and fresh fruit flavours have often been remarkable. Since output now exceeds that of Brunello, others, too, have emerged with what qualifies as one of Tuscany's most satisfying red wines. A few producers use the appellation for bigger, sturdier reds, sometimes aged in *barriques*.

Zone: Slopes in the vast commune of Montalcino in Siena province. Dry red. Grape: Brunello di Montalcino. Yld 70/100, Alc 12, Acd 0.5, Ag 1 yr.

Moscadello di Montalcino (DOC 1985)

DOC, rather than a revival, represents a reincarnation of this once prized sweet wine. The original Moscadelletto vine, probably a mutation of Moscato, was known in Montalcino in the Middle Ages, though due to a susceptibility to disease, it has practically disappeared. In its place has come Moscato Bianco, the base of Asti Spumante. Villa Banfi came up with something reminiscent of aromatic, bubbly Moscato d'Asti, though its Moscadello di Montalcino has not been nearly as successful. Banfi has also made a richer *liquoroso* type called simply "B" that is more impressive. But purists argue that neither has much in common with the tenuous Moscadelletto that the poet Redi recommended to the ladies. Ironically, the authentic Moscadelleto vine is no longer approved, but Il Poggione, for one, nurses its tender shoots along for use in a lightly bubbly amber wine that in its rustic way might be described as divine.

Zone: Slopes in the vast commune of Montalcino in Siena province. Sweet white, also frizzante. Grapes: Moscato Bianco, other whites up to 15%. Yld 65/100, Alc 10.5 (res sugar min 3.5%), Acd 0.5.
Liquoroso Fortified sweet white. Grapes: As above but passito. Yld 65/100, Alc 19 (res sugar 3%), Acd 0.5, Ag 6 mths from fortification.

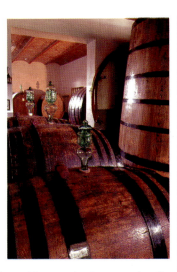

Other wines of note

Many estates make vdt, often using Brunello aged in *barriques*. Villa Banfi introduced Cabernet, Chardonnay, and Sauvignon, increasingly used by others. Producers can make Chianti Colli Senesi, though few bother. Adjacent to Montalcino in the province of Grosseto is Monte Antico with a Sangiovese-based red of notable quality from Castello di Monte Antico. Car magnate Lee Iacocca has an estate there, whose name, Villa Nicola, is used on labels of Rosso di Montalcino shipped to the USA.

ESTATES/GROWERS

(All estates are in the commune of Montalcino.)

Altesino. Director Claudio Basla and winemakers Angelo Solci and Pietro Rivella produce fine Brunello and Rosso from 14 ha at Altesino and 6 ha at Montosoli. The vdt Palazzo Altesi uses carbonic maceration and *barriques* to give Brunello supple, fruity qualities similar to Burgundy. Alte d'Altesi combines Brunello with Cabernet Sauvignon. Also notable are Bianco di Montosoli vdt and a Moscadello passito called Ambro d'Altesi.

Argiano. From the remaining 20 ha of vines on this once huge estate of the Gaetani Lovatelli family near Sant'Angelo in Colle, Cinzano is again making notable Brunello under Maurizio Castelli.

Baricci. From 3 ha in the vaunted vineyards of Colombaio di Montosoli, Nello Baricci makes sometimes excellent Brunello and good Rosso.

Biondi Santi-Il Greppo. The estate where Brunello was born has been described as Italy's first *grand cru*. Still, despite prices that attract awe, envy, and outrage, financial problems prompted the family to form a company to handle the commerce of Biondi Santi wines. In 1989 a controlling interest

Above: Franco Biondi Santi and his Il Greppo estate, where Brunello di Montalcino was first produced by his grandfather and where bottles of wine dating back to the 1891 and 1888 vintages still rest in the cellars.

passed from Calogero Calì (a prominent estate owner in Chianti Classico) to Pierluigi Tagliabue of the neighbouring Poggio Salvi estate. Some saw the move as the end of an institution, but Franco Biondi Santi and son Jacopo remained in charge at Il Greppo, making their singular Brunello as though nothing had changed. The estate, named after the steep banks on the property, lies 2 km southeast of Montalcino along a lane lined by century old cypresses. The villa, with its quaint mix of architecture, has a cellar where old vintages – including the remaining bottles of 1888 and 1891, the latter still for sale – are locked away in a vault. Bottles are recorked every 25 years after being topped up with wine from the same vintage. An adjacent new cellar holds such concessions to modernity as stainless steel tanks and a pneumatic press, which recently replaced a hand-operated wooden *torchio*. About 20 ha of Brunello are planted at Il Greppo at 400-500 m, as well as at the nearby estate of Pieri. Vines trained in a low spurred cordon are widely spaced (2,222 per ha) but yields are held below permitted levels by close pruning and thinning. Recently a superior clone of Brunello, known as BBS11, was isolated in the vineyards and will be grafted throughout under a rotation method. Choice plots, oriented towards the south in soils of *galestro*, are identified by names: Chiusa, Greppo, Greppino, Pievecchia, Scarnaquoia, and Pieri. Biondi Santi's Brunello *annata* is made from vines 10-25 years old, only from good vintages ('84, '76, and '72 were declassified). Brunello riserva comes from vines over 25 years old and only when quality is superior. Production rarely exceeds 50,000 bottles, including at most 15,000 *riserva*. Recent releases carry prices

close to top Bordeaux, as critics often note. Yet after apparent lapses in the 1970s, Biondi Santi has made Brunello in the 1980s with the old complexity and depth but with better balance and more approachable style than in the past – factors behind recent high ratings.

Camigliano. From 60 ha around the hamlet of Camigliano in the hottest part of the zone, the Ghezzi family makes Brunello whose muscles lack coordination.

Campogiovanni. Good Brunello from the estate with 6.8 ha of vines near Sant'Angelo in Colle owned by San Felice of Chianti Classico.

Canalicchio di Sopra. From 4.5 ha at Canalicchio, Primo Pacenti makes sound Brunello and Rosso. The property was split with brother Rosildo Pacenti, who labels his Brunello simply Canalicchio.

Canalicchio di Sotto. From 3 ha, Silvano and Maurizio Lambardi make Brunello and Rosso.

Capanna-Cencione. From 10 ha near Montosoli, the Cencioni family makes good Brunello and Rosso.

Capanna di Santa Restituta-Fattoi e Minocci.

Caprili. Alfo Bartolommei was among Montalcino's first farmers to bottle Brunello and Rosso from 7 ha near Santa Restituta, a terrain whose excellence shows in the wines.

Casale del Bosco. From 45 ha in the northwestern part of the zone, Silvio and Emilia Nardi make Brunello and Rosso.

Casanova. From 12 ha above Torrenieri, the Neri family makes steadily improving Brunello and Rosso.

Case Basse. From 6.3 ha at Villa Santa Restituta, Milanese stockbroker Gianfranco Soldera makes the Brunello which has won most recent acclaim,

noted for exceptional concentration of components balanced by smooth, almost voluptuous fruit. The Rosso also stands out, as does the recent vdt called Intistieti, pure Brunello from the estate's finest plot.

Castelgiocondo. The vast estate around the ancient castle is owned by the Frescobaldi family. It has the largest spread of Brunello vines – 160 of its 220 ha – but production centres on a selection from the 45-ha Riguardo area. Brunello shows supple, fruity traits, as does the highly drinkable Rosso Campo ai Sassi. Production conducted by Luciano Boarino goes into various vdt, including the oak-kissed Sauvignon Blanc Vergena, which qualifies as Predicato del Selvante.

Castiglion del Bosco. The hamlet of Castiglione del Bosco surrounded by woods has 35 ha split between Poggio La Vigna and the Badia Ardenga area. Winemaker Maurizio Castelli has notably improved recent Brunello and Rosso.

Cerbaiona. From less than 1.5 ha at Cerbaiona, Diego Molinari makes good Brunello and Rosso.

Col d'Orcia. Piedmont's Cinzano owns this estate at Sant'Angelo with 69 ha of vines. Manager Edoardo Virano and consultant Maurizio Castelli have renewed cellars and vineyards with the aim of bringing Brunello to top levels. Also good Rosso and Chianti Colli Senesi Gineprone, plus Moscadello, Vin Santo, and a *novello* called Novembrino.

Colle al Matrichese-Poderi Emilio Costanti. Emilio Costanti's Brunello of the 1960s and early 1970s often outclassed the field, combining size and staying power with grace. Nephews Andrea and Riccardo Costanti and winemaker Vittorio Fiore uphold the status with Brunello from 7 ha at Villa Il Colle, comprising Paretaio, Vignanova, Baiocco, and Piano, single vineyard *riserva* that each fill a 30-hl cask. Annual production of 20,000 bottles includes a bit of red vdt

Vermiglio and good Chianti Colli Senesi.

Cottimello-Eredi Fuligni. From 3.5 ha adjacent to Canalicchio, Maria Flora Fuligni and Roberto Guerrini have been improving Brunello and Rosso.

Fattoria dei Barbi-Proprietà Colombini. In the 1950s Giovanni Colombini revived the family wine tradition and at times rivalled neighbour Tancredi Biondi Santi's Brunello. Today, his daughter Francesca Colombini Cinelli and her daugher Donatella are the most ambitious promoters of Montalcino and its wines; among initiatives is the annual Barbi Colombini International Award for literature about Montalcino. The wines from 34 ha occasionally match the hype, though some Brunello in the 1970s and early 1980s did poorly in tastings. There have been signs of an upturn under winemaker Giancarlo Arrigoni with fine '85 and '88 vintages, led by the Vigna del Fiore from a 2-ha plot. The Barbi vineyards, 17 plots which range from 170-500 m, show varying results in a host of wines. Notable are a Rosso di Montalcino Sole dei Barbi, a red vdt Brusco dei Barbi (rich Sangiovese given youthful tone by *governo*), the similar, late-harvested Bruscone dei Barbi, the white Bianco del Beato, and good Vin Santo. All wines are served with tasty produce of the farm at the Taverna dei Barbi on the premises.

Il Casello. From 7 ha at Sant'Angelo in Colle belonging to the Franceschi family of Tenuta Il Poggione, Pierluigi Talenti makes Brunello and Rosso.

Il Greppone Mazzi. The estate adjacent to Biondi Santi's Il Greppo is used by the Folonari family of Ruffino for good Brunello from 8 ha.

Il Marroneto. A gem of a Brunello from a farm that the Mori family is gradually expanding toward 1.5 ha.

Il Poggiolo. From 4 ha southwest of Montalcino, the Cosimi family makes respected Brunello and Rosso.

La Chiesa di Santa Restituta. Lombardian Roberto Bellini and oenologist Pietro Rivella make improving Brunello and Rosso from 16.5 ha of some of Montalcino's best terrain around this ancient church.

La Fortuna. The Zannoni family is expanding vineyards east of Montalcino to 9 ha to increase quantities of already fine Brunello and good Rosso.

La Gerla. From 4 ha at Montosoli, Milanese owner Sergio Rossi and winemaker Vittorio Fiore produce Brunello and Rosso of emerging class.

La Magia. From 16 ha of high vineyards near Poggio Civitella, the South Tyrolean Schwarz family makes Brunello and Rosso.

La Poderina.

Lisini. After ups and downs in the 1970s, the Fattoria di Sant'Angelo in Colle is clearly on the rise again as the Lisini brothers and winemaker Franco Bernabei hone stylish Brunello and Rosso from 12 ha.

Mastrojanni. From 12 ha of the Podere Loreto at Castelnuovo dell'Abate, Romans Gabriele and Antonio Mastrojanni and Venetian winemaker Pino Zardetto produce increasingly impressive Brunello and Rosso.

Pertimali.

Poggio Antico. From 20 ha on high slopes between Montalcino and Sant'Angelo in Colle, improving Brunello and Rosso, along with Brunello vdt Altero. All are served with wild boar at the estate's restaurant.

Poggio Salvi. The estate of Pierluigi Tagliabue has 11 ha of Brunello and Rosso made under supervision of his business partners the Biondi Santi.

San Carlo.

San Filippo dei Comunali. From 5 ha near the church of San Filippo Neri east of Montalcino, Ermanno Rosi makes good Brunello and Rosso.

Talenti-Pian di Conte. Pierluigi Talenti (of Il Poggione) has his own estate with 2.7 ha for first-rate Brunello and Rosso.

Tenuta Caparzo. Milanese manager Nuccio Turone and oenologist Vittorio Fiore make Brunello, Rosso, and vdt from 16 ha adjacent to Altesino and 6.5 ha at Montosoli (source of the praised single vineyard Brunello La Casa). The vdt red Ca' del Pazzo combines Brunello and Cabernet in *barriques*. The barrel-fermented Le Grance first proved Montalcino's potential might with Chardonnay.

Tenuta Il Poggione. Manager-winemaker Pierluigi Talenti built the solid reputation of this estate owned by Clemente and Roberto Franceschi by producing Brunello and Rosso of constant class. Talenti, retiring to his own Pian di Conte as Fabrizio Bindocci takes over, credits success to ideally situated vineyards – 51 ha at 150-450 m around Sant'Angelo in Colle – and careful selection. Wines not up to standard are sold in bulk. That is why over the last 20 years Il Poggione has shown exemplary consistency, making good Brunello even in '84, '76, and '72, and always at reasonable price. The fine Rosso is an even better bargain. The estate also makes a bit of the true (fizzy golden-amber) Moscadello.

Val di Cava.

Val di Suga. Milanese Lionello Marchesi's first Tuscan wine estate (also Trerose in Montepulciano, La Capraia in Chianti Classico) has 23 ha northeast of Montalcino, source of respected Brunello and Rosso.

Villa Banfi. The largest importer of wine in the United States has established its main Italian estate under eminent oenologist Ezio Rivella, who shares winemaking with Swiss born Pablo Hari. Despite early doubts about the colossal project, Villa Banfi has brought Montalcino money and jobs while broadening local concepts of winemaking. Though the original aim was a split between premium and popular wines mainly for the US market, Banfi has opted for prestige with some of the best modern Brunello, good Rosso Centine, and an array of vdt that has found favour in Italy and Europe. The estate occupies 2,850 ha of slopes between 250-400 m rising from the Orcia valley below Pian delle Mura (now Castello Banfi) and Sant'Angelo Scalo (site of its high tech cellars) north past the hamlet of Tavernelle. Vineyards, 80% irrigated from artificial lakes, cover 800 ha: 150 in Brunello, 160

in Cabernets, 140 in Chardonnay, 120 in Moscato, 60 in Sauvignon Blanc – along with Pinot Grigio, Sémillon, Pinot Nero, Montepulciano, and Syrah. All varieties are planted at different altitudes to favour ripening at intervals for even results. Vine training is Casarsa designed for mechanical harvesting, but most grapes are picked by hand. Moscadello in a fizzy version similar to Moscato d'Asti has proved less popular than expected; a rich *passito* is called simply "B". Vdt aged in French barrels are a Cabernet Sauvignon Tavernelle, Chardonnay Fontanelle, and the unusual Castello Banfi which blends Brunello and Cabernet with Pinot Nero. Pinot Grigio is called San Angelo, Sauvignon Blanc Fumaio. Brunello grapes are also used in the successful *novello* called Santa Costanza. The restored Castello Banfi houses a wine museum and hospitality quarters. Plans for a restaurant, hotel, and golf course there have been delayed.

WINE HOUSES/MERCHANTS

(Brunello must be vinified in the commune of Montalcino, though several houses sell the wine under their labels. These include Luigi Cecchi.)

Left: Pablo Hari is the Swiss-born oenologist who makes wines at Villa Banfi (below) with director Ezio Rivella. Despite the cellars' large scale, the emphasis is on premium wines that go beyond Brunello to include Chardonnay and Cabernet.

Wines of Montepulciano

The town of Montepulciano meanders up a spur dominating the Chiana valley on whose broad southwestern slopes lie the vineyards of Vino Nobile, the doyen of Tuscan wines. The steep and winding main street resembles a Renaissance parade route along which men of the various *contrade* brave the heat of August to see who can roll a wine cask to the top first. The joke is that the old barrels are better suited to rolling than ageing a wine that long typified the antique Tuscan style. Still, in a town that was still a vinous backwater in the early 1980s, much commendable activity is taking place, and Vino Nobile, after what seemed an interminable lapse, has regained some of its former glory. Wines were first documented here in the eighth century, though Etruscans earlier grew vines in the environs, as did Romans, who named the hill Mons Politianus. The traditional Sienese stronghold eventually came under Florentine influence, as Montepulciano's poet laureate Poliziano (Politian) befriended Lorenzo de' Medici. He bestowed favours on a town whose gracious churches and *palazzi* earned it the accolade of "the pearl of the 1500s". Its red wine also inspired outsiders. Papal bottler Sante Lancerio described it as fit for lords, but Francesco Redi went further in 1685 when he proclaimed "Montepulciano of all wines is king". The term Nobile came into use in the eighteenth century, in reference to the wine and the nobles who consumed it. The red of Montepulciano was a bona fide aristocrat when Chianti still strived for recognition, a good two centuries before Brunello di Montalcino was even invented. But today, though Vino Nobile can match Chianti Classico in prestige and price, it is clearly outclassed on both counts by Brunello. This challenge from its neighbour across the hills has spurred producers to improve Vino Nobile, while drawing inspiration from Rosso di Montalcino for their useful alternative of Rosso di Montepulciano DOC. Besides the further options of Chianti and Bianco Vergine della Valdichiana, some estates make convincing table wines. But most emphasize Vino Nobile, whose title and historical credentials are

unmatched even by Brunello. The two are sometimes twinned, like Barolo and Barbaresco, but differences in the Tuscan DOCGs are more pronounced. Both are based on clones of Sangiovese, but Brunello stands alone while Vino Nobile's Prugnolo Gentile plays the key role in a composite that includes optional white varieties. Also, despite their proximity, the communes of Montalcino and Montepulciano have notable variations in climate and soil. Only rarely does Vino Nobile match Brunello's heroic dimensions, yet at its best it shows some of the latter's structure with the complexity and finesse of reserve Chianti – a combination that ought to make it as noble as a Tuscan wine could be.

Vino Nobile di Montepulciano (DOCG 1981, DOC 1966)

As if living with age-old legends hadn't been trying enough, Vino Nobile was put on the spot in 1983 as the first DOCG wine on the market. As expected, the debut was a flop. Some critics noted that little had changed since the old days when faulty fermentations and long ageing in decrepit casks caused the wine to fade before its time. But since then Vino Nobile has taken a rapid turn for the better, thanks mainly to a new generation of producers and an influx of oenologists and money from outside. Wines from perhaps a dozen estates seem fresher and better balanced than

before, with more depth of colour, bouquet, and flavour and some of that polish that promises durability. Then, again, a series of fine vintages through the 1980s has aided the cause of drinkability even among backward producers, whose ranks, however, seem to be diminishing. There is evidence, too, that the tasting commissions have become stricter, rejecting wines whose eccentricities used to represent the norm.

Not that Vino Nobile is in danger of becoming uniform, for telling differences remain among the 40 or so producers, mostly estates. Yet, despite conflicting ambitions and personal rivalries that may date back ages, many

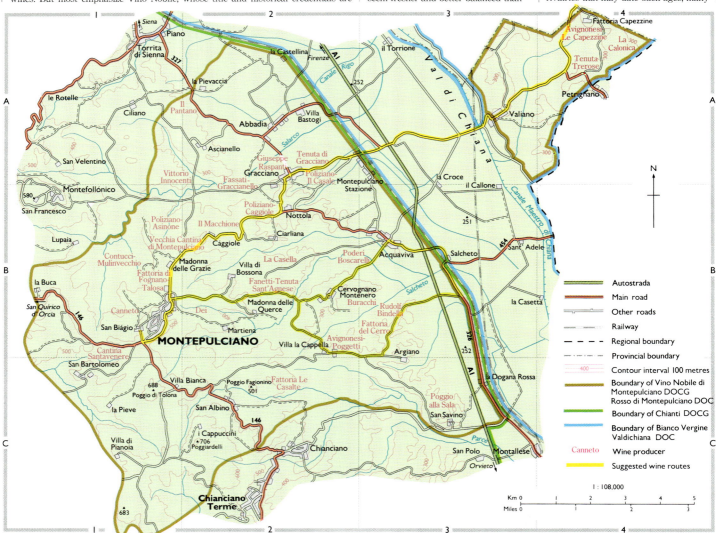

producers seem convinced that the wine's fortunes are on the rise and that higher standards will benefit all. Most belong to the consortium which supervises production of an average of 1.5 million bottles a year – much less than half of the potential from the 740 ha of registered vineyards. The new alternative of Rosso di Montepulciano gave them the chance to select their best grapes for Vino Nobile. Prugnolo Gentile could stand alone, though its youthful harshness is alleviated by the softening effect of Canaiolo and the traditional Mammolo is often included to enhance bouquet. Until last year, the blend required at least 10% of white varieties, which could range as high as 25% if the full dose of Trebbiano, Malvasia, and Grechetto – here known as Pulcinculo – were included. But a wise alteration made white grapes optional, gratifying to those winemakers who had already ignored them.

Progressives now prevail over traditionalists, yet some *cantine* are still lined with ancient chestnut casks, even if owners boast less about their attributes than before. Periodic replacement of the now prevalent Slavonian oak casks is considered a necessity by the better winemakers, some of whom also use *barriques* in an era of inspired if not always clearly focused experimentation. But the old-style Vino Nobile isn't gone forever. Aged bottles from Bologna Buonsignori, Contucci, Tenuta di Gracciano, and Fanetti, when not spirited away before their time, sometimes took on aristocratic airs, an effeteness reminiscent of certain tired Pauillacs. But even when enjoyable, they tended to vary so radically from one vintage – or even one bottle – to the next that it was hard to determine a Vino Nobile personality or define any one house's style. In the 1970s, Poderi Boscarelli emerged quietly with wines of depth and vigour that the others seemed to lack. Then came Avignonesi, with Vino Nobile and other modern wines that redefined the overworked adjective elegant. The once lacklustre Poliziano ranks as the most improved estate, rivalled by Contucci, an ancient family house that finally has broken the conservative mould. Outside investments have built such names as Trerose, Fattoria del Cerro, Fattoria di Fognano, and Fassati. Such small producers as Bindella and Le Casalte also have made an impact. But the dominant force remains the Vecchia Cantina di Montepulciano, whose more than 300 members could produce about half of Vino Nobile and a major share of the other wines. Thanks to tight quality controls, the cooperative's mass production is commendable. Yet wines carrying the Vecchia Cantina and merchants' labels may be found in

Above: the town of Montepulciano is noted for its Renaissance architecture, exemplified by the Palazzo Comunale (left), and its regal Vino Nobile, whose vineyards generally face southwest towards the Chiana valley on slopes where Romans and Etruscans grew vines. The term Nobile came into use two centuries ago to describe the wine and the nobles who drank it.

supermarkets and other retail outlets at prices that undercut the others, preventing them from arriving at the lofty levels of Brunello. For the time being, at least, Vino Nobile is among the best values in Tuscan wine.

Vineyard growth, if steady, has not been nearly as rapid as in Montalcino, so Montepulciano has space to expand. Most vines are planted on gradual, open slopes oriented towards the southeast between the heights of the town and the Valdichiana. The Vino Nobile consortium has taken the lead in Tuscany in studies of vine performance in various soils and microclimates. This research has distinguished five areas of predilection in the prevalent clays and sands of the Chiana basin, whose ancient lakes and streams left deposits of marine sediments and organic matter. Here are the five areas broken

down by villages with estates or vineyards of note:
Argiano, taking in Argiano (Avignonesi's Poggetti, Fattoria del Cerro, Bindella), Cervognano (Boscarelli, Buracchi), Madonna della Querce (Fanetti), and Acquaviva.
Caggiole, taking in Caggiole (Poliziano's Caggiole, Il Macchione), Ascianello (Il Pantano, Innocenti), Ciarliana (La Casella), Gracciano (Fassati's Graccianello, Raspanti, Tenuta di Gracciano, Poliziano).
Canneto, taking in Canneto (Canneto), Pietrose (Contucci's Mulinvecchio, Fattoria Fognano-Talosa, Poliziano's Asinone), and Bossano.
Casalte, taking in Casalte (Le Casalte, Martiena (Dei), and Paterno.
Valiano, taking in only Valiano (Avignonesi's Le Capezzine, Trerose, La Calonica).

Experts seem to agree that wines from the reddish terrain of Argiano often show superior balance and finesse. Those from the high slopes of Canneto and Pietrose are noted for bouquet, while those from the lower, hotter reaches of Gracciano are known for ample body and structure. Valiano, across the valley, has shown excellent potential from emerging estates. Though vineyard rankings are still distant, at least a basis exists, as producers strive to make Vino Nobile truly worthy of the name.

Zone: Slopes from 250-600 m in the commune of Montepulciano in Siena province. Dry red. Grapes: Prugnolo Gentile 60-80%, Canaiolo Nero 10-20%, other varieties up to 20%, though no more than 10% white. Yld 56/80 (52/80 after ageing). Alc 12.5, Acd 0.5, Ag 2 yrs in oak or chestnut casks; riserva 3 yrs.

Rosso di Montepulciano (1989)

The new appellation gives producers a chance to declassify Vino Nobile into a lighter red to drink young, though ideas vary about how fresh and youthful the wine should be. Some may follow the lines of Sarmento or *vino novello*. But others, including a few who are preparing special vineyards, plan to follow the example of the best Rosso di Montalcino in wines of some depth that benefit from a couple years of ageing.

Zone: Slopes at no higher than 600 m in the commune of Montepulciano in Siena province. Vineyards may correspond with those of Vino Nobile or may be registered separately. Dry red. Grapes: Sangiovese (Prugnolo Gentile) 60-80%, Canaiolo Nero 10-20%, other varieties up to 20%, though no more than 10% white. Yld 70/100, Alc 11, Acd 0.5, Ag 6 mths.

Other wines of note

Though Chianti Colli Senesi or simply Chianti is always secondary to Vino Nobile, some producers make good examples at reasonable price. Several others make Bianco Vergine and lightweight vdt. A few, relying on Prugnolo Gentile or Cabernet, Chardonnay, and Sauvignon, have turned out first-class vdt cited below.

ESTATES/GROWERS

(All estates are in the commune of Montepulciano. Those cited without comment are recommended for Vino Nobile.)

Avignonesi. The new image of Vino Nobile owes much to this dynamic young house whose studied array of wines is rarely rivalled for class and whose packaging is unequalled for design. Winemaker Ettore Falvo, who runs the firm with brothers Alberto and Leonardo, has headquarters in the Avignonesi palazzo in Montepulciano. Grapes come from three estates: the 15-ha Poggetti and 6-ha Le Capezzine, used for Vino Nobile, Rosso di Montepulciano, Chianti, and the red vdt Grifi (which combines local varieties with Cabernet), and the 60-ha La Selva, planted mainly in white varieties with Cabernet Sauvignon and Merlot. Production includes good Bianco Vergine and dry Malvasia vdt, as well as a Chardonnay called Il Marzocco and a Sauvignon Blanc called Il Vignola, which rank with the finest varietals of central Italy. The house pride is its minuscule output of Vin Santo known as Occhio del Pernice, which if not exactly typical, is generally noted as best of breed.

Rudolf Bindella. On his estate of Vallocaia at Argiano, Swiss importer Bindella makes first-rate Vino Nobile. In preparation is a pure Prugnolo vdt to be called Vallocaia He is also developing estates in Chianti Classico.

Buracchi.

Top: Ettore Falvo, shown with his son, is the winemaker at Avignonesi, a house that has led the revival in the wines of Montepulciano. Centre: vineyards for Vino Nobile di Montepulciano. Bottom: bottles in the shop in Montepulciano where Avignonesi has headquarters for wines made from the vineyards of three estates.

Canneto.

Cantina Santavenere.

Contucci. Alamanno Contucci, who heads the consortium, has gradually revised his once traditional style in wine from 21 ha at his Mulinvecchio farm at Pietrose, just north of the town. Recent bottlings of Vino Nobile riserva aged in cellars at his family's Renaissance palazzo on the Piazza Grande have been convincing. Also Chianti and Vin Santo.

Dei.

Fanetti. Adamo Fanetti, a pioneer bottler of Vino Nobile, set the standards here from the 1920s to the 1970s. Son Giuseppe continues the tradition from 18 ha of choice vineyards at the Tenuta Sant'Agnese, though the wines, including Chianti and vdt, are now rarely remarkable.

Fassati. The firm owned by Fabat or Fazi-Battaglia group added 35 ha of vineyards at Graccianello and built new cellars where winemaker Amedeo Esposito produces sound Vino Nobile and Chianti.

Fattoria del Cerro. SAI Agricola, the agriculture branch of a large insurance firm, has been making some of the best Vino Nobile and Chianti from 117 ha of this estate near Acquaviva. Part of the production is sold under the Cantine Baiocchi label.

Fattoria di Fognano-Talosa. From 35 ha at Fognano on the northern edge of Montepulciano, the firm managed by Ottorino De Angelis makes sound Vino Nobile, exemplified by the single vineyard Talosa, and Chianti.

Fattoria Le Casalte. Paola Silvestri makes good Vino Nobile and Chianti from 8 ha at Casalte.

Il Macchione-Francavilla Agricola.

Il Pantano.

Vittorio Innocenti.

La Calonica. From 30 ha near Valiano, Fernando Cattani makes good Vino Nobile and Bianco Vergine.

La Casella. From 5 ha, Alfio Carpini makes sound Vino Nobile.

Poderi Boscarelli. From 9 ha of choice land at Cervognano, Paola De

Ferrari Corradi makes Vino Nobile that has often ranked with the best over the last two decades, along with good Chianti Colli Senesi. Winemaker Maurizio Castelli helped devise the excellent Prugnolo *barrique* vdt called Boscarelli.

Poggio alla Sala. The estate near San Savino has changed owners.

Poliziano. The dynamic Federico Carletti has built the estate named after the town's favourite son into a leader in Montepulciano. From more than 80 ha of vines around the cellars at Gracciano, as well as at Caggiole and at the higher Asinone plot at Pietrose, Carletti and Maurizio Castelli make admirable Vino Nobile, good Chianti, Bianco Vergine, and Vin Santo. The impressive vdt are named after Poliziano's poems Elegìa (a pure Sangiovese) and Le Stanze (based on Cabernet). Carletti has designated new vineyards for Rosso di Montepulciano. The estate uses the second label of Carletti della Giovampaola.

Giuseppe Raspanti & Figli. Good Vino Nobile from Gracciano.

Tenuta di Gracciano. The Della Seta Ferrari Corbelli family makes sometimes impressive Vino Nobile.

Tenuta Trerose. Milanese businessman Lionello Marchesi established this estate at Valiano with more than 40 ha for what is designed to be Vino Nobile second to none. The first vintage, '85, was promising, as was the barrel-fermented Chardonnay Salterio.

WINE HOUSES/MERCHANTS

Gattavecchi. Quality seems to be improving from this established house. *(Vino Nobile must be vinified and aged within the commune of Montepulciano, though bottlers outside the zone include Luigi Cecchi, Melini, Bigi, Granducato.)*

COOPERATIVES

Vecchia Cantina di Montepulciano. The zone's largest producer groups some 300 growers with more than 1,000 ha of vines. Director Aldo Trabalzini has insisted on clear quality standards for Vino Nobile, though the cellars also produce large amounts of Chianti, Bianco Vergine, and vdt.

Wines of Arezzo's hills

The province of Arezzo, which claims most of the upper Arno valley renowned in centuries past for sweet whites, rarely distinguishes itself with Chianti. Not because certain slopes along the Pratomagno and Monti del Chianti lack the propensity, but because so few growers seem dedicated to quality. Things seem to have changed little since 1903, when a reliable text described Aretini reds (then not called Chianti) as coarse and bitter. The same book noted that whites of Cortona in the Valdichiana were appreciated as far away as Switzerland. But the province of Arezzo for the most part remains a strangely underdeveloped corner of the wine world. The few exceptions have distanced themselves from the rest of the field, none so dynamically as Villa Cilnia on the edge of Arezzo or the Vino Nobile house of Avignonesi with its whites of the Valdichiana.

Chianti Colli Aretini

Few producers mention the zone on labels, knowing that the name conveys little to outsiders. The usual theme is youthful drinkability, but since Chianti here often turns out harsh, even if intended to be fleeting, few producers have more than a local following. Still, some estates seem to be trying to follow the lead of Villa Cilnia and Giovanni Bianchi who gives all his wines modern style. Local tastings have even uncovered an occasional Chianti of some depth, belying age as deftly as some *riserve* wines of adjacent Classico.

Zone: Slopes around Arezzo and 13 other communes in its province along the upper Arno valley between the Monti del Chianti and Pratomagno ranges, extending south into the Ambra valley adjacent to Chianti Classico and up to the northern edge of the Valdichiana. Dry red. Grapes: Sangiovese 75-90%, Canaiolo Nero 5-10%, Trebbiano Toscano/Malvasia del Chianti 5-10%, other reds up to 10%. Yld 70/100, Alc 11.5; riserva 12.5, Acd 0.5-0.75, Ag 6 mths; riserva 3 yrs.

Bianco Vergine Valdichiana (1972)

Etruscans made white wine on the easy inclines of the Chiana valley, launching a tradition that defied Tuscany's usual pre-eminence of reds. The wine's delicate almondy qualities were more noted in times past than they are today, perhaps because so much Bianco Vergine is boringly chaste. Still, amidst the cooperative output which seems aimed at providing a cheaper alternative to Galestro, the estate bottlings of Baldetti, Fattoria di Manzano, and especially Avignonesi seem almost seductive. *Vergine* refers either to the pure state the musts are in after separation from the skins before vinification or the practice of drawing wine from the vat before fermentation is complete, leaving it *frizzante*. But interpretations of virginity can be rather loose hereabouts, except among fine olive oils, which qualify as extra.

Zone: Rolling hills of the Chiana valley extending from the edge of Arezzo south between Cortona and Montepulciano as far as Chiusi and including six communes in Arezzo province and four in Siena. Dry white, sometimes lightly amabile or frizzante. Grapes: Trebbiano Toscano 70-85%, Malvasia del Chianti 10-20%, other whites 5-10%. Yld 91/130, Alc 11, Acd 0.6, Ag 5 mths.

Other wines of note

The unclassified wines of Avignonesi and Villa Cilnia take prizes for originality, though Fattoria di Manzano also has some unique bottles. Most Chianti producers make a house white and most Bianco Vergine producers a house red, sometimes of real interest.

ESTATES/GROWERS

Avignonesi-La Selva, Cignano di Cortona (AR). The noted Vino Nobile house has 60 ha of vines below Cortona where it makes Bianco Vergine and white vdt described under Montepulciano.

Mario Baldetti, Terontola (AR). Good Bianco Vergine.

Aldo Casagni, Rigutino (AR). From 10 ha, Bianco Vergine, good vdt Rosato di Rigutino, and fine but scarce Vin Santo.

Fattoria dell'Albereto, Subbiano (AR). Good Chianti Colli Aretini.

Fattoria di Manzano, Manzano di Cortona (AR). From 40 ha, Massimo D'Alessandro makes Bianco Vergine and vdt, including the youthful Vigna del Vescovo from Gamay and Ciliegiolo.

I Selvatici, Montevarchi (AR). Chianti.

Montepetrognano, Quarata (AR). From 7 ha, the Cherici family makes Chianti Montepetrognano and Caparbio.

San Fabiano, Arezzo. From 50 ha at the edge of Arezzo, the Conti Borghini Baldovinetti make a traditional type of Chianti.

Savoia Aosta, San Giustino Valdarno (AR). From vineyards on his Tenuta del Borro, Amadeo di Savoia, Duca d'Aosta, of the former Italian royal family, produces modest Chianti and vdt which he sells with a range of farm products.

Villa Cilnia, Pieve a' Bagnoro Montoncello (AR). Milanese Giovanni Bianchi built a cellar on the edge of Arezzo in the 1970s, added outside varieties to 36 ha of vines, and created a unique array of wines. Unlike most others, his Chianti Colli Aretini is full, round, and easy to drink. Vdt whites include the perfumed Poggio Garbato and the barrel-aged dry Campo del Sasso, and sweet Sassolato (all variations of Chardonnay, Trebbiano and Malvasia). A Chardonnay qualifies as Predicato del Muschio. There is also fizzy white Le Bizze and rosé Poggio Cicaleto, both from red grapes. Vdt reds are Vocato, from Chianti grapes, and Le Vignacce, which blends Cabernet Sauvignon with Brunello and Montepulciano in what may be Tuscany's most original *barrique* wine to date.

Villa La Selva, Monte Benichi (AR). The Carpini family and oenologist Vittorio Fiore make sound Chianti and Vin Santo.

COOPERATIVES

CS di Cortona, Camucia di Cortona (AR). From 520 growers comes some 80,000 hl of wine a year, Bianco Vergine and vdt.

Cantina Vini Tipici dell'Aretino, Ponte a Chiani (AR). Chianti and Bianco Vergine.

THE COASTAL FLANK

The coastal flank consists of three sectors: the northwest, the maritime hills, and Grosseto's Maremma. The wines of coastal Tuscany had been long obscured by the greater glories of the central hills, even if the evidence is that Etruscans made wine at points along the Ligurian and Tyrrhenian seas before they established vineyards inland. Wines of the coastal flank received recognition with a host of DOCs, though had it not been for Sassicaia, doubts might have persisted that the mild climes had any special aptitude for wine. Lately, growers from the border of Liguria to the edge of Latium have been rediscovering an ancient avocation for viticulture.

Wines of the northwest

The Apennines, which hug the coast through Liguria, begin their course inland in northwestern Tuscany through the Tosco-Emiliano range and the towering Alpi Apuani. Etruscans planted vines in the Apuan hills around what became the marble-quarrying centres of Massa and Carrara, though today's wines from those maritime climes rarely sell beyond the beach resorts of Versilia. Proudly independent Lucca has long coveted tasty reds from its verdant hills and the white of Montecarlo, which alone among the wines of northwestern Tuscany has an international reputation. The recent DOC of Colli di Luni, centred in Liguria, includes a small area in Tuscany.

Candia dei Colli Apuani (1981)

This white is rarely seen outside the area, though the soft, scented Candia of Scurtarola is worth looking for.

Zone: A strip of hills extending from the border of Liguria past Carrara and Massa to Montignoso between the Apuan Alps and the Via Aurelia. Candia is a village near

Massa. Dry to lightly amabile white. Grapes: Vermentino Bianco 70-80%, Albarola 10-20%, Trebbiano Toscano up to 20%, Malvasia del Chianti up to 5%. Yld 56/80, Alc 11.5, Acd 0.55.

Colline Lucchesi (Rosso 1968, Bianco 1986)

The Chianti-like *rosso* of Lucca's olive-cloaked hills has long been noted for its youthful drinkability, though some vintages keep nicely for a few years. The *bianco* has yet to distinguish itself.

Zone: Hills between 100-500 m east and west of the Serchio valley in the communes of Lucca, Capannori, and Porcari in Lucca province.
Rosso Dry red. Grapes: Sangiovese 45-60%, Canaiolo 8-15%, Trebbiano Toscano 10-15%, Ciliegiolo/Colorino 5-15%, Vermentino/Malvasia Toscana 5-10%. Yld 84/120, Alc 11.5, Acd 0.55.
Bianco Dry white. Grapes: Trebbiano Toscano 50-70%, Greco/Grechetto 5-15%, Vermentino Bianco 5-15%; Malvasia del Chianti up to 5%. Yld 77/110, Alc 11, Acd 0.5.

Montecarlo (Bianco 1969, Rosso 1986)

Montecarlo got a head start on other Tuscan whites by complementing the pedestrian Trebbiano with a host of interesting varieties which give it touches of colour, aroma, and suave personality. Fattoria del Buonamico set a precedent with class now rivalled by others. The Lucca area's most impressive reds also come from the town, though the best are vdt.

Zone: Low slopes oriented towards the south around the hilltop town of Montecarlo and parts of the communes of Altopascio, Capannori, and Porcari in Lucca province.
Bianco Dry white. Grapes: Trebbiano Toscano 60-70%, Sémillon/Pinot Grigio/Pinot Bianco/Vermentino/ Sauvignon/Roussanne 30-40%. Yld 70/100, Alc 11.5, Acd 0.5.
Rosso Dry red. Grapes: Sangiovese 50-75%, Canaiolo Nero 5-15%, Ciliegiolo/Colorino/ Malvasia Nera/Syrah 10-20%. Yld 70/100, Alc 11.5, Acd 0.55.

Other wines of note

Montecarlo's red wines occasionally surpass the whites, as long confirmed by Fattoria del Buonamico's Rosso di Cercatoia, a cousin of Chianti with the style of a Burgundy, and more recently Carmignani's opulent Sassonero.

ESTATES/GROWERS

Carmignani G. "Fuso", Montecarlo (LU). "Fuso" Carmignani injects soul into Montecarlo Bianco, as well as vdt red Sassonero from Sangiovese, Syrah, and Malvasia Nera, and white Pietrachiara, all from 4 ha of vines.
Cerruglio-Attilio Tori, Montecarlo (LU). Montecarlo Bianco and Rosso.
Fattoria del Buonamico, Montecarlo (LU). Distinguished Montecarlo Bianco and Rosso from 15 ha are surpassed by winemaker Vasco Grassi's Rosso di Cercatoia, a vdt from Sangiovese and other varieties.
Fattoria di Fubbiano, San Gennaro (LU). From 12 ha, respected Colline Lucchesi Rosso and Bianco.
Fattoria Maionchi, Montecarlo (LU). Good Rosso delle Colline Lucchesi.
Fattoria Michi, Montecarlo (LU). From 17 ha good Montecarlo Bianco and a personable white vdt from Roussanne.
Romano Franceschini, Montecarlo (LU). The proprietor of Viareggio's fine restaurant Romano makes Montecarlo Bianco at his home town.
Il Colle, Porcari (LU). Good Rosso delle Colline Lucchesi.
La Badiola, San Pancrazio (LU). Promising new Rosso delle Colline Lucchesi Vigna Flora.
Scurtarola, Massa. Pierpaolo Lorieri is a dedicated producer of the rare Candia dei Colli Apuani.
Tenuta di Maria Teresa, San Martino di Vignale (LU). Vittorio Rossi di Montelera (of Piedmont's Martini & Rossi) is developing Colline Lucchesi DOC wines at this lovely villa-estate.
Vigna del Greppo, Montecarlo (LU). Good Montecarlo Bianco and Rosso.

Wines of the maritime hills from Pisa to Elba

Sassicaia stands out among the wines of the coastal hills in the provinces of Pisa and Livorno. The status of what ranks as Italy's premier Cabernet has been bolstered by the rise of two nearby estates in the Bolgheri oasis: Grattamacco and Ornellaia. Signs of potential elsewhere along the coast have been confined mainly to table wines that break the Sangiovese-Trebbiano mould by using Cabernet and other varieties. The area's classified wines rarely show much, starting with Pisa's versions of Chianti and Trebbiano in Chianti Colline Pisane and Bianco Pisano di San Torpè, and skipping south past Livorno, Italy's busiest port, into the northern Maremma and across the waters to Elba. But, at least, it is now known that outstanding dry wines, not just red but white, can be made in the maritime hills.

Chianti Colline Pisane

The mild nature of these sunny hills is conducive to what are often the lightest and shortest lived wines of the seven Chianti zones, though now and then a *riserva* of some stature provides the exception.

Zone: Low hills south of the Arno between San Miniato and Casciana Terme and including eight other communes in Pisa province. Dry red. Grapes: Sangiovese 75-90%, Canaiolo Nero 5-10%, Trebbiano Toscano/Malvasia del Chianti 5-10%. Yld 70/100, Alc 11.5; riserva 12.5, Acd 0.5-0.75, Ag 6 mths; riserva 3 yrs.

Bianco Pisano di San Torpè (1980)

The summertime white of Pisa's lowlands was noted as long ago as Roman times, though the modern version has little to distinguish it from the rest of the Trebbiano clan. Vin Santo is popular locally.

Zone: Plains along the Arno between Cascina and San Miniato, extending south into low hills around Casciana Terme and Terricciola in 17 communes in Pisa province and Collesalvetti in Livorno. Dry white. Grapes: Trebbiano Toscano at least 75%, other whites up to 25%. Yld 84/120, Alc 11, Acd 0.55.
Vin Santo Amber dessert wine, secco or amabile. Grapes: As bianco but semidried. Yld 42/120, Alc 17, Acd 0.6, Ag 4 yrs in *caratelli* no larger than 2 hl in *vin santo* lofts.

Montescudaio (1977)

The breezy red and white wines of these arid hills are so appreciated locally that they are rarely seen elsewhere, though Fattoria di Sorbaiano's single vineyard Rosso del Miniere and barrel-fermented Lucestraia Bianco have attracted notice. Vin Santo is rare.

Zone: Hills north and south of the Cecina river between the towns of Cecina and Volterra in the communes of Montescudaio and six others in Pisa province.
Bianco Dry white. Grapes: Trebbiano Toscano 70-85%, Malvasia del Chianti/ Vermentino 15-30%, other whites up to 10%. Yld 84/120, Alc 11.5, Acd 0.6.
Rosso Dry red. Grapes: Sangiovese 65-85%, Trebbiano Toscano/Malvasia del Chianti 15-25%, other reds up to 10%. Yld 77/110, Alc 11.5, Acd 0.5.
Vin Santo Amber dessert wine. Grapes: As bianco but semidried. Yld 42/120, Alc 17, Acd 0.6, Ag 3 yrs in *caratelli* no larger than 2 hl in *vin santo* lofts.

Bolgheri (1984)

Perhaps intimidated by the grandeur of Sassicaia (which remains a vdt), other growers here obtained a DOC for white and rosé. Antinori's Rosé di Bolgheri from the Vigneto Scalabrone and Grattamacco give the appellation credibility, but Sassicaia and Ornellaia are outside DOC.

Zone: The gradually sloping coastal plain south of the village of Bolgheri between the Via Aurelia and the Colline Metallifere in the commune of Castagneto Carducci in Livorno province.
Bianco Dry white. Grapes: Trebbiano Toscano 75-90%, Vermentino 10-25%, other whites up to 15%. Yld 70/100, Alc 10.5, Acd 0.55.
Rosato Dry rosé. Grapes: Sangiovese 80-95%, Canaiolo 5-20%, other reds up to 15%. Yld 70/100, Alc 10.5, Acd 0.55.

Elba (1967)

Italy's third largest island – after Sicily and Sardinia – Elba has been noted since Etruscan times for what Pliny the Elder described as *vini ferax*, wines of sturdy character said to derive from the iron-rich soil. Napoleon apparently liked the taste, since he encouraged new vineyards during his exile there. Portoferraio and Marciana were noted for full-bodied whites from Procanico and Biancone and rich reds from Sangioveto. Today's versions, which rely more on productive strains of Trebbiano and Sangiovese, tend to be lighter to satisfy tourists who consume far more than the island produces. Still, a few growers – Acquabona, Tenuta La Chiusa, Podere L'Isolella, and Arrighi, among them – make dry wines of character. The traditional sweet red Aleatico and golden Moscato are rare.

Zone: The island of Elba in Livorno province.
Bianco Dry white, also spumante naturale. Grapes: Procanico/Trebbiano Toscano, other whites up to 10%. Yld 67.5/90, Alc 11, Acd 0.55-0.7.

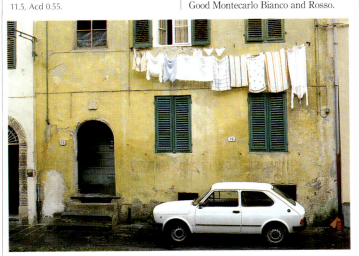

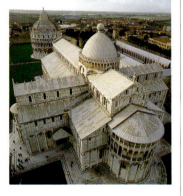

Left and below: the Piazza dei Miracoli at Pisa with the Cathedral and leaning tower. The city in the lower Arno plain is a centre of tourism and learning, though its province takes in a series of hills where the wines of Colline Pisane, San Torpè, and Montescudaio are produced.

Rosso Dry red. Grapes: Sangiovese at least 75%, Canaiolo Nero/Trebbiano Toscano/Biancone up to 25%. Yld 63/90, Alc 12, Acd 0.5-0.7.

Other wines of note

DOC has been approved for Val di Cornia in the communes of Campiglia Marittima, Suvereto, San Vincenzo, and Piombino in the province of Livorno. The *rosso* and *rosato* would be based on Sangiovese, the *bianco* on Trebbiano and Vermentino. Producers there already make good vdt: a light white called Corniello and red and white that may carry the name Ghimbergo, if approved by a tasting commission. Bianco di Nugola is a recognized vdt near Livorno. But the finest wines of the coast are the unclassified trio from the villages of Bolgheri and Castagneto Carducci: Sassicaia, Grattamacco, and Ornellaia (*see* below). In Pisa's hills the Tenuta di Ghizzano makes the admirable red Veneroso from Sangiovese and Cabernet Sauvignon. Elba's pride had been the sweet red Aleatico di Portoferraio, probably at its modern best from Enrico Terloni. Capraia and Pianosa, other islands of the Tuscan archipelago, make simple, tasty wines.

ESTATES/GROWERS

Acquabona, Portoferraio, Elba (LI). Rejuvenated estate emerging with good Elba DOC.

Arrighi, Porto Azzurro, Elba (LI).

From 3 ha, Sergio Arrighi maks good Elba DOC served at the family's Belmare hotel restaurant.

Jacopo Banti, Campiglia Marittima (LI). Good vdt white Corniello and red Ciliegiolo from the Val di Cornia.

Fattoria di Piedivilla, San Pietro Belvedere (PI). Chianti and Bianco Pisano di San Torpè.

Fattoria di Sant'Ermo, Casciana Terme (PI). Chianti Colline Pisane and Bianco Pisano di San Torpè as well as vdt.

Fattoria Usiglian del Vescovo, Palaia (PI). Chianti.

Grattamacco, Castagneto Carducci (LI). Pier Mario Meletti Cavallari has turned a rundown farm into a nationally recognized estate. First came Grattamacco Bianco, proof that Trebbiano and Malvasia can show class when yields are drastically reduced. Grattamacco also makes some Bolgheri DOC. But the outstanding wine from what will soon be 7.5 ha of vines is Grattamacco Rosso – Sangiovese and Malvasia Nera with Cabernet Sauvignon – a vdt that can stand proudly alongside Sassicaia.

Le Macchiole, Bolgheri (LI). From 5 ha, improving Bolgheri DOC.

Marchesi L. & P. Antinori, Bolgheri (LI). The vast Belvedere farm with about 50 ha of vines is the source of popular Bolgheri Rosato, including Vigneto Scalabrone which blends Sangiovese and Cabernet.

Ornellaia, Bolgheri (LI). Lodovico Antinori quietly developed this estate on the upper reaches of the family property next to Sassicaia, and in 1988 issued white Poggio alle Gazze from Sauvignon Blanc with Sémillon and red Ornellaia from Cabernet Sauvignon, Merlot, and Cabernet Franc. California's André Tchelistcheff designed the futuristic cellars and 25 ha of vineyards carved out of sloping pastures and woodland that had never been planted in vines. Other expert advisers have been viticulturist Mario Fregoni and Antinori winemaker Giacomo Tachis. Tchelistcheff, who called the ecosystem practically ideal in vineyards surrounded by woods at 200-300 m heights 15 km from the coast, said that unique mixes of clones of noble varieties create wines that are different and distinguished. French oenologist Jacques Puisais advised resident winemaker Federico Staderini in making the white Poggio alle Gazze from 1988 that drew high praise from experts. The red, which Antinori insists is not an imitation of Sassicaia (Merlot sets it apart), showed signs of becoming equally illustrious.

Podere Morazzano, Montescudaio (PI). Rosso and Rosato di Morazzano vdt.

Poggio Cosmiano, Peccioli (PI). The estate of the Principi Aldobrandini family produces Bianco Pisano San Torpè and vdt.

Sassicaia-Tenuta San Guido, Bolgheri (LI). In 1944, Mario Incisa della Rocchetta planted cuttings from Château Lafite-Rothschild on a hillside called Castiglioncello to see how Cabernet would do amidst the Tyrrhenian brush. Early wines were coarse, practically undrinkable, but each vintage the Marchese laid away some bottles that with time began to show style. One admirer was nephew Piero Antinori, who with oenologist Giacomo Tachis and Emile Peynaud of Bordeaux offered suggestions for ageing what was one of the first and certainly the most influential modern Italian wine in *barriques*. The first 3,000 bottles were issued by Antinori in 1968 under the name of a *podere* on the vast San Guido estate: Sassicaia, which refers to the *sassi* (stones) that abound in the calcareous terrain. In the 1970s, the wine won prestige in blind tastings in which it was taken either for a top Bordeaux or a top California Cabernet but rarely for an Italian. It quickly became a legend, rationed to followers in Europe and North America, where some devotees call it simply "Sass". Since Mario Incisa's death in 1983, son Niccolò has shifted the bottling to Bolgheri, while taking personal control of selling the annual average of 100,000 bottles. Vineyards have been expanded to 23 ha in three units. The 1.6-ha Castiglioncello lies about 15 km from the sea at altitudes of 330-350 m. Sassicaia di Sotto and adjacent Mandrioli cover 9 ha, Aianova 12.5 ha in plots 7-8 km from the sea at altitudes of 60-90 m. The mix is now about 75% Cabernet Sauvignon and 25% Cabernet Franc in vines that average 30 years old

at Castiglioncello and about 20 years in the lower plots. Sassicaia's consistency (the only vintage missed in two decades was 1973) is due to the regular maritime climate and low yields of about 30 hl/ha from vines trained in short double cordon. Fermentation takes place in stainless steel tanks with maceration on the skins for 12-14 days, followed by 18-22 months in *barriques* of French and Yugoslavian oak in air conditioned cellars.

Sorbaiano, Montecatini Val di Cecina (PI). From 12 ha, Febo Picciolini and winemaker Vittorio Fiore have given new style to Montescudaio DOC with the single vineyard Rosso del Miniere and barrel-fermented Lucestraia Bianco, along with traditional Vin Santo.

Tenuta di Ghizzano, Ghizzano di Peccioli (PI). The Venerosi Pesciolini family with the aid of Pier Mario

Meletti Cavallari (*see* Grattamacco) makes an impressive red vdt Veneroso from Sangiovese and Cabernet Sauvignon.

Tenuta La Chiusa, Magazzini, Elba (LI). From 5 ha of seaside vineyards, Giuliana Foresi makes Elba DOCs, exemplified by a full-bodied *rosso*.

Enrico Tirloni, Lacona, Elba (LI). Good Elba Rosso and an opulent Aleatico di Portoferraio from Podere L'Isolella.

Top: Sassicaia became a legend and a prototype for modern Italian red wines as the first Cabernet to be aged in French barriques. Above: owner Niccolò Incisa della Rocchetta outside his villa on the Tenuta San Guido at Bolgheri. Centre: ripe grapes ready for harvesting. Left: barrels for ageing the wine. Bottom: vineyards in the Bianco di Pitigliano zone.

Wines of Grosseto's Maremma

The province of Grosseto is known for its seaside resorts – Punta Ala, Castiglione della Pescaia, the isle of Giglio, and the Argentario peninsula with its harbours of Porto Ercole and Porto Santo Stefano. But the real Maremma lies inland, around the solitary towns where boar have roamed since Etruscan times. The Scansano and Pitigliano DOC zones overlap in the heart of Etruria amidst vineyards that stand out as oases of green against the summer tans of the hillsides. Their wines, like those of Parrina from a knoll above the Argentario, have won over vacationers while gaining some outside attention. But evidence exists that the Maremma is capable of grander things.

Morellino di Scansano (1978)

Sangiovese, which may stand alone as Morellino from around the hill town of Scansano, develops personality of its own in the Maremma. The name is a diminutive of *morello*, which refers to the wine's blackish hue, even if most modern versions tend more towards a rosy glowed ruby. The wine's growing success seems to rely on innate goodness that gives even the rough country types – still a majority – a certain appeal. Erik Banti has used French barrels to lend his single vineyard wines touches of class. Still, despite the hype that might have us believe that this is the next Brunello, Morellino has a long way to go to rival its neighbour from up the Ombrone valley at Montalcino.

Zone: Hills southeast of Grosseto between the Ombrone and Albegna valleys, extending from the Via Aurelia east past Scansano, the centre, to Roccalbegna and Magliano in seven communes in the province. Dry red. Grapes: Sangiovese, other reds up to 15%.Yld 84/120, Alc 11.5, riserva 12, Acd 0.5, Ag riserva 2 yrs (1 in wood).

Bianco di Pitigliano (1966)

If this white qualifies as a stand-in for Orvieto, it's because there is more than a vague similarity between the two. The town of Pitigliano also sits dramatically atop a tufaceous mesa into whose underpinnings wine cellars had been carved since prehistoric times. For that matter the mix of grapes is almost identical. But as a wine Bianco di Pitigliano resembles Orvieto more in content than in class. So far only La Stellata's Lunaia seems to have achieved regular style.

Zone: Rocky slopes interrupted by gorges around the towns of Pitigliano and Sorano, extending from the border with Latium through Manciano and across the Albegna valley to Scansano in Grosseto province. Dry white. Grapes: Trebbiano Toscano/Procanico 65-70%, Greco (Grechetto)/Malvasia Bianca Toscana/Verdello 30-35% together but no more than 15% each. Yld 87.5/125, Alc 11.5, Acd 0.55-0.7.

Parrina (1971)

The pleasant wines of Parrina were fixtures on the Argentario even before

the resort moved up-market. Still, the steady good value from the Spinola estate of La Parrina keeps the trio as popular in country *trattorie* as aboard the jet set's yachts.

Zone: Slopes of Poggio di Leccio around the village of La Parrina, overlooking the Argentario peninsula in the commune of Orbetello in Grosseto province.

Bianco Dry white. Grapes: Trebbiano Toscano/Procanico, Ansonica/Malvasia del Chianti up to 20%. Yld 84/120, Alc 11.5, Acd 0.5.

Rosso Dry red. Grapes: Sangiovese, Canaiolo Nero/Montepulciano/Colorino up to 20%. Yld 77/110, Alc 11.5; riserva 12.5, Acd 0.5, Ag riserva 3 yrs.

Rosato Dry rosé. Grapes: As rosso. Yld 77/110, Alc 11, Acd 0.5.

Other wines of note

The once respected Ansonica or Anzonica (Sicily's Inzolia) is now found mainly on the isle of Giglio, where it makes a golden to amber wine whose full flavour makes it good with fish soup. Another rarity is Alicante (from

the Spanish Granacha family), best from Erik Banti. The Meleta estate makes an original range of vdt. Sound red, white, and rosé vdt of the Maremma are made here and there, though like the recognized vdt of Montecucco they are nearly all drunk locally.

ESTATES/GROWERS

Erik Banti, Montemerano (GR). From 10.5 ha of vines, Erik Banti makes fine Morellino di Scansano *crus* Ciabatta, Aquilaia, and Piaggie, as well as a spicy, rich Alicante that outshines most of its Cannonau cousins from Sardinia.

Above: the wine town of Pitigliano near the border with Latium is perched dramatically on a mesa of tufaceous rock. Left: Sovana, a town of Etruscan origin.

The wines are served at his enoteca-trattoria L'Antico Frantoio.

Bargagli, Scansano (GR). Bargaglino Bianco di Pitigliano.

Coliberto, Massa Marittima (GR). New estate with promising vdt red Morello and white Coliberto di Coliberto.

Fattoria Le Pupille, Magliano in Toscana (GR). Morellino di Scansano.

La Stellata, Manciano (GR). From 4 ha, Clara Divizia and Manlio Giorni make the most acclaimed Bianco di Pitigliano under the name Lunaia.

Mantellassi, Magliano in Toscana (GR). Ezio Mantellassi makes sound Morellino di Scansano at his Podere Banditaccia.

Meleta, Roccatederighi (GR). Swiss owner Peter Max Suter has built new cellars where winemaker Marco Stefanini develops the good vdt Rosso

della Rocca and Lucertolo Bianco.
Motta, Alberese (GR). Emerging estate with good Morellino di Scansano.
Sellari-Franceschini, Scansano (GR). Morellino di Scansano.
Tenuta La Parrina, Albinia (GR). Sound quality in Parrina DOC "Vino Etrusco" from 60 ha on the estate of Franca Spinola.

COOPERATIVES

Consorzio Vini Toscani Montepescali, Montepescali (GR). Good value in Maremma vdt *bianco* and *rosso*.
CS Cooperativa di Pitigliano, Pitigliano (GR). Tuscany's largest cooperative groups most of Pitigliano's 1,000 growers with some 1,500 ha of vines for reliable Bianco di Pitigliano, including a kosher type for the town's prominent Jewish community, as well as vdt.
Cantina Cooperativa del Morellino di Scansano, Scansano (GR). From growers with 300 ha of vines, Morellino di Scansano, Bianco di Pitigliano, and vdt.

Travel Information

Above: Drying reeds for demijohn bases and baskets at Sovana in Grosseto province.

RESTAURANTS/HOTELS

(In addition to places cited, many wine estates and farms rent rooms and provide meals under a system known as Agriturismo.)

Da Delfina, 50042 Carmignano (FI). Tel (055)8718074. At Artimino, Carlo Cioni follows mother Delfina's recipes for refined home cooking served with Carmignano and other choice wines.
Vicolo del Contento, 52020 Castelfranco di Sopra (AR). Tel (055)9149277. Angelo and Lina Redditi offer excellent value in creative Tuscan dishes and deftly chosen wines from the region and beyond.
La Tenda Rossa, 50020 Cerbaia (FI). Tel 055)826132. In a quiet town on the edge of Chianti Classico, Silvano Santandrea provides top echelon food and wines with prices to match.
Arnolfo, 53034 Colle di Val d'Elsa (SI). Tel (0577)920549. Young Gaetano Trovato has brought élan to a cellar with ingenious dishes and a studied array of wines from Tuscany and other places at sensible prices.
La Biscondola, 50024 Mercatale Val di Pesa (FI). Tel (055)821381. Choice Florentine beefsteak on a terrace in the woods of Chianti Classico.
La Cucina di Edgardo, 53024 Montalcino (SI). Tel (0577)848232. Edgardo and Franca Sandoli give imaginative touches to local dishes with top wines.

La Chiusa, 53040 Montefollonico (SI). Tel (0577)669668. Dania Luccherini's natural master touch with Sienese country cooking has brought fame to this gracious restaurant with rooms and a view of Montepulciano. Husband Umberto serves up wine, wisdom, and weighty bills.
Al Vipore, 55100 Pieve Santo Stefano (LU). Tel (0583)59245. Cesare Casella has kept the family tone of this country trattoria with a view while garnishing traditional Luccan food and wine with genial whims.
La Mora, 55029 Ponte a Moriano (LU). Tel (0583)57109. Sauro Brunicardi and family lend touches of elegance to the wholesome food of the Garfagnana, while offering a formidable array of wines from the adjoining *enoteca*.
Antica Posta, 50026 San Casciano in Val di Pesa (FI). Tel (055)820116. Alessandro Panzani and chef Stefano Chiesura provide some of Tuscany's most inspired modern dishes studiously matched with wines.
La Cisterna, 53037 San Gimignano (SI). Tel (0577)940328. Charming hotel in the centre of town with grand views over the vineyards and acceptable food.
Gambero Rosso, 57027 San Vincenzo (LI). Tel (0565)701021. Fulvio and Emanuela Pierangelini have created one of the finest seafood restaurants of the

Tyrrhenian in a bright setting overlooking the port.
L'Amorosa, 53048 Sinalunga (SI). Tel (0577)679497. Carlo Citterio has turned this hamlet into a romantic retreat with a menu nicely balanced between old and new, good wines (including his own), and restful rooms.
Romano, 55049 Viareggio (LU). Tel. (0584)31382. In a resort famous for good restaurants, Romano and Franca Franceschini have established this point of reference for seafood and white wine, including their own Montecarlo.

WINE SHOPS/ENOTECHE

Siena's Enoteca Italiana in the Fortezza Medicea, known as the national wine library, has a gallery of bottles and a pleasant bar for sampling. Other public *enoteche* are in the Fortezza at Montalcino, at Carmignano, and at Terricciola in the Colline Pisane. The wine museum in the Poggio Reale villa at Rufina is worth a visit. The Enoteca Pinchiorri in Florence has what may be the greatest contemporary collection of wine from around the world, available to guests at the fine restaurant. A number of wine shops around Tuscany offer commendable choices, among them:
Enoteca Trinci, Agliana near Pistoia.
Enoteca Nebraska, Camaiore near Viareggio. With food.
Enoteca Porrini, Castiglione della Pescaia.

Bottiglieria Bussotti, Florence.
Enoteca Internazionale De Rham, Florence.
Enoteca Ombrone, Grosseto. With food.
Enoteca Gallo Nero, Greve in Chianti. Most Chianti Classico.
Il Gusto, Lucca.
Wine Club, Pescia.
Enoteca Peri, San Giovanni Valdarno.
Le Bollicine, Siena. With food.
Puntodivino, Viareggio. With food.

PLACES OF INTEREST

Tuscany takes time to get to know. Florence alone requires a week or so just to scratch its Renaissance surface. When you add Pisa, Lucca, Siena, Prato, Arezzo, and other urban centres of culture, who has time for a tour of the wine country? Well, it has been said that rural Tuscany is itself a work of art, an attestation to a people's love of the land that has reached the level of genius. It's a privilege just to look at the sculpted hills with their olives, vineyards, and woods; exploring them can be an unforgettable adventure. But be prepared to negotiate more curves and grades than appear on any map, and remember that it takes at least twice as long to get from Point A to Point B as it would anywhere else.

The best times to visit Tuscany are in spring, when wild flowers bloom and there is soft *pecorino* cheese with fresh *fave* (broad beans) to go with young Chianti, and autumn, when the air is perfumed with fermenting wine and wooded hillsides of burnished reds and amber provide mushrooms and game. Summers are pleasant in the hills, but in July and August the beaches from Versilia to Argentario are packed and the cities, especially Florence, swelter and function at half speed. Some prefer the cold months, when they have the museums to themselves, and the odour of wood smoke promises good things roasting on open hearths. But since the concept of wine tourism is still

rudimentary here, improvisation is often more rewarding than methodical planning. Visits to Carmignano, Rufina and Pomino, Lucca and Montecarlo, Bolgheri, Scansano, Pitigliano, and the island of Elba are recommended, in addition to the following.

Chianti Classico. The wine road known as La Chiantigiana (SS 222) runs from Florence through Greve, Panzano, and Castellina to Siena. A complete tour takes in Radda, Gaiole, Brolio, Castelnuovo Berardenga, Vagliagli, and San Casciano, not forgetting Badia a Coltibuono to the east and Badia a Passignano to the west. Each September Greve hosts a wine fair sponsored by the Gallo Nero consortium.

Montalcino and Montepulciano. The hill towns lie 25 km from each other across the moors of Siena province. Montalcino provides a medieval backdrop to the vineyards of Brunello. Montepulciano offers Vino Nobile in a Renaissance setting. In between is the town of Pienza which supplies them both with well-aged *pecorino* cheese.

San Gimignano. Once there were 72 towers; now there are 14. But tourists still flock to the Manhattan of Tuscany, which does almost as brisk a trade in Vernaccia as it does in souvenirs. Even when traffic is elbow to elbow, the town has something irresistible about it.

Above left: doorway in Montepulciano characteristic of the Renaissance period. Above right: vegetable market in Florence. Below: vineyards surrounding the ramparts of San Gimignano.

Umbria

Capital: Perugia.
Provinces: Perugia (PG), Terni (TR).
Area: 8,456 square kilometres (sixteenth).
Population: 817,000 (seventeenth).

Above: a vineyard in the Orvieto Classico zone.

The green hills of Umbria, which match Tuscany's for splendour, also rival their aptitude for wine. Though squeezed by the Apennines, Umbria has been sculpted by the Tiber and its tributaries into an often gentle upland with lime-rich soils and cool conditions that exalt noble varieties. Yet, with the exception of Orvieto, which Tuscans continue to regard as a colony, Umbria's vinous potential has barely been tapped.

The long enduring peasant wine tradition is fading as an ambitious development program establishes DOC zones (soon to be eight) over most of the territory deemed favourable to vines. The recent record of 15 percent DOC exceeds the national average. But take away Orvieto, and the other zones account for five percent of the remaining total – comparable to rates in southern regions which make mainly blending wines. This criticism may seem unduly harsh, but it is frustrating to note that Umbria's wine, like its fine olive oil, holds a lowly position in the farm economy, far surpassed by grains, livestock, and tobacco. About half of the region's wine is now handled by cooperatives or consortiums.

Premium production has failed to develop as expected. But where it has results have been impressive, indicating that what Umbria lacks to become a force in fine wine is individual initiative.

Orvieto opened world markets, but other winemakers, accustomed to having their customers come to them, have rarely followed. Despite the advantages of being at the heart of the peninsula with access to major road and rail routes and a steady tourist trade, Umbria and its wine remain largely outside Italy's mainstream. This is the only region that does not form part of the national border, and the only one south of the Alps with no outlet to the sea. Within these cosy confines Umbrians remain almost mystically serene. Like their beloved Francis of Assisi, they haven't let prosperity corrupt their basic values or the symbiosis with nature that has come to be regarded as an Umbrian birthright.

Admirers of bona fide country food and wine know that they can eat and drink as well here as anywhere in Italy. The rarefied ambience seems to endow things that grow with harmony and grace. Maybe this good fortune accounts for the nonchalant attitude about wine, for, as insiders know, even the most rudimentary of them can be exhilarating when tasted before the August heat or a mouldy cask take their toll. They insist that this rustic goodness is best savoured on the spot, and they have a point, but only a die-hard would pretend that Umbrian wines don't travel.

The legend of Orvieto has travelled far and wide for centuries, though what was originally a sweet golden wine prized at the papal court in Rome and beyond has lately become a polished dry white. The transition from antique to modern created problems with image for a while, but Orvieto Classico seems to have re-established its world class commercial attributes. White wines dominate in Umbria, accounting for four-fifths of the DOC. Yet the most convincing proof of class has come from Lungarotti at Torgiano, whose Rubesco riserva can match the classic reds of Tuscany (or Piedmont or Bordeaux) for elegance and long life. Montefalco's mighty Sagrantino reinforces the case for Umbrian reds.

Wine has been made here since pre-Roman times, when the Etruscans and Umbri, who gave the region its name, held territories on either side of the Tiber. As evidence, Etruscans left wine paraphernalia in tombs from Perugia to Orvieto. The conquering Romans found Umbrian wines too fleeting for imperial tastes. Not until the late Middle Ages and the Renaissance, when the Umbrian towns reached heights of glory, did wines rate written attention. Those of Spoleto, Todi, Assisi, Narni, Spello, Montefalco, Terni, and Spello attracted favourable notice, but Orvieto monopolized the praise.

Umbria is often likened to Tuscany, due to striking physical and cultural similarities, as well as to Latium, due to the eternal links of the Tiber and Flaminian Way. Yet Umbrians keep their distance from both,

sometimes seeming aloof and resentful about being paired and compared with their more ostentatious neighbours. So far, they have managed to keep their sanctuary, with its verdant woods and fields and medieval towns, more faithfully intact than the others. The question is, can they do so with their wines? The answer might be found, aptly enough, in Orvieto. After witnessing extremes of old and new within a generation, winemakers there seem to be plotting a future in the middle ground, striving for contemporary style without sacrificing the spontaneous grace with which Umbrian wines have been so generously endowed.

Umbria's Vineyards

As testimony to tradition, nearly half of Umbria's vineyards remained in mixed culture in the late 1980s, with vines often trained onto trees. But rapid renewal in DOC zones is in monoculture using vertical systems on wires strung between cement poles. Most training is in variations on cordon, including the *doppio capovolto* (double arch) in Orvieto.

The emphasis is on improved clones of traditional vines, which range beyond central Italy's standards to take in Garganega, Tocai, Barbera, Merlot, and Gamay. Most white varieties are variations on Trebbiano, though not all are certified family members. Procanico is, but the old mainstay of Orvieto has lost ground to Trebbiano Toscano, which accounts for about half of the region's white vines. Still, since Procanico gives Orvieto more structure, ageing potential, and general class, it seems due for a comeback. Another worthy but neglected native is Trebbiano Spoletino. But the rising star among whites is Grechetto, which holds its own against the surge of Chardonnay and Sauvignon.

Sangiovese dominates red varieties, backed by Ciliegiolo, Canaiolo, and Montepulciano, but some producers find the native Sagrantino more inspiring. Others prefer Merlot, Cabernet, even Pinot Noir. Among the oddities planted here and there are Piedmont's Dolcetto and Nebbiolo. The following varieties are associated primarily with Umbria.

Drupeggio. Local name for Canaiolo Bianco, this figures in the Orvieto blend, though it has faded due to low yields and questions about class.

Grechetto. Considered native despite a name that seems to link it to the Greco-Trebbiano family. Its compact bunches make whites of marked personality, but still more clonal selection is needed to bring out its best. Originally prominent at Todi, it is gaining ground elsewhere around Perugia and at Orvieto, where it is also called Norchiello. Grown in eastern Tuscany (as Pulcinculo) and in northern Latium (as Greghetto).

Sagrantino. The most distinguished of Umbria's red wine vines is being revived around Montefalco after fading from favour due to low yields. Whether the variety is native or imported long ago is uncertain, but it is increasingly touted for class. Sagrantino makes wines of power and personality, both in the sweet *passito* and in dry, wood-aged types.

Trebbiano or **Trebbianino Spoletino**. This distinctive clone is named after Spoleto in whose hills it historically made a white of more than usual Trebbiano character. But since it ripens late, the more precocious and productive Trebbiano Toscano has upstaged it.

Verdello. Productive component of Orvieto, Torgiano, and Colli Trasimeno white blends, it is appreciated for ample alcohol and acidity. It may be related to Verdicchio, but is not the same as Sicily's Verdello.

Other varieties

Other varieties recommended or approved in Umbria include:

For red (or rosé): Barbera, Cabernet Franc, Cabernet Sauvignon, Canaiolo Nero, Cesanese Comune, Ciliegiolo, Colorino, Dolcetto, Gamay, Merlot, Montepulciano, Pinot Nero, Sangiovese, Vernaccia Nera.

For white: Biancame, Canaiolo Bianco, Garganega, Malvasia Bianca di Candia, Malvasia del Chianti, Pecorino, Pinot Bianco, Riesling Italico, Tocai Friulano, Verdicchio Bianco, Vernaccia di San Gimignano.

Left: Orvieto's white wines have DOC status in dry and sweet versions, though dark varieties are also grown for sometimes impressive local reds.

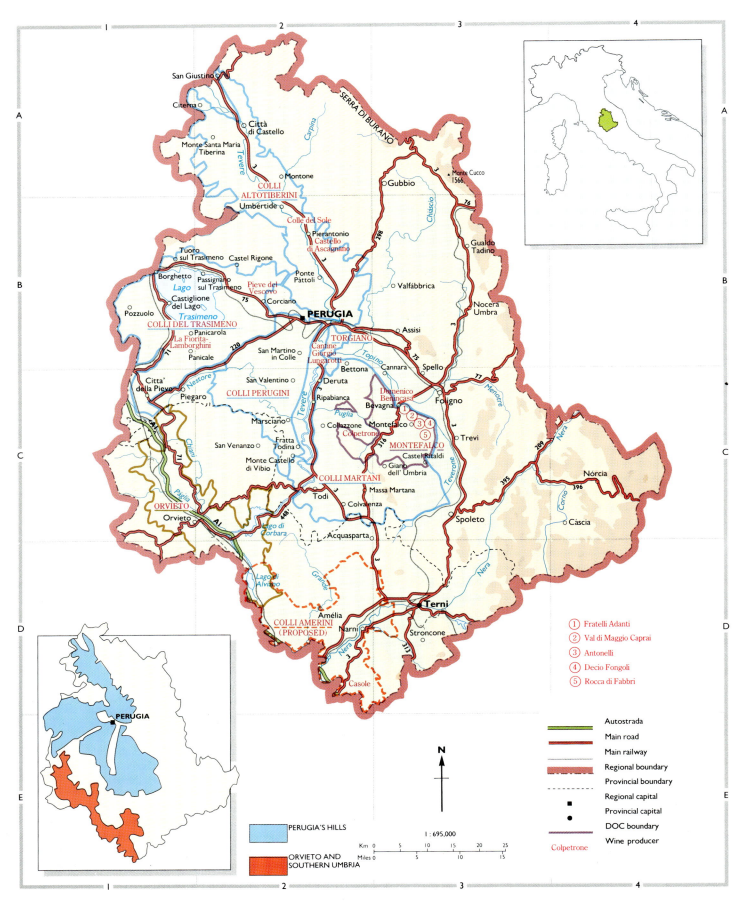

San Giustino

Citerna

Città
di Castello

Monte Santa Maria
Tiberina

Montone

SERRA DI BURANO

Gubbio

Monte Cucco
1566.

COLLI
ALTOTIBERINI

Umbèrtide

Colle del Sole

Pierantonio
Castello
di Ascagnano

Gualdo
Tadino

Tuoro
sul Trasimeno

Castel Rigone

Ponte
Páttoli

Valfábbrica

Nocera
Umbra

Borghetto

Passignano
sul Trasimeno

Pieve del
Vescovo

Lago

Corciano

Castiglione
del Lago

Pozzuolo

Trasimeno

PERUGIA

Assisi

COLLI DEL TRASIMENO

Panicarola

TORGIANO

La Fiorita-
Lamborghini

San Martino
in Colle

Cantine
Giorgio
Lungarotti

Topino

Spello

Panicale

Bettona

Cannara

Città
della Pieve

Nestore

San Valentino

COLLI PERUGINI

Deruta

Domenico
Benincasa

Foligno

Menore

Piegaro

Ripabianca

Puglia

Bevagna

① Fratelli Adanti

Marsciano

Collazzone

Montefalco

② Val di Maggio Caprai

San Venanzo

Fratta
Todina

Colpetrone

MONTEFALCO

Trevi

③ Antonelli

Monte Castello
di Vibio

Castel Ritaldi

④ Decio Fongoli

Chiani

Giano
dell' Umbria

Nórcia

⑤ Rocca di Fabbri

COLLI MARTANI

ORVIETO

Orvieto

Todi

Massa Martana

Teverone

Corno

Colvalenza

Paglia

A1

Lago di
Corbara

Acquasparta

Spoleto

Cáscia

Nera

Nera

Lago di
Alviano

Grande

Nera

Terni

Amélia

Narni

Stroncone

COLLI AMERINI
(PROPOSED)

Nera

Casole

N

1 : 695,000

Km 0   5   10   15   20   25

Miles 0   5   10   15

① Fratelli Adanti

② Val di Maggio Caprai

③ Antonelli

④ Decio Fongoli

⑤ Rocca di Fabbri

PERUGIA

PERUGIA'S HILLS

ORVIETO AND
SOUTHERN UMBRIA

Autostrada

Main road

Main railway

Regional boundary

Provincial boundary

Regional capital

Provincial capital

DOC boundary

Wine producer

Colpetrone

Umbria's Wine Zones

The Apennines envelope Umbria in a verdant upland at the heart of the peninsula, blessed with abundant water in lakes, rivers, and springs, but without an outlet to the sea. Yet the Tyrrhenian influence is decisive, since the Umbro-Marchigiano Apennines to the north and east form a wall and watershed from which the Tiber and its tributaries flow towards Rome, opening paths for weather patterns from the south and west. The mountains, which peak at around 1,700 metres in the Sibillini and Reatini ranges to the southeast, drop quickly into hills and high plains formed by streams and ancient lakes, of which Trasimeno is Italy's fourth largest. At points Umbria's gentle slopes have terrains and microclimates suited to the highest levels of viticulture, if rarely used for such. Most vineyards are in calcareous clay and sand, rich in limestone in places where, as growers may point out, the chalky colour is similar to that of Champagne. Since the entire region lies above 100 metres (though only 30 percent is above 500 metres), rainfall is ample in the cold months and summers are sunny but cooled by breezes, meaning that vineyards rarely become overheated and the normal drought lacks the damaging intensity felt nearer the sea.

Perugia's hills

Perugia's six DOC zones lie in or near the Tiber and Topino valleys and around Lake Trasimeno. Colli Altotiberini, which covers often steep hills along the Tiber north of Perugia, makes wines noted for freshness, especially rosé. Colli del Trasimeno surrounds the shallow lake which mirrors a mild influence on medium-bodied reds from rolling fluvial land to the southwest and zesty whites from steeper hills to the east. Torgiano, across the Tiber from Perugia, covers low slopes (180-300 metres) of sandy, calcareous clay on a tufaceous base. Its relatively warm climate favours enviable consistency in structured reds and full, fragrant whites. Colli Perugini, west of the Tiber between Perugia and Todi, rarely realizes its potential for red and white wines. Montefalco, overlapped by the new Colli Martani zone, is noted for the powerful red Sagrantino from soils of marly clay and sandy schists, though white Grechetto also shows class in the Martana massif's cool microclimates.

Orvieto and southern Umbria

Orvieto Classico lies within a broad basin of slopes webbed by gullies on either side of the Paglia and Tiber rivers in calcareous soils whose beige tones are bleached almost white during the summer drought. The heat within this *conca* is tempered by breezes wafting up the valleys and across the Tiber reservoir of Lake Corbara. Normal autumn damp induces fog and the botrytis cinerea that gives sweet wines extra dimensions. Orvieto's historical sites lay mainly around the town, which rests atop one of several mesas of volcanic origin towering over the Paglia's right bank. Most recent planting has been on slopes facing south and west along the Paglia's left bank and around Lake Corbara. Though soils range from loose sand to heavy clay, deposits of lime and marine fossils are quality factors not only for the Orvieto varieties but for such recent arrivals as Chardonnay, Sauvignon, and Pinot Nero. The sector of Orvieto north of the Classico area is high and not heavily planted. Latium's share is in prevalently volcanic soil, rendering wines closer in character to Lake Bolsena's Est! Est!! Est!!! than Orvieto Classico. The recent Colli Amerini zone extends east of the Tiber and along the Nera valley towards Terni through sunny hills so far noted for tasty country wines.

Above: La Badia, a medieval abbey on the edge of Orvieto, houses a hotel and restaurant as well as cellars for wines from adjacent vineyards.

Wines of Perugia

Perugia could be a wine centre of renown. Three DOC zones – Colli Altotiberini, Colli Perugini, and Torgiano – reach almost to the city limits. Another three – Colli Trasimeno, Montefalco, and Colli Martani – lie just beyond the circumventing hills. Assisi, which has no DOC but deserves one, is visible from the town's ramparts. Yet producers in a province with vinicultural potential perhaps comparable to adjacent Siena have done surprisingly little to exploit it. Only one winery in the entire area enjoys a wide reputation for excellence, Lungarotti, a name better known in world wine circles than are any of Perugia's official appellations. Other estates have emerged beyond the region, notably Adanti's Arquata and Caprai's Val di Maggio in Montefalco and Lamborghini's La Fiorita in Colli del Trasimeno. But most winemakers seem to prefer the ease and security of catering to local tastes, which means that Perugians drink enviably well, if often a bit rustically, and pay precious little for the privilege.

Colli Altotiberini (1980)

The wines of these bucolic hills were praised by Pliny the Younger, who summered at a villa overlooking the Tiber. But rather than striving for recognition, producers seem happy to supply friends and relatives with wines that are eminently easy to toss back. The once renowned *bianco* is now rarely more than zippy. The *rosso* (thanks to Merlot) is softer and fruitier than most country reds. But the best is often the *rosato*, which from Colle del Sole is a persuasive blush wine.

Zone: Hills along both sides of the Upper Tiber Valley from the border with Tuscany past Città di Castello and Umbertide to the outskirts of Perugia, taking in eight communes in the province.

Bianco Dry white. Grapes: Trebbiano Toscano 75-90%, Malvasia del Chianti up to 10%; other whites up to 15%. Yld 77/110, Alc 10.5, Acd 0.6.

Rosso Dry red. Grapes: Sangiovese 55-70%, Merlot 10-20%, Trebbiano Toscano/Malvasia del Chianti up to 10%; other varieties up to 15%. Yld 77/110, Alc 11.5, Acd 0.6.
Rosato Dry rosé. Grapes: As rosso. Yld 77/110, Alc 11.5, Acd 0.6.

Colli del Trasimeno (1972)
The broad basin of central Italy's largest lake has enough vineyards to rank a distant second to Orvieto in volume among Umbria's DOCs, but the wines of Trasimeno, good as they often are, have never made the impact expected of them. The better whites can compare with Orvieto or Torgiano. The red, which may include Gamay, has a supple fruitiness most attractive when young. Lamborghini and Pieve del Vescovo are reliable producers.

Zone: Hills surrounding Lake Trasimeno, taking in nine communes in Perugia province.
Bianco Dry white. Grapes: Trebbiano Toscano 60-80%, Malvasia del Chianti/Verdicchio/Verdello/Grechetto up to 40%. Yld 87.5/120, Alc 11, Acd 0.55.
Rosso Dry red. Grapes: Sangiovese 60-80%, Ciliegiolo/Gamay up to 40%; Trebbiano Toscano/Malvasia del Chianti up to 20%. Yld 87.5/120, Alc 11.5, Acd 0.55.

Torgiano (1968)
The Torre di Giano (Tower of Janus, the two-faced Roman god of gates and the namesake of January) dominates the graceful skyline of this hill town that boasts Umbria's first and in a gem-like way its foremost DOC. Gem-like because the reputation has belonged to Giorgio Lungarotti from the start, even if other producers may use the name and occasionally do. The standard *rosso* and *bianco* are wines of sound quality and reasonable price, though the Lungarotti brands of Rubesco and Torre di Giano are better known than the official appellation. International status was built on Rubesco *riserva* Monticchio, whose best aged vintages (1971, 1975) have been compared with top *crus* of Bordeaux. The Torre di Giano *riserva* Il Pino was one of Italy's first modern wood-aged whites of real style. A special DOCG has been requested for Torgiano Rosso riserva.

Zone: Low hills east of the Tiber in the commune of Torgiano, extending from just southeast of Perugia, through the villages of Miralduolo and Brufa and across the Chiascio stream as far south as Ponte Nuovo.
Bianco Dry white. Grapes: Trebbiano Toscano 50-70%, Grechetto 15-35%; Malvasia Toscana/Malvasia di Candia (non aromatic)/Verdello up to 15%. Yld 81/125, Alc 11.5, Acd 0.5-0.7.
Rosso Dry red, also riserva. Grapes: Sangiovese 50-70%, Canaiolo 15-30%; Trebbiano Toscano up to 10%, Ciliegiolo/Montepulciano up to 10%. Yld 78/120, Alc 12; riserva 12.5, Acd 0.5-0.7, Ag riserva 3 yrs.

Colli Perugini (1982)
The panoramic hills across the Tiber from Torgiano are higher and cooler and would seem to offer even more exciting prospects for heightened aromas and flavours in both red and white wines. But most have that homespun goodness that is better suited to sales in demijohn than bottle. Despite DOC, producers seem to have had greater incentive to excel a century ago, when the Conti Faina at Collelungo built a series of underground galleries in stone to age wines. Today, one of Italy's most extraordinary wine cellars is not in use.

Zone: Hills west of the Tiber extending from the outskirts of Perugia south almost to Todi, taking in six communes in Perugia province and San Venanzo in Terni.
Bianco Dry white. Grapes: Trebbiano Toscano 65-85%, Verdicchio/Grechetto/Garganega 15-35%; Malvasia del Chianti up to 10%. Yld 84/120, Alc 11, Acd 0.5.
Rosso Dry red. Grapes: Sangiovese 65-85%, Montepulciano/Ciliegiolo/Barbera 15-35%; Merlot up to 10%. Yld 84/120, Alc 11.5, Acd 0.55.
Rosato Dry rosé. Grapes: As rosso. Yld 72/120, Alc 11.5, Acd 0.55.

Colli Martani (1989)
The newest of Perugia's DOCs would seem to hold promise, since good country wines are a tradition in the peaceful uplands between Todi and Foligno. But it remains to be seen if producers will take up the challenge to make wines of real class. Of the three varietals, Grechetto from the environs of Bevagna and Todi seems to offer the brightest prospects.

Zone: Hills of the Martana massif between the Tiber and Topino-Clitunno valleys, extending from Bettona as far south as Spoleto and taking in Gualdo Cattaneo, Giano dell'Umbria, and parts of 12 other communes in Perugia province. The territory overlaps the smaller Montefalco DOC zone. Grechetto from the commune of Todi may be called Classico.
Grechetto Dry white. Grapes: Grechetto; other whites up to 15%. Yld 77/110, Alc 12, Acd 0.5.
Trebbiano Dry white. Grapes: Trebbiano Toscano; other whites up to 15%. Yld 84/120, Alc 11, Acd 0.5.
Sangiovese Dry red, also riserva. Grapes: Sangiovese; other reds up to 15%. Yld 84/120, Alc 11.5; riserva 12, Acd 0.5, Ag 1 yr; riserva 2 yrs (1 in wood).

Montefalco (1980)
Montefalco is one Perugian DOC whose fortunes are on the rise, though not so much for its rather anonymous red as for its singular Sagrantino. Traditionally a sweet *passito* that seemed on the verge of expiring little more than a decade ago, Sagrantino has been born again as a dry red of assertive, if hard to restrain, personality. Not even its most fervent devotees seem to know much about Sagrantino's background, but the cult that surrounds this lusty red has spread beyond Umbria's borders. Though depicted as ancient and indigenous, records of its presence on Montefalco's heights date only to the last century. So whether it is native or was brought from Catalonia or Piedmont or was introduced by Saracens, as legends relate, isn't known. The name may refer to the Sacrament, since having been sweet it was cultivated by Franciscans for use in religious rites. Recent emphasis has been on the dry, whose voluptuous body but sometimes staggering strength recall Amarone. But some insist that true Sagrantino is *passito* of soaring richness tempered by a light tannic bite. Since techniques are still evolving, questions remain not only about typology but about durability and whether the wine will ever be as grand as its admirers submit. Several estates on the slopes dominating the Clitunno plain between Foligno and Spoleto have risen from obscurity over the last decade, none more gallantly than Adanti, which excels with both styles of Sagrantino and other wines. Other worthy producers include Arnaldo Caprai, Antonelli, Colpetrone, and Bea. Montefalco Rosso, if often tasty, is too variable to define. The advent of Colli Martani adds the option of making the zone's sometimes impressive Grechetto DOC.

Zone: Slopes around the lofty town of Montefalco and parts of Bevagna, Castel Ritardi, Giano dell'Umbria, and Gualdo Cattaneo in Perugia province. Colli Martani overlaps the zone.
Rosso Dry red. Grapes: Sangiovese 65-75%, Trebbiano Toscano 15-20%, Sagrantino 5-10%; Ciliegiolo/Montepulciano/Merlot/Barbera/Malvasia del Chianti up to 15%. Yld 91/130, Alc 11.5, Acd 0.6.
Sagrantino Dry red. Grapes: Sagrantino; Trebbiano Toscano up to 5%. Yld 52/80, Alc 12.5, Acd 0.55.
Sagrantino passito Sweet red. Grapes: As Sagrantino but semidried or passito. Yld 36/80, Alc 14, Acd 0.6, Ag 1 yr.

Other wines of note
The province of Perugia abounds in unclassified wines, a few sleek and modern, many more roughly individualistic. Among dry reds, Adanti's Rosso d'Arquata, Lungarotti's San Giorgio and Cabernet, and Veneri's Merlot di Spello stand out. Curiosities include the inky sweet Vernaccia di Cannara, Nebbiolo and Dolcetto from Gubbio, and an aptly named Scacciadiavoli (chase away devils) from Foligno. Among whites, Lungarotti and Adanti again come to the fore, the former with Chardonnay, *spumanti*, and the unique Solleone, the latter with Grechetto and Bianco d'Arquata. Both produce fine Vin Santo, which is invariably sweet in Umbria, where an annual batch is made by nearly every farm family. There are several good examples of Grechetto dell'Umbria vdt, some of which will qualify under the new Colli Martani DOC. Why Assisi has never capitalized on its famous name by requesting a DOC is hard to say, since the red, white, and rosé from Tili and Sasso Rosso are well above the classified norm.

ESTATES/GROWERS

Fratelli Adanti, Bevagna (PG). From 18 ha of vines at a place called Arquata, a talented winemaker named Alvaro has pushed Adanti to the forefront in the Montefalco zone with fine Sagrantino, both dry and *passito*, and a decent Rosso DOC. But the house pride is Rosso d'Arquata, a vdt from Barbera, Canaiolo, Merlot, and Cabernet, that ranks as one of central Italy's most original and enjoyable red wines. Adanti also makes good Vin Santo and the area's best dry whites: a pure Grechetto and Grechetto with Trebbiano in the long lived Bianco d'Arquata.
Antonelli, Montefalco (PG). From 10 ha of vines, Montefalco DOC, including

fine Sagrantino, as well as Grechetto.

Paolo Bea, Montefalco (PG). Tiny production of Montefalco DOC includes a titanic Sagrantino *passito*.

Domenico Benincasa, Bevagna (PG). Montefalco DOCs and vdt from 45 ha.

Castello di Ascagnano, Pierantonio di Umbertide (PG). From 36 ha of vines, Colli Altotiberini DOC and *spumanti*.

Colle del Sole, Pierantonio di Umbertide (PG). From 30 ha of vines, Carlo Polidori and daughter Lauretta produce Colli Altotiberini DOC, led by a fine *rosato*, and a good red vdt known as Rubino.

Colpetrone, Gualdo Cattaneo (PG). Filippo Fabbri's tiny production of Montefalco DOC includes sometimes impressive Sagrantino.

Fattoria Belvedere, Castiglione del Lago (PG). Colli del Trasimeno DOC.

Decio Fongoli, San Marco di Montefalco (PG). From 10 ha, occasionally fine Sagrantino di Montefalco.

La Fiorita, Panicale (PG). Ferruccio Lamborghini, the retired car mogul, runs this expensive hobby estate with 75 ha of vines for Colli del Trasimeno DOC (led by the red Sangue di Miura), rosé vdt, and *spumante*.

La Querciolana, Panicale (PG). Colli del Trasimeno DOC under the Grifo di Boldrino label.

Morolli, Petrignano del Lago (PG). Colli del Trasimeno DOC.

Silvio Nardi, San Giustino (PG). Colli Altotiberini DOC.

Pieve del Vescovo, Corciano (PG). Good Colli del Trasimeno DOC from the vineyards of Il Lucciaio.

Rocca di Fabbri, Montefalco (PG). From 92 ha, Montefalco DOC and vdt, including Grechetto dell'Umbria.

Sasso Rosso, Capodacqua (PG). Tasty Assisi vdt.

Fratelli Sportoletti, Spello (PG). From 20 ha, Grechetto dell'Umbria and Assisi vdt.

Silvestro Sposini, Marsciano (PG). Colli Perugini DOC and vdt under the Castello di San Valentino label.

Tili, Capodacqua (PG). From 13 ha, Assisi vdt and a good Grechetto dell'Umbria.

Ugo Vagniluca, Frontignano di Todi (PG). From 20 ha, Castello di Almonte red and Grechetto di Todi vdt.

Val di Maggio-Arnaldo Caprai, Montefalco (PG). From 25 ha, Montefalco DOCs, including a fine, dry Sagrantino, plus Grechetto dell'Umbria vdt and bubbly wines.

Ruggero Veneri, Spello (PG). Small production of Merlot and Gran Merlot di Spello vdt, among the best of that varietal in central Italy.

Villa Antica, Città della Pieve (PG). From 20 ha at the estate owned by the Di Lauro family, Vittorio Fiore makes Colli del Trasimeno DOC plus Orvieto Classico from bought in grapes.

WINE HOUSES/MERCHANTS

Cantine Giorgio Lungarotti, Torgiano (PG). Giorgio Lungarotti's compound of family land holdings and cellars constitutes Umbria's most illustrious wine house, noted for Torgiano DOCs, an array of red and white vdt, and *spumanti*. Drawing almost entirely from about 250 ha of company vines, Lungarotti and step-daughter Maria Teresa Severini run the operation with technical director Angelo Valentini and consulting oenologist Corrado Cantarelli. More than half of the annual 270,000 cases produced is exported. The early reputation was built on Torgiano DOC Rubesco, whose *riserva* from the 12-ha Monticchio plot ranks among Italy's most dignified aged reds, as well as the white Torre di Giano, which reaches heights in the wood-aged *riserva* from the 10-ha Il Pino vineyard. The line includes vdt red Rosciano, white

Buffaloro, and rosé Castel Grifone, along with sweet Vin Santo. In the 1970s, Lungarotti introduced Cabernet Sauvignon, first in a varietal vdt from vineyards at Miralduolo, then blended with Torgiano varieties in the more convincing San Giorgio. There is also a Pinot Grigio, but Chardonnay is the up-and-coming white, used both in a barrel-aged still version and blended with Pinot Noir in Lungarotti Brut *champenoise* and Rondò tank *spumante*. Solleone is a unique aperitif wine made by *solera*.

COOPERATIVES

CS del Trasimeno, Castiglione del Lago (PG). From growers with 900 ha, Colli del Trasimeno DOC and vdt.

CS Colli Perugini, Marsciano (PG). Colli Perugini DOC.

CS dei Colli Spoletini, Petrognano (PG). Montefalco and Colli Martani DOC and vdt.

Co.Vi.P., Ponte Pattoli (PG). Consortium of cooperatives bottles wine from all six Perugia DOC zones.

CS Tudernum, Todi (PG). From 650 ha, Grechetto di Todi and other vdt.

Wines of Orvieto and southern Umbria

The province of Terni has had just one DOC, Orvieto, though that accounts for two-thirds of Umbria's classified wine. Orvieto's penchant for vines has been known since pre-Roman times, though only recently has its potential for wines other than the legendary *abboccato* been actively explored. Orvieto doesn't stand alone in the province. DOC has been advanced for Colli Amerini, in hills along the Tiber and its tributary the Nera, which flows past Terni, Narni, and Amelia to Orte. Those towns had been noted for their wine in the past, but it remains to be seen if the new DOC will raise standards above recent lackadaisical levels.

Orvieto (1971)

Orvieto looms majestically atop a bluff whose broad shoulders seem to have borne the destiny of Umbrian wine since the Etruscans carved cellars out of the town's underlying tufa. Mythical status dates to the late Middle Ages, when Pinturicchio and Luca Signorelli demanded rations of golden wine as partial payment for paintings in the Cathedral. Lofty endorsements also came from popes, who used Orvieto as a retreat when the Holy Seat at Rome got too hot for comfort. None was more devoted than Gregory XVI, whose will stipulated that his body be washed with Orvieto before his funeral. The soft *abboccato* must have been supreme when autumn mists in the Paglia-Tiber basin affected the grapes with botrytis cinerea. The wine, long identified with the squat, straw-based *pulcinella* flask, stayed sweet and more or less golden until after World War II. DOC encouraged new vineyards and cellars, which hastened the conversion to a dry white. Soon the *pulcinella*, like the

Chianti flask, was phased out for being too unwieldy on rapid-fire bottling lines and unsuited to the wine's clean-cut image. But even customers who found flavourless, odourless, colourless whites easy to swallow soon realized that the new Orvieto in standard bottles was one of a growing crowd.

The comeback, if quicker than expected, is by no means complete. Quality has improved steadily in Orvieto Classico, whose vineyards really are superior to the others. Dry wines from top producers show class, though the real surprises have come in sweet types, whose shining examples reek nobly of botrytis. But while rebuilding markets for both types, producers and bottlers have failed to mount the concerted drive needed to put the name Orvieto Classico back at the forefront of Italian wine. They have, however, requested DOCG, which, even if approved, is no guarantee of brilliance. What lacks in Orvieto, apart from unity, is a confirmed leader. Antinori could easily assume the

Left: the golden wines of Orvieto have been praised by popes and poets alike.

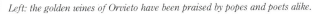

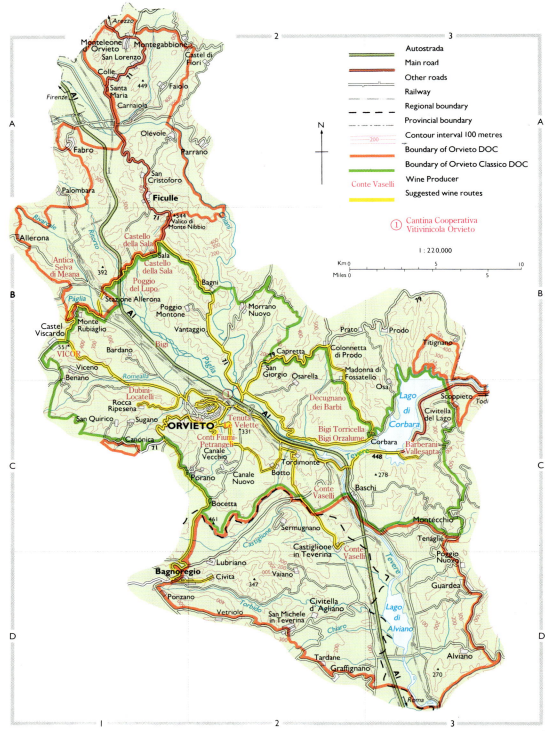

Legend:
- Autostrada
- Main road
- Other roads
- Railway
- Regional boundary
- Provincial boundary
- Contour interval 100 metres
- — 200 —
- Boundary of Orvieto DOC
- Boundary of Orvieto Classico DOC
- *Conte Vaselli* Wine Producer
- Suggested wine routes

① Cantina Cooperativa Vitivinicola Orvieto

1 : 220,000

Km 0 .... 5 10
Miles 0 5

several leading growers insist that the future of Orvieto be native. They are pointing at Procanico and Grechetto, whose personalities are enhanced by lower yields and picking at peaks of ripeness. Though dry types predominate, evidence mounts that Orvieto's ultimate expression is as a sweet wine with at least a hint of botrytis. Best examples to date have been Decugnano dei Barbi's Pourriture Noble, Barberani's Calcaia, and Antinori's non-DOC Muffato della Sala. Historical sweetness apparently was not just a matter of taste, but a natural phenomenon having to do with soils and yeasts and the cool tufa caves where the wine was made. Giovanni Dubini, who resigned as director of the Orvieto Classico consortium to concentrate on his own estate, noted that even if fermentation takes place without selected yeasts or temperature control, the finished wine will contain some residual sugar. Lately, though, the traditional *abboccato* has been supplemented by sweeter versions under the recent EEC-approved definitions of *amabile* and *dolce*, terms which appear on labels.

Zone: Hills between 100-500 m surrounding the town of Orvieto traversed by the Paglia river and its tributary the Astrone to the northwest as far as Monteleone di Orvieto and by the Tiber to the southeast as far as Alviano, taking in 11 communes in Terni province and five, including Bagnoregio, in Latium's province of Viterbo. The Classico area lies at the centre along both sides of the Paglia and adjacent to Lake Corbara between Baschi and Civitella del Lago, excluding the northern tier along the Astrone and the southern sector in Latium. Secco, abboccato, amabile, or dolce. Grapes: Procanico/Trebbiano Toscano 40-65%, Verdello 15-25%, Grechetto/Drupeggio and other whites 20-30%; Malvasia Toscana up to 20%. Yld 71.5/110, Alc 11.5 (abboccato res sugar 4-12 gr/l; amabile 12-45 gr/l; dolce min 45 gr/l), Acd 0.5.

Colli Amerini (Proposed DOC)

Approval is near for four wines from this large but scarcely noted zone: Bianco (from Trebbiano Toscano with others), Rosso, and Rosato (both from Sangiovese with others), and Malvasia.

Other wines of note

Among many unclassified wines of Orvieto, Antinori's innovations at Castello della Sala have drawn wide acclaim. Bigi's Marrano is also admirable. Many producers make red vdt. Noteworthy are Decugnano dei Barbi's Decugnano Rosso, Conte Vaselli's Santa Giulia, and Lago di Corbara, a recognized vdt at its best from Barberani. Decugnano dei Barbi pioneered in the area with *champenoise*. Two estates of note are Castello di Montoro and Casole.

mantle, but so far the best efforts at Castello della Sala have gone into table wines more glamorous and costly than the DOC. Bigi has made fine single vineyard wines, but the firm's industrial scale works against prestige. Two estates have emerged impressively, though neither has yet acquired the requisite charisma. Decugnano dei Barbi's versions of Orvieto Classico, if admired, are considered atypical. Barberani-Vallesanta sells most of its fine Orvieto and table wines abroad.

Among producers and bottlers, who number less than 30, ideas vary widely over what Orvieto ought to be. Many of the zone's 750 growers belong to cooperatives, which account for about two-thirds of production, sold either under their own labels or under those of private firms. Bottlers have long been dominated by Tuscan houses, which offer Orvieto Classico as a white alternative to Chianti. Some make their own Orvieto, at least in part, or supervise winemaking from purchased grapes. Antinori buys to supplement

production from Castello della Sala. Melini is supplied by Bigi, both part of the Gruppo Italiano Vini. Rocca delle Macìe makes wine from a local estate. Oenologists from Ruffino, Ricasoli, and Cecchi are among those who control sources in the zone. Barbi, a family firm in Lombardy which owns the Decugnano dei Barbi estate, also bottles Orvieto as a *négociant*.

There is reason to suspect that the unauthorized Chardonnay, Pinots, and Sauvignon have been used to brighten the motley array of local varieties. But

ESTATES/GROWERS

Antica Selva di Meana, Allerona (TR). Orvieto Classico DOC.

Barberani-Vallesanta, Baschi (TR). From 25 ha above Lake Corbara, Luigi Barberani and winemaker Maurizio Castelli produce Orvieto Classico and vdt under the Barberani and Vallesanta labels. The single vineyard Castagnolo exemplifies modern dry Orvieto Classico. Pulicchio shows style as *amabile*. Calcaia advances the noble cause of botrytis. A barrel-aged Sauvignon called Pommaio shows promise.

Casole, Otrìcoli (TR). Elio and Alberto Cuccarini, aided by Trentino's Salvatore Maule, make Casole Bianco and Rosso vdt at this emerging estate.

Castello della Sala, Sala (TR). Antinori's Umbrian castle with 130 ha of vines has become Orvieto's nerve centre under estate director Renzo Cottarella. Wines labelled Castello della Sala are vdt, led by Cervaro della Sala (Chardonnay and Grechetto fermented and aged on the lees in small barrels) and Borro della Sala "Fumé" (Sauvignon Blanc and Procanico). Cottarella and oenologist Giacomo Tachis have developed Muffato della Sala, a botrytised sweet wine from Sauvignon, Grechetto, and Drupeggio. A sweet Gewürztraminer is also promising. Red wines from Pinot Noir and other varieties are under consideration. Orvieto Classico from 45 ha (including the single vineyard Campogrande) is supplemented by purchased grapes and wine sold under the Antinori trademark.

Castello di Montoro, Montoro Umbro (TR). From 150 ha at the estate near Narni, the Patrizi Montoro family makes a noted *rosso* and other vdt.

Conte Vaselli, Castiglione in Teverina (VT). The property's 130 ha of vines is centred in Latium but extends into Orvieto Classico, where the vdt Santa Giùlia is produced from Sangiovese and various foreign varieties, a sometimes impressive once noted for long ageing.

Conti Fiumi-Petrangeli, Orvieto (TR). Orvieto Classico and red vdt served at their restaurant La Badia.

Decugnano dei Barbi, Orvieto (TR). From 18 ha near Lake Corbara, Claudio and Marina Barbi make Orvieto of singular style. The botrytised Pourriture Noble set a precedent for others. The *champenoise* Decugnano Brut, which combines Chardonnay with local varieties, is aged in an ancient grotto on the estate.

Dubini-Locatelli, Orvieto (TR). Giovanni Dubini and family in 1988 began vinifying the entire production from 18 ha at Rocca Ripesena in promising Orvieto Classico under the Palazzone label.

Poggio del Lupo, Allerona (TR).

Orvieto Classico.

Tenuta Le Velette, Orvieto (TR). From 95 ha, improving Orvieto Classico and vdt.

WINE HOUSES/MERCHANTS

Bigi, Orvieto (TR). The firm, founded by Tuscan Luigi Bigi in 1881, is now owned by Gruppo Italiano Vini. It draws from 70 ha for Orvieto Classico, though production of more than 3 million cases a year includes the DOC Est! Est!! Est!!! and Aleatico di Gradoli from Latium as well as vdt. The single-vineyard Torricella (dry) and Orzalume (sweet) exemplified Orvieto in the mid-1980s, though other producers now match their class. The vdt Marrano is a barrel-aged pure Grechetto from the Orzalume vineyard.

(Prominent bottlers of Orvieto Classico DOC from outside the zone include Ruffino, Melini, Barone Ricasoli, Luigi Cecchi, and Rocca delle Macìe, all of Tuscany, and Barbi of Lombardy.)

COOPERATIVES

VICOR, Castel Viscardo (TR). Orvieto Classico and vdt.

Cantina Colli Amerini, Fornole di Amelia (TR). Orvieto Classico and vdt of the Colli Amerini.

Cantina Cooperativa Vitivinicola Orvieto, Orvieto (TR). The largest producer of Orvieto Classico bottles its best under the trademark Cardeto.

Travel Information

RESTAURANTS/HOTELS

Buca di San Francesco, 06081 Assisi (PG). Tel (075)812204. Giovanni and Graziella Betti mix tradition and creativity in dishes deftly matched with wines from Umbria and beyond.

Enoteca Altotiberina, 06012 Città di Castello (PG). Tel (075)8553089. Colli Altotiberini wines with tasty rustic food and pizza at bargain prices.

Villa Roncalli, 06034 Foligno (PG). Tel (0742)670291. Sandra Scolastra's dishes are unmatched for authentic flavours, served in a splendid dining room with wines chosen by husband Angelo and daughter Maria Luisa. The villa on the edge of Foligno also has rooms.

Vissani, 05023 Lago di Corbara-Baschi (TR). Tel (0744)950206. Giancarlo Vissani, probably Italy's most provocative restaurateur, invents menus artistically prepared by his wife and served in the inner sanctum of a lakeside refuge-bunker with rooms. The wine list is astounding for its choices from nearly everywhere but Orvieto. Be prepared to pay dearly for an unforgettable experience, though a stripped-down version of the menu can be tasted in the "outer" eatery known as **Il Padrino**.

La Badia, 05018 Orvieto (TR). Tel (0763)90359. A medieval abbey and elite hotel with pool amidst olives and vines. Orvieto and red wine from Conti Fiumi-Petrangeli go with good country fare.

Villa Ciconia, 05018 Orvieto (TR). Tel (0763)90677. The villa-hotel with gardens epitomizes Umbria's antique style in an attractive dining room where local dishes are complemented by fish and a studied array of wines.

Le Tre Vaselle, 06089 Torgiano (PG). Tel (075)982447. Few hotels combine the antique and modern as elegantly as this inn owned by the Lungarotti family, whose wines enhance the refined country cooking.

WINE SHOPS/ENOTECHE

Enoteca Provinciale, Via Rocchi 16, Perugia. A complete array of the province's wines in central Perugia.

Enoteca Vino Vino, Corso Vecchio 201, Terni. Also shops at Orvieto and Rieti in Latium. Renzo Franceschini has collected a bit of the best of everything from Umbria to the Napa Valley in his three *enoteche*.

PLACES OF INTEREST

The obligatory stop on any wine tour is Orvieto, which is also the easiest place to reach, since it towers over the Autostrada del Sole and the Rome-Florence railway line. Sipping cool white wine on a shaded terrace while studying the Duomo's splendid façade is an experience not easily forgotten, nor is the sweeping view of Orvieto at sunset from the road to Bolsena. But, then, nearly all of the "green heart of Italy" is a pleasure to behold. Remnants of ancient civilizations – Umbri, Etruscans, Romans – offer insights into the past, though the region's dominant themes are medieval architecture and Renaissance art. Perugia and Assisi abound in both, as do the nearby towns of Todi, Spello, Gubbio, and Spoleto (with its Festival of the Two Worlds in June and July). Wine buffs often make their headquarters at Le Tre Vaselle at Torgiano, which has the added attraction of a truly enlightening Museo del Vino. Suggested excursions include Lake Trasimeno, the upper Tiber valley, and Norcia, famous for black truffles. The best times to visit are late spring and autumn, though summers are pleasantly warm and winters may appeal to travellers willing to put up with a little cold and damp for the privilege of having mystic Umbria almost to themselves.

Latium (Lazio)

Capital: Roma (Rome).
Provinces: Frosinone (FR), Latina (LT), Rieti (RI), Roma (RM),
Viterbo (VT).
Area: 17,203 (ninth).
Population: 5,102,000 (third).

Among the world's metropolises, Rome may rank as the leading wine town. Apart from the burden of administering the mammoth national industry, Rome probably has more vineyards and makes more wine than any other major city. Within its confines are parts of four DOC zones – Frascati, Marino, Colli Albani, and Cerveteri – and within its province lie seven others. Yet such distinctions have a way of being overlooked by a citizenry which sometimes seems to have been resting on its laurels since Rome was the centre of the universe.

But perhaps Romans can be forgiven. Ancient achievements with viticulture were so prodigious that they overshadow later events. Yet Rome has rarely been deprived of vinous moments. In the late Middle Ages and early Renaissance, the papal court comprised a circle of connoisseurs who knew the wines of other Italian regions and France as well as the Campagna Romana. In the sixteenth century, Pope Paul III banned French wine, while his bottler, Sante Lancerio, followed the Pontiff's palate to compile the most authoritative text on Italian vineyards of the time. Through the centuries, Rome's poets composed odes to the Castelli Romani's wines, among which Frascati reigned supreme. But lately Rome's status as a wine town seems to have become somewhat watered down. The politicians, diplomats, and bureaucrats, who crowd restaurants with tourists, tend to favour wines from other regions. Even real Romans – as opposed to the resident hordes who have created the city's eternal traffic jam – might boast that *er mejo vino* is Frascati or Marino while sipping Friulian whites or Tuscan reds.

Latium (or Lazio) overflows with white wine, which in central Italy's most productive region accounts for an unparalleled 90 percent of the total. Yet, despite the international renown of Frascati and the assertively titled Est! Est!! Est!!! di Montefiascone, the region's wines are stuck with an everyday image and prices to match. To foreigners, the name Latium means little in relation to wine or much of anything else. Rome overshadows the region which was pieced together as five provinces with no recent record of homogeneity. In pre-Roman days, Etruscans inhabited the territory northwest of the Tiber, Sabines the hills to the northeast. Aequi, Volsci, Hernici, and Samnites prevailed in the Apennines, and Latins held sway in the coastal south. The southern and eastern elements formed a Latin League, which was united with Etruria in the early Roman Republic and later became the core of the Empire. But when Rome fell and Longobards and Byzantines contested the territory, people of the outlying areas went their own ways. The districts were divided among the great aristocratic families who fought against each other long after the sixteenth century, when the region was incorporated in the pontifical state. But Latium as a functioning political unit is a rather loose modern concept.

Lack of identity may explain why Latium's wine industry, which is made up nearly two thirds of cooperatives, lacks the vibrancy so evident in other important wine regions. Curiously, Latium's most esteemed wines are red, but they are confined to a trio – Fiorano, Colle Picchioni, and Torre Ercolana – all of which contain Cabernet and Merlot. Serious producers of white wine seem caught in a bind. Many feel that the prevalent Malvasia and Trebbiano represent a heritage that should be maintained against the universal drive towards Chardonnay. But most whites of Latium have been transformed beyond recognition.

In the old days, the lush, green vineyards of the Castelli Romani produced soft, fleshy, golden to light amber wines whose full flavours flowed winningly with the pungently spicy *cucina romana*. But those wines were so flimsy that they often failed to survive the short trip into Rome. The new oenology has rendered pale, balanced, pure whites that can be shipped with confidence anywhere, whether in standard bottles with corks or in large bottles with metal caps. But their success on world markets – notably in Germany, Britain, and America – seems to rely on low price. In Latium, too, most growers are obsessed with volume, and since yields soar in the Castelli Romani and the adjacent flatlands, something similar to Frascati is always available as a bargain.

Some producers manage to bring out the unmistakable personality that select clones of Malvasia can express when yields are controlled. Yet only a few have managed to win the prestige that commands rewarding prices. The world's wine raters rarely find Latium's whites exciting. Even at home they have lost their faithful followings. Real Romans, so it seems, preferred the golden oldies.

Latium's Vineyards

Viticulture has been in a state of flux for decades here, becoming modern after centuries in which rustic training systems prevailed. The shift to monoculture brought a decline in vineyards from 98,000 hectares to about 65,000 over the last decade, but output has increased slightly due to planting in irrigated plains and the advent of high trellises. Ancient Roman viticulture, so meticulously described by Cato the Censor and Columella, was more influenced by Etruscans than Greeks, whose head-trained vines never caught on here as they did further south. The Romans developed vertical training systems that evolved into cordon and Guyot, which now prevail in the hills, though remnants of Etruscan tree training abound.

The Castelli Romani, focal point of the region's wine, developed a system known as *canocchia*, which involves training onto cane poles with vine density as high as 10,000 per hectare. But that has given way to more efficient wide spacing in Guyot and Cazanave. *Tendone* is also used in the Castelli, but quality producers prefer vertical systems. Except in the plains of Aprilia, vineyards are fragmentized throughout Latium, the result of the breaking up of vast feudal domains into small plots. Frascati has 2,556 registered growers with 2,820 hectares. For most of them vineyards are a part-time occupation, since more than half the plots consist of less than half a hectare and only seven Frascati estates have 30 hectares or more.

More than 200 varieties are still in use in Latium, but only a dozen or so have much importance. Various members of the Trebbiano and Malvasia families mingle everywhere. Trebbiano Toscano had been gaining for years to rival Malvasia Bianca di Candia in volume if not in space. But recently the less productive but more typical Malvasia del Lazio has made a small comeback among Castelli Romani producers who seek character in their whites. The admirable native red Cesanese has barely held its own over the years, first against an influx of Sangiovese and Montepulciano, more recently against the Cabernets and Merlot that had begun to distinguish themselves on an elite scale decades ago. Foreign white varieties have begun to make their presence felt as well, although

the most likely to succeed, Chardonnay, does not have official approval anywhere yet, nor do the promising Sauvignon Blanc and Sémillon. The following varieties are associated primarily with Latium.

Abbuoto. Used along with San Giuseppe Nero and Negroamaro in the rare red Cècubo, the modern version of the Roman Caecuban.

Bellone. Pliny the Elder described its predecessor as "all juice", which may explain its popularity in the Castelli Romani and Capena.

Cesanese. Latium's one distinguished red variety has two clones: Cesanese Comune and the smaller-berried Cesanese di Affile, which makes finer wines. They may be interchanged in the three DOCs of the Ciociaria hills, where they apparently evolved from the ancient Alveola. They also serve as back-ups in the reds of Cerveteri, Cori, and Velletri.

Malvasia del Lazio or **Malvasia Puntinata**. The Castelli Romani's traditional Malvasia has lost ground to Malvasia Bianca di Candia and Trebbiano Toscano, but some producers are bringing it back as the source of the most typical Frascati and other whites.

Moscato di Terracina. Local Muscat once renowned for the sweet golden wine of Terracina but consumed more often now as a table grape.

Nero Buono di Cori. Local variety used in the blend of red Cori DOC.

Trebbiano Giallo. This member of the Greco-Trebbiano family figures

Above: vineyards at Cisterna di Latina at the edge of the Alban hills where the Velletri, Cori, and Aprilia DOC zones meet.

in blends of many whites, though less prominently than before. Synonyms are Greco, or Rossetto at Lake Bolsena. It is also planted around Verona.

Trebbiano Verde. The variety used sparingly in Castelli Romani whites seems to be the same as Umbria's Trebbiano Spoletino.

Other varieties

Other varieties recommended or approved in Latium include:

For red (or rosé): Aleatico, Alicante, Barbera, Bombino Nero, Cabernet Franc, Cabernet Sauvignon, Canaiolo Nero, Carignano, Ciliegiolo, Grechetto Rosso, Greco Nero, Merlot, Montepulciano, Olivella Nera or Sciascinoso, Pinot Nero, Sangiovese, Syrah.

For white: Bonvino (Bombino Bianco), Grechetto, Malvasia del Chianti, Montonico Bianco, Moscato Bianco, Mostosa, Passerina, Pecorino, Pinot Bianco, Riesling Italico, Tocai Friulano, Trebbiano di Soave, Trebbiano Romagnolo, Trebbiano Toscano, Verdello, Verdicchio Bianco, Vernaccia di San Gimignano.

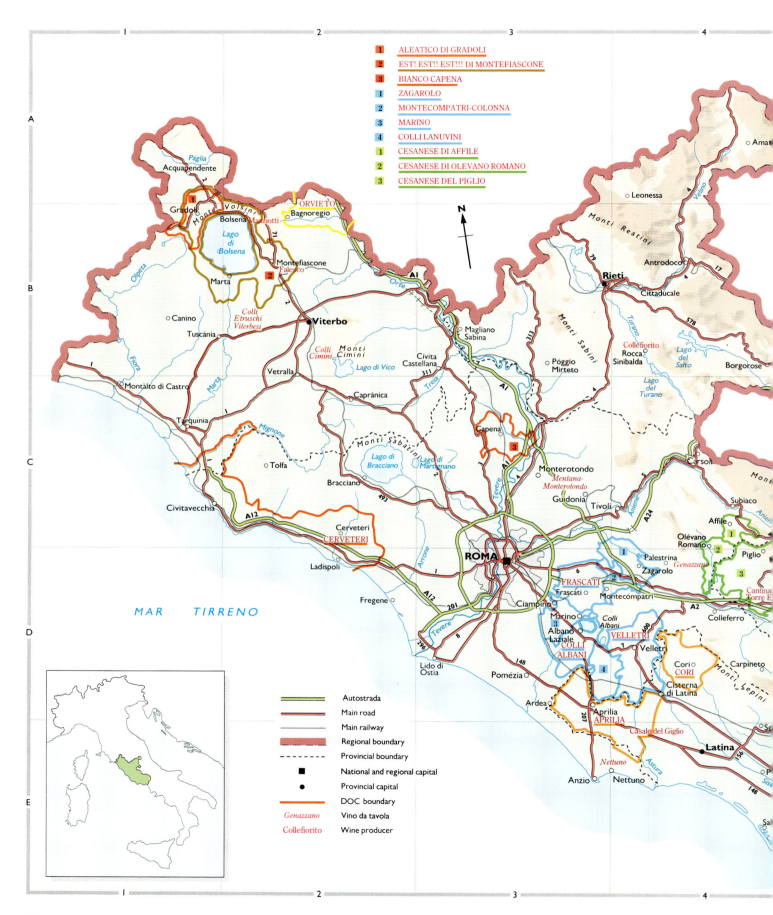

1 ALEATICO DI GRADOLI
2 EST! EST!! EST!!! DI MONTEFIASCONE
3 BIANCO CAPENA
1 ZAGAROLO
2 MONTECOMPATRI-COLONNA
3 MARINO
4 COLLI LANUVINI
1 CESANESE DI AFFILE
2 CESANESE DI OLEVANO ROMANO
3 CESANESE DEL PIGLIO

MAR TIRRENO

Autostrada
Main road
Main railway
Regional boundary
Provincial boundary
National and regional capital
Provincial capital
DOC boundary
Genazzano Vino da tavola
Collefiorito Wine producer

Latium's Wine Zones

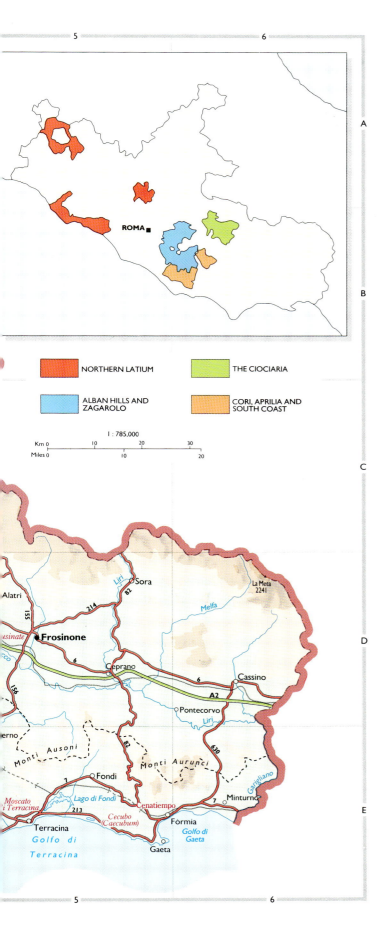

Latium touches all the other five central regions, with whom it shares an inventory of vines. But physically it has more in common with southern neighbour Campania, since both have flourishing volcanic soils and full-fledged Tyrrhenian climates held in check by the Apennines. Yet while Campania has dissipated vinous potential, Latium has exploited its easier contours (54 percent hills, 20 percent plains) to become central Italy's largest source of wine. From 327 kilometres of coast (comprising the Ponza isles in the Gulf of Gaeta), the region sprawls over plains and across the Tiber, Aniene, and Sacco valleys through hills of irregular form and diverse geological origins. Climate varies from hot and dry along the coast to increasingly cooler and damper in the interior, where the normal summer drought rarely creates problems. Vines grow everywhere short of the Apennines, whose regional peak is the 2,216-metre Monte Terminillo. In antiquity, the hot southern coast produced the heady Caecuban and Falernian. But later Romans came to prefer soft whites from the hills, notably from around the craters of Vulsino (Lake Bolsena), Cimino (Lago di Vico), Sabatino (Lake Bracciano), and, above all, Albano (the Colli Albani or Castelli Romani). Today only the Alban hills and Lake Bolsena are major vineyard zones, while such unlikely places as the Pontine lowlands around Aprilia abound in trellised vines.

The north: Bolsena, Cerveteri, Capena, and the Sabine hills

Lake Bolsena is surrounded by tufaceous slopes with vineyards planted in loose basalt of notable fertility. Although Montefiascone stakes claims to Est! Est!! Est!!!, the best Trebbiano and Malvasia come from around the town of Bolsena, where vines bask in the sun reflecting off the lake. The bit of Aleatico thrives around Gradoli on the steep northwestern shores. Cerveteri's warm, dry coastal hills consist mainly of calcareous clay mixed with volcanic residue from the heights of the Tolfa hills, conditions that seem better suited to the red from Sangiovese and Montepulciano than the run-of-the-mill white. Capena on slopes tapering eastwards towards the Tiber has elements and wines similar to those of Frascati. The cool Sabine hills, whose rocky terrain is mixed with calcareous and sandy clays, have scarcely exploited potential for fragrant, zesty wines.

The Castelli Romani, Colli Albani, and Zagarolo

The six DOC zones of the Alban hills wrap three quarters of the way around the flanks of the great Tuscolano volcano that formed five small craters still partly visible in the lakes of Albano and Nemi. The northern part of the hills are known as the Castelli Romani, the central and southern parts as the Colli Albani, though either name may be applied generally. Soils are prevalently loose basalt or tufaceous clay, though vineyards stretch into low hills where alluvial elements can be a factor. Frascati must come from soils of volcanic origin rich in potassium and phosphorous and low in nitrogen and chalk – standards applied to the hills' DOCs in general. Key quality factors are altitude and exposure. Frascati and Montecompatri-Colonna are slightly cooler and damper than the rest, due to northerly positions and greater distance from the sea. This accounts for a fruity buoyancy in wines from vineyards at heights of 200-400 metres. Much of Marino and Colli Albani cover low slopes (100-250 metres) exposed to the west, where wines were normally corpulent, though early picking and mass vinification have made them mostly dry and light. Cabernet and Merlot can do well in Marino and even in the lower, hotter Campagna Romagna, as proven by Fiorano. The southerly Colli Lanuvini and Velletri tend to be hotter and drier, but high vineyards (300-400 metres) can still make fragrant, fruity wines. Zagarolo covers low hills between the Alban and Prenestini ranges in soils mixed between volcanic and calcareous clays. The bit of wine made there is practically identical to whites of the Castelli Romani.

The Ciociaria hills

Vineyards on slopes oriented towards the Sacco valley to the southwest range from 350 metres to nearly 700 metres high in the three Cesanese DOC zones. The wall of the Ernici and Affilani ranges holds the Tyrrhenian influence in check in mild microclimates with ample ventilation. The terrain of calcareous clay and dolomitic rock is used mainly for red varieties, including Barbera, Cabernet, and Merlot, though white wines could probably do as well.

Cori, Aprilia, and the south

Cori extends from the Lepini range into lower slopes where calcareous clay and volcanic soils mix. Moderately warm, dry conditions could favour wine of some depth, but the DOC white and red are the standard light styles. Aprilia covers plains mainly of sandy or gravelly alluvial soil of volcanic residue. Canopies of irrigated vineyards in Trebbiano, Merlot, and Sangiovese are more noted for quantity than quality. The hot, dry coastal hills of Terracina and Formia were known historically for heavy wines – ie Caecuban and Moscato di Terracina – but vineyards today are used mainly for bulk or blending wines or table grapes.

Wines of northern Latium

The Tiber splits northern Latium into two diverse sectors. To the east lie the Sabine reaches of the Apennines in the province of Rieti. To the west lie the crater lakes of Bolsena, Vico, and Bracciano, and the southern flank of the coastal Maremma in the provinces of Viterbo and part of Roma. Though wines are made throughout the territory, still often in grottos carved into the tufaceous cliffs, the DOCs are limited to the western sector. Vineyards of the fabled Est! Est!! Est!!! di Montefiascone surround the crater of Bolsena, which also harbours the Aleatico vines of Gradoli. Nearly adjacent is the part of Orvieto that protrudes into Latium (Orvieto DOC is discussed in Umbria). The Cerveteri zone extends through coastal hills in the Etruscan lands known as Tuscia. Bianco Capena covers the hills just north of Rome between the Tiber and Lake Bracciano. Rieti is the only province of central Italy without a DOC. Some attribute this deprivation to lack of initiative, others to lack of aptitude. The Romans low regard for Sabine vineyards prompted their joke about the ancient Sabine: "Who would drink a leaden wine from a golden cup?". But tastes in those days favoured syrupy wines from the warm coastal vineyards over fresher, lighter growths from the hills.

Aleatico di Gradoli (1972)

The once revered Aleatico vine survives in this lakeside sanctuary where it makes an aromatic purple dessert wine. The regular version is soft and fruity when young, though the *liquoroso* has enough poise to serve as a sort of poor man's port.

Zone: Volcanic slopes on the northwestern edge of Lake Bolsena in the communes of Gradoli, Grotte di Castro, Latera, and San Lorenzo Nuovo in Viterbo province. Sweet red, also liquoroso. Grape: Aleatico. Liquoroso usually comes from semidried or passito grapes. Yld 63/90, Alc 12 (res sugar 2.5%); liquoroso 17.5 (res sugar 2.5%), Acd 0.45, Ag 6 mths.

Est! Est!! Est!!! di Montefiascone (1966)

The tale of the German bishop (or prince) named Fugger (or Defuk) and his wine scout Martin who inscribed the frenzied message on the wall of an inn at Montefiascone in 1111 has been partly debunked. Local historians say the man was probably a knight named Deuc who left the army of Emperor Henry V at Montefiascone and died there two years later. Though Montefiascone's wines were cited in ensuing centuries, the reference was mainly to sweet golden Moscato or Moscatellone rather than the pallid Trebbiano-Malvasia of today. Nor did reliable texts mention the term Est! Est!!

Est!!! until quite recently. But whether the exclamations were Martin's or strokes of contemporary hype, they are the outstanding feature of this otherwise modest white. The touristy container is the squat *pulcianella* flask, though the best wines – Falesco and Mazziotti – are issued in standard bottles.

Zone: Volcanic slopes surrounding Lake Bolsena in the communes of Montefiascone, Bolsena, San Lorenzo Nuovo, Grotte di Castro, Gradoli, Capodimonte, and Marta in Viterbo province. Dry or abboccato white. Grapes: Procanico/Trebbiano Toscano 65%, Malvasia Bianca Toscana 20%, Rossetto (Trebbiano Giallo) 15%. Yld 91/130, Alc 11, Acd 0.5-0.7.

Cerveteri (1975)

Cerveteri, the ancient Caere, was a centre of the Etruscans, whose viticulture probably influenced the early Romans more than any other. Today, a dizzying melange of varieties makes the ordinary white Cerveteri, which in these coastal resorts has proved to be more popular than the *rosso* version which might rank as one of Latium's worthier DOC reds.

Zone: An elongated tract of hills in the Tolfa range, extending along the coast from the outskirts of Rome to the northwestern point of Roma province, taking in the communes of Cerveteri, Ladispoli, Santa Marinella, Tolfa, Allumiere, Civitavecchia, and Tarquinia.

Bianco Dry white, also abboccato. Grapes: Trebbiano Toscano/Trebbiano Romagnolo/Trebbiano Giallo at least 50%, Malvasia di Candia/Malvasia del Lazio up to 35%, Bellone/Bombino/Tocai/Verdicchio up to 15%. Yld 108/150, Alc 11, Acd 0.45.

Rosso Dry red. Grapes: Sangiovese and Montepulciano at least 60% (no less than 25% each), Cesanese up to 25%, Carignano/Canaiolo Nero/Barbera up to 30%. Yld 95/140, Alc 12, Acd 0.5.

Bianco Capena (1975)

Rome's northern environs were noted for wine in antiquity, even if the Romans considered Veian, the wine of Etruscan Veii, to be a sort of *deuxième cru*. The luxuriant vineyards around adjacent Capena were praised by Cicero. They are fewer and less famous today, yet the pleasant Bianco Capena can compare with most of the Castelli Romani.

Zone: Hills due north of Rome between the Via Flaminia and the Tiber in the communes of Capena, Morlupo, Fiano Romano, and Castelnuovo di Porto in Roma province. Dry or abboccato white, also superiore. Grapes: Malvasia di Candia/Malvasia del Lazio/Malvasia Toscana up to 55%, Trebbiano Toscano/Trebbiano Romagnolo/Trebbiano Giallo at least 25%, Bellone/Bombino up to 20%. Yld 112/160, Alc 11; superiore 12 (abboccato res sugar 4-20 gr/l), Acd 0.45.

Other wines of note

Good local wines abound in northern Latium, though most are sold in demijohns or large bottles with metal caps. Travellers may come across such recognized vdt as Bolsena Rosso and Grechetto di Gradoli from around Lake Bolsena, Colli Cimini and Colli Etruschi Viterbese from around Lago di Vico. From the outskirts of Rome come the wines of Mentana-Monterotondo and some respected reds: the mellow Baccanale from Campagnano di Roma, the sturdier Torre in Pietra, and the opulent Maccarese (grown on seaside flats adjacent to Fiumicino airport). But urban sprawl seems to be phasing them out. Wines of the Sabine hills may be called Colli Sabini, though the most intriguing bottles of Rieti's province come from the Collefiorito estate at Rocca Sinibalda.

ESTATES/GROWERS

Collefiorito, Rocca Sinibalda (RI). From 5 ha of vines near the heights of this fortress town, Englishman Colin Fraser makes appealingly light vdt led by a fragrant Pinot Bianco called Rigogolo. He combines Sangiovese and Montepulciano in the red Nibbio and rosé Cardellino.

Mazziotti, Bolsena (VT). Italo Mazziotti was the first producer to lend a credible modern image to Est Est Est (his labels avoid the exclamation marks) with fresh, balanced wine from his 20-ha Colle Bonvino plot in a choice position facing Lake Bolsena.

WINE HOUSES/MERCHANTS

Falesco, Montefiascone (VT). Riccardo Cottarella, oenologist in Orvieto, makes an Est! Est!! Est!!! of unexpected substance at his emerging winery.

COOPERATIVES

CS Cooperativa Cerveteri, Cerveteri (RM). Huge production includes Cerveteri DOC and vdt.

CS Cooperativa Feronia, Feronia (RM). Respectable Bianco Capena DOC and vdt.

CS Cooperativa Gradoli, Gradoli (VT). Aleatico di Gradoli DOC and vdt.

Cantina di Montefiascone, Montefiascone (VT). Est! Est!! Est!!! and vdt Colli Etruschi.

Wines of the Castelli Romani, Colli Albani, and Zagarolo

The Alban hills produce four-fifths of Latium's classified wine, nearly all of it white, in six zones that coil anticlockwise around the volcanic mass from Montecompatri-Colonna in the north to Velletri in the south. Although the names are used interchangeably, Castelli Romani originally applied to the area around Frascati, brightest of the constellation of hill towns, while Colli Albani denoted the slopes that culminate around the crater lakes of Albano and Nemi. The heights, with their ample woods and vineyards have been a mecca for Romans since imperial times. In the Middle Ages, woodsmen in the forest of Tusculum built huts of *frascata*, the brushwood that gave Frascati its name and the local wines their symbol: the *frasca* (the branch) hung over the door of taverns when the new vintage was ready. Villas built during the Renaissance and baroque periods reached heights of splendour, notably in Frascati. Popes still summer at their palace in Castelgandolfo. Much of the area once consisted of vast feudal domains belonging to Rome's aristocracy, but land reform broke them up into farms so fragmented that there are few real wine estates in the hills and few growers who make a living from vineyards alone. Most sell grapes directly to cooperatives or large private cellars, since the once thriving market for farmers' wines has all but disappeared.

In the old days the Castelli's social centres were the simple *osterie*, where the house wine could be stretched through a Sunday afternoon to accompany almost anything from a game of *scoppa* or *bocce* to a snack of *porchetta*, roast suckling pig wedged between crusty slabs of country bread. *Cantine* were often carved into grottos where wine was drawn fresh from giant chestnut casks. Visitors filled demijohns and flasks with wines of Frascati, Marino, Montecompatri, from vineyards around the lakes of Albano and Nemi and below the towns strung along the Appian Way as far as Velletri, where the road descends toward the Pontine Marshes. Zagarolo, the neighbour to the northeast on the lower slopes of the Prenestina range, was almost like one of the family. The rustic charm of the Alban hills can still be enjoyed on the back roads through the chestnut woods or the side streets of the remotest villages, but each year it seems that yet more greenery is sacrificed to Rome's insidious expansion.

In Rome, the Castelli wines no longer stand unchallenged. Not long ago, the open whites served in hour-glass carafes with lead stamps to verify the measure – litre, half, or quarter – were almost invariably passed off as Frascati, whether they came from there or not. Roman jokes about watered down wine were all too often to the point. Since many of the city's *osterie* were owned by Castelli wine producers who set prices attractively low to encourage sales, the only way they could make a profit was to add water. Customers developed the habit of mixing wines with other soft drinks to make them more palatable. But as Romans became more affluent, they switched to trustier bottles from other places. The Castelli wines have never recovered, but markets abroad seem to have more than made up for the losses. Frascati led the export boom of the 1970s made possible by hot bottling to counter the effects of oxidation to which wines from Malvasia and Trebbiano are so prone. Large bottles of pasteurized wines became the norm through the world. Lately cold treatments have prevailed, restoring fruit and fragrance in balanced, modern wines, led by the brand names of Fontana Candida and Gotto d'Oro. But the practice of price cutting has kept the wines of the Castelli more popular than prestigious.

Frascati (1966)

Frascati's pre-eminence among local wines was built on the fame of the hill town that gave it its name and also on the ample space for vineyards on the gentle slopes that roll northwards into the Campagna Romana. More than half of the Castelli Romani's DOC wine originates in the zone, whose somewhat cooler, damper conditions in fine, dark soil account for generally superior quality. Frascati has been described as the locomotive of the Castelli's wine train, yet even some loyalists seem surprised that its next scheduled destination is DOCG. (Then again, they might reason if Albana di Romagna made it that far, why not Frascati?). Today's stereotype Frascati is dry and clear with a purity of line that can be attributed to the ascendancy of Trebbiano Toscano, though the more persuasive Superiore versions – Conte Zandotti, Villa Simone, Fontana Candida's Santa Teresa, Colli di Catone's Colle Gaio – have a gentle harmony that seems more in tune with the traditional Malvasia. In the not so distant past, much Frascati was a softly medium dry *abboccato*, though the really prized version was the refinedly sweet *cannellino*, especially when it took on nuances of botrytis cinerea. Most current *cannellino* is insipid, though a few producers seem intent on a revival.

Zone: The northern sector of the Castelli Romani in Roma province around the towns of Frascati, Grottaferrata, Monteporzio Catone, and Montecompatri, extending north across the Roma-Napoli stretch of the Autostrada del Sole through lower slopes as far as the Via Casalina in the commune of Roma. Dry white, also amabile, cannellino or dolce, superiore, and spumante. Grapes: Malvasia Bianca di Candia/Trebbiano Toscano at least 70%; Malvasia del Lazio/Greco up to 30%. Cannellino comes from very ripe grapes preferably affected by botrytis cinerea. Yld 105/150, Alc 11 (amabile res sugar 1-3%; cannellino or dolce 3-6%); superiore 11.5 (res sugar 3-6%), Acd 0.45.

Montecompatri-Colonna (1973)

The zone, practically an adjunct of Frascati, makes a little similar wine appreciated locally. It may carry the full name or that of either town.

Zone: The northeast corner of the Castelli Romani on either side of the Roma-Napoli stretch of the Autostrada del Sole in the communes of Montecompatri, Colonna and parts of Rocca Priora and Zagarolo in Roma province. Dry or lightly amabile white. Grapes: Malvasia Bianca di Candia/Malvasia Puntinata up to 70%, Trebbiano Toscano/Trebbiano Verde/Trebbiano Giallo at least 30%; Bellone/Bonvino up to 10%. Yld 108/150, Alc 11.5; superiore 12.5, Acd 0.45.

Marino (1970)

Marino has a nostalgic following among local cognoscenti who remember it as being softer and broader and deeper in colour than Frascati, closer to the old-style Castelli whites. But for years now most Marino has been made by the Gotto d'Oro cooperative and is barely distinguishable from the cellar's Frascati. Both are admirably balanced modern whites, but nothing more. Marino has an exception, though, Paola Di Mauro's Colle Picchioni Oro, which combines some of the old strength of character with a certain finesse acquired with a year or two of age.

Zone: In the western sector of the Castelli Romani, extending from the towns of Marino and Castelgandolfo down across the Via Appia Antica onto lower slopes in the commune of Roma. Dry white, also amabile and spumante. Grapes: Malvasia Rossa (Malvasia Bianca di Candia) up to 60%, Trebbiano Toscano/Trebbiano Verde/Trebbiano Giallo 25-55%, Malvasia del Lazio (Malvasia Puntinata) 15-45%; Bonvino/Cacchione up to 10%. Yld 115.5/165, Alc 11; superiore 11.5, Acd 0.45.

Left: vines in the Marino DOC zone of the Castelli Romani.

Colli Albani (1970)

This ranks second to Frascati in volume among the DOCs, though wines produced mainly in cooperatives tend to be anonymous if attractively priced.

Zone: Slopes in the western sector of the Colli Albani, extending from around Lake Albano and the communes of Albano Laziale, Castelgandolfo, and Ariccia on the Via Appia Antica southwest into the communes of Roma and Pomezia in Roma province. Dry white, also abboccato, amabile, dolce, and spumante. Grapes: Malvasia Rossa (Malvasia Bianca di Candia)

up to 60%, Trebbiano Toscano/Trebbiano Romagnolo/Trebbiano Giallo/Trebbiano di Soave 25-50%, Malvasia del Lazio (Malvasia Puntinata) 5-45%; other whites up to 10%. Yld 115.5/165, Alc 11; superiore 11.5. Acd 0.45.

Colli Lanuvini (1971)

Though production is limited in this zone with some of the warmest, driest slopes of the hills, wines made by several producers have shown improving style and general class surpassed only in the cooler reaches of

Frascati. Monte Giove, Antenore Baldassari, and the La Selva and San Tommaso cooperatives all make commendable wines.

Zone: The southwestern sector of the Colli Albani on slopes extending from Lake Nemi and Genzano on the Via Appia Antica south past Lanuvio almost to Aprilia in Roma province. Dry white, also amabile. Grapes: Malvasia Bianca di Candia/Malvasia Puntinata up to 70%, Trebbiano Toscano/Trebbiano Verde/Trebbiano Giallo at least 30%; Bellone/Bonvino up to 10%. Yld 101/140, Alc 11.5, Acd 0.45.

Velletri (1972)

The lone DOC red of the hills comes in two versions, though the dry is usually preferred to the *amabile*, which seems hopelessly out of step with modern tastes. The white fits the Colli Albani stereotype, though Villa Clemens lends it a touch of class.

Zone: Southeastern slopes of the Colli Albani, extending from the rim of Monte Artemisio between Lake Nemi and Lariano south through communes of Velletri in Roma province and Cisterna in Latina.

Bianco Dry white, sometimes amabile or

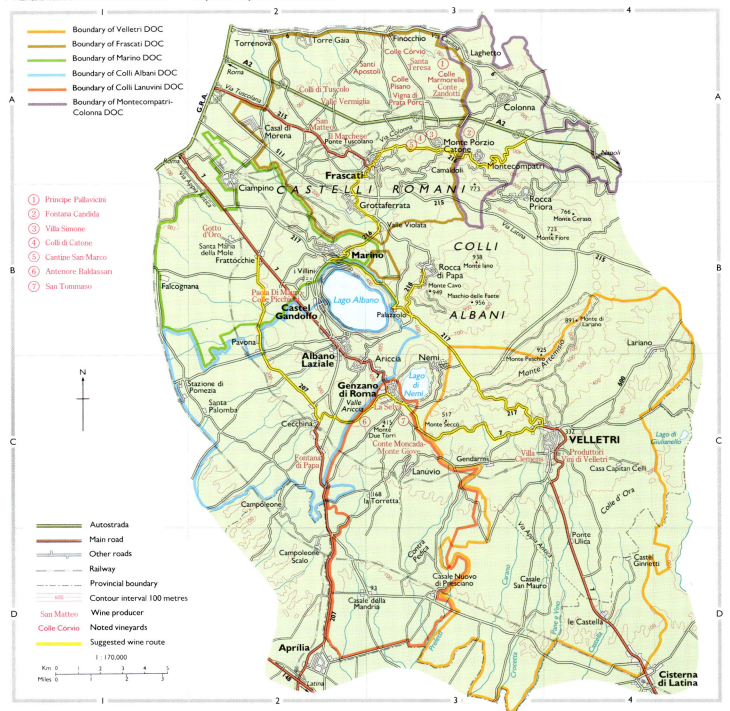

dolce, also spumante. Grapes: Malvasia Bianca di Candia/Malvasia Puntinata up to 70%, Trebbiano Toscano/Trebbiano Verde/Trebbiano Giallo at least 30%; Bellone/Bonvino up to 10%. Yld 112/160, Alc 11 (amabile res sugar 4-20 gr/l and dolce min 20 gr/l); secco superiore 11.5, Acd 0.45.

Rosso Dry red, rarely amabile. Grapes: Sangiovese 20-45%, Montepulciano 30-35%, Cesanese Comune/Cesanese di Affile at least 15%; Bombino Nero/Merlot/Ciliegiolo up to 10%. Yld 104/160, Alc 12; riserva 12.5 (res sugar amabile and amabile riserva 4-20 gr/l), Acd 0.5, Ag riserva 2 yrs.

Zagarolo (1973)

The little DOC wine made in the zone is hardly distinguishable from its neighbours in the Castelli Romani, though it is rarely seen in bottle.

Zone: Low hills northeast of the Castelli Romani in the valley beneath the Prenestini range of the Apennines in the communes of Zagarolo and Gallicano nel Lazio in Roma province. Dry white, also amabile. Grapes: Malvasia Bianca di Candia/Malvasia Puntinata up to 70%, Trebbiano Toscano/Trebbiano Verde/Trebbiano Giallo at least 30%; Bellone/Bonvino up to 10%. Yld 108/150, Alc 11.5; superiore 12.5, Acd 0.45.

Other wines of note

The Castelli Romani and environs produce more table wines than DOC, much of it in light white or pink beverages or red *vini novelli*. But there are some wines of real class from the area, first among them the vaunted vdt of Fiorano and more recently the Colle Picchioni red.

ESTATES/GROWERS

Antenore Baldassari, Genzano (RM). Good Colli Lanuvini DOC.

Conte Moncada-Monte Giove, Lanuvio (RM). Colli Lanuvini DOC that ranks among the best estate wines of the hills.

Conte Zandotti-Tenimento San Paolo, Via Colle Mattia, Roma. Enrico Massimo Zandotti continues a family tradition of Frascati begun in 1734, though he and oenologist Ivo Straffi have adapted mostly modern methods to the cellars carved into the vaults of an ancient Roman water cistern beneath the fortified San Paolo villa. The 25 ha of vines are used only for dry Frascati Superiore of unerring dignity.

Paola Di Mauro-Colle Picchioni, Frattocchie di Marino (RM). From less than 4 ha of vines, Paola Di Mauro and son Armando make Marino DOC and red vdt Colle Picchioni that have made the estate the most admired of the hills. Prized among the tiny production is the Marino Oro, one of the most sumptuous of Castelli whites, and the authoritative red Vigna del Vassallo based on Merlot and Cabernet.

Fiorano, Via di Fioranello, Roma. On just 2.5 ha of flat land along the ancient Appian Way on the outskirts of Rome, Alberico Boncompagni Ludovisi, the reclusive Prince of Venosa, continues to make some of Latium's finest wines in a most unlikely place. With the help of consulting oenologist Tancredi Biondi Santi, he planted classic Bordeaux varieties decades ago for what has become the legendary Fiorano Rosso (from Merlot and Cabernet) and Sémillon for a white of exquisitely

subtle sweetness. Fiorano Bianco from Malvasia di Candia usually outclasses whites from the more suitable terrain of the Castelli Romani.

Il Marchese, Frascati (RM). Good Frascati Superiore from 40 ha of vines.

Panfilio Nati, Zagarolo (RM). From 10.5 ha, a suggestion of Zagarolo DOC.

Principe Pallavicini, Colonna (RM). From 55 ha, good Frascati Superiore (including Vigne di Valpignola) and vdt under the Marmorelle label.

Villa Simone, Monteporzio Catone

Top: the town of Nemi which overlooks a crater lake in the Colli Albani. Bottom: gladioli growing near Cisterna in Latina province.

(RM). Piero Costantini, who owns the respected *enoteca* in Rome, selects from 6 ha of vines to make some of the finest Frascati Superiore, including the single vineyard Vigneto Filonardi, and a little rare *cannellino*.

WINE HOUSES/MERCHANTS

Cantine San Marco, Monteporzio Catone (RM). Frascati Superiore DOC.

Colli di Catone, Monteporzio Catone (RM). Antonio Pulcini makes consistently good Frascati Superiore under the Colli di Catone, Villa Catone, and Villa Porziana labels. His two special versions of Frascati both come from pure Malvasia; one is issued in a frosted bottle and the other, the single vineyard Colle Gaio, is made only in good years from low yielding vines.

Colli di Tuscolo, Vermicino (RM). Large production of Frascati includes Superiore under the De Sanctis and Vigneti Carlo Micara labels, plus vdt.

Fontana Candida, Frascati (RM). The zone's largest private winery, with production of more than 60,000 hl a year, is part of the Gruppo Italiano Vini. Amidst vast production of Frascati Superiore emerges the single vineyard Santa Teresa, selected by winemaker Francesco Bardi from a 10-ha plot. It ranks consistently among the top whites of the Castelli.

San Matteo, Frascati (RM). Long respected Frascati Superiore.

Villa Clemens, Velletri (RM). Indefatigable consulting oenologist Ivo Straffi, who has lent style to wines of the hills for years, recently founded his own winery where he makes exemplary Velletri Bianco and Frascati DOC, as well as a red vdt known as Zeus.

COOPERATIVES

CS Cooperativa Colli Albani, Ariccia (RM). Large production of Colli Albani and Marino DOC under the Fontana di Papa label.

CS Cooperativa Gotto d'Oro, Frattocchie di Marino (RM). From growers with 1,100 ha of vines, winemaker Manlio Erba realizes consistent quality in Frascati and Marino DOC under the Gotto d'Oro label.

Cooperativa La Selva, Genzano (RM). Commendable Colli Lanuvini.

CS Cooperativa San Tommaso, Genzano (RM). Good Colli Lanuvini DOC.

Consorzio Produttori Vini di Velletri, Velletri (RM). Large output of Velletri DOC and vdt.

Società Cooperativa Gabinia, Zagarolo (RM). Zagarolo DOC.

Wines of the Ciociaria

The Ciociaria looms to the left of the Roma-Napoli *autostrada* as it follows the Sacco valley from Valmontone past Frosinone. The hills are noted for the strikingly poised towns of Anagni and Alatri, but the Ciociaria's legend was built on its country life. The hardy hill people are depicted as eating some of Latium's tastiest food (such as *pasta alla ciociara* with a sauce of bacon and sausage) and drinking its boldest red wine (fleshy Cesanese). In the old days – which could cover most of the 20 centuries since Pliny the Elder described a similar wine from the area – Cesanese was normally sweet and bubbly, best to drink young when fruity and fragrant. Lately, most has been made dry and still, showing a voluptuous warmth that might be likened to that of Amarone. But Cesanese has lost ground as the peasantry has been steadily absorbed by industry. The Ciociaria's bottled mineral water (Fiuggi) is better known than its wine.

Cesanese di Olevano Romano (1973)
The little Cesanese from this zone issues from the cooperative, which makes much more dry wine than sweet or bubbly. Its reputation is local.

Zone: South facing slopes in a valley between the Prenestini and Ernici ranges of the Apennines in the communes of Olevano Romano and Gennazzano in Roma province. Dry red, also amabile or dolce, frizzante or spumante. Grapes: Cesanese di Affile/Cesanese Comune; Sangiovese/Montepulciano/Barbera/Trebbiano Toscano (Passerano)/Bombino Bianco (Ottenese) up to 10%. Yld 81/125, Alc 12 (amabile res sugar 1.1-3.5%; dolce min 3.5%, though fermented alc min 10%), Acd 0.55.

Cesanese di Affile (1973)
This Cesanese from the highest vineyards of the Ciociaria might have been the most authentic of the three DOCs, but most growers have abandoned vineyards so in recent years none has been made.

Zone: High slopes of the Affilani range of the Apennines around Affile, Roiate, and Arcinazzo Romano in Roma province. (The production code is the same as that of Cesanese di Olevano Romano).

Cesanese del Piglio (1973)
This is the one Cesanese of some renown, thanks to the initiative of the admirable cooperative which has built markets beyond Rome. The emphasis is on the dry type, which can improve with a bit of ageing, as can the bubbly *amabile* from Massimi Berucci.

Zone: South facing slopes of the Ernici range of the Apennines in Frosinone province, descending from the heights around the communes of Piglio, Serrone, and Acuto down between Paliano and Anagni to the valley floor. (The production code is the same as that of Cesanese di Olevano Romano).

Other wines of note
The Ciociaria is still a source of rustic wines from Cesanese, Barbera, and white varieties that can be surprisingly tasty when sampled locally. Yet one wine of the hills, the red Torre Ercolana from Colacicchi, enjoys lofty status in Rome and beyond. Recognized vdt include those from the town of Genazzano and from around Frosinone, which may be called Frusinate.

ESTATES/GROWERS

Antonio Bertacco, Paliano (FR). Small output of good Cesanese del Piglio.

Cantina Colacicchi, Anagni (FR). From 3.5 ha of vines, Bruno Colacicchi manages to make just 8,000-9,000 bottles a year of Torre Ercolana from Cabernet and Merlot with Cesanese aged in casks. The wine, invented by his uncle Luigi Colacicchi, an orchestra conductor, is one of the region's most sought after bottlings. Torre Ercolana and the bit of Romagnano Bianco from Malvasia are sold exclusively by Trimani of Rome.

Massimi Berucci, Piglio (FR). Small production of Cesanese at its best under the name of Casal Cervino.

COOPERATIVES

CS Cesanese, Olevano Romano (RM). Cesanese di Olevano Romano and vdt.

CS Cesanese del Piglio, Piglio (FR). Sound quality in Cesanese del Piglio DOC.

Wines of Cori, Aprilia, and the south

The province of Latina extends from the edge of the Colli Albani down across the Pontine plains to the Circeo peninsula and along the coast past Terracina and Gaeta. The ancient Romans preferred the southeastern coastal hills for their Caecuban and Falernian, but modern growers favour more convenient vineyards on reclaimed marshland to the northwest. Still, it isn't fair to say that Latium's wines reach lows in Aprilia's plains, because what producers there lack in natural endowments they often make up for in industriousness. The Monti Lepini furnished the Romans with the popular Setian, from a town now called Sezze, along with the not so well known wines of Cori, which is today the only recognized zone of the range.

Cori (1971)
The white is nearly identical to adjacent Velletri, though the red is distinguished by a local variety known as Nero Buono di Cori. Little of either is produced.

Zone: Hills at the northwestern edge of the Monti Lepini extending into the Teppia valley in the communes of Cori and Cisterna in Latina province.

Bianco Dry white, also amabile or dolce. Grapes: Malvasia di Candia up to 70%, Trebbiano Toscano up to 40%; Trebbiano Giallo/Bellone up to 30%. Yld 112/160, Alc 11, Acd 0.45.

Rosso Dry red. Grapes: Montepulciano 40-60%, Nero Buono di Cori 20-40%, Cesanese 10-30%. Yld 112/160, Alc 11.5, Acd 0.5.

Below: the Cori DOC zone with the Lepini range in the background.

Aprilia (1966)

Italian farmers returning from Tunisia a half century ago planted vineyards in lowlands that had never shown an aptitude for wine, yet in recent times Aprilia's clean, balanced Trebbiano and respectably fruity Merlot have found commercial outlets as far afield as America. Production is centred in cooperatives, though the model estate of Casale del Giglio comes closest to producing wines of class.

Zone: The Pontine plains between the Colli Albani and the coast in the communes of Aprilia, Cisterna, and Latina in the latter province and Nettuno in Roma.

Merlot Dry red. Grapes: Merlot; other reds up to 5%. Yld 91/140, Alc 12, Acd 0.5.

Sangiovese Dry rosé. Grapes: Sangiovese; other reds up to 5%. Yld 84/140, Alc 11.5, Acd 0.5.

Trebbiano Dry white. Grapes: Trebbiano; other whites up to 5%. Yld 90/150, Alc 11, Acd 0.45.

Other wines of note

High yields enable the Pontine plains to turn out masses of ordinary vdt and growing amounts of white and bubbly. Wines of local interest are made in the resorts of Circeo and on the Ponza isles, where the simple white goes well with fish. Terracina's slopes render a bit of golden Moscato, but the once revered vineyards of Caecuban near Formia have been reduced to token offerings of Cècubo, mainly from one producer.

ESTATES/GROWERS

Casale del Giglio, Borgo Montello (LT). Dino Santarelli and family use 180 ha of vineyards to lead the field in Aprilia with a refined Trebbiano called Satrico and a slick Merlot. An experimental genetic engineering project, followed by scholars, is studying new varieties and new training methods on 30 ha.

Prato di Coppola, Borgo Sabotino (LT). Circeo red, white, and rosé vdt.

WINE HOUSES/MERCHANTS

F. Cenatiempo & C., Formia (LT). Persistent producer of Cècubo (from Abbuoto, San Giuseppe, Negroamaro), and Falernian, both vdt of full size and colour and acceptable style.

Tres Tabernae, Cisterna (LT). Aprilia DOC.

COOPERATIVES

Cooperativa Enotria, Aprilia (LT). From growers with nearly 900 ha of vines, Aprilia DOC and vdt.

CS Cooperativa Colli del Cavaliere, Aprilia (LT). Large producer of Aprilia DOC and vdt.

CS di Cori, Cori (LT). Cori DOC under the Cincinnato brand.

Travel Information

RESTAURANTS/HOTELS

Da Picchietto, 01023 Bolsena (VT). Tel (0761)799158. Trattoria with homemade pasta, grilled eels and other lake fish, and Est! Est!! Est!!!.

Da Nazareno, 00052 Cerveteri (RM). Tel (06)9952382. Family place with good local dishes and fresh seafood, Cerveteri and other wines.

Cacciani, 00044 Frascati (RM). Tel (06)9420378. The Cacciani brothers provide a shady terrace on which to enjoy a well-rounded menu with the best of the Castelli wines and others.

La Vecchia Osteria, 00030 Làbico (RM). Tel (06)9510032. In this inn on the Via Casalina between the Castelli Romani and Ciociaria, Antonello Colonna offers creative dishes and an equally inspired national wine list.

Fontana Candida-Da Micara, 00040 Monte Porzio Catone (RM). Tel (06)9425714. The Micara family offers tasty Roman cooking with the good house Frascati and other wines.

Pino al Mare, 00050 Santa Severa (RM). Tel (0766)740027. Modern seaside hotel with restaurant noted for fresh fish and white wines.

Laocoonte-Da Rocco, 04029 Sperlonga (LT). Tel (0771)54122. Fresh fish artfully prepared in this lovely village on a rock overlooking the sea.

Da Benito, 00049 Velletri (RM). Tel (06)9632220. Fresh seafood is the speciality, but *porcini* mushrooms, *pecorino* cheese, and wild strawberries from Velletri's hills also appear on menus here and at **Da Benito al Bosco**, located in a nearby wood, with the added attraction of quiet rooms.

PLACES OF INTEREST

Most visitors to Latium begin or end their tours in Rome, capital of art, history, and religion, as well as a unique theatre of life. The Eternal City has its own guides, which need no additions here, though it should be noted that Rome has some excellent *enoteche* – Trimani, Cavour, Costantini, Al Parlamento, L'Antica Vasca, Arte del Bere, Fratelli Roffi Isabelli, among them – and several restaurants, though not many, with world class wine lists. The obligatory wine tour is the Castelli Romani. The Cerveteri zone and Lake Bolsena have Etruscan remnants. Admirers of antiquity might also enjoy checking out the places where the Romans grew Caecuban and Falernian, along the coast between Gaeta and northern Campania.

The Alban hills and Ciociaria. The hills haven't lost all their magic, though they are hardly the oases of peace they used to be. Frascati has lush vineyards, patrician villas, and the ruins of Roman Tusculum. Castelgandolfo has the Pope's summer palace. Marino holds a harvest festival in October when a fountain spouts wine. The crater lakes of Albano and Nemi mirror the hills' volcanic origins. Rocca di Papa provides monumental views over the Roman countryside. Velletri and Nemi have autumn woods full of chestnuts and wild mushrooms. Everywhere are restaurants designed for weekend crowds, though guests can dine in more tranquility on weekdays. Easy access to the Autostrada del Sole and the busy Appian Way have turned stretches of the hills into an extension of Rome's suburbs. So you may need to get off the main roads to witness what's left of their charm. Across the valley to the east are the Ciociaria hills, whose heights remain more rustically intact. The drive from Palestrina, with its Temple of Fortune, to Anagni, with its Duomo, takes in the Cesanese zones.

Cerveteri. The DOC zone comprises major Etruscan sites at Cerveteri and Tarquinia, as well as the seaside resorts of Ladispoli, Santa Severa, and Santa Marinella, and the port of Civitavecchia. The ancient city of Caere has vanished, but the Banditaccia necropolis north of Cerveteri contains tombs with works of Etruscan art. Relics from Tarquinia's necropolis are displayed at a museum in the Palazzo Vitelleschi.

Lake Bolsena. The high walls of the crater afford sweeping views over Italy's largest volcanic lake and the countryside of Tuscia with its vivid reminders of the Etruscan past. East of the lake in the Orvieto DOC zone is the medieval village of Civita di Bagnoregio.

Left: Latium's coast near where the ancient Romans made Caecuban.

Above: the Solopaca wine zone in Campania lies in the foothills of the Apennines northeast of Caserta.

Southern Peninsula

The heel, toe, and ankle of the Italian boot, lapped by the mystic waters of the Mediterranean, may be the most intriguing of cartographic images. But if the map suggests an odyssey, wanderers should be warned that even if the routes around these antique lands are easier to follow than in Homer's time, the events which occur along them are not always easier to comprehend.

Wine's fate figures prominently among the mysteries. The south's sunny hillsides take kindly to vines, as attested by evidence of winemaking here since the Bronze Age. Many peoples, from the Oscans and Greeks to the Swabians and Bourbons, embellished the noble tradition, only to have modern man tarnish the image by his indifference.

The ancients marvelled over the southern peninsula's aptitude for vines. When Phoenician traders arrived in Apulia around 2000 BC, they supposedly found an active, if rustic wine industry. As the cult of Dionysus spread through the colonies of what are now Apulia, Calabria, Basilicata, Campania, and Sicily, the Greek historian Herodotus referred to this part of Italy as Oenotria, the land of wine. The Romans looked to Campania Felix for the fabled Falernum, though they voiced similar praise for the wines of Tarentum, in what is now Apulia.

But over time the odes to Oenotria have lost their resonance, for in no other part of Italy has such obvious potential been squandered or left untapped. Despite technological advances, the status of southern wine seems to have declined since the fall of the Kingdom of Naples and the Two Sicilies in 1860. DOC is rarely more than a joke in the deep south, which manages to classify less than two percent of its wine. Triumphs of winemaking in the Mezzogiorno are all the more laudable for their scarcity. To excel requires more than skill and dedication, it takes the courage to defy the status quo, to navigate upstream against a torrent of mediocrity. Those who succeed are a breed apart.

Other Italians decry the south's chronic deficiencies: the indolence and corruption that channels improvement funds to the underworld. The most publicized elements are Sicily's Mafia, Calabria's 'ndrangheta, and Campania's Camorra, though it is said that much of southern Italy is under criminal control. When times are bad, growers may blame their plight on politicians and bureaucrats. But whatever the cause, wine's incongruities in these southerly regions glare like the midday sun.

Overproduction takes a share of the blame. Generations of farmers, often aided by EEC grants and subsidies, planted trouble-free grape varieties that rewarded them with bountiful crops. Most became blending wines, rich in alcohol, body, and colour – inexpensive boosters welcomed in northern Italy, France, and West Germany. But excess is only one reason why southern winemakers rarely excel. Distance is another. Many parts of the south could produce fine wines, but local customers used to buying demijohns rarely demand bottles. Without the proof of a tradition of excellence at home, it is hard to get a foothold in elite markets in faraway Milan or Munich, let alone half way around the globe. Responsible producers are increasingly establishing their own vineyards or finding ways to improve the quality of the grapes they buy. The concept of estate or single vineyard wines is catching on slowly after generations in which growers and producers functioned separately, both paying more attention to the alcohol potential of the grapes than to their balance of components.

Yet it should be emphasized that each of these steadfastly diverse regions has its own nature and its own attitudes about wine. Apulia's plains produce more wine than any other region, a volume that far surpasses the bounds of reason. The quantities turned out in the hills of Basilicata, Campania, and Calabria would be moderate if only the overall quality was higher. Still, the notion that the Mezzogiorno's vineyards are suited only to blending wines is nonsense. For even if blenders still flourish on the hot flats, they are rightly overshadowed by wines from the Apennines, whose slopes can be as cool as alpine meadows.

Microclimates, like ingredients of soil, vary markedly from place to place in the southern peninsula, determined by the influences of mountains and sea. The factors behind the quality of hill wines are altitude and exposure to sun and breezes. The key to the maritime wines is proximity to the water – and it makes a difference whether the sea is the Adriatic, Ionian, or Tyrrhenian, each of which has prevailing currents and winds from as far away as the Balkans or the Sahara.

But in the end the decisive element is human. In the past, traditions of winemaking had a way of deviating from one valley to the next. Today, for all the age-old quaintness expressed in methods, customs, and choice of vines, most southern wines are made following modern concepts, often in large private wineries or cooperatives. As a consequence those qualities that set a local wine apart are often missing. But when they are there, the wines of Italy's south can be as distinctive as any of Europe.

Below: the village of Casalabate, south of Brindisi, is in Apulia's Squinzano DOC zone. This coast has served as a gateway to Greece since antiquity.

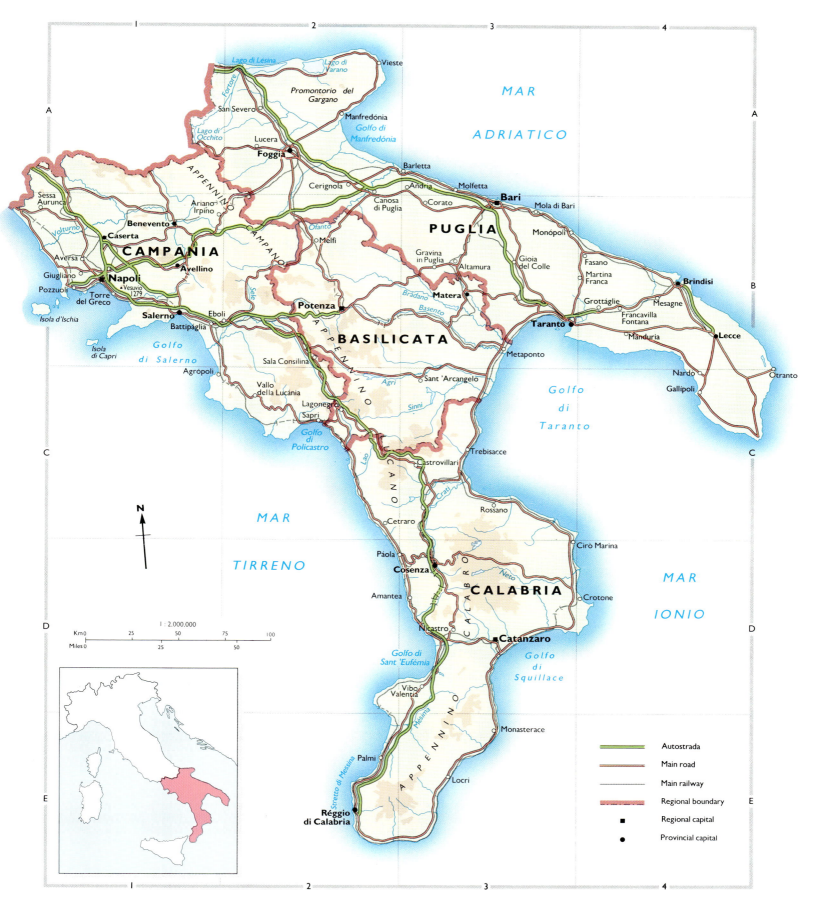

Autostrada
Main road
Main railway
Regional boundary
Regional capital
Provincial capital

Apulia (Puglia)

Capital: Bari.
Provinces: Bari (BA), Brindisi (BR), Foggia (FG), Lecce (LE), Taranto (TA).
Area: 19,347 square kilometres (seventh).
Population: 4,005,000 (seventh).

Apulia (or Puglia) is the colossus of Italian viticulture, producing more grapes and more wine than any other region. An average production of 11,900,000 hectolitres (swollen to 14,380,000 hectolitres in 1986, the all-time high for a region) surpasses the output of West Germany and all but six other countries. Apulia fits the description of "Europe's wine cellar", though that title no longer carries much distinction.

Named after the Apuli, an Oscan tribe among the many early peoples to have settled there, Apulia's rolling plains had been a sanctuary for the vine and the olive since the time of the Phoenicians and Greeks. The Romans praised above all the wines of Tarentum, where, according to the poet Horace, "spring is eternal". Even after the fall of the Roman empire, Apulia remained one of Italy's few active wine regions. Through constant occupation – from Byzantines and Saracens to Longobards, Goths, Normans, Swabians, Venetians, Aragonese, and Bourbons – Apulia persisted as Italy's most bountiful source of wine and olive oil.

The problem is that demand for the blending wines of Salento and the Capitanata dropped dramatically in the 1980s, so the region vowed to put the accent on premium wines. But promises were not backed by action. Apulia increased output in the 1980s to outstrip Sicily as the most prolific wine region. But to do so growers had to force yields upwards, since Apulia has much less space devoted to wine grapes than Sicily.

Abundance is obviously hard to resist on these easy-to-work plains, where grapes generate greater profits than in any other region.

The statistics also refute the wine establishment's oaths to honour quality, vows that seem cynical in a region that annually distilled much more wine than it classified. Since DOC represents a mere fraction of Apulia's prodigious production, one might wonder what happens to the 98.5 percent that isn't classified. Blending wine shipments have dwindled and distillation has declined. True, much grape juice is concentrated into the rectified musts that Italians are supposed to use instead of sugar to give their wines strength. Also Apulians drink more wine than any other southerners, including unclassified whites from the Murge and rosés and reds from Salento which easily outclass most DOCs. But even allowing for a fair amount of *vino da tavola* sold in bottles or, more frequently, in demijohns, that still leaves a lot of those nearly 1.2 billion litres a year unaccounted for.

Critics may ask why Apulia rates as many DOCs as Tuscany when it makes a sixth as much classified wine. The resultant lack of credibility has meant that the leading DOCs – Castel del Monte, Locorotondo, San Severo, Martina Franca, Salice Salentino – have made little impact elsewhere. The other good wines that are made here remain even more remote. With a few exceptions, producers have been reluctant to make the sacrifices that could make their wines more prominent in Italy.

Still some hard-won progress has been made. The Leone De Castris family, which for more than three centuries produced bulk wine on the Salento peninsula, pioneered with bottles in 1929. A half century of effort has built some international markets for wines that merit wider esteem. Other private wineries can also point to modest success – Conti Zecca, Cosimo Taurino, Giuseppe Calò, and Attilio Simonini's Favonio, to mention a few. Rivera, in collaboration with Gancia of Piedmont, has produced wines from an array of varieties on the Murge plateau, showing that greater heights are well within Apulia's reach.

The region has respected wine research centres at Barletta and Bari. But their guidance, however well intended, seems to have done little for general quality, though yields have risen steadily since phylloxera. The bulk of production is centred in cooperatives which only rarely concentrate on premium quality. Unless this mentality changes – as well it might under growing pressure – the goal of selling 30-40 percent of Apulia's wine in bottle in the 1990s seems remote.

Overproduction is not just a modern problem. In 1884, after stretches of Apulia's plains had been transformed from a granary to a winery, R. De Cesare, an authority on the region's viticulutre, expressed "great doubts about the future of the oenological industry" if the increase in wine production did not correspond with its improvement. One can only wonder what he might have to say about Europe's wine cellar today.

Apulia's Vineyards

Apulia has fewer vineyards than Sicily but often makes more wine. Still, though average yields of 90 hectolitres per hectare are the highest in the south, that rate is surpassed by the Abruzzi, Emilia-Romagna, Veneto,

Left: the Rivera winery makes some of the region's most respected wines at the Torrebianco estate in Bari province.

and Trentino-Alto Adige. Vineyards are ubiquitous, though the greatest concentrations are in the flattest areas: the Capitanata to the north, Terra di Bari in the centre, and Salento to the southeast.

Apulia boasts the largest array of vine varieties in the south, a substantial base of natives bolstered by such intriguing outsiders as Primitivo (known elsewhere as Zinfandel) and, more recently, Chardonnay, the Pinots, Sauvignon Blanc, and Cabernet. Red wine varieties dominate white by about four to one. The heavyweights make the inky blending wines of Salento: Negroamaro (the sixth most planted Italian variety with nearly 40,000 hectares), Primitivo (eighth with about 30,000 hectares), and Malvasia Nera (with about 10,000 hectares). The respected Uva di Troia is grown mainly in the north. The trend, however, is towards white varieties, both native and foreign. Verdeca is the leading white with about 7,000 hectares planted, followed by its partner in the Itria valley, Bianco d'Alessano. Bombino Bianco and Trebbiano Toscano are well distributed in the north. Malvasia Bianca, which is found nearly everywhere, is the base of most Salento whites.

Most vineyards are in the head-trained *alberello*, which has prevailed since Greek times in Salento and the Itria valley, the traditional sources of blending wines. In the central hills, vertical systems are more prevalent because they promote slower ripening and superior aromas in premium wines. The *tendone* or trellis system is also used for wine grapes, but unless controlled it promotes quantity at the expense of quality. The Casarsa system is gaining since it permits mechanized harvesting.

The following varieties are associated primarily with Apulia.

Bianco d'Alessano. Though said to be an ancient vine of Salento, its modern home is the Itria valley, where it combines with Verdeca to lend a golden hint to such DOCs as Locorotondo and Martina Franca.

Bombino Bianco. Once Apulia's most abundant white variety, noted for soft, neutral wines, it has lost ground to the more productive Trebbiano Toscano. Though its origins are uncertain, Bombino, whose synonyms include Bambino, Bonvino or Buonvino, and Colatamburo, seems related to Romagna's Pagedebit and Abruzzi's Campolese.

Bombino Nero. The dark counterpart of Bombino Bianco. Grapes from this prolific vine ripen unevenly, so are better suited to rosé – ie Castel del Monte Rosato – than red wine.

Impigno. The pillar of Ostuni Bianco DOC was dubbed Impigno (stress-free) from the nickname of a local farmer at the turn of the century.

Malvasia Nera di Brindisi/Lecce. These similar clones of dark Malvasia contribute to the aromas and flavours of Salento's numerous red wines, usually as minor partners in blends with Negroamaro.

Moscato di Trani or **Moscato Reale**. This selection of white Moscato is the official source of the Moscato di Trani DOC, though growers often include the native Moscatello Selvatico, which contributes a pronounced aroma.

Negroamaro or **Negro Amaro**. Black and bitter, as the name states, Salento's preferred variety gives generous yields on the hot plains. Though traditionally a source of blending wine, when treated with respect it can make distinctive reds and exquisite rosé on its own.

Ottavianello. A rare Italian example of the Midi's everyday Cinsaut arrived in Apulia via the Campanian town of Ottaviano. It makes a light cherry-red wine as Ostuni Ottavianello DOC.

Pampanuto. An indigenous variety used in blends, such as Castel del Monte Bianco DOC, but rarely on its own due to low natural acidity.

Primitivo. The origins of this much discussed vine are uncertain, though evidence points to the Austro-Hungarian empire. It was in Apulia by the seventeenth century when Benedictine friars at Gioia del Colle called it Primitivo or Primativo due to its early ripening. This, along with its strength, made its wines ideal for blending with late ripening northern reds. As Apulia's second most planted variety, it also makes dry and sweet wines under Manduria and Gioia del Colle DOCs. It is related to California's Zinfandel, which apparently arrived there via Hungary.

Above: vines trained on high trellises in the Castel del Monte zone supply grapes for the area's white wine.

Ampelographers note a similarity to the Plavina of Yugoslavia's Dalmatia and are studying a possible link to Austria's Roter Veltliner.

Susumaniello. A native of Dalmatia, it is appreciated around Brindisi in blends, thanks to its bright ruby violet colour and good acidity.

Uva di Troia. Though seemingly linked to the Apulian town of Troia, experts say the name refers to Troy in Asia Minor, from which it was brought by the ancient Greeks. One of southern Italy's most persuasive red varieties, it is the base of several DOCs, notably Castel del Monte Rosso. Synonyms include Sumarello and Uva della Marina.

Verdeca. Apparently a native of the Itria valley, Apulia's most popular white variety makes green-tinted wines of rather neutral aroma and flavour. This makes it useful as a base for vermouth or in blends, usually with Bianco d'Alessano in the DOCs of Locorotondo and Martina Franca.

Other varieties

Other varieties recommended or approved in Apulia include:

For red (or rosé): Aglianico, Ancellota, Barbera, Cabernet Franc, Cabernet Sauvignon, Ciliegiolo, Lacrima, Lambrusco Maestri, Malbec, Merlot, Montepulciano, Notar Domenico, Somarello, Piedirosso, Pinot Nero.

For white: Asprinio, Chardonnay, Cococciola, Fiano, Francavilla or Francavidda, Garganega, Greco, Incrocio Manzoni 6.0.13, Malvasia del Chianti, Montonico Bianco, Moscato Bianco, Mostosa, Pinot Bianco, Riesling Italico, Riesling Renano, Sauvignon, Sémillon, Traminer Aromatico, Trebbiano Giallo, Trebbiano Romagnolo, Trebbiano Toscano, Vermentino.

Apulia's Wine Zones

The elongated region of Apulia forms the so-called spur (the Gargano promontory) and heel (the Salento peninsula) of the Italian boot, extending to the nation's easternmost point at Capo d'Otranto. Apulia is Italy's flattest region, with 53 percent of its area taken up by plains, 45 percent low plateaux or hills, and only two percent (Italy's lowest) mountains. It has 830 kilometres of coastline (including the Trémiti isles) on the Adriatic and Ionian Seas. Eighty percent of Apulia (the largest proportion) is given over to agriculture, dominated by vines, olives, and cereal crops. The Salento peninsula and the Bari and Capitanata plains to the north are the principal vineyard areas of Europe's most prolific wine region, though even the higher terrain of the Murge plateau is heavily planted with vines. Though known for hot, dry summers, variations in weather are caused by air currents from the Adriatic crossing the heights of Le Murge and Gargano to meet the wall of the Apennines. Generally, however, rain is scarce from mid-spring to early autumn, so irrigation from both underground water supplies and reservoirs in the Apennines is extensive. Rainfall is heaviest in Le Murge, though even in Salento the clash of Adriatic and Ionian breezes brings occasional storms, including hail. Still, throughout Apulia drought remains the main deterrent to habitual overproduction.

The northern plains: La Capitanata

Vineyards and grainfields alternate in the Capitanata plain and Daunia hills where the play of breezes between the Adriatic and the Apennines tempers the usually torrid summer weather. The mixture of calcareous clay and sand spawns light whites and middleweight reds in the San Severo, Lucera, Orta Nova, and Cerignola DOCs, though worthy wines have been made by Favonio and Torre Quarto.

Bari's plain and central plateau: Terra di Bari and Le Murge

The undulating plateau called Le Murge provides Apulia's best conditions in the Castel del Monte zone, though viticulture is less prolific there than in the coastal Terra di Bari, where Moscato di Trani and the reds of Barletta and Canosa originate. The plateau's mild climate favours both novel white varieties and traditional reds and rosés. Castel del Monte's better vineyards lie in reddish brown soil accumulated in pockets of limestone at 300-680 metres.

The trulli district

The low hills, valleys, and gorges of the southeastern Murge and Itria valley are typified by red soil on a calcareous base. Though hot, clashing currents from the Adriatic and Ionian can result in summer rainfall, favouring ample production of the white Locorotondo and Martina DOCs and the light red and white of Ostuni. At Gioia del Colle red varieties dominate in conditions similar to Castel del Monte.

The Salento peninsula

The vast plain gives way to the gentle rises known as Tavoliere di Lecce, Murge Tarantine, Terra d'Otranto, and Murge Salentine, but the nine DOC zones lie mainly to the north and west of the peninsula on flat land typified by red soil on a calcareous base. Though hot and dry in summer, desert-like cool nights retard ripening and encourage aromas in certain wines. Drought is a frequent problem but the summer heat may be broken by violent storms caused by warm Ionian winds meeting cooler Adriatic air. Conditions favour dark varieties for reds and rosés, though some success has been reported with whites.

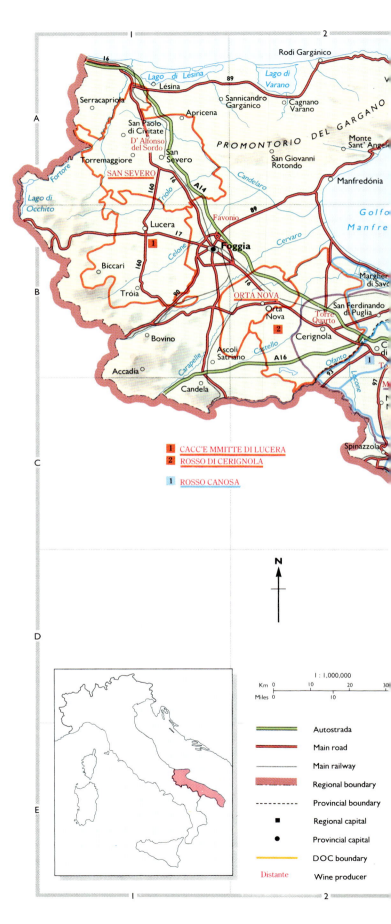

1 CACC'E MMITTE DI LUCERA
2 ROSSO DI CERIGNOLA

1 ROSSO CANOSA

N

1 : 1,000,000

| Km | 0 | | 10 | | 20 | 30 |
| Miles | 0 | | | 10 | | |

Autostrada
Main road
Main railway
Regional boundary
Provincial boundary
Regional capital
Provincial capital
DOC boundary
Distante   Wine producer

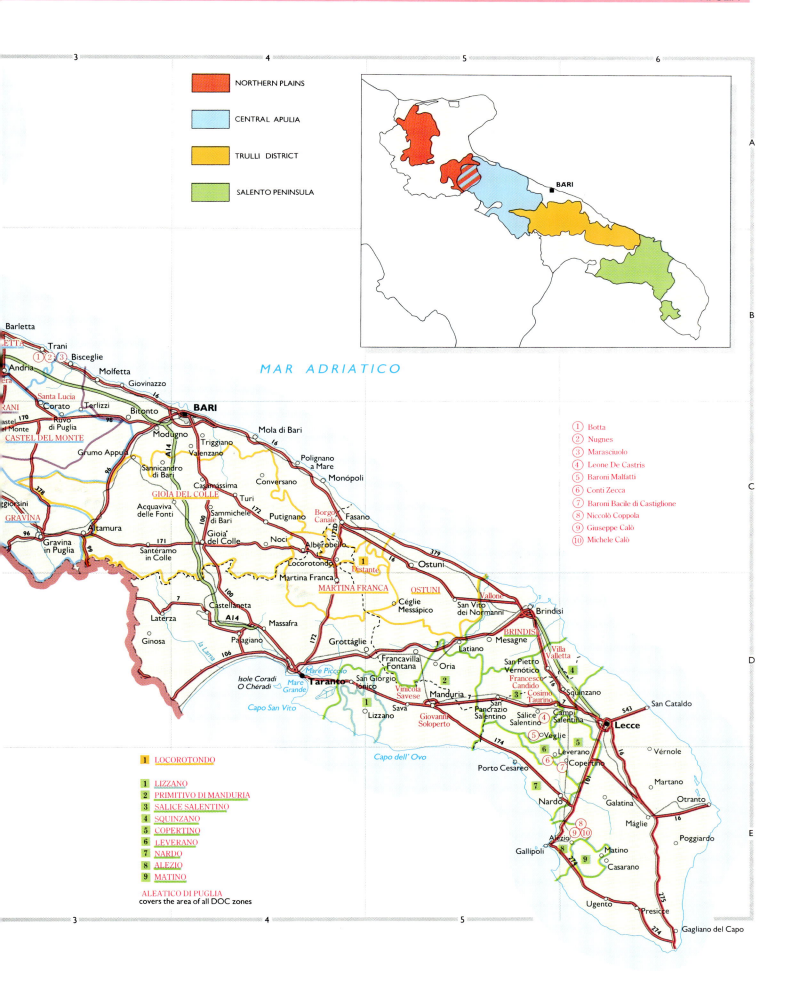

NORTHERN PLAINS

CENTRAL APULIA

TRULLI DISTRICT

SALENTO PENINSULA

BARI

MAR ADRIATICO

Barletta
Trani
① ② ③ Bisceglie
Andra
Molfetta
Giovinazzo
Santa Lucia
Corato Terlizzi
Castel del Monte
CASTEL DEL MONTE
Ruvo
di Puglia   Bitonto
170
98
BARI
Modugno
Grumo Appula
Triggiano
Mola di Bari
A14
Valenzano
Sannicandro
di Bari
16
Casamássima
Polignano
a Mare
Conversano
Monópoli
GIOIA DEL COLLE
Turi
Acquaviva
delle Fonti
Sammichele
di Bari
Putignano
GRAVINA
172
Borgo
Canale
Fasano
giorsini
Altamura
Gioia'
del Colle
Noci
Alberobello
379
GRAVINA
96
171
Santéramo
in Colle
Locorotondo
16
Ostuni
Gravina
in Puglia
100
Distante
Martina Franca
7
MARTINA FRANCA
OSTUNI
378
Castellaneta
Céglie
Messápico
San Vito
dei Normanni
Vallone
Brindisi
A14
Massafra
100
Laterza
172
Grottáglie
Latiano
BRINDISI
Ginosa
106
Palagiano
Francavilla
Fontana
Oria
Mesagne
Villa
Valletta
la Lama
Mare Piccolo
San Giorgio
Jonico
2
San Pietro
Vernótico
4
Isole Coradi
O Chéradi
Mare
Grande
Taranto
Vinicola
Savese
Manduria
Francesco
Candido
Squinzano
1
Capo San Vito
1
Sava
3
Cosimo
Taurino
San
Pancrazio
Salentino
7
Campi
Salentina
San Cataldo
543
Lizzano
Giovanni
Soloperto
4
Sálice
Salentino
Véglie
Lecce
Capo dell' Ovo
5
6
5
Leverano
Vérnole
6
7
Copertino
Nardo
7
Porto Cesareo
Martano
Galatina
Otranto
8
Alézio
9 10
Máglie
16
Gallipoli
8
Matino
Poggiardo
9
Casarano
275
Ugento
Presicce
274
Gagliano del Capo

① Botta
② Nugnes
③ Marasciuolo
④ Leone De Castris
⑤ Baroni Malfatti
⑥ Conti Zecca
⑦ Baroni Bacile di Castiglione
⑧ Niccolò Coppola
⑨ Giuseppe Calò
⑩ Michele Calò

1 LOCOROTONDO

1 LIZZANO
2 PRIMITIVO DI MANDURIA
3 SALICE SALENTINO
4 SQUINZANO
5 COPERTINO
6 LEVERANO
7 NARDO
8 ALEZIO
9 MATINO

ALEATICO DI PUGLIA
covers the area of all DOC zones

The regional DOC

Aleatico di Puglia (1973)
This fine red dessert wine comes almost exclusively from the province of Bari, so moves are afoot to revoke the regionwide DOC and confine the minuscule production to the original area. The *dolce naturale* is medium sweet. The richer *liquoroso* is usually made from grapes dried on racks to concentrate the sugar.

Zone: All five provinces of Apulia, though the little Aleatico that still remains is planted mainly around Gioia del Colle south of Bari.
Dolce naturale Sweet red, also riserva. Grapes: Aleatico; Negroamaro/Malvasia Nera/Primitivo up to 15%. Yld 52/80, Alc 15 (res sugar 2%), Acd 0.4, Ag riserva 3 yrs.
Liquoroso Sweet red, also riserva. Grapes: As dolce naturale, though it may use dried grapes or be fortified with alcohol. Yld 52/80, Alc 18.5 (res sugar 2.5%), Acd 0.4, Ag riserva 3 yrs.

Wines of the northern plains: La Capitanata

Discriminating drinkers might agree with critics that northern Apulia's plains are better suited to grain than vines, for few wines here show inherent class. The workhorse varieties of Trebbiano, Bombino Bianco, Montepulciano, and Sangiovese are used for everyday wines. The DOCs, dominated by San Severo, at best are clean, balanced, and free of pretension. Exceptions are the non-DOC Favonio and Torre Quarto, whose wines come primarily from vines of French origin.

San Severo (1968)
The region's most prolific DOC in unremarkable red, rosé, and white, though they can be tasty and offer good value.

Zone: Plains in Foggia province, mainly the commune of San Severo and seven others.
Bianco Dry white, also spumante. Grapes: Bombino Bianco/Trebbiano Toscano 40-60% each; Malvasia Bianca/Verdeca up to 20%. Yld 98/140, Alc 11, Acd 0.45-0.65.
Rosso Dry red. Grapes: Montepulciano; Sangiovese up to 30%. Yld 84/120, Alc 11.5, Acd 0.45-0.65.
Rosato Dry rosé. Grapes: As rosso. Yld 84/120, Alc 11.5, Acd 0.45-0.65.

Cacc'e Mmitte di Lucera (1976)
The name in dialect refers to the custom of adding grapes to the wine fermenting in vat and drawing off the surplus to drink. This makes sense, as youth is the main attribute of this simple red.

Zone: Plains in Foggia province, mainly the communes of Lucera, Biccari, and Troia. Dry red. Grapes: Uva di Troia 35-60%; Montepulciano/Sangiovese/Malvasia Nera 25-35%; Bombino Bianco/Malvasia del Chianti 15-30%. Yld 91/140, Alc 11.5, Acd 0.45.

Orta Nova (1984)
Unheeded red and rosé.

Zone: Plains in Foggia province, mainly the communes of Orta Nova, Ordona, and parts of four others.
Rosso Dry red. Grapes: Sangiovese; Uva di Troia/Montepulciano up to 40%, Lambrusco Maestri/Trebbiano Toscano up to 10%. Yld 105/150, Alc 12, Acd 0.45.
Rosato Dry rosé. Grapes: As rosso. Yld 97.5/150, Alc 11.5, Acd 0.45.

Below: a well near Lecce in Salento is a welcome source of water on the hot, dry plains. Far right: many Castel del Monte vineyards lie in pockets of reddish soil on a limestone base.

Rosso di Cerignola (1974)
Potentially interesting but rarely seen red from the gallant Uva di Troia.

Zone: Plains in Foggia province, mainly the commune of Cerignola and three others. Dry red, also riserva. Grapes: Uva di Troia at least 55%; Negroamaro 15-30%; Sangiovese/Barbera/Malbec/Montepulciano/Trebbiano Toscano up to 15%. Yld 98/140, Alc 12; riserva 13, Acd 0.5, Ag riserva 2 yrs in wood.

Other wines of note
Few of the many unclassified wines of northern Apulia deserve a mention since they follow the overworked patterns of light and bubbly. But two estates stand out with wines recognized for virtues that have gone well beyond the norm: Favonio and Torre Quarto (*see* below).

ESTATES/GROWERS

Favonio-Attilio Simonini, Località Donadone, Foggia. Veneto native Attilio Simonini pioneered outside varieties here with an enviably limited production from 16 ha of Cabernet Franc, Chardonnay, Pinot Bianco, Pinot Rosso, and Trebbiano Toscano, all vdt of the Capitanata. Studied vineyard methods (including drip irrigation), early picking, and deft cellar techniques result in lively, flowery whites and full, balanced reds that rarely reveal their southern origins.
Aldo Pugliese, San Severo (FG). San Severo DOC.
Torre Quarto, Cerignola (FG). This vast estate was once owned by the Dukes of Rochefoucauld, who founded the winery in 1847 and planted Malbec from their native France. More recently the property was owned by the Cirillo-Farrusi family, who made the notably long-lived Torre Quarto Rosso from Malbec and Uva di Troia, as well as white and rosé vdt. Its purchase by ERSAP, the regional development board, has now left its future uncertain.
Torricelli, Cerignola (FG). Rosso di Cerignola DOC.

WINE HOUSES/MERCHANTS

Cantine D'Alfonso del Sordo, Contrada Sant'Antonio, San Severo (FG). Top-ranked producer of San Severo DOC, in part from own vines.
Federico II, Lucera (FG). San Severo DOC and vdt.

COOPERATIVES

CS Svevo, Lucera (FG). Large producer of Cacc'e Mmitte di Lucera DOC and vdt from more than 400 growers.

Below: the name and symbol of the Castel del Monte DOC zone come from the striking 13th-century castle with its eight octagonal towers.

Wines of central Apulia

The province of Bari boasts favourable conditions for premium wine in the heights of Le Murge and even at points along the coastal plain known as Terra di Bari. In the thirteenth century Emperor Frederick II built Castel del Monte (which lends its name to the area's leading DOC), and surrounded the castle with vineyards, realizing that the reddish soil deposited between the strata of grey rock on the arid plateau promised character. This quality is best illustrated by the modern wine house of Rivera with its studied Castel del Monte DOCs and fashionable white table wines.

Rosso Barletta (1977)

Uva di Troia, which may be used exclusively, enables this red named after the bustling little port of Barletta. Though good young, the *invecchiato* may improve for 5-6 years.

Zone: Coastal plains and low hills in the communes of Barletta, Andria, and Trani in Bari province, and parts of two others in Foggia. Dry red, also invecchiato. Grapes: Uva di Troia; Montepulciano/Sangiovese up to 30%, Malbec up to 10%. Yld 105/150, Alc 12, Acd 0.5, Ag invecchiato 2 yrs (1 in wood).

Rosso Canosa (1979)

From Canosa, the Roman town of Canusium, once famous for its wine, comes this obscure red nearly identical to Castel del Monte Rosso. It may also be labelled Canusium.

Zone: Hills in the commune of Canosa di Puglia in Bari province. Dry red, also riserva. Grapes: Uva di Troia; Montepulciano up to 35%, Sangiovese up to 15%, other varieties up to 5%. Yld 98/140, Alc 12; riserva 13, Acd 0.5, Ag riserva 2 yrs (1 in wood).

Moscato di Trani (1975)

Golden dessert wine from Moscato grapes traditionally grown around the coastal town of Trani. Rich in aroma, flavour and texture, this precariously rare sweet wine is one of the southern peninsula's finest.

Zone: Coastal plains and Le Murge inland from Trani, taking in parts of nine other communes in Bari province and two in Foggia.
Dolce naturale Sweet white. Grapes: Moscato di Trani or Moscato Reale; other whites up to 15%. Yld 78/120, Alc 15 (res sugar min 2%), Acd 0.45, Ag 5 mths.
Liquoroso Sweet white. Grapes: As dolce naturale, though the base wine may be fortified with alcohol. Yld 78/120, Alc 18 (res sugar min 2%), Acd 0.45, Ag 1 yr.

Castel del Monte (1971)

Apulia's most impressive DOC wines originate in this zone of rocky, arid inclines where only certain pockets have enough soil for vines. The *rosato* is one of Italy's most popular pink – or blush – wines, but the *rosso* is grander. The *riserva* with its deep colour and opulent tone can age splendidly, notably in Rivera's Il Falcone. The white is bland but pleasantly so. Producers have asked to add wines from Chardonnay, Pinot Bianco, Sauvignon, Pinot Nero (red and white), and Aglianico (red and rosé) to the list.

Zone: Undulating hills of Le Murge around Castel del Monte between Bitonto, Andria, Minervino Murge, and seven other communes in Bari province.
Bianco Dry white. Grapes: Pampanuto; other whites up to 35%.Yld 105/150, Alc 11, Acd 0.45.
Rosso Dry red, also riserva. Grapes: Uva di Troia; Sangiovese/Montepulciano/Aglianico/ Pinot Nero up to 35%. Yld 98/140, Alc 12; riserva 12.5, Acd 0.45, Ag riserva 3 yrs (1 in wood).
Rosato Dry rosé. Grapes: Bombino Nero; Uva di Troia/Montepulciano/Aglianico/Pinot Nero up to 35%. Yld 91/140, Alc 11, Acd 0.4.

Gravina (1984)

Vineyards around Gravina near the border with Basilicata produce this little known white, whether dry or slightly sweet.

Zone: Hills of Le Murge in Bari province, based in the communes of Gravina in Puglia, Altamura, and two others. Dry white, also amabile. Grapes: Malvasia del Chianti 40-65%, Greco di Tufo/Bianco di Alessano 35-60%; Bombino Bianco/Trebbiano Toscano/Verdeca up to 10%. Yld 105/150, Alc 11 (amabile res sugar 4-20 gr/l), Acd 0.5.

Other wines of note

Rivera, backed by investment from Fratelli Gancia of Piedmont, is leading central Apulia into a future of renewed hope with admirably sleek and balanced whites from Sauvignon and Pinot Bianco. Gancia at its own Tenute Torrebianco makes impressive Chardonnays called Preludio No 1 and Cantico. Cordon training and reduced yields, combined with deft vinification, have set an example for other Apulians to follow.

ESTATES/GROWERS

Bruno-Tenuta Torre d'Isola, Minervino Murge (BA). Castel del Monte DOC.
G. Jatta, Ruvo di Puglia (BA). Castel del Monte DOC.
Santa Lucia, Corato (BA). Emerging estate with Castel del Monte DOC.
Fratelli Nugnes, Trani (BA). Small production of refined Moscato di Trani Dolce Naturale DOC.
Tenuta Torrebianco, Andria (BA). Gancia's new estate with 100 ha of irrigated vines made its debut with Chardonnay table wines called Preludio No 1 and Cantico, the latest creations of consultant Giorgio Grai. Vineyards at 200 m include 44 ha in Chardonnay, 10 in Aglianico and others in coolest zones planted in Sauvignon Blanc, Pinot Bianco, and Pinot Nero.

WINE HOUSES/MERCHANTS

Felice Botta, Trani (BA). Aleatico del Puglia, Castel del Monte, and Moscato di Trani DOC.
Chiddo Vini, Bitonto (BA). Castel del Monte DOC and vdt.
Gennaro Marasciuolo, Trani (BA). Fine Moscato di Trani, plus Castel del Monte DOC and vdt.
Rivera, Andria (BA). Carlo De Corato was already making Castel del Monte's best rosé and red (Il Falcone) when Gancia acquired half ownership and pushed the manager-winemaker towards new horizons. Rivera's Pinot and Sauvignon vdt, in part from grapes grown at the Torrebianco estate, have been winning prizes. The same white varietals, plus a rosé from Aglianico, use the trademark Vigna al Monte.
Vinicola Palumbo, Rutigliano (BA). Castel del Monte DOC and vdt.

COOPERATIVES

CS di Barletta, Barletta (BA). Good Rosso Barletta plus vdt and sparkling.
Cooperativa Agraria Nicola Rossi, Canosa (BA). Rosso Canosa and vdt.

Wines of the trulli district: the Itria valley, Gioia del Colle, and Ostuni

South of Bari, near the provincial borders with Taranto and Brindisi, the Murge tapers into valleys and gorges carved by the Itria river in a district known above all for the *trulli* stone dwellings. This has become a centre of modern white wine production, exemplified by the DOCs of Locorotondo and Martina Franca. But in the past, wines from Verdeca and Bianco d'Alessano grapes were used for blending and as a base for vermouth. On the fringes of the *trulli* district lie Gioia del Colle, a hill town where red wine prevails and the picturesque whitewashed town of Ostuni with its peculiar red and white wines.

Gioia del Colle (1987)

This DOC honours a wine heritage in a hill town almost as pretty as its name. Primitivo, which was first noted here in Apulia, may also be called Primitivo di Gioia. Aleatico is at its best in the surrounding hills. The other wines have yet to show their colours, but the promise is there.

Zone: Hills around Gioia del Colle and 15 neighbouring communes in Bari province.
Bianco Dry white. Grapes: Trebbiano Toscano with other whites at 30-50%. Yld 78/130, Alc 10.5, Acd 0.5.
Rosso Dry red. Grapes: Primitivo 50-60%, Montepulciano/Sangiovese/Negroamaro 40-50%; Malvasia Nera up to 10%. Yld 84/120, Alc 11.5, Acd 0.45.
Rosato Dry rosé. Grapes: As rosso. Yld 72/120, Alc 11, Acd 0.5.
Aleatico Sweet red, also riserva and liquoroso dolce. Grapes: Aleatico; Negroamaro/Malvasia Nera/Primitivo up to 15%. Yld 52/80, Alc 15 (riserva res sugar 2%); liquoroso dolce 18.5 (res sugar 2.5%), Acd 0.45, Ag 5 mths; riserva 2 yrs (1 in wood).
Primitivo Dry red, also amabile and riserva. Grape: Primitivo. Yld 52/80, Alc 13 (amabile and amabile riserva res sugar max 10 gr/l); riserva 14, Acd 0.45, Ag riserva 2 yrs.

Locorotondo (1969)

Sometimes hailed as Apulia's premier white, though you may have to search for character. Still, its subtle fruit and almondy finish usually go well with fish. The *spumante* is increasingly popular.

Zone: Slopes in the communes of Locorotondo, Cisternino, and Fasano in Bari and Brindisi provinces. Dry white, also spumante. Grapes: Verdeca 50-65%, Bianco di Alessano 35-50%; Fiano/Bombino Bianco/Malvasia Toscana up to 5%. Yld 91/130, Alc 11, Acd 0.45-0.65.

Martina Franca or Martina (1969)

Named after one of Apulia's most attractive hill towns, Martina Franca is a near twin of Locorotondo.

Zone: Slopes around Martina Franca and Alberobello and parts of three other communes in the provinces of Taranto, Brindisi, and Bari. Dry white, also spumante. Grapes: Verdeca 50-65%, Bianco di Alessano 35-50%; Fiano/Bombino Bianco/Malvasia Toscana up to 5%. Yld 91/130, Alc 11, Acd 0.45.

Ostuni (1972)

Individuality rather than class distinguishes the fragile Bianco and cherry-coloured Ottavianello from this antique town northwest of Brindisi. The grape varieties of Impigno and Ottavianello (France's Cinsaut) are unique to this zone.

Zone: Coastal hills and plains around Ostuni and six other communes in Brindisi province.
Bianco Dry white. Grapes: Impigno 50-85%, Francavilla 15-50%; Bianco d'Alessano/Verdeca up to 10%. Yld 77/110, Alc 11, Acd 0.45.
Ottavianello Dry red. Grapes: Ottavianello; Negroamaro/Malvasia Nera/Notar Domenico/Susumaniello up to 15%. Yld 77/110, Alc 11.5, Acd 0.5.

Other wines of note

Numerous table wines are made in the area, mainly bubbly whites for summer sipping.

WINE HOUSES/MERCHANTS

Borgo Canale, Selva di Fasano (BR). Good Locorotondo and Martina Franca DOCs, as well as vdt.
Cantina Calella, Locorotondo (BA). Locorotondo DOC and vdt.
Distante Vini, Cisternino (BR). Admirable quality in Locorotondo, Martina Franca, Brindisi DOCs, and vdt.
Lippolis, Alberobello (BA). Martina Franca and Aglianico del Vulture DOC, as well as vdt.
Miali, Martina Franca (TA). Castel del Monte, Martina Franca, and Aglianico del Vulture DOC, as well as vdt.

COOPERATIVES

CS Cooperativa di Alberobello, Alberobello (BA). Martina Franca DOC and vdt.
CS Cooperativa di Locorotondo, Locorotondo (BA). Admired group of nearly 1,300 growers producing 120,000 hl, notably Locorotondo DOC, including *spumante*, in addition to red, white, and rosé vdt.
CS di Ostuni, Ostuni (BR). Ostuni DOC.

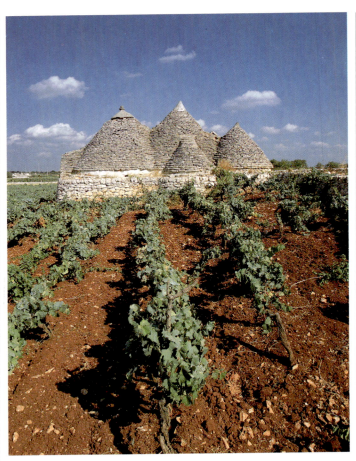

Above: the curious trulli *stone dwellings around Locorotondo are surrounded by neat rows of vines.*

Wines of Salento

Southeast of the *trulli* district the Murge opens onto the Salento peninsula, a plain stretching beyond Brindisi, Taranto, and Lecce to Italy's eastern extremes at Otranto and the Cape of Santa Maria Leuca. The scenery, the clusters of cactus and stands of palms shading whitewashed villages and farms surrounded by stone walls, could pass for North African were it not for the vines extending in neat rows of verdigris across the brick-red soil. Salento is the blending vat of the potent Primitivo, Negroamaro, and Malvasia Nera that lent body and soul to northern reds. But producers who would have them stand on their own have had to struggle to prove that reds of such power can also show grace. Some of Italy's finest rosés are crafted here by an intricate process that first involves maceration with the skins before about half the must is drawn off and fermented into wines of coral, roseate, and salmon hues. These exquisitely dry predecessors of the New World's often dulcet blush wines have not had the success they deserve outside Apulia. They are almost invariably superior to Salento's whites.

Primitivo di Manduria (1975)

Apulia's archetypal blending wine is occasionally tamed into a gentle giant which, whether opulently dry or potently sweet, bears a family resemblance to California's Zinfandel. But Apulians have not matched Californians' skill at giving finesse to this early ripening variety. The natural versions are usually good after a year when they still have a deep violet colour. The fortified version can take on some smoothness and complexity, with hints of orange after 4-5 years. Leading producers are Vinicola Savese and Soloperto, who draw from the zone's best vineyards around Sava and Manduria. Potential production has increased, but it is reliably estimated that only 10,000-12,000 bottles of DOC are sold a year.

Zone: Plains and gentle hills of the Murge Tarantine, mainly in Manduria and Sava and including 14 other communes in Taranto and Brindisi provinces. Grape: Primitivo.
Secco Dry red. Yld 63/90, Alc 14, Acd 0.5, Ag 9 mths.
Amabile Semisweet red. Yld 63/90, Alc 14 (res sugar max 10 gr/l), Acd 0.5, Ag 9 mths.
Dolce naturale Sweet red. Yld 63/90, Alc 16 (res sugar 3%), Acd 0.5, Ag 9 mths.

Liquoroso secco Dry fortified. Yld 63/90, Alc 18 (res sugar 1.5%), Acd 0.5, Ag 2 yrs.
Liquoroso dolce naturale Sweet fortified. Yld 63/90, Alc 17.5 (res sugar 2.5%), Acd 0.5, Ag 2 yrs.

Lizzano (1989)
The latest in the network of Salento DOCs, Lizzano's six types add new but unproved options to the peninsula's array of wines.
  Zone: Plains and low hills of the Murge Tarantine in the communes of Lizzano, Faggiano, and part of Taranto.
Bianco Dry white. Grapes: Trebbiano Toscano 40-60%, Chardonnay/Pinot Bianco min 30%, Sauvignon/Bianco di Alessano up to 25%, Malvasia Bianca Lunga up to 10%. Yld 104/160, Alc 10.5, Acd 0.55.
Rosso Dry red. Grapes: Negroamaro 60-80%, Montepulciano/Sangiovese/Bombino Nero/ Pinot Nero up to 40%, Malvasia Nera di Brindisi or Lecce up to 10%. Yld 98/140, Alc 12, Acd 0.5.
Rosato Dry rosé. Grapes: As rosso. Yld 91/140, Alc 12, Acd 0.55.
Malvasia Nera Dry red. Grapes: Malvasia Nera di Brindisi or Lecce 85%, Negroamaro/ Montepulciano/Sangiovese/Pinot Nero up to 15%. Yld 98/140, Alc 12, Acd 0.5.
Negroamaro rosso Dry red. Grapes: Negroamaro 85%, Malvasia Nera di Brindisi or Lecce/Montepulciano/Sangiovese/Pinot Nero up to 15%. Yld 98/140, Alc 12, Acd 0.5.
Negroamaro rosato Dry rosé. Grapes: As Negroamaro rosso. Yld 91/140, Alc 12, Acd 0.55.

Brindisi (1980)
The red can be among Salento's best, notably in the long-lived *riserva* known as Patriglione from Cosimo Taurino. The *rosato* is pleasant at best.
  Zone: Plains and low hills in the communes of Brindisi and Mesagne.
Rosso Dry red, also riserva. Grapes: Negroamaro; Malvasia Nera di Brindisi/ Susumaniello/Montepulciano up to 30%,

Sangiovese up to 10%. Yld 105/150, Alc 12; riserva 12.5, Acd 0.5, Ag riserva 2 yrs.
Rosato Dry rosé. Grapes: As rosso. Yld 105/150, Alc 12, Acd 0.5.

Salice Salentino (1976)
The most prominent of Salento's DOCs, due to consistent quality in wines from Leone De Castris and Cosimo Taurino. The *rosso* is rich in colour and robust, but with age an inviting mellowness offsets the bitter undertone. The *rosato* can be fresh and flowery or, with time, fairly deep and complex and in either case among the most distinctive of Italian rosés. Producers have asked to include Aleatico, Chardonnay, Pinot Bianco, and a *bianco* in the DOC, while requesting other changes such as a red *novello* and *rosato spumante*.
  Zone: Plains in Lecce and Brindisi provinces, mainly the communes of Salice Salentino and six others.
Rosso Dry red, also riserva. Grapes: Negroamaro; Malvasia Nera di Brindisi or Lecce up to 20%. Yld 84/120, Alc 12.5, Acd 0.5, Ag 8 mths; riserva 2 yrs (1 in wood).
Rosato Dry rosé, also prodotto invecchiato. Grapes: As rosso. Yld 48/120, Alc 12, Acd 0.5, Ag 8 mths; prodotto invecchiato 1 yr.

Squinzano (1976)
This once vaunted source of blending wines makes a sometimes convincing *rosso* and a *rosato* from the juice of only 30% of the weight of the grapes. Villa Valletta is the best-known producer.
  Zone: Plains in Lecce province in the communes of Squinzano, San Pietro Vernotico, and seven others.
Rosso Dry red, also riserva. Grapes: Negroamaro; Malvasia Nera di Brindisi or Lecce up to 30%, Sangiovese up to 15%. Yld 98/140, Alc 12.5, Acd 0.5, Ag riserva 2 yrs (6 mths in wood).
Rosato Dry rosé. Grapes: As rosso. Yld 42/140, Alc 12.5, Acd 0.5.

Leverano (1980)
The first white Salento DOC is hardly worth the distinction, but the *rosato* and the even more stylish *rosso* from the Vigna del Saraceno of Conti Zecca stand with Salento's finest.
  Zone: Plains in the commune of Leverano in Lecce province.
Bianco Dry white. Grapes: Malvasia Bianca; Bombino Bianco/Trebbiano Toscano up to 35%. Yld 97.5/150, Alc 11, Acd 0.5.
Rosso Dry red, also riserva. Grapes: Negroamaro; Malvasia Nera di Lecce/ Sangiovese/Montepulciano up to 35%, Malvasia Bianca up to 10%. Yld 105/150, Alc 12; riserva 12.5, Acd 0.5, Ag riserva 2 yrs.
Rosato Dry rosé. Grapes: As rosso. Yld 67.5/150, Alc 11.5, Acd 0.5.

Copertino (1977)
Sturdy *rosso* and *rosato* from the heart of Salento, led by the estate wines of Barone Bacile di Castiglione.
  Zone: Plains in Lecce province, mainly the commune of Copertino and five others.
Rosso Dry red, also riserva. Grapes: Negroamaro; Malvasia Nera di Brindisi or Lecce/Montepulciano up to 30%, Sangiovese up to 15%. Yld 98/140, Alc 12; riserva 12.5, Acd 0.5, Ag riserva 2 yrs.
Rosato Dry rosé. Grapes: As rosso. Yld 49/140, Alc 12, Acd 0.45.

Nardò (1987)
A newer addition to Salento's DOC list, Nardò's *rosso* and *rosato* risk being lost in the crowd.
  Zone: Plains in Lecce province, mainly the communes of Nardò and Porto Cesareo.
Rosso Dry red, also riserva. Grapes: Negroamaro; Malvasia Nera di Brindisi or Lecce/Montepulciano up to 20%. Yld 126/180, Alc 11.5; riserva 12.5, Acd 0.5, Ag riserva 2 yrs.
Rosato Dry rosé. Grapes: As rosso. Yld 81/180, Alc 11.5, Acd 0.5.

Alezio (1983)
Though the zone east of Gallipoli has proven quality potential for *rosso* and *rosato*, so far its best wines are the vdt from Calò.
  Zone: Plains in Lecce province, mainly the commune of Alezio and three others.
Rosso Dry red, also riserva. Grapes: Negroamaro; Malvasia Nera di Lecce/Sangiovese/ Montepulciano up to 20%. Yld 98/140, Alc 12; riserva 12.5, Acd 0.5, Ag riserva 2 yrs.
Rosato Dry rosé. Grapes: As rosso. Yld 49/140, Alc 12, Acd 0.55.

Matino (1971)
Salento's earliest DOC has never made an impact with its uninspiring *rosso* and *rosato* from the easternmost vineyards of Italy.
  Zone: Plains in Lecce province, mainly the commune of Matino and parts of seven others.
Rosso Dry red. Grapes: Negroamaro; Malvasia Nera/Sangiovese up to 30%. Yld 84/120, Alc 11.5, Acd 0.5.
Rosato Dry rosé. Grapes: As rosso. Yld 78/120, Alc 11.5, Acd 0.45.

Other wines of note
A number of Salento's better wines are not DOC but fall either under the noted vdt category of Rosso, Rosato, or Bianco di Salento or else carry their own colours. Among the reds, Calò's Quarantale and Taurino's Notarpanaro are admired. Leone De Castris began selling Five Roses in the 1930s as Italy's first bottled rosé, distinguished by a unique capacity to age. Calò's Rosa del Golfo is the pride of Salento's pink wines. Among non-DOC sweet wines, Leone De Castris's Negrino has port-like attributes. Some efforts with sparkling wines, dry and sweet, have been commendable, though so far markets are largely local.

ESTATES/GROWERS

Barone Bacile di Castiglione, Copertino (LE). Copertino DOC and vdt from 200 ha.
Francesco Candido, San Donaci (BR). Salice Salentino and a bit of Aleatico di Puglia DOC, as well as a convincing red vdt called Cappello di Prete.
Niccolò Coppola, Alezio (LE). Good Alezio DOC from the San Nicola Li Cuti vineyards, as well as Salento vdt.
Leone De Castris, Salice Salentino (LE). Salvatore Leone De Castris, lawyer and professor of economics as well as a winemaker, has built this large, ultramodern winery into a leader in southern Italy, notable for consistent quality and value. From more than 400 ha of vines come fine Salice Salentino DOC, along with the legendary rosé vdt known as Five Roses. The firm also produces Locorotondo DOC, Negrino and an array of sparkling wines. One of Italy's largest private wineries.
Cosimo Taurino, Guagnano (LE). Cosimo Taurino, a pharmacist, is one of

263

Right: date palms guard a farm gate at Salice Salentino near Lecce.

Salento's most skilled and dedicated producers. From 70 ha of vines he and oenologist Severino Garofano make the long-lived Brindisi DOC Patriglione and Notarpanaro vdt and some of the best Salice Salentino DOC. Also admirable are Chardonnay and Salento vdt.

Agricola Vallone, Brindisi. Vittoria and Maria Teresa Vallone own this estate with 140 ha producing fine Brindisi and Salice Salentino DOCs from the Vigna Flaminio, as well as Sauvignon del Salento and other vdt.

Conti Zecca, Leverano (LE). Leverano DOC from the Vigna del Saraceno and the Salento vdt labelled Donna Marzia originate in the 300 ha of vines owned by the Zecca family. Alcibiade Zecca, whose family has made wine since the 16th century, runs this vast operation with enlightened skill.

WINE HOUSES/MERCHANTS

Giuseppe Calò & Figlio, Alezio (LE). From a carefully supervised team of local growers, Giuseppe Calò and son Mino select grapes for Rosa del Golfo, which from the Scaliere Mazzì vineyard is sometimes cited as Italy's finest rosé. Also admirable are the red Portulano (in particular the *riserva* Quarantale) and white Bolina – all Salento vdt.

Michele Calò & Figli, Tuglie (LE). Alezio DOC and Salento vdt.

Baroni Malfatti, Veglie (LE). Large family winery with control over 150 ha of vines producing Salice Salentino DOC and Salento vdt.

Renna, Squinzano (LE). Squinzano DOC and vdt.

Vinicola Savese, Sava (TA). The Pichierri brothers make some of the best Primitivo di Manduria DOC.

Giovanni Soloperto, Manduria (TA). Primitivo di Manduria DOC and Salento vdt, partly from own vines.

Antica Casa Vinicola Antonio Valletta, San Pietro Vernotico (BR). Squinzano and Martina Franca DOC under trademark Villa Valletta, in part from 110 ha. Also *spumante* and vdt.

Venturi, Copertino (LE). Copertino and Leverano DOCs plus vdt.

Vignali, Galatone (LE). Salice Salentino and Locorotondo DOCs.

COOPERATIVES

CS Cooperativa di Copertino, Copertino (LE). Huge production includes good Copertino DOC.

CS Cooperativa, Leverano (LE). Leverano DOC and Salento vdt.

CS di Salento, Sannicola (LE). Alezio and Primitivo di Manduria DOC.

CS di Squinzano, Squinzano (LE). Squinzano DOC and Salento vdt.

Travel Information

RESTAURANTS/HOTELS

Il Poeta Contadino, 70011 Alberobello (BA). Tel (080)721917. Good regional dishes and inspired wine list.

Del Corso, Corso Federico di Svevia 76, 70022 Altamura (BA). Tel (080)841453. Excellent Apulian food, outstanding cellar.

Ostello di Federico, Castel del Monte, 70031 Andria (BA). Tel (0883)83043. Restful hotel beside the castle with simple regional dishes.

Bacco, Via Sipontina 10, 70051 Barletta (BA). Tel (0883)38398. Creative offerings of traditional dishes and seafood.

Vecchia Canosa, 70053 Canosa (BA). Tel (0883)963074. Tasty local cooking in rustic surroundings.

Cicolella, Viale 24 Maggio 60, 71100 Foggia. Tel (0881)3890. Comfortable hotel with good regional and national food and wines. **Cicolella in Fiera** is the branch at fairgrounds.

Marechiaro, 73014 Gallipoli (LE). Tel (0833)476143. The freshest seafood and Salento wines on a pier in the Ionian.

Gino e Gianni, Via 4 Finite 2, 73100 Lecce. Tel (0832)45888. Artistic regional dishes, notably fish, with good range of wines.

La Pergola, 73050 Santa Maria al Bagno (LE). Tel (0833)823008. Simply prepared fresh fish in abundance at reasonable prices.

Fagiano, 72010 Selva di Fasano (BR). Tel (080)799157. Eclectic range of food and wines in a handsome villa; summer dining in the garden.

Sierra Silvana, 72010 Selva di Fasano (BR). Tel (080)799322. Rooms in individual pavilions amidst gardens with good views, and pool and tennis courts.

WINE SHOPS/ENOTECHE

Enoteca Gianni Dell'Olio, 71042 Cerignola (FG).

Enoteca Internazionale, Via Cesare Battisti 23, 73100 Lecce. Oustanding range of Apulian, Italian, and foreign wines and spirits, also served by the glass with light dishes.

PLACES OF INTEREST

Though sometimes referred to by inobservant travellers as Italy's gateway to Greece, Apulia possesses perhaps more unheralded treasures of art and architecture than any other region of Italy. The landscape is for the most part unspectacular plains, plateaux, and gorges, but Puglia's towns are filled with revelations, remnants of Greeks, Romans, Saracens, Normans, Swabians, and Spaniards, among others. The cathedrals in the wine towns of Barletta and Trani are Romanesque masterpieces.

Castel del Monte. Octagonal fortress with eight towers built by Emperor Frederick II in 1240 on a rise dominating the plateau west of Bari. Described by the intrepid traveller R.W. Apple Jr. as "probably the finest castle in all of Italy". Namesake of Apulia's best DOC zone.

The Gargano massif. Adjacent to the Capitanata plain is the spur of the Italian boot, a promontory with white cliffs dropping to the sea and forests covering the heights. Quiet beaches in May, June, and September.

Salento. The Ionian and Adriatic flank one of Italy's most extensive expanses of vines on the heel of the boot. The towns of Otranto and Gallipoli have Grecian charm. The cities of Taranto and Brindisi combine the antique with the modern. But the jewel of Salento is Lecce, a monument to baroque architecture.

The trulli. The Itria valley is a fairyland of these curious domed dwellings, whose origins have been attributed to diverse sources from prehistoric tribes to the Rosicrucians. Alberobello is the capital of the *trulli*, but not to be missed are Gioia del Colle, Martina Franca, Cisternino, Locorotondo, or Ostuni, gleaming white towns surrounded by olive groves and vineyards. The *grotte* at Castellana are the most impressive of Apulia's many caves.

Campania

Capital: Napoli (Naples).
Provinces: Avellino (AV), Benevento (BN), Caserta (CE), Napoli (NA), Salerno (SA).
Area: 13,595 square kilometres (twelfth).
Population: 5,650,000 (second).

When writers search for nice things to say about Campania's wines, they tend either to rave about the scenic vineyards or lapse into past glories described by the likes of Horace, Virgil, and Pliny the Elder. Modern achievements are so rare that it would not be too far-fetched to say that the region's commendable winemakers (at least on a commercial level) can be counted on one's fingers. More than half of the potential 1.8 million bottles of DOC wine annually comes from a single family firm, Mastroberardino. Repeated references to that name might seem obsequious, but where else in Italy does one producer so clearly stand apart from the crowd? Or, viewed in another way, where else in Italy is the crowd so exasperatingly inert?

The maddening thing about this mediocrity is that there is no obvious excuse for it. Even laziness and indifference don't explain why viticultural potential exploited so honourably in the past is now all but ignored. Grapes and wine account for less than five percent of agricultural income in the region with the lowest percentage of DOC. But not just premium wine is neglected. Campania is one of the few regions that imports more wine than it exports. It may be that its hillsides are difficult to work or that its fields are needed for crops to feed the teeming population, but if anything the obstacles seem fewer here than in other regions where accomplishments with wine have been far greater.

Campania had been famous for its wines through most of its chequered history. The Romans called it "Campania felix", which may appear to mean happy countryside because of the way crops thrive in the volcanic earth with its ample water and sunshine. But in fact the name is derived from Campani, the inhabitants of Capua who were there when the Greeks introduced vines around the Bay of Naples. The Roman favourite Falernian grew along the northern coast near what is now Mondragone. The wines of Vesuvius, Avellino, Sorrento, and the islands of Ischia and Capri were also honoured by the ancients. Pope Paul III's bottler Sante Lancerio in his sixteenth-century chronicles raved about the wines of the Kingdom of Naples. He devoted more attention to this realm – and, in particular its wines from Greco – than to any other part of Italy. This reputation persisted into the nineteenth century, but the fall of the Kingdom of the Two Sicilies in 1860 foreboded a decline that still shows only feeble signs of recovery.

The Greeks and Romans, who raised viticulture to enviable levels in hot, fertile coastal zones, might be amazed to learn that Campania's finest wines today come from the cool, wooded uplands of Irpinia around the city of Avellino. But the international success of Fiano di Avellino, Greco di Tufo, and Taurasi is due to Mastroberardino, whose presence has also elevated the status of Vesuvius. Palatable wines are also made on the island of Ischia, around the northern town of Solopaca, on the Cilento promontory, in several sites along the Amalfi coast and even in the coastal hills where Falernian originated. Other areas in Campania have promise that isn't being exploited.

If any of those places lie along the Tyrrhenian, however, we will never know what might have been, for the coast from Baia Domizia on the border with Latium southeast to Sorrento is now lined by squalid high rise blocks and smoke spewing factories. Right in the middle of this bleak setting, overlooking the bay that awed the ancients with its images of heaven and hell, sits Naples, Babylon of paradise lost.

Above: the Greco di Tufo zone with the Mastroberardino estate in the distance.

Campania's Vineyards

Campania is home to several of Italy's esteemed "archaeological vines", among them the Avellino trio of Aglianico (for Taurasi), Fiano, and Greco di Tufo, and the Falanghina of Falerno and Capri. In the past vines were trained up trees and poles, spilling over pergolas, roofs, and any other available appendage while achieving growth that amazed outsiders. The Etruscans trained Asprinio vines up poplar trees in the fertile soil around Aversa. A slightly modified version is still seen in which high wires are strung between trees in the so-called *alberata aversana*.

Today most vineyards are arranged in neat rows on the hillsides. Vertical training dominates, with several variations. In the cool Avellino area, the so-called Guyot avellinese leaves grapes suspended beneath the lower wire to absorb heat from the earth. In the plains, the trellised *tendone* is used for both high-yield wine grapes and table grapes. The *alberello* (bush) system is often seen as well. On the stone-walled terraces of Amalfi, Capri, and Sorrento a localized pergola consists of columns supporting wooden beams set in quadrangles over which vines sprawl picturesquely – strikingly similar to those of mountainous Valle d'Aosta.

Despite the well-known fertility of its volcanic and alluvial soils,

Above: terraced vineyards on the steep hillsides of the Amalfi coast have been trained over pergolas since classical times.

Campania's average yields of wine are relatively low, largely because many vineyards are being abandoned and others are planted in places where little else will grow.

Aglianico, source of several DOC reds, is described in the introduction, *see* page 16, since Basilicata lays equal claim to it. Sciascinoso (also known as Olivella due to its grapes' resemblance to olives) is a key component of Vesuvio Rosso and is used in blends elsewhere and in Latium. The following varieties are associated primarily with Campania.

Asprinio. The Etruscans, who planted this species of *Vitis silvestres* in the flatlands around Aversa, used grapes from its high vines mainly for vinegar. But eventually its tart, spritzy white wines became the joy of Naples. Recently Asprinio or Asprino has fallen from favour, though new plantings point to a modest comeback in sparkling wines.

Biancolella. A useful back-up variety in the DOC whites of Capri and Ischia, where it also makes an impressive table wine on its own.

Coda di Volpe. Pliny the Elder dubbed this *Cauda vulpium* (fox tail) after the form of the clusters. A key to Vesuvio Bianco DOC, it can also be used in Greco di Tufo. Also known as Caprettone and Pallegrello.

Falanghina. Possibly of Greek origin (as Falanghina Greco), it may have been the vine of the Romans' white Falernian. Now the source of the DOC whites of Falerno del Massico and Capri, this extremely late ripening variety is attracting attention elsewhere in the south in wines of pronounced personality.

Fiano. Known as *Vitis apiana* to the ancient Romans due to its attractiveness to bees (*apis*), Fiano grown around Avellino is considered one of Italy's most distinctive white varieties. But its low yields have prevented extensive plantings elsewhere.

Forastera. The mainstay of Ischia Bianco. Some sources say it was brought to the island from Sardinia and Corsica two centuries ago.

Greco di Tufo. This clone descended from the ancient Greek varieties makes one of southern Italy's finest whites near Avellino. The once prominent Greco family is still evident elsewhere in Campania – in Greco del Vesuvio, Greco d'Ischia, and Greco di Somma among others.

Guarnaccia. The main grape of Ischia Rosso DOC, it is often known elsewhere as Alicante. Guarnaccia is related to Sardinia's Cannonau in the family known in Spain as Granacha and in France as Grenache. Campania also has a bit of white Guarnaccia.

Piedirosso or **Palombina** or **Pere'e Palummo**. An admired dark variety plays a key role in the DOC reds of Capri, Vesuvio (where it is called Palombina), and Ischia (where it is called Per'e Palummo). The name means "red feet" in reference to the colour of its stalks. Other synonyms include Piede di Colombo (dove's foot).

Other varieties

The prevalent outside varieties are Sangiovese and Trebbiano Toscano, main components of Solopaca Rosso and Bianco DOC, followed by Barbera, which is popular in blends. Apulia's Verdeca is the key to Vesuvio Bianco and its Primitivo has become DOC under Falerno del Massico. Other varieties recommended or approved in Campania include: For red (or rosé): Aleatico, Cesanese Comune, Greco Nero, Lambrusco Maestri, Malvasia Nera, Merlot, Montepulciano, Uva di Troia. For white: Bombino Bianco, Malvasia di Candia, Mantonico or Montonico Bianco, Moscato Bianco, San Lunardo.

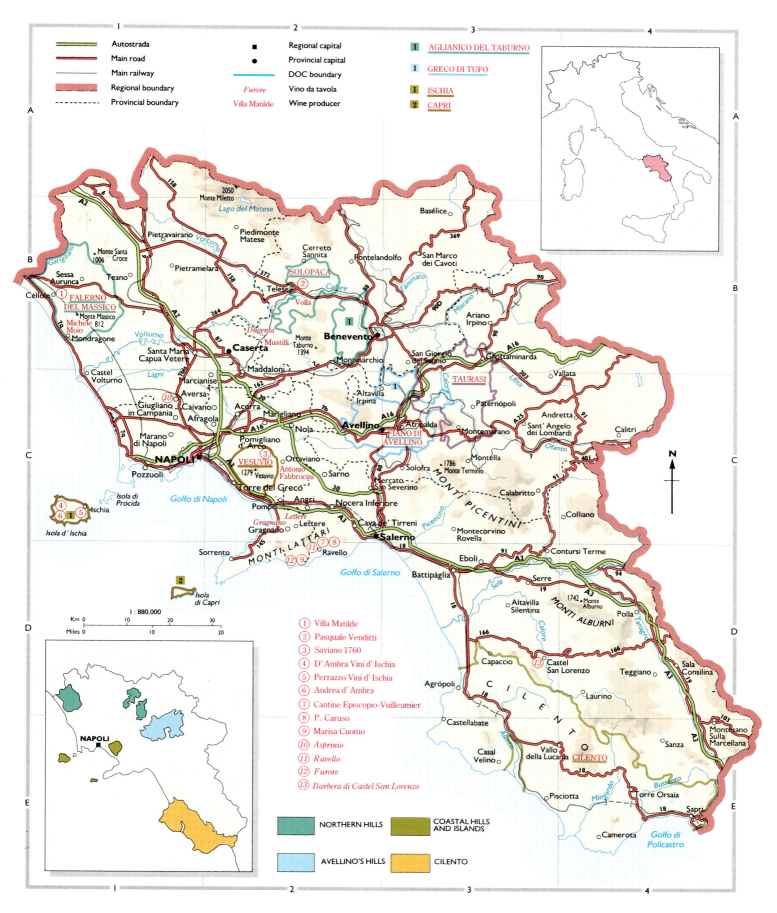

Autostrada
Main road
Main railway
Regional boundary
Provincial boundary

■ Regional capital
● Provincial capital
── DOC boundary
Furore Vino da tavola
Villa Matilde Wine producer

1 AGLIANICO DEL TABURNO
1 GRECO DI TUFO
1 ISCHIA
2 CAPRI

1 Villa Matilde
2 Pasquale Venditti
3 Saviano 1760
4 D' Ambra Vini d' Ischia
5 Perrazzo Vini d' Ischia
6 Andrea d' Ambra
7 Cantine Episcopio-Vuilleumier
8 P. Caruso
9 Marisa Cuomo
10 *Asprinio*
11 *Ravello*
12 *Furore*
13 *Barbera di Castel San Lorenzo*

1 : 880,000

Km 0   10   20   30
Miles 0   10   20

NAPOLI

NORTHERN HILLS
COASTAL HILLS AND ISLANDS
AVELLINO'S HILLS
CILENTO

Campania's Wine Zones

Campania packs uncommon productivity into a compact space between the cool heights of the Apennines and the sun-drenched Tyrrhenian coast, whose 460 kilometres include the islands of Ischia and Capri. From the hillsides beyond Naples' urban sprawl come lavish supplies of vegetables, fruit, and cereals, and wine from its once prized vineyards is often just another commodity. More than half of the region's area consists of luxuriant hills from 100-500 metres above sea level carved in irregular patterns by the Volturno and Calore rivers draining the Campano Apennines to the northeast and the Sele draining the Cilento range to the southeast. The masses of Vesuvius and the Lattari mountains between Sorrento and Salerno influence often bizarre changes in weather around the Bay of Naples and the central interior. Where contours are rugged, hillsides were often terraced in the past, though most modern vineyards are laid out on gradual slopes. The climate is highly variable, ranging from hot and dry near the sea to cooler and damper as the height of the terrain increases in the interior. Drought can be a factor along the coast, but most hilly zones have ample precipitation, sometimes suffering from excessive rain and hail.

The northern hills

The high vineyards of Benevento's Sannite and Taburno ranges consist largely of clay mixed with volcanic residue and limestone, though the Calore river has washed rich alluvial soil into the valley around Solopaca, where vineyards make light whites from Trebbiano and medium-weight reds from Sangiovese. The high Taburno zone is cooled by fresh breezes, with ample rainfall even in summer, so the Aglianico there has potential similar to Avellino's Taurasi. The volcanic slopes of the Falerno del Massico zone in the Aurunci mountains have warm, dry conditions where Aglianico develops good body but less bouquet than in higher vineyards, though Falanghina can show unusual depth for a white.

Irpinia, Avellino's hills

The high vineyards of Avellino's wooded Irpinia hills lie north and east of the city in soil of volcanic origin. Greco di Tufo has compact tufaceous earth of calcareous clay mixed with sand, though the classical vineyards of Fiano and Taurasi have looser soil with more limestone. The Chiusano massif with its peak at the 1,422-metre Monte Tuoro influences weather in the Taurasi zone, where most vineyards are on slopes along the Calore river valley. The best vineyards of all three DOCs lie between 400-700 metres where the cool conditions favour slow ripening. Sharp variations in day-night temperatures contribute to full aromas in white wines and rich, complex bouquet in Taurasi. Greco grapes are usually harvested in late September, followed by Fiano, and finally Aglianico, which has been picked as late as December in the snow.

The coastal hills and islands

The northern coasts of the Bay of Naples are made up of black volcanic earth in the DOC zones of Ischia and Vesuvio. Hot, dry conditions around the Bay favour robust reds, but growers cater to the local preference for light whites. By contrast the Ittari range of the Sorrentine peninsula (re-emerging at Capri) consists of calcareous rock which had to be terraced to support vines. High points above Sorrento and Amalfi can produce well-scented wines of any colour, as evident in certain bottlings of Ravello and the few remaining reds of Gragnano and Lettere.

Cilento

Rocky hillsides make viticulture a challenge, though the calcareous soil and mild interior climate favour robust reds and hearty rosés from Aglianico and Primitivo.

Below: tobacco is an important crop at Solopaca in Benevento province.

Above: bringing in the harvest in Solopaca.
Left: brush covers slopes of the Massico massif near to where the Romans kept vineyards for Falernian.

Wines of the north: Falerno, Solopaca, and Taburno

Northern Campania is dominated by the Apennines and their foothills, running from the borders with Latium and Molise southeast past Benevento above the broad valleys of the Volturno river and its tributary the Calore. The previously unheralded Solopaca has attracted some attention in Italy, as has the still limited output of Falerno del Massico. Aglianico del Taburno, or simply Taburno, is so far a little known quantity, though the promise is there.

Falerno del Massico (1989)

Falernian has been revived in its original zone in coastal hills near the Latium border in three modern wines that probably bear little resemblance to the Roman favourite. The *rosso*, based on Aglianico, has shown class from certain producers as a full-bodied wine that benefits from a few years of ageing. The *bianco*, from the intriguing Falanghina, holds similar promise. Primitivo in one of its rare appearances outside Apulia shows power from Michele Moio.

Zone: The slopes of Monte Massico and surrounding hills between the communes of Mondragone and Sessa Aurunca and including three others in Caserta province.
Bianco Dry white. Grape: Falanghina. Yld 70/100, Alc 11, Acd 0.5.
Rosso Dry red, also riserva or vecchio. Grapes: Aglianico 60-80%, Piedirosso 20-40%; Primitivo/Barbera up to 20%. Yld 70/100, Alc 12.5, Acd 0.6, Ag 1 yr; riserva or vecchio 2 yrs (1 in wood).

Primitivo Dry to slightly sweet red, also riserva or vecchio. Grapes: Primitivo; Aglianico/Piedirosso/Barbera up to 15%. Yld 70/100, Alc 13, Acd 0.6, Ag 1 yr; riserva or vecchio 2 yrs (1 in wood).

Solopaca (1974)

Though wine has been made for centuries in this fertile valley in the shadow of Monte Alto Rotondo, it was rarely noted for its class. Nor does modern reliance on the overworked Trebbiano and Sangiovese raise hopes for great things in the future. Yet a few producers – Venditti and Volla first among them – make wines pleasant enough to have attracted attention beyond Campania.

Zone: The Calore river valley between the Taburno and Sannite ranges in the commune of Solopaca and ten others in Benevento province.
Bianco Dry white. Grapes: Trebbiano Toscano 50-70% and Malvasia di Candia 20-40%; Malvasia Toscana/Coda di Volpe/other whites up to 10%. Yld 105/150, Alc 12, Acd 0.45.
Rosso Dry red. Grapes: Sangiovese 45-60%, Piedirosso 20-25%, Aglianico 10-20%; Sciascinoso/other reds up to 10%. Yld 91/130, Alc 11.5, Acd 0.45.

Aglianico del Taburno or Taburno (1987)

The wooded hills to the east of Monte Alto Rotondo in the Taburno massif near Benevento seem to offer the right conditions for Aglianico, though little evidence is available in bottle.

Zone: Slopes of the Taburno range south of the Calore river in the communes of Monte Taburno, Torrecuso, and ten others in Benevento province.
Rosso Dry red, also riserva. Grapes: Aglianico; Piedirosso/Sciascinoso/Sangiovese up to 15%. Yld 91/130, Alc 11.5, Acd 0.5, Ag 1 yr; riserva 3 yrs.
Rosato Dry rosé. Grapes: As rosso. Yld 91/130, Alc 11.5, Acd 0.5, Ag 5 mths.

Other wines of note

Most unclassified wine from the northern hills is drunk locally or sold in bulk. Reds, whether thick and heavy or light and thin, tend to be rustic, though bottles from producers of the calibre of Mustilli, Venditti, and Villa Matilde rise above the norm while offering good value. Whites and rosés, if not heavy and oxidized, may well be nondescript and *frizzante*.

ESTATES/GROWERS

Michele Moio, Mondragone (CE). Heavyweight Primitivo will come under Falerno del Massico DOC.
Mustilli, Sant'Agata dei Goti (BN). Family operation with good vdt from typical Campania varieties under the Santa Croce label. White Falanghina stands high beside Aglianico and Greco.
Pasquale Venditti, Castelvenere (BN). Improving quality in Solopaca DOC and red and white vdt.
Villa Matilde, Cellole (CE). Good Falerno del Massico DOC and vdt.
Volla, Solopaca (BN). Maria Teresa Perlingieri, with admirable devotion, produces fine Solopaca Rosso DOC from 8 ha of vines.

WINE HOUSES/MERCHANTS

Ocone, Ponte (BN). Solopaca DOC and vdt.

COOPERATIVES

La Guardiense, Guardia Sanframondi (BN). Large producer of Solopaca DOC, vdt and *spumante* from growers with nearly 1,500 ha of vines.
CS di Solopaca, Solopaca (BN). Solopaca DOC and vdt of Sannio.

Wines of Avellino: Fiano, Greco, and Taurasi

The Romans enjoyed the wines of Avellino (Abellinum) on the Appian Way, though they probably found the hills of Hirpinia (from the Sabine "hirpus" meaning wolf) too wild for practical viticulture. Much later a thriving wine industry developed in what is known in Italy as Irpinia, only to be devastated by phylloxera in the 1920s and 1930s and crippled by the earthquakes of 1980. If Irpinia is the most prestigious wine area of Campania – or indeed of the Mezzogiorno – credit is due to the Mastroberardino family and their dogged faith in the antique vines of Fiano, Greco, and Aglianico. Today Fiano di Avellino and Greco di Tufo are thoroughly contemporary dry white wines, but with character that distinguishes them from the commoners that abound elsewhere. Taurasi has been called "the Barolo of the south", and it does have traits in common with Piedmont's regal red. Irpinia's climate, terrain, and vegetation bear striking resemblances to those of the Langhe hills around Alba, where Nebbiolo ripens with equal stubborness in the late autumn mists. Taurasi and Barolo age with similar grace, but in the end they stand apart from each other with patrician aloofness.

Fiano di Avellino (1978)

Some experts regard this as the most distinguished dry white of Italy's south, noting subtle hints of pear and spices in its delicate aroma and toasted hazelnuts in its lingering flavour. Fiano from Mastroberardino has been known to age well for 3-6 years or more, gaining depth and complexity that belie the myth that Italian whites are by nature fragile; their Vignadora from Montefalcione stands out from its few competitors. The classical Fiano vineyards lie around the village of Lapio northeast of Avellino. Wine from there may be referred to as Fiano di Lapio. The Roman name "Apianum" may also be used on labels.

Zone: Hills completely surrounding Avellino and including 25 other communes in its province. Dry white. Grapes: Fiano; Greco/Coda di Volpe/Trebbiano Toscano up to 15%. Yld 70/100, Alc 11.5, Acd 0.5.

Greco di Tufo (1970)

A rival to Fiano in class, Greco is preferred by some for purer sensations of fruit and a crisper flavour that finishes with a suggestion of toasted almonds. It can age nearly as well as Fiano, though it may be most impressive within two or three years as an accompaniment to fish. The vine, a clone of the Greco introduced by the Greeks, thrives in the tufaceous volcanic soil around the hillside villages of Tufo, Santa Paolina, Montefusco, and Chianche. In a decidedly uncompetitive field, Greco di Tufo leads all Campania DOCs in volume with 4,000 hl a year, nearly all from Mastroberardino, whose single vineyard Vignadangelo is the classic example. A *spumante* version is occasionally seen locally.

Zone: Hills due north of Avellino surrounding the village of Tufo and including seven other communes in the province. Dry white, also spumante. Grapes: Greco di Tufo; Coda di Volpe up to 15%. Yld 70/100, Alc 11.5, Acd 0.5.

Taurasi (1970)

One of Italy's most admired red wines, Taurasi has a noted capacity for ageing due to its powerful structure and ample tannin and extract that derive from extremely late ripening Aglianico grapes. A wine of full ruby colour when young, with age it takes on hints of mahogany while developing remarkable nuance in bouquet and depth of flavour. The legend is Mastroberardino's 1968 *riserva*, which is still going strong, though some recent vintages have shown attractive roundness and balance within four years of the harvest. Mastroberardino's single vineyard Radici made its debut in 1986 with what seemed to be an added dimension in bouquet. Though Piedirosso,

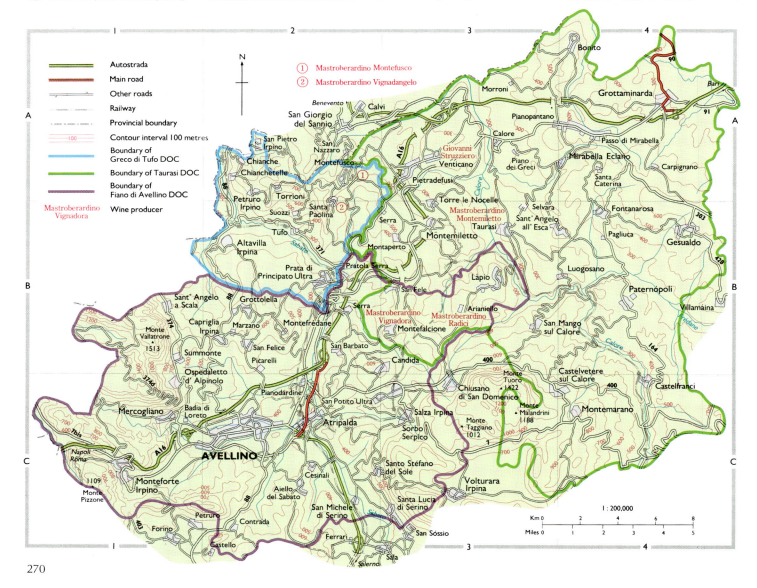

Sangiovese, and Barbera may be included in the blend, the leading winemakers stick to pure Aglianico, aged for a year or two in large Slavonian oak casks before bottling.

Zone: Hills surrounding the village of Taurasi northeast of Avellino and taking in 16 other communes in its province. Dry red, also riserva. Grapes: Aglianico; Piedirosso/Sangiovese/Barbera up to 30%. Yld 77/110, Alc 12, Acd 0.6, Ag 3 yrs (1 in wood); riserva 4 yrs (1 in wood).

Other wines of note

Mastroberardino uses Aglianico for its Lacrimarosa rosé, as well as the recent Plinius, a well structured white which includes some Coda di Volpe grapes. Most other wines of Irpinia are sold locally in large bottles or demijohns.

ESTATES/GROWERS

Mastroberardino, Atripalda (AV). The south's most admired producer traces a family tradition dating back to the early 1700s, though the firm was founded in 1878. Brothers Antonio (Tonino) and Walter Mastroberardino and sons Carlo and Paolo continue to outclass their limited competition with Fiano, Greco, and Taurasi. They have given new life to Vesuvio Lacryma Christi DOC, while devising the refined vdt Lacrimarosa and Plinius. The operation has a neat division of labour: Tonino winemaker, Walter sales manager, Paolo vineyard operations, Carlo international marketing. Their average output of 900,000 bottles of DOC is about half of Campania's classified production, but since not all declared wine is sold as such, Mastroberardino has a near monopoly of the region's premium market.

Cellars were renovated and expanded after being destroyed in the earthquakes of 1980. The tragedy, which prompted them to install ultramodern equipment, signalled a shift in the philosophy and style behind their white Fiano and Greco, which until 1982 were aged in wood, but are now made in temperature-controlled stainless steel tanks. Formerly the wine house purchased all grapes, but 12 years ago it formed an agricultural branch and acquired about 100 ha of land in the hills north and east of Avellino. Vineyards have been planted on plots abandoned after phylloxera but known to have been superior a half century ago. Properties include the 10-ha Vignadora at Montefalcione for Fiano; the 40-ha Vignadangelo at Santa Paolina and 8 ha at Montefusco for Greco; a 30-ha estate near Lapio, which comprises the Radici plot for Taurasi and 13 ha at Montemiletto, mainly for Aglianico. Another 150 ha remain under contract with local growers. Vines proliferate in the fertile soil, so pruning and thinning are aimed at maintaining yields of Greco and Aglianico to 35-40 hl/ha. The unfruitful Fiano rarely reaches 35 hl/ha. All wines are made at Atripalda, though estate bottling is planned.

Giovanni Struzziero, Venticano (AV). Emerging winemaker with sometimes impressive Fiano, Greco, and above all Taurasi DOC.

Vadiaperti, Montefredane (AV). Fiano di Avellino DOC.

Wines of the coastal hills and islands

"I only wish the wines of Naples could really compare in quality with the landscape", wrote Charles G. Bode in *Wines of Italy* in 1956. Since both have deteriorated, he might find them more compatible today. A few may be better now than they were then, but exceptions can hardly excuse most examples of what passes for *vino* in Naples and environs. Two of the three DOCs – Ischia and Vesuvio, but by no means Capri – provide an occasional taste of what might have been were winemaking as serious an endeavour as it had been in times long past. Pleasant surprises can pop up among table wines from the Sorrentine and Amalfi hills, whose terraced vineyards are among Italy's most picturesque. But like that most Neapolitan of wines, the fizzy white Asprinio from the flatlands to the north around Aversa, their futures are increasingly in doubt.

Ischia (1966)

The honour of becoming Italy's second DOC clearly didn't inspire Ischia's winemakers, whose output has decreased in recent years. The small amount of red can be soothingly tasty, the regular white is a decent fish wine, and the *bianco superiore* could be just what the name suggests. But the top producer, D'Ambra, prefers to put its best efforts into table wines.

Zone: Volcanic slopes on the island of Ischia in the communes of Barano, Casamicciola Terme, Forio, Lacco Ameno, and Serrara Fontana in Napoli province.
Bianco Dry white. Grapes: Forastera 65%, Biancolella 20%, other whites 15%. Yld 72/100, Alc 11, Acd 0.5-0.6.
Bianco superiore Dry white. Grapes: Forastera 50%, Biancolella 40%, San Lunardo 10%. Yld 56/80, Alc 12, Acd 0.45-0.55.
Rosso Dry red. Grapes: Guarnaccia 50%, Piedirosso (Per'e Palummo) 40%, Barbera 10%. Yld 72/100, Alc 11.5, Acd 0.5-0.65.

Vesuvio (1983)

Vines had reached enviable heights in the cindery soil of Vesuvius even before lava buried Pompeii in AD 79. Since ancient times its wines' fortunes have been as capricious as the volcano's eruptions. Lacryma Christi became one of Italy's most imitated wines. But the imitators rarely agreed on what they were imitating so "Christ's Tears" became a loosely interpreted joke. DOC has begun to put things back in order, thanks to the leadership of Mastroberardino, whose mellow red and fine-tuned white come from vineyards in the best part of the zone around the town of Boscotrecase. Variations on the DOC theme are confusingly intricate. Vesuvio applies to the basic white, rosé, and red, while Lacryma Christi del Vesuvio (abbreviated LCV below) applies to four versions (plus three sparkling).

Zone: The lower slopes of the mountain in 15 communes in Napoli province.
Rosso Dry red. Grapes: Piedirosso; Sciascinoso up to 50%, Aglianico up to 20%. Yld 70/100, Alc 10.5, Acd 0.5.
LCV rosso Dry red, also spumante. Grapes: As rosso. Yld 65/100, Alc 12, Acd 0.5.
Rosato Dry rosé. Grapes: As rosso. Yld 70/100, Alc 10.5, Acd 0.5.
LCV rosato Dry rosé, also spumante. Grapes: As rosso. Yld 65/100, Alc 12, Acd 0.5.
Bianco Dry white. Grapes: Verdeca; Coda di Volpe up to 65%, Falanghina/Greco up to 20%. Yld 70/100, Alc 11, Acd 0.45.
LCV bianco Dry white, also spumante. Grapes: As bianco. Yld 65/100, Alc 12, Acd 0.5.
LCV liquoroso Fortified white. Grapes: As bianco. Yld 65/100, Alc 12, Acd 0.5.

Capri (1977)

Capri's calcareous soil could produce wines of class, none more so than the white from Falanghina. But as hardly anybody on the prosperous island can spare the time or space to grow grapes any longer, a bottle of authentic Capri DOC is hard to come by.

Zone: The extremely limited vineyards on the island in Napoli province.
Bianco Dry white. Grapes: Falanghina with Greco up to 50%; Biancolella up to 20%. Yld 84/120, Alc 11, Acd 0.5.
Rosso Dry red. Grapes: Piedirosso; other varieties up to 20%. Yld 91/130, Alc 11.5, Acd 0.45.

Above: Leading winemaker Antonio Mastroberardino and son Carlo conduct a tasting beneath the gaze of their forebears at their Atripalda winery in Avellino province.

Other wines of note

Few wines produced beside Campania's sea have official credentials. If most such *vini da tavola* should be studiously avoided, there are a few which equal or surpass DOC standards. The best examples are in D'Ambra's unclassified range from Ischia: dry white Biancolella (from Tenuta Frassitelli) and Forastera; the red Per'e Palummo (from Vigneto Montecorvo); the champagne-method Kalimera (from Biancolella and Chardonnay); and the sweet Amber Drops. The Amalfi coast boasts Ravello's thriving red, white, and rosé, which can be nearly as charming as the views of the trellised vineyards stepping down the slopes on rocky terraces to the gulf of Salerno. The village of Furore also makes wines of some interest, though many vineyards of the Sorrentine peninsula have been abandoned or replaced by buildings. Perhaps the saddest victims are the red wines of Lettere and Gragnano, from hillside towns with the misfortune of lying on the Naples' side of the range, where urban development is most dreadful. Both wines had been proposed by growers as candidates for DOC, but only Lettere has persisted with its bid. Lettere, whether ruby, purple, or cherry pink, was invariably fizzy and easy to drink in its youth. Gragnano, purple and frothily medium-dry, seems rarer than ever, even on the hillsides where its remaining vineyards grow.

ESTATES/GROWERS

Andrea D'Ambra, Serrara Fontana, Ischia (NA). From a small vineyard on Ischia, oenologist Andrea D'Ambra makes the *champenoise* Kalimera in the D'Ambra Vini d'Ischia range.
Antonio Fabbrocini, Terzigno (NA). Lacryma Christi del Vesuvio DOC.
Antonio Pentangelo, Lettere (NA). Small production of Lettere vdt.

WINE HOUSES/MERCHANTS

Cantine Episcopio-Pasquale Vuilleumier, Ravello (SA). Good Ravello red, white, and rosé vdt under the Episcopio label.
P. Caruso, Ravello (SA). Pleasant Ravello red, white, and rosé vdt called Vino Gran Caruso.
Marisa Cuomo, Furore (SA). Divina Costiera vdt.
D'Ambra Vini d'Ischia, Forio d'Ischia (NA). After a lapse in quality and prestige, the late Mario D'Ambra injected new life into the island's top winery, which has been continued by the family's younger generation. Their thoroughly modern revival has brought new style to Ischia DOC and, even more notably, to vdt created by Andrea D'Ambra.
Perrazzo Vini d'Ischia, Ischia Porto (NA). Ischia DOC and vdt.
Saviano 1760, Ottaviano (NA). Vesuvio DOC and vdt, including a bit of Gragnano.

Wines of Cilento

Southeast of Salerno, across the alluvial plain of the Sele river from Eboli, lies Cilento, a promontory of low mountains whose savage beauty remains unchanged from when the Greeks built their colony of Paestum on the edge of it. Vines have to struggle on these rocky hillsides, though wines from Aglianico and Primitivo can show more breadth and depth than any others south of Avellino.

Cilento (1989)

Approval has been granted for four types of wine, including a red from Aglianico in an area that was historically part of Lucania or Basilicata.

Zone: A vast tract of hills along Campania's southern coast between Agropoli and the border of Basilicata on the Gulf of Policastro and covering 60 communes in Salerno province.
Aglianico Dry red. Grapes: Aglianico; other reds up to 15%. Yld 70/100, Alc 12, Acd 0.6 Ag 1 yr.
Rosso Dry red. Grapes: Aglianico 60–75%, Piedirosso/Primitivo 15–20%, Barbera 10–20%; other reds up to 10%. Yld 70/100, Alc 11.5, Acd 0.6.
Rosato Dry rosé. Grapes: Sangiovese 70–80%, Aglianico 10–15%, Primitivo/Piedirosso 10–15%. Yld 50/100, Alc 11, Acd 0.6.

Bianco Dry white. Grapes: Fiano 60–65%, Trebbiano Toscano 20–30%, Greco Bianco/Malvasia Bianca 10–15%; other whites up to 10%.

COOPERATIVES

CS del Cilento, Rutino (SA). Cilento DOC.

Travel Information

Above: the ancient hillside town of Ravello is celebrated for its views and its wines from surrounding vineyards.

Right: sheep grazing in the Lattari hills behind Amalfi.

Left: the region's green and flourishing plains have produced an abundance of fruit, vegetables, and grains since Roman times.

RESTAURANTS/HOTELS

Trattoria Da Gemma, 84011 Amalfi (SA). Tel (089)871345. Family trattoria with tasty fish dishes, good wines.
Trattoria Martella, Via Chiesa Conservatorio 10, 83100 Avellino. Tel (0825)31117. Genuine mountain cooking with fine Avellino wines.
La Capannina, 80073 Capri (NA). Tel (081)8370732. Fine food with a sound choice of local and national wines, warm hospitality.
Le Ginestre, Via Vesuvio 7, 80056 Ercolano (NA). Tel (081)7395206. Country cooking with wines of Vesuvio, Gragnano, Lettere.
Giardini Eden, 80070 Ischia Ponte (NA). Tel. (081)993909. Peaceful setting for fish and vegetable specialities with wines of Ischia.
Dante's Tavern, 82016 Montesarchio (BN). Tel (0824)834360. Good local food and wines with an unexpected French accent.
Hotel Caruso Belvedere, 84010 Ravello (SA). Tel (089)857111. Tasty food in a gorgeous setting with Gran Caruso house wines.

Hotel Palumbo, 84010 Ravello (SA). Tel (089)857244. Luxury hotel with magnificent views, good food and Episcopio house wines.
Don Alfonso 1890, 80064 Sant'Agata sui Due Golfi, Massa Lubrense (NA). Tel (081)8780026. Campania's top-rated restaurant offers choice seafood and intelligently selected wines and spirits in an unforgettable setting.
La Favorita-o'Parrucchiano, Corso Italia 71, 80067 Sorrento (NA). Tel (081)8781321. Vast array of regional dishes and wines served on the veranda.

PLACES OF INTEREST

Campania has many attractions for tourists: history, art, music, seaside resorts, and some of Italy's most dramatic scenery. But if wine is the subject, students would be better off elsewhere – with the possible exception of a scholarly visit to the Mastroberardino winery at Atripalda. Still, even if nobody goes to Capri or Amalfi to study the vineyards, there is nothing to stop them from enjoying the wines while marvelling over the views. The following are things to see in or near the wine zones:
Ischia. The island is the most wine conscious of Campania's resorts. The vineyards of towering Monte Epomeo are uniquely picturesque.
Massico. Around this mountain near Mondragone in northern Campania grew the vines for the Roman Falernian, today revived as the DOC Falerno del Massico.
Paestum. On the edge of the Cilento massif in the southeast stand the largely intact Greek temples of Paestum.
Ravello. The precariously terraced vineyards around this fairytale hilltown make the most persuasive wines of the Amalfi coast.
Vesuvius, Pompeii, and Herculanum. The importance of wine to the ancients can be seen in the recently discovered cellar where the art of winemaking had reached remarkably sophisticated levels more than 2,000 years ago. The enormous painting devoted to the cult of Dionysus in Pompeii's Villa dei Misteri is equally revealing.

Basilicata

Capital: Potenza.
Provinces: Matera (MT), Potenza (PZ).
Area: 9,992 square kilometres (fourteenth).
Population: 619,000 (eighteenth).

Above: the Matera plain in Basilicata rises towards forested hills.

Basilicata has been known for its wines since the sixth or seventh century BC when the Greeks planted what came to be known as Aglianico and other vines. But grape growing is still often at the subsistence level – like the production of olive oil and fruit, and grazing of livestock – in what has been historically one of Italy's poorest regions. The Romans called the region Lucania; the name Basilicata was bestowed later by the Byzantines. The names were – and are – used alternately, though Basilicata became official in 1932.

Until not long ago Basilicata was little more than a vinous adjunct of Apulia, supplying its neighbour with discreet quantities of Aglianico and other wines for blending. Enterprising Apulians might have been slow to admit it, but Aglianico from the volcanic heights of Monte Vulture was more often than not the best of the wines they bottled as their own. Then in 1971 Aglianico del Vulture won a DOC and almost reluctantly producers in the zone began bottling and selling it. Over the years it has won less acclaim than it deserves, but at least its makers have the satisfaction of knowing that Aglianico del Vulture can reach heights to which Apulian reds can only aspire.

Basilicata still has only one DOC, the least of any region, and with a potential million bottles a year Aglianico del Vulture accounts for less than two percent of the region's wine. It may be that these uplands are suited to more and greater things, but growers have a becoming modesty that may be due to a long heritage of hardship, of coaxing crops from the desolate heights. It is not rare for growers to pick grapes in November, since Aglianico ripens late. If their reward is hard won praise for what is one of Italy's finest red wines, it won't go to their heads.

The region's vineyards are divided in patterns that seem practically medieval. Even in the Vulture zone the 1,192 registered DOC plots average just over a hectare each. This fragmentation and the task of working vines by hand on slopes so steep that some are accessible only by foot or with mules have led to a steady decline in production from high vineyards. Some growers have gone north to find work; others have retired without successors. Two decades ago the dirt road from Rionero to Ripacandida wound through a sloping garden of vines, planted most intensely on the sheer terrain of San Savino, which still is responsible for the zone's best wine. Today the buckling asphalt bisects an untidy patchwork of brush which each year claims more vines.

Meanwhile, new vineyards are being planted on the gentler inclines around Venosa, where only Aglianico from exceptional plots can approach the finesse of wines from Rionero and Barile. So far the resulting decline in grape quality has been compensated by improved oenology. But as the zone's leading winemaker Donato D'Angelo cautions, that process can't go on much longer. So the wine houses, which have always depended on close relations with growers, may have to acquire their own vineyards. That break with tradition would not be such a challenge if vineyard specialists weren't a dying breed. Aglianico del Vulture deserves a better fate, but unless current trends can be reversed, it seems destined to remain a solitary aristocrat.

Basilicata's Vineyards

Uniquely among the southern regions Basilicata has no grape varieties of its own, but Aglianico is so firmly entrenched on the slopes of Monte Vulture that it has earned native status. Though Campania shares this noble vine, it probably arrived in Basilicata first, brought by the Greeks between the seventh and sixth centuries BC.

In the Vulture zone, as in most of Basilicata, vines are trained vertically using variations of Guyot. On the steep slopes around Rionero and Barile new growth is normally supported by cane poles with the clusters kept below the first wire to benefit from the heat reflecting off the soil. Though patterns vary, rows are usually about a metre apart and vines may be spaced as little as half a metre from each other, resulting in as many as 20,000 per hectare – a density rarely equalled anywhere. On the easier slopes around Venosa, vines are trained higher and spacing is wider to permit machine cultivation.

In the warmer flatlands around Metaponto, training is often in *alberello* or *tendone* as in neighbouring Apulia. Basilicata's average wine

yields are 28 hectolitres per hectare, Italy's lowest, though this may be because many registered vineyards are no longer in use.

Alongside Aglianico and the larger but less prized Aglianicone are other varieties, such as dark and light Malvasia that rate being described as "di Basilicata". Asprinio is as admired here as in its native Campania. The rest is a mix of southern vines and a curious array of newcomers from the north and abroad, a few of which are promising. Varieties recommended or approved in Basilicata also include:

For red (or rosé): Aleatico, Bombino Nero, Ciliegiolo, Malvasia Nera di Basilicata, Montepulciano, Primitivo, Sangiovese.

For white: Asprinio, Bombino Bianco, Chardonnay, Fiano, Malvasia Bianca di Basilicata, Moscato Bianco, Pinot Grigio, Trebbiano Toscano.

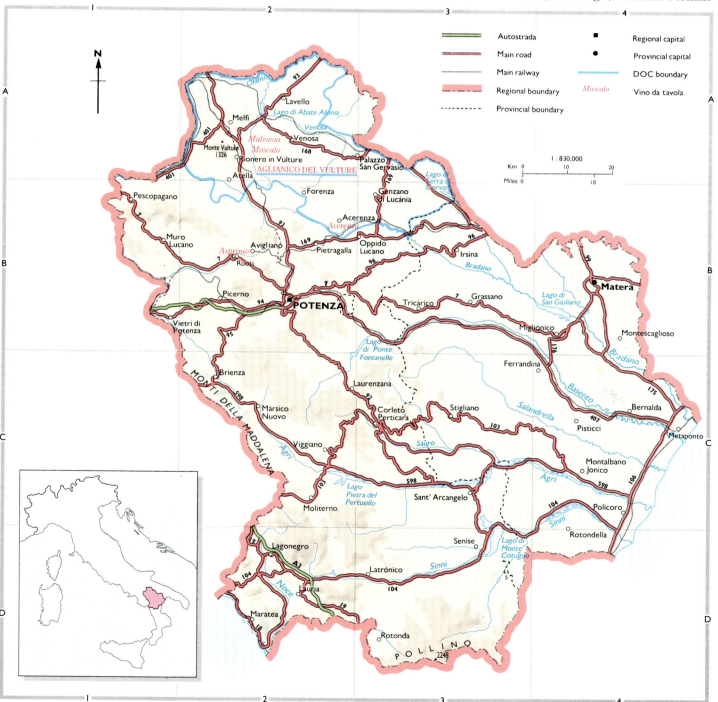

Basilicata's Wine Zones

Above: Aglianico vines in Vulture are planted close together and supported by canes.

Basilicata is a sprawling upland enclosed by Apulia, Campania, and Calabria at the heart of the southern peninsula with only a short stretch of coast along the Ionian Sea and a precipitous outlet on the Tyrrhenian. The region is so dominated by the Lucanian Apennines and their barren plateaux that only eight percent qualifies as plains: the valleys and reclaimed marshland along the Ionian. The Aglianico del Vulture zone covers high ground in the extreme north of the region. Most other vineyards lie towards Matera along river valleys and in seaside plains around Metaponto. Climate varies to extremes. The Apennines block warm Tyrrhenian currents from the west, but the uplands are exposed to winds that blow in from the Balkans across the Adriatic Sea and Apulia. Potenza, at 800 metres, is often the coldest Italian city – winter and summer. Rainfall is heavy in the mountains, where snow is normal from December to March. The hills around Matera are milder and drier. The Ionian coast, exposed to North African currents, is arid and hot.

Monte Vulture

The zone has two distinct geological areas, one on the steep eastern side of the volcano and the other on the high plains around Venosa reaching to Apulia's border. The slopes of Monte Vulture were derived from lava which reached depths of four metres in places. The powdery dark brown soil on a tufaceous base is rich in potassium. To the east the clay is often too heavy for vines, though some stretches close to Venosa are rich in calcium and nitrogen. The climate is among the most severe of any Italian DOC zone, due to average heights of about 600 metres on Monte Vulture and about 500 metres on the Venosa plateau. Winters can be cold and it is often damp in the spring. A period of hot, dry weather is usually broken by rain, which can be useful in late summer but harmful if it falls heavily before or during the late October harvest of Aglianico.

Matera and the Ionian plains

Most vineyards are planted along the Bradano, Basento, Agri, and Sinni river valleys and in the reclaimed marshland around Metaponto. Climate ranges from moderate in the hills above 100 metres to hot in the plains, with more rain at higher altitudes. Red wines from Aglianico and Montepulciano can be robust but rarely refined, while whites from Malvasia and Trebbiano are usually light and lacking character.

Wines of Basilicata

Aglianico del Vulture (1971)

Though basically dry in both young and aged versions, Aglianico may be *amabile*, or *spumante* which is also usually sweet. The dry wine is typically hard and closed in its first year or two, with a hint of blackberry in colour and flavour. With age it turns more ruby and garnet as it mellows and expands in bouquet. The *vecchio* and *riserva* from certain vintages can age well for 7-10 years, sometimes much more. Fratelli D'Angelo stands out among several commendable producers.

Of the three prime vineyard areas, San Savino, between Rionero and Ripacandida, often produces the most elegant Aglianico. Though dense plantings were extensive in the past, they now cover no more than 30 ha, lying between 560-670 m in two sectors: La Mezzana, below the road, and Piano dell'Altare above. The second area lies east of Barile in two nearly adjacent sectors: Gorizza, of about 15 ha, and Macarico, somewhat larger. Vineyards in small plots interspersed with olives lie on slopes between 500-600 m generally exposed to the southeast. Wines can rival those of San Savino, often with a shade more alcohol. The third area lies southeast of Venosa on the plateau at Masseria Sant'Angelo, formerly a large estate now divided between growers. The rise known as Serra Dolente, at about 430 m, produces Aglianico of body, structure, and full flavour prized in blends. East of Venosa and Masseria Sant'Angelo is the zone's heaviest concentration of vines, though wines from these often irrigated vineyards are sold mainly in bulk in Apulia and Campania.

Zone: Slopes of Monte Vulture, notably the communes of Rionero in Vulture and Barile, as well as on the high plateau to the east around Venosa. The large zone also takes in 12 other communes in Potenza province. Dry red, also vecchio and riserva. Grape: Aglianico. Yld 70/100, Alc 11.5; vecchio and riserva 12.5, Acd 0.6, Ag 1 yr; vecchio 3 yrs (2 in wood), riserva 5 yrs (2 in wood).
Amabile Sweet red. Yld 70/100, Alc 11.5 (res sugar max 10%), Acd 0.6, Ag 1 yr.
Spumante Sparkling red, usually sweet. Yld 70/100, Alc 11.5, Acd 0.6.

Other wines of note

Aglianico doesn't stand entirely alone in Basilicata. The Vulture area produces remarkably fragrant Moscato and Malvasia, which are usually sweet and bubbly but show enough personality to be candidates for *Vini tipici*, if not DOC. Production of the once prized Moscato from the town of Ginestra is sadly in decline. Fizzy white Asprinio is a speciality of Ruoti near the border with Campania, though that is also becoming rarer. Down towards the Ionian coast in the small part of Basilicata that qualifies as flat, decent table wines are made from Aglianico, Sangiovese, Montepulciano, and varieties from adjacent Apulia.

ESTATES/GROWERS

Donato Botte, Barile (PZ). Aglianico DOC and Moscato.
Giuseppe Botte, Barile (PZ). Aglianico DOC.
Fattoria La Vigna-Carbone, Melfi (PZ). Aglianico DOC.

WINE HOUSES/MERCHANTS

Fratelli D'Angelo, Rionero in Vulture (PZ). Brothers Donato and Lucio D'Angelo have transformed their family winery into the undisputed leader in Basilicata, with Aglianico that ranks with the finest reds of southern Italy. Current production ranges from 13,000-15,000 cases of Aglianico DOC a year, plus quantities of sparkling Moscato and Malvasia. Donato D'Angelo, a graduate of the wine school at Conegliano (Veneto), experiments tirelessly with the aim of raising Aglianico to new levels. He succeeded with Canneto, a selection of Aglianico from 1985, 1987, and 1988 aged in small barrels. This vdt showed such impressive harmony and depth that production may exceed 20,000 bottles from exceptional years. The family owns no vineyards but selects from growers in the best areas around Rionero and Barile and the Sant'Angelo area of Venosa. Donato D'Angelo is convinced that Moscato also has potential for greater recognition due to its exceptional aromatic qualities.
Armando Martino, Rionero in Vulture (PZ). Aglianico DOC, Malvasia and Moscato *spumanti*.
Fratelli Napolitano, Rionero in Vulture (PZ). Aglianico DOC, Malvasia, Moscato, and Aleatico.
Paternoster, Barile (PZ). Sound quality in Aglianico DOC, Malvasia, Moscato, and *spumante*.
Francesco Sasso, Rionero in Vulture (PZ). Good Aglianico DOC and Malvasia.

COOPERATIVES

Consorzio Viticoltori Associati del Vulture, Barile (PZ). From a large network of growers, Aglianico DOC and other wines.
CS di Metapontino, Metaponto (MT). Metapontum and Montepulciano di Basilicata vdt.
Società Cooperativa Vinicola del Vulture, Rionero in Vulture (PZ). Aglianico DOC, *spumante* and vdt.
Riforma Fondiaria di Venosa, Venosa (PZ). Aglianico DOC, Malvasia and Moscato.

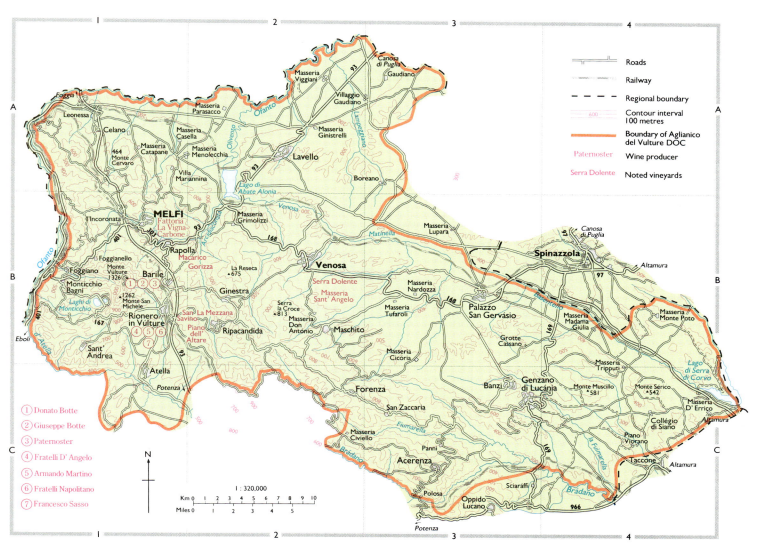

Key to map:
- Roads
- Railway
- Regional boundary
- 600 — Contour interval 100 metres
- Boundary of Aglianico del Vulture DOC
- **Paternoster** Wine producer
- *Serra Dolente* Noted vineyards

① Donato Botte
② Giuseppe Botte
③ Paternoster
④ Fratelli D' Angelo
⑤ Armando Martino
⑥ Fratelli Napolitano
⑦ Francesco Sasso

1 : 320,000

N

Travel Information

RESTAURANTS/HOTELS

Il Castagneto, 85025 Melfi (PZ). Tel (0972)24363. Homemade pasta, grilled meat and game with local wines.
Marziano, 85020 Monticchio Laghi (PZ). Tel (0972)731027. Good food and pretty views of the Monticchio lakes and forests.
La Pergola, 85020 Rionero in Vulture (PZ). Tel (0972)72119. Modest hotel and restaurant with tasty local dishes.

PLACES OF INTEREST

Monte Vulture provides a focal point for an off-the-beaten-track wine tour. The noted cellars of Aglianico are at Rionero and Barile on the southeastern slopes of the volcano. Nearby are the little lakes of Monticchio with an abbey set amidst the forest. Barile, where wine is still kept in caves hollowed out of the tufa centuries ago, holds a festival to celebrate Aglianico and roasted chestnuts in October.

Left: the countryside around the extinct volcano of Monte Vulture has sloping vineyards that produce the renowned red wine Aglianico del Vulture.

277

Calabria

Capital: Catanzaro.
Provinces: Catanzaro (CZ), Cosenza (CS), Reggio di Calabria (RC).
Area: 15,080 square kilometres (tenth).
Population: 2,130,000 (tenth).

Calabrian wine must have had an illustrious past, since so many winemakers have chosen to live in it. There do seem to have been some proud moments. One legend has it that vineyards along the Ionian coast inspired the Greeks to coin the term Oenotria (land of wine). Another recounts how Calabrian athletes toasted triumphs in early Olympiads with Krimisa, the alleged forerunner of Cirò. There are more, but by now most tales are as tarnished as Calabria's old-fashioned wines, which tend to turn brown even sooner than their neighbours'.

Still, legends are more soothing to listen to than are dire warnings about wine's future. Anyway, as traditionalists insist, if the customers come back, why change? The wonder of it is that the customers come back. The explanation seems to be that Calabria produces less wine than its inhabitants (and numerous summer tourists) consume, so its limited bottles (or more often demijohns) have a captive clientele. Wine plays a minor role in the economy, outperformed by olive oil, citrus fruits, grain, and those vegetables (tomatoes, peppers, eggplant) that give the diet its Mediterranean zeal.

The shame of it is that Calabria could do so much more with wine, for its handsome uplands have the temperate conditions that suit almost any kind of vine. As the only remaining wine of renown, Cirò takes a giant share of credit – or blame – for the status quo. Yet, despite the legends that surround it, Cirò has not always enjoyed supremacy. It isn't certain if it actually succeeded Krimisa or when, though the two do have points in common. Both originated along the Ionian between the Greek garden spots of Kroton and Sybaris (now the port of Crotone and the Sibari plain). Both are primarily red. Krimisa is also referred to as Cremisa which means crimson in Italian. Red Cirò derives from Gaglioppo, which may (or may not) have been there in Krimisa's time.

Below: the rugged landscape of Calabria is arid along the seacoasts and heavily forested in the mountains with little arable land.

Chroniclers from Roman times to the Risorgimento mentioned the region's wines, but most frequently from Tyrrhenian ports, which were more accessible than Ionian. A century ago Calabria supplied some of Italy's best red blending wines and Cirò was one of the better known. Centuries of abuse left the region miserably poor and corrupt, influencing emigrants to leave in droves for the Americas. Some remembered their region's wines and when they could afford to buy bottles from home, Cirò, with its catchy name, was an obvious choice. It was probably about then that the legends were recalled (or invented).

Cirò has no doubt influenced Calabria's preference for reds over whites by unparalleled margins of more than eight to one. It should be noted, though, that *rosso* here refers to various shades from the bright ruby of a good young Cirò or Savuto to the rose and cherry hues of the highland wines of Pollino and Donnici to the amber crimson shadings most of them acquire with a little bit of age.

Those few Calabrian producers who seem aware of the growing international demand for white wine have had second thoughts. In Cirò, new emphasis has been given to the DOC white from the admirable Greco Bianco. (A different Greco also makes an uncommon sweet wine around the southern town of Bianco, though in token quantities). Today most research here is with white varieties that take in an array of the international elite. But experiments are few and far between. So are those producers who call themselves progressives at the risk of being branded as spendthrifts or traitors to the comfortable cause of living in the past.

Calabria's Vineyards

The predominance of vines for red wine in Calabria is led by the mysterious Gaglioppo, which covers more than 7,000 hectares, or about a quarter of the vineyard area. Like other ancient varieties, Gaglioppo varies confusingly in typology and name. The blending partners of Greco Nero and Magliocco between them nearly equal Gaglioppo. Such outsiders as Sicily's Nerello duo and Sangiovese are also in wide use. The foremost white variety is Greco Bianco, though Trebbiano Toscano is also gaining.

Except in Cirò and certain coastal areas, vineyards were always part of the family farm, so plots are fragmented, averaging little more than a hectare each. By now most have been converted from mixed cropping to monoculture. The Greek inspired *alberello* (bush) training is still common, though vertical systems, sometimes localized, are also used. The trellised *tendone* has increased productivity in hot areas, including Cirò, though overall yields in Calabria's often steep vineyards are among Italy's lowest.

Aware that the domination of red varieties is out of step with market demands, Calabrian officials are experimenting with Chardonnay, Pinot Bianco, Riesling, Traminer Aromatico, and Sauvignon around Cosenza. Merlot and Cabernet also have shown promise. But the mainstays remain the following traditional varieties.

Gaglioppo. An antique vine, whether native or of Greek origin, is the chief variety of Cirò and most other reds. The name represents a confusing range of diverse types, however. Gaglioppo is often blended with other dark and white varieties in wines of pale hues, though certain clones can make rich, deeply coloured reds alone. Experts are studying a possible link with Aglianico, which it is called in places. In various forms it is known as Arvino, Lacrima Nera, Magliocco, and Mantonico Nero.

Greco Bianco. The Greco introduced by the Greeks may have been the progenitor of those vines known as Grechetto, Grecanico, etc., though parentage is uncertain. White Greco shows style here both in dry wines, such as Cirò Bianco, and sweet, exemplified by Greco di Bianco, though the name applies to different clones and possibly even unrelated vines.

Greco Nero. Despite the name, there is some dispute over whether its origins are Greek or Calabrian. Here it usually plays a supporting role with Gaglioppo, though it can make decent red wines on its own. Also

Above: vineyards on the Sila massif share the slopes with crops, forests, and pastures.

planted in Sardinia, Sicily, and Campania. Known locally as Marsigliana.

Lacrima Nera. *See* Gaglioppo.

Magliocco Canino. This dark variety often figures in blends with Gaglioppo, to which it seems to be related.

Mantonico or **Montonico Bianco**. The antique Mantonico or Montonico (Greek for prophetic) is grown around Bianco on the Ionian Sea, where it makes a sherry-like wine. An apparently unrelated vine of the same name is common around Cosenza. Some say Mantonico came from the Abruzzi, where it is now rare. Mantonico Nero is a synonym for Gaglioppo.

Other varieties

The tradition of sweet wines has long favoured Moscato varieties (mainly Bianco but also Zibibbo and even the red Moscato d'Amburgo), as well as various types of Malvasia. The Sicilian Nerello Mascalese and Cappuccio are the main varieties of Lamezia Rosso DOC. Reggio di Calabria's local red Pellaro is based on Alicante (Garnacha), which, curiously enough, is not authorized in the region. Other varieties recommended or approved Calabria include:

For red (or rosé): Barbera, Cabernet Franc, Cabernet Sauvignon, Calabrese, Castiglione, Malvasia Nera di Brindisi, Merlot, Nocera, Pecorello, Prunesta, Sangiovese.

For white: Chardonnay, Guardavalle, Guarnaccia Bianca, Incrocio Manzoni 6.0.13 (Riesling Pinot Bianco), Malvasia Bianca, Pinot Bianco, Riesling Italico, Riesling Renano, Sémillon, Traminer Aromatico.

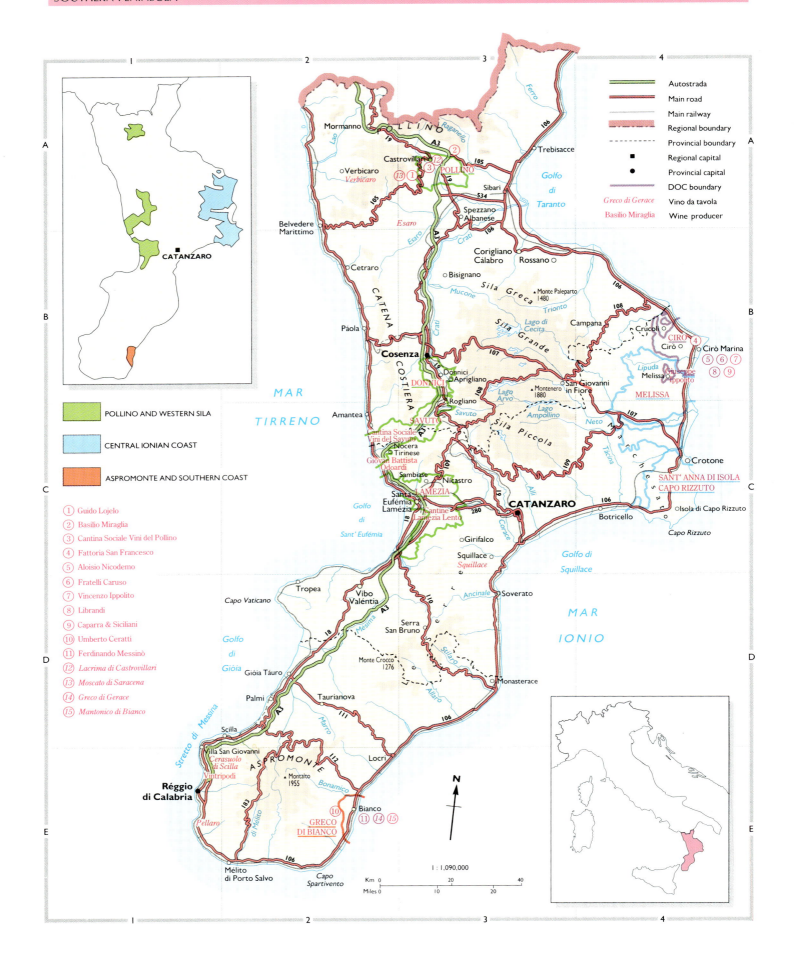

MAR
TIRRENO

POLLINO AND WESTERN SILA

CENTRAL IONIAN COAST

ASPROMONTE AND SOUTHERN COAST

1 Guido Lojelo
2 Basilio Miraglia
3 Cantina Sociale Vini del Pollino
4 Fattoria San Francesco
5 Aloisio Nicodemo
6 Fratelli Caruso
7 Vincenzo Ippolito
8 Librandi
9 Caparra & Siciliani
10 Umberto Ceratti
11 Ferdinando Messinò
12 Lacrima di Castrovillari
13 Moscato di Saracena
14 Greco di Gerace
15 Mantonico di Bianco

Autostrada
Main road
Main railway
Regional boundary
Provincial boundary
Regional capital
Provincial capital
DOC boundary
Greco di Gerace   Vino da tavola
Basilio Miraglia   Wine producer

CATANZARO

MAR
IONIO

1 : 1,090,000

Km 0   20   40
Miles 0   10   20

N

Calabria's Wine Zones

The southernmost point of the Italian peninsula, the toe of the boot, Calabria was historically cut off from Basilicata and the north by the Pollino range and from Sicily by the Straits of Messina. The Apennines dominate the landscape. With more than 90 percent covered by steep highlands and 742 kilometres of mostly rugged coasts on the Tyrrhenian and Ionian seas, the region is rather cramped for vineyard space. The mountains extend from the Pollino wall into the Tyrrhenian coastal chain, which is split off from the Sila massif in the centre by the Crati and Savuto river valleys. The range called Le Serre further south links the sprawling Sila with the hulk of Aspromonte at the toe of the boot. The only lowlands are near the coasts: the plains of Sibari, Sant'Eufemia, and Gioia Tauro, and the rolling Marchesato between Cirò and Catanzaro. The vineyards host a myriad of microclimates. Points along the Ionian coast in the direct line of the *maestrelle* winds from Africa are practically subtropical, whereas the heights of the Sila and Aspromonte are nearly alpine. High vineyards, which often get rain in summer, also face the risk of spring frosts. Even normally arid coastal areas may be relieved by summer storms caused by clashes of maritime and mountain currents.

Pollino, the Sila, and Lamezia

Pollino covers a sloping plateau on the southern face of the mountain range with loose, well-drained soil of clay mixed with marl and sandstone. Donnici and Savuto on the steep, often terraced western inclines of the Sila have similar soils. All three zones have sunny summers with sharp day-night temperature variations and rainy spells. Winters are cold and damp, often with snow. Pollino is warmed by currents from the Gulf of Taranto. Donnici has a fairly severe climate, as does the upper part of Savuto, though the lower valley benefits from the Tyrrhenian influence. Red wines, chiefly from Gaglioppo, are fragrant and fresh in these climes. Lamezia in the Sant'Eufemia plain has alluvial soil mixed with gravel and sand in maritime conditions: cool winters, rainy springs and hot, dry summers.

The central Ionian coast

Cirò lies east of the Sila in coastal hills webbed by ravines and gullies. Some slopes are terraced to prevent loose soil of clay mixed with sand and marl from sliding downhill. Adjacent Melissa is generally lower, extending into the rolling hills of the Marchesato. Sant'Anna di Isola Capo Rizzuto lies to the southeast of the Marchesato, partly in alluvial soil on a sand and gravel base. The area has cool, damp winters and hot to torrid summers with extended droughts, though Cirò's higher vineyards benefit from milder temperatures and occasional showers. Gaglioppo dominates here, though like Greco Bianco it is picked early to maintain acidity.

Aspromonte and the southern coast

Aspromonte's scattered vineyards are mainly on plateaux or terraces within view of the sea. Greco grapes develop ample sugar and extract in hot, dry conditions at Bianco near the Ionian. On the milder western side the terrain is rugged along the Straits of Messina around Reggio and Scilla, but the plains towards Palmi and Gioia Tauro on the Calabrian Riviera support extensive vineyards. Red wines and dark rosés are made from Alicante and other varieties.

Right: the Pollino mountains in the background give their name to the high wine zone around Castrovillari.

Wines of Pollino and the western Sila

Pale red wines enjoy virtual exclusivity in the high vineyards of Pollino, Donnici, and Savuto, though their youthful fragrance and freshness suggest that these zones are as well suited to white varieties as the dominant Gaglioppo and Greco Nero. Still, though defined as *rosso*, in body and colour they are usually closer to *chiaretto* or *cerasuolo*. This habitual lightness is due less to the cool climate than to brief maceration with the skins during fermentation and the inclusion of white grapes in the blends – up to 20-25 percent. Most grapes or new wines are sold locally and bottles of DOC are rarely seen. Sadly, some outstanding vineyards have been abandoned, so potential has been lost. Lamezia is a case apart, since its ordinary red comes from the hot seaside plains southwest of the Sila.

Pollino (1975)
A mountain quaffing wine which varies in colour from pale ruby to cherry, though it can be stronger than it appears. The sturdier *superiore* version can be aged, though oxidation is a recurrent problem.

Zone: Hills in the southern flank of the Pollino range opening eastwards towards the Sibari plain in the communes of Castrovillari, Frascineto, San Basile, Saracena, Cassano Ionio, and Civita in Cosenza province. Dry red, also superiore. Grapes: Gaglioppo 60-80%, Greco Nero up to 40%; Malvasia Bianca/Mantonico Bianco/Guarnaccia Bianca up to 20%. Yld 77/110, Alc 12; superiore 12.5, Acd 0.5, Ag superiore 2 yrs.

Donnici (1975)
Cosenza's local red can be bracingly light, usually *chiaretto* in style, and best young and fresh. When dark varieties are used alone, Donnici can combine size and colour with grace. But vineyards in these lovely hills are being abandoned, so the wine is ever rarer.

Zone: Hills on the western flank of the Sila Grande extending from the southern outskirts of Cosenza through nine other communes in its province. Dry red. Grapes: Gaglioppo 60-90%, Greco Nero 10-20%; Malvasia Bianca/Mantonico Bianco/Pecorello up to 20%. Yld 84/120, Alc 12, Acd 0.5.

Savuto (1975)
Potentially the best of Calabria's mountain reds, though styles vary from the ruby *superiore* to a pale cherry version. The small production is based in this picturesque valley's warmer lower reaches amidst olive groves near the Tyrrhenian, but the best vineyards are on the terraced high slopes around Rogliano where wines can improve for five or six years from some vintages due to greater strength and body. Unfortunately, they are almost never seen commercially.

Zone: Steep hills along the Savuto river valley and Tyrrhenian coast taking in 14 communes in Cosenza province and six in Catanzaro. Dry red, also superiore. Grapes: Gaglioppo 35-45%, Greco Nero/Nerello Cappuccio/Magliocco Canino 30-40%, Sangiovese up to 10%, Malvasia Bianca/Pecorello up to 25%. Yld 77/110, Alc 12; superiore 12.5, Acd 0.5, Ag superiore 2 yrs.

Lamezia (1979)
The Sila is merely a backdrop to the low vineyards around Lamezia Terme and Nicastro. The combination of a balmy Tyrrhenian climate and the Sicilian Nerello varieties in the blend results in a red of little character.

Zone: Plains and low hills overlooking the Gulf of Sant'Eufemia, taking in Lamezia Terme and eight other communes in Catanzaro province. Dry red. Grapes: Nerello Mascalese/Nerello Cappuccio 30-50%, Gaglioppo 25-35%, Greco Nero 25-35%; other varieties up to 5%. Yld 84/120, Alc 12, Acd 0.5.

Other wines of note
Special wines in these mountain areas are ever rarer and need to be searched out. Worth the trouble in the Pollino zone is the traditional Moscato di Saracena from semidried Moscatello grapes; of the several producers, Guido Lojelo stands out. Castrovillari was

once renowned for Lacrima, which derives from the clone of Gaglioppo and other varieties. The Alìa family serves two versions at their fine restaurant: one pale garnet red, the other cherry pink, both with full blossomed bouquet and flavour. Recognized red and white vdt carry the names of Esaro (a river north of Cosenza) and Verbicaro (a town in the Tyrrhenian coastal chain). Experiments by the regional agricultural development board with Chardonnay, Merlot, Cabernet, Incrocio Manzoni 6.0.13, and Greco Bianco have proved successful in the hills around Cosenza, though commercial production may take time.

ESTATES/GROWERS

Istituto Professionale di Stato per l'Agricoltura F. Todaro, Rende and Scigliano (CS). Two branches of the agricultural school sell wines from their own vineyards, including Savuto DOC, Esaro, and Verbicaro.
Guido Lojelo, Saracena (CS). A retired professor makes a little precious Moscato di Saracena.
Basilio Miraglia, Frascineto (CS). Pollino DOC and vdt.
Giovan Battista Odoardi, Nocera Tirinese (CZ). Odoardi, a physician and a rare progressive winemaker, has 60 ha of model vineyards in the Savuto zone. His promising wines still need refining. Savuto DOC is tasty young but fragile. Red, white, and rosé table wines labelled Scavigna are popular locally. The sweet Valeo from a mystery strain of Moscato has a wild, almost foxy aroma, though some admire its peculiarity.

WINE HOUSES/MERCHANTS

Pasquale Bozzo, Donnici Inferiore (CS). Donnici DOC and vdt, partly from own vines.

COOPERATIVES

CS Vini del Pollino, Castrovillari (CS). Good value Pollino DOC and vdt.
Cantine Lamezia Lento, Lamezia Terme (CZ). Lamezia DOC and vdt.
CS Vini del Savuto-Dr. Giambattista Longo, Savuto di Cleto (CS). Savuto DOC and vdt.

Right: the town of Cirò is in the centre of the Classico zone and a base for several wineries.

Wines of the central Ionian coast

Nearly half of Calabria's wine originates in the eastern foothills of the Sila and coastal plains of the Marchesato. The vast majority is red from Gaglioppo, the mainstay of Cirò Rosso. Only in this part of Calabria do dry whites have status, chiefly in the Cirò from Greco Bianco. The DOC wines of neighbouring Melissa echo Cirò's typology. Sant'Anna di Isola Capo Rizzuto is exceedingly hard to find.

Cirò (1969)

Cirò still stakes its reputation more on myths than its merits. DOC drew new attention to the name and brought incentives to improve, but few producers have made the necessary improvements. Gaglioppo thrives in the Classico area of these coastal hills, though its character is too variable to define. Growers rarely restrain yields in a way that would lead to real quality. Earlier picking and new cellar techniques have improved balance in both red and white wines and reduced the red's tendency to oxidize, though only the *riserva* from top vintages can be aged beyond 3-4 years. Classico applies to *rosso* only. The *rosato* has local appeal. The *bianco* from Greco Bianco, with subtle floral aromas and fruity flavours, can be persuasive when made well. The wines of Ippolito, Aloisio, Librandi, Enotria, and Caparra & Siciliani are fairly consistent. The Siciliani family's

Fattoria di San Francesco wins praise, though its Cirò Classico still isn't quite the stuff of which legends are made.

Zone: Low hills facing the Ionian Sea in the communes of Cirò and Cirò Marina (the Classico area) and parts of Crucoli and Melissa in Catanzaro province.
Bianco Dry white. Grapes: Greco Bianco; Trebbiano Toscano up to 10%. Yld 97/135, Alc 12, Acd 0.55-0.85.
Rosso Dry red, also riserva. Grapes: Gaglioppo; Trebbiano Toscano/Greco Bianco up to 5%. Yld 80/115, Alc 13.5, Acd 0.45-0.8, Ag 9 mths; riserva 3 yrs.
Rosato Dry rosé. Grapes: As rosso. Yld 80/115, Alc 13.5, Acd 0.45-0.8.

Melissa (1979)

The red and white wines of this adjacent zone resemble Cirò but don't match its best. Sold locally, they represent good value.

Zone: The low hills of the Marchesato inland from the coast beween Cirò and

Crotone in the commune of Melissa and 13 others in Catanzaro province.
Bianco Dry white. Grapes: Greco Bianco 80-95%, Trebbiano Toscano/Malvasia Bianca 5-20%. Yld 84/120, Alc 11.5, Acd 0.5.
Rosso Dry red, also superiore. Grapes: Gaglioppo 75-95%, Greco Nero/Greco Bianco/Trebbiano Toscano/Malvasia Bianca 5-25%. Yld 77/110, Alc 12.5; superiore 13, Acd 0.5, Ag superiore 2 yrs.

Sant'Anna di Isola Capo Rizzuto (1979)

As the name reveals, Isola di Capo Rizzuto was once an island but it is now a quiet town surrounded by reclaimed marshland which produces limited quantities of nondescript red or rosé called Sant'Anna.

Zone: The low hills and coastal plains of the Marchesato inland from Capes Colonna and Rizzuto in the communes of Isola di Capo Rizzuto, Crotone, and Cutro in Catanzaro province. Dry red or rosé. Grapes: Gaglioppo 40-60%, Nocera/Nerello Mascalese/Nerello Cappuccio 40-60%; Malvasia Bianca/Greco Bianco up to 35%. Yld 84/120, Alc 12, Acd 0.6.

Other wines of note

Commercial production outside DOC is focused on dry vdt, most sold locally. Some Cirò producers have been

working on new-style wines, such as the simply stated Bianco di Calabria of Fattoria San Francesco. The town of Squillace south of Catanzaro has a delicate white that has always been best when drunk on the spot.

ESTATES/GROWERS

Aloisio Nicodemo, Cirò Marina (CZ). Good Cirò from the Tenute Pirainetto sold under the brand name Aloisio.
Fattoria San Francesco, Cirò (CZ). The Siciliani family has made the ancient San Francesco estate with more than 100 ha of vineyards its base for praised Cirò *rosso*, *rosato*, and *bianco*.

WINE HOUSES/MERCHANTS

Fratelli Caruso, Cirò Marina (CZ). Cirò DOC and vdt.
Giuseppe Ippolito, Torre Melissa (CZ). Melissa DOC.

Vincenzo Ippolito, Cirò Marina (CZ). Brothers Antonio and Salvatore Ippolito make good Cirò DOC and vdt, in part from 70 ha of family vines.
Librandi, Cirò Marina (CZ). Traditional style in Cirò DOC and vdt, in part from proprietor Antonio Cataldo Librandi's own vines.

COOPERATIVES

Caparra & Siciliani, Cirò Marina (CZ). From growers with more than 200 ha of vines, Cirò DOC of sound class and value.
Enotria Produttori Agricoli Associati, Cirò Marina (CZ). Cirò DOC from some 70 growers.
CS Sant'Anna, Isola di Capo Rizzuto (CZ). Sant'Anna di Isola Capo Rizzuto DOC and vdt.
CS Cooperativa Torre Melissa, Torre Melissa (CZ). Cirò and Melissa DOC, plus vdt.

Wines of Aspromonte and the southern coasts

Aspromonte's harsh inclines are best known as hideouts for bandits and kidnappers whose "anonymous sequesters" seem to be the handiwork of a branch of the *'ndrangheta*. But here and there on the lower slopes a vineyard turns out a wine that is too good to hide. The Greco from the Ionian town of Bianco ranks among Italy's elite dessert wines, though so little is made that admirers would like to keep it secret. Elsewhere on the massif and in the hills and valleys to the north, only vdt are produced.

Greco di Bianco (1980)

The remote seaside town of Bianco lends its name to this entrancing honey-coloured to amber sweet wine whose hints of citrus and herbs on the nose and palate are unparalleled. Made from partially dried Greco Bianco grapes, it combines natural strength and richness of flavour with tongue-caressing softness. The best DOC producer, Ceratti, immerses grapes in boiling water before crushing to stabilize the wine without the normal use of sulphur. The traditional name Greco di Gerace is still used on unclassified bottlings of Ferdinando Messinò, whose wine can surpass the others with more intense bouquet and greater length of flavour.

Zone: Hills behind the Ionian coastal town of Bianco including part of the commune of Casignana in Reggio di Calabria province. Sweet white. Grapes: Greco Bianco; other whites up to 5%. Grapes are partly dried before crushing. Yld 45/100, Alc 17 (res sugar min 3%), Acd 0.6, Ag 1 yr.

Other wines of note

The town of Bianco is also known for its unclassified Greco di Gerace and Mantonico di Bianco, a dry to slightly sweet sherry-like white with an almondy undertone. From Pellaro on the cape just south of Reggio comes a red from Alicante with a cherry colour that belies its strength. Alicante also

figures in Cerasuolo di Scilla, a bright pink wine from the ancient Scylla at the top of the Straits of Messina. The Calabrian Riviera towns of Palma and Gioia Tauro produce light red and rosé which are enjoyed locally.

ESTATES/GROWERS

Umberto Ceratti, Caraffa di Bianco (RC). Brothers Adolfo and Stefano Ceratti continue the tradition of father Umberto with the exquisite Greco di Bianco DOC, along with a bit of Mantonico di Bianco.
Ferdinando Messinò, Bianco (RC). Messinò at his tiny estate produces Bianco's finest wine, the unclassified Greco di Gerace, along with convincing Mantonico di Bianco.
Vincenzo Oliva, Pellaro (RC). Pellaro vdt.

WINE HOUSES/MERCHANTS

Vintripodi, Archi (RC). Vdt of Pellaro, Arghillà and "della Magna Grecia".

COOPERATIVES

Cooperativa Agricola Calabro Ionica Bianchese (CACIB), Bianco (RC). Greco di Bianco DOC and Mantonico di Bianco.

Travel Information

RESTAURANTS/HOTELS

Villa Franca, 89034 Bovalino Marina (RC). Tel (0964)61402. Fresh produce from land and sea, carefully prepared at reasonable prices.
Alìa, 87012 Castrovillari (CS). Tel (0981)46370. Lucia, Pinuccio, and Gaetano Alìa's quintessential Mediterranean cooking has brought deserved recognition to this fine restaurant. Wines include the family's own Lacrima di Castrovillari and other well-chosen regional wines.
Il Camino, 88071 Cirò (CZ). Tel (0962)32197. Tasty country cooking with Cirò. Good pizza.
La Calavrisella, Via Gerolamo De Rada 11A, 87100 Cosenza. Tel (0984)28012. Authentic specialities of Cosenza with Calabrian wines.
L'Aragosta, 88047 Marina di Nocera Tirinese (CZ). Tel (0968)91535. Fresh seafood with wines from Savuto.

PLACES OF INTEREST

Calabria's main attractions are its scenic mountains and sea. The Sila massif between Cosenza and the Ionian has been called "Little Switzerland" because of the alpine aspects of its forests and lakes. On its slopes are the DOC zones of Donnici and Savuto, more notable for their scenery than their wines. The town of Cirò lies between the ancient towns of Sybaris and Kroton, though modern Sibari and Crotone retain little of their Grecian glory. The extensive coastline varies from precipitous (most of the western and southern coasts) to languid (the northeastern Ionian), but avoid visiting in July and August when beaches are crowded.

Below: Calabria remains rooted in its past, isolated as it is by geography and distance from the rest of Italy.

283

Above: the mountains in Sardinia's undeveloped interior are cloaked with cork oaks.

The Islands

Sardinians and Sicilians dislike having their islands depicted as twins. They may remind you that the distance across the Tyrrhenian from Cagliari to Palermo is greater than from Rome to Venice or that remote points – Sardinia's isle of Asinara and Sicily's Capo Passero – are farther apart than the Dolomites and Vesuvius. But even more conspicuous than the physical distances are the cultural and spiritual divides between the Mediterranean's two largest islands.

Still, they do have some things in common. They have shared the fate of peoples who live in strategically important places of being periodically dominated by foreigners. These intrusions have been endured from the earliest times up until the last century, when both became incorporated into the Italian state. Over time the islanders developed systems of largely passive self-defence, their own patterns of speech, customs, and attitudes that remain inscrutable to outsiders.

Their insularity sets them apart from each other and to an even greater degree from other Italians. Most islanders speak Italian, but many also speak Sardo or Sicilian, which are languages apart. That is one reason why they were among the five regions granted special statutes to deal with problems of communication and economic development.

Their wines reflect this autonomy. No other Italians have retained such idiosyncracy in grape varieties or, until recently, in ways of vinifying them. Climate has a lot to do with the selection. Sicily and Sardinia are the only parts of Italy that enjoy more than seven hours of sunshine on average a day. Even though it is a myth that the islands are ubiquitously hot, there is rarely any deterrent to full ripening of grapes when moisture is adequate. Historically both regions specialized in strong, often fortified wines that seemed to voice the Mediterranean's natural accent. Sicily became tied to the fluctuating fortunes of Marsala and Sardinia was linked to the peculiar likes of Cannonau and Vernaccia di Oristano. Both islands grew Moscato and Malvasia, though, needless to say, each made different styles of wine. Here, as elsewhere in the Mezzogiorno, blending wines were growers' bread and butter.

Then came the revolution that was to have made Sicily and Sardinia into models of modern oenology. And, indeed, it might be stated that over the last 25 years winemaking has evolved more radically here than anywhere else in the world – but it might be added that previously little

had changed since the Risorgimento. In both regions farmers were paid subsidies to plant vineyards using more rational (ie productive) methods and varieties. Cooperative cellars were equipped to process wines of moderate strength and standard scents and flavours. As market trends became apparent, the emphasis has been placed increasingly on dry white, often bubbly, wines. But on the islands, as elsewhere in the Mezzogiorno, this strategy hasn't quite worked.

Sicily, which has the most vineyards of any Italian region, is second to Apulia in terms of average wine production. Sardinia is in the middle range among regions in both categories. Few producers on either island pay much heed to DOC; cooperatives dominate, accounting for 90 percent of Sicily's output and about 60 percent in Sardinia. Some make admirable wines that command respectable prices, but the qualities of others are lost in the nebulous masses of wine that can't be sold even at cost. With markets for blending wines fluctuating, distillation had been the easy solution for producers until the EEC clamped down. So it might be hoped that those cellars which had produced wine expressly for distillation (they abound in Sicily) will be forced to change their ways or opt out.

Individual enterprise gets a strong endorsement here, since the most admired estates and wineries in both Sardinia and Sicily are privately owned. Some make dry table wines which dispel the myth that excellence cannot be achieved in these climes. Yet evidence persists that the sunny maritime conditions lend themselves naturally to dessert and aperitif wines. For even when given contemporary polish, the grandest wines of the islands exude old-fashioned strength of character.

Above: with a coastline of 1,850 km, Sardinia is the Mediterranean's and Italy's second largest island. Right: ruins of ancient nuraghi *abound in Sardinia.*

Sardinia (Sardegna)

Capital: Cagliari.
Provinces: Cagliari (CA), Nuoro (NU), Oristano (OR), Sassari (SS).
Area: 24,090 square kilometres (third).
Population: 1,638,000 (twelfth).

Confronting Sardinian wines is a bit like shopping in a street bazaar. Amidst the cheap novelties and antiques of dubious pedigree, you might find a real work of art. Then again, shoppers with conventional tastes would be better off somewhere else.

Wine is just one of the curiosities that have earned the island autonomy. Sardinia is geologically one of the oldest parts of Italy and geographically the most remote. Its eccentricity is rooted in its long history. The earliest human inhabitants might have walked there, not across the 180 kilometres of water that now separate Sardinia from the mainland but over the isthmuses that 150 millennia or so ago linked it to what are now Corsica, Elba, and Tuscany. The most insular of islanders still have their own language, Sardo, a neo-Latin tongue spiced with Spanish, Basque, and Arabic, though the dialect in the northern Gallura is more closely related to Corsican.

Its isolated position has meant that much of Sardinia's background has remained mysterious. It still isn't known why the stone towers called *nuraghi* were built or even how the island got its name (it may have come from the Shardane, a mysterious tribe from Asia Minor). Another puzzle is why Sardinians, blessed with Italy's most extensive sea coast (1,850 kilometres including the islands), remained hill people – shepherds, farmers, woodsmen, and brigands – from the Stone Age almost to the present.

Sardinians made wine as early as the eighth century BC, when itinerant Phoenician traders showed them what were then the tricks of the trade. During the subsequent incursions of Carthaginians, Romans, Vandals, Byzantines, Moslems, Genoese, and Pisans, vintages were rarely recorded, but viticulture was given a boost by the arrival in the thirteenth-century of Spain's would-be *conquistadores*. (No one has ever really conquered Sardinia, but some stayed long enough to learn that

Below: the rugged and rocky landscape of the Gallura peninsula in the north.

they could not coax the natives down from the hills). The Aragonese stayed longer than most, giving the island's wines a Spanish tang that they never lost, even after the House of Savoy proclaimed the Kingdom of Sardinia in 1720 and then brought it into the Kingdom of Italy in 1860.

Using mainly Iberian grape varieties, Sardinians crafted wines that somewhat resembled sherry (Vernaccia di Oristano and Nasco), port (sweet red Cannonau, Girò, and Monica) and madeira (Malvasia di Bosa and Cagliari). These oddities came to epitomize Sardinian taste, which once seemed as unchanging as the *nuraghi*. Then a couple of decades ago word reached the island that the world's wine drinkers wanted light, fresh wines. Growers were recruited into cooperatives which with amazing haste built modern plants to meet the demand. Curiously, the purest example of the new breed of wine comes from what may be Sardinia's oldest grape variety, Nuragus, grown with the highest permitted yields of all DOCs in the Campidano plains above Cagliari. A dry white occasionally described as antiseptic, Nuragus, like most Sardinian novelties, now marches with southern Italy's faceless legions.

Producers of modern wines are reluctant to admit that an image of class is hard to build on an assembly line, while producers of traditional wines have been slow to adopt scientific methods. Both could learn from Sella & Mosca, whose vast estate near Alghero might be considered a proving ground for the future of Sardinian wine. The firm had problems a few years ago when it produced new-wave light wines, similar in style, if more consistent, than those turned out by the big cooperatives. But when Sella & Mosca put the emphasis on character – Torbato Terre Bianche, Anghelu Ruju, Tanca Farrà – its fortunes quickly improved.

Most Sardinian wine, including much of the DOC, is made on the Campidano plains, but other areas, Alghero in particular, make wines of more distinction. The Tirso river basin is the home of the classic Vernaccia di Oristano. The eastern hills provide mighty Cannonau. The Planargia hills on the west coast make a solitary Malvasia. The northern Gallura peninsula takes pride in its Vermentino.

Sardinia's record with DOC is better than the southern standard, but whether classified or not, the island's wines are hard to sell. Perhaps the name Sardegna, already applied to four varietal DOC wines – Cannonau, Monica, Moscato, and Vermentino – could be usefully applied to the other 14 zones, most of whose names are unrecognizable elsewhere. But Sardinia's real treasures could only appeal to wine drinkers willing to sort through the orthodox in search of the bizarre.

Sardinia's Vineyards

The grape varieties grown in Sardinia are a curious array of relics from different epochs. Some were selected for force of character, essential for traditional dessert and aperitif wines. Others were chosen for the inherent strength that by the late nineteenth century had made Sardinia an important source of blending wines (a role it has largely relinquished to Apulia and Sicily). Several are indigenous, but most arrived from distant parts of the Mediterranean, principally Spain.

Even after phylloxera, Sardinia retained its traditional varieties, though vineyards were almost totally converted to monoculture. The traditional head-trained *alberello* still prevails, but vertical systems are used increasingly in the hills. Many new vineyards, mainly in the Campidano and around Oristano, have been planted in flat, dry areas using trellises and irrigation, which favour quantity over quality. Several estates have extensive vineyards, but most plots are owned by farmers who consign grapes to local cooperatives or sell them to private wineries.

Vineyards for red and white wine are about evenly split, though trends favour the latter. The leading white variety is the prolific Nuragus, which occupies about a third of the vineyard space, followed at a distance by Vermentino which has become a full-fledged native despite Spanish origins. Cannonau is the foremost vine for red wines with about a fifth of the total vineyards, followed by Monica and Carignano with about ten percent each. The following varieties remain (in an Italian context) uniquely or primarily Sardinian.

Bovale. Of Spanish origin (Bobal or Monastrell), Bovale Sardo is the source of the lean red DOCs Campidano di Terralba and Mandrolisai. Known locally as Muristellu. Bovale Grande is sometimes known as Nièddera. As with the Sardo it is widely planted, but used mainly in blends.

Cannonau or **Cannonao**. The Sardinian version of Spain's Granacha, or the Midi's Grenache, the world's most widely planted variety. It takes on styles of its own here in potent reds, both dry and sweet, under Cannonau di Sardegna DOC. It is also used for rosé and even white table wines. Cannonau is linked to Campania's Guarnaccia and other vines called Granaccia elsewhere. The term Alicante is also used in Italy for vines and wines of the Granacha family.

Carignano. The Carignan, native of Spain but more common in France (where it is the most popular red variety) and California, is planted primarily in the southwestern corner of Sardinia and the isles of Sant'Antioco and San Pietro. There it makes red and rosé DOC wines called Carignano del Sulcis. Also known as Uva di Spagna.

Girò. Brought from Spain in around 1400, this worthy but unproductive and now rare variety is used for vaguely port-like reds under Girò di Cagliari DOC.

Malvasia Sarda or **di Sardegna**. A distinct strain of Malvasia probably brought from Greece by the Byzantines. It shows suave personality in the Malvasia DOCs of Bosa and Cagliari.

Monica. Native of Spain, though its parentage is uncertain, this once popular but fading variety makes supple red wines, which are usually dry as Monica di Sardegna DOC and only rarely sweet as Monica di Cagliari DOC.

Nasco. Apparently indigenous to the island, this ancient vine is used in the Campidano for both softly dry and sweet whites under Nasco di Cagliari DOC.

Nièddera. *See* Bovale.

Nuragus. Reputedly of Phoenician origin (though some say it is native), the vine is named after the *nuraghi*, the island's prehistoric stone towers. Grapes are used mainly for the neutral white Nuragus di Cagliari DOC.

Torbato. This rare vine, possibly related to France's Tourbat, was brought from Spain in around 1500. Planted at Alghero, it makes Sardinia's finest dry whites.

Vernaccia di Oristano. Though legends surround its origins, the vine is probably indigenous to the Tirso valley, where it makes the most typical of Sardinian wines, Vernaccia di Oristano. Another theory is that it was planted by the ancient Romans, but it is clearly not related to any other vine called Vernaccia.

Other varieties

Recently, Chardonnay has been planted, though it hasn't been approved yet. Other varieties recommended or approved in Sardinia include:

For red (or rosé): Aglianico, Albaranzeuli Nero, Aleatico, Alicante Bouschet, Ancellota, Barbera, Barbera Sarda, Bombino Nero, Cabernet Franc, Cabernet Sauvignon, Caddiu, Cagniulari, Canaiolo Nero, Caricagiola, Dolcetto, Gaglioppo, Greco Nero or Grego Nieddu, Malvasia Nera, Merlot, Montepulciano, Nebbiolo, Nieddu Mannu, Pascale di Cagliari, Pinot Nero, Sangiovese.

For white: Albaranzeuli Bianco, Arvesiniadu, Biancolella, Clairette, Falanghina, Forastera, Garganega, Malvasia di Candia, Moscato Bianco, Pinot Bianco, Pinot Grigio, Retagliado Bianco, Riesling Italico, Riesling Renano, Sauvignon Blanc, Semidano, Traminer Aromatico, Trebbiano Romagnolo, Trebbiano Toscano, Vernaccia di San Gimignano.

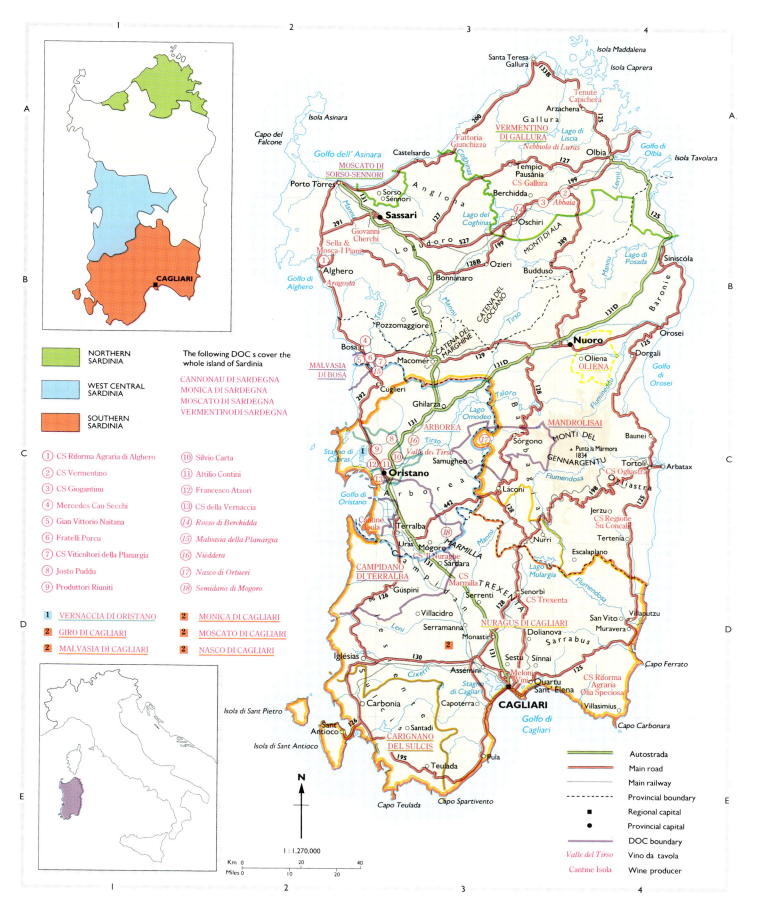

NORTHERN SARDINIA

WEST CENTRAL SARDINIA

SOUTHERN SARDINIA

The following DOCs cover the whole island of Sardinia

CANNONAU DI SARDEGNA
MONICA DI SARDEGNA
MOSCATO DI SARDEGNA
VERMENTNODI SARDEGNA

① CS Riforma Agraria di Alghero
② CS Vermentino
③ CS Giogantinu
④ Mercedes Cau Secchi
⑤ Gian Vittorio Naitana
⑥ Fratelli Porcu
⑦ CS Viticoltori della Planargia
⑧ Josto Puddu
⑨ Produttori Riuniti
⑩ Silvio Carta
⑪ Attilio Contini
⑫ Francesco Atzori
⑬ CS della Vernaccia
⑭ Rosso di Berchidda
⑮ Malvasia della Planargia
⑯ Nièddera
⑰ Nasco di Ortueri
⑱ Semidano di Mogoro

1 VERNACCIA DI ORISTANO
2 GIRO DI CAGLIARI
2 MALVASIA DI CAGLIARI
2 MONICA DI CAGLIARI
2 MOSCATO DI CAGLIARI
2 NASCO DI CAGLIARI

N

1 : 1,270,000

Km 0   20   40
Miles 0   10   20

━━━ Autostrada
━━━ Main road
━━━ Main railway
- - - Provincial boundary
■ Regional capital
● Provincial capital
━━━ DOC boundary
Valle del Tirso Vino da tavola
Cantine Isola Wine producer

Sardinia's Wine Zones

Sardinia and Corsica were once part of a mountain range that existed before the Alps and Apennines were formed and then settled to become the Mediterranean's second and third largest islands (after Sicily). Today the two are narrowly divided by the Strait of Bonifacio. About 85 percent of Sardinia is hills, plateaux, or mountains, where the granite or volcanic rock has been smoothed by erosion and is covered mainly by pastures, brush, and woods. This higher terrain is well suited to vinegrowing, but the potential is rarely realized. Most vineyards are planted at lower levels, notably in the rolling hills and flatlands of the Campidano between Cagliari and Oristano and the plains of Alghero. Sardinia's mid-Mediterranean position affords ample sunshine, though temperatures vary between the warm southern and western sides of the island, exposed to winds across the Sardinian Sea from North Africa, and the higher eastern and northern sectors, influenced by cooler Tyrrhenian currents. Strong winds can damage vines, so low *alberello* training was traditionally employed and new vineyards are often planted with hills or trees as natural windbreaks. Drought can be a problem; annual rainfall is modest, varying from 450 millimetres along the southern coast to 700 millimetres in the high interior, so many recent vineyards have been irrigated.

The north: Gallura, Anglona, and Alghero

In the Gallura and Anglona hills most vineyards lie at altitudes of 300-500 metres in granite-based soil mixed with sand, limestone, and clay. Gallura is heavily wooded and fairly cool with adequate humidity, favouring white wines from Vermentino and Moscato of ample acidity and fragrance. In the high vineyards around Tempio Pausania and Monti yields are modest from vertical or head-trained vines. The Anglona hills are slightly warmer and drier with conditions well suited to both red (mainly Cannonau) and white wines. The plain north of Alghero between the Nurra and Anglona hills is partly reclaimed marshland whose soil varies from volcanic grey to alluvial sand and gravel to reddish calcareous, each giving different styles of wine. Conditions are hot and dry, so many vineyards are trellised to delay ripening of fresh, balanced whites from Torbato and Vermentino grapes and fleshy, smooth reds, mainly from Cannonau. Potentially high yields must be limited to guarantee good quality.

The eastern hills: Cannonau and Mandrolisai

The Gennargentu massif is the axis of Cannonau, whose vineyards in the surrounding hills are cooled by winds from the northeast. Conditions range from mildly hot and dry in the coastal hills of Baronìe, Ogliastra, and Sarrabus to cooler and slightly damper in the higher interior of the Barbagia. Mandrolisai in the Barbagia is a red wine based on Bovale Sardo and Cannonau. Yields are generally low from predominantly head-trained vines planted on crumbling granite mixed with chalk, sand, clay, or volcanic deposits.

West central Sardinia: Planargia and Oristano

Each wine zone has distinct conditions. Malvasia di Bosa comes from the often steep Planargia hills with its volcanic soil of calcareous clay and mild climate in which grapes from head-trained vines become concentrated from low yields in hot, dry years. Vernaccia di Oristano grows in the Tirso basin where the alluvial sand and gravel is rich in lime and the climate is often hot and dry, ideal for the full ripening of grapes from head-trained vines. The Arborea and Terralba zones overlap in sandflats and reclaimed marshland, though some vineyards extend into the low hills. Vines for dry wines from Nuragus, Trebbiano, Bovale, and Sangiovese are trained vertically or increasingly trellised for higher yields.

The south: Cagliari's Campidano and Sulcis

The Campidano extends northwest from Cagliari to Oristano through a corridor between the Marmilla-Trexenta and Iglesiente hills. The dominant Nuragus is often planted in fertile soil, while vines for dry red Monica and Cannonau do better in sparer hillside sites. Sulcis, Sardinia's southwest corner, and the islands of Sant'Antioco and San Pietro, have prevalently sandy clay soils. Winds from Africa are tempered as they cross the Sardinian Sea, but Cagliari is still one of the hottest places in Italy. The climate seems best suited to dessert or aperitif wines, such as Malvasia, Girò, Nasco, and Moscato. The dry Nuragus and the Carignano of Sulcis thrive in the heat but produce wines of little character.

Below: vineyards in the Gallura hills around Tempio Pausania produce mainly Vermentino grapes for white wine.

The regional DOCs

Cannonau di Sardegna (1972)
Sardinia's potent red can come in many different styles, but the basic dry version seems to be gaining ground while the historically more prominent sweet and fortified types can scarcely hold their own. Cannonau's sometimes pale garnet to mahogany colour can be deceptive, for even the *secco* (the lightest style) is no shrinking violet. After a year in barrel it has the warmth and humour of an older red; only rarely does it need much further ageing. The richer and more durable *amabile*, *dolce*, and *liquoroso* are made from partially dried grapes that contribute not only greater strength and/or sweetness but also a darker ruby to garnet colour. The poet Gabriele D'Annunzio gave the Cannonau of Oliena the nickname Nepente (from the opium-like nepenthe

of the ancient Greeks), but since he was a teetotaler he was merely observing the effects of the wine on his Roman colleague Trilussa. The *rosato* has the attributes of an afterthought. Though it can be reminiscent of rosés from the Rhône it's a long way from its Grenache-based cousin Tavel.

Zone: Entire island but most production is based in the Barbagia, Baronie, and Ogliastra hills in Nuoro province (wine from the communes of Oliena and Orgosolo may be called Oliena or Nepente di Oliena); in the Sarrabus hills in the eastern part of Cagliari province (wine from the communes of Muravera, San Vito, Villaputzo, and Villasimius may be called Capo Ferrato); and from the Anglona hills and the plains above Alghero in Sassari province.
Rosso Dry red, also amabile and riserva. Grapes: Cannonau; Bovale Grande/Bovale Sardo/Carignano/Pascale di Cagliari/Monica up to 10%/Vernaccia di San Gimignano up to 5%. Yld 72/110, Alc 13.5, Acd 0.4, Ag 1 yr in wood; riserva 3 yrs (1 in wood).
Rosato Rosé, also amabile. Grapes: As rosso. Yld 72/110, Alc 13.5, Acd 0.4.
Superiore naturale Dry red, also amabile and dolce. Grapes: As rosso but semidried or passito. Yld 72/110, Alc 15 (amabile res sugar 10-25 gr/l and dolce min 2%.), Acd 0.4, Ag 2 yrs in wood.
Liquoroso Fortified red, also secco and dolce naturale. Grapes: As rosso but semidried or passito. Yld 72/110, Alc 18 (secco res sugar max 10 gr/l and dolce naturale min 50 gr/l), Acd 0.35, Ag 1 yr in wood.

Monica di Sardegna (1972)
This typically dry style of Monica is more admired in Sardinia than the usually sweet Monica di Cagliari DOC, but neither are often seen elsewhere. Usually soft and fairly light in body, its youthful ruby colour darkens towards purple with age, though even the *superiore* isn't a marathon runner.

Zone: Entire island but most is grown in the Campidano. Dry or semisweet red, also frizzante naturale and superiore. Grapes: Monica; other reds up to 15%. Yld 105/150, Alc 11; superiore 12.5, Acd 0.45, Ag 6 mths; superiore 1 yr in wood.

Moscato di Sardegna (1980)
This *spumante* has never been produced in quantity, though its delicate aroma and fruity sweetness seem to give it potential.

Zone: Entire island but most is grown in the Anglona and Gallura hills to the north. The term Tempio Pausania (or Tempio) may be used for wines from that commune, Gallura for wines from the northern promontory. Sparkling sweet white. Grapes: Moscato Bianco; other whites up to 10%. Yld 91/130, Alc 11.5 (res sugar 3.5%), Acd 0.5.

Vermentino di Sardegna (1989)
Though not yet established, this Vermentino, whether dry, sweet, or sparkling, promises to join the legions of faceless whites – if growers meet the agreed yields of 130 hl/ha. Those who show restraint may manage to express traditional character.

Zone: Entire island but most is grown in the north. Dry white, also amabile and spumante. Grapes: Vermentino; other whites up to 15%. Yld 130/200, Alc 10.5 (amabile res sugar from 4-20 gr/l); spumante 11, Acd 0.45.

CANNONAU DI SARDEGNA PRODUCERS

The following producers specialize in Cannonau di Sardegna, much of which is made in the eastern part of the island where there are no other classified wines. Producers of Monica, Moscato, and Vermentino di Sardegna generally make other DOCs and are mentioned under the appropriate zone.

COOPERATIVES

CS della Riforma Agraria Olia Speciosa, Castiadas (CA). The cellars in the Sarrabus area east of Cagliari produce a good Cannonau di Sardegna Capo Ferrato, as well as vdt.
CS di Dorgali, Dorgali (NU). From the Baronie hills overlooking the Gulf of Orosei, this is one of the biggest and best producers of Cannonau in various types of DOC as well as the non-DOC Cannonau di Dorgali, and other vdt.
CS Regione Su Concali, Jerzu (NU). Large producer of Cannonau DOC under the Jerzu trademark, along with vdt from growers in the Ogliastra and Barbagia hills.
CS di Oliena, Oliena (NU). The cellars in the Barbagia hills produce a respected Cannonau di Sardegna "Nepente di Oliena".
CS Ogliastra, Tortolì (NU). Good Cannonau DOC and vdt from the Ogliastra hills.

Wines of the north: Gallura, Sassari, and Alghero

Northern Sardinia is more renowned for its seaside resorts than its vineyards, though visitors to the Costa Smeralda seem to enjoy the local whites with fresh rock lobster (*aragosta*). A popular choice is Vermentino, whose colourful character is best expressed in the cool hills of the Gallura peninsula around Tempio Pausania. Sardinia's most fragrant Moscato originates in the Gallura and Anglona hills north of Sassari. There are only two DOCs – Vermentino di Gallura and Moscato di Sorso-Sennori – but most of the recently classified Vermentino and Moscato di Sardegna also seem destined to grow here. One of northern Sardinia's worst kept secrets is that its best wines are not DOC, notably from Sella & Mosca among others. The woods of Gallura are also Italy's prime source of cork.

Vermentino di Gallura (1975)
Like other Italian whites, Vermentino has been toned down for modern palates, apparently to improve its marketability. But, thanks to Sardinian obstinacy, the heroic style has not been entirely squandered. Vermentino of strong character can be tasted in the *superiore* from the Giogantinu cooperative and the Aghiloia from the Vermentino cooperative, which also makes a good modern wine called

S'Eleme. Also respected is the single vineyard Vigne di Piras from the CS Gallura.

Zone: Hills of the Gallura peninsula, taking in 17 communes in Sassari province and two in Nuoro. Dry white, also superiore. Grapes: Vermentino; other whites up to 5%. Yld 98/140, Alc 12; superiore 13.5, Acd 0.45.

Moscato di Sorso-Sennori (1972)

Sassari's traditional sweet Moscato is the colour of honey and, when fortified, almost as sweet, but there is barely enough of this aromatic nectar to meet local demand.

Zone: Low coastal hills in the communes of Sorso and Sennori in Sassari province. Sweet white, also liquoroso dolce. Grape: Moscato Bianco. Yld 54/90, Alc 15 (res sugar 2%); liquoroso dolce 19 (res sugar 3%), Acd 0.35, Ag 5 mths.

Other wines of note

Good modern Vermentino is made outside the aegis of DOC, at Alghero and at nearby Usini by Giovanni

Cherchi. Sella & Mosca makes some of Sardinia's finest table wines at Alghero with white Torbato, red Tanca Farrà and sweet red Anghelu Ruju (*see* below). Curiosities are Cherchi's red Cagnulari, from an ancient vine of that name and the CS Gallura's Nebbiolo di Luras. Reds based on the Pascale vine are Rosso di Berchidda from the Giogantinu cooperative and Abbaìa from the CS del Vermentino, which uses the same variety in its rosé Thaòra.

ESTATES/GROWERS

Giovanni Cherchi, Usini (SS). Small grower with fine Vermentino di Usini from the Tuvaoes vineyard and the unique red Cagnulari, both vdt.
Fattoria Giunchizza, Trinità di Agultu (SS). Vermentino di Gallura.
Sella & Mosca, Alghero (SS). Founded in 1899 by Piedmontese Emilio Sella and Edgardo Mosca, who began by converting marshland into vineyards.

The firm is now one of Italy's largest modern wine estates and the long-time quality leader in Sardinia. Sella & Mosca increasingly emphasizes premium production under director Mario Consorte. The range of non-DOC wines comes entirely from 400 ha of vineyards known as I Piani in reference to the plains north of Alghero where the island's first trellised vines were planted. The best-sellers are Vermentino, rosé (from Cannonau), and Cannonau di Alghero. Torbato di Alghero, a dry white made in still and sparkling versions, reaches new heights in Terre Bianche (named after the vineyard's chalky white soil). The red Tanca Farrà is an original blend of Cannonau with Cabernet Sauvignon. Cannonau reaches its zenith in a sweet wine, Anghelu Ruju (Red Angel) named after a prehistoric burial site discovered on the property. Grapes are partly dried on cane matting before undergoing a process that results in Italy's closest rival to fine port.

Tenute Capichera, Arzachena (SS). Emerging estate with good Vermentino di Gallura.

COOPERATIVES

CS Giogantinu, Berchidda (SS). Distinctive Vermentino di Gallura *superiore* under Giogantinu trademark, plus vdt.
CS del Vermentino, Monti (SS). The huge output includes the respected Vermentino di Gallura S'Eleme and Aghiloia superiore, along with the vdt red Abbaìa and rosé Thaòra table wines.
CS della Riforma Agraria di Alghero, Santa Maria La Palma (SS). Production focuses on Aragosta vdt from Vermentino.
CS Gallura, Tempio Pausania (SS). Fine Vermentino di Gallura from Vigne di Piras and Moscato di Sardegna DOC along with vdt, including a rare Nebbiolo di Luras.

Below: throughout their history the islanders have resisted changes imposed by outsiders while upholding their traditional ways of life.

Wines of the Planargia, Mandrolisai, and Oristano

West central Sardinia boasts two of Italy's best aperitif wines in the rare Malvasia di Bosa and the once cherished Vernaccia di Oristano. Both have been compared – perhaps too often – with sherry, though, as experts insist, each speaks fluent Sardinian with only a trace of a Spanish accent. The grape varieties are Sardinian and the stages of the long vinification and ageing processes follow local patterns. There is a strong maritime influence on the vineyards of each, but the similarities end there; Vernaccia di Oristano comes from the broad Tirso river basin and Malvasia di Bosa from the steep Planargia hills to the north. The non-DOC Malvasia della Planargia can equal that of Bosa. Mandrolisai is off by itself in rocky hills at the centre of the island, where its red and rosé have their own sort of character. The other DOCs of the area – Terralba and Arborea – are disappointingly common. But, two choice unclassified wines, Semidano di Mogoro and Nasco di Ortueri, show what can be accomplished when large cooperatives recognize something special in their masses of grapes.

Malvasia di Bosa (1972)

Of Italy's many Malvasie this is one of the most recherché, especially in the pale golden *secco* version. Like Malvasia di Cagliari, this comes from the Sardinian strain of white Malvasia. Though both have flavours reminiscent of dried hazelnuts and green olives, Malvasia di Bosa is often more delicate and refined in fragrance. The *dolce* and *liquoroso* are bolder but less distinctive. Production is small on the steep, chalky slopes of the Planargia, where styles vary from one producer to the next. For example, some let the wines develop *flor* as they age in barrels (*see* Vernaccia di Oristano), but others wouldn't hear of it. This means that no two wines are ever the same. Malvasia di Bosa from the Campeda vineyards of Salvatore Deriu Mocci was long noted as the finest, though certain small producers, including those of the non-DOC Malvasia della Planargia, are now highly regarded.

Zone: The Planargia hills along the coast

south of Bosa, taking in the communes of Magomadas, Modolo, Tresnuraghes and three others in Nuoro and Oristano provinces. Grape: Malvasia Sarda.
Secco Dry aperitif white. Yld 56/80, Alc 15 (res sugar max 0.5%), Acd 0.35, Ag 2 yrs.
Dolce naturale Sweet aperitif white. Yld 56/80, Alc 15 (res sugar min 2%), Acd 0.35, Ag 2 yrs.
Liquoroso secco Dry fortified white. Yld 56/80, Alc 17.5 (res sugar max 1%), Acd 0.35, Ag 2 yrs.
Liquoroso dolce naturale Sweet fortified white. Yld 56/80, Alc 17.5 (res sugar min 2.5%), Acd 0.35, Ag 2 yrs.

Mandrolisai (1982)

Mandrolisai is the name of a section of the barren Barbagia hills at the centre of the island where Bovale Sardo grapes are combined with Cannonau in pleasant light red and rosé. Most is to drink young, though the red *superiore* is sturdy enough to last a few years.

Zone: The Barbagia hills of central Sardinia between the Gennargentu mountains and

Above: cork is still an important crop for farmers in the hill country.

Lake Omodeo, including Sorgono and five other communes in Nuoro province, and Samugheo in Oristano.

Rosso Dry red, also superiore. Grapes: Bovale Sardo at least 35%, Cannonau 20-35%, Monica 20-35%; other varieties up to 10%. Yld 84/120, Alc 11.5; superiore 12.5, Acd 0.45, Ag superiore 2 yrs (1 in wood).

Rosato Dry rosé. Grapes: As rosso. Yld 78/120, Alc 11.5, Acd 0.45.

Vernaccia di Oristano (1971)

This Vernaccia has been recorded since at least the 16th century, when it was enjoyed on the Italian mainland and even as far away as Greece. However, this most typically Sardinian wine, through no obvious fault of its own, now seems out of step with the times. But it still has a few admirers in Sardinia who drink it as an aperitif or with traditional dishes. Vernaccia vines are trained low in the Tirso flatlands where grapes soak up heat from the sandy limestone soil, giving the wine the strength and sustenance to undergo a long and involved process of vinification and ageing. The very ripe grapes are made into wine with high natural alcohol, which is aged in small barrels in *magazzini* (brick buildings with openings to let in air and sunlight). Since the barrels are never full, a veil of yeast known as *flor* forms over the wine, preventing spoilage while

influencing the development of bouquet and flavour. Since this practice is common in southeastern Spain, Vernaccia develops what is often described as a "sherry-like character". The differences in grapes, climate, and the absence of the *solera* process of educating young wines with older ones (normal for sherry), set Vernaccia di Oristano apart. Truest to type are the natural versions, particularly the thoroughly wood-aged *superiore* and *riserva* from Contini, both endowed with nuances of toasted nuts, spices, and faded flowers that heighten with ageing as the wine loses its sharp, bitter edges. The fortified types, whether dry or sweet, are softer and richer but less distinctive.

Zone: The Tirso river basin and flatlands around the Stagno di Cabras lagoon north of Oristano and including 14 other communes in its province. Dry aperitif white, also superiore, riserva, liquoroso and liquoroso secco. Grape: Vernaccia di Oristano. Yld 52/65, Alc 15; liquoroso 16.5 (res sugar 50-80 gr/l); liquoroso secco 18 (res sugar max 40 gr/l), Acd 0.5, Ag 2 yrs in wood; superiore 3 yrs in wood; riserva 4 yrs in wood.

Arborea (1987)

Although too recent to verify, this DOC promises little more than lightweight Sangiovese and Trebbiano, with which Italy is already inundated.

Zone: Though it is named after the town of Arborea, vineyards cover the plains and low hills of many communes in Oristano province.

Sangiovese Dry red, also rosé. Grapes: Sangiovese at least 85%; other reds. Rosato from grapes vinified after separation from skins. Yld 126/180, Alc 11, Acd 0.45.

Trebbiano Dry white, also amabile amd frizzante naturale. Grapes: Trebbiano Romagnolo/Trebbiano Toscano at least 85%; other whites. Yld 126/180, Alc 10.5, Acd 0.45.

Campidano di Terralba or Terralba (1976)

Ruby to crimson wine of little size or weight. It can be refreshing young.

Zone: A large tract of rolling plains and low hills in the northern part of the Campidano, including Terralba and 22 other communes in Oristano and Cagliari provinces. Dry red. Grapes: Bovale Sardo/Bovale di Spagna; Pascale di Cagliari/Greco Nero/Monica up to 20%. Yld 105/150, Alc 11.5, Acd 0.45, Ag 5 mths.

Other wines of note

Of the many unclassified wines of west central Sardinia, only a few are known elsewhere. These include table wines of the Tirso valley, such as the red and rosé Nièddera made by Vernaccia producers, and the light and bubbly concoctions of the various cooperatives. But amidst the ordinary some gems

emerge. One is the vital and gentle aperitif wine, Malvasia della Planargia from Naitana. Two large cooperatives offer rarities: the dry but softly seductive white Semidano di Mogoro from the cellars of Il Nuraghe and the subtly sweet Nasco di Ortueri from Samugheo.

ESTATES/GROWERS

Francesco Atzori, Cabras (OR). Vernaccia di Oristano DOC and Nièddera red vdt.

Mercedes Cau Sechi, Bosa (NU). Malvasia di Bosa DOC.

Gian Vittorio Naitana, Magomadas (NU). Fine Malvasia della Planargia vdt from 1.5 ha, including single plots of Vigna Murapiscados, Vigna Su Filigalzu, and Vigna Giagonìa. The wine, not aged long enough to qualify as Malvasia di Bosa DOC, is selected by the wine writer Gilberto Arru.

Fratelli Porcu, Modolo (NU). Tiny production of Malvasia di Bosa DOC.

Produttori Riuniti, Baratili San Pietro (OR). Vernaccia di Oristano from 50 ha of vineyards.

WINE HOUSES/MERCHANTS

Cantine Isola, Terralba (OR). Cannonau di Sardegna and a range of sparkling wines.

Silvio Carta, Baratili San Pietro (OR). Good Vernaccia di Oristano.

Attilio Contini, Cabras (OR). Admired as the top producer of Vernaccia di Oristano, mostly from 70 ha of family vineyards around the Stagno di Cabras. The firm, founded late in the last century, is owned and operated by brothers Antonio, Paolo, and Salvatore Contini. Certain *riserva* bottlings of Vernaccia di Oristano reach heights rarely matched by similar wines in Italy. Vdt include a rosé from Nièddera and a light dry white called Contina from Vernaccia.

Josto Puddu, San Vero Milis (OR). Vernaccia di Oristano DOC, Malvasia della Planargia, and vdt, including red Nièddera and white Semidano, in part from own vineyards.

COOPERATIVES

CS fra Vitivinicoltori della Planargia, Flussio (NU). Malvasia di Bosa DOC and semisweet Malvasia della Planargia spumante.

CS Il Nuraghe, Mogoro (OR). Major producer of Nuragus di Cagliari and other DOC and vdt from growers with more than 1,200 ha. But the gem of this large cooperative is the rare white Semidano di Mogoro.

CS della Vernaccia, Oristano. Large production of Vernaccia di Oristano DOC under the trademark Sardinian Gold.

CS di Samugheo, Samugheo (OR). DOC wines of Mandrolisai and the Campidano, plus Nasco di Ortueri under the Tormedusa label. High vineyards with old vines in calcareous soil yield this exquisitely sweet amber wine that outclasses any Nasco di Cagliari DOC.

CS del Campidano di Terralba, Terralba (OR). DOC and vdt from growers with nearly 1,000 ha of own vines.

Wines of Cagliari's Campidano and Sulcis

The rolling Campidano plain northwest of the capital is Sardinia's wine barrel. More than half of the region's wine originates in the province of Cagliari, much of which is DOC for the six wines that carry its name after the varietal, as well as the zones of Carignano del Sulcis and part of Arborea. Of the classified wines, only the dry white Nuragus is produced in any quantity. The other Cagliari DOCs are either aperitif or dessert wines that can be special – in particular the uniquely Sardinian Girò and Nasco – but, like others of the type, they seem to be losing popularity in the vineyards and in the marketplace. Here, as in so many of Italy's "easy" vineyard areas, producers are concentrating increasingly on volume production of light bubbly wines. Winemaking in the Campidano and adjacent hills is dominated by cooperatives, many of them large. However, there is also some experimentation underway with noble varieties that show promise on hillside vineyard sites.

Girò di Cagliari (1972)

This light but worthy stand-in for port is in danger of extinction, so what little there is must be treasured. The suave *dolce naturale* is easy on the palate, though fans of Girò seem to prefer the more intense flavours of the *liquoroso riserva*. Dry types are permitted but rarely seen.

Zone: Cagliari province and several communes in Oristano, though the minuscule production is based in the Campidano. Grape: Giro, possibly semidried or passito.

Dolce naturale Sweet red. Yld 72/120, Alc 14.5 (res sugar min 2.5%), Acd 0.4, Ag 9 mths.

Secco Dry red. Yld 72/120, Alc 14 (res sugar max 0.5%), Acd 0.4, Ag 9 mths.

Liquoroso Fortified red, also dolce naturale, secco, and riserva. Yld 72/110, Alc 14; dolce naturale and secco 17.5 (dolce naturale res sugar min 2.5% and secco max 1%), Acd 0.35, Ag 9 mths; riserva 2 yrs (1 in wood).

Malvasia di Cagliari (1972)

A golden to amber-coloured Malvasia, whose tenuous bouquet and almondy flavour show best as a dry aperitif. Sweet and fortified versions are also allowed.

Zone: Cagliari province and several communes in Oristano, though the small production is based in the Campidano. Grape: Malvasia Sarda, possibly semidried or passito.

Secco Dry white. Yld 72/110, Alc 14 (res sugar max 0.5%), Acd 0.45, Ag 9 mths.

Dolce Sweet white. Yld 72/110, Alc 14 (res sugar min 2%), Acd 0.45, Ag 9 mths.

Liquoroso Fortified white, also secco, dolce naturale, and riserva. Yld 72/110, Alc 14; secco and dolce naturale 17.5 (secco res sugar max 1% and dolce naturale min 2%), Acd 0.35, Ag 9 mths; riserva 2 yrs (1 in wood).

Monica di Cagliari (1972)

This red wine comes from grapes naturally concentrated by growing on low vines. Unlike its counterpart Monica di Sardegna, the Cagliari version is almost invariably sweet, though dry is also permitted. Its light ruby colour takes on hints of orange with time, though only the *liquoroso riserva* is suited to long ageing.

Zone: Cagliari province and several communes in Oristano, though the small production is based in the Campidano.

Grape: Monica, possibly semidried or passito.

Dolce naturale Sweet red. Yld 72/110, Alc 14.5 (res sugar min 2.5%), Acd 0.4, Ag 9 mths.

Secco Dry red. Yld 72/110, Alc 14 (res sugar max 0.5%), Acd 0.4, Ag 9 mths.

Liquoroso Fortified red, also dolce naturale, secco, and riserva. Yld 72/110, Alc 14; dolce naturale and secco 17.5 (dolce naturale res sugar min 2.5% and secco max 1%), Acd 0.3, Ag 9 mths; riserva 2 yrs (1 in wood).

Moscato di Cagliari (1972)

A golden dessert wine of soaring aroma, which becomes even more intense in the aged *liquoroso riserva*.

Zone: Cagliari province and several communes in Oristano, though the small production is based in the Campidano. Grape: Moscato Bianco, possibly semidried or passito.

Dolce naturale Sweet white. Yld 72/110, Alc 16 (res sugar min 3%), Acd 0.4, Ag 5 mths.

Liquoroso dolce naturale Fortified sweet white, also riserva. Yld 72/110, Alc 17.5 (res sugar min 2.5%), Acd 0.35, Ag 5 mths; riserva 1 yr.

Nasco di Cagliari (1972)

Nasco grows only in Sardinia, where it makes pale golden to light amber wines of exquisitely subdued personality. Nasco can be distinctive as a sweet and fortified wine with traits reminiscent of tawny port, but connoisseurs seem to prefer it with a delicate medium dry flavour.

Zone: Cagliari province and several communes in Oristano, though the small production is based in the Campidano. Grape: Nasco, possibly semidried or passito.

Dolce naturale Slightly sweet white. Yld 72/110, Alc 14.5 (res sugar min 2.5%), Acd 0.4, Ag 9 mths.

Secco Dry white. Yld 72/110, Alc 14 (res sugar max 0.5%), Acd 0.4, Ag 9 mths.

Liquoroso Fortified white, also dolce naturale, secco, and riserva. Yld 72/110, Alc 14; dolce naturale and secco 17.5 (dolce naturale res sugar min 2.5% and secco max 1%), Acd 0.35, Ag 9 mths; riserva 2 yrs (1 in wood).

Nuragus di Cagliari (1975)

It seems a cruel twist of fate that Nuragus, possibly introduced by the Phoenicians and named after the *nuraghi*, the prehistoric stone towers, has become a white wine that typifies the tastelessness of modern mass wine production. But, the vine's popularity seems always to have been based more on abundance than class. The potent, amber, old-style Nuragus was so harsh it was usually diluted with water. Nuragus di Cagliari boasts the highest consented yields of any DOC – 140 hl/ha, with the possibility of 20% more in "exceptional" years. Those who take advantage of this make wines showing all the personality of mineral water with perhaps a twist of lemon, but a cold glass of the *frizzante* can be thirst-quenching on a hot summer day. The *amabile* is rarely seen.

Zone: Cagliari province and numerous communes in Oristano and Nuoro with production concentrated in the Campidano. Dry white, also amabile and frizzante. Grapes: Nuragus 85-95%, Trebbiano Toscano or Romagnolo/Vermentino/Clairette/ Semidano 5-15%. Yld 140/200, Alc 10.5, Acd 0.45.

Carignano del Sulcis (1975)

In Italy the Spanish/French Carignan is prominent only in the hilly vineyards of Sulcis, as the Carthaginians named the promontory and islands of Sant'Antioco and San Pietro. Though it used to make strong blending wines, Carignano has been toned down into a mildly interesting DOC. The *rosso* is grapey when young, but it is sturdy enough to mellow with two or three years of age as *invecchiato*. The modest *rosato* is best young.

Zone: The southwest corner of Sardinia in the hills around Capo Teulada and including the islands of Sant'Antioco and San Pietro in 15 communes in Cagliari province.

Rosso Dry red, also invecchiato. Grapes: Carignano; Monica/Pascale/Alicante Bouschet up to 15%. Yld 104/160, Alc 11.5, Acd 0.45, Ag 5 mths; invecchiato 11 mths.

Rosato Dry rosé, also invecchiato. Grapes: As rosso. Yld 88/160, Alc 11.5, Acd 0.45, Ag 5 mths; invecchiato 11 mths.

Other wines of note

Most producers make table wines and *spumanti*, though rarely of any more than local interest. The Consorzio Interprovinciale per la Frutticoltura is working on improving Sardinian varieties and testing outsiders, such as Chardonnay, Sauvignon, the Cabernets, and Pinots. Limited quantities of new-style wine are sold at the cellars at Villasor.

ESTATES/GROWERS

Meloni Vini, Selargius (CA). DOC wines of Cagliari, plus Cannonau and Vermentino di Sardegna from 250 ha of

WINE HOUSES/MERCHANTS

Zedda Piras, Cagliari. Cagliari DOC and vdt.

COOPERATIVES

CS di Dolianova, Dolianova (CA). Huge production includes good Cannonau and Monica di Sardegna, Cagliari DOC, and vdt from the Parteolla area of the Campidano.

CS Marmilla, Sanluri (CA). Cellars managed by oenologist Enzo Biondo, with more than 1,800 growers in the Marmilla hills. Good Cagliari DOCs, Cannonau and Monica di Sardegna, and vdt carrying the Marmilla trademark.

CS di Santadi, Santadi (CA). Good Carignano del Sulcis DOC and vdt.

CS di Sant'Antioco, Sant'Antioco (CA). Large output includes Carignano del Sulcis and Monica di Sardegna DOC and vdt.

CS della Trexenta, Senorbi (CA). Sound Nuragus di Cagliari DOC and vdt from the Trexenta hills.

CS del Campidano di Serramanna, Serramanna (CA). Large volume of Cagliari and Sardegna DOC as well as vdt.

CS di Villacidro, Villacidro (CA). Cagliari DOC and vdt.

Below: the Sardinian diet is based on an array of pastas, pastries, stews, game, poultry, cheeses and a variety of bread. The Campidano in the south is the island's richest agricultural area and the centre of wine production.

Travel Information

RESTAURANTS/HOTELS

La Lepanto, 07041 Alghero (SS). Tel (079)979116. Waterfront hotel with good restaurant serving regional dishes, including *aragosta* (rock lobster). Wide range of wines.

Grazia Deledda, 07021 Arzachena (SS). Tel (0789)98988. Creative touches with Sardinian fish and meat dishes in a refined setting. Good wine list. Smart rooms with views over Baia Sardinia.

Dal Corsaro, Viale Regina Margherita 28, 09124 Cagliari. Tel (070)664318. The capital's most admired restaurant offers an impressive range of regional dishes and wines.

Hotel Is Morus, 09010 Santa Margherita di Pula (CA). Tel (070)921424. Inviting seaside hotel surrounded by pine trees with good leisure facilities and a fine restaurant specializing in seafood.

Su Gologone, 08025 Oliena (NU). Tel (0784)287512. Warmly rustic hotel with tasty hill country food cooked on the open hearth. Hearty Cannonau and other local wines.

Il Faro, Via Bellini 25, 09170 Oristano. Tel (0783)70002. Oristano's best restaurant raises traditional Sardinian food to new heights.

Da Franco, 07020 Palau (SS). Tel (0789) 709558. First-rate regional and national dishes and wines served on a terrace overlooking the fishing port.

Canne al Vento-da Brancaccio, 07028 Santa Teresa Gallura (SS). Tel (0789)754219. Simpatico family place with good local food and wines.

WINE SHOPS/ENOTECHE

Antica Enoteca Cagliaritana, Scaletta Santa Chiara 21, 09124 Cagliari. Impressive range of Sardinian, Italian, and foreign wines and spirits.

PLACES OF INTEREST

Despite the development of seaside resorts, much of Sardinia's coast remains as unspoiled as is its remote, herb-scented interior. Those places that remain untouched by urban development and tourism have retained customs, crafts, and cooking that provide a rare glimpse of the past. The island is still one of Italy's best places to escape to for peace and quiet, especially between September and June when the jet set has gone elsewhere.

Regular flights and a ferry service link the Italian mainland with Cagliari and Olbia near the Costa Smeralda.

Gallura and the Costa Smeralda. Gallura in northernmost Sardinia is a wooded promontory whose rocky coasts and isles harbour the ultra-chic playground of the Costa Smeralda in the resorts of Arzachena, Porto Cervo, Baia Sardinia, and Cala di Volpe. Worth visiting are the ports of Santa Teresa Gallura and Palau, and the the Maddalena Archipelago, including the isle of Caprera with the house and tomb of Giuseppe Garibaldi.

The Gennargentu mountains. South of Nuoro is the Gennargentu massif, whose rugged heights, the lair of Sardinia's legendary bandits and kidnappers, provide sweeping views over eastern Sardinia. Most Cannonau vineyards lie in the surrounding Barbagia, Ogliastra, and Sarrabus hills. Along the coastal cliffs between Cala Gonone and Arbatax are caves where some of the Mediterranean's last surviving seals live.

The Nuraghi. Curious remnants of Sardinia's past are the *nuraghi*, the round stone towers built without mortar in prehistoric times. Examples are the group at Serra Orrios east of Nuoro and the Nuraghi Losa, Santa Barbara, and Sant'Antine between Oristano and Sassari.

Sicily (Sicilia)

Capital: Palermo.
Provinces: Agrigento (AG), Caltanissetta (CL), Catania (CT), Enna (EN), Messina (ME), Palermo (PA), Ragusa (RG), Siracusa (SR), Trapani (TP).
Area: 25,708 square kilometres (first).
Population: 5,084,000 (fourth).

Sicily emblemizes the Mediterranean in its jagged coasts, seething volcanos, and stony hillsides, where olives, grain, citrus fruits, herbs, and vines proliferate in the sun. The largest island in the sea retains indelible souvenirs of not always friendly visits from virtually all the peoples who surrounded it: Phoenicians, Carthaginians, Greeks, Saracens, Arabs, as well as the Romans and other Europeans. Yet, though it has served all too often as a target for all-comers, Sicily has never adjusted comfortably to its role as a Mediterranean melting pot. As a blending vat it has come up with some curious *cuvées*, not all of them under the name Marsala.

It seems odd that Italy's largest region with the most vineyards and from some vintages the most wine has the lowest per capita consumption, but Sicilians have lived with contradictions since the days of Magna Graecia. The Greeks, who first called the island Trinacria because of its triangular shape, later gave it its lasting name after the Siculi hill people. A flourishing wine trade developed from the Greek cities of Syracuse, with its prized Pollio, and Akragas (Agrigento), as well as from Taormina on the slopes of Mount Etna. But the Romans, despite Julius Caesar's fondness for the sweet Mamertino, converted much of the island's rolling contours into grainfields. The Vandals and Goths did nothing for the cause of wine before it became taboo under the Moslems, who for centuries dried grapes into raisins that came to be known in Italy as "uva sultana" in tribute to the sultans. Normans, Swabians, and Bourbons set the stage for the revival, which came about in the late eighteenth century when the English created Marsala and made Sicily a prime source of fortified wines.

The island's reputation for sweet wines was enhanced further by Moscato di Pantelleria and Malvasia delle Lipari, though dessert and aperitif wines are too often ignored in the region's rush to promote the light and bright. Overall Sicily's modern wines seem the south's most reliable, even if the whites, a growing majority, often lack identity and the reds can lack polish. DOC hasn't caught on in Sicily (only accounting for 2.5 percent of the total), but the region sets its own standards, awarding a "Q" for quality on labels of wines that meet the requirements.

Although nine-tenths of the wine is made by cooperatives, eight out of every ten bottles sold come from private cellars or estates. With few exceptions, the prestige wines are made by independent producers: Corvo, Regaleali, Florio, Pellegrino, Rapitalà, Donnafugata, Hauner, and Vecchio Samperi. These and a few others give Sicilian oenology a quality level to admire, evidence that some elements of the outsized industry have taken to heart the cryptic slogan "Il corraggio della qualità". Well, it does take courage to limit production and strive for class in a hot region whose reputation and earnings were built on wines of power in abundance. But beyond the usual southern barriers to success, honest producers have to live with the innuendos that link all things Sicilian to the Mafia.

The prime example of Sicily's drive to improve the quality and image of its wine was the rescue of Marsala. An act of courage not devoid of desperation, the recent overhaul of the obsolete production code seems to have pointed a once luminous fortified wine back on the road to salvation. But even when attacked by critics, Marsala remained Sicily's pride and joy. Then as now it dominates DOC production and the port

Above: Sicilian cooking is known for its flavours of sun and sea in the many types of fresh fish available in the markets. Below: fishing is a mainstay of Sicily's economy.

that gave it its name is one of Italy's busiest wine centres.

The plains that become rolling hills towards Marsala's eastern horizon support what must be the world's most prodigious stand of vines, making Trapani the volume leader among Italy's 94 provinces. The adjacent province of Agrigento, which has no DOC, is also a major contributor to the surfeit of wine absorbed largely through distillation over the last decade. Huge quantities of grapes from the western provinces are made into musts and concentrates to increase the strength of Italian wines, since northern producers may not use sugar for such purposes, as many would prefer to do. Meanwhile, on the eastern side of the island, which boasts Etna and five other of the nine DOCs, vineyards have diminished despite the theoretical advantages offered by higher and cooler positions.

Sicilian wine promotions reverberate with the term quality, yet bottles of real class represent a mere fraction of the products derived from the masses of grapes. Even admirers of Sicily's recent progress may punctuate the "Q" for quality with a question mark.

Sicily's Vineyards

Sicily has the most vineyards of any region, marked by an extraordinary density of vines in Trapani province and much of Agrigento. However, Sicily is second to Apulia in the production of wine as well as table grapes, which in both regions are a major source of "wine" for distillation. Sicilian vineyards have been transformed almost entirely to monoculture. But today only about half the space is devoted to the once preponderant head-training for low yields which in the heat produced grapes for strong dessert or aperitif wines or for blending. Many new vineyards are in irrigated vertical or trellised systems with generous yields best suited to light, dry, prevalently white, table wines.

Despite changing patterns, Sicilian growers favour traditional vines, which if not indigenous have been planted since ancient times. White varieties dominate by nearly three to one. Catarratto Bianco, prominent in Marsala and Alcamo, is by far the most popular variety, covering some 85,000 hectares, or more than 40 percent of the island's vineyard area. It ranks as Italy's third most planted variety after Trebbiano and Sangiovese. The exception to the native preference is Trebbiano Toscano, which has taken second position among white vines, well ahead of Grillo, Inzolia, Grecanico, Carricante, and the Muscat table/wine grape Zibibbo. Trebbiano's rise is easily explained; its average yields more than triple those of Catarratto, so in less than a third of the space it produces about the same amount of wine.

Calabrese (or Nero d'Avola), which can make wines of class, is the chief dark variety with more than 25,000 hectares planted, followed closely by the Nerello subvarieties of Mascalese and Cappuccio. Perricone is the other native dark grape of note, holding its own against such imports as Sangiovese and Barbera.

The following varieties are associated either exclusively or primarily with Sicily.

Ansonica or **Anzonica**. *See* Inzolia.

Calabrese or **Nero d'Avola**. Despite apparent Calabrian origins, this generous variety is Sicily's first choice for red wine. Its aristocratic class shines through in Corvo's Duca Enrico and Regaleali's Rosso del Conte. Though it makes amply robust wines on its own, its strength and colour are also useful in blends. The names Calabrese and Nero d'Avola are interchangeable. Known in dialect as Calavrisi.

Carricante. Chief variety of the Etna Bianco DOC, where it thrives in the volcanic soil. Also called Catanese Bianco.

Catarratto Bianco. This ancient vine has two subvarieties in Lucido and the more common Comune. The mainstay of Alcamo DOC, Catarratto combines good body and strength with fairly bland character, making it a favoured base for Marsala and Vermouth. It plays a secondary role in Etna Bianco DOC and the white Corvo and Regaleali.

Above: Frappato di Vittoria vines are grown around the town of Vittoria mainly for use in a cherry-hued wine called Cerasuolo.

Damaschino. Possibly of Syrian origin (the name refers to Damascus). This vine has lost ground due to lack of acidity and strength, but when well guided it makes whites of finesse.

Frappato di Vittoria. Part of the blend of Cerasuolo di Vittoria DOC, Frappato produces pale red wines with surprising vigour and durability.

Grecanico or **Grecanico Dorato**. Apparently of Greek origin, this once prized vine has diminished as a source of light but fresh and firmly textured white table wines in western Sicily.

Grillo. Believed to have come from Apulia in the last century, Grillo was once the preferred grape for Marsala, and still is attributed greater character than the more prolific Catarratto.

Inzolia or **Insolia**. This apparently indigenous variety is valued in dry table wines of suave character (Corvo and Regaleali) and in the modern blend of Marsala, though it tends to be fragile. Also called Ansonica or Anzonica in Sicily and in Tuscany. Known locally as 'Nzolia.

Malvasia di Lipari. Brought to the Aeolian or Lipari isles by the Greeks in the sixth century BC, this strain of Malvasia developed unique character in the volcanic soil. After nearing extinction, the wine has enjoyed a modest revival in Malvasia delle Lipari DOC.

Nerello. Nerello Mascalese and Cappuccio together rank second to Calabrese in popularity among Sicily's red varieties. The Mascalese shows class in both DOC and table wines. The lesser Cappuccio is used mainly in blends.

Nero d'Avola. *See* Calabrese.

Perricone or **Pignatello**. Vigour, colour, and strength make this useful in blends and in varietal wines called Pignatello.

Zibibbo. This large-berried Moscato or Moscatellone originated in North Africa as Muscat d'Alexandria. Usually a table grape, it turns up often in sweet wines, notably Moscato di Pantelleria DOC.

Other varieties

Sicily's emphasis on white wines has led to an influx of varieties still not officially recognised, such as Sauvignon, Pinot Bianco and Grigio, and Chardonnay. The Cabernets, Merlot, and Pinot Nero are also present, and there is even a bit of Lambrusco and Niebbolo grown. Other varieties recommended or approved in Sicily include:

For red (or rosé): Alicante, Barbera, Cabernet, Catanese Nero, Corinto Nero or Passolina di Lipari, Gaglioppo, Mantonico or Montonico Nero, Nocera, Sangiovese.

For white: Albanello, Mantonico or Montonico Bianco, Minnella Bianca, Moscato Bianco, Moscato Giallo, Trebbiano Toscano, Verdello.

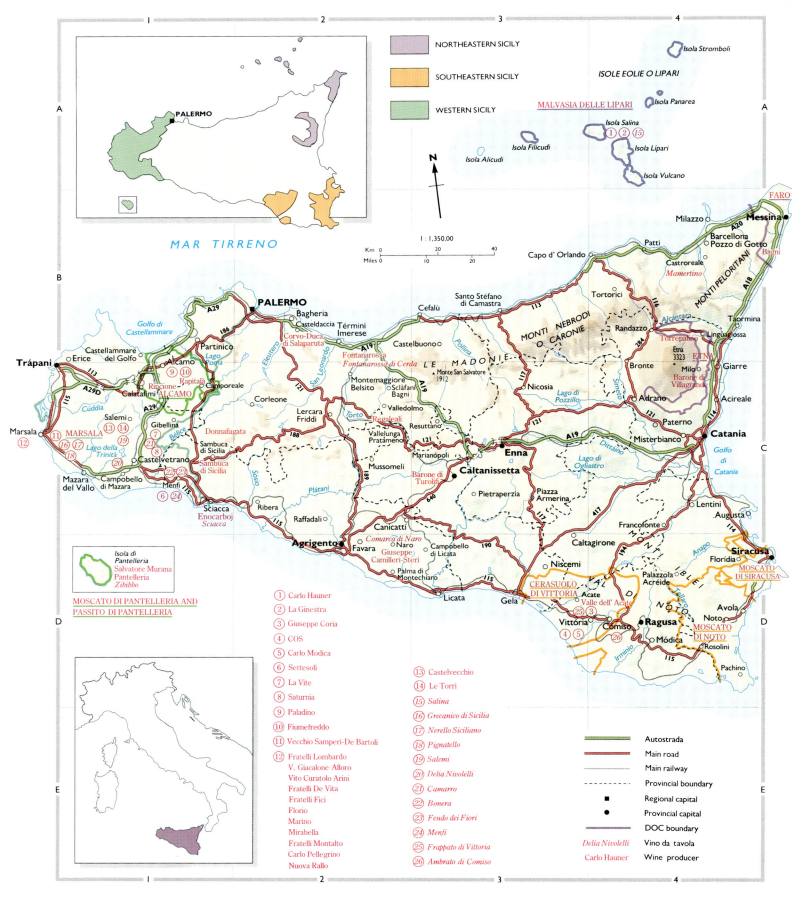

I : 1,350,00

Km 0   20   40
Miles 0   10   20

NORTHEASTERN SICILY

SOUTHEASTERN SICILY

WESTERN SICILY

ISOLE EOLIE O LIPARI

MALVASIA DELLE LIPARI

MOSCATO DI PANTELLERIA AND
PASSITO DI PANTELLERIA

Isola di
Pantelleria
Salvatore Murana
Pantelleria
Zibibbo

① Carlo Hauner
② La Ginestra
③ Giuseppe Coria
④ COS
⑤ Carlo Modica
⑥ Settesoli
⑦ La Vite
⑧ Saturnia
⑨ Paladino
⑩ Fiumefreddo
⑪ Vecchio Samperi-De Bartoli
⑫ Fratelli Lombardo
     V. Giacalone Alloro
     Vito Curatolo Arini
     Fratelli De Vita
     Fratelli Fici
     Florio
     Marino
     Mirabella
     Fratelli Montalto
     Carlo Pellegrino
     Nuova Rallo

⑬ Castelvecchio
⑭ Le Torri
⑮ Salina
⑯ Grecanico di Sicilia
⑰ Nerello Siciliano
⑱ Pignatello
⑲ Salemi
⑳ Delia Nivolelli
㉑ Camarro
㉒ Bonera
㉓ Feudo dei Fiori
㉔ Menfi
㉕ Frappato di Vittoria
㉖ Ambrato di Comiso

Autostrada
Main road
Main railway
Provincial boundary
■ Regional capital
● Provincial capital
DOC boundary
Delia Nivolelli   Vino da tavola
Carlo Hauner   Wine producer

Sicily's Wine Zones

Sicily, separated from the Italian peninsula by the Straits of Messina, is the Mediterranean's largest and most populous island, as well as the midpoint between east and west. The triangular main island is the axis of a constellation that includes Pantelleria and Ustica, as well as the Lipari (Aeolian), Egadi, and Pelagie groups. The region has 1,500 kilometres of coastline on the Tyrrhenian, Ionian, and Sicilian seas (the latter flanked by the Maltese and Sicilian channels). The southern side of the main island is almost entirely arid hills, where irrigated vineyards are surrounded by brush, scrub, and cactus. The north is dominated by the Sicilian Apennines, whose pastures and grain fields give way to woods towards the east in the heights of the Nebrodi chain and the mass of Etna at 3,340 metres. Etna is one of three active volcanos – along with Stromboli and Vulcano in the Lipari isles – and much of Sicily's soil is of volcanic origin. Only 15 percent of the land lies below 100 metres – mainly around Catania, Capo Passero, and Gela, as well as much of the province of Trapani, which produces Marsala and enormous quantities of blending and table wines. The southern and eastern zones around Marsala, Agrigento, and Ragusa are in the direct line of winds from Africa. Rainfall is scant between June and September, so drought is a frequent problem, which explains why about half the region's vineyards are irrigated. The hills to the north and east are cooler and damper, but still blessed with ample sunshine for slow, even ripening of grapes. The mountains in the northeast get plenty of rain and snow. The highest peaks are usually snow-capped through the winter.

The northeast: Etna, Messina, and Lipari

Etna's vineyards lie in volcanic soil at a height of 300-700 metres in Sicily's coolest DOC zone overlooking Catania, which is often Italy's hottest city. Favoured by sunshine and gentle breezes, Etna's head-trained Carricante vines can make whites of good fruit and acidity, but reds from Nerello Mascalese are rarely inspiring. The slopes of the adjacent Peloritani range above Messina hardly ever match their potential in the red Faro DOC, also from Nerello. Lipari is a world apart. The Aeolian islands have plenty of home-made wine, though the only commercial Malvasia comes from Salina. There head-trained vines in the ash grey soil make rich Malvasia both *naturale* and *passito*, with aromas which epitomize the Mediterranean ambience.

The southeast: Siracusa and Ragusa

The arid plains and lower slopes of the Monti Iblei between Siracusa and Gela produce mainly blending wines or heady *vini da tavola* from head-trained vines in chalky clay soil. The rich Moscato di Noto and cherry-coloured Cerasuolo di Vittoria DOCs account for a fraction of the total production.

Central and southern Sicily: Agrigento and Caltanissetta

Irrigation has made the hot slopes of Agrigento province a major source of both table grapes and wine from trellised or vertical-trained vines, though quality is rarely noteworthy except around Sciacca and Ribera to the west and in the Comarca di Naro plateau. The cool altitudes at the island's centre provide prime conditions for vines, notably in the tufaceous clay and limestone soil of the Regaleali estate at 500-700 metres.

Above: vineyards in the hot southeastern part of the island are most noted for the Moscato of Siracusa and Noto.

The west: Marsala and Alcamo

The rolling plains and low hills of Trapani province support Italy's largest expanse of vines: for Marsala and Alcamo DOCs as well as table and blending wines. The Marsala zone has two basic types of terrain. In the classical area – extending from the coast between Paceco and Mazara del Vallo eastwards to Calatafimi, Salemi, and Castelvetrano – a pale reddish brown soil prevails, known locally as *sciare* in reference to aridness and low yields. Only low vertical or head training is permitted in the hot, dry climate, resulting in concentrated wines from the prevalent Catarratto as well as Grillo and Inzolia, and the red Perricone and Calabrese. To the east in the higher ground around Gibellina, and Partanna, siliceous clay prevails in more humid and fertile land where larger yields produce grapes of less substance. The Alcamo zone is rich in clay and limestone, favouring rather bland whites from Catarratto.

The island of Pantelleria

On the remote island of Pantelleria, head-trained Zibibbo vines for Moscato are planted in the traces of arable land along the rocky coast where the residue of some 50 extinct volcanos has collected with sand and pebbles in hollows and declivities. Plots of low, stunted vines are protected by stone walls against winds from the Sahara, which are tamed slightly by crossing 70 kilometres of sea. Yields are low and sugar and extract high, accounting for the unmatched richness of the island's Moscato.

Wines of the northeast: Lipari, Messina, and Etna

Perhaps the most awe-inspiring of Italy's views can be enjoyed from the Calabrian Riviera on a clear winter day: a sweeping panorama from the volcano of Stromboli in the Aeolian or Lipari islands to the Straits of Messina with snow-covered Etna in the background. It is hardly surprising that northeastern Sicily's historical background is shrouded in myth. Local lore has it that young Bacchus planted a vine and squeezed its grapes into the first wine at the foot of Etna and that Julius Caesar's preferred tipple was Mamertino from the hills above Milazzo. Modern winemaking seems far less imaginative than the ancient. Etna, Sicily's first DOC, has never reached the heights, and Faro, Messina's once towering red, has all but collapsed. The revival of the long-suffering Malvasia delle Lipari is largely the work of a Milanese designer named Carlo Hauner, who has fashioned it into a contemporary legend.

Malvasia delle Lipari (1974)

This inimitable Malvasia from vines brought to the Aeolian isles by the Greeks was clearly in decline before Carlo Hauner staged his one-man revival that has encouraged others to follow. Hauner's regular Capo Salina and stronger, sweeter *passito* vie for attention among admirers, though experts often prefer the former. Both its orangish-amber colour and its beguiling bouquet are reminiscent of ripe apricots, though underlying sensations include citrus fruits and the herbs and flowers that spring from the isle's volcanic soil. The *liquoroso* is rarely seen.

Zone: All isles of the Lipari archipelago with the small production based in Salina. Sweet white. Grapes: Malvasia di Lipari with 5-8% Corinto Nero, possibly semidried or passito. Yld 63/90, Alc 11.5 (fermented alc min 8%), Acd 0.4.
Passito or **dolce naturale** Sweet white. Yld 40/90, Alc 18 (res sugar min 6%), Acd 0.4, Ag 9 mths.
Liquoroso Fortified version. Yld 54/90, Alc 20 (res sugar min 6%), Acd 0.4, Ag 6 mths.

Faro (1977)

This wine, once nearly as famous as the lighthouse it is named after, is a shadow of its former self. A shame, since those who remember its more active days insist that it was one of Sicily's most illuminating reds. The wine from Bagni (*see* over) is well worth seeking out.

Zone: Slopes in the commune of Messina extending from Capo Peloro with its lighthouse ("faro") at the top of the Straits southwest to the base of Monte Poverello. Dry red. Grapes: Nerello Mascalese 45-60%, Nerello Cappuccio 15-30%, Nocera 5-10%; Calabrese/Gaglioppo/Sangiovese up to 15%. Yld 70/100, Alc 12, Acd 0.5, Ag 1 yr.

Etna (1968)

The theory that the soil around active volcanos is ideal for vines gets a tepid endorsement on Etna, where today's wines, though produced in some quantity, never equal the grandeur of the setting. The red can be firm and tasty in its early years, but the rosé

from the same grapes seems but a pale afterthought. The best of Etna is often the *bianco superiore*, which relies almost exclusively on Carricante. It shows polish from the Barone di Villagrande which has long been the zone's leading producer.

Zone: Slopes of the volcano in a high altitude strip forming a semicircle around the eastern side, extending from Randazzo on the north through Linguaglossa, Sant'Alfio, and Nicolosi to Paternò on the south, and taking in 14 other communes in Catania province. Bianco superiore comes only from the commune of Milo.
Bianco Dry white. Grapes: Carricante at least 60% with Catarratto Bianco Comune or Lucido; Trebbiano/Minnella Bianca/other whites up to 15%. Yld 63/90, Alc 11.5, Acd 0.6-0.75.
Bianco superiore Dry white. Grapes: Carricante min 80% with Catarratto Bianco Comune or Lucido; Trebbiano/Minnella Bianca/other whites. Yld 63/90, Alc 12, Acd 0.55-0.7.
Rosso Dry red. Grapes: Nerello Mascalese at least 80% with Nerello Cappuccio; whites up to 10%. Yld 63/90, Alc 12.5, Acd 0.55-0.7.
Rosato Dry rosé. Grapes: As rosso. Yld 63/90, Alc 12.5, Acd 0.55-0.7.

Other wines of note

Most growers in the Lipari isles make dry table wines, of which Carlo Hauner's Salina Rosso and Bianco are pleasant examples. Token quantities of amber, slightly sweet Mamertino are made from whites at the state-run Cantina Sperimentale at Milazzo. Many producers of Etna DOC also make vdt, as well as sparkling and dessert wines, though rarely of special note.

ESTATES/GROWERS

Bagni, Santa Margherita di Messina (ME). Practically exclusive production of Faro DOC from a 2 ha plot owned by Giacomo Currò.
Carlo Hauner, Lingua di Salina (ME). A Milanese designer arrived as a tourist in 1963 and bought a farm where he could paint and make wine. It took time and patience to build up his vineyards to 22 ha and master the intricacies of the peculiar local Malvasia, but Hauner

has emerged with one of Italy's most acclaimed dessert wines and proof that connoisseurs will pay a high price for the truly unique.

WINE HOUSES/MERCHANTS

Barone di Villagrande, Milo (CT). From high vineyards on the southern slopes, Carlo Nicolosi Asmundo produces Etna DOC, including an admired *bianco superiore*.
Cantine Colosi, Messina. Pietro Colosi makes impressive Malvasia delle Lipari, along with the vdt Salina Rosso and Bianco.

COOPERATIVES

Cooperativa La Ginestra, Malfa (ME). Small group of growers on the isle of Salina makes a good, if rustic, Malvasia delle Lipari.
CS Torrepalino, Solicchiata (CT). Etna DOC and vdt from growers with 165 ha.

Below top: lemon trees growing around Noto in Siracusa province. Bottom: vineyards for Etna's Bianco Superiore are planted only at Milo where the estate of Barone di Villagrande is the leading producer.

Wines of the southeast: Siracusa, Noto, and Vittoria

This hot corner of Sicily was once noted for opulent Moscato and unexpectedly potent cherry-coloured table wines, but like the glories of Magna Graecia they have now been reduced to remnants. Producers also find it hard to sell the once prized blending wines from Pachino in the plains between Capo Passero and Monti Iblei. But curiosity seekers should be amused by the creations of Giuseppe Coria, whose cellars at Vittoria hold some of Italy's most unusual wines.

Moscato di Siracusa (1973)

The DOC requires a wine of yellow to old gold colour with amber tints, a delicate and characteristic aroma, and a sweet, velvety flavour, but since none has been produced for years there is no way of confirming the description. Grecian Syracuse is well worth a visit, but not for its wine.

Zone: Coastal hills in the commune of Siracusa. Sweet white. Grape: Moscato Bianco, possibly semidried or passito. Yld 49/70, Alc 16.5 (res sugar min 2.5%), Acd 0.5.

Moscato di Noto (1974)

Only a few hundred bottles of this luscious sweet wine are made, most of them on an experimental basis at the state-sponsored cellars at Noto.

Zone: Hills in the communes of Noto, Rosolini, Pachino, and Avola all in Siracusa province. Grape: Moscato Bianco.

Naturale Sweet white. Yld 81/125, Alc 11.5 (res sugar max 3.5%), Acd 0.45.

Spumante Sweet sparkling white. Yld 81/125, Alc 13 (res sugar max 3.5%), Acd 0.5.

Liquoroso Fortified sweet white. Yld 81/125, Alc 22 (natural alc min 16% before fortification, after which 6% max may remain in res sugar), Acd 0.4. Ag 5 mths.

Cerasuolo di Vittoria (1973)

This typical local wine is named for its cherry-red colour, which makes it look like a dark rosé though it has more strength and stamina than most. It goes well when young with white meat such as veal or poultry.

Zone: Hills inland from the coast between Ragusa and Gela, based in Vittoria and including four other communes in Ragusa province, Caltagirone and Licodia Eubea in Catania province, and Gela and Niscemi in Caltanissetta. Dry red. Grapes: Frappato at least 40% with Calabrese up to 60%; Grosso Nero/Nerello Mascalese up to 10%. Yld 65/100, Alc 13, Acd 0.5.

Other wines of note

The most remarkable wines of the area are made by Giuseppe Coria at Vittoria (see below), though the environs of that DOC zone were once among the most prolific and prized vineyard areas of Sicily. Today, good local wines can be found around the towns of Acate, Niscemi, Mazzarone, and Caltagirone, but none are publicized outside the area. The once noted Ambrato di Comiso, a sweet amber wine made from Frappato grapes whose musts are partly reduced by cooking, is rarely seen. Nor is there much evidence of Frappato di Vittoria, a dry red from the same grapes that is sometimes aged into a maderized aperitif wine. The plains around Pachino make decent vdt, including Luparello, from Calabrese grapes which is aged in wood to become one of Italy's most virile rosés.

ESTATES/GROWERS

Giuseppe Coria, Vittoria (RG). A retired army colonel is one of Sicily's most inspired winemakers with creations from 3 ha of vines at Villa Fontane. They include a rich Moscato; the aged Solicchiato Bianco from semidried grapes; and the even more durable reddish-amber Stravecchio Siciliano from Cerasuolo. Decades in casks make the *stravecchio* ever more luxuriant. Perpetuo is a wine drawn from the same barrel each year, after which it is topped up with the latest vintage in the *solera* style. Coria's Cerasuolo di Villa Fontane is slightly stronger than the DOC version.

COS, Vittoria (RG). An emerging estate carries the initials of its owners' last names – Cilia, Occhipinti Strano – on the labels of an impressive Cerasuolo di Vittoria DOC.

WINE HOUSES/MERCHANTS

Cantina Sperimentale di Noto, Noto (SR). The state-run oenological research centre bottles some Moscato di Noto DOC.

Carlo Modica, Vittoria (RG). Good Cerasuolo di Vittoria DOC.

COOPERATIVES

CS Valle dell'Acate, Acate (RG). Good Cerasuolo di Vittoria DOC and vdt from cellars supervised by Giuseppe Coria.

Below: vines in the province of Agrigento an area centred around a Greek city and its temple ruins.

Wines of central and southern Sicily

Some of Sicily's fine wines – and a lot of notoriously inferior products – comes from the sun-soaked central and southern slopes. None of the provinces of Agrigento, Caltanissetta, and Enna has a DOC of its own, though Caltanissetta claims a corner of Cerasuolo di Vittoria. That province also produces the well publicized Libecchio and claims a share of the region's leading estate in Regaleali, where the Tasca d'Almerita family has proved that Sicily's highlands can make dry wines as fragrant, complex, and suave as those from several latitudes further north. If Enna's isolated heights have little to offer, Agrigento's arid contours contribute greatly to the island's surpluses with "wines" from table grapes that are often made expressly for EEC subsidized distillation. But among that province's massive output there are a number of worthy vdt sold under the brands of Settesoli, Bonera, Feudo dei Fiori, and Steri from the Comarca di Naro.

ESTATES/GROWERS

Regaleali/Conte Tasca d'Almerita, Vallelunga (CL). More than two decades ago Giuseppe Tasca began devoting his efforts to improving the wine on his Regaleali estate, a former feudal domain straddling the provinces of Caltanissetta and Palermo. He reasoned that microclimates at heights of 500-700 m would be similar to those on the lower slopes of the Alps and central Apennines. Vineyards were replanted and expanded (now almost 300 ha) and cellars revitalized. Three generations of the Tasca family now contribute to production of first-rate dry vdt. The whites are exemplified by Nozze d'Oro, which emphasizes Sauvignon Blanc over Inzolia in a wine of size and depth with fresh aromas and flavours. The reds and rosé are made from Nerello Mascalese and Perricone, which reach full-blown style in the aristocratic Rosso del Conte from the Casavecchia vineyards.
Giuseppe Camilleri, Naro (AG). On 17 ha of the fertile Comarca di Naro plateau, Camilleri grows Lambrusco and Barbera alongside Nero d'Avola for Steri Rosso and the singular Riserva

Speciale. Trebbiano, Inzolia, and Vernaccia di San Gimignano make a fresh, tasty white.

WINE HOUSES/MERCHANTS

Barone di Turolifi, Caltanissetta. Fratelli Averna, producers of a noted Amaro, also make the well-publicized Libecchio Bianco and Rosso vdt with a label designed by the famous Sicilian artist Renato Guttuso.

COOPERATIVES

CS Settesoli, Menfi (AG). Immense production from growers with 4,000 ha of vines includes the red, white, and rosé Menfi vdt that carry the admirable Settesoli trademark, as well as the respectable Feudo dei Fiori and Bonera brands. Director Diego Planeta is also president of the Regional Institute of Vines and Wine.
CS Sambuca di Sicilia, Sambuca di Sicilia (AG). Cellaro red, white, and rosé vdt head the large production.
CS Enocarboj, Sciacca (AG). Large output of vdt sold under the Carboj and Anteo brands.

Above: the traditional and modern faces of winemaking at the Regaleali estate straddling the provinces of Palermo and Caltanissetta.

Wines of western Sicily and Pantelleria

Well over half of Sicily's wine originates in the hills between Palermo and the western tip of Cape Lilibeo with the old port of Marsala that lends its name to the island's only credible wine legend. Marsala leads Sicily's DOCs in prestige as well as volume. The vineyards that surround the town contribute a vital share to the volume that makes Trapani the most prolific of Italy's 94 provinces and Marsala one of the busiest ports for wine shipments to northern Italy and France. The province's two other classified wines also have gained some prominence, Alcamo for its flinty dry white and the island of Pantelleria for its wickedly rich Moscato. But DOC is only part of the story, for the majority of Sicily's good dry table wines are made in the provinces of Trapani and Palermo, whose premier house, Duca di Salaparuta, is better known as Corvo. Its wines from grapes selected in choice vineyards around the island have given Sicilian oenology a modern image.

Alcamo or Bianco Alcamo (1972)
Some producers defy the norm and make white wines of respectable class and character – notably the estates of Rapitalà and Rincione – though there is little to commend most of the others beyond the wishy washy sort of purity that automatically qualifies it as a good fish wine in Sicily.
   Zone: Hills around the town of Alcamo overlooking the Gulf of Castellamare between Monreale and Calatafimi and including 11 other communes in Trapani and Palermo provinces. Dry white. Grapes: Catarratto Bianco Comune/Catarratto Bianco Lucido; Damaschino/Grecanico/Trebbiano Toscano up to 20%. Yld 84/120, Alc 11.5, Acd .45.

Marsala (1969)
The ancient port of Marsala, whose name derives from the Arab Marsah-el-Allah, is the capital of Sicilian viniculture, though its low-rise industrial-style *cantine* give it more the appearance of an old factory town than a wine mecca. Not long ago, the name Marsala was little more than a joke among serious drinkers who scoffed at its connection with flavourings alien to wine. But lately *vergine* and *superiore* versions from certain houses have regained some of the early status.
   This Sicilian classic can trace its roots to antiquity, since the Romans used cooked musts to make similar sweet wines. The influence of the long

Spanish rule is also evident with traditional ageing methods similar to that of sherry. But it was an Englishman, John Woodhouse from Liverpool, who devised the basic methods for Marsala and created an international market for the fortified wines which he began shipping to Britain in 1773. He was joined by compatriots whose names – Ingham and Whitaker – still appear on labels, though Italians led by Vincenzo Florio have dominated the industry since the mid-1800s. Among Marsala's famous devotees were Lord Nelson, who supplied it to his Mediterranean fleet, and Garibaldi, who praised the sweet type when he landed in Sicily at the start of his drive to unite Italy. But its real achievement was winning a place of honour alongside port, sherry, and madeira in Regency and Victorian England, where prized versions were identified by initials as SOM (Superior Old Marsala), LP (London Particular), and GD (Garibaldi Dolce).

A century ago, Marsala was Italy's best-known wine abroad, even if it was sometimes passed off as the more prestigious madeira. But gradually Marsala lost ground as a sipping wine, though it remained indispensable in the kitchen in dishes ranging from veal escalope to zabaglione. Its inimitably assertive flavour has inspired blends with the likes of eggs, coffee, and marzipan in creamy sweet concoctions that all but destroyed its reputation as a serious wine. Only over the last couple of decades has authentic Marsala regained its place at Italian tables, though it still has a lot of lost ground to make up internationally on sherry and port. The DOC was a starting point for recovery, but its regulations didn't go far enough. So a small group of producers, showing foresight and drive unprecedented in the Mezzogiorno's wine industry, worked behind the scenes to restore its image, finally bringing about a reform that took effect in 1986.

The rules restrict vinification, ageing, and bottling to the DOC zone, requiring also that concentrated or cooked musts and alcohol for fortification be derived only from the prescribed grape varieties grown there. Previously, parts of the provinces of Palermo and Agrigento were included in the growing zone, and wines were often aged and bottled away from the island (mainly in Piedmont where vermouth firms also handled Marsala). It is the only Italian wine to specify bottling in the DOC zone – and this requirement has been contested by the EEC. Also new are the descriptions *oro* (gold), *ambra* (amber), and *rubino* (ruby). *Oro* and *ambra*, both based on white grapes, prevail in wines that turn from honey-yellow to burnished gold to deep amber as they

age. Of the prescribed grape varieties, Catarratto dominates, though Grillo is considered the classic grape. The rarely seen *rubino* revives the historic use of dark varieties in wines that show a deep ruby hue in their youth but turn more amber with age.

The new law also did away with the DOC category of Marsala Speciali, which had applied to the flavoured types. It does allow for the popular egg or zabaglione style known as *cremovo* to state on labels "cremovo zabaione vino aromatizzato" or "cremovo vino aromatizzato" if it contains at least 80% Marsala. Products which contain 60% or more may put on the label "preparato con l'impiego di vino Marsala", citing the type. If made with less than 60%, the product may still list Marsala among the ingredients.

Production and ageing methods for DOC Marsala vary according to type, though the rules wisely allow some flexibility for houses to express personal styles. Processes are intricate, even for the basic *fine*, which requires no wood ageing and is used mainly for cooking or blending. For example, the use of concentrated musts, and what are known as *cotto* (cooked musts) and *sifone* or *mistella* (a blend of sweet musts and wine alcohol) are strictly defined (*see* right). But the key to a fine Marsala is ageing, which is done in locally made oak barrels stacked in rows reaching almost to the rafters in the well-ventilated, above ground *cantine*. Some wines are kept for a decade or longer in barrels to become

lieviti, or cultures for blending. Producers express many individual styles in the dry, semisweet, and sweet versions of *superiore* and its *riserva*, and in the always dry *vergine* or *soleras*. Some of the latter is made through a process similar to the Jerez *solera* method of fractional blending of younger wines with older, but most Marsala Vergine relies on combining wines of different ages from different barrels. The dry *superiore riserva* is often the smoothest type of Marsala, though the most distinctive is the *vergine* or *soleras*, with its hints of spices, vanilla, citrus fruits, and that curious combination of burnt caramel and wood.

Marsala production has levelled off at about 225,000 hl, barely enough to rank in the top ten of DOC wines in volume, where years ago it was usually third or fourth. Of the potential 187,500 cases, however, much is *fine* sold in bulk for making the flavoured types. Production of the aged *superiore* and *vergine* remain limited. Florio is the largest house, though among the big firms Pellegrino and Rallo seem the most admired. But none matches the image built by Marco De Bartoli, whose token quantities from his Vecchio Samperi estate have won wide critical acclaim.

Zone: A vast area of plains and tapered hills extending from the port of Marsala through much of Trapani province, excluding the communes of Alcamo, Favignana (the Egadi isles), and Pantelleria. Production is concentrated in Marsala, where most houses have their cellars. Grapes: For oro and ambra

of all types Grillo/Catarratto(all clones)/ Inzolia/Damaschino. Max yld for base wine 75/100; For rubino of all types Perricone/ Calabrese/Nerello Mascalese, any or all above whites up to 30%. Max yld reds for base wine 67.5/90.

Fine May be oro, ambra, or rubino, also secco, semisecco, and dolce. May also be called Italy Particular (IP). Sifone and concentrated musts are used in all types but cotto is permitted only in ambra. Yld *see* grapes, Alc 17*, Acd 0.35, Ag 1 yr.
Superiore May be oro, ambra, or rubino, also secco, semisecco, dolce, and riserva. May also be called Superior Old Marsala (SOM), London Particular (LP) and Garibaldi Dolce (GD). Sifone and concentrated musts are used in all types but cotto is permitted only in ambra. Yld *see* grapes, Alc 18*, Acd 0.35, Ag 2 yrs in wood; riserva 4 yrs in wood.
Vergine or **soleras** May be oro, ambra, or rubino, also secco, stravecchio, and riserva. Fortified with wine alcohol, but no concentrated must, cotto or sifone is permitted. Yld *see* grapes, Alc 18*, Acd 0.35, Ag 5 yrs in wood; stravecchio or riserva 10 yrs. in wood.
* Secco res sugar less than 40 gr/l, semisecco 40-100 gr/l and dolce more than 100 gr/l.

Moscato di Pantelleria and Passito di Pantelleria (1971)

The most ornate of Italy's many Moscatos comes from the sun-scorched volcanic isle of Pantelleria, which lies closer to Tunisia than to the rest of Sicily. The exotic surroundings have inspired myths since the Phoenicians first arrived with Zibibbo vines and began dedicating their sweet ambrosias

Above: barrel ageing is essential in the making of fine Marsala. Left: Marco De Bartoli has built his small Vecchio Samperi estate into one of Marsala's most admired producers.

303

to Tanit, the goddess of love. The wind-withered vines of this variety of Moscato or Moscatellone produce plump, sugar-laden grapes that are dried in the sun to concentrate for the *passito* versions (also Italy's most prized raisins). The Agricoltori Associati cooperative makes a slightly sweet *spumante* called Solimano, though its star is a *passito extra* called Tanit that exudes opulence. Marco De Bartoli's *passito naturalmente dolce* called Bukkuram matches sweetness with grace in an uncommonly seductive dessert wine. Although the DOC defines a dizzying array of sweet golden to amber nectars, the other versions are rarely seen.

Zone: The island of Pantelleria in Trapani province. Grape: Zibibbo, possibly semidried or passito.

Naturale Sweet white, also spumante, naturalmente dolce and liquoroso. Yld 49/70, Alc 12.5*; naturalmente dolce 17.5*, Acd 0.45.

Passito Sweet white, also naturalmente dolce, liquoroso and extra. Yld 28/70, Alc 14*; liquoroso 21.5*; extra 23.9*, Acd 0.4, Ag extra 1 yr.

* Naturale fermented alc incl res sugar min 8% and naturalmente dolce min 13%. Passito fermented alc min 14% plus 11% res sugar; liquoroso fermented alc incl res sugar min 15%; extra min 15.5%.

Other wines of note

Sicily's best known brand is Corvo, as applied to the dry white and red vdt of Duca di Salaparuta, as well as sparkling and sweet wines and a revelation in the Duca Enrico red. Marco De Bartoli's Vecchio Samperi and sweet Inzolia di Samperi have brought new style to Marsala's wines. Fresh, dry vdt have gained prominence, none more than Donnafugata, though Rincione, Draceno, Cellaro, Cerdèse, and Conte di Salemi are other brands that offer good quality at a reasonable price. Varietal whites come from Grecanico and Damaschino and reds from Pignatello. Most Marsala firms also make vdt and *spumanti*, as well as sweet wines, brandy, and liqueurs. Much Moscato from Pantelleria and elsewhere is blended into commercial Vin Santo and other sweet wines sold in large bottles with metal caps.

ESTATES/GROWERS

Donnafugata, Contessa Entellina (PA). Gabriella Anca Rallo and her husband Giacomo, of the noted Marsala family, make some of Sicily's most stylish dry vdt at their new cellars, drawing from 70 ha of vineyards in the high Belice valley south of Palermo. The prize-winning Donnafugata Bianco and Rosso combine typical Sicilian varieties with outsiders which lend aroma and character. The single vineyard Vigna di

Above: the Doric temple at Segesta dates back to the year 430 BC.

Gabri white comes entirely from Anzonia. The winery also produces rosé, some Chardonnay and the novel white Damaskino from the ancient Damaschino variety.

Fontanarossa, Cerda (PA). Source of Cerdèse red, white, and rosé vdt.

Fratelli Lombardo, Marsala (TP). Good Marsala Superiore DOC and other wines mainly from 425 ha of own vines.

Salvatore Murana, Pantelleria (PA). A grower making Moscato di Pantelleria and vdt from his small production.

Rapitalà, Camporeale (PA). The estate in the Alcamo zone is owned by the Adelkam corporation and run by Frenchman Contes Hugues de la Gatinais and Sicilian wife Gigi. From 150 ha of vines at an altitude of 300-535 m they produce 125,000 cases of Alcamo DOC of an uncommon depth and nuance, as well as 40,000 cases of Rapitalà Rosso vdt.

Rincione, Calatafimi (TP). Pietro Paolo Papè, Principe di Valdina, selects from 120 ha of vines to make bright, modern wines: a flowery Alcamo DOC plus Rincione Bianco, Rosso, and Rosato vdt.

Vecchio Samperi-De Bartoli, Marsala (TP). Marco De Bartoli, the bright, amiable ambassador of Marsala, has revolutionized his 15 ha Vecchio Samperi estate to produce the most admired wines of western Sicily. After serving as *enotecnico* at noted Marsala houses, De Bartoli went out on his own in 1978, and issued Vecchio Samperi, almost a Marsala Solera but not fortified with alcohol. His limited production of 20-year-old Vecchio Samperi and Marsala Superiore Riserva have raised the long tradition to new heights. He also makes a sweet white wine called Inzolia di Samperi from the Vigna Miscia, and a dry Josephine Doré.

De Bartoli buys grapes on Pantelleria and dries them there for his velvety Moscato Passito called Bukkuram.

WINE HOUSES/MERCHANTS

V. Giacalone Alloro, Marsala (TP). Large and respected Marsala house.

Vito Curatolo Arini, Marsala (TP). Sound Marsala DOC from a house founded in 1875.

Duca di Salaparuta, Casteldaccia (PA). Founded in 1824 by Edoardo Alliata di Villafranca, the firm is now owned by the Ente Siciliano per la Promozione Industriale, which has made it the region's standard-bearer. Its Corvo wines are respected for class and consistency and account for nearly 10 million bottles a year, of which about 40% is exported. Grapes from various parts of the island are fastidiously selected by chief winemaker Franco Giacosa and vinified in the new computerized cellars at Casteldaccia. The whites – Prima Goccia and the delicate Colomba Platino – come from Inzolia, Trebbiano, and Catarratto, the red Vino Fiore from Nerello Mascalese, Perricone, and Nero d'Avola. From the 1984 vintage came a new wine called Duca Enrico, a pure Nero d'Avola from high vineyards in east central Sicily. After ageing to perfection in small barrels, it laid to rest any lingering doubts that Sicily can make dry red wines of grace and complexity from native grape varieties. The house also produces sparkling wines, the Marsala-like Stravecchio di Sicilia, and the unique fortified red Ala, which is aged in bitter cherry wood.

Fratelli De Vita, Marsala (TP). Marsala DOC.

Fratelli Fici, Marsala (TP). Sound range includes a fine Marsala Vergine.

Florio, Marsala (TP). In 1833 Vincenzo Florio began the enterprise that earned him the title "king of Marsala" as he outpaced the English pioneers. In 1929 the firm became part of the Cinzano group, incorporating the original Woodhouse and Ingham (whose names are still used on labels) into what is now called S.A.V.I. Florio & Co. The largest producer of Marsala DOC with more than 300,000 cases, Florio's complete range is headed by the semisweet ACI 1840 and bone dry Riserva Egadi, both *superiore*. Brandy and liqueurs are also produced.

Marino Grandi Vini Siciliani, Marsala (TP). Marsala and Alcamo DOC and dry vdt: white Verdello Siciliano and red Nerello Siciliano.

Mirabella, Marsala (TP). A relatively young but dynamic firm with an admirable Marsala Vergine. The firm also uses the Cudia brand.

Fratelli Montalto, Marsala (TP). Alcamo and Marsala DOC and vdt.

Carlo Pellegrino, Marsala (TP). Founded in 1880, the firm makes some of the best Marsala Superiore, as well as vdt from Grecanico and Pignatello.

Nuova Rallo, Marsala (TP). Founded in 1860, this is one of the most respected Marsala houses, with 120 ha of vines contributing to 90,000 cases of DOC and a significant production of vdt and *spumante*. Marsala Vergine 1860 stands out in the distinguished range.

COOPERATIVES

Cooperativa Agricola Fiumefreddo, Alcamo (TP). Alcamo DOC and vdt.

CS Paladino, Alcamo (TP). Alcamo DOC and vdt.

Agricoltori Associati di Pantelleria, Pantelleria (TP). Some 1,300 growers supply grapes to the largest producer of Moscato di Pantelleria DOC. Specialities are the Passito Extra called Tanit and the *spumante* known as Solimano.

Cooperativa Agricoltori Saturnia, Partanna (TP). Red, white, and rosé vdt under the Draceno label.

CS La Vite, Partanna (TP). Red and white vdt under the Donzelle label.

Cooperativa Agricola Aurora, Salemi (TP). Alcamo DOC and vdt under the Castelvecchio trademark.

Cooperativa Agricola Le Torri, Salemi (TP). Large production of refreshing vdt, led by the white Conte di Salemi.

Consorzio Agrario Provinciale di Trapani, Trapani. Vdt under the Segesta and Trabino trademarks.

Travel Information

RESTAURANTS/HOTELS

La Funtanazza, 91011 Alcamo (TP), at Monte Bonifato 6 km south of town. Tel (0924)25314. Fine country food and friendly service in a hillside hotel with views over Alcamo and the Gulf of Castellamare.

Filippino, 98055 Isola di Lipari (ME). Tel (090)9811002. Lipari's renowned restaurant serves fresh fish and Sicilian wines on a seaside terrace.

Zio Ciccio, 91025 Marsala (TP). Tel (0923)981962. Seaside restaurant offers fish fresh from the boat with the best Sicilian whites.

Mazzarò Sea Palace, 98030 Mazzarò (ME). Tel (0942)24004. Deluxe hotel on the bay of Taormina with its own beach and heated pool.

Hotel Cossyra, Contrada Mùrsia, 91017 Pantelleria (TP). Tel (0923) 911154. Pleasant hotel with beach, pool, tennis court, and a good restaurant with fish and other island specialities.

Alberto, Via Ghibellina 95, 98100 Messina. Tel (090)710711. Traditional Messina dishes and novelties. Good local wines.

Jonico'a Rutta e Ciauli, Riviera Dionisio il Grande 194, 96100 Siracusa. Tel (0931)65540. Perched on a cliff overlooking the Ionian Sea, the restaurant serves good Sicilian specialities with well-chosen wines.

Trattoria Minosse, Via Mirabella 6, 96100 Siracusa. Tel (0931)66366. Family place in Ortigia, the heart of the old city, with tasty vegetable and fish dishes.

Giova Rosy Senior, 98039 Taormina (ME). Tel (0942)24411. Impeccably prepared fresh pasta and fish served on a shady terrace.

PLACES OF INTEREST

Sicilians haven't yet realized the tourist potential of their wealth of vineyards. Marsala's are awe-inspiring for their expanse; Etna's are breathtaking for their positions and views; Lipari's and Pantelleria's are intriguing for their sheer tenacity. But most tourists come to Sicily for the glories of the antique Mediterranean world and the sun and sea. The Greek heritage is unsurpassed in Italy, and there are more than enough Roman, Arab, Norman, and other artefacts to keep scholars busy. Regular ferries connect Calabria's Villa San Giovanni and Messina. There is also a ferry service from Naples, Genoa, and Cagliari to Palermo, Catania, and Trapani. Daily flights link Palermo and Catania with other Italian and major European cities.

Agrigento. The ancient Greek town of Akragas shouldn't be missed for its Valley of the Temples at sunset. Wander into the old towns in the pastel hills to see the island as Giuseppe Tomasi di Lampedusa depicted it in his novel based on Sicilian history, *The Leopard*.

Etna and Taormina. The ascent of Mount Etna by car, cable car, or foot is memorable, especially if the volcano is erupting. On clear days there are views halfway across Sicily and over the water to Lipari and Calabria. The medieval town of Taormina, between mountain and sea, is the fashionable place to stop before and after the climb.

Lipari (Aeolian isles). The seven isles have volcanos, black sand beaches, and crystal clear waters with unusual marine life. Wine lovers might find the Malvasia of Hauner worth the trip to Salina. Regular ferry service links Lipari with Milazzo and Messina, as well as other ports.

Marsala. Despite the drab industrial appearance of the port, the cellars can be interesting. The largest, Florio (*see* page 304), has a wine museum and gives regular guided tours, though any can be visited by appointment. A drive from Marsala northeast to Segesta, then south to Selinus (Selinunte) and back takes in two of Sicily's finest Greek temples and its most impressive stretch of vines.

Pantelleria. The sun-scorched island is an exotic hideaway with black beaches, fresh fish, sweet Moscato, and a scent of the nearby Arab world. In summer there are regular ferries and flights from Trapani and Palermo.

Siracusa and Noto. Ancient Syracuse, the home of Archimedes, was the pride of Magna Graecia. Remnants of the city which rivalled Athens for splendour are seen everywhere in and around it. This corner of Sicily is also noted for baroque architecture, which embellishes the *palazzi* in Siracusa's Ortigia quarter and in the wine town of Noto to the southwest.

Below: the name Marsala is Arabic in origin: the town is most noted for its fortified wines and as the port where Garibaldi landed in 1860.

Glossary

Abboccato Lightly sweet, mouth filling.

Acidità Acidity, in total or fixed acids as opposed to volatile acids (*acidità volatile* or acetic acid, which impart a sour taste and a vinegary odour).

Acidulo Acidulous, crisp or sharp in flavour from high acidity.

Alberello Bush, in reference to a low, either staked or free standing vine formed by head training. Most common in the south, but fading.

Alcool Alcohol, as expressed by percent of volume on labels. *Alcool svolto* is developed through partial fermentation, usually in sweet wines.

Amabile Literally "amiable" to describe medium sweet wines, usually but not always with more residual sugar than *abboccato* and less than *dolce*.

Amaro Bitter, applied to a type of liqueur and to describe the flavour of certain wines, though the terms *amarognolo* or *ammandorlato*, denoting a toasted almond sort of bitterness, are more complimentary.

Ambra or **ambrato** The amber or burnished gold to light brown colour of certain well-aged wines, such as Marsala, where Ambra is a specific type.

Annata Year of vintage.

Aroma The ample scent of young, fruity wines, often white.

Aromatico Refers to wine of pronounced aroma, ie Moscato or Riesling.

Asciutto Bone dry for still wines, though in *spumante* it is moderately sweet.

Assaggio or **degustazione** Tasting.

Azienda agricola/agraria/vitivinicola Farm or estate which by law may not purchase more than half the grapes or wine sold under its labels and may only use terms for estate bottling on products of its own vines.

Barrique Small oak barrel often of French origin used increasingly for ageing.

Bianco White.

Botte Cask or barrel (also called *fusto*). A *bottaio* is a barrel maker.

Bottiglia Bottle.

Bouquet The term, as in French and English, describes the odour of a mature wine.

Bricco Piedmontese term for a vineyard at the crest of a hill. Also *bric*.

Brut Dry sparkling wine. Extra Brut signifies very dry, as in *pas dosé* or *nature*·wines without the final dose of liqueur.

Cantina Cellar or winery.

Cantina sociale or **cooperativa** Cooperative winery.

Capitel A privileged vineyard site in Verona's hills.

Carato A small barrel, sometimes used as a synonym for *barrique*. *Caratello* is the smaller barrel traditionally used for ageing Vin Santo.

Casa vinicola or **azienda vinicola** Wine house or merchant (*commerciante*) whose production comes mainly from purchased grapes.

Cascina Farmhouse, often used for estate or vineyard in the northwest.

Castello The term for castle in theory can only be used on labels of DOC/DOCG wines, though exceptions are seen.

Cerasuolo Cherry red, used to describe certain rosé wines.

Champenois or **metodo champenois** The Champagne method, though the term *méthode champenoise* or translations are to be restricted to French sparkling wines in the EEC, so *metodo classico* or *metodo tradizionale* are usual in Italy.

Charmat or **metodo charmat** The French-originated method (also known as *cuve close*) of fermenting sparkling wine in sealed tanks, or *autoclave*. *Charmat lungo* is a prolonged fermentation of a wine in contact with the lees to approximate the effect of *champenoise*.

Chiaretto A traditional term for claret used to describe certain rosé wines.

Chilogrammo Kilogram (1,000 grams), the basic measure of weight used in Italy, where it is also known as kilo. Abbreviated as kg in text.

Classico Area of historical note within a broader zone (eg Chianti Classico, Soave Classico) and the wine from there, which is often – but not necessarily – superior to the rest. Also applied to sparkling wines by the Champagne method as *metodo classico*.

Colle or **Collina** Hill, plural *colli* or *colline*.

Commerciante Merchant house or bottler that works primarily with purchased grapes or wines.

Consorzio Voluntary consortium of producers authorised to supervise and control production as well as to promote wine.

Cordone Cordon, the classic system of training vines onto wires strung between poles, also called *spalliera*.

Crémant The French term for softly sparkling wine is also used in Italy.

Cru The French term not permitted on Italian labels is often used to describe distinct vineyards or areas, since there is no single equivalent in Italian.

DOC Wine of controlled origin (*see* Laws and Labels).

DOCG Wine of controlled and guaranteed origin (*see* Laws and Labels).

Dolce Sweet, usually for wines with the highest degree of residual sugar.

Dry When describing sparkling wine, also as extra dry, it refers to lightly sweet rather than the truly dry brut or extra brut.

Enologia Oenology, the science of wine. *Enologo*, for oenologist or winemaker, may also apply to a wine expert. *Enotecnico* is a qualification for a graduate of a five-year course at a technical school of oenology.

Enoteca Wine collection in reference to a place where it is displayed and usually sold. Italy's earliest *enoteche* were the Roman *tabernae vinariae*.

Etichetta label.

Ettaro Hectare, equivalent to 2.471 acres, the standard measure of vineyard area in Italy. Abbreviated as ha in text.

Ettolitro Hectolitre, or 100 litres, the usual measure of bulk wine volume in Italy. Abbreviated as hl in text.

Fattoria A farm or estate, originally applied mainly in central Italy to a property of some size consisting of several *poderi* (*see* Podere).

Fermentazione Fermentation, as applied to both the primary (or alcoholic) and secondary, which for still wines is usually the malolactic. Sparkling wines may state *fermentazione naturale* on labels if they have acquired carbon dioxide gas through natural processes.

Fiasco Flask, ie the straw-based bulbous Chianti container that has become ever rarer. Another popular flask was Orvieto's squat *pulcinella*.

Frizzante Lightly bubbly or *pétillant* in a category now specified as having less pressure than *spumante*. *Frizzantino* refers to a barely noticeable prickle.

Governo The once popular *governo all'uso toscano*, a secondary fermentation induced by adding semidried grapes or musts to the wine, typified the old Chianti which often had a brisk, slightly *pétillant* flavour.

Granato Garnet, a colour often used to describe red wines after ageing.

Gusto Flavour (not in the English sense of "gusto", however).

Imbottigliato da/messo in bottiglia da Bottled by, when followed by a term for grape grower or property with vineyards (often with the indication "all'origine") the wine should be estate bottled.

Invecchiato Aged, sometimes used as a qualifying term under DOC to specify a length of time. Ageing or *invecchiamento* is abbreviated as Ag in the Atlas.

Liquoroso Wine of high alcohol grade usually, but not always, fortified.

Litro Litre, the basic liquid measure in Italy, equivalent to 1.76 UK pints or 1.057 US quarts. Bottle sizes are usually expressed in millilitres, the standard size being 750 ml or three-quarters of a litre.

Macerazione carbonica Carbonic maceration, a partial fermentation process of whole grapes in sealed containers under pressure of their self-generated carbon dioxide gas, used mainly for *vino novello*.

Marchio Trademark, *registrato* or *depositato* means the brand is registered.

Marsalato or **maderizzato** Refers to wines which through slow oxidation take on flavours reminiscent of Marsala or Madeira, favourable when controlled in aperitif or dessert wines, undesirable in most dry table wines.

Maso A holding often used to describe an estate or vineyard in Trentino and the Verona area.

Masseria An estate or farm used most often in the southern peninsula.

Metodo classico or **tradizionale** See champenois.

Morbido Soft, used to describe wines with round, mellow flavour.

Mosto Must or grape juice. *Mosto concentrato* is concentrated for blending, *mosto cotto* (cooked for use in Marsala), *mosto fiore* (free run juice from softly crushed grapes, used for white wine).

Oro Gold, in wines of deep yellow colour, specifically in a type of Marsala.

Paglierino The pale straw colour often used to describe young whites.

Passito Strong, usually sweet wine from semidried, or *passito*, grapes. Called *flétri* in French-speaking Valle d'Aosta.

Pastoso Mellow, medium dry wine.

Pergola Vine training system using pole arms or arbours, most noted as the *pergola trentina* of the upper Adige valley.

Podere Farm or estate, usually small (*see* Fattoria).

Poggio Hill.

Profumo Odour or scent.

QbA The initials for *Qualitätswein bestimmter Anbaugebiete*, the German equivalent to DOC, is permitted for classified wines of Alto Adige.

Quintale Quintal or 100 kilograms, the usual measure of grape weight per hectare in Italy, though as of 1990 the EEC required use of kilograms or metric tons (*see* Tonnellata).

Recioto Term used mainly around Verona for strong wine from semidried grapes, often sweet but also dry (as in Amarone).

Resa Yield, as applied to both grapes and wine.

Riserva Reserve, applied only to DOC or DOCG wines aged for a specific length of time. *Riserva speciale* denotes longer ageing.

Ronco The Friulian term for a terraced vineyard (plural *ronchi*) is often used in wine names. Also used occasionally in Romagna and elsewhere.

Rosato Rosé or pink wine.

Rosso Red.

Rubino The ruby colour noted often in young red wine.

Sapore Flavour.

Secco Dry in still wines, but quite sweet in sparkling wines. *Semisecco* refers to medium dry or semisweet.

Solera or **soleras** Fractional blending by topping up wines ageing in barrels with younger ones, used for sherry in Spain, from where it was introduced to Sardinia and Sicily. Soleras is a type of Marsala.

Sommelier The French term is used for wine waiters or restaurateurs who often belong to the active Associazione Italiana Sommeliers.

Sorì Piedmontese for the part of a slope best exposed to the midday sun and most favourable to vines. Often used with a vineyard name. Also *sörì*.

Spumante Sparkling wine, dry or sweet, with no less than three atmospheres of pressure, produced by fermentation either in bottle or sealed tank methods. The German term *Sekt* may be used in Alto Adige.

Superiore Denotes a DOC wine that meets standards above the norm (higher alcohol, longer ageing) or, in some cases (eg Sangiovese di Romagna) from a certain area, though conditions vary.

Tappo di sughero Cork top. *Sa di tappo* means the wine is corked.

Tendone System of high trellised vine training used mainly on hot plains.

Tenuta Estate or farm.

Tonnellata The metric ton or 1,000 kilograms is to replace the quintale (100 kilograms) to measure grape weight in Italy.

Uva Grape. A bunch of grapes is *grappolo d'uva*.

Uvaggio A mixture of grape varieties, as in a composite wine such as Chianti.

Vecchio Old. certain DOC wines may carry the term after a set length of ageing. *Stravecchio*, very old, is used more often for spirits than wine.

Vendemmia The grape harvest.

Vigna or **vigneto** Vineyard.

Vignaiolo/viticoltore/coltivatore Terms for grape growers who may also be wine producers.

Vino da arrosto Robust, aged red wine that goes with roast meats, eg Barolo, Brunello.

Vino da taglio Blending wine, usually strong and red.

Vino da tavola Table wine, applied to most wines that don't qualify as DOC. Much of what is abbreviated as vdt in the text is *Vino da tavola a indicazione geografica*, which can include fine wines (*see* Laws and Labels).

Vino novello New wine, usually red, like the French *nouveau*. By law it must be bottled within the year of harvest.

Vini tipici Recently created category for wines typical of certain defined geographical areas (*see* Laws and Labels).

Vite Grapevine. *Viticoltura* is viticulture.

Vitigno Vine or grape variety. The term *monovitigno*, or sometimes *varietale*, is used to describe wine from a single variety.

Vitis vinifera The vine species from which most wine is made, though there are several families and thousands of distinct varieties.

Vivace Lively, a synonym for *frizzante* used to describe lightly bubbly wines.

VQPRD The EEC initials for quality wine produced in determined regions, as applied to DOC/DOCG. VSQPRD is used for sparkling wine in the category.

Zuccheri Sugars. Residual sugars are known as *residui*. *Zuccheraggio* is the term for chaptalization, the adding of sugar to musts to increase a wine's alcohol content.

BIBLIOGRAPHY

Burton Anderson, *The Mitchell Beazley Pocket Guide to Italian Wines*, revised edition, Mitchell Beazley: London, 1987.

Burton Anderson, *Vino, The Wines and Winemakers of Italy*, Little, Brown & Co: Boston, 1980.

R.W. Apple Jr., *Apple's Europe*, Atheneum: New York, 1986.

Nicola Dante Basile, *Il Vino in Italia*, Edizione del Sole 24 Ore: Milan, 1988.

Nicolas Belfrage, *Life Beyond Lambrusco*, Sidgwick & Jackson: London, 1985.

Alexis Bespaloff, *The New Frank Schoonmaker Encyclopedia of Wine*, Morrow: New York, 1988.

Alexis Bespaloff, *New Signet Book of Wine*, New American Library: New York, 1986.

Charles G. Bode, *Wines of Italy*, Peter Owen: London 1956; Dover: New York, 1974.

Gianfranco Bolognesi, *I Vini del Sole Romagna*, Editori del Sole: Milan, 1983.

Samuel Chamberlain, *Italian Bouquet*, Gourmet: New York, 1973.

Oz Clarke, *Webster's Wine Price Guide*, Websters/Mitchell Beazley: London, 1989.

Oz Clarke, *Wine Factfinder and Taste Guide*, Websters/Mitchell Beazley: London, 1989.

Philip Dallas, *Italian Wines*, Faber: London, 1983.

De Agostini, *Grande Atlante d'Italia*, Istituto Geografico De Agostini: Novara, 1987.

Riccardo Di Corato, *2214 Vini d'Italia*, Sonzogno: Milan, 1975.

Riccardo Di Corato, *Guida all'Italia dei Vini*, Touring Club Italiano: Milan, 1985.

Sandro Doglio, *Mangiare e Bere in Piemonte e in Valle d'Aosta*, City 2: Genoa, 1987.

Lorenzo Fantini, *Monografia sulla viticoltura ed enologia nella Provincia di Cuneo*, reprinted, Ordine dei Cavalieri del Tartufo e dei Vini di Alba, 1973.

Walter Filiputti, *Terre, Vigne & Vini del Friuli-Venezia Giulia*, Gianfranco Angelico Benvenuto: Udine, 1983.

Robert Finigan, *Essentials of Wine*, Knopf: New York, 1987.

Raymond Flower, *Chianti*, revised edition, Croom Helm: London, 1988.

Mario Fregoni, *Storia Antica sulle Origini della Vite e della Viticoltura*, to be published.

Mario Fregoni, *Viticoltura Generale*, Reda: Rome, 1985.

Gambero Rosso Vini d'Italia, revised edition, Le Guide del Gambero: Rome, 1989.

David Gleave, *The Wines of Italy*, Salamander: London, 1989.

Victor Hazan, *Italian Wine*, Alfred A. Knopf: New York, 1982.

Edward Hyams, *Dionysus, A Social History of the Wine Vine*, Sidgwick & Jackson: London, 1987.

Hugh Johnson, *The Story of Wine*, Mitchell Beazley: London, 1989.

Hugh Johnson, *The World Atlas of Wine*, 3rd edition, Mitchell Beazley: London, 1986.

Hugh Johnson, *Wine Companion*, 2nd edition, Mitchell Beazley: London, 1987.

La Guida d'Italia 1990, Le Guide dell'Espresso: Milan, 1989.

Alexis Lichine, *Encyclopedia of Wines & Spirits*, 4th edition, Cassell: London, 1985; Knopf: New York, 1985.

Michelin Italia 1990, Michelin Italiana: Milan, 1990.

Stefano Milioni, *Catalogo Generale dei Vini d'Italia 1987-1988*, Union: Rome, 1987.

Sandro Mondini, *I Vitigni Stranieri da Vino Coltivati in Italia*, G. Barbera: Florence, 1903.

E. Ottavi and A. Marescalchi, *Vade-Mecum del Commerciante di Uva e di Vini in Italia*, 2nd edition, Ottavi: Casale Monferrato, 1903.

Luigi Papo & Anna Pesenti, *Il Marsala*, Fabbri Editori: Milan, 1986.

Robert M. Parker Jr., *Wine Buyer's Guide*, revised edition, Dorling Kindersley: London, 1989; Simon & Schuster: New York, 1989.

Lamberto Paronetto, *Il Magnifico Chianti*, Enostampa: Verona, 1967.

Lamberto Paronetto et al, *Guida ai Vini d'Italia*, Arnoldo Mondadori: Milan, 1980.

Emanuele Pellucci, *Brunello di Montalcino*, 2nd edition, Pellucci: Florence, 1986.

Emanuele Pellucci, *Vino Nobile di Montepulciano*, Pellucci: Fiesole, 1985.

Emile Peynaud, *Knowing and Making Wine*, John Wiley: New York, 1984.

Emile Peynaud, *The Taste of Wine*, Macdonald & Co: London, 1987.

Antonio Piccinardi, *I Ristoranti di Bell'Italia*, Giorgio Mondadori: Milan, 1980.

Antonio Piccinardi & James Johnson, *The Gourmet's Tour of Italy*, New York Graphic Society/ Little, Brown & Co: New York, 1987.

Antonio Piccinardi & Gianni Sassi, *Berealto*, Arnoldo Mondadori: Milan, 1986.

Piero Pittaro & Lisio Plozner, *L'Uva e Il Vino*, Magnus Edizioni: Udine, 1982.

Jens Priewe, *Italiens Grosse Weine*, Sewald: Herford, Germany, 1987.

Virgilio Pronzati, *Guida alle Cantine e ai Vini di Liguria*, City 2: Genoa, 1987.

Renato Ratti, *Conoscere i Vini d'Italia*, AEB: Brescia, 1985.

Adriano Ravegnani, *I Cento Vini d'Italia*, Longanesi & Co: Milan, 1979.

Cyril Ray, *The New Book of Italian Wines*, Sidgwick & Jackson: London, 1982.

Cyril Ray, *The Wines of Italy*, McGraw-Hill: London, 1966.

Giuseppe Aldo di Ricaldone, *La Collezione Ampelografica Incisa (1792-1871)*, Camera Commercio di Asti: Asti, 1974.

Rivista di Viticoltura e di Enologia, *Disciplinari di Produzione Vini a Denominazione di Origine Controllata*, vols I-III, Casa Editrice Scarpis: Conegliano Veneto, 1968, 1971, 1979.

Jancis Robinson, *Vines, Grapes and Wines*, Mitchell Beazley: London, 1986.

Waverley Root, *The Food of Italy*, Atheneum: New York, 1971.

E.T. Salmon, *The Making of Roman Italy*, Thames & Hudson: London, 1982.

Mario Soldati, *Vino al Vino*, vols I-II, Arnoldo Mondadori: Milan, 1969, 1971.

Marco Trimani, *Brindare Italiano*, Fabbri Editori: Milan, 1984.

Marco Trimani, *Guida ai Vini d'Italia*, Editori Riuniti: Rome, 1984.

Luigi Veronelli, *I Vignaioli Storici*, vols I-IV, Mediolanum Editori Associati: Milan, 1986, 1987, 1990.

Luigi Veronelli, *Le Cantine di Veronelli*, Arnoldo Mondadori: Milan.

Luigi Veronelli, *I Ristoranti di Veronelli*, Fortune Italia: Milan.

Luigi Veronelli, *Catalogo dei Vini d'Italia*, various editions.

Sheldon & Pauline Wasserman, *Italy's Noble Red Wines*, New Century: Piscataway, NJ, 1985.

Faith Heller Willinger, *Eating in Italy*, Hearst Books: New York, 1989.

Index and Gazetteer

Note: the index includes references to all DOC wines, vineyards, estates and growers, wine houses and merchants, cooperatives, as well as important towns and villages. Map and grid references are given with the page number of the main reference in the text in numerical order as follows: Amorosa 196 C3, 216. All German place names in the South Tyrol are cross-referenced with the Italian town names.

Where different town names share the same name they are distinguished by the following abbreviations: Ab *Abruzzi*; Bas *Basilicata*; Cal *Calabria*; Cam *Campania*; E-R *Emilia-Romagna*; F-VG *Friuli-Venezia Giulia*; Lat *Latium*; Lig *Liguria*; Lom *Lombardy*; Mar *Marches*; Mol *Molise*; Pie *Piedmont*; Sar *Sardinia*; Si *Sicily*; T-AA *Trentino-Alto Adige*; Tus *Tuscany*; Umb *Umbria*; VdA *Valle d'Aosta*; Ven *Veneto*.

ACKNOWLEDGMENTS

Many persons have contributed to the realization of this book. First among them was the late Renato Ratti, whose maps of the vineyards of Barolo and Barbaresco and Italy's wine sectors inspired my own work. Special gratitude goes to Mario Fregoni who was generous with source material and the wisdom that has brought him so propitiously to lead the national DOC committee. Much practical information, and some revealing insights, were supplied by numerous wine-makers mentioned in the text.

The editorial team, headed by Chris Foulkes, met challenges with professional poise, though no one showed more patience than Alison Melvin, who besides putting my Americanisms into proper English managed to bridge the consider-able gap between Soho and Oliveto. Also Gaye Allen designed the book. Alan Williams witnessed vinous Italy's extremes in capturing its essence in his photos. My wife Nancy, daughter Gaia, and son Benjamin stood by me with spirit and understanding.

Some others who deserve much more than a mention are the following: Primo Barelli; Gianfranco Bolognesi; Giorgio Bombi; Dino Boscarato; Vittorio Braga; Vincenzo Buonassisi; Teodoro Bugari; Antonio Calò; Franco Colombani; Giam-pietro Comolli; Pasquale Di Lena; Peter Dipoli; Renzo Franceschini; Laura Furlan; the late Louis Iacucci; Hugh Johnson; James Johnson; Roberto Macaluso; Antonio Maggiore; Gilberto Nardi; Tom O'Toole; Cesare Pillon; Fabrizio Pedrolli; Riccardo Riccardi; Lamberto Ridolfi; Pierluigi Rogate; Doreen Schmid; Franco Solari; Angelo Solci; Piero Solci; Nazzareno Strinati; Marco Trimani; Adrian Webster.

The following organizations supplied useful information:
Associazione Enotecnici Italiani; Associazione Italiana Sommeliers; Camera di Commercio Provincia di Bolzano; Camera di Commercio Provincia di Cuneo; Comitato Vitivinicolo Trentino; Ente Sviluppo nelle Marche; and the agricultural departments of the regions of Campania, Molise, Piedmont, Apulia, Umbria, and Valle d'Aosta.

Picture Credits
All photographs by Alan Williams except for the following.
Michael Holford p. 11; Edoardo Fornaci p. 211; John Heseltine pp. 284/285, 286, 287, 292, 293, 295.

"What are you thinking about, Emily?"

He turned over suddenly on his back and studied me through sleep-narrowed eyes.

"Oh, nothing," I hedged, and tried not to give myself away. Then as he still stared and smiled through the slanting sunshine I broke down and confessed. "Well, us, then—if you must know."

"Of course I must—"

He spoke casually, but he broke off and the look in his eyes turned me suddenly shy and confused, though it was what I had hoped I might see in them some time. Day after day I had searched them for that look. Now there was no doubt, and the age-old instinct to flee was upon me. I sprang up, scattering my books and paints and brushes in every direction.

"Hey, wait," he called. "You know—it's funny, I was thinking about us, too—especially you."

His arms were strong and hard and warm about me. His breath was warm, too, on my cheek, and the smell of sunburnt grass was all about him and will always overwhelm me with the memory of that moment. . . .

And Now Tomorrow

by

Rachel Field

ace books

A Division of Charter Communications Inc.
A GROSSET & DUNLAP COMPANY
360 Park Avenue South
New York, New York 10010

First ACE Printing: December 1978

An ACE Book

Published by arrangement with
Macmillan Publishing Co., Inc.

Printed in U.S.A.

TO

ROSALIE STEWART

WHOSE FRIENDSHIP BEGAN

"AT THE JUNCTION"

And Now Tomorrow

CHAPTER ONE

IT WAS YEARS since I had set foot in the ell storeroom. But yesterday Aunt Em sent me there on an errand, and the souvenirs I came upon have disturbed me ever since, teasing my mind with memories that persist like fragments of old tunes.

There is a fascination in places that hold our past in safe keeping. We are drawn to them, often against our will. For the past is a shadow grown greater than its substance, and shadows have power to mock and betray us to the end of our days. I knew it yesterday in that hour I spent in the storeroom's dusty chillness, half dreading, half courting the pangs which each well remembered object brought.

So we sigh, perhaps, at the mute and stringless guitar with its knot of yellow ribbon bleached pale as a dandelion gone to seed. So we smile at the tarnished medal that set the heart pounding under the dress folds where it was once pinned. So we tremble or flush again at the flimsy favors and dance programs with their little dangling pencils and scribbled names.

"Now *who* was he?" we ask ourselves, puzzling over

some illegible name. "I must have liked him very much to save him the first and the last dance."

And the old photographs in albums and boxes! It takes fortitude to meet the direct gaze of a child whose face is one's own in innocent embryo. It is hard to believe that the shy young woman with the sealskin muff is one's mother at nineteen beside a thin, merry-eyed young man whose features bear a faint resemblance to one's father. Their youth and gaiety are caught fast on this bit of cardboard all these years after that winter day when they sat for their pictures at the Junction photographer's. Here am I, a child of two between them, and here again at four with my arms about year-old Janice and the clipped French poodle Bon-Bon pressing close to my knees. That was the summer I first remember the big lawns and trees and high-ceilinged rooms of Peace-Pipe and all the curious New England relatives who peered at us. They asked questions that must be answered politely in English, not the French which Bon-Bon and I understood most easily. He and I still look bewildered in the picture, but Janice is completely at ease in her embroidered Paris dress and bonnet. Yes, there we are—Bon-Bon who has been still for years now under the thorn tree at the foot of the garden; Janice whose round baby eyes give no hint of the defiance I was to see there at our last meeting, and I, who will never again fit into those slippers with crossed straps or face a camera or the world with so steadfast a look.

Once when I was a child Father told me of a great scientist who could take a single bone in his hands and from that reconstruct the whole skeleton of the animal to which it had belonged. I wondered, standing alone in that jumble of possessions, among dangling clothes, old books, and discarded furniture, whether there might be anyone wise enough to reconstruct from these remnants the likeness of a family. Yet perhaps out of such very clutter some pattern does emerge if one has the insight to ferret out the faults and virtues, the hopes and shortcomings, the loves and loyalties of one such household. Merek Vance would have the wisdom and patience to do that if anyone could. But Merek Vance is three thousand miles away and busy with research of a very different sort. Besides, he would only smile and shrug in the way I know so well, and say that the ell storeroom and its contents are my problem.

He knows that I do not like problems, that I have sometimes lacked courage to accept the challenge of those that belong peculiarly to me. I shunned problems whether they took the form of choosing between a sleigh-ride party and a trip to Boston, or happened to be inside an arithmetic book and concerned men papering imaginary rooms or digging wells that required an exact knowledge of yards and feet and fractions. The same inner panic seized me yesterday when I opened a worn algebra and met those dread specters of my schooldays, a and b and their mysterious companion x that for me always remained an unknown quantity. Well, I know now that this unknown quantity is something to be reckoned with outside the covers of an algebra. I have learned that it can rise up out of nowhere to change the sum total of our lives.

There were plenty of old schoolbooks on the storeroom shelves, books with Janice's name and mine on thumb-marked fly leaves. In one I had written in a prim vertical hand the familiar jargon:

September 19th, 1921

Emily Blair is my name,
America my nation,
Blairstown, Mass., my dwelling place,
And heaven my destination.

I must have been fourteen when I penned that, barely a dozen years ago. Yet "heaven" is a word I seldom write or take for granted nowadays. In this year 1933 I am not so confident of my dwelling place or my destination.

Another book that bore my name was a Latin grammar, with penciled jottings on margins and exercises on folded sheets of paper. I used to be rather good at Latin, though it never occurred to me then that truth or meaning might lie behind the phrases I labored to translate. But as I pored over the pages again they began to take on life and significance. Once, I realized, people had used this tongue to speak to one another, to write words warm with affection or heavy with despair. A phrase held me as I turned the pages: "Forsan et haec olim meminisse juvabit." My lips repeated the words. I wrestled with their meaning as one struggles to move the key in some rusty lock. At last I had it: "Perhaps it will be pleasant to remember even these things." I knew then that it was not some whim of chance that had sent me to the storeroom, that had guided my hand to that book and my eye to that particular phrase.

In the life of each of us, I told myself, there comes a time when we must pause to look back and see by what straight or twisting ways we have arrived at the place where we find ourselves. Instinct is not enough, and even hope is not enough. We must have eyes to see where we missed this turn or that, and where we struggled through dark thickets that threatened to confound us. I know that I have arrived at such a time.

Some day, it may be, I shall tie a handkerchief round my hair and take a broom and duster and set to work clearing out the storeroom. But I must take stock of myself before I am ready for that. I rebelled against returning to this house and the querulous wants of a tired old woman and a middle-aged man with time heavy on their hands. But I am rebellious no longer. Old times, old feelings, old hurts, old loves, and old losses must be sorted and weighed and put in order as well as outworn mementoes. We cannot simply close the door upon them and forget what lies behind it. We cannot let bitterness gather there like a layer of dust.

I fumble awkwardly for words as I sit here at this desk where I have so often dashed off schoolgirl essays full of glib phrases; where I have penned letters marred with self-pity and despair. I am done with all that now. Once I considered myself a very important person in my own world. Now I know that I matter less perhaps in the scheme of things than the tireless, pollen-dusted bee; than the mole, delving in darkness; than the inchworm that measures its infinitesimal length on a grass-blade.

I don't pretend to know what I believe beyond this—that nothing which lives and breathes and has its appointed course under the sun can be altogether insignificant. Some trace remains of what we have been, of what we tried to be, even as the star-shaped petals of the apple blossom lie hidden at its core; even as the seed a bird scatters in flight may grow into the tree which shall later shelter other birds. And so, those whose names I write here—Aunt Em, Uncle Wallace, Janice, Harry, Old Jo and young Jo

Kelly, Maggie, Dr. Weeks, Merek Vance, and I—all of us are changed in some measure, each because of the others. Our flesh and blood, our nerves and veins and senses have responded under this old roof to forces and currents that we shall never be able to explain. We are scattered now, and what we did and what we said will be forgotten soon. It will fade into the unreality of old photographs, like those I stared at yesterday in the storeroom.

I shall begin with the river because without it there would have been no busy Blairstown, with its bridges above and below the falls; there would have been no mills and no bleacheries, no pulsing machinery, no smoking chimneys gaunt against the winter sky or thrusting their darkened tops through summer's dominant green. There would be no reason for trains between Boston and Portland to stop at the brick station with its black-lettered sign above the familiar trademark of the Indian War Bonnet and Pipe and the words that encircle them: "Peace-Pipe Industries."

No one thought it an ironical name until lately. Four generations of American households have known the pipe and feathers and the legend they carry on sheets and pillowcases and towels the country over: "Peace-Pipe for Quality." It was Great-grandfather Blair who made famous those four words and the product of his mill. But it was a hundred years before his time that the first Blair had made his peace with the Wawickett Indians. Their name alone has survived them in the bright, rushing waters of the river where they fished and paddled their canoes.

More than anything else in Blairstown; more even than this big stone house that rose on the foundations of the first unpretentious family farm, the river is bound up with my childhood. I cannot remember my first sight of it, for I was less than two when Father and Mother brought me back from France to be displayed to my New England relatives. Father used to swear that even then the river had a queer power over me. He would stand me on the bridges and lift me up in his arms, and I would stare, spellbound, at the torrent of shining water that fell endlessly, and at the fierce steaming, churning whiteness of the rapids below. In other summers when we returned and Janice was the baby to be held aloft, I would stand peering through gaps in the stonework, never tiring of the liquid drama that went on without beginning or end.

Father was amused and tolerant of my passion for the river, and Aunt Em openly gloated over my preference, but Mother did not seem altogether pleased. She died before I was seven, and so she must always remain for me a dim figure in rustling skirts, with a voice that kept unpredictable accents and cadences because she had learned to speak first in Polish. If we children happened to be with her when we crossed the bridges, she always hurried us over, ignoring my pleas for "just one more little look." Only once I remember prevailing upon her to pause there, and I have never forgotten the occasion. She stayed so quiet at my side that her silence at last made me curious. Though I was young to notice such things, I was struck by the expression of her face as I peered up into it. She was not looking either at me or at the seething water. Instead she stayed still as stone staring over at the mills and the chimneys and the small brick and wood houses where the mill hands and their families lived. Her eyes had grown dark in the soft, pale oval of her face. They held a remoteness that chilled me.

"Mama!" I tugged at her hand. "Don't look over there at the ugly side."

My words brought her eyes back to me, and she answered in her slow, rich voice that blurred softly where words met.

"So you feel shame for that already, my little Emily! But don't worry. You are safe on your side of the river. You're all Blair."

I was to hear that last remark many times afterward. But as often as it has been said, I can never hear it without thinking of that day on the bridge when my early complacency met its first shock. There we stood together, hand in hand, yet we had hurt each other. The river, shining in the summer sun, and the smoky bulk of the mills with those small crowded houses and yards full of washing, were somehow all part of what had come between us.

Often and often I think of it, until sometimes the Wawickett River becomes more than a hurrying stream that has furnished the power for Peace-Pipe Industries and brought prosperity to our family. It has become a symbol to me, as it must have been to my mother that day. For in spite of its bridges the river did then and does now mark the boundary between secure and precarious living; between the humble and the proud. Some may cross from one side to the other as my mother did; as young Jo Kelly was to do years after. And there are a few, like me, who stand on the span of its bridges, knowing that we belong to both—troubled and uncertain because we cannot renounce all of one side for all of the other.

CHAPTER TWO

"ALWAYS DO WHAT'S EXPECTED of you, Emily," Father used to say, watching me with eyes narrowed in a habit acquired by years of painting. "I never learned the trick, but it saves a lot of trouble in the end."

No, Father never did what was expected of him, but perhaps it wasn't altogether his fault. Everyone expected almost too much of Father, and he was born wanting to please everyone he met. He made people happy too easily; and by the same token he disappointed them, because no one can please everybody all the time. He was the oldest of those three Blairs, the handsome, clever one of the family. Aunt Em came next to him—tall, and serious and distinguished-looking even before she was full-grown. She had inherited the Blair shrewdness for business, along with the Blair stubborn streak and the Blair energy. It's a pity that her passion for activity couldn't have been directed as successfully as the Wawickett River's forces had been harnessed into power for the mills. Uncle Wallace came last in order of age and importance, a position he has maintained ever since.

9

Always he has been referred to as "the other Blair brother." He has never seemed to resent this. I think it's all he ever wanted to be. A pleasant, uncommunicative man, contented with the mill routine, occasional business trips, his golf, and his collections of stamps, Uncle Wallace has fitted himself into the scheme of life to which he was born better than any of us. He hasn't Aunt Em's will to fight against the current. He asked little of life and has paid the penalty of those who ask that; for even that little has been taken away from him.

But with Father it was different always. His good looks and gifts marked him from boyhood. Yet he managed, miraculously, not to be spoiled, and he was never taken in by himself. Therein lay his salvation. It was also the reason why he never became a first-rate artist. Tolerant of others' work, he was ruthless when it came to judging his own. And so his vigor and friendship poured out in all directions, enriching those whose genius bore the fruit he was often the first to recognize. In the memoirs of his contemporaries, painters, writers, and musicians living in those more leisurely years of the early 1900's, Father's name slips in and out like some comforting and casual tune. I like to come upon it and know that he mattered more than the canvases that bear his name in the corner and that will never bring a price worth mentioning.

"Want to come in the studio and play being a model?" Those were words I loved to hear, and I always sprang to answer the invitation. Father had a flair for catching likeness. The best things he painted are portraits of Mother and of us as children. I never tired of sitting for him in the high, littered studios he made so completely his own, whether he inhabited them for a year or a month. I can see his big left thumb hooked into the hole of the palette where he had squeezed brilliant daubs of vermilion and cobalt and burnt sienna. His right hand held the long brushes with a strength and delicacy I shall never forget. He seldom talked when he painted, but he used to hum in deep, contented monotony like bees in an apple orchard in May. That pleasant rumble is bound up in my mind with Father and his studio. It will always be part of the smell of turpentine and linseed oil and the tobacco in the pipe he smoked; part of the image of a tall man with eyes as blue as his paint-spattered smock.

Janice can barely recall the studio days, though she says she remembers the afternoon receptions and evening gatherings when we would be carried from bed in our nightgowns to be displayed to the guests. I was never the success that Janice used to be on these occasions, though I was much more dependable when plates of refreshments were entrusted to our passing. Janice needed no encouragement to dance in her white nightgown and red slippers. She was always applauded; and no wonder, for she was a captivating sprite with her fair hair tumbled on her shoulders and falling into her eyes that shone as dark and bright as blackberries. She was the despair of those who tried to catch her on canvas, for she was changeable as quicksilver. I was considered quaint and paintable with my solemn blue eyes and brown straight bangs.

"That one," people would remark, "is her grandfather Blair all over again. Too bad she couldn't have been a boy to carry on the family name as well as the family features."

Once again Father had failed in what was expected of him. Having married a Polish girl worker in the mills and having abandoned the family business, at least he might have provided a son instead of two daughters. But he didn't seem to mind, and from the day I was brought back to wear the Blair christening robe and be called by her name, Aunt Em accepted the marriage and Mother.

"You couldn't wonder he fell for her," Maggie told me once when I questioned her about that match which had been the talk of the county. "When a Polack girl's beautiful she puts the come-hither on a man once and for all."

"The come-hither, Maggie?" I persisted, for I was still very young and curious. "What's that?"

"You'll know right enough some day."

That was all I could ever get out of Maggie on the subject, but I know now how it must have been that day when my father saw my mother sliding down a long patch of ice by the mill gates. The story has taken on the quality of a legend all these years afterward. It was closing time, and the workers were thronging out in the November dusk, chattering and jostling one another as I have seen them so often at that hour, a human torrent of youth and animal high spirits. Skirts were longer in those days, and there were shawls and braids and thick coils of hair instead of berets and bright scarfs over permanently waved, bobbed heads. But the effect must have been much the same then as now. Father had been out of college for several years, and the mill routine had been growing more and more irksome. His heart wasn't in the business. Besides, he was already set on his painting. In the mill workers he saw living models that he longed to put on canvas. I don't mean that he was indifferent to some Polish or Lithuanian girl's good looks, any more than the other men in the office. But he had an artist's eye for line and color as well as masculine appreciation of a curved body, full lips, or trim ankles.

It was fate, or destiny, or just plain good luck that singled Mother out from the rest that winter day. The closing whistle had blown, and Father stood by a window watching the girls hurrying through the mill yard. Ice had formed round one of the exhaust pipes. There was a smooth frozen stretch below it. Suddenly a girl broke away from the rest and took it in one long, graceful slide. It was the most simple, spontaneous response that he had ever seen, he said afterward. Though he couldn't see her face for the gathering twilight, he couldn't forget the free sure motion of her body, with arms held out to keep the balance true, or the way her warm breath streamed out in the chillness under a red knitted shawl that wrapped her head like the crest on a woodpecker.

That was how it began—strange and improbable enough to be the climax of some old-fashioned romance in paper covers. Father must have been born a romantic, but he must have had his share of the Blair persistence to carry the courtship through. Certainly Mother gave him very small encouragement. She had scruples against accepting attentions from the mill owner's obviously admiring son. Lots of girls had set their caps for Father, and he was well aware of that. It made him cautious at picnics and dances and house parties. Perhaps it made him all the more vulnerable to this girl with her foreign name and speech and her self-guarded beauty. Even more than the heavy coils of light brown hair, the soft oval face and wide-set dark eyes, it was this quality of personal dignity in her that must have stirred and held him.

Well, in love there's no choosing, and Father and Mother were ready for love and each other. I shall never know when they first answered the summons; when they first guessed what had taken possession of their separate lives, drawing them so surely and inexorably together. I shall never be able to conjure up what passed between them during the months when each struggled to keep an impossible freedom. But I can picture how it may have been as they met, day after day, while the building vibrated about them and the mill machinery throbbed like a gigantic pulse. It must have seemed almost a magnified echo of their own pulses and the beating of their two quickened hearts. Yes, that is how I like to think it may have been—shuttles weaving, bobbins twisting, threads like millions of humming harp strings, fine-spun about them. And so they became part of the pattern of life, which may not vary its design, though the two who give themselves to its making are always new.

Afterward, when Aunt Em had accepted the marriage, she made rather a point of stressing Mother's background. Polish, yes, but far from the ordinary run of mill girls. Helena Jeretska came of good stock. Her father had been a music teacher, and her mother had had a fair education. Both had died in a typhoid epidemic shortly after landing in Boston, and another immigrant family of quite a different type had taken the child and brought her up with their own. Somehow they had drifted to Blairstown and the mills. Mother had gone to work there at seventeen.

"Oh, yes," I can almost hear Aunt Em saying, "she's quite pretty, almost beautiful in a different sort of way. I think Elliott expects to spend his life painting her. Well, naturally, it's hard to have him go so far away, but Paris is the place for artists. It's not as if the business had ever been congenial to him, and Wallace and I can do our part. Peace-Pipe Mills have always been family-run, and I trust they always will be."

It never took Aunt Em long to recover from any shock. I wasn't born till two years after she met that one, but I've seen her take a good many since. I know the set of her head and lips and the old rallying phrases she summons for times of need. Only lately have I known her to admit defeat, and she has never accepted it. Even now with her once active body stiff and restricted of motion, I can tell that she believes in the power of her own will to accomplish the inevitable. I am reminded of a picture in an old history book—King Canute sitting in state with salt waves breaking about his feet, commanding the tide to turn back.

Aunt Em will resist the encroaching tides of change right up to her last breath, and I love her for it. For all the difference in our ages she is younger than I in some respects. She has not learned what I am only just now beginning to understand—that no matter how hard and faithfully we may try we can never compensate another for some lack in his or her life.

In my own case this sense of obligation came about naturally through the circumstances that followed Mother's tragic death the summer I was seven. She had been fatally injured in a motor accident that spring in Paris, and Father moved in a daze of despair during those days when doctors and nurses fought hopelessly to keep her alive. Father was like a stranger to Janice and me for a long time. His new black coat didn't smell comfortingly of paint and tobacco, and we were glad when men came to crate the canvases and pack furniture and when our things were put in trunks and sent to the ship that would take us back to America. We missed Mama, but our minds were full of the thought of Peace-Pipe. We longed to see how our big brown poodle, Bon-Bon, looked after a winter without us. We wanted to be back before the lilacs were past blooming and in plenty of time to pick wild strawberries in the meadows on the outskirts of town. Father seemed to care little for important things like that, though he was very indulgent of us on the crossing.

One occasion on the voyage I recall with peculiar distinctness. It was the night of the captain's dinner, and Father had promised that I might sit up later than my usual bedtime to watch the people in evening dress go down to the dining saloon. I was ready long before the dinner hour, and to quiet my impatience Father took me on deck. We sat very close together watching the last fiery shreds of cloud dim as the steamer throbbed on tirelessly through darkening water. It was exciting as if Father and I had escaped to some far and secret place. The tones of his deep voice when he spoke to me out of the dimness were all part of that night, giving emphasis to his words.

He had been speaking of Peace-Pipe and Aunt Em when suddenly his tone changed.

"This summer won't be like the others," he said. "You and Janice are going to be Aunt Em's little girls from now on."

I must have trembled or crept closer, for he added quickly:

"Of course you'll always belong most to me, but you mustn't ever let Aunt Em think that. She needs you, and you'll try hard to make her happy, won't you?"

So I promised, filled with a pleasant glow of responsibility. Yet it seemed a queer thing to me then, as it does to me now, that anyone should have to try hard for happiness.

CHAPTER THREE

THERE IS ONE DAY I recollect most clearly from that summer of our return, because it was my seventh birthday and because it was my first meeting with Harry Collins.

From its start the early August day was mine. I ran out barefoot into a world of dew and opening flowers; of robins making little watery calls and splashing at the rim of the lily pool. I measured my seven-year-old height against the vigorous green of hollyhocks by the fence; but, stretch as I might, I could not reach the lowest pink rosette. By the side door a huge old snowball bush bent double under its load of green and white. I crept beneath and felt the cool shock of dew upon me from shaken branches. Myriads of bees were filling it with sound. As I crouched there in the morning stillness they seemed louder and more insistent than I have ever heard them since. That tireless sound made me think of the water going over the Falls; like the throbbing mill machinery when it came distantly from across the river.

Butterflies and birds were everywhere as well as bees. Droning or darting or drifting, they passed me on invisible currents of air. I was aware of them wherever I moved. There was an intensity to their busyness that made me a little in awe of them. They went about their work as if the world were coming to an end at sunset. I think something of the fierce urgency of their frail bodies must have been imparted to my young self that day to make me remember the shape and color and sound of each moment as I do these years afterward.

The trumpet vine that covered the side porch is gone now, but I can still see the miraculous spinning of a hummingbird above it. I knew that its wings were a rainbow whirl because they revolved so fast, yet they gave an illusion of stillness, and the long bill seemed held fast to the magnet of a trumpet flower. I stood there, elated and alone, with my bare feet rooted to wet earth. Some vigorous, sweet essence of summer and sun flowed through me in that moment of breathless watching.

"Happy birthday, Em'ly," Janice called down from an upper window, and the spell was shattered.

Then breakfast, with waffles and honey and packages to open, claimed me. Father had gone to Boston, but he had promised to be back on an afternoon train in time for my party. I knew there would be more presents in his arms, and meantime there were plenty to keep me busy—a new doll and carriage and a boat with sails that could really put to sea in the waters of the lily pool. I much preferred it to the blue enamel locket that had belonged to Aunt Em when she was a little girl, but, remembering my promise to Father, I tried to let her think that was my favorite present.

Uncle Wallace let us walk to the bridge with him, and when we returned Old Jo Kelly and young Jo, his grandson, were waiting to wish me happy birthday. They lived in quarters over the stable. Old Jo had been gardener on the place as long as Father could remember. He had a bouquet of flowers for me, and young Jo had brought three alley marbles and a tin soldier.

"You can play he's captain," he suggested when he saw the new boat. "He don't stand very good alone, but you can lash him to the mast."

We wanted young Jo to play with the new boat, but he went off to help his grandfather haul fertilizer. They worked side by side, those two, the best of cronies for all the sixty-odd years' difference between them. Young Jo's parents had died when he was a baby, and he had always lived with his grandfather.

Even then there was something to be reckoned with about young Jo Kelly. Gay and good-natured though he was for the most part, he could summon up furies that were terrifying to behold. I have seen his blue eyes darken and his lips turn white when he pleaded with his grandfather not to set traps for the moles that were ruining our lawns. His hands were clever at unfastening traps. If rabbits or squirrels or mice could have given testimonials, then young Jo Kelly's name would surely have been blessed. Aunt Em, I remember, once had a long conversation with him on the subject of ridding the place of English sparrows. He listened quietly through her explanation that they were noisy, dirty pests who drove the songbirds away. But her arguments left him unconvinced.

"Sparrows are just as human as any other kind of bird," he told her firmly, and for once Aunt Em had no answer.

My party began on the stroke of four when the Parker twins, Nancy and Joan, appeared, bringing their cousin who had arrived that morning. His name was Harry Collins, and he was older than the rest of us by several years. I can see him now as he looked coming up our drive in his white sailor suit with a twin on either side in pink and blue dresses. The sun made his sandy hair look redder than it really was, and he walked easily with an air of being on very good terms with the world. The twins carried gifts, conspicuously displayed, but he came empty-handed.

"Hello," he called when they were within hailing distance, and I saw that his eyes were hazel with gold flecks that matched the freckles on his nose. "How old are you?" he demanded pleasantly.

"Seven today," I explained.

"Seven's nice," he encouraged me. "Wait till you get to be ten."

"Are you ten?" I ventured.

"Well, practically," he amended.

"Not till after Christmas," the twins chorused. "You only have a right to say you're *going-on ten*."

"'Practically' means the same thing," he insisted, and once more he smiled at me.

When Harry Collins smiled one seldom questioned his statements. He turned a not very expert handspring on the grass while we four little girls watched admiringly. If he made a mistake he somehow convinced you that it had been intentional, merely a delightful variation from the usual pattern.

We were joined just then by Jim and Lolly Wood from across the Square, and by the time I had opened their presents young Jo Kelly had appeared from the back garden, more scrubbed and combed than I had ever seen him.

"Who's the kid?" Harry Collins eyed Jo critically.

I felt uncertain just how to explain him. Young Jo Kelly, we had always taken for granted without classification. Yet I knew that he did not usually rate parties.

"Oh, he lives down there," I answered evasively, pointing vaguely in the direction of the garden.

I was glad that Maggie and Aunt Em appeared just then to supervise a hunt for presents hidden in the shrubbery. After that we played hide-and-seek, and it was then that I found the injured chipmunk under the big hemlock.

Bon-Bon, our French poodle, really made the discovery. I heard his excited barks, and by the time I reached him the tawny ball of fur with dark and light stripes was electric with fright. My first impulse was to pick it up, but Bon-Bon's behavior made me hesitate. I seized him by the collar instead, and it took all my strength to hold him back. The others ran up, attracted by the barkings and my cries. Harry Collins reached us first and bent over the chipmunk, which had begun to make terrified chitterings and to bare sharp little teeth.

"Gee, look at it spit!" he cried. "Get him in a box quick, and then we'll have a pet squirrel."

But Harry had reckoned without young Jo Kelly.

"You leave that chipmunk be," he ordered. "Can't you see it's hurt?"

"Then it'll be all the better in a box. We can crack nuts for it, and—"

Young Jo pulled him away.

"Don't you touch him," he said. "They always die if you shut 'em up."

"He'll die if the dog gets him."

"Sure," Jo was growing exasperated. "We've got to get him back up there."

He pointed to the hemlock, but just then Bon-Bon made another lunge, and I all but lost my grip on his collar. When I looked up again I saw a brown fist double and strike out. It thudded against Harry Collins' face, and though he was so much bigger than young Jo, the sudden surprise of the blow made him stagger back. The next moment Jo stooped down, stuffed the chipmunk into the front of his shirt and made for the lower branches of the hemlock. Up and up he went, hand over hand, while we all watched from below and I still clung to Bon-Bon.

"He hit Harry," the twins kept saying. "He hit him right in the face, at a party too."

"Jo Kelly's got no business coming to parties, anyhow," I heard Lolly Wood protesting. "His grandfather's just your gardener, isn't he?"

The dog's barking gave me an excuse not to answer, and Aunt Em was calling as she hurried to us across the lawn: "Children, children, what on earth is all the racket about? Leave that dog, Emily, and come here."

But I hung on. I wasn't going to let Bon-Bon leap against the tree while young Jo was balanced precariously up there among the spiked boughs. He had climbed to a place where he could brace his feet between two branches and while he held on with one hand I saw him fumbling in his shirt with the other. I saw him take something out and reach up and up with the branch he clung to sagging under his hold. Suddenly he gave a sharp cry and then he was slipping and clutching frantically to keep his hold. Before any of us could move or cry out he came crashing through a shower of twigs and green needles to lie in a heap at our feet.

Everyone began to cry and run after that. I let Bon-Bon

go free and dashed off to hunt for Old Jo Kelly. By the time I had found him and we reached the hemlock tree again Maggie had taken charge with wet cloths and spirits of ammonia.

My birthday party ended with less festivity than it had begun. We were hustled off to the arbor to eat our ice cream and cake with strict orders to keep out of the house and not to ask questions.

"Send them home as soon as you can, Maggie," we heard Aunt Em say. "Mr. Elliot's just back and I've sent him after Dr. Wells."

We gulped great spoonfuls of ice cream and talked in excited whispers. Later we stood at the gate in a subdued little group.

"Goodbye," the twins said politely. "It was a nice party, and we had a lovely time."

"You asked us from four to six, and it's only a quarter to," Lolly Wood said reproachfully as they turned to go.

"So long, kid," Harry Collins laughed through the fence at me. "I'll be seeing you."

"My birthday'll be next," Janice was saying beside me. "You won't have another for a whole year."

"Mine's not over yet," I reminded her.

But I felt low-spirited because the party had been spoiled before it was over and because young Jo had been hurt. The sun had slipped to the level of the lawns, lighting them to a strange clear green, deeper than the emerald in Aunt Em's ring. The frogs had begun to grunt in their deep guttural under the lily pads in the pool, and birds made sleepy-sounding calls that filled me with a sadness I could not explain or share. Morning with its shimmering promise seemed years ago. I did not care when Janice pounced on a forgotten package and claimed it for her own.

Upstairs in the room where they had carried young Jo I could hear the murmur of voices and sometimes a long, whimpering cry. Then it grew suddenly quieter and a queer, sweetish smell drifted down to us.

"Emily! Janice! Where are you?" Aunt En was calling us as she followed Dr. Weeks out to his car. We ran to her with questions, and she comforted us.

"Young Jo's going to be all right," she explained. "The doctor has just been setting his leg where he broke it. No, it didn't hurt Jo much—he had a whiff of chloroform, and he slept till the splints were on. We'll keep him in the spare room till he's able to be up and about."

We were allowed to say good night to young Jo later, conversing through the door. He looked no bigger than a chipmunk himself in the middle of the big carved walnut bed. His voice came faintly from between the pillows.

"He bir ne," young Jo explained. "I reached to put him in that hole and he up and bit my thumb."

"That was mean," I said, "when you were only trying to save him."

"Oh, he didn't mean no harm." Jo would never let a word be spoken against anything in fur or feathers. "Chipmunks just get rattled."

Maggie was unusually short when she put Janice and me to bed that night. Her temper had been tried by the afternoon, between the extra work of the party and caring for an unexpected invalid. She seemed inclined to blame me for being the cause of the catastrophe, and she made few responses to our chatter, hurrying us through baths and prayers.

"Now, then, no more mischief," she warned us sternly.
"There's been plenty for one day."

"What's mischief, Maggie?" Janice demanded from her bed.

She looked so pretty with her yellow hair shaken round her ruffled gown and her eyes dark and shining in her flushed face that Maggie couldn't stay altogether grim.

"Now, Miss Janice," she remonstrated, "you know what I mean, so you needn't put on the innocent airs. You just remember the mother of mischief's no bigger than a midge's wing."

Janice fell asleep before darkness filled the room. But I watched it creep over the familiar pieces of furniture. I hid my head under the covers when it took my clothes draped over a chair and turned them into terrifying shapes. Outside, the frogs sounded very loud and insistent. Suddenly I wanted Father to come and tell me that everything was all right. I remembered in that moment that Father had not appeared in that moment according to his promise. In the excitement I had forgotten that. Surely he must be back by now. I began to feel very sorry for myself lying awake up there in the darkness. I slipped from bed and felt my way across the room. The doorknob eluded me. I fumbled for it in panic, and tears overwhelmed me before my hands felt the reassuring cold brass.

Downstairs lights were bright, and I could hear voices coming from the back parlor. My bare feet made no noise, and although I was breathing hard I managed to smother my sobs. When I reached the portieres I paused, fearing that there might be visitors. I knew Aunt Em would be mortified to have me burst in on guests, so I listened though I knew that that, too, was strictly against rules.

"But what if there is a war over there?" Uncle Wallace was saying. "That's no reason for you to get mixed up in it."

"Thank your lucky stars you're here with the children, not caught over in the midst of it," Aunt Em's voice broke in.

"Besides"—it was Uncle Wallace speaking again—"they all say it can't possibly last more than three or four weeks."

I heard Father give an impatient grunt before he spoke.

"Believe what you want to," he answered. "I happen to know what France and now England too have got ahead. Everyone talked war last year, but no one thought it would come so soon. It's happened, and I know where I belong."

"But, Elliott"—Aunt Em's voice sounded as if she were trying hard not to cry—"you can't really mean what you're saying. There's nothing to take you there and everything to keep you here: your work, your children, and—"

"And Peace-Pipe!" Father gave a short laugh that had no fun in it. "No, Em, the mills will go on, the way they always have. And the children will grow the way children always do, whether I'm here or not. As for my work which you so kindly mention, you know as well as I do that I'm no great shakes of a painter, and ever since I lost Helena—"

He stopped, and there was a sudden silence.

I decided that the time for my entrance had arrived.

"Father!" I cried, and burst through the portières. "It's my birthday, and you forgot to come up and wish me many happy returns."

CHAPTER FOUR

OCTOBER TOOK OVER New England with a fierce brightness I had never known before. After those first frosty nights the hills round Blairstown were a riot of color. It seemed to me that the orange and red and yellow and russet trees stood out in the strong fall sunshine like the bright daubs of wet paint Father used to squeeze on his palette. But whenever I looked across the river the brilliance was subdued by a haze of smoke from Peace-Pipe chimneys.

It was then that I first noticed how swiftly night comes to New England mill towns. Even before the sun drops its fiery red ball, the smoke has settled down to make a mock twilight of its own. It seemed to me then, as it does still, that night came less from the sky than from those great chimneys across the river. It was as if the great throbbing presence, breathing out smoke and steam, had power to hasten night and shorten day. If Father had stayed with us I might have talked to him of this, and then the fancy would have taken less hold upon my imagination. But Father had left for France soon after my birthday, and we were full of the importance of his going. People listened with a flattering attention not usually given to children when we explained his absence.

"My father's a poilu," Janice would announce to every-one we met. "He's a soldier in the war."

"But not exactly a soldier," a year or so later I was to supplement out of my fund of information. "He's an artist, and he paints ships and guns and airplanes so they won't get hit. He's in the camouflage division."

I felt superior, knowing such a difficult word and what it meant. I took pride in using it at school when teachers called on me to recite for visitors. It was a private school, not the public primary school young Jo Kelly attended.

He had spent a month in our guest room and those weeks had made him part of the family. He and I were always full of secret projects, and when he returned to the rooms above the stable I missed him. Aunt Em had grown very fond of the little boy with his unpredictable ways and quaint manner of speech. I heard her tell Maggie that she would have kept him there for good except that Old Jo would have been too lonely without him.

There's a proverb that says "every house is a world," and so it was with ours. It kept pace in its smaller way with the world that was rocking and reeling overseas. Horror and shock and fear came with the newspaper that lay each morning and evening on the doorstep. "Boche," "Hun," "atrocities," "dugouts," "bombardment"—these and other words lost their strangeness, we heard them discussed so often. Aunt Em organized committees that fall, and each had something to do with the war. There were evening meetings when men and women filled our parlors on either side of the hall and overflowed into the dining room and back study. Speakers came to talk about relief work in France and Belgium and Poland. Janice and I crouched in our night clothes on the landing to hear snatches of the talk. The German army, we learned, had marched through Belgium and France, almost as far as Paris, and they had blown up whole towns and shelled cathedrals and done things which must be terrible because of the queer, hushed way people spoke of "atrocities" and because they evaded definite explanations of the word. We gathered little by little that it was all the fault of the Kaiser with his fierce upturned mustaches. He had started the war, and so we were allowed to scratch his picture with pins whenever we came across it in the newspapers. Gradually we grew used to Father's absence, though his soft felt hat still hung on the hall rack, and his paints and brushes and canvases were not disturbed in the third-floor studio. Thanksgiving was hardly over and the last of the mammoth turkey making its exit in hash before snow fell and we began to practice Christmas carols.

Janice, young Jo, and I wavered in eager, ill matched chorus as we played in the winter-shrouded garden or poured pails of water on a slope behind the house to turn it into a glassy, frozen slide. We sang "O little town of Bethlehem, how still we see thee lie," and "It came upon the midnight clear" and my favorite "O Tannenbaum." Father always used to wake us with that one on Christmas morning. Only now the German words had been banished. But I knew the new ones by heart:

O hemlock tree! O hemlock tree! how faithful are thy
       branches!
   Green not alone in summer time,
   But in the winter's frost and rime!
O hemlock tree! O hemlock tree! how faithful are thy
       branches!

I loved those words because I could understand them. Standing there under our snowy hemlock where young Jo had fallen on my birthday, I felt almost that I had made the words up through myself. They seemed so true and right as I stared up through branches darkly green against the clear, December skies. All the maples and beeches and elms were swept bare of leaves, and the old apple trees behind the garden looked more twisted than ever in their wintry nakedness. But the hemlock was richly alive in every needle. It was good that this should be so, and that there was a song to fit it.

Young Jo Kelly and I were united by a tremendous secret. We knew that there wasn't any Santa Claus.

Janice still believed that he came with his reindeer and squeezed down chimneys. We were hardened realists and knew better. But we also knew that to the adult world our faith in the legend was appealing. Older people thought they deceived us with their sly references to the jovial Saint and their hurried hiding of presents when we appeared. Young Jo and I discussed it seriously and decided not to disillusion them even though it required constant watchfulness to keep up our end of the fantasy.

"I've known for a whole year," he boasted when I dared to voice my suspicions. "I kind of thought Gran'pa was fooling me, so I fixed a way to find out for sure; and I did all right."

"How, Jo?"

"Oh, I hung up one stocking same's he said to. Then I hung the other one where Gran'pa didn't know. I figured if there really was a Santa Claus he could find it anywhere."

"Well," I persisted, "and was it empty in the morning?"

"You bet it was."

"You two stop whispering," Janice complained when we compared notes in skepticism. "'Tisn't polite to whisper in front of people, and I'll tell Maggie and Aunt Em on you."

"All right. Go ahead and tell them," I urged her. "And then I'll tell who dropped the silver spoon they can't find down the hall register."

Two days before Christmas Aunt Em and I walked home through the winter twilight after the exercises at my school. There had been Christmas carols and a tree, and I had recited a French poem without faltering once. Aunt Em said she was proud that I remembered every word, and that I could be heard to the back row of chairs. She said it was a pity when children were shy and mumbled their words. I can remember exactly how she looked that afternoon, tall and straight in her sealskin coat. In spite of the cold air her long face stayed the color of my white coral beads and her smooth brown hair exactly matched the fur of her collar and the small toque she wore. She seemed years older than the other children's mothers, yet she must have been only thirty-five. Our school exercises had taken on importance simply by her presence. I noticed that the teachers looked to her for approval when each carol or poem had been safely accomplished. Used to her as I was, I had had a sense that day of her place in the community. She did not need to wear bright colors or stylish clothes to be the most distinguished visitor.

"There will be another Christmas tree for you to see tomorrow," Aunt Em told me as we turned in at our gate. "It's going to be over at the mills, and you can go with me if you'd like to."

"Across the river?" I was instantly curious.

Janice had run out to meet us.

"Doesn't Santa Claus cross the bridges?" she wanted to know.

"Of course, dear," Aunt Em explained. "But so many more people live over there that we must try to help him."

"But," Janice broke in, "he remembers everyone except the bad children. Are there more bad ones over there?"

"Certainly not!" Aunt Em answered hurriedly. "Now run upstairs, both of you, and get ready for supper."

That other Christmas tree across the river, I shall remember as long as I recall anything out of those years.

It stood on a wooden platform that had been raised in the center of the mill yard with the long brick buildings on all four sides. On that day before Christmas the closing whistle had blown at four-thirty instead of six o'clock. When Aunt Em, Uncle Wallace and I reached the gates all the machinery was silent, and the great open space was already teeming with workers and their families. I found myself peering into old faces wrinkled as walnuts under shawls or shapeless caps. There were women with babies in their arms and children of all sizes pressing at their skirts, and trooping from the buildings where machinery loomed gigantic against lighted windows, came the mill hands, men, women, and young girls. Although the workers chattered together in languages I could not understand, they smiled at me and stepped back to make room for us to reach the platform.

"This is Elliott's older daughter," Aunt Em introduced me to the group of men on the platform. I made my curtsy and stood quietly beside her, secretly glad that Janice had been considered too young to take part in such an occasion. I tried to stand as straight as Aunt Em in my blue broadcloth coat with the squirrel fur and the round muff that kept my hands warm.

A band with banners that bore the familiar Indian's head and Peace-Pipe name had begun to play a march, and over the deep rhythm of the drums I asked Uncle Wallace when the tree would be lighted.

"Pretty soon now. Want to turn on the switch?"

I nodded eagerly, and he lifted me on a chair and put the electric button attached to a long cord in my hand. I wasn't to press it, he cautioned, till he gave me the signal. I suppose that wait could not have lasted more than ten minutes, but it seemed hours to me perched high above the close-packed crowd, hoping that nothing would go wrong in my part of the ceremonies. First the Catholic priest rose and made a prayer in Latin, and then our minister followed him with another that had to do with Bethlehem and with Peace-Pipe and the Blair family. After that the mill band played "Adeste Fideles," and then it was my turn to make those green and fragrant branches come to life.

As I pressed the button a deep murmur rose in admiration, and heads were lifted to the tree. All the faces were touched by the light from that glowing pyramid of quivering tinsel and colored bulbs like miraculous fruit. I tilted my head back till I could see the topmost star, set so high that it cleared the smoke that still hung low over the yard and mill buildings.

"Now for the presents," I heard Aunt Em say to Mr. Parker, who was the twins' father and also the mill manager, "I must say I'll be glad when they've been distributed."

"Don't worry, Miss Blair," he promised. "We've got more than enough, and everything's well in hand."

Just then a big red-coated Santa Claus appeared, jingling bells and shouting to invisible reindeer that were supposed to have been left outside the gates. He carried a pack on his shoulders, and his white beard waggled unsteadily with every word he spoke.

"Merry Christmas, one and all!" he began. "This here tree's not big enough to hold what I've brought for the folks at Peace-Pipe. So you'll have to line up and come and get your presents. No pushing, if you please. Plenty for all, and keep your places in line. Strike up, boys." And he waved to the band leader.

He took his place just below the platform, and though I could not see much of his face there was a familiar ring to his voice that puzzled me till I recognized it as belonging to Mr. Dolan, the big Irish night watchman. The band was playing another march, and the distribution of gifts had begun. The hand trucks that wheeled cotton from the storehouse had been loaded with filled baskets and hundreds of red mesh stockings that each contained an orange and an apple, a bag of chocolates, a sugar Santa Claus, and a striped peppermint candy cane. Baskets, with chicken legs and celery tops protruding, as well as each red stocking were identical as pins in a paper. I turned to Aunt Em with shocked surprise.

"But where are the presents?" I asked under cover of the music and the noise of marshaling the long lines into military order.

"Why, right here," she whispered, and then turned

back to her place. She was bowing and smiling as the long line moved forward below the platform.

I stared dizzily down at the hands that reached out for the baskets and the stockings, moving along in an endless stream. I felt cold and disappointed and hollow under my coat. All the magical glow of Christmas had slipped away into monotony. It might have been a grocery store, I thought, except for the lighted tree that everyone seemed to have forgotten except me.

"Aren't there going to be any *real* presents?" I tried once more to distract Aunt Em.

Mr. Parker heard me, and they exchanged an amused look.

"What's the matter with these, Emily?" He bent down and pinched my cold cheek. "A chicken dinner and plenty of candy looks pretty good to me. How about you? Want me to get you one of those stockings?"

But I shook my head. My feet had turned to chill clods, and my eyes swam with weariness. Even if I closed them I could still see the stockings and baskets being handed out. The band had paused to rest, and only the drum thumped on to keep feet moving in time. I drew closer to Aunt Em and plucked at her sleeve. She turned to speak to me, and as she did so a sudden commotion began below us.

There was a break in the slow-moving, orderly line. Then something thudded against the platform. More thuds and ripping sounds followed. One of the candy-filled stockings came hurtling and spilled open at my feet. I saw a man's arms gesturing darkly above the crowd. His voice came hoarse and shrill above the drumbeats.

"Merry Christmas—yah—I rather have job back, not this—"

I could see the man who spoke. He was dark and thick-set, and his black hair had fallen across his eyes. Beside him stood a woman tugging at his waving arms and a little girl and boy. The girl's face was buried in the woman's skirt, but the boy did not turn his face away. His lips were pressed together in a thin line, and his eyes looked directly at me from below the platform. Something about his un-flinching look terrified me more than the man's strange, wild voice crying out again in broken, accusing words.

"You give charitee for Christmas—no want—I rather work—" For a moment the voice was muffled, then it broke out again. "No eat your dinner—we starve first. Chicken an' candy—yah—an' other time you throw me out an' no care!"

They overpowered him at last.

"What you care so long your mill run an' your damn whistle blow?" he shouted back as they dragged him away.

"Merry Christmas—sure—I got hell of Merry Christmas—"

The band struck up loudly and drowned out the rest of his words. Aunt Em's hand tightened on mine. I could feel its cold tenseness through her gloves. Below us the line had closed in again as if nothing had interrupted the ceremonies. But the red candy stocking was still lying where it had fallen at my feet with bits of broken candy like splinters of glass. The shouted words still rang in my ears. They made me shiver and feel afraid.

"What was the matter with that man?" I asked Aunt Em when all the baskets had been given out and we were following Uncle Wallace into his office.

"Try not to think about it," she answered me. "He wasn't—well, he wasn't quite himself."

I was not satisfied.

"He didn't like us," I persisted. "Why didn't he? And why did he throw the things away?"

I heard Aunt Em put in a question and Mr. Parker answer her.

"Vancovitch is the name—good worker, but a crank. Never know when something'll set him off. Had to drop him a couple of months ago, but the wife was sick and there's a family. We thought, seeing it was Christmas, we'd let them in for the distribution. Well, we'll have to tighten up on rules next year. Too bad, but you see where sentiment gets us."

I was very quiet all the way home. The lights and the river and the Christmas wreaths had lost something of their wonder. My happy confidence in gifts and carols and the spirit of good will had been shaken.

"What's a crank, Aunt Em?" I broke silence at last.

We had taken our places at the supper table, and I saw her lay down her spoon and hesitate before she answered.

"Oh"—her eyes met Uncle Wallace's across the table—"it's—well—bad feelings about things that get the better of people sometimes. Go on with your soup, dear."

"That man over at the mill," I persisted, "someone said that's what he is."

"I know, but never mind."

"Now, Em," Uncle Wallace unexpectedly took my part in the discussion, "you can't put the child off like that. She was there and she heard it all, so you'd better answer her questions."

Aunt Em frowned and sighed before she spoke.

"Well then, if you have to remember what happened at

the mill party this afternoon, just say to yourself that sometimes people get all twisted up in their minds about other people—"

"About us? He acted as if he hated us, and he meant me too."

A hurt look came into her eyes, but she went on quietly.

"We can't expect to be praised and liked all the time, no matter if we try to do what seems right to us. You'll find that out, Emily, the older you grow. Sometimes people can't see our side, and sometimes, I suppose, they think we can't see theirs."

Long after I had hung up my stocking beside Janice's by the fireplace, I lay awake in bed remembering another stocking of flimsy red mesh, seeing the shadow of waving arms, hearing a voice that shouted accusing words, the more frightening because they had been half understood. I have heard others like them since then, but I have never learned to be indifferent to hatred and bitterness, on whichever side of the river they may have been spoken.

CHAPTER FIVE

JANICE AND I grew into long-legged schoolgirls in those war-shadowed years. But there was little jubilation in our household when Armistice Day came, for Father had died of pneumonia at a base hospital in France two years earlier. Already his name appeared in memorials at the mill and the church; and the bronze tablet above our pew bore the inscription:

> To the glory of God, and the memory of Elliott Blair, who served in war in order that peace might be preserved, and who died in France, March 12, 1916.
>
> "There is a way which seemeth right to a man, but the ends thereof are the ways of death."

Somehow I could never connect this father who had become a hero with the humorous, easy-going one of the old studio days. His personality grew dim and brittle like the twisted tubes of paint and the dried colors on the palette he would never hold again.

The years were long and separate then, one from another, though now they blur and mingle in my mind. They have run together the way raindrops will on a pane of window glass.

It is strange to remember how Janice and I lived through them side by side, and yet how surely we grew farther and farther apart with each one that passed. We shared the same room till we had reached our teens. We read the same books, practiced at the same piano and went to school and parties together. But always our thoughts and feelings moved in separate paths.

It disturbed Aunt Em's faith in family ties that we two sisters should have so little in common. There had been a deep and close relationship always between herself and her brothers. We were happy, though, in our different ways with trips to Boston for concerts and plays and shopping, and dancing and painting and music lessons besides our school work. I managed to keep at the head of my class, and Janice slipped along in hers.

"It's really a shame to keep Emily in a school like this," I overheard a teacher say to Aunt Em once. I was in the next room sketching a medieval castle on the blackboard to illustrate tomorrow's lesson. "She needs more competition. Have you ever thought of sending her to Blairstown High School?"

"To public school?" I caught a note of shocked surprise in Aunt Em's response.

"I ought not to suggest your changing." The teacher was new at school and evidently worried at what she had said. "I'd probably lose my job tomorrow if you quoted me, but I've watched Emily, and—well, if you're from the best family in a town like this, you get to taking a good deal for granted, to lose initiative. I'd like to see Emily have to exert herself, and she would if she had to hold her own with some of those Polish and Russian and Irish youngsters that are trying to be something better than mill hands."

"I can think of worse things they could be." I knew from Aunt Em's voice how her back must have stiffened. "Certainly you won't find many mills as progressive as ours—"

Other voices broke in just then, and I heard no more. But I have always been grateful to that teacher whose name I have forgotten. The next September I was allowed to enter Blairstown High School in the face of disapproval from most of our relatives. Cousin Eunice Blair was particularly vehement on the subject when she came to attend the fall directors' meeting.

"You know it doesn't look right, Em, a girl in her position going to public school. People will think you're either poor or peculiar. If you had any sense you'd be sending her to boarding school this year to make good social contacts."

"I like high school," I repeated stubbornly. "If I can make geometry and Latin up by June I can graduate with the class of 1925."

"That's the year you ought to 'come out,'" Cousin Eunice reminded me. "You're sixteen now and not bad-looking if Em had any sense about dressing you. I was planning to give a dance for you in Boston this Christmas if Em and Wallace felt like sharing expenses."

"I'd rather be in the Christmas play," I told her. "We're doing 'Everyman' and I'm trying for the lead though there's a girl named Angeletta Rossi who may get the most votes because she's almost as good as a real actress. She's planning to be one some day."

"I suppose boys are going to take part in this play too?" Cousin Eunice eyed me sharply across the table.

"Oh, yes! Young Jo Kelly's been selected already for the prologue."

"Well," Cousin Eunice turned to Aunt Em with raised eyebrows, "Elliott had plenty of queer ideas, but at least he kept his wife out of the mills once he married her. You seem to be doing your best to put his daughter back there. I suppose you'll go to see this play, Em, and enjoy watching some Pole or Lithuanian boy making love to your niece?"

"She can't," I protested. "It isn't that kind of play. It's an old English morality—"

"Call it what you want to, facts are facts, aren't they, Wallace?"

Uncle Wallace, when directly appealed to, took my side.

"It never did me any harm to rub up against the workers' families when I was a boy. Makes it easier for me to deal with the men now because we went to school together. Plenty of them still call me by my first name."

"A man can afford that kind of thing," Cousin Eunice reminded him, "but it cheapens a girl. And they didn't take advantage of it then, the way they do now. There's too much of this 'I'm as good and better than you are' spirit, and that's what leads to trouble, like the kind they're having at Fenwick and Low's plant."

"I certainly don't like the sound of that," Uncle Wallace put in. "And this big strike they've called at Fall River doesn't look as if it could be staved off."

"You'd better keep a firm hand if you don't want one starting here—"

"Oh, not at Peace-Pipe," Aunt Em protested. "We're not like those big impersonal plants where they've lost touch with the workers as individuals. There's a different spirit here."

I was grateful that the conversation had taken this turn, and that I no longer need be the target for criticism.

"Spirit's all right," Cousin Eunice was going on, "but what matters is profit. A mill that's going full tilt and making money doesn't have to worry about trouble with its hands. If the war could just have lasted a few months longer the way we expected it to," Cousin Eunice sighed, "then we wouldn't have been left with all that surplus stock to get rid of."

"Yes," Uncle Wallace agreed as he lighted his cigar. "We ought not to have put in that extra equipment and laid in so much cotton at skyrocket prices. It was against my better judgment, but with those Army contracts it seemed all right."

"Oh, please—" Aunt Em's voice shook. "I can't bear to think of the war that way—in profit and losses. It seems like betraying Elliott. Surely things must get back to normal soon?"

I left them discussing mill problems round the fire, for Maggie had come to tell me that young Jo Kelly was waiting for me. We climbed the stairs to the room that had been Father's studio and was now my study. The easel had been pushed into a corner, and all the unframed canvases were stacked face against the wall like children in disgrace. We spread our books and papers under the lamp on the old flat-topped table, and Jo helped me with my geometry and I checked his outline of Burke's "Speech on Conciliation." Then we heard each other recite speeches from "Everyman." Jo knew his lines, but he kept making careless mistakes. I could tell that something was on his mind.

"Jo," I said at last, "what makes you frown like that? You haven't walked to school with me for nearly a week now. Is anything wrong?"

His eyes avoided mine.

"Well, no." He shifted in his chair and began to sort out his books and papers. "I got a lot of things to do, that's all."

But it was more than that, and we both knew it. I leaned across the table and made him face me.

"Would you be sorry if I got the part in 'Everyman' instead of Angeletta?" I asked.

He flushed.

"I think Angie's better," he said finally. "I'd rather see her act it even if she can't get as good a costume as you could. It's just fun to you, but she really cares."

There was a long, uncomfortable silence between us broken only by the big maple tree outside tapping its twigs at the dark windowpane.

"It's got nothing to do with Angie," he went on. "I like you better when it comes to that, only—"

"Only you wish I'd stayed at private school," I interrupted. "And you wish you didn't have to live over here on our side of the river, don't you?"

"Maybe I do and maybe I don't. I guess you just have to find out some time where you belong."

He gathered up his books and turned to go.

"Listen, Jo," I begged. "If you think Angeletta wants

the part so much, I could always pretend I've got a cold and not try out for the play."

He turned on me harshly.

"She doesn't want you to *give* her the part."

"How would she know?"

"You couldn't fool her. No, you've got to see a thing through once you start it."

After his footsteps had clattered into silence on the uncarpeted back stairs I sat a long while over the open books. But I couldn't go on studying. Janice had begun to play the piano downstairs, and the music came up to me thinned and saddened by distance and my own inner hurt. Jo had only made more clear what I had felt for some weeks past. It was all very well for me to go to high school, but when the doors closed I walked alone in my direction while the rest streamed back across the bridges to a world into which I could not follow them, any more than they could follow me into mine.

IT WAS THE SPRING OF 1928, a few months before my twenty-first birthday, that I fell in love. I had returned from a winter in Boston with Cousin Eunice Blair, going to art school by day and to dances by night. I knew that I was a disappointment to Cousin Eunice because I could not center my interest upon anyone in particular.

"You can't go on this way indefinitely," she used to warn me. "I was married to your cousin John Blair before I was your age."

"Oh, I'm not in any hurry," I would tell her. "There's nobody special yet."

"Well, there ought to be," she would lament. "That comes of an old maid like Em bringing you up. Not that Em isn't a remarkable woman, but then what woman wants to be remarkable? She'll make an old maid of you yet. Heaven knows she'll never do that to Janice. No, it wouldn't surprise me if Janice married and settled down ahead of you. She's a handful now, I'll admit. But when I was young they used to say wanton kittens make sober cats."

At eighteen Janice was certainly soft and pretty as a kitten and as gay. She liked men and made no effort to conceal the fact. Her irresponsibility drove Aunt Em and Maggie distracted, but it was difficult to stay annoyed with her for long. I had been born with a strong sense of possessiveness, and Aunt Em's methodical training had only intensified my respect for personal property. But nothing was sacred to Janice. She had a genius for losing whatever she borrowed, and she borrowed every article I owned. In those years I was always finding myself left with one ear-ring, or a dress minus its belt, or a glove or stocking without its mate. So it was with a certain relief that I looked forward to that summer when she would be in Europe with the Parker twins. It would be a pleasant change to come back to a room where for the next six months my belongings would stay as I placed them; where I could count on the clothes I expected to wear being in closet and drawers, not on a sister's back.

"I hope you won't find it too quiet here after Boston," Aunt Em said that night of my return while the house was recovering from the flurry of Janice's departure. "You'll have the little car," Aunt Em went on. "It's been put in order for you, and most of the dents Janice put in it have been taken out. That and your painting ought to keep you fairly busy."

"By the way," Uncle Wallace suggested, "they tell me they want to start an evening class in designing over in the new Recreation Building. Maybe Emily'd like to take it over and pass on some of the things she's been learning?" Aunt Em became enthusiastic immediately. The Recreation Center where mill workers could take up weaving and pottery and dressmaking, and where certain evenings were devoted to games and dancing, was her pet project. She had fought for it against the criticism of certain directors and townspeople who felt it was unnecessary. Mill workers, they claimed, were not what they had been before the war, and shorter hours and higher wages ate up a large share of the profits. Still prosperity was in the air. A brief, false boom dominated all industry again, and the stock market rose higher and higher. The figures on the ticker tape made older men like Uncle Wallace and Mr. Parker shake their heads and wonder where it would end, and younger men plunge heavily into buying on margin. There was no more talk of Peace-Pipe dividends being passed. If quarterly profits didn't quite come up to expectations company stock holdings could easily be shifted to meet obligations. I hardly realized this at the time, for the talk of the mills was involved with the coming presidential election. If Mr. Hoover were elected it appeared that business and industry must continue to prosper.

But such matters were far from uppermost in my mind that spring night as I strolled down to the Recreation Center after supper. Aunt Em had a group of committee-women in the parlor, Uncle Wallace was busy in his study, and suddenly the evening stretched long before me.

Outside, the earthy April darkness made me feel lonely and restless. Buds showed on the beech trees where the street lights struck them, and I could smell the damp sweetness of the flowers Old Jo Kelly had under the cold frames behind the house. I saw a flashlight moving round the grape arbor and knew that he must be prowling about on his nightly rounds. In the uncertain light he looked more stooped and knotty than I remembered. I noticed as he came nearer that he moved stiffly as if he were some antiquated member of the mole family with whom I had al-ways associated him.

"Nice night, Miss Emily," he answered my greeting.

"Not the kind to walk alone."

"Well, you're alone, too," I reminded him.

"Oh, me! That's been my way so long I don't look for any other, but it's not the right pattern to follow, all the same. Two by two, it was meant to be since the animals went into the Ark. It's a queer thing," Old Jo went on, "to raise a family and lose them all one way or another."

"Except young Jo," I reminded him. "What's he up to, these days?"

"To no good, Miss Emily. That's one sure thing."

I had asked the question casually, and the sharpness of his answer startled me. Before I could put another ques-tion to him he was going on.

"I had to turn the boy out, and it comes hard to do that to your own grandson, but I couldn't let him go on biting the hand that's fed us all these years. He's down there now." He turned and pointed in the direction of the mill chimneys, dark across the river. "Making trouble. He got these views, you see, very mistaken views."

"Oh, well," I tried to comfort him, "Jo maybe thinks differently from you about a lot of things, but he couldn't ever be bad or wild."

"No, Jo's a good boy, that's the pity of it. I'd rather see him dead and buried like Mollie and the rest than going the way he's going. I tell you, Miss Emily, there's bad things brewing down there, and Jo's at the core of it all because he can't see straight."

"What sort of things?" I persisted.

"All this talk—organize, organize, that's all he and those

cronies of his can think about, and unions and wages and closed shop and walk-outs and strikes. I know where it's going to end when all the talk turns into fists and bricks and blackjacks."

"Oh," I refused to take his dire predictions seriously, "what's a little talk? Besides there's never been any trouble at our mills."

"Well, I hope you're right. I'm too old to understand such things, but Jo's got the gift of talk, like my father that was killed in the Dublin riots. It's a dangerous gift. You'd swear black was white if he wanted you should think so. I can't sleep nights for thinking my Jo's there in Peace-Pipe Mills with a squint in his mind that no spectacles can cure."

"Don't worry." I was growing impatient at his talk, and the night was too fine to hear an old voice croaking beside me. "After young Jo's been working in the mills awhile he'll think differently about a lot of things."

"There's no getting round facts," he went on as I opened the gate. "The world's the same's it's always been and there's just two kinds of people in it—the haves and the have-nots. Mix 'em up, and they'll start right in all over again and be the same."

I was glad to be out of the sound of Old Jo's voice, which had a rusty insistence, like a cricket's plaint. Yet he had roused my curiosity about his grandson. It must have been a serious difference to cause a break like that between them.

Dr. Weeks was leaving his house when I passed. I hailed him as he opened the door of his car and threw in his familiar bag of instruments. Any car that belonged to the

Doctor took on his look of shabby, dogged activity, no matter how spruce and factory-finished it had appeared a few weeks before. I smiled at the mud-spattered wheels and hood, the fenders whose scars of battle he had been too busy to have repaired. Off in the outlying country, people used to swear that they knew the sound of Dr. Weeks' engine coming over rough roads at night to answer some urgent summons. I have no doubt they did, for certainly there was some nervous, quick response between that machine and the man who guided it.

"Yes," he answered me after we had exchanged greetings, "I've got a busy night over on the mill side of town. Pneumonia case that looks bad, and a baby due before morning."

"You have got a lot on your hands," I said. "It'll be tomorrow when you get back."

"Well," he agreed, "always plenty doing over there. Someone coming or someone going, that's the way it is."

"Aunt Em says you ought to have an assistant now your practice has grown so."

"Now I'm not so young as I was," he corrected me. "That's what she really means. Well, maybe I will if I can find the right youngster. I've got my eye on a couple of interns right now. Good to see you back again, Emily. You're planning to take the summer easy. You're a bit on the thin side, and it wouldn't do you any harm to take on a few more pounds. Not that you'll follow that piece of advice, I suppose?"

I laughed and shook my head as he studied me intently.

"You grow more like your father and Em every time I see you," he was going on. "Yes, you're Em all over again in modern dress. She wasn't much older than you the year I came to practice in Blairstown, and I thought— Oh, well, never mind what I thought—"

He gave an apologetic laugh that ended in a sigh as he got in and started the engine. Something about the way he spoke made me remember certain remarks I had heard about how Dr. Weeks had wanted to marry Aunt Em years ago. I wondered if the rumor were true, and why nothing had ever come of it. There he was driving off to his round of night visits, alone and past middle age, and there was Aunt Em surrounded by a ladies' committee discussing some good work or other. Somehow spring nights are apt to make the waste of human capacity for love and fulfillment seem more poignant then than at other seasons of the year. Or perhaps it only came of my being back in the limits of a smaller community. One felt somehow more aware of human relationships.

"A little town is like a lantern," Maggie Flynn used to say with a shrewd pursing of her lips. "Nothing's hid away from sight."

It may have been some intimate quality of the night, or my own heightened senses that made me unusually receptive to my surroundings. Each familiar house and yard I passed, each tree and fence and postbox arrested me as if I were marking them for the first and last time. Perhaps the river mist had something to do with what I felt; perhaps it was only a sudden sense of place such as all of us have experienced at some time or other. I only know that all this was part of that night in April which must forever punctuate my life, as an exclamation point stands out boldly on the page of a book.

The Wawickett River was swollen with spring rains. I

could hear the noise of its waters going over the dam long before I set foot on the upper bridge, as if it were a human presence hailing me. I could not see the torrent rushing under me. But I felt the power that charged it, that seemed stronger than the span of bridge that ordinarily rose so high above it, and that was so bound to me from child-hood. My cheeks and hair grew damp with misty spray. A chill wildness was in the atmosphere, so strong and fresh and full of vigor that even the smell of chemicals and ma-chinery and factory smoke could not overpower it.

In that misty stretch between the two sides, I felt that time did not count. It was as if the bridge had become a sort of no man's land where the past and present might meet and mingle as they do sometimes in our dreams. It would not have surprised me to find my own father swing-ing towards me with his long, easy strides, or my mother leaning at the rail with a child pressed against her skirts. Now I know that the future was there, too, that every step I took brought me nearer to it.

The clamor of the rushing water had taken all other sounds. I heard no footsteps, my own or those that must have been coming behind me. So I was startled when a man passed by me, then stopped and hesitated as if uncer-tain whether to speak or not. When he did I realized that he was not the mill hand I had taken him to be.

"Are you Emily Blair?" His voice was young and pleasant.

"Why, yes," I stopped short. "Yes, I'm Emily Blair, but I don't know who you are?"

"We met at a party." He laughed. "You were seven years old and it lasted from four to six."

"Wait a minute." My mind raced back as I tried to

catch at a name that eluded me. "Then you must be the Parker twins' cousin. I've forgotten your name, but I remember you didn't bring me any present."

This time we both laughed.

"Harry Collins—do you remember now? I've been working in your mills since January. Stopped to see you just now, and they said I'd find you if I walked this way. I guess your uncle forgot to tell you I was coming over after dinner. Do you really have to go over to the Recreation Building?"

"No, it was just something to do."

"Let's go back then." We turned and fell into step together. "We'll sit in your parlor and look at the family photograph album."

"Oh"—I shook my head and drops of mist ran off my hair—"we can't do that because Aunt Em and her committee are there, and besides there isn't any family album."

That wasn't a funny remark, and yet it made us laugh. I know now that we laughed because we had both been lonely on a spring night.

CHAPTER SEVEN

How CAN I TELL of that summer except to say that I shall never meet its like again? There may be others more fair, others more busy and full of contentment, but never one so charged with the warm swift current of love when first it takes over an untried heart. The response in me was unpredictable. Sometimes I was restless as the dragonflies that hovered over our lily pool, their wings a shimmer of impatience. On others I was wary and withdrawn as one of our garden moles guarding his secret ways. But whatever the mood I no longer slept or woke or went about my business with the old self-sufficiency. It was Harry Collins this, and Harry Collins that, day in and day out. Nothing made sense without him, and I didn't care who knew it.

To love and be wise, they say, is impossible. They say, too, that if you love you are the slave, and if you are loved you are the master. It was like that with Harry Collins and me from the first night of my return. He had only to beckon and up I sprang, one leap ahead of myself. Foolish—of course it was, but past my power to have it otherwise. Maggie Flynn used to shake her head when she saw me hurrying downstairs to meet him, or dressing for the country-club dances as if my very life depended on being ready an hour before it was time to start.

"Come now, Miss Emily, have patience," she would say. "There's all the time in the world and some left over." And when her words failed to halt me she would add slyly, "Ah, well, the feet go to the place where the heart is."

I was always making some excuse to drive by the mills, hoping for a glimpse of Harry's head bent over a desk, or his familiar figure striding across the mill yard. Even when I stayed on our side of the river I would look over a dozen times an hour wondering if he were thinking of me at that precise moment. I was in love, no doubt of that.

There is an old sketchbook of mine in the ell storeroom that always brings back that summer, especially a certain water color which I pass over quickly. Some time perhaps I shall be able to look impersonally at the painted shape of a tilted thorn tree in a field with the outline of a low hill beyond. I shall look and not feel memory stirring too sharp for me to bear. For though the sketch is only half finished it still keeps something of the magic of an afternoon in midsummer. There in the corner the brush strokes end abruptly because I looked up and caught Harry's eyes, and after that—no more reaching for paint and brushes, nothing to do or say but to be aware each of the other.

On summer Saturdays the mills closed at noon, and often Harry and I would drive with a picnic basket over to a place on the outskirts of town. It has changed since then. Only the river is the way it used to be, tranquil and broad after its plunge over Peace-Pipe dam. It flowed there quiet and free of barriers and factory grime, between marshy meadows that spread out below Blairstown. Those marshes are drained now of their cattails and their shallow pools that used to make sunsets more fiery in the irregular small patches they reflected. Gone are the thorn trees and alder thickets, cleared to make room for a parkway and real estate development. Cheap bungalows like rows of painted boxes multiply where field larks used to rise singing from sunburnt grass that was just the color of Harry Collins' hair.

But I, too, am changed. For I have been drained of a certain bright assurance that love can stay secure; cleared of old hopes and confidences by the ruthlessness of experience. But on one July Saturday not a doubt clouded my mind or heart.

I was waiting in the car for Harry by the mill gates when the noon whistle blew. It was sweet to my ears that day, for all its shrillness, and I heard it as wives and sweethearts of mill hands must have heard it, knowing it meant a man's step at the door and a precious half-day to be shared in sunshine and warmth together. He climbed in beside me, so good to see in the heather mixture sweater that was my favorite because it duplicated the little flecks of brown and green in his hazel eyes. We drove for a few miles on the main turnpike and then turned the car into a dusty, unfrequented road that narrowed to a pair of overgrown wheel ruts that ended by clumps of fireweed and the cellar of a burned-out house. Here on the flat, sunny doorstep we sat and ate the sandwiches and cookies I had brought, and drank some sour, red wine that Harry had wheedled one of the Italian mill hands into selling him.

"It's supposed to be Chianti," Harry explained. "Pretty poor imitation, but beggars can't be choosers in Prohibition times. Roselli didn't want to let me have this for fear it would get out he was making it in his woodshed. It's a farce, this Eighteenth Amendment."

"I know," I agreed, trying not to pucker my lips over the wine. "Last winter in Boston all the men carried hip flasks to dances, and some of the girls brought bottles, too."

"Women don't understand about drinking." Harry leaned back and lit a cigarette. "Oh, not this mild sort of thing." He waved at the wine disguised in a catsup bottle, and went on, "Not that I've been drunk often, but just enough to know."

"How does it make you feel?"

"Oh, sort of equal to anything. It's as if nothing were hard or impossible any more. Kind of like a god until you pass out."

"I've only had enough to feel like giggling a lot," I told him. "And once, in the middle of a parry last winter, I wanted to cry and cry about nothing in particular."

Harry laughed.

"You're funny, Emmy," he said, and I loved the way that nickname sounded on his lips. "Funny, but I like you."

"You're funny, too," I told him, "and I like you."

"I can read you like a book," he went on. "You're really a very pleasant and easy book to read, though no girl likes to be told that for some strange reason." He yawned and put out his cigarette. "And now, with your permission, I'll take my after-luncheon nap and you can paint a picture, but not of me."

He turned over on the grass, his face buried in his folded arms to keep the flies away.

I set out my water colors and opened my sketchbook to

a fresh page, and my fingers began marking out the scene before me, the tilted thorn tree and the tawny patch of field, the familiar hump of hill beyond. My hands worked surely with pencil and brushes and paints, yet my eyes would keep turning to where Harry lay stretched, long-legged and strong of body, in the sun. So still and relaxed he lay, yet so full of vigor and life, that I could almost mark the swift stir of blood in the veins of his freckled hands and arms where the fine hairs were yellower than on his sandy head. Under the white cotton material of his shirt his chest rose and fell, rose and fell, with unbroken regularity. I paused in my painting, and my cheeks began to burn with something far more potent than that home-brewed wine.

"What are you thinking about, Emily?"

He turned over suddenly on his back and studied me through sleep-narrowed eyes.

"Oh, nothing," I hedged, and tried not to give myself away. Then as he still stared and smiled through the slant-ing sunshine I broke down and confessed. "Well, us, then—if you must know."

"Of course I must—"

He spoke casually, but he broke off and the look in his eyes turned me suddenly shy and confused, though it was what I had hoped I might see in them some time. Day after day I had searched them for that look. Now there was no doubt, and the age-old instinct to flee was upon me. I sprang up, scattering my book and paints and brushes in every direction. I might have been Daphne in flight, my feet suddenly taking root, hair turning into laurel leaves before the onrush of the pursuer.

"Hey, wait." There was nothing of ancient Greece in

his words, but I would not have exchanged them for all the sonnets in creation. "You know—it's funny, I was thinking about us, too—especially you."

His arms were strong and hard and warm about me. His breath was warm, too, on my cheek, and the smell of sunburnt grass was all about him and will always overwhelm me with the memory of that moment.

I had been kissed before. What girl of my age hasn't? But this was different. Whatever I can think of him now—and I have thought plenty, both good and bad, since that day—I can never forget the strength and sweetness of his lips.

He held me close—how long, I shall never know, for time was our friend that day and there was no mill whistle to sound and only a kindly, gradual setting in of twilight after the pink went out of the sky and the marshy pools lost their reflected fire.

"Harry," I remember I faltered at last, "does it mean that you and I—that we—"

He nodded and held me closer.

"And we can tell them—tonight?"

"If you want to. But I'd just as soon we kept it to ourselves a little longer."

"They'll know, whether we say a word or not. They'll see it on my face. Oh, Harry, I didn't know, I wasn't sure —about you, I mean. I was always sure about me."

CHAPTER EIGHT

WE MOVED THROUGH those first few weeks of our engagement, Harry and I, like swimmers carried effortlessly by a current that was stronger than we. I say "we," but I can speak only for myself. It is all a warm daze to me now, pricked with moments of awareness that I recall, as if I had not lived them but had read them in the pages of some book.

So I tell myself that the tall girl in the gray organdy with the coral trimmings was really I, and that it was indeed my own quick breathing that made the lace quiver as I pinned it down with the pearl circlet Aunt Em had given me for my twenty-first birthday and engagement present. There were heliotrope and mignonette and a moss rose in a vase, I remember. Their fragrance was almost stifling as my sleeve brushed them when I leaned across the bureau to take a last look at myself before going down for the garden party which was to announce my great news as well as my coming of age.

The dress had arrived that morning from Boston, and I hoped that I looked my best in it. But would Harry like ir? Would he be proud of me in the soft gray clinging folds and notice that the coral bands and sash brought brighter color to my cheeks? If approval did not immediately show in his eyes, then it would not matter who else might praise me. I touched the ring on my left hand for reassurance before I went downstairs. Harry had bought it for me the day before with apologies for the smallness of the stone. He would be paying for it from his salary envelope for months to come, and I knew he couldn't afford it. Even a very little diamond cost far too much for a young man just starting in any business. I had tried to scold him for his extravagance, but my protests had been lost in happiness.

All the guests at my birthday party that afternoon would see it on my finger. They would hear that Harry Collins and I were engaged to be married, and our love would be a secret thing no longer. That made me feel shy and serious. But I wanted them all to know. I wanted to hear their congratulations and see the curious, searching look in the eyes that watched us. Already I knew that look. I had seen it in Aunt Em's eyes and Maggie's, and even in Uncle Wallace's. I had stared at engaged couples in the same way myself. Curiosity and envy mingled in that look—the older eyes might be tired and practical, but there was a certain envy and approval there, as if they would like to be young and in love all over again; and younger eyes were awed and shy in their appraisal, hoping that the miracle would not be denied them. So Harry and I became symbols to those friends and neighbors who gathered in the garden or moved about the lawns under the maple and beech trees. I felt that we were, and the knowledge only deepened my happiness. Whether Harry knew or felt what I did, I cannot say; but his hand was warm on mine and his eyes approving as we went from group to group.

Aunt Em was in her element, welcoming guests and answering questions.

"Well, no, it wasn't exactly a surprise," I could hear her saying from the bench under the copper beech tree, "except that having Emily old enough to think about being married does come as a surprise of course. Why, it seems only yesterday it was her seventh birthday party and she and Janice and Harry and the twins were all playing hide-and-seek together and stuffing themselves on ice cream and angel cake." Then as she moved on to another group I would catch variations of the same theme. "Yes, we're delighted, and the best part is we shan't be losing her. With Harry in the mills Wallace and I needn't worry about Peace-Pipe going out of the family; and Harry being John Parker's cousin makes it all the more suitable."

Somehow it always came back to that word "suitable" as people discussed our engagement and beamed upon us while refreshments were served at the tables that dotted the lawns. I had done what was expected of me just as Father had advised me to do years ago. His words had lain long forgotten in my mind, but now they came back to me. Father had confessed that he had never learned the trick himself. Perhaps if he had he would have been beside us that afternoon. I found myself suddenly thinking of my mother, and I wondered if any of the friends and neighbors gathered there to wish me well were thinking of her too. Or had she never really counted much in their world on this side of the river?

"Well," I heard one woman say to another later as I

passed, "Em must be glad about this match. No making the best of it the way she had to with the other one. Elliott certainly took a chance marrying a mill girl, but she made a good wife and mother."

"Em will certainly draw a long breath when she sees her other niece settled." A different voice chimed in. "I was saying last night Emily wouldn't have had half the show this summer with that younger sister around. She's always had the beaux, so I guess she can afford to let Emily go down the aisle first."

I couldn't help feeling relieved that I had not had to share these weeks with Janice. Not that I was jealous of her popularity, but it was pleasant to make my plans without having to consider hers. Just then I caught Harry's eyes upon me across a group of people, and I answered the secret signal of his smile.

"And don't I know I'm lucky!" I could hear his voice responding to other voices. "When I think that I almost took a job in Boston last March instead of coming here—it makes me believe in fate or whatever you want to call it."

No matter how sure I was of his love, I listened hungrily for such words as I went through the ritual of thanks.

"Oh, how nice of you to say so! Well, of course, I think he is. Yes, isn't it wonderful, he's come to work at Peace-Pipe."

Over and over my lips repeated the polite formulas; the threadbare words that somehow seem new by reason of their personal significance.

"Oh, thank you! I'm so glad you're glad about us. Why, no, we haven't made any plans yet. It's pretty soon to set a date, and Harry's busy learning the business. Maybe next summer."

People I scarcely knew suddenly kissed me and wished me well with an interest I had never guessed before, and the married women embarrassed me with attentions. I tried to be more outgoing in my response to them. I felt especially sorry that day for old maids. Maybe it wasn't so much that as relief that I felt. I saw a fate from which I had escaped. Even Aunt Em, handsome and gracious in her mauve lace, was less herself than someone I might have become in time except for this miracle. A wave of pity for all that she had missed came over me, and I stopped to squeeze her hand.

"Not getting too tired, Emily?" she asked, smiling back at my eager protests. "Oh, there's old Mrs. Norwood just coming up the path. Do run down and meet her."

I seem to be watching myself and listening these five years afterward with the detachment of experience, as if I were looking through the wrong end of an opera glass. How small and immature I was then; how fearful that I might not fulfill all expectations! How much, I wonder, did I really feel? I had not suffered then in the flesh or in the heart. But now, because I know what such pain can be, have I the right to say that love was less than it seemed to me that afternoon?

Twilight was coming across the lawns. The golden afternoon light softened to dusky greenness, and the shadows round the tree trunks were reaching out to meet one another. Beyond the gates Old Jo Kelly and another man were helping guests into their cars. Only a few late-comers lingered, and Maggie and extra hired servants were already discreetly carrying in trays and chairs. John Parker and several other men had stopped by to collect their wives and daughters, and they lingered on the steps talking to Uncle Wallace. The rich fragrance of their cigars mingled with the scent of drooping flowers. It was good to feel the presence of men after all the chatter and feminine bustle.

Harry had left to drive some friends of Aunt Em's home. Already I felt incomplete without him as I wandered uncertainly about the littered grounds. There is something a little sad about the end of a party; all the laughter and activity is over, but it has not yet taken on the perspective of memory. The paper napkins lie strewn underfoot; the glasses are warm and sticky, and plates bear remnants of the pride they once held. A dish of ice cream and cake had been upset on the grass and an army of ants were attacking it with the precision of a trained battalion. Down by the lily pool the frogs were making their familiar guttural. All sounds became intensified for me in that interval. It was as if something warned me, saying: "Listen, listen while you can."

Then I saw a figure moving by the old hemlock, and I recognized young Jo Kelly. He waved to me, but when he made no effort to come nearer I went down to him. It was weeks since I had seen him, and we had not exchanged words all that summer.

"Jo," I called, "come up and have some of my party. There's lots of food left."

But he only grinned and shook his head.

"No, thanks," he told me. "Just wanted to wish you luck on the day."

He smiled at me, and when his thin face broke into those familiar merry lines the past seemed suddenly to rise up between us. I felt it drawing us together with links we had both forgotten. Just for a moment I forgot that young Jo disapproved of our family; that he had been denounced by Aunt Em and Uncle Wallace and Old Jo as a traitor to the mills and Peace-Pipe traditions. I felt only the old bonds of childhood, the memory of treats and fears and secrets we had shared together under the old hemlock where we were standing now.

"Jo"—I put out my hand and he took it—"I'm so glad you came today: it's like old times."

"Yes." His voice always startled me by sounding more slow and deep than I had remembered. "That's why I almost didn't come."

"But it's good to remember old times. I only wish—"

"I know," he cut me short, and his smile faded. "You wish I'd remember them oftener. Well, I've had that all out with Grandfather. He sees things your way and I see them mine. I guess it can't ever be different. Don't you tell him I was here, will you?"

"Why, no, if you ask me not to. But it would please him to know you came."

"That's why. He'd start getting his hopes up about me, and I'd just go and disappoint him again."

"Jo," I said, "I don't pretend to know what's made things different from the way they used to be. It's something you feel about the mills, I know that much, and that you think we're to blame—"

"No." He shook his head, and the hair fell over his forehead just as it used to, so that he looked once more like a stubborn pony with rough, dark forelocks. "It's not as simple as all that, and I don't blame you folks except you all think everything'll go on same's it did in your grandfather's day."

"Well, he started Peace-Pipe, didn't he? There wouldn't be any mills or work for all of you down there if he hadn't."

"Sure." Jo smiled the patient kind of smile one gives to a child. "Remember those snowballs we used to roll down the back slope when we were kids? You started with one in your fist, and then it kept rolling up more and more; and pretty soon it got bigger'n you were, and there it was pulling you along instead of the other way round. I tell you that grandfather of yours started a snowball you're going to have trouble keeping up with, one of these days."

The pupils of young Jo's blue eyes had grown enormous and dark, the way they used to get when he stood up to debate on the high-school team.

"Maybe you read what happened over in Fall River last month?" he went on.

"You mean that textile strike?" I hadn't bothered to read about it, but I had heard Uncle Wallace and Aunt Em discussing it with Harry.

"That's what I mean. If it can happen in one place, it can in another."

"Oh, but not here!" I was surprised to catch a quality in my own voice that suggested Aunt Em. "We never have trouble at Peace-Pipe, and besides conditions were terrible in that plant. Even Uncle Wallace said the workers had some justification though no strike is ever the right answer, and Harry Collins says—"

I broke off because I couldn't remember Harry's exact words and because just the mention of his name distracted my mind from other subjects. "Mr. Collins and I are going to be married, Jo," I went on, "maybe you heard?"

"No." He shook his head before he smiled and put out

his hand. "Well, I guess everybody's pleased. He seems a nice fellow all right. Here's hoping you'll be happy."

"Thank you, Jo. I'm glad you came up so I could tell you about it myself. Funny, isn't it, that he came to my other party, the time you broke your leg falling out of this tree—because the hurt chipmunk bit you, remember?"

"I remember all right. It was nice being laid up here in the big house. You were all real good to me. Well, good luck, Emily. I'll have to practice calling you Mrs. Collins soon."

"Oh, there's plenty of time for that," I protested, but it pleased me to hear him say the name. "You'll be getting married yourself one of these days, and I'll be congratulating you."

His lips drew together in a thin line, and once more he shook his dark head.

"It's wonderful being in love," I persisted. "You wait and see."

"I'll wait." There was a note of bitterness in his voice as he turned away in the twilight that was all about us. "Being in love's kind of a luxury for some of us. Can't afford to think too much about it."

Before I could reply he had turned away, leaving me feeling hurt and uncertain. Barriers not of my raising were between us once more, and I was glad when he wheeled back and returned to my side again.

"Look," he said out of the dimness. "I don't suppose you'd like a puppy for a present? It's lonesome up here since Janice's spaniel got run over, and you haven't had a dog since Bon-Bon died. That hound of mine's got a litter of six, and I have to get rid of them by tomorrow. They're not beauties, but I'll pick the least objectionable if you'll take it off my hands."

"Of course I will, Jo. You and I may disagree on a lot of things, but I'll always trust you to pick out a good dog. I suppose it's got a long tail?"

"Well, yes. There isn't much choice when it comes to that, but you can have the one with the fewest different colors."

We laughed together, and I watched him out of sight before I went back to wait for the honk of the car bringing Harry to me again.

CHAPTER NINE

NEW YEAR'S EVE, 1928, slid into 1929 while Harry smiled at me across the living room at Peace-Pipe and the candles made little reddish glints in the sherry glass he held high. I never took my eyes from his face while the clock chimed and the bells outside rang through a cold January drizzle. I needed the reassurance of his eyes. Good as the old year had been to us, I wanted the new one to be even better and more completely our own. Janice, standing between Uncle Wallace and Dr. Weeks in her silver Paris dress that made her look like a bob-haired angel from a Christmas tree, watched us with amused tolerance.

"Those two," she laughed, "you can see they're making plans for 1929 before 1928 has breathed its last, and after the way Emmy's been sentimentalizing all day about what happened to her in this year."

"I'm glad she's a sentimentalist," Harry championed me. "It's an old-fashioned trait, and I love it in her. Go ahead and make pets out of old junk and old years all you want to, darling, only don't neglect me."

"A likely chance of that." Janice laughed.

She had come back in November, prettier than ever and more full of life. I had dreaded her return because I had wanted nothing to change and Janice always brought change and commotion. Yet I found the readjustment less difficult than I had expected. Janice envied me my new status. I could tell that she had not thought me capable of attracting a man like Harry Collins. Then, too, the months of traveling without Maggie to keep order had given her more consideration for other people's possessions. I, for my part, was less irritated by petty pilferings and trivialities. Only what concerned Harry could touch me deeply. Looking back to it now, I wonder how long we might have stayed so if what lay ahead had been longer in coming; if it had not come at all?

The penalty of love, I suppose, must always be the fear of losing it. So old a motif, yet to each of us new with personal significance at one time or another. Love and fear, I was aware of them both that night as I had not been on other New Years.

"There," I heard Janice sigh. "That's over for one year." She turned to Harry when the last toast had been drunk. "I hope Emily warned you about all the family rituals you'll be in for when you marry a Blair."

"She did," he whispered back, "and so far I'm doing all right."

"Well, you wait," she warned, "they have a way of piling up on you."

Our little gathering broke up soon after midnight, for Dr. Weeks had late visits to make and Harry was driving home with him because of the rain.

"Happy New Year again," the Doctor said as he struggled into his overcoat. "But you youngsters listen to me.

There's an epidemic going the rounds and it's no respecter of persons. I've got some pretty sick patients over there across the river."

"You mean in the Mill Infirmary?" Aunt Em was anxious.

"In the Infirmary and out of it," he told her. "And it's not all plain flu either. There are a couple of cases of such high temperatures I suspect meningitis."

I didn't bother much about the word then, though now it seems incredible that there could ever have been a time that I did not know it.

"That sounds serious, Will." Aunt Em followed him to the door all concerned and full of questions. "You don't really think—"

"I'll know more by tomorrow, Em; but frankly I don't like the look of things. Keep the girls away from dances and picture shows and make them eat and rest sensibly if you can. Emily'd better stop going down to her art classes in the Recreation Center for a bit. Just for precaution's sake, you understand, though germs don't keep to one side of the river once they get headway."

His predictions were right as it turned out. By mid-January the Mill Infirmary and the town hospital were taxed to capacity. In spite of extra medical help from Boston Dr. Weeks hardly knew what it was to snatch an hour of uninterrupted sleep. For me the only personal hardship of the epidemic was my promise not to drive to the mills to meet Harry when the five o'clock whistle blew.

A sort of gloom hung over Peace-Pipe that January which I resented because I could not always keep my own well-being clear of it.

"You know, Emmy," Harry said one night, "they've had me checking up on last year's orders and the year before that, and there's been a steady decline. I can't understand it with the stock market soaring. Why, with General Electric and Telephone and U.S. Steel going up, the textile and cotton industries ought to be right on top too. If I only had a few thousand dollars to invest I could make a neat little turnover. Sometimes I can't help wishing—"

"Oh, darling"—I wouldn't let him finish the sentence—"don't wish you hadn't come to Peace-Pipe! I get cold all over when I think how it would have been if you hadn't. If you want to leave the mills after we're married you can try something different. But they'll be raising your salary soon, and Uncle Wallace and Mr. Parker are going to make you an assistant manager before long. I know I can talk Aunt Em into a June wedding instead of a fall one, once this epidemic gets over and done with."

"Oh, I suppose I'll stick." Harry shrugged and lit another cigarette. "Lots of the men in my class would envy me the start I've got here, but when I think what I could do with a little money and a rising market—"

"I wish I had some of my own," I told him. "It's a nuisance having it all tied up in the mills, though I never wanted more than my allowance before. Maybe when we're married they'll give me some outright, and then you can do what you want with it. You tell the market not to go any higher till after June."

"All right," he grinned and kissed me, "I'll use my influence with Wall Street, and you use yours on the family. You don't think you could fix it up for April, do you—just a year from the night we met?"

Somehow when Harry said things like that I didn't know how I could bear so much happiness. I never took being wanted for granted, then or now. There should have been something to tell me of the precipice before the earth crumbled under my feet. Why are we humans less forewarned than the wild ducks who heed the summons of frost even though summer sun lies warm upon their feathers?

Janice had set her heart on going to a Valentine dance at the Country Club, and she begged me to persuade Aunt Em and Dr. Weeks to let us go. January had been a long, cold month with little social activity in Blairstown because of the epidemic.

"It's seemed like a whole solid month of day-after-Christmases to me," Janice had sighed. "I'll have to break out some way soon or go mad."

Dr. Weeks did waive his taboos. The club dances were small and select, and the epidemic seemed definitely on the wane. We felt suddenly festive as we set off, and even Maggie fell into the spirit of the evening as she helped me on with my wraps.

"Choose a groom on a horse," she told us, "and a bride at a dance and you can't go wrong."

"Sorry about the horse, Maggie," Harry teased her from the steps. "But I think there's something in what you say."

We did seem to be a part of a special rhythm when we danced together that night. I had wakened in the morning feeling tired and heavy, and my head had ached all day. But suddenly I felt light and elated and charged with an inner current of happiness that tingled in every nerve and fiber. Somehow that night I couldn't make myself believe in death or pain or despair. Other people might know them, but not Harry Collins and Emily Blair moving together in a close-wrapped mantle of well-being.

"Harry," I whispered once when the music stopped and we waited while the rest clapped for an encore. "I'm almost afraid to be so happy. You don't think—"

His arm tightened around me. "It's fatal to think about being happy. You just are, or you're not, that's all there is to that."

But he was wrong. Too much good fortune can make you smug and unaware. Happiness should be like an oasis, the greener for the desert that surrounds it.

It was three by the clock in the Square as we drove back through the deserted town. Rain was falling, and there was no sign of morning in the east.

"Good night, my sweet." Harry kissed me and turned on the doorstep with a laugh that ended in a yawn.

The drip of cold rain in the darkness and those four words he had spoken became one to me as I stood watching him go down the path—fond, casual words that were never meant to be weighted down with the importance I gave them. Yet all those days and weeks and months and years afterward my heart echoed them. If they became distorted and magnified out of all proportion, the fault is mine and mine alone. For I had no right to cling to them as I did because my need of their reassurance was so great. Yet I am not the first, and I shall not be the last, to try to make a bowstring into an anchor chain.

CHAPTER TEN

"THANK YOU, I understand. I know you've done everything you could, and it's no use. But thanks just the same."

I was to say that so many times in the next two years that I lost count. The words would rise almost mechanically to my lips, and though they might vary, the theme was always the same. As time went on I even became confused as to whether the current specialist delivering the verdict happened to be in Boston or New York, in Baltimore or Chicago. Sometimes as I waited for my turn, the past would creep up and betray me with false reassurance. I would stare incredulously at the newspaper I might be reading and ask myself what I was doing here in a strange city, in a strange doctor's reception room, under the impersonal cheerful eye of a starched attendant and the curious glances of other patients.

Well, I had stood it as long as I could. I was through with doctors' offices and hospital clinics. No one could say that I hadn't given them every chance. Even Aunt Em would have to admit that I had cooperated with the doctors and their treatments. In the beginning I had even hoped. This business of hoping was going to die hard with Aunt Em and with Harry. But they would have to see my side. They couldn't make me go on and on with this weary, humiliating round. I must convince them somehow, once I got back. What had made my exit different that day was that the doctor had not tried to be kind.

"Well," he had said, "we've given it a fair trial, and frankly there's nothing more I can do. I might as well be honest with you."

"I know," I said, wishing I could have been sure that my voice kept steady. "I understand—"

He stopped me with a quick gesture and turned to speak into the telephone beside him. I sat in the chair opposite and stared at the colored reproductions of French moderns on the walls—a Renoir girl, pink and full-blown as a rose; a Degas dancer bending to her ballet slipper; a pot of flowers on a window sill that would bloom forever because van Gogh had seen it so on another morning. Someone had chosen those paintings, I suppose, because they were so far removed from pain and weariness of spirit and medical paraphernalia. It was a good theory, yet one that I resented. Somehow a blank wall was more appropriate when one sat waiting for what one had traveled so far and been through so much probing and pains to learn.

"Then you think it's hopeless?" I leaned across the desk when he put back the telephone and turned to me again.

"I've learned not to use that word, Miss Blair. In the medical profession there's always the chance one may be wrong. I only say that I don't seem able to help you. Let's see how long it's been." He held out a sheaf of typed reports that the nurse had brought from the files. "H'm-m,

February, 1929, and you've been to Chase in Chicago; Mack and Thomas in New York; Ricker in Baltimore and—"

"Do we need to go into the medical who's who?"

I had felt no surprise or resentment at his words. They had been said to me with variations so often before, that I could meet them almost before they had been spoken. What I did feel was a sudden relief, a sense almost as if I had come to the wall of a dead-end street. I need not struggle to find a way out. I saw that he was studying me with an expression I knew to be the usual forerunner of farewell salvos of good advice.

"Please," I said, reaching for my things, "would you mind *not* telling me I have a lot to be thankful for, or that I must never let myself be handicapped, or that everybody has adjustments to make of some kind? I'll meet this in my own way as long as I have to, but I'd rather not be reminded that it could be worse than it is."

So there I was once more in the long bleak waiting room of the North Station with an hour to kill before I could board the Blairstown train. The ticket windows and benches and every postcard and candy bar on display were familiar to me as the suitcase at my feet with E. B. in black letters and all the dents and scratches that two years of traveling in close companionship had put there. I had packed it in haste. A blue tassel from my dressing gown had got left outside. I needn't have been in such a frenzy after I left the doctor's office that noon. Certainly I should have known there wasn't a train between the 12:53 and the 3:19. But somehow flight had been my only thought, not flight as I had known it before, pushing on to what lay ahead. This was to be a deliberate flight into the past where I might face what must be faced as soon as possible, without pity and without false hopes.

The coffee stand was deserted, as I went over and sat on one of the revolving stools. I didn't really want the coffee I ordered, but I had found that time passes more quickly if one goes through the motions of eating and drinking. My own reflection stared back at me from the looking glass above the counter. In the strong, unflattering light I studied my face critically, searching for some sign of outward change. I was still young and attractive enough at twenty-four to be noticed when I traveled alone. Only a certain tenseness and anxiety of expression betrayed me at times.

"Why, Emily Blair," the Parker twins and others were always telling me, "with your looks and brains you don't have to worry. It isn't as if anybody'd guess you had a thing wrong with you."

I knew they meant to be kind. I couldn't explain that it was the little clumsinesses and petty irritations that hurt my pride.

I knew that going back to Blairstown empty of hope wasn't going to be easy. But facts had to be faced. I should have to convince Aunt Em that I couldn't go on with this being shunted from specialist to specialist. And Harry—I must make him understand, too, about the loneliness and despair that only his presence had the power to ease. When I had been back for week ends of late he had seemed preoccupied and constrained, and his letter of day before yesterday had left me feeling somehow unsatisfied. I took it out of my bag and spread the single sheet on the counter before me, trying to find some crumb of reassurance there that might have gone unnoticed on other readings. I was like a child shaking an empty candy box, in hope that some sweet may have miraculously remained.

My Dear [it began]:

Your letters put me to shame for my sins of omission, but honestly this week has been the worst since the market hit bottom in '29. If you've read the papers you know what the mills are up against. You're lucky to be out of it with the whole place about as cheerful as the tomb of the Capulets. Orders practically nil and the United Textile gang cutting up— Well, maybe something can be worked out before the next Directors' meeting.

I'm sorry the treatments aren't going better. But don't let them get you down, Emmy—I have a feeling you're on the right track this time. So don't hurry it and have any regrets. It's been a long pull, I know, but you've been grand, and I needn't remind you of the sort of person you are.

I turned the page with a pang. It was one of those times when I could have managed with a large dose of praise.

Your idea about my driving up for the Harvard-Dartmouth game next week sounds good, but Janice has got herself and the car all dated up. Wish I could see my way to getting a secondhand car of my own. Funny to think we ever talked about such a thing as a raise. Well, my sweet, it's late, and the whistle blows as usual tomorrow morning; and we pretend to be busy, with prosperity just around the corner. Sorry you won't be back for your aunt's birthday. Let me know when to expect you here if I can't get on for the game.

Love,
HARRY

I folded the paper and put it back into the envelope. There was no reason to feel as I did about that letter.

Words were not Harry's strong point, and I knew that he was genuinely worried about the mill situation. But if he had simply scrawled across the page, "Miss you like all creation, darling," or something like it I'd have felt a good deal better. Surely he must know that it was as much for his sake as my own that I had forced myself to try one cure after another. I had fought to keep our love on the old footing. It mustn't be hurt because I had been hurt. Yet when I saw people watching us together I guessed what was in their minds.

A man had seated himself at the lunch counter, and I could see in the mirror that he was studying me curiously. I felt annoyed because his look was so frank and impersonal for all its intentness. I stared back at him in the mirror, but he continued his survey without concern. I noticed that he was on the youngish side of thirty and his clothes, while not exactly shabby, were obviously not the sort that Harry or other men I knew wore. Yet there was a kind of distinction about the man that cheap tailoring could not conceal. His head was well set, and his high cheekbones made his rather pale, dark-browed face seem broader than it really was. His eyes looked black at first because of their dark lashes and large pupils, but they were actually gray, and his hands were unusually flexible and well kept. You felt they had been scrubbed and scoured almost to the bone.

Well, I thought, there's still twenty minutes to train time. I might as well walk up and down the platform as sit here and be Exhibit A to a total stranger!

I pushed away my cup and saucer and felt for change in my bag. My fingers must have been cold, for the dime slipped out of them and rolled along the floor like a runaway drop of quicksilver before a man's foot stopped its course.

"Oh, thank you, thanks very much," I murmured as the long, white fingers held it out to me. But I didn't allow my eyes above the range of the second coat button.

The first editions of the afternoon papers had just come in. I stopped by the news stand and bought one, arrested by a familiar name in larger type. "Oldest Textile Plant in New England Threatened. Peace-Pipe Industries and United Textile Workers Clash on Demands. Employees in Mass Meeting Tonight."

Tonight. Why, that was Aunt Em's birthday. I noticed the date on the newspaper. My own preoccupation had made me forget. Now I would be there for the celebration that always took place. But it wouldn't be a very festive one with this news. Perhaps I ought to wire that I was on my way. I started towards the telegraph office before I decided that it would mean more if I surprised Aunt Em. So I went on through the gate, set down my suitcase, and stood there on the platform, reading the headlines and the finer print in the news story beneath them.

"Move to organize local union main issue in textile fight. Proposed ten per cent wage cut attacked by Joseph Kelly, Jr."

Joseph Kelly, Jr. I read the name twice before I realized that this was young Jo. Young Jo Kelly with those mistaken views of his that never seemed to have anything to do with the kind and pleasant person he really was. But this was treason, throwing dynamite at Peace-Pipe, at us—

I felt a hand laid without warning on my arm, and then I was pushed so roughly that I almost lost balance. I would have fallen if I had not been held firm and fast. I turned with words of furious protest on my lips, but I never said them. At that same instant a heavily loaded station truck bore down within a few inches. The piled trunks teetered as it swerved its course, and the man steering it glared and made frantic motions at me. Only after it had passed did I turn to see who was responsible for my still being whole.

"Oh!" I knew that I was stammering because it embarrassed me to find that my rescuer was also my companion of the coffee stand. Apparently I couldn't escape from him, whoever he was. This time I knew that explanations were in order. "Thanks again," I said. "I couldn't hear it coming. You see I'm—deaf; I don't hear a thing."

I knew that I must look at him because he would be making some sort of answer and I must follow the motions of his lips. I could feel the color creeping over my face and neck with the effort it had been to get the words out.

He did not seem startled by what I had told him. He smiled a rather slow, grave smile as if he were acknowledging something of which he was already aware.

"I know," he said simply, touched his hat, and walked away without once looking back.

It wasn't until I was in my seat and the train just getting clear of the dingy outskirts of the city, that I found myself thinking about his answer, and wondering how he could have been so sure.

CHAPTER ELEVEN

BY THE TIME my train neared Blairstown a steady rain was blurring the window panes and the early twilight of October had set in. The station and the familiar mill sign with the Indian Chief's head and legendary pipe of peace looked dingier than I remembered. The bitter tang of all mill towns was in the air as I left the stuffy car. The keenness of river damp and smoke and the faint suggestion of chemicals mingled with every breath I drew. It clung to buildings and houses and was part of every bush and tree and signpost as the smell of mice and dust, old clothes and old books belongs to an attic; as chalk and ink are part of any schoolroom since time began. Perhaps I was more aware of it than most, for ever since the deafness had come upon me my sense of smell had been sharpened. I had come to depend upon it, almost as an animal does for its very existence.

One other passenger was alighting at the station, a man from the car ahead. As he turned into the light I recognized him for my companion of the coffee stand, the same who had rescued me from the baggage truck. He had put on his raincoat, and though his hat was over his eyes I knew him by his walk and the sharp, strongly set jaw. I felt annoyed that he should be here in Blairstown, walking with an easy assurance as if the place and he were on familiar terms. I was further annoyed when I saw him hail the one and only station taxi, which I had been planning to take. It served me right for not wiring the house to have Janice meet me. Of course I could ask the station agent to call another cab, but that always meant explanations and talk and I felt in no mood to study moving lips and think up appropriate replies to questions.

"The walk won't do me any harm," I decided, "and I've carried heavier suitcases than this one."

There is something about falling rain that crystallizes thought—at least so it is for me. It is as if seeds of emotion long dormant in my mind must stir at that moist summons even as their earthy counterparts do. So the chill drops on my face were both a goad and a caress that night as I plodded on through the grimy no man's land which always seems to surround stations in any community. It was a good mile and a half to the house, and I had plenty of time to think. The reaction of the day's strain had already set in. I had been facing that decision so long. The past two years seemed longer, looking back upon them, than all the years that had gone before. Certain days and nights rose to mock me, more vivid because of the rain with which they must always be associated.

It had been raining the day that I first realized my plight. I had been aware of myself lying helpless on my bed in the room at the head of the stairs. My body had felt miraculously free of pain, and though I was still very weak I had been able to turn it a little. I could follow a figure in starched white who moved about my room. I had wondered vaguely why she did not speak to me, though she made me comfortable without words and smiled as she anticipated my needs. She had left the room on some errand, I remember, and I had lain quiet watching the familiar pattern of bare branches and falling rain beyond the windows. Painstakingly as only those who have emerged from illness can do, I had studied the furniture and reassured myself that every chair and picture and article on my bureau was in its place. I could find nothing amiss, and yet through the haze of my own weakness I had sensed that all was not as it should have been. It had taken the rain outside to give me the clue. A tin roof covered the porch below the western windows, and always, even in a mild summer shower, the drops had made a pleasant din that could swell to frantic volume in heavier downpours. That had been the false note in the picture—my eyes saw falling water and my ears heard nothing. Presentiment turned me cold under the warmth of the bedclothes. I had known then what I must do and I called upon every shred of strength left in me to accomplish it.

My knees buckled under me, and the effort to crawl those few yards over the carpet made me break out into a sweat. But I reached the window at last. It had been left open a little and I thrust my hand into the wetness. The water struck me with an icy chill, and I knew that my eyes had not deceived me. Rain was coming down in slanting shafts, bounding and splashing on the roof below, and yet I might have been in a padded cell for all the sound I heard.

The nurse found me there, and I don't remember how she got me back to bed. Later I knew Aunt Em was holding one of my hands, and Dr. Weeks the other. They tried to smile and act reassuringly, but they were trying so hard it was worse than if tears were running down their cheeks. Their lips kept moving and I knew they must be speaking to each other. There they were so close I could feel their breath, and not a sound reached me. The more I strained, the more I felt a queer numbness in my ears. It was like having been turned to a wooden puppet suddenly in the midst of live actors.

I could feel my own lips beginning to move, to form words that my mind was saying over and over.

"I can't hear you," I said, and I turned to the Doctor and held him fast with my eyes. "I'm deaf—that's the truth, isn't it?"

I shall always be grateful to Dr. Weeks for not hedging. His eyes held mine steadily and he gave a long, affirmative nod. After Aunt Em left us alone he went over to my desk and wrote down the answer to another question I had not asked.

"You have been very ill," I read. "The meningitis infection has affected your ears, but we hope not permanently."

I think I shall always be able to see the shape of those jerky penciled letters, though the realization of what had happened came slowly, in little ways. Returning to Blairstown that day brought back all the hurts and bitternesses, as if those memories were actually keeping step with me through the rain.

Especially I quickened my pace past the town hall at the edge of the Square. I could never pass it without the humiliation of a certain day when I had gone there to renew my driver's license and returned without it. It was the summer after my illness and I was just beginning to read lips. I still missed a good many words unless people spoke slowly and remembered not to turn away as they talked. But that inspector had made me understand without any difficulty. Then there was the book of rules with the special paragraph about physical impediments. I couldn't very well ignore that. It didn't do any good to protest that I had a good driving record, and that there was nothing wrong with my eyes and other faculties. Those ten minutes are among the most painful I have ever endured. The inspector didn't relish them any more than I. He was red with embarrassment when he handed me back my old license with an apologetic headshake.

I might have got one somewhere else. Usually there are ways of getting by rules. But I never had the heart to try again. Besides, everyone in Blairstown knew what had happened to me, so what would have been the use? Yes, I thought splashing through a deep puddle to get past the building, that was the trouble with small towns, one was too much a part of them ever to escape from one's self. Association stalked one at every corner. There was no deceiving the next-door neighbors. No matter how brave a show one might stage for their benefit.

"A little town is like a lantern," Maggie Flynn used to say. "Nothing's hid from sight."

Across the river the mill lights showed through the rain. Several of the buildings were half dark, which I knew meant small shifts and no great rush of business. Even if I had not heard it from Harry or read it in the papers, the spacing of those lights would have told me how steadily business had slackened month by month since November, 1929. A panic in Wall Street had seemed a little thing compared to the personal calamity that had overtaken me.

But now in 1931 I was beginning to realize a financial collapse could seriously affect the sort of security I had always taken for granted. Uncle Wallace and Mr. Parker discussed bank loans with Aunt Em and returned from business conferences in New York and Washington with long faces. Harry no longer spoke wistfully of dabbling in the market.

"Guess it was lucky for me I couldn't afford to buy any securities on margin," he had admitted more than once.

He had come back considerably sobered by his last college reunion. So many of his class were out of jobs, and the rest worried about the unemployment situation. He had been reckoned fortunate to be kept on at all.

"Don't think I'm fool enough not to know where I'd be if you and I weren't going to be married," he had reminded me a little bitterly one day.

"Please, dear," I had begged, "don't say things like that. You'd got your start at Peace-Pipe before we met, and Uncle Wallace and Mr. Parker both think you have real ability once you know the business from the bottom up—"

"By that time the bottom will have dropped out and there won't be any top most likely," he had answered with a shrug. Then, seeing that his words had hurt me, he had slipped an arm round my shoulders and rubbed his cheek against mine. "Don't take what I say personally, Emmy, I've got a prize in you and I know it—only I could make good in the business if I had the chance."

He had gone on to tell me of certain innovations he was eager to see made in the mill products. There was a trend towards cheaper, less conservative merchandise, and he felt that Peace-Pipe might as well begin to meet the demand.

"Who's buying sheets and towels nowadays?" he pointed out. "It's girls your age getting married and setting up homes on a shoestring. Well, they're going to get the most goods they can for their money, and to hell with quality. Put on fancy borders and plenty of color and do it up in smart wrappers, and the orders'll come in. It's worth trying, but get the company to see it! Peace-Pipe Mills will go on turning out the same old line, and the buying public will let them go bury themselves under their own surplus stock."

Harry's arguments made sense, but when I tried to back him up I met the same stone wall of conservatism. Uncle Wallace and Aunt Em, Mr. Parker and the directors couldn't seem to see things in any but the old terms. They were proud of their standards, and they instinctively fought against any radical changes in methods and products.

"If we can just hold out!" they always ended by saying. "Business is bound to start on the upswing soon. We've weathered other panics and depressions. Quality always wins out in the long run."

My deafness spared me much of the discussions, but no one with eyes to see and read could fail to note the signs and portents. Other New England textile centers were becoming ghost towns, operating on skeleton shifts or shut down completely like mining towns where the vein of precious ore is dwindling, and the pulse of prosperity has slowed down. I never thought it could be so with Blairstown, yet I saw the first unmistakable signs that day. Still, I saw them as someone watching from behind the security of a windowpane sees falling snow, not as one feels who has ever been caught in a blizzard.

I was drenched through by the time I turned up our driveway. The shades were not drawn, and lamplight within shone on the wet lawn. I could see Great-grand-father Blair's portrait over the fireplace and the comb-back Windsor chairs that were more admired than sat upon silhouetted against the windowpanes. Chrysanthemums in russet and copper gave back reflected brightness on the center table. Across the hall mahogany, white damask and polished silver were as they had always been ever since I could remember, and Maggie Flynn moved from table to sideboard in her immemorial black and white. Order and comfort and tradition waited there. Once I stepped across the threshold they would take me in hand again. It is strange to look in upon the life of a household to which one has belonged when it is continuing its activity without one. I was not expected, and the household was preparing to celebrate Aunt Em's birthday as usual. I saw extra places for guests, the best china service, and the pre-Prohibition sherry in readiness. My return would not alter it except by one place more, hastily set at the table. We are less indispensable than we think, even to those we love.

I wonder if soldiers feel like this, I thought standing out there in the rain. I wonder if they feel, coming back from some unsuccessful campaign, that maybe a place and people could go on just as well without them.

Foolish to make such comparisons. What did I know about soldiers?

But at least, I kept on thinking as I reached for the cold knob of the front door, at least if they're beaten they don't have to bring back the news of their own de-feat. Their families would have heard of that first, and

I've got to tell mine that doctor number nine—or is it eleven?—has failed.

I must have frightened Maggie and Aunt Em, for they ran out and took my wet things and brought me a glass of sherry before they started to scold me for walking up from the station.

"Please, Aunt Em," I said when Maggie had hurried upstairs to draw a hot bath, "please don't ask a lot of questions. I'll tell you everything tomorrow, but just tonight I don't feel as if—"

One of the things I minded most about being deaf was never feeling sure of my voice. It would have been a comfort to know that it kept steady. I guess it didn't then because Aunt Em's expression changed to that scared, helpless one I knew so well.

"You're tired, dear," she comforted as she drew me over to the fire. "You shouldn't have walked so far and carried that heavy suitcase in all the rain."

"Don't try to be kind," I could feel my throat tightening with every word. It made me hard and curt with her as I hadn't meant to be. "We might as well face the music—" I broke off and shrugged. It helped to hide what I was really feeling. "Music that even I can hear."

I saw her wince, though she tried to act as if she hadn't understood what I meant.

"Well"—she straightened her shoulders and smiled in the encouraging way that I had come to dread—"suppose these treatments haven't helped you as much as we hoped. Dr. Lowe isn't the only ear specialist left. There are others we haven't tried."

"We're not going to try any more." Her eyes dropped before the determination she met in mine. I knew I was hurting her, but I couldn't stop. I'd been through too much in the last weeks to try to make things easy for myself or anyone else. "We can't go on this way any longer, hoping like fools and catching at straws. I'm deaf—stone-deaf. I always will be and that's that."

I turned and started for the hall, but she caught my arm. I could feel her trembling under her best, black taffeta dress.

"We mustn't be hasty, dear," she tried to soothe me; "and besides, there's Harry. You must give it more time for his sake as much as your own."

"It was for Harry's sake I tried this last doctor," I reminded her. "Except for him I couldn't go on. He's all I've got, and when we're together—"

I saw her face relax with relief at that.

"You'll feel different about this when you've talked everything over with Harry. He's coming for dinner tonight. It'll be a real birthday for me now you're back, even if things aren't looking very bright down at the mills. I suppose you've seen the papers?"

I nodded in sudden contrition.

"I don't know what we're heading for, and if the worst element here gets mixed up with a lot of professional trouble makers . . . I'm worried, Emily—nothing like this ever started at Peace-Pipe before."

She had never turned to me in just that way before. I realized suddenly all she had been keeping out of the cheerful letters she had written me.

"I'm sorry," I told her. "I didn't mean to unload everything that was on my mind, but somehow—tonight—"

She turned, and I knew that Maggie had spoken to her from the hall.

"Your bath's ready," she relayed the message, "and Maggie says she's laid out your dry things. Cousin Eunice is in the guest room."

I sighed as I gathered up my wet hat and soggy purse.

"Anyone else coming?" I asked.

"No, just a family party. We can play bridge afterwards. Oh, I forgot to tell you, Dr. Weeks is taking on an assistant, and he's coming too."

"What did you say?" I thought I had failed to catch her words, though I knew the motions of her lips so well I seldom had to ask her to repeat.

"An assistant, and I'm thankful he's got someone to take a little of the work off his shoulders. I haven't met the young man yet. He's just out of his hospital training and considered very promising. Will's been interested in him for some time now. He asked to bring him here tonight. Run along and dress now, dear, you've got nearly an hour."

CHAPTER TWELVE

I FELT ANYTHING but festive as I came downstairs in a last year's dress that Maggie had laid out for me. Janice had made use of it during my absence. The clasp of the belt was bent, and she had taken off the rhinestone shoulder clips and forgotten to put them back. Without them it looked drab and spiritless, the way I felt. But perhaps Harry wouldn't care what I had on, so long as we need no longer be separated. I could see him standing by the fire, and I tried to make him look up and catch my eye instead of listening to Aunt Em and Cousin Eunice. Cousin Eunice was pointing to the headlines I had already seen in the evening paper, and from Harry's expression I guessed that she was giving him her opinion of the mill trouble. He seemed tired, though his face lightened in quick response when I called his name.

"Harry, Harry darling," I was clinging to him, with my lips against the sandy crispness of his hair. "I had to come back. I couldn't stand another hour of it and— Oh, dear, why can't we just be by ourselves somewhere?"

I hung back at the door, trying to prolong the moment.

I saw then what I hadn't noticed at first, that he was in evening clothes, a formality that a family birthday dinner would not have rated. So, he was going somewhere afterward. I must have shown my surprise, for he rolled his eyes at me and sighed.

"The Catons are giving a dance," he explained. "I promised to drive over with Janice and help out with some of their house guests. Of course if I'd known you were coming I wouldn't have said yes. Why don't you come along too?"

"No." I shook my head and tried not to look disappointed. "I'd just be an extra girl. It's all right, only of course I can't help wishing—"

I broke off partly because Maggie was opening the front door to Dr. Weeks and his companion. As Maggie moved away with their hats and coats the hall light shone full upon the newcomer. For the fourth time that day I was seeing the man of the coffee stand and the railway platforms. This time there was no turning away or snubbing him.

"Emily, this is a surprise." I tried to give no sign as Dr. Weeks went through the introductions. "Well, here's one for you. My associate, Dr. Vance. Merek, this is Emily Blair, though I told you she wouldn't be here tonight."

I had expected him to make small talk of our earlier meetings, but he merely acknowledged the Doctor's introduction with a handshake before he went into the other room.

"Nice fellow," Harry said as we followed them in. "Doesn't have much to say for himself the few times we've met. Guess he knows his business though. He's over at the mills a lot, taking over all that end of the practice. It was getting too much for the old man."

I kept close to Harry. The old sense of happiness in his presence flooded me once more. Everything was going to be all right, I told myself, as I sat beside him sipping the sherry that Aunt Em poured sparingly into the cut glasses that went with the decanter. Harry touched his glass to mine and smiled. I could not hear the little answering clink, but the gesture went to my heart. I didn't begrudge Janice her entrance in a new green dress the color of spring grass. She was looking prettier than ever. Her fair bobbed head shone under the lamplight and her face had that flowerlike tenacity that always surprised me after an absence. She had matured in the last couple of months. Her eyes were less soft and childish, and there was a new set to her mouth and chin. She stood with her glass high, talking animatedly to the young Doctor. Their heads were turned away so I couldn't have read their lips if I had wanted to know what they were saying. I wasn't particularly interested, but I watched to see if she could throw her usual spell over him, or if he would continue to scrutinize her as he had me earlier in the day. He appeared to be listening intently and yet, as I watched them, I saw his eyes leave her face; and though he nodded in response to some remark I knew that he was watching Harry Collins and me. There was something disturbing in his glance. I slipped my arm through Harry's, and the firelight caught the stone on the ring he had given me. I felt sure young Dr. Vance must have noticed it on the third finger of my left hand. He seemed to notice everything and to be stowing it away in some invisible filing cabinet of his mind.

I don't remember much about that meal except that it

was the usual party fare, served in Maggie's best style on
the best Dresden china. The evening paper had disappeared,
I noticed, before we went in to the table, and all mention
of the mill troubles was avoided. We had pumpkin pie
made from Grandmother Blair's recipe and I knew that
Aunt Em must be telling Dr. Vance all that went into its
making. He sat at her right and seemed always listening,
seldom speaking, whenever I glanced that way. I sat quietly
between Harry and Dr. Weeks, hungry and tired and glad
to be back. The despair of the day seemed to retreat to
the other side of the curtains that shut out the fall night.

It was time to drink toasts in cider made from the apples
on the old trees below the garden. Dr. Weeks rose and
lifted his glass towards Aunt Em at her end of the table.
There was that quietly fond look in his eyes that always
made me feel a little sad.

"Well," he began, and I knew beforehand what the
toast would be, "to you, Emily, because there's no one like
you."

Aunt Em accepted it with her usual little deprecating
headshake.

"I'm afraid you're prejudiced, Will," she said, as she
had said on every birthday since I could remember. Then
she lifted her glass, and I saw her hand tremble a little as
she held it out. "Here's to Peace-Pipe," she began, and
again I didn't have to follow her lips to know the toast she
was making, "To Peace-Pipe—past, present, and future."

We drank coffee before the living-room fire, and I
found myself on the sofa between Cousin Eunice and Dr.
Vance. It wasn't an easy position with Cousin Eunice leaning across me to make conversation with the stranger in
our midst. Cousin Eunice never minded asking personal

questions. I was glad that for once they were not being directed at me.

"Vance," she said, weighing his name as if it had been some commodity she was appraising. "I don't suppose by any chance you're related to the Milton branch?"

"No," he told her, and I thought I saw a faint flicker of amusement in his expression. "My family name was spelled differently."

"Really." Cousin Eunice peered at him suspiciously.

"Yes," he went on, "it used to be Vancovitch, so you see those Milton Vances wouldn't claim me."

Cousin Eunice showed her surprise. She wasn't used to people with names like that, people who were obviously unimpressed by the sort of background she admired.

"Well, I always make it a point to ask," Cousin Eunice rallied with a shrug. "It's such a small world, and somehow I never can understand people changing their names, except by marriage of course. Mine was Pratt before I married into the Blair family."

"Any relation to the Pratt smelting and iron works in Pennsylvania?" Again I thought I detected a grim amusement about his lips.

"Oh, no, we belong to the Massachusetts branch," she told him emphatically.

"Well, the world's so small I thought I'd ask." He gave no sign beyond a slightly lifted eyebrow, but I knew he was speaking for my benefit. "I was out there working last summer."

"In the iron and smelting works?" I could see that Cousin Eunice was growing more disapproving with every remark, and that it pleased him to lead her on.

"Why, yes, in a way. I was making a survey of industrial diseases."

"Oh, I see, how interesting! Do you play contract?" Already Cousin Eunice's eyes were upon the card table being set up in the alcove.

He shook his head and watched her move over to it. I was rather sorry he didn't play because bridge was one of my accomplishments. Deafness didn't interfere with it and I had come to be a good player. I wanted to show him what I could do with cards, and now there would be no chance. The four older ones would have their table, and after Harry and Janice left for the dance I would have this strange young doctor on my hands. Aunt Em was beckoning me over to the table, but I smiled and shook my head. I wouldn't have kept her from her game, knowing how she enjoyed it.

Janice went over and tinkered the radio. I knew it must be dance music from the way her shoulders swayed in time and from the annoyed frown on Aunt Em's face. She was trying to catch Janice's eye to make her turn it off. But before she had managed that Janice had caught Harry by the arm and they had begun to dance. I watched them, indifferently at first, and then with a sudden sense of hurt. They needn't have started in so soon; they were going to have the rest of the evening for dancing.

"Come," Harry was bending over me and reaching out his hands. "Come on, dear, here's one you know: 'Two Hearts in Waltz Time.' Let's take a turn."

Yes, I remembered. They had played it that night of the Valentine party. We had danced and danced to it with big red hearts for favors. I wasn't likely to forget that tune to the end of my days.

His arms were strong about me, and though I fumbled at the start I managed to get into the swing. I was so used to following his steps that it wasn't as hard as I had expected. I thought we were doing rather well, and I stopped straining to keep the rhythm. As we passed by the sofa I looked up and saw that Dr. Vance was watching us with that frank curiosity that had annoyed me earlier in the day. What annoyed me even more was that I caught a look of pity in his eyes before he let them drop once more to the book he had picked up from the table. I turned quickly to Harry's face for reassurance. But it was not there. He was given over completely to guiding me, and I knew in that moment that all spontaneity had gone out of our motions. I lost step just then and fumbled in sudden confusion.

"Oh, I'm sorry," I apologized. "My fault."

"No, mine," Harry denied politely. "It's because we haven't tried dancing together for so long. You're not bad, Emily, really you're not."

"Well, I'm certainly not very good." I tried to laugh it off as I spoke, but couldn't have sounded very convincing. "Remember what Dr. Johnson said—at least I think it was Dr. Johnson—about the dog walking on his hind legs: the wonder wasn't that he could do it gracefully, but that he could do it at all!"

"She shouldn't say things like that, should she, Dr. Vance?" Harry turned to him after he had motioned Janice to shut the radio off. "We'll have to get you to prescribe for her when she's difficult."

It irritated me that Harry should have drawn our guest into the talk, and I must have shown it.

"You don't like to make compromises, do you, Miss Blair?"

I pretended not to have caught his words, and there was some satisfaction in making him repeat them.

"I hate compromises, if you must know!" I flashed back. "I hate them almost as much as I do doctors' office manners and their puns."

"If I promise never to make any in your hearing—" he began.

But I cut him short. "In my *hearing*, did you say?"

"Well, what if I did?" He compelled me to go on with the conversation, though anyone could see that I wanted to get away. "I'm not afraid to mention your deafness the way everyone else around here seems to be."

I don't remember what answer I made, but I went over to the bridge table and stayed a long time watching the players. They didn't guess that the cards were a blur before my eyes. I felt hot inwardly at the bluntness of that remark, even more at the truth that lay behind it.

When it was time for Janice and Harry to leave for the Catons' dance I followed them into the hall, determined to seem gayer than I felt as I watched them drive off. Ridiculous to feel forlorn and left out with Harry's kiss warm on my lips and the reassurance that he would be over the next evening. Yet I could not shake myself free of my earlier mood. As I closed the front door, I turned and found Dr. Vance standing behind me.

"Good night," he held out his hand. "I've just been thanking your aunt for letting me come to her birthday party, and it's been nice meeting you again."

"Again?" I repeated. "Oh, you mean the North Station. That wasn't exactly my idea of a meeting."

"Or mine." He shrugged and smiled before he went on. "But as a matter of fact we'd met before that."

"In some doctor's office, I suppose. I've wasted so much time in one or another these last two years I can't keep track of them all."

He let the remark pass.

"No," he said, without reaching for his hat and coat, "it happened right here in Blairstown. There was a Christmas party down at the mills and you stood on the platform holding a little muff about the size of that." He put his two fists together as he spoke. "You must have been seven or maybe eight."

"Seven," I told him. "Yes, I remember. There was— some sort of trouble, wasn't there?"

He nodded.

"My father staged a little demonstration. He'd been laid off and he wasn't in the mood to appreciate Santa Claus."

Once more he gave me one of his long, disquieting looks.

"Oh!" I said lamely. "Then your father must have been the one who—"

"Yes, he was the one. Our name was Vancovitch then. They changed it after we left Blairstown. My father's dead," he added, "he died of lead poisoning in a plant near Newark. You needn't be afraid he'll turn up with a grudge."

"I suppose you can carry it on for him," I said. "It's just the perfect time for you to come back with all this labor trouble starting."

I saw him flush and knew that my words had hit the mark I meant them to.

"I guess I deserved that," he answered. "I hadn't meant

to tell you. It was an impulse, and I ought to know by this time it's a mistake to yield to them." He hesitated before he went on again. "Well, I might as well explain that I came because Dr. Weeks asked me to. We owe a lot to him from years back. He saved my mother's life, and he helped me through college and medical school. I don't know any other way of paying him back."

"Oh," I said, feeling very small, "I see."

"And there are other reasons, too . . ." Even without hearing the tones of his voice I felt the sureness go out of his manner. "This place never brought us anything but misery and hard luck. It's come to stand for everything I hated and struggled to escape from, and I knew it would stay like that always unless I came back and gave it the best I have to offer. You have to turn the tables on the past sometimes if you don't want it to play tricks on you."

He bent to pick up his things, and suddenly I found myself trying to keep him from going.

"I'm sorry I said what I did," I told him. "I've had rather a bad day, and I took some of my feelings out on you. You kept turning up, you see, and it bothered me the way you seemed to know all about me."

He scarcely seemed to notice my apology as he stood there looking in at the living room—at the firelight on the drawn brocade curtains; at the flowers and ornaments and books and the family portraits hanging in their places. I could tell that he was taking in every detail in a special kind of way, not like the casual observer.

"It's a funny feeling"—he turned to me at last with a quick shrug—"being on this side of your front door. When I was a kid I used to pass this house and wonder what it must be like inside. Well, now I've found out."

"And is everything the way you expected it to be?"

"Why, yes!" His eyes went back to the room and the group about the card table before they returned to me. "Yes, it's the way I expected—all except you."

I didn't want to press him, but curiosity got the better of me at last.

"Oh, so I don't run true to form?"

"No," he told me, "you 'wear your rue with a difference.'"

"My what?" I thought I must have mistaken the word.

"Rue," he repeated, "in case it matters. You know, Miss Blair, I can't help liking you in spite of my disapproval. Good night."

He was out of the front door before I could answer. I went back to the fire and tried to go on with the piece of knitting I had begun. But I kept losing count of stitches, and at last I put down my work and went to the shelf where the dictionary was always kept. I took it down and turned to the *r*'s. "Rue," I read, "an herb with a bitter taste; to lament, or regret."

CHAPTER THIRTEEN

IT HAD NEVER occurred to me that Harry and I could ever quarrel, and yet we did, the day after my return. The afternoon had been beautiful after the rain, and that somehow made the sharp, barbed words the more hard to reconcile. Everything shone in a late October brilliance that was like a coat of clear lacquer laid on the familiar hills and roadsides. The bright, washed air held a faint edge of frost, and the far smoke of bonfires and a delicate spice of fallen apples mingled with every breath I drew. It was like drinking some rare, ethereal wine, such as gods might have brewed in the days of faith and innocence. I felt renewed as I rode beside Harry in the open roadster. Yesterday's despair had fallen away like dried scales.

"Harry," I begged as we drove back along the turnpike after a trip to the cider mill, "let's turn off here and walk to the burned-out house. I haven't been there since the day we had our picnic there and you told me—"

Looking back now, I can see that he had no wish to go there; but I persuaded him against his excuses. Before we had gone far on the wheel ruts I began to notice changes.

The scrub oak and elder and sumac bushes had been ruth-lessly cleared, and trenches dug in the marshes on either side. I cried out in protest as I had done as a child when what I treasured lay spoiled before my eyes. A rough, un-painted shack had been set up on the foundations of the ruined house, and workmen's tools were all about.

"Oh, Harry," I cried, "it's not ours any more!"

He kept his head turned away so I couldn't tell what his response might be. I caught at his arm and made him face me.

"Just see what they've done to it, dear. And I always hoped we could own this place some day. I never thought of it being sold to someone else and changed."

But he didn't answer with the fond, reassuring look I had expected. Instead he frowned and drew away his arm.

"Oh, don't be so dramatic about it, Emmy," he said shortly. "Things are bound to change."

His words were chilling. The brightness of the day sud-denly went out for me though the sun still lay warm on the distant marshes, making broken mirrors of all the little irregular pools. There was something more than casual annoyance in his rebuke, and because I was hurt I did not let it pass as I should have done.

"And people change, too," I reminded him. "You're dif-ferent, Harry. I've felt it ever since last night."

"Oh, Lord, if you're going to get edgy because I didn't know you were coming and because I'd made a date—"

I cut him short.

"I'm not getting edgy as you call it. It's only—" I saw his face grow remote and blurred through the tears I was determined not to shed. "It's only that you seem to be holding me off at arms' length. You won't let me get *to* you any more, and when two people love each other and are going to be married . . . You haven't forgotten we're going to be married, have you, dear?"

I tried to make it light and ironical, but I think my voice must have given away the desperation behind my words.

"Now, Emmy, that's not fair—"

"But you never mention it any more?"

"Well, how can I? Look what I'm making, and look at what's happening at the mills. It would be a fine time to ask for a raise so we can be married. Besides your aunt has other plans. She's been telling me about a doctor up in Montreal who's had a lot of luck with cases like yours, and—"

It came like a slap in the face, and I turned on him furiously.

"Don't you use that word about me, ever again," I said. "Whatever else you call me, I'm not a case. There aren't going to be any more doctors and treatments. I told Aunt Em that last night, and I'm telling you now, so it won't do any good to try and humor me along. I've put through two years it's going to take me the rest of my life to forget. They're over, and I've come back to marry you and be the best wife I know how to be. I have a terrible handicap, and we both know it. But I'll do everything in my power so it won't be too hard for you. It might even make us closer because it makes me even more yours. You do see how it is. Tell me you do, Harry, or I just can't go on. I can't—"

He held me close and tried to soothe me.

"You mustn't get all worked up like this. We have to be practical, you know. Calm down a little and be sensible."

"I've tried to be, Harry, but when you start talking about waiting it's like asking someone who's starving to wait while you set the table with the best linen and china—"

"Someone has to think about the dollars and cents. We can't live without them, not the way you're used to living."

That hurt me as it always hurts a woman to be told she's an expensive proposition.

"Just because I've had everything done for me doesn't mean I can't get along without lots of things I've been used to. The only thing I can't face doing without is you. We can manage with what I have. I know we can."

"Everything your father left you and Janice is tied up in the mills, and I don't suppose you know what Peace-Pipe Industries is bringing a share right now?"

"No, I don't know and I don't care. With my allowance and what you're making we'd have more than a lot of couples start on."

"Please." He pointed off behind the shack and put his finger to his lips. "I think someone's coming. Let's not stand here arguing any longer."

I followed him back along the narrow wheel ruts, fighting off the crowding tears of hurt and humiliation. I tried to tell myself that men were stubborn about accepting financial help from a girl or her family. I had been brought up to feel that this was a trait to be admired. Perhaps I had gone too far with my plans. I had rather flung them at his head, but I had a right to discuss the future that we were going to share. It couldn't be a crime to say what one felt to the man one was going to marry. Perhaps I had been foolish and impetuous. Maggie had always warned me against rushing headlong into things.

"Least said, soonest mended," she used to tell me.

We reached the parked car, and Harry took his place beside me. But his eyes avoided mine and I knew he resented what I had said.

The sun was going down behind the broken, rough-backed line of western hills. Soon the sky would be a welter of flame above the dark chimneys of Peace-Pipe Mills. Once there had been a time when the shape of trees and hills and the molten drama of a sun's exit would have been enough to lift my heart and spirits. But that time was gone. My happiness was bound too closely to the happiness of another to be stirred in the old, impersonal way. I felt baffled and alone as we drove back through the miracle of a fall sunset over a New England mill town.

"Harry," I said as the car drew up by the steps, "don't feel annoyed with me. I've been waiting so long for this afternoon all to ourselves, and we can't let anything spoil it."

"Oh, forget it, Emmy." He reached for a cigarette and offered me one.

But I shook my head. I couldn't dismiss it as lightly as that.

"No, dear," I went on, "I meant every word I said about us and not waiting. Maybe I ought to have had more pride than to say them. I don't know what's become of my pride lately. It just seems to melt away when you love someone."

"I meant what I said, too, Emmy." He puffed hard at the cigarette and kept his eyes from meeting mine. "God knows, you're a thousand times too good for me and I know it, but—"

"Oh, Harry, please!" I cut him short. "I'm selfish and headstrong and impetuous, but I do love you so. It makes me impatient and stupid sometimes."

He put his fingers over my lips and would not let me go on.

After he had left I wandered about the garden and the path that led to the made-over stable and the apple trees behind it. Bridget, the dog that young Jo Kelly had presented me with the day of my engagement party, came rushing out of the toolhouse to greet me. It was comforting to feel the thrash of her regrettably long tail against my legs and the wet softness of her tongue on my fingers. "That dog," Aunt Em and Maggie called her, and we had all given up hope of classifying her as to breed. But she made up for discrepancies of appearance by exuberance of spirit and a devotion to me that was almost an embarrassment at times. Everything about Bridget was at variance— her body long and rangy; her coat the silky kind that should have belonged to a lap dog; her ears drooped limply, while her tail flaunted its length like the banner of some fantastic lost cause. I smiled in spite of my own preoccupation to see her trotting before me through the dusk. Her nose pointed toward the woodyard at the foot of the orchard, but she kept looking back to make sure that I was following.

Suddenly I saw her start forward, all wagging animation. She forgot to look back at me, and I lost her for a moment in the dimness. Then I came closer and saw the reason for her excitement. A man was moving about in the woodyard, a shabby figure with a shock of dark upstanding hair. I knew it for young Jo Kelly even though our woodpile was the last place in Blairstown where I might have expected to find him. I could not see his face for the failing light, but I stood behind one of the old apple trees and watched him leave off splitting a big log to bend and caress the dog. She leaped upon him, and even though I could not hear her whines of welcome the pantomime of her joy was deeply affecting. Watching those two, I wondered what it was that he had—this power to kindle the affections of a dog, or to stir his own kind to confidence and courage. Even those who held him an enemy had to like him. He possessed some quality one couldn't name that made difference of opinion seem unimportant. I was glad that Bridget had led me there just at that moment. I wanted to call his name and feel his thin, quick fingers in mine again. I could have taken comfort talking to young Jo there by the woodpile even though so much had happened in the last two years to send us in opposite directions.

But the dusk was too thick to make it possible for me to follow his lips. So I stood there watching him through the gap between crooked apple branches. He was lifting and piling the wood he had split, and I knew as if he had told me that this was his way of helping lighten the work that must be growing too heavy for his grandfather. I knew that Aunt Em worried about Old Jo's stubborn carrying on of duties, refusing all assistance. I guessed that young Jo must also have the old man on his mind, though they were still unreconciled.

He set the last piece in place and wiped his forehead with the sleeve of his coat. Then he straightened his shoulders and stood still a moment looking up towards the house where lights shone yellow in all the familiar rooms. I wondered if he remembered the big carved bed in the spare room where he had spent those weeks of convalescence in his childhood, or if he had shed completely our side of the river.

I saw him bend to pat the dog he had given me before he swung himself over the fence and disappeared down the back road. Perhaps he was already on his way to talk to some group of workers, to urge them to organize and call a strike as he had done at the last mass meeting. Yet here was the wood he had split and piled to keep our fires burning. So ironic a situation was past my comprehension. But, whether it made sense or not, seeing young Jo Kelly there had given me back for a moment the old happy sense of confidence that used to surround my childhood. It was as if he and I shared a secret once more, the way we used to before the river had come to flow so irrevocably between us.

Bridget had returned to my side. She kept her nose pressed close to my ankles as I went up the dark driveway. I felt grateful for her warm and living presence. Night always intensified the isolation which deafness had brought. Well I knew the truth behind the old saying: "The day has eyes, the night has ears."

CHAPTER FOURTEEN

THE DIRECTORS of Peace-Pipe Industries always met on the first day of November and the last day of April, dates which punctuated the year for Aunt Em and Uncle Wallace. I could not recall a time when they had not reckoned happenings as before or after spring or fall meeting. Of recent years my long absences from Blairstown had lessened the importance of these occasions for me. This year, however, the November meeting loomed large on the calendar, for the future of Peace-Pipe Industries hung in the balance. None of us liked to admit the seriousness of the situation. But we all knew that the strike agitation was far from idle talk; that a walk-out might be called on short notice. Warnings had been given, and the issues could hardly lie dormant much longer. We knew that representatives of the United Textile Workers would present their case to the Board. We knew the demands—dropping of the proposed 10 per cent wage cut, reinstatement of certain workers who had been laid off, and recognition of a local union to be organized by Peace-Pipe employees. We knew, too, what the Directors felt about all these issues.

They would never make concessions, particularly on the matter of organizing.

"It's the end of Peace-Pipe if we give in an inch," Uncle Wallace had said plenty of times, and Aunt Em and Mr. Parker and the rest were in complete agreement. "When a company has operated for over half a century it doesn't have to be told how to run a business. There wouldn't be any mills today without the stockholders' money, and it's time some of us took a stand to see their rights protected. Who carries the losses in times like these, I'd like to know."

"Still, it might be wise to make a few concessions," Harry Collins sometimes ventured to remind them. "They don't want to call a strike when business is practically at a standstill. The best time to get what they want is when it's booming and they can hold you up on orders—"

"Hold us up, yes, that's exactly what they're planning to do. Bandit methods, and you needn't try to cover it up with the sort of talk they use. I'm surprised, Harry, that you'll even suggest our listening to their demands. They've got to be curbed right at the start of things."

"I'm not taking their side," Harry would argue, "but I do know we can't take care of what little business we have left without experienced mill hands. We have to meet competition, and it's stiffer than ever right now. There have to be compromises on both sides—"

"There you go again!" Uncle Wallace and Mr. Parker always reacted violently to that word. "Compromise—it only means giving in by inches, and you ought to know it. Look at what happened at Danforth Mills and Still River. If they'd had any backbone it wouldn't have come to wholesale walk-outs and the disgrace of calling for the State militia. We'll never let it come to that at Peace-Pipe.

The United Textile group needn't think they can frighten us by waving the big stick."

A year before, even six months ago, I would not have bothered about such discussions. I would not have strained to make out what they were saying about the mills. Now it had become important to me because the state of Peace-Pipe Industries had come to have bearing on the future I waited so impatiently to share with Harry. It was like studying a new language, the terms were so strange; and I hesitated to show my ignorance. I didn't want to keep asking what this word meant or that. Often it was difficult to follow discussions that grew heated and full of interruptions. Each person who joined in made it harder for me to follow. I had learned from past experience not to keep asking to have remarks repeated. In the days when I was first struggling to read lips I used to be reminded of the circus jugglers who could keep a number of balls going in the air at once. It seemed to me that to follow the talk of two or more people required as keen an eye and agility of mind.

So I read all I could find about the mill activities in the paper, and I questioned Harry whenever he was in the mood to be expansive. Although he came and went as usual and was with us at the dinner table night after night, he and I were alone together less often. At any other time I might have accused him of maneuvering it so; but his interest in the business was genuine, and Aunt Em and Uncle Wallace turned to him with their problems as they had never done before. I accepted a certain tension and preoccupation, telling myself that I must be patient till after the Directors' meeting. I began to live up to that date and long to have it over. Neither Harry nor I alluded to our differences of the day after my return. I regretted having been so impulsive on the subject of our marriage. He must be the first to speak of it. After all, I reasoned, lying awake in my bed, waiting for morning to show between the branches of the copper beech tree by my eastern window, after all there were other matters as important as my own personal happiness.

"It will all come right in the night," Maggie Flynn had always assured Janice and me when we were little and in need of comfort. I had believed her implicitly then, and the habit of faith in tomorrow persisted in me as I think it must in all of us to the end of our days.

And so the first of November came round and Aunt Em and the others went down to the Wawickett House where Directors' meetings had been held in the long private drawing room where Janice and the Parker twins and I used to take dancing lessons years before. Board members from Boston would come on the ten o'clock train, and the meeting would last till midafternoon. It was a gray day of low-hanging clouds. Smoke from across the river mingled with the damp and lay like wet dust that could not settle to the ground.

"Ugh!" Janice shivered as we ate lunch together. "Nice cheerful weather, just the kind to put everyone in good humor down there at the Wawickett House. I'm going to date up somebody and clear out."

I had half a mind to ask her to take me along, but before I knew it she had slipped away in the little car. I had never felt close to Janice, and now more than ever we seemed separated by a wall of cold glass through which we motioned to each other. For all that, I felt a new warmth in her when she was off her guard. Yet with it there was a tension I had never suspected in her. In the old days she had been gay and casual in all her relations with others. Now she took offense easily; blazed away at some unintentional slight, or grew moody and aloof for no apparent reason. Aunt Em had noticed the change and commented upon it.

"I can't make out what's come over Janice," she said. "I offered to send her to New York last month; but she said she'd rather stay here, though Heaven knows the child has always complained that Blairstown's too dull to suit her. If there were any eligible young men about I'd think she was in love."

I put on my raincoat and walked for an hour through the gray afternoon, with no objective but to kill time and avoid sodden leaves that had washed down from lawns and driveways. Even Bridget seemed affected by the atmosphere. She made no excited foragings with stiffened tail and wriggling body. She stayed at my heels, closer than a shadow.

This isn't living, I thought as I moved on aimlessly through the dampness. It's no better than doctors' waiting rooms. I can't fit into the old ruts any more or make new ones with Harry.

I felt suddenly alien in this town where I had grown up. It was not the refuge I had thought to find in my hour of need. I felt like someone who returns to knock at the doors of the past, only to find them closed. It was in this mood that I came back to find Dr. Vance sitting by the living-room fire.

He was the last person I cared to see, and my irritation was plain. That morning I had been sorting out some sketches I had made months before with an idea of developing them into textile patterns. I wished that I had not left them spread about on the table, for I saw that Dr. Vance had been studying them while he waited. He held one in his hand as he rose to greet me.

"Aunt Em is still at the Directors' meeting," I told him without cordiality. "There's no telling how long it will last."

"I know," he said; "that's the reason I came today. I wanted to see you, not your aunt."

If Maggie had announced him I might have had a chance to escape, but I was caught now.

"I took a look at these." He held out the sketch and indicated the others. "They seemed to be out on exhibition. I take it they're yours."

"Yes, they're mine. Am I supposed to ask you what you think of them?"

"Well, since you seem so eager for my opinion"—he squinted at the one he held and reached for the others— "I rather expected they'd be worse."

"You overwhelm me."

I rose stiffly and gathered the sheaf into the portfolio. He didn't offer to give back the one he had, so I held out my hand for it. But he took no notice of the gesture.

"This is the only one you really pulled off," he went on. "The design's good, but it would be more effective if you reversed the dark and light."

His suggestion was right. I wondered why I hadn't realized it before. But I had no intention of letting him see that I agreed.

"You're pretty cocksure about a lot of things, aren't you, Dr. Vance?" I said.

"Maybe." He gave back the sketch as he spoke. "I never

could see much point in saying what I didn't think. Now these things of yours are so good they ought to be a whole lot better. But you never bothered to work them through. That's the trouble with girls like you—"

"Just what do you mean when you say 'girls like you'?" I broke in.

He shrugged and reached for a cigarette.

"Plenty of money, plenty of talent; good looks, too much doting family and too many distractions. I think that about covers it."

Maggie appeared just then with the tea tray. She seemed pleased that I had a caller. I noticed that she had trimmed the crusts off the sandwiches, an infallible sign of her approval. But I did not smile as she set it on a low table before me. I wished that Maggie had been less eager to offer hospitality.

"That goes to the spot." Dr. Vance held out his cup to be refilled. "I had an emergency appendix to do this morning and a couple of visits out in the country, so I skipped lunch."

I found myself looking at his hands, noticing again how strong and flexible they were, the fingers long, with slightly flattened tips. I could visualize them manipulating some sharp, delicate instrument. In my scrutiny I forgot to watch his lips.

"Look!" He was leaning across the tea table, forcing me to follow his words. "We got off to a bad start again today. Let's forget it and begin all over, because the sooner we do the easier it will be for both of us. I came because I wanted to see you alone. I'm going to talk to you, and you're going to listen whether you want to or not."

My hand shook as I set down the cup. I started to rise,

and I might have managed to bolt from the room if the tea table had not hemmed me in.

"No." He went on speaking without taking his eyes from mine. "It's this way. I'm a doctor; and if I saw some-one going round dragging one foot, and I knew I could do something about it, don't you think it would be a crime if I just let him go on limping?"

"That would depend," I answered evasively, "on how the person felt."

"You know what I'm driving at—I mean you and your deafness."

"That's my trouble, isn't it? I'd rather not talk about it, if you don't mind."

"But if I can help you—"

"You can't. Please just finish your tea and go—" Once more I tried to get up, but somehow I couldn't force my-self from the chair.

"You can't put me off like this." He was leaning for-ward, and his face had sharpened with intensity.

"Why did you have to come here?" I hoped my voice was as bitter as the feeling behind it. "Why couldn't you leave me alone? I'm not asking for pity from you or any-one."

But he shook his head.

"Yes, you are," he said, "—not in words, maybe, but there are other ways. When you strain to catch what people are saying, and when you miss something and that look comes into your face, you're asking for it."

"Why do you say such things to me? Do you think I lost my hearing on purpose?"

He shook his head once more.

"Please get this straight, Miss Blair. You mustn't confuse help with pity, just because you confuse love with it."

I rose and started for the door, but I felt his strong thin hands on my arms as he pulled me back. I wanted to shake them off, yet I was too startled to free myself. He made me look at him while he went on.

"You must listen. After that it will be up to you. No, don't speak. It's this way—I've helped cure people who'd been deaf longer than you have." Once more I struggled to move away, and once more his grip tightened. "It's nothing you ever tried—it's a sort of discovery another doctor and I stumbled on. I won't try to tell you in medical terms; you wouldn't understand them, and besides we're still experimenting. But we're not quacks. We're both full-fledged doctors and we know we're on the right track."

I twisted free of him at last and began gathering up my things. I wouldn't give him the satisfaction of further argument. Better to ignore the subject, I decided. But I hadn't counted on Dr. Vance's persistence. I felt like the wedding guest who had no choice once the Ancient Mariner with his glittering eye had singled him out for victim. It didn't matter how many times I told him the specialists I'd been to and that they'd all given me up as a hopeless case. He just kept right on telling me more about this discovery of his. It seemed he and this other doctor had come on it accidentally when they were treating some steel workers for gland deficiency. Two of the men were stone-deaf, and after the treatments had been going on for some weeks they began to feel sensation in their ears.

"They showed so much improvement that we knew it couldn't have been just fool luck," he told me. "We had something, so we went on experimenting at the hospital clinic all last winter. The staff there let us work with a group of deaf patients, and I don't mind telling you we got results—three complete cures and definite response in all the other cases, even ones where the auditory nerves seemed permanently dead. We never had a chance to try it where the ears had been affected by meningitis. That's why, when I heard about you, I thought—"

"That I'd make another guinea pig to experiment on? No, thank you, Dr. Vance. I should think you'd have known how I'd feel without asking me."

I saw his face redden at that, and I was glad if I had hurt him.

"Many things are lost for want of asking," he said. "That's a proverb my father brought with him from Europe. I've found it worth remembering."

"Well, once and for all then," I told him, "my answer is 'No.' When I came back from Boston that day we met I'd made up my mind there would be no more doctors for me and no more experimenting. I've come home to make the best of things as they are, and—and I have other plans."

"That means you're going to marry Collins soon, I suppose?"

"We've been engaged for some time—"

"I know, and long engagements are apt to be risky." His eyes were uncomfortably keen in their scrutiny.

"Not when people really love each other," I said shortly.

"Maybe. I don't pretend to be an authority on that subject. Still, I've noticed that being in love isn't necessarily a permanent state."

"Just what do you mean?" I wasn't going to let a remark like that pass.

"Oh, only that marriage is the sort of business that demands all the faculties."

"You needn't have said that to me."

I felt my knees begin to shake, and I pressed my hands tight together so that he might not see how they were trembling.

"No," he admitted, "I needn't have, but you don't seem to think much of the pleasantries that successful doctors cultivate. I'll never be a successful one for that reason; apt to be on the blunt side. All right then, I'll finish what I started to say—just because you can't *hear* is no reason for you not to *see*."

He was in the hall, looking for his hat, and now it was my turn to go after him and call him back.

"I've been brought up to say 'Thank you,' even for things I don't want," I found myself telling him. "I needn't have been rude just because you were."

"It's all right by me." He smiled and took up his hat. "Call me any name you want to, only I can't understand your not being interested enough to give what I'm offering you a try. There's nothing to lose and everything to gain."

"But I tell you I can't afford to hope any more. For the last two years I've been chained to hope. Now I've broken free, you can't make me a prisoner again."

"We're all prisoners of hope some way or other, aren't we?"

"More fools then!"

"Well, maybe." He raised his shoulders once more in the expressive, half-foreign shrug. "People called Columbus a fool once, and Pasteur and a good many others I could mention. If you and I hoped a little we'd be in good company. But never mind, thanks for the tea."

"If I could be sure—" I began.

He wheeled about and cut me short.

"Who's sure of anything in this world?" Even without hearing the tones of his voice I was aware of the scorn behind his words. "I'm not a salesman. I didn't come here to give you guarantees and a lot of high-pressured talk. I don't offer you anything but a chance. Of course you needn't take it."

A car turned into our driveway as he opened the front door. I saw the nearing headlights brighten wet branches to gaunt silver in the instant of passing. Then they fell into darkness again.

"Well, goodbye," he was saying. "My office hours are from two to four every afternoon except Friday, and I can always be seen by appointment."

He was gone before the car drew up at the steps. I felt grateful that I should not have to explain his presence to Aunt Em and Cousin Eunice as they came stiffly up the steps. They looked old and worn in different ways—Aunt Em peaked and grim, Cousin Eunice pouting and saggy and protesting. I was glad to busy myself replenishing the fire and pouring fresh tea.

"Aunt Em," I said, as I brought her a cup, "you look all in. Did you get anywhere at the meeting?"

"We got as far as a deadlock," she told me grimly between swallows. "Began with it and ended with it."

CHAPTER FIFTEEN

On the desk before me as I write is a small wooden box, painted blue and patterned in quaint, bright designs. The colors are softer than they must once have been, like the eyes of those who have lived long and seen much. Many hands have left their mark upon the wood. The grain shows through in places, especially where the worn brass key fits into the little lock. That small blue box is like no other object in my room though it must be older than Grandmother Blair's pine chest, or the cherry bureau, older than the glass dolphin vases that came round the Horn by barkentine. The box, also, has crossed stormy seas. The hands that fashioned it and traced the delicate shapes of hearts and birds and flowers would have faltered, perhaps, in the laying on of those clear colors if they could have guessed how far their handiwork was to travel. Yet for me and for Merek Vance it has come to stand for all that we shared together in those months after my return.

I remember the first time I saw it incongruously set between a card index and a prescription pad on the top of a battered desk. It caught my eye because it seemed to be the one personal touch in the office Vance had fitted up for himself in a back room of Dr. Weeks' shabby old frame house just off the Square.

"I won't give in and let him experiment on me," I had vowed, resolutely turning about-face whenever I found my feet taking me in that direction. "I won't be fool enough to go through all the misery and disappointment again. He needn't think he can make me."

But all the time I knew a day would come when weakness would overtake me. Try my best, I couldn't put what he had said out of my mind.

"You mustn't confuse help with pity," he had told me, "just because you confuse love with it."

How had he dared to talk like that of love? He couldn't mean that pity had any part in what Harry felt for me. Yet perhaps he saw what my love and need of love would not let me see.

"Just because you can't hear is no reason for you not to see."

He had said that, too, and I wished that I could forget it and the look that he had given me as he spoke.

"Being in love isn't necessarily a permanent state." I tried not to let myself remember those words and others that tormented me like thorns driven inward upon my mind and heart. "Marriage is the sort of business that demands all the faculties."

I knew that he was using my own fears as a means to break down my resistance to his plan, and I hated him for it. Yet for all my antagonism to the man himself I could not doubt his sincerity. He knew the vulnerable spot in me as surely as if his long fingers had touched a hidden spring of pain. I recoiled from his probings, though I was powerless to resist them. I hated him for having let drop those pebbles of doubt and fear into the deep pool of my consciousness. They had stirred ripples that spread and widened to engulf me as ripples will grow large long after the object that woke them has disappeared from sight. And the more I struggled against his offer of help, the more certain I became that I should find myself accepting it.

Sitting here alone at my desk, thinking back to that time and all that I felt for Harry Collins, I am shaken by the memory. For it is a memory now, not the frantic, feverish urge that goaded me then.

Love, when it comes for the first time, has the fierce and bewildering beat of spring in its pulses. Such ecstasy and despair are not to be reckoned with in terms of sanity and reason. The foolish and wise are equally at its mercy. Let no one doubt its power to exalt or betray, for it can rise renewed from bludgeonings or shrivel at a single breath. I think we were not meant to endure its rigors for more than a brief span. I am grateful to be free of its toils. Yet when I see that it has laid its bright, infallible mark upon some boy or girl, some man or woman, I feel a kind of inner comradeship. The terrible, sweet pain flows back, though the one whose presence could once inflict it is a stranger to me now.

But I must return to the small blue box. There I was, reaching out my hands to it for comfort, in that bare, plain office I had avoided so long. Across the desk I knew that Dr. Vance must be watching me with satisfaction, because I had not held out against him. It was my place to open the conversation, to explain my presence there after so emphatic a refusal. I turned the box about in my hands, tracing the design self-consciously with cold fingers while

I tried to summon the words that proved to be unnecessary.

At such tense moments it often happens, as it happened to me then, that some insignificant object will become for-ever linked to our extremity. We must recall the exact shape of a leaf whose shadow fell across the blind of a sick-room; the scroll on the handle of a spoon our fingers gripped in the numbness of despair, the lace that edged the handkerchief we pressed to our lips to hide their trem-bling. I studied that little box almost without being aware of what I was doing. Yet the shape and colors of that painted design will stay with me as long as memory itself. It had been done with the same intricate, tender care that went into the fashioning of some medieval missal book, yet it also suggested a prim valentine. Two hearts held the center of the lid, with a painted needle and twist of thread joining them together. Stiff birds and spotted butterflies hovered at the corners, and a flowery garland encircled the whole. There were initials below the lock and fine lettering in a script I could not read. One felt the love that had gone into the making of that little box. A sense of other lives seemed to radiate from the very grain of the wood, as if one could feel the hands that had held it reach-ing out and touching one's own in turn.

I looked up at last, though my hands still held the box.

"Well," I began lamely, "here I am."

The eyes that met mine across the desk were intent, but kinder than I had ever seen them. To my surprise I saw that Dr. Vance was not gloating over my capitulation.

"So you like my little box," he said, as if it were the most natural thing for me to be sitting there in his make-shift office. "It happens to be my one and only family heirloom, and I'm rather attached to it."

"It's very old, isn't it?" I didn't know what else to say.

"I think so. My mother always said it had been in her family. It held the few trinkets she brought with her to America. Sometimes she'd let me play with it, or my sister, if we'd promise to be careful. I can remember seeing my mother take it in her hands, the way you did just now. I used to watch her and wonder why her eyes would look the way they did when she held it. I know now it took her back to the old days when she was young and the prettiest girl in her village, before she had to worry about winter and coal for the fire, and Father getting laid off and one or the other of us sick or needing something she couldn't give us."

"What do the letters say?" I asked. "It looks like a motto."

"It is," he told me, "in Lithuanian that I can't read. But my mother told me once what it means—that's where the needle and thread come in. It says, 'Love is like the eye of a needle.'"

"That's a queer saying."

"Yes, she had to explain it to me. The eye of a needle is a small thing, she used to say, but without it we could make nothing to keep us warm against the chills of winter."

"Why, that's beautiful!"

I found myself touching the letters that neither of us could read, in sudden recognition. It was as if a long procession of other women were speaking to me across time and space in some universal language.

"Then you believe it's true?" he asked.

"Of course. Don't you?"

"I haven't had a chance to prove it yet."

"Everything can't be proved." I was surprised that I could talk this way to a man I hardly knew, one who had antagonized me from our first meeting. "Some things you just feel first and prove afterward."

He gave me one of his swift reassuring smiles.

"And you were the girl who wanted a guarantee that I could cure her," he reminded me.

"Yes," I admitted, "there are times when it's not easy to live up to what we believe." I was provoked that I should be giving myself and my feelings away like this. I certainly hadn't lived up to my plan of keeping the visit a cool impersonal one.

He must have felt the change in me, for before I had a chance to go on he leaned across the desk and spoke earnestly.

"I'm not asking you to believe that I can help you," he was saying, "but only that I want to do it."

"All right." I didn't trust myself to say more. "When do we start?"

For answer he rose and left the room while I waited, as I had waited in other, more handsomely furnished offices.

"There's still time to go," I reminded myself as I measured the few feet of space between me and the hall door. I could be outside and away before the larger hand on the cheap alarm clock moved a fraction of the way to the next minute. Yet I knew that I would not go. And then he was coming towards me, carrying familiar paraphernalia.

"Oh," I said, "an injection. I've had plenty of those."

"You know," he said as he handled his instruments, "it's a funny thing, but you've never asked me whether it would hurt or not. I've been expecting you to."

It was my turn to shrug.

"Do I have to do everything you expect me to?" I asked. "Besides," I added, "pain wasn't the point, was it?"

"No, but it's a usual question."

He gave me another of his direct, searching looks.

"I'm going to ask you to give me your word that you'll see this through," he said. "It may take longer than either of us can guess, so I'd like to hear you say it."

"Don't you trust me?"

"Not altogether." I saw his eyes turn to the window that looked towards the mill chimneys and the span of the upper bridge. "I come from over there," he went on. "That's where I really belong, and I don't feel sure of myself or you or anyone else on this side of the river, except of course Dr. Weeks."

"My mother came from over there, too," I found myself saying.

He nodded.

"I know," he said. "I used to hear them tell about her when I was little. She's a sort of legend, like the Cinderella story that girls who are plain and lonely and overworked have to believe in or they couldn't keep going. I never thought I'd be talking like this to her daughter."

I thought that it was even stranger that I should be there, letting him do what I had vowed I would never submit to again.

"Isn't it enough that I've come here?" I said bitterly. "Do I have to take some kind of oath on the Bible or one of your pet medical books?"

He held the needle up to the light and squinted at it before he answered.

"All right then," he said. "Let's not be melodramatic about it. You're here, and I'm ready to begin."

I reached for the little blue box, and he smiled to see me do so.

"That'll do instead of a book," he said before he went to work.

Afterward I walked in the fall sunshine trying to forget that the old disturbing routine had begun again. Well, I had given my word, and I would keep it. I would not miss a visit, but he need not think that he could make me hope against all my doubts and prejudices.

I hardly noticed where I was walking till I found myself halfway across the bridge where I had stood so often as a child; where my mother and I had stood together all those years ago. "Don't worry," she had said. "You're safe on your side of the river. You're all Blair." But I wasn't all Blair, and I didn't feel that I belonged anywhere in particular. Had my mother felt so sometimes, I wondered. Had old differences, old standards, and old loyalties overwhelmed her time and again as she stood where I was standing now? Surely it must have been so, though she had not had to stand here alone. A man's arm or a child's clinging fingers must make one feel more secure, I thought. Or did they twist the heartstrings into a more difficult, intricate tangle? I should never know that now.

The small blue box, for all its association with another woman, had given my mother back to me in a new image. I realized that for years I had confused her with the portrait of a beautiful woman in the ruffles and pompadour of two decades ago that an artist more famous than my father had painted. His brush had also made a legend of her even as Vance had said she was a legend to the people living over there in the crowded mill houses, to girls who tended bobbin and loom. It came to me then that I must be part of the legend, too, because I was her daughter. Perhaps they hated or envied me for that. I thought of the Christmas party for the mill workers that winter day when a man had sworn and shaken his fist; of a half-grown boy who had stared curiously at my little squirrel muff, and remembered it years later. It made me feel suddenly lonely and afraid.

"It will be different once Harry and I are married, and we will be married just as soon as this trouble at the mills is over."

It comforted me to tell myself that, even though I knew that the mill trouble had only just begun. From where I stood I could see a line of shabby figures, three or four men and a couple of women, stationed by Peace-Pipe gates. Hour after hour now they were there. They moved mechanically because it was easier than standing still on tired feet. Harry had told me that they were union supporters who had been dropped from the pay roll. Other workers were being dropped each week while the deadlock between the union and the mill grew more bitter; while futile negotiations went on and on without either side giving way on a single point. I could see the white placards they carried on sticks. When one or another of the picketers turned to reverse pace I could even make out a word or two: "Organized Labor," "Rights," "Unfair."

"Most of them don't like to picket," Harry had told me a few days before. "It's a protest now, but it's going to be a lot more than that if the union decides to call a walk-out."

So I turned back, but I couldn't put those distant figures with their white placards out of my mind. It ought to have been a simple, easy thing to cross over and talk with that little group. Yet I knew they would have distrusted such a gesture of camaraderie. Instinctively they would have thought there must be some motive behind my coming, and we should all have drawn back into our separate shells like cautious snails. It would only have ended in our talking about the weather, that safe conversational refuge to people who are on their guard. Even if one of them had been young Jo Kelly, I could not hope that it might have been otherwise.

Only children, I thought, can play and talk together without this self-imposed constraint. And even children's eyes are quick to note the difference between a patched sweater and a squirrel muff. They recognize the outward symbols and are more wary than we guess. I found myself wondering when I had first been made aware of the invisible barriers that are so much more formidable than those of brick and stone and barbed wire.

CHAPTER SIXTEEN

JANICE AND I seldom saw each other except at mealtime, and even these meetings were apt to be occasional.

"I don't know when or where or what the child eats, most of the time," Aunt Em had sighed in the early days of my return. "I always seem to meet her going out or coming in to get ready to go somewhere else. I've given up asking questions."

"Oh," I reminded her, "Janice has always been on the go. That's nothing new."

I had given the conversation no further thought. For years now Janice and I had moved independently of each other except for occasional clashes, or when we rallied our forces to put through some mutually dreaded family gathering. So it was a surprise to find Janice alone in the living room that afternoon when I returned from my first visit to Dr. Vance. She sat hunched in a corner of the sofa with a fashion magazine open beside her. But she was not absorbed in its pages. She looked limp and woebegone, and I saw that she had been crying.

"Janice," I said, dropping down on the sofa, "what's the matter? Has anything happened?"

She shook her head and pushed back a lock of moist, fair hair.

"Is it something I can do anything about?" I tried again.

"You can let me alone!" She frowned as she spoke. "I guess I have a right to be unhappy sometimes, haven't I? That's not just your own private privilege."

She lowered her head, and there I sat, so close that my skirt brushed hers, yet cut off completely as I always was when people turned their faces from me. I waited a moment before I touched her shoulder.

"What do you mean by that? If I've said or done anything lately—I haven't meant to be difficult, honestly I haven't."

"There you go getting personal." I could scarcely follow the words because her lips were quivering.

"But you said—" I broke off and tried again. "I'm sorry, Janice; I don't know what for, but I'm sorry anyway."

"Oh, all right, let's leave it at that, and don't start trying to cheer me up with the 'Into each life some rain must fall' line. I'm not in the mood."

"I don't feel in the mood for quoting either. But I know how it can be sometimes. I really do know, Janice."

"You can't know because you're you and I'm me. You're considered an admirable character, Emily."

"Well, you needn't throw it at me like that. I certainly don't feel admirable most of the time."

"Oh," she shrugged, "you know what I mean. You've got resources and strength of character, and people depend on you."

"And I suppose you think it's been easy." I felt suddenly bitter and hurt as if she were accusing me of being a prude. "I suppose you think I've enjoyed being cut off from everything these last two years, having to struggle to make out what people around me were saying?"

"I didn't say it had been easy, Emily, so don't get touchy the way you always do if anyone mentions your deafness. I only meant that at least people give you credit for keeping your chin up. Now me—I'm supposed to be the life of the party when there *is* a party; and when there isn't one I'm expected to be happy and have fun—in a nice way, of course."

"But, Janice," I protested, "you have everything—"

"That's what *you* think!" she broke in. "But don't get the idea that I always act the way I feel, or that I like myself much. If you want to know, I hate myself."

"Well, I don't think there's anything very strange about that. Most of us do a lot of the time." I tried to comfort her because I saw that she was genuinely unhappy. "I guess we all need someone else to make us know we matter. I know I couldn't have gone on if it hadn't been for Harry; there wouldn't have been any reason to. I tell myself it must have been meant that Harry and I should meet and fall in love just when we did—before this happened to me. It frightens me sometimes to think how different it might have been—"

She gave me a long, startled look, and her eyes were dark with misery.

"Don't, Emily," she said, "don't say that."

I was touched and surprised by her solicitude.

"It's because I've been miserable and lonely, too," I went on, "that I can tell when you are. It's—it's sort of like the least common denominator in arithmetic, something shared by both. I can't explain very well, but you must know what I mean."

She did not speak, and so I went on.

"You need to fall in love," I told her. "That's all that's wrong with you."

She gave me another of those startled looks, then turned away so quickly that I only half caught the words on her lips. I couldn't be sure, but it seemed to me that she said, "Oh, God!" before she got up and began gathering together her scattered possessions. She gave an unusual amount of care to collecting her hat and coat and bag. I remembered that long afterward because it wasn't like Janice to be so methodical. She kept her eyes from meeting mine, but I saw that her hands shook as she folded her gloves.

After Janice had gone I stayed on in the living room thinking of what she had said while I watched darkness swallow up the lawn and the beeches and maples. It had been disturbing to come so close to what was on Janice's mind, as if a door had been opened a chink and then shut quickly again to hide what lay behind. I thought how anyone looking in at the window might well have supposed that we two were exchanging intimate confidences, yet those few broken words had left me baffled. The misery I had seen in her face was no momentary mood of boredom or futility.

I found myself remembering Janice as a child, what a nuisance she had been, always borrowing and breaking or losing my playthings, telling tales on me, and getting in the way of my plans. Still when her curved red mouth had drawn down forlornly and tears had gathered in her dark eyes I had always forgotten my annoyance and tried to make her smile again. Lightheartedness was her gift, and she wore it like a ribbon in her hair. No matter how little we shared in common or how we might disagree, I could not bear to see her wearing sackcloth and ashes.

Presently Maggie appeared in her trim black and white to switch on the lights and set the rooms in order for the evening. I watched her moving about with the same unhurried precision that had been part of that rite ever since my childhood. She did not notice me till she came over to pick up the magazine Janice had let fall to the floor.

"I didn't know you were in, Miss Emily," she answered my greetings, "or I'd have brought you a cup of tea. It's not too late for one now if you want it."

But I shook my head.

"Maggie," I said as I watched her putting things to rights, "what's happened to all of us in this house?"

"I don't know what you mean except some of us aren't getting any younger, and the same can be said for these sofa cushions. They're a disgrace, and I've been after Miss Blair to do something about them for months back."

"I didn't mean the sofa cushions, Maggie. It's just we all seem unhappy and pulling away from each other. Even Janice doesn't have a good time any more. She was crying when I came in awhile ago."

"Oh, Miss Janice!" Maggie reached for another pillow and shook it vigorously into plumpness. "Well, I expect she's got reasons of her own."

She moved over to the table and began sorting out magazines and newspapers. Conversation with Maggie never meant suspended action. If necessary one followed her about to continue it. I had a feeling she wished to avoid more questions, but I was determined not to let the subject drop.

"Maggie," I began again as she started for the hall, "you

know more about all of us in this house than we know about ourselves, but you never take advantage of what you've heard or seen the way some would. It's more than just being well trained; it's a sort of gift you have, almost like second sight."

"There's nothing to it," she protested with an uneasy glance under my scrutiny. "Nothing out of the way, I mean. I guess anybody that's worked thirty-eight years in one place gets on to signs and portents. I never listened at keyholes or read what wasn't intended for me, but I can't help knowing things. I guess it's just people don't remember I'm around, that's all. They get used to me along with the furniture. Except they need me for something I might be that sofa or chair."

"Haven't you ever wanted to go away or try another place in all these years?" I asked curiously.

"Why should I? I'd just be doing the same things somewhere else."

I looked about the familiar high-ceilinged room and beyond her to the long hall and the other rooms opening from it.

"It's a big house," I said, "as houses go. But isn't it rather a small place to make a world of?"

"Oh, I wouldn't say that, Miss Emily." She gave me one of her rare smiles, as if I were a little girl again asking her foolish questions. "World or no world, it's been plenty to tackle. All I ask is I don't live to see it break up in front of my eyes."

"You mean if this trouble at the mills gets worse—"

"Now, Miss Emily, don't take my word to mean anything. I've got to get back to the kitchen now and help with dinner."

"You'll never join a domestic workers' union, Maggie, I can see that." I laughed. "You don't believe in closed shop for kitchens, do you?"

"And don't you give me any of that union rigmarole round here," she retorted. "There's a few of us left in this town that haven't seen fit to go on strike. I should live to be told how many hours a day I'll work!"

I rose and patted her shoulder.

"I guess Uncle Wallace and Harry wish there were more like you down at Peace-Pipe," I told her. "It looks bad and getting worse all the time. I wish it hadn't come just now to delay my wedding. It's hard to be patient when you're in love, Maggie, and when things keep coming in between—"

"I expect so, Miss Emily. Not that I know much about it first hand. Love's one kind of broom that never swept me off my feet. Maybe I've missed a lot—plenty of tears anyhow. There!" She broke off and pointed to the nearest window. "Mr. Harry's been at that curtain cord again. Hardly a week goes by I don't have to pick out those knots he ties in them. If I met them in Jericho I'd know he'd been fidgeting around."

"I'll pick them out. He doesn't know when he does it, Maggie, he has so much on his mind."

She opened her mouth as if to speak, but evidently changed her mind and turned away. When Maggie disapproved of anyone or anything you could tell by the set of her shoulders and the way she walked, as if she were treading on the unspoken words of criticism.

"Watch out for Maggie when she stalks," I had told Harry once, and I couldn't help thinking of that when she disappeared down the hall.

CHAPTER SEVENTEEN

I HAD NOT EXPECTED to meet young Jo Kelly coming down the Doctor's steps a few days later as I turned up the path. But there he was, and there was I with Bridget leaping between us in frantic greeting. He smiled at me across her brown, excited body.

"Hello, Jo," I said. "I'm glad to see you, even if Bridget doesn't give me much chance to say so. How do you think she looks for a lady going on five?"

He bent to pet and examine her with that reassuring touch that made all animals his no matter who their official owners might be.

"Pretty fair," he answered in the slow-spoken way that was so easy for me to follow. "Better since you've been back to give her some exercise. She was getting a bit too fat."

"The same can't be said of you, Jo."

He had always been thin, but now his boyish slightness had settled into gaunt maturity. His eyes were as blue and candid as I remembered them under their dark brows; but his cheekbones showed too prominently, and his mouth was firmer and less merry.

"Oh, I'm all right," he assured me. "I just stopped by the Doctor's to get some medicine for a friend of mine." He patted the sagging pocket of his shabby Mackinaw and glanced towards the window of Vance's office. "Blairstown's lucky to get some one like him," he went on, "young and up to the minute in his line. They mostly stay in the big cities."

In his manner there was nothing to suggest differences of opinion or constraint between us. He was, as he had always been, completely without self-consciousness. Watching him, I felt that this lack of pretense and personal importance was what distinguished him from other people. It was a positive rather than a negative quality that gave him the power of which he seemed least aware. It is strange to remember now how we stood there by the Doctor's steps and talked together. The November wind came up from the river with an edge on it that made one feel winter at the bones though the sun shone through bare branches of maple and elms. Change was in the air about us as it stirred behind our talk. I often think back to that day and the words that wove back and forth like shuttles carrying the frail threads of thought between us to make a pattern which it was beyond our power to alter.

"Oh, Jo," I found myself saying, "why do things have to be this way? Do you have to stir up all this trouble at the mills and work against us and talk as if we were criminals?"

He hesitated before he answered, and he kept on stroking the dog's coat with those thin, kind fingers of his.

"You've got me all wrong, Emily," he said, and I was glad that he called me by my first name in the old familiar way. "I was afraid you would. I can't work up hard feelings for any of you folks. I'm on my side of the fence and you're on yours, that's all."

"But, Jo, can't you look over the fence and see our side?"

"That goes for you, too." He gave me one of his long, slow smiles as he spoke. "Still, I guess I can't expect you to see very far."

"Why not? There's nothing wrong with my eyes."

"But you've always had this thing they call security. You've never known what it was to wonder where your next meal was coming from, or a new pair of shoes or a place to sleep nights—"

"Maybe not, but there are other kinds of security that matter more."

"I know what you mean. Still, you try doing without a few of those things I mentioned and you'll understand better. You'll know what we're fighting for."

"There won't be much sense to higher wages and shorter hours if this strike of yours ties Peace-Pipe up all winter. What business there is will go to other mills, if ours has to shut down."

He shrugged and straightened his thin shoulders. "Well, I don't blame you for seeing it that way. Stockholders are bound to feel differently about it."

"They take the biggest losses when times are bad." I found myself bringing out all the arguments I had heard Uncle Wallace and Mr. Perkins and Aunt Em use. But they seemed suddenly inadequate under Jo Kelly's direct gaze.

"Sure," he answered, "and they take the profits when it's the other way round. Don't forget that part."

"But, Jo, it's always been different at Peace-Pipe. You

can't stand there and tell me that our family has ever prof-
iteered. You know it's one of the best run mills in New
England and it's done everything for its workers—look at
the Infirmary and Recreation Building, the night classes,
and the band concerts in summer. Our family's always
tried to take a personal interest. Why, Aunt Em's worrying right now about what she ought to do for Christmas.
Even with this strike talk she doesn't want to give up the
food baskets and presents. She says there'll be all the more
need, and she won't let her own feelings stand in the way;
only it's against her principles—"

"She means all right, Emily." His forehead puckered
into the lines I knew so well. "Your aunt's one of the finest
ever. That's why I wish she didn't have to get so hurt
about this. But Christmas baskets and recreation buildings
and night classes are something else again. Can't you see
we don't want to be done *for*? We want to do for ourselves and those we love—"

He broke off and bent over Bridget again as if he found
it difficult to get out what he was trying to say. I lost his
next words and had to ask him to repeat them.

"I beg your pardon, Jo, I didn't quite catch what you
said."

"No matter," he told me. "I haven't got any business
talking about love."

"Why haven't you, Jo? Why shouldn't people talk
about loving and being loved? This trouble at the mills
hasn't made things any easier for Harry Collins and me—
If anyone had told me I'd have to go on waiting like
this—" I broke off, not trusting myself to say more.

He turned to me with such quick sympathy in his eyes
that I felt almost as if we were children again. It eased me

to have spoken the words. We met once more on the old footing of our childhood, when we had shared punishments and secrets together.

"I'm sorry," he said simply, "real sorry. But don't worry about waiting. The way I figure it, you have to wait or fight for things that matter in this world."

"I guess so," I managed to answer. "It's the only world we know anything about, after all."

I tried to smile and he did, too, but neither of us made much success of it. We stood there a moment without speaking; and I saw that he was looking away, over towards the mill chimneys, and his face stayed grave and set.

"No," he went on at last. "It isn't conditions we're fighting for. I guess they're fair enough as mills go, and it isn't just the pay and the hours either. But we've got a right to organize—it's our only guarantee for the future. Whatever anybody says about this union, it means a hell of a lot to most of us."

"It can't work miracles," I argued, snatching at what I had heard from this one and that. "A union can't bring prosperity back overnight or make the public want to buy what mills like ours are making. There are too many doing business, Uncle Wallace says. That's what makes all this cutthroat competition."

"That's true," he admitted. "But give us a chance and maybe we could prove a unionized mill could do better for both sides. Ever hear of collective bargaining?"

I shook my head.

"How would I hear anything?" I reminded him bitterly. "No one goes out of the way to explain things to me. It's too much trouble. See those sparrows over there picking up a crumb here and another one there? That's how it is if you're deaf. You just have to pick up what you can, and you learn not to ask too many questions. It annoys people."

"Well, at least you *try* to understand. That's more than the rest of them do over on your side of the river. Now take this collective bargaining. Suppose you got in a tight place some time and needed a lawyer. You'd want to be able to hire one, wouldn't you? Sure you would. It's the same thing, sort of—I've got a grievance, so I go to the foreman or maybe somebody higher up about it. Maybe I get listened to and maybe I don't, but it's a pretty safe bet I get laid off at the end of the week. Too many waiting to step into my shoes. Well, that's where a union comes in. I tell you we've got to stand up for the ones that are getting bad breaks, not just in Peace-Pipe. I mean the ones behind the machines all over everywhere."

"It sounds all right," I told him, "if it works. But Uncle Wallace and the rest say it's plain highway robbery the way the unions are holding them up at gun's point. He says— Oh, well, what's the use? I'll never be able to know who's right and who's wrong. I try to understand, but even the words don't make sense. I'm not sure I know what a scab is exactly—"

"A scab." Young Jo smiled suddenly in spite of our seriousness. "Why, that's just another name for a strike-breaker—sort of polite way of saying the other fellow steals your pants while you're in swimming. Do you get me?"

I had to laugh too, and I was glad to break the tension. He could care enough to fight for something he believed in, and still joke about it. He hadn't changed his ways, and somehow that was a comfort to me.

"Thanks," I said, as I turned to go up the steps, "I'll remember."

He grinned, but before he moved away he came closer and touched my arm.

"How's Grandpa?" he asked. "I didn't like the looks of him last time I got sight. He won't speak to me any more, you know, and I kind of worry about him down there all alone."

"Oh," I explained, "he's about the same. His rheumatism's worse when it rains. But he sleeps at the big house now. He didn't want to move up, but Aunt Em and Dr. Will made him. It seems queer to have those rooms over the old stable empty after all these years."

"Thanks," he said. "I'll feel better about him nights. If he ever—" He broke off and shrugged helplessly. "But I guess it wouldn't do any good to send for me. He thinks I'm a mad dog biting the hand that's fed us. I wish he didn't have to see it that way."

"So do I," I said. "I'm glad we met. It did me good to talk to you, Jo. You make it feel like old times, and I guess we all need to remember old times no matter what happens to us."

There were no other patients waiting, so I went on through the connecting door to Dr. Vance's office.

"Your aunt's asked me for Thanksgiving dinner next week," he said, looking up from his preparations. "I thought I'd better find out if you had any objections before I accepted."

"Why should I have any?"

"I don't know, but you might. It's hard to get under this veneer of politeness of yours."

"Politeness?" I smiled. "I've been more rude to you than anyone I've ever met in my life."

But he shook his head.

"Let's call it 'honest,'" he corrected. "I think you are that down here; but up at your place I'm never quite sure. You're still making your curtsies and speeches the way you've been taught. You must have had the social graces dinned into you pretty hard when you were little, or they wouldn't come so naturally to you now. You put me in mind of something I read in a book once when I was a kid. It was about Marie Antoinette going to the guillotine, and how she stepped on the executioner's foot and begged his pardon—"

"Are you comparing me to Marie Antoinette?"

He smiled at me sheepishly.

"Well, you belong to the royal family of Blairstown, don't you?"

"And just where do you come in?" I asked.

Resentment flooded me in a hot wave. I felt it brightening my cheeks, blurring my eyes. The jab of the needle brought me to my senses, and his face suddenly cleared before me. He was no longer smiling, and his eyes had that dark intentness which had first made me notice him that day in the station.

"Just where do I come in?" He was repeating my question. "Darned if I wouldn't like to know."

CHAPTER EIGHTEEN

THE PEACE-PIPE MILLS STRIKE is past history now. I suppose it will never be reckoned of importance to industrial history, for it was a poor one as strikes go, ill timed and insignificant. But for Blairstown and for us it marked the end of an era, as if a page had been turned forever on a familiar way of life. Just now I rummaged in my desk and found a sheaf of newspaper clippings neatly sorted and labeled. The print is already beginning to fade, and the paper growing brittle though the dates are so recent: December, 1931; January, February, and March, 1932. Our strike seldom made the front-page headlines of Boston or New York; only local papers carried full day-to-day accounts of its progress. I have been trying to reread the columns of print over again, but the words mean less than the scenes and faces that crowd my memory.

"You'll never get it straight, Emmy," Harry said impatiently once when I questioned him about some issue. "Can't you stay on the side of town where you belong?"

I have never quite understood all the intricacies involved; the bitter issues; the compromises that each side proposed only to be rejected by the other in the long battle that was never won—that has turned Blairstown into the ghost of a prosperous manufacturing center. Some claim that it was already doomed and the strike mercifully shortened its slow decline. Others believe that the industry was deliberately betrayed and tricked into its own suicide. No one can say with certainty, least of all I, caught in the crosscurrents of family loyalty and sudden awareness of another way of life. Something I could not define was stirring in me in those months, feeding on my own loneliness and frustration. For the strike was somehow a symbol of my own inner conflict; as if I had become a human counterpart of the bridge which joined the two sides of our river without ever making them one.

"I don't see how this could have happened to Peace-Pipe," I said to Harry the first day I looked across and saw the stark shapes of the chimneys without a wisp of smoke curling from them. "I thought it was only talk. I didn't believe that words could do so much. They won't make the wheels of a mill go round."

"No, but they can stop them," he reminded me simply.

Harry Collins had criticized many things about the policy and product of the mills long before the strike threatened. He had argued for a compromise on the union demands at the early stages of negotiations, but when it came to the final test he sided with the Directors.

"At least we haven't been disappointed in Harry," Uncle Wallace told Aunt Em. "I won't deny I was worried about his attitude awhile back. From the way he talked I was afraid he might be turning radical. But he's got too much good sound sense to be taken in by that sort of talk."

"I thought we could count on Harry," she agreed. "After all, when he and Emily are married he'll be taking over more of the business. His future's tied up with Peace-Pipe, and he knows it."

"Maybe we should give the boy more chance to try some of his ideas about putting out a cheaper line of goods," Uncle Wallace went on. "Parker and I have held him back, but maybe he's right and we're in a manufacturing rut. Once we get clear of this mess we might let him branch out a bit. How'd that suit you, Emily?"

I smiled and nodded my assent. But I couldn't let them guess that Harry seldom confided his ambitions to me, business or otherwise. I tried to let them think all was well between us because I had to believe it was. Always when we were together there was that subtle constraint, but when we were apart I could make excuses for Harry. I could convince myself that he loved and needed me as I loved and needed him.

It's different with a man, I would reason; he doesn't have to make his whole world of a single person.

Perhaps I should never have found out how wrong it was of me to do just that if the strike had not happened when it did. Against my will I was made aware of it. It dominated the town like a cloud, larger and darker than the smoke one which had always hung over Peace-Pipe. Although I was shut off from sound and the normal exchange of talk I felt the change all about me. I saw bitterness tighten men's and women's lips; I saw hunger and fear in their eyes. Even the groups of children at their games moved less freely, as if they reflected something of the grimness and dared not give themselves completely to play.

I shuffle through the clippings on my desk, and the familiar words of the headlines rise up before me: "Peace-Pipe Negotiations Fail"; "Strike Threatens"; "Mediation Hope Abandoned"; "Mill Directors, Union and A.F. of L. Representatives in Deadlock"; "No Compromise, Company Officials Reaffirm"; "Union Issues Ultimatum"; "Walkout in 24 Hours As Truce Period Nears End"; "Strike Called for Tomorrow"; "Oldest New England Textile Plant Stands Firm"; "Nonunion Workers Assured Police Protection As Company Prepares to Reopen"; "United Textile Union Pledges Support at Mass Meeting"; "Eighth Day of Blairstown Strike"; "Sixteenth Day of Strike," and so on. I hardly need the words to recall those days. They will be with me always because I was part of them.

Even now, a year away from it all, I cannot forget the picketers by the mill gates or huddled for warmth close to the fires that burned in buckets, idle men waiting to take their turns. I cannot forget the women with shawls and empty shopping bags who stood patiently for hours where supplies were distributed; the half-grown boys and girls who haunted the railroad yards and tracks to pounce on an occasional scattered nugget of coal. I cannot forget seeing children fighting over discarded wooden crates and bits of kindling wood, dragging what they had salvaged home on sleds after the first fall of snow. I know that there were longer lines than these in other industrial centers and in the big cities that winter of 1932. I read about them in the papers between appeals to the public to spend more liberally and hasten the return to what was optimistically called "normalcy." But I did not see those jobless with my own eyes. And there was this difference—hunger and cold and resentment were new to Blairstown. There had been hard times before, but not this twilight of dogged bitterness as the days went on and on.

Janice showed more interest in the mill situation than I had expected. Indeed she was almost vehement in her sentiments, denouncing the workers wholesale till we all lost patience. It seemed in some strange way to have become an issue of personal concern to her, though it was months later that I learned the reason why.

"Good Lord, Janice!" Harry said one night at dinner after she had finished a particularly violent outburst. "You'd better shut up and cool off."

"What do they want anyway?" Her soft lips hardened, and she tossed back her fair hair.

"I guess they want just as much out of life as you and I do." It surprised me to find myself answering her. "The trouble is," I went on, "it's so easy to say 'they.' We're 'they' to the mill hands, and they're 'they' to us. That's when we stop being real people and turn into classes."

I broke off, having said more than I had meant to, but if I had risen up with a hammer in one hand and a sickle in the other I could not have startled the group about the table more.

"Well," Janice exclaimed, "I must say Emily sounds like a union agitator or Jo Kelly out on his soapbox!"

"And I say you girls better stop talking about what you don't know the first thing about," Harry reproved. "It's bad enough having to take the strike and the talk all day at the mills without getting it served with dinner. Isn't that so, Mr. Blair?" He appealed to Uncle Wallace, who of course agreed.

Aunt Em showed more tolerance than I had expected,

but her bewilderment and concern were hard to see. She had hoped for a miracle right up to the walk-out, and she continued to pray for some impossible settlement that would satisfy both sides.

"You mustn't take the mill trouble so hard, Em," Dr. Weeks told her a week or two after it had started, when he stopped in for a cup of tea one afternoon. "Strikes seem to be the order of the day now everywhere, so you needn't feel it's a disgrace. In fact it's like an industrial epidemic breaking out all over the country. Might be a good thing in the end, I suppose, but the symptoms are pretty painful."

"It's what lies behind the symptoms, Will," she pointed out. "As a doctor you ought to know that's what matters."

She looked stricken in those days, not only for herself but for all the generations of Blairs whose lives had gone into the building of Peace-Pipe. It hurt her to feel that the long record of harmony between mill owners and mill workers had been broken.

"We always felt personally responsible for our workers," she told me over and over again. "Any family in need was free to come to us for help, and we did what we could, either from the mill funds or our own pocketbooks."

"I know," I would answer. "But nowadays I guess people prefer their own pocketbooks. I mean"—I groped to recall what young Jo Kelly had said on the Doctor's doorstep—"they don't want to be done for if they can do for themselves."

She looked at me as if I had struck her a blow.

"Why, Emily," she said, "you don't mean to tell me you think they're in the right about this strike?"

I sighed and shook my head.

"Oh, Aunt Em," I said, "how can I know what I think? I don't know where I stand any more. I wish I'd listened more when I could; but it's more than just hearing. . . . I'm trying to find out how they feel about it, that's all. I can't help wondering how it would be if I worked down there the way some of the girls and boys I went to high school with are doing. And after all, Mother was a mill hand before she married Father."

Aunt Em stiffened at that. I realized that I had made a mistake to link her name with the present. She and my father belonged to the past that had taken on the mellow haze that removed it from present-day reality and vexing problems.

"Your mother was a very unusual woman, Emily," Aunt Em reproved me gently. "If she were alive today I haven't a doubt she'd feel worse about this trouble at the mills than any of us."

I wished that I could feel as sure about that as Aunt Em did, but I said no more.

"I'll get Harry to talk sense to you," she went on presently as if she were distracting a child from playing with some dangerous toy. "It's hard on you both to have all this trouble on your minds when you ought to be making your wedding plans instead. I'd hoped to see you two married right after the New Year. We could do with a little festivity in the family for a change, and I'm not at all sure Harry's right about thinking it wouldn't look well at a time like this."

"You've—been talking to him about it lately?" I felt my throat tighten, and I hoped I didn't sound too eager.

"Why not, dear? I'm worried about the mills, but that's a small thing compared to your happiness. I can't change this—this terrible handicap you have to meet, but at least you needn't go on waiting. I can't see that a quiet little home wedding would be out of place, but Harry does seem to feel we shouldn't make plans till the strike's settled . . ."

"I suppose you offered to give us enough to live on?"

"Well, why shouldn't I? There's enough for that even if most of what we have is tied up in the mills. But there's some insurance of your father's that your Uncle Wallace and I always planned to turn over to you and Janice when you married. With that and what Harry makes you two should be able to manage. I told him that, but he seems to have a lot of pride about accepting anything from us. I don't altogether agree with him, still I have to admire his attitude."

"I wouldn't care where we lived," I told her. "Those rooms over the old stable are just going to waste now old Jo's moved up here to the big house. They wouldn't be half bad with fresh paper and paint."

"Well, you and Harry talk it over. You can convince him if anyone can."

She smiled at me and turned back to the letter she was writing. But her remarks had made me restless. Personal concerns forced the mill trouble into the back of my mind. I decided to go down and have a look at those rooms again before the light dwindled into December darkness.

I pulled on my old leather windbreaker and started down the path with Bridget pressing close at my ankles. It was windy and chill outdoors. Bare branches were raking dull skies and the winter sun looked like tarnished silver in the west. Yet a glow of anticipation warmed me. It took so little to set me planning in the shy, determined way that no woman can resist. As I came in sight of the stable and the windows showing square and blank above, I saw them not as they were, but as they might be, gay with curtains of flowered chintz, and yellow-paned with lamplight. I felt for the key that was always kept on a beam halfway up the stairs and let myself in at the door that opened on the small kitchen.

Everything looked mute and impersonal in its ordered bareness though the simple furniture that Old Jo and his grandson had used for so many years had not been removed. Oilcloth was on the table and thick blue and white china in the cupboards, even an old almanac hung between stove and sink. The small sitting room beyond was more cheerful because the late light slanted through the western windows. I stood in the center of the worn carpet with Bridget beside me and studied every detail. It was a small but well proportioned room with built-in shelves that already I saw filled with Harry's books and mine. A Franklin stove would replace the old airtight iron one. I could fairly see the firelight on my desk and favorite chairs; on Grandmother Blair's pine chest and the cherry bureau that was the color of russet apples. Yes, I decided the place between the windows would be just wide enough to hold it. I moved over to make certain of the space, and as I did so I automatically straightened the window shades.

"Well," I said to myself, "that's funny."

There were knots in the dangling cords, and it took me a moment to realize why I had noticed them. Then I remembered how I had picked out just such knots from the curtain cords in the living-room windows only a short time before.

"Mr. Harry's been at those cords again," Maggie had

said. "If I met those knots in Jericho I'd know he'd been fidgeting around."

Her words came back to me as I stood there alone in the deserted room. I told myself it was foolish to think twice about such a trivial thing, and even more foolish to take the time and trouble to pick them out. It was almost dark when I had the cords free of the last one. I hardly glanced into the small adjoining bedroom as I hurried away, locking the door behind me.

CHAPTER NINETEEN

THE STRAIN of the mill situation was beginning to tell on Uncle Wallace. When Harry dropped in later that evening I saw that he too looked tense and tired. Peace-Pipe had been shut down for ten days though negotiations still continued in the hope that some means of reopening might be found. Every day of bickering was time lost on the orders still waiting to be filled. There were few enough of those, but contracts were contracts and business must be kept, what there was left of it.

"Harry!" I hurried over to meet him by the door, but I could tell by his look that his mind was anywhere but on me and the questions I had been wanting all day to ask him. The eagerness and joy I had felt at sight of him slipped away before his preoccupation.

"You'll have to get along without each other for a day or two, Emily." Uncle Wallace touched my arm to draw my attention to what he was saying. "Harry's going to Boston with me tomorrow."

"Oh, do you have to go?" I protested.

"Well, it's not China, Emmy!" he teased. "Your uncle

needs me to go over figures with some men at the bank there, and I must say I shan't mind getting away from Blairstown for a bit. You don't know what it's like down at the mills these days with the machinery stopped and pickets everywhere you look."

"It's not very cheerful round here either," I reminded him. "I've a good mind to go to Boston myself. I might have more chance to see you there than I've had here lately."

He smiled, but shook his head emphatically at the same time.

"This is business," he told me, "and you'd better get used to the idea of not tagging along. I'm not joking," he went on; "it's serious business. Money's tight everywhere, and we've got to convince our backers we're a good bet for another loan."

"But Peace-Pipe doesn't have to borrow money to keep going, does it?"

"That's about what it amounts to," he admitted. "The banks have always controlled a certain amount of the stock, but we're going to need more to tide us over this. . . . Even if the mill can get under way again by January— and it doesn't look too promising right now—we won't break even this year, to put it mildly. Don't worry and screw up your forehead like that. It's not becoming."

It was no use asking him more questions. He resented having to explain what he believed I could never under-stand. I felt like a child being told to look pleasant, please, and be seen and not heard. It wasn't so much his impa-tience that hurt me. I was used to trying people's patience, even Harry's. What hurt me was that he seemed relieved to be going away while I must get on as best I could till his return. I sat beside him on the sofa. His arm was about me, but that did not bring him closer.

What is it? I thought. What has come between us? I don't matter to him any more. There's no use pretending to myself that I do.

He must have felt me shiver, for he patted my shoulder.

"Cold?" His lips formed the word carefully, so he would not have to repeat it.

I shook my head.

"No. I guess I'm just missing you already, dear."

"I'll be back before you know I've gone."

How could I tell him what had chilled me? I wanted him so much, too much. Other girls, other women loved other men, and they had not waited as I had through interminable months and years. Love was never meant to be like this, dammed up in oneself because the floodgates were locked from the outside. The pressure was growing too heavy for me to bear. Why couldn't I say to him simply and honestly: "Harry, you do want me still, don't you, my darling? You must, or I can't go on, for nothing has meaning or reality for me except you." But I knew why I could not say those words. I was afraid—afraid of losing what I had by asking for more.

He shifted his position and pulled himself up.

"Well, I must be getting back," he said. "We'll be taking the early train tomorrow, and I must pack before I turn in. Besides, I have to pick up some things I left over at the Parkers'."

"You'll be roped into cards," I told him. "Janice is over there now. They wanted me to fill in, but I knew they'd put me at a table of misfits."

"Well, I'll only look in for a minute," he said. "Glad

you warned me. Goodbye, dear. Get a good rest. You look tired."

"That means I'm definitely not at my best," I tried to laugh as I watched him go down the steps.

But I knew he would be up late at cards. The twins would see to that. I wished suddenly that I had gone even though I hated pretending to enjoy myself.

So I turned back to the living room feeling as deserted as it looked. The fire burned in cheerful unconcern of empty chairs about it. Aunt Em and Uncle Wallace had both gone to their rooms, and Bridget and I were left to keep each other company. It was half past nine, and I must hunt for the detective story I had begun yesterday. I didn't care who had killed the adventuress in the night club; but no matter, it might make me sleepy to read awhile by the fire.

I don't know how long after that Bridget roused herself from the rug and stood listening with lifted head. I always knew when someone was coming by the way her ears pointed and her throat rippled making the rumbling warnings I could not hear. She moved towards the hall, and I rose and followed her. Peering through the narrow glass panes by the door, I saw a man coming up the steps, and I recognized Merek Vance. The light over the entrance shone full on his face as I let him in.

"Sorry," he explained. "I wouldn't have bothered you so late, but I'm having car trouble. My engine stopped dead just below your drive, and I can't get it started. If I could use your telephone—"

"Of course." I let him into the study.

When he returned presently, he shrugged and frowned. "I can't get any answer from the garage," he told me. "The man on duty must be out or asleep, and the hotel says they can't say when they can send a taxi. I wish Dr. Weeks wasn't off in his car. I've got an emergency call out on the Ridgeville Road."

"You can borrow ours," I said, "if Janice didn't drive it over to the Parkers."

"Thanks." He didn't bother with protests or further explanations. "It would save a lot of time and sometimes minutes count."

"I'll show you the way," I said, and caught up my coat.

It was dark going down to the made-over stable, but I knew every inch of the way. He held my arm, and I could feel the firm grip of his fingers and his breath warm beside me in the cold night air.

"Here." I saw with relief that the little roadster was in its place. "The keys are probably in. She usually leaves them. Yes, she did, thank goodness."

I felt for the light switch and turned on the ignition. I could feel the engine begin to throb and, as it started, a sudden impulse overtook me not to go back to the house. He took his place behind the wheel, but instead of getting out I turned to him.

"Let me go, too," I said. "I haven't anything else to do. I know the car better than you do even if I don't drive it any more, and I can wait while you make your visit."

"Well"—I could just make out the motion of his lips in the light from the dashboard—"I can't say how long I'll be. Your family won't worry?"

"They'll think I've gone to bed. Please don't make me go back to that book I was trying to read. I won't be a bother to you, really I won't."

He nodded and began backing the car out. He stopped

for a moment by his own to collect his bag, which he set on the floor between us. I couldn't help thinking that no matter how the times and methods changed, those limp, worn leather bags were the universal badges of the medical profession. Instinctively I would have distrusted a doctor who carried a new, shiny one. The very scratches and stains and rubbed places gave one reassurance as if each were a scar of mortal combat.

It was strange to be riding beside Merek Vance at such an hour in the little car that had taken me on so many pleasure jaunts in the past, that must always be associated with that summer of my engagement to Harry before my own personal disaster. A car, especially at night, with everything dark but the round, luminous dials and the beams of the headlights, may become a complete small world to those inside it. We take on its dimensions as if it were our larger shell. Its power seems to come from ourselves. It seemed so that night as we put the town behind us. The air rushed by, sharper for the open country that lay beyond the range of our lights on the pale cement of the road ahead. I could not see Merek Vance's face clearly. He was a shadowy shape in the overcoat that smelled faintly of wool and tobacco and other scents I could not classify. His hands held the wheel with an easy grip. If he had spoken I should have had no way of knowing what he said, and if I had spoken to him I could not have read his answer in the dimness. So for a little while there was no need to talk.

I found myself thinking back to my first meeting with Merek Vance. It was strange that I trusted him as I did in spite of my prejudices. Though I would not admit it to myself, I had come to count on those visits to his bare little office to break the monotony of days that were empty and meaningless as days have never been before or since. It was well into December by then, nearly two months since the treatments had begun. At first I had been afraid of detection, but no one took notice of my walks with Bridget. Our family intimacy with Dr. Weeks made it seem a natural thing if I happened to be seen entering or leaving his place. He, of course, knew the reason for my coming. But he asked no questions and I could trust him to deal with Aunt Em if she became suspicious. The middle-aged nurse who answered the telephone and helped with patients was equally trustworthy and closemouthed. Dr. Vance saw most of his patients in the evening or at the hospital clinics, so that I met few. I had no more faith than I had had the day of my return that he could help my hearing. He knew that and did not try to convert me. We had given our word to each other, and once the bargain was made he would keep to his end of it. He made no personal issue of the experiments, only now and then his eagerness betrayed him as he went through the routine of tests in the hope of some sign of improvement. And there was this to be said for Merek Vance: he did not put me off with excuses or avoid conversation because my deafness made it difficult. He continued to be frank, almost ruthless about my hearing.

"Deaf people strain too much," he told me once, "except for the ones who pretend they hear when they don't. After all, half the world hears what it wants to hear, and the other half doesn't bother to do anything about it."

"And what about you?" I cornered him.

"Oh," he shrugged, "I'm a doctor. I needn't remind you what you think about them, though I could, for I happen to have a good memory. But honestly, now, think back a few years: did you ever really listen?"

"Of course I did," I insisted. "And I would again if I had the chance."

"I doubt it." He shook his head. "And I'm not setting myself to be better than average when it comes to that. We none of us hear all we might."

CHAPTER TWENTY

FROM THE MOMENT we set out in the car something outside myself seemed to take me in hand. I had a sense of being in a play, given a part to act in which I had not been rehearsed. Mine was not an important role in that drama of life and death, but I have reason to remember it well.

We turned off the main road into what was hardly more than two wheel ruts. Presently I made out the shape of a house dwarfed by the larger shape of a barn behind it. Four squares of windowpane were yellow in the darkness, and someone must have heard the sound of our engine, for as we came to a stop a door opened and a man's figure showed sharply in silhouette. Merek Vance reached for his bag and got out. He came over to my side and motioned me to join him. I had expected to stay in the car; but there was no chance for argument, so I followed him to the door. After the cold night air the room in which I found myself seemed crowded and stifling. It was evidently the kitchen of a farmhouse, for a large coal stove filled one side and a sink with a primitive sort of pump the other. I remember a table covered with a red cloth, set with thick dishes, and people about it: a shrunken old man in a faded bathrobe; an old woman with a sleeping baby in her arms; a half-grown boy bent over a book, and a little girl of three or four who stared at me over the shapeless form of a rag doll.

The man who had let us in scarcely noticed me. His eyes were fixed on Merek Vance, and he talked so rapidly that I gave up trying to read his lips. I felt sure that he must be speaking in broken English, and that was almost impossible for me to follow. From his stocky strong build and his quick gesturings I guessed that he might be Italian. Vance's back was towards me, so I could not tell what he might be saying as he removed his overcoat and warmed his hands at the stove.

He must have made some explanation of my presence, for the old woman looked up and nodded as she eyed me curiously. She motioned to the boy to give me his chair. I smiled uncertainly as I took it and beckoned the little girl to show me her doll. While I was fashioning my handkerchief into an apron for it, the two men went into another room and were gone some time. I felt as if I had been suddenly set down in a foreign country, completely cut off from communication except by gestures. Once or twice the old woman addressed remarks to the old man or boy, but I could make nothing of them. The little girl had lost her first shyness. She let me set her on my lap. She was not pretty, but neatly made and charming with her dark eyes and clear, pale skin. I had not held a child for so long that I was startled by the light firmness of her body. I could feel the delicate bones under her dress and her heart beating quick as a bird's when you hold it in your hands. She found the bright flowers on the scarf I had tied over my hair, and I marveled at the gentle curiosity of her touch. So intent were we that I did not see the door open until she turned quickly and slid from my lap.

She ran to a woman who had come in with Vance, and tugged at her skirts, holding up the doll with my handkerchief and making shy motions in my direction. The woman did not turn at once because she was listening intently to Vance. Something about her caught my attention immediately. I could see that she was young and slight, and the droop of her shoulders showed that she was very tired. Her hair wrapped her head in smooth blackness, and the line of her throat was long and graceful. Even without seeing her face I could feel the intensity of her listening and speaking. Then she turned, and I recognized Angeletta Rossi, my old classmate, the girl who had won all the debates and played the lead in high-school plays. I hadn't thought of her in the seven years since we had marched up to receive our diplomas and the class history had predicted that I would paint pictures and she would win fame on the stage. We stared at each other across the cluttered room, and I knew that she must be remembering, too.

"Angie," I began awkwardly, "I didn't know you lived here."

"Why should you know?" I had no difficulty in understanding her as she flung the words to me over the child's upturned face. "Why should you know?" she repeated with a defiant lift of her shoulders. "We've gone an awful long ways since Blairstown High. Well—" The spirit died out of her face that had grown sharp and pale, though the features were as I remembered them—clear-cut and arresting. "Well, I can't blame you for what's happened to me."

"Mamma!" I caught the word on the little girl's lips.

"Is she yours, Angie?"

Angeletta looked down at the child and nodded.

"This one, too," she said, and pointed to the baby in the old woman's lap. "And the one in there—" She broke off, and her eyes went back to the door of the room behind the kitchen from which she and Vance and the man who must be her husband had just come. I saw her face grow peaked as she spoke, and she looked at Merek Vance in a way I can't forget.

I turned to him, too, for I couldn't go on staring at her. He met the question I did not put into words.

"Yes," he told me from the sink, where he had poured out a steaming basin of water from the kettle. "The little fellow in there's pretty sick. If I could have got him over to the hospital yesterday or even this morning—" He broke off with an expressive gesture.

"What is it?"

"Infection of the middle ear. It's spread to the mastoid bone." He was rolling up his sleeves as he spoke. "I can't take any chances with the temperature he's running."

"What are you going to do?"

"Open it. Operate."

"Here?" I glanced incredulously about the kitchen.

He nodded shortly.

"Won't be the first time I've done it, or the last. Look, have you got a flashlight out there? I left mine behind when we changed cars."

I asked no further questions but went out to fumble in the pocket of the car. Luckily I found the flashlight under a clutter of maps, driving gloves, and old letters with directions scrawled on the envelopes. As I hurried up the path I had a sense of being part of that house which I had never so much as passed till that night. The lighted windows were no longer bright, impersonal panes of glass to me. Some new and powerful force joined me to those rooms and to the people in them.

When I returned to the kitchen it was already a changed room. Merek Vance had taken it over, and the freshness of outside air blew in through an open window. Chairs had been pushed back against the walls. The old couple, the baby, and the little girl were gone; and Angeletta, too, had disappeared. The half-grown boy was busy pumping and carrying water from sink to stove while the man with the stocky body and dark face was scrubbing furiously at the bare wood of the table where the red cloth and dishes had been. Vance still stood at the sink, turning his head from one to another. I could not follow what he said, but I knew he must be giving directions from the way they moved and listened. Standing there in the doorway, like a spectator at a play, I felt suddenly useless and afraid. I looked down at my hands holding the flashlight and they seemed oddly inadequate. What good could they do in such a crisis, I thought. What had they ever done except hold pens and paintbrushes and unimportant paraphernalia?

Just then Merek Vance noticed me and came over.

"Good!" He nodded as he saw the light. "You'd better not stay around if you're the kind that faints easily; but if you're not . . . Want to help?"

"Of course, but how can I?" I touched my ears to remind him.

"You won't need anything but your hands," he reassured me. "Think you could hold the light steady for me? All right, I'd rather not ask Mrs. Gallo; it's hard on a mother—this sort of business . . . She's keeping up well though. Funny you should know each other, but I'm glad you do. Maybe you can talk to her while I'm in there with the boy. She's under enough strain without seeing him take the anesthetic. Lucky I have enough to see us through."

Angeletta came back presently bringing some aprons over her arm. Vance selected the plainest one of the lot and put it on as unconcernedly as if it had been his white surgeon's coat. He moved with unhurried precision, setting out the contents of his bag on a clean towel.

"Angie!" I reached out to take the apron she handed me, a cheap cotton print covered with incongruously gay flowers. Exactly the kind I thought that one would choose not to wear on such an occasion. "Angie," I tried again lamely, "I'm so sorry . . ."

Her eyes met mine with a glazed, expressionless look as she reached to help me put it on. I hoped I could make her feel my sympathy, but it was hard to find words.

"You don't mind my being here, do you?"

She shook her head and bent to fasten the apron strings.

"Because if you do—I'll keep out of the way. I'd never have barged in like this if I'd known; but now I'm here I want to help. I guess there isn't anyone wants to help more than I do because the Doctor says the trouble's in his ears, and I'm deaf, Angie, did you know that?"

"He told me." She jerked her head towards Vance, who was standing over the stove, clouds of steam rising about him from the heating water. "I didn't know before."

I followed her into the bedroom beyond. It was untidy and badly lighted. Bedclothes and garments seemed to be everywhere, and the large sagging bed was only half made. In a crib beside it I made out the small shape of a child whose head showed round and dark against the pillow. His face was turned away, but I saw the rapid rise and fall of his chest before Angeletta bent over him. A crucifix and rosary beads hung from a nail on the wall, and a candle in a red glass cup burned under a likeness of the Virgin and Child above the bed. Although it was a poorly painted flimsy bit of tin the little shrine lent a kind of dignity to the room. Angeletta, bending over her child, took on the ageless quality of an old master in terms of living flesh so that she seemed the personification of all women of all time.

Seven years ago last June, Angeletta and I had marched up the aisle to receive our high-school diplomas. We had been a little awed and grave because the familiar doors were closing behind us, yet flushed and eager, too, because others were opening on what was going to be wonderful—maybe. Angeletta had been eager and lovely that day with a kind of glow under her skin, and her eyes big and bright as a child's on Christmas morning. I guess I must have looked that way, too, though it's hard to tell about oneself. Well, we would never be like that again, that much was certain. In her shapeless house dress and with her anxious gaunt face Angeletta looked years older than I. She was poor, but she was alive as I knew I had never been in those years between. Life had stirred in her, and through her it was going on to be part of the endless procession of the future. So much had happened to her while I had stayed tight-rolled as a bulb in the security of some dusty shelf, away from the rains and the frost, from the magnetic forces of earth and sun.

I wished that I could tell Angeletta what I was feeling as we stood in that shabby room. But she wouldn't have listened or believed me. I knew, without her saying a word, that she was envying the comfort and security that mattered so little to me. The little boy's head burrowed into the hollow between her breasts. Her thin, strong arms tightened about the curve of his body. I flattened my own against my sides that I might be less aware of their emptiness as we waited there together.

But I had no more time to think or feel, once Vance summoned me to the kitchen.

"You needn't look," he told me. "Just stand here by this knothole on the floor board and keep the light as steady as you can."

I took my place, grateful that I could become a pair of hands, nothing more.

Though I was aware of the figures about the table, I did not look at the faces or try to follow the motions of lips. Even the child's relaxed small body wrapped in a sheet became less real to me than Merek Vance's hands in their rubber gloves reaching for this or that instrument. I marveled that they could move without a tremor or a second's hesitancy. The cloying smell of ether grew stronger as the moments passed, and steam and more potent scents mingled with the heat from the kerosene lamps. I saw a thin line of red widen as the scalpel took its course. I had never guessed that there could be such sure precision as this that I saw with my own eyes.

The flashlight seemed to weigh more each moment. I ached from the effort of holding it steady. My hands felt numb, and I must ease now one hand, now the other. That circle of light became the only reality to me, and at last even Vance's hands were blurs. I clenched my teeth and set my feet more firmly on the reassuring hardness of the floor. Then I lost even that sensation. My whole body and mind were projected into that clear beam of light that I must keep from wavering.

I came to with a start, and the room suddenly cleared about me. The man and the boy were lifting the limp figure, and Angeletta was wheeling the crib in to receive it. The floor was strewn with soaked swabs and cotton, and the sheet that covered the table was no longer white. Merek Vance was standing by the sink peeling off the gloves he had worn. I still held the flashlight, but suddenly my hands began to shake so that it fell to the floor.

It must have made a loud noise, for Vance looked up and nodded to me across the room. Just that and nothing more, yet the gesture reassured me as no words could have done. His face, under a shining mask of sweat, looked sharpened with weariness.

I found one of the kitchen chairs and sank down in it gratefully. I was trembling by that time, not only my hands but my knees and lips as well. It amazed me to see how methodically he went on with his washing, and how he gathered up his instruments and counted and put them away according to routine. My experience with doctors had been confined to hospitals and offices with modern equipment and able assistants at hand. The sort of discipline and skill that could meet emergency alone in the kitchen of a run-down farm was something I had never encountered till that night. I had stood at the edge of a miracle, and even so I could not altogether credit what I had seen.

Vance was through with his scrubbing and sorting at last. But there were still directions to give, and he would not leave till he made sure that the child was reacting favorably. Angeletta came out from the bedroom with him when it was time to leave, and I saw him pat her shoulder reassuringly. As he turned to put on his coat she looked about the kitchen for me and then came over.

"I've got to thank you," she began, "for what you did. I won't forget it—ever."

"Oh, it wasn't anything, Angie; anybody could have held a flashlight. But I'm glad I could help, and he's going to be all right. I'm sure he is."

I saw the muscles of her throat working, and I knew that what she was trying to say came hard.

"I'm sorry I acted the way I did," she began. "But seeing you sort of brought things back. I wanted to make something of myself once and do things that count—" She broke off and looked about the kitchen before she threw out her expressive hands in a futile gesture.

"Don't feel that way about it, Angie," I told her. "Those things that we thought counted then don't seem so much to me now."

She gave me a long searching look.

"I always thought you had it easy," she said, "but I guess I was wrong. I can see you've had it tough, too, in your way. Well, goodbye."

"Goodbye." I took her hand at the door. "I'll be over again soon to see how he's getting along."

I kept thinking of what she had said, as I sat beside

Vance on the drive back. I was glad that the bitterness had gone out of her face; that we were friends once more and she no longer made me the symbol of what she had missed in life. I remembered the rich clear tones of Angeletta's voice from high-school dramatics, and I wondered if the warmth and sweetness had gone out of it along with her freshness and bloom. "We've gone an awful long ways since Blairstown High," she had said, and I couldn't deny that. But it was something that we could still find each other and talk, not as two untried girls, but as one woman to another. I had Merek Vance to thank for that. It was strange that it should be so; that I must ask him to tell me more about Angeletta who had sat beside me and shared confidences through those other years.

I felt his hand reach out and touch mine, almost as if he knew what I had been thinking. It seemed the most natural thing in the world for him to do that, and the quick, light pressure of his fingers made me know that all was well.

The hands of the clock on the dashboard pointed to a quarter past two. The little car had no heater, and the winter air came in at every crack and crevice. It felt not only cold, but leaden as if it were weighted down with the coming day. The stars were still out, but their brilliance was dulled by early morning damp. It was that interval before the tug of the sun begins to be felt in the east. Even though I could see nothing beyond the straight beams of our headlights I felt that we were trespassers, as if the earth were half resentful of those who were not dead or asleep.

Just before we reached the town limits the lights of an all-night diner loomed ahead like a cheerful beacon. I felt glad when Vance turned the car into the place. My feet were numb, and my teeth chattering, as I got out and followed him inside. The crude brightness of the diner and its heavy rich smells of coffee and frying food were exactly what I needed at that moment. The glaring nickel fittings seemed actually beautiful to me as we sat down at a small table. It was empty except for the man behind the counter in his spattered white coat and two men who were hunched over another table at the far end of the narrow place.

Vance ordered coffee, and we drank it eagerly from thick white china mugs. I could see the color coming back into his face as he relaxed over the hot drink. His hands were steadier than mine as he lighted our cigarettes.

"You've certainly got grit," he said after he had taken a long puff. "It's a little late to say 'Thank you,' but I want to, especially for not fainting."

"You said I wasn't the fainting kind. I had to prove it. But tell me—about the little boy: will he be all right?"

"Unless there are complications—yes. I'll run over at noon and see how he's coming along. He's a tough little fellow, fortunately, except for badly infected tonsils which we'll have to watch. I suspect they made the trouble, and of course if I'd been called earlier it wouldn't have been necessary to operate. But it was the only chance he had."

"Would he have been deaf if you hadn't?" I asked.

"No," he told me simply, "he'd have been dead. The infection spreads fast with children. It would have reached the brain."

"Oh," I said, "I didn't know. I could only think about his ears—because of mine, I suppose."

The coffee was thawing my chilled body and nerves. The whole excursion had been so strange that it seemed the least strange part of it all to be sitting at a quarter of three in the morning in the hot, brightly lighted roadside diner with Merek Vance. I hadn't felt so alive and at my ease in weeks—years, it seemed; and I knew with a queer conviction over which I had no control that I should always trust Merek Vance after that night. In little ways he might irritate me; we would disagree often, of that I had no doubt; but in the essentials he would not disappoint me. His very ruthlessness was no longer something to be shunned. I recognized it now for the steel beam that keeps the whole structure of a house in place. I was at a sudden loss for words though I felt a deep inner gratitude flow out towards him across the white-topped table.

"Are you ever afraid," I asked, "when you start to operate, the way you had to tonight?"

He did not dismiss the question as foolish curiosity, but considered it thoughtfully between puffs of his cigarette.

"Well, I can't say I relish it," he admitted. "I'm not a born surgeon. I'd always rather leave the cutting to some one who is. I can do it when I have to, and it's the only way sometimes. They'll have a drug perfected soon that will check about 90 per cent of the mastoid and 'strep' infections at the start. It's going to revolutionize treatments when it's ready." His eyes took on new life and light as he spoke, and the tension and weariness was draining out of his face as he went on. "That's what really interests me: preventive medicine."

"I suppose there's a cure for everything under the sun," I said, "if it could be found."

"That's a pretty large order," he reminded me with a smile. "Back in medical school one of the professors always began his lectures on mental and nervous diseases by saying, 'Give me any plague but the plague of the heart.' I forget where the quotation came from, but that was the gist of it anyway. Of course Freud and Jung and that school think they've found the answer, and maybe they have—" He broke off and shrugged expressively.

"But you don't agree?"

"I haven't the right to express an opinion because I could never meddle with people's minds and brains. I'm mortally afraid of that, more than cutting living tissue or sawing bones. Besides, I haven't the knack of drawing people out. I get out of patience and show it; funny too, when I've got more patience than most for laboratory work and experiment. I always say," he smiled again as he put out his cigarette, "if you can talk to patients you're a doctor; if you can get patients to talk to you—you're a psychiatrist."

The food we had ordered arrived just then, and nothing ever smelled more delicious to me than those plates of crisp brown bacon and golden scrambled eggs. The pile of buttered toast melted before our hunger. We did not speak again for some moments, but Merek Vance nodded his approval of my appetite. He ordered more coffee and leaned back contentedly in his chair when our plates were cleared.

"Funny thing," he said, "your going over there with me tonight. Of course I didn't know what I was in for when we started, or I'd never have let you come along. It was queer, too, your knowing the mother back in school. I'd have thought she was years older than you; but she's had a hard time of it—the husband was laid off at the mills months ago. He told me he'd go back as a strikebreaker if he got the chance. His people own that farm, but they're likely to lose it any time, I gather. They're the kind that never get ahead somehow, like my father and mother—different race, but the same type. I can recognize it."

I found myself telling him of Angeletta and the school plays; of her striking looks and her ability. He sat there quietly opposite me, but as I talked it seemed as if he were studying me more than listening to the words I said. I broke off in the middle of a sentence and cornered him.

"Why do you look at me like that?" I asked. "What are you thinking about me?"

He shrugged, but he did not hesitate.

"I was thinking what a pity it was you weren't born poor," he said. I opened my mouth to protest, but he went on before I could stop him. "I don't mean just the money part—it's more the little comfortable rut of easy prosperity you were born into, that you'll be going on in if you marry the man you're engaged to."

"I love Harry Collins." I could feel the color rising in my cheeks, and my heart stirred as I said his name; yet even as I said it I had to admit to myself that for the last few hours I had not given him a thought. He was not part of what had happened that night. Other people's lives had come between, and I had not missed his presence until that moment. I knew, too, that he would disapprove of this strange experience. I should not be able to share it with him as I was sharing it now with Merek Vance. So I protested more firmly because I felt I had been disloyal to Harry.

"I love Harry Collins," I repeated, "and the only happiness I want is the kind of life we'll have together, whether you approve of it or not."

"All right," he nodded. "If that's what you want, I hope you'll get it; but I still think—what I think. . . . I didn't expect to like you, but I've changed my mind. You've got qualities I hate to see going to waste."

"Such as?" I faced him challengingly.

Again he shrugged and smiled.

"The trouble with you is you were meant to be a prop, and you're trying to make yourself believe you're a vine. Usually it's the other way round: the weak think they're the strong ones. Maybe that's why they get their way so often. Well, I say a person can't be a rock and a barnacle at the same time. And who wants to be a barnacle?"

Before I could answer, the two men who had been sitting at the other end of the diner passed close to our table; and to my surprise I recognized Jo Kelly. I do not think he noticed us. If he did he gave no sign as he went out. I must have shown my surprise, for Merek Vance answered my look.

"You never know where you'll run into Jo Kelly nowadays," he said. "I couldn't place that man with him; one of the union crowd, probably."

"An agitator?" I asked.

"Well," he smiled tolerantly, "personally I think 'investigator' is a better word to use."

"Then you're with Jo Kelly on this union business?"

"I'm for unions, yes; but they're not a religion with me the way they are with him. I can't feel that they're going to solve everything, because the trouble goes deeper than that. . . . At best they're only a step in the right direction. My father was like Jo: he believed in causes too hard and in what they were going to accomplish. There have to be people like that—but you'll hardly ever find a reformer that doesn't die pretty bitter and disillusioned. I saw my father go that way, and I made up my mind then I wouldn't mix up with groups or organizations. I'd try and see things as straight as I could for myself, and stick to them in my own way and work on my own. . . . I guess I'm what you'd call a rank individualist."

"And yet a doctor has to follow rules and conform to codes that are all accepted and laid out by a group," I pointed out.

"The rules of life and death are what everyone has to conform to," he reminded me. "We just try to outwit death, the way I had to tonight. I admit, though, it's not as simple as I make it sound."

I did not press the discussion further. Something I had learned in a literature class years before came knocking at my mind. I remembered it word for word: "Eagles commonly fly alone; they are crows and starlings that flock together." I found myself studying him across the table as if I had never really seen his dark, sharp-featured face and his keen, restless eyes before.

"I—I beg your pardon." I realized that he had been speaking to me and I must ask him to repeat the words. So easy had it been for me to talk with him for the past half-hour that I had forgotten my deafness.

"I was speaking as a doctor," he told me. "The man at the counter started the canned music just now, and I wondered if you had any sensation yet."

I shook my head.

"Only a kind of vibration that I can feel from the floor boards under my feet and at the back of my chair; nothing here"—I touched my ears. "You're wasting your time with me, you know. . . . Aren't you tired of your part of the bargain?"

It was his turn to shake his head.

"I've got faith enough for the two of us, and besides we've only just started." He lit another cigarette before he went on. "I'm going to cure you; only I can't guarantee you're always going to hear the things you want to hear, you know."

"I want to hear everything," I told him. "I can take the bitter with the sweet."

"I can think of a lot of things a woman would just as soon not hear," he went on, "—things like a child crying for what she can't give it, or a man's discouraged step on the stairs and his key fumbling for the lock when he's had too much to drink, and words that turn love into something pretty cheap and rotten. . . . I don't suppose you ever stopped to think it could be like that for you?"

"Why should I think of such things?"

"Sorry, I shouldn't have reminded you." He took up the bill and felt for change in his pocket. "But somehow tonight I've found myself talking to you as if you weren't one of the Blairstown Blairs."

His smile took the edge off those words. I followed him out into the chillness and once more the little car was taking us back through the unfamiliarity of early morning. The pale globes of street lamps were set at long intervals, and our house showed at last a faint, unlit shape as we turned into the driveway. I felt for the purse I had caught up when we left the house, thankful that my key was in it. I should not need to rouse the household.

We did not speak as we left the car in the old stable. Perhaps it was because I was more keyed up than I realized, or because my sense of smell had grown sharper since I had had to depend more upon it, that I felt certain we two were not alone there. There was no light anywhere in the dimness, yet the impression would not leave me as I waited for Vance to collect his bag. A faint whiff of cigarette smoke suddenly made me know that I had not been mistaken. Neither Vance nor I was smoking, and besides this scent came from above, in the rooms I had visited. As I turned to go out I passed close to the wooden stairs, and something made me reach up and feel for the key. But my fingers found only the empty nail where I had so lately hung it.

CHAPTER TWENTY-ONE

IT WAS MIDMORNING when I woke. The experience of the night before had the quality of a dream, vivid, yet unreal. Merek Vance's car was no longer in front of the house, and I could almost believe that it had never stalled there. Yet when I came downstairs to beg a belated cup of coffee from Maggie, I guessed that Aunt Em already knew something of my adventure. She looked up from a pile of mail she was sorting to eye me curiously.

"I don't wonder you slept late. From what that young doctor tells me you two certainly put through a pretty strenuous time of it."

"Oh," I said, trying to sound casual, "so Dr. Vance has been here and stolen my thunder."

"He came with a mechanic to get his car while we were having breakfast, so he had a cup of coffee with us. Janice had just been telling me about noticing that the car was gone when she came back from the Parkers', and we didn't know what to make of it."

"It's a funny thing she'd notice it was gone," I said.

"Well, she did," Aunt Em went on. "We were just

trying to figure it out when Dr. Vance stopped to explain. I must say he was pleasanter than he's been the other times I've seen him. He's always seemed a morose, cold young man to me before, but he thanked me very nicely for the loan of the car and praised you and what you did to help. Whatever possessed you to go?"

Maggie brought my coffee just then, so I postponed answering for a moment.

"I don't know what made me," I told her; "it was just one of those impulses we can't account for. But I thought he might have trouble with the car, and of course we didn't know till we got to the place how serious it was. I wish you'd seen how he operated on that child, right on the kitchen table without any equipment except what he had in his bag. I'll never forget it."

"He said you turned to and helped as cool as could be."

"I was frightened, though, more frightened than I've ever been in my life. Of course I couldn't really do much. I just held the flashlight and tried to keep it steady while he worked. He was wonderful, Aunt Em; if that child pulls through, Dr. Vance deserves all the credit. But he didn't make anything of it."

"Why should he? That's all in a day's work for a doctor; but I'm glad he appreciated what you did. I'm thankful he didn't expose you to anything contagious."

I smiled and helped myself to more coffee. Aunt Em was trying so hard to overcome her prejudices. She was transparent as a child in some ways, and I knew Merek Vance must have said the right thing.

"Your uncle's left already," she went on. "He and Harry and Mr. Parker took the early train. I wish they hadn't all three gone at the same time in case anything new develops at the mills. Old Jo's laid up again. I made him go back to bed after he'd got the furnace going. I don't know what we're going to do this winter if he and the furnace give out at the same time."

Janice's door stood open half an hour later as I passed, and there she sat on the floor surrounded by a jungle of multi-colored dresses draped over chairs, bed, and lounge—all she possessed with several of mine added to the collection.

"What's up?" I asked, pausing at the door. She started and stared at me keenly before she answered.

"I'm going to May Lowell's coming-out party in Waltham," she told me. "Florence Eaton just wrote they could put me up, and I thought I might as well go as stick the week end out here."

"Well, why not?" I felt indifferent to her plan, though not to the clothes she evidently counted on borrowing. "But I'm not lending you the green chiffon or the Burgundy taffeta. They're going right back in my closet where they came from." I removed them firmly from the rest. "And you'd better not count on seeing Harry. He's going to be up to his ears in work."

"Who said anything about Harry?" She rose and began to fumble in a bureau drawer. "I wasn't going to sneak off with your dresses," she went on when she turned back to me again. "They can rot on their hangers for all of me. I was just trying to see if I could fix over my old blue net some way so I won't be ashamed to appear in public. You needn't always jump to conclusions, Emily; and people that go chasing all over the country with strange doctors at all hours of the night and morning needn't hand out advice!"

Her eyes narrowed and I saw that she looked tired and on edge. Her hands shook as she bent to fold the blue net and lay it in the open suitcase. Then she flung back her soft curls and faced me again.

"Oh, yes," she went on, "we heard all about your errand of mercy at the breakfast table. It sounded almost too good to be true—like an unpublished chapter of Florence Nightingale or something."

"Don't forget," I reminded her, "that the car belongs to me as much as it does to you even if I don't use it very often. And by the way, I don't see how you happened to notice it was gone when you came back. You couldn't have seen way down to the old stable from the house."

A look of defiance sprang up in her eyes. They darkened as they always used to when she was a child facing some moment of reckoning. She mumbled something that I couldn't follow.

"What's that you say?" I persisted. "You know I can't make out a word when you turn your head away."

"Well, then"—she wheeled about and formed her words with exaggerated care—"I went down there to see if the keys were in the car. I was afraid I might have left them in. When I saw it was gone I didn't know what to think. I almost called the police."

"It's certainly something new for you to start worrying about the car keys. You know you always leave them in."

She shrugged her slim shoulders under the yellow sweater that so exactly matched the color of her hair. But her eyes and mouth were sullen as she turned back to her sorting and packing. I could see that the subject was closed as far as she was concerned.

I collected my windbreaker and beret and started downstairs again. In the hall I met Maggie cleaning the carpets. Maggie was having what was alluded to in the household as "one of her off days." I could tell from the set of her head and shoulders and the way she bore down on the handle of the vacuum cleaner that her mind was even busier than her body.

"Well, Maggie," I said as she stopped to let me by, "I suppose you heard about last night."

"Yes," she nodded, "I heard, and I say good for the both of you."

I was surprised that she didn't scold me. I had expected at least one vigorous reprimand.

"And when you see him," she went on, "you'd best tell him to come by and take a look at Old Jo. He's a bundle of knots this morning that'll take more than those sticky mustard plasters of his to untie."

"Why not telephone Dr. Weeks?" I suggested.

"It's not Dr. Weeks I mean." She stood with her arms about the vacuum cleaner, making something impressive and antique of its black polished handle. "No," she repeated, eyeing me shrewdly as she spoke, "it's the young doctor I'm after. No reflection on old brooms, but a new one sweeps clean."

"All right, Maggie, I can leave word at his office when I'm out walking Bridget. But why didn't you speak to him yourself when he stopped this morning?"

Again she gave me a keen look.

"I thought it would come better from you," she said, "and I reckoned you'd be seeing him same as usual."

"But, Maggie," I began, "what makes you think—"

Once more she looked at me. It was the way she used to look when we were children and all our most carefully guarded secrets turned out to be old stories to her. While I hesitated she laid her forefinger to her lips and smiled reassuringly.

"I don't have to think, Miss Emily," she said; "I just know. You can't live with people like I've lived with all of you Blairs and not have an eye to what's going on, or a nose for what's in the air. No." She shook her head as I opened my lips to protest. "Don't say a word, then I won't have to."

I stood there without a word, watching her as she stooped and began coiling the long cord of the vacuum and fitting it into place. There was something so final and oracular about Maggie's statements that one had no need of answers or arguments. She was, as she had told me before, like a familiar piece of furniture. We flung ourselves upon her as we might on the chairs or sofa, counting on her being where we expected to find her. We took her presence for granted, and that was her hold over us. I did not know how she knew what I thought I had kept from everyone. I should never know, and I was torn between scolding her and flinging myself into her arms. So I did neither, and she appeared to expect nothing more from me.

"Maggie," I said at last as if we had not spoken, "do you think we should get in touch with young Jo before we call in Dr. Vance?"

"That's up to you, Miss Emily. But Old Jo won't see him, the way things are. If he could slip in and tinker with the furnace I must say it would be a help. Nobody knows how to work it like those two do. It's kind of ticklish to get him in without his grandpa or Miss Blair knowing, but I could sneak him down cellar if he came the back way.

The boy's good-hearted if he is always mixed up with the wrong sides of things."

"I'll tell him if I can track him down. You don't think, do you, Maggie, that he ever comes up here to the old stable?"

"Not that I know of, Miss Emily. What makes you ask that?"

"Oh, I just wondered."

I knew it was too early to find Merek Vance at his office. He would be busy at the clinic till noon and then off on visits for another hour at least. But I would walk awhile first and perhaps find young Jo Kelly over by the union headquarters, which had been temporarily set up in a vacant building not far from the railroad station.

It was one of those raw December days when the sun has a metallic quality to its shining and even a distant red barn looks dull in the unlit distance. One feels the weight of coming snow as if it were a burden on the heart. Now and then a hard, icy flake touched my cheek or lay on my coat sleeve. The softly feathered kind would come later, and the bleakness of bare trees, stark buildings, and brown yards would be smothered in white by night. But these forerunners seemed to me like the difficult scanty tears of old, old people.

The excitement and accomplishment of the night before were gone. I no longer felt the energy that had warmed me then, and the faces of the people I met did nothing to lift my spirits. As I neared the railroad station I saw groups of children along the tracks and about the yards collecting bits of coal to carry home in dirty flour bags or boxes or toy express wagons. It was the noon period between morning and afternoon school sessions, when they should have been home eating dinner or out in the playgrounds. But there they were, as busy as the brown sparrows in the Square.

The station agent stood on the platform as I passed and, when he saw me watching them, he gave me an apologetic sidewise look.

"Morning, Miss Blair." He came over as I paused. "Feels like we'll get snow tonight. Have to keep an eye on these kids from the mill or they'll try and root up the ties to cart home. Still, it's one way to get the place picked clean as a wishbone, and what can I do about it?" He shrugged and shifted his tobacco.

"What can anybody do?" I said, and stared severely at the Indian Chief on the **Peace-Pipe** sign as if he might volunteer advice.

At that moment Bridget stiffened beside me, and I turned just in time to see a small, shabby boy take aim with a sling shot. The station agent ducked, and I caught the dog's collar and held her firmly. Something flew past us, and a dent appeared in the painted profile of the sign. I saw that other dents had pitted the signboard, and several letters of the legend "Peace-pipe for Quality" were mutilated. At any other time I would have smiled over that exhibition of marksmanship, but that day I felt chilled and hurt, as if the stone or bit of coal had struck me, too.

"Fresh, that's what!" The station agent returned to me after making threatening gestures towards the little group as it scattered. "Can't trust one of them behind your back. That sign sure is a tempting target for the little rascals though. Well, kids will be kids, poor little devils."

I slipped the leash on Bridget and continued my way.

Several figures were lounging about the door of the dingy brick building where the union had set up its headquarters. They eyed me curiously as I came up to the entrance, and it seemed to me that they drew closer together as if they instinctively distrusted my coming. A woman in the little group nudged the man beside her, and I was certain that I made out the shape of my name on several lips. I had come too far to turn back, however, much as I wanted to hurry in the opposite direction. By the steps I stopped short and singled out the most familiar face, one of the workers I had often seen loading trucks in the mill grounds.

"Good morning," I began. "I'm looking for Jo Kelly, and I thought I might find him here."

The man touched his cap and nodded a bit nervously, I thought.

"Guess Jo's inside," he said. "I'll see."

They came out of the building together presently.

"What's the matter?" Jo asked without ceremony. "Is it Grandpa?"

I nodded as he fell into step beside me. We walked away together, and it seemed to me that I could feel the curious eyes fixed on my back. I realized that it had been rash of me to go there, that Jo would be held to account later.

"I've got to talk to you," I said. "If you can spare a few moments let's go in the station."

He followed me into the empty waiting room, and Bridget jumped on the wooden bench between us, her head flattened against Jo's trouser leg where his knee bones pushed sharply through the worn material.

"I don't mean to worry you about it," I said, "but he's pretty badly crippled, and we think Dr. Vance ought to see him. I thought I'd tell you first, and then you can have a talk with the Doctor yourself when he's made an examination."

"Why, sure," he agreed, and went on stroking the dog mechanically. "I think you couldn't do better. I don't suppose he's—changed about me any? No. Well, I guess I can't expect it, but I sure wish there was something I could do."

"Old Jo's in no shape to work with the furnace," I told him, "but he will get up and try. Maggie says it's acting up again, and no one but you knows how to handle it. She said she'd sneak you down cellar if you'd take a look at it. I hate to ask favors of you, Jo, but if you could—"

He smiled, and his teeth showed white and sharp as Bridget's.

"Why, don't mention it," he grinned. "I'll be over later —maybe I'd better make it after dark in case Grandpa had an eye out the window. Just needs a little humoring or a new grate maybe. Sure I can count on Maggie?"

"It was her idea to ask you," I said. "Maybe I shouldn't have come down here looking for you. I didn't think it might be hard for you to explain to—to your friends."

"Don't worry about that, Emily."

"I promise not to do it again, only you'd better let me know some way I can reach you if I have to."

He went over to the other side of the waiting room, scribbled something on a telegraph blank and brought it back to me.

"You send word down there," he explained, "and they'll know where I am. Don't forget now, if you need me."

"I won't forget."

I spoke then of Angeletta.

"Must be a couple of years since I saw her," he commented. "I'd like to help her some way if I could. But Gallo's got no use for me. He always thought I was sweet on Angie."

"I used to think you were in high school."

He shook his dark head emphatically.

"I had plenty of foolish notions then," he admitted, "but that wasn't one of them. Well, you tell Maggie to keep an eye out so's she can sneak me in. Look here, this dog's coat seems kind of poor to me. Try a spoonful of malt every day, and a lump of sulphur in her drinking water won't hurt any either. So long."

The expected snow had begun to fall in thin flakes by the time I reached the Doctor's steps. I felt glad of the shabby warmth of the office while I waited for his return. The small blue box stood on top of a pile of papers and medical reports on his desk. I reached for it and touched the painted flowers and hearts and inscription with my finger tips. Our house was crowded with old things, objects good and bad, yet none of them comforted me as this did whenever I took it in my hands.

Merek Vance came in presently, shaking snow from his collar and hair, looking more boyish than I had seen him in many visits. He stood warming his hands at the radiator and eyeing me intently.

"You look tired," he said. "Was last night too much for you?"

I shook my head.

"No, not last night--it's this town. I can't help feeling when I walk around that it's been struck by some blight."

"It's not the only place that has been," he answered. "From what I hear of the big cities, they're worse off."

"How's the Gallo boy?" I asked, glad to change the subject.

"He's coming along splendidly. We made a good clean job of it last night. The visiting nurse is going over there to change the dressing and check up on his temperature." He peered at me more closely before he went on. "You're not used to such strenuous evenings. No wonder you're tired today."

"Oh," I sighed, "being tired isn't what I mind. It's things you can't do anything about that get you down. It seems worth while to do what you did last night. At the time I couldn't feel anything mattered except your pulling that child through so he'd go on living and breathing. But afterwards—don't you ever say to yourself 'What for?' "

"Well, suppose I do?" he asked in turn.

"Last night it seemed wonderful to save a child's life," I persisted, "and then this morning I saw a lot of children grubbing and fighting over little lumps of coal along the railroad tracks. I suppose that was what started me thinking. . . . You know for most of them there'll never be enough coal or food or clothes or anything else to go round. I don't see how you can reconcile it—patching people up, curing them of one thing to be ready for something worse. Doesn't it seem pretty futile to you? Isn't it almost like operating on a condemned man so he'll be in good shape for hanging?"

He did not seem to mind my tirade. He went on warming his hands and watching me across the little space that divided us.

"Yes, there are times when a doctor feels like that," he said at last. "Maybe it's because you've just come round to taking notice, that it's knocked you all of a heap. I suppose

I got used to the inconsistencies you mentioned and to the waste of human beings earlier than most do. I'm not reconciled to it, as you say, and I never will be. I look at it differently, that's all."

"How?" I leaned forward in my chair, and my hands still pressed the small blue box.

"You're thinking in the plural," he went on, "and a doctor like me learns to think in terms of the singular—one person at a time and do what you can for him. We have to forget mass tragedy in relieving one human being. Lucky thing it's that way, or we wouldn't be able to take it most of the time."

He was busy after that with preparations that were now a familiar routine to us both. I submitted to my part absently, hardly aware until I felt that brief prick of the needle that another treatment was over. But before I had collected my things to go he stopped me.

"Do you mind if I ask a favor," he said, and I thought he seemed hesitant, embarrassed as I had never known him to be before. "It's my birthday, and it's bad luck, I've always heard, to drink one's own health. I wasn't going to notice the day, but I seemed to feel the need of telling someone; and I hope you don't mind."

Before I could offer my congratulations he disappeared and returned with a bottle and two glasses.

"This is very old port," he explained; "but we mustn't take any chances with the law, so as your doctor I shall prescribe for you first."

He laughed and scribbled quickly on his office pad. I took the page he tore off and read what he had written there. My name came first, then some unintelligible medical shorthand and below that the familiar words: "To be taken as directed. M. Vance. December 11th, 1931." I have that bit of paper yet, though I have no need to refresh my memory.

"Now that you've prescribed," I smiled back at him as he poured the wine carefully so that not a drop should spill, "I suppose I'd better be deciding on a toast. If you were Dr. Weeks I'd say, 'Your health,' and if you were Janice I'd say, 'Happy days.' But I'm a little puzzled about you."

"I could do with health and happiness as well as anyone, and I'm just entering my thirty-third year, if that's any clue." He held out the little glass as he spoke.

I took it, but still I hesitated.

"Here's to your not being sorry you came back to Blairstown," I said at last, and took the first sip.

"And here's the same to you, Emily Blair."

We drank our port without further toasts, and I thought how strange it was that I, of all people, should have been the one to wish him well on his thirty-second birthday. I went back through the years to another December afternoon. I had been seven then, so he must have been fourteen at that Christmas party when I had first felt myself the target of bitterness even as the Indian Chief's head had been earlier that day.

"You've gone a long way since then." I must have spoken my thoughts, for he looked at me questioningly with raised brows. "I was just thinking of the mill Christmas party," I explained. "You remember the one I mean?"

He nodded, and I went on.

"I don't seem to have got very far, at least not the way you have. Last night you said I was in a comfortable little rut, and you're probably right."

"Did I? Well, there are a lot of worse places to be than ruts. And I don't know how far I've gone when it comes to that. A good many people might think I'd doubled back on my tracks and landed where I started from."

I squinted at the wine in my glass before I answered.

"I think coming back to a place takes a special sort of perspective," I told him, "unless, of course, one comes back to gloat."

He followed me to the door and promised to visit Old Jo Kelly as soon as office hours were over. As I turned to go he touched my arm to attract my attention.

"Maybe you're right," he said, "about my coming back to Blairstown. I thought it was all my wanting to help Dr. Weeks out; but perhaps I did want to do a little gloating, though I wouldn't admit it to myself before."

CHAPTER TWENTY-TWO

Uncle Wallace and Harry returned from Boston looking graver than when they had left, and Mr. Parker stayed on for more conferences with Directors and bank executives.

"It's the same story everywhere," Uncle Wallace told us, "only worse in New Bedford and Fall River. Even down South they're feeling the pinch. Business isn't dull, it's just plain dead."

I tried to catch all I could, and for once Harry seemed ready to explain the situation in terms that I could grasp.

"The banks aren't going to refuse, are they?" I asked him. "They won't withdraw their backing or loans, or whatever you call it?"

"Banks are tightening up everywhere," he told me as we sat by the fire after Sunday dinner, while Uncle Wallace and Aunt Em talked and went over reports in the study. "The bankers that Peace-Pipe has always dealt with didn't exactly turn us down, but they're not taking any chances with their money."

"How do you mean, dear? Make it easy for me to understand if you can?"

He was unusually patient with me that afternoon, and I tried to ask as few questions as possible. My head ached with the strain of reading his lips, with piecing together facts when I lost words here and there and tried to follow without asking for repetitions.

The situation was simple enough when I got to the bottom of it. The banks would continue their backing and even make additional loans if they could have assurance that our mill would reopen by the first of the year.

"It's a fair enough proposition," Harry admitted; "the only trouble is we're pressed for time. The union's got us in a tight spot—just where they want to keep us till we have to come round to their terms. That's what they're counting on."

"Can't you put it up to the workers themselves? This way it's as if both sides were starving each other out. There'll be nothing left of the business if it goes on like this."

"You're right, there won't be. That's why we've got to reopen, strike or no strike. If we recognize their union, that means accepting a new wage scale. We'd be filling orders at a loss if we met their demands. They're beginning to feel the pinch down there now—"

"I know, Harry, I know. Even over here I can feel how much worse things are this week than last, and with Christmas coming and all—something's got to be done. But what?"

I searched his face, but found no optimism there.

"The banks agree with us there's only one stand to take. Mill hands who want work can come back at wages we can pay; those who don't— Well," he shrugged expressively, "they'll just have to stay outside the gates and let the union worry about them. We can get all the help we need; too many out of work in this town, and plenty of others if it comes to that."

"You mean you'll call in strikebreakers—scabs?"

I had never used the word before except to young Jo Kelly. I saw Harry's surprise at my mention of the term.

"Why, yes," he admitted, "that's about what it amounts to. I'm not saying there won't be trouble, but we've tried every other way since the walk-out."

"Trouble?" I asked. "Even more than now?"

"They may put up a fight. Still a picket line wouldn't make much show if we called in the State militia—" He broke off, seeing the horrified look on my face. "Now don't you start worrying, Emmy. Of course we hope it won't come to that. We want to keep things peaceful if we can."

I could not speak for a minute. I sat there on the sofa beside him and tried to remember all that I had ever read about strike violence and militia being called out in other plants. There was a newsreel I had seen once where officers with raised clubs bore down on men and women who retreated before them like a dark wave, and there were blurred newspaper prints of crowds being scattered by tear-gas bombs. I wondered if Harry could be thinking beyond the words he said.

"And if Peace-Pipe didn't reopen—for a while, I mean?"

I could see that he was growing tired of my questions before he answered.

"It's got to," he told me. "It's got to reopen or go under. Do you know how much we're losing every day the plant's idle? No? Well, I can get you the figures in case you're interested. The money doesn't roll in of itself, you know."

"But it's awful to talk about it like that," I protested, and I could feel tears gathering in my eyes. "I can't seem to put money first, not ahead of the people over there. Maybe I feel differently about it because I went to school with some of them. I can't just call them mill hands and let it go at that. They've got their side, too, and when I see the children—"

"There you go sentimentalizing." His mouth hardened as he spoke, and he turned on me accusingly. "You asked for facts, and I'm giving them to you. You've got to stop mixing up in what you don't know the first thing about, and you've got to stop middle-of-the-night errands of mercy with strange doctors."

I was so startled I had no answer ready. How could he have heard about my visit to the Gallo family so soon after his return? I had meant to tell him of it myself.

"Oh," I began lamely, "you've heard about that—"

"Yes, I heard. Things like that get around."

I felt myself growing hot, hurt by his criticism and worried because I did not wish to have him question me further about Merek Vance.

"If you ran into Janice in Boston," I said, "and she told you—well, you know how she exaggerates . . ."

I scarcely thought what I was saying until he rose and went to the window as if he did not want to meet my eyes. So Janice had told him. I could imagine that she had made the most of the incident.

"It wasn't anything I planned to do, Harry." I rose and went over to where he stood, toying with the shade cord in his preoccupied way. "And Dr. Vance didn't ask me to. I just went along when he borrowed the car. . . . I can't see why you should be annoyed about it."

I slipped my hand through his arm and tried to make him look at me. But he was unresponsive to my touch.

"Please, Harry," I begged foolishly because I felt so completely cut off from contact. He could put me miles away simply by keeping his face averted. "I never thought you'd mind my going. You don't really, do you?"

He turned around at last, and though he smiled I felt no reassurance behind it.

"It's not whether I mind or not, Emmy," he said, forming the words emphatically so that I could not possibly mistake them. "But you must remember you can't afford to get talked about. You're not just anybody in this town. Your family's been behind Peace-Pipe for generations. You're part of it and everything it stands for, don't forget that."

"I don't forget," I began, "but it seems to me there's a lot that none of us understand yet. What was right in the business fifty years ago, even ten years ago, may be all wrong now." I saw his eyes grow cold behind the little flecks of golden light that I loved even more than his tilted brows and humorous mouth, and I hurried on before he could turn away. "I don't pretend to know anything, but I'm honestly trying to see both sides. A business can grow too big for a family to run, like—like a snowball you roll till it gets bigger than you are." It surprised me to find myself repeating the very words young Jo had said. "That old Indian in his war feathers has seen a lot of changes since he came to be our trademark."

"And a lot of good will and respect are behind him, and

money, too," he reminded me. "I may have criticized the
kind of goods we've been turning out, and I still think
we're behind the times in lots of ways; but Peace-Pipe's
never let down on quality, and I'd be pretty proud of the
product of the mill if I were you."

I realized that it was useless to go on with a discussion
that was only drawing us further apart. It hurt and puzzled
me that he should resent my interest, that he should make
such an issue of my visit to the sick child of a worker's
family. He made me feel almost as disloyal as if I had
joined the picket line across the river. I was relieved when
he proposed going out for a drive.

Because it was Sunday afternoon the town seemed mo-
mentarily to have shed its blight. There were no shabby
lines of men and women about the mill gates, and the mo-
tionless machinery and smokeless chimneys were less op-
pressive than in the weekday idleness. The snow which
usually took on a gray film of smoke as it fell had stayed
white. The town looked its best with sharp roof lines and
bare trees and lawns softened into prim beauty. We kept
to the main road which had been cleared and drove north
towards the dark ridges of hills. With the town behind us
I breathed more freely. The little car took the miles, almost as if it had invisible wings. No one ever drove a car
better than Harry. He and the engine always seemed to
merge like perfectly matched partners in some rhythm of
their own. Since my deafness I had become more than ever
conscious of such mechanical harmony. I felt the tension
ease between us, and I relaxed beside him and gave myself
to the moment. If he had reached out and taken my hand
just then, I think I might have been completely happy.

Even without that I forgot to be troubled and afraid.

Christmas was only ten days off, and the feel of it was in the air. Red barns were warmed to brightness on the side where the low sun struck. Apple trees in orchards were stubbornly crooked to the clear pale sky and clumps of hemlock invading rough pastures were purple-dark against the snow. Now and then a wreath showed at some window or door, and Christmas greens and bunches of scarlet berries had been set out for sale at the roadside. Just before we turned to drive back I signaled Harry to stop at one of these stands.

"I must have a bunch," I told him; "I know Aunt Em has ordered our wreaths months ago, but these are somehow special."

He drew up obligingly while I got out to make my selection. My reason told me that the berries could not possibly be as brilliant as they seemed. It was the slantwise, winter light in that hour before sunset that laid a curious shine upon them. It was as if each and every round red ball had been dipped in glory. If only one could keep them so always, I thought, along with moments that are kindled by a look or a word or a smile from someone we love! I bought a miniature Christmas wreath, no bigger than my two fists. It would be too small to make a showing among the laurel festoons and wreaths of holly and ground pine that always filled our house. But I decided it was exactly the size to hang on a doctor's door.

Harry smiled tolerantly as I carried my purchases back to the car, and we drove home through the December sunset with the chimneys of Peace-Pipe black shapes against clouds of feathered flame.

There was a light at Dr. Weeks' house as we passed, a single oblong of brightness in the wing where Merek

Vance had his office. I could picture him at his desk. It seemed right and natural to think of him there. I was startled to remember how short a time it was since he had come to Blairstown. But then it was not as if he were a stranger. Peace-Pipe was in his past, too, even as it was in mine. The shadow of those black chimneys, the bitter smoke from their throats, and the pulse of humming mill machinery had somehow marked us both long ago. We were both a part of the "product of the mill." Harry had flung that phrase at me a little while before, and I had thought little of those five familiar words; but suddenly they took on life and significance for me as the scarlet berries had taken on strange brightness by the roadside. Peace-Pipe had made me the sort of person I was. By the same token Merek Vance was what he was because of those difficult years of resentment his childhood had known across the river and its bridges.

"Peace-Pipe for Quality," another well known phrase, leaped to my mind. I hoped it applied to me. But I wasn't sure of myself as I was of him. I found myself smiling to think how vehemently the dark sharp-featured man behind that lighted window would deny the charge.

CHAPTER TWENTY-THREE

MIRACLES ARE OUT of fashion nowadays. Or perhaps it is only that they have been explained away from us. Radios and newsreels and words have shorn them of their mystery. Yet to each of us, I think, a miracle is given at some time in our lives. We may not choose the moment it shall be revealed or the form it shall take. We may not even realize till long afterward that it was our privilege to be part of one. Our minds may betray the wonder that our hearts accept. I fought against the miracle that was to be mine, but there was no denying it when it came to me.

I must tell of it in my own way, though my words will make a poor showing to those who ask for explanations in technical phraseology. In the medical world much has been written about the Vance treatment of deafness and restoration of impaired nerve cells. His formula and method of injection has been widely publicized in the last year, hailed as one of the greatest contributions to medical science and a boon to humanity. Already it is being put to practical test by doctors in hospitals and clinics all over the country, and reports of even greater uses to which it may be applied are continually appearing. But of these I may not write even if it were in my power to master the terms. These seem to have no part in the visits I made to the bare, poorly equipped office during those months which were to change the whole course of my life.

Whenever I come upon the familiar letters in print, "Merek Vance, M.D."—and I come upon them often nowadays in magazines and newspapers, I must stop and convince myself that they belong to the man whose faith and determination dominated that shabby room and all who entered it. But the printed name has less reality for me than the remembrance of an alert face that could darken to disapproval or light up in sudden sympathy. The medical journals with their impressive accounts of his discovery seem vague and impersonal compared to the makeshift rack of test tubes with their homemade labels, the long, skillful fingers that handled them, and the prick of a needle whose power I once dared to doubt. It frightens me a little to read of that doctor and his achievement. But when I remember his eyes watching me across the battered desk I am reassured. I have faltered under the directness of his look and the uncompromising words he has spoken, but they have had power over me in the past, and they will have power to hurt and strengthen me again.

That blind man in the Bible whose sight was restored to him had no explanation to offer in testimonial. He could only stand and stare and repeat, "I was blind, now I see." That is how it was with me. Whatever I am or may become, I shall never be as I was before. For I am no longer shut off from the sweet and the harsh sounds of earth. The simple, terrible impact of spoken words is mine once more, and I shall never take the gift for granted. Even though I should live to be an old, old woman I doubt that I can ever be unshaken by the first splashing of rain, by the tender clamor of bird calls in early morning, and the pulse of unseen crickets hailing frost. I shall fall silent sometimes in the midst of eager voices, knowing that the wonder of voice answering to human voice is too much for me to bear. I must listen then, not to what the voices are saying, but to the silence that once made me its prisoner. Sometimes, it may be that I shall see a look in other eyes, a listening look that I shall recognize; before which I shall be humble and kind.

I have not thanked Merek Vance for what he has done for me. We do not thank the sun for rising or the air for letting us breathe it. Besides, if I tried to thank him he would only shrug his shoulders and lift his dark brows in the way I know so well. But this much he did say once, and I have not forgotten it:

"No matter how many people the injections might have helped," he told me, "I could never have taken any satisfaction if I'd failed with you. It would have been bitter—like isolating the germ that had killed your wife or your child."

But I am far ahead of myself. What happens to people is the story. What they think about while it is happening to them is something else.

The day after my drive with Harry I woke feeling restless, weighed down with a mood of despair which I could not shake off. I felt as I used to feel in my childhood when the door of a closet closed upon me and I found myself half smothered by the folds of heavy garments. Only when I pushed my way through them and fumbled for the doorknob would the unreasoning panic leave me. Since there

was no such simple way out of my depression, I decided
to go to Boston on the pretext of Christmas shopping. I
must get away from the fear and futility that hung over
Blairstown even if I could not get away from myself. I
didn't care whether I inconvenienced Vance by missing
treatments. I had never had any real faith in them. Those
visits to the little office, I told myself, had merely been
something to do each day, nothing more. I would put an
end to them with the new year. Merek Vance couldn't
hold me to a promise he had forced upon me.

So I scribbled a hurried note and left it with the little
wreath on my way to the train. Vance would find it in the
mailbox when he returned from the clinic, and by that
time I would be gone. Harry would be working late over
mill reports that night. He had told me not to expect him
for supper. Aunt Em seemed glad to have me go.

"Do you good to get away, dear," she said. "A day's
shopping always used to set me up when I was your age.
Just enjoy yourself and forget all about mill trouble. But
don't let Eunice know how worried we are about Peace-
Pipe, whatever you do. You just tell her that everything's
going to be all right after New Year's when the mill reopens."

I promised and tried to put Blairstown behind me once
I had boarded the train. But that was easier said than done.
It was an express from the north, crowded with Christmas
shoppers and students going home for the holidays. The
stir of festivity that surged through the car had no power
to lift my spirits. Bundles fell from overhead racks; skates,
suitcases, and armfuls of country greens overflowed the
aisles, fellow passengers smiled and nodded and were gay
and good-humored about me. But I could not shed my own

preoccupation. I stayed dull and quiet as a snail might withdraw into the narrow world of its own shell.

The exuberance was more than I could face after a while, and I closed my eyes against it. Let them think I slept. I felt too tired to strain at reading the lips of strangers. There was no need to pretend that I caught the friendly greetings of the season, especially as I was in no mood to respond in kind.

Perhaps I really did doze off for a minute or two. I shall never know. But suddenly I was aware of sound, or what seemed to be sound above the vibration of the train. I found myself sitting bolt upright on the plush seat with a queer chill at my spine. My bag fell to the floor and as I bent mechanically to recover it I lost the odd sensation in my ears.

"It's being on a train," I reasoned. "Vibration can play tricks like this sometimes."

I remembered that in the past I had once or twice been betrayed into imagining that I heard when I traveled on trains. The doctors had tried to explain the affiliation between different nerve responses and the tie between sound and motion. They had even been interested enough to try other mechanical stimulation. I had spent many hours being tested with intricate machines in one office or another. I had even been taken up in an airplane on several occasions because some cases of deafness had been benefited by altitude and vibration. Knowing how these experiments had failed, I argued myself into apathy once more. There was no recurrence of the sensation I had seemed to feel, and yet I knew that something had suggested music to me —a faint thread of sound that was not part of the motion and throb of the engine.

I must have dreamed it, I decided; and yet I could not put it from my mind so lightly. In the last year I had accepted my deafness so completely that I could not remember once a dream which had given sound back to me.

And then I turned and stared down the car. There a few seats behind me a group of college boys and girls were crowded among suitcases and bags, and I saw one of the boys playing an accordion. It opened and shrank under his hands and he swayed to the music he must be making.

What of it? I argued inwardly. He's playing now, and you can't hear him. What makes you think you did before?

I hurried through the North Station, trying not to remember the last time I had waited there. Cousin Eunice was out for the afternoon playing bridge. I left my bag and walked away from her narrow red brick house that held no charm of pleasant association for me. The air blew strong as I crossed the Public Gardens towards the stores on Boylston Street. It felt clean and fresh on my face, though the remnants of snow beside the paths were gray with city smoke. Christmas stirred all about me; children in bright coats feeding pigeons and brown sparrows; skaters on the frozen pond, and a shivering Salvation Army Santa Claus with his tripod and kettle. I dropped a coin in it as I passed, and presently I was part of the crowd of shoppers. It was exhilarating to be in stores again, though such expeditions always taxed my power of concentration. I was more than ever aware of my handicap when customers jostled me to one side. It was difficult to make my wants known to busy salesgirls who had a way of turning their heads in another direction as I strained to catch their answers to questions. But I managed my purchases at last and completed the list of purchases Aunt Em had given me. Suddenly I found my arms full of packages and my head throbbing with the effort I had made to secure them.

I walked past my reflection in a looking-glass panel and smiled to see that I looked like all the other bundle-laden shoppers. To see me no one would have guessed how little festivity I felt. It was only midafternoon; but already twilight was settling over the city, and the brightness of decorated windows accentuated the early December dark. I made my way to the edge of the sidewalk and went on, letting the home-going crowd take me in the direction of Copley Square. I had no reason for returning to Cousin Eunice's house before dinnertime, and I thought a walk might help me to face the barrage of her questions. So I moved on without objective. The city sights and smells brought back associations with every block. All the futile visits to doctors' offices returned to haunt me as I recognized this landmark or that—the florist's at the corner where bunched violets kept their fragrance longer; the blind man with his magazine and newspaper stand; the pet shop window with its never failing crop of round, luster-eyed puppies. I did not pause to tap at that pane of plate glass as others were doing. Back in Blairstown, Bridget would be missing me, I knew, whether anyone else did or not.

It seemed to me that beggars and street venders were more in evidence than usual. I tried not to notice them, shivering at the curb among their tawdry wares. The contrast from corner to corner took me by surprise: on one, stacks of spruce and fir trees and greens making the air pungent with spice; and across the way, black headlines that newsboys held high—"Financier Commits Suicide, Bankruptcy Hinted," "Market Hits New Low for Year,"

"Third Largest Mass. Woolen Mill Closes." If Harry had been there walking beside me I should not have read the headlines. Or, if I had read them, their import would not have made me shiver under the warmth of my sealskin coat.

Ugh! Let me get away from headlines and people selling things I don't want to buy! I thought as I stepped off the curb and started across the street.

Usually I was timid in traffic, overcautious because of my deafness. I thought I was careful then; but I must have been more preoccupied than I realized, for suddenly I stopped short trembling from head to foot. Once more I was conscious of sound. This time there could be no doubt. A horn honked shrilly and brakes screeched at the same instant a truck shuddered to a stop so close beside me I could feel the throbbing heat of the motor. I stood there smiling foolishly into the furious, frightened face of the driver. I can see him yet, glaring at me over the wheel, while I continued to stand and smile as if he had saved my life instead of so nearly crushing it out of existence. Just as well, perhaps, that I couldn't hear the names he was calling me. His frantic gesturings finally brought me to my senses.

I don't know how I made my way across the street. I only know that I was still smiling long after I had reached safety. My knees went weak then, and my hands shook so that I could hardly keep my bundles from scattering. I found the refuge of a bench and sank down on it. I must have made a spectacle of myself, surrounded by gayly wrapped packages, with tears streaming down my cheeks for any passer-by to see. But I didn't care who saw me there. I didn't care what anyone thought. It didn't seem incongruous that a strident motor horn had been the means of revealing the miracle that I could no longer deny.

I have no idea how long I sat huddled on that cold bench in the city twilight, shaken with sobs and oblivious to the curious looks of those who passed. Maybe it feels like that to die and be lifted out of time and the infirmities of flesh and spirit. Or perhaps that realization of well-being only comes when we who have given up hope suddenly feel its living stir within us, as Aaron's rod put out leaf and bud for a sign.

And so I walked back through the dusk with my bundles. Silhouettes of Christmas wreaths showed dark against all the lighted windowpanes in the houses I passed. My face was stiff with drying tears, and I scarcely knew how my feet took me along the streets. But I no longer felt alone. I turned once, half expecting to see Merek Vance at my elbow. He had dragged me back from unheard danger before, and now, miles away from the congested street crossing, he had saved me once again. He would be keeping office hours at his desk in the familiar room. I knew that, and yet it seemed to me that I could feel his hand warm and reassuring on my arm.

I stood a moment by the flight of stone steps, bracing myself against the chill iron railing before I went in to face Cousin Eunice. My ears were dull and lifeless again. It might be days or hours before they quickened to sound once more, and I would hear it again. Yet the signal had come.

CHAPTER TWENTY-FOUR

THAT WAS A STRANGE and wakeful night in Cousin Eunice's spare bedroom. I tried to read myself to sleep, but the words on the pages I turned had less reality than the pattern of the flowered wallpaper. I put out the light at last and lay, tense and wide-eyed in the darkness, my mind churning over and over all the happenings of the day. It had begun gray and tight-fisted as some knob of bud on a winter tree, and then it had changed miraculously like the tiny dried flowers we children used to watch expand to color and beauty in a bowl of water. Yes, it had bloomed like that for me.

Although there had been no recurrence of sound since afternoon, I was certain of what I had heard. I felt certain, too, of a subtle change in my ears. Silence muffled them again, but the dullness was gone. It was as if a telephone wire, long disconnected, had suddenly become charged with a live current. It startled me, too, to realize that in spite of my stubborn refusal to believe in or hope for a cure, something secret and strong in me had managed to keep faith all along. I must have clung to it unconsciously even while my lips uttered their denials. So I drifted off to sleep at last with morning a thin gray behind the near-by chimneys; with happiness wrapping me more warm and light than Cousin Eunice's best eiderdown quilt.

"No, I can't stay," I told her at breakfast. "I must take the next train."

"Always on the go, you young people," she reproved across the silver coffee service. "No stability or sense about you. It's as if you were all too busy tracking down happiness ever to meet up with it. I always gave you credit for wanting to marry and settle down, but lately you act as flighty as Janice."

Her keen eyes scrutinized me from her puffy, well preserved face.

"Well," she went on. "I suppose I shouldn't blame you for wanting to get back to Harry. Heaven knows, long engagements are trying enough without all you've had to put up with beside. I guess you two wish you had some of the money that's been thrown away on ear specialists these last years. It would come in handy to start housekeeping."

I lifted my coffee cup and nodded over its gold rim.

"This is lovely china, Cousin Eunice." I touched the porcelain admiringly as I spoke. "Coffee tastes better out of these cups than any I know."

Praise of her possessions usually mollified her, but that day she couldn't be distracted.

"There's the paper," she said. "Maybe you have the courage to read it. Frankly I haven't; nothing but bank failures and mill shutdowns and suicides. With all this unfortunate business at Peace-Pipe and dividends going to be passed again—I don't know what we're coming to. Do you?"

"Harry and Uncle Wallace are too worried to talk much," I hedged. "But the mills are going to reopen—that's all I know."

"I can't see why they're not making money," she persisted. "After all, it's not as if Peace-Pipe were manufacturing luxury goods, like silk or perfumery or fancy linens. People all over this country have to sleep and wash themselves, so there's always a demand for sheets and pillowcases and towels."

I found myself thinking of the Gallo family huddled round the kitchen stove and of the gaunt, grimy faces I had seen at street curb and park the day before.

"I guess there are plenty of people nowadays who'd think a clean sheet or a towel was a luxury," I reminded her.

Without waiting for her answer I set down my cup, and rose from the table.

In my impatience to be on my way to Blairstown I reached the station nearly an hour before traintime. But that day I did not mind the bleakness of the waiting room with all its earlier associations. The smell of varnished wood and cinders, of wet wool and rubber from overcoats and galoshes could not depress me even on so dark and moist a morning. I had felt elated as the taxi brought me through a gray drizzle that slanted in from the water front. The traffic had been hopelessly snarled in the maze of narrow, crowded streets. Sleet filmed the sidewalks and glazed the umbrellas that clustered like jungles of strange mushrooms by subway entrances and street crossings. Yet they did not seem grotesque to me that dark December morning. My heart bore up my body. I felt that curious whetting of the senses, that inner quickening that is the nearest thing to pure joy. I moved in a kind of glow of my own making. It seemed to me that people felt and responded to it. The taxi driver smiled as he helped me out. The porter who carried my bags and the ticket seller also relaxed their tense, pre-holiday expression and I was aware that those who waited on near-by benches eyed me with less impersonal stares. It had not been like that since the summer of my engagement when my happiness had brimmed over and flowed out in every direction.

"You don't see many happy-looking folks nowadays," Maggie had said once. "It's a treat to pass somebody that don't look down in the mouth or out-and-out sour."

Maggie would guess the truth as soon as I crossed the threshold. Her wise gray eyes would find me out though neither of us spoke a word. Yes, Maggie and Bridget would know by some common gift of insight that they possessed, and I could trust them not to betray me.

As I waited on the wooden bench with my bag and purchases I found myself thinking of Merek Vance. It occurred to me for the first time since my flight that he might well have resented my leaving town without warning. I had only missed one day, to be sure, but my note had been curt. He must have sensed the irritation behind the hastily scribbled words. If only I might rush to one of the telephone booths and call him by long distance! Since that was still impossible I tried to think how I could make amends before I reached Blairstown. I must prepare him for the news I was bringing. So I hurried over to the telegraph stand and reached for a form. It was difficult to frame my message. Care must be taken of the wording since the local operators sometimes took far too personal an interest in the wires received and delivered. I stared about me in search of words, and my eyes noticed a sign that recommended the season's greetings and listed a variety of hackneyed suggestions. None of these suited my particular need, but I seized the idea and began to write on the yellow blank:

DR. MEREK VANCE
COURT HOUSE SQUARE
BLAIRSTOWN, MASS.

O COME ALL YE FAITHFUL JOYFUL AND TRIUMPHANT STOP RETURNING IMMEDIATELY.

E. BLAIR

The operator counted out the words mechanically. Her pencil hung questioningly over the "O," but I shook my head at her suggested pruning and attempt to change "ye" to "you." Whatever changes it might suffer, I told myself, Merek Vance would be able to translate the carol into medical terms.

I glanced at the clock as I crossed the waiting room. It was seven minutes before ten. I tried to calculate the time it would take for my wire to reach its destination. I could see the messenger boy crossing the Square in his rainy-day slicker and cap, ringing the Doctor's bell, and waiting with his pencil and receipt slip in hand. Perhaps Vance would be on his way out to the car. I could see him pause in his hat and overcoat while he tore the yellow envelope open. Or if he had already left on his rounds I could picture it lying among the other papers on his desk.

I thought of Harry, and my throat went dry, trying to summon words to tell him that evening when we should be alone. The station became a blur while I clung to the moment that lay ahead.

"Harry," I would say. "Harry darling, we've had so much bad luck, you and I. Do you think you could bear something else—something wonderful for a change?"

The thought of hearing his voice once more turned me faint for an instant. It might be many more weeks or months, but I could wait for that. Everything was going to be as it had been before, only better, a thousand times better. This unacknowledged chill that had lain between us since my return to Blairstown would vanish like mist under a noonday sun. Nothing in the world, it seemed, not even the trouble at Peace-Pipe, had power to dim our happiness.

In the women's waiting room I found a lone Gideon Bible chained to a table, and I began to turn the pages as I used to do on days when I felt the need of some sign from heaven. That was how I came upon the verse in the book of Proverbs. "Hope deferred maketh the heart sick: but when the desire cometh, it is a tree of life."

"A tree of life." . . . I could feel those very branches stirring to live green in the core of my being. I stood there shaken before the truth of those words. I tremble now as I set them down upon this sheet of paper, for they were like an echo of my own heart, of all hearts beating and hoping through time and space.

I had just settled myself by the car window when a porter passed, his arms weighed down with familiar luggage. I recognized a hatbox bearing my initials, Janice's suitcase, and a little gray overnight bag I had given her on her last birthday. She went by before I could reach out and touch her arm. Her eyes were on the porter and a seat he had found for her far down the car. But I could see her profile under a new green hat. It was tilted like a fallen leaf on the bright waves of her hair. Her cheeks were rosy from haste and moist with damp. She must have been hurrying to catch the train, and haste was always becoming to Janice. No wonder people turned to watch her. No wonder that men especially forgot subjects they were discussing when she came within range.

If I were a man, I told myself, I'd certainly be attracted to Janice—not me. I wonder she hasn't married long ago. She's had plenty of chances to. . . . Maybe she knows more than she lets on about love and men and—oh, well, she can take care of herself, I guess. But she ought to fall in love and be happy. She'd be different then. Maybe we could get to know each other if we didn't have to live under the same roof and always have to be on guard against being sisters. I want Janice to be happy. I've never wanted it as much as I do today.

I was tempted to rise and go to her, but already the seat beside me was filled and all my things on the overhead rack would have to be shifted. Besides, I needed to be alone for a little while longer. I needed to hold fast to my happiness that day, though I had enough and to spare for Janice and that whole carload of people. So I sat on in my place while the train sped away from the city, past towns and farms, whose streets and buildings I recognized through the December drizzle and my own sense of well-being.

Yes, I admitted, I had been overcritical of Janice lately. The habit had grown on me since my deafness. I suppose personal bitterness and anxiety had intensified petty irritations from pinpricks into deep wounds. Doubt of myself had made me resent qualities in her which under ordinary circumstances I should never have envied. Now that I could dare to look ahead and count on all my faculties again I felt a wave of affection and tenderness overwhelm me as if Janice were once more the little sister I must humor and help even when she was most trying. Memories of our childhood stirred to the rhythm of the train. Janice had been afraid of spiders, and it used to make me feel proud and protective to walk ahead when we explored wood paths and brush them away. Once we were going to be angels and wear halos and wings in a Christmas tableau; and, the day before, I had come down with bronchitis and been put to bed. Janice was all dressed and ready when suddenly she refused to go without me. I could see her still in the trailing white robe with the homemade halo slightly askew on her fair curls. There was the time she had sent me the bunch of violets when I won the high-school debating contest. That had been in midwinter, and it must have taken her allowance for two weeks to buy that little bunch. I felt contrite, remembering things like that. They mattered more than the antagonism that had followed. Suppose we had gone our separate ways and become strangers to each other—there would be time enough to change that. The next visit she made I would let her have the pick of my closet. Now that everything was going to be all right, I could afford to be generous.

Sitting there, close to the misted windowpane beyond which a wet and frosty world slid by, I gave myself up to good resolutions as I used to do in my childhood on the last day of an old year. I made mental lists to follow: I would be more tolerant of Janice; I would be less demanding of Harry while the mill trouble took so much of his time; I would not keep asking for tangible proof of his devotion; I would be more thoughtful of Aunt Em, less impatient of her set ways and unasked advice; I would try to be more sympathetic to Uncle Wallace and his blind acceptance of the business creeds of his youth; I would try harder to understand Jo Kelly and his convictions even if they didn't fit in with family loyalties, and I would show my gratefulness to Merek Vance by admitting that I had been wrong to doubt his power to help me. It is easy to be generous and forgiving when we are in danger or when we are tingling with happiness as I was in that hour and a half.

We were nearing Springwood, two stops before Blairstown, when I saw Janice reaching her bags down from the rack. It surprised me to see her doing that because usually she was anything but forehanded. As the train slowed down and the station platform came into view I was even more startled to see her moving towards the door. I half rose in my seat to go to her, but the aisle was full of alighting passengers.

Oh, well, I thought, she'll be back again. She'll notice her mistake the minute she's off the train. It's not like Janice, though, to be so absent-minded.

I rubbed a clear place on the steam-filmed glass and stared out at the station platform where the drama of welcomes and goodbyes was in full swing. Cars and busses were parked close, their tops shiny with wet. Little groups of people were hurrying to one or another, exchanging handshakes and embraces, surrendering luggage as they climbed in.

And then I saw Janice. She was standing alone with her things about her. I could tell that she was looking anxiously up and down, searching the wooden platform and the waiting cars. I pressed close to the window and pulled at my glove. I would signal to her by tapping with my ring. But just as I raised it to strike the glass something stopped me, and my hand dropped to my lap. I saw her wave, and there down at the end of the line of cars I recognized our little green roadster. The glass was filming again. I cleared it to make sure I wasn't mistaken. There might be other such cars, but not one with our license plates, not one with Harry Collins at the wheel. He had climbed out and was coming down the platform with his long, easy strides. His hat was pulled over his eyes, but I caught the line of his chin and the familiar shape of his hand, tossing away a cigarette. He was beside her as the train began to move. I pressed my face to the cold pane and saw him stoop to pick up her bags before the station shut them out of my sight.

CHAPTER TWENTY-FIVE

I WAS AT HOME at last and in my own room. I had come directly from the station, not stopping at the Doctor's as I had planned. It seemed to me that I had not drawn a free breath since the train had pulled away from the platform at Springwood. Mechanically I had collected my things, left the car, and hailed the Blairstown station taxicab. But all the time I moved without sense of feeling. My chest felt tight as if it had been frozen over.

I won't believe it, I insisted again and again. That wasn't Janice I saw on the train; that wasn't Harry waiting for her back there in Springwood.

But I knew what I had seen. I didn't deceive myself.

I went downstairs at last, leaving the unopened packages as I had tumbled them in the hall. Maggie wanted to bring me lunch on a tray, but I told her I had eaten on the train.

"Where's Janice?" I asked her, trying to appear casual. "Isn't she back yet?"

"Not that I know of, Miss Emily. Your aunt said tonight or maybe tomorrow. She wasn't sure, and we didn't expect you back this early."

She may have said more. I do not know what, for I turned away. Bridget pushed her body against my legs and nuzzled my fingers with her moist nose. I scratched the soft place behind her ears, hardly feeling what I did. Then I reached for my raincoat and umbrella and let her follow me outside. Through the slanting drizzle I made my way down the drive to the stable. It was foolish for me to go there, but I had to see with my own eyes that the car was gone.

Old Jo Kelly was hobbling about among his tools and flowerpots under the stairs. He tried to straighten his bent back when he saw me there. I came in out of the wet and stood beside him, watching his misshapen old hands sorting out dried bulbs and seed packets. His pipe was between his lips, and the tang of the tobacco he smoked lay strong on the damp air. I inhaled it with my own difficult breaths. The scent will stay with me always whenever I recall that afternoon and my own stress.

He said something by way of greeting, but I made no effort to catch the words from his lips.

"Jo," I said finally mustering my own as I leaned against the workbench, "where's the little car?"

"Mr. Harry come after it this morning early. I give him the keys myself."

"Mr. Harry?" I made him repeat the name to be certain. "What did he want it for?" I persisted.

"He didn't say, Miss Emily, and I didn't ask him. Maybe I'd ought to have, now you mention it. But he always makes free and easy with what he pleases round here."

"Yes," I answered out of the chillness that had taken me, "he does that."

I started for the stairs, but as I reached for the hidden

key on the beam I felt old Jo's hand on my arm. His eyes were searching mine anxiously.

"Miss Emily," he began, "you mustn't mind my asking —but those rooms up there—I've got them on my mind lately. You don't go up often, do you?"

"I've been there just once since you moved out," I told him. "That was—let me think—about two weeks ago. What makes you ask?"

The lines deepened on his face. I had not realized that there were so many. But then I had not looked at him closely for a long, long time—not really looked as I was looking now.

"Well," he admitted at last, "I haven't said nothing to the rest about it, but I've got a feeling—something's going on up there. Tell you the truth, Miss Emily, I'm afraid it's Jo. If I thought he was up to mischief there, stirring up more mill trouble with those cronies of his . . ."

He said more, but in trying to keep his lips steady I lost what followed. However, I had made out enough. Ironical, I thought, the two of us standing there in the made-over stable, afraid to put our fear into actual words.

"I don't believe Jo would set foot up there," I told him. "He's too honest to make use of a place that doesn't belong to him. Don't doubt young Jo: he wouldn't do that to you or us."

Old Jo relaxed a little, as if he were leaning on the comfort of my words. He knocked his cold pipe on a near-by beam and watched me take out the key.

"I hope you're right," he said. "I'll try to believe the best. But someone's been up there, and who'd know where to find the key except Jo?"

"Suppose I keep this." I slipped the one I held into my

pocket. "There's another one on that nail. You take that and say nothing for the present. We'll both feel easier, and it's probably nothing to worry about. We may be mistaken."

I left him and went out into the rain, feeling the hard, cold shape of the key in my pocket; feeling a still more hard, more cold inner weight. So I plodded through the wet, across the Square, trying to shake off my dread, trying to believe that there would be a reason for what I had seen. Some simple, easy explanation to make me limp with thankfulness—that was all I asked, yet more than I expected.

Merek Vance was in his office. I saw him hurry to the door as I crossed the porch. Before I knew it he had half pushed me into the old leather chair and was standing over me. There was more color on his cheeks than I had ever seen there, and his eyes searched and held mine before he spoke.

"I've been waiting for you," he began, pointing to the telegram which lay open on his desk. "Ever since this came I've been expecting you."

I made some foolish excuse about having had to go home first, and then I tried to collect myself to tell him about yesterday. But already it seemed remote and unreal. I might have been telling him of someone in a play that I had seen long ago from the last row of the gallery. I was glad for once that I could not hear my own voice, which must have sounded dull and lifeless. I cannot remember the words I summoned, though I tried to explain exactly what had happened without missing a detail that might prove helpful. He jotted down a note occasionally, and now and then questioned me about such things as length of sensation, the volume of sound and whether my ears had felt further stimulation from my train journey that day. He was all doctor as he listened and wrote and observed. Yet I was conscious, under his professional alertness, of pride and elation. Once I could have shared in that. It would have flowed from us to meet and flood the dingy room.

"Well"—he looked up from the paper and smiled at me—"we've done it! Of course we've got a long way to go yet; this is just the beginning. There'll have to be tests, much more thorough ones than I could give you here even if I had decent equipment. But we've proved the nerves are responding to the treatment. You feel sensation now where there was nothing before."

"Yes," I told him, and I wondered if my voice sounded as empty as I felt, "my ears are alive now. You've done that where all the other doctors failed. . . . Even when I wouldn't help you by believing you could, you did it."

"You always believed," he said, "you wouldn't have come here all these weeks if you hadn't. None of those arguments you put up ever fooled me. You talked yourself into being brave, like a scared child who makes up ghosts because he's afraid of real ones. I liked you better for that . . ."

I let my eyes leave his face for a moment before I spoke again. His eyes were too bright and searching.

"How long," I began, deliberately shifting the subject to a more practical angle, "how long do you think it will be before I can really hear?"

"I can't make predictions," he answered. "Every case is different in response, and it may be months before we can get those nerves to function without artificial stimulus.

You're younger than any of those we experimented on, and I told you in the beginning I'd never worked with deafness that came as the result of meningitis. I'll need more advice and a chance to discuss this with the group in Baltimore. I want to get down there as soon as I can leave —next week, maybe. In the meantime I'll increase the injections as much as I dare and arrange with Dr. Weeks to give them to you while I'm gone. But I'm not rushing this. You'll have to go on being patient awhile longer. It means too damned much to us both to take any chances now."

"All right," I said. "I haven't asked you to hurry things, have I?"

"No," he admitted, "not in words you haven't. But there's something you're not telling me. . . . That wire you sent—I've sat here with it in front of me ever since it came. You were happy when you sent it. What's come over you now?"

I shrugged and turned away. I couldn't trust myself to answer him. I would escape from the office before he forced me into admissions. As I reached the door I felt his hands on my shoulders. He wheeled me about and made me face him.

"Joyful and triumphant," he said. "Yes, you certainly look it."

I tried to twist away; but he kept his hold, and it was easier at last to look at him than to feel his eyes upon me.

"I just wrote that to fool the telegraph operator," I explained lamely. "I needed something that sounded like the season's greetings, and yet that you'd understand. It's not worth making such a fuss about."

"You were happy when you sent that wire," he persisted, "and you're anything but happy now. I think I have a right to know the reason."

"I've told you everything you have a right to know."

" 'Everything' is a pretty big word—a doctor learns not to use it as often as other people do." He was leaning forward, still holding me by the shoulders, and his face was so close to mine I could feel the warmth of his breath as he spoke. "Well, I suppose I can't make you tell me if you don't want to. It might just happen that I have my own theory about what's hurt you."

"Who said anything about being hurt—" I began, but he cut me short.

"Maybe you've found out what you were bound to sooner or later. That's it, isn't it?"

I faltered under the directness of his look. I tried to keep my eyes on the floor, but again he forced me to lift them.

"I'm going now," I said. "Please don't keep me. I'm rather tired and—"

But he went on as if he had not heard me. He spoke slowly so that I should not miss a syllable.

"I've been expecting this. The wonder to me is that you didn't find out before. It would have to be now though. I'm sorry for that part."

"I don't know what you're driving at." I lied desperately, but he must have felt me trembling.

"Oh, yes, you know, Emily Blair." His hands dropped from my shoulders. "We both know. I've known ever since that first time I came to your house, the night of your aunt's birthday."

Anger rose in me like a swift and fiery tide. The room

retreated in a haze, and only his face was clear in that moment. I struck at it with all the force I could summon. It was a shock to feel the hardness of his cheekbone taking the blow. We both started back and stood staring numbly at each other. The blood tingled in my hand and color came sharp and red on the cheek that I had struck.

Somehow I was free of the place and walking across the Square with rain and tears mingling on my face. Bridget nudged at my heels in a worried way, and my hands were still shaking. It came over me then what I had done. Never since I was old enough to remember had I reached out to strike someone. And I had committed this physical violence against Merek Vance to whom I should have been more grateful than to anyone in the world. I set my teeth and turned to recross the Square.

The office door was open, and he had gone back to his desk. I saw that the folder containing the record of my case was open before him and he was already adding more notes to it. He looked up and smiled as I stood there in the door. But one cheek was still undeniably redder than the other. I went straight to the desk before he had a chance to move.

"I'm sorry," I said. "I came back to tell you so. I never struck anyone before. I don't know what possessed me."

He laid down his pen and closed the folder.

"That's all right," he said. "I didn't think you had it in you to forget the proprieties so completely. It's a very healthy sign. That's that, and let's forget it."

"I can't forget that easily. It makes me afraid of myself. . . . But when you said what you did—it came over me in a rush. You know too much about me. You've always known too much, and I hated you for it."

He gave the shrug that I had come to know so well.

"It's not that I know too much. It's that you insisted on knowing so little."

I felt myself flushing under the impact of his words. All my hard, frantic love for Harry was laid bare suddenly. I saw it in that moment for the pitiful, hopeless thing it had been. I had made a crutch of that love that had once been a free and ardent urge between us. My need had betrayed me into making a fool of myself. Bitterness overwhelmed me again, shutting out the momentary flash of truth that had been revealed. Before I could speak Merek Vance had come from the desk to my side.

"Don't try to think yet," he told me. "You've had a shock, two in twenty-four hours. You must give yourself time. No one can tell you what to do. I'd be the last to try, and this—this other thing is out of my line. But I'll see you through as much as anyone can."

"Thank you," I said. "We seem to have forgotten what I came for. You haven't given me the injection."

He smiled, and the tension was broken by familiar routine.

"I'd like to go a little farther before we do any talking," he said when he was through. "I must have a chance to discuss it with some of the rest at the hospital, and then we'll put you through more tests. I know it's asking a lot of you to wait."

"I'll wait," I promised. "At least I won't say anything without giving you warning. When we made that bargain we didn't mention a time limit. I was a lot more certain of myself then: I wouldn't be so ready to make bargains now."

A great weariness overcame me, and I turned without

a word of goodbye and started for the door. But before I reached it his arms were about me. I felt the hard muscles under the cloth of his coat, and I was too tired and shaken to protest. I was crying convulsively against him, my tears shutting out his face so that whatever he may have said I knew nothing of it. I knew only the comfort of his strength, and the surprise of his kiss, strong and compelling on my lips.

And then I was leaning against the door frame and his face was growing clear again. He must have put his handkerchief into my hands, for I was wiping my eyes with it and drawing longer breaths. He no longer held me except with his eyes. His lips were moving, and at last I could follow their motions.

"I'm not sorry," he was saying, "not any more than you were when you struck me. So now we're even."

CHAPTER TWENTY-SIX

No HARDY PERENNIAL has the enduring quality of hope. Cut it to the roots, stamp it underfoot, let frost and fire work their will, and still some valiant shoot will push, to grow again on such scanty fare as it can find. Only time and the cruel quicklime of fact can destroy that stubborn urgency.

So it was with me in the days that followed. Even as I recrossed the wet and leafless Square I let hope soften my suspicions. I struggled against my doubts, turning over a dozen possible explanations for that meeting at Springwood station, discarding them and starting all over again as a lost traveler will make frantic dashes in every direction, only to double back on his own tracks and be no better off for his effort. I could not face what I feared. I must make excuses and believe those fears would all be explained.

Vance had had no right to say what he had said. He had had no right to kiss me in that sudden disquieting way. I could still feel the warmth and pressure of his lips on mine as I hurried home through the wet. I tried to shake off the memory. Yet, there was comfort in it and a lingering glow. I had not been as angry as I should have been, I told myself. But then, he had not been angry at the blow I had struck him. Perhaps, as he had said, that made us even. When you have reason to doubt the man you love another man's kiss may seem a poor substitute, but it can bolster up a woman's pride. We may want only the love that is denied; but to know that we continue to be desirable is a prop to which we cling, and cling we must to whatever our hearts can lay hold on.

A taxi was moving out of the driveway as I came in sight of the house, and I saw Janice's coat and the new green hat flung down carelessly in the hall. Her door was open as I passed by to go to my room. She stood at the bureau, brushing her hair, and under the hanging light it stood out from her face like a bright fan. In spite of all that I was feeling I had to notice that. She turned when she saw me in the mirror and waved the brush by way of greeting.

"When did you get back?" I asked, pausing in the doorway.

"Just now," she said, and turned back to the mirror again.

"On the train?" I persisted. "I thought there wasn't one at this hour."

She laid down the brush with a gesture of impatience, and even though I strained to catch the motion of her lips I could not make out what she was saying.

"I beg your pardon," I said, "I didn't quite—"

This time she wheeled about sharply and came nearer.

"I said"—she spoke with exaggerated distinctness to make me realize the trouble I was causing her—"I said the three-fifty-seven was an hour late. Christmas seems to have thrown them all off schedule."

"I'm just back from Boston myself," I told her, "I went up yesterday to shop, and I came back on the ten-forty-five this morning."

I kept my eyes fixed on her face, and it seemed to me that her lips tightened and the pupils of her eyes grew wider. But she gave no other sign of interest.

"Too bad I didn't know," she said, shaking the hair from her face with apparent unconcern. "We could have come back together."

"Yes," I went on, "if we'd known we might have had the car sent to meet us somewhere along the way—at Springwood station. A lot of people were being met there."

She turned abruptly and went back to the bureau. She took care that I should not see her face, but when she lifted the brush again I saw her knuckles stand out white and sharp.

"You know"—my throat was dry, and I braced myself against the door frame, grateful for the hardness of the wood at my back—"there was someone who looked like you on the train this morning. You must have a double, Janice."

I tried to laugh, casually, but I doubt if I managed to sound convincing. She shrugged and went on brushing her hair. I did not wait for an answer, though I was certain my words had made her uneasy.

Once I had closed the door of my own room I felt suddenly limp and shaken. But I was determined to keep my doubts in check until I had given Harry a chance to explain. I wasn't naturally suspicious. I hated people who were always imagining that others were scheming and plotting behind their backs. I remembered reading somewhere that deafness did that to its victims. Perhaps this had crept upon me without my knowing; perhaps I was no exception to the rule. Love only intensified bitterness and doubt as it had the power to magnify happiness. I stood there in my wet coat and hat and pressed my hands together, palm to palm, the way I used to when I said my prayers. I found myself praying again, not so much out of belief as out of my need.

"O God," I prayed, "don't let this happen. Please let me be wrong in what I think. Please make it right somehow, and don't let me lose Harry."

I remember just how I stood there, making that frantic petition over and over in the dim familiarity of my room. Looking back to it now, I neither smile nor sigh. It seems as futile to me as an earlier prayer I made asking God to change the course of the Mississippi River because I had been wrong in answering a geography question back in third grade. There are things beyond the power of prayer to change. I know that now. I have learned that we can pray for ourselves alone. Whatever God we believe in, whatever name He goes by, we cannot ask that things or people be changed to suit our needs. We may ask only to have strength to do our best, no matter how often we fall short of that.

I switched on the light at last and began to take off my wet things. As I did so I caught sight of myself in the mirror and was startled at my own reflection. Rain and tears and all the varying emotions of the last twenty-four hours had changed me. I saw myself in that moment as I might look in ten, in fifteen years, as Aunt Em had appeared to me in my childhood. The resemblance between us was more marked than ever, and I faltered before it. Did Harry Collins see me like that and falter, too, before a future he had given his word to share?

I won't look middle-aged yet, I vowed as I stared into the glass. I'm young still; whether I feel young or not, I mean to look it.

So I went to the closet and took out the blue crepe dress that deepened the color of my eyes. I brushed my hair fiercely till it took on luster again. I parted it smoothly and let it wave back to a soft roll at the nape of my neck. Harry had always praised my pallor. He never encouraged me to use rouge, but that night I added a faint color to my cheeks and made my lips more full and red before I went downstairs.

"Why, Emily," Aunt Em greeted me, "you certainly put through your shopping quickly. How well you look, dear! The trip must have done you good."

I smiled and breathed more easily. I was glad that I had deceived her. It gave me more confidence, and I began hurriedly delivering messages from Cousin Eunice. We sat there by the fire, waiting for Uncle Wallace's return and Maggie's summons to dinner. I took up a piece of knitting I had begun, a child's sweater for Angeletta's little girl. The yarn was Christmas red in the lamplight, and the stitches formed with mechanical precision, like little marching soldiers under my fingers.

Uncle Wallace was in a surprisingly bad humor that night. He was growing more worried about the mill reopening and recent cancellations of orders. He had asked the banks for an extension of time, and this had been refused. He would have to make a hurried trip the next day to New York, where a group of textile manufacturers were meeting.

"Where's Harry?" he demanded across the dinner table. "A fine day he chose to be away—just when I needed him."

I could feel my heart set up a sudden hammering. I looked at Janice, but her eyes were on her plate. I laid down my knife and fork carefully so that my fingers would not betray me by shaking.

"The girls are just back from Boston," Aunt Em was explaining from her end of the table; "they wouldn't know."

"He took the little car," I spoke up then. "It was gone when I came back and Old Jo told me Harry had been by for it."

Janice worried a bit of bread into crumbs but gave no other sign.

"Well," Uncle Wallace went on, "he'll be bringing it back soon, I hope. I left a message with his landlady and the Parkers to have him come and see me when he turns up. I have to go over some important letters with him to-night."

We were having our coffee by the living-room fire when Harry walked in. I was the last to see him because my back was to the door. He was wearing his old tweeds and the sweater I had knitted for him long ago, the one with tawny flecks that matched his freckles and the lights in his eyes. His hair curled from the dampness, and the room seemed suddenly alive and full of his presence. Janice set down her cup as he came in and went over to the piano. I saw her shuffling through music sheets in apparent preoccupation.

He came over and stood behind my chair. His hands were warm on my shoulders, and his lips brushed the back of my neck, lightly, swiftly, just behind my ears. I twisted my head and tried to smile up at him in easy greeting. He was speaking above me to Uncle Wallace, and I could not follow the motions of his lips. Aunt Em poured him a cup of coffee, and he came round to sit on the sofa and drink it.

I must put all my mind on what he says, I told myself. I can't afford to miss a word, but I mustn't seem too interested. I must be as natural as I can be.

"I'm sorry, sir," he was answering some question from Uncle Wallace, "I thought they'd tell you I drove over to Biddeford to see Hawkins about those orders. Things were so quiet this week it seemed a good time to go."

Biddeford, I thought; that's a hundred miles in the opposite direction from Springwood. It doesn't make sense.

Uncle Wallace was speaking, but I dared not take my eyes from Harry's face. He sat listening, a trifle uneasily, I thought, for he reached absent-mindedly to add sugar to his cup though he had already dropped in two lumps.

"Of course, if I'd known you were leaving for New York tomorrow I wouldn't have gone," Harry went on. "I borrowed the little car. I knew you wouldn't mind with the girls both away. Good thing I did, too; the carburetor was acting up, and Janice had let the oil get low. I had it checked over so the day wasn't altogether wasted."

"Where did you have it fixed?" I found myself asking. "In Biddeford?"

Harry looked surprised at my interest. Neither he nor the others seemed to remember that the little car had originally been mine.

"Oh, some garage along the way. I can't remember just where. But it's set now for another thousand miles."

Janice came over from the piano and poured herself another cup of coffee. Her back was towards me, yet I felt, rather than saw, that she was trying to convey something to him without resorting to words. His eyes were upon her over the rim of his cup. I was aware suddenly of a current of communication between them, a tenseness that each was trying to keep in check. My hands went cold in my lap as I watched them. I knew then for certain what I had fought against believing since morning. I knew— because love is plain to those who have ever known it.

How long? I wondered with an inner numbness spreading over me. How long has it been since I—since he—since they . . .

But even in my own mind I could not finish the question.

A hand was on my arm. Aunt Em was trying to attract my attention. I forced myself to follow the motion of her lips.

"Oh, yes, Aunt Em!" I started up. "I have the things you wanted. I'll bring them down."

When I returned Harry had gone into the study with Uncle Wallace, and Janice was at the piano again. I felt the vibration of music in the room and though no tune emerged I heard for the third time a distinct sound in my ears. It was clearer than before, and I made a mental note to tell Dr. Vance on my next visit.

"Piano," I would tell him to write in his notes. "Definite response, and more sustained sensation."

I sorted out the various packages for Aunt Em and gave her the sales slips methodically.

"I'm sorry I couldn't find a better match for blanket binding," I explained, "but this was the nearest shade. I bought an extra yard just in case you ran short. If you'll excuse me, Aunt Em, I think I'll go to bed now. I won't wait till Harry's through talking business. Tell him I have a headache from shopping and trains. I'll be all right tomorrow."

I did not wait for her answer. She would only offer aspirin and sympathy, and I had no need of either. Upstairs I slipped out of my dress into my outdoor things and down the back stairs. The flashlight I felt for was in its place on the entry shelf. I followed the little circle of light it made on the steps and graveled drive.

The rain was over; the moon struggling to clear a path among blowing clouds, an old moon toiling through space. I watched it above me and thought that it had never seemed so far, so impersonal on its timeless course.

It was dark in the old stable, but my flashlight showed me the two cars in their places. The small one was mud-splashed, the windshield still misty except for the half-circle the wiper had kept clear. I slid into the empty seat, letting the beam of light search into every corner. The dashboard pocket held the usual collection of old maps, gloves, matches, and sun glasses. I closed it wearily, hardly knowing what I had expected to find. Then, as I turned to leave, the light showed a bit of cardboard wedged between the door and running board. It proved to be a parking ticket, damp and torn, but with printing still distinguishable. "Springwood Gar—" I made out, and a penciled number below.

So I had not been mistaken! I stuffed the telltale fragment into my pocket and sank back on the seat. Up to that moment I had believed that I might be wrong. Now that there could be no more doubt I grew numb and hollow. Life died out of me then. I let the torch grow dark in my hands. I could not think. I could not feel. I just sat there as still as some inanimate fixture of the car.

Then I was outside once more, my hands fumbling with the fastenings of the door. A shower of icy drops from a wet low-hanging branch shocked me as they drenched my face. I stopped short on the graveled path and stood staring up at the house with its lighted windows yellow in the darkness. There were the kitchen panes, the broad bow windows of the living room, and the two set on either side of Uncle Wallace's desk in the study. Above it my own were bright, and Janice's also lit. I saw others grow bright and knew that Maggie must be making her evening rounds, turning down bed covers. I could smell the tang of woodsmoke from the chimney. It came strong and fragrant to meet me, and I guessed that someone had just thrown a fresh log on the living-room fire. An old Windsor chair showed its sturdy shape in silhouette against the hall window. It had stood in that exact spot ever since I could remember, and I marked it as one might mark a familiar beacon.

Yes, I thought, everything is in its place. How ordered and substantial the house and its furnishings appear to someone looking in from the outside as I am looking now! A stranger might even think that the people in those rooms moved and acted according to the same well ordered pattern of living.

I sighed and shivered, knowing that I myself had been deceived into thinking so until a few hours ago. Well, I knew how wrong I had been. For Janice and Harry and me at least, the pattern had shifted precariously. I would open the back door and go up the stairs. I would return to those rooms and continue to put on the accustomed habits of nights and days. They must not know that I knew—not yet.

CHAPTER TWENTY-SEVEN

THE HOLIDAYS STRETCHED before me in festive mockery. They would have been difficult enough that year with the mill trouble heavy over us all. I might have been equal to that, but to put a false front on my own despair took all the strength I could muster. Christmas, like spring water, has its source in the heart, and when the heart is frozen or dried up nothing can flow out in a flood of joyous response. Yet one must not betray traditions of good will and joy to the world, no matter how little one may share them.

I don't know how successful a performance I gave. I only know that I ached dully from the effort I was making. My lips stayed set in a determined smile. I seemed to be carrying myself about, like the stiff wooden figures that ventriloquists manipulate into semblance of life and animation, speaking words for them as they jerk the painted jaws and head. So I went through the days with the cards to be sent and received, with presents leaving and arriving bright in seals and labels that read, "Merry Christmas," "Please do not open till December 25th."

I can recall the very pattern of the brightly printed papers we used for our gifts that year. I can see the stars and bells, the sleigh and reindeer and red-coated figures of the designs, the snow sprinkled over the surface in large conventional dots. Janice never could wrap presents without cutting the paper too short or wrinkling it at the corners, and Aunt Em had little knack with her hands and less patience with stickers and seals. From the time I had been old enough to be trusted with scissors and ribbon, the task had fallen to me. I had taken pride in my skill, in the neat way I could fold and fit objects to paper with the least possible waste of materials. So, though I could summon no feeling for these pre-holiday rites, my hands still reached mechanically to perform them. Package after package, box after box took on perennial gayety under my fingers; little silver bells and miniature candles and holly sprigs nestled into tinsel and ribbon as I worked at the long table in the back entry.

The Christmas tree kept me company, waiting to be set up according to custom in the bay window on the afternoon of the 24th. It was cooler out there in the entry, and fewer needles would fall than in the heated rooms. I had to endure the bitter spiciness it shed as I worked. Sometimes if my skirt brushed a branch in passing the fragrance engulfed me, and I would lay down the scissors and ribbons because the memory of other Christmases would stir in spite of all I could do to put them from me. Happiness remembered in pain is like that, I think: we magnify it till it tricks us like a desert mirage.

So the waiting tree became a symbol of my own heart. I felt that year as if I were trimming an inner, secret tree that no one saw, working with feverish zeal to hide the bare, stark branches with a load of deceptive tinsel.

The days might have been less difficult if Merek Vance had not gone away from Blairstown. Ostensibly he left to spend the holidays with his sister in New York, but Dr. Weeks and I both knew the reason for his trip—consultations with medical associates there and in Baltimore. His brief-case bulged with pages of notes on my case history, exhaustive comments, and day-to-day observations on the treatments and my reactions to them. I was amazed and a little awed when he showed me the minute details he had so painstakingly charted. I stared at the closely written pages, and it seemed that they must contain the records of a lifetime. Yet it was just short of three months since my first visit to his office.

"Yes," I found myself agreeing to his plans, "I will go on to Baltimore or New York, or wherever you arrange for the further tests and examinations; but I'm glad there's no need of that just yet."

That last visit was unsatisfactory, too full of exhaustive details and instructions. We met in Dr. Weeks' office, and I missed the familiar intimacy of the smaller one. Dr. Weeks' presence also made me self-conscious. He had known, of course, about the experiment, but he had had no part in it before. His close friendship with our family kept me from being entirely at my ease. He would continue the treatments during Vance's absence, and I dreaded that. I feared that I might in some way betray what was on my mind and heart. With Merek Vance it was different. I had never been able to hide anything from him, yet I knew any admission I might make was in safe keeping. He cared nothing for the Blairs and their family relationships. I think I had been aware of this from our first meeting and it had lent a kind of confidence to our friendship. Yes, I had to admit that I should miss him, that I had come to depend on him more than I realized till then.

There was so much technical discussion between the two doctors that I gave up trying to follow it. I let them talk and test and work over me as if I were a lay figure on which they experimented. All the time I sat there in bleak misery, going over the inescapable fact that I must meet and face.

"Janice loves Harry. Harry loves Janice." Those three words beat on and on in my brain. They had the rhythm of childish ones we used to chalk on sidewalks in grade-school days: So-and-so loves So-and-so, with a crudely drawn heart encircling the names to give greater emphasis. But now it was real, not make-believe, love to tease a playmate. In the adult world to which I suddenly realized we all belonged, I supposed a triangle would be substituted for the outline of a heart. Well, after all, what was a triangle but a heart with the grace taken out of it?

I opened my eyes, hardly realizing that I had closed them. Merek Vance was touching my arm, and his eyes were kind and full of concern.

"You're tired," he was saying, "we've kept you at it too long. But there were so many directions. Dr. Weeks wants to be sure about everything."

"Yes, you'll be in my hands, Emily." The older man smiled and wiped his spectacles. "Can you put up with me for a couple of weeks?" I nodded and patted his hand. "We don't want any setbacks, you and I," he was going on. "We've got a lot to live up to now. . . . I still can't quite credit the facts, and when I think what your cure is going to mean to the profession—well, it's all I can do not to shout from the housetop."

"You'd better not let him," Vance put in quickly. "We're agreed on keeping still awhile longer, aren't we?"

I nodded listlessly.

"All right, I've kept medical secrets before, and I can now," Dr. Weeks promised. "But I must say I don't see how you can do it, Emily. Think what a Christmas it would make for your aunt and for Harry. . . . You young people have a good deal more restraint than I gave you credit for."

Vance followed me out to the steps, and we both stood there without speaking. It was an awkward interval because we were thinking back to what had happened on our last meeting. I had struck him, and he had kissed me. In those seconds when we had yielded to our impulses we had been completely ourselves as we had never been before, as perhaps we should never be again. Neither of us put out a hand. I think now that we were too close in that moment for such a conventional exchange of courtesies.

"Goodbye," I said at last. "I guess I ought to try and say 'Thank you'; but that seems foolish and stupid, and I've been foolish and stupid enough already."

"Oh, we'll just say you're human in spite of being a Blairstown Blair and you haven't one speck of complacency about you. . . . That's more than I can say for myself and a lot of other people."

I flushed under his praise, tried to start down the steps, and then came back.

"Goodbye," I said, and added grimly, "I'm glad you didn't wish me a merry Christmas."

"Why should I? That's one thing you're almost certain

not to have. But I hope you won't mind my thinking of you on the day, because if you ask me not to I might have to break my word."

I did not answer, and he did not seem to expect me to.

"You'll surely be back the first week in January?" I said, and he nodded his assurance. "But that's next year," I reminded him as I turned to go.

"If you count by the calendars, yes; but I never do it that way."

"How do you count time then?"

"By accomplishment, I guess, or by growth; that makes it much easier to reckon things. . . . According to that, you and I have known each other more years than we're old."

I knew he was standing there watching me go down the path between the barberry bushes. I knew he wanted me to look back, but I felt it would be easier to go without that. Then his hand was on my arm. I stopped reluctantly because I hated goodbyes, and because already I felt abandoned by the one person from whom I had nothing to hide. I tried to keep my eyes from his. I knew mine would betray me, no matter what contradictory words I might summon. As I turned I saw that he held something out to me. It was the blue box that had belonged to his mother, the one I had reached for in those first difficult visits. He said nothing as he laid it in my hands.

"Oh, no!" I shook my head in vehement protest. "You mustn't do that. . . . You said it was your one family heirloom. I couldn't take it, not after what you told me—"

But he, too, shook his head.

"You can't turn down a Christmas present," he told me. "I want you to have it. Ever since the first time I saw it in your hands I knew it belonged there. A man may have made it; but that needle and thread, and that motto, are for a woman."

I stood there not knowing how to answer him, and so he went on again, taking my silence for disapproval that I did not feel.

"Call it a present from my mother if you want to. She'd have liked you to have it. At least she would, once she'd come to know you."

Tears sprang to my eyes, so that I could not see his face. One splashed on the gay roses, and another on the hearts before I could look up again and follow what he was saying.

"I'm not a sentimentalist about my mother," he was going on. "She wasn't a saint, and I knew it. She was stubborn and proud like you. She went through hell, too—not your kind exactly. . . . Love's simpler over on that side of the river, and all mixed up with hunger and drudgery and physical pain. But hell's in the same latitude, no matter how we get there. She'd have known what to say to you now, the way I can't. That's why I want you to have this— to see you through the new year."

Still I stood there, holding his gift, too worn and miserable to speak.

"Thank you," I managed to tell him at last, and I spoke primly in words that came back from formulas of my childhood: "It's just what I needed."

He couldn't help smiling at that, and I smiled too because I must have sounded so politely incongruous.

CHAPTER TWENTY-EIGHT

I HAD WRITTEN a note to young Jo Kelly asking him to drive out to Angeletta's place with presents for the children. I had no license to drive the car, so I could not go alone; and besides I felt the need of Jo's company. He met me as I had asked him to at the foot of the garden, and we set off with boxes and packages piled about us. He sat with a doll carriage on his knees and a carton of groceries at his feet. Bridget had squirmed into the space between us and tucked her head into the crook of his arm. We had ordered her to go back to the house, but finally her persistence won us over.

It always comforted me to feel the wheel under my hands and the reassuring vibration of the engine. It gave me back a sense of lost confidence to be driving the car again over the familiar roads leading out of town. We left early in the afternoon, but already the light seemed thin and waning. Tomorrow would be the winter solstice, and one felt the reluctance of the sun to stay even for its shortest span. Rains had washed what remained of snow into irregular patches on fields and pastures. There was a clearness to the outlines of bare trees and bushes as if their twigs had been whittled into sharp relief by wind and frost. In hollows by frozen brooks and ponds the willows showed a purplish tinge at their tips and the far hills were humped in a long procession of darker purple against the sky. The air felt keen, not windy or damp with hint of coming snow, but still and cold, so that the smoke from chimneys mounted visibly in dark smudges. Few people were out. We had the roads practically to ourselves once we were clear of town, except for an occasional truck or a half-chilled rabbit that scuttled across our way.

Neither Jo nor I made any attempt at talk. I had to keep my eyes on the road, and he seemed glad to relax in the seat beside me with the presents and Bridget his only concerns. He had looked tired when we met, and I noticed that his old Mackinaw was still doing duty instead of the overcoat he should have worn in such bleak weather. His hands were bare, and I was glad he kept one on Bridget's warm fur. Still, there was something strong and alive about him, a driving force that seemed charged by an inner dynamo. One sees the same spirit in birds and small animals that defy winter and its rigors. One cannot pity them, for they give the illusion of having chosen their own difficult way; of preferring scanty fare and cold to comfort and easy existence.

Yes, I thought as we drove on, Jo has always been like that, going his own way, believing what he had to believe no matter how unpopular it's made him. He'll never fit into any pattern for long; but wherever he goes people take a sort of answering spark from him, the way animals do. He might have been like St. Francis in another period.

The Gallo kitchen was warm and cluttered and full of

people. Garlic and strong cheese mingled with the scent of evergreen from a small tree that stood brave in popcorn and fringed-paper garlands. I was glad that I had brought some bells and brightly wrapped candies to add to its decorations. The shy little girl with the enormous eyes had not forgotten me, and Angeletta beamed and made us welcome, shifting the baby to her other arm as she cleared two chairs by the big table. Her husband and father-in-law were out in the barn. Presently Jo went out to join them while Angeletta and the old woman helped sort and put away the things I had brought. The little girl played with the new carriage, and the boy whose operation I had witnessed sat in a wooden packing box and watched us with bright, squirrel-like eyes. His bandages were off, but he still had the peaked, bluish look of a convalescent.

"He's doing good," Angeletta assured me, "but he can't hear right yet—" She stopped short and flushed, fearing that she had been treading on dangerous ground.

"He will though before long," I told her. "Dr. Vance says he's made a remarkable recovery. I knitted him a cap that he can pull down over his ears when he's able to go out. You're sure to have a happy Christmas, Angeletta, when you look at him and think what might have been."

"Yes," she nodded, and reached out with her free hand to touch his round, dark head. "Yes, times are pretty bad, but I guess they could be a lot worse. You shouldn't have brought all those things, but I won't say we can't use them. It was real good of you to come, and I'm glad you brought Jo Kelly. Maybe he can make my Peter feel better. We had to sell the cow last week and we all felt awful bad."

I could think of nothing comforting to say in the face of such elemental loss.

"Thank God I can nurse the baby," she went on. "Peter talked to the union about us, and they say they'll give us some canned milk for the kids. It'll help out, but it don't taste the same; and we sure miss Bossy."

The old woman lighted the oil lamp over the sink and busied herself with the pots on the stove while I talked to Angeletta over the little girl who had climbed on my lap again.

"Angie," I said, "I know this is going to be a bad winter for you all, but it's worse for those in town. At least you don't have to go out with the children and pick up bits of coal from the tracks. You've got some wood cut, and some potatoes and winter vegetables in the cellar. That's more than they can count on."

"I know," she nodded. "If it wasn't for Peter's folks I don't know where we'd be. Do you think"—she leaned forward in her chair, and her eyes were large and anxious in her gaunt face—"do you think the mills will reopen and Peter can get on the old shift again?"

I faltered under the question, knowing what my answer must be.

"You'll have to ask Jo Kelly," I hedged. "He knows more than I do. The mills are going to reopen after New Year's, but I'm afraid there's bound to be even more trouble then. The men on strike won't be taken back on the terms they want, and you know what that may mean, Angeletta?"

"If the company puts scabs in, there sure will be worse trouble." Her eyes widened and rolled expressively. "But they wouldn't do that, would they? They just want to scare the men into making terms."

I sighed and hesitated as I straightened the ribbon on the child's brown hair.

"I'm afraid it's more than talk," I said. "You know there'll be plenty ready to go back on any terms. Too many families are feeling the pinch now."

"I'd ought to know that!" Her lips tightened grimly as she spoke. "That's where they've got us, and it's where they want to keep us. I don't care what you or anyone else says."

There it was, I thought, the word "they" that we all took refuge in. It would always crop up to foster hate and misunderstanding on both sides. Already I could feel Angeletta withdrawing from me, distrustful and wary.

"You know," I reminded her, "my mother worked as a mill hand when she was young. I never forget that."

"That's all right to say, but you never had to stand up eight hours tending the bobbins or looms. Your folks own Peace-Pipe; I guess you don't forget that either."

"No," I admitted, "I don't. It makes a difference—that's the trouble with me: I have to see both sides and so I just seem to be caught between."

She shifted the baby to her other arm before she went on.

"It's easier to see two sides if you're not worrying about what you'll make your next meal of or if your man can weather another week of it."

"I know that—at least I'm beginning to know a little better. Don't be too hard on me, Angeletta: it's not going to be exactly a merry Christmas for us either. I needed to come and see you and the children. It can't hurt any of us to let them have fun with the things I brought. I liked knitting the sweater and the cap and finding the toys. You don't mind their having them from me?"

It was strange to be pleading my cause like that, battering against the wall of her pride and bitterness. But Angeletta and I had always liked each other, and the children's eyes turning to the packages helped more than any words of mine. The men came in presently, their breath frosty in the warm room. I was glad of their return, and we all drank a glass of homemade wine that the old man brought out from some mysterious place of hiding. I choked a little over mine, but it warmed me for the trip back in the winter twilight.

I let Jo take the wheel for the drive home. It had turned colder, and I was grateful for Bridget's warmth beside me. The car seemed empty without the oddly shaped parcels that had crowded it on our way out. I dreaded returning to the big house and the part I must play there. Suspicion was a hateful thing to me, and I resented the need to be furtive and watchful of each move that Janice or Harry might make. Out there in the Gallo kitchen I had been able to forget for a little. At least, if I had not exactly forgotten, the dull ache and despair had retreated while I talked and entered into the problems of their existence. Now the pain sharpened once more as I turned towards Blairstown. Another family dinner must be faced, another evening must be endured. If Harry came I would be trying to appear natural and at ease. Yet all the time I would be watching for some betrayal if he glanced towards Janice or if she brushed his hand in passing. If he did not appear, if Janice were away or left the house with some flimsy excuse, I must torture myself with fears that might or might not be well founded. I sighed and shrank deeper into my coat as

I watched the minute hand of the lighted clock on the dashboard move on towards half past five. It would have been a comfort to talk to Jo Kelly there beside me. I felt a great need of that, and though he knew so little really of my life, and I of his, yet the pull of the old associations always drew us together in spite of our differing worlds.

"Jo," I spoke as I saw the brightly lighted windows of the roadside diner just ahead. "How about stopping here for a cup of coffee?"

He swung the car in and parked it obediently near by. A loaded truck had stopped too. We could see two men seated at the counter, but otherwise the place was deserted. I saw young Jo notice that before he followed me in. We took the corner table, where Merek Vance and I had sat at a far later hour.

"I shouldn't have asked you to come in here with me," I said after my first sip of coffee. "I'm not exactly the company you want to be seen with nowadays, am I?"

He smiled across the table, but he did not deny the charge. It was a new sensation to feel that I must apologize for my presence; to feel that there were those who would consider me an undesirable companion.

"I guess your friends don't think very highly of me, Jo," I went on, "and I wouldn't want to get you into trouble."

"I'm used to taking care of myself," he answered shortly.

"But you don't belong just to yourself, at least not any more," I pointed out. "You seem to stand for a lot of people. You'd have some explaining to do if any of your union friends happened to walk in here now and saw us sitting like this?"

"Maybe," he admitted, and this time he did not smile.

"Jo"—I set down my half-empty cup and reached for a cigarette—"where's it going to end? One side or the other has got to give in, and it won't be the Peace-Pipe Directors. I know that much."

The tired lines of his face that had relaxed a little over the coffee and cigarettes, sharpened again as he looked up.

No one could look into young Jo Kelly's eyes without trusting him, I thought, while I waited for his answer.

"It all depends on how many of us can hold out," he told me, "and for how long."

"But, Jo, even if your union and their sympathizers help out with funds there are months of winter ahead for all those families like the Gallos. You saw what I saw over there this afternoon, and they're luckier than most. . . . How can you expect them to hold out on nothing?"

"That's what we're up against," he said. He rose then and went over to a big machine that dealt out popular music. I saw him put in some coins, and I felt the place vibrate to sound before he returned to the table. My ears were already so much more sensitive that I could make out the steady blaring of jazz though I could not yet recognize tunes as I listened. Mentally I made a note to tell Merek Vance of this and my response to the machine.

"Thought our voices might carry over to the counter," Jo explained when he returned to his place. "Can't run the chance of any one thinking I talk out of turn. The noise won't bother you any, and I can hear you through it. Go ahead."

"It's you I'm asking, Jo." He shrugged wearily and shook his head. "Well," I went on, "at least tell me this:

there won't be violence when the mill reopens. Your pickets won't start that kind of trouble, will they?"

Again his face seemed to shrink into old, anxious lines, and only his eyes stayed young and eager.

"Not if I can stop it," he told me at last. "I've never believed that force and fists won anything in the long run. I'm doing all I can to keep this strike a clean one. They listen to me now, but I can't guarantee they will later—"

A spasm of coughing shook him, and I missed the rest of his words.

"You mean," I asked, "that they may get out of hand when Peace-Pipe reopens?"

He nodded.

"It'll take them one way or the other then. Plenty will turn scab and go back: half a loaf's better than nothing, they figure. I have a hunch Peter Gallo will go that way. Those that stick to their guns—well, you can't blame them for pulling the trigger, can you?"

I shook my head. Tears rose to my eyes because I felt suddenly very tired and baffled.

"I don't blame anybody for anything," I faltered across the white-topped table. "I'm very unhappy, Jo. No," I hurried on to forestall the question he might be going to ask. "No, I can't tell you why. It's nothing you could do anything about. But somehow when you're unhappy you draw other people's unhappinesses and troubles to you. I suppose it's like reaching out to like, because it used to be the other way round when I was happy. Do you know what I mean?"

I don't know what he may have answered. My eyes were too wet to see his face except as a blur. But I felt the quick response of his hand on mine, and I was grateful for that pressure. It had helped to say even so little to him. Sometimes a sudden rush of tears sharpens the sight as a quick shower clears the air of impurities. I looked straight into Jo Kelly's eyes and saw my own face mirrored in the shining darkness of those pupils. I wondered if he were seeing his face in mine, and if he felt reassured as I did by the reflection. When I forget Jo Kelly's eyes giving me back myself, I shall be past remembering anything that matters.

We talked on there under the hard, glaring lights of the roadside diner. It was always easy for me to follow him, perhaps because we had grown up together and I knew his way of speech so well. Then, too, he always listened intently and gave himself completely to the other person. I think that was one reason why people turned to him as they did. I wish I could recall word for word all that he told me. At the time I seemed to understand the issues and problems that had bewildered me for so long. He made me see Peace-Pipe strike in simple terms, not in a confusing jumble of technical phrases and abbreviations that stood for this labor organization or that. But now only a few of his words return to me. They stir in my consciousness all these months afterward, like last year's leaves from some tree we shall never see putting out new ones in the spring.

"Men with wives and kids can't be expected to think as far ahead as someone like me," I remember he said. "To-day matters more than any tomorrow to them. It's bound to be that way when you've got a family to do for. That's why it's up to me to do more than the rest about holding on and speaking up. You're not the first to ask about the union letting us down, maybe even selling us out. It's happened before, and it might again. Still, I figure what's right stays right, no matter how many knocks it gets."

"But that's the hard part," I broke in, "to feel sure you know what's right! I get pulled in so many directions. I keep remembering what Maggie used to tell us when we were little: 'There's not the thickness of a penny between good and evil!'"

We both smiled at that, remembering the times she had quoted it to us when we used to raise childish arguments if she caught us red-handed in some misdemeanor. It seemed years since Jo and I had felt as close as we did that afternoon. It comforts me now to remember that it was so. If we had guessed all that lay ahead I think we couldn't have made better use of that half-hour together. The men left the counter and went out to their truck. We watched its tail lights dwindle to red specks in the darkness and then go out like sparks. One or two other customers came in, but they stayed at the counter; and after quick glances at them Jo relaxed and we could go on talking.

"Whatever happens"—his words come back to me now with a queer twinge of pain—"we've made a dent that may count next time. It takes a lot of hammering to break through any wall or any system."

"If the men only didn't hate us so!" I told him. "At least that's what Uncle Wallace says. And then he says they'll come round and want to be friendly. . . . Why do they have to be so inconsistent?"

"That's because they're like a bunch of kids." He surprised me by a kind of tolerant wisdom, as if he were already years older than his cronies. "A lot of them haven't ever stopped going to grade school in their feelings: an apple for teacher one day and wanting to burn the schoolhouse down the next. That's why it's so hard to organize them and make them stay organized."

Our coffee cups had been empty for a long time, but still we sat on, reluctant to leave and go our separate ways. I felt that he was clinging to the mood and the moment even as I was.

"Well, it's good we can still keep on being friends," I told him before I gathered up my things to leave.

"Yes," he agreed. And then he added with the nearest approach to bitterness that he ever expressed: "Plenty of people are your friends till you need them."

It was six o'clock by the big lighted timepiece above the door. I glanced at it and pushed back my chair.

"Remember I'm trying to see your side, too, Jo," I said. "But it's hard being tied so fast to the other, and—and being deaf doesn't help, you know."

He leaned across the table as if he must make me feel the words that I have cherished ever since.

"I wish a lot of people who can hear would try as hard to understand," he said. "You've never been deaf to me."

CHAPTER TWENTY-NINE

I NEED NOT HAVE dreaded that Christmas so, for as it turned out our household was far from festive when the day arrived. Aunt Em was the cause of this, and she never knew that her accident and suffering helped me through the holidays as nothing else could have done. It happened at dusk of Christmas Eve. She had been out, winding up a few last errands, and had walked back from the shopping district across the Square. Aunt Em always preferred to walk when distance was not too great. She prided herself on her activity and independence, and her energy and endurance had become a byword with all the family.

"Aunt Em can run me ragged in an hour," Janice used to complain.

And I would agree on that subject.

"Too bad they can't put her in the picket line," Harry had laughed during the first days of the strike. "There'd be no wearing her down if she believed in the cause."

Poor Aunt Em, it seems strange to think that we ever made such jokes about her; that so short a time ago she came and went as she pleased on legs that are helpless now under the striped afghan.

None of us will ever know exactly how it happened. The day had been one of doors opening and shutting and the confusion of arrivals and departures. Janice was off in the car, and I had been late going to Dr. Weeks for my treatment. He had been delayed and had kept me longer than usual, fussing over the latest instructions from Merek Vance. These had been to double the strength of the injections, and he had been anxious to do so with as little discomfort as possible.

"We'd better skip the treatments tomorrow," I said as I left. "It's hardly a day I can slip over here unnoticed. Besides you'll be with us for dinner."

There were lights in the church that faced the Square, and I knew the greens must be up for the evening service. Behind the bare branches of elms and maples I could see the strong reds and yellows and blues of the stained-glass windows that had been familiar to me since childhood. There was the one of Christ blessing little children given in memory of Grandmother Blair, and the one about the parable of the loaves and fishes in memory of Grandfather Blair, and the one above the chancel given by Aunt Em and Uncle Wallace after my father's death in memory of him and the other Blairstown men who had lost their lives in France. Acting on an impulse I made Bridget's leash fast to a post and slipped into the empty church. The sexton was just finishing with the decorations at the far end of the long aisle, and the fragrance of fir and spruce boughs met me in spicy warmth as I pushed open the door. The glowing scarlet of poinsettia plants was like tongues of flame under the chancel lights. The rest of the church was dim, the organ pipes mounting tall and golden into the shadowy arches. Just so they had looked to me in the days when my head hardly showed above our pew top; just so had the Christmas greens smelled then, aromatic and rich to my nostrils. I sank down in a back pew, hoping to ease the tightness that had held me fast for days; but the old faith and assurance of childhood would not come out of the dimness to take me again.

As I rose to go I stood a moment before my father's bronze tablet with its inscription beginning, "To the glory of God, and the memory of Elliott Blair." Because I felt a great need of my father, I read and reread these words. But they only made him seem farther away. So I turned at last and tiptoed out, knowing that if he could have returned on Christmas Eve the years would have made me more of a stranger to him than he was to me.

It was almost dark when I reached our driveway, and I was annoyed by Bridget's behavior. She kept tugging at the leash, butting her head against my legs and trying to dash off towards the garden. I did my best to discipline her, but she only grew more insistent as I tried to drag her up the steps. At last I gave in and followed her lead. That was how I came upon Aunt Em, a helpless and crumpled heap by the side doorsteps.

I have a confused memory of what happened after that: of Maggie and Old Jo Kelly and myself carrying her into the entry between us; of the sharpness of spirits of ammonia and brandy spilled in the effort to get them past Aunt Em's set lips while we waited for Dr. Will; of awkward attempts to remove wraps and warm her icy hands. The Christmas tree still stood there waiting to be set up and decorated. I saw Aunt Em's eyes turn towards it as I lifted her head to a pillow. Her face was distorted with pain, but she turned her eyes to the tree and then to me.

I knew she was making wordless apology for such a catastrophe on Christmas Eve.

Catastrophe it surely was—a far more serious fall than we guessed until we saw Dr. Will's face as he worked over her. Maggie and I gave ourselves up to following directions, Maggie at the telephone and I running up and down stairs bringing blankets and robes and more pillows. It was a broken hip, Dr. Will managed to tell me when he could take me aside for a moment. He suspected it was a compound fracture that had not been helped by Aunt Em's struggles to rise and our clumsy efforts to carry her in. She must be taken to the hospital at once for X-rays before a cast could be put on. If only Merek Vance were within call . . .

I was thinking that, too, as I did the few simple things I could before the ambulance arrived and as I sat on the little folding seat beside the stretcher. I held Aunt Em's cold hand, and tried to be reassuring though I winced in sympathy at every turn and jolt of the short journey. Aunt Em had protested feebly when Dr. Weeks had mentioned the hospital. She wasn't used to having her wishes overruled, but she had given in finally. It was touching to me to see her dependence on him. Even in the stress of those moments I realized that she counted on him as more than a doctor and more than a friend. But for myself I suddenly felt lost and alone, knowing that Merek Vance would not be waiting for us at the hospital in his white coat, with his skillful, hard-scrubbed hands ready to do their best for us.

The Blair Memorial Hospital and Clinic had been built and endowed by Grandfather Blair; yet curiously enough none of our family had ever made use of it before that night. The resident doctor and staff of nurses couldn't do enough for Aunt Em's comfort. Indeed, the whole machinery of the place was presently revolving about her. I know that pleased her even in the midst of her pain. It seemed to give her back an old assurance in family traditions. I hoped that the present and its problems would retreat for her and she could rest for a while on the old formula of the past.

"But how did she do it?" Uncle Wallace kept asking as he and I waited in the impersonal cheerfulness of the visitors' reception room. He had returned from the mill just in time to see the ambulance leaving the driveway and had hurried on to join me at the hospital.

"She went out to do some errands," I told him, "and coming back she slipped on the side steps. You know how the eaves drip and the water freezes after the sun goes down. We don't know how long she'd been lying there."

"It would have to happen on Christmas Eve." Uncle Wallace shook his head and relighted the cigar that kept going out as we waited there together. "Em's bound to blame herself for spoiling the holiday for the rest of us. Seems to me they're taking longer than they should with those X-rays."

I looked at the clock in the hall outside and saw that it was exactly seven minutes since she had been carried into the X-ray room. I reached for a current magazine and turned the pages with determined absorption. In that next hour and a half I knew the pictures of every article and story by heart and all the products advertised on the pages. I knew the pattern of the chintz curtains as if I had designed them, and I had counted over and over the colored bulbs on a small Christmas tree the nurses had set up in the window: nine white; six orange; six green; three blue, and eleven red bulbs—twelve if you counted the one that didn't light up.

Twice the nurses came in and called Uncle Wallace to the telephone. Once the call was from Janice, wanting to know if she should come over to the hospital. I was grateful that he told her to stay at home and take any messages that might come. The other call was from Harry, wanting to know what he could do to help. I wished that Uncle Wallace had urged him to join us. I wished that Harry had come without asking. I think if he had appeared just then I might have forgotten everything but the comfort of his presence. Perhaps I might have broken down and told him that I was going to hear again. There is no telling what I might have said to him in those moments of tension in the hospital waiting room. But he did not come, and at last Uncle Wallace and I were relieved of our anxiety.

Aunt Em's broken hip had been set. It was a serious break, and there were complications. But everything had been done, and she was sleeping from the anesthetic. We could see her in the morning.

"She was worrying about you all and—Christmas," Dr. Weeks told us with a tired smile. "You know how Em is—thinking of everybody and everything except herself. That tree was on her mind, Emily, so I promised to remind you. She seemed relieved, almost as if she were superstitious about it being trimmed and in the bay window where it's always stood."

I nodded my reassurance.

"It'll be up and lighted before midnight. I'll do everything right—the way she likes it to be."

We drove back with Dr. Weeks, and he came in for a glass of port. I knew when he accepted the offer of a drink that he must be worn out from the ordeal. I guessed that it was the first time he had ever been asked to attend Aunt Em, and that the strain had been greater than he would admit. He looked old and frail as I helped him into his overcoat.

"Merek Vance should have been here today." We were alone in the hall, and he spoke as if he were answering my thoughts. "Stone's an able doctor, but all the time we were putting on that cast I knew who would have made a better job of it. If you'd feel easier to send for him tonight to take over the case, don't consider my feelings. He'd drop everything to come. I guess you know that."

"Yes," I said, "I know."

For a moment I was tempted to accept the offer. I hesitated, then I shook my head.

"No," I told him, and laid my hand on his coat sleeve. "You've done your best for Aunt Em. I'm satisfied with that, and we haven't any right to send for him now just because it would bolster us up. He'd come if we called him. I haven't a doubt of that. But these experiments he's made that we've been part of—they matter too much. Don't mention the accident when you write or wire. You knew what he had in him before I did; but now I know. Go home now and get some rest. You look all in."

I was the last one astir in the house that Christmas Eve. As I moved about the empty rooms the despair of the morning and the tension of later hours left me. Perhaps it was not that they left me but rather they merged into one of those intervals of quiet which lie between the breaking and gathering of waves at sea. The curtains were drawn against the winter dark, the wood in the fireplace no longer burned in active flame but glowed with an incandescent rose that still kept the shape of the logs which would presently crumble to ashes. In its accustomed place on the table in the bay window another Christmas tree had joined its green to the ghosts of other such trees that had stood there. I seemed to see them stretching back to my childhood in a long unbroken procession. There was comfort for me in the enduring sense of that continuity. I could understand why Aunt Em had remembered about it even in the midst of her own pain.

We Blairs, in common with other New England families, prided ourselves on saving possessions that might be used from year to year. Each December the familiar box with its carefully written label was brought out of the storeroom, and each January it returned to wait for another holiday to come round. I knew even before I lifted the cover just how the colored globes and gilded cones, the wax figures and neatly wound balls of tinsel would look inside. Only the small white tapers in their tin sockets had been reluctantly discarded some years before in favor of electric lights.

"I suppose we had to come to it some time," Aunt Em had sighed over the substitution. "I'll miss the smell of the candles among the needles, even if my mind will be more at rest and I'll dare to leave the room for five minutes the way I never could before. Still, there's nothing can ever take the place of candlelight. Tapers may be dangerous, but maybe that's what makes them do whatever it is they do to us."

But nothing else had been discarded from the box of decorations. Some even dated back to Christmases when

Aunt Em and Uncle Wallace and my father were children. There were cunningly carved and painted figures of the Nativity which Grandfather Blair had brought back from a momentous journey to Oberammergau. There were tiny scarlet toadstools with painted spots, like none that grew in our woods. They were souvenirs from a walking trip my father had made in the Black Forest during his college days. There were miniature bone reindeer and sledges from Lapland and two exquisite wax angels with gilt wings and yellow hair that looked as Janice used to look when she took part in Christmas tableaux. The wax on the face of one had run, the wing of another was broken, but no tree would look complete in our living room until they were hung high in the bristling green. Some of the tinsel had tarnished, but it still glittered as I wound it through the branches, better than the too bright artificial snow and blinding brilliance of new finery. I had to stand on a chair to set the star in its place on the topmost branch. I might have waited for Harry to put it there next day, but I was superstitious about having every ornament in place before I went upstairs. And that star meant more than all the rest, because my father had drawn and cut it from cardboard and gilded it with his own paints for my first Christmas tree in a studio in Brussels. It was always kept wrapped in cotton, and each year as I lifted it out I felt again the poignancy of survival—the power of such frail things to survive the hands that have fashioned them.

As I unwrapped each trinket and treasure and hung them up, I felt the tightness easing in myself. Whether it was natural reaction from my long strain and the new anxiety over Aunt Em, or whether some intangible peace of the season actually did lay hold upon my tired nerves and troubled mind, I shall never know. But I felt quieted, more at rest than I had been since I had stared out of the train window at Springwood station.

There might still be a way out of what I feared. I could not doubt what I had seen. I could not dismiss it as an ugly dream or deny the blow which had struck me down at the moment when I had been most defenseless. But I had loved Harry too long not to cling to that love as those who drown at sea are found still clutching some bit of wreckage.

I must give Harry a chance, so I argued to myself. Suppose he did love Janice now: it might be a transient, fleeting urge that would pass or burn itself out. He might even come to love me more for this strange madness. I had read of such things, of women who lost a man's love temporarily only to be rewarded by a deeper bond. If my love were strong enough and I were wise enough to wait and take no immediate issue, perhaps it might be so with me. I had little knowledge of other men. Harry Collins had been my whole existence in the last years. I had been young and inexperienced when we met, and I felt even more so now. If only we had not listened to reason; if only we had dared to be reckless and happy, then perhaps the terrible gulf of my deafness would not have widened between us. Those long absences, the discouraging verdicts of doctors, the strain of reunions and partings—I realized what they had meant to us both. Harry had been lonely and restless, ready to be caught and betrayed. And Janice had been restless, too. . . . I could make allowances for Harry, but not for Janice. No, I told myself bitterly, that was something I could never reconcile.

Bridget nudged at my ankles as I went into the hall. I

had forgotten her in my preoccupation with the box of ornaments and the tree. I opened the front door and let her out for a late run. But I did not follow her into the cold. I stood in the open door and waited for her to return. The porch light was on above me, and beyond the circle of warmth it made the lawn spread shadowy and dim. Winter stars shone icy-bright between the branches of the copper beeches—almost as brilliant and symmetrical, they seemed, as those I had just hung on the tree. Yet I was not thinking so much of Christmas stars as I was of that other night when Merek Vance had come to our door asking for help. Just so I had stood there on the top step, and he below me under the dome of light. My mind raced back to that night when his decisiveness and skill had saved Angeletta's little boy; when I had felt my last barrier of prejudice go down before his power. It had marked the turning point in our friendship. I knew that if he had been standing there again I should have taken strength from his presence.

Why had I fought so desperately against his help? I could find no answer as I stared out into the frost-gripped world.

Maybe it's some blind instinct, I thought, something that makes us resist what we're really reaching out to find. Or perhaps it's just nature: winter always fights the spring.

CHAPTER THIRTY

Two HOURS MORE and it would be another year—1932. All day in odd moments I had been trying to accustom myself to the change. Tomorrow when I dated letters or paid bills I would substitute a new figure for the old. Yet I knew that even the simple act of shifting numerals would confound me. I would forget the change and go back laboriously to correct the mistake I had made.

"Always remember, children," a teacher whose name I had forgotten used to tell us, "every day is a new year. We needn't wait for the first of January."

But I hadn't been able to believe her, not even in third grade. As time went on it became harder to put on a new year and shuffle off the familiar habit of the old. One grew used to years, like garments. At least one knew where the holes and patched places were; one had learned not to strain threadbare folds past endurance. A new year felt stiff and semifitted as one tried to move in it without self-consciousness. It was like dresses that used to be made to allow for growth, too sturdy and voluminous and reaching to boot tops. Only time and hard use would accomplish the fitting, and I did not look forward to that inevitable process. A silly, feminine whim, I decided, and tried to put it from me as I turned once more to the pile of letters and telegrams on my desk to be answered.

"Thank you for your note and the flowers. I can't tell you how much it meant to Aunt Em to know that you were thinking of her. She wants me to say that she is on the road to recovery, but I am afraid she has no idea how long and painful a road it may be . . ." I found my pen writing the same sentence over and over, like the refrain of a song. "It was a serious fracture, and any such accident at her age is serious . . ." I crossed out the first "serious" and substituted "difficult"--not that repetitions would matter to the recipient of the letter, but I must not lapse into the form-letter habit. "She is out of immediate danger now, and everything is being done for her comfort. We hope to bring her back from the hospital in an ambulance tomorrow. When she is able to have visitors I will let you know. Thanking you again for the flowers and your messages, and with best wishes for a happy new year in which Aunt Em joins me, . . ."

I laid the letter with others in addressed envelopes and gathered the sheaf to take downstairs for mailing. It was ten o'clock by the big Blair clock in the hall. I noticed the hour as I went by, and the booming of the strokes sounded in my ears, though not yet clear and sharp; but the surprise of hearing such sounds still shook me. I would find myself stopping short, trembling in sudden recognition. Human voices still eluded me, though I was beginning to catch blurred words now and again, and the radio could send its mechanical tones farther into my consciousness. I had caught myself starting up to turn off the machine several times in the last few days. But I had managed to stop the gesture before it betrayed me.

In that week between Christmas and New Year's Eve I had had little time to indulge in personal worry. My own problems retreated before the immediate concern for Aunt Em. I had been grateful for this as I was grateful for the activity that filled each hour. Down to the hospital after breakfast; mail to be sorted and read to Aunt Em; long lists of errands to be done; back to the house again; meals to be discussed with Maggie; visitors to be seen and reassured; flowers to be arranged; conferences with doctors and nurses; letters to be answered in any spare moment and late into the night—the whole ordered routine of life suddenly turned from its natural course.

"Take it easy, Aunt Em," I would beg as I sat by the hospital bed and tried to follow the accumulation of worries that had been churning in her mind through hours of wakefulness. "Things are going all right at the house, at least as right as they can be without you."

"I know," she would say, moving her head restlessly on the pillow. "I know it's foolish to think a house and a family can't get along without you. Maybe this came to show me how vain I'd been about running things my own way."

"Now, Aunt Em," I would protest, "that's not what I meant. We just want to make things easy so you can relax and get well sooner."

The futile words would go on and on every day. But it was easier for me to cope with them than to answer her on the subject of Harry and me. She had too much time to lie and make plans. I faltered inwardly whenever she started to talk about my wedding.

"There'll be time for that when you're better," I would urge. "Let's put New Year's through first and see the mills reopened."

But it was difficult to distract her, even with the mill problems. It was almost as if, in her unaccustomed state of weakness, she sensed the panic and tension I was trying to hide.

"There's never plenty of time," she kept insisting. "Waiting, when there's no need to wait, is one of the unpardonable sins; and I'm not going to be the cause of it. Maybe we were wrong to send you from doctor to doctor: I realize that more now I've had a dose of being at their mercy. . . . Well, be that as it may, you and Harry must go ahead and make your plans. There's money in the bank deposited in your name—five thousand dollars in cash from that annuity your father left, and the same for Janice later. Wallace can tell you more about it. Harry's not making much, I know, but you'll have enough to help out till times improve—if they ever do."

It had seemed doubly ironic to me, this talk of money put at my disposal in the bank. Somehow the older generation always felt it could buy happiness for one. I had tried to sound pleased as I thanked her, but I don't know how well I succeeded. I found myself thinking of a dozen such conversations I had had with Aunt Em, as I came down the stairs with the letters.

In the hall I saw Harry's hat and his overcoat flung down on the sofa near Janice's gray fur coat. I stopped short and leaned against the newel post. My heart quickened its beating, partly because I had not expected Harry to come for another hour and partly because those two garments flung down together set an edge to the pain that stayed like a dull ache behind all my activities. Harry had stopped at the hospital that afternoon to see Aunt Em, and he had promised he would be over later in the evening.

"No, Emmy, I can't come for dinner," he had told me when he left, "but I'll be over before midnight with a bottle I've been saving. Don't ask me where I got it in these times."

I had hoped that Janice would go to the annual New Year's Eve dance at the country club. I had counted on being alone with Harry. He had been considerate and full of helpfulness to me of late. It had almost seemed that we could find our way back to each other if only we could have the chance. Yes, the seed of hope in me had dared to put out a stubborn tendril of green. I stood there irresolute by the hall table with the letters still in my hands. Uncle Wallace was alone in his study. The door was open, and I could see him bent over his stamp album, absorbed in his cataloguing of series. Across the hall, Janice and Harry had the living room all to themselves. How long, I wondered, since he had tossed down his coat and gone in there? An hour, perhaps, or maybe only ten minutes, and what were they saying to each other? I mustn't look suspicious when I joined them. There must be no hint of that in my manner.

I had no intention of spying on them when I peered into the hall mirror. My impulse was to make sure of my own looks. It was only when I saw the two in the living room that I realized my opportunity to play eavesdropper, for the mirror revealed them to me while I myself could keep clear of its reflection. If I had had my hearing and had stood there, unseen but deliberately listening, I should have been no more guilty than I was at that moment. For the deaf learn to listen with their eyes, and I must take my chance. I was past being honorable as I strained to catch the movements of their reflected lips.

Janice sat on the low chair by the fire. Her arms hugged her knees; her hands clasped tight together. I knew instinctively that she longed to fling them about Harry's neck. It must be taking all her will power to keep those few feet away from him. He stood by the fireplace, looking down at her, and the lamplight was strong on his face so that I had no difficulty in following his words.

"Janice, stop going all over it again. Don't you know I hate myself for what I've let us into?"

"We couldn't help ourselves, Harry." She lifted her face to his, and I saw she was struggling against tears. "We didn't want to fall in love. God knows, we tried to fight it at first . . ."

"Maybe we could have tried harder." I saw him stiffen as she reached out a hand to him. "No, darling, don't touch me—not here, not in this house. . . . I know what I'm putting you through."

"But we can't drift on like this. Waiting isn't going to make it easier for her or for us. It's getting too much for me—nights like this when we . . ." She let her head fall on her arms. Her curls quivered in the lamplight as sobs took her.

I saw Harry reach out and then resolutely draw back his hand. There was distress and longing on his face that I had never seen there before. I knew then that they were suffering in their way as I had suffered in mine. But they were together in their misery, and I was alone. I knew I ought to go in to them then and there without further subterfuge and spying. I was no better than they at that moment. Yet

I stayed rigid, pressing my body against the table to steady my trembling.

"I was sure she guessed something," Janice was going on, her wet face lifted once more towards his, "just before Christmas. She must have seen us together, and then the keys disappearing—but lately she's acted . . ." Her head went down again, and I missed her muffled words.

"I can't do it," he was answering. "I can't tell her yet."

Janice faced him again, and for once tears and hopelessness made her ugly.

"Harry," she said, and her lips were firm as they put the question: "If Emily could hear, it would be different, wouldn't it? You'd make the break?"

"But she is deaf." He shrugged helplessly before he went on. "That's why I can't. You don't know what it's like to be loved and not be able to return it. And I did love her once, Janice, even if I know now I made a mistake."

"You needn't make another!" She was on her feet then, moving towards him.

He held her off at arms' length.

"I know Emily better than you do." I could see the muscles of his throat working. "If we take away the one thing she feels she's got to live for—she might be desperate enough to do something . . ."

"How about my being desperate, Harry?"

"I know. . . . Don't think I don't, but you and I haven't her kind of strength. Emily's like Peace-Pipe goods—a hundred per cent quality. . . . I can't live up to her and that's why I'm afraid . . ."

They drew closer then. Love and fear and misery were too much for them to resist any longer. I saw her head go down against his tweed coat. His face was hidden in the tumbled fairness of her hair. I moved away from the table, and turned from the mirror that had revealed too much. My heart still hammered frantically, but the rest of me had gone numb. I tried to think as I stood, still clutching the sheaf of letters in my hands. I knew that I ought to go into that room and face them once and for all. A woman in a book or a play would have done that, but I wasn't behind footlights or between the pages of a book. I felt incapable of words or actions as if I had been thrown over some precipice and were not quite sure whether I were alive or dead. . . .

They were seated at opposite ends of the sofa when I finally made my way to the living-room door. Janice's hair was only slightly disordered, and only the dark brightness of her eyes betrayed her recent tears. Harry sprang up a little too quickly, I thought; but except for that and a certain tension in his smile there was nothing in their manner to give them away. My hands began to shake as I stood there before them, and the letters spilled to the floor.

"Oh!" I apologized. "I'm sorry—stupid of me."

Harry was on his knees helping to pick them up. Our faces were on a level as we stooped to recover the scattered envelopes.

"Good Lord, Emmy," he said as he gathered them up, "what a lot of letters! . . . No wonder you look all in. Let's not wait for midnight to open that bottle I brought."

I nodded and made my way to the nearest chair.

"All right," I told him. "I could do with a drink now."

I held out my hands to the heat of the fire, and I did not look beyond my own fingers. Harry must have gone to the kitchen for glasses, and perhaps Janice helped him bring them in. I have no recollection of that. But presently we were all by the fire again and Uncle Wallace had joined us.

"Don't look as if you were seeing a ghost, sir," Harry was grinning as he showed the label on a bottle of champagne. "Just pretend I set the clock back to pre-Volstead days. It was a present, and there won't be enough to hurt us. If we ever needed to drink to prosperity being just round the corner, we do tonight."

"I guess you're right, my boy," Uncle Wallace agreed. "Careful how you handle that cork."

They were too absorbed to notice my silence or that I started, too, at the sudden loud pop that announced the successful uncorking. It seemed ironical that I should hear that sound distinctly above the pounding of blood in my ears.

"Well, then," Uncle Wallace held his glass high. "Here's to the New Year and better business—"

Janice tossed back her hair impatiently. "Here's to us!" she interrupted.

I could scarcely taste the champagne as I tried to keep the glass steady in both hands. I dared not trust myself to look at Janice and Harry, though I knew they must be keeping up the pretense of talk. But if they noticed my preoccupation they did nothing to rouse me from it.

I must do something, my mind seemed to be telling me from a great distance off. I must think what to say to them. I can't just sit like this from now till midnight.

I shall always be grateful to the Parker twins and their escorts for bursting in upon us as they did. They stopped on their way to the dance, stirring the atmosphere of our

living room as if by invisible brooms. We were caught up
in a flurry of embraces and introductions, for the young
men turned out to be holiday house guests. I remember
mechanically shaking the hands they extended, and hoping
that the chill of my fingers would not be commented upon.
The chattering Parker twins and their young men, whose
names I made no attempt to master, were certainly a god-
send to me. I have been thankful ever since for the diver-
sion they created. A group of people always made me retreat into silence. I sat in their midst making no effort to
join in.

"Emily!" It was one of the Parker twins who touched
my arm and appealed directly to me at last. "I think you
might help us out. You haven't said a word one way or
the other."

I forced my mind back to her and what she was saying
—something about the dance and wanting us to go with
them. Club dances were deadly unless one made sure of
one's own party. It wasn't fair of Janice and Harry to
desert them like this.

"And you come, too," she added as an afterthought.
"Even if you don't want to dance it's better than sticking
around here on New Year's Eve."

"Why, of course," I told her, "Janice ought to go. I
thought she was planning to, and if Harry's staying here
on my account—"

He must have been listening for he came over at that.

"Now, Emily"—he laid his hand on mine, and I tried
not to tremble under his touch—"don't you let yourself be
persuaded. It won't kill us to see the New Year in here.
I'm not backing down on a promise."

But I saw Janice's eyes on his face. I could feel their

eagerness to be free of this room and of me. I knew those club dances. There were plenty of opportunities for a couple to slip away to a parked car. Even those who stayed on the crowded dance floor could be isolated by the music, severed from unwelcome talk to an outsider. I knew they were both ready to snatch at any moments together. Let them go. Let them get out of the house on any pretext while I tried to muster the remnants of my defense.

"Please go," I repeated, "both of you. I've had a pretty hard day, so count me out. You know dragging me to a dance isn't a treat to me or—or anyone else."

Harry tried to protest, but I cut him short. Janice was already hurrying upstairs to change her dress, and as far as the others were concerned the matter was settled.

"Emmy"—even in his relief at the chance to escape, Harry seemed reluctant to desert me—"I hate to go off like this and leave you alone on New Year's Eve. You've had a bad week to put through at the hospital and all. You ought to have a little fun yourself—"

"Fun!" I repeated, and choked suddenly over the word.

"I can come back if you want me to," Harry insisted. "I'll go over with them now and slip off just before midnight."

But I put him off hastily. I manufactured an excuse to go upstairs as they were leaving, though I watched the cars' headlights whiten the driveway and then become indistinguishable from other hurrying specks of light on the dark road. Once they were out of sight I went downstairs again—for no reason in particular.

The house seemed empty, hollow as some discarded shell. Yet the living room was still too full of Janice and Harry as I moved about, setting it to rights in a kind of determined frenzy. There was no need for me to straighten the hearthrug and magazines, to shake the sofa cushions into smoothness and collect scattered ash trays. Maggie would be up to do that long before breakfast. Yet I found it necessary to keep active.

Across the hall Uncle Wallace turned off the study light and appeared in the doorway. He had a new detective novel under his arm, one that Aunt Em had rejected from the books sent to her at the hospital. He smiled sheepishly as he saw my eyes upon the title.

"Yes, I've taken to murder mysteries," he said. "Find them easier to sleep on than the newspapers nowadays. Why didn't you go with the rest? . . . Or maybe Harry's coming back for you?"

"No, Uncle Wallace," I said, "I didn't feel—exactly in the mood for—festivity."

He peered at me a little anxiously, as if he were looking through new spectacles, and seemed bewildered by the change he saw.

"But it's all wrong for a girl like you to be here alone on New Year's Eve. I'm not feeling too gay myself with Em laid up and with Peace-Pipe sitting like a ton of bricks on my mind; but I'll see the New Year in with you, if you want me to."

I was touched by his concern. Uncle Wallace liked life to flow along in the conventional pattern to which he was accustomed. I suddenly realized that I belonged to the pattern of his existence. He thought of me as young and happy and carefree, and here I was upsetting all his theories of fitness. I reached out and took his hand.

"The New Year will come in whether we sit up for it or not," I said.

"Yes," he admitted, "but you shouldn't be feeling that way about it, not at your age."

"What's age got to do with our feelings, Uncle Wallace?"

"Well, I don't know." He frowned uncertainly. "I guess I'm too old to cope with change—been used to walking on solid ground too long; now it's slipping under me, and I can't seem to keep my balance."

I had no comfort to offer him. We stood awkwardly by the fire, each of us alone with our fears and uncertainties, each of us dreading the New Year which every moment brought nearer.

When he had gone to his room, I still kept up my aimless activity. Feeling had begun to return, not only to my body, but to my mind. As the numbness lessened, a deep, inner conviction began to take form. No matter what I had seen; no matter how much I knew, I wouldn't let Harry go. Until one admitted defeat one was never really beaten. Janice had her weapons, and I had mine. She might seem to have the more powerful ones, but I would make my very handicap serve me. Harry had admitted he could not take advantage of my deafness. I had been foolish to send them off to the dance. But at least I had not given myself away. I would rally my scattered forces and accept the challenge. Tomorrow I would take the offensive.

A cold rush of air made me turn just then to find Merek Vance in the doorway. I was too startled to speak or move as he came forward in his old ulster and felt hat. He did not pause to remove either before he reached me. His hands felt icy on my shoulders as he held me off and searched my face, smiling as he did so.

"Don't look as if I were a ghost," he said. "Your front

door was unlocked. I've been driving all day to get here, and I'm half frozen; but I'll come to life in a moment. Didn't want to wire you for fear I might spoil some plan you'd made. Don't tell me you're all alone?"

When I nodded he threw off his coat and hat and went to the fire.

"That's better than I dared expect." He held out his hands to the heat of the one remaining log. I saw then that he was shaking with cold.

I brought out the sherry from the sideboard.

"You look as if you could do with something stronger, but this is the best I can find. Here, I'll pour it."

It was queer to have my hands steadier than his as I filled the glass. While he drank it I put more wood on the fire and blew it into flame. It was several minutes before either of us spoke. I did not look at him while I bent to the fire, yet I knew his eyes were upon me. I could feel their probing.

"Why didn't you send for me?" he asked when I looked up at last. "Why didn't you let me know about your aunt's accident? It's a queer thing I'd have to hear of it from one of my patients across the river."

"You couldn't have come in time to set the bone," I told him, "and besides Dr. Weeks and I felt what you were doing in Baltimore was more important. We knew you'd leave everything to come."

His expression relaxed at that. The color was coming back to his lips, though he still crouched close to the fire as if he could never thaw out. I answered his questions about Aunt Em, trying to sound as accurate and medical as I could.

"You don't look as if you'd had any dinner," I said. "Better let me see what I can find in the ice box."

He shook his head impatiently.

"Never mind that. . . . Tell me about Emily Blair." His eyes held me with their disconcerting keenness. "You've had a tough stretch to put through alone. I had a feeling I should have come back before this—a hunch that you needed me."

"Oh, I managed all right," I told him evasively.

"Yes," he smiled as he continued to scrutinize me. "I can see you're in fine form. You look as if you'd been left out all night in a January thaw. How's the reaction to sound: clearer, less spasmodic?"

He went to the piano and played a few bars, keeping his eyes on my face as he did so.

"The Unfinished Symphony," I recognized the familiar theme, and he nodded and let his hands drop from the keys. "I never knew you could play the piano."

"I can't unfortunately. My childhood didn't include music lessons. But I got free tickets to concerts occasionally when I was in college. My sister and I went to one in Carnegie Hall last week. They played the Debussy 'Drowned Cathedral.' It made me think of you."

"Of me. . . . Why?"

"Indirectly, of course. It's as if you'd been engulfed by a lot of things—conventions and systems and people that were muffling you. It's only now and then that I know you're really there under it all; that I can hear the real person coming through, like those bells under water in the music—"

"Sometimes I feel like that."

I had not meant to answer him. My words came as a surprise to me.

He turned to the watch on his wrist and held it out for me to read. The hands pointed to a quarter before twelve.

"There's a lot to talk to you about between now and midnight," he went on. "Not that I can crowd it all into these few minutes, because I'll need hours of explaining when I try to tell you what the doctors think about your case. They're still checking over my notes and charts, and they'll work with us from now on. We did a lot of experimenting, too. They've even started a special clinic for research and experiments. I helped them organize it, and two doctors I know are in charge. Nothing's been made public yet, but they're convinced we're on the track of big things. And it won't stop with ears: if one set of impaired nerves can be stimulated by my formula, why not others? Think of the possibilities—"

"I wonder they let you come back here to Blairstown."

"They brought a lot of pressure to keep me there, but I said no, for the present. We'll need a couple more times before I'm ready to have you go through their tests, and I want to have you past this daily injection stage. I'm increasing the strength tomorrow and gradually working up—"

"Wait," I cut him short. "I have something to say about that."

My voice and manner must have given him some warning, for the eager excitement left his face. The anxiety in his eyes was disconcerting. I could not look at him directly and say what must be said.

"I'm through," I told him. "I'm not coming to you for any more treatments."

Once I had got those words out, I dared to face him

again. His whole body had stiffened, and the line of his jaw had grown hard.

"There's no need for staying here on my account," I went on. "You can go back to that clinic."

"You don't know what you're saying, Emily. You're not cured yet. We haven't reached a point where those nerves will go on without artificial stimulation. This is the most critical stage of all, and it would be fatal to stop the injections. I wouldn't answer for the consequences."

"You mean," I went on, "that I'd go back to where I was before you began? I'd be deaf again?"

He nodded, and I blundered on.

"I tell you I can't go on, bargain or no bargain. You proved what you wanted to prove through me. If I choose to stay deaf—well, that's my business whether you understand it or not."

"I understand all right." He turned from me and walked to the window. He stayed there, quietly staring out between the half-drawn curtains. Then he came back. Once more his hands gripped my shoulders. He forced me to look up, to follow what he was saying. "So you'd rather be weak for Harry Collins than strong for me? That's the answer, isn't it?"

I felt the scorn behind his clear, accusing eyes. I could feel myself withering under his contempt.

"Can't you ever leave me alone?" I tried to twist free of his hold. "I'm through, I tell you. You can find plenty of other deaf people to experiment on."

"We're not talking about other people. Leave them out of this. And leave Harry Collins out, too. I thought you were over this madness. I gave you credit for having some pride!"

I was shaking now under his grip. His fingers that looked so thin and supple were strong as steel and charged with a vitality that I was powerless to resist.

"Pride doesn't stand much chance with love," I managed to falter. "But I wouldn't expect you to know about that."

"No." He bent closer, and I felt the heat of his breath on my face as he spoke. "And I hope I'll never know about that kind of love. You want to turn love into a crutch. Dead wood to lean on because you're not brave enough or honest enough to accept the truth. You love someone. All right. Maybe he loved you once, but he doesn't any more. He loves someone else. All right. Nothing so remarkable about that. Stop being a snob about your own feelings."

"It's not fair to say such things. I—"

"Are you being fair to yourself, or to me?"

"I'll do what I want with my life. It doesn't happen to concern you."

"But it does, no matter how you deny it." His hands suddenly dropped from my aching shoulders, and he pushed me away from him. "I don't know why I thought you were worth bothering about. I might have guessed you were one of the life-owes-me people. Life owes me a living, life owes me happiness, life owes me love . . . Well, you owe life something—and you owe me something when it comes to that. And I don't mean money."

He turned away abruptly and strode over to the chair where he had laid his hat and coat. I made no move to speak or to follow him. I felt nothing except a pounding of blood at my temples, a blurring of the familiar objects in the room.

And then, suddenly, I was aware of sound: bells were ringing outside and whistles shrilling. They were echoing in me, in my ears that had been dead so long to the noisy welcome of a new year. I must have cried out at the new sensation. I must have run to the window and thrown it open involuntarily. For there we were, side by side, leaning out to the cold and the wild clamor.

His arm was about me, and we stood there, listening together without moving, without speaking till the peak of sound had passed.

He closed the window and turned to me at last.

"Well," he said, "I came to wish you a happy new year; but there's no use in that now—you'd rather have the old one—"

"No, no." I found myself clinging to him in frantic appeal. Tears were pouring down my face, and I made no effort to check their flow. "Don't say that. . . . I was a fool to think I could give back what you've given me. It's not that easy, is it? I'll be down again tomorrow—I mean to-day."

CHAPTER THIRTY-ONE

STRANGE TO WAKE to the Peace-Pipe whistle on the morning set for the mills' reopening. It was just short of three years since I had heard that long shrill blast, for it had been silent in the weeks after my hearing began to return. I started up in bed, shivering under the covers at the challenge of that distant summons. Never again, I knew, would I take the sound for granted.

I thought of all those who must be listening to it at that moment under the roofs of Blairstown: women looking anxiously at their men who started fires of broken crates and salvaged coal; women who put coffee on to boil and sliced bread as thin as they dared for a noon dinner pail; children huddled close under old quilts, watching with bright, curious eyes while they whispered together.

"There's the whistle. . . . Hear it?"

"Papa going back to work, you think?"

"He told Mamma '*No*' last night, but he's putting on his pants and shoes. What you bet we get stew for supper?"

"There's going to be men with guns by the mill gates, real honest-to-gosh guns, and things they throw that make you cough and cry. Ma says we got to go the long way round to school. We might get hurt if the picket line starts to rush 'em. She says there's no telling what to expect. Come on, let's get up."

I thought of Uncle Wallace dressing in his room at the end of the hall, slipping the folds of his tie into a careful knot, trying to look as if this were any day and not one to be reckoned with in Peace-Pipe history. I thought of Aunt Em lying helpless in her cast, straining her ears at every real or imagined sound. Whatever happened or did not happen, she would believe we were keeping important facts from her. She would lie there rigid and uncompromising, feeling that somehow she had helped to betray Peace-Pipe Mills by falling and breaking her hip. I thought of Old Jo Kelly wrestling with the furnace in the cellar, his crippled hands and stiff knees stubbornly responding to his will while he tried not to remember a boy's small alert figure following him about on other winter mornings. I thought of young Jo, too, rousing himself in some room across the river, his eyes more dark than blue, his shoulders defiant under the old Mackinaw. I thought of Merek Vance in his makeshift office, quietly sorting and filling his doctor's bag with extra bandages and antidotes that might be needed if a hurry call came. I thought of Harry Collins—but no, I would try not to think of him, not once all day.

Uncle Wallace had begun his second cup of coffee when I reached the dining room. The morning paper was open beside him, but I made no reference to the headlines in heavy type, "Mill Reopens Today Under Armed Guard."

"Aunt Em had a fair night," I reported as I took my

place. "Of course she's beginning to worry. She wants the paper as soon as you're through with it."

"I'll take it up before I leave. We must keep her reassured, Emily. I know I can count on you for that."

"Yes, Uncle Wallace. How—how much in the way of trouble do you expect?"

"That's hard to say, but we're not taking chances. If there should be any attempt at violence we're prepared to meet it."

"With more violence?"

He evaded my question and went on after a moment.

"I want you and Janice to keep away from that part of town for the present. Better stay on this side of the river till we have things well in hand. The weather prediction is for snow today. That's to our advantage."

"Yes," I said, "snow's hard on a picket line, especially if shoes happen to need mending."

Uncle Wallace looked grim as he folded his napkin.

"Emily," he reproved, "I don't doubt your good intentions, but your sympathies are running away with you. You've had too little experience to take a long view of the situation."

"I've never worked behind a loom or tended the bobbin machinery," I reminded him. "I've never tried to live on a mill hand's wages."

"You've never tried to run a mill so that wages could be paid—remember that, too." He rose from the table and pushed back his chair. "You don't realize we're obligated all round, to our stockholders as well as our workers. We have to take a firm hand now, or else . . ."

His shoulders sagged expressively.

"Or else what?" I persisted.

"Close down—be taken over by a receivership. . . . It would amount to the same thing as far as we're concerned. God knows, Peace-Pipe's never compromised with its product or its principles, and we won't be bullied into it by a bunch of paid organizers that have shut down bigger mills than ours. There are plenty of workers to fill the shifts, and we mean to see they're protected. Well, don't worry, and don't let Em get worked up about it. By the way, this house is freezing again. Old Jo must be having more trouble with the furnace. Better get someone in to help him."

Maggie was in anything but a good humor when I approached her on the subject. Yes, she admitted, the house was cold, upstairs and down, but that was no reason for a trained nurse to go round sniffling and wearing a sweater over her uniform and demanding hot tea or coffee every hour. She'd be warm if she kept as busy as she was paid to be. Old Jo was doing his best. He wasn't fit to be up and tinkering with the furnace. He'd be the next to take to his bed, and then it would be even worse. That substitute boy always managed to do the wrong things with dampers and drafts. We'd have to worry along somehow while the cold snap lasted.

So that first week in January began—a week that grew more tense as each day passed. Snow fell intermittently, but brought no relief from the cold. The hard, tight flakes took on a grayish tinge before they reached the ground. After the recent smokeless weeks I had half forgotten that familiar heaviness on the air. Once more the chimneys of Peace-Pipe dominated the town with clouds of their own making. Wherever I went, whatever I did, I was conscious of that; and though I did not cross the bridges I felt the distant throb of machinery. Morning, noon, and night, I found myself straining to catch the sound of the mill whistle. Those were the times to be dreaded, I knew, when gates opened or closed on arriving and departing workers; when the line of picketers pressed closer and the armed guard left off lounging about the mill yard.

"We're satisfied with the way order is being kept." That was all I could find out from Uncle Wallace, and Harry was uncommunicative on the hurried visits he made to the house. Both were nervous and on edge through those days. Neither could be drawn into talk.

Except for Merek Vance I should have known less of the situation than if I had been with Cousin Eunice in Boston. He did not evade my questions as he increased his injections and made daily notes on my improvement. I was glad to avoid references to my outburst of New Year's Eve, and he tactfully made no mention of it. It was good to reach his office each afternoon when I left Aunt Em and the big house on a pretext of errands or a breath of fresh air. I relaxed in the worn leather chair whose broken springs and resulting hollows I knew so well. The weight of fear and uncertainty that kept me tense, even when I slept, would lift gradually as we talked across the desk.

"The weather and Jo Kelly are keeping things reasonably quiet so far," he told me by Wednesday. "But I've been through a couple of strikes before this, and I'm not making any predictions."

He had had an emergency call or two. A few flying bricks had found their marks. There had been bruises to be treated, some stitches taken, a broken wrist to be set, but nothing serious yet.

"Dr. Weeks and I are more afraid of another flu epidemic," he admitted. "A lot of the picketers are home with chills and fever, and every other family's been scrimping on food. No wonder a good half of the strikers couldn't hold out and turned scab. That makes the ones that stick more bitter."

"Bitter about—us, you mean?"

"Yes, of course, but there's plenty being lavished on the union, too. They feel they could have made a stronger stand with more financial help. Claim they're taking the brunt of the strike and the union hasn't lived up to its promises of backing. I guess there's more than a little truth in it. The United Textile Workers group is pretty well involved right now with Fall River and New Bedford and some of the bigger plants. It's going to take all the organization's funds to win those, and they naturally count more than a small family-owned mill like Peace-Pipe."

"I see. . . . Then you think the strikers will be squeezed out or just have to accept the old terms."

He shrugged.

"Looks that way now, but things can change overnight in situations like this. The strike should never have been called to my way of thinking, not with business lagging the way it is and banks withdrawing funds all over the country. Well, I'm no prophet and I'm no industrialist; I'll have to stick to patching up broken heads."

"What about Jo Kelly?"

"So far he's the spokesman and keeping things clean. But I suspect there's an element that would like to see him out and put on a show of their own. He's done a good job, but this feeling that the union may be up to some double-crossing is bound to react on him."

"Jo Kelly hasn't a mean streak in him," I said. "I've never known him to bear a personal grudge to anyone. People must feel that and trust him the way animals do."

"Yes, he's one of the finest. I only hope he'll watch his step. . . . I saw him last night, and he was asking for you. He seemed worried about your aunt."

By Thursday Uncle Wallace looked more cheerful, and the Blairstown newspaper ran an editorial complimenting the Directors of Peace Pipe Industries on their firm stand. "The traditions of quality and integrity have not been sacrificed," it read. "When all efforts at negotiations failed the company did not stoop to compromise. 'We will continue to give work to those who want it,' Mr. W. J. Perkins was quoted as saying in an interview to the press yesterday, 'and we have taken measures to protect our returning workers. We never have been, and we never will be, dictated to by an element which must eventually defeat its own ends by exorbitant demands and high-handed methods.' Other industrial plants may well watch and benefit by the stand which Peace-Pipe directors have taken."

That night Maggie told me that Old Jo Kelly had given out. Dr. Weeks had ordered him to bed that afternoon and had personally seen to the order being carried out. It was a heavy cold, and the Doctor was taking no chances of pneumonia. He had given the old man a sleeping powder to keep him quiet, and Maggie had promised to keep an eye on him.

"The nurse won't, that's one sure thing," Maggie had remarked grimly. "Said she couldn't run the risk of any contagion for your aunt. Now all we need is for the furnace to act up."

She came to me later that evening with a queer expression on her face.

"I've got an idea young Jo's been down cellar," she told me. "About half an hour ago I thought I heard coal being shoveled. Then the heat started coming up good in the registers. When I got a chance to go down just now the ashes was taken out and the fire fixed to last through the night. There was something chalked on the floor. It said: 'Back in morning. Don't worry.' I don't know who else could have done that but him. He's got a good heart, I'll say that for the boy."

"Yes," I agreed, "he always manages to find out if we're sick or in trouble. But I hope he'll be careful—"

I broke off, remembering the precautions he had taken when we stopped at the roadside diner. I was tempted to leave a note for him by the furnace, but decided against that. He probably wanted no notice taken of his visits. Later there would be a chance to thank him.

Harry had not appeared at the house for several days, and I had seen almost nothing of Janice except for hurried glimpses of her figure flitting through the hall or at the wheel of the car. The mill situation had reassured me somewhat about their chances of meeting. Ever since New Year's Eve I had tried not to think of what must be said when the moment came for me to speak out. By day I could take refuge in activity. It was at night in my own room that I was at the mercy of my own emotions. Bitterness would overwhelm me as I lay wakeful through the long hours of darkness and chill half-light. I no longer deluded myself with hope. At least I fought it in my consciousness. But during brief snatches of sleep it would lay insidious hold upon me once more. Then I would believe that the reality had been the dream; that Harry Collins and I had never been separated. So I came to dread sleep and its treachery.

By Friday of that week the strain was growing more than I could hide. My nerves were like fiddlestrings taut to the point of breaking. The muscles of my face stayed stiffly set, and my eyes were glazed with sleeplessness. In spite of my efforts at cheerfulness Aunt Em noticed the change in me and worried each time I came into her room. Even Uncle Wallace commented upon the dark circles under my eyes.

"Don't take things so hard, Emily," he cautioned. "Your aunt's getting along as well as we can expect. A few days more, and we'll feel we've turned the corner with this mill trouble. There was only a little demonstration yesterday when we opened the gates; a few pickets tried to rush the lines, nothing really serious. Of course we'll keep the guard on awhile longer, but there's no cause for you to worry so."

Merek Vance alone made no remarks about my appearance. He seemed to take the outward signs of my feeling as a natural reaction. Indeed we talked little together on my visits, which were briefer than usual and devoted entirely to the routine of injections, sound tests, and note taking. He knew when to speak and when to keep silence. I was grateful for that and asked nothing more of him.

I had come in out of the cold that Friday afternoon to find Janice moving restlessly about the living room, and the radio giving out such a blare of sound that even I recoiled from it. I flung down my wraps and hurried in, words of involuntary protest rising to my lips.

"Janice," I cried, "tune that thing down or stop it!"

I hardly realized what I had said until I caught the expression on Janice's face; her start of incredulous surprise.

"Well!" She gave me a long, curious look. "You're certainly the last person in this house I'd expect to complain about a little music!"

"Oh, never mind me—but you might remember there's sickness in this house."

She hunched her shoulders and moved to turn off the radio switch.

"Oh, all right then, have it your way, only stop staring at me like that. You can have the whole place to yourself. I don't want it."

"Janice, wait, you've got to listen to me."

I found myself moving across the room to her. She stopped reluctantly in the act of gathering up some scattered possessions. The color went out of her face though she tried to appear unconcerned.

"What's come over you anyhow, Emily?"

My throat felt dry, and my head throbbed. I knew I could not keep hold of myself any longer.

"How do you think I knew the radio was on?" I asked her.

"I'm sure I don't know." She shrugged again. "But it doesn't matter, does it?"

"It happens to matter a lot to me," I went on without taking my eyes from her face. "I could *hear* it—that's why. You can ask Dr. Vance if you don't believe me."

"What's he got to do with it?"

"He's cured me. At least I'm on the way to being cured."

"But—that doesn't seem possible . . ." Her eyes grew wider, and I saw sudden fear start up in them. "I mean we'd—we'd have noticed it."

"I took pains you shouldn't. I had reasons—and I wanted to be sure first. I'd been disappointed so many times before, I was afraid to hope, and now"—I knew my voice must have broken before I forced myself to go on—"now there isn't any point to that."

Either she missed my meaning or she was determined not to show that she sensed it.

"Why, it's wonderful, Emily!" she began. "You certainly ought to feel happy."

She reached out her hands to me, but I drew back.

"How can you stand there and say that to me, after—after—"

I could not trust myself to go on for a moment. We stood there facing each other, alert and wary.

"What did you expect me to say? I can't make you out."

"Can't you? I shouldn't have thought that would be hard to do, especially for you and Harry. You thought you were playing safe, I suppose. Perhaps you thought I didn't see and feel other things just because I couldn't hear what you said."

Janice's hair had loosened and tumbled into her eyes. She pushed it back with a little defiant gesture before she answered.

"All right," she said. "Why didn't you speak up instead of spying on us? I was all for telling you. God knows I was. But Harry was so afraid of his job and Aunt Em feeling the way she does about you two marrying; and then you came back and made him feel you couldn't go on living without him. What could I do? I didn't want to love him, Emily, and he didn't want to love me. We tried not to—at first. It's the truth, whether you believe it or not."

"That's going to be a great comfort." I was beginning to tremble in spite of my effort to keep calm. The room was retreating in a haze about us. Such a fierce rush of words struggled in me that I felt I should go down under their weight.

It was then that I felt a hand on my arm. I turned to find Maggie at my side. Her face was crumpled with excitement and fear. Her breath came short under her black dress.

"Miss Emily! Miss Janice! Come quick: there's trouble —right at our back door. Some kind of a fight, I think. A brick went through the pantry window, and there's a lot of noise. You'd better call the police."

Janice started for the telephone as I followed Maggie down the hall. I could hear sounds now. Voices were shouting, and there were thuds at the back door. I reached out to unbolt it, but Maggie tried to hold me back.

"Miss Emily, please! Wait till the police get here. Whatever it is, they sound awful rough to me."

"I'm going to find out." I pushed her aside.

"It's all right to talk brave," she protested, "but this isn't any time for fool's courage."

I don't remember how I got the door open. I must have switched on the light that illuminated the steps and the path that led from the cellar entrance. I seemed to be part of some drama thrown on the black and white of a motion picture screen. Three men retreated before me down the steps, moving towards two other men bent over another figure stretched out on the frost-whitened driveway. They were only a few yards away, but before I could reach them

I felt Bridget brush by me, her ears stiff, her body flattened to the ground. The men tried to push her away, but she stood over the sprawled shape, quivering and sniffing and giving long, shrill howls that even I could hear.

The men were speaking to me, but I could not follow them. One tried to stop me as I came close to the little group. I shook him off and went on. I think I knew even before I recognized the familiar Mackinaw jacket that Jo Kelly lay limp at my feet.

"Jo! Jo!" I could feel myself repeating his name incoherently over and over as I gathered his head into my lap.

"Careful, Miss Blair," one of the men was cautioning, his face so close to mine that I could not miss the warning. "He's hurt. . . . A brick must have caught him right there —you can see."

He pointed to the spot where the bone showed white under the soaked hair. Already I could feel a sticky warmth on my hands and the smell of blood from an open wound. I could not look at the place. I kept my eyes on the mouth whose lines I knew so well; on the thin sensitive hands that Bridget was licking in frantic appeal. I took one of his wrists in my hands and tried to find the reassuring beat of his pulse before I turned once more to the man who had spoken to me.

"Get Dr. Vance," I told him. "Take the little car. The keys will be in it. Bring him back with you as fast as you can. Hurry!"

Maggie had come out with a blanket and pillows. We eased them under him and made him as comfortable as we could, crouching there in the cold. I managed to make out fragments of what the men were saying. I even put in a question or two of my own.

"He sure got an awful slug from the looks . . ."

"We told him to keep away from here. Just this morning I says to him, 'Jo, we know you're on the level, we don't ask questions, but you better stay on your own side of the river if you want to keep out of trouble.' And then he had to come up here again tonight."

"But he was only helping us out," I faltered, "with the furnace. See, there's the ashes he must have been carrying out when they—"

"Yes." Another man came closer and joined in. "And there's his flashlight. They must of got him when he come out. Wisht we'd got here in time to head him off."

"But everyone trusted Jo Kelly." I turned from one to another of the faces about me. "You did, didn't you? Who could have wanted to hurt him?"

"Well," one of the men hesitated before he answered, "you see there's been feeling lately. Some said he was trying to double-cross us. Might even turn scab himself next. They been watching him pretty close, so when he started to sneak up here they didn't wait to ask questions. But I guess they didn't mean to do more'n put a scare in him."

"He always did have one foot in trouble from the day he was born." Maggie had returned with a bottle of brandy and a spoon. She was trying to get a few drops between his lips. Her hands kept steady, but her face was distorted with tears. It was the one and only time I had ever seen Maggie cry. "You wait till the police get here," she was saying. "They'll get to the bottom of this."

The five men drew together then and began to whisper. They hesitated and pulled their caps over their eyes.

"Look!" One of them touched me on the shoulder and glanced furtively down the drive. "We'd better scram, or they might pin this on us. The police won't worry about who done it if they can find someone to lock up. It don't seem right to clear out this way, but he'd be the first to tell us to. There's a car now."

I dared not shift my position to stop them as they disappeared into the back garden. Jo's head felt so heavy on the pillow that I ached from the effort to keep it steady. Maggie had forced a little more brandy between his lips. The air was full of that strong, sharp smell. His eyelids quivered faintly, but he gave no other sign. I wondered, as we waited there beside him, if Maggie were remembering my seventh birthday party and young Jo lying as limp and white under the old hemlock tree.

CHAPTER THIRTY-TWO

THE BARE, SHEDLIKE HALL where rallies, revival meetings, and occasional dances were held was already crowded when I reached it through the dripping grayness of a January thaw. I hesitated for a moment, searching the group of men, young and old, who stood by the open doors. They stared at me and then uneasily at one another. Evidently I had not been expected, for no one seemed ready to take the initiative about seating me. At last a young man came forward. He nodded awkwardly, and I recognized him as the one who had been chief spokesman when we worked over Jo Kelly's limp body two nights ago.

Only two nights ago, that's all it was. I had to stop and tell myself that all over again, before I answered his nod with one of guarded recognition.

He turned and beckoned me up the long aisle, signaling to some one many rows in front. I followed him, keeping my eyes on the floor boards, wishing that I might have stayed inconspicuously near the doors. People moved closer together on one of the benches; a woman lifted a child to her lap, and I crowded past knees to reach the vacant place. I could feel eyes regarding me, especially women's eyes under hatbrims and woolen shawls. Even though I could not hear it, I felt the ripple of curious interest my presence had created. The man beside me sat stiffly, staring straight before him. I could feel the hard muscular strength of his body under the cheap material of his suit. His thick, blunt-fingered hands looked out of place in idleness on his knees. On my other side a girl in a checked coat and tilted beret dabbed more powder on her nose from a ten-cent-store compact. Her hair was as black and shining as the flimsy patent leather shoes she wore. I saw her eying my wrist watch appraisingly when I pushed back my glove to see the time.

Ten minutes before three. I sighed and hoped that they would begin on time. I must force myself to look up at the platform. The sooner I did that, the easier it would be. There were several rows of heads between, but I could find gaps to peer through. Yes, there were the simple uncompromising lines of the box whose shape I had dreaded to see. I was glad they had covered it with an American flag. Maybe some people might object. Jo Kelly had never served in the army or navy. The battle he had fought would never earn him a patriotic memorial. But I couldn't help thinking of the little printed labels pasted on articles one bought: "Made in America." It seemed to me that young Jo had a right to those words and to the flag that he used to help Old Jo raise and lower on our pole each Fourth of July and Memorial Day.

There were only a few floral tributes. But then it was January. Flowers were scarce and prices high. A big, gaudy wreath, reminiscent of those that heralded the opening of some new store, minus the gold streamer with the legend "Success," had been prominently placed. I guessed that it had been sent by the local chapter of the Textile Workers Union. There were several other less spectacular offerings that I knew must represent collections of quarters and dime contributions. That was all except for the red roses I had sent, standing in an ugly tin container on a wooden table.

A group of twelve men mounted the platform steps. They moved self-consciously, and I guessed that they must be trying to keep their shoes from squeaking. Yet there was a kind of clumsy dignity in their bearing that made up for the varied suits they wore. I noticed that they had all managed to put on white shirts and dark ties out of respect to the occasion. They seated themselves on folding chairs at one side of the platform. Those on the other side, closer to the coffin, were soon filled. I recognized a young priest, Father Fergus, from the Catholic church across the river and the Methodist minister, old Dr. Ellis, whose service to the mill families had included all denominations for the last twenty years. It was going to be an unorthodox service, I gathered. Evidently there would be eulogies from others too, for there were three strangers, who must be officials from the union or the labor organizations. A woman whose face I could not see had taken her place at an upright piano flanked by two anemic-looking potted palms. The figures on the platform rose, and we all struggled to our feet.

"Mine eyes have seen the glory of the coming of the Lord:
  He is trampling out the vintage where the grapes of wrath
    are stored."

The whole place was pulsating with the sound of many voices. The strong, stirring rhythm beat all about me in waves, so that I hardly knew how much of it I was hearing, how much of it I was feeling. I clutched the seat in front to steady myself against the torrent of music; against the familiar words that were returning in me with a new significance. I had learned them years ago when we used to march into the high-school auditorium. Some of those men and women about me must have marched to them then, as young Jo Kelly and I had done. And now we were singing for him. No, I thought, not for him but for ourselves, gathered there bewildered and unreconciled to his death.

"He has sounded forth the trumpet that shall never call retreat;
   He is sifting out the hearts of men before his judgment seat."

Terrible words and true, whether one believed in an Old Testament judgment seat or not. "Sifting out the hearts of men": I trembled at these words, remembering the shortcomings of my own heart taking the easy way of least resistance through all those past weeks and months of testing. But I had no doubts about Jo's heart. His had been whole and honest and free of compromise. He had given the best he had always—and for what? For a Cause that already seemed lost; for personal loyalties that had brought about his betrayal. I could see his slumped body lying on our gravel path, defenseless against the assault of those he had counted as his friends; his life snuffed out in bitterness and humiliation.

We slid back into our cramped places, and the service went on. I did not try to follow what they were saying up there on the platform, beyond bowing my head with

the others when prayers were being said. It was too difficult to fix my eyes on the moving lips, and my mind was
too full of the past to focus on the reality of this present
scene. I had never realized fully how close the ties were
between us. We had shared so much, without ever demanding anything of each other. It was a kind of love, I
thought, that one didn't recognize as love till one suddenly
found oneself without it. Jo and I had argued and dis-
agreed. We had taken our different ways and still counted
each upon the other. Something was gone out of my life
now. I should have to rely on the memory of it.

The eulogies were being spoken. One of the strange
men had taken his place beside the table. My roses quivered in the vase beside him when he pounded with heavy
emphasis. Women were crying all around me. The faces
of near-by men looked grim and set as they listened. Already, I felt, they were beginning to make a symbol of
Jo Kelly. I could imagine that union orator charging them
not to forget what he had stood for. But I couldn't bring
myself to think of him that way, perhaps because I had
never seen him in the picket line or addressing some group
of workers from a soapbox.

It was over at last. Men and women began to mount the
steps to the platform and move on in a long, quiet line. I
had no wish to join them and turned to make my way out
of the building. Now and again a familiar face passed, and
I acknowledged it with recognition. The hall was stifling
with close-packed bodies and damp clothing. I thought I
should never make my escape; but I was free at last. The
moist coolness of the outside air was good to breathe as
I reached the doors. It was then that I felt a touch on my

arm, and looked up to find Merek Vance beside me. I was glad to let him lead me out to his car.

"I thought you must be there," he said, "though I couldn't see you for the crowd. They hadn't figured on so many coming, not even on a Sunday. I'll drive you back after I've stopped at the hospital."

The streets were almost deserted as we drove on. The suspended activity of Sunday was over Blairstown. Across the river the sky was clearing behind Peace-Pipe chimneys. I was glad that they had chosen a Sunday for Jo's service. It meant that men and women who had returned to work could pay their last respects.

"I can't go back to the house, not yet," I said when Vance rejoined me after his errand at the hospital. "I'll have to get myself in hand first. Aunt Em's upset enough over all this without her finding out I went to the funeral."

"Then they didn't know you were there?"

Merek Vance sat back in the seat beside me, his hands resting laxly on the wheel. I had never seen those supple, strong hands of his so still. His face looked drawn, and there was a tired sag to his mouth.

"No," I explained. "No one knew I was going, but I had to be there. After all, Jo would be alive now except for trying to help us out with the furnace. Old Jo was too sick to leave his bed, and Uncle Wallace said he couldn't go—not in his position and with the union taking charge instead of having a service at the church. Well, Jo won't know I went, but at least I'll know one of us was there. I'm glad you went, too." Again I searched his face, struck by a defeated weariness I had not seen there before. "You look so tired," I added, "as if you hadn't slept since the accident."

"A doctor grows used to losing sleep," he reminded me. "But he never grows used to losing a patient."

"You did everything you could."

"It wasn't enough. Perhaps if we could have sent for a brain surgeon from Boston . . . But there wasn't time for that. The only chance he had was an emergency operation, and we lost."

"You tried. I know you'd have given everything you had to save him."

He gave me a wry smile and spread his hands in a futile gesture.

"That's a great comfort, knowing that all the study and skill it's taken years to learn can't cope with what a well aimed brick or club can do. Makes a doctor feel like giving up the human system and mending boilers or cracked cylinders."

I stared back at him incredulously. It was my turn to speak out in sudden protest.

"You can't say a thing like that! You haven't any right to, after what you've done for me!"

"And look how happy it's made you! Why, only the other night you were begging me to give up the treatments. You wanted to be deaf again."

"Forget what I said then, and I'll try and forget what you said just now. Besides, you told me once you couldn't guarantee to make me happy."

"I had my nerve going on to you about happiness."

"Maybe happiness isn't as important as we think." I said. "Most of us talk too much about it. I don't remember Jo Kelly mentioning happiness often. I guess he managed to get along without it, or maybe what he believed in made up for that. We'll never know now."

Impulsively I reached out my hand to his—partly to comfort him and partly because I also needed comfort.

"I'll never be reconciled to Jo's going out like that," I found myself saying. "I'll never be able to look at Bridget without wishing he'd stuck to animals and left human beings and their troubles alone. He had so little to call his own, not even a place where he could keep one of the dogs he was always picking up and having to give away."

Merek Vance did not smile at my words.

"You know," he said presently, "there's a sort of greatness about being as inconsistent as Jo Kelly was."

We were silent after that, sitting there together in the car, each of us thinking his own thoughts. The afternoon was slipping into twilight, and a low mist was coming up from the river, chill and faintly bitter with a hint of chemicals and smoke. Nothing new or strange in that. Time and again Jo Kelly must have felt it as he crossed one bridge or another at this hour.

CHAPTER THIRTY-THREE

WE SAT TOGETHER on the sofa with the fire burning before us and the curtains drawn for the night. Somehow we had put through the ordeal of Sunday night supper, with Harry making desperate efforts to appear interested in food and what Uncle Wallace was saying; with Janice restless and furtive over her untouched plate. Harry must have insisted on her going upstairs, for she had seemed reluctant to leave us alone. There had been a frantic, defiant appeal in her eyes as she turned away.

It had to come some time, I told myself, watching Harry put out one cigarette and then nervously light another at his end of the sofa. I suppose it might as well be tonight; only Jo Kelly's funeral was enough to go through for one day.

He leaned toward me in the firelight, and I saw the fear and misery in his eyes. His mouth that I had loved for its full-lipped, easy laughter had fallen into ineffectual lines. All the humor and charm of his face seemed to have been lost. Or perhaps I was seeing what I had determined not to see there before.

"Emmy," he began, "there isn't any name you could call me that I haven't called myself. You've got to believe that, even if I can't expect you to understand . . ."

He broke off and waited for me to help him out.

"Then Janice has told you? That makes it easier for me."

"It's wonderful about your hearing. I can't believe it yet. You deserve that—only why couldn't you have let us in on it? Why all this secrecy?"

"I didn't trust myself or Dr. Vance at first. You know what I'd been through with doctors."

"Yes, I know. How long has this taken?"

"I've been having the injections ever since I came back last fall, but it's been so gradual I could hardly feel the change till lately. Then I really began to hear sounds. Dr. Vance can't promise how long it will be before I'm cured; before I can hear voices clearly and all that people are saying, without reading lips too. I thought I couldn't wait for that, but now I'm not—so impatient, Harry. There doesn't seem to be the same reason to hurry."

He turned away at that. I could see him struggling to find words for what he was trying to say.

"Love's a hell of a thing, Emmy. You don't need me to tell you that."

"There's no good in trying to find the reason for its going," I said, "or in going back to set the exact moment when it went. Let's say as little as we can about it."

"But you must believe that I still care about you. It's just that I didn't know till—till a few months ago what it was to feel this other way."

The muscles in his throat were working quickly. I could have no doubts as to his genuine distress. I looked away for a moment before I could bring myself to answer.

"There's only one kind of love I want, Harry, and you can't give it to me. I was stupid and stubborn not to realize how it was, long ago. But you see I'd come to depend on it so. It's a pity two people can't fall out of love at the same time, the way they fall into it."

"Oh, God, Emmy, don't! I've made such a mess of everything. I wanted not to hurt you, and I've only made things worse for us all."

His head dropped to his hands. I longed to reach out and touch his thick, springy hair. But it was too late for that now. After a while he straightened his shoulders and went on.

"If I'd had any sense or spirit I'd have cleared out long ago."

"With or without Janice?" I put the question to him bluntly.

"Don't ask me." He spread his hands in a hopeless gesture. "I don't know where I'm going or what I'm doing, between the mills and the strike and my job and wanting to love you and loving Janice. I'm not blaming anyone but myself. That's the hardest part."

I twisted the ring he had given me, watching the firelight bring little flecks of brightness into the stone. It was going to seem queer to take it off, almost like losing the finger that had worn it so long.

"We're all to blame in different ways," I told him at last. "You and Janice didn't play fair with me, and I didn't with you when I found I was going to hear again. We all thought it was easier to be a little dishonest than to hurt someone a lot.

"Harry," I began after another long pause, "we might

as well be practical. You and Janice want to be married as soon as possible, don't you?" He started to speak, but once more the pulse in his throat beat visibly; and I did not wait for his words. "All right then. How are you going to do it?"

The lines in his forehead deepened. His face grew bleak.

"If I could find another job— But it's the same story everywhere: mills shutting down all over the country and business just about paralyzed. I've been around. I've seen the fellows behind desks, going through the motions and scared stiff the ax is going to catch them next. I tell you, Emmy, I'd be up against it to find a file clerk's job at twenty a week right now. And Hoover has the nerve to start a 'Don't Hoard—Spend Now' campaign right in the middle of a depression."

"I know. . . . Well, how about your going away for a while?"

He shook his head forlornly.

"It's no time for me to leave the mills. Besides, if I did there probably wouldn't be a job for me to come back to. If your family didn't fire me—and they'd have a right to— Peace-Pipe may not come through these next months."

"That's a chance we'll all be taking," I reminded him. "There'll be a lot of explaining to do. Aunt Em is going to take this hard. But she'll have to accept it, once you two are married. I'll handle her the best way I can, if you'll only go away."

"Don't be noble, Emmy! I can't take that too."

"I'm not being noble. It's not nobility to accept facts. The way things are now, we're all three miserable. Well, subtract one person, and that leaves two who might be happy if they had a chance. I mean you and Janice. But you can't stay in Blairstown, not for a while anyway. People will talk too much, and I couldn't bear it seeing you here together every day."

"And what could we go away on? You know how I'm fixed for money, and Janice hasn't any of her own."

"There'll be some money in the bank in her name if you go there tomorrow. Don't ask any questions. It's not enough to last forever, but it will see you through for a while."

"But we can't do that, not on your money! I've got some pride left."

"Don't you think it's a little late in the day to talk about pride?" He winced under the bitterness behind my words. I hurried on before he could make further protests. "Besides, Janice has as much right to that money as I. It came from my father and she'd be having her share in a few years anyway."

"But, Emmy, I tell you we can't do it. I'd borrow the money—it isn't that: it's you, making this possible—"

I felt suddenly very tired, as if my strength and determination were about to desert me. I had lived up to this so long that there was a sense of relief in knowing it was almost over.

"Please, Harry," I went on, "please listen. Don't make things harder than they are already. Money's the least part of this. It came from Peace-Pipe Mills, and I don't want any share of them now. I've seen too much lately, and I've felt too much. A few days ago I wouldn't have lifted a finger to help you and Janice. I was willing to play dog-in-the-manger to keep you two from having what I couldn't have for myself."

"You had a right to feel that way, Emily."

"After you've seen someone die—someone eager and

alive like Jo Kelly—it shakes the spitefulness out of you and the self-pity. I'm beginning to learn that feeling sorry for yourself is a pretty expensive luxury."

"No one could accuse you of that. You've taken more than your share of jolts without a whimper."

"Maybe I didn't whimper in public, but I had ways of my own." I rose, and he rose, too. His arm reached out, but I stiffened myself against the impulse to lean against him once more. "Here," I said, and I laid the ring in his palm. "Don't tell me to keep it. I'd feel better if you turned it in for old gold, though. I'd rather not think of someone else wearing it. And, Harry, you tell Janice whatever you want to about the money. Make up any excuse, but don't tell her it was mine. It mustn't be one more hurdle between us. I'd rather not see her now. She'll understand that."

I know he followed me to the hall. I think he called to me as I started up the stairs. But I didn't look back. I didn't pause to draw a long breath till I had reached my room. Maggie was there, going through her evening routine of turning down bedcovers.

"Miss Emily," she began, "that dog of yours has been pawing at the spread again. She's too smart, that one, for comfort."

"Oh, now, Maggie," I protested, "you know she never jumps on furniture. She's been trained not to."

"She's trained herself to twist her claws in the fringe and drag it down where she can make a fine soft nest. If you don't believe me, look at the hairs on it."

I refused to take an interest in Bridget's accomplishments, and Maggie went on with her folding and straightening. I slumped down at my desk and shuffled through a pile of letters. I had no wish for conversation just then, but still Maggie lingered, obviously manufacturing unnecessary tasks.

"Miss Emily," she began again, touching my arm to draw my attention. "I took the liberty of telling Old Jo you went to the funeral. I was sure that's where you were going. It isn't often I break out about what I'm not supposed to know. But I was sitting with him this afternoon while it was going on, and I couldn't think of no other way to give him comfort. I think you'd ought to tell him about it tomorrow. It's taken him hard—his mind feeling one way about young Jo and his heart another."

"All right, Maggie, I'll see him tomorrow. I wish he wouldn't take it this way."

"I've tried to talk him out of it. 'Jo,' I says, 'you stop calling that grandson of yours stubborn. Maybe we're the stubborn ones, you and me. Maybe our minds have got stiff along with our knees, and we won't give in to it.' But he just lays there and says nothing makes sense any more."

I laid down the letters and sat looking up into that plain face, whose blunt features had been familiar to me for longer than I could remember. Looking at Maggie Flynn always made me feel young and inexperienced. That was strange, I thought, remembering that for nearly forty years her life had been lived vicariously through ours. Yet she possessed some secret formula, like that of the ancient alchemists, for turning our little triumphs, our weaknesses, and our shortcomings into wisdom.

"Lots of things don't make sense to me any more," I told her. "Right and wrong and tragedy and happiness—I can't seem to tell where one begins and the other ends nowadays."

"Maybe we're not supposed to," she said, folding her

arms over the bedspread she held. " 'Tisn't as easy as sorting out linen from cotton or real silver from plated."

I had no answer for that, though there was much that I could have found to say to her that night. She made no move to go, and I saw she was looking at my hands. Her eyes were on the finger that looked bare now without Harry's ring.

"You're tired, Miss Emily," she said at last, "and no wonder. I've known a long time how things were and how they'd have to end. It wasn't for me to speak out, and it wouldn't have done the least good if I had. But I keep right on seeing what I see, and I tell you you're alive now —like no one else around here is."

"What—what do you mean, Maggie? Haven't I always been alive?"

Her forehead puckered into deeper grooves above the rims of her spectacles.

"Oh, yes, in a way, I guess," she admitted, "but just middling. You put me in mind of that climbing rose used to be by the front porch. Just kind of held its own there, nothing more. Soil was too rich for it, not enough grit and sand to make it take hold. Once it got moved over where it had to turn to and do for itself, it started to pick up and bloom. You remember what it's like now every summer?"

"Yes," I said, "I remember. Good night, Maggie."

CHAPTER THIRTY-FOUR

I DID NOT KNOW that my visit to the ell storeroom would take me so far into the past. I did not guess how painful I should find some of the going. But I have doubled back on my tracks at last and caught up with the present. When I have set the last word on paper I shall have no need to open that door again upon the accumulated souvenirs and possessions. I shall no longer be haunted by what lies dusty and discarded behind it.

It has not been easy, these months since I returned from the silent shore where deafness had kept me so long. Once I thought that regaining my hearing would solve all my problems, but now I know it has only made me more aware of them.

"He that hath ears to hear, let him hear." I say that over and over to myself each day. For it is not enough to listen with restored ears. I must listen with a restored mind and heart as well. That is my particular obligation; the only payment I can make for a gift that was lost and returned to me. I must listen to the sounds of earth and to the voices of men and women as if I were hearing them for the first and the last time.

I had to come back to Blairstown to rid myself of its hold. It may be different for those who live in big cities, yet even there one cannot escape the pangs of recognition. Landmarks are everywhere under the sun. Here, it seemed to me, I could not find a house or a tree or a postbox without some personal association. Each was like a tombstone marking some memory I wanted to forget: here he kissed me; here we met by chance; here we were happy; here I stumbled crying past that fence post. Walking the streets of Blairstown was a daily penance for me when I first returned after the six months I spent working and undergoing further treatments in the hospital in New York.

Just now I have been in to settle Aunt Em for the night. We have played our evening game of double Canfield on the table by her couch, and I have blessed for the thousandth time the human ingenuity that went into the evolution of a pack of playing cards. Just so we sat the afternoon when I told her of my break with Harry Collins. It came as the second shock to her that day, for Dr. Weeks had been the one to tell her of my cure. A shock of joy; a shock of pain. I was glad that I had let him bring her the good news first. I needed all my strength to meet her questions and protests. I can see her pale, dry fingers now with the familiar rings as she shuffled the cards and laid them out in formation.

"Emily dear," she had said across the table and the black and red of the suits her hands were sorting, "if anything could make me rise up from this bed and go down on my knees it would be what I've heard today. There's nothing that young Dr. Vance could ask that I wouldn't give him for what he's given you and all of us. I can't get over it yet, that he should have been the one when all the rest failed. But there must be some queer kind of pattern behind it: his coming from across the river; his father that crazy troublemaker at the mills. It's—it's shaken me."

I tried to explain about Merek Vance and his discovery, and all that it might mean to the world of medicine. But she had not been able to think beyond what it had done for me. Her gratitude and relief must keep turning back to that and to her plans for my future.

"I don't question your keeping these treatments secret, dear," she said, and there had been the shadow of reproach in her eyes. "You've been through so much strain and disappointment I can understand how you might feel you couldn't take me into your confidence. But Dr. Weeks says no one but you three knew—not even Harry. I don't see how you could have helped telling him, the man you're going to marry."

The moment had come. I swallowed hard and kept my eyes fixed on the cards spread out on the table. I remember I even reached out and moved a black seven to a red eight before I answered.

"I'm not going to marry Harry Collins," I said before I could trust myself to look up. "That's what I came to tell you."

It was easier once the words were spoken. One thing I have learned in all these months. What we dread to face is always simpler than we expect. It may be more painful, more bitter, but always simpler.

The hardest part was that she blamed herself as much as she blamed Harry and Janice. For days she brooded on it, and I could do nothing to ease her. Even now, though she is beginning to be reconciled to the inevitable, I think she still believes she might have prevented what happened if she had been farsighted enough. Aunt Em has never learned to accept compromise in any form. The code she has laid down for herself is inflexible. She cannot understand any deviation from it in those she loves.

"I should have known," she said over and over in those days after the first shock of revelation; "I should have sensed trouble ahead. I ought to have seen that you and Harry were married as soon as you recovered from that terrible illness. Instead I urged you from one doctor to another. It doesn't excuse me that I thought I was doing it for the best. I should have known somehow—"

"But, Aunt Em," I would protest wearily. "How could you possibly have known? How could any of us know? Love isn't predictable. It's an unknown quantity. I counted on it too much. Maybe that's why this had to happen. But at least we don't have to keep saying, 'If only we'd done this or hadn't done that!'"

"Oh, Emily, if you weren't so brave about it all!"

"Please, I'm not brave, Aunt Em. I'm just trying to be practical. It's worse to go over and over things. I don't believe love can ever be patched together again, once it's broken, and I'm not going to spend the rest of my life torturing myself by fitting the pieces together."

"I can't help thinking how different it might have been if your father and mother had lived. They would have known what to do. They wouldn't have failed you the way I have."

"I'm not so sure of that," I had to remind her. "You always did the best you could for Janice and me when we were little. When we grew up we had to go our separate ways. It wasn't any fault of yours if we didn't do what you expected of us."

I remember thinking, as I said those words, of the words my father had spoken years ago on the boat that brought us back from France.

"Always do what's expected of you, little Emily. I never did."

Certainly I had not lived up to his advice. I wondered if he could have guessed, holding my small, untried hand in his, how difficult it would be for me to benefit by his warning.

I remembered how he had also charged me to be happy for Aunt Em's sake; to make up to her for what she had missed in her life. Unconsciously I realized that obligation had stayed with me through the years. I had tried to live for her satisfaction as well as for my own. At first it had been natural and easy. The pattern of our lives had followed much the same course. I had acted and reacted as she might have done. She had approved of my engagement to Harry Collins because he was the suitable sort of young man she might have married in her own youth. Yet, subtly, imperceptibly our patterns had begun to vary. Against my will I had broken through mine and left her hurt and baffled. Perhaps, I thought, Janice's particular brand of ruthlessness was kinder in the end.

I found it almost impossible to speak of Janice in the days immediately following that hurried marriage in a near-by city. I had thought that we were strangers, but I could have met losing Harry to a stranger with more fortitude. Old associations, old grudges, and old jealousies were always rising up to confound me. Yet family condemnation of her was so fierce that I was forced to defend her sometimes. The intensity of Aunt Em's bitterness centered on Janice. Harry had been weak and faithless, but Janice had deliberately preyed upon his weaknesses and set out to steal him from me. Aunt Em's vocabulary failed her when she tried to give full vent to her feelings about Janice's betrayal.

"It was bad enough for Harry," she kept insisting, "after all we've done for him, here and at the mills, to let himself be swept off his feet while you were away trying to get back your hearing. But he wouldn't have fallen into the trap if it hadn't been deliberately set. There's no getting round that. I thought Janice was just young and careless and on the flighty side, and all the time she was bad— bad through and through. There's no other name for it."

"Please, let's leave Janice out of this," I would plead. "I'm beginning to understand that we can't fight against our feelings sometimes. It only makes them grow stronger than we are in the end. And let's be honest about one thing—love isn't something that can be trapped and caught. You can't steal it from someone unless that person has lost it already. I didn't want to believe that. But I've had to."

Merek Vance was the only one I could turn to without having to be constantly on my guard. With him I could talk without restraint or say nothing as I might feel inclined. My reactions to sound were steadily increasing with each treatment. I was beginning to hear voices more or less clearly now, though I missed many words unless I depended upon the motion of lips.

"We'll have to give you daily blindfold tests," he used to say with a smile. "You were always so clever at lip reading you fooled most people into thinking you could hear, and now you'll be fooling yourself."

I remember the day of the big demonstration down by

the mill gates and how we were together in his office when the police-car sirens shrilled and the distant crackle of gun-fire came in sharp staccato from across the river. We looked at each other, knowing that what we had feared was happening. He laid down the needle and syringe and reached for his bag. He did not speak, but I saw him quickly slipping in extra paraphernalia before he started away.

"You're going down there?" I asked. "Let me go, too." But I had to obey when he shook his head. I watched him run down the path to his car and drive away leaving me more alone and useless than I had ever felt in my life before.

I must have waited hours in his office, moving restlessly from chair to window, only to repeat the process a few moments later. Twilight came, the street lamps went on outside, but still I made no move to go or to turn on the light by the desk. The firing had stopped across the river. I strained my ears against the stillness. But the emergency searchlight in the mill yard had begun to sweep the dark like some ominous white finger.

"What! Still here!" Vance stumbled against me in the dimness.

He snapped the lights on quickly and I saw that his face was grave. One cheek showed a large bluish bruise.

"That's nothing," he answered my look. "I took a couple of cracks intended for someone else. I should have worn my white coat and looked more like a doctor." He tried to smile without much success before he went on. "Scab trouble again, and a pretty general free-for-all. Picket line charged the shift coming out, and the guard tried to scare them. They fired in the air mostly, but a few picketers were hit and plenty of others beaten up and gassed. It's a bad business, and we haven't seen the end of it."

I knew he was speaking the truth then, and I know even more surely now with Peace-Pipe Industries shut down for the last six months and the workers' houses clustered about it half empty of occupants. The mill whistle no longer punctuates the day into ordered periods of morning, noon, and night. The chimneys rise gaunt against smokeless skies, and no pulse of machinery beats behind brick walls and windows. The Wawickett River flows on unhindered below the bridges, its dams open now since there is no need of its power. I have read of ghost towns, and I am reminded of such as I take my daily walks across the river. But it seems less like that to me than like some deserted beehive that once swarmed and hummed with activity.

I do not pretend to understand all that has gone into the failure of Peace-Pipe Mills. Uncle Wallace and the directors blame the strike for paralyzing production at a critical time. Those more sympathetic to union demands insist that recognition by the company would have saved the mills from discord and disintegration. Others merely shrug and lay the whole collapse to business conditions which are slowly but surely shutting down other industries all over the country. All I know is that something living and vital went out of the mills after those last bitter spurts of spirit by the strikers and the harsh violence that went into curbing them. I only know that business dwindled, diverted to larger companies, and that the banks finally withdrew their backing. Peace-Pipe had gone into receivership, and there are rumors that it will soon be consolidated with one of the great cotton and textile companies that control a score of smaller units.

The trademark of the Indian in his proud feathers with his legend of "Peace-Pipe for Quality," if he survives at all, will no longer stand for the ideals of a family-dominated industry. Already that painted image on the board by the railroad station is beginning to show signs of the times. His paint is peeling and dented, and he seems, in more ways than one, the symbol of a vanishing race. I want no part of him or what he has stood for, and yet I am glad I shall not be here to see his final humiliation. For to me he will always belong to the years that changed my life and the lives of all of us who lived through them in Blairstown. Hardly anyone mentions young Jo Kelly now. But down there in the dingy frame houses where women hang out their lines of washing and stand patiently for donations of food and coal, where men pick up any chance at an odd job and wait grimly for something to turn up, down there I think he is remembered for what he was and what he tried to be. I know that for me he will always be there, a solitary, unseen picket keeping faith by the mill gates.

Merek Vance and I talked of Jo Kelly and of Blairstown on our last meeting many months ago. It was late spring in New York, and we sat together in a little park near the hospital where I had gone at his urging. There must be further tests and examinations by a group of specialists who were organizing a clinic to develop and perfect the Vance method of stimulating impaired nerve cells. He had persuaded me to go there after a long session of arguments. I had wanted to stay at home. It had seemed like running away from my own problems and associations just when I had begun to meet their challenge. But once more his firm insistence had overcome my prejudices. I know now that he was wiser than I.

"You need more help than I could give you even if I stayed on to see you through," he had said, handing me a sheaf of wires all urgently summoning him to work with his associates at important medical centers. "I can't very well refuse to accept such offers, now we've proved the cure is effective. You helped me to prove that, and it's up to you to go on contributing yourself—so, don't start that argument about not wanting to act the guinea pig. We've had that all out before. Besides, you can work with other deaf patients. The clinic will keep you so busy you won't have time to think, and that's what you need right now, whether you know it or not."

So I gave in and let Merek Vance arrange for my stay at the hospital when he left to take up his new duties. I had to fortify myself against wistful looks and disapproval at home. Aunt Em was well enough for Dr. Weeks and Maggie to care for her, though it was evident that she would not regain full use of her legs. The fracture had mended, but she would never again move without stiffness or pain, and her heart must be guarded against the strain of exertion. She would be a semi-invalid for the rest of her life. We all knew it, and so we all avoided acknowledging the fact.

Uncle Wallace had been against my leaving, but he accepted it finally. Peace-Pipe Mills and the shadow of failure that was gradually engulfing them were the only realities for him in those days before the final shutdown. It was Maggie Flynn who stood by me in the decision to go.

I think if I had weakened at the last moment she would have taken her broom in hand and swept me out of the front door.

"You've had trouble enough here," she had said as she helped me with my packing. "I don't mean there can't be plenty of it for anybody anywhere, but you're too young to go into storage yet. Time enough for that when you're old like me and used to the smell of camphor and moth balls."

She had smiled grimly as she spoke, but I noticed that she kept her eyes lowered.

"It's not that I want to run away from what has to be faced, Maggie," I tried to explain. "I'm past minding the gossip or the looks or knowing that people know—about Harry Collins and me. That's over and done with now. I'll come back when I've done all I can to help at the hospital. Blairstown hasn't seen the last of me yet."

Maggie had listened, her long arms continuing to smooth and fold a dress of mine to fit my trunk. I can see her now, standing stiff and unyielding on the worn roses of my bedroom carpet. She seemed, as she had told me herself, like a part of the furniture. When she spoke, it was almost as if a familiar table or chair had passed judgment upon me after years of silence.

"You'll be back maybe, but not to stay. This town doesn't fit people same's it used to. You and Dr. Vance now—you're both grown too big for it, and folks can't squeeze back into clothes they've outgrown, no matter how hard they may try to."

So I had gone away to plunge into the experience of work that was new and often difficult for me to accomplish. I was to be a volunteer worker in the clinic in exchange for the care I was to receive. It wasn't easy for me to adjust to long hours or to taking orders like any other unskilled probationer. I was clumsy and stupid at first, unused to the routine and the following of even simple rules. But the doctors and nurses were patient with my ineptitudes, and after the early weeks of adjustment I began to improve. For the first time in my life I was paying my own way with hard work.

Looking back to that period in the hospital clinic, I realize that my services must have been far more on the debit than the credit side of the ledger. I think that only medical curiosity in my case and Vance's influence kept me on. But I tried as I had never tried to succeed at anything before. I was interviewed for hours by visiting doctors and put through long and exhausting tests. I helped with case histories and filing reports, and I made myself useful with the deaf patients who came for the injections. I was best at that, especially with timid children or the confused older people who had not learned to read lips. Perhaps the fact that I was myself still a little dazed and bewildered made a bond between us. In time the staff came to recognize that and to let me deal with patients in my own way. They accepted me after a fashion, though I never achieved skill or efficiency.

In those months I saw Merek Vance whenever he came to the hospital for consultations. But these were infrequent, for he was dividing his services between several medical units. Once he asked me to appear before a large group of doctors at a conference where he was to deliver a lecture. I dreaded the ordeal and the questions which I must meet.

"It's the penalty for being my prize patient," he smiled when he came to take me to the meeting. "But we'll celebrate when it's over. We'll have dinner afterwards and a whole evening to ourselves. You're working too hard, I'm afraid, but it's becoming to you. No, I don't mean your hat and dress, though I approve of them. I'm glad you wore blue. I've always liked you in it."

It pleased and surprised me to have him say that. I hadn't thought he noticed what I put on.

When Merek Vance rose to speak I felt as I had felt on that winter night in Angeletta's kitchen. Once more he was in command, and once more he carried assurance with him. Seeing him there among others of his profession I was more than ever conscious of his quiet authority. He looked young, almost boyish, beside the doctors who crowded the auditorium. The light from the reading desk where he had spread out his notes edged his thin face, making the features stand out in sharp relief: the dark brows and wide-set eyes; the high cheekbones, the full, expressive lips and prominent chin. He seemed charged with vigor and intelligence that brought a quiver of response from his listeners the moment he began to speak.

There were no easy words of introduction. He plunged headlong into his subject with a kind of impatient exuberance that had no time to waste on trivialities. Sometimes he paused to elaborate on his notes with quick, lucid explanations and concrete examples. Unknown phrases and medical terms confused me again and again, but always the sense of the words and the power of the voice that carried them swept me along.

Sitting there in my seat below the platform, I felt awed

and alone. It was as if I had lost Merek Vance and the bare little Blairstown office forever. Once we had shared it, but now he had gone on—it frightened me to think how far. He could not escape from the dignity of accomplishment which would be recognized wherever he went. Once, long ago, I had stood on another platform, a little girl holding a squirrel muff, and he had been a shabby, long-legged boy looking up from the crowd below in the mill yard.

Queer, I thought, the way things work out. But Aunt Em was right. There's a sort of pattern behind it all.

I was glad that I had remembered. It didn't seem to matter that our positions had been reversed in the years between.

After the meeting was over and I had been through my part of the questions and open discussion that followed, Merek Vance and I drove to a small Italian restaurant near the Medical School where he had studied. We sat outside under a striped awning, our table a part of the sidewalk so that we could have reached out and touched passers-by without moving from our places.

"Thanks for this afternoon," he said. "You did me proud. I hope you didn't mind too much."

I watched his strong hands breaking one of the chunks of crisp bread, and I must have smiled, for he turned to me with a curious tilt to his brows.

"What are you thinking to make you look like that?"

"Oh, only that you've done about everything except box my ears, and you must have wanted to do that a good many times. I guess you'll never have a more difficult patient than I've been."

"I'm not making any predictions," he laughed. "Here comes the soup. If it's not as good as it used to be I'll know for certain I'm growing old and critical."

We had progressed to coffee before he showed me the telegram with the offer from the Pacific Coast. I knew he was watching me intently as I read and reread the words. Here was recognition and opportunity that come to few: his own laboratory and assistants for further research; financial endowment for the future if he would join the staff of a great western medical center.

"Well," he asked when I handed back the slip of paper, "what do you think I should do about it?"

I started at his words.

"You're asking me?" I stammered. "Why should you when you've always seemed so sure where you were going?"

"But I am asking you," he persisted. "I think I've earned the right to know how you feel."

"I don't see how you could refuse. It means everything for your future and a chance to go on without worrying over a practice." I smiled as I pushed back my coffee cup, and went on: "Speaking from personal experience, I doubt if you'd be very successful at that. You're apt to forget to send your patients their bills."

That had come to be a joke between us. He acknowledged it with his lips, but his eyes stayed grave. We said little as we jolted uptown on a lumbering green bus. We did not return at once to the apartment house near the hospital where I had taken a room. The night stayed warm and soft with spring and river mist. We found an empty bench under a plane tree that was just putting out new leaves.

"It feels like Blairstown tonight," I said when we had settled ourselves. "I mean there's the same smoke and grit mixed with river damp."

"Yes," he agreed, "and across the Hudson there are plenty of factories full of workers wondering what's ahead for them. It's like that everywhere. I've seen a lot of mill towns since I've been traveling around. You'll find they're all pretty much alike, whatever they produce: same chimneys, same smoke, same whistles, same river, mostly, dividing the two sides of town."

I have remembered his words. I have thought of them often as I crossed the bridges over the Wawickett since my return.

"Peace-Pipe Mills are closing soon," I told him. "I suppose you heard. That means Aunt Em and Uncle Wallace are going to need me till they grow more used to the change. It won't be easy to fit into their ways again, but I'm going back. Not just for them—there are things I have to see through for myself. No one can do it for me."

This time he did not question my decision.

"All right," he said, "go back. You'll have to lay the ghosts in your own way. I know all about that. You helped me get rid of mine. You didn't know that day in the North Station when the baggage truck nearly ran you down how close I was to turning tail. Seeing you put me on my mettle; made me want to lick the town and what it had done to me and my family. I hated you that day, and yet your deafness was a challenge I couldn't resist."

After that we were silent. Perhaps because there was so much I wanted to say I found that words were difficult to summon. I think, too, that unconsciously we were both missing the familiar boundaries of the little Blairstown office. Always before, even when we had talked most intimately, most honestly together, we had not been alone. Harry Collins had been there with us. His presence had dominated my life for so long, and now suddenly it was gone. The knowledge made me shy and constrained as I had never been with Merek Vance before.

"It seems queer," he spoke as if he knew my thoughts, "not to be jotting notes down on that folder marked 'Emily Blair.' I—" His arm pressed closer between my shoulder and the wooden bench rail. "I can't help missing that even though I'm glad you're well over the bad stretch. It'll be easier going from now on."

I knew what he was trying to say and that it was for me to speak first on a subject I had avoided.

"I suppose you know that Harry—that they're living in Pennsylvania," I said. "He got work in some smelting and iron company."

Vance nodded.

"As a matter of fact I saw them both when I was out that way a month ago. They had a pretty tough time of it for a while. But they've stuck together and they're happy —because they're right for each other."

"Yes," I answered. "I don't resent that the way I used to. It's as if I were someone else who felt like that once."

"You can't keep scar tissue from growing over," he reminded me; "inside or outside, it's the same."

"I'm glad they went away from Blairstown," I said. "Janice never fitted in. Her roots aren't there the way mine will always be."

His shoulders jerked in the familiar shrug of impatience. Once more he turned on me with the old ruthlessness.

"There you go!" He burst out. "As if roots were all that mattered!"

"Well," I protested, "you'll have to admit they're rather important."

"Of course they are, but so are branches. I'd say the farther a tree grew away from its roots the more life it had in it. And that goes for people too."

"Meaning . . . me?"

"Yes, meaning you." His arm tightened about me. "It's been a fight all the way for both of us and I'm not letting you settle back now. I know what you've been up against . . . half smothered with comfort and conventionality . . . too much background and not enough room to turn round in and face the present or the future. Any mill worker's daughter had a better chance to come through alive than you had. I have to give you credit for that. Maybe it was your deafness that kept you from being completely caught. If you hadn't had that to meet and if you'd married the man you loved when you wanted to—"

"Please," I begged, "let's not talk about that."

But he cut me short.

"I've earned the right to talk about love or anything else to you. I'm through keeping hands off your life and your feelings. I had to keep still about a lot of things before. It wasn't easy to sit back and see you dominated by a shadow. Yes, you were clinging to a shadow though you wouldn't admit it."

"I know, now," I told him. "But it's harder to shake off shadows than realities sometimes. That's one reason why I know I must go back to Blairstown. You're right about roots and branches. I'll do my best to grow in the right direction."

"And I'll make sure that you do." I could not see his face in the darkness, yet I knew the expression that would be on his lips and behind his eyes. "Go on back to that old house and those old people," he urged. "I want you to. I can wait while you prove to yourself that you're no longer part of them. We'll know, both of us, when you're free for tomorrow."

We must have spoken other words after that, but I do not recall them. I remember rather the lights on the Jersey shore as I saw them over his shoulder; the moisture of river mist turning to rain; the strong swift pressure of his lips on mine as he left me at my doorsteps and strode away down the lengths of wet asphalt.

Even then I did not know as I watched him out of sight how great was to be my need of him at every turn. I did not dare to believe that he might also come to have such need of me. But these months have made me know that he does and that we must go on together.

Tonight, sitting in a room that seems suddenly to belong to someone else, I shall lay away these pages, for they have answered their purpose. Perhaps it was foolish to imagine that the first quarter of one's life should be recorded. Memories will withdraw into their right perspective if we let them have their way. On the desk before me is a long railroad ticket stamped with the names of many places. These are strange to me, all but the last one which I know from the familiar post mark on the letters I have watched for week after week. Once I might have faltered before such a transplanting. But that was yesterday. Now I am ready for tomorrow.

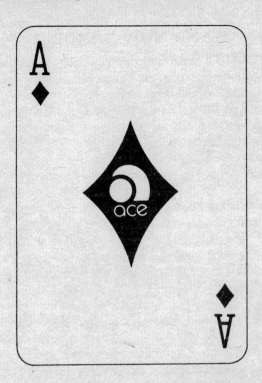

There are a lot more
where this one came from!

Don't Miss these Ace Romance Bestsellers!

————#75157 **SAVAGE SURRENDER** $1.95
The million-copy bestseller by Natasha Peters,
author of Dangerous Obsession.

————#29802 **GOLD MOUNTAIN** $1.95

————#88965 **WILD VALLEY** $1.95
Two vivid and exciting novels by
Phoenix Island author, Charlotte Paul.

————#80040 **TENDER TORMENT** $1.95
A sweeping romantic saga in the
Dangerous Obsession tradition.

Available wherever paperbacks are sold or use this coupon.

D.E. Stevenson Romances

"Finding a re-issued novel by D. E. Stevenson is like coming upon a Tiffany lamp in Woolworth's. It is not 'nostalgia'; it is the real thing."

—THE NEW YORK TIMES BOOK REVIEW

Enter the world of D. E. Stevenson in these delightful romantic novels:

AMBERWELL
THE BAKER'S DAUGHTER
BEL LAMINGTON
THE BLUE SAPPHIRE
CELIA'S HOUSE
THE ENCHANTED ISLE
GERALD AND ELIZABETH
GREEN MONEY
THE HOUSE ON THE CLIFF
KATE HARDY
THE MUSGRAVES
SPRING MAGIC
SUMMERHILLS
THE TALL STRANGER

ROMANTIC SUSPENSE

Discover ACE's exciting new line of exotic romantic suspense novels by award-winning author Anne Worboys:

THE LION OF DELOS

RENDEZVOUS WITH FEAR

THE WAY OF THE TAMARISK

Coming soon:

THE BARRANCOURT DESTINY